OLD TESTAMENT PSEUDEPIGRAPHA

Old Testament Pseudepigrapha
More Noncanonical Scriptures

VOLUME ONE

Edited by

Richard Bauckham

James R. Davila

Alexander Panayotov

William B. Eerdmans Publishing Company

Grand Rapids, Michigan / Cambridge, U.K.

Published 2013 by
Wm. B. Eerdmans Publishing Co.
2140 Oak Industrial Drive N.E., Grand Rapids, Michigan 49505 /
P.O. Box 163, Cambridge CB3 9PU U.K.

Printed in the United States of America

19 18 17 16 15 14 13 7 6 5 4 3 2 1

Library of Congress Cataloging-in-Publication Data

Bible. Apocrypha. English. 2013.
Old Testament pseudepigrapha : more noncanonical scriptures /
edited by Richard Bauckham, James R. Davila, Alexander Panayotov.
volumes cm
Includes bibliographical references and index.
ISBN 978-0-8028-2739-5 (cloth: alk. paper)
1. Apocryphal books (Old Testament) I. Bauckham, Richard.
II. Davila, James R., 1960- III. Panayotov, Alexander. IV. Title.

BS1692 2013
229'.91052 — dc23

2013022754

www.eerdmans.com

Dedicated to
Johann Albert Fabricius, on the three hundredth anniversary
of the publication of his *Codex Pseudepigraphus*
Veteris Testamenti (1713)
and to
Robert Henry Charles, on the hundredth anniversary
of the publication of his *The Apocrypha and*
Pseudepigrapha of the Old Testament in English (1913)

Contents

Foreword: The Fundamental Importance of an Expansive Collection of "Old Testament Pseudepigrapha"

With the *Old Testament Pseudepigrapha: More Noncanonical Scriptures,* Professor Richard Bauckham, Professor James R. Davila, and Dr. Alexander Panayotov enhance the historic collections of early Jewish and "Christian" sacred texts. Their work is high on the list of the most important publications in biblical studies over the past twenty-five years.

Historic Collections

The lost worlds of the early Scriptures were explored from the early 1700s until the present through collections edited by Fabricius, Migne, Kautzsch, Charles, James, Riessler, Kahana (and the more recent and popular collection by Hartom), Hammershaimb, Sacchi, Diez Macho, Dupont-Sommer with Philonenko, Kümmel with Lichtenberger (*Jüdische Schriften aus hellenistisch-römischer Zeit*), Sparks, and the editor of and contributors to *The Old Testament Pseudepigrapha* (*OTP*).[1]

The Italian Rabbi Azariah de Rossi (ca. 1511-77), in *Meor Enayim* ("The Light of the Eyes"), apparently inaugurated the search for the "lost" Jewish Scriptures. When he states that the early Jews imagined that the sun enters and exits through "portals" (166-67), he may be influenced by the *Books of Enoch*. Interest in a collection of Jewish apocryphal works may be foreshadowed in 1698-99, when Johann Ernest Grabe published the *Testaments of the Twelve Patriarchs* and portions of *1 Enoch*. Clearly, the modern study of the "Old Testament Pseudepigrapha" began in 1713 with Johann Albert Fabricius's publication of *Codex Pseudepigraphus Veteris Testamenti*.[2] This monumental work, consisting of more than 300 documents or quotations, mirrors the search for knowledge inspirited by the Renaissance and the exploration of a "canon" and Scripture stimulated by the Reformation.

One might be able to comprehend why theologians do not include in their study of antiquity the many works in the pseudepigrapha. Although 1 (Ethiopic) Enoch and Jubilees are in the Ethiopic canon, the pseudepigrapha are not preserved in the Jewish, Roman Catholic, Greek (and Russian) Orthodox, or Protestant biblical canons. There has never been an excuse for scholars or historians to ignore, let alone denigrate, the pseudepigrapha, in a historical and theological study of Early Judaism and Early Christianity.

The editors mentioned in the first paragraph published collections of pseudepigrapha that gradually revealed a new paradigm: As scholars focus on reconstructing Early Judaism (300 B.C.E. to 220 C.E.) and Early Christianity (26?-400 C.E.?), they must be unusu-

1. Many of these are discussed in greater detail in the Introduction to this volume by Bauckham and Davila.

2. J. A. Fabricius, *Codex pseudepigraphus Veteris Testamenti* (Hamburg and Leipzig, 1713 [2nd ed. Hamburg, 1723]).

ally circumspect in using words like "canon" and "extra-canonical." Due to the dedication and sacrifice of hundreds of experts, the ancient land of Sacred Scripture is no longer *terra incognita.*

Anachronistic Nomenclature

Throughout the world, scholars use terms like "canon," "noncanonical," "apocryphal," "pseudepigraphical," and "Bible," while warning that such terms are anachronistic in the study of Judaism and Christianity in antiquity. To be relegated to the pit of collapsed assumptions for historians (and theologians) of Early Judaism and Early Christianity are the elevation of "canon" and the denigration of "noncanonical."

The terms "orthodoxy" and "heresy" are also problematic.[3] While we might perceive a "proto-orthodoxy" in the second century C.E. in Justin, Melito, and Irenaeus, we need to agree that "heresy" often precedes orthodoxy and that talking about a proto-orthodoxy is possible only by assuming an elevation of orthodoxy by the fourth-century Church. Retrospection may be permitted; but it should be admitted. Perceiving the evolution of a *regula fidei* is more historically sensitive.

Here we emphasize that the Jewish sacred writings composed before the Mishnah and Tosefta must not be branded as "non-canonical," as if there were a recognized closed canon. They are fundamental to a perception and reconstruction of the vastly different concepts within Judaism before 70 C.E. and the matrix of Christian Origins. The formerly misperceived works do not represent an inferior type of Judaism that was on the fringes of a putative "Orthodox Judaism." Later triumphant institutions, like Rabbinic Judaism and Christian Orthodoxy, enabled the survival of great (and conceivably the greatest) traditions and Scriptures; but too often it was at the exclusion of many early documents Jews and Christians once deemed to be replete with God's message for the faithful on earth.

These early documents not included in the canon are called "pseudepigrapha." When experts use this term they assume readers will comprehend that there is no closed canon in early Judaism, that many early Jews and Christians may have considered the documents Scripture, and that they are not "false" compositions (*pace* Fabricius).

Leading scholars do not brand Early Judaism as "Late Judaism," and avoid the term "Christian" for Jesus' early followers, recognizing that "Christians" in Acts 11:26 may be a term of derision and is certainly not synonymous with that concept in 325 C.E. and later.

Now, historians tend to agree that the Dead Sea Scrolls do not represent a sect living in isolation from a putative "normative Judaism." The Dead Sea Scrolls are a collection of writings with more than one provenience. Some works found at Qumran and Masada were composed or copied clearly in Jerusalem (many of the biblical scrolls) and others probably in Galilee (some of the *Books of Enoch*). Recent archaeological discoveries in Lower Galilee prove the cultural similarity and connectedness of Galilee with Judea, especially after the Hasmonean conquests.

3. The observation that "heresy" sometimes in many places antedates "orthodoxy" and the inappropriateness of these anachronistic terms in the study of Christian Origins was demonstrated by W. Bauer in his *Orthodoxy and Heresy in Earliest Christianity* (edited by R. A. Kraft and G. Krodel; Philadelphia: Fortress Press, 1979).

Shared Judaism

A shared Land promised to Jews, a common Pentateuch, the Decalogue, ethnicity, the *Shema*, purity, and monotheism united most Jews. Thus, we may imagine sects and groups related to an "established Judaism" centralized in Jerusalem and the Temple. The Jewish apocryphal works help us also perceive a "shared Judaism," since Sadducees, Pharisees, Essenes, the Baptist groups, the Enoch groups, the Zealots, the Samaritans, and the Palestinian Jesus Movement shared many concepts and the earliest confessions.

Describing the Old Testament Pseudepigrapha

When the *Old Testament Pseudepigrapha* (*OTP*)[4] was heralded as a classic, notably in the *Times* and *New York Times*, and in the leading biblical journals, few scholars seemed concerned that some worthy compositions were excluded. Some experts even suggested that there was a putative core or "canon" to the *OTP* and that some works should not be included because they were expanded by "Christians" (then numerous scholars thought it easy to distinguish between "Jewish" and "Christian" passages). Too many critics incorrectly assumed not only that there was a canon of pseudepigrapha but that the biblical canon was closed long before 400 C.E.; now we know that debates over the canonicity of certain books continued by Jews and Christians long after the fourth century C.E. The 1980s was a period when many scholars were shocked with the so-called expanded collection, missing the point that the great R. H. Charles had created a fictional collection that represented works certainly not in the category of Old Testament pseudepigrapha (e.g. *Pirke Abot*) and drew attention to documents of interest to his English colleagues in Oxford. It remains inexplicable why Charles did not include many documents known to him and highlighted later by M. R. James.

By 1990, I was convinced that more texts should have been included in the *OTP*. I imagined that 5 *Maccabees* could be a medieval redaction of a lost early Jewish work or a collection of ancient Jewish traditions. It is good that I did not include it; recent research has shown me that 5 *Maccabees* is merely a Syriac translation of book 6 of Josephus' *Jewish War*, the earliest copy of which is found with this title in the sixth- or seventh-century C.E. manuscript Codex Ambrosianus B.21, the oldest copy of the complete Syriac Bible. Along with a team of advisors, I did not want to mislead scholars by including pseudepigrapha that were "pagan" (though attention was drawn to them); these works did not help us obtain a more pristine perception of the complex world of Judaism (and Christian Origins) prior to the Mishnah. We shunned away from including documents that antedated 300 B.C.E. or were composed after the fourth century C.E. (unless they possibly contained otherwise lost Jewish traditions). Thus, our primary focus was the creative world of Second Temple Judaism and "Jesus' Judaism."

Since the 1970s, when the *OTP* was taking shape, I have published my opinion that more works should be included in the Old Testament pseudepigrapha (this is not the place to reiterate my point that most share: "The Old Testament" can be misleading and even disturbing [yes; it reflects Christian confessions]). My fundamental criterion was to collect *texts or traditions* that antedate Mishnah and (almost always) postdate *Tanach* (even though

4. James H. Charlesworth, ed., *The Old Testament Pseudepigrapha*, vol. 1, *Apocalyptic Literature and Testaments*, vol. 2, *Expansions of the "Old Testament" and Legends, Wisdom and Philosophical Literature, Prayers, Psalms, and Odes, Fragments of Lost Judeo-Hellenistic Works* (Garden City, N.Y.: Doubleday, 1983, 1985).

since 1985 we have perceived that Daniel postdates *1 Enoch* 1-36). Documents composed by Jews before the Mishnah (c. 200-220 C.E.), even if edited by later Jews or Christians, must be included; and later compositions that preserve early Jewish traditions should be brought to the attention of scholars. From this collection of pseudepigrapha, the *OTP*, scholars can refer to a collection of ancient Jewish documents or Scriptures, clarify those on which they would ground reflections, and stipulate what criteria enabled them to make such choices in the attempt to comprehend the creative world of Second Temple Judaism.

Inclusiveness

If we placard what should be read to comprehend Early Judaism (300 B.C.E. to 220 C.E.) and the Origins of "Christianity" then we must be inclusive in a corpus, and point to other collections, such as the Old Testament Apocrypha, the Dead Sea Scrolls, the Jewish Magical Papyri, the vast number of inscriptions, Philo of Alexandria, and Josephus. We should also recognize that Acts 1–12 is one of the best descriptions of life in Jerusalem when the day, month, and year were regulated by the liturgical ceremonies and festivals celebrated in the Temple.

In the past, I listed three books that should also be included in this broad category represented by the Old Testament pseudepigrapha; I prefaced my comments by drawing attention to a new category. The Old Testament pseudepigrapha may now be labeled "the biblical pseudepigrapha." That term helps us distinguish the corpus in the *OTP* from "the Qumran pseudepigrapha"; that is, pseudepigraphical writings known only since 1947 and found only in the Qumran Caves. For many years, I have suggested that at least three books should be considered part of the biblical pseudepigrapha (= Old Testament pseudepigrapha) or an appendix to the *OTP*.

First, the *Book of Giants* should be included within the Old Testament pseudepigrapha or biblical pseudepigrapha. It is not a Qumran sectarian composition, and was known before the discovery of the Dead Sea Scrolls; therefore, it should not be placed only among the Qumran pseudepigrapha. It was revered by the Manicheans, and the *Midrash of Shemhazai and Aza'el* is clearly familiar with traditions from it. Only fragments of the Aramaic original have been found in Qumran Caves I, II, IV, and VI. These fragments help us comprehend the original work in distinction to its later redaction. The *Book of Giants* is clearly Jewish and certainly antedates the first century C.E. We need focused research on ascertaining more precisely the date and provenience of this challenging document. It is certain that the *Book of Giants* is a very early Jewish work that represents the culture of Second Temple period (see Stuckenbruck, *Book of Giants*, p. viii).[5]

Second, the *Apocalypse of Elchasai* should be included in the Old Testament pseudepigrapha or biblical pseudepigrapha. It is an apocalypse composed by a Jew, conceivably by an early-second-century Jew who was deeply influenced by ideas found in the New Testament (see Luttikhuizen, *Revelation of Elchasai*).[6] The book was revered as divine revelation by the Elkesaites who lived on the eastern side of the Jordan River. The *Apocalypse of Elchasai* contains traditions that enrich our perceptions of the origins of such works as the *Odes of Solomon* and the *Testaments of the Twelve Patriarchs*.

5. Loren T. Stuckenbruck, *The Book of Giants from Qumran: Texts, Translation and Commentary* (TSAJ 63; Tübingen: Mohr Siebeck, 1997).

6. Gerhard P. Luttikhuizen, *The Revelation of Elchasai: Investigations into the Evidence of a Mesopotamian Jewish Apocalypse of the Second Century and Its Reception by Judeo-Christian Propagandists* (TSAJ 8; Tübingen: Mohr, 1985).

Third, the *Apocalypse of Pseudo-Methodius*, extant in Greek, Latin, and Syriac, should be included in the corpus. Although it is late, dating from the seventh century C.E., it appears to preserve some otherwise lost ancient Jewish ideas, concepts, and traditions (see esp. Reinink, *Die syrische Apokalypse des Pseudo-Methodius*).[7] The work is a history of the world from Adam until the end of time. It thus provides a fresh perspective from which to study the creative histories preserved in such documents as 1 Maccabees, 2 Maccabees, Josephus' works, *Jubilees*, *Pseudo-Philo*, and the summaries of history found in *1 Enoch* and other apocalyptic compositions.

These three works not found in the *OTP* or other collections should be studied carefully when one explores the world of the pseudepigrapha. Other works also should be included in an appendix of the *OTP*, notably *The History of Joseph* (see Isaac's translation of the Ethiopic version in *JSP*)[8] and the early Jewish apocalypses preserved in the Mani Codex.[9] For decades, I contemplated adding these compositions in an expanded edition of the biblical pseudepigrapha or Old Testament pseudepigrapha.

Now, thanks to the leadership of Bauckham and Davila, and with the assistance of Panayotov, a work appears that includes more pseudepigrapha that should be brought into perspective as we explore the ancient world, and especially the *sacra scriptura* that shaped the minds of Hillel, Jesus, Paul, as well as Tertullian, Origen, Eusebius, and Jerome—and many Jewish sages including Maimonides. The collection contains about 100 documents.

Scholars will debate the criteria for inclusion, and certainly no one should imagine that all these texts are important for reconstructing the world of the Righteous Teacher, Hillel, Jesus, Paul, Gamaliel, Johanan ben Zakkai, and the Evangelists. The whole collection, however, does mirror the unparalleled influence of the Bible on Western culture and thought. They are a key to a better perception of the reception of the Bible (*Wirkungsgeschichte*)—an increasing interest of specialists. One also should keep an eye open for the "pseudepigraphical texts" preserved in unedited Ethiopic manuscripts and collections of Old Irish apocryphal works but not included in *OTP* or the two new volumes.

Old Testament Pseudepigrapha: More Noncanonical Scriptures is a treasure trove. It brings to the attention of all today documents purporting to be ancient and to be composed in honor of a biblical sage or by a biblical luminary. Pseudepigraphers might condemn scholars today for putting their names on books that contain insights and words learned from teachers and others. They would be aghast that some scholars today think that attributing one's writing to the spirit, genius, or inspiration of a biblical luminary is "false-writing." Yet, we today would need to respond by pointing out that some pseudepigraphical authors deliberately tried to dupe the reader; for examples, the author of 2 Peter claims to be Peter and assumes his authority, and the author of the *Letter of Lentilus* perpetuated a false, and medieval, description of Jesus.[10] Surely, no one should confuse such false claims with attributing inspiration to and honoring an ancient luminary, like Enoch,

7. G. J. Reinink, *Die syrische Apokalypse des Pseudo-Methodius* (CSCO 540-41, Scriptores Syri 220-21; Leuven: Peeters, 1993).

8. E. Isaac, "The Ethiopic History of Joseph: Translation with Introduction and Notes," *JSP* 3 (1990): 3-125. Since Isaac's publication the Syriac original behind the Ethiopic version has been identified by Kristian Heal and it is translated by him in this volume.

9. See John C. Reeves, *Heralds of That Good Realm: Syro-Mesopotamina Gnosis and Jewish Traditions* (Nag Hammadi and Manichaean Studies 41; Leiden: Brill, 1996).

10. See James H. Charlesworth, *Authentic Apocrypha: False and Genuine Christian Apocrypha* (North Richland Hills, Texas: BIBAL Press, 1998).

the perfect one, who was seventh after Adam and did not die but is with God (Gen 5:21-24; *1 Enoch* [a library of compositions that spans almost four centuries], *2 Enoch*, the *Coptic Enoch Apocryphon, 3 Enoch*).

One should now only praise the work and skill of all who contributed to and edited this massive collection. It highlights the singular importance of the Old Testament pseudepigrapha (and the *OTP*), is also presented in two volumes, and calls for all scholars to re-assess the perceptions and conclusions they inherited. In a preface to the *OTP*, Samuel Sandmel wrote: "By the strangest quirk of fate respecting literature that I know of, large numbers of writings by Jews were completely lost from the transmitted Jewish heritage." Now, we have two sets of collections that help point to that vast heritage; but let us not forget that many writings are probably lost forever, like the *Apocalypse of Lamech*, or preserved only in fragments, such as the *Apocryphon of Joseph* (not in either collection but in the Princeton DSS Project series).

Many of the pseudepigrapha were considered sacred by numerous Jews and Christians. For many centuries, influential experts considered some of them authentic; that is, for example, the *Psalms of Solomon* and the *Odes of Solomon* were composed by Solomon, as were Proverbs and the Song of Songs (pseudepigrapha canonized within the Old Testament). Is that not sufficient reason to read and include them in our research and reflection? Should we not treasure them as another indication of the enduring human search for the creating Creator?

James H. Charlesworth
Princeton and
Ramat haSharon, Israel

Introduction

by Richard Bauckham and James R. Davila

The "Old Testament pseudepigrapha," as the term is now commonly used, are ancient books that claim to be written by a character in the Old Testament or set in the same time period as the Old Testament and recount narratives related to it, but which do not belong to the Jewish, Catholic, Orthodox, or Protestant biblical canons. They include apocalypses (angelic revelations to prophets and sages such as Enoch, Moses, and Ezra); magical, oracular, and mantic works attributed to prophets and sages such as Solomon, the Sibyl, and Jeremiah; testaments put in the mouths of Old Testament characters such as Job and the twelve sons of Jacob at the end of their lives; songs and poetry attributed to Old Testament characters, especially David; "rewritten scripture" that retells stories known from the Old Testament from the fall of Adam and Eve to the deaths of the Maccabean martyrs; legends and tales set in the Old Testament period and usually, although not always, involving Old Testament characters; and various other obscure and intriguing works. This volume is a new collection of Old Testament pseudepigrapha.

Terminology

For readers to make sense of what follows, a few terms need to be defined at the outset. "Old Testament" is a Christian phrase, referring first and foremost to the collection of twenty-four "scriptures" found in what Jews call the "Hebrew Bible." The term "scripture" is a Latin term that means simply "writing," but it translates Hebrew and Greek words that were used in ancient Judaism and earliest Christianity in certain contexts to mean a book with sacred (specifically prophetic) authority and considered to be divinely revealed. The scriptures in the Hebrew Bible are written in Hebrew (with a few scattered chapters and verses in Aramaic) and they include, first, the *Torah*, or five books of Moses; second, the *Nevi'im*, or Prophets, comprising both the "former prophets" or historical books of Joshua, Judges, 1-2 Samuel and 1-2 Kings and the "latter prophets," the books of Isaiah, Jeremiah and Ezekiel, as well as the book of the twelve "minor" (i.e., shorter) prophets; and third, the *Ketuvim* or Writings, the remaining books: Psalms, Job, Proverbs, the Five Scrolls (Ruth, Song of Songs, Ecclesiastes, Lamentations, and Daniel), Ezra, Nehemiah, and 1-2 Chronicles. The Catholic Old Testament contains the same books in a different order but also includes thirteen additional documents, some as separate books and some as expansions within books of the Hebrew Bible. These are known as "Deuterocanonical" works to Catholics, whereas Jews and Protestants refer to them as the Old Testament "Apocrypha."[1]

---

1. The additional documents are the Epistle of Jeremiah, Tobit, Judith, 1 Esdras, Additions to Esther, The Prayer of Azariah and the Song of the Three Youths, Susanna, Bel and the Dragon, 1 Baruch, Ben Sira (Ecclesiasticus), The Wisdom of Solomon, and 1-2 Maccabees. The book of 3 Maccabees is also included in

The Protestant Old Testament is the same as the Jewish Hebrew Bible, again, with a different ordering of the books, while the Old Testament of the Eastern Orthodox branch of Christianity is, apart from the inclusion of 3 Maccabees, the same as that of Catholics.

It thus becomes clear immediately that the Old Testament does not have a universally accepted "canon."[2] This is a Greek term that originally meant a "reed," then by extension a "measuring rod," and by further extension a collection of authoritative books against which one could measure religious doctrine to establish if it was sound.[3] Although faiths in the biblical tradition agree that there is a corpus of authoritative scriptures taken from the religious literature of ancient Israel, there is considerable disagreement on what belongs and does not belong in that corpus. Indeed, there is even disagreement on what to call this collection of scriptures. Christians refer to it as the "Old Testament," an archaic term for what we would call an "old covenant" or, better, "old treaty," that is, the covenant or treaty made at Mount Sinai between God and Israel. Christian tradition regards it as "old" in contrast with the "new covenant" with God mediated by Jesus and the "New Testament," the Christian Greek scriptures associated with this new covenant. "Old Testament" is thus a highly confessional and, to Jews, a rather demeaning title. The Jewish equivalents are "Hebrew Bible" or *Tanach*.[4] This is a far more neutral and descriptive term and therefore it is the one normally used by modern scholars. But for reasons explained below, we continue to use the phrase "Old Testament pseudepigrapha" here with the realization that it is highly unsatisfactory on this and other counts.

This leaves us with the odd word "pseudepigrapha," the plural form of "pseudepigraphon," a Greek term whose literal meaning is "false-" or perhaps more charitably "fictional writing." As already noted, in current usage an "Old Testament pseudepigraphon" is a book that falsely claims to be written by an Old Testament character or to give an accurate account of events set in the Old Testament period, events that may or may not be mentioned in the Old Testament itself. This usage is ancient: the fourth-century church historian Eusebius of Caesarea informs us in *Hist. Eccl.* 6.12 that in the early third century,

---

the Orthodox canon. The books of 2 Esdras, The Prayer of Manasseh, and 3-4 Maccabees are often bound with the Apocrypha in modern Bibles, but they are not technically part of the Apocrypha and are generally assigned to the Old Testament pseudepigrapha (this despite the canonical status of 3 Maccabees for the Orthodox Church). The term "Apocrypha," which means "hidden (books)," goes back at least to the second century C.E., when the church father Irenaeus used it to refer to the vast number of spurious "hidden" or "secret" writings used by the Marcosian heretics (*Haer.* 1.20.1), although the texts in question seem to be what we would today call New Testament apocrypha (see n. 6 below). References to "apocryphal" Old Testament books (i.e., Old Testament pseudepigrapha) go back at least to Origen of Alexandria in the first half of the third century (e.g., *Comm. Matt.* 10.18.60; *Ep. Afr.* 13).

2. The Ethiopian Church uniquely includes the books of *1 Enoch* and *Jubilees* in its Old Testament canon. Both books survive complete only in Ge'ez, the Ethiopic language of this Church, and elsewhere both books are considered noncanonical even though the books portray themselves as prophetic revelations, respectively, to the biblical sages Enoch and Moses. The fact that *1 Enoch* 1:9 (from the Book of the Watchers) is quoted as a genuine prophecy in the New Testament book of Jude, vv. 14-15, and that *Jubilees* is quoted in the Damascus Document (a sectarian Dead Sea Scroll), xvi 2-4, as an authoritative source for predictions about future biblical history hints that in antiquity their status as scripture may have been accepted rather more widely than today.

3. See Lee Martin McDonald and James A. Sanders, *The Canon Debate* (Peabody, Mass.: Hendrickson, 2002) for an important collection of essays on the origin and early history of the biblical canon.

4. *Tanach* is an acronym made from the first letters of the Hebrew words *Torah*, *Nevi'im*, and *Ketuvim* (see above). Some scholars have adopted the term "First Testament" in order to avoid the potentially derogatory implications of "Old."

Serapion, bishop of Antioch, referred to books forged in the names of the apostles, notably the *Gospel of Peter*, as *pseudepigrapha* or "fictional writings." Nevertheless, its usage for our corpus of texts is highly problematical, as is uniformly agreed by specialists.

It is worthwhile at this point to reflect a little on these books called "Old Testament pseudepigrapha," starting from first principles and attempting to understand them on their own terms, without the theological baggage and conventions in which they have become mired over the centuries. Let us begin by observing that in antiquity there were a great many books about what we may call the "revelatory history" of ancient Israel, books either attributed to specific figures associated with the traditions about God's dealings with Israel or presenting events associated with those traditions. Presumably at least sometimes these books were written by the person to whom they were attributed and some of these events actually happened as described, but that does not really matter for our purposes.

In the course of time some of these books became widely understood to have a special authority associated more or less with prophetic revelation. That is, they were believed to be revealed by God to prophets such as Moses, David, Isaiah, Jeremiah, etc., and thus to be on some level divinely inspired.[5] Many of those books came to be accepted as having this special revelatory authority by very widespread faith communities and ultimately entered one or more biblical canons. But for our purposes as historians the distinction between these authoritative or canonical books and the very many other ancient books devoted to the revelatory history of ancient Israel (i.e., what is now conventionally but unhelpfully called the "pseudepigrapha") is only of tangential interest, chiefly for historical insights into the theologies of these faith communities. All of these books, canonical or not, are of historical value on some level, even if considerable work is required to appreciate that value. A book attributed to, say, Moses but actually composed by an anonymous Jew in the Hellenistic period tells us nothing about Moses but may tell us any number of interesting things about Jews in the second century B.C.E. and what they thought about Moses. By the same token, few if any of these books provide the historian with raw material easily transmuted into a straightforward historical account. Modern biblical criticism has, for example, rendered a simple belief that Moses wrote the Pentateuch highly dubious. It is clear that many authors contributed to the "five books of Moses" over a very long time, and any use of the Pentateuch by historians must take this research into account and approach the text for history with considerable critical caution.

Moreover, there is simply no "magic bullet" (such as date of composition, authorship, genre, etc.) which allows us as historians rather than theologians to distinguish between canonical ancient revelatory books and noncanonical ones. It is technically correct to call the noncanonical ones "pseudepigrapha" in that scholars agree that these texts are "fictional writings," but it ignores the fact that many books in the major biblical canons are equally fictional. Although the books of Enoch were not written by the patriarch Enoch, neither was the biblical book of Deuteronomy dictated by Moses nor the biblical book of Daniel written by a sixth-century-B.C.E. sage named Daniel in Babylonia, nor did the events narrated in the book of Judith actually happen. From the historian's perspective, therefore, there is no reason to distinguish fictional writings outside the major canons

5. For informed speculation on how some of the individual books in the Hebrew Bible and the Apocrypha acquired this authoritative status, see Eugene Ulrich, "From Literature to Scripture: Reflections on the Growth of a Text's Authoritativeness," *DSD* 10 (2003): 3-25.

from those within one or more of these canons and to give the former the rather condescending title "pseudepigrapha." Nevertheless, we reluctantly retain the term for the writings we have collected here, again, for reasons explained below. As will also be noted below, some publications still use the term "apocrypha" for these writings, but we find it clearer to retain that term solely for the Old Testament Apocrypha as defined above.[6]

All this said, the canonical or non-canonical status of these books has been a significant factor in the history of their transmission, affecting how and how much they were copied as well how often they were quoted and for which purposes, and this status must be taken into account by the historian when considering such questions.

The Composition, Transmission, and Study of the Old Testament Pseudepigrapha

Old Testament pseudepigrapha were being composed as early as pre-exilic ancient Israel, presumably at the time when some of the Old Testament itself was being written. The earliest surviving Old Testament pseudepigraphon is the *Balaam Text from Deir ʿAllā*, a collection of polytheistic oracles written in the name of the seer Balaam (who also appears in the Hebrew Bible) and recovered in Jordan in an archaeological excavation. It is written in a language closely related to Hebrew and Aramaic, but not to be identified with either, and the surviving fragmentary copy was inscribed on a plaster wall around 700 B.C.E. The Hebrew Bible itself refers to and quotes from many more such works that are now lost, including, for example, the epic and elegiac poetry of the Book of the Wars of Yahweh and the Book of the Righteous; royal chronicles in the Books of the Chronicles of the Kings of Israel and the Book of the Chronicles of the Kings of Judah; and the Laments over the fallen King Josiah attributed to the prophet Jeremiah.

In the Second Temple period, pseudepigrapha continued to be composed by Jews in Hebrew, Aramaic, and Greek. Some of those in Hebrew and Aramaic were translated into Greek, and these Greek translations continued to receive some attention from Christian scribes from late antiquity into the early Middle Ages. In time, Christians too began to compose pseudepigrapha in Greek. In the early centuries C.E., Jews began to lose interest in their pseudepigrapha, with the result that the Hebrew and Aramaic texts of many of these books ceased to be copied and so were lost, some entirely and some being transmitted thereafter only by Christians in a Greek translation or secondary translations based on a (frequently also lost) Greek translation. Surviving Jewish pseudepigrapha in Greek include the *Letter of Aristeas*, 3-4 Maccabees (all three original Greek compositions) and the *Psalms of Solomon* (translated from Hebrew). Surviving Christian Greek pseudepigrapha include the *Testaments of the Twelve Patriarchs* (based at least in part on older Jewish texts in Aramaic and Hebrew) and the *Testament of Solomon* (composed in Greek). In the cases of other pseudepigrapha composed in Greek, such as *Joseph and Aseneth*, the

---

6. There are also many ancient books outside the New Testament canon which share genres of New Testament books (gospels, acts of apostles, letters to churches, apocalypses) and claim the authority of the apostles or other figures associated with earliest Christianity. These as a group are referred to as "New Testament apocrypha," even though for consistency's sake they perhaps ought to be called New Testament pseudepigrapha. But the latter term is never used and any attempt to impose a full consistency of terminology on the noncanonical biblical literature would be impractical at this stage. An extensive collection of New Testament apocrypha in English translation has been edited by J. K. Elliott in *The Apocryphal New Testament: A Collection of Apocryphal Christian Literature in an English Translation* (Oxford: Clarendon, 1993).

Testament of Job, and the *Testament of Abraham*, it is disputed whether they are Jewish or Christian compositions.

As time passed, Christians too focused more on their canonical scriptures and showed less interest in preserving pseudepigraphic ones. The result was that many ancient Greek pseudepigrapha, whether written by Jews or Christians and whether composed in or translated into Greek, survived only or mainly in secondary translations into regional church languages. In the West, some pseudepigrapha, such as *4 Ezra* and the *Vision of Ezra*, were translated into Latin. The church in Anatolia and Iraq translated works such as *4 Ezra* and *2 Baruch* into Syriac, an important Christian dialect of Aramaic. Egyptian Christians translated other works, including an *Apocalypse of Elijah*, the book of *2 Enoch*, and another *Enoch Apocryphon* into Coptic, a late dialect of the ancient Egyptian language written in an adapted Greek alphabet rather than hieroglyphics. Armenian Christians developed a writing system for their own language, again, based on the Greek alphabet, and numerous pseudepigrapha were translated from Greek or Syriac into Armenian, including *4 Ezra*, the *Questions of the Queen of Sheba to Solomon*, and the *Seventh Vision of Daniel*. The Ethiopic Church developed a writing system for the Ge'ez language, based on the Old South Arabian script, and translated a number of important pseudepigrapha, mostly or entirely from Greek versions, including the books of *1 Enoch* and *Jubilees*. (Small sections of the Greek of these two works also survived in quotations by Byzantine writers and in manuscripts later recovered archaeologically, and portions of Latin translations of the Greek versions survived as well.) Greek-speaking Christian missionaries in the ninth century used the Greek alphabet as the basis for a script for the Old Slavonic language, leading to translations from Greek of *2 Enoch* and the *Ladder of Jacob*. Some pseudepigrapha were even translated into languages such as Arabic, Judeo-Arabic (Arabic written in Hebrew letters), Georgian, Old Irish, and even Manichean Iranian and Turkic. And in addition to translating older works, the Christians of late antiquity also occasionally composed pseudepigrapha in their regional languages. For example, *5 Ezra* may have been composed in Latin and the *History of Joseph* was probably originally written in Syriac.

Relatively few manuscripts of Old Testament pseudepigrapha copied by Christians in Christian languages survive from before the ninth century. But from the tenth century on, the number of manuscripts of such works increases dramatically, and most of our manuscript evidence for many of these documents comes from after this date, often long after. Often the text of such works has been carelessly copied or deliberately edited and not infrequently a document survives in manuscripts whose texts differ so much that we must regard them as different editions.

Meanwhile, despite their relative lack of interest, Jews did not ignore such texts entirely. There is some evidence that Jewish pseudepigrapha continued to be copied and even composed well after this time. A geniza (a repository for worn manuscripts bearing the name of God) associated with the Ben Ezra Synagogue in Cairo was discovered by European explorers in the late nineteenth century to contain many thousands of manuscripts, some dating back to the early Middle Ages. Among these have been recovered early medieval fragments of a work known as *Aramaic Levi*, a major source behind one of the Greek *Testaments of the Twelve Patriarchs*; of the *Ladder of Jacob* in Hebrew (perhaps translated from an original Greek text); of noncanonical Psalms in Hebrew attributed to David; of the Hebrew magical handbooks called the *Book of the Mysteries* and *The Sword of Moses*; of a Hebrew *Apocalypse of Elijah*; and of a Hebrew *Apocalypse of Zerubbabel*. Complete late medieval manuscripts of the last four survive as well. The wealth of evidence for the reception, transmission, and use of Old Testament pseudepigrapha in both Christian and Jewish circles from late antiquity through the Middle Ages is in need of much more attention from scholars.[7]

These Old Testament pseudepigrapha are representative examples, but many more survive from antiquity and we know of many other such texts that are now lost but which are quoted or mentioned by later writers. Some of those that do survive, whether complete or only in fragments or quotations, are published in this volume or are slated to be published in its forthcoming companion volume. Others have been published in earlier collections that will be discussed below. Old Testament pseudepigrapha continued to be composed through the Middle Ages and even up to the present. Eventually some of those that have survived began to come to the attention of the Renaissance scholars who devoted their lives to the recovery, editing, and critical study of the literature of antiquity. The history of the rediscovery of the Old Testament pseudepigrapha in the early Renaissance remains for the most part to be written,[8] but a few illustrative examples may be useful here.

Such pseudepigrapha as were known to these scholars survived in part or in full either in Greek or Latin versions, whatever their original language. The Latin book of 2 Esdras contained the books of *4-6 Ezra* treated as a single work and was widely disseminated. The thirteenth-century Franciscan philosopher Roger Bacon defended its authenticity and appealed to chapter 6:42-52 to demonstrate that the oceans covered only one-seventh of the earth's surface. In the late fifteenth century, Christopher Columbus drew on the same passage to convince Ferdinand and Isabella that his proposed trip to the Indies was feasible.[9] The *Testaments of the Twelve Patriarchs* were brought from Greece to England in 1242 in a tenth-century Greek manuscript that was translated into Latin by Robert Grosseteste. His translation was widely disseminated.[10] The book of *1 Enoc*h was almost entirely lost to the West. Although some quotations of the Greek version of the early part of it (the Book of the Watchers) survived in the work of the Byzantine chronographer George Syncellus, and a Latin translation of *1 Enoch* may have existed at some point, early Renaissance scholars knew of it primarily from the Greek quotation in the New Testament Epistle of Jude and some allusions in early patristic writers. Reportedly, in the late fifteenth century the Christian Cabalist Pico della Mirandola purchased a complete copy of the *Book of Enoch* at great expense. This seems highly unlikely, although it is possible that he had some acquaintance with the much later Hebrew book now known as *3 Enoch*. Pico himself quoted the passage in 2 Esdras 14:46 which refers to the seventy esoteric scriptural books restored to Ezra by divine revelation, and he claimed to have purchased Latin versions of them which he carefully studied. Which books these actually were remains unclear.[11]

---

7. Some important discussions both of broad methodological problems and of the transmission of specific pseudepigrapha during this period can be found in James C. VanderKam and William Adler, eds., *The Jewish Apocalyptic Heritage in Early Christianity* (CRINT 3.4; Assen/Minneapolis, Minn.: Van Gorcum/Fortress, 1996) and Robert Alan Kraft, *Exploring the Scripturesque: Jewish Texts and Their Christian Contexts* (JSJSup 137; Leiden: Brill, 2009).

8. The reception history of the book of 2 Esdras is a happy exception to this generalization: it is covered in detail by Alastair Hamilton in *The Apocryphal Apocalypse: The Reception of the Second Book of Esdras (4 Ezra) from the Renaissance to the Enlightenment* (Oxford: Clarendon, 1999).

9. *Ibid.*, 27-29.

10. M. De Jonge, "Robert Grosseteste and the Testaments of the Twelve Patriarchs," *JTS* N.S. 42 (1991): 115-25.

11. Nathaniel Schmidt, "Traces of Early Acquaintance in Europe with the Book of Enoch," *JAOS* 42 (1922): 44-52.

In the early 1580s the English scholar and magus John Dee undertook an experiment with his "scryer," who went by the name of Edward Kelley, to try to acquire otherwise inaccessible knowledge by means of invoking and interrogating angels. Kelley, by peering into his "seer stone," mediated numerous conversations between these angels and Dee, and Dee left detailed transcripts of these encounters. He was told that the lost books of Esdras were still in the hands of the Jews. He was also told that he would be shown the lost books of Enoch quoted by Jude, but there is no record of this happening. Instead, the angels dictated a lengthy revelatory book called *Liber Loagaeth*, which was to restore all the lost holy books. Unfortunately, it is written in an "angelic" language (called "Enochian" by later followers of Dee) and, apart from a word or two here and there, no translation was ever forthcoming.[12]

Despite these and other setbacks, some real progress was made in the search for the lost Enochic literature with Joseph Scaliger's publication of Syncellus's Greek excerpts of the Book of the Watchers (part of the book of *1 Enoch*) in 1606, which effectively reintroduced them to the West. Scaliger's edition generated much discussion and led in turn to Johann Ernest Grabe's 1698-99 Greek edition and Latin translation of both the *Testaments of the Twelve Patriarchs* and the then extant fragments of *1 Enoch*.[13]

During this period a gradual recognition developed that these documents were not actually composed by their reputed authors and in fact were written much later than the times when those authors were said to have lived. Grabe, for example, had a very sensible discussion of the authorship of the *Testaments* in which he argued that it was a pre-Christian Jewish work with Christian interpolations, a position still maintained by some today. The authenticity of 2 Esdras had been stridently debated since the time of the fifth-century church father Jerome, but a critical mass of serious historical-critical work on it developed in the late seventeenth century and Grabe and others confirmed that it was a late pseudepigraphon.[14] A century earlier Johannes Opsopoeus, capitalizing on important text-critical work done on the recently-recovered first eight books of the Greek *Sibylline Oracles*, demonstrated on historical-critical and philological grounds that these *Oracles* must be after-the-fact prophecies from the Hellenistic period.[15]

The first modern collection of Old Testament pseudepigrapha was published in the early eighteenth century by the prolific German polymath Johann Albert Fabricius, who also published, among many other things, vast histories of Greek and Latin literature and an edition of New Testament apocrypha. Fabricius has the perhaps dubious honor of tying the term "pseudepigrapha" to these noncanonical Old Testament texts, seemingly inextricably, and in his two volumes of Old Testament pseudepigrapha, entitled *Codex pseudepigraphus Veteris Testamenti*, he published Latin translations (or the Latin texts) of

---

12. Joseph H. Peterson, ed., *John Dee's Five Books of Mystery: Original Sourcebook of Enochian Magic* (York Beach, Maine: Weiser, 2003), 31-32, 354-55.

13. Ariel Hessayon, "Og King of Bashan, Enoch and the Books of Enoch: Extra-Canonical Texts and Interpretations of Genesis 6:1-4," in *Scripture and Scholarship in Early Modern England* (ed. Ariel Hessayon and Nicholas Keene; Aldershot, England: Ashgate, 2006), 5-40, esp. pp. 31-40.

14. Hamilton, *Apocryphal Apocalypse*, 225-48.

15. Anthony Grafton, "Higher Criticism Ancient and Modern: The Lamentable Deaths of Hermes and the Sibyls," in *The Uses of Greek and Latin: Historical Essays* (ed. A. C. Dionisotti, Anthony Grafton, and Jill Kraye; London: Warburg Institute, University of London, 1988), 155-70, esp. pp. 165-70. These conclusions about the date of the Sibylline Oracles were also reinforced in the late seventeenth century. See Hamilton, *Apocryphal Apocalypse*, 243.

more than three hundred documents or quotations of documents.[16] Among them were the Latin text of *2 Esdras* and the surviving Greek texts of the *Testaments of the Twelve Patriarchs, 1 Enoch*, and the *Sibylline Oracles*. (The term *pseudepigraphus* was not a neutral one for Fabricius; he makes it clear in the volume that he considered the works therein to be fraudulent tales worthy only of universal contempt.) Many of his texts are included in later collections, although many other pseudepigrapha were recovered only after his time. Between the time of Fabricius's publication and the mid-nineteenth century there were no further attempts at a systematic collection of pseudepigrapha, although some work was done on individual books, particularly on the Ethiopic text of *1 Enoch,* which was reintroduced to the West in 1773 by the Scottish explorer James Bruce. In the second half of the nineteenth century, J. P. Migne published a translation of Old Testament "apocrypha" (i.e., pseudepigrapha) and New Testament apocrypha in French, and numerous other studies of individual pseudepigrapha preserved in many different languages were published by many different scholars.[17] In 1891 William John Deane published a volume that introduced and discussed many of the texts that were known at the time, although it only occasionally translated excerpts of these texts.[18] The next attempt at a systematic collection came at the beginning of the twentieth century, when E. Kautsch published his German translation of Old Testament Apocrypha and pseudepigrapha.[19] His volume of pseudepigrapha was much less comprehensive than Fabricius's collection but it included works unknown to Fabricius. R. H. Charles edited two volumes of translations of Old Testament Apocrypha and pseudepigrapha into English in 1913, his collection of pseudepigrapha being somewhat larger than Kautzsch's.[20] And in 1920, M. R. James published *The Lost Apocrypha of the Old Testament*, which collected references to and quotations from otherwise lost Old Testament pseudepigrapha.[21]

With the onset of the First World War the study of the pseudepigrapha languished,

---

16. J. A. Fabricius, *Codex pseudepigraphus Veteris Testamenti* (Hamburg and Leipzig, 1713 [2nd ed. Hamburg, 1723]). See Annette Yoshiko Reed, "The Modern Invention of 'Old Testament Pseudepigrapha,'" *JTS* N.S. 60 (2009): 403-36 for an authoritative treatment of Fabricius's contribution to pseudepigrapha studies and its historical context in the Renaissance.

17. J. P. Migne, *Dictionnaire des apocryphes, ou, collection de tous les livres apocryphes relatifs à l'Ancien et au Nouveau Testament* (Paris, 1856-58). For a survey of scholarly research on the Old Testament pseudepigrapha from Fabricius to the 1970s, see James H. Charlesworth, "A History of Pseudepigrapha Research: The Re-emerging Importance of the Pseudepigrapha," *ANRW* II.19.1 (Berlin/New York, 1979): 54-88.

18. William John Deane, *Pseudepigrapha: An Account of Certain Apocryphal Sacred Writings of the Jews and Early Christians* (Edinburgh: T.&T. Clark, 1891). Deane covered the *Psalms of Solomon, 1 Enoch*, the *Assumption of Moses, 2 Baruch*, the *Testaments of the Twelve Patriarchs, Jubilees*, the *Ascension of Isaiah*, and the *Sibylline Oracles*.

19. E. Kautzsch, ed., *Die Apokryphen und Pseudepigraphen des Alten Testaments* (2 vols.; Tübingen: Mohr Siebeck, 1900). Kautzsch translated all the books covered by Deane (except that only excerpts of the *Ascension of Isaiah* are included as the putative original core Jewish work, the *Martyrdom of Isaiah*). In addition he included the *Letter of Aristeas, 4 Maccebees, 4 Ezra, 3 Baruch*, and the *Life of Adam and Eve*.

20. R. H. Charles, ed., *The Apocrypha and Pseudepigrapha of the Old Testament in English: With Introductions and Critical and Explanatory Notes to the Several Books* (2 vols.; Oxford: Clarendon, 1913). Charles translated all the books in Kautzsch's corpus and added *2 Enoch, Ahiqar*, and the highly dubious additions of *Pirqe Avot*, a tractate from the Mishnah, and the Cairo Geniza fragments of the Damascus Document ("a Zadokite Work"), a legal document with no attribution to an Old Testament character or setting. Fragments of this document were later found among the Dead Sea Scrolls and it is now known to be a Qumran sectarian text.

21. M. R. James, *The Lost Apocrypha of the Old Testament: Their Titles and Fragments* (London: SPCK, 1920).

with relatively few publications in the next half-century, although two major manuscript discoveries in the 1940s ultimately fueled a new interest. The Dead Sea Scrolls, found in caves near the Wadi Qumran, comprised a massive library of Jewish texts from around the turn of the Era in Hebrew, Aramaic, and Greek. Among them were very poorly preserved manuscripts of the original Hebrew of *Jubilees*; of the original Aramaic of some of the books included in *1 Enoch*; of *Aramaic Levi*, known already from the Cairo Geniza; and of another Enochic Aramaic work called the *Book of Giants*, known from Medieval Manichaean manuscript fragments. Small fragments of numerous other pseudepigrapha associated with the Hebrew Bible were also found at Qumran, confirming that much of this ancient literature has been lost.[22] At around the same time the Coptic Gnostic library of texts recovered from Nag Hammadi in upper Egypt brought to light a number of otherwise lost Old Testament pseudepigrapha and New Testament apocrypha, some of which had been known from references to them by ancient authors.[23]

It took time for these new discoveries to translate into momentum in the field, and research on the pseudepigrapha only began to pick up again in the 1970s. This decade inaugurated a monograph series with Brill, the *Studia in Veteris Testamenti Pseudepigrapha*, with a major introduction to the Greek pseudepigrapha by A.-M. Denis,[24] as well as the German translation and commentary series *Jüdische Schriften aus hellenistisch-römischer Zeit*, with many volumes on individual pseudepigrapha. An important bibliographic survey by James H. Charlesworth also appeared in this decade.[25] The founding of the *Journal for the Study of Judaism in the Persian, Hellenistic and Roman Period* in 1970 also provided a new venue for pseudepigrapha studies.[26]

The true renaissance of the field came about in the 1980s with the publication of two major collections in English. In 1984, the Clarendon Press published a new and extensively expanded and updated successor to Charles's *Pseudepigrapha* volume, edited by H. F. D. Sparks. And the largest and most influential collection is, of course, the two volumes edited by Charlesworth in 1983-86, which contain translations of forty-eight substantially complete texts and another sixteen texts that survive only in quotations or very fragmentary manuscripts.[27] The Sparks and Charlesworth collections are the giants in the

---

22. Major English translations of the Dead Sea Scrolls include Florentino García Martínez, *The Dead Sea Scrolls Translated: The Qumran Texts in English* (2nd ed.; Leiden: Brill, 1997) and Geza Vermes, *The Complete Dead Sea Scrolls in English* (Rev. ed.; London/New York: Penguin, 2004).

23. Major English translations of the Nag Hammadi library include James M. Robinson, ed., *The Nag Hammadi Library in English* (3rd ed.; San Francisco: Harper & Row, 1988) and Marvin Meyer, ed., *The Nag Hammadi Scriptures: The International Edition* (New York: HarperOne, 2007). Other earlier manuscript discoveries also provided new information about already-known pseudepigrapha. For example, large portions of the Greek translation of *1 Enoch* were recovered from a grave in Egypt in 1887-88 and in the Chester Beatty collection of Greek manuscripts in the early twentieth century. A few fragments of the *Apocryphon of Ezekiel* were also found in the latter. In the late nineteenth century the Egyptian site of Oxyrhynchus produced a vast mass of manuscripts from which were recovered small fragments of the (original?) Greek versions of *2 Baruch*, *6 Ezra*, and the Greek text of *1 Enoch*.

24. Albert-Marie Denis, *Introduction aux pseudépigraphes grecs d'ancien Testament* (SVTP 1; Leiden: Brill, 1970). The same publisher began the *Pseudepigrapha Veteris Testamenti Graecae* series in 1964.

25. James H. Charlesworth et al., *The Pseudepigrapha and Modern Research, with a Supplement* (Chico, Calif.: Scholars Press, 1981 [1st ed. Missoula, Mont.: Scholars Press, 1976]).

26. For a survey of the state of pseudepigrapha studies in the early 1970s, see James H. Charlesworth, "The Renaissance of Pseudepigrapha Studies: The SBL Pseudepigrapha Project," *JSJ* 2 (1971): 107-14.

27. H. F. D. Sparks, *The Apocryphal Old Testament* (Oxford: Clarendon, 1984); James H. Charlesworth, ed., *The Old Testament Pseudepigrapha*, vol. 1, *Apocalyptic Literature and Testaments*, vol. 2, *Expansions of*

field upon whose shoulders the current project stands. They brought the Old Testament pseudepigrapha into popular consciousness and generated and influenced an enormous amount of scholarly study.[28]

Since the early 1980s the study of the pseudepigrapha has burgeoned. Innumerable articles and monographs have been published on both specific texts and wider issues. The *Journal for the Study of the Pseudepigrapha* was founded in 1988. Brepols Publishers inaugurated the Corpus Christianorum Series Apocryphorum, which publishes editions and French translations of Old Testament pseudepigrapha and New Testament apocrypha, in 1983, and Walter de Gruyter Publishers have been producing volumes of a new commentary series, Commentaries on Early Jewish Literature, since 2003. Denis's introduction has been republished in a second, vastly expanded edition.[29] And two new major bibliographic resources have been published as well: Haelewyck's *Clavis Apocryphorum veteris testamenti* provides details of editions and translations of a vast number of texts and DiTommaso's *A Bibliography of Pseudepigrapha Research 1850-1999* lists virtually all scholarly publications on a similar range of texts.[30]

This Collection

It was in this rich atmosphere of scholarly accomplishment that the More Old Testament Pseudepigrapha Project was conceived in 2002, when it became clear to the chief editors that a new collection of Old Testament pseudepigrapha was urgently needed.[31] Most of the texts in this volume and the one that is to follow have not been included in any other recent collection of pseudepigrapha.[32] The texts represent a wide range of genres and origins. Many of them are complete or substantially complete, but a number are fragmentary, either because the manuscripts in which they survive are very poorly preserved or because they are entirely lost apart from references and quotations in the works of later writers.[33] Some of the works in our corpus are already well known by specialists but not by the general public. These include, for example, *Aramaic Levi*, the *Book of Giants*, *The Book of the Mysteries*, the *Cave of Treasures*, and the *Eighth Book of Moses*. Some texts were published some time ago but are not even widely known among specialists interested in such things. Examples are the Greek *Apocryphon of Jacob and Joseph*, the *Tiburtine Sibyl*, the Arabic *Surid Legend* of the post-Flood building of the Egyptian pyramids, and the Syriac *History of Joseph*. (A translation of the latter in a secondary Ethiopic version was

the "Old Testament" and Legends, Wisdom and Philosophical Literature, Prayers, Psalms, and Odes, Fragments of Lost Judeo-Hellenistic Works (Garden City, N.Y.: Doubleday, 1983, 1985). A perceptive combined review of both editions was published by Kraft in 1988 and is reprinted with additions in *Exploring the Scripturesque*, 93-106.

28. Collections of Old Testament pseudepigrapha have also been published in numerous other modern languages, including Spanish, Italian, French, Modern Hebrew, Modern Greek, Danish, and Japanese.

29. Denis, ed., *Introduction à la littérature religieuse judéo-hellénistique: Pseudépigraphes de l'Ancien Testament* (2 vols.; Turnhout: Brepols, 2000).

30. J.-C. Haelewyck, *Clavis Apocryphorum veteris testamenti* (Brepols: Turnhout, 1998); Lorenzo DiTommaso, *A Bibliography of Pseudepigrapha Research 1850-1999* (JSPSup 39; Sheffield, England: Sheffield Academic Press, 2001).

31. The More Old Testament Pseudepigrapha Project was supported by a generous research grant from the Leverhulme Trust which allowed the Project to hire co-editor Dr. Alexander Panayotov as a research fellow for three years from 2005 to 2008.

32. Fabricius included some of them in his collection.

33. The independent existence of the works apparently behind some of these quotation fragments is speculative, but we judged the case for these at least to be worth presenting.

published by Ephraim Isaac in the *Journal for the Study of the Pseudepigrapha* in 1990. The Syriac original had been published in the nineteenth century, but was only recently rediscovered by Kristian Heal.) Some of the texts, but not many, were first published or even first discovered only after the Sparks and Charlesworth collections had been published. These include the Aramaic *Song of the Lamb*, the Hebrew *Revelation of Gabriel*, a number of texts and fragments from the Cairo Geniza, and the very new and as yet unpublished Coptic fragments of *2 Enoch*.

The previous collections of pseudepigrapha, going all the way back to that by Fabricius, have set various precedents and laid out various templates for how to organize and present the texts. The editors of this collection have taken this background into account, with special attention to the recent monumental volumes edited by Sparks and Charlesworth, in order to provide a compendium that is intelligible both to specialists in cognate fields and to the general public, while advancing our understanding of the current state of the question and maintaining the integrity of the work for specialists in noncanonical biblical literature.

Deciding on a title for this collection proved to be a surprisingly difficult task, and the title we eventually settled on, *Old Testament Pseudepigrapha: More Noncanonical Scriptures*, requires some explanation. The observant reader will note a missing word that distinguishes our title from that of the Charlesworth corpus: ours omits the definite article. We leave it off to make clear that this is not a definitive collection. There is no canon of Old Testament pseudepigrapha. Further delving into archaeological sites, museum and library collections, and old journals will doubtless uncover more texts and in all likelihood will lead to someone publishing more volumes than the two planned by us at present.[34] We retain "Old Testament," first, because combined with "Pseudepigrapha" it will evoke the Charlesworth volumes in the minds of much of our nonspecialist audience and so provide them immediately with a familiar context. Second, the term "Old Testament" is, for better or for worse, more broadly known and understood by the public than "Hebrew Bible." We use it here, of course, without any reference to the traditional theological agenda behind it. Third, "Old Testament" is a more accurate designation in that many of the texts were either composed or transmitted by Christians and were thus regarded as relating to the Old Testament rather than the Hebrew Bible, and some of the texts retell stories from the Old Testament Apocrypha and so are not technically pseudepigrapha of the Hebrew Bible. We retain "Pseudepigrapha" despite its unsatisfactory associations, because none of the proposed replacement terms ("parabiblical literature," "parascriptural literature," "scripturesque remnants," etc.) yet commands general acceptance or is as widely recognized by the public. As for the subtitle, the "More" indicates that this collection is additional to the Charlesworth corpus, not a re-publication or a replacement. And "Noncanonical Scriptures" aims at clarifying the subject of the book for those not immediately familiar with the idea of "pseudepigrapha." The title is an unsatisfactory compromise, but anything more precise would be more cumbersome, less clear to nonspecialists, and would have to resort to jargon whose value remains debated.

Our overall criteria for inclusion in our new pseudepigrapha corpus are somewhat more flexible, but at the same time more focused, than those that underlie the editions

34. Moreover, Old Testament pseudepigrapha continued to be produced throughout the Middle Ages and into the modern era. Collections of these later texts would be a valuable addition to our and the other collections of earlier texts.

of Sparks and Charlesworth. Notably, our principles for the selection of the texts to be published are formulated in an attempt to understand them on their own terms and not principally as background to the New Testament. First, with a few exceptions to be noted, we are limiting the corpus to texts for which a reasonable—if not necessarily conclusive—case can be made for a date of composition before the rise of Islam in the early seventh century C.E. The rise of Islam is one of the traditional cutoff points for the end of antiquity (the others are the fall of Rome ca. 400 and the reign of Charlemagne ca. 800), and we have chosen it mainly because the number of relevant texts rapidly increases after this and including them would make the corpus unworkably large. They are better dealt with as a corpus of medieval pseudepigrapha, a project we leave to others. Neither Sparks nor Charlesworth gives a specific upper cutoff date for their collections, although the range of probable dates of their texts is not dissimilar to ours.

Second, as for provenance, we are including texts of any origin, including Jewish, Christian, or indigenous polytheistic (i.e., "pagan") works. The Charlesworth volumes focused on Jewish texts or texts that preserved "ideas possibly characteristic of Early Judaism," as Charlesworth notes in his Editor's Preface (p. xv). In his Foreword, George W. MacRae characterizes the corpus as "ancient Jewish and Jewish-Christian documents" (p. ix). And Charlesworth, in his Introduction for the General Reader, characterizes them as revelatory writings "often attributed to ideal figures in Israel's past" and often based on Old Testament themes and narratives, which "with the exception of Ahiqar, are Jewish or Christian" and either date to between 200 B.C.E. to 200 C.E. or, if later, "apparently preserve, albeit in an edited form, Jewish traditions that date from that period" (p. xxv). The assumption seems thus to be that on some level the texts usually contain "Jewish traditions," whereas this is not a criterion for our new corpus of texts. Our approach is more similar to that of Sparks, who "thought it best to abandon the concept of 'background literature' entirely" and whose "single criterion for inclusion has been whether or not any particular item is attributed to (or is primarily concerned with the history or activities of) an Old Testament character (or characters)" (p. xv). We differ from Sparks, however, and follow Charlesworth in including both works of pagan origin and works about pagan figures such as the seers Hystaspes and the Sibyl whose setting is in the Old Testament period and who were, one might say, "adopted" into the biblical tradition by Jews and Christians.[35]

The determination of the provenance of a text, specifically whether it is Jewish, Christian, or other (e.g., indigenous polytheistic or Samaritan), is often a far from straightforward process. Texts surviving only in manuscripts of clearly Jewish origin can uncontroversially be assigned a Jewish provenance. The position of the editors is that texts found only in Christian manuscripts that circulated in Christian circles should be thought of as Christian compositions unless a convincing positive case can be made for a different origin. In other words, we should understand the texts first in the social context of their earliest surviving manuscripts and move backwards from there only on the basis of positive evidence. Evidence for Jewish origin may include internal evidence for a pre-Christian date combined with informed interest on Jewish matters; compelling linguistic evidence for original composition in Hebrew; and a consistent pattern of sympathetic in-

35. Other such works would include *Ahiqar*, a court tale about an Assyrian sage published in the Charlesworth corpus, and *Zostrianos*, an apocalypse in the name of the Iranian prophet Zoroaster found in the Nag Hammadi library.

terest in Jewish ritual and *halakha* and Jewish ethnic and national interests. Contributors to this project were encouraged to keep these issues in mind, but in the end attributions of provenance were the decisions of the individual contributors translating the individual texts. Documents such as the *Balaam Text from Deir Alla*, the *Eighth Book of Moses*, and the *Phylactery of Moses* are assigned an indigenous polytheistic provenance on the basis of their archaeological or textual context and their content.[36] The collection does not aim to determine provenance conclusively in every case.

Third, for purely practical reasons we exclude for the most part texts that fit best in and survive only in other thematically coherent or traditional collections of works that have been treated (or deserve treatment) on their own terms. These include the Old Testament Apocrypha, the Dead Sea Scrolls, the Coptic Gnostic works of the Nag Hammadi library, the ancient Greco-Egyptian mystical works of the Hermetic corpus, the Greco-Egyptian incantations of the Greek Magical Papyri, and the Jewish mystical texts known as the Hekhalot Literature. Most of these are already available in at least one good English translation.[37] We do include one substantial text from the Greek Magical Papyri, the *Eighth Book of Moses*, because, although this corpus of texts is available in an excellent English translation, we felt that study of this particular document would benefit from an introduction and translation that treated it specifically as a biblical pseudepigraphon. We also include a few texts of which fragments have been found among the Dead Sea Scrolls (*Aramaic Levi*, *Hebrew Naphtali* traditions, an exorcistic *Song of David*, and the *Book of Giants*), but only when the texts are also known from much later medieval manuscripts.

Fourth, we are not including texts published already in the Sparks or Charlesworth volumes unless we have important new manuscript data or we believe that the text requires a new treatment for other reasons. We draw on new or previously unused manuscript data for our publication of fragments of the *Life of Adam and Eve* (Coptic), the *Horarium of Adam* (Arabic, Georgian, Syriac), the *Treatise of Shem* (Aramaic and Judeo-Arabic), *2 Enoch* (Coptic), the *Ladder of Jacob* (Hebrew), the *Testament of Job* (Coptic), and the *Testament of Solomon* (the Greek Vienna manuscript, the earliest manuscript, which is of considerable interest on its own terms). We revisit the *Assumption/Testament of Moses* and *Apocryphon of Ezekiel* with new fragments. We publish a longer and earlier version of the Latin *Vision of Ezra*. The short books of *5-6 Ezra* were translated by Bruce Metzger as part of *4 Ezra* in the Charlesworth corpus but were given no introduction. We include them treated as works in their own right. We also include a translation of Armenian *4 Ezra* as a work in itself, since it is of considerable interest for the history of the interpretation of this ancient apocalypse.

Fifth, we have included a number of texts that were written in the form we have them

---

36. For a comprehensive treatment of issues of provenance, see James R. Davila, *The Provenance of the Pseudepigrapha: Jewish, Christian, or Other?* (JSJSup 105; Leiden: Brill, 2005). For a brief popular article covering the same ground, see Davila, "The Old Testament Pseudepigrapha as Background to the New Testament," *ExpTim* 117 (2005): 53-57.

37. Translations of the Apocrypha are available in many Bibles. Translations of the Dead Sea Scrolls and the Nag Hammadi library have been noted above. For the Hermetic corpus and the Greek Magical Papyri, see Brian P. Copenhaver, *Hermetica: The Greek Corpus Hermeticum and the Latin Asclepius in a New English Translation, with Notes and Introduction* (Cambridge: Cambridge University Press, 1992) and Hans Dieter Betz, ed., *The Greek Magical Papyri in Translation, Including the Demotic Spells* (2nd ed.; Chicago: University of Chicago Press, 1985). For English translations of the Hekhalot literature see P. Alexander, "3 (Hebrew Apocalypse of) Enoch," in *OTP* 1:223-315, and James R. Davila, *Hekhalot Literature in Translation: Major Texts of Merkavah Mysticism* (Supplements to the Journal of Jewish Thought and Philosophy 20; Leiden: Brill, 2013).

well after the early seventh century, but which clearly either preserve earlier material or have a close relationship with such material. These include the *Cave of Treasures*; the *Palaea Historica*; nine Hebrew and Aramaic texts containing visions of hell and paradise collected and translated by Moses Gaster in 1893 and retranslated by Helen Spurling here; and the *Treatise of the Vessels*, a Hebrew work of undetermined date which tells legends about where certain leaders at the time of the Babylonian destruction of the First Temple hid the Temple vessels and paraphernalia and which has notable parallels to the Qumran Copper Scroll and ancient folklore about the Temple treasures.

Sixth is the problem of in what order to present the texts. There are two precedents in earlier collections. Fabricius and Sparks listed them by the name of the relevant Old Testament character in the traditional biblical chronological order, whereas Kautzsch, Charles, and Charlesworth arranged them according to genre, then by name of character in the biblical order. For a number of reasons we have chosen to follow the precedent of Fabricius and Sparks. In practical terms this gave us flexibility to publish a volume once we had received a sufficient number of contributions, although we did give some attention as well to balancing the content of the two volumes. This approach also leaves the number of volumes open-ended, although at present we do not have plans to publish more than two. In addition listing the texts this way sidesteps the problem of establishing the genre of a text (a matter that can become complex and is best left to a nuanced discussion in the introduction to each document). This biblical ordering by name (or in some cases, event) does not serve for thematic texts that cover a long span of biblical history and deal with many characters or which are set primarily in an eschatological framework. We have relegated such thematic texts to their own separate section of the collection and ordered them according to the period of time they cover.[38]

Importance of This Collection

Old Testament pseudepigrapha are of value and importance across a range of areas both of general interest and of academic study and research. In the modern period they have been studied mainly by scholars and students interested either in the Jewish history and religion of the late Second Temple period (from ca. 200 B.C.E. to 135 C.E.) or in Christian origins and the New Testament. It is, of course, their importance for our understanding of Judaism that has made them also of considerable importance for New Testament studies, since it was in the context of late Second Temple Judaism that Christianity originated and developed in the earliest period. Those of the Old Testament pseudepigrapha that are Jewish works from before 135 C.E. constitute one of the five major bodies of extant Jewish literature from that period (the others are the Dead Sea Scrolls, some of the Old Testament Apocrypha, and the works of Josephus and Philo). They have, for example, helped us to appreciate better the diversity of Jewish belief and practice in that period. They have also helped to make increasingly clear how Jewish the New Testament writings are and how they relate to the spectrum of sorts of Judaism that composed the Jewish world of that period. Within New Testament studies, they have sometimes been abused by scholars who have merely plundered them for parallels to the language and ideas of the New Testament writing. They must, of course, be properly understood in their literary integrity and in

38. The *Cave of Treasures* and the *Palaea Historica* both begin with creation; the *Quotations of Lost Books in the Hebrew Bible* are set in the pre-exilic period of Israel's history; and the *Hebrew Visions of Hell and Paradise* deal mainly with eschatology.

their context in early Judaism before they can function usefully as evidence for the Jewish context in which Jesus lived and in which Christianity originated and developed. But, understood in that way, they can do much to illuminate those very Jewish documents that comprise the New Testament.[39]

It would be easy to list a substantial body of Old Testament pseudepigrapha that all or almost all scholars agree are Jewish works of that period,[40] but there are others, included in the major collections (such as Charlesworth's), whose date and provenance are uncertain and disputed. Some of these have been treated by many scholars as important resources for the study of late Second Temple Judaism and earliest Christianity but have been treated with much more reserve by other scholars.[41] Much more work on the affinities and textual transmission of such works still needs to be done.

Within the present collection (both this volume and the forthcoming second volume) there are some texts whose relevance to the study of Judaism up to 135 C.E. and of Christian origins and early development is clear. These are works whose early Jewish provenance is well established. They include *Aramaic Levi*, the Hebrew fragments of the *Testament of Naphtali*, the *Book of Giants*, and the fragments of the *Apocryphon of Ezekiel*. There are others whose editors and translators in the present collection argue probably originated within late Second Temple Judaism, including the *Songs of David*, the *Nine and a Half Tribes*, the *Coptic Jeremiah Apocryphon*, the *Horarium of Adam*, the pseudo-Philonic *Sermons on Jonah, Samson and God*, and the fragments of the *Greek Apocalypse of Elijah* and of *the Testament of Moses*. These arguments require discussion and assessment by other scholars, especially since, like many of the texts in the present collection, they have so far received very little attention from scholars. There are also works that, while as such they are of later origin, likely contain sources or traditions that date from the Second Temple period. These include the *Book of Noah*, the *Aramaic Song of the Lamb*, and the *Hebrew Visions of Heaven and Hell*. Of course, only with considerable caution and methodological awareness can the evidence of such works be utilized in the study of Second Temple Judaism. Also noteworthy in this connection is the fact that the present collection includes new textual evidence for works whose early Jewish provenance has been widely accepted but is also seriously disputed: the Coptic fragments of the *Testament of Job*, the *Life of Adam and Eve*, and *2 Enoch*.

Since scholarly interest in Old Testament pseudepigrapha has focused very largely on their importance for the study of Second Temple Judaism and earliest Christianity, previ-

39. See Richard Bauckham, "The Relevance of Extra-Canonical Jewish Texts to New Testament Study," in *Hearing the New Testament: Strategies for Interpretation* (ed. Joel B. Green; Grand Rapids, Mich.: Eerdmans, 2010), 65-84. A recent collection of essays relating various Old Testament pseudepigrapha to New Testament texts is *The Pseudepigrapha and Christian Origins: Essays from the Studiorum Novi Testamenti Societas* (ed. Gerbern S. Oegema and James H. Charlesworth; T. & T. Clark Jewish and Christian Texts Series; London: T. & T. Clark, 2008).

40. *1 Enoch, Jubilees, Testament of Moses, 4 Ezra, 2 Baruch,* Pseudo-Philo's *Liber Antiquitatum Biblicarum, Letter of Aristeas, 3 Maccabees, 4 Maccabees, Sibylline Oracles* book 3, *Psalms of Solomon* is a minimal list.

41. Davila, *The Provenance of the Pseudepigrapha*, building on the work of Robert Kraft, develops a methodology for distinguishing works of early Jewish provenance, and concludes that a number of Old Testament pseudepigrapha that are widely treated as early Jewish may well be of originally Christian provenance (e.g., *Testament of Abraham, Testament of Job, Joseph and Aseneth*). See also Richard Bauckham, "The Continuing Quest for the Provenance of Old Testament Pseudepigrapha," in *The Pseudepigrapha* (ed. Oegema and Charlesworth), 9-29.

ous collections of Old Testament pseudepigrapha have tended to prioritize those works that arguably date from that period, while often including also admittedly later works that may contain earlier sources or traditions. There has probably also been a tendency for scholars working on Old Testament pseudepigraphal texts to be optimistic in their arguments for an early date and Jewish provenance, whether of the works themselves or of their sources, and insufficiently attentive to aspects of the texts that might suggest a later date and/or Christian provenance. The present collection is different, in that importance for the study of Second Temple Judaism and the New Testament has not been a criterion for including texts in the collection. The editors have taken a much broader view of the value and importance of Old Testament pseudepigrapha.

Such a broader view is necessary partly because the transmission and writing of Old Testament pseudepigrapha continued without any obvious break at the end of the first century C.E. or in the early part of the second. Certainly there were major developments that could not but have some impact on the transmission and writing of Old Testament pseudepigrapha. The destruction of the Jerusalem Temple in 70 C.E. and the failure of the second great Jewish revolt against Rome in 135 CE were traumatic events that permanently affected the character of Judaism, while the gradual rise of rabbinic Judaism to dominance accompanied decreasing diversity in the Jewish world. The gradual "parting of the ways" between Judaism and Christianity in the same period (a process whose chronology and significance continues to be a topic of scholarly debate)[42] also changed the nature of the contexts in which Old Testament pseudepigrapha were transmitted and composed. Some of the Old Testament pseudepigrapha of Christian origin and some of those adapted by Christian editors bear the marks of that great division. One further factor was the growing awareness of canonical limits defining the Hebrew Bible or, as Christians now called it, the Old Testament (though, again, there is scholarly debate about the process of canonization). In both Judaism and Christianity this could not but affect the status of Old Testament pseudepigraphal writings, but it certainly did not put an end either to their use or to their composition.

In the case of Christianity in the early centuries—the so-called patristic period—the importance of Old Testament pseudepigrapha has often been underestimated. It remains a remarkable fact that almost all of such works that were composed in the Second Temple period have reached us only because they were used and copied by Christians (pseudepigraphal works included among the Dead Sea Scrolls are, of course, exceptions, as are a few Geniza texts, such as *Aramaic Levi*). With regard to those works we should remember that, therefore, they represent essentially a Christian selection of Old Testament pseudepigrapha from the Second Temple period. Notably absent are works of interpretation of Torah (halakah) of the kind that we do find among the Dead Sea Scrolls (for example, the Temple Scroll, which is a Mosaic pseudepigraphon). Christians had no use for Jewish halakah (though some was preserved in *Jubilees*, which interested them for other reasons). Another casualty of Christian selection may be prophetic or apocalyptic works that emphasized a strongly militant form of messianic expectation (such as we find in the *War Scroll* from Qumran), whereas Christians did preserve Jewish works of eschatological prophecy whose messianic expectations could more easily be related to belief in Jesus as the Messiah (these included some of the Enochic literature as well as *2 Baruch* and

42. Adam H. Becker and Annette Yoshiko Reed, eds., *The Ways That Never Parted: Jews and Christians in Late Antiquity and the Early Middle Ages* (TSAJ 95; Tübingen: Mohr Siebeck, 2003).

4 Ezra). Early Christians certainly seem to have had a considerable appetite for para-biblical stories about Old Testament characters, which many of the Old Testament pseudepigrapha from the Second Temple period provided, just as they also valued a growing body of extra-canonical literature about Jesus and the apostles.

Old Testament pseudepigrapha were more valued by Christians at some times and in some contexts than others. Scholars and theologians of Alexandria—Clement, Origen, Didymus the Blind—knew a remarkably wide range of such works and quoted them even when, at the same time, they cast doubts on their authority. The present collection includes some works that we only know because they quote or allude to them (the *Book of the Covenant*, the *Dispute over Abraham*, the *Greek Apocalypse of Elijah*). The Christian chronographers, beginning with Julius Africanus, were interested in works that provided them with resources for ancient history, and could make use of some Old Testament pseudepigrapha without regarding them as Scripture, in the same way that they used the *Antiquities* of Josephus.[43] Christian writers, especially from the late fourth century onwards (following the 39th Festal Letter of Athanasius, 367 C.E.), were often concerned to insist on the canon of the Old and New Testaments as defining the only authoritative Scriptures of the Catholic Church and in that connection they condemned apocryphal works of all kinds. But nevertheless some Old Testament pseudepigrapha continued to be copied and remained popular even through the Middle Ages in both the Latin West and the Greek East,[44] not to mention the Old Irish tradition and the diverse linguistic-cultural traditions of eastern Christianity—Armenian, Syriac, Arabic, Coptic, Ethiopic—which have preserved many such works that have been lost in their original Semitic or Greek versions. Though occasionally such works were regarded as canonical (such as *1 Enoch* and *Jubilees* in the Ethiopian Orthodox church), in most cases they must have been regarded as interesting or instructive even though not Scripture. In addition to preserving Old Testament pseudepigrapha from the Second Temple period, we should remember that Christians sometimes revised and edited such works to a greater or lesser extent.

Moreover, Christians actively continued the tradition of writing Old Testament pseudepigrapha. (The earliest such Christian writing is probably the *Ascension of Isaiah*, which may be as early as the end of the first century.) Of the works included in the present collection, at least the following (and probably more) were composed by Christian authors from the second to the sixth centuries: the *Apocryphon of Seth*, the *Story of Melchizedek*, the *Syriac History of Joseph*, the *Tiburtine Sibyl*, the *Questions of the Queen of Sheba*, *Jeremiah's Prophecy to Passhur*, the *Relics of Zechariah*, *5 Ezra*, *6 Ezra*, *6*, *7* and *8 Maccabees*, the *Cave of Treasures*, the *Seventh Vision of Daniel*, and the various other apocalyptic works ascribed to Daniel. Some of the major genres of the older pseudepigrapha are represented here: rewritten Scripture, Sibylline prophecy, historical-eschatological apocalypses, expansions of Old Testament narrative. In many ways Christians continued to write the *same kind* of Old Testament pseudepigrapha as had been written by Jewish authors in

---

43. William Adler, "Jacob of Edessa and the Jewish Pseudepigrapha in Syriac Chronography," in *Tracing the Threads: Studies in the Vitality of Jewish Pseudepigrapha* (ed. John C. Reeves; SBLEJL 6; Atlanta, Ga.: Scholars Press, 1994), 143-71; idem, *Time Immemorial: Archaic History and Its Sources in Christian Chronography from Julius Africanus to George Syncellus* (Dumbarton Oaks Studies 26; Washington, D.C.: Dunbarton Oaks Research Library, 1989).

44. For example, the *Life of Adam and Eve* was well known in medieval Europe: see Brian Murdoch, *The Apocryphal Adam and Eve in Medieval Europe: Vernacular Translations and Adaptations of the* Vita Adae et Evae (Oxford: Oxford University Press, 2009).

the Second Temple period. They continued to do so through the medieval period, and the limitation of the present collection largely to texts dating from before 600 C.E. is an artificial but a necessary convenience, precisely because so many other, later works would have to be included if we had not imposed such a limit.

At this point, it is worth noting that the distinction between Old Testament pseudepigrapha and New Testament apocrypha can be somewhat misleading, because some of the latter are also the same kind of literature as Old Testament pseudepigrapha from the Second Temple period, differing only in being ascribed to a figure from the New Testament. Christian apocalypses ascribed to Peter, Paul or the Virgin Mary are no less continuous with older apocalyptic writings than are those ascribed to Daniel or Ezra. Similarly, works such as the *Protevangelium of James* and the *Infancy Gospel of Thomas* are expansions of New Testament narrative[45] just as the *Story of Melchizedek* and *Joseph and Aseneth* are of Old Testament narrative. The Old/New boundary is entirely absent in the case of the *Apocryphon of Seth*, an expansion of New Testament narrative ascribed to an extremely ancient figure of the Old Testament!

Although there is much evidence of the use and composition of Old Testament pseudepigrapha by Christians in the patristic period, there are as yet no studies that attempt a general picture of the ways in which these books were used and by whom. Were they (or some of them) known largely only to scholars or to monks, or were they (or some of them) widely known through liturgical or catechetical use? Were some of them read largely for entertainment? Should we think of them as popular or learned literature (and which belong to which category)? Were some of them confined to heterodox or marginal groups? Did any of them feature in doctrinal disputes? To what extent were they accorded scriptural status in some contexts? Which of them were the more popular and why? Did they influence the exegesis of the Bible in preaching or commentaries? How far were some of them preserved as part of the hagiographical tradition? How far were developing views of the other world and the fate of the dead influenced by some of them? Are they reflected at all in the Christian art of this period? We know the answer to some of these questions in the case of particular pseudepigraphal works,[46] but the broad picture remains very uncertain. Further study is likely to reveal a quite complex picture of a diversity of uses of different pseudepigraphal works in a variety of contexts.

Whereas there is undoubtedly much continuity between the Old Testament pseudepigrapha of the Second Temple period and those of the patristic period in Christianity, discerning such continuity in the Jewish tradition is more problematic. From the surviving literature it would be quite easy to conclude that after 135 C.E. Jews neither continued to copy and use the already existing Old Testament pseudepigrapha (almost all of which, as we have noticed, were preserved by Christians) nor continued to write such works,

---

45. On the latter, see Tony Chartrand-Burke, "Completing the Gospel: *The Infancy Gospel of Thomas* as a Supplement to the Gospel of Luke," in *The Reception and Interpretation of the Bible in Late Antiquity* (ed. Lorenzo DiTommaso and Lucian Turcescu; Bible in Ancient Christianity 6; Leiden: Brill, 2008), 111-19.

46. See the valuable essays in *The Jewish Apocalyptic Heritage in Early Christianity*. Other significant studies include Gary A. Anderson, *The Genesis of Perfection: Adam and Eve in Jewish and Christian Imagination* (Louisville, Ky.: Westminster John Knox, 2001); Daniel C. Harlow, *The Greek* Apocalypse of Baruch *(3 Baruch) in Hellenistic Judaism and Early Christianity* (SVTP 12; Leiden: Brill, 1996); Annette Yoshiko Reed, *Fallen Angels and the History of Judaism and Christianity* (Cambridge: Cambridge University Press, 2005); Daniel Joslyn-Siemiatkoski, *Christian Memories of the Maccabean Martyrs* (New York: Palgrave Macmillan, 2009).

beginning to do so again only after ca. 500 C.E., when the later Jewish apocalypses began to be written (such as *3 Enoch, Visions of Ezekiel, Sefer Zerubbabel,* and the *Hebrew Apocalypse of Elijah,* though the dates of all these works are quite uncertain). Yet these works themselves often display continuity of genre and content with the Jewish literature of the Second Temple period. Although we should not underestimate the degree of literary exchange between Jews and Christians (we know that some Jewish works preserved by Christians were reclaimed and even translated into Hebrew in the medieval period), it is not plausible to account for such continuity solely or even largely in that way. Furthermore there are other Jewish works of the late antique and medieval periods that certainly preserve material from a much earlier period, some of it close to the content of known Old Testament pseudepigrapha from the Second Temple period, even though precise sources cannot be identified. (For this phenomenon within works in the present collection, see the *Book of Noah, Midrash Vayissa'u,* the *Hebrew Visions of Heaven and Hell,* and the *Midrash of Shemihazai and Azael*). There is also the possibility that some Old Testament pseudepigrapha preserved by Christians are originally Jewish works from the second to fourth centuries (of the works in the present collection, the *Latin Vision of Ezra* is one such possibility). Nevertheless the absence of Jewish manuscripts of or attestations of nearly all of late Second Temple Jewish literature remains puzzling. Continuity there must have been, but in what circles and by what channels is not yet clear.

Within biblical scholarship there is a fast developing interest in the *Wirkungsgeschichte* ("history of effects") of the biblical texts. The Old Testament pseudepigrapha—whether Jewish or Christian or of as yet uncertain provenance—deserve their place in this. Especially the works that belong in the category of "rewritten Scripture" are important evidence of the way the narratives of the Old Testament were re-appropriated, understood, and interpreted from the late Second Temple period onwards. These works preserve traditions of exegesis that developed to answer questions about the biblical text—to explain apparent difficulties in the text, to fill in gaps in the narratives, to forge connections between some narratives and others—by the ingenious exercise of literary and historical imagination as well as biblical learning.[47] They are exercises in biblical interpretation in a mode very different from formal midrash or commentary (the biblical text is not distinguished and the exegetical questions and reasoning are very often hidden), a mode that is likely to have been of much wider appeal to a popular audience. This is a category of pseudepigrapha that was probably not usually seen as competing with canonical Scripture, but was acceptable as an aid to understanding Scripture, rather as the Targums were in the Jewish tradition. To the well-known examples of rewritten Scripture from the Second Temple period—*Jubilees*, Pseudo-Philo's *Liber Antiquitatum Biblicarum*, Josephus' *Antiquities*—the present collection adds major later examples, including the *Syriac History of Joseph*, the *Coptic Jeremiah Apocryphon*, the *Cave of Treasures*, the *Palaea Historica* (so important as a compendium of such interpretation that we have included it despite its post-600 date), the later books of *Maccabees,* and *Midrash Vayissa'u*. These offer scholars and students the opportunity to study the phenomenon of "rewriting Scripture" over a much longer period than most studies have so far attempted.

The line between "rewritten Scripture" and expansions of Scripture, i.e., stories about

47. James L. Kugel, *Traditions of the Bible: A Guide to the Bible As It Was at the Start of the Common Era* (Cambridge, Mass.: Harvard University Press, 1998), chapter 1, is a good introduction. The rest of the book is a rich collection of the interpretative traditions that gathered around each phase of the biblical narrative.

biblical characters that are attached to the biblical narrative at only one point in that narrative, is not a very strict one. Some such expansions answer the same kind of exegetical questions that are often implicit in rewritten Scripture. For example, the *Questions of the Queen of Sheba* satisfies the curiosity of the reader of 1 Kings 10:2-3 by detailing what questions the Queen asked and how Solomon answered them. Similar works in the present collection include *Eldad and Modad*, the *Aramaic Song of the Lamb*, *Jeremiah's Prophecy to Passhur*, the *Manasseh Apocryphon*, and *Adam Octipartite*. These also have their place in the history of biblical interpretation.

A distinctive ingredient in the present collection is a kind of Old Testament pseudepigraphal literature—magical literature—that has been represented in previous collections only by the *Testament of Solomon* and the *Prayer of Jacob*. Our collection includes a variety of such works attributed to David and Solomon, well known respectively as exorcist and wise magician—the *Exorcistic Psalms of David*, the *Seledromion of David and Solomon*, the *Hygromancy of Solomon*, and a newly edited version of the *Testament of Solomon*—as well as the *Eighth Book of Moses*, which concerns the magical use of the divine name, the *Sword of Moses* (*Harba di-Moshe*), the *Book of Mysteries (Sefer ha-Razim)*, the *Adjuration of Elijah*, and the *Phylactery of Moses*. There is rich material here for the study of ancient and medieval magic.

An important feature of both Jewish and Christian religion in the ancient and medieval periods was the imaginative construction of the "other world"—the ascending sequence of heavens, with their various contents and angelic inhabitants, culminating in the throne-room of God in the highest heaven, and the places of the dead, paradise and hell, whether already populated with the dead or awaiting the dead after the last judgment.[48] The imagining of such places was richly funded by a genre of apocalypse in which a seer is taken on a tour of these other-worldly locations. Such apocalypses (including in the Christian tradition some attributed to New Testament figures: Peter, Paul, the Virgin Mary) were very popular, no doubt partly because there is so little of this kind within the Jewish and Christian scriptural canons. This may also be the reason why, despite their claim to authoritative revelation, they seem not usually to have been suppressed by religious authorities. The present collection contains some important examples of the genre, including some little-known ones. They include *2 Enoch* (the important new Coptic fragments), the *Latin Vision of Ezra* (a longer and older version), the *Visions of Ezekiel*, the *Hebrew Visions of Heaven and Hell*, the *Seven Heavens Apocryphon* (generically not exactly an apocalypse), and the fragments of the *Greek Apocalypse of Elijah*.

Another type of apocalypse of which many examples were written over an even longer period (from the second century B.C.E. to at least the late Middle Ages) is the eschatological apocalypse in which the events of the end of history are foreseen, with or without

48. See especially Martha Himmelfarb, *Tours of Hell: An Apocalyptic Form in Jewish and Christian Literature* (Philadelphia, Pa.: University of Pennsylvania Press, 1983); idem, *Ascent to Heaven in Jewish and Christian Apocalypses* (Oxford: Oxford University Press, 1993); Richard Bauckham, *The Fate of the Dead: Studies on the Jewish and Christian Apocalypses* (NovTSup 93; Leiden: Brill, 1998); Jane Ralls Baun, *Tales from Another Byzantium: Celestial Journey and Local Community in the Medieval Greek Apocrypha* (Cambridge: Cambridge University Press, 2007); Tobias Niklas, Joseph Verheyden, Erik M. M. Eynikel and Florentino García Martínez, eds., *Other Worlds and Their Relation to This World: Early Jewish and Ancient Christian Traditions* (JSJSup 143; Leiden: Brill, 2010); Markus Bockmuehl and Guy G. Stroumsa, eds., *Paradise in Antiquity: Jewish and Christian Views* (Cambridge: Cambridge University Press, 2010).

a long section of largely *post eventum* prophecies of events that lead up to the end.[49] To this tradition belong, within the present collection, the various apocalypses of Daniel, the *Hebrew Apocalypse of Elijah*, and *Sefer Zerubbabel*. Closely related are works of eschatological prophecy (to be distinguished generically from apocalypses)—*5 Ezra, 6 Ezra*, and perhaps the *Nine and a Half Tribes*—and Sibylline oracles, a genre that continued popular throughout the Middle Ages,[50] here represented by the *Greek Tiburtine Sibyl*. These works remind us that both Judaism and Christianity, for most of their history, recurrently, if not usually, featured an imminent eschatological expectation, which was often related to a perception that the course of history was reaching a critical moment.

The Second Volume

The More Old Testament Pseudepigrapha Project remains a work in progress and, although most of the content for the companion volume to this one is set, the contents may change between now and the publication of that volume. More texts may surface and closer examination of texts now tentatively slated for volume two may lead us to omit some of them. The following is our current list of texts to be included in volume two.

Horarium of Adam (Arabic, Georgian, Syriac)
Apocalypses of Adam, Sethel, Shem, Enosh, and Enoch (quoted in the Life of Mani)
Book of (the Angel) Baruch (quoted by Hippolytus)
Treatise of Shem (Aramaic and Judeo-Arabic fragments)
2 Enoch (Coptic fragments)
Enoch Apocryphon (Coptic)
Book of Giants (Aramaic and Manichaean versions, with the Hebrew Midrash of Shemihazai and Azael)
Book of the Mysteries (Sefer Ha-Razim)
Surid Legend
Abraham Apocryphon (quoted by Vettius Valens)
Ladder of Jacob (Hebrew fragment)
Apocryphon of Jacob and Joseph
Testament of Naphtali (Hebrew fragments)
Joseph and Aseneth Apocryphon (quoted by Origen)
Oracle of Hystaspes (quotations)
Testament and Assumption of Moses (quotation fragments)
Phylactery of Moses
Words of Gad the Seer
Testament of Solomon (Vienna Manuscript)
Apocalypse of Elijah (Hebrew)
Apocalypse of Elijah (Greek quotation fragments)
Adjuration of Elijah (Sheva Eliyyahu)
Manasseh Apocryphon (embedded in Didascalia Apostolorum)

---

49. See Paul J. Alexander, *The Byzantine Apocalyptic Tradition* (Berkeley, Calif.: University of California Press, 1985); John C. Reeves, *Trajectories in Near Eastern Apocalyptic: A Postrabbinic Jewish Apocalypse Reader* (SBLRBS 45; Atlanta, Ga.: Society of Biblical Literature, 2005); Lorenzo DiTommaso, *The Book of Daniel and the Apocryphal Daniel Literature* (SVTP 20; Leiden: Brill, 2005).

50. Anke Holdenried, *The Sibyl and Her Scribes: Manuscripts and Interpretation of the Latin Sibylla Tiburtina c. 1050-1500* (Aldershot: Ashgate, 2006).

Jeremiah Apocryphon
Baruch (quoted by Cyprian)
Visions of Ezekiel
Apocalypses of Daniel (Greek)
Apocalypse of Daniel (Syriac)
Danielic Prognostica
Oracles of Daniel
4 Ezra (Armenian translation)
6 Maccabees
7 Maccabees
8 Maccabees (embedded in the Chronicle of Malalas)

Revelation of Gabriel
Pseudo-Philonic Sermons on Jonah, Samson, and God
Apocryphon of the Seven Heavens
Signs of the Judgment
Quotations from unidentified Old Testament-related works
Alleged quotations from the Old Testament not found in extant texts

Conclusion

The Old Testament pseudepigrapha are an important and much neglected part of the biblical tradition. The earliest of them were written down at the same time and in the same geographic area as the Hebrew Bible, and some are even cited therein. They continued to be composed and copied throughout antiquity and the Middle Ages and, indeed, new pseudepigrapha are still being written in the modern era. The corpus being published in these two volumes adds a great many texts to those already known from earlier collections, most notably those of Sparks and Charlesworth, and together with them provides the reader with virtually all known surviving pseudepigrapha written before the rise of Islam. Some of these compositions provide us with fascinating background material to the New Testament. Others are a rich source of information on the reception history of the Hebrew Bible by Jews, Christians, and pagans through late antiquity. They frequently give us different perspectives from those found in writings of the same period which later acquired an authoritative status in Judaism (the rabbinic literature) and Christianity (the patristic literature). Together they present us with the sacred legends and spiritual reflections of numerous long-dead authors whose works were lost, neglected, or suppressed for many centuries. By making these documents available in excellent English translations and authoritative but accessible introductions we aim both to promote more scholarly study of them and to bring them to the attention of the vast lay audience who appreciate such treasures. We hope you enjoy them.

Abbreviations

Unless listed below, all abbreviations used in this volume are found in *The SBL Handbook of Style* (ed. Patrick H. Alexander et al.; Peabody, Mass.: Hendrickson, 1999).

BHM	Adolph Jellinek. *Bet ha-Midrasch*. 6 vols. 3rd ed. Jerusalem: Wahrmann, 1967.
CPVT	Johannes Albertus Fabricius. *Codex Pseudepigraphus Veteris Testamenti, Collectus Castigatus, Testimoniisque, Censuris & Animadversionibus illustratu*. Hamburg and Leipzig: Chr. Liebezeit, 1713.
CšD	*Songs of David* from the Cairo Geniza
Evv	English versions
GMPT	Hans Dieter Betz, ed. *The Greek Magical Papyri in Translation: Including the Demotic Spells*. Chicago: University of Chicago Press, 1986. 2nd ed. 1992.
MosesVIII	*Eighth Book of Moses*
OTPMNS	Richard Bauckham, James R. Davila, Alexander Panayotov. *The Old Testament Pseudepigrapha: More Noncanonical Scriptures*. Grand Rapids, Mich.: Eerdmans, 2013.
7Dan	*Seventh Vision of Daniel*
ShR	*Sefer ha-Razim* (*The Book of the Mysteries*)
SpTh	*Cave of Treasures* (*Spelunca Thesaurorum*)
Syr. Hist. Jos.	*Syriac History of Joseph*
VisRevDan	*Vision and Revelation of the Prophet Daniel*

Sigla

[text]	Square brackets indicate damaged, illegible, or missing text, whether restorable or unrecoverable.
(text)	Parentheses or round brackets indicate words added by the translator for clarity.

<text>	Pointed brackets indicate a correction or emendation made to a text by the translator.
{text}	Braces enclose dittographies (double writings) or other erroneous readings in a manuscript or text.
{...}	Braces containing three ellipsis points indicate that a textual tradition (i.e., involving more than one manuscript) has lost one or more words in transmission and that the original reading cannot be reconstructed with any confidence.

I. Texts Ordered according to Biblical Chronology

Adam Octipartite/Septipartite

A new translation and introduction

by Grant Macaskill

with a contribution by Eamon Greenwood

Adam Octipartite (which also occurs in a Septipartite version, as discussed below) is a short unit that elaborates the description of man's creation from the dust of the earth in Gen 2:7, describing how God made Adam from eight elements of the world and cataloguing which parts of Adam's composition are derived from each of these. The accounts often also describe the character traits caused by the predominance of each element. Finally, the description of Adam's creation is followed by the story of the origins of his name, which is derived from the four cardinal points of the compass, or the stars from which these points derive their names.

The tradition is never found in self-contained accounts, but is always integrated into larger works, most commonly the *question-answer* or *conversation* texts that developed in monastic circles and which circulated more generally for educational purposes among medieval Christians. Latin versions, for example, are found in manuscripts of the *Joca Monachorum* ("monkish jokes" or "riddles") tradition, and Church Slavonic versions are found in *The Conversation of the Three Hierarchs, The Constitution of the [Holy] Words* and *Razumnik* (Wisdom). The context determines whether the account is introduced with a question. Despite a measure of fluidity in specific details, there is sufficient consistency for us to identify a definite tradition behind the various textual witnesses.

There is a tendency among scholars to see Adam Octipartite/Septipartite as a progressively Christianized version of a narrative originating within ancient Judaism, since a form of the tradition is represented in *2 Enoch* 30. My own view is that this may be mistaken, since the manuscripts of *2 Enoch* are late (fourteenth to seventeenth century) and show signs of the collapsing of different versions of Adam Octipartite/Septipartite (as noted below).

Manuscripts and Original Language

The tradition that describes Adam's creation from seven or eight elements is widespread in Western texts from the seventh century onwards, with almost all of the witnesses demonstrably dependent upon the earlier Latin texts.[1] Of the dependent traditions, represented in numerous different languages, the earliest are those of the Irish versions, also translated in this volume. A parallel tradition in the Eastern context is also found, rep-

1. See Max Förster, "Adams Erschaffung und Namengebung: Ein lateinisches Fragment des s.g. slawischen Henoch," *Archiv für Religionswissenschaft* 2 (1908): 477-529. See also C. Böttrich, *Adam als Mikrokosmos: Eine Untersuchung zum slavischen Henochbuch* (Frankfurt am Main: Peter Lang, 1995), esp. pp. 59-82. Böttrich provides a very useful collection of the most important texts in this appendix, including some of those that reflect this tradition of man being made from four sods of earth; his work is indispensable for anyone intending to do further research on Adam Octipartite.

resented only by a number of Church Slavonic texts in various dialects, dating from the twelfth to eighteenth centuries.

The presence of the tradition in such diverse linguistic contexts almost certainly requires a Greek (rather than a Latin) original. Moreover, as will become clear from the discussion below, the strong connection of the tradition with "question-answer" type texts suggests that it may have originated in Greek monastic circles, in which such texts were popular and from which they were commonly translated into other languages.

1. Latin Texts

The very earliest Latin manuscripts of Adam Octipartite bear witness to the existence of two types of the account (see Table 1), based on the elements that are listed. In fact, one of the early manuscripts (Codex Vaticanus Latinus Reginae Christianae 846[2]) contains both versions, back to back. In addition to the differences between the lists of elements, the two types also vary in the way in which they list the elements and what is derived from them. Type A lists each element and derivative together (e.g., "a measure of sea, from which are formed tears") while Type B has two lists, one of the elements, the other of the derivatives. The overlap between the two types confirms that they have developed from a common source, and almost certainly Type A is closer to this, since it is unlikely that Christian tradents would have removed the references to the Light of the World and Christ.

TABLE 1

TYPE A		TYPE B*	
Element	**Part of Man**	**Element**	**Part of Man**
Dirt	Whole body/flesh	Earth	Flesh
Sea	Tears	Sea	Blood
Fire	Warmth	Sun	Eyes
Wind	Breath	Wind	Breath
Dew	Sweat	Stones	Bones
Flowers	Colors of Eyes	Holy Spirit	Spirit placed in man
Grass	Hair	Light of the World	Christ
Cloud	Mind/Thought	Clouds	Thoughts

* For the sake of comparison I have changed the order of the elements in the table for Type B. The order should be 1. Earth. 2. Sea. 3. Sun. 4. Clouds. 5. Wind. 6. Stones. 7. Holy Spirit. 8. Light of the World.

In fact, the earliest manuscript we have of Adam Octipartite displays a text of Type A. This is the seventh-century manuscript No. 1083 held in the Town Library, Sélestat (Schlettstadt). It is one of the manuscripts of the *Joca Monachorum*, a family of question-answer[3] texts of the kind popular in medieval Christianity.[4] These texts contain collections of riddles, questions and answers, probably derived from Byzantine Greek sources,[5]

2. This is a compendium text, mainly containing legal material pertaining to Salic law.

3. "Joca monachorum" is literally "monastic jokes," though "riddles" would perhaps translate *joca* rather better.

4. See Erik Wahlgren, "A Swedish-Latin Parallel to the 'Joca Monachorum,'" *Modern Philology* 6.3 (1939): 239-45.

5. See Walther Suchier, *L'Enfant Sage (das Gespräch des Kaisers Hadrian mit dem klugen Kinde Epitus)*

and have their own rather unstable transmission history. Various examples of *Joca Monachorum* exist and these vary from one another, often substantially. In addition to being our oldest witness to Adam Octipartite, Sélestat 1083 is interesting because it introduces Adam as being made from seven elements, though it goes on to list eight. This may be because the first element, dirt, is meant to function inclusively: the opening of the account reads, "Adam from seven *measures*[6] was made. A measure of dirt, because of dirt he is formed." Whether or not such an inclusive function can be given to the first element, the reading suggests that the account stands in a tradition within which Adam's composition could be understood in Septipartite (not Octipartite) terms. This is a feature that recurs in the later Irish and Slavonic versions.

The ninth-century manuscript Codex Vaticanus Latinus Reginae Christianae 846 is the earliest to present the Type B text, which is the most common in the Latin texts. This manuscript is paralleled rather closely by another ninth-century manuscript, Ms 15 of the Cathedral Library, Cologne (Kölner Dombibliothek). While the texts are fairly similar, the specific words used for each element vary somewhat.

The tenth-century Manuscript 326 of Corpus Christi College, Cambridge, is of particular importance as it seems to preserve the text form most closely replicated in the Irish texts. The manuscript itself contains a fairly random collection of material,[7] and the Adam Octipartite account is written in a different hand to the material that precedes and follows it, in red ink. There is no narrative context for the account, which clearly now has a certain autonomy and stability. Yet, there are traces of the question-answer form remaining in the account. It begins with the question, "Tell me brother, from what was Adam formed?" The answer begins with the words, "I say to you ..." These traces indicate the importance that the question-answer tradition must have played in the transmission of the idea.

To these early Latin texts of Adam Octipartite, we can compare the evidence of several later manuscripts: Vienna Imperial Library (Wien Hofbibliothek) Cod. lat 1118 fol 81b-82a (thirteenth century); Zürich Town Library (Zürich Stadtbibliotek) C.101/467, fol. 51b (fifteenth century); Bodleian Library: Ashmole 1285, fol. 4a-4b (thirteenth century) and Rawlinson C.499, fol. 153a (fifteenth century). These manuscripts are fairly consistent with one another in terms of their content but vary widely in the specific choice of words used. Amidst the diversity, however, it is possible to identify loosely defined families, with the manuscripts from mainland Europe generally closer to one another than to those from Britain, and vice versa.[8] This, however, is as close to constructing a stemma as we may probably safely come, given the level of variation.

Before we conclude our discussion of the Latin manuscripts, it is worth noting the texts that integrate the Adam Octipartite tradition into the *Life of Adam and Eve*. The fourteenth- and fifteenth-century manuscripts published by J. H. Mozely[9] display this

(Dresden: Gesellschaft für Romanische Literatur, 1910), esp. pp. 3-12. See also his *Das mittellateinische Gespräch Adrian et Epictitus nebst verwandten Texten (Joca monachorum)* (Tübingen: Max Niehmeyer Verlag, 1955). Suchier's studies are a basic starting point for research into these instructional question-answer documents and contain the key texts.

6. The Latin translated as "measure" here is *pondus/ponderis*.

7. See M. R. James, *A Descriptive Catalogue of the Manuscripts of Corpus Christi College, Cambridge* (Cambridge: Cambridge University Press, 1912), 2:144-45.

8. For this, see Förster's critical listing of variants, "Adams Erschaffung," 479-81.

9. J. H. Mozley, "The 'Vita Adae,'" *JTS* 30 (1929): 121-49. The manuscripts he lists are: Arundel 326, Royal 8 Fxvi, Harleian 526, Lambeth 352, Harleian 275, Harlein 2432, St John's Cambridge 176, and Corpus Christi Cambridge 275. See also Meyer, "Vita Adae et Evae. Herausgegeben und erläutert," *Abhandlungen*

tendency, although the level of integration is limited to our account being tagged onto the end of the primary narrative. The main reason for mentioning these manuscripts, though, is precisely this integration of Adam Octipartite into the primary Adam literature, a phenomenon not seen until this period and only seen in the manuscripts preserved in England. They are interesting also, however, because they exhibit a tendency for the various constituent parts of the account (cosmic elements, body parts, significance of the balance of elements) to be collapsed together, rather than listed in progressive sections of the account. Thus we read:

> The first part was of the dust of the earth, from which was made his flesh, and thereby he was sluggish. The next part was of the sea, from which was made his blood, and thereby he was aimless and fleeing...[10]

2. *Slavonic Texts*

The Adam Octipartite/Septipartite tradition is widespread in the Slavonic literature, probably to an extent greater than reflected here, since a number of manuscripts containing it remain unpublished. Indeed, the Bulgarian scholar Annisava Miltenova has recently identified more than thirty manuscript witnesses to the Adam Octipartite/Septipartite tradition, many of which are unpublished.[11] Without direct access to the Russian libraries, in particular, the discussion that follows will inevitably be less thorough than I would have wished, but a fair sense of the issues may still be gained.

While some of the witnesses to the tradition are found in *compendia*-type texts (*sborniki*) and present the account in a more autonomous form, sometimes integrated into larger narratives, it is also widely found in question-answer texts, particularly the family of texts containing the *Conversation of the Three Hierarchs* and another family containing a parallel question-answer text, *Razumnik* (Wisdom). In the former, Basil the Great, Gregory the Theologian (Nazianzus) and John the Theologian—the three greatest theologians according to the Orthodox tradition—are presented as having a conversation, within which (in some texts) the topics of Adam's creation and of his name are discussed, along with much else. In the latter text we encounter very similar material, but it is not ascribed to the conversation between the three saints, instead simply being given in question-answer form. Recent research by Miltenova has demonstrated the presence of the tradition also in a third text known as *The Constitution of the [Holy] Words*, which overlaps with—and is often confused with—the *Conversation of the Three Hierarchs* (the same three characters are involved).[12] The various witnesses to *The Constitution of the [Holy] Words* are, in fact, the oldest of the texts to preserve Adam Octipartite/Septipartite in Slavonic, with manuscripts dating back to the twelfth century. Obviously the boundary

---

der philosophisch-philologischen Classe der königlich bayerischen Akademie der Wissenschaften, vol. 14,3 (1878): 187-250.

10. Translation, B. Custis. Online: http://www2.iath.virginia.edu/anderson/vita/english/vita.lat.html.

11. A. A. Miltenova, *Erotapokriseis: Sŭchineniata ot kratki vŭprosi i otgovori v starobŭlgarskata literatura* (Sofia: Damian Lakov, 2004), 200-236. See also her briefer English article, "Slavonic Erotapokriseis: Sources, Transmission, and Morphology of the Genre," forthcoming in *The Old Testament Apocrypha in the Slavonic Tradition: Continuity and Diversity*, edited by Christfried Böttrich, Lorenzo DiTommaso, and Marina Swoboda, Texts and Studies in Ancient Judaism (Tübingen: Mohr Siebeck, 2009). I am grateful to Christfried Böttrich for sharing the pre-publication version of this.

12. See Miltenova, "Slavonic Erotapokriseis."

between the three groups of texts is rather permeable. For this reason, I will simply refer to all of these texts as "the *Conversation*" in what follows.

Most of the manuscripts of the *Conversation* that contain some form of our tradition present it in its Octipartite form, in the Type B form noted in our discussion of the Latin texts. The Slavonic manuscripts broadly parallel the Latin texts but with more fluidity, both in the list of elements themselves and, indeed, in the macrostructure of the account, with sections of the account sometimes left out. Alongside these, however, are texts that present a Septipartite version of the account. The sixteenth-century manuscript No. 794 in the Trinity St. Sergius Monastery Library contains one such witness, listing man as being made from seven elements:

> Question: from how many parts did God make Adam? The first part was his body from the earth. The second were his bones from stone. The third part his eyes from the sea. Fourth, his thoughts were from the motion of angels. Fifth, his soul and breathing from the wind. Sixth, his reason from the clouds of heaven. Seventh, his blood from dew and from sun.[13]

While the septipartite nature of Man's composition and the absence of a reference to the Light of the World may suggest a more rudimentary text,[14] one rather closer to the earliest of the Latin texts noted above, closer examination suggests that this text is, in fact, a later development, representing a conflation of the Type A and Type B texts or traditions. Unlike the other texts we have studied so far, this text does not have a one-to-one correspondence of natural elements to components of Adam's composition. Instead, in the fifth case we find both his soul and his breathing being made of the wind[15] and in the seventh, his blood is made from both the dew and the sun. These seem to be conflations of elements that we have encountered in other texts. More significantly, we here have two elements being connected to some form of thought (clouds and angels), which is a duplication not seen in the Latin Septipartite texts, and that seems to indicate a measure of confusion. This confusion seems to have arisen from interference between the two text types identified in the oldest Latin manuscripts. These aspects of the texts suggest the presence in the Slavic environment of both of the traditions seen in the Latin context, with interference occurring between them. This indicates that at least two forms of the tradition crossed the boundary into the Slavonic environment from the prior Greek one, a situation paralleling both the Latin and Irish evidence and rendering problematic all attempts at construction of stemmata.[16]

Alongside the texts of the *Conversation,* Adam Octipartite is found in a number of compendium texts. In several of these (e.g., Rumjancev Sbornik No. 370, leaf 147-177) it

---

13. Another manuscript parallels this one closely, though not precisely. The text is noted by R. Nachtigall, "Ein Beitrag zu den Forschungen über die sogennante 'Beseda Trech Svjatitelej' (Gespräch dreier Heiligen)" in *Archiv für Slavische Philologie* 23 (1901): 81-83, and reads:

Question: from what did God make Adam? Answer: from seven parts. 1. His body from the earth. 2. His bones from stone. 3. His blood from dew and from sun. 4. His breath from wind, his soul from the Spirit of God. 5. His understanding from clouds. 6. His eyes from sea. 7. His thought from the motion of angels.

14. So Förster, "Adam's Erschaffung," esp. pp. 500-501.

15. Though this could be Slavonic punning on breath and soul.

16. This conclusion is also independently reached by Miltenova, *Erotapokriseis*, whose work I came across only after finishing the first draft of this chapter.

has been integrated into the larger narrative of the creation and of Satan's temptation of Adam and Eve, but in one or two others, it is an autonomous account, with headings that vary ("Concerning the Body"; "How God Created Adam"; "Concerning How Many Parts Adam Was Made of"). Where it has been integrated into the larger story of the Garden, we find only the bare list of Adam's composition from the eight elements; the discussion of the balance of these elements is not found.

3. *Irish Texts*

In Old Irish, the Adam Octipartite tradition is found as a narrative in three manuscripts (British Museum Additional 4783, f.7; British Museum Egerton 136, f. 74b; British Museum Egerton 1782 f. 45b). While these follow quite closely the text of the Latin Corpus Christi manuscript, discussed above, BM Add. 4783 and BM Egerton 1782 depart from this by presenting man as made from seven elements.[17] Interestingly, though, the list of elements in these is of the Type B seen in the Latin manuscripts. Moreover, BM Egerton 1782 identifies the Light of the World with the Holy Spirit, demonstrating a dependence upon the Octipartite tradition and a collapsing of these two originally distinct components.

The account of the origin of Adam's name is missing from all of these texts, though it is found elsewhere in the Old Irish corpus, in *Lebor Gabála,* and is reflected in *Saltair na Rann.* In fact, the link between Adam's name and the four cardinal points is a regularly encountered distinctive of Irish exegesis.[18]

In addition to these narrative texts, we also find the idea that Adam was made from eight *pondera* in the earliest recension of a text known as *The Evernew Tongue* (*An Tenga Bithnua*), a question-answer text that narrates the conversation between a group of eastern kings and bishops and the spirit of the apostle Philip. This text is old, with the earliest recension of the Irish text probably dating to the tenth century. It blends narrative traditions, such as the account of Adam's creation, with apocalyptic accounts of heavenly geography and descriptions of the afterlife. The interesting point is that, once again, the Adam Octipartite account is linked to the question-answer tradition. *The Evernew Tongue* also displays an explicitly Christological reading of the tradition. Immediately following the description of Adam's composition, Philip explains that the whole creation rose in Christ, linking Adam's microcosmic nature with Christ's cosmic redemption through his own body. As I will suggest below, this may well be the theological gravity of the entire tradition, even if left unwritten in most manuscripts.

4. *Adam Octipartite and 2 Enoch*

This brings us, at last, to the thorny question of the relationship between Adam Octipartite/Septipartite and the creation story found in 2 *En.* 30:8-9. *Second Enoch* is an apoca-

17. The text is corrected and completed by Whitley Stokes to present Adam as being made from eight elements. *Three Irish Glossaries: Cormac's glossary, Codex A (From a manuscript in the library of the Royal Irish Academy), O'Davoren's glossary (from a manuscript in the library of the British Museum), and a glossary to the calendar of Oingus the Culdee (from a manuscript in the library of Trinity College, Dublin)* (London: Williams and Norgate, 1862), xl.

18. R. E. McNally writes, "The same derivation is to be found in so many seventh- and eighth-century Irish works that it has almost become a characteristic of Irish Bible exegesis." *The Bible in the Early Middle Ages* (Westminster: Newman Press, 1959), 26.

lyptic text, probably of Jewish origin,[19] but preserved only in Church Slavonic. There are broadly two recensions, a longer and a shorter one, with the longer containing a good deal of material, at various points of the narrative, not found in the shorter one.

In *2 Enoch* 30:8-9 we find, first of all, a septipartite account of Adam's composition:

> His flesh from earth; his blood from dew and from the sun; his eyes from the bottomless sea; his bones from stone; his reason from the mobility of angels and from clouds; his veins and hair from grass of the earth; his spirit from my spirit and from wind. And I gave him 7 properties: hearing to the flesh; sight to the eyes; smell to the spirit; touch to the veins; taste to the blood; to the bones—endurance; to the reason—sweetness.[20]

Thus we have two lists of seven: one of Adam's constituent elements and the other of his senses. This is followed by a creation poem:

> Behold, I have thought up an ingenious poem to write:
>
> From visible and invisible substances I created man. From both his natures come both death and life. And (as my) image he knows the word like (no) other creature. But even at his greatest he is small, and again at his smallest he is great.
>
> And on the earth I assigned him to be a second angel, honoured and great and glorious.[21] (30:10-11)

After more is said on the uniqueness of Adam's glory, the account then continues with the story of his naming:

> And I assigned to him a name from the four components: From east—(A), from West—(D), from North—(A), from South—(M). And I assigned to him four special stars, and called his name Adam.[22] (30:12-13)

Several points are worth noting as we begin to consider the relationship of this text to Adam Octipartite/Septipartite. First, there is considerable overlap with the septipartite texts found in the *Conversation* tradition: again, we have mention of dew here and also find two elements connected with reason (angels and clouds). Behind this, though, there are differences. Where the *Conversation* texts list both "reason" and "thoughts," linking these independently to "clouds" and "angels," here the two elements are linked to a singular component of Adam's composition: reason. Second, we have also here the reappearance of an element not seen since the earliest of the Latin texts, "grass," which forms Adam's veins and hair.[23] Third, we also encounter here God's spirit, which is connected to the wind as the source of Adam's breath. This represents only a partial parallel with the earliest of the Latin texts, where only the wind is mentioned, but does parallel the later

19. F. I. Andersen, "2 (Slavonic Apocalypse of) Enoch," in *OTP*, 1:150.

20. Andersen, "2 Enoch," 150.

21. Andersen, "2 Enoch," 150, 152.

22. Andersen, "2 Enoch," 152.

23. In both Greek and Latin the terms for capillaries and hair are etymologically linked and are very similar; this may represent an expansion based on some confusion arising from this.

Octipartite texts, in which the Spirit features (though is not linked to the wind).[24] Fourth, the list of properties given to each element of man's composition and the poem on Adam's nature are not found in the Adam Octipartite texts.[25]

It is widely held that what we have here is an ancient Jewish text, probably originating in Alexandria. This text would have been transmitted through later Judaism into Byzantine circles and from there into the Slavonic environment. Along the way, it would have seeded ideas into Christian monastic circles that were subsequently developed into the Adam Octipartite tradition. This view is seen in Förster's classic study of the Adam Octipartite texts,[26] is taken up in Herbert and McNamara's discussion of Irish texts,[27] and has recently been effectively argued by Böttrich.[28]

This idea can certainly not be easily discounted and remains a distinct possibility, but I have elsewhere registered concerns with it[29] and remain uneasy about ascribing antiquity to this portion of the text of *2 Enoch*. Briefly, the following issues may be noted:[30]

1. This material is found only in the four manuscripts of the longer recension (one of which is a duplicate of another). This should not be regarded as a fatal objection, since the text may have been abbreviated as well as lengthened, but it should at least make us wary. It is simply undeniable that *2 Enoch* was subject to a great deal of redactional activity—the levels of inconsistency between the manuscript witnesses demonstrate this—and so we must be open to the possibility that this material was a late addition to the text.
2. There is a great deal of evidence of redactional activity throughout the creation account in the longer recension and a fair amount of confusion even among the small number of manuscripts that attest the longer recension.
3. While Man's dignity as the bearer of God's image is reflected throughout *2 Enoch*, as the basis for much of its ethics, nothing more is said that relates specifically to the septipartite nature of his composition, so that claims for this part of the creation story to be well-integrated into the rest of the book must be regarded as modest, at best.
4. The fact that we have duplication of certain elements in the *2 Enoch* account ("blood from dew and sun"; "reason from the mobility of angels and clouds"; "veins and hair from grass"; "spirit from my spirit and wind") may suggest the collapsing of elements from the Adam Octipartite tradition into one another, with interference from an Adam Septipartite tradition.

---

24. The interplay of Spirit and wind/breath is, of course, seen in Genesis 2:7.

25. The elevated status and angelic glory of Adam is, however, a popular idea in both early Judaism and early Christianity. See Alexander Golitzin, "Recovering the 'Glory of Adam': 'Divine Light' Traditions in the Dead Sea Scrolls and the Christian Ascetical Literature of Fourth-Century Syro-Mesopotamia," in *The Dead Sea Scrolls as Background to Postbiblical Judaism and Early Christianity: Papers from an International Conference at St Andrews in 2001* (ed. James R. Davila; STDJ 46; Leiden: Brill, 2003), 275-308.

26. Förster, "Adam's Erschaffung."

27. Màíre Herbert and Martín McNamara, *Irish Biblical Apocrypha* (Edinburgh: T.&T. Clark, 1989), 1.

28. See his *Adam als Mikrokosmos.*

29. G. Macaskill, *Revealed Wisdom and Inaugurated Eschatology in Ancient Judaism and Early Christianity* (JSJSup 115; Leiden: Brill, 2007), 196-240.

30. I explore these problems in more depth in my article, "2 Enoch: Manuscripts, Recensions and Original Language," in *New Directions in the Study of 2 Enoch: No Longer Slavonic Only* (Studia Judaeoslavica 4; ed. A. Orlov, G. Boccaccini, and J. Zurawski; Leiden/Boston: Brill, 2012), 83-102.

Taken together, these concerns mean that we should be open to an alternative theory of the relationship of these texts. It seems entirely possible that the Adam Octipartite/ Septipartite tradition originated in Christian monastic circles, in the Greek traditions that lay behind the *Joca Monachorum*. From here it may have been transmitted through monastic channels, circulating in different forms capable of interfering with one another and alongside pseudepigraphal texts such as *2 Enoch* which were also transmitted in this environment. In the fluid redactional environments of the Byzantine and Slavonic contexts a form of this text may have been introduced to the creation account of *2 Enoch,* possibly because the Adam Octipartite/Septipartite tradition was so well known that it would have been regarded as an omission for it not to be found here. The septipartite form of the myth would be most appropriate to *2 Enoch,* since the creation account has a number of structural features based around the number seven; also, the absence of a reference to the Light of the World here may have seemed more appropriate to an ostensibly pre-Christian creation account.

Which of these theories is correct remains to be proved. Perhaps, though, a final conclusion on the matter is simply beyond our ability to reach.

Theological Significance

Obviously, this whole tradition represents an expansion of the biblical portrayal of man as made from the dust of the earth (Gen 2:7). This portrayal is, of course, also developed in other traditions, such as the one that describes Adam as being formed from sods of earth from different parts of the world, found in certain rabbinic texts, such as *Targum Pseudo-Jonathan* and *Pirqe R. El.* 11 and paralleled by numerous Christian texts.[31] Those texts seem concerned to link Adam to the totality of humanity, since what is emphasised is the connection of the ground upon which all humans live to the first man. Thus, the text of *Pirqe Rabbi Eliezer*, noted above, reads:

> If a man should come from the east to the west, or from the west to the east, and his time comes to depart from the world then the earth shall not say, The dust of thy body is not mine, return to the place whence thou wast created. But (this circumstance) teaches thee that in every place where a man goes or comes, and his end approaches when he must depart from the world, thence is the dust of his body and there it returns to the dust.[32]

By contrast, the Adam Octipartite/Septipartite tradition emphasizes much more the link between Adam and the rest of creation, essentially portraying Adam as a microcosm of creation.[33] While this may simply involve a reflection on Man's status as the image bearer, the contact point between the divine and the created, it also seems to have acquired a distinct connection with redemptive Christology. Thus, we find mentioned the Holy Spirit which is placed in man and the Light of the World, which is interpreted as Christ. This may well pick up on the teaching of the New Testament, notably Romans 5–8,

---

31. See my article "The Creation of Man in *2 (Slavonic) Enoch* and Christian Tradition," in *XIXth Congress of the International Organization for the Study of the Old Testament (IOSOT), Ljubljana 16-20 July 2007, Congress Volume (*ed. André Lemaire; Leiden: Brill, 2010), 399-422. Also, see D. Wasserstein, "The Creation of Adam and the Apocrypha in Early Ireland," *Proceedings of the Royal Irish Academy* 88 (1988): 1-18.

32. Friedlander, *Pirke de Rabbi Eliezer*, 76.

33. As in the title of Böttrich's book, *Adam als Mikrokosmos*.

which portrays Jesus as a second Adam, redeeming not just humanity but the whole of the creation that fell with (or in) Adam. This link between the constitution of Adam's body and the redemption of the cosmos through the Incarnation is most clearly expressed in *The Evernew Tongue*:

> All the world rose with Him, for the nature of all the elements dwelt in the body which Jesus assumed.[34]

It is not simply that Christ redeemed humankind, that "the whole of the divine was united to the whole of humanity through the single hypostasis [of the Logos],"[35] but that through this union there was also effected a redemption of all creation:

> For it was the good pleasure of the Father that in him should all the fullness dwell and through him to reconcile *all things* unto himself, having made peace through the blood of his cross; through him, I say, whether things upon the earth, or things in the heavens. (Col 1:19-20; my emphasis)

Such a tradition could explain why in Christian texts there is such an interest in the link not simply between Adam and "global soil," but between Adam and the elements of creation: as the Logos took to himself a human nature, he was taking a nature inherently linked to the rest of creation as a whole. Within Judaism, such a notion of a redemptive *microcosm* was arguably much more closely connected to the temple than to Adam.[36]

Christological associations of the creation of Adam are further brought out in texts such as the Irish *Saltair na Rann* which explicitly link the fate of Adam's body to Christ's redemptive work. Here Adam's corpse is carried by the Flood to Jerusalem; the head remains at the gate to the city while the body lies in the soil in which the Cross is planted.[37]

Notes on the Translations

Faced with such a widespread and inconsistent tradition, it is impossible to establish a best critical reading and, indeed, such a reading would be misleading in suggesting a certain level of consistency. The translations, therefore, will follow specific manuscript witnesses and discuss variants against these. In the case of the Latin, the translation will primarily follow the Vatican manuscript. Not only is this the earliest to bear witness to the Adam Octipartite tradition (the Sélestat manuscript presents Adam as being made from seven elements, even though it goes on to list 8), it also contains both early types of the account (A and B), allowing some appreciation of the differences and similarities between them.

34. *The Evernew Tongue,* paragraph 13. Whitley Stokes, "The Evernew Tongue," *Ériu* 2 (1905): 105. See also paragraph 11, which immediately precedes the Octipartite discussion of the constitution of man (Stokes, "Evernew Tongue," 103): "For every material and every element and every nature which is seen in the world were all combined in the Body in which Christ arose, that is, in the body of every human being."

35. Maximus the Confessor, *Doctrina partium de incarnatione Verbi* 11.1. Translation from Jaroslav Pelikan, *The Spirit of Eastern Christendom (600-1700)* (Chicago: University of Chicago Press, 1974; paperback edition, 1977), 80.

36. On this point, see William P. Brown, *The Ethos of the Cosmos: The Genesis of Moral Imagination in the Bible* (Grand Rapids, Mich.: Eerdmans, 1998), 35-131.

37. Herbert and McNamara, *Irish Biblical Apocrypha,* 16. This tradition is, of course, quite widely found.

To this translation, however, I will append the story of the naming of Adam from the Corpus Christi manuscript. This account may well be a later form of the story than that attested in the Vatican text, but it is also fuller and is reflected in many later texts, including those in other languages. For these reasons, it is functionally important to present this version in our translation. Again, comparison of this account with the different version found in the Vatican manuscript will allow some appreciation of the diversity and fluidity that characterizes this tradition.

In the case of the Slavonic version, the translation will follow RNB No. 11/1088. This is the earliest of the versions of the story to be found in the compendia-type texts, and is a good witness to the form of the tradition that is essentially presented as a story in its own right. Although there are earlier texts (listed and discussed by Miltenova), I have avoided using these for the translation as they do not represent the more autonomous text-form found in the compendia. The discussion of variant readings here will be less thorough than I would like, but a satisfactory discussion of such a complex and disparate tradition would, in truth, require a book-length treatment. Of the Slavonic manuscripts provided in Table 2, the three St. Petersburg texts are the most important for our purposes, as they represent the more autonomous form of our text. The first two texts do not inform my translation, but are listed as the earliest witnesses to the Conversation (*Constitution of the [Holy] Words)* tradition in Slavonic. The Rumjancev manuscript contains the story integrated into the wider narrative of creation and fall, while the Trinity St. Sergius manuscript is another witness to the *Conversation.* A key discussion of the *Conversation* texts is found in R. Nachtigall, "Ein Beitrag zu den Forschungen über die sogenannte 'Beseda Trech Svjatitelej' (Gespräch dreier Heiligen)," in *Archiv für Slavische Philologie* 23 (1901): 1-95; 24 (1902): 321-408; 26 (1904): 472-477. The most thorough study of the *Conversation* tradition in Slavonic is now that of Miltenova.[38]

The translation of the Irish version, provided by Eamon Greenwood, is based on British Museum manuscript Additional 4783. I have added some brief notes to his translation.

The following tables present the most relevant manuscripts of the texts, with publication details listed in the table notes, where possible:

TABLE 2: LATIN TEXTS

Location	Catalogue Listing	Date
Vatican	Codex Vaticanus Latinus Reginae Christianae 846, f.106b*	9th Century
Cathedral Library, Cologne (Kölner Dombibliothek)	Hs. 15†	9th Century
Corpus Christi College, Cambridge	Manuscript 326, l. 135‡	10th Century
Vienna Imperial Library (Wien Hofbibliothek)	Cod. lat 1118 fol 81b-82a**	13th Century
Bodleian Library	Ashmole 1285, fol. 4a-4b††	13th Century

38. Miltenova, *Erotapokriseis.* The work as a whole is relevant, but the key discussion of Adam literature is found on pp. 200-236.

Location	Catalogue Listing	Date
Zürich Town Library (Zürich Stadtbibliotek)	C.101/467, fol. 51b‡‡	15th Century
Bodleian Library	Rawlinson C.499, fol. 153a***	15th Century

* Published by W. Schmitz, *Miscellanea Tironiana: Aus dem Codex Vaticanus Latinus Reginae 846* (Leipzig: B. G. Teubner, 1896), 35.

† Published by Suchier, *L'Enfant Sage*, 279.

‡ Published by Förster, "Adam's Erschaffung," 479-81.

** Published by J. Haupt, *Zeitschrift für deutsches Alterthum* 23 (Leipzig: Weidmannsche Buchhandlung, 1880), 356.

†† Variants in Förster, "Adam's Erschaffung," 479-81.

‡‡ Variants in Förster, "Adam's Erschaffung," 479-81.

*** Variants in Förster, "Adam's Erschaffung," 479-81.

TABLE 3: SLAVONIC TEXTS

Location	Catalogue Listing	Date
St. Catherine Monastery, Sinai	Apostle No. 39 Fragment	12th Century
Vienna National Library	Cod. Slav. 12 (originating from the Chilandar Monastery) fols. 161a-165b*	13th Century
St. Petersburg, National Library of Russia (RNB)	Kyrillo-Belozersk Collection No. 11/1088, l. 279-280†	15th Century
Trinity St. Sergius Library	No. 794 l. 335-344‡	15th Century
St. Petersburg, National Library of Russia (RNB)	Kyrillo-Belozersk Collection No. 22/1099, l. 517**	16th Century
St. Petersburg, National Library of Russia (RNB)	Coleveck Collection, No. 653/711, l. 59††	16th Century
Rumjancev Museum	Sbornik No. 370, l. 147-177 (17th century)‡‡	17th Century

* Published by Miltenova, *Erotapokriseis*, 204-206.

† V. V. Mil'kov, *Drevnerusskie Apokrify* (St. Petersburg: Institute of Russian Christian Humanities, 1999), 442-44.

‡ N. Tichonravov, *Pamjatniki Otrečennoj Russkoj Literatury*, 2:448-49. On pp. 443-44 in this volume, Tichonravov also reproduces the fifteenth-century Serbian Grigorovič manuscript.

** Mil'kov, *Drevnerusskie Apokrify*, 445-47.

†† Mil'kov, *Drevnerusskie Apokrify*, 448-49.

‡‡ A. N. Pypin, "Ložnyja i Otrečennyja Knigi Russkoj Stariny," in G. G. Kušelevym-Bezborodko, *Pamjatniki Starinnoj Russkoj Literatury*, 3:12-14 (St. Petersburg: P. A. Kuliša, 1862; reprint in the series Slavistic Printings and Reprintings, Paris: Mouton, 1970).

TABLE 4: IRISH TEXTS*

Location	Catalogue Listing	Date
British Museum	BM Additional 4783 f.7†	15th Century
British Museum	BM Egerton 136, folio 74b	17th Century (1631 C.E.)
British Museum	BM Egerton 1782, fol 45b	16th Century (1517 C.E.)

* For a discussion of each of these manuscripts, see R. Flower, *Catalogue of Irish Manuscripts in the British Museum,* vol. 2 (London: The Trustees of the British Museum, 1926).

† Whitley Stokes, *Three Irish Glossaries,* xl-xli.

Bibliography

Andersen, Francis I. "2 (Slavonic Apocalypse of) Enoch," in *OTP* 1:91-221.

Böttrich, Christfried. *Adam als Mikrokosmos: Eine Untersuchung zum slavischen Henochbuch.* Frankfurt am Main: Peter Lang, 1995.

Brown, William P. *The Ethos of the Cosmos: The Genesis of Moral Imagination in the Bible.* Grand Rapids, Mich.: Eerdmans, 1998.

Flower, Robin. *Catalogue of Irish Manuscripts in the British Museum.* Volume 2. London: The Trustees of the British Museum, 1926.

Förster, Max. "Adams Erschaffung und Namengebung: Ein lateinisches Fragment des s.g. slawischen Henoch." *Archiv für Religionswissenschaft* 2 (1908): 477-529.

Friedlander, Gerald. *Pirke de Rabbi Eliezer: The Chapters of Rabbi Eliezer the Great.* Fourth edition. New York: Sepher-Hermon Press, 1981.

Golitzin, Alexander. "Recovering the 'Glory of Adam': 'Divine Light' Traditions in the Dead Sea Scrolls and the Christian Ascetical Literature of Fourth-Century Syro-Mesopotamia." Pages 275-308 in *The Dead Sea Scrolls as Background to Postbiblical Judaism and Early Christianity: Papers from an International Conference at St. Andrews in 2001.* Edited by James R. Davila. STDJ 46. Leiden: Brill, 2003.

Herbert, Màíre, and Martín McNamara. *Irish Biblical Apocrypha.* Edinburgh: T.&T. Clark, 1989.

James, Montague Rhodes. *A Descriptive Catalogue of the Manuscripts of Corpus Christi College, Cambridge.* Volume 2. Cambridge: Cambridge University Press, 1912.

Macaskill, Grant. "The Creation of Man in 2 *(Slavonic) Enoch* and Christian Tradition." Pages 399-422 in *Congress Volume, Ljubljana 2007 (XIXth Congress of the International Organization for the Study of the Old Testament [IOSOT], Ljubljana 16-20 July 2007).* Edited by André Lemaire. Leiden: Brill, 2010.

__________. *Revealed Wisdom and Inaugurated Eschatology in Ancient Judaism and Early Christianity.* JSJSup 115; Leiden: Brill, 2007.

__________. "2 Enoch: Manuscripts, Recensions and Original Language," "2 Enoch: Manuscripts, Recensions and Original Language," pages 83-102 in *New Directions in the Study of 2 Enoch: No Longer Slavonic Only.* Edited by A. Orlov, G. Boccaccini and J. Zurawski. Studia Judaeoslavica 4. Leiden/Boston: Brill, 2012.

Maher, Michael. *Targum Pseudo-Jonathan: Genesis. Translated, with Introduction and Notes.* The Aramaic Bible, Vol. 1b. Edinburgh: T.&T. Clark, 1992.

McNally, Robert E. *The Bible in the Early Middle Ages.* Westminster: Newman Press, 1959.

Meyer, Wilhelm, "Vita Adae et Evae. Herausgegeben und erläutert." *Abhandlungen der philosophisch-philologischen Classe der königlich bayerischen Akademie der Wissenschaften.* Vol. 14,3 (1878): 187-250.

Mil'kov, V. V. *Drevnerusskie Apokrify*. St. Petersburg: Institute of Russian Christian Humanities, 1999.

Miltenova, Annisava A. *Erotapokriseis: Sŭchineniata ot kratki vŭprosi i otgovori v starobŭlgarskata literatura*. Sofia: Damian Lakov, 2004.

__________. "Slavonic Erotapokriseis: Sources, Transmission, and Morphology of the Genre." Pages 279-301 in *The Old Testament Apocrypha in the Slavonic Tradition: Continuity and Diversity*. Edited by Christfried Böttrich, Lorenzi DiTommaso, and Marina Swoboda. TSAJ 140. Tübingen: Mohr Siebeck, 2011.

Mozley, J. H. "The 'Vita Adae.'" *JTS* 30 (1929): 121-149.

Pypin, A. N. "Ložnyja i Otrečennyja Knigi Russkoj Stariny." Pages 12-14 in *Pamjatniki Starinnoj Russkoj Literatur.* Volume 3. Edited by G. G. Kušelevym-Bezborodko. St. Petersburg: P. A. Kuliša, 1862 (reprint in the series *Slavistic Printings and Reprintings,* Paris: Mouton, 1970).

Schmitz, W. *Miscellanea Tironiana: Aus dem Codex Vaticanus Latinus Reginae 846*. Leipzig: B. G. Teubner, 1896.

Stokes, Whitley. "The Evernew Tongue." *Ériu* 2 (1905): 96-162.

__________. *Three Irish Glossaries: Cormac's glossary, Codex A (From a manuscript in the library of the Royal Irish Academy), O'Davoren's glossary (from a manuscript in the library of the British Museum), and a glossary to the calendar of Oingus the Culdee (from a manuscript in the library of Trinity College, Dublin)*. London: Williams and Norgate, 1862.

Suchier, Walther. *L'Enfant Sage (das Gespräch des Kaisers Hadrian mit dem klugen Kinde Epitus)*. Dresden: Gesellschaft für Romanische Literatur, 1910.

__________. *Das mittellateinische Gespräch Adrian et Epictitus nebst verwandten Texten (Joca monachorum)*. Tübingen: Max Niehmeyer Verlag, 1955.

Tichonravov, N. *Pamjatniki Otrečennoj Russkoj Literatury*. Volume 2. St Petersburg: V' Tip. Obshchestvenaia pol'za, 1863.

Wahlgren, Erik. "A Swedish-Latin Parallel to the 'Joca Monachorum.'" *Modern Philology* 6.3 (1939): 239-245.

Wasserstein, David. "The Creation of Adam and the Apocrypha in Early Ireland." *Proceedings of the Royal Irish Academy* 88 (1988): 1-18.

Adam Octipartite

Translation: Adam Octipartite (Latin)

Now the first man[a] was made of eight[b] parts.[c] The first part of the soil of the earth; the second of the sea; the third of sun; the fourth of the clouds of the sky; the fifth of the wind; the sixth of the stones; the seventh of the Holy Spirit; the eighth of the light of the world.

Now this is its interpretation. It is said that from the soil of the earth is formed his flesh. The second, it is said, is of sea, from which is his blood. The third is of the sun, from which are his eyes, which are the lamp of the body. Fourth: from the clouds of the sky are formed his thoughts. The fifth is of wind, which is his inhalation and exhalation. The sixth is of stones, from which are his bones. The seventh is of the Holy Spirit, which God has placed in man. The eighth is of the Light of the World, which being interpreted, (is Christ).[d, e]

This is its interpretation. Man, who of these is formed, cannot be procreated apart from these eight parts, but one of these will predominate in each person's nature.[f] If, for example, the soil of the earth predominates, he will be made sluggish in his works;[g] if the

---

a. This phrase parallels the Jewish stock expression, *Adam ha-rishon*. Might this point to a Jewish origin? Such a conclusion is probably rash, since it neglects the extent to which Jewish traditions, and thus expressions, were transmitted in Christian contexts.

b. There is a parallel tradition, discussed above, that has Adam formed from seven elements (hence Adam Septipartite).

c. The passage is introduced in various ways. Sometimes, as here, this is with a statement, but often it is with some variation of the question "of what (or 'from whence') was Adam made?"

d. The Vatican manuscript lacks the words "is Christ," but these are found in parallel manuscripts.

e. The manuscripts vary throughout this paragraph in wording, but the elements are consistently represented. There is a striking parallel in the *Prose Edda,* where the elements of the earth derived from the body of the giant Ymir largely match those found here (including, most remarkably, the derivation of the clouds from Ymir's brain). The parallel is lacking from the older *Poetic Edda* and it may be that Snorri modified his sources in the light of the Adam Octipartite traditions, in keeping with the Christianizing developments of the *Prose Edda.*

f. An awkward sentence is found in most of the manuscripts, but is absent from the Cambridge text (and from the Irish texts that seem to be dependent on it, or on a related manuscript). The first part of the sentence is straightforward, despite some variation between the manuscripts: man is formed of these eight elements and from no others. The second half of the sentence is less straightforward and the manuscripts part company more severely, probably indicating the struggle that the scribes themselves had with the phrase. The Cologne manuscript reads "one of these will predominate in each person," while the Vatican manuscript has a slightly garbled version of this that speaks of deficiency rather than excess (*subtrahit* rather than *supertrahit*), which clashes with the rest of the account. Later manuscripts insert a reference to the individual's character, and this seems to be the underlying idea: the character or nature of a man will be decided by which of the elements predominates. My translation is rather loose, in order to capture this implied meaning.

g. The manuscripts show some confusion here. Vatican, as presented above, reads, "He will be sluggish

sea, he will be wise and deep. If the sun, however, he will be bright and attractive;[a] if the clouds of the sky, he will be in every way light and exuberant. If the wind predominates, he will be swift and hot-headed. If the stones of the earth predominate, he will be hard to look upon[b] or to deal with[c] and will be avaricious. If the Holy Spirit predominates, he will in every part (of the earth) follow the reign of Adam.[d] [If the light of the world predominates, he will be chosen of all, faithful and bright.][e]

Of eight measures he is made. A measure of earth: from this is formed the flesh. A measure of sea: from this salt[f] will be tears. A measure of fire: from this [is] hot breath. A measure of wind: from this [is] cold. A measure of sun:[g] from which [is] the variety of eyes. A measure of moon:[h] from this are different kinds of hair. A measure of cloud: from this is the stability of thought. A measure of dew: from this is sweat.

Since the world was formed of four parts, therefore also four stars were constituted in heaven. From the four is derived the name of Adam. The first star, in the East, is called Anatholi. The second star, in the West, is called Dosi. The third star, in the North, is called Artus. The fourth star, in the South, is called Mesimorion.[i] From these four stars he takes the four letters, that is: from the star Anatholi he takes A; from the star Dosi he takes D; from the star Artus he takes A; from the star Mesemorion he takes M. And he has the name Adam.

---

in his works"; Cologne reads, "He will be sluggish in all the earth." The Corpus Christi manuscript probably preserves the best reading: "He will be sluggish in every part." This reads well and the Latin employed can best account for the variant readings in the other manuscripts.

a. The Latin terms used here seem positive, but perhaps we should see a contrast with "wise and deep," suggesting vanity.

b. The manuscripts vary widely at this point. All begin with the adjective "hard" (*durus*) and follow this with one or more gerundives. While these vary from manuscript to manuscript, they all denote some kind of personal encounter (e.g., "seeing," "hearing," "beseeching"). The structure is awkward; clearly it caused problems for tradents or scribes, since so many variations are found, but the sense is clear: this person's presence will not be pleasant for anyone to be in and dealing with him will be difficult.

c. Not all manuscripts have a second gerundive at this point (see previous footnote).

d. The manuscripts vary here. This phrase is missing in the Cambridge manuscript, which simply reads, "He will be handsome and beautiful and full of the Divine Scripture." The Cologne manuscript presents Adam as "in all the earth a second God, good and virtuous and full of Holy Scripture." This is a significant parallel to the material in 2 *Enoch* 30.

e. This phrase is absent from the Vatican manuscript, but is found, with some variation, in Cologne and Cambridge.

f. Compare Vatican to Sélestat: the latter has "salt" as an adjective in agreement with tears.

g. Sélestat here reads "floris" ("flower"). The Vatican reading ("sun") probably reflects an alteration to bring the text into better agreement with the Type B text.

h. Sélestat here reads "feni" (grass). This makes better sense, as an image, than does the mention of the moon in the Vatican text.

i. This is a corruption of "Mesembria." Interestingly, this name was also used in antiquity and medieval times for the Black Sea coastal town known today as Nesebar (in Bulgaria).

Appendix: The Naming of Adam (Cambridge Corpus Christi)

And when God had made Adam, and he yet had no name, he called four angels to him: Michael, Gabriel, Uriel and Raphael, to whom he said, "Find for him a name." Michael lived in the east and saw the star that is called Anatole, saw it, and took the letter A from it and took it to God. Gabriel lived in the west and saw the star called Dysis, took the letter D from it to God. Raphael lived in the north, where he saw the star that is called Arctus, and took from it the letter A and took it to God. Uriel lived in the South and saw the star called Mesembria; he saw there the letter A, which he took to God. Then God said to Uriel, "Read the letters." And Uriel said: Adam. And the Lord said, This will be his name.[a]

a. The witnesses vary in their accounts of the naming of Adam. The Vatican manuscript, in common with all of the pre-tenth-century manuscripts, including those of the *Joca Monachorum,* simply has Adam named after the four cardinal points, though these texts tend to link this to the tradition that Adam was made from four sods of earth. The story of the sending out of the angels is not found in these texts. The manuscripts from the tenth century onwards vary in their witness, but increasingly tend to narrate the story of the sending out of the four angels.

Translation: Adam Octipartite (Slavonic)

Concerning the body. The body of man was created from four elements, it is said: from fire, heat; and from air, cold; from earth, dryness; and from water, moisture.[a] But it is elsewhere written that Adam was created from eight parts. First from earth, [his] body. Second from the Red Sea,[b] [his] blood. Third from the sun, [his] eyes. Fourth from the wind, the breath of [his] life/soul. Fifth from the cloud, [his] thought, good and evil. Sixth from stones, [his] bones. Seventh from the Holy Spirit, which was placed in man for righteousness/truth and part of eternal light, which is Christ; Eighth part from Christ himself,[c] which is the Breath of Life.[d]

When God made Adam and he had no name, God called four angels and said to them, "Find a name for him." The angel Michael went to the East and saw there the star that is called Naphola[e] and took from it the "A." Gabriel went to the South and saw there the star which is called Mashim[f] and took from it the "D." Uriel went to the North and saw the star called Brion and took from it the "M."[g] Raphael went to the West and saw the star called Ador[h] and took from it the "E."[i] And they appeared before God and said of the gifts they consecrated, that by number they made the name Adam. The Lord said, "This will be his name." And all the angels said, "Lord, have mercy upon us."

---

a. The ancient notion of man being made from four elements continues to circulate alongside the distinctive Octipartite tradition.

b. An interesting feature of the Slavonic texts is the tendency to specify that the sea in question is the Red Sea.

c. A reference to the Light of the World has been lost in this manuscript, but continues to be seen in most of the Slavonic witnesses. Interestingly, the word for light, *sveta,* can also mean "world," which leads to confusion in some manuscripts.

d. The Slavonic manuscripts do not discuss the balance of elements in the same way as do the Latin. This manuscript, in fact, entirely lacks any mention of attributes associated with the various elements. Such a discussion is found, however, in the sixteenth-century manuscript RNB Cobr. No. 22/1099, though it is substantially different from the form found in the Latin texts:

"From the earth is taken the attribute of each part. From the sea, kindness. From the sun, beauty. From the clouds, lightness and rebellious thought. From the wind, envy. From the Holy Spirit, every blessing. And from the light of this world is kindness."

e. The names of the stars and their connections to Adam's name clearly become problematic for the Slavic scribes. All of the Slavonic texts reflect some level of confusion over this. The best reading is probably that found in the fifteenth-century Serbian manuscript of the *Conversation* published by Tichonravov, *Pamjatniki,* 2:444, which is correct but for its listing of Mesembria as "Cevria." This, though, is a predictable form of Mesembria, which would contract to Sembria with the *mb* subsequently mutating to a *v* (I am grateful to A. Panayotov for highlighting this fact). That we have at least one largely correct version of the story confirms that the confusion arose as the story was being transmitted within the Slavonic context.

In the base text for our translation, RNB 11/1088, "Naphola" is a corrupted version of "Anatole," from which the "A" may be taken. It is common in Church Slavonic manuscripts to find such confusion of *t, th and ph.*

f. "Mashim" is a corruption of "Dysis." The scribes have also confused the location of the stars: this star should be located in the West.

g. "Brion" is clearly an abbreviated version of "Mesembrion." Again, the star has migrated: this time from the South to the North.

h. "Ador" has taken the place of "Arctus."

i. We find an "E" here where we would expect an "A." The error is unique to this manuscript, but illustrates nicely the confusion experienced by the Slavic scribes.

Translation: Adam Octipartite (Irish)

(Translation provided by Eamon Greenwood. Notes by Grant Macaskill)

It is worthwhile knowing how Adam was made up. Adam was made up of eight parts.[a]

The first part was of earth, the second of sea, the third of sun, the fourth of clouds, the fifth of wind, the sixth of stone, the seventh of the Holy Spirit [and the eighth of the light of the world].[b]

Earth made up Adam's body, sea made up his blood, sun made up his face, clouds [...], wind made up his breath, stone made up his bones, the Holy Spirit made up his soul and the light of the world made up his goodness as a person.

If earth should be the dominant element in a person's make-up, then he will be lazy. If this element is the sea, he will be flighty. If this element is the sun, he will be lively and engaging. If this element is the clouds, he will be of no account. If this element is the wind, he will be blustery to all. If this element is stone, he will be overweening, thieving and greedy. If this element is the Holy Spirit, he will be lively, engaging and full of all the good things of Scripture. If this element is the light of the world, he will be easy to love and sensible.[c]

---

a. The Irish text (BM 4783) here reads "vii." Stokes, *Three Irish Glossaries*, xl, corrects this to "viii."

b. This phrase is added by Whitley Stokes, *Three Irish Glossaries*, xl, and has been included here by Dr. Greenwood. The description of the attributes given by the elements confirms that the text is dependent upon an Octipartite tradition. Interestingly, BM Egerton 1782, which also presents Adam as being made from seven elements, lists the final element as being "from the Light of the World," and then proceeds to specify that this element is the Holy Spirit. The text thus constitutes a conflation of elements from the Octipartite tradition and further supports the case that the Irish texts are dependent upon this.

c. The account of Adam's name is not found in the Irish texts of Adam Octipartite, but it is widely found in that tradition (see the discussion above, in the introduction).

The Life of Adam and Eve (Coptic Fragments)
A new translation and introduction

by Simon J. Gathercole

The *Life of Adam and Eve* (or *Apocalypse of Moses*) recounts some legendary events in the life of Adam and Eve after their expulsion from the Garden of Eden. The contents of the surviving texts vary considerably among themselves but it is agreed that the earliest extant form of the text is the Greek, probably in its short recension. The date of composition of this work is debated, but could be as early as the first or second century C.E. There is also much debate over whether it is of Jewish or Christian provenance.

Versions deriving ultimately from the Greek in Latin, Armenian, Georgian and Slavonic (in some cases, versions in a loose sense) are widely known. In addition to the Greek and Latin texts, Fuchs noted the Slavonic,[1] Wells and Johnson the Armenian and Slavonic.[2] Fernández Marcos[3] and Denis, in the first edition of his *Introduction*, mentioned the Armenian, Slavonic and one of the Coptic texts;[4] the magisterial second edition has a fuller discussion.[5] Whittaker, however, adds the Georgian, but does not include the Coptic fragments.[6] As far as the actual content of the fragments is concerned, Anderson and Stone only include more complete versions in their *Synopsis* and so do not reproduce and translate the Coptic texts, though there is an invaluable treatment in Stone's *History*.[7] Similar information about the text is also presented by de Jonge and Tromp in their introduction to the literature.[8] The Coptic texts of the two fragments were published some time ago, but in rather obscure places, and one of them (the Fayyumic) has not hitherto been translated. As such, an accessible translation of both Coptic fragments is a desideratum, especially as one of the fragments may in fact be the oldest text of the *Life of Adam and Eve* extant in any language.

---

1. E. Kautzsch, ed., *Die Apokryphen und Pseudepigraphen des alten Testaments* (Tübingen: Mohr Siebeck, 1900), 2:506-509.
2. L. S. A. Wells, "The Books of Adam and Eve," in *APOT*, 2:125; M. D. Johnson, "Life of Adam and Eve," in *OTP*, 1:250.
3. N. Fernández Marcos, "Vida de Adam y Eva (Apocalypsis de Moises)," in A. Díez Macho, ed., *Apócrifos del Antiguo Testamento* (Madrid: Ediciónes Cristiandad, 1984-1987), 2:332 n. 6.
4. A.-M. Denis, *Introduction aux pseudépigraphes grecs d'ancien testament* (SVTP 1; Leiden: Brill, 1970), 3-6.
5. A.-M. Denis, *Introduction à la littérature religieuse judéo-hellénistique*, 2 vols. (Turnhout: Brepols, 2000), 1:16-17. This second edition was produced in collaboration with, among others, J.-C. Haelewyck, who provides information about the texts and two notes on related evidence in his *Clavis apocryphorum Veteris Testamenti* (Corpus Christianorum; Turnhout: Brepols, 1998).
6. M. Whittaker, "The Life of Adam and Eve," in *AOT*, 144-145.
7. M. E. Stone, *A History of the Literature of Adam and Eve* (SBLEJL 3; Atlanta, Ga.: Scholars Press, 1992), 39-41.
8. M. de Jonge and Johannes Tromp, *The Life of Adam and Eve and Related Literature* (Guides to Apocrypha and Pseudepigrapha; Sheffield: Sheffield Academic Press, 1997), 17.

Contents

We have observed that the *Life of Adam and Eve* taken as a whole narrates the experience of the protoplasts after their expulsion from Paradise.[9] The Greek version announces in a preface that the account was revealed by God to Moses on Mount Sinai when he received the tablets of the Law, hence the alternative title, the *Apocalypse of Moses*. The work in its Greek form begins with the death of Abel and the birth of Seth and the other sons and daughters (1:1–5:1).[10] Thereafter, the book is taken up with the final days of Adam, in which he first gives Seth a brief account of the fall (7-8), and then requests that Eve and Seth go to the edge of paradise to plead for mercy for him (9:3). They do this, and receive a revelation from Michael who then tells them to return (10-13). Adam instructs Eve (14) to recount to the children the story of their fall, expulsion and repentance (15-30). After that, on the day before he dies, Eve laments and Adam gives his final instructions (31); the next day she again confesses her sin in despair and an angel tells her to get up and see his soul ascend because he has now died (32). Eve receives a vision of angels praying for Adam, which she then shows to Seth (33-36). Adam's soul is taken to the Acherusian Lake and his body buried (37-42).

The material in the Coptic fragments consists of the end of Eve's report of the fall (28:3–29:6, in the Berlin fragment), and the day before and day of Adam's death (31:3–32:2, in the Rylands fragment).

Manuscripts

As has already been noted, there are two Coptic witnesses to the *Life of Adam and Eve* in two different dialects. Both are extremely fragmentary:

1. *Fayyumic version.*[11] Text in Classical Fayyumic Coptic[12] on both sides of a single papyrus leaf, 12 cm high by 24 cm wide, in 2 columns. Both sides of the leaf are missing text at the top and the bottom. Leipoldt provides a "Schriftprobe" in his own handwriting, which shows the text to be written in uncials, or a later form of biblical majuscule (i.e., written entirely in capital letters). Provenance unknown. It was catalogued by Leipoldt as P3212, when it was in the Royal (later, National) Museum in Berlin. It is currently kept in Berlin's Egyptian Museum. It contains, as already mentioned, parts of 28:3–29:6.

2. *Sahidic version.*[13] Text in Sahidic Coptic on both sides of a single parchment leaf, 5 cm high x 13.5 cm wide, in 2 columns. All four columns are almost complete. The text, according to Crum, is written in "small square uncials." Its exact provenance is unknown.[14]

---

9. See notes 2 and 6 above for conveniently available English translations.

10. The chapter numbers here are those conventionally assigned to the Greek version.

11. Original Publication: J. Leipoldt, "Bruchstück einer Mosesapokalypse (faiiumisch)," in idem, ed. Ägyptische Urkunden aus den königlichen Museen zu Berlin, published by Generalverwaltung. Koptische Urkunden, vol. 1 (Berlin, 1904), 171-172 = no. 181.

12. According to the standard criteria, this text is probably written in "Classical" Fayyumic. See the summary in W.-P. Funk, "Der Anfang des Johannesevangeliums auf Faijumisch," *Archiv für Papyrusforschung* 34 (1988): 33-42 (34). One example of the evidence is the long 'e' in *nēf* (as opposed to *nef*, which one would expect in early Fayyumic) in *Recto*, col. 2, line 11.

13. Original Publication: W. E. Crum, *Catalogue of the Coptic Manuscripts in the Collection of the John Rylands Library* (Manchester: Manchester University Press, 1909), 40; §84.

14. Crum, *Catalogue*, vii-viii, comments that the collection might be described—with qualifications—as coming from "the neighbourhood of Ashmunain," but the facts that (a) the collection (which is Crum's "collection B") came from two different dealers, and that (b) it contains some Fayyumic material, mean that a single provenance for all the manuscripts is by no means certain.

It is held in the John Rylands Library, Manchester, catalogued as Coptic MS 84, and contains parts of 31:3–32:2.

Date

For the Sahidic fragment, Crum tentatively gives a possible date of the sixth to seventh century: he places a question mark alongside his sixth-seventh century date in a list which is in any case entitled "Approximate dates."[15] As is often the case with Coptic manuscripts, the date is very difficult to determine, but if Crum is correct, this Sahidic text would be the earliest witness to the *Life of Adam and Eve.*[16] Leipoldt makes no attempt to date the Berlin papyrus.

Stone draws attention to the extensive use of Adam and Eve traditions in the Coptic *Discourse on Abbaton*, attributed to Timothy, Bishop of Alexandria (whose episcopacy ran ca. 380-385), suggesting that this may provide a *terminus ad quem* for a Coptic version of the *Life of Adam and Eve.*[17] Stone assumes that this work presupposes an Adam book in Coptic, but even if this is the case, there is no overlap of any substance with our Coptic fragments. It is possible that, if it is genuine, this work *might* provide a terminus ad quem for a Coptic version of the *Life of Adam and Eve*, though this would not necessarily apply to either of our translations.[18]

Original Language

Although the possibility remains that there is inner-Coptic translation here, the overwhelming probability is that both Coptic fragments here are separate translations from Greek.[19]

---

15. Crum, *Catalogue*, 241. He notes the similarity in script to Brit. Mus. Catal. Pl. 8, no. 171.

16. W. Nagel, *La Vie Grecque d'Adam et Ève, Apocalypse de Moïse* (Dissertation, University of Strasbourg, 1974), 2:102.

17. Stone, *History*, 40. For the *Discourse*, see E. A. W. Budge, *Coptic Martyrdoms in the Dialect of Upper Egypt* (London: The British Museum, 1914), 225-249 (Coptic text) and 474-496 (ET).

18. Stone again mentions (*History*, 141) that "Burmester pointed out the use of the Coptic Adam book in *The Mysteries of the Apostle John and of the Holy Virgin*." However, Burmester does not quite say this; he merely remarks that a particular motif in *Mysteries* goes back not to Egyptian mythology (as Budge had supposed) but to an early form of the Adam book. It may well be the case, however, that *Mysteries* does presuppose a form of the Adam book in Coptic (Denis, *Introduction*[2], 1:17). Further, an Arabic text found in the Coptic monastery of St. Pishoi may attest to the existence of a Coptic version: see O. H. E. Burmester, *Koptische Handschriften I: Die Handschriftenfragmente der Staats- und Universitätsbibliothek Hamburg* (Verzeichnis der orientalischen Handschriften in Deutschland XXI; Wiesbaden: Frans Steiner, 1975), 305. However, Burmester's announcement that he would publish the text in the *Bullétin de la Société de l'archéologie copte* 22 was not fulfilled: the following issue of the *Bullétin* announced Burmester's death.

19. Both fragments contain a good proportion of Greek loan words. In the Berlin fragment: *alla*; *angelos* (x3); *paradisos* (Gk *paradeisos*, but which can also be spelled *paradisos* already in Gk); *kata*; *keleusis*; *palin* (x2); *garpos* (Gk *karpos*; x2); *kasia*; *klatos* (Gk *klados*); *libanos*; *chalbane* (Gk *chalbanē*). In the Rylands fragment: *tote* (x2); *gar*; *alla*; *apanta* (Gk *apantaō*); *despotēs*; *apili* (Gk *apeileō*); *metanoia* (x2); *paraba* (Gk *parabainō*).

Bibliography

FIRST PUBLICATIONS

Leipoldt, J. "Bruchstück einer Mosesapokalypse (faiiumisch)." Pages 171-172 = no. 181 in idem, ed., *Ägyptische Urkunden aus den königlichen Museen ZM Berlin,* Vol. 1. Berlin: Generalverwaltung. Koptische Urkunden, 1904.

Crum, W. E. Page 40; §84 in *Catalogue of the Coptic Manuscripts in the Collection of the John Rylands Library*. Manchester: Manchester University Press, 1909.

ADDITIONAL RELATED LITERATURE

Anderson, G. A., and M. E. Stone, eds. *A Synopsis of the Books of Adam and Eve,* Second Revised Edition. SBLEJL 17; Atlanta, Ga.: Scholars Press, 1999.

de Jonge, M., and J. Tromp. *The Life of Adam and Eve and Related Literature*. Sheffield: Sheffield Academic Press, 1997.

Nagel, W. *La Vie Grecque d'Adam et Ève, Apocalypse de Moïse.* Dissertation, University of Strasbourg, 1974.

Sharpe, J. L. *Prolegomena to the Establishment of the Critical Text of the Greek Apocalypse of Moses*. Dissertation, Duke University, 1969.

Stone, M. E. *A History of the Literature of Adam and Eve*. SBLEJL 3. Atlanta, Ga.: Scholars Press, 1992.

Tromp, J. *The Life of Adam and Eve in Greek: A Critical Edition*. PVTG 6. Leiden: Brill, 2005.

The Life of Adam and Eve (Coptic Fragments)

Berlin fragment

28:3 ... the (?) ... and ... to [gu]ard the tree which ... because of you, [lest] you eat
Gen 3:22 from it, [and be] immortal for ever.

28:4 But on ... when you have come out from ... knowledge, and you are (?) ....

29:1 ... said ... [ang]els so that they might ... us out of paradise. They cried out, saying, in terrifying voices, "Go forth, according to the command of God."[a]

29:2 And Adam your father wept before the angels.[b] They said to him, "What do you [want us to do for you]?"[c]

29:3 ... Again... he cried out ... to the angels, saying, "My lords,[d] if you ..., then allow ... fruit, figs to harvest, figs, fragrant fruit so that when I ..."[e]

29:4-5 ... one (?) ... cassia ... he gave them ... not again.

29:6 He took (?) ... choosing some ... and some branches and frankincense ... gal[ba]num,[f] he ...

---

a. This sentence "They cried out, saying, in terrifying voices, 'Go forth, according to the command of God.'" is not found elsewhere in the textual tradition.

b. Some Greek MSS add "before/in paradise" to the reference to the angels; some omit both. The Coptic here agrees with Gk MSS *p*, *h* and *e*. See the *apparatus criticus* in Tromp, *The Life of Adam and Eve in Greek*, 155. In the notes here, the system of letters designating Greek manuscripts is that of Tromp.

c. The end of the question is as found in Gk, arm and geo versions.

d. Only Gk MS *e* has "my lords."

e. While the fig-leaves are, following Gen 3:7, an important component in many of the versions (Gk 20:4; 21-22 arm slav; 44:2b geo), only this Coptic text has figs in this context.

f. The spices and seeds mentioned vary considerably in the different versions. For the Greek evidence, see Tromp, *The Greek Life of Adam and Eve*, 157; see further Anderson/Stone, *Synopsis*, 73 (+ 73E). Cassia is not mentioned, to my knowledge, in the other versions.

Rylands fragment

31:2 "[H]ow many more years will I have to live? Do not conceal [the] matter from me,[a] my [l]ord[b] Adam, chosen one of God."[c]

31:3 Then [A]dam sa[id] to Eve, ... Adam. He said, "When I die, do not [to]uch me in my place {my place} until the Lord[d] send and speak to you (pl.) about me.

31:4 For he will not forget me, but will seek ... ... gave it[e] to me because I[f] do not know how I will meet the Lord of all, whether God will threaten me or have mercy upon me." Then she arose ...

32:2 ... mercy and greatness.[g] Grant repentance to me,[h] for [I] have sinned in [your] presence. I [ent]reat you, Fat[her], [...]er,[i] [grant] repenta[nce to me].

---

a. None of the other versions have "Do not conceal [the] matter from me."

b. The phrase "my lord" here is paralleled only in Gk MSS *q* and *z*. Elsewhere in the versions, it is a relatively frequent way for Eve to address Adam. See 3:2c geo; 19:2 lat; 20:2a lat geo; 2:2 (Gk)//23:2 (lat arm geo); 9:2 (Gk)//35:2 arm geo. The chapter numbering and versification here (and henceforth) follows that in Anderson & Stone, *Synopsis*.

c. This title of Adam is found elsewhere in, e.g., 21:2 arm geo.

d. Reference to "the Lord" is not paralleled in the Greek manuscript tradition. The closest are *b, q* and *z* which have "angel of the Lord"; other Gk MSS have "(the) angel."

e. Crum provides this as an alternative reading, and prints *tamo* ("said") in the main text. The parallel versions suggest that *taas* ("gave") is correct, however.

f. Perhaps reading the Greek *oidamen* ("we know") as two words (*oida men*).

g. Eve addresses God as "father of mercies" in Gk MSS *m* and *r* here.

h. There is some ambiguity in biblical references to "granting repentance" (e.g., 2 Tim 2:25) as to whether the phrase means granting the ability to repent, or granting an opportunity to repent. In the versions of the *Life of Adam and Eve*, however, the sense is rather that of God hearing favourably a prayer of repentance and forgiving the sinner.

i. The Coptic word begins with *ref-*, which when prefixed to a verb turns the verb into an adjective of agency. Crum suggests "merciful father" (*lit.* "father doing mercy").

The Book of the Covenant

A new translation and introduction

by James VanderKam

Didymus, often called Didymus the Blind (313-98 C.E.), lived in Alexandria where he composed a number of works in the Greek language. In his corpus, he makes numerous references to extra-canonical writings, among which is one he calls *Hē biblos tēs diathēkēs* ("The Book of the Covenant"). Apart from one use of it in his *Commentary on Job*, all of the certain references are in his *Commentary on Genesis*, which is preserved only to Gen 17:3-6. It is likely that he also employed the *Book of the Covenant* in the latter parts of the work on Genesis which are not available at present as the allusion in the Job commentary (relating the scene in Job 1 to the one in Genesis 22) suggests.

Pierre Nautin, who published an edition of Didymus's *Commentary on Genesis*, briefly analyzed the five references to the *Book of the Covenant* and concluded that the work in question was the *Book of Jubilees* on the grounds that three of the five references (1, 4, 5) found parallels in *Jubilees*. While he did not exclude the possibility there was another work that included all the material in the five references, he believed the most likely explanation was that Didymus had a lapse of memory and mistakenly thought he had read numbers 2 and 3 as well in *Jubilees*, due to the similarity in subject matter.[1] Dieter and Ulrike Hagedorn later identified a sixth reference to the *Book of the Covenant* in Didymus's *Commentary on Job* and, with Nautin, thought he meant by it a version of the *Book of Jubilees* "oder stand ihnen zumindest sehr nahe."[2]

In the most comprehensive study of the material from the *Book of the Covenant*, Dieter Lührmann summarized the brief history of scholarship on the subject, presented the Greek excerpts, translated and commented upon them.[3] He did the same for Didymus's use of the *Ascension of Isaiah* and the *Apocalypse of Elijah*. As Lührmann noted, Didymus admits that he did not know Hebrew, yet he refers to Jewish works that were available in Alexandria in the fourth century and that had apparently been received by Christians for some time. He never, for example, stops to explain to the readers what the noncanonical works from which he takes information are—as if they would be aware of

1. Nautin, *Didyme l'Aveugle Sur la Genèse I*, 28-29. There he lists the passages and adduces the parallels from *Jubilees* for the first, fourth, and fifth of them. For numbers 2 and 3, which lack parallels in *Jubilees*, he finds similarities in an Ethiopic work *The Conflict of Adam and Eve with Satan*, a Christian composition that may have used *Jubilees* as a source (see Stone, *A History of the Literature of Adam and Eve*, 98-100). Didymus's commentary is preserved in one of the eight codices containing his and Origen writings, found in a cave near Tura in Egypt in 1941.

2. "or it at least stands very near to it." "Kritisches zum Hiobkommentar Didymus' des Blinden," 60. The editor of the Commentary on Job, A. Henrichs, had translated the title of the work to which he referred as "das (Alte) Testament" (*Didymos der Blinde Kommentar zu Hiob [Tura-Papyrus]*, part I, *Kommentar zu Hiob Kap. 1-4*, 41).

3. "Alttestamentliche Pseudepigraphen," 231-49.

them—though he does occasionally express misgivings about them (see 1, 5, 6; cf. 2). In his presentation of the sections in which Didymus appeals to the *Book of the Covenant*, Lührmann kept the thesis of Nautin and the Hagedorns that the work is *Jubilees* in the foreground but eventually rejected it, and in this he certainly appears to be correct. There are indeed several parallels between what Didymus attributes to the *Book of the Covenant* and the contents of *Jubilees*, but similar information is found elsewhere as well and nothing specifically ties any of the notices to *Jubilees*. Moreover, in some cases Didymus claims material for the *Book of the Covenant* that is not found in *Jubilees* (passages 2 and 3). The *Book of the Covenant* was probably a work that, like *Jubilees*, filled in some of the gaps left in Genesis, even though it was not *Jubilees* itself.

In no one of the six certain references to the *Book of the Covenant* does Didymus quote it directly. His practice is to adduce information from it or allude to it in summary fashion.

Bibliography

Hagedorn, D., and U. Hagedorn. "Kritisches zum Hiobkommentar Didymus' des Blinden." *ZPE* 67 (1987): 59-78.

Henrichs, A. *Didymos der Blinde Kommentar zu Hiob (Tura-Papyrus)*, part I, *Kommentar zu Hiob Kap. 1-4*. Papyrologische Texte und Abhandlungen 1. Bonn: Rudolf Habelt Verlag GMBH, 1968. The edition of Didymus's *Commentary on Job*.

Kugel, J. *Traditions of the Bible: A Guide to the Bible As It Was at the Start of the Common Era*. Cambridge/London: Harvard University Press, 1998.

Lührmann, D. "Alttestamentliche Pseudepigraphen bei Didymos von Alexandrien." *ZAW* 104 (1992): 231-49.

Nautin, P. *Didyme l'Aveugle Sur la Genèse I*. SC 233. Paris: Les éditions du Cerf, 1976.

__________. *Didyme l'Aveugle Sur la Genèse II*. SC 244. Paris: Les éditions du Cerf, 1978. The edition of Didymus's *Commentary on Genesis*.

Stone, M. *A History of the Literature of Adam and Eve*. *SBLEJL* 3. Atlanta, Ga.: Scholars Press, 1992.

VanderKam, J. *The Book of Jubilees*. 2 volumes. CSCO 510-11, Scriptores Aethiopici 87-88. Leuven: Peeters, 1989. The first volume contains the ancient versions available at the time of publication, the second an English translation of them.

The Book of the Covenant[a]

Passage 1 (118, 29–119, 2: on Gen 4:1-2)

If one is willing to admit the Book of the Covenant, he will find in it by how much time the one preceded the other.

Comment: Here Didymus is interested in the question how long a time elapsed between the births of Cain and Abel—how much older Adam and Eve's first son was than their second. Genesis fails to provide any chronological details, noting only that Abel was born later (literally, "she [Eve] added to bear"). Didymus does not divulge how the *Book of the Covenant* answers the query; he simply invites readers to consult it if they are curious about the matter and are willing to accept what it has to say. *Jubilees*, which regularly dates events within a week of years (a seven-year period), places Cain's birth between years of the world 64 and 70, that of Abel between 71 and 77 (4:1-2). The Byzantine chronographer George Syncellus specifies the year 70 for Cain and 77 for Abel.

Passage 2 (121, 22-27: on Gen 4:5)

Regarding which one could mention what emerges from the Book of the Cov-
1 Kgs 18:38; 2 Chr 7:1 enant in which it is written that, when fire descended from heaven, it received (the) properly offered sacrifices, from which, it seems, Cain recognized that the fire did not fall upon his while that of Abel was consumed by it.

Comment: Genesis 4:4-5 relate cryptically that the Lord "had regard for Abel and his offering, but for Cain and his offering he had no regard." The text says nothing about how the divine evaluation of the two sacrifices was communicated to the brothers, although they were obviously aware of it. The *Book of Jubilees* is no less reticent than Genesis about the matter. In 4:2 the Angel of the Presence who narrates the action to Moses discloses only that he and his colleagues accepted Abel's sacrifice but not that of Cain and that Cain killed his brother as a result. There are early sources that attempt to explain the divine decision and how it was conveyed to the brothers; such expansions of the brief scriptural text appear to have been fairly widespread and took several forms.[b]

a. The text of the *Commentary on Genesis* translated here is that of Nautin, *Didyme l'Aveugle Sur la Genèse I* (SC 233; Paris: Les éditions du Cerf, 1976). The numbers in parentheses are the page and line numbers in this edition.

b. See Kugel, *Traditions of the Bible*, 150-52, for examples. Lührmann ("Alttestamentliche Pseudepigraphen," 241) noted that a close parallel to what Didymus found in the *Book of the*

Passage 3 (126, 24-26: on Gen 4:8)

This is in fact not difficult, for if it was not with iron, it could still have taken place with either stone or wood—a matter about which the Book of the Covenant offered a hint.

Comment: Genesis 4:8 says that, while they were in the field, Cain "rose up against his brother Abel, and killed him." A natural question for the inquiring reader is how he murdered his brother, but Genesis does not name the instrument he used. The *Book of the Covenant* speaks darkly or offers hints about the tool involved, according to Didymus. *Jubilees* 4:4 reports the homicide, without details about the instrument Cain used, but later, when dealing with the death of Cain, it says that his house collapsed on him and its stones killed him: "for with a stone he had killed Abel and, by a just judgment, he was killed with a stone"[a] (4:31; the event was the reason for the law providing that a killer be executed with the instrument with which he had murdered his fellow [4:32; cf. Lev 24:17-20]). The motif of the stone and the law attached to it are more widespread than in *Jubilees*.[b] If Didymus is saying that the *Book of the Covenant* was not clear about the instrument Cain employed, he would not have been referring to *Jubilees*, which is unambiguous about the matter.[c]

Passage 4 (142, 28–143, 3: on Cain's death)

It is said in the Book of the Covenant that Cain was unintentionally killed by Lamech, for a wall he was building overturned on him, while Cain, who thus was killed unintentionally, was behind it.

Comment: Genesis neglects to tell about the death of Cain. The last one hears of him is when he goes away from the presence of the Lord and lives in the land of Nod (Gen 4:16). Again Didymus calls upon the *Book of the Covenant* to fill the gap left by the scriptural account. As noted above, *Jub.* 4:31 indicates that Cain died when his house fell on him, with a stone delivering the fatal blow. The *Book of the Covenant*, however, connects Cain's death with Lamech. It apparently understands the "man" of Lamech's song as a reference to Cain—not an unnatural assumption since he mentions Cain in the next sentence: "I have killed a man for wounding me, a young man for striking me. If Cain is avenged sevenfold, truly Lamech seventy-sevenfold" (4:23b-24).[d] The passage offers another indication that the *Book of the Covenant* is unlikely to have been *Jubilees*.

Passage 5 (149, 5-8: on Gen 5:24)

If one is willing to read the Book of the Covenant, he will know that it is said he was taken (into) the garden.[e] And to know this, even if it does not come from an unimpeachable book, is not absurd.

Covenant is present in 1 Kgs 18:38 (fire falling from heaven and consuming Elijah's burnt offering and everything near it). See also the sources in Kugel, *Traditions of the Bible*, 159 (where he mentions this passage from Didymus).

a. Translations of *Jubilees* are from VanderKam, *The Book of Jubilees*, 2:30-31.

b. See Kugel, *Traditions of the Bible*, 166-67.

c. As Lührmann wrote ("Alttestamentliche Pseudepigraphen," 241), the problem with positing that Cain used an iron weapon is that iron was not invented until Gen 4:22. Hence Didymus had to deal with the issue.

d. See Kugel, *Traditions of the Bible*, 167 (where he mentions this passage from Didymus).

e. Or "Paradise."

Comment: Genesis 5:24 offers these cryptic words about Enoch: "Enoch walked with God; then he was no more, because God took him." One might wonder where God transported him, but Genesis does not answer the question. *Jubilees* 4:23 relates: "He was taken from human society, and we led him into the garden of Eden for (his) greatness and honor. Now he is there writing down the judgment and condemnation of the world and all the wickedness of mankind." In this instance, *Jubilees* does agree with what is, according to Didymus, in the *Book of the Covenant*. Lührmann objected that the name of the place is different (paradise/garden of Eden), but the distinction is hardly compelling.[a]

Passage 6 (*Commentary on Job* 6, 17-24: comments on Job 1)[b]

He [the devil] put in motion the last scheme of the demand for surrender, thinking that by this means he could move him from applying his virtue, a tactic he also used on the patriarch Abraham, if one is willing to accept the Book of the Covenant.

Commentary: In the Job commentary, Didymus deals with the similarity between the satan's approach to Job and to Abraham, as explained in the *Book of the Covenant*. Since his *Commentary on Genesis* is preserved only through Gen 17:3-6, the Aqedah is not covered; but the Job commentary implies that Didymus may have employed the *Book of the Covenant* also in connection with Genesis 22. *Jubilees* presents the story of the binding of Isaac in a Joban framework: Mastema, not the Lord, is the one responsible ultimately for the command that Abraham sacrifice his son (see 17:15–18:19, especially 17:16; 18:12). In the context Didymus does not designate the opponent as Mastema, but otherwise the *Book of the Covenant* seems to understand the Genesis 22 story within the same framework as *Jubilees* does. It should be added, nevertheless, that *Jubilees* was not the only ancient source to depict the Aqedah in Joban terms. Another clear example is 4Q225 from Qumran.[c]

a. Lührmann, "Alttestamentliche Pseudepigraphen," 242. He also cited Didymus's comment on Acts 8:39 where the Spirit snatches Philip away after he baptizes the Ethiopian eunuch; the latter did not see him again. Didymus says this agrees with what is said about Enoch's being moved from one place to another without the text saying where. He writes that in the apocrypha it is said that the place was paradise. Lührmann thought the *Book of the Covenant* was also the source here, though Didymus did not identify it explicitly ("Alttestamentliche Pseudepigraphen," 242-43).

b. For the text, see Albert Henrichs, *Didymos der Blinde Kommentar zu Hiob (Tura-Papyrus)*, part I, *Kommentar zu Hiob Kap. 1-4*. The designation "6, 17-24" refers to the page and line numbers of the text in Henrichs's edition.

c. Lührmann also adduces a passage from the Catena of Nicephorus where there is an expansion on the story of the tower of Babel, an expansion attributed to "the Covenant" ("Alttestamentliche Pseudepigraphen," 244). Whether the work was the same as the *Book of the Covenant* to which Didymus refers is not clear, though it offers similar material. It reads: "... they spent 43 years building (it). Its height was 5433 cubits and two palms. Its width was about 203 bricks. The height of the brick was a third of one brick. The extent of one wall was 13 stades and of the other 30" (VanderKam, *The Book of Jubilees*, 2.355; for the Greek text, see 1.267). The passage is a reproduction of *Jub.* 10:21.

The Apocryphon of Seth

A new translation and introduction

by Alexander Toepel

The *Liber apocryphus nomine Seth*, "Apocryphal Book in the name of Seth", is known exclusively from a lengthy quotation in a spurious Latin commentary upon the Gospel of Matthew.[1] This work, commonly known as *Opus imperfectum in Matthaeum*, until the sixteenth century C.E. was believed to have been authored by John Chrysostom. Its authenticity was first called into question by Erasmus of Rotterdam, and since then an Arian author writing in the fifth century in or around Constantinople has been singled out as the most probable source of the commentary.[2] *Opus imperfectum in Matthaeum* is characterized by a great leniency towards pseudepigraphal writings which borders upon a blurring of the biblical canon. In this context noncanonical writings are especially sought out for an elucidation and augmentation of the canonical text, and it is in this respect that the *Liber apocryphus nomine Seth* makes its appearance.

Contents

The *Liber apocryphus* seems to have been a comparatively short text which is concerned with the pre-history of the magi visiting the newborn Jesus. Its contents are summarized by the author of the *Opus imperfectum*, who quotes the book in connection with an exegesis of the canonical birth-story in Matt 2:1-12. The account begins with a reference to a "certain scripture" (*quadam scriptura*), presumably the *Liber apocryphus*, which tells of a tribe living in the outermost East in the vicinity of the world-surrounding *oceanus*. This tribe is later identified with the magi, who are given to celestial observation and the safeguarding of the apocryphal book in question. More precisely, they expect the appearance of a certain star, for which they are looking out over generations. The star is finally seen; upon this the magi travel to Judaea, where the canonical narrative sets in. After returning to their home country they proclaim Christ; finally they are baptized by the apostle Thomas. At this point the author of the *Opus imperfectum* resumes his/her own work with a lengthy discussion of the value and fallaciousness of astrology.

---

1. In Jacques-Paul Migne's edition (PG 56, 637) it bears the subtitle *Mons Victorialis* "the victorious mountain/mountain of victories". On this motif, cf. below.

2. Cf. Christiane Schmidt, "Opus imperfectum in Matthaeum," in *Lexikon der antiken christlichen Literatur* (ed. Siegmar Döpp and Wilhelm Geerlings; 3rd ed. 2002; Freiburg im Breisgau: Herder), 527. Joop van Banning and Franz Mali, "Opus imperfectum in Matthaeum" in *Theologische Realenzyklopädie* (ed. Gerhard Müller; Berlin: De Gruyter, 1995), 25:305. Brent C. Landau, *The Sages and the Star-Child. An Introduction to the* Revelation of the Magi, *An Ancient Christian Apocryphon* (Unpublished Ph.D. thesis; Harvard University, 2008), 139-142. Joop van Banning, *Opus Imperfectum in Matthaeum. Praefatio* (CCSL 87B; Turnhout: Brepols, 1988), p. V, believes the book to originate more specifically from one of the Danube provinces of the Roman empire, such as Illyricum, Dacia or Moesia.

Manuscripts and Versions

The author of the *Opus imperfectum* obviously had first-hand knowledge of this apocryphal book, but he or she does not seem to quote *verbatim*; rather his/her account gives the impression of an abbreviated form which seeks to summarize all the important points while leaving out things considered to be superfluous or known through the canonical text. There is no independent textual evidence for the *Liber apocryphus*, which means that its textual history is identical with, and reduced to, the textual history of the *Opus imperfectum*, of which it forms a part. The textual tradition of the latter work has been studied extensively by Joop van Banning, who distinguishes altogether four families of texts, all in the Latin language.[3] This classification goes back to work by Friedrich Kauffmann[4] who in 1909 identified a group of mainly Carolingian manuscripts, one of mainly French manuscripts from the twelfth century and one of mainly English ones from the thirteenth century. In 1974 a fourth group of manuscripts of Italian and Spanish provenance was discovered by Joseph Lemarié and Raymond Étaix,[5] which is counted as the third family by van Banning due to its date between Kauffmann's French and English families, the fourth one in van Banning's system being Kauffmann's English subgroup.

Editions of the *Opus imperfectum* go back to an early date with the *editio princeps* having been printed in 1487 as part of an edition of the works of John Chrysostom. This was followed by editions of the Benedictine monks of Santa Justina in Padua (Venice 1503), Andreas Cratander (Basel 1525) and Erasmus of Rotterdam (Basel 1530). The latter published a revised edition in Paris 1536, which was reprinted in Basel 1539. Jacques-Paul Migne's edition in volume 56 of the Patrologia Graeca goes back to an edition of the works of John Chrysostom by Bernard de Montfaucon from 1724; it does not represent any substantial improvement over against Erasmus' edition from 1536.[6]

Genre and Structure

Due to the abbreviated form of the text in the *Opus imperfectum* attempts at determining its literary character have to remain tentative. There is on the one hand a reference to an actual book going back to Seth (it is not clear whether this book is identical with the account quoted by the author of the *Opus imperfectum*), which calls to mind similar texts claiming to be revelations given by Adam to his son Seth.[7] As these revelations assume the shape of a testament of Adam, it is possible that the *Liber apocryphus* originally belonged to the same literary genre, i.e., Testaments of the Patriarchs.[8] On the other hand the text is obviously linked with the birth of Jesus and seeks to give an account of the origins and further adventures of the magi. In this respect it might be seen as akin to other pseude-

3. Cf. van Banning, *Opus Imperfectum*, XI-XIII.

4. *Zur Textgeschichte des Opus imperfectum in Matthaeum* (Festschrift der Universität Kiel zur Feier des Geburtsfestes Seiner Majestät des Kaisers und Königs Wilhelm II.; Kiel: Lipsis & Tischer, 1909).

5. "Fragments inédits de l'Opus Imperfectum in Matthaeum," *Revue Bénédictine* 84 (1974): 278-300.

6. Cf. van Banning, *Opus Imperfectum*, CCCXXXI-CCCXLVIII.

7. Cf. Giuseppe Messina, "Una presunta profezia di Zoroastro sulla venuto del Messia," *Bib* 14 (1933): 178-79. Apart from the actual *Testament of Adam*, on which cf. Stephen E. Robinson, "Testament of Adam," in *OTP*, 1:989-92, the Greek *Apocalypse of Moses* and Latin *Vita Adae et Evae* present Seth as recipient and tradent of special revelations concerning the salvation of Adam; cf. *Ap. Mos.* 38:4; 42:3 and *L.A.E.* 25:1–29:3; 46:3; 47:2-3; 51:3-9.

8. This would fit well with the text's Christian character, which corresponds to the Christian origins of the genre; cf. Robert A. Kugler, *The Testaments of the Twelve Patriarchs* (Guides to Apocrypha and Pseudepigrapha; Sheffield: Sheffield Academic Press, 2001), 35-38, summarizing work by Marinus de Jonge.

pigraphal infancy narratives and therefore could, following Helmut Koester's assessment of the noncanonical infancy gospels, be classified as an aretalogy.[9] The latter alternative seems validated insofar as the *Liber apocryphus* does not contain a prophecy or revelatory testament in the strict sense but rather tells of the prehistory and aftermath of an episode from the childhood of Jesus as related in the New Testament. It gains additional weight by the fact that already in the canonical infancy narrative the magi's visit serves an aretalogical purpose: The new-born Jesus is put into one line with Persian and Roman emperors, at whose birth astrologers were present and unusual celestial phenomena made their appearance.[10]

Date and Provenance

As concerns the date of the *Liber apocryphus* a terminus ante quem is fixed by its use in the *Opus imperfectum* in the fifth century C.E. A terminus post quem is given by the fact that the text seems to presuppose a Christianization of earlier Hellenistic-Persian oracles (cf. on this below) such as can be found in Justin Martyr, *Apol.* 1:20:1; 1:44:12; Clem. Alex., *Strom.* 5:43:1-3 and Lact., *Div. Inst.* 7:15:19; 7:17:16; 7:18:2.[11] This would result in a possible origin of the *Liber apocryphus* in the third or fourth century C.E. A further subdivision can be achieved, if the final episode concerning the apostle Thomas baptizing the magi is seen as a redactional element added to a more original account of the magi's visit to Bethlehem. In that case the text's core might well go back into the second century.[12] The geographical background of the work is not quite as clear. On the one hand the text does not seem to have been distributed widely, since it is only known to the author of the *Opus Imperfectum*; this would point to an origin in the vicinity of Constantinople with Greek or even Latin as the original language. On the other hand, some of the book's traditions are known from later Syriac sources as well, and furthermore the subtitle *Mons Victorialis* seems to go back to the misunderstanding of a Syriac term.[13] This has led some researchers to assume a common source of Syriac provenance which would have been abbreviated by the author of the *Opus Imperfectum* while being expanded in later Syriac works.[14]

9. On the literary genre of the pseudepigraphal infancy gospels cf. Helmut Koester, "Ein Jesus und vier ursprüngliche Evangeliengattungen," in Helmut Koester and James M. Robinson, *Entwicklungslinien durch die Welt des frühen Christentums* (Tübingen: Mohr, 1971), 178-79.

10. Cf. Ulrich Luz, *Das Evangelium nach Matthäus* (Evangelisch-Katholischer Kommentar zum Neuen Testament I/1; Einsiedeln and Neukirchen-Vluyn: Benziger Verlag and Neukirchener Verlag, 1985), 1:120. For *religionsgeschichtliche* parallels see Martin Hengel and Helmut Merkel, "Die Magier aus dem Osten und die Flucht nach Ägypten (Mt 2) im Rahmen der antiken Religionsgeschichte und der Theologie des Matthäus," in *Orientierung an Jesus. Zur Theologie der Synoptiker* (ed. Paul Hoffmann; Freiburg im Breisgau: Herder, 1973), 139-69 (extensive bibliography on pp. 166-69); Klaus Berger and Carsten Colpe, *Religionsgeschichtliches Textbuch zum Neuen Testament* (Texte zum Neuen Testament, 1; Göttingen: Vandenhoeck & Ruprecht, 1987), 114-15.

11. Cf. A.-M. Denis et al., *Introduction à la littérature religieuse judéo-hellénistique* (Turnhout: Brepols, 2000), 2:1185-89; Messina, "Una presunta profezia," 187-189, 198.

12. Cf. Landau, *Sages*, 175-201 and the graph on p. 19.

13. Cf. on this below.

14. Cf. Wilhelm Bousset, *Hauptprobleme der Gnosis* (FRLANT, 10; Göttingen: Vandenhoeck & Ruprecht, 1907), 380-81; Jacques Duchesne-Guillemin, "Die Magier in Bethlehem und Mithras als Erlöser?" in *ZDMG* 111 (1961): 472. Landau, *Sages*, 165-70, 201-20.

Literary Context

A first clue to the book's literary context and sources is given by the Iranian elements present within it. In the Latin manuscript tradition the book bears a subtitle *Mons Victorialis*, "the victorious mountain/mountain of victories." This term refers most likely to the world-mountain *Harā B^{e}r^{e}zaitī*, more commonly known as "Alborz," of Zoroastrian lore. This cosmic mountain range is described in *Yasht* 10:50 as luminous; a Syriac term *tura naziḥa*, "luminous mountain" is indeed known from *Cave of Treasures* 6:23, and insofar as the root *nzḥ* can have the meaning "victorious," as well as "luminous," the Latin *mons victorialis* seems to be a mistranslation of the Syriac phrase.[15] The tribesmen residing in the outermost East are explicitly identified as *magi*, who praise God "in silence and with a low voice"; this apparently refers to the silent, murmuring way of reciting sacred texts, which was considered characteristic of Zoroastrian priests in Greco-Roman antiquity.[16] The phrase *post messem trituratoriam* "after the hay harvest" is identified by Geo Widengren as the designation of a Zoroastrian feast day.[17] The Magi, who ascend the *mons victorialis* on this occasion, go to a cave nearby a fountain surrounded by trees. This brings immediately to mind the literary description of a Mithraic grotto in Porphyrius, *de antro nymph.* §6, as well as the depiction of trees representing the seven planets in archaeological remains of the Mithraic mystery cult.[18]

Given this strong presence of Iranian elements within the *Liber apocryphus* it is tempting to locate the text within a Persian environment or at least to trace literary or oral sources of Iranian origin.[19] However, since Hellenistic times Persian traditions were widely received in the Greek and Latin-speaking world, including Christian authors of late antiquity such as Justin Martyr, Clement of Alexandria and Lactantius. Iranian elements such as the mountain and cave, therefore, do not necessarily point to an origin in Persia; they can as well be elements of a much broader stream of Hellenized Iranian lore current in the early centuries of the Common Era.

This is confirmed by the fact that the *Liber apocryphus* contains other elements which are exclusively known from Jewish or Christian authors. The idea that Seth and his descendants possess a special revelatory knowledge based upon astronomy is found in Josephus, *A.J.* 1:70-71.[20] The idea of sages residing in the East near to the earth-encircling ocean is known from the Syriac *Cave of Treasures* 27:6-11, where an apocryphal fourth son

15. Cf. my *Die Adam- und Sethlegenden im Syrischen* Buch der Schatzhöhle (CSCO 618; Subsidia 119; Louvain: Peeters, 2006), 230 with n. 47 and the literature quoted there. Messina, "Una presunta profezia," 197, sees a connection with the middle-Persian term *vrθragan* "victorious," which is an epithet of the Zoroastrian savior; still, the Latin term retains a distinct "colorito iranico" (*ibid.*, 196).

16. Cf. Geo Widengren, *Die Religionen Irans* (Die Religionen der Menschheit, 14; Stuttgart: Kohlhammer, 1965), 207, 250 and the references in Joseph Bidez and Franz Cumont, *Les mages hellénises* (Paris: Soc. d'Éd. Les Belles Lettres, 1973), 2:285-86. It is, however, possible, that the silent prayer of the Magi in the *Liber apocryphus* is meant to emphasize their mystical inclinations as well; cf. Widengren, *Religionen*, 211 with n. 16. The two explanations do not seem to exclude each other.

17. Cf. *ibid.*, 207 n. 1 with reference to Richard Reitzenstein, *Die Vorgeschichte der christlichen Taufe* (Leipzig: Teubner, 1929), 379.

18. Cf. Widengren, *Religionen*, 207; Alexander Toepel, "Planetary Demons in Early Jewish Literature," *JSP* 14 (2005): 231-33, esp. p. 233.

19. This is done by Geo Widengren, *Religionen*, 207, as well as by Wilhelm Bousset, *Hauptprobleme*, 380-381, who regard the *Liber apocryphus* as essentially Iranian in character.

20. Cf. Gerrit J. Reinink, "Das Land «Seiris» (Šir) und das Volk der Serer in jüdischen und christlichen Traditionen," *JSJ* 6 (1975): 72.

of Noah by the name of Yonton makes his appearance.[21] Yonton is said to have lived near the *okeanos* and taught his stellar wisdom to Nimrod. The latter one, however, as well as Balaam, is frequently identified with Zoroaster in Christian texts of the third to eighth centuries C.E.[22] Over against this the allegedly Iranian elements in the *Liber apocryphus* are not present in Zoroastrian tradition proper;[23] they most likely stem from a syncretistic environment such as is attested by the Mithraic mysteries, the Oracles of Hystaspes and similar phenomena.

It seems therefore safe to put the *Liber apocryphus* within a context of applying Hellenized Iranian lore to Christ, as can be observed from the second century onward. An elaborate version of the material contained within the present text can be found in the eighth-century anonymous Syriac work commonly known as the *Chronicle of Zuqnīn* or "Chronicle of Pseudo-Dionysius of Tel-Mahre."[24] Since there are marked differences between the latter's account and the *Liber apocryphus*, a common source has been assumed, which was abbreviated by the *Liber apocryphus* and expanded by the *Chronicle of Zuqnīn*.[25]

In the Latin West the book exercised a certain influence through its incorporation into the *Legenda aurea* of Jacobus de Voragine (end of thirteenth century), who refers to its content, without mentioning the source, in the context of Epiphany. The East-Syrian (Nestorian) Church, which knows of twelve magi visiting the new-born Christ,[26] owes this knowledge via the *Chronicle of Zuqnīn* likewise to the *Liber apocryphus* or a related account.

Bibliography

EDITION

Migne, Jacques Paul. *S.P.N. Joannis Chrysostomi opera omnia quae exstant*. PG 56. Paris: Migne, 1859: 601-946. [*Liber apocryphus nomine Seth*, 637-38.]

STUDIES

Banning, Joop van. *Opus Imperfectum in Matthaeum. Praefatio*. CCSL 87B. Turnhout: Brepols, 1988. (Extensive bibliography.)

21. On this figure and its *religionsgeschichtliche* background cf. Stephen Gero, "The Legend of the Fourth Son of Noah," *HTR* 73 (1980): 321-30 and Alexander Toepel, "Yonton Revisited: A Case Study in the Reception of Hellenistic Science within Early Judaism," *HTR* 99 (2006): 235-45.

22. Cf. Messina, "Una presunta profezia," 180-185; Su-Min Ri, *Commentaire de la Caverne des Trésors. Étude sur l'histoire du texte et de ses sources* (CSCO 581, Subsidia 103; Louvain: Peeters, 2000), 354-56 .

23. Cf. Duchesne-Guillemin, *ZDMG* 111 (1961): 469-75.

24. On the work and its date cf. generally Ignacio Ortiz de Urbina, *Patrologia Syriaca* (Rome: Pont. Inst. Orient. Stud., 2nd ed., 1965), 211. The relevant Syriac text is available in *Chronicon pseudo-Dionysianum vulgo dictum* (ed. Jean-Baptiste Chabot; CSCO, 121; Script. Syri 3,1 [= 66]; Louvain: Durbecq, 1949), 1:45-70. An English translation is to be found in Landau, *Sages*, 75-136.

25. Cf. Duchesne-Guillemin, in *ZDMG* 111 (1961): 472. The early-13th-century Nestorian bishop Solomon of Basra, who in his *Book of the Bee* has preserved similar traditions, most likely took them over from the *Chronicle of Zuqnīn* and therefore cannot be regarded as an independent witness, as Bousset, *Hauptprobleme*, 379, 381 has it. Unlike earlier scholars, Brent Landau is not convinced that the *Chronicle of Zuqnīn* substantially reworks an earlier version; cf. his *Sages*, 165-70. In that case the Syriac text contained in the chronicle would be identical with *Liber apocryphus nomine Seth*.

26. Cf. Adolf Rücker (ed. and transl.), "Zwei nestorianische Hymnen über die Magier," *OrChr* n.s. 10 (1920): 33-55.

Duchesne-Guillemin, Jacques. "Die Magier in Bethlehem und Mithras als Erlöser?" *ZDMG* 111 (1961): 469-75.

Landau, Brent Christopher. *The Sages and the Star-Child. An Introduction to the* Revelation of the Magi, *An Ancient Christian Apocryphon*. Unpublished Ph.D. thesis. Harvard University, 2008.

Messina, Giuseppe. "Una presunta profezia di Zoroastro sulla venuto del Messia." *Bib* 14 (1933): 170-98.

Monneret de Villard, Ugo. *Le leggende orientali sui magi evangelici*. Studi e Testi 163. Vatican City: Biblioteca Apostolica Vaticana, 1952.

Sieben, Hermann-Josef. "Opus imperfectum in Matthaeum." *Dictionnaire de Spiritualité*. Paris: Beauchesne, 1974: 8:362-69.

Widengren, Geo. *Iranisch-semitische Kulturbegegnung in parthischer Zeit*. Cologne: Westdeutscher Verlag, 1960.

The Apocryphon of Seth

Apocryphal book in the name of Seth—The mountain of victories. I heard some relate from a certain scripture, albeit not wholly reliable, which is nonetheless not destroying faith, but rather pleasing, that there was a certain tribe residing in the furthermost East, opposite the Ocean, among whom a certain scripture is passed on, written in the name of Seth, about the appearance of this star and in which way those presents were offered. (This book) has come down through generations of studious men, fathers relating it to their sons. Thus they chose themselves some twelve from among their most studious, who were lovers of celestial mysteries and put themselves to looking out for that star. If one of them died, his son or someone of his relatives who was found to be of the same inclinations, was put in place of the deceased. In their own language, however, they were called "magi," because they glorified God in silence and with a low voice. Now these went up each single year after the hay harvest to some mountain in this area which in their language is called "mountain of victories," having within it a kind of cave in the rock, fountains and choice trees of the most pleasant kind. After having gone up there and washing themselves they prayed and praised God in silence for three days. Thus they did in each single generation, always wondering whether in their own generation this blessed star might rise. Finally it appeared to them descending upon this mountain of victories, having within it the shape of a small boy and above it the likeness of a cross. Then (the star) spoke to them, taught them and commanded them to go to Judaea. On their way, however, the star preceded them for half a year and never was there food or drink lacking in their bags. The rest of the deeds now, which are told about them, are briefly laid down in the gospel. When they had returned, however, they kept serving and glorifying God with great zeal, as before, preached to everybody in their tribe and educated many. Later, when after the Lord's resurrection the apostle Thomas came into that province, they adhered to him and, having been baptized by him, became co-workers in his proclamation.

Matt 2:2

Matt 2:11

Matt 2:9; Clem. Alex., *Strom.* 1:24:163; Plutarch, *Life of Timoleon* §8; Diod. Sic., *Bibl. Hist.* 16:66:3; Vergil, *Aeneid* 2:692-697

Matt 2:1-12

The Book of Noah
A new translation and introduction

by Martha Himmelfarb

The text translated here is the introduction to a Hebrew medical work from ninth- or tenth-century Byzantine Italy, the *Book of Asaph*.[1] The narrative genre of the passage and its association with a biblical hero set it apart from the work to which it is prefaced, and its striking similarity to a passage in the *Book of Jubilees*, a work of the second century B.C.E., gives good reason to believe that it is of greater antiquity than the rest of the *Book of Asaph*.

The title "Book of Noah" goes back to Adolph Jellinek, who published the passage together with two other brief passages about Noah drawn from magical works under that title in 1855.[2] There are several references to a Book of Noah in texts of the Second Temple period,[3] but no such work has survived. Some scholars doubt that one ever existed,[4] but others have attempted to reconstruct its contents on the basis of the references and passages about the career of Noah in Second Temple works.[5] Below I suggest that the source that the author/compiler of the *Book of Asaph* used for the "Book of Noah" was not *Jubilees* itself but a no longer extant work on which *Jubilees* drew. The existence of such a work has implications for the discussion of the ancient "Book of Noah," though the work need not have been restricted to materials about Noah.

The "Book of Noah" recounts the angel Raphael's revelation to Noah of a book of remedies for the diseases that afflict Noah's descendants as a result of their sins, which are instigated by evil spirits (2). The "Book of Noah" does not explain where the evil spirits come from, but *Jubilees* identifies them as the spirits of the sons of the Watchers (*Jub.* 10:5), the angels who descended to earth and took human wives with disastrous

---

1. For this dating and provenance, Elinor Leiber, "Asaf's *Book of Medicines*: A Hebrew Encyclopedia of Greek and Jewish Medicine, Possibly Compiled in Byzantium on an Indian Model," *Dumbarton Oaks Papers* 38: *Symposium on Byzantine Medicine* (ed. John Scarborough; Washington, D.C.: Dumbarton Oaks, 1984), 233-49.

2. Jellinek, *BHM*, 3:155-56.

3. *Jub.* 8:11, 10:13-14, 21:10; *Genesis Apocryphon* col. 5, line 29; *Aramaic Levi Document* §57.

4. See, e.g., Cana Werman, "Qumran and the Book of Noah," in *Pseudepigraphic Perspectives: The Apocrypha and Pseudepigrapha in Light of the Dead Sea Scrolls*, ed. Esther G. Chazon and Michael E. Stone, (STDJ 31: Leiden: Brill, 1999), 171-81; and Devorah Dimant, "Two 'Scientific' Fictions: The So-Called *Book of Noah* and the Alleged Quotation of *Jubilees* in CD 16:3-4," in *Studies in the Hebrew Bible, Qumran, and the Septuagint Presented to Eugene Ulrich*, ed. Peter W. Flint, Emanuel Tov, and James C. VanderKam (VTSup 101; Leiden: Brill, 2006), 230-49.

5. The sources include the *Aramaic Levi Document*, the *Genesis Apocryphon*, and *1 Enoch*, particularly the *Parables of Enoch* (*1 Enoch* 37-71) and chapters 106-7. For recent attempts at reconstruction, see, e.g., Florentino García Martínez, *Qumran and Apocalyptic: Studies on the Aramaic Texts from Qumran* (STDJ 9; Leiden: Brill, 1992), 24-44; Wayne Baxter, "Noachic Traditions and the *Book of Noah*," *JSP* 15 (2006): 179-94; and Michael E. Stone, "The Book(s) Attributed to Noah," *DSD* 13 (2006): 4-23.

results. In response to Noah's sacrifice and prayer (5) God sends the angel Raphael to imprison most of the evil spirits (6-7). But Raphael leaves one-tenth of the spirits free to continue their attacks (8); thus it is clear that humanity will continue to be afflicted by disease. Raphael then gives Noah a book containing herbal remedies for the illnesses human beings will endure and sends the princes of the spirits to explain the remedies (9-10). The book that Noah receives becomes the source of all medical wisdom world over (11).

The many similarities of the "Book of Noah" to *Jub.* 10:1-14 led Jellinek to describe the "Book of Noah" as a remnant of the lost Hebrew original of *Jubilees.*[6] Yet even a cursory comparison of the passage from *Jubilees* and the "Book of Noah" reveals significant differences between them. Thus, for example, the "Book of Noah" refers to the evil spirits as "the spirits of the bastards" (2); this insulting designation appears not in *Jubilees,* however, but in the even more ancient *Book of the Watchers* (*1 En.* 10:9). In the "Book of Noah" Noah sacrifices and prays, but the words of the prayer are not reported (5); *Jubilees,* however, does not mention a sacrifice but includes the content of the prayer (*Jub.* 10:3-6). *Jubilees* describes God's decision to leave a tenth of the evil spirits free to continue their attacks on humanity as a response to the request of Mastemah, their leader (*Jub.* 10:7-9), while the "Book of Noah" reports that Raphael allowed a tenth of the spirits to remain free without mention of Mastemah's request (8).

Several of the differences between *Jubilees* and the "Book of Noah" reflect the medical concerns of the *Book of Asaph.* In the "Book of Noah" the afflictions caused by the evil spirits consist of illness and physical problems (2, 4), while in *Jubilees* the afflictions are as much spiritual as physical (*Jub.* 10:1-2, 10). The "Book of Noah" attributes the imprisonment of the evil spirits and the revelation of the book of remedies to the angel Raphael, whose name means "God heals" (6-9); *Jubilees*'s narrator, the angel of the presence, claims that he and other anonymous angels performed these tasks (*Jub.* 10:11-12).[7] So too the "Book of Noah" offers a list of the parts of the plants to be used in the remedies of the angelic book (9-10), while *Jubilees* merely notes that the remedies involve plants (*Jub.* 10:12).[8]

The complete *Book of Jubilees* has come down to us only in Ethiopic translation; the original Hebrew is known from fragments found among the Dead Sea Scrolls, which, unfortunately, do not include the passage discussed here. But though the relevant Hebrew has not survived, the differences between *Jubilees* and the "Book of Noah" just noted show that the "Book of Noah" can hardly be a fragment of the Hebrew *Jubilees.* A more plausible explanation for the similarities and differences is that the "Book of Noah" is a revision of the passage from *Jubilees* that places greater emphasis on disease and herbal medicine for the purposes of the *Book of Asaph.*[9]

6. Jellinek, *BHM,* 3:xxx-xxxi.

7. *Jubilees* reports that God ordered one of the angels, no name given, to reveal the remedies to Noah (*Jub.* 10:10), but the angelic narrator uses the first-person plural to describe the fulfillment of the command (*Jub.* 10:12).

8. On the differences, see Martha Himmelfarb, "Some Echoes of *Jubilees* in Medieval Hebrew Literature," *Tracing the Threads: Studies in the Vitality of the Jewish Pseudepigrapha* (ed. John C. Reeves; SBLEJL 6; Atlanta, Ga.: Scholars Press, 1994), 130-31.

9. This is the position of Devorah Dimant, "'The Fallen Angels' in the Dead Sea Scrolls and in the Apocrypha and Pseudepigraphic Books Related to Them" (Ph.D. diss., Hebrew University of Jerusalem, 1974) (Heb.), 128-30, as cited by Michael Segal, *The Book of* Jubilees*: Rewritten Bible, Redaction, Ideology and Theology* (JSJSup 117; Leiden: Brill, 2007), 171 n. 8; I have not seen Dimant's dissertation.

Attractive though this suggestion is, however, there is reason for caution. Medieval Hebrew works such as *Midrash Aggadah* and *Midrash Tadshe* know material from *Jubilees*, but the passages on which they draw appear also in the work of the Byzantine chronographers.[10] The chronographers did not know *Jubilees* directly but made use of a collection of excerpts from the Greek versions of ancient Jewish and Christian works that contained material of interest to them.[11] Given the overlap between the medieval Hebrew works and the chronographies and the absence of other evidence for the survival of the Hebrew of *Jubilees* into the Middle Ages, it seems likely that the medieval Hebrew works drew on the collection of excerpts used by the chronographers, which they translated back into Hebrew, rather than on the Hebrew original of *Jubilees*.[12]

The passage about the book of remedies may well have formed part of the Greek collection. Although it does not appear in any of the chronographies, Syncellus alludes to the story.[13] Yet two terms in the "Book of Noah" make it unlikely that it is based on an excerpt from *Jubilees* in Greek. The "Book of Noah" uses the phrase "*bêt mišpat*," "place of judgment," to mean prison. The meaning "prison" is attested in the Dead Sea Scrolls (1QpHab 8.2), but in medieval Hebrew the phrase is used to mean "court."[14] Thus the phrase seems unlikely to be the work of a medieval Jew translating a Greek version of *Jubilees* back into Hebrew. So too "Mastemah" is unlikely in a text translated from Greek by a medieval Jew. The abstract noun "*maśṭēmâ*," "hostility," appears twice in the Bible (Hos 9:7-8) and more frequently in the Scrolls.[15] But in *Jubilees* "the Prince of Mastemah" is the leader of the evil spirits who plays a role at many points in the narrative, including the affliction of Noah's sons, where, however, he is referred to without the title "prince" (*Jub.* 10:8). The name together with the title appears in at least two other ancient Jewish works as well.[16] Syncellus also preserves a form of the name in a passage in which he

---

Segal himself argues for direct dependence of the "Book of Noah" on *Jubilees* (*Book of* Jubilees, 170-74). Segal's claims for the preservation in the "Book of Noah" of concerns and language that make sense only in the context of *Jubilees* do not seem decisive to me. In relation to his claim that the transmission of the book from Noah to Shem reflects the interests of *Jubilees*, see the discussion of chains of transmission in rabbinic literature, Hekhalot texts, and Hebrew magical texts including the "Book of Noah" in Michael D. Swartz, "Book and Tradition in Hekhalot and Magical Literatures," *Journal of Jewish Thought and Philosophy* 3 (1994): 189-229; on the "Book of Noah," 214-16.

10. Himmelfarb, "Some Echoes," 115-26.

11. William Adler, *Time Immemorial: Archaic History and Its Sources in Christian Chronography from Julius Africanus to George Syncellus* (Dumbarton Oaks Studies 26; Washington, D.C.: Dumbarton Oaks, 1989), 159-231, with a convenient summary, 229-31.

12. A possible exception is the list of names of wives of the patriarchs that appears not in *Midrash Aggadah* and *Midrash Tadshe* but in three different medieval works (Himmelfarb, "Some Echoes," 126-27).

13. For the text of Syncellus, Alden A. Mosshammer, ed., *Georgii Syncelli Ecloga Chronographica* (Leipzig: Teubner, 1984), 27.33–28.9. For a translation, William Adler and Paul Tuffin, *The Chronography of George Synkellos: A Byzantine Chronicle of Universal History from the Creation* (Oxford: Oxford University Press, 2002), 37.

14. Yehoshua M. Grintz, *Chapters in the History of the Second Temple Times* (Hebrew; Jerusalem: Makor, 1999), 127 n. 51, and for *Pesher Habakkuk*, A. M. Habermann, *'Edah We-'Eduth: Three Scrolls from the Judaean Desert, the Legacy of a Community* (Hebrew; Jerusalem: Mahbaroth Le-Sifruth, 1952), 52 n. 2.

15. For references and discussion, J. W. van Henten, "Mastemah," *DDD*, 1033-35; Michael Mach, "Demons," in *Encyclopedia of the Dead Sea Scrolls* (ed. Lawrence H. Schiffman and James C. VanderKam; New York: Oxford University Press, 2000), 1:189-92.

16. He plays a role in six passages in *Jubilees*; see Esther Eshel, "Mastema's Attempt on Moses' Life in the 'Pseudo-Jubilees' Text from Masada," *DSD* 10 (2003): 359-64, esp. pp. 362-63. The "Prince of Mastemah" appears also in two fragmentary texts, 4Q225 and the text from Masada discussed by Eshel in the article just

reports *Jubilees*' treatment of the near sacrifice of Isaac (*Jub.* 17:15-16); he refers to the figure who, according to *Jubilees*, prompts God to initiate the test of Abraham as "Mastipham, the leader of the demons."[17] Yet it is unlikely that a medieval Jew translating from Greek into Hebrew would recognize "Mastipham" as "Mastemah," although it is possible that earlier manuscripts now lost to us had the name in a less corrupt and more recognizable form.

The "Book of Noah," then, probably did not draw on a Greek version of a passage from *Jubilees* as *Midrash Aggadah* and *Midrash Tadshe* appear to have done. It is possible that the original Hebrew of *Jub.* 10:1-14, perhaps somehow excerpted from *Jubilees*, was transmitted into the Middle Ages and revised by the author/compiler of the *Book of Asaph*. But it seems to me more likely that the *Book of Asaph* made use not of the passage from *Jubilees* but of a source used by *Jubilees*. No such source has survived, but comparison of the "Book of Noah" and *Jub.* 10:1-14 gives some grounds for thinking one existed. The name "Mastemah" or "Prince of Mastemah" is indeed characteristic of *Jubilees*, but, as already noted, it appeared in other ancient texts as well. The description of the evil spirits as "the spirits of the bastards" in the "Book of Noah" points away from *Jubilees* as the source since the offspring of the Watchers are called bastards in the *Book of the Watchers* but never in *Jubilees*. Furthermore, some of the differences between the "Book of Noah" and *Jubilees* could be explained as the effort of the author of *Jubilees* to adapt the source to his picture of the world.[18] At one point, at least, *Jubilees* appears to have played down information contained in a common source that it found distasteful. In the "Book of Noah," it is the princes of the evil spirits who still remain on earth who teach Noah the remedies (10). In *Jubilees* it is the angelic narrator and his associates who teach the remedies (*Jub.* 10:12). It seems unlikely that the "Book of Noah" would have added such a problematic pedigree for the remedies to its source. More likely both *Jubilees* and the "Book of Noah" used a source that made the princes of the evil spirits the teachers, but only *Jubilees* found that claim intolerable. Above I suggested that the interest of the "Book of Noah" in the parts of plants to be used for remedies, an interest absent in *Jubilees*, reflected the medical interests of the *Book of Asaph*. It is also possible that *Jubilees* played down a common source's details about the use of plants for healing because of the magical associations of such use; the *Book of the Watchers* includes among the types of dangerous knowledge revealed to humanity by the Watchers "spells and the cutting of roots" (*1 En.* 8:3).[19]

If the text on which the "Book of Noah" drew was not *Jubilees* itself but a source of *Jubilees*, it would not be the only such source to leave its traces in the Middle Ages. The medieval work known as *Midrash Vayissa'u* appears to have drawn on an account of the wars of Jacob and his sons against the Amorites and Esau that stands behind the accounts in *Jubilees* and the *Testament of Judah*, and the medieval Hebrew *Testament of Naphtali* may reflect use of a source of the ancient Greek *Testament of Naphtali*.[20]

---

cited. In 4Q225 the subject is the binding of Isaac; in the text from Masada, Eshel argues that the narrative reports the attempt on Moses' life on his return to Egypt described in Exod 4:24-26.

17. Mosshammer, *Georgii Syncelli Ecloga Chronographica*, 116.23-24, Adler and Tuffin, *Chronography*, 144. Syncellus here, as at some other points, refers to *Jubilees* as the *Little Genesis*.

18. Himmelfarb, "Some Echoes," 131-32.

19. The translation is that of George W. E. Nickelsburg and James C. VanderKam, *1 Enoch: A New Translation* (Minneapolis, Minn.: Fortress, 2004).

20. Himmelfarb, "Some Echoes," 128. *Midrash Vayissa'u* is translated in this volume. The fragments of

Firm conclusions about the nature of the relationship of the "Book of Noah" to the *Book of Jubilees* are impossible at this stage of our knowledge, but we can say with some confidence that the "Book of Noah" draws on a Hebrew text of the second century B.C.E. or even earlier. As more scholarly attention is devoted to the transmission of texts and traditions of the Second Temple period into the Middle Ages and the reclamation by medieval Jews of what they took to be Jewish traditions found in Christian hands, we may be able to come to a fuller understanding of the relationship between the "Book of Noah" and ancient Jewish tradition.

The text translated here is Jellinek's transcription from the Munich manuscript of the *Book of Asaph*.[21] The *Book of Asaph* has still not been published in its entirety. The "Book of Noah" is among the sample passages from the *Book of Asaph* that Süssman Muntner includes in his introduction to the work. He uses both the Oxford and the Munich manuscripts and compares them to other manuscripts.[22] But because he does not indicate clearly which manuscript he is drawing on at each point, I prefer to use Jellinek's text. The differences are quite small.

Bibliography

Dimant, Devorah. "Two 'Scientific' Fictions: The So-Called *Book of Noah* and the Alleged Quotation of *Jubilees* in CD 16:3-4." Pages 230-49 in *Studies in the Hebrew Bible, Qumran, and the Septuagint Presented to Eugene Ulrich*. Edited by Peter W. Flint, Emanuel Tov, and James C. VanderKam. VTSup 101. Leiden: Brill, 2006.

Himmelfarb, Martha. "Some Echoes of *Jubilees* in Medieval Hebrew Literature." Pages 115-41 in *Tracing the Threads: Studies in the Vitality of the Jewish Pseudepigrapha*. Edited by John C. Reeves. SBLEJL 6. Atlanta, Ga.: Scholars Press, 1994.

Lieber, Elinor. "Asaf's *Book of Medicines*: A Hebrew Encyclopedia of Greek and Jewish Medicine, Possibly Compiled in Byzantium on an Indian Model." Pages 223-49 in *Dumbarton Oaks Papers* 38: *Symposium on Byzantine Medicine*. Edited by John Scarborough. Washington, D.C.: Dumbarton Oaks, 1984.

Segal, Michael. *The Book of* Jubilees*: Rewritten Bible, Redaction, Ideology and Theology*. JSJSup 117. Leiden: Brill, 2007.

Sharbach, Rebecca. "The Rebirth of a Book." Pages 113-33 in *Noah and His Book(s)*, ed. Stone et al.

Stone, Michael E. "The Book(s) Attributed to Noah." *DSD* 13 (2006): 4-23.

__________. "The Book(s) Attributed to Noah." Pages 7-25 in *Noah and His Book(s)*, ed. Stone et al.

Hebrew Naphtali will appear in volume two. It is also worth noting that Michael Segal has recently argued that the author of *Jubilees* drew on a variety of written sources for the narrative of his work (*Book of* Jubilees); these sources account for the points of tension between the narrative and the legal and chronological framework or even contradiction that appear from time to time in *Jubilees*. Segal does not, however, understand *Jub.* 10:1-14 as reworking a written source about the afflictions of Noah's sons, as I suggest. He sees it rather as an effort to adapt Enochic traditions about the significance of the descent of the Watchers to *Jubilees*' view that the angels, and thus Mastemah and the forces of evil too, date back to creation (*Book of* Jubilees, 169-80, 265-66). As noted above (n. 9), he argues that the "Book of Noah" is directly dependent on the passage from *Jubilees* (*Book of* Jubilees, 170-74).

21. Jellinek, *BHM*, 3:xxx n.2.

22. Süssman Muntner, *Introduction to the Book of Assaph the Physician* (Hebrew; Jerusalem: Geniza, 1957).

Stone, Michael, Aryeh Amihay, Vered Hillel (eds.). *Noah and His Book(s)*. Atlanta, Ga.: Society of Biblical Literature, 2010.

Swartz, Michael D. "Book and Tradition in Hekhalot and Magical Literatures." *Journal of Jewish Thought and Philosophy* 3 (1994): 189-229.

The Book of Noah

1. This is the book of remedies that the ancient sages copied from the book of Shem the son of Noah, which was handed down to Noah on Mt. Lubar, one of the mountains of Ararat, after the flood. 2. For in those days and at that time the spirits of the bastards began to attack Noah's children to lead them astray and to make them err, to injure them and to strike them with sicknesses and pains and with all kinds of illness that kill and destroy human beings. 3. Then all the children of Noah together with their children came and reported their afflictions to Noah their father and told him about the pains their children endured. 4. And Noah became frightened, for he realized that they were suffering all kinds of sicknesses and diseases because of human transgression and their sinful ways.

5. Then Noah sanctified his children and the members of his household together with his house. He approached the altar and offered sacrifices, and he prayed to God and supplicated him. 6. (God) sent one of the angels of the presence from among the holy ones, Raphael by name, to imprison[a] the spirits of the bastards from under the heavens so that they would not corrupt human beings anymore. 7. The angel did so, imprisoning them in the place of judgment. 8. But he left one out of ten to go about on earth before the Prince of Mastemah, to punish the evil doers, to afflict and torture them with all kinds of illness and diseases and to afflict them with pains.

9. The angel told (him) the remedies for the afflictions of humanity and all kinds of remedies for healing with trees of the earth and vegetation of the soil and their roots. 10. And he sent the princes of the spirits who remained to show Noah and to explain to him why the trees for remedies were created with all their sprouts, greenery, grasses, roots, and seeds, and to teach him all their curative properties for healing and for life. 11. And Noah wrote these words in a book and gave them to Shem, his oldest son. The ancient wise men copied from this book and wrote many books, each one in his own language ...

a. Reading *lkl'* instead of *lklh*. The proper form of the infinitive for the verb *klh* is *lklwt* ("to complete"). More important, the verb *kl'* appears in the next sentence ("imprisoning").

The Apocryphon of Eber

A new translation and introduction

by James VanderKam

The patriarch Eber is mentioned in two chapters in Genesis. In 10:21 the author, in introducing the line of Noah's son Shem, writes: "To Shem also, the father of all the children of Eber, the elder brother of Japheth, children were born." A few verses later (v. 24) the reader learns that Shem's grandson Shelah became the father of Eber and: "To Eber were born two sons: the name of the one was Peleg, for in his days the earth was divided, and his brother's name was Joktan" (v. 25). The further genealogy of Shem's line in Genesis 11 takes due note of Eber. Eber, born when his father Shelah was thirty years of age, himself became the father of Peleg at age thirty-four. In the next 430 years of his life he had other sons and daughters (11:14-17). These seemingly arid genealogical notes actually contained within them several points of interest for interpreters, not least of which was the fact that the chronology for Eber's life entailed that it overlapped with the time when the tower of Babel was built and destroyed.

There is no surviving text that bears the name *Apocryphon of Eber*, but Gilles Dorival has made a case that there was a work, possibly Jewish, revolving (at least in part) around Eber (Dorival prefers the spelling Heber) and that it has left its mark on early Christian literature.[1] His case runs as follows.[2] In Patristic and Byzantine sources, Heber/Eber appears a number of times in connection with a series of topics. For example, it was widely recognized that his name was connected with the Hebrew word for *Hebrew ('ēḇer/'iḇrît)*, a fact that raised questions regarding the history of the language and its fate during the confusion of tongues at Babel. His son Peleg's name (division) was also related to the tower story, particularly the dispersion and division of the earth associated with it. Was Eber prophetic in so naming his son? What was Eber's role when the tower was under construction and was he punished with the others? Dorival finds that the sources offer conflicting opinions on several of these points; in them Heber/Eber:

- "plays a role in the story of the tower construction or he plays no role;
- is the only one named in the episode or Nimrod and/or 72 chiefs are named;
- plays a positive role in the tower episode or he plays a negative role;
- is rewarded or he receives no reward for his actions at that fateful time."

Dorival finds that Christian writers were aware of such differences but did not always choose just one of the options and thus introduced a measure of incoherence into their accounts.

1. Dorival, "Le patriarche Héber et la tour de Babel," 181-201.
2. The following paragraphs are a summary of Dorival, "Le patriarche Héber et la tour de Babel," 183-94.

He next investigates Jewish sources to determine how they handle Eber. The ones he surveys are *Jubilees*, *Sibylline Oracles* 3, Philo (who wrote a tractate on the tower but does not deal with Eber), Pseudo-Philo's *Biblical Antiquities*, Josephus, and rabbinic texts (they introduce the notion of the academy of Shem and Eber where the ways of God were taught). He finds they have little to offer, although they do cast some light on a couple of points. First, *Jub.* 8:7 says that Eber married Azurad, the daughter of Nebrod (Nimrod) who according to other accounts was the leader of the tower project. The book thus supplies a key link that brings Eber into closer connection with the tower.[3] Second, Pseudo-Philo mentions the chiefs involved in the construction, although it does not give the number (see *L.A.B.* 6-7). The total of 72 arose from the number of nations. Third, the prophetic gift enjoyed by Eber in naming his son Peleg is not mentioned in *Jubilees* but is attested in rabbinic texts.

So, there were important traditions about Eber in Jewish texts, but the fuller story about him appears in Christian works. Was the story a Christian invention? Dorival argues that five texts, all written at nearly the same time (the fourth century), document the existence of a work regarding Eber. The reports by Diodore of Tarsus, Epiphanius of Salamis, John Chrysostom (twice), and Pseudo-Eustathius of Antioch about the post-diluvian patriarch share these main traits:

- "Eber alone among the people of his time refused to join in building the tower.
- He was rewarded by escaping the confusion of languages.
- He preserved the original Hebrew language and transmitted it to his descendants, among whom was Abraham."

Dorival observes that in four of the texts some distrust of the information is expressed through terms such as *isōs* ("probably"), *legousi* ("they say"), *legetai* ("it is said"), and *logos echei* ("a report has it"). He thinks two reasons are possible for this attitude: either the authors depend on informers who are not Christians (Jews?), or they reproduce information contained in a writing of uncertain status (an apocryphon?). In view of the poor relations between Jews and Christians in the fourth century, he finds the latter explanation preferable. There probably was an apocryphon dealing with Eber; it was circulating in the fourth century and may go back to a still earlier time.

Dorival thinks the four authors he discusses worked independently of one another. Consequently, the legend of Eber is attested for Antioch (Diodore and Chrysostom) and possibly various other places including Palestine and Egypt (Epiphanius). The work could be a Jewish composition, though no such book has survived; also, Jewish authors who mentioned Eber emphasized other positive traits he displayed.

Dorival concludes by suggesting that the Synopsis of Pseudo-Athanasius (second half of the fifth century or the sixth) may preserve a vague reference to a writing about Eber. In paragraphs 74-76 the writer lists the contested books of the Old Testament, the Old Testament apocrypha, the contested books of the New Testament, and the New Testament apocrypha. The list of Old Testament apocrypha includes fourteen books and ends by mentioning "pseudepigrapha"—a term apparently synonymous with "apocrypha." The

3. The chronology in *Jubilees* dates the marriage of Eber and Azurad to the year of the world 1564 (8:7) and the beginning of the tower construction to 1590-96 (10:20), so the project clearly took place during Eber's lifetime as did the subsequent dispersal (dated to the year 1639; see *Jub.* 10:27).

second in the list of the apocrypha (after *Enoch*) is a work called *Patriarchs*. Although its contents are unknown, Dorival thinks the title leads one to believe it was concerned with all the patriarchs and hence could have contained a section on Eber.[4]

In view of the slim evidence for such a work, one should be cautious in positing its existence. Yet, one must admit that it would not be surprising if there were a composition about a scriptural character who, though described so briefly in Genesis, was intriguing enough to attract fairly widespread interest and curiosity.

Bibliography

Dorival, Gilles. "Le patriarche Héber et la tour de Babel: un apocryphe disparu?" Pages 181-201 in *Poussières de christianisme et de judaïsme antiques: Études réunités en l'honneur de Jean-Daniel Kaestli et Éric Junod*. Edited by Albert Frey and Rémi Gounelle. Lausanne: Éditions du Zébre, 2007.

Petit, Françoise. *La chaîne sur la Genèse. Édition intégrale II Chapitres 4 à 11*. Tradition Exegetica Graeca 2. Leuven: Peeters, 1993.

4. Dorival, "Le patriarche Héber et la tour de Babel," 200-201.

The Apocryphon of Eber[a]

Text 1: Diodore of Tarsus (died ca. 390 C.E.), Fragment 168[b]

After becoming the father of Peleg, Eber lived 209 years, had sons and daughters, and died. If Eber lived 209 years after becoming the father of Peleg, if Peleg became the father of Reu in the 134th year of his life, while the tower building occurred during Peleg's (life), it is evident that Eber was alive then and departed (this) life many years after the tower building. Accordingly, the Hebrew language took its name from Eber—a language that was preserved when all the others were divided into different sounds because he probably did not agree with the others in the enterprise of tower building.

Comment: The numbers of years—209 in Eber's life from the time he had Peleg to his death and 134 in Peleg's when he first became a father—seem to have resulted when data for the two men were switched. According to both the MT and LXX, Peleg lived 209 years after he had his first son (Gen 11:19), and Eber was 34 (MT) or 134 (LXX) when Peleg was born (11:16).[c] The point does not affect the overall force of Diodore's argument since, in whatever order they occur, the numbers are simply added. In the MT, Eber lived 430 years after Peleg's birth, in the LXX 370 (11:17). Either would comfortably encompass the tower episode.

Dorival highlights the word *isōs* (here translated "probably") as suggesting either that Diodore had originated the interpretation and was presenting it cautiously or, more likely, that he took it from a source that he did not view as entirely reliable.[d]

Text 2: Epiphanius of Salamis (ca. 315-403 C.E.; cited by Michael Glycas, *Annales* II, 242, 7-11)

Moreover, the great Epiphanius too speaks in this way about these matters: After the flood (came) the tower. At that time (lived) Heber, the ancestor of the Hebrews, who, they say, not wishing to join the others who were building the tower, continued in his own language. A descendant of his was Abraham, and from him [Eber] also came the Hebrew language. Josephus too says the same things as these people. Though they also do this, Theodore says Adam's descendants used the Syriac language.

---

a. The Greek texts translated are the ones printed in Dorival, "Le patriarche Héber et la tour de Babel," 194-99.

b. For a similar but shorter text, see #858 (without attribution) in Petit, ed., *La chaîne sur la Genèse*, 213-14.

c. Dorival, "Le patriarche Héber et la tour de Babel," 195.

d. Dorival, "Le patriarche Héber et la tour de Babel," 195-96.

Comment: Dorival notes that Epiphanius refers to "they say (*legousi*)" and thus indicates a source for this report—whether oral or written. He also points out that Epiphanius misrepresents Josephus who fails to mention Eber in his version of the tower story (*Ant.* 1.109-21).[a]

Text 3: Chrysostom (ca. 347-407 C.E.)
Preface to the Synopsis of the Old and New Testament

To learn from where the Jewish race was produced, it is necessary to say a few words. After Adam, Seth was born, then Enosh, then the others for many generations. Then (came) Noah at whose time, when humanity were corrupt, the flood (took place). When the flood ended, he alone emerged from the ark (and) with his three sons filled the earth. From his generation in turn many were born. After they became numerous, they decided to build a tower that would reach to the sky. When God observed their plan, he confused their languages and split the one into many. As a result it became necessary for those who could not understand one another not to live together. This was the reason they were dispersed everywhere in the world. It is said that in the confusing of languages Eber, the ancestor of the Jews, did not wish to join them in the endeavor. He alone continued to maintain his own language, receiving honor for his excellent judgment. A descendant of his was Abraham. For this reason the language of the Jews is called Hebrew, after Eber.

Comment: Chrysostom studied under Diodore and could have derived the information from him, but, as Dorival observes, he could also have used the source common to Diodore and Epiphanius, whether oral or written (note Chrysostom's *legetai,* "it is said"). There are several phrases that he shares with Diodore; his account is less similar to Epiphanius's paragraph.[b]

Text 4: Chrysostom, *Synopsis of Genesis*

... (these were) the descendants from Noah to Peleg who received this name from the division of the earth in his time. For at that time they built the tower, for which reason the place was called Babylon, that is, confusion, since their languages were confused there. A report has it that Eber, Peleg's father, did not agree with the others regarding the building of the tower and therefore there was no change of language for him. Rather he continued having a pure speech and from him it received its name. For because Eber had this name, it was called Hebrew. This is also a very weighty indication that Hebrew is older than all the languages. The reason is that before the languages were confused, all used this one. This Eber is an ancestor of Abraham.

Comment: In this report that parallels the one above, Chrysostom uses the expression *logos echei*, "a report has it," again signaling a source, possibly written.[c]

---

a. Dorival, "Le patriarche Héber et la tour de Babel," 196.
b. Dorival, "Le patriarche Héber et la tour de Babel," 198.
c. Dorival, "Le patriarche Héber et la tour de Babel," 198.

Text 5: Pseudo-Eustathius of Antioch, *Commentary on the Hexameron* (second half of the fifth century C.E. or the sixth)

The son of Shelah was Eber from whom (come) the Hebrews who have preserved the ancient Hebrew language. Since Eber did not take part in building the tower, he did not change his language.

Comment: The information resembles that in the previous reports, but the writer does not allude to a source for it.[a]

a. Dorival, “Le patriarche Héber et la tour de Babel,” 199.

The Dispute over Abraham
A new translation and introduction

by Richard Bauckham

In his *Homilies on Luke* (preached in 233-234 C.E.),[1] Origen refers to an apocryphal account (which he anticipates not all his readers will be willing to accept as an authority) in which Abraham's eternal fate is disputed between two angels, one of righteousness and one of wickedness. Apparently each of the angels has a band of others with him and each band claims Abraham for themselves. Although Origen does not explicitly say that the contest takes place at Abraham's death and concerns the fate of his soul, the fact that he does say that it concerns his salvation or perdition strongly implies that.

We have this work of Origen only in Jerome's Latin translation, and it may well be that the original was somewhat fuller, since the tendency of the Latin translations of Origen is to slur over, if not to eliminate such apocryphal quotations.[2] The extant texts of the two known pseudepigraphic works associated with Abraham, the *Testament* and the *Apocalypse*, contain nothing corresponding to this allusion. The former contains a quite different account of the taking of Abraham's soul to heaven at his death (A20; B14), while the suggestion that Origen makes a confused reference to the *Testament*'s account of the weighing of the deeds of a departed soul shown to Abraham in a vision by Michael (A13:9-14),[3] is unconvincing because this passage is so divergent from what Origen says,[4] and also because, as we shall see, there are much closer parallels to the scenario Origen depicts.

Klaus Berger has collected and discussed a series of later Christian texts that describe how the human soul, at death, encounters good and evil angels who contend for its possession.[5] Two of these are of particular importance for comparison with our text. The first is from the *Homily* of John of Thessalonica (bishop of Thessalonica some time between 610 and 649) *on the Dormition of the Virgin Mary*. The other is a passage in the Syriac *Apocalypse of Paul*. (The corresponding passage in the long Latin version of the *Apocalypse of Paul* [13-14], which generally preserves the content of the original, fifth-century Greek apocalypse, lacks the motif of conflict between the good and evil angels. This is

1. On the date, see Crouzel, Fournier and Périchon, *Origène: Homélies sur S. Luc,* 79-81.

2. James, *Lost Apocrypha*, 16. Crouzel, Fournier and Périchon, *Origène: Homélies sur S. Luc,* 85-87, defend Jerome, to a large extent, against Rufinus's charge that he corrected and abbreviated the text to conform it to orthodoxy, but allow that Jerome made minor changes to Origen's text.

3. James, *The Testament*, 14-26. He argues that Origen confused this passage with the account of the contest for the body of Moses in the *Testament of Moses* (cf. Jude 9).

4. Dale C. Allison, *Testament of Abraham* (Commentaries on Early Jewish Literature; Berlin: Walter de Gruyter, 2003), 37, comments that James's "argument, to my knowledge, has convinced no one."

5. Berger, "Der Streit."

lacking also in the very abbreviated version of this passage in the extant Greek *Apocalypse of Paul*, but is likely to belong to the original form of the work.[6])

Homily of John of Thessalonica on the Dormition of Mary (chapter 5)

For two angels come to meet each human being: one an angel of righteousness and one of wickedness, and they encounter him at the moment of death. And when death besieges the soul with anguish, the two angels come and grasp his body. If he is someone who has done works of righteousness, the angel of righteousness rejoices over him, because the wicked one has nothing in that person. Then several angels come to the soul, singing before him all the way to the place of the just. Then the angel of wickedness is grieved, because he has no share in him. But if the person is found to be one who has done evil deeds, that angel rejoices, and brings with him other wicked spirits, and they lay hold of the soul and pluck it out for themselves. Then the angel of righteousness grieves deeply.[7]

Syriac Apocalypse of Paul

[In a preceding section Paul has been shown "those angels in whom there is no mercy, who are sent after the souls of sinners," and "angels of righteousness, who are sent after the souls of the righteous."]

Then I said unto him [the angel who guides Paul through the other world]: "O my Lord, wilt thou not grant that I may see in what manner the souls of the righteous and of the wicked depart out of this world?" and he said unto me: "Paul, look down, and see the thing which thou requestest." And I looked, and saw, and beheld one of the sons of men fallen nigh unto death. And the angel said unto me: "This is a just one, and righteous in all his works." And I saw every thing which he did for God standing before him, in the hour of his departure from the world.... And there approached him wicked angels (when a righteous one departs, they do not find a place by him), and those good angels ruled over that righteous one. And they drew out of him the soul, while alluring it with rest.... Then that soul was carried from the body; and they inquired about its health; and they took delight with it in love.... And there came to meet it he who was its guardian in its life, and said to it: "O soul of mine, be of good courage, and be joyful, and I will rejoice over thee, that thou hast done the will of our Lord, all the days of thy life; and I carried thy good works, by day and by night, before God." And while I was beholding these things, that spirit was lifted up from the earth, that it might ascend to heaven. And there went out to meet it wicked powers, those that are under heaven. And there reached it the spirit of error, and said: "Whither does thou presume, O soul? And art thou running that thou mayest enter heaven? Stop, that we may see; perhaps there is in thee something that belongs to us, that we may narrate a little." And that soul was bound there; and there was a fight

---

6. The motif is also found in the Ethiopic *Apocalypse of Gorgorios* (translation in Wolf Leslau, *Falasha Anthology* [Yale Judaica Series 6; New Haven: Yale University Press, 1951], 77-91, here 81-82), which is probably dependent on the *Apocalypse of Paul*. See also the Ethiopic *Book of the Angels* (translation in Leslau, *Falasha Anthology*, 50-56, here 52-54).

7. Translation from Brian E. Daley, *On the Dormition of Mary: Early Patristic Homilies* (Crestwood, New York: St. Vladimir's Seminary Press, 1998), 52. The Greek text is in Aurelio de Santos Otero, *Los Evangelios Apócrifos* (BAC 148; Madrid: La Editorial Catolica, 1988), 614.

between the good angels and the evil angels. And when that spirit of deception saw, it bewailed with a loud voice, and said: "Woe unto thee, O soul, that we have found in thee nothing of ours! and lo, all the angels and the spirits are helping thee against us; and behold, these all are with thee; thou hast passed out from us." And there went forth another spirit, the spirit of the Tempter, and the spirit of fornication; and they came to meet it; and when they saw it, they wept over it, and said: "How has this soul escaped from us? It did the will of God on earth, and behold, the angels help it and pass it, and pass it along from us." And all the principalities and evil spirits came to meet it, even unto it; and they did not find in it anything that was from them; and they were not able to do anything to it; and they gnashed their teeth upon that soul, and said: "How hast thou escaped from us?" And the angel which conducted it in life answered and said unto them: "Return, O ye mortified ones; ye have no way of access to it; with many artifices ye enticed, when it was on earth, and it did not listen to you."[8]

[The text goes on to describe the reception of the righteous soul in heaven and what happens when a wicked soul departs from the body.]

The following parallels with Origen's apocryphal allusion should be noticed. In the *Homily on the Dormition*, there are initially two angels, one of righteousness and one of wickedness, exactly as in the most likely reading of Origen's text. But then, as in Origen, there are also two groups of angels, aligned respectively with the angel of righteousness and the angel of wickedness. In the Syriac *Apocalypse of Paul*, the situation is rather more complex, but, as well as two groups of angels, there is one good angel with a special role, the soul's guardian angel during its life, and, on the other side, there is "the spirit of error," later joined by "the spirit of fornication." However, what is especially notable, because it is lacking in the *Homily on the Dormition*, as well as in most of the other texts which transmit the same tradition, is the "fight" over the soul between the two groups of angels, corresponding with the "dispute" between the two angels in Origen. These parallels confirm that very probably the narrative to which Origen alludes recounted what happened at Abraham's death. I have reproduced at length that portion of the Syriac *Apocalypse of Paul* that deals with the fate of a righteous soul up to the point when it is taken up to heaven because it shows how Origen's brief summary could allude to a fairly extended narrative.

The work to which Origen alludes is unlikely to have been the source of this and other later Christian accounts of angels meeting the soul at death, because in Origen's apocryphon the motif is applied specifically to Abraham, a righteous person, whereas the other texts describe in turn what happens to a righteous person and, by contrast, to a wicked person (or in the alternative order). In fact, Origen himself seems to have known something like those accounts, as the following passage from a later work, his sermon on Psalm 36 (Evv 37), suggests:

Then, in the time of tribulation, "the Lord will help them and snatch them away and remove them from sinners" [Ps 36 (Evv 37):40], not only from human sinners, but also from the hostile powers, precisely at the time when the soul is separated from the

8. Translation from Justin Perkins, "The Revelation of the Blessed Apostle Paul, Translated from an Ancient Syriac Manuscript," *JAOS* 8 (1864): 183-212, here 191-92. A critical edition of the Syriac text, with a Latin translation, was published by G. Ricciotti, "Apocalypsis Pauli Syriace iuxta codices vaticanos," *Orientalia* 2 (1933): 1-24, 120-49. Ricciotti's edition is based on two manuscripts different from the one translated by Perkins.

> body, and sinful demons, adverse powers and the spirits of this air, rush to meet it, wishing to detain and to possess it for themselves, if they recognize anything of their works and deeds in it. For the prince of this world and the powers of the air come to every soul when it leaves this world, and see if they can find anything of their own. If they find avarice, it belongs to their portion. If they find anger or extravagance or envy or any similar vice, it belongs to their portion and they claim it for themselves and draw it to themselves and carry it away to the portion of sinners. But if anyone imitates the one who said, "Behold, the prince of this world is coming and he will find nothing in me" [John 14:30], if anyone keeps watch over themselves in this way, those sinners [the demons] come, and, when they seek in them but do not find the things that are theirs, they will nevertheless try by means of violence to carry them away towards their portion, but the Lord will snatch them away from the sinners. Perhaps it is for this reason that we are commanded to pray, "but deliver us from evil" [Matt 6:13].[9]

Here there is only one band of angels, the wicked ones, while God himself performs the task elsewhere attributed to the good angels. But this may well be because Origen has adapted the material to suit the use he is making of it to comment on the words of the psalm, where it is the Lord who delivers the righteous from sinners.

A final text whose relationship to our Abraham apocryphon needs to be considered is *4QVisions of Amram*, of which we have fragments from five manuscripts in Aramaic from Qumran Cave 4. It could equally well be called the Testament of Amram, because it relates what Amram, the father of Moses and Aaron, said to his sons on the day of his death. Part of the content is the account of a vision, which took place some time before Amram's death, in which he saw two angels engaged in a dispute over him. They are the two chief angels, the Prince of darkness, who rules over all the sons of darkness, and the Prince of light, who rules over all the sons of light. One of the names of the former is Melchiresha' and one of the latter's names was almost certainly Melchizedek, though the name has not survived in the manuscripts we have. This is what survives of their contest:

> [I saw watchers] in my vision, the dream-vision, and behold two (of them) were disputing over me and were saying [ ] and they were engaged in a great contest over me. And I asked them, "Who are you who are thus trying [to exercise auth]ority[.... over me?" And they answered me, saying, "We have been put in p]ower, and we rule over all humanity." And they said to me, "By which of us do yo[u choose to be ruled?" (4Q544 [VisAmr^{b} ar] 1 9-12).[10]

The dispute between the two angels, good and wicked, over Amram certainly corresponds closely to Origen's summary of the Abraham apocryphon, and J. T. Milik proposed that *4QVisions of Amram* was actually the work to which Origen refers. The name Amram could easily have been miscopied as the better known Abraham.[11] Berger responded to Milik, arguing plausibly that the wider tradition, found in many later texts, about the

9. Origen, *Hom. Ps.* 5.7 (on Ps 36 [Evv 37]): my translation from the Latin text in Emmanuela Prinzivalli, *Origene: Omelie sui Salmi: Homiliae in Psalmos XXXVI – XXXVII – XXXVIII* (Biblioteca Patristica 18; Florence: Nardini Editore, 1991), 242. Prinzivalli dates these homilies to ca. 245 (14-17).

10. Translation adapted from Paul J. Kobelski, *Melchizedek and Melchireša'* (CBQMS 10; Washington, D.C.: Catholic Biblical Association of America, 1981), 27.

11. Milik, "4Q Visions de 'Amram," 86-89.

angels who encounter the soul at death, makes it unnecessary to correct the text of Origen, since both *4QVisions of Amram* and Origen's apocryphon could be related within a broader tradition without direct literary dependence between them. Berger saw *4QVisions of Amram* as the first record of a tradition that continued into Christian apocalyptic works such as the Syriac *Apocalypse of Paul.*[12]

Milik assumed and Berger seems not to question that the dispute in *4QVisions of Amram* relates to Amram's fate at death,[13] but the surviving texts really give no grounds for supposing this. The vision took place in Hebron, after which Amram returned to Egypt, and so some time before his death. The dispute seems to be over Amram's allegiance during life. He is asked to choose which of the angels is to rule over him. In the Christian texts that describe the encounter with the angels at death, the person is never given such a choice. Of course, it is possible that a subsequent part of *4QVisions of Amram,* not preserved in the Qumran fragments, described what happened at Amram's death, but the text as we have it is significantly less like Origen's allusion than is the Syriac Apocalypse of Paul, which also features a dispute ("a fight between the good angels and the evil angels").

Most likely Origen's allusion is to an otherwise unknown work which described a contest between angels for Abraham's soul at his death. It may have been an extended narrative around the death of Abraham, like the *Testament of Abraham,* or it may have been a work that ranged more widely over the patriarchal history, an example of rewritten Bible like *Jubilees.*

Bibliography

EDITIONS AND TRANSLATIONS

Crouzel, Henri, François Fournier and Pierre Périchon. Pages 414-17 in *Origène: Homélies sur S. Luc.* SC 87. Paris: Éditions du Cerf, 1962. (Latin text and French translation)

Lienhard, Joseph T. Page 143 in *Origen: Homilies on Luke: Fragments on Luke.* FC 94. Washington, D.C.: Catholic University of America Press, 1996. (English translation)

Rauer, Max. Page 197 in *Origenes Werke: IX: Die Homilien zu Lukas in der Übersetzung des Hieronymus und die Grieschischen Reste der Homilien und des Lukas-Kommentars.* 2nd edition. GCS. Berlin: Akademie-Verlag, 1959. (Critical edition of the Latin text)

Sieben, Herrmann-Josef. Pages 348-49 in *Origenes: In Lucam Homiliae: Homilien zum Lukasevangelium.* Vol. 2. Fontes Christiani 4/2. Freiburg: Herder, 1992. (Latin text and German translation)

STUDIES

Berger, Klaus. "Der Streit des guten und des bösen Engels um die Seele." *JSJ* 4 (1973): 1-18.

James, Montague Rhodes. Pages 16-17 in *The Lost Apocrypha of the Old Testament.* London: SPCK, 1920.

__________. Pages 14-26 in *The Testament of Abraham.* TS 2/2. Cambridge: Cambridge University Press, 1892.

Milik, Józef Tadeusz. "4Q Visions de 'Amram et une citation d'Origène." *RB* 79 (1972): 77-97.

---

12. On the relationship of Jude 9 and other texts about the dispute over the body of Moses to this tradition, see Richard Bauckham, *Jude and the Relatives of Jesus in the Early Church* (Edinburgh: T.&T. Clark, 1990), 245-49.

13. So also Kobelski, *Melchizedek,* 24, 77.

The Dispute over Abraham

We read—at least if one is willing to accept a writing of this kind—**that the angel of righteousness and the angel of wickedness[a] disputed over the salvation or perdition of Abraham, each of the bands claiming him for their own company.** But if it displeases anyone, they should go to the book called *The Shepherd*, and there they will find that two angels attend on every human being: a wicked angel, who exhorts them to everything evil, and a good angel, who encourages them to everything that is best.[b] Elsewhere too it is written that two angels stand beside a human being, one for good and the other for evil.

(Origen, *Hom. Luc.* 35.3)

---

a. The Latin (*iustitiae et iniquitatis angelos*) could refer to more than one angel in each category, but the context in Origen's argument favors a reference to one angel of each type.

b. Hermas, *Mand.* 6.2.1. Origen considered *The Shepherd* of Hermas an inspired work (*Comm. Rom.* 10.31).

The Inquiry of Abraham
(A Possible Allusion to the *Apocalypse of Abraham*)
A new translation and introduction

by Richard Bauckham

Niceta, bishop of Remesiana (present-day Bela Palanka, near Niš, in Serbia) (d. ca. 414), refers disapprovingly to a noncanonical writing he calls the *Inquisitio Abrahae* in the course of his book in defense of congregational hymn singing in church.[1] (Some of the scribes were evidently even more disapproving and excised this reference from the copies they made of Niceta's work.) In the context of the reference Niceta claims that Moses was the first person to introduce the singing of hymns to God, referring to the Song at the Sea in Exodus 15. Niceta anticipates that someone might think the honour should go to Abraham, because in the work he calls the *Inquisitio Abrahae* Abraham is said to have sung along with the animals, the springs of water and the elements. Niceta does not object to the idea that such creatures sing praises to God: later in this work he says that the psalmist (in Ps 150:6) is "urging everyone and everything to praise God" (chap. 7). His objection to the *Inquisitio Abrahae* would seem to be, not that the work is heretical in its teaching, but simply that it is noncanonical and so its information is not reliable. Abraham was not the first to engage in choral hymn singing; Moses was.

This work may be one of which we have otherwise no knowledge. But it is worth exploring three possible identifications of it. How we should translate (or amend) the title *Inquisitio Abrahae* will vary according to these options.

(1) Hardly a year after the *editio princeps* of this work of Niceta was published,[2] M. R. James published a typically ingenious explanation of Niceta's apocryphal reference.[3] He identified it as the *Testament of Adam*, taking *Inquisitio Abrahae* to be a corruption of *Dispositio Adae*. He correctly pointed out that the Latin *dispositio* is a good translation of the Greek *diathēkē* ("testament"). The first part of the *Testament of Adam*, known as the *Horarium*, lists the hours of the day and the night, indicating which of the creatures praises God at each hour. In the (probably original) Syriac version they include the animals, the birds, the fish, the waters, the fountains, and the waters above the heaven, the fire and all the lower depths, the cherubim, the heavenly powers, the angels and all human beings. No Latin version of the *Horarium* is known, but Niceta could probably have read Greek. However, this raises a problem for James's argument. There are two extant Greek versions of the *Horarium*. One of these, a highly abbreviated version, is attributed to Adam in the chronicle of the eleventh-century Byzantine writer George Cedrenus. We do not know what his source was or in what language it was. The other Greek version is extant in six manuscripts, all dating from the fifteenth to the seventeenth centuries, in none of which

1. It is known variously as *De psalmodiae bono* and *De utilitate hymnorum*.

2. Burn, *Niceta*.

3. James, "Notes."

is it called the *Testament of Adam* or associated with Adam.[4] We should also note that the title *Testament of Adam* does not occur in any of the Greek lists of apocryphal works.[5] Thus we cannot be at all sure that a *Testament of Adam* in Greek existed as such in Niceta's time. It could still be the case that Niceta's reference, as corrected by James, is the sole surviving evidence of the *Testament of Adam*, so entitled, either in Greek or in Latin.[6]

However, there is another difficulty with James's proposal. James knew the text of Niceta in the edition of Burn, where the crucial description of the apocryphon says that it pretended that "the animals themselves (*ipsa animalia*) and the springs of water and the elements sang." The later edition by Turner prefers an alternative reading not known to Burn: "he himself [i.e., Abraham] and the animals (*ipse et animalia*) and the springs of water and the elements sang."[7] This reading is certainly to be preferred because it fits the context in Niceta's argument much better. Niceta has been arguing that Moses was the first human being to introduce choral hymn singing. It would not be relevant to cite, as an ostensibly earlier example, a case in which only non-human creatures sang. The *Testament of Adam* does allocate an hour to the praises of human beings, but Adam himself is not explicitly said to have sung. The match with Niceta's reference is weak.

(2) It is possible that Niceta refers to the same book about Abraham that Origen mentions in his *Homilies on Luke* 35.2. (In this volume we have entitled that work *The Dispute over Abraham.*) The Latin title Niceta cites, *Inquisitio Abrahae*, could be translated: *The Interrogation of Abraham*, and could refer to the process of interrogation by evil angels that Abraham had to undergo at his death. Though Origen's brief summary refers only to a dispute between the righteous and evil angels for possession of Abraham, more detailed descriptions of such a contest (such as that in the Syriac *Apocalypse of Paul*) include such an interrogation. The difficulty with this suggestion is that it would require the interrogation to be a sufficiently major part of the work for the whole work to be named after it.

(3) Finally, perhaps the best case can be made for identifying Niceta's *Inquisitio Abrahae* with the work generally known as the *Apocalypse of Abraham*, extant only in Old Slavonic but considered by most scholars to have originated as a Jewish writing from ca. 100 C.E. In this work Abraham recites a lengthy song of praise to God (13:8-21). A reference to an actual hymn of this kind suits the context of Niceta's reference within his argument, since the Old Testament examples he considers are the Song at the Sea (Exod 15), the Song of Deborah (Judg 5) and the Song of Moses (Deut 32). He goes on to discuss the Psalms of David. His mind is on, not just references to people singing praise to God, but examples of actual hymns.

In the *Apocalypse of Abraham* Abraham is taken up to the heavenly throne-room by the angel Yahoel, who teaches him the song he is to sing when he arrives there and sings it along with him. The song is not his alone:

> And while I was still reciting the song, the edge of the fire which was on the expanse rose up on high. And I heard a voice like the roaring of the sea, and it did not cease because of the fire. And as the fire rose up, soaring higher, I saw under the fire a throne

---

4. For these details about the Greek versions, see Robinson, *Testament*, chapter 4.

5. Michael E. Stone, *A History of the Literature of Adam and Eve* (SBLEJL 3; Atlanta, Ga.: Scholars Press, 1992), 75-81. It may be listed in the chronicle of Samuel of Ani (Armenian historian) as one of the books introduced into Armenia by Nestorian missionaries in 590 C.E.

6. Cf. Robinson, *Testament*, 13-14.

7. See Turner, "Niceta," 234, 243-244.

> [made] of fire and the many-eyed Wheels, and they are reciting the song. And under the throne [I saw] four singing fiery Living Creatures (18:1-3).[8]

The text goes on to describe the four living creatures. The *animalia* of Niceta's text may be, not earthly animals, but these heavenly ones,[9] who sing with Abraham the same heavenly song.

This does not explain why Niceta mentions "the springs of water and the elements," but there are some obscure passages in the *Apocalypse of Abraham*'s account of Abraham in heaven that might account for them:[10]

> And behold, in this light a fire was kindled [and there was] a crowd of many people in male likeness. They were all changing in appearance and likeness, running and being transformed and bowing and shouting in a language the words of which I did not know (15:6-7).

> ... behold, a fire was coming towards us round about, and a sound was in the fire like a sound of many waters, like a sound of the sea in its uproar (17:1).

> And above the Wheels there was the throne which I had seen. And it was covered with fire and the fire encircled it round about, and an indescribable light surrounded the fiery people. And I heard the sound of their qedusha like the voice of a single man (18:13-14).[11]

What then of the title *Inquisitio Abrahae*? In the later chapters of the *Apocalypse of Abraham* Abraham is shown many things in visions, and like many another apocalyptic seer, he is continually asking his angel guide questions about what he sees (20:7; 22:1, 3; 23:9, 12, 14; 25:3; 26:1; 27:6; 28:2; 29:1, 7). With reference to these, the work could be called *The Inquiry of Abraham*, by analogy with such works as the *Questions of Bartholomew*, the Armenian *Questions of Ezra*, and the *Questions of Mary*.

In view of the fact that the *Apocalypse of Abraham* survives only in Slavonic, it is noteworthy that Niceta's episcopal see was in the heart of the Balkans, close to the modern border between Serbia and Bulgaria. Ryszard Rubinkiewicz thinks that the *Apocalypse of Abraham* was most likely translated into Old Church Slavonic, along with many other texts in Greek, during the reign of the emperor Simeon of Bulgaria (893-927). He writes that it is "fully realistic to assume that a Greek text of the Apocalypse of Abraham still existed in the Balkans as late as the ninth century."[12]

This case for identifying the work Niceta knew with the *Apocalypse of Abraham* is far from conclusive, but remains a tantalizing possibility.

---

8. Translation from Alexander Kulik, *Retroverting Slavonic Pseudepigrapha: Toward the Original of the* Apocalypse of Abraham (SBLTCS 3; Atlanta, Ga.: Society of Biblical Literature, 2004), 23-24.

9. *Animalia* is the term used in the Vulgate of Ezekiel 1 and Revelation 4.

10. Note also the extended passage about the four elements in 7:1-10, where Abraham is demonstrating to his father that the elements are not gods. It would be appropriate if, on his ascension to heaven, Abraham were to witness these elements actually worshiping God, and so it is possible that in the original text there was something more explicit along these lines.

11. Translations from Kulik, *Retroverting*, 22, 24.

12. Ryszard Rubinkiewicz, "Apocalypse of Abraham," *OTP*, 1:683-705, here 686; see also his n. 25.

Bibliography

TEXT AND TRANSLATION

Burn, Andrew Eubank. Pages 70-71 in *Niceta of Remesiana: His Life and Works*. Cambridge: Cambridge University Press, 1905. (*editio princeps*)

Turner, Cuthbert Hamilton. "Niceta of Remesiana II." *JTS* 24 (1923): 225-252, here 234-235, 243-244. (Critical edition of the Latin text)

Walsh, Gerald G., Bernard M. Peebles, Rudolph E. Morris and J. Reginald O'Donnell. Pages 3-76 in *Niceta of Remesiana: Writings; Sulpicius Severus: Writings; Vincent of Lerins: Commonitories; Prosper of Aquitaine: Grace and Free Will*. FC 7. New York: Fathers of the Church, Inc., 1949. (English translation on pp. 67-68)

STUDIES

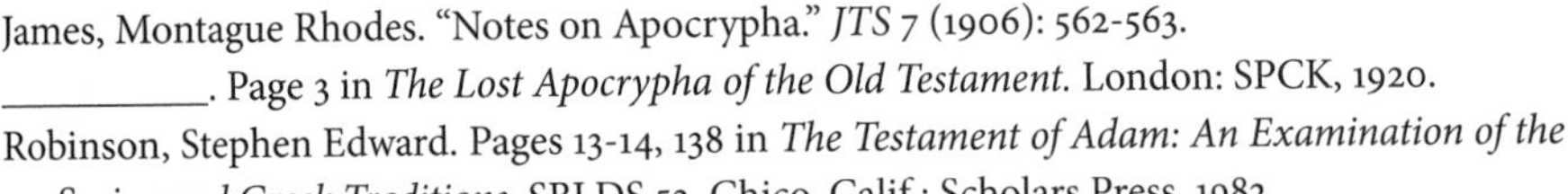

James, Montague Rhodes. "Notes on Apocrypha." *JTS* 7 (1906): 562-563.

__________. Page 3 in *The Lost Apocrypha of the Old Testament*. London: SPCK, 1920.

Robinson, Stephen Edward. Pages 13-14, 138 in *The Testament of Adam: An Examination of the Syriac and Greek Traditions*. SBLDS 52. Chico, Calif.: Scholars Press, 1982.

The Inquiry of Abraham

If we ask who first introduced this kind of singing, we shall find that it was none other than Moses, who sang a remarkable song to God when, after Egypt had been struck by the ten plagues and Pharaoh had drowned, the people went out rejoicing to the wilderness by an unprecedented route through the sea. Moses sang, "Let us sing to the Lord for he has been gloriously exalted." **Now that volume that is entitled *The Inquiry of Abraham*,[a] in which it is pretended that he himself and the animals[b] and the springs of water and the elements sang, should not be thoughtlessly accepted, seeing that that book is of no credit and rests on no authority.**[c] Therefore Moses, the leader of the tribes of Israel, was the first to institute choirs. He separated the men and the women into two groups, and, with himself and his sister leading, he taught them to sing to God the song of triumph. Later Deborah, a woman of distinction, is found in the book of Judges performing the same ministry. But Moses himself, when he was about to depart from the body, again sang a terrifying canticle, in Deuteronomy, which he left in written form to the people as a sort of testament, so that the tribes of Israel should know what and what kind of funeral rites awaited them when they abandoned God.

(Niceta of Remesiana, *De Psalmodiae Bono* 3)

---

a. Another possible translation is *The Interrogation of Abraham.*

b. "he himself and the animals" is the reading of MS R; MSS AV have "the animals themselves."

c. Several MSS omit this sentence.

The Story of Melchizedek with the Melchizedek Legend from the *Chronicon Paschale*

A new translation and introduction

by Pierluigi Piovanelli

The *Story of Melchizedek*, written in Greek and attributed to Athanasius, patriarch of Alexandria (ca. 295-373 C.E.), is an extremely popular work from late antiquity that provides a short account of the origins and early life of the otherwise elusive priest-king of Salem prior to his meeting with Abraham (Gen 14:18-20).[1] The original Greek text was translated into all of the languages of the Christian Orient (Coptic, Syriac, Arabic, Ethiopic, Armenian, Georgian, Slavonic, and Romanian) and incorporated in a slightly different form into the Greek *Palaea Historica*, a ninth-century compendium of biblical history from Adam to David which was also translated into Slavonic and Romanian.[2] Moreover, the *Story of Melchizedek* became a significant source of inspiration for the topography of the Holy Land and for Coptic and Byzantine iconography.[3]

Contents

According to Pseudo-Athanasius, a certain Melchi, king of Salem, son of Salaad and grandson of queen Salem, was married to a woman also named Salem and had two sons, Melĉhi Jr. and Melchizedek. When the latter, "having raised his eyes to the heaven," had a revelation of "the true God," the king decided to sacrifice him to his idols "in the *dōdekátheon*," i.e., "the temple of the Twelve Gods." Melchizedek, however, was saved by his mother and, as a consequence, Melchi had no choice but to immolate his other son along with eight hundred and three boys. When he realized what was going on, Melchizedek was so distressed that he escaped to the top of Mount Tabor, where he prayed to the Lord that all of the people who assisted in the sacrifice might die. God heard him and "all the family of Melchizedek together with the whole city" were swallowed up and disappeared completely. At that sight, Melchizedek lost his mind and isolated himself in the forest. "He went into the depths of the forest, and remained there, for seven years, naked, as when he emerged from his mother's womb; and his fingernails became a span long, the hair of his head (hung) down to his loins, and his back became like a tortoise-shell.

1. See, in general, Robinson, "The Apocryphal Story," 26-28; Denis, *Introduction*, 1:215-16; Dochhorn, "Die Historia de Melchisedech," 7-16; Böttrich, *Geschichte Melchisedeks*, 1-6.

2. On the parabiblical traditions incorporated into Byzantine compilations, see David Flusser, "*Palaea Historica*: An Unknown Source of Biblical Legends," in *Studies in Aggadah and Folk-Literature* (ed. Joseph Heinemann and David Noy; ScrHier 22; Jerusalem: Magness, 1971), 48-79; Christfried Böttrich, "Palaea/Paleja. Ein byzantinisch-slavischer Beitrag zu den europäischen Historienbibeln," in *Fragmentarisches Wörterbuch. Beiträge zur biblischen Exegese und christlichen Theologie. Horst Balz zum 70. Geburtstag* (ed. Kerstin Schiffner, Klaus Wengst, and Werner Zager; Stuttgart: Kohlhammer, 2007), 304-13, as well as William Adler's introduction to his translation of the *Palaea Historica* in the present volume.

3. See the section on "Cultural Influence" below.

Berries were his nourishment, and his drink was the dew which he lapped up" (9:3-6). Seven years later, the voice of God ordered Abraham to go up on Mount Tabor, find the wild Melchizedek, and "shave him, pare his nails, clothe him, and be blessed by him." So he did and Melchizedek, three days later, anointed and blessed Abraham, to whom he also gave his new and definitive name. This is the reason why—says the Lord—Melchizedek is "without father, without mother, without genealogy, having neither beginning of days nor end of life, but made like the Son of God, he remains a priest perpetually" (Heb 7:3). Then, when he met Abraham for the second time and gave him the wine and the bread, "he was 'made like the Son of God,' but not according to grace. And thus he became the first type of the bloodless sacrifice of the Savior, pointing to the Holy Offering. Therefore he says, 'You are a priest forever according to the order of Melchizedek' (Ps 110:4)."

Manuscripts and Versions

Jan Dochhorn, who is preparing a new edition of the Greek text of the *Story of Melchizedek*, has recently provided a list of twenty-nine Greek manuscripts copied between the eleventh and the nineteenth centuries, the majority of which are unpublished.[4] We can infer from the scant descriptions provided by the catalogues of manuscripts that the text circulated in at least three different recensions.

1. As a pseudo-Athanasian work preserved in fourteen codices, including the most ancient one, the manuscript Paris, Bibliothèque nationale de France, Gr. 1336 (previously known as Regius 2570 = our MS *R*), from the eleventh century, whose variant readings have been selectively published by Jacques-Paul Migne.[5] This is the text that was initially printed in the *Editio Commeliniana* of Athanasius's works, published in Heidelberg, in 1600-01, and subsequently reprinted in the different editions of the writings of the Alexandrian patriarch published throughout the seventeenth and eighteenth centuries.[6] Johannes Albertus Fabricius took it from the Parisian edition of Bernard de Montfaucon, published in 1698, and included it, along with other apocryphal traditions and texts about Melchizedek, in his famous *Codex Pseudepigraphus Veteris Testamenti*, published in Hamburg and Leipzig, in 1713.[7] Then, in 1857 Migne reprinted it in the twenty-eighth volume of the *Patrologia Graeca* with the addition of a selection of variant readings taken from the manuscripts Paris, Bibliothèque nationale de France, Gr. 1336, mentioned above, and Gr. 1190 (previously known as Colbertinus 5108 = our MS *C*), written in 1568.[8] The text edited by Migne has become the standard version of the *Story of Melchizedek*, which

4. Dochhorn, "Die Historia de Melchisedech," 17-21; cf. Haelewyck, *Clavis*, 64 (the *Story of Melchizedek*) and 219 (the *Palaea Historica*).

5. Migne, "Historia de Melchisedec," 525-30.

6. Conveniently listed by Dochhorn, "Die Historia de Melchisedech," 16 n. 23; Böttrich, *Geschichte Melchisedeks*, 7-8.

7. Fabricius, *CPVT*, 311-20 (the *Story of Melchizedek*), 320-322 (Sudas's entry on Melchizedek), 322-25 (the Melchizedek story from the *Chronicon Paschale*), 325-26 (excerpts from the works of Michael Glycas and George Cedrenus) and 326-28 (quotations on the names of Melchizedek's parents taken from the *Yosippon*, Epiphanius's *Panarion*, and an Arabic exegetical chain on Genesis 9). A free English rendering of the texts collected by Fabricius can be found in Baring-Gould, *Legends*, 235-41.

8. Migne, "Historia de Melchisedec." The same author provided a relatively free translation of the *Story of Melchizedek* into French in the second volume of his *Dictionnaire des Apocryphes*, published in 1858.

was republished by Dochhorn,[9] and translated into English and German.[10] It will also serve as basic text for the present translation.

2. As an anonymous work copied in at least six or seven manuscripts,[11] one of which, the sixteenth-century Paris, Bibliothèque nationale de France, Gr. 1083 (= our MS *P*), has been published by Dochhorn.[12] An abridged version of this kind of text was also copied, in the thirteenth century, on the back of segments 5-6 of the famous Joshua Roll, one of the most remarkable Byzantine illuminated manuscripts of the Biblioteca Apostolica Vaticana (Palat. Gr. 431), which is devoted to the first twelve chapters of the Book of Joshua. It was published and translated into German by Peter Schreiner, in 1999.[13]
3. Finally, another anonymous rewriting *Concerning Melchizedek* was included in the *Palaea Historica*, chapters 32–38 and 40:1-2, and copied in at least seven manuscripts. It was initially published in 1893 by Afanasiĭ Vassiliev,[14] who used the manuscripts Vienna, Österreichische Nationalbibliothek, Theol. Gr. 247, of the sixteenth century, and Biblioteca Apostolica Vaticana, Othobonianus Gr. 205, of the fifteenth century. This recension has now been republished by Dochhorn,[15] who has also added some variant readings taken from the manuscript Paris, Bibliothèque nationale de France, Gr. 37, written in 1558. Vassiliev's text with Dochhorn's improvements has subsequently been translated into German and English.[16]

A similar variety of recensions is found among the different primary and secondary translations of the *Story of Melchizedek*.[17] Thus, many are unambiguously attributed to Athanasius. These include: the Arabic, the Slavonic, the Romanian, and the Armenian versions (the latter being included in the Armenian *Synaxarium*); a Syriac fragment (Biblioteca Apostolica Vaticana, Vat. Syr. 159, ff. 241^{v}-242^{r}); a scholion to Gen 14:17-20 found in an Arabic Catena to the Pentateuch, as well as the new Georgian translation made from the Russian, in 1782. The Ethiopic and the old Georgian versions are apparently anonymous, while the *Palaea Historica* has been translated into Slavonic and Romanian. Moreover, a liturgical use of the episode of the meeting with Abraham and his blessing by Melchizedek is attested by a Coptic (Sahidic) fragment of a "Prayer over the bread" (Bibliothèque nationale de France, Copte 129^{20}, f. 136^{rv}) and what seems to be its Bohairic

9. Dochhorn, "Die Historia de Melchisedech," 27-33.

10. See Robinson, "The Apocryphal Story," 28-31; Böttrich, *Geschichte Melchisedeks*, 85-105.

11. Actually, the short text entitled *Wonderful narration of an absolutely trustworthy elder about Melchizedek* copied in the manuscript of the Biblioteca Apostolica Vaticana, Othobonianus Gr. 441 (= Dochhorn's ms. n. 21), written in 1477, looks more like an independent copy of the Melchizedek text found in the *Chronicon Paschale* (see below, the section on "Aims, Sources, and Closely Related Texts") than another form of the *Story of Melchizedek*.

12. Dochhorn, "Die Historia de Melchisedech," 42-46.

13. Schreiner, "Die Prachthandschrift als Gebrauchsgegenstand," 47-50; cf. Böttrich, *Geschichte Melchisedeks*, 10-11 and 117-120.

14. Vassiliev, "Palaea historica," 206-14.

15. Dochhorn, "Die Historia de Melchisedech," 33-40.

16. See Böttrich, *Geschichte Melchisedeks*, 105-16, and Adler's translation of the *Palaea Historica* in the present volume.

17. For further information and bibliography, see Dochhorn, "Die Historia de Melchisedech," 21-23; Böttrich, *Geschichte Melchisedeks*, 16-29. Dochhorn, "Die Historia de Melchisedech," 23-27, has also re-edited and translated the two Coptic fragments, while Böttrich, *Geschichte Melchisedeks*, 121-35, provides useful German translations of the main versions.

equivalent (Cambridge, University Library, Ll, 6, 32, ff. 68r-71v). Such a liturgical habit, though discontinued by the Coptic Church, has been preserved by Ethiopian Christianity. Thus, the Ethiopic version of a similar "Prayer over the breaking of the bread" is present in both the manuscript tradition and the printed editions of the Ethiopic *First Anaphora of St. Gregory*.[18] Interestingly enough, the Ethiopic text of the passage quoted in this Eucharistic prayer is slightly different from the full text of the *Discourse on Melchizedek*, that is, the Ethiopic version of the *Story of Melchizedek*, which is extant in three copies: two complete (Bibliothèque nationale de France, Abb. 94, and Berlin, Staatsbibliothek Preussischer Kulturbesitz, Peterm. II Nachtr. 40) and one fragmentary (Bibliothèque nationale de France, Abb. 156).[19] A closer philological comparison reveals that the first of these was probably translated from the Arabic together with the rest of the Ethiopic Missal, while the second seems to be an earlier translation from the Greek,[20] possibly one of the various homilies on Melchizedek included in the *Qērillos*, the Aksumite anthology of Christological writings of Cyril of Alexandria and other Fathers of the Church that was translated into Ethiopic in the second half of the fifth century.[21] Thus, the old Ethiopic version of the *Story of Melchizedek* should play—as is usually the case for Ethiopic texts translated from the Greek—a major role in the hypothetical reconstruction of its lost, late antique original.

Original Text

Before grappling with the plot and the nature of the *Story of Melchizedek*, we should try to ascertain what its original profile was and which recension, if any, has better preserved its primary features. On the one hand, a certain number of elements found in the text of the *Palaea Historica* appear to be quite secondary. This is clearly the case for three main narrative modifications introduced by the narrator of the *Palaea*.

1. In 2:2 and 6:2, the *Palaea Historica* has replaced the mention of *tò dōdekátheon*, "the temple of the Twelve Gods," where king Melchi was accustomed to sacrificing to his gods, with a generic reference to "the great god Cronus and the rest of the gods" (33.2). Actually, such a compound name—well attested in the few published manuscripts of the Athanasian and the anonymous Greek recensions, to which we can also add the Ethiopic version—was originally meant to designate a sanctuary devoted to the Twelve Olympians, as in the case of a votive inscription from the

18. As insightfully acknowledged by Euringer, "Un frammento di Midrasch."

19. Still unpublished.

20. Contrary to what was suggested in Cowley, *Ethiopian Biblical Interpretation*, 25; Piovanelli, "Les aventures des apocryphes," 214 n. 60.

21. Cyril's two homilies on Melchizedek have been published by August Dillmann, "Cyrilli de Melchisedec homilia prior [et] altera," in idem, *Chrestomathia Aethiopica* (Leipzig: Weigel, 1866), 88-98; translated into German by Sebastian Euringer, "Übersetzung der Homilien des Cyrillus von Alexandrien, des Severus von Synnada und des Theodotus von Ancyra in Dillmanns 'Chrestomathia Aethiopica,'" *Or* 12 (1943): 113-34 (at 114-27); and reedited by Bernd M. Weischer, *Qērellos*. Vol. IV,3: *Traktate des Severianos von Gabala, Gregorios Thaumaturgos und Kyrillos von Alexandrien* (Äthiopistische Forschungen 7; Wiesbaden: Harrassowitz, 1970), 82-117. Concerning the reception of Melchizedek's figure in Ethiopia, see, in general, Bausi, "Melchizedek." On the other *Discourse on Melchizedek*, attributed to an unspecified "Orthodox" author, but identical with the anonymous text inserted into the *Chronicon Paschale*, see below, the section on "Aims, Sources, and Closely Related Texts." One should note that the Ethiopic versions of the *Story of Melchizedek*, Cyril's *First* and *Second Homily on Melchizedek*, and the *Discourse on Melchizedek* were copied together in ms. Abb. 94, written in the fifteenth or the sixteenth century.

island of Cos (Inscr. Cos 43, col. II, lines 7-8). In the apologetic context of the *Story of Melchizedek* it probably refers to their role as patrons of the twelve months and rulers of the signs of the zodiac, an association that originated in ancient Egypt and subsequently gained wide acceptance in the Greco-Roman world.[22] Therefore, the narrator seems to suggest that, even if king Melchi worships "the signs of heaven" as gods, in contrast to his son, he is unable to understand that they "make clear ... that their creator rests above them" (3:4), while the substitution of the Twelve Gods with Cronus simply obliterates the subtle irony of the original story.

2. Likewise, in 7:3 the *Palaea Historica* does not have Melchizedek ascending Mount Tabor—he will escape there only after the complete destruction of his city (36.2), but rather, standing "opposite the city upon the mountain now called the Mount of Olives," a mountain he called by that name (*elaiōn*) "because he found mercy (*eleos*) there" (35.4-5; 38.2). Such a secondary identification is clearly meant to suggest that Salem, Melchizedek's city, is none other than Jerusalem, which is generally acknowledged in Jewish and Christian traditions,[23] while one of the most original features of the *Story of Melchizedek* is the fact that it locates Salem in lower Galilee, in close proximity to Mount Tabor.
3. Finally, in the *Palaea Historica* and (probably independently) the Coptic-Ethiopic "Prayer over the (breaking of the) bread," it is Abraham who receives the order to bring "the bread, the wine, and the oil" (31.4; 36.4) for the (Eucharistic) offering that Melchizedek will make on the top of Mount Tabor before sharing with the patriarch his first civilized meal since the destruction of his city (37.4-9). This is not the case in the other recensions of the *Story of Melchizedek*, in which the two episodes of the meeting of Abraham and Melchizedek and the Eucharistic offering are clearly distinct. Firstly, it is only three days later that the priest-king of Salem comes down from Mount Tabor "carrying a horn of oil" in order to bless Abraham and confer upon him his full and "perfected" name (12:1-2; cf. Gen 17:5). Then, after a certain amount of time has elapsed, when Abraham is "returning from the slaughter of the kings" (cf. Gen 14:17; Heb 7:1) Melchizedek gives him "a cup of pure wine in which he had put a piece of bread," thus anticipating both "the bloodless sacrifice of the Savior" and his special priestly role (13:1-4; cf. *Palaea* 46.4-7). As a result, in both cases Melchizedek plays a determining role as the religious practitioner who initiates Abraham into more advanced forms of (Christian) faith.[24] The opposite can be seen in the *Palaea Historica*, where the narrator seems to downplay such a "baptismal" role, instead adapting a story originally focused on Melchizedek as the prototype of the Christian priest to the new Abrahamic setting of his or her narrative.

---

22. See Charlotte R. Long, *The Twelve Gods of Greece and Rome* (EPRO 107; Leiden: Brill, 1987). Moreover, according to the story related in the medieval Hebrew compilation of the *Sefer ha-Yashar*, "Terah (i.e., Abraham's father) had twelve gods of large size, made of wood and stone, after the twelve months (of the year)" (9:8), "standing there (i.e., in Terah's house) in their temples" (11:16, translated by [Moses Samuel], *Sefer ha-Yašar, or The Book of Jasher* [Salt Lake City: J. H. Parry & Co., 1887], 20 and 25).

23. See Ps 76:2; 1QapGen 22.13; Josephus, *J.W.* 6.438 and *A.J.* 1.180-81. Cf. Bardy, "Melchisédech dans la tradition," 506-507 n. 4; Simon, "Melchisédech dans la polémique," 61; Robinson, "The Apocryphal Story," 33; Böttrich, *Geschichte Melchisedeks*, 85-86.

24. See the insightful comments of Simon, "Melchisédech dans la polémique," 77.

On the other hand, some features of the published Athanasian recension, as it has been edited by Migne, seem to be secondary as well.

1. The attribution to Athanasius, unsupported not only by a significant part of the Greek manuscript tradition, but also by the Ethiopic and old Georgian versions, is probably the first of these derivative elements. Such an illustrious pseudonymous identity has also been used to legitimize, among their Egyptian and Ethiopian Christian readers, the Arabic and Ethiopic collections of the *Testaments of the Three Patriarchs*.[25] In both cases, however, this attribution does not provide any direct or indirect information about the origins of the writings posthumously placed under the authorship of the Alexandrian pope.[26]
2. Another example of secondary development is the gloss added to Melchizedek's Eucharistic offering to Abraham: "(a cup of pure wine in which he had put a piece of bread) which is called a *boukákraton* to the present day" (13:1). The reading "pure wine" is a conjecture on the part of Dochhorn, while the commentary "which is called a *boukákraton*" (from *boukká*, "piece," and *ákraton*, "pure wine")[27] is only found in Greek MS *R*. In the Middle Ages, the Eucharistic practice of dipping a piece of consecrated bread into the wine, while forbidden in the West, was relatively common among Orthodox and other Eastern Christians. "Pure wine," however, was apparently only used in the Armenian liturgy,[28] a peculiarity that certainly does not suffice, by itself, to demonstrate that the *Story of Melchizedek* originated in an Armenian milieu. As for the additional clue provided by the denomination *boukákraton* of the Eucharistic chalice, it only confirms that a learned medieval scribe anticipated a modern scholarly interpretation of the text.

All things considered, it would seem reasonable to conclude that the Greek manuscripts of the pseudo-Athanasian recension, especially when they are supported by the Ethiopic version, have better preserved the original text of the *Story of Melchizedek*, while the narrator of the *Palaea Historica* has considerably reworked it, as he or she was accustomed to doing with the sources he or she used, in a creative way. This does not mean that we can trust any detail of the pseudo-Athanasian text as Migne or Dochhorn have edited it. However, while waiting for a more exhaustive and truly critical edition, this is still the best approximation of the original text to which we have access.

Aims, Sources, and Closely Related Texts

A great deal of thanks is owed to Stephen R. Robinson for having rescued such a fascinating text from oblivion in 1987. In order to do that, however, he perhaps placed too much emphasis on the use of Jewish written sources and oral traditions—essentially, a

25. As noted by Böttrich, *Geschichte Melchisedeks*, 6-7. Cf. Martin Heide, *Die Testamente Isaaks und Jakobs. Edition und Übersetzung der arabischen und äthiopischen Versionen* (Äthiopistische Forschungen 56; Wiesbaden: Harrassowitz, 2000), 15. It is, then, rather telling that the Ethiopic version of the *Story of Melchizedek* is *not* attributed to Athanasius.

26. The attribution of authorship to Athanasius may have been inspired by the final reference explicitly made to the three hundred and eighteen "holy Fathers" who attended the first Council of Nicaea in 14:1-2, a figure to which Athanasius bore testimony in his *Synodal Letter to the Bishops of Africa* 2, written about 369.

27. See, e.g., Dochhorn, "Die Historia de Melchisedech," 33 n. 63.

28. Thus Euringer, "Un frammento di Midrasch," 60.

few episodes belonging to the cycle of Abrahamic legends[29]—which were readily available, in biblical and parabiblical literature, not to mention through personal contact and discussion, to every late antique Christian author.[30] Actually, the *Story of Melchizedek* is a perfect example of an Old Testament pseudepigraphon that contains too many explicitly Christian elements to be considered of Jewish origin.[31] The first part of the text is all but extolling the figure of Melchizedek at the expense of Abraham. Actually, its aim is simply to provide a narrative explanation for the absence of any mention of Melchizedek's family in the Hebrew Bible, for his status as king of Salem, and for his faith in God. The interlude of Melchizedek's madness prepares for the intervention of Abraham, who delivers the "man of God" from his fate and helps him to reintegrate into human society. As for the goal of the second part of the story, it is not to demonstrate, this time, the superiority of Abraham over Melchizedek, but instead, to show that the mysterious priest-king of Salem is no longer a stranger to the patriarch and to explain why Melchizedek, full of gratitude, is going to bless his new friend[32] and, following this, to receive him with an appropriate offering of wine and bread that makes him a true priest of God Most High.[33]

Filling in the blanks of biblical episodes and solving the contradictions, apparent or

---

29. For the different versions of Abraham's discovery of monotheism, the ensuing confrontation with his father Terah, and the death of his brother Haran, accidentally or intentionally burnt alive, see *Jubilees* 12; *Apocalypse of Abraham* 7-8; *Gen. Rab.* 38:13, and the passages of the *Sefer ha-Yashar* mentioned above (n. 22).

30. Robinson, "The Apocryphal Story," 31-33 and 34-36, now followed by Böttrich, *Geschichte Melchisedeks*, 62-65, while previous scholarship (Lévy, "Légendes judéo-chrétiennes," 197-99; James, *The Lost Apocrypha*, 17-18; Jérôme, *Das geschichtliche Melchisedech-Bild*, 19-21; Bardy, "Melchisédech dans la tradition," 40-42; Wuttke, *Melchisedech, der Priesterkönig*, 39-40; Simon, "Melchisédech dans la polémique," 70-91) had stressed the obviously Christian nature of the *Story of Melchizedek*, an interpretation also shared by Poorthuis, "Enoch and Melchizedek," 110-19.

31. Eloquent examples of this category of Christian parabiblical texts are provided by James R. Davila, *The Provenance of the Pseudepigrapha: Jewish, Christian, or Other?* (JSJSup 105; Leiden: Brill, 2005) and Pierluigi Piovanelli, "In Praise of 'The Default Position,' or Reassessing the Christian Reception of the Jewish Pseudepigraphic Heritage," *NedTT* 61 (2007): 233-50.

32. Interestingly enough, according to Philo Melchizedek rejoices over Abraham's victory because, "as the (Pythagorean) proverb says, 'friends share all things'" and offers a sacrifice on behalf of *all* those who followed the patriarch in his punitive expedition (*Abr.* 235). Moreover, in Philo's opinion Melchizedek's priesthood was "instinctively learned and self-taught" (*automathēs kaì autodídaktos*) (*Congr.* 99). However, unlike the *Story of Melchizedek*, in his allegorical reading of Gen 14:18-20 Philo identifies Melchizedek with the "priestly Logos" (*lógos hiereús*) (*Leg.* 3.79-82).

33. Other clues that, in Robinson's opinion, could point to a Jewish source—such as Melchizedek's ministering the Holy Offering to Abraham *and* "to his people as well, who were three hundred and eighteen men" (13:1, 4), and his description as a nazirite ("The Apocryphal Story," 34-35)—are perfectly at home and explainable in a Christian context. Thus, for example, concerning the Christological value of the number 318 found in Gen 14:14, as early as the first quarter of the second century the Christian author of the *Epistle of Barnabas* would be able to claim that "Abraham, the first to perform circumcision, was looking ahead in the spirit to Jesus when he circumcised. For he received the firm teachings of the three letters. For it says, 'Abraham circumcised eighteen and three hundred men from his household' (cf. Gen 14:14; 17:23-27). What knowledge, then, was given to him? Notice that he first mentions the eighteen and then, after a pause, the three hundred. The number eighteen [in Greek] consists of an Iota [I], 10, and an Eta [E], 8. There you have Jesus. And because the cross was about to have grace in the letter Tau [T], he next gives the three hundred, Tau. And so he shows the name Jesus by the first two letters, and the cross by the other" (9:7-8, translated by Bart D. Ehrman, *The Apostolic Fathers.* Volume II [LCL 25; Cambridge, Mass.: Harvard University Press, 2003], 45). Concerning Melchizedek's ascetic lifestyle (recently reexamined by Böttrich, "Melchisedek Naziraios"; idem, *Geschichte Melchisedeks*, 54-62), it is difficult to dissociate it from a typology that points to the figures to come of John the Baptist and Christian anchorites.

real, between different versions of the same story has always been one of the *raisons d'être* of rewriting biblical narratives. In the case of the *Story of Melchizedek*, the narrator's goal was to create an account that would provide a satisfactory explanation for the intriguing pictures of the king-priest of Salem which are found in Gen 14:18-20; Ps 110:4, and Heb 7:1-10. In doing so, he or she was trying to address an exegetical problem that dates back to the end of the Second Temple period, that is, the special status granted to the mysterious biblical character of Melchizedek, whose miraculous birth was described in *2 En.* 71-72 and whose role as eschatological avenger and heavenly savior was celebrated in the Qumran pesher *11QMelchizedek* (11Q13), the traditions of the Jewish Christian sect founded by Theodotus of Byzantium,[34] the Nag Hammadi apocalyptic tractate *Melchizedek* (NHC IX,1), and other Gnostic texts.[35] It would be naive, however, to think that this kind of belief was limited to the periphery of ancient Judaism and early Christianity. With the ascetic Hierakas, who lived in Egypt at the end of the third and the beginning of the fourth century, the idea of a divinized Melchizedek found its way into Egyptian Greek and/or Coptic-speaking monastic milieus,[36] where traces of discussions concerning Melchizedek's controversial nature are still apparent at the beginning of the fifth century and later, especially among the monks of Scetis (Wadi El Natrun). Finally, patriarchs Theophilus (385-412 C.E.) and Cyril of Alexandria (412-444 C.E.) had to personally intervene in order to dispel such (from their point of view) heterodox doctrines.

Monastic culture, being the true heir of Jewish, Jewish Christian, and Gnostic apocalyptic traditions,[37] is the background against which we should try to understand the original message of the *Story of Melchizedek*. With regard to this connection, Marcel Simon's conclusions are, more than seventy years later, still topical. This great scholar from Strasburg was able to explain the Galilean setting of the narrative as the result of a northern localization of the city of Salem in proximity to Aenon, the place where, according to John 3:23 ("Aenon near Salim"), John had been baptizing. The famous pilgrim Egeria visited

34. According to Pseudo-Tertullian's *Against All Heresies* 8, "After him (i.e., Theodotus of Byzantium), appeared another heretic (called) Theodotus, who introduced another sect; he too affirms that the Christ is merely a human being, conceived by the Holy Spirit and born of the virgin Mary, who is, nonetheless, inferior to Melchizedek because the Scripture says about the Christ, 'You are a priest forever according to the order of Melchizedek' (Ps 110:4). For (he says that) this Melchizedek, by a special grace, is a heavenly power, and what the Christ does for human beings, having become their intercessor and advocate (*deprecator et advocatus ipsorum factus*), Melchizedek does for the heavenly angels and powers. For he is to such a point superior to the Christ that he is 'without father, without mother, without genealogy, whose beginning and end are neither understood nor understandable' (Heb 7:3)."

35. On these and other Second Temple Jewish and early Christian texts and traditions, see especially the useful syntheses of Fred L. Horton Jr., *The Melchizedek Tradition: A Critical Examination of the Sources to the Fifth Century A.D. and in the Epistle to the Hebrews* (SNTSMS 30; Cambridge: Cambridge University Press, 1976); Claudio Gianotto, *Melchisedek e la sua tipologia. Tradizioni giudaiche, cristiane e gnostiche (sec. II a.C. - sec. III d.C.)* (Supplementi alla Rivista biblica 12; Brescia: Paideia, 1984); Birger A. Pearson, "The Figure of Melchizedek in Gnostic Literature," in idem, *Gnosticism, Judaism, and Egyptian Christianity* (2nd ed.; SAC; Philadelphia, Pa.: Fortress, 2006), 108-23; idem, "Melchizedek in Early Judaism, Christianity, and Gnosticism," in *Biblical Figures Outside the Bible* (ed. Michael E. Stone and Theodore A. Bergren; Harrisburg, Pa.: Trinity, 1998), 176-202; Piovanelli, "Much to Say."

36. According to Epiphanius of Salamis, who is our only source of information about him, Hierakas had come to the conclusion that not only is Melchizedek similar to the Christ, but also that he should be identified with the Holy Spirit (*Pan.* 55.5; 67.1-8).

37. See especially David Frankfurter, "The Legacy of Jewish Apocalypses in Early Christianity: Regional Trajectories," in *The Jewish Apocalyptic Heritage in Early Christianity* (ed. James C. VanderKam and William Adler; CRINT 3.4; Minneapolis, Minn.: Fortress; Assen: Van Gorcum, 1996), 129-200.

both sites in February-March 384 C.E. and was shown the *Opu Melchisedech* church in Sedima/Salem, which is built on the hillock on the top of which "Melchizedek offered God pure offerings of bread and wine," the foundations of his palace, the road to the river Jordan on which he met Abraham, as well as, just "two hundred yards away," John the Baptist's spring of water and pool which was still used to baptize the inhabitants of the village.[38] Simon even wondered if a member of the local clergy, especially the extremely learned "holy presbyter" in charge of the place, could not be identified as the author of the *Story of Melchizedek*.[39] It is more significant, however, that Simon was also able to demonstrate that Melchizedek's priestly acts prefigure both the Eucharist *and* the baptism and that he himself has become the ideal archetype of both the Christ *and* John the Baptist, "the most illustrious of all the anchorites."[40] This modification of the perspective of the Epistle to the Hebrews was probably the price to pay in order to bring the wild and controversial figure of the priest-king of Salem under complete control and firmly back to earth.

The successful attempt made by the author of the *Story of Melchizedek* to write down, most likely at the end of the fourth or the beginning of the fifth century, a biography of the priest-king of Salem in human and "historical" terms corresponds to a more general trend aiming at the domestication of Melchizedek and, through him, of some of his ascetic supporters. Strange though it may seem, more so than theological discourses, new apocryphal stories proved to be the most effective means of—paraphrasing Marcel Poorthuis—abandoning Melchizedek as a disturbing heavenly intermediary.[41] Thus, similar biographical developments about Melchizedek were included in popular late antique and early medieval texts such as the Syriac *Cave of Treasures* and the Arabic and Ethiopic *Conflict of Adam and Eve with Satan*.[42] The most intriguing parallel to the *Story of Melchizedek* is, however, offered by a short discourse *On Melchizedek* based on the teachings of an anonymous "elder," secondarily inserted in the *Chronicon Paschale*, a Byzantine chronicle summarizing human history from the creation of Adam to the twentieth year of the reign of the emperor Heraclius (610-641 C.E.). The existence of an Ethiopic version of this discourse as part of the *Qērillos* patristic anthology, translated directly from the Greek at a date earlier than that of the *Chronicon Paschale*, demonstrates that it was originally written, perhaps in the first half of the fifth century, as an autonomous piece of literature.[43]

38. John C. Wilkinson, *Egeria's Travels to the Holy Land* (2nd ed.; Jerusalem: Ariel; Warminster, U.K.: Aris & Phillips, 1981), 108-11 (chaps. 13-14).

39. Simon, "Melchisédech dans la polémique," 81.

40. Simon, "Melchisédech dans la polémique," 76-78 and 80-81.

41. Poorthuis, "Enoch and Melchizedek," 115. The same author identifies five stages in the changing Jewish and Christian perception of the biblical priest-king of Salem: (1) "the Jewish interpretation of Melchizedek as an intermediary"; (2) "the Christian appropriation of Melchizedek"; (3) "the Jewish reaction to Christian appropriation of Melchizedek"; (4) "the Christian abandonment of Melchizedek as an intermediary"; (5) "a Jewish rehabilitation of Melchizedek." In his opinion, the *Story of Melchizedek* fits perfectly into the fourth of these stages (117 n. 64).

42. See especially Böttrich, *Geschichte Melchisedeks*, 30-35.

43. The Greek text can be found in Fabricius, *CPVT*, 32-325 (taken from Charles du Fresne, sieur du Cange's 1689 edition of the *Chronicon Paschale*, and translated into English by Baring-Gould, *Legends*, 238-39), and Migne, "Πασχάλιον," 175-78 (reproducing the text of the 1832 edition of Dindorf, *Chronicon Paschale*). For a possible Greek manuscript of the discourse *On Melchizedek* alone, see above, n. 11. The Ethiopic version was published by Weischer, "Die äthiopischen Psalmen- und Qērlosfragmente," 142-43 (Ethiopic text), 152-53 (German translation) and 158 (Addenda). The German scholar, however, unaware of the original Greek text, thought that it was but a medieval translation from the Arabic. Only a few scholars have mentioned the discourse, and always *en passant*; among them, Bardy, "Melchisédech dans la

Melchizedek is described here as "a man from the tribe of Ham" chosen by God for his righteousness, separated from his people, and made king of Salem (explicitly identified with Jerusalem) and priest of the Most High even before his meeting with Abraham. On his way back from his expedition against king Chedorlaomer and his allies, the patriarch is entitled to see Melchizedek only after "he had passed over the Jordan, which is—as the text clearly puts it—a symbol of the baptism" (74:10),[44] while the fully human priest-king of Salem becomes the prototype of the Savior and a symbol of God's promise to the nations. Thus, in the end, although he has lost the highly prestigious status of a heavenly power in charge of judging the fallen angels and other eschatological duties, the role Melchizedek plays in the economy of redemption will nonetheless remain important, and his position among the heroes and heroines of biblical memory comfortable.

Cultural Influence

The late antique *Story of Melchizedek* has exerted a certain influence on different areas of medieval Christian culture, beginning with iconography. Its earliest traces are to be located in the illuminated folios of three Byzantine manuscripts of the Octateuch dating from the eleventh century, in which has been added, on the background of a more conventional representation of the meeting of Abraham and Melchizedek inspired by Gen 14:18-20, a scene depicting Abraham summoning a long-bearded Melchizedek who emerges from his cave.[45] A similar picture of the priest-king of Salem is displayed on the wall paintings representing the same biblical episode in three Egyptian churches dating from the twelfth and the thirteenth centuries, in which Melchizedek is portrayed as a half naked hermit living in a cave and offering a chalice to Abraham.[46] It is, however, in the manuscript tradition of the *Palaea Historica* that one can find the most impressive series of illuminations of the *Story of Melchizedek*: two vignettes in a Russian codex dating from 1477, as well as two sixteenth-century Greek manuscripts, containing six and nineteen sketches respectively.[47] Moreover, the same version of the *Palaea* was used, at the end of the fifteenth century, by the Cretan poet Georgious Chumnos in his verse paraphrase of Genesis and Exodus in vernacular Greek.[48] The reports of Christian pilgrims who, in the tenth century, started identifying the Galilean Mt. Tabor or its foot with the place where Melchizedek blessed Abraham, are equally late. After this, the Russian abbot Daniil, in 1106-07, and the Greek monk John Phokas, in 1177 or 1185, were even able to visit the actual cave in which, they

---

tradition," 42-43; Simon, "Melchisédech dans la polémique," 74 and 77; Böttrich, *Geschichte Melchisedeks*, 63 n. 336.

44. On this typological interpretation, see Everett Ferguson, *Baptism in the Early Church: History, Theology, and Liturgy in the First Five Centuries* (Grand Rapids, Mich.: Eerdmans, 2009), 221 and 402-403.

45. Biblioteca Apostolica Vaticana, Gr. 746, f. 68[r], and Gr. 747, f. 36[v]; Smyrna, Evangelical School A.1 (currently lost), f. 28[r]. See Böttrich, *Geschichte Melchisedeks*, 49-50 (discussion) and 145 (pictures).

46. Paintings of Dayr Anba Antuniyus (Red Sea), studied by Leroy, "Le programme décoratif," and Van Moorsel, "A Different Melchisedech?" and reexamined, together with those of Saint Macarius in Dayr Abu Maqar and the Church of the Virgin in Dayr al-Baramus (Wadi an-Natrun), by Van Loon, *The Gate of Heaven*; eadem, "Priester van God de Allerhoogste"; eadem, "The Meeting of Abraham and Melchizedek."

47. Pskov, Tolkovaja Paleja, ff. 79[rv]; Saint Catherine's Monastery, Mount Sinai, Ms. 1187, ff. 50[v]-61[r]; London, British Library, Add. 40724. See Robinson, "The Apocryphal Story," 36; Böttrich, *Geschichte Melchisedeks*, 50-51 (discussion) and 146-54 (pictures).

48. Edited and translated into English by Marshall, *Old Testament Legends*, 56-72. See Böttrich, *Geschichte Melchisedeks*, 46 (discussion) and 142-45 (Marshall's translation).

believed, the priest-king of Salem lived his solitary life. A small cave church was eventually rebuilt on the site in the nineteenth century.[49]

Finally, the *Story of Melchizedek* has also left a durable imprint on the Ethiopian liturgy[50] and the tradition of biblical commentaries. Thus, for example, the *andemta* commentary[51] to *Filkesius* (i.e., a collection of questions and answers on monastic life ascribed to the Syriac author Philoxenus of Mabbug) attributes to a certain "Mark" (the Hermit?), who "was a Greek, an Egyptian" and wrote "a book concerning the reply to the ones who say that Melchizedek is the Son of God," the following opinion, "The descent and tribal division of the tribe of Ham (cf. *On Melchizedek* 74:1, 14) is not written in the Torah, but he (Melchizedek) had a mother and father. Hasel begat Salem, Salem begat Melki, Melki begat a further Melki and Melchizedek. Their mother is called Sälima. Their father used to worship idols (cf. *Story of Melchizedek* 1:1-2:1)."[52]

This Translation

Due to the absence of a reliable critical edition of the Greek text of the *Story of Melchizedek*, this translation is based on the eclectic text edited by Migne and republished by Dochhorn.[53] As a result, the English translation offered here will not differ too much from the excellent work, also based on Migne's edition, previously published by Robinson. In the footnotes, however, the reader will, for the first time, be able to find a selection of the most significant variant readings from manuscripts *R* and *C* (used by Migne), together with the newly published *P* (edited by Dochhorn), as well as the *Palaea* (edited by Vassiliev and Dochhorn, translated by Adler) and the earliest editions of the *Story of Melchizedek* (republished by Fabricius). The discourse *On Melchizedek* is translated from the Greek text edited by Dindorf and republished by Migne. The footnotes also contain translations of a few variant readings taken from the edition of the Ethiopic version published by Weischer.[54]

Bibliography

Bardy, Gustave. "Melchisédech dans la tradition patristique." *RB* 35 (1926): 496-509; 36 (1927): 25-45.

---

49. See Simon, "Melchisédech dans la polémique," 79-80; Robinson, "The Apocryphal Story," 38; Pringle, *The Churches of the Crusader Kingdom*, 83-85; Böttrich, *Geschichte Melchisedeks*, 41-44 and 47 (discussion), 140-42 (German translation of Daniil and John Phokas's reports) and 155-57 (pictures of Mt. Tabor and the cave church of St. Melchizedek); idem, "Die 'Geschichte Melchisedeks,'" 201-205.

50. See above, n. 18.

51. *Andem*, "or," is the technical Amharic term that introduces a new, alternative explanation into the exegetical chain. See Kirsten Stoffregen-Pedersen and Tedros Abraha, "Andemta," *Encyclopaedia Aethiopica* 1 (2003): 258-59.

52. Cowley's translation (*Ethiopian Biblical Interpretation*, 25), slightly modified.

53. For practical reasons, following the example of Böttrich, *Geschichte Melchisedeks*, and in spite of its rather arbitrary nature, Dochhorn's subdivision of the text into chapters and verses has been adopted here.

54. Last but not least, it is a very pleasant task for me to warmly thank the various colleagues and friends who have helped me to complete the present translation, especially Richard Bauckham and James Davila, for their willingness to include these two fascinating texts in their anthology of Old Testament Pseudepigrapha and allowing me to take more time than had been agreed upon; Christfried Böttrich, for promptly sending me a copy of his wonderful German translation and commentary, along with other useful works, as soon as they were published, thus saving me from omitting things and making additional mistakes; and Robert Edwards, for copyediting my English text as competently and sensitively as ever.

Baring-Gould, Sabine. *Legends of the Patriarchs and Prophets and Other Old Testament Characters from Various Sources.* New York: Millar & Co., 1884.

Bausi, Alssandro. "Melchizedek." *Encyclopaedia Aethiopica* 3 (2007): 914-916.

Böttrich, Christfried. "Die 'Geschichte Melchisedeks' (*HistMelch*) im slavischen Kulturkreis." Pages 163-207 in *Old Testament Apocrypha in the Slavonic Tradition: Continuity and Diversity.* Edited by Lorenzo DiTommaso and Christfried Böttrich, with the assistance of Marina Swoboda. TSAJ 140. Tübingen: Mohr Siebeck, 2010.

__________. *Geschichte Melchisedeks.* JSHRZ.NF 2.1. Gütersloh: Gütersloher Verlagshaus, 2010.

__________. "Melchisedek Naziraios. Beobachtungen zur apokryphen 'Geschichte Melchisedeks' (HistMelch)." Pages 17-38 in *Mein Haus wird ein Bethaus für alle Völker genannt werden (Jes 56,7). Judentum seit der Zeit des Zweiten Tempels in Geschichte, Literatur und Kult. Festschrift für Thomas Willi zum 65. Geburtstag.* Edited by Julia Männchen, in collaboration with Torsten Reiprich. Neukirchen-Vluyn: Neukirchener Verlag, 2007.

Cowley, Roger W. *Ethiopian Biblical Interpretation: A Study in Exegetical Tradition and Hermeneutics.* University of Cambridge Oriental Publications 38. Cambridge and New York: Cambridge University Press, 1988.

Denis, Albert-Marie et al. *Introduction à la littérature religieuse judéo-hellénistique.* 2 vols. Turnhout: Brepols, 2000.

Dindorf, Ludwig August. *Chronicon Paschale.* Vol. I. Scriptorum Historiae Byzantinae. Bonn: Weber, 1832.

Dochhorn, Jan. "Die Historia de Melchisedech (Hist Melch). Einführung, editorischer Vorbericht und Editiones praeliminares." *Mus* 117 (2004): 7-48.

Euringer, Sebastian. "Un frammento di Midrasch di Melchisedech nella Liturgia dell'Osanna etiopica." *Rassegna di Studi Etiopici* 3 (1943): 50-60.

Fabricius, Johannes Albertus. "Narratio Apocrypha de Melchisedecho." Pages 311-320 in *CPVT.*

Haelewyck, Jean-Claude. *Clavis Apocryphorum Veteris Testamenti.* Corpus Christianorum. Turnhout: Brepols, 1998.

James, Montague Rhodes. *The Lost Apocrypha of the Old Testament: Their Titles and Fragments.* Translations of Early Documents 1,14. London and New York: Society for Promoting Christian Knowledge, 1920.

Jérôme, Franz Josef. *Das geschichtliche Melchisedech-Bild und seine Bedeutung im Hebräerbriefe.* Freiburg im Breisgau: Benzinger, 1920.

Leroy, Jules. "Le programme décoratif de l'église de Saint-Antoine du désert de la mer Rouge." *BIFAO* 76 (1976): 347-379.

Lévy, Israël. "Légendes judéo-chrétiennes." *RÉJ* 8 (1884): 197-205.

Marshall, Frederick H. *Old Testament Legends from a Greek Poem on Genesis and Exodus by Georgious Chumnos.* Cambridge: Cambridge University Press, 1925.

Migne, Jacques-Paul. "Historia de Melchisedec." PG 28 (1857): 523-530.

__________. "Melchisédech." In *Dictionnaire des Apocryphes, ou Collection de tous les livres apocryphes relatifs à l'Ancien et au Nouveau Testament,* 2:583-588. Paris: Migne, 1858.

__________. "Πασχάλιον seu Chronicon Paschale, a mundo condito ad Heraclii imp. annum XX." PG 92 (1860): 9-1160.

Piovanelli, Pierluigi. "Les aventures des apocryphes en Éthiopie." *Apocrypha* 4 (1993): 197-224.

__________. "'Much to Say and Hard to Explain': Melchizedek in Early Christian Literature, Theology, and Controversy." Pages 411-429 in *New Perspectives on 2 Enoch: No Longer Sla-*

vonic Only. Edited by Andrei A. Orlov and Gabriele Boccaccini, in association with Jason Zurawski. Studia Judaeoslavica 4. Leiden: Brill, 2012.

Poorthuis, Marcel. "Enoch and Melchizedek in Judaism and Christianity: A Study in Intermediaries." Pages 97-120 in *Saints and Role Models in Judaism and Christianity*. Edited by Joshua Schwartz and Marcel Poorthuis. Jewish and Christian Perspectives Series 7. Leiden: Brill, 2004.

Pringle, Deny. *The Churches of the Crusader Kingdom of Jerusalem: A Corpus. Volume II: L-Z (Excluding Tyre)*. Cambridge: Cambridge University Press, 1998.

Robinson, Stephen R. "The Apocryphal Story of Melchizedek." *JSJ* 18 (1987): 26-39.

Schreiner, Peter. "Die Prachthandschrift als Gebrauchsgegenstand: theologische und wirtschaftsgeschichtliche Notizen auf dem Verso des Josua-Rotulus (Vat. Palat. gr. 431)." *AÖAW. PH* 134 (1997-99): 43-62.

Simon, Marcel. "Melchisédech dans la polémique entre juifs et chrétiens et dans la légende." *RHPR* 17 (1937): 58-93. Reprinted in idem, *Recherches d'histoire judéo-chrétienne*, 101-126. Études juives 6. Paris and La Haye: Mouton & Co., 1962.

Van Loon, Gertrud J. M. *The Gate of Heaven: Wall Paintings with Old Testament Scenes in the Altar Room and the Hurus of Coptic Churches*. Publications de l'Institut historique-archéologique néerlandais de Stamboul 85. Istanbul: Netherlands Institute for the Near East, 1999.

__________. "The Meeting of Abraham and Melchizedek and the Communion of the Apostles." In *Coptic Studies on the Threshold of a New Millennium: Proceedings of the Seventh International Congress of Coptic Studies, Leiden, August 27–September 2, 2000*, 2:1373-1392. Edited by Mat Immerzeel and Jacques van der Vliet. OLA 133. Leuven: Peeters, 2004.

__________. "Priester van God de Allerhoogste. Iconografische en iconologische aspecten van de ontmoeting van Abraham." *Journal of Eastern Christian Studies* 53 (2001): 5-29.

Van Moorsel, Paul P. V. "A Different Melchisedech? Some Iconographical Remarks." Pages 329-342 in *ΘΕΜΕΛΙΑ. Spätantike und koptologische Studien Peter Grossmann zum 65. Geburtstag*. Edited by Martin Krause and Sofia Schaten. Sprachen und Kulturen des Christlichen Orients 3. Wiesbaden: Reichert Verlag, 1998.

Vassiliev, Afanasiĭ. "Palaea historica." In *Anecdota Graeco-Byzantina. Pars prior*, 188-292. Moscow: Universitas Cæsarea, 1893.

Weischer, Bernd M. "Die äthiopischen Psalmen- und Qērlosfragmente in Erevan / Armenien." *OrChr* 53 (1969): 113-158.

Wuttke, Gottfried. *Melchisedech, der Priesterkönig von Salem. Eine Studie zur Geschichte der Exegese*. BZNW 5. Giessen: Töpelmann, 1927.

The Story of Melchizedek

Melchizedek's discovery of monotheism

1 [1]At that time, there was a queen named Salem after the name of the city. [2]She
gave birth to Salaad. [3]And Salaad begat Melchi. [4]Melchi took a wife named Salem after her.[a] [5]And she bore him two sons, one called Melchi and the other
Melchizedek.[b] **2** [1]Their father was a pagan, wicked, and offering sacrifices to
the idols.[c] [2]And the appropriate time arrived for him to sacrifice to the idols, for
he was sacrificing in the temple of the Twelve Gods.[d] [3]King Melchi said to his
son Melchizedek, "Take some young men with you, go to the herd, and bring
me seven calves,[e] that we may sacrifice to the gods." **3** [1]As Melchizedek therefore went out, a divine thought occurred to him on the road. [2]Having raised his
eyes to heaven, he gazed upon the sun and considered the moon and the stars.
[3]While he was meditating within himself, he said, "If someone made the heaven,
the earth, the sea, and the stars, to him should the sacrifice be offered, to their
creator. [4]The signs of heaven make it clear to me that their creator rests above
them, incorruptible, invisible, immortal, being the only God in heaven and on
earth, who knows the thoughts[f] of hearts. [5]He is the true God; to him should the

---

a. Either the city or Melchi's grandmother.

b. Thus the beginning of Migne's printed text. The few manuscripts already published read: "Salem was named after the name of the city of Salom. Salem gave birth to Melchel [first hand, 'Melchizedek'], and Melchel [idem] begat two sons, one called Melchel, as his father, and the other called Melchizedek. The father preferred the one who had his name, Melchel, and the mother preferred the son who had the same name [sic], Melchizedek," MS *R*; "King Melchiel begat two sons, one called Melchiel, as his father, and the other called Melchizedek. Their father preferred the elder son, Melchiel, while their mother preferred the younger, Melchizedek," MS *C* (note the anticipation of the motif of parental penchants mentioned below, 5:3-7); "Asel begat Asal, and Asal begat Melchel. Melchel was a pagan, wicked, and offering sacrifices to the idols. He begat two sons, and called the first Melchel and the second Melchizedek," MS *P*. In the *Palaea*, the names of the king and his two sons are, respectively, "Josedek," "Sedek," and "Melchi" (32.2-3).

c. "Their father was a king of the pagans [read *Hellēnōn*], offering wicked sacrifices to the idols," MS *R*. In MS *P* this sentence is anticipated by 1:4 (see the previous note).

d. The "temple of the Twelve Gods," mentioned here and below (6:2), is *tò dōdekátheon*, a compound name that was originally meant to designate a sanctuary devoted to the Twelve Olympians and that probably refers here to their role as patrons of the twelve months and rulers of the zodiac signs. In the *Palaea*, the Twelve Gods are replaced by "the great god Cronus and the rest of the gods" (33.2).

e. In the *Palaea*, Melchi is charged with bringing "seventy bulls" back from "Galilee" (33.2).

f. Thus Dochhorn, following MS *R*; "the blasphemies," Migne.

sacrifice be offered.[a] [6]I will go back to my father and beg for his pardon. Perhaps he will listen to me."

The sacrifice of one of the king's sons

4 [1]So Melchizedek returned bringing nothing. [2]Seeing him, his father asked him, "Where are the calves?" [3]And Melchizedek replied to him, "Do not be angry, O father king, but listen to me." [4]He said, "What you have to say, say it quickly!" [5]And Melchizedek said, "Come, the sacrifice that we have to offer, let us not offer to these gods, for these do not seem to me to be gods. Rather, let us offer a sacrifice to the one who rests above the heavens, for he is the supreme God."[b] [6]But his father became angry and said to him, "Go, bring what I told you, or you will not live." **5** [1]As soon as Melchizedek went back to the herd, Melchi, the king of Salem, approached Salem, his wife, and said to her, "Come let us offer one of our sons as a sacrifice." [2]When his wife heard this, she wept bitterly, [3]for she knew that the king was looking for a pretext to kill Melchizedek because he had criticized him about the sacrifice. [4]The queen lamented and said, "Ah me, I have labored and toiled in vain!"[c] [5]But seeing her, the king said to her, "Do not weep, but come let us cast lots, and if the lot falls to me, I will choose the one I wish and will offer him as a sacrifice to our gods. But if the lot falls to you, choose the one you wish and protect him." [6]He said that thinking that he would hold possession of the one of his wife.[d] [7]But when they cast the lot, it fell to the queen who chose Melchizedek whom she loved. [8]And the king of Salem, defeated by his wife, prepared the son who had fallen to him for the sacrifice, for he was afraid to offend his gods.[e] **6** [1]Melchizedek arrived bringing the seven calves, [2]while the father, taking the son who had fallen to him, went into the shrine of the idols in the temple of the Twelve Gods. [3]Five hundred and three boys went together to the sacrifice offered by their own fathers, and three hundred[f] others offered by their mothers, with countless cattle and sheep. And the sacrifice was ready. **7** [1]Salem, however, the mother of Melchizedek, who was sitting in her house, cried out in a loud voice and said to Melchizedek, "Do you not weep for your brother because he goes to be slaughtered after so much toil?" [2]And when he heard this from her, he wept and said to his[g] mother, "How long am I going

---

a. The discovery of monotheism through the observation of the regularity of natural, especially astronomical, phenomena plays a key role in Second Temple and rabbinic traditions and stories about the vocation of the patriarch Abraham (cf. *Jub.* 12:16-18; *Apoc. Ab.* 7:7-11; *Gen. Rab.* 38:13). The underlying presupposition is that "since the creation of the world his (i.e., God's) eternal power and divine nature, invisible though they are, have been understood and seen through the things he has made," as Paul puts it in Rom 1:20 (NRSV).

b. Literally, "God of gods."

c. Cf. 1 Thess 3:5; Phil 2:16; 6 Ezra 16:45.

d. "That he would hold possession of the one of his wife," according to MS *R*, or "that the lot would not fall to his wife," according to MS *C*, against the corrupt reading of the printed editions reproduced by Migne, "that he would hold possession (of him thanks) to the priest," which Robinson freely renders, "(thinking) to obtain his aims by means of the priest."

e. "For he was afraid to offend his gods," according to MSS *R* and *C*, followed by Migne, but absent from MS *P* and the earliest printed editions.

f. Read *triakósioi* with MSS *R*, *C*, and Migne (omitted by the first editors).

g. Read *autoû* as in the printed editions and Migne.

to need those who are here?" [3]And rising up he ascended Mount Tabor,[a] [4]while his mother rising up went into the temple of the idols to see her own son and her whole people before the slaughter.

Melchizedek's madness after the annihilation of his family

8 [1]As for Melchizedek, after he ascended Mount Tabor, he bent his knees and said, [2]"Oh God, the Lord of all, creator of heaven and earth, I beseech you, the only true God. [3]Hear me in this hour and order that for all those who were present at the sacrifice of my brother Melchi the place may become like Hades and devour them." [4]And God heard Melchizedek, and immediately the earth opened its mouth wide and devoured them, all the family of Melchizedek together with the entire city; [5]neither man, nor altar, nor temple, nor animal, nor any trace of the whole city remained, but everything was swallowed up. **9** [1]Melchizedek came down from Mount Tabor. [2]But when he saw that God had heard him, he returned to the mountain in great fear. [3]He went deep into the forest, and remained there for seven years,[b] [4]naked as when he emerged from his mother's womb; [5]and his fingernails became a span long, the hair of his head (hung) down to his loins,[c] and his back became like a tortoise-shell. [6]Berries[d] were his nourishment, and his drink was the dew, which he lapped up.

Melchizedek's rescue by Abraham

10 [1]After seven years,[e] a voice[f] came to Abraham, saying, "Abraham, Abraham." [2]And Abraham replied, "My Lord!" [3]And he said, "Saddle your donkey, carry precious clothes and a razor,[g] go up on Mount Tabor, [4]and cry out three times, 'Man of God!' [5]And a wild man will rise up. [6]Do not be afraid of him, but shave him, pare his nails, clothe him,[h] and be blessed by him." **11** [1]And Abraham did as the Lord had commanded him: he went up to Mount Tabor, stood by the

---

a. In the *Palaea*, the identification of the mountain which Melchizedek initially climbs with "the Mount of Olives" (35:4; 38:2) clearly betrays the narrator's conviction that Melchizedek's city is Jerusalem. It is only after the complete destruction of Salem that Melchizedek flees to a mountain called *Tabúrion* (36:2), a name apparently derived from an adjectival form like *thabórion* which is found in MS *P*.

b. Thus Migne (and Dochhorn), following MS *R* (joined now by MS *P*); "for 60 years," MS *C*; "for forty years," according to the *Palaea* (36:3; 37:7).

c. The earliest editions omit "as when he had come out from his mother's womb; and his fingernails became a span long, the hair of his head" and read "naked from his belly to his loins." According to MS *P*, Melchizedek's hair hung down "to his feet."

d. Greek *akródrua* means "fruits grown on upper branches of trees," especially "hard-shelled fruits."

e. MS *C* reads, once again, "60 years."

f. MS *P* adds "from heaven."

g. "A razor," according to MS *R* and the *Palaea* (36:4), while the earliest editions read "and make a sacrifice," to which MS *C* adds "to the Lord, your God" (MS *P* omits "carry precious clothes and a razor"). Note that in the *Palaea* it is Abraham who also brings "the bread and the wine" (ibid.). This is also the case in the Coptic ("bread, wine, and water," Sahidic; "a vessel of bread and a vessel of wine," Bohairic) and the Ethiopic ("a basket of bread and an amphora of wine") Eucharistic prayers.

h. Instead of "shave him, pare his nails, clothe him," MS *C* reads "cut his hair, cut his nails, kiss him."

depths of the forest, [2]and cried out three times, "Man of God!" [3]And Melchizedek rose up. Abraham saw him and was afraid. [4]Melchizedek said to him, "Do not be afraid, but tell me who you are and what you are seeking." [5]And Abraham replied, "The Lord commanded me to shave you, cut your nails,[a] clothe you, and be blessed by you." [6]And Melchizedek said to him, "Do as the Lord has commanded you." [7]And Abraham did as the Lord had commanded him.

Abraham's blessing by Melchizedek

12 [1]Melchizedek came down from Mount Tabor three days later carrying a horn of oil, and confirming the word of God, he blessed Abraham,[b] saying, [2]"Blessed are you by the Most High God, and henceforth your name will be perfected:[c] your name will no longer be Abram, but your name will be perfect, (i.e.) Abraham."[d]

The reasons for Melchizedek's anonymity

[3]And again a voice came to Abraham. [4]And he asked, "What is it, my Lord?"
[5]And the Lord said to him, "Because no one of the family of Melchizedek has
survived on earth, for this reason he will be called *without father, without moth-*
er, without genealogy, having neither beginning of days nor end of life, but made
Heb 7:3 *like the Son of God, he remains a priest perpetually.* [6]I have loved him as I have
loved my beloved Son, because he kept my commandments,[e] and he will keep
them forever." [7]Therefore one should not think that he has no beginning of days
because he does not know when he was born, or his genealogy, or his father, or
his mother. This is the reason why he is said to be *without father, without mother,*
without genealogy. [8]And because he is well pleasing to God, *he remains a priest*
perpetually.

Melchizedek's second meeting with Abraham (and its typology)

13 [1]Then, when Melchizedek *met Abraham as he was returning from the slaugh-*
Heb 7:1 *ter of the kings,* he gave him a cup of pure wine[f] in which he had put a piece of

---

a. The earliest editions omit, "cut your nails."

b. In the *Palaea*, Abraham and Melchizedek seem to remain on the top of Mount Tabor, where they make a Eucharistic offering (37:8-9); then, after Melchizedek has told "everything about himself" (38:1-2), Abraham gives him a tenth "from his household" (38:6-8) and is blessed by him (40:1).

c. MS *P* omits "and henceforth your name will be perfected" and reads "a voice from heaven came to Abraham, saying," thus attributing the discourse that follows to God.

d. The earliest editions omit "your name will no longer be Abram, but your name will be perfect, (i.e.) Abraham." Here Melchizedek is anticipating the change of Abraham's name by God in Gen 17:5. Also note that the suggested interpretation of Abraham's name is neither "the father of a multitude of nations" (Gen 17:4-5, followed by *Palaea* 31.2-3) nor "the friend of God" (Jas 2:23). The *Palaea* summarizes the content of the blessing—Melchizedek "[invoked him (i.e., Abraham) by name], blessed him as a son, and on his own foretold a blessing on his offspring" (40:1)—and brings the story to an end with the mention that "from that day Abraham continued coming to be blessed by Melchizedek" (ibid.).

e. This is where the text of MS *P* ends.

f. Adopting Dochhorn's conjecture, which combines the readings of the printed texts ("a cup of pure [wine]") and MS *R* ("a cup of wine [in which he had] secretly [put]").

bread—which is called a *boukákraton*[a] to the present day—, and to his people as
well, who were three hundred and eighteen men.[b] [2]In this way he was *made like
the Son of God,* but not according to grace. [3]And thus he[c] became the first type of
the bloodless sacrifice of the Savior, pointing to the Holy Offering.[d] [4]Therefore
he says, *You are a priest forever according to the order of Melchizedek*, because Ps 110:4
he became a type of the Holy Offering, as he gave it to Abraham and the three
hundred and eighteen. **14** [1]So also, at that time, the holy Fathers, who taught the
faith aright, were found in the city of Nicaea. [2]Their number is, according to the
likeness of the patriarch Abraham, three hundred and eighteen holy bishops in
the assembly.

[3]And glory is due to our God now and always, forever and ever.[e] Amen.

---

a. Thus MS *R* (followed by Migne), while the earliest editions and the Ethiopic version omit the commentary, "which is called a *boukákraton*." The latter is a rare compound name made of *boukká*, "piece," and *ákraton*, "pure wine."

b. Cf. Gen 14:14. Here Melchizedek provides a feast for *all* those who followed Abraham to the battle against Chedorlaomer and his allies, as in 1QapGen 22.15; Philo, *Abr.* 235; Josephus, *A.J.* 1.181.

c. "Melchizedek," MS *C.*

d. "(Bringing to the Holy Offering) bread, wine, and water, showing the three-fold hypostatic power," MS *C.*

e. The earliest editions omit the final invocation.

APPENDIX

On Melchizedek from the *Chronicon Paschale*

Melchizedek's Hamitic origins

74 [1]A certain elder[a] used to say of Melchizedek, and to maintain strongly, that he was a man from the tribe of Ham[b] who, having been found to be a holy child in his tribe, pleased God. [2]And God moved him from his own to the land beyond the Jordan, in the same way as he had moved Abraham from the country of the Chaldeans.[c] [3]Because this man was holy and righteous, he became a priest of the Most High God, offering bread, wine, and holy prayers to the Most High God. [4]And he prayed on behalf of his tribe, saying, "Lord, you have removed me from my tribe,[d] and have had mercy on me; have mercy on them too." [5]And the Lord replied to him, "I will save them when I call my Son out of Egypt."[e] This is the promise that God made to Melchizedek.

Melchizedek's only meeting with Abraham (and its typology)

[6]That elder also used to mention that, at that time, it happened that Lot was taken captive from the land of Sodom by some of the men of Chedorlaomer,[f] and that Abraham had pursued and destroyed them, delivering from their hands all of the prisoners, including Lot, the son of his brother Haran.[g] [7]Therefore[h] Abraham said within himself, "Lord, if in my days you send your angel[i] upon the earth, grant me to see that day!" [8]And God replied to him, "No, but I will show you the type of that day: go down and cross the Jordan River, and you will

---

a. Eth. adds "and knowledgeable in the law of the Lord."

b. This is apparently, with the prologue to the Slavonic version of the *Story of Melchizedek*, the only case of identification of Melchizedek as a Hamite, probably because, according to the Table of Nations of Gen 10, Ham is the father of Canaan (Gen 10:6) and the grandfather of the Jebusites (Gen 10:16), the latter being the ancestors of the first inhabitants of Jerusalem (cf. Josh 15:63; Judg 1:21; 2 Sam 5:6-8; 1 Chr 11:4).

c. Instead of "from the country of the Chaldeans" Eth. reads "from his country."

d. In place of "you have removed me from my tribe" Eth. reads "you have turned me away from the knowledge of the devil."

e. Cf. Hos 11:1; Matt 2:15. This means that even people of non-Semitic lineage will finally be saved by Jesus.

f. The king of Elam is called here "Gothōllogomōr" ("Kadologomor," "Kaladogomor," or "Kālodogomor" in Eth.), a variant of the Greek rendering of his name in the Septuagint (Gen 14:1, 4-5, 9, 17).

g. Cf. Gen 14:12-16. Instead of "including Lot, the son of his brother Haran" Eth. reads "from the slaughter of the kings."

h. Eth. adds "and, as it is written, Melchizedek came to meet him, but before they meet."

i. In the Eth. it is "your word."

see the type[a] of that day." [9]Therefore Abraham crossed the Jordan River with his
army, and Melchizedek rose up to meet him, inspired by the Holy Spirit,[b] carrying in his hands the bread of the Eucharist and the cup of blessing.[c] [10]Abraham,
however, did not see Melchizedek before he had passed over the Jordan, which
is a symbol of the baptism.[d] [11]Abraham, then, seeing Melchizedek coming to
meet him with the bread of the Eucharist and the cup of blessing, fell on his face
upon the earth and adored, for he had seen the day of the Lord[e] and was glad.
[12]After he met him, Melchizedek, king of Jerusalem, priest of the Most High
God, blessed Abraham *and said, "Blessed be Abraham by the Most High God, the
creator of heaven and earth;* [13]*and blessed be the Most High God, who has delivered your enemies into your hand." And Abraham gave him a tenth of all.*[f] Gen 14:19-20

The truth about Melchizedek

[14]Therefore[g] Melchizedek was a man from the tribe of Ham, who was removed
from his tribe to the country of the Canaanites,[h] to the land beyond the Jordan, to the city of Salem, where we have even seen his quarter.[i] [15]He became
the priest of the Most High God, according to the Scriptures,[j] *without father,
without mother, without genealogy*, and was established in the village of Salem, Heb 7:3
which means "peace." [16]The apostle Paul mentions him when he writes to the
Hebrews,[k] *The Lord has sworn and will not change his mind, "You are a priest
forever, according to the order of Melchizedek."* [17]*About him we have much to say,* Ps 110:4 | Heb 5:11
but it is the elder who spoke the truth.[l]

Inscription[m]

[18]How great is this Melchizedek, the priest of the Most High God, who takes a
tenth of those who are priests according to the Law of Moses.[n] [19]He is not only
the king of peace and justice, but also priest of the Most High God, made like the Heb 7:2
Son of God, who did not receive the priesthood from the succession of other

---

a. Eth. reads "the glory."

b. Eth. omits "inspired by the Holy Spirit."

c. Eth. adds "and he blessed Abraham."

d. As implied by *4 Bar.* 6:23 and clearly stated by Origen (who paraphrases 1 Cor 10:1-2) in his *Comm. Jo.* 6.44-45 and *Hom. Jes. Nav.* 4-5.

e. Melchizedek is depicted here as the true prototype of Jesus.

f. Eth. omits 74:12-13.

g. Eth. adds "truly and certainly."

h. As if the Canaanites were not, according to the Table of Nations, of Hamitic stock! Eth. omits "to the country of the Canaanites."

i. In place of "where we have even seen his quarter" Eth. anticipates here "whose interpretation is 'peace.'"

j. Instead of "according to the Scriptures" Eth. reads "as the blessed Paul says."

k. Actually, what follows is a direct citation of Ps 110:4, a passage that is never quoted in full in the Epistle to the Hebrews (cf. Heb 5:6; 7:17).

l. Eth. omits 74:16-21 and comes to an end with "Melchizedek was from the people of Canaan."

m. In this *epígramma*, made of a series of four short sentences that all begin with *hoûtós estin ho…*, "this is the (one who)…," Melchizedek's priestly functions anticipate the cultic role that the author of the Epistle to the Hebrews attributes to Jesus.

n. I.e., the Levitical priests. Cf. Heb 7:4-10.

priests, nor did he transmit it to other priests.[a] [20]He is the one who did not prescribe rites according to the Law of Moses, but performed them with other, better symbols. [21]He is the one who blessed the patriarch Abraham, the one *without father, without mother, without genealogy,* the only priest and king to be
Heb 7:3 *made like the Son of God* and to have received the honor of being the herald of such good things.

a. Cf. Heb 7:13-16.

The Syriac History of Joseph
A new translation and introduction

by Kristian S. Heal

The *Syriac History of Joseph* is a dramatic prose retelling of the story of the Old Testament patriarch Joseph, beginning with his dreams and ending with his death (Gen 37, 39–47, 50), but omitting Jacob's blessing upon both Joseph's and his own children (Gen 48–49). The narrative is rich in expansions, many of which contain Jewish elements. The work is attributed to Basil of Caesarea in each of its five known manuscript witnesses (CPG 2987). This attribution is certainly spurious.[1] However, the work is no less important for not coming from the pen of the famous Cappadocian since it embodies an influential and early stratum of the significant corpus of Syriac Joseph texts.

Editions and Manuscripts

The *editio princeps* of the *Syriac History of Joseph* was published in two parts, the first in 1893 by Magnus Weinberg and the second in 1895 by Samuel Wolf Link.[2] This edition was based on Berlin Syriac 74 (Sachau 9), a parchment codex written in an East Syriac hand dated to A.D. 1695. Pages are wanting at both the beginning and end, and elsewhere throughout the manuscript. The "History of Joseph," which begins on folio 24r and comprises twenty-eight leaves, is the seventh item in this miscellany of apocryphal and hagiographical works.[3] The loss of a single leaf after the current folio 37 caused a lacuna to the most important narrative expansion in the text, and thus to the published edition of this work. This gap has now been filled, and the complete episode is found in the present translation.[4]

Four additional manuscript witnesses of this work have been identified since it was

1. Most recently, Sebastian Brock affirmed that the text is "wrongly attributed to Basil" ("Dramatic Dialogue Poems," in H.J.W. Drijvers et al., eds., *IV Symposium Syriacum, 1984*, Orientalia Christiana Analecta 229 [Roma: Pontificio Istituto Orientale, 1987], 135-47, specifically, p. 140 n. 16). The question of Basil's authorship is discussed at greater length (and dismissed) in Magnus Weinberg, *Die Geschichte Josefs angeblich verfasst von Basilius dem Grossen aus Cäsarea* (Halle: Druck von H. Itzkowski, 1893), 12-15. This attribution is not found in the Ethiopic and Latin versions, though it is found in the Arabic. On Basil's works in Syriac, see David G. K.Taylor, *The Syriac Versions of the* De Spiritu Sancto *by Basil of Caesarea*, CSCO 577 (Leuven: Peeters, 1999), ix-xix. According to the *Clavis Patrum Graecorum* this is the only work spuriously attributed to Basil in Syriac (Maurice Geerard, et al., *Clavis Patrum Graecorum*, 5 vols. [Turnhout: Brepols, 1974-87], 2:177-78).

2. Weinberg, *Geschichte Josefs;* Samuel Wolf Link, *Die Geschichte Josefs angeblich verfasst von Basilius dem Grossen aus Cäsarea* (Berlin: H. Itskowski, 1895). I have a new edition in preparation.

3. Eduard Sachau, *Verzeichniss der syrischen Handschriften der Königlichen Bibliothek zu Berlin*, 2 vols. (Berlin: A. Asher & Co., 1899), 284.

4. An edition and annotated translation of the complete episode is found in my "A Missing Leaf from the *Syriac History of Joseph*" (forthcoming).

first published, two in the British Library, a third in the Bibliothèque Nationale in Paris, and the fourth in the library of the Chaldean Archbishop of Tehran.[5] I use the following sigla to refer to these manuscripts in the translation:

B Berlin Syriac 74 (Sachau 9), folios 24r-52v.
L London, British Library Oriental 4528, folios 3v–26r (A.D. 1737).[6]
M London, British Library Oriental 2316, folios 176r–82v (fragmentary, seventeenth or eighteenth century).[7]
P Paris, Bibliothèque Nationale Syriac 309, folios 10r-51v (A.D. 1869).[8]
T Tehran, Fonds Issayi 18 (*olim* Neesan 8), f. 182v–214r (eighteenth century).[9]

Arabic (H 113), Latin, and Ethiopic (H 113) versions of the *Syriac History* are attested in the manuscripts.[10] Georg Graf has identified several manuscripts containing the Christian Arabic (Garshuni) version.[11] For example, Cambridge University Library Additional 2886, an eighteenth-century West-Syrian collection of saints' lives in Garshuni, contains the *History of Joseph* attributed to Basil the Great as its fourth item.[12] A Latin version of the *Syriac History* was discovered by Frederic Faverty in a manuscript in the Vienna National Library (Codex 4739, ff. 234r–250v).[13] The *explicit* of the translation notes that it was made by a Spaniard called Alphonsus Bonihominius in A.D. 1336.[14] The Ethiopic version is found in a fifteenth-century manuscript filmed by the Hill Museum and Manu-

5. Alain Desreumaux refers to only four known witnesses to the text in his "Esquisse d'une liste d'œuvres apocryphes syriaques," in M. Debié et al., eds., *Les apocryphes syriaques* (Études syriaques 2; Paris: Geuthner, 2005), 217-25, specifically, p. 219; he did not appear to be aware of the London or Paris manuscripts when he brought to light the Tehran witness to this text in his "Un manuscript syriaque de Téhéran contenant des apocryphes," *Apocrypha* 5 (1994): 137-64, specifically 162. Robert Phenix, who seems unaware of Desreumaux's work, mentions only the Berlin and Paris manuscripts (*The Sermons on Joseph of Balai of Qenneshrin* [Tübingen: Mohr Siebeck, 2008], p. 102).

6. George Margoliouth, *Descriptive List of Syriac and Karshuni Mss. in the British Museum Acquired Since 1873* (London: Longmans & Co., 1899), 47.

7. Margoliouth, *Descriptive List*, 9.

8. Chabot, "Les manuscrits syriaques de la Bibliothèque Nationale acquis depuis 1874," *Journal Asiatique* 8 (1896): 8-9.

9. Desreumaux, "Un manuscrit syriaque de Téhéran."

10. Note that Denis et al. only knew of the Ethiopic version of the *Syriac History* (Albert-Marie Denis et al., *Introduction à la littérature religieuse judéo-hellénistique,* 2 vols. [Turnhout: Brepols, 2000], 1:346). A later attempt by Haelewyck to describe systematically the apocryphal Joseph texts proved successful in linking the Ethiopic version to its Arabic *Vorlage*, though not to the Syriac original (Jean-Claude Haelewyck, *Clavis apocryphorum Veteris Testamenti* [Turnhout: Brepols, 1998], 113). I bring all of the pieces together in my "Identifying the Syriac Vorlage of the Ethiopic *History of Joseph*," in *Malphono w-Rabo d-Malphone: Studies in Honor of Sebastian P. Brock* (ed. George Kiraz; Piscataway: Gorgias, 2008), 205-10.

11. Georg Graf, *Geschichte der christlichen arabischen Literatur,* 5 vols., Studi e Testi, 118, 133, 146, 147, 172 (Vatican City: Bibl. Apost. Vaticana, 1944-53), 1:205-6.

12. William Wright, *A Catalogue of the Syriac Manuscripts in the Library of the University of Cambridge,* 2 vols. (Cambridge: Cambridge University Press, 1901; repr. Piscataway, NJ: Gorgias, 2002), 736.

13. Frederic Everett Faverty, "The Story of Joseph and Potiphar's Wife in Mediaeval Literature," *Harvard Studies and Notes in Philology and Literature* 13 (1931): 81-127, specifically pp. 122-25.

14. Faverty gives a transcription of the exchange of letters between Potiphar's wife and Joseph, noting that the Latin version fills the lacuna in Weinberg's edition. He goes on to conclude from a comparison of the Latin text and Weinberg's edition that "The incidents in the Latin and Syrian excerpts are the same" (Faverty, "Joseph and Potiphar's Wife," 123-25). Faverty also notes ("Joseph and Potiphar's Wife," 123) that another extract of this Latin version is given by A. Mussafia (*Über die Quelle des altfranzösischen*

script Library (EMML 1939, folios 124r-168r).[15] A translation, with a provisional study, of the Ethiopic version was published in 1990 by Ephraim Isaac as the sixth issue of the *Journal for the Study of the Pseudepigrapha.*[16]

The *Syriac History* is our primary witness to this narrative. Despite claims to the contrary,[17] the Latin and Ethiopic versions were each derived from an Arabic exemplar, which was, in turn, translated from a Syriac original. Thus, while the versions have their value,[18] I do not make reference to them in the translation that follows. Nor has any sustainable case been put forward for the existence of a *Vorlage* for the *Syriac History of Joseph.* All of our evidence points to this work being an original Syriac composition, a point which is discussed further below.

The present translation is based on the published edition by Weinberg and Link, together with the edition of the missing leaf mentioned above.[19] Recourse is made to other manuscript witnesses only in cases where the published edition is unclear, damaged or missing text.

Genre and Structure

The *Syriac History of Joseph* retells a biblical story with narrative expansions, and thus it may usefully be categorized in the genre of "rewritten Bible." However, a few words need to be added about the structure and formal characteristics of the work to supplement a generic designation that is far from unproblematic.[20] The *Syriac History* follows the biblical sequence with some omissions and expansions. Many of the expansions involve the addition of speeches and small mimetic details. Some expansions appear to be imaginative, and some interpretative, while others appear to be incorporating the extra-biblical traditions about the story of Joseph known by the author. Some of the expansions exhibit an awareness of the whole biblical narrative. Throughout, there is an absence of homiletic material. There are no clear indications that the author is pursuing any particular apologetic aims.

Unlike later Syriac retellings, the *Syriac History* does not exhibit a self-conscious relationship to scripture—there is no indication that the auditor is expected to be aware of the biblical text, nor are there explicit indications of the presupposition of, or allusions to scripture. The *Syriac History* is thus a fluent freestanding composition woven from

---

Dolopathos [Vienna, 1865], 20-22), though he gives no indication that Mussafia knew of the *Vorlage* of the Latin text (I have yet to inspect this work).

15. Getatchew Haile and William Macomber, *A Catalogue of Ethiopian Manuscripts Microfilmed for the Ethiopian Manuscript Microfilm Library*, 12 vols. (Collegeville, Minn.: Hill Monastic Manuscript Library, 1975-), 5:429.

16. Ephraim Isaac, "The Ethiopic *History of Joseph*," *JSP* 6 (1990): 3-125. Isaac's confusion about the *Vorlage* of this text is resolved in my "Identifying the Syriac *Vorlage*."

17. See my "Identifying the Syriac *Vorlage*."

18. The Ethiopic version, for example, contains a number of unique Jewish traditions (examples are given below).

19. Reference to the published Syriac edition by part (I, II) and page number is included in the translation below (see n. 2 above for bibliography).

20. In what follows I am engaging with the generic features that Philip Alexander deduces for texts classified as "Rewritten Bible" (Philip S. Alexander, "Retelling the Old Testament," in D. A. Carson and H.G.M. Williamson, eds., *It Is Written: Scripture Citing Scripture. Essays in Honour of Barnabas Lindars, SSF*, 99-121 [Cambridge: Cambridge University Press, 1988]).

the biblical narrative, imaginative and interpretative expansions, and other contemporary traditions.

Date and Provenance

There is an absence of distinctively Christian themes and elements in the *Syriac History*. At the same time, the text's strong affinity to certain early Jewish texts and traditions has long been acknowledged. Examples of the influence of Jewish traditions are adduced by Weinberg[21] and Link.[22] Desreumaux seems to accept the text's Jewish origin without question, listing it along with other Syriac Jewish pseudepigrapha.[23] And beyond this, Ephraim Isaac has argued that the text, in its Ethiopic version, is actually the product of Second Temple Judaism.[24] Though a full study of Jewish sources in the *Syriac History* lies beyond the scope of this introduction, it is useful to review the connections that have been suggested thus far.[25]

Several of the claims for Jewish dependency are far from compelling, and will not be considered in any detail.[26] Other parallels that have been suggested are found only in the Ethiopic version and not in the *Syriac History*.[27] Nevertheless, there are five parallels which are suggestive of Jewish influence, and these are worth reviewing in more detail. In addition, a further three parallels seem to me to be clear examples of dependency or a shared source. These deserve closer consideration since any strong signs of Jewish influence will give more credence to those parallels which are reasonable but inconclusive.

1. In the *Syriac History* Reuben claims that he is unable to read the bill of sale because he has weak eyes "like my mother" (*Syr. Hist. Jos.* 44:11).[28] Already in LXX Gen 29:17 we find the idea that Leah's eyes were weak. An exegetical expansion in the Targum of this verse draws on the tradition that Leah was originally betrothed to Esau and "became bleary eyed with weeping, for she had prayed God not to be given to the

---

21. Weinberg, *Geschichte Josefs*, 8-10.

22. Link, *Geschichte Josefs*, 6.

23. Desreumaux, "Esquisse d'une liste d'œuvres apocryphes syriaques," 219.

24. He restates this position throughout his introduction: "The *History of Joseph* is full of many well-known rabbinic haggadic insights about the life of Joseph. ... Several ideas alluded to in the *History* reflect the theology of the late Second Temple period. ... It is my view that the Ethiopic *History of Joseph* is based, even if not directly, on one or more ancient Jewish works" (Isaac, "Ethiopic *History*," 28, 36, 40).

25. A list of fifteen examples is given in Isaac, "Ethiopic *History*," 28-32. Weinberg lists seven items in *Geschichte Josefs*, 9-10. Link gives five additional items in *Geschichte Josefs*, 7. Davila also points out two parallels to Jewish traditions in his synopsis of the Joseph narrative as treated in Ephrem's *Commentary on Genesis*, one of which is also applicable to the *Syriac History* (James R. Davila, *The Provenance of the Pseudepigrapha: Jewish, Christian, or Other?* [JSPSup 105; Leiden: Brill, 2005], 98-101).

26. I. Epithets applied to Joseph (Isaac, "Ethiopic *History*," 29, 74, with reference to *Midr. ha-Gadol* 37:27; 39:10; and cf. *Syr. Hist. Jos.* 25:3); II. High price paid by Potiphar for Joseph (Isaac, "Ethiopic *History*," 30, citing *Sefer Hayyashar* giving sale price of 400 silver pieces; *Syr. Hist. Jos.* 14:1 says 300); III. Period of Jacob's mourning (Isaac, "Ethiopic *History*," 30, equates twenty-two years of *Midr. ha-Gadol* 37:34 with the twenty years of *Syr. Hist. Jos.* 13:11); IV. Location of Potiphar during Gen 39:11-12 (*Syr. Hist. Jos.* 17:5 and Isaac, "Ethiopic *History*," 31, 63 say Potiphar was meeting with Pharaoh; *b. Sotah* 36b says he was at the Egyptian Nile Festival).

27. I. Joseph's steward is a Hebrew (Isaac, "Ethiopic *History*," 32); II. Joseph mentions that Abraham was delivered from Nimrod's fire (Isaac, "Ethiopic *History*," 29, 50-51).

28. In the Ethiopic version the malady is claimed by Judah (Isaac, "Ethiopic *History*," 97).

evil Esau" (*Tg. Ps.-J.* 29:17).[29] However, though the Jewish tradition developed a creative explanation to explain the state of Leah's weak eyes, we find no reference to this explanation in the *Syriac History*, only the statement that Leah's eyes were weak. In fact, to this extent the *Syriac History* is simply reproducing the language of the Peshitta version of Gen 29:17. Thus Isaac's suggestion of Jewish influence at this point, though attractive, is tenuous at best.[30]

2. The *Syriac History*, followed by the Ethiopic version, distinguishes the sons of the handmaidens as a separate group, who are determined to bring about Joseph's demise (*Syr. Hist. Jos.* 5:2). The sons of the handmaidens are also set apart in certain Jewish texts (*Pirqe R. El.* 38; *Gen. Rab.* 84:7).[31] This seems to be an entirely plausible connection. However, because the sons of the handmaidens are already delineated as a group in the biblical account (Gen 37:2) it is also possible that such a development came about in the two traditions independently.
3. Whereas in the *Syriac History* and the Ethiopic version an angel guides Joseph in the Wilderness (*Syr. Hist. Jos.* 4:8), Isaac cites Jewish sources in which three angels lead Joseph to his brothers (*Midr. ha-Gadol* 37:15-16; *Gen. Rab.* 84:14). Other Jewish sources specifically identify this guide as the angel Gabriel (*Tg. Ps.-J.* 37.15; *Pirqe R. El.* 38).[32] Nevertheless, despite the differences in the number of angels, it seems likely that the *Syriac History* is adopting a Jewish tradition at this point, and in doing so stands apart from the rest of the Syriac tradition.
4. In the *Syriac History* Jacob refers to Joseph as "the fairest of his brothers and the likeness of his father" (*Syr. Hist. Jos.* 33:15). Likewise in Jewish sources, Joseph is called the likeness of his father (*Gen. Rab.* 84:8). This is a straightforward and reasonable connection.[33]
5. In both the Syriac History (*Syr. Hist. Jos.* 41:7, 43:3) and Jewish sources (*Gen. Rab.* 92:8), Benjamin's brothers call him the son of a thief (cf. Gen. 31:18) when he is caught with the cup in his sack. This seems an entirely reasonable case for dependency upon Jewish sources.[34]
6. The first of the more compelling connections with the Jewish tradition is the link suggested by Isaac between the seduction narrative in the Ethiopic version and that in Jewish sources.[35] In this instance, the *Syriac History* actually agrees with the Jewish sources more precisely. In the Ethiopic version Joseph's mistress offers to make Joseph her husband, apparently in order to remove Joseph's perceived concerns about the difference in their status.[36] This offer is also extended to Joseph in the *Syriac History* (*Syr. Hist. Jos.* 15:7). However, in this text she actually offers to kill her husband in order to counter Joseph's unwillingness to offend his master, a startling offer also found in one Jewish source (*Syr. Hist. Jos.* 15:14; *Gen. Rab.* 87:5). What is

---

29. I cite the translation of James L. Kugel given in *Traditions of the Bible* (Cambridge, Mass.: Harvard University Press, 1998), 381.

30. Isaac refers to an extended version of the Jewish exegetical expansion (*Tanh. Vayyese* 4; cf. Isaac, "Ethiopic *History*," 29, 97).

31. Isaac, "Ethiopic *History*," 29; Weinberg, *Geschichte Josefs*, 9.

32. Isaac, "Ethiopic *History*," 30; Weinberg, *Geschichte Josefs*, 9, 39.

33. Weinberg, *Geschichte Josefs*, 9.

34. Weinberg, *Geschichte Josefs*, 9; Link, *Geschichte Josefs*, 7.

35. Isaac, "Ethiopic *History*," 30-31, 59-63.

36. Isaac, "Ethiopic *History*," 60, 62.

distinctive about the *Syriac History* is that Potiphar's wife specifies poison as her preferred method of homicide. Interestingly, the offer of marriage as well as the poison are both also mentioned in the *Testament of Joseph*, a text otherwise unattested in the Syriac tradition (*T. Jos.* 5:1). However, it would be problematic to assert this as a connection with Jewish tradition.

7. In both *Syriac History* and Jewish sources Joseph uses his goblet to divine variously the brothers' misdeeds and also to seat them in order (*Syr. Hist. Jos.* 36:1-11, 45:1-17; *Gen. Rab.* 92:5, 93:7; *Tg. Ps.-J.* 43:33; *Tanh. Wayyigash* 4).[37] This appears to be a definite point of contact between the traditions.[38]
8. Finally, *Syriac History* contains several references to Judah's fearsome strength, a motif that is expanded upon in the Ethiopic version.[39] When Joseph sends his steward to bring back the brothers after having secreted his cup in Benjamin's sack, he warns the steward about the inordinate strength Judah has when his chest hairs stand on end, and gives him instructions to avoid this eventuality (*Syr. Hist. Jos.* 39:3). This reference seems to stem from Jewish sources, and offers a clear point of connection (cf. *Midr. ha-Gadol* 44:18; *Gen. Rab.* 93:6-7).

Cumulatively, these connections suggest a close affinity with Jewish sources, and a possible Jewish provenance. However, being able to identify Jewish elements in the text does not settle the question of the text's origin. Sebastian Brock has demonstrated that it is not unusual for texts from the early Syriac tradition, which are certainly Christian compositions, to be nevertheless peppered with Jewish traditions.[40] More recently, James Davila has advised caution in attributing Jewish authorship to texts that are preserved in the Christian tradition simply on the basis of the fact that there are no clear Christian markers. With particular reference to Ephrem the Syrian he observes that "Christians had access to Jewish exegesis and were capable of drawing on it freely. Allusions to Jewish exegetical traditions are by no means proof of Jewish authorship."[41]

Thus it is certainly not insignificant that several of the distinctive features of the *Syriac History* also appear in Ephrem's rendering of the Joseph story in his *Commentary on Genesis* (though in a deliberately developed form), such as the return of Potiphar's wife and the use of the cup for divination (as mentioned above).[42] At the same time, Ephrem's account contains just a few distinctively Christian themes, such as the symbolism of Jacob

37. This last reference is translated in Kugel, *Traditions of the Bible*, 481.

38. Weinberg, *Geschichte Josefs*, 9; Link, *Geschichte Josefs*, 7; Isaac, "Ethiopic *History*," 31; Davila, *Provenance of the Pseudepigrapha*, 100. As Davila notes, this motif also appears in Ephrem the Syrian's *Commentary on Genesis* (cf. Edward G. Mathews and Joseph P. Amar, *St. Ephrem the Syrian: Selected Prose Works*, Fathers of the Church 91 [Washington, D.C.: Catholic University of America Press, 1994], 193 n. 546).

39. Cf. Isaac, "Ethiopic *History*," 31-32, 81.

40. Brock, "Jewish Traditions in Syriac Sources," *JJS* 30 (1979): 212-32.

41. Davila, *Provenance of the Pseudepigrapha*, 103.

42. Näf, following Weinberg's earlier study, gave priority to Ephrem's *Commentary on Genesis* (Heinrich Näf, *Syrische Josef-Gedichte: Mit Uebersetzung des Gedichts von Narsai und Proben aus Balai und Jaqob von Sarug* [Zurich: Buchdruckerei A. Schwarzenbach, 1923], 84). To counter this position I would point in particular to the return of Potiphar's wife scene in Ephrem, which has all the appearance of being an exegetical recasting of the scene as presented in the *Syriac History*. On which, see my *Tradition and Transformation: Genesis 37 and 39 in Early Syriac Sources*, Monographs of the Peshitta Institute, Leiden (Leiden: Brill, forthcoming).

crossing his hands when blessing Ephraim and Manasseh, an episode that is absent from the *Syriac History*.[43]

The case for considering the *Syriac History* as an early Syriac composition is further advanced when we observe that this text does seem to have some quite clear rhetorical connections with early Syriac literature. Importantly, the *Syriac History* uses the language of the Peshitta version of Genesis, even when the text is being reworked. Also, certain passages seem to be evoking New Testament language, though this is often subtle, and needs to be teased out from particular expressions.[44]

In addition to echoes of the Christian Syriac canon, we can also detect the influence of the *Acts of Thomas*, a third-century Syriac text, in an expansion added to the *Syriac History's* construal of the circumstances of Joseph's sale to the merchants. This point deserves a little more attention.[45] Specifically, the merchants' emphasis on both ensuring that Joseph is indeed a slave, as well as ensuring that they have appropriate proof of purchase suggests a more intimate link between this text and the second chapter of the *Acts of Thomas* than has hitherto been noticed.[46] It seems that the two new elements in Joseph's sale are directly influenced by the text of the *Acts of Thomas*. In both texts we learn the name of the merchant(s), in both the newly made slave is asked if he is truly a slave, in both he answers yes, in both the merchants receive a bill of sale from the supposed owner(s), and in both the bill of sale mentions the name(s) of the owner(s), the slave, and the merchant(s). The only difference in content is that the bill of sale in the *Syriac History* includes the price of the sale. The particular term used for the bill of sale is also the same in the two texts.[47] This term is not used later in the tradition, however, which further suggests that the borrowing may have been deliberate, rather than reflecting actual contemporary commercial language.[48]

Evidence for the *terminus ante quem* of this text can be deduced from its place in

43. R.M. Tonneau, *Sancti Ephraem Syri in Genesim et in Exodum Commentarii*, CSCO 152 (Louvain: L. Durbecq, 1955), 110 (§XLI.4).

44. For example, on hearing the second dream, the brothers' initial reaction is visceral: "anger entered into them" (*Syr. Hist. Jos.* 2.9). The verbal link with the betrayal of Jesus by Judas (John 13:27) would not have escaped the notice of those listening to this story. In the Syriac tradition, Judas is seen as the very epitome of Satan's work—as Ephrem says in the *Hymns on Paradise*, "though Satan's history is a long one, it is summed up in the Iscariot" (Sebastian Brock, *Ephrem the Syrian: Hymns on Paradise* [Crestwood, NY: St. Vladimir's Seminary Press, 1998], 187 [Hymn XV.15]).

45. I have used the translation and commentary in A. F. J. Klijn, *The Acts of Thomas: Introduction, Text, and Commentary* (2nd ed.; NovTSup 108; Leiden: Brill, 2003).

46. In his commentary, Klijn was principally concerned to understand why Thomas was, like Joseph, sold for twenty pieces of silver, rather than the thirty, which would have connected him more intimately with the sale of Jesus by Judas. He was attracted to the idea of this latter connection, and is somewhat reticent to make a connection between this scene and Gen 37, which is perhaps why he did not search further into the Syriac Joseph texts (Klijn, *Acts of Thomas*, 21-22). Klijn notes that in the Sachau manuscript of the acts Thomas is indeed sold for thirty pieces of silver. However, he concludes that "the influence of Gen. 37, 28 cannot be excluded according to which Joseph has been sold for twenty pieces of silver" (Klijn, *Acts of Thomas*, 21-22).

47. In the *Syriac History* the term is extended to a deed or document "of slavery" (*Syr. Hist. Jos.* 8:17; 16:4). Klijn briefly discusses the term in *Acts of Thomas*, 22; see also Sebastian Brock, "Dinah in a Syriac Poem on Joseph," in *Semitic Studies in Honour of Edward Ullendorff* (ed. G. Khan; Leiden: Brill, 2005), 222-35, specifically, p. 229 n. 15.

48. In the homilies on Joseph attributed to Narsai, for example, the bill of sale is called a *pethqa*, "a slip of paper, letter" (used 8 times). This Greek term is briefly discussed in Brock, "Dinah in a Syriac Dialogue Poem on Joseph," 229 n. 15. Brock also discusses another Greek term used for the bill of sale in which he

the larger corpus of Syriac Joseph materials.[49] There is clear evidence for the partial and wholesale reuse of the *Syriac History* in subsequent verse homilies on Joseph.[50] This influence is most clearly seen in the pair of narrative homilies on Joseph variously attributed in the manuscripts to Narsai (d. 502) and Jacob of Serug (d. 521).[51] Among the numerous examples that could be cited, the dependence of this pair of homilies on the *Syriac History* is clearly seen in the recasting of the narrative expansion describing the encounter of Potiphar and his wife with the newly elevated Joseph. That these homilies survived in both the East and West Syriac manuscript traditions also suggests that they were composed before the doctrinal split in the late fifth century.[52]

The cumulative effect of this and other evidence indicates that the *Syriac History* is an original composition, written in Syriac in a Christian context. The text can be dated to the early fifth century.[53] At the same time, however, we must acknowledge that the text contains several significant and unique narrative expansions, some of which have demonstrable parallels to early Jewish sources, suggesting that we must carefully distinguish between the date of the composition of the text and the development of a given motif contained within that text.[54]

Literary Context

The variety and vibrancy of the early Syriac reception of the Bible have only recently come into focus. Problem-centered exegesis is rare in this period. Rather what we find predominately are biblical episodes retold in prose and verse.[55] Often these verse homilies are comprised of imagined dialogic exchanges between biblical figures, such as Joseph and Potiphar's wife.[56] However, we also find numerous examples of extensive narrative poems treating single episodes, such as Elijah and the widow of Sarepta, or a series of episodes, such as the narrative homilies on Joseph.[57] Very occasionally we find a dramatic prose narrative standing behind the verse rendering, such as is the case with the *Syriac History*.

---

gives references to mercantile usage found in papyri (Brock, "Dinah in a Syriac Poem on Joseph," 228, esp. n. 14).

49. A useful outline of this corpus is found in Brock, "Dinah in a Syriac Poem on Joseph," 222-24.

50. The work of documenting the influence of this text on the later tradition was begun in earnest by Heinrich Näf (*Syrische Josef-Gedichte*, 85; and examples in preceding history of motifs section). Particular motifs are traced more fully in Heal, *Tradition and Transformation*.

51. Paul Bedjan, ed., *Homiliae Mar Narsetis in Joseph* (Paris; Leipzig: Harrassowitz, 1901).

52. Brock notes the survival of dialogue poems in both East and West Syriac manuscripts as suggestive of pre-doctrinal-split dating ("Dramatic Dialogue Poems," 35).

53. Weinberg argued for a late-fourth-century dating (*Geschichte Josefs*, 11-12). However, Brock employs linguistic evidence, in particular the use of Greek vocabulary, to argue that the *Syriac History* should be dated to the fifth rather than the fourth century ("Dinah in a Syriac Poem on Joseph," 222-23, esp. n. 4).

54. Thus we must acknowledge that a late text may preserve an earlier incarnation of a particular motif. On this problem, see Geza Vermes, *Scripture and Tradition in Judaism: Haggadic Studies* (StPB 4; Leiden: Brill, 1983), 1-10; and, more generally on the problem of tracing exegetical motifs, see James L. Kugel, *In Potiphar's House: The Interpretative Life of Biblical Texts* (2nd ed.; Cambridge, Mass.: Harvard University Press, 1994), 247-270.

55. Lucas van Rompay, "The Christian Syriac Tradition of Interpretation," in Magne Sæbø (ed.), *Hebrew Bible/Old Testament: The History of Its Interpretation.* Volume 1: *From the Beginnings to the Middle Ages (until 1300)*, 611-41 (Göttingen: Vandenhoeck & Ruprecht, 1996).

56. For example, see Sebastian Brock, "Joseph and Potiphar's Wife (Genesis 39): Two Anonymous Dispute Poems," in *Syriac Polemics: Studies in Honour of Gerrit Jan Reinink* (ed. W. J. van Bekkum et al.; Leuven: Peeters, 2007), 41-58.

57. Bibliography found in Brock, "Dramatic Dialogue Poems."

We have cases in which a prose homily on a given theme is found alongside closely related verse homilies on the same theme.[58] The *Syriac History* can usefully be read within this complex of prose narratives, dialogue poems and narrative poems.[59]

Bibliography

Brock, Sebastian P. "Dinah in a Syriac Poem on Joseph." Pages 222-35 in *Semitic Studies in Honour of Edward Ullendorff*. Edited by G. Khan. Leiden: Brill, 2005.

__________. "Dramatic Dialogue Poems." Pages 135-47 in *IV Symposium Syriacum, 1984*. Edited by H. J. W. Drijvers et al. OrChAn 229. Rome: Pontificio Istituto Orientale, 1987.

Desreumaux, Alain. "Esquisse d'une liste d'œuvres apocryphes syriaques." Pages 217-25 in *Les apocryphes syriaques*. Edited by M. Debié et al. Études syriaques 2. Paris: Geuthner, 2005.

__________. "Un manuscript syriaque de Téhéran contenant des apocryphes." *Apocrypha* 5 (1994): 137-64.

Faverty, Frederic Everett. "The Story of Joseph and Potiphar's Wife in Mediaeval Literature." *Harvard Studies and Notes in Philology and Literature* 13 (1931): 81-127.

Heal, Kristian S. "Identifying the Syriac Vorlage of the Ethiopic *History of Joseph*." Pages 205-10 in *Malphono w-Rabo d-Malphone: Studies in Honor of Sebastian P. Brock*. Edited by George Kiraz. Piscataway: Gorgias Press, 2008.

__________. "Joseph as a Type of Christ in the Syriac Tradition." *Brigham Young University Studies* 41, no. 1 (2002): 29-49.

__________. "Joseph in the Syriac Tradition: A Review of the Sources." Forthcoming.

__________. "A Missing Leaf from the *Syriac History of Joseph*." Forthcoming.

__________. "Reworking the Biblical Text in the Dramatic Dialogue Poems on the Old Testament Patriarch Joseph." In *The Peshitta: Its Use in Literature and Liturgy*, 87-98. Edited by Bas Ter Haar Romeny. Monographs of the Peshitta Institute. Leiden. Leiden: Brill, 2007.

__________. *Tradition and Transformation: Genesis 37 and 39 in Early Syriac Sources*. Monographs of the Peshitta Institute. Leiden. Leiden: Brill. Forthcoming.

Isaac, Ephraim. "The Ethiopic *History of Joseph*." *JSP* 6 (1990): 3-125.

Link, Samuel Wolf. *Die Geschichte Josefs angeblich verfasst von Basilius dem Grossen aus Cäsarea*. Berlin: H. Itskowski, 1895.

Näf, Heinrich. *Syrische Josef-Gedichte: Mit Uebersetzung des Gedichts von Narsai und Proben aus Balai und Jaqob von Sarug*. Zurich: Buchdruckerei A. Schwarzenbach, 1923.

Phenix, Robert R. *The Sermons on Joseph of Balai of Qenneshrin*. Tübingen: Mohr Siebeck, 2008.

Weinberg, Magnus. *Die Geschichte Josefs angeblich verfasst von Basilius dem Grossen aus Cäsarea*. Halle: Druck von H. Itzkowski, 1893.

58. Sebastian Brock, "An Anonymous Syriac Homily on Abraham (Gen. 22)," OLP 12 (1981): 225-60.

59. Discussed more fully in Heal, *Tradition and Transformation*.

The Syriac History of Joseph

(**I.17**) Again, with the aid of God, we write the story of Joseph, son of Jacob that was composed by Mar Basil of Caesarea. Our Lord, aid me with your mercy, amen.

Gen 35:23-26; 37:2-4 **The family of Jacob**

1 [1]The blessed Jacob took to wife two free-born women and two handmaidens,
and he begat from them twelve sons: [2]Reuben and Simeon, and Levi and Judah, and Issachar and Zebulon, the sons of Leah; [3]and Joseph and Benjamin of
Rachel; [4]and Gad and Asher of Zilpah, the handmaiden of Leah; [5]and Dan and
Gen 35:23-26 Naphtali of Bilhah, the handmaiden of Rachel. [6]And their father Jacob loved
Joseph more than all of his sons, and he made a long-sleeved coat for him and
clothed him. [7]And when his brothers saw that their father loved Joseph more
than them they were filled with an especial envy for Joseph. [8]And they hated
him severely.

Gen 37:5-10a **The dreams of Joseph**

2 [1]And Joseph saw a dream and he related it to his brothers. [2]And he said to
them, "My brothers, hear the dream that I saw. I saw in my dream that all of us
were in the field and your sheaves bowed down to my sheaf." [3]And his brothers
said to him, "So then, shall you indeed reign over us, or shall you indeed rule
over us and all of us will gather together and bow down to you?" [4]And their enmity increased against him. [5]But Joseph continued and he saw a second dream.
[6]And when all of his brothers were gathered at the side of Jacob their father,
Joseph told them: [7]"Hear again, oh my brothers, another dream that I have seen.
I saw that the sun and the moon and eleven stars came and bowed down before
me." [8]And when the brothers heard the second dream, anger entered into them
(**I.18**) and they covered him with rage,[a] and they plotted to kill him. [9]And they
said to Jacob their father, "Did you hear what your son Joseph said? Or perhaps
you are glad that you hear his dreams? For behold, twice he said to us that he saw
in his dream that we would bow down to him. [10]He did not even reverence your
old age, nor was he ashamed to say rashly in your presence that he saw in his
dream that you will bow down before him. [11]Even concerning the lights which
are in heaven, he was so bold as to say that, 'they bowed down to me.'"

---

a. Reading with L. B and T read, "they wore anger against him."

Jacob's reaction to the dreams Gen 37:10b-11

3 [1]And when Jacob heard the words of his sons, he perceived that their wickedness increased against Joseph. [2]And Jacob rebuked Joseph and said to him, "What is this that you saying? Or, perhaps (you think) you will really reign over us and I and your brothers will bow down before you? Be quiet! So that I will no longer hear your voice when you speak in this way." [3]But Jacob was amazed and wondered at the dreams of Joseph. [4]And he said to himself, "These dreams that have been seen by my son Joseph, they are not false dreams, rather they are true dreams. He has been shown them by God and something great will be done by God with Joseph."

Jacob sends the brothers out to the flocks Gen 37:12

[5]And when Jacob saw his sons gathering together, one to another, he perceived that they were contriving something evil against Joseph because they had been shaken up by the dreams of Joseph. [6]And Jacob said to them, "What you have done is not right, my sons, that you sent your children out with the flocks and you stayed here in your dwellings—your children are yet youngsters and are not practiced in going after the flocks, but send your children to me." [7]And they hearkened to the word of their father, and they went out and went together. [8]But Joseph stayed with Jacob, and Benjamin his brother was (only) little and did not have strength to come in and go out before Jacob.

Joseph is sent out to the brothers Gen 37:13-17

4 (I.19) [1]Now after many days that the brothers of Joseph were in the wilderness with the flocks, and not one of them returned to Jacob, nor did they send home for food, [2]Jacob said to Joseph, "The (lack of) news of your brothers is not pleasing to my ears, my son. For behold, not one of them has come (back for) forty days, and they have not sent (anyone back) to fetch food for them. Perhaps one of them has fallen ill, or perhaps something terrible has happened to them. [3]So arouse yourself, my son, and take food and go out to your brothers. [4]But do not linger with them—for I will remain worrying about you—lest something happen to you, and you add further distress and anxiety to your father—the grief of your mother is enough for me—because, I know that not all of them love you from the day they heard your dreams. [5]And may God, He who was with Abraham and Isaac, may He be with you, and may that angel, which brought me up from the East and was a support to me, go with you." [6]And when his father Jacob had prayed, Joseph arose, loaded the food and went out to go to his brothers.

[7]And when he had passed through Shechem and did not find them there, he wandered in the wilderness. [8]And behold, an angel of God came to him in the form of an old man, and he said to him, "What are you looking for, young man?" [9]And Joseph said to him, "I am looking for my brothers, the sons of Jacob." [10]And the angel said, "They departed from here and went to Dothan. Come with me and I will show you." [11]And Joseph went with the angel, and from afar he showed him and said, "Behold, your brothers. Go in peace, and may the God of your fathers be with you."

Gen 37:18-22 **The brothers see Joseph and plan to kill him**

5 1At that time, they were gathered together and eating bread. 2And when they
lifted up their eyes and saw him coming, the sons of the handmaidens were embittered against him and they plotted to kill him. 3But Reuben spoke up and said,
"My brothers, you should not do this great and terrible thing and sin against
God; for he is our flesh and blood." 4And they said to Reuben, "You are the first
born of us all and our head and leader, yet this rash one was not ashamed to
say in your presence, 'You will bow down to me.' Don't be a protector to him!
5Come, let us kill this dreamer and we will see what (**I.20**) will become of his
Gen 49:9 dreams." 6But Judah, the lion's whelp, said to them, "Whosoever stretches out
his hand against him today will die." 7And they all said, "This one will not live."
And they sought to wage war and kill one another. 8But, when Reuben and Judah saw that their wickedness waxed stronger, they said to them, "Then do not
kill him with your hands! Behold, there is an empty cistern without any water in
it. Throw him in it, and let him die there suffering from hunger and thirst. You
should not bespatter your hands with his blood." 9And this matter was agreed
upon by all of them.

Gen 37:23-25a **Joseph arrives, is attacked, and thrown in the cistern**

6 1Now when Joseph reached them, and asked after their welfare, the sons of the handmaidens rose against him with cursing and mocking. 2And they fell upon him like wild animals, and they stripped off the coat with which he had been clothed and threw him into the cistern naked. 3And they sat down to eat and to drink from that which Joseph had brought with him for them, laughing and rejoicing. 4And each one of them was standing and mocking him in the cistern, ridiculing him and saying, "We bow down to you, my lord king! Where now are those sheaves that bowed down to your sheaf? Where are the sun and the moon and the eleven stars that bowed down to you? 5For behold, you have been thrust down into the pit by the sheaves and the luminaries." 6And with these words the sons of the handmaidens were mocking him. 7Whereas he Joseph had been stripped and thrown down inside the pit.

8And from within the cistern he prayed a prayer that was full of grief and suffering, and his eyes were filled with tears while he spoke: 9"Oh God of Abraham and Isaac and of my father Jacob, send salvation, you my Lord, to your servant, and do not let go of me that I should suffer this bitter affliction and die from hunger and thirst and nakedness! 10Have pity, you my Lord, on the old age of our father Jacob, and act favorably to him and receive his petition on my behalf! 11Yea, my Lord, send aid for me, as your grace is accustomed to do. There is no God apart from you. 12You my Lord made the heaven and the earth and the seas and all that is (**I.21**) in them; you my Lord saved Isaac from the knife, and Abraham his father did not kill him; you delivered our father Jacob from the hands of his brother Esau. So also now my Lord, send to your servant Joseph salvation, and deliver me from this bitter and terrible event."

Gen 37:22b **Reuben plans to rescue Joseph**

7 1Reuben gazed down into the cistern, and he felt pity for him, and he spoke with him and said, "Don't be sad, my brother Joseph, and don't kill yourself. 2For as soon as all of them go out with the flocks I will pull you up, and I will send you to our father." [3]And Joseph said to him, "Oh my brother Reuben, may this thing truly come by your hands! By the God of our father Jacob, may this thing really be done!" [4]And Reuben said to his brothers, "Behold, I will look around the land for pasture for the flocks. However, you should go out with the flocks, and let Judah stay behind in the land country." [5]And his brothers said to him, "We will do your bidding." [6]But to Judah he said, "Judah, my brother, watch over the boy that they do not kill him."

The merchants appear and the brothers decide to sell Joseph Gen 37:25-27

8 [1]Now, while they were sitting down in the early morning, behold, a caravan of camels came from Gilead. [2]And when they saw it, they said to one another, "Behold, Arab merchants going down to Egypt. [3]Come, let's sell Joseph to them as a slave, (that is) if Judah commands us." [4]But Judah said to them, "If it were acceptable in your eyes, I would persuade you to let us send him to his father, but if not, this is better for you and him than that he suffer inside the cistern and die from hunger."

Judah negotiates the sale, but intends to save Joseph Gen 37:28

[5]And when the merchants reached them, Judah said to them, "Where are you men from, and what are your camels carrying and to where are you making ready to go?" [6]And they said, "We are Arabs and we are going down to Egypt and our camels are carrying balms and balsam and terebinth berries and almonds." [7]And Judah said to them, "We have a certain slave boy, and all the time he leaves the flocks and runs away from us. [8]So, now that you are going down to Egypt, take him with you, and you shall sell him in Egypt. [9]But write and bring back (word) with you to us regarding who bought him from you in Egypt." **(I.22)** [10]And Judah was determined to go down and to save him.

Judah tells his plan to Joseph

[11]And they pulled him up from the pit and Judah took him aside from his brothers, and he comforted him and said to him, "I am not able to help you here in the wilderness, nor am I able to save you from the hands of the sons of the handmaidens. [12]But, go down like a slave to Egypt with these merchants, and I and your father Jacob will come down and bring you up from there, and (thus) you will not die inside this pit. See, my brother, what they have done to me because of you." [13]Joseph rejoiced greatly that he had come up from the pit, and he said to Judah, "The God who sent me aid and lifted me out of the pit, He will send help for me to the midst of Egypt."

The merchants purchase Joseph and receive a bill of sale Gen 37:28

[14]Now when the merchants saw that Joseph's appearance was beautiful and fair and pleasant, they loved him like themselves. [15]And they questioned him and said to him, "Are you a slave boy?" [16]But Joseph was (too) afraid of his brothers to say about himself that he was a free man. And he said to the merchants, "Yes my Lords, I am a slave." [17]And the merchants bought Joseph from his brothers for twenty pieces of silver, and they said to the brothers, "Sit down and write for

us a document of slavery." [18]And they wrote for them, "We are ten and we have sold to these merchants, to Hakaneh and to Mesebleha and Rabakare,[a] a slave boy whose name is Joseph—I Reuben and Simeon and Levi, and Judah, and Issachar, and Zebulon, and Naphtali, and Dan, and Gad, and Asher—for twenty silver coins." [19]But Reuben was not with them when they sold him. [20]And the merchants set him up on a camel and they made straight for Egypt.

Gen 37:29-30 **Reuben returns and laments**

9 [1]Now when Reuben came to the pit, and when he had looked for Joseph and could not find him inside the pit, he rent his garments while weeping with grief and mourning and wailing: [2]"Woe is me, Woe is me, because of you my brother Joseph. [3]Woe be to the deceitful men, the murderers of their brother. Woe be to the great wickedness that you have done, for the like of it has not been heard in the whole land, from Cain the murderer until now, that a man killed his brother, except you only. [4]Woe is me because of you my brother Joseph. Woe be to the old age of your father. [5]Where is his body? Come, show me now how we look at our father **(I.23)** Jacob? And what reply do you have to give to him when he asks you, 'Where is my son Joseph?'" [6]And the brothers said to Reuben, "Don't cry, Reuben, our brother, and don't kill yourself because of Joseph: for we did not really kill him as you said. [7]We actually sold him to Arab merchants for twenty silver pieces, and behold, (here are) two coins, your portion of his sale price." [8]And Reuben wept when he heard that his brother had been sold like a slave, and he said, "Woe to your old age Jacob, all the days of your life, for your sons have broken the staff of your old age, and they have extinguished the lamp of your light. It would have been much better for you if you never had sons."

Gen 37:31-32 **The brothers plan to fool Jacob with the bloodied coat**

10 [1]And his brothers said to him, "Behold we have that variegated coat. Come, let us slay a kid over it and spatter (the coat) with its blood, and we will take it and go to Jacob, and we will say to him, 'We found this coat in the wilderness of Dothan and it looks to us like Joseph's one.' And as soon as he sees it he will believe that a wild beast has devoured him, and we will be cleared of all charge." [2]And straight away they hastened and brought a kid, and they slew (it) over the coat of Joseph and spattered (the coat) with its blood. [3]And they said to one another, "Now, who from among us will take (the coat) before our father Jacob?" [4]And Reuben said to them, "You committed the iniquity and sin—you sold that free-born son into slavery—you go in and receive the curses of that aged just one." [5]And not one of the sons of Leah wanted to go in, but Dan and Asher, the sons of the handmaidens, took (the coat) and entered in before Jacob.

Gen 37:32-33 **The coat is brought in to Jacob**

11 [1]And as soon as he saw them he was startled and greeted them eagerly, and he spoke up and said to them, "Where is my son Joseph?" [2]And they said to Jacob, "You, by your own hands have killed our brother Joseph. Did you indeed

---

a. The names of the merchants are found (with slight variation) in manuscripts B (f. 28b), M (f. 179a), P (f. 16b), and T (f. 186a); but not in L (f. 6b).

not know that there are wild animals that maul people in the wilderness? [3]And because of this fact we were not able to come and fetch food for ourselves these forty days. **(I.24)** But you sent a child out by himself into the ravaging wilderness! [4]Yesterday, when we were passing through the wilderness of Dothan we found the coat spattered with blood and cast aside in the wilderness, and his body was eaten by animals."

Jacob sees the coat and mourns and laments Joseph's death Gen 37:34

12 [1]And they spread out the coat in front of Jacob, and when he saw it, the light of his eyes grew dim, and the strength of his limbs vanished away. [2]And he raved[a] because of grief and distress, and he rent his clothes, and he sprinkled his face and his head with ashes, and he tore at the white hair of his old age. [3]And he collapsed upon the coat of Joseph, and he wept upon it with bitter grief, and he mourned and cried out. [4]And he offered up lamentations of grief because of Joseph, and he said, "Woe is me, woe is me because of you my son Joseph. Woe is me because of my beloved and my dear one. Woe is me because of you, the light of my eyes and the staff of my old age; woe is me because of you, the joy of my heart and encourager of my soul; woe is me my son, because of your beauty and because of your fairness and looks. Woe is me my son, because of your good dreams and your excellent visions. [5]Blessed is your mother Rachel, my son, who is not alive to see the destruction of your youth; blessed is she, my son, and how beloved of God, for her eyes have not seen your coat spattered with your own blood—she, my son, truly she is blessed. [6]But woe be to the old age of your father and to your brother Benjamin—[7]I have looked for you my son that you might set your hands upon my eyes in the day of my death. I expected to have my eyes shut and be laid out by your hands, and (that) you would prepare the old age of your father for burial.

Jacob calls on Rachel as he laments Gen 37:34

[8]Who will go and say to your mother Rachel, "Come, come out from the grave and see your son, your firstborn son, the son of your vows, his body eaten by wild animals. That fair and beloved one was not buried, nor was that cherished one enshrouded"? [9]Come Rachel, go out into the wilderness, and gather up the limbs of your cherished one. [10]Oh Rachel, the belly of wild beasts is his grave. [11]Rachel, Rachel, come, come out from the grave,[b] and lament **(I.25)** and cry out over the youth of your beloved, and the mountains will weep with you, and the hills will lament over the ruin of my old age. [12]Why were sons required by you
Rachel, beloved of Jacob? For you said, "Grant me sons or I die." [13]Come, rejoice Gen 30:1
in the banquet of adversities that your son Joseph has made for you! Come, lay out the gifts in this feast! [14]Alas, Rachel, for how bitter and miserable and full of grief and lamentation is this bridal chamber that he (Joseph) interwove for me. [15]You Rachel and your son lie down and sleep, and I and Benjamin will mourn

a. Reading with B, P and T. Manuscript L reads, "he became blind"; while M reads, "he was terrified."

b. Lit., "house of the dead."

and lament all the days of our lives. [16]Joseph, my dear one, you have broken your father, and there is no remedy for his disease, and no medicine for his wound."

Gen 37:34 **Jacob puts on sackcloth and continues his lament**

[17]And Jacob arose and took off his robes and put on the sackcloth of mourning and threw himself down on top of Joseph's coat, weeping over him with great grief. [18]And with the words of his sorrow he said, "The heaven and the earth will weep over my son Joseph, (as will) the sun and the moon and the stars that he saw in his dream bowing down to him. [19]Weep over my son Joseph, my friends and neighbors! [20]The alive and the dead will weep over my son; the alive with your father Jacob and the dead with Rachel your mother. [21]They will not weep over you alone my son, but (also) over the old age of your father and the light of his eyes that grew dim and over the staff of his old age which was broken. [22]Oh my son Joseph, if wild animals truly have ravaged your body and your beauty, the God of your father will destroy them; [23]but if, my son, men have taken you away from me, my old age will not depart from life until my eyes look upon the affliction and the oppression that (comes upon them because of) your injustice— because they have been so rash and have acted to despoil the beauty of your modesty.

[24]"Who is it who has separated you from the tender care of your father? [25]My dear one, who is it who snatched you from the company of your beloved Benjamin? [26]What will I do for your brother, my son, for he moans and weeps for you like a young dove? [27]And when he approaches me, he demands of me, saying, 'Where is my brother Joseph, my father? Where did you send him? How long until **(I.26)** my brother Joseph comes?' [28]And in the evening, he awakens grief for you in my heart so that all through the night tears will overflow from my eyes. And he asks, 'Has Joseph come, my father?' [29]If I say to him, 'he has come, my son,' he will ask of me, 'where is he? that I may go and see him?' [30]Woe to the old age of your father, my son Joseph, for how does my life suffer on account of the grief that is for you! [31]Oh my son, may the God of your father make me worthy to see you before the day of my death, so that you may put your hands upon the eyes of your father." [32]And Jacob reduced all of his loved ones and his dear ones and his sons and daughters-in-law to weeping.

Gen 37:35 **Jacob's family attempt to comfort him**

13 [1]And after seven days, all of his sons and daughters-in-law and the local elders gathered around him to console him and to give him some food, but he declined. [2]And he said to them, "Why am I still alive, an old man who was troubled by evil days? [3]For twenty years I suffered with the flocks for the sake of Rachel the mother of Joseph, being afflicted by both summer and winter. And in her death she left behind two sons for me—Joseph, who was not yet of age, and Benjamin on the day of her death—and my old age has been wearied with the upbringing of the two of them. [4]And behold, Joseph has broken me by his death, and Benjamin darkens my eyes when he begs me every day for his brother—of what advantage to me is a life full of sorrows?" [5]And Jacob went twenty days without eating food, the number of years that he was with the flocks. [6]And he did not see his son Joseph until the light of his eyes had grown dim, and the strength of his limbs had vanished away.

The brothers weep and are worried because of their father's grief Gen 37:35

[7]And the brothers of Joseph wept and were in great grief and in distress over the old age of their father. [8]And they said to each other, "Woe be to us from the God of heaven because of the thing that we have done to our father. [9]Do you indeed think that God will not repay us for his tears and his sorrow and the anxiety of his old age? He will truly repay us with a terrible punishment because of him! [10]But woe to us (because of) the curses and the groans of the heart and the tears of his eyes!"

[11]And Jacob was **(I.27)** clothed with sackcloth upon his body for twenty years. [12]And he would spread out the coat of Joseph before him, and every day he would wet it with his tears and would cling to it and kiss it.

Joseph is sold to Potiphar Gen 37:36; 39:1-6a

14 [1]And the merchants took Joseph down to Egypt and sold him for three hundred pieces of silver to Potiphar, the head of Pharaoh's eunuchs. [2]And God was with Joseph, and he granted him mercy in the eyes of his master. [3]And (Potiphar) loved him like his own self because he saw that God blessed his whole household because of Joseph. [4]And he made him chief and ruler over all his house—over his servants and his handmaidens and over his possessions. [5]And he said to Joseph, "See, I have put into your hands everything that I have, and there is not in Pharaoh's house a man greater than your master, and there is none in my entire house greater than you. [6]Behold, I give into your hands power over everything except your mistress, for you are her servant." [7]And God blessed the Egyptian and all his house.

Joseph's first encounter with Potiphar's wife Gen 39:6b-9

15 [1]Now, as Joseph came and went his mistress watched him, for his appearance was fine and fair and there was no one like him in all of Egypt. [2]And she loved him in her heart and the fire of desire for him was kindled within her. [3]And she called out to him, "Joseph." [4]And he entered beside her, and she commanded him to come into her private room, and she embraced and kissed him and caressed him, and said to him, "You are my servant and I am your mistress. I have power to do with you anything that is pleasing in my eyes." [5]And Joseph said to her, "Truly I am your servant and you are my mistress and anything that is pleasing to your eyes I will do: You command me like a mistress (and) I will serve you like a slave." [6]And his mistress said to him, "Far be it from you to be a slave to me. Rather, be like a lord to me and I will be like a maidservant to you. For, it is right for you to be my head and I will be like the wife of your youth. [7]Take me, come, lie with me and instead of a servant I will make you a lord, **(I.28)** for to you lordship and freedom are fitting, but to your mistress servitude and obedience."

[8]And when Joseph heard these sayings from his mistress, he was exceedingly afraid, and the color of his face changed, and he was saddened and grieved. [9]And he answered and said to his mistress, "The God of Heaven forbids me to do this thing, to lie with you and dishonor the bed of my master, who has committed all things into my hands—he said to me, 'I make you ruler over everything I have, except your mistress.' [10]And now, behold, you want me to sleep with you; it is a great wrong."

[11]But she spoke with him further, "These things are (really) sought by you;

for by the flurry of your words I am enslaved by you. [12]For, men are usually the ones seducing and persuading women in order to sleep with them, and not women the men. [13]For I know in my heart that you also earnestly desire to sleep with me, but you stand in awe (of me)— have I not humbled myself before you? [14]And if you are afraid of your master, by the life of Pharaoh, I swear to you that as soon as you do my will, I will lay out for him a deadly poison. And you will be my husband without fear."

[15]And Joseph trembled even more, and he said, "My master treated me kindly and gave me authority over his household. Now, how can I repay the kindness he did for me with evil? [16]Then God would not deliver me from bondage and return me beneath the wings of my father, the just man Jacob." [17]And he said to his mistress, "The whole lineage of his fathers, and I, hold fast to purity and chastity and we fear God (too much) to behave shamefully or commit fornication. For, God judges those who commit adultery, and murderers, with fire. [18]And now Satan schemes to do away with you by the murder of my master. [19]And now, my mistress, hear my words and be patient and the God of my fathers will take care of this business."

Gen 39:10

Potiphar's wife tries repeatedly to seduce Joseph

16 [1]However, she would adorn herself everyday with regal clothes and would perfume her body with choice perfumes. [2]But Joseph was very strong and resisted the desire of his body. [3]But she continued to increase her lack of restraint, **(I.29)** swearing by the life of Pharaoh, "Whether you are willing or not, it is not in your power to get yourself out of doing my will. [4]By the crown of Pharaoh, king of Egypt, I swear that I will write a deed of freedom for you and I will tear into pieces the deed of slavery. [5]Lie with me Joseph and be a freeman.

[6]"Woe to your beauty, Joseph, for you are not a wise man. Your beauty is great, but you do not have wisdom, (as can be seen from) the fact that every (other) man yearns for freedom and to escape from slavery, but you, you love slavery and loathe freedom. [7]Now if you are afraid of sin as you say, take as much silver and gold as you wish and give it to the poor, and God will forgive your folly. [8]Behold, I give you your freedom and want you to become a lord, but you have no sense in you." [9]And Joseph continually restrained himself and strove against his desire, and Satan continually stirred up and troubled the Egyptian woman. [10]But, even though she petitioned him every day he would not submit to her.

Gen 39:11-15

Joseph's last encounter with Potiphar's wife

17 [1]On one of the days she called him, and he went up to her and entered into her private room. [2]And she grabbed hold of him securely and said to him, "I can no longer bear for you to say to me in my own house that you will not do my will. [3]For, you have set me alight with desire for you, and with the fire of love for you. [4]I have no more patience for you. You must choose one of these two things for yourself. [5]All of the slaves and servant women are outside and your lord is in Pharaoh's house, and there is no one else here. [6]Come, lie with me and be a freeman. [7]But if you won't, by the life of Pharaoh, I will say before (Potiphar) that 'the servant entered in upon me in order to lie with me.' [8]Now choose that which is better in your eyes."

[9]And (Joseph) said, "The God who sent me aid and brought me up from the cistern, he will send me redemption. [10]For I know that God will not despise the tears and prayers of my father Jacob. [11]For I will never lie with you nor will I defile (**I.30**) my body in the mire of fornication." [12]And when his mistress heard these words, Satan entered into her, and she rushed forward and grabbed him tightly and clung on to his clothes. [13]Now when Joseph saw her boldness he feared fornication and shook at her wantonness, and he left his clothes in her hand and escaped from her. [14]And she immediately cried out and screamed, and when the men of the house heard they all gathered around. [15]And she said to them, "Grab him, grab him, that insolent fellow, grab him hold tightly, that Hebrew slave, until his master comes from Pharaoh's house. [16]So that I say to him, 'This insolent one entered in upon me and sought to mock me and ventured to besmear your bed.'" [17]And the Egyptian men ran and bound Joseph with harsh bonds.

Joseph is accused of attempted rape Gen 39:16-20

18 [1]And when Joseph's master entered the house, she added further to her mad rage and she cried out and said to him, [2]"I will not remain in the house, nor will I speak with your servant again, because I am a noblewoman and I did not come to commit fornication in your house. [3]Come and see what I have endured: for this base fellow bought with silver left all the wives of his fellow slaves, and ventured forth and entered in upon me to mock me—and (would have) if I had not grabbed him tightly. [4]When he heard that I screamed he was afraid and he left his clothes in my hands and went out. [5]By the life of Pharaoh, make him leave your house and sell this insolent slave, because he does not have reverence for you and he does not fear you and he seeks to besmear your bed." [6]And when his lord heard these words he was really astounded and amazed, and he was exceedingly upset because of him. [7]And he led Joseph and threw him in prison.

Joseph in prison Gen 39:21-23

19 [1]Then God made the head of the prison look upon Joseph with compassion, and he committed all the prisoners into his hands. [2]And God blessed the head of the prison because of Joseph.

Pharaoh's butler and baker are thrown in prison and have dreams Gen 40:1-8

[3]After Joseph had been in the prison for a little while, (**I.31**) two of the servants of Pharaoh, the king of Egypt, acted foolishly: the head baker and the head butler. [4]And Pharaoh was angry with the two of them and he confined them in the prison where Joseph was confined. [5]And Joseph ministered to them. [6]And both of them saw dreams in the same night and they were frightened by the dreams that they saw, and their faces were saddened. [7]And Joseph came to them in the morning and saw that their faces were saddened and he said to them, "What is your news today, men, and why are your faces saddened?" [8]They said to him, "This very night we saw dreams and we are very shaken up by them, and we don't have an interpreter of dreams." [9]Joseph said to them, "All these dreams and their interpretations are of God. Tell me your dreams."

Gen 40:9-15

Joseph interprets the butler's dream

[10]The head butler said, "I saw in my dream, and behold a vine was in front of me and on the vine were three branches, and its leaves shot forth, and the grape clusters grew ripe. [11]And I saw that I took the gold cup that the king drinks from, and I ran rapidly and plucked a bunch of grapes and squeezed them into the Pharaoh's cup, and I placed the cup in his hand and he took it from me and drank." [12]Joseph said, "Hear the interpretation of the dream: the three branches are three days, and after three days Pharaoh will remember you and send and have you taken out of prison. [13]And you will stand before him and hold out the cup for him as was your custom formerly. [14]But see that you remember me before Pharaoh, because I really was stolen away from my father, and I am not a slave but I am a freeman from the nobles of the Hebrews. [15]And now, what is more, I did not commit any sin that would cause that they throw me in prison—so, treat me kindly, and get me out from here!"

Gen 40:16-19

Joseph interprets the baker's dream

[16]And when the chief baker heard that he had interpreted the dream of his friend favorably, he also said to Joseph, "And also I saw in my dream, and behold three baskets that are set upon my head and are filled with all the food for Pharaoh, and a bird came down and ate from the baskets and there was no one to drive it away." [17]And Joseph said to him, "This is (**I. 32**) the interpretation of your dream: The three baskets are three days. [18]After three days Pharaoh will behead you and will hang you from a tree, and a bird will eat your flesh, and there will be no one to drive it away from you."

Gen 40:20-23

The dreams are fulfilled as interpreted

20 [1]Then, after three days, it was Pharaoh's birthday and he prepared a great feast, and sent and called for all his servants and all his nobles. [2]And he remembered his servants who were confined in prison, and he sent and brought them out. [3]And appointed the chief butler to his former position, and he gave the cup into Pharaoh's hands, and the chief baker he hung from a tree just as he had interpreted their dreams for them. [4]But the chief butler forgot Joseph and did not remember him.

Gen 41:1-8

Pharaoh has two dreams and is distressed

21 [1]Now, after Joseph had been in prison two years, the king saw two dreams in one night. [2]In his dream he saw (that) he was standing by the great river of Egypt, and behold seven fine fat cows were grazing by the river. [3]And there came up from within the river seven other cows that were lean and of poor appearance, and the poor cows ate the fat ones, and they went inside them, though it was not clear that they went inside them. [4]And again, he saw seven ears of wheat on one stalk that were full and fine, and behold, seven others rose up after them that were afflicted by a withering wind and were small and mean, and they swallowed up the seven others. [5]And when Pharaoh awoke, he was in a severe state of distress, and he sent and called all the wise men and soothsayers that were in Egypt, but none were able to give Pharaoh the interpretation of his dreams. [6]And Pharaoh was furious with them and his anger heightened.

The butler remembers Joseph Gen 41:9-13

[7]Now, when the chief butler saw that the king was troubled and perplexed he remembered Joseph, and came to Pharaoh and knelt before him and said, "Forgive the folly of your servant my lord, because I mention my crime today. [8]When the chief baker and I were confined in prison we saw dreams, and there was there (**I.33**) a certain Hebrew. [9]He interpreted our dreams, and your majesty ordered just as he had interpreted, and he will interpret your dreams."

Joseph is summoned and he interprets Pharaoh's dreams Gen 41:14-32

22 [1]And he immediately sent trustworthy men after Joseph, and they quickly went out from his presence and brought Joseph out from the prison. [2]And he cut his hair and they bathed him, and he changed his clothes and they brought him before Pharaoh. [3]And (Joseph) knelt before Pharaoh, and when Pharaoh saw Joseph he wondered greatly at him. [4]And Pharaoh related his dreams to Joseph, and Joseph said to Pharaoh, "The two dreams are one. [5]God showed you what he is about to do: The seven fat cows are seven good years that will come about in the world, the like of which there has never been in the land of Egypt. [6]And the seven mean cows are seven mean years, the like of which there has never been in the land. [7]Behold, there will be seven good years in the land the like of which there has never been, and after them there will be seven years of famine throughout the whole land the like of which there has never been in the land.

Joseph advises Pharaoh Gen 41:33-36

[8]Now let my lord king do the thing his servant shall say in his presence: See to getting a wise man unlike any in all the land of Egypt and let trustworthy men go out with him and let them gather grain. [9]Have them lay aside one fifth of the harvest in storehouses in every town throughout the land of Egypt during each of the seven abundant years, and let it be kept for those seven years of famine—and the people will live and not die from the famine. [10]God has shown you what he is about to do, and I have revealed and shown to you the interpretation of your dreams."

Pharaoh makes Joseph a ruler in Egypt Gen 41:37-45

23 [1]And Pharaoh said to his faithful servants, "Where can (such) a man of understanding be found who possesses the spirit of God?" [2]And Pharaoh said to Joseph, "Since God has revealed to you all these things I have no other trustworthy man like you in my entire kingdom. [3]You shall be over my whole household and over my servants, and my maidservants, and my freemen and my nobles. [4]And you shall be a chief and ruler over the whole land of Egypt, and only my royal throne (**I.34**) shall be greater than you." [5]And Pharaoh took his signet ring from his hand and placed it on the hand of Joseph, and he set a necklace of gold upon his neck, and he clothed him with royal robes.

[6]And Pharaoh said to Joseph in the presence of all of the free- and noblemen of his kingdom, "See that today I have made you the ruler over all the land of Egypt and there is none greater than you in my entire kingdom. [7]You are the head and ruler of the house of Pharaoh and I have given life and death into your hands." [8]And Pharaoh commanded his faithful servants, "Bring Joseph the four-

horsed chariot." [9]And he had Joseph sit upon it beside him, and he ordered that he go throughout the whole of Egypt and that they cry out before him saying, "This is the father and ruler of the house of Pharaoh." [10]And the fear of Joseph fell upon all of the free and noble men of the house of Pharaoh. [11]And he gave Joseph a wife, the daughter of Potiphar the priest.

Potiphar learns of Joseph's new position

24 [1]Now when Potiphar, Joseph's (former) master, saw the honor that had been granted to Joseph he was exceedingly afraid. [2]And he said to his wife, "You have brought all these terrible things upon me. [3]You dishonored me, and made me a disgrace and an object of derision before all my friends, and before Pharaoh and all his nobles. [4]How will I show my face before Joseph? For behold, he has been made father and ruler of the house of Pharaoh. [5]I knew from the very first day that Joseph was not a slave, and because of this I made him the ruler of all I had. [6]And Joseph did not commit any offense against you. Instead you in your unseemliness yearned for his beauty, and he like a free man let go of his garment and fled from you: For if he had been assaulting you, you would have left your clothes in his hands. [7]And because I knew this fact about this matter I did not beat him, nor scourge him." [8]And his wife said to him, "Truly I have sinned and wronged him; but now, don't be upset, for I will appease him, and he will honor you more than all of your friends, and he will make you a great man, and a ruler over all the freemen and nobles of Pharaoh."

Potiphar's wife writes a letter to Joseph

25 [1]And she wrote a letter, and sealed it with her signet ring, and sent it to Joseph. [2]Now she wrote as follows, "From the debauched and immodest and shameless woman, the shamefaced one, the one humbled by her hateful works, your maidservant, reverencing your greatness. [3]To the pure and clean and chaste and humble man, the son of free men, lover of chastity and purity, the wise man, who is full of the fear of his God, who guards his chastity, and flees from wickedness and sin, the valiant hero and warrior, greetings. [4]No one can blame me that I longed for your beauty, my lord; for who does not desire the light and hate the darkness, or love the daytime and flee from the night? [5]Who, my lord, does not long for the pearl,[a] and labour diligently to acquire it? [6]And there are many people, my lord, who for its sake dive into the sea, and are drowned in it, and become food for sea creatures; and there is no one who finds fault with them, for everyone works hard to possess that thing which is best. [7]Yea, my lord, if Pharaoh the king, and the free men and nobles of Egypt longed for the beauty of my lord, and his wisdom, I, my lord, who am a base woman, with a bad name, and shamefaced, how could I not have longed for the fair beauty of my lord? [8]But I adjure my lord, by the God of his fathers and by the authority of his greatness, that you forgive your handmaiden her offense. [9]And may he be merciful to the servant of my lord—and so that I do not do away with myself for fear of my lord, let him send me words of consolation and comfort, and also to the servant of

a. Cf. *Syr. Hist. Jos.* 36:16, where Joseph, as yet unknown to the brothers, describes himself as a pearl.

my lord, for behold, he has fled and is hiding in the inner rooms because of his shame and his fear. 10Yea, my lord, I beseech you, bring about joy for us today that we may rejoice with you, in your elevation to greatness, with all Egypt, in the new lord who has been made for her."

Joseph replies in a letter to Potiphar's wife

26 1And Joseph made haste, and wrote and sent (a letter) to his (former) mistress (saying), "To the honorable woman, full of modesty, to the daughter of freemen, far from blame, my own mother, who, lo, conceived me with her love and gave birth to me with her compassion. 2My lady, be joyful and exult, and rejoice and glorify God, for He gave honor to your son, and an exalted position to your beloved. 3And for whom is the pride and joy, if not for you and for my father? 4You are the mistress of all the free women that are in Egypt, and my father the head of all the freemen of Pharaoh's house. 5And that you may believe my word, behold, I have sent you magnificent clothes—dress yourselves and come to me."

Potiphar and his wife are received and honored by Joseph

27 1And when his (former) mistress received his letter she was overjoyed, both she and her husband. 2And they put on the robes that Joseph sent to them and they went to greet him. 3And when they entered his presence both of them fell on their faces and bowed down before him. 4And he commanded them to arise, and Joseph ordered his servants and they placed seats for them. 5And Joseph received them joyfully. 6And he had them sit down before him, and he rejoiced with them and laughed and glorified God. 7And he spoke up and said to his (former) mistress, "I greatly appreciate your kindness towards me." 8And he praised her before all of the free and noble men of the king's house. 9And he gave her gifts and sent her away with honor to her house. 10And his (former) master he elevated above all of the freemen and nobles of Pharaoh's house.

Joseph prepares for the famine Gen 41:47-49

28 1And during those seven years of plenty Joseph took wise men and Egyptian scribes with him and went out to gather grain like the sand of the sea. 2And there were never seen in the land storehouses like those that Joseph built.

The famine begins Gen 41:53-57

3And the seven years of plenty passed away, and the seven years of famine came. 4And there was a great famine throughout the whole land just as Joseph said. 5And the Egyptians gathered together and came in to Pharaoh, and they said to him, "We are your servants, do not let us die from the famine. Give us food that we may eat and live." 6And Pharaoh said to them, "Go to Joseph, and whatever he says to you, do." 7And the Egyptians went to Joseph and bowed down and said to him, "Have mercy upon your servants and give us food that we and our wives and our children may eat and not die." 8And Joseph opened the storehouses and began to sell to whoever came to him to buy. 9And the famine gained strength in the land.

Gen 42:1-5 Jacob sends his sons to Egypt

29 (**II.9**) 1And when Jacob heard that there was grain in Egypt, he called to his sons and said to them, "Don't be afraid of the famine, my sons, for behold, according to what I have heard from many people there is grain in Egypt. 2The man who presides over it is good and merciful, and he sells to everyone who goes to him. 3Just take some money with you, and go down and buy food, and we shall eat and not die from the famine." 4Ten of the brothers of Joseph went down to Egypt, but Benjamin stayed with his father.

Gen 42:6 The brothers come before Joseph

5When they entered into Egypt and saw the glory and honor of Joseph as he sat upon the royal throne with all the free and noble ones of Egypt standing in his presence they were exceedingly afraid. 6And they did not know, nor did they recall their brother Joseph. 7And they all approached and fell down on their faces and bowed down before Joseph.

Gen 42:7-16 Joseph recognizes his brothers and accuses them

30 1When Joseph saw them he praised God and said, "Glory be to you Oh God of my fathers, for behold, the dreams that I saw about the sheaves were true." 2And Joseph commanded his servants and they made them get up from the ground. 3And Joseph looked at them angrily, and he spoke with them and said to them, "Where have you men come from? And from which land and from what place are you? And for what reason have you come to the land of Egypt? 4I see that you are mighty men, men of powerful strength—and (**II.10**) you have been especially chosen from your land, and have entered into Egypt as spies to spy out and see the bounties of the kingdom of Egypt." 5And an interpreter was translating the words of Joseph for them.

6When his brothers heard the words that he spoke to them they were terribly afraid—like men condemned to die. 7Then he was even more severe with them, and he said to them, "I know from your faces that you are deceitful and treacherous men. 8And behold, God has cast you into the hands of Egyptians that they might exact vengeance from you because of your wicked deeds." 9And Judah spoke with him and said to him, "No my lord, your servants are not spies, nor have we ever done anything wrong. 10Rather, my lord, we are upright men, and we are sons of one just man. 11He begat twelve sons; behold, ten of us are before our lord, one went out into the wilderness, and a terrible wild beast devoured him, and lo the youngest of us all is with our father." 12Joseph said, "Truly you are treacherous and deceitful men. 13But, by the life of Pharaoh, I swear to you that you will not escape from my hands until I discover all of the wicked things that you have done."

Gen 42:22-24; 43:30 Reuben chastises the brothers

14And when he heard Joseph, Reuben said to his brothers, "Do you not realize that God has delivered you into the hands of this man that he may avenge against you the wicked and sinful deed you perpetrated against Joseph? 15Did I not say to you, 'Don't commit this sin against the child'? 16Or, did you not think that God would repay you for the sin against him, and deliver you into the hands of evil men just as you delivered your free-born brother into slavery? [17]And if God forgave you for the sin against Joseph, he will not forget, nor forgive you for the sadness, and the sorrow, and the distress, and the sackcloth that your father wore upon his body lo these twenty years."

[18]Now when Joseph heard what Reuben said to his brothers about him and about his father it grieved him almost to death. He hastened and went inside (**II.11**) his private room and wept bitterly, and said, "Woe is me because of you, oh our father Jacob. [19]For your son is clothed in royal robes; but you, you wear sackcloth upon your body because of me. [20]Behold, twenty years have your children troubled your old age and darkened the light of your eyes. How good it would have been for you not to have ever had children."

Joseph throws the brothers into prison Gen 42:17; 43:31

31 [1]And when he had wept greatly and washed his face and come out, he sat down upon his throne and spoke with them again. [2]And he said to them, "Since you don't wish to tell me the truth, I will confine you to a dark pit and you shall never see the light again." [3]And Joseph sent them to prison. [4]And he sent one of his servants with them who knew Hebrew, and he said to him, "As soon as you have thrown them in the pit, sit down just above them and listen to their words and write them all down."

[5]And when they fell into the pit, Reuben said to them, "You threw Joseph inside a pit, but there was light in there. Now behold, God has cast us into a pitch-black pit, so that you can't see each other's faces. [6]Where now is the coat upon which you slaughtered the goat's kid, and besmeared it with its blood, and with it you broke the heart of our father Jacob? [7]Did I not tell you, O sons of handmaids?" [8]And Judah said to them, "If not for me, you would have indeed killed him. Now mourn for your lives."

Joseph summons the brothers again Gen 42:18-20, 24

32 [1]And after they had been in the pit for three days Joseph sent and had them brought up, and he said to them, "I fear the God of Heaven: For, perhaps your father truly is a just man—and for his sake I brought you out of prison. [2]But, one of you will stay behind inside the pit, and you shall take food and go to your father. [3]Now bring your younger brother with you to me straight away, and have your father write that you truly are his children. [4]Then by the life of Pharaoh I swear to you that as soon as my eyes see (**II.12**) your brother and I receive the response from your father, I will immediately release your brother that is confined, and I will give you grain and all of you will go in peace to your father—only you must bring your younger brother with you. [5]Now, take heed, don't delay, or your brother will die in prison." [6]And he had Simeon bound in his presence and cast him into prison, because there was none among the brothers whom Joseph loved like Simeon.

The money in the sack Gen 42:25-28

33 [1]And Joseph said to his steward, "Fill their sacks with grain and place each one's money bag inside his load." [2]And he did just what Joseph had commanded him. And they left Egypt, and when they reached the inn they opened up their loads and found their money in their loads and they were greatly afraid.

Gen 42:29-38; 43:6-7

The brothers return to Jacob

3And when they had arrived and come in before Jacob their father, they related to him everything that happened to them. 4And when he heard that Simeon was imprisoned, he poured ashes on his head and cried out and wept, and he said, "Woe be to your father Jacob all the days of his life: For everywhere you go, one of you is lost. 5I sent Joseph to the flock, and you said that a wild beast devoured him. 6And you went down to Egypt and have imprisoned Simeon. 7And little by little I will be deprived of you (all), and not one of you will be left by me in the day of my death to put his hand upon my eyes, but you will cause my old age to go down exceedingly sorrowfully into **(II.13)** the grave.

8"Why was it necessary for you to say, 'We have a younger brother'?" 9Judah said, "We entered the man's presence—we approached him according to the practice and bowed down to him, and as soon as he saw our faces the color of his face changed, and he spoke with us in a frightful fury and said to us, 'You are spies, and you are all not one (family), but you have really been chosen to be spies.' 10Then we said to him, 'We are all brothers and we have a single upright father and one younger brother with him.' 11And he confined us in prison for three days, and were it not for (Benjamin) he really would not have brought us out. 12And he swore to us by the life of Pharaoh saying, 'As soon as your father writes to me saying that you are truly all his children and my eyes see your younger brother, I will immediately release Simeon, and will give you food and you will go up in peace to your father.'" 13Jacob said to them, "I will not send my son Benjamin away. 14Rachel bore me two sons. 15Joseph—the fairest of his brothers and the likeness of his father—is no longer and Simeon is no longer. 16And if Benjamin also leaves me, behold, everything is over for me."

Gen 43:15, 7-13

Jacob agrees to send Benjamin to Egypt

34 1When that food that they brought from Egypt had disappeared, and their children and their wives were suffering from hunger, their children came to the aged Jacob beseeching him for bread. 2And they were all weeping before him and crying out and saying, "Oh grandfather of ours, give us bread!" 3And Jacob heard their cries while they wept and the tears were flowing from his eyes **(II.14)**, and he said to his sons, "I am no longer able to bear the sound of your children weeping before me from hunger. 4Up! Go down to Egypt and fetch grain for your children, and see about Simeon." 5His sons said to him, "We cannot possibly see that man's face without Benjamin being with us." 6And Judah said to his father, "Hand Benjamin over to me, and if I do not bring him back and have him stand before you, I will be sinful to you all the days of my life. 7And God will be with me that I may protect him." 8And Jacob said to him, "Well then, take with you the original money and take some extra money. 9And take from every good thing of the land to the man, the lord of Egypt. 10And may El Shaddai grant you mercy in his eyes that he may receive my son Benjamin peaceably."

Gen 43:15

The brothers return to Egypt with Benjamin

11And Jacob embraced Benjamin and caressed him and kissed him and spoke to him while crying and shedding tears—and Jacob wept greatly for all his sons with words of his grief. 12And he prayed over Benjamin and said to him, "Go in peace, my son, and may God be with you, and may he grant you mercy before the lord of Egypt and bring you back quickly to the side of your father. [13]And in seeing you I will forget all those former things, and may my ears hear your voice talking with me when you go up from Egypt and your brothers with you." [14]And when Jacob had prayed over them, they led off Benjamin and went down to Egypt. [15]And when they reached Egypt, Judah took Benjamin by the hand and they bowed down to Joseph.

Joseph receives Benjamin Gen 43:16-28

35 [3]And when Joseph saw his brother Benjamin he rejoiced exceedingly. [4]And he smiled on them and laughed. [5]And Joseph said to his steward, "Go, receive those men, and honor them and give them water to bathe their feet, and take them to their brother, and prepare a meal: for they will be dining with me today." [6]And the steward did just as Joseph told him.

(II.15) [7]And when Joseph entered to dine, they all drew near and bowed down to Joseph. [8]And Joseph said to them, "Is this the younger brother you told me about?" [9]Judah said to him, "Indeed my lord, this is your servant." [10]And Joseph put his right hand upon Benjamin's head and blessed him, and said to him, "May the God of your father bless you my son." [11]And Joseph said to him, "Is your aged father alive?" [12]And he said, "He is alive and well and he bows down to your majesty and also prays for your life. [13]And behold, my lord, the gift that he sent to your majesty."

Joseph uses his divining cup to seat the brothers Gen 43:33-34

36 [1]And Joseph took from them the thing that his father sent to him, and when the feast was ready, he said to his steward, "Bring me the cup with which I drink." [2]And he took the cup and stared at them and they were afraid. [3]And the Egyptians and his brothers were standing[a] in his presence. [4]And he knocked on the cup with his finger and he stared at them and said, "Reuben." [5]And he said, "Here I am, your servant." [6]And he said to him, "According to what the cup says to me, you are head and first-born of all your brothers. [7]Come over and be seated at the head." [8]And he knocked on the cup again and said, "Simeon, be seated next to Reuben. [9]And you Levi, after Simeon, and Judah after Levi." [10]And he did likewise to all of them. [11]And when the ten of them were seated one after the other according to their order, an amazed stupor fell upon the Egyptians, and the brothers feared exceedingly. [12]And he stared at them and shook his head at them, and they were like dead men from their fear.

[13]And Joseph said to his brother Benjamin, "You boy, you don't have a brother among them to be seated next to, so pass over, and sit by yourself." [14]And Joseph said to them, "Men, woe to you that your other brother is not now among you. [15]Were it not so, there would be no company as good as yours. [16]That brother of yours that was like a pearl among you, and the light and the sun of all of you, to which **(II.16)** of you did that brother of yours resemble? [17]And they all trembled and no one was able to say anything to him in return. [18]And Judah said to him, "none of us are like him, my lord. [19]Behold, Benjamin is his brother from the

a. Lit. "standing on their legs."

(same) father and from the (same) mother. [20]But he, my lord, was much fairer in his appearance." [21]And they ate the bread, which was bitter because of their fear. [22]And Joseph gave them each equal portions, but to Benjamin his brother he gave a larger portion of the food from his table than all of them. [23]And again, they wondered and were amazed.

Gen 43:34

Benjamin talks to Joseph about his brother

37 [1]And when Benjamin was merry with wine he said to Joseph, "My lord, I only had one brother, but our father sent him with my brothers to the flocks, and he didn't come back anymore. [2]Behold, our father has had twenty years of wearing sackcloth on his flesh because of him, and the light of his eyes has darkened from weeping, and the strength of his limbs has failed. [3]And he wails and laments over him just as though he had died today. [4]And he will not stop, my lord, because he sees the coat spattered with blood laid out before him. [5]Now I petition your majesty, my lord, that you knock on the cup, the revealer of hidden things, to see whether a wild beast ate him or men killed him." [6]And when Joseph heard these words from his brother he was grieved over the old age of his father, and he was not able to endure without weeping. [7]And he arose and entered into his private room and wept bitterly. [8]And he washed his face and came out. [9]And his brothers said to Benjamin, "O Insolent one! Be silent around us, so that we may go up from Egypt in peace. [10]It is now twenty years ago that your brother was eaten by a wild beast, and you, like a simpleton, you ask about him!" [11]But when Joseph knocked and laughed and stared at them, they died from fright. [12]And he said to Benjamin, "Your brother is alive, young man. [13]A beast did not (**II.17**) eat him, neither did men kill him, and when you come down again to get food I will tell you where your brother is."

Gen 44:1-3

The brothers return to Canaan

38 [1]Joseph said to his steward, "Fill their sacks with food, put the cup in the load of this boy, and urge them to leave Egypt." [2]And the steward did just as he was commanded. [3]And Joseph said to them, "Go in peace, and ask fervently after the welfare of your father from me." [4]And they bowed down before him on the ground and left by night. [5]And they loaded their beasts with produce and left Egypt. [6]And they said one to another, "Egypt and all its food is cursed! [7]May famine and pestilence and all such terrible things come upon it, and may we never again enter sorcerer-ridden Egypt—for truly devils spoke by this man and he did everything by sorcery."

Gen 44:4-5

Joseph sends his steward after the brothers

39 [1]And when they had journeyed far from Egypt, Joseph said to his steward, "Take forty men with you and chase after the Hebrew men. [2]Shout at them from afar, and they will tremble and weaken their strength with your threatening words, and trouble them boisterously, and take away their reason by your threats. [3]Watch out and be careful of the hairy man Judah, because if he is provoked to anger and the separate hairs on his chest stand on end, all Egypt will be accounted as nothing in his eyes. [4]See that you don't underestimate them, because they are warriors, and men of strength."

The steward accuses the brothers Gen 44:6-13

40 [1]And while (the brothers) were traveling along talking with one another, Joseph's steward and the men of Egypt fell upon them suddenly. [2]And the steward cried out to them from a great distance, "Wait, wait you deceitful and lying men! Wait you impostors and thieves, who have troubled the whole of Egypt with the thing that you have done. [3]Woe unto you for the wicked way that you have repaid us (**II.18**)—for you dared to steal the cup with which the king practiced divination just as you saw with your (own) eyes. [4]For it reveals to him hidden things and shows him what he wants. [5]Truly, it was not for grain that you came down to Egypt; rather you had heard in your land about the cup and you came down because of it—and you are sorcerers who know about divination. [6]Now like thieves you left in the night and fled."

[7]And the Egyptians accused them, and they trembled and were afraid, and they mourned for themselves. [8]And Judah spoke with the steward and said to him, "Do not sin against God, my lord, and revile your servants, for your servants are not thieves or sorcerers. [9]Far be it from us to dare to do such things as those, after you all honored us and acted kindly towards us, and your lord had us dine with him and received us with honor. [10]Far be it from us to be so presumptuous! [11]Behold, my lord, we and our loads and all that we have are before you. [12]Search, my lord, and see, and with whomever is found the cup, he shall be killed immediately, and we will all be slaves to your lord."

[12]And they rushed forward and took down their loads and opened their sacks in the man's presence. [13]And he began to search in Reuben's load, and on until Benjamin, but he didn't make a find. [14]Then their faces brightened, and they were encouraged. [15]And the steward said to them, "You are victorious, men, and have (done) no evil thing. [16]Put back your burdens upon your beasts, and go in peace, and forgive me that I made you out to be thieves." [17]But they all assembled together and besought him that he would also search Benjamin's load, saying, "Perhaps after a little your mind will be troubled and you will say, 'Perhaps the cup was put by them in that other load.'" [18]And they pressed him, saying, "Search this load also."

[19]And then he thrust in his hand and felt the cup (**II.19**) inside the sack and his face that was gloomy gladdened and he laughed, and lifted up the cup wrapped in a covering. [20]And when they saw the cup they died from fear, and the strength of their bodies drained away. [21]And the power of their mighty strength was broken, and their knees buckled, and the light of their eyes was darkened. [22]And the steward said to them, "Woe unto you men. [23]You have done a great evil to yourselves this day, and you shall die a terrible death at the harsh judgment that the Egyptians shall bring out upon you. [24]Load your burdens upon your beasts and get up to go!" [25]But they were not able to load the burdens on their beasts because their strength failed from terror.

The steward brings the brothers back to Joseph

41 [1]And while they were going along they were accusing Benjamin, saying to him, "Indeed you are the son of a thief, and the brother of that liar! [2]What is this you have done to us? [3]The man honored you more than all of us and he sat you down on his right hand at his table and he had you eat from all the good things

of his kingdom. [4]Why have you subjected us to mockery and this very hour you will have us killed in the midst of Egypt? [5]Why was this cup sought by you now? [6]You and your mother and your brother are a scandal to the sons of Jacob.
Gen 31:34-35 [7]Your mother stole the idols that her father worshipped, and your brother used to say, 'I shall be a king over you!' [8] and you have caused us to perish among the Egyptians." [9]And the steward was listening to their words so that he might relate them to Joseph.

Gen 44:14-15 Joseph reviles the brothers

42 [1]And when they entered Egypt they found Joseph sitting upon his royal throne and the freemen and nobles of Pharaoh standing before him. [2]And when his brothers approached him they fell upon their faces and bowed down before him. [3]And he commanded and had them get up from the ground. [4]And he roared at them angrily and spoke to them with fury, and he said to them, "Did I not say to you, oh men, from the very first day that I saw your faces that you were liars and thieves and spies? [5]But you said to me, (**II.20**) 'No my lord, rather we are free men and trustworthy and true men, and we have a just father.' [6]You deceived me with your craftiness! [7]I had you enter into my house and had you eat food at my table, and I gave you grain, and you stole the cup with which I divine, and you fled in the night. [8]Now I know of the terrible wicked things done by you; and this day those things have thrown you down into my hands."

Gen 44:16-34; 45:2 Judah pleads for Benjamin's release

43 [1]And his brothers, the sons of the handmaids, said to him, "Oh good lord, have pity upon your servants! [2]Not all of us have acted foolishly, my lord—just one, and he did this wicked thing. [3]His mother and his brother also used to behave dishonestly, my lord." [4]Then Judah restrained them and they were silent, and Judah opened his mouth and said to Joseph, "My lord, I petition your majesty that you command your servant to speak before you." [5]And Joseph said to him, "Speak that which you desire." [6]And Judah said to him, "Now, my lord, because the cup has been found in the load of this boy all of us are guilty, and we are all condemned to death. [7]By that God who gave you greatness and wisdom and knowledge, and set you apart inside the womb of your mother to be lord and ruler over all Egypt, perform (an act of) righteousness before God and have pity upon the infirmity of that aged just man, and send the boy to his father, and we, all of us, will be slaves to your majesty. [8]The heavens and the earth bear witness with me, my lord, that our father is a just and righteous man—God has spoken with him more than twenty times, and kings have come down to him and spoke with him." [9]And the Egyptians were afraid when they heard these things. [10]"And this boy is the living breath of that aged man, and if he is separated from him he will die immediately from his grief, because he is the light of his eyes and the staff of his old age. [11]And I gave myself as surety for him, for the boy, and I said to my father, 'If I do not bring him back to you, (**II.21**) I will sin against you all the days of my life.' [12]Behold, my lord, we are ten. Let us stay in his stead and let him go up to his father. [13]Whatever your majesty commands, do to your servants. [14]Truly we have sinned and have gone astray."

[15]Joseph said to Judah, "I see that you have a great love for this young thief."

[16]And Joseph said to Benjamin his brother, "Tell me, boy, did you steal the cup by yourself or were all of them aware of it?" [17]And weeping, Benjamin swore to Joseph, "By the God of our father Jacob, no! By the soul of Rachel, no! By that hour that my brother Joseph was separated from me, no! I do not know who stole the cup, or who it was who put it in my load." [18]And it distressed Joseph and he was not able to go on without weeping, and he entered into his private room and cried bitterly. [19]Then he washed his face and came out.

Enter the merchants who bought and sold Joseph

44 [1]Then, behold those merchants who bought Joseph from his brothers entered in and bowed down before Joseph. [2]And they said to him, "Twenty years ago, when we were crossing through the desert at Dothan, we came across men who were tending flocks. [3]They said to us, Oh Arab men, buy this man that we have, because he runs away from the flock every day. [4]And we purchased (him) from them for twenty pieces of silver, and we sold him for three hundred pieces of silver." [5]And when Joseph heard he praised God and said, "Glory be to you Oh God! [6]For, everything that has happened to your servant is gathered together and come and is standing before my eyes." [7]And Joseph took his bill of sale from the merchants—that which they had written for the merchants—and he showed it to his brothers, and he said to them, "Is there any among you a man who reads Hebrew?" [8]And they said, "Yes, my lord, Reuben." [9]And when he had opened out the document, he found that his name was written first. [10]And Joseph said to him, "Read!" [11]And Reuben said (**II.22**), "Truly, by your life, my lord, my eyes are soft just like my mother, and your servant is not able to read."

Joseph uses his divining cup to tell of the brothers' misdeeds

45 [1]Joseph said to his steward, "Since these men don't want to tell the truth in front of me, bring me the cup. [2]And he took the cup and knocked on it with his finger and put it to his ear and laughed. [3]And he said, "Reuben!" [4]And he said, "Here I am, your servant." [5](Joseph) said, "Hear what that the cup said to me about you: You slept with your father's wife and besmeared his bed. [6]How come you did not fear God, that you would dare to do this thing? [7]For behold, you said to me that your father is a just and righteous man—you deserve death." [8]And again, he knocked on the cup and said, "Simeon and Levi, the two of you have done something terribly bad—because of one woman you laid waste to the city of Shechem." [9]And he knocked again and said, "You, Judah, I had thought that you were a just man—you slept with your daughter-in-law after your two sons had died." [10]And the Egyptians were standing about in astonishment.

[11]And again, he knocked on the cup and color of his face changed and he smote his thigh and stared at them and said, "Woe men, Oh that I had not seen your faces, for how many terrible things have you done! [12]You are not worthy for mercy to come upon you. [13]Indeed you are unjust, and wicked and execrable men. [14]Where has this thing ever been heard of, that brothers sold their brother, and slew a kid upon his coat and bespattered it with blood and brought it in and showed it to their father? [15]Did you not fear God that you could sell your brother into slavery? [16]And your brother is alive and well, but your father is clothed with sackcloth upon his flesh and mourns for him! [17]And behold, these merchants

who bought him from you, God sent them to be your accusers." [18]And Joseph brought a man and said to him, "Read the document (**II.23**) in their presence." [19]And he read what was written in it as follows, "We, Reuben, and Simeon, and Levi, and Judah, and Gad, and Issachar, and Zebulon, and Dan, and Naphtali, and Asher, we ten brothers sold the slave called Joseph to the Arab merchants for twenty pieces of silver." [20]And Joseph shouted at them in a harsh voice, and said to them, "The men deserving to die are you." [21]And their arms became feeble, and they fell upon their faces before him, and collapsed as if dead from their fear.

Gen 45:1-15

Joseph reveals himself to his brothers

46 [1]And when Joseph saw them sprawled in front of him like dead men, he was moved with compassion over them, and more especially because of his brother Benjamin. [2]And he commanded and had them arise from the ground, and he comforted them and said to them, "Take courage, and don't be afraid, for I am your brother Joseph, and I saw the dreams and related (them) to you. [3]And behold, you have seen with your own eyes that my dreams were true. [4]Behold, you are in the place of your sheaves and you have bowed down to me; and the sun is our father Jacob, who will come down and see me; and the moon is Pharaoh the king; and the eleven stars are you. [5]I am he whom you threw in the dried-out cistern, and I am he whom you sold to the Arabs." [6]Joseph was relating (these things), and they were reeling from their fear and their terror. [7]And he embraced Benjamin and kissed him and caressed him, and said to him, "Is our father Jacob, my beloved, alive, for how long is the time that he mourned over me!"

Gen 45:16-20

Joseph presents his brothers to Pharaoh

47 [1]And Joseph went in to Pharaoh and said to him, "My lord, my eleven brothers have come to me." [2]And Pharaoh rejoiced greatly when he heard that he was Joseph the son of Jacob, because Pharaoh had heard of the fame of Jacob the Hebrew a long time ago. [3]And Pharaoh said to Joseph, "Send trustworthy men immediately, and they shall take wagons and beasts with them, and they shall load upon them your father and all the people of his house (**II.24**) and they shall come down to us."

Gen 45:21-24

The brothers return to Canaan

48 [1]And (Joseph) clothed Benjamin in magnificent royal robes, and he sent to his father ten suits of magnificent clothing, and ten asses loaded with all the good things of Egypt. [2]And he sent to his father the same chariot upon which Joseph rode, that he might ride and come to him. [3]And the trustworthy and venerable men and the honorable elders from Pharaoh's court went up after Jacob. [4]And Joseph said to his brothers, "Don't contend with each other on the way, and don't make fools of yourselves in front of the Egyptians who are with you." [5]And he commanded Benjamin his brother and said to him, "Ask after the welfare of our father, and declare to him everything that I have done to your brothers, and see that you don't delay from coming."

Jacob is told that Joseph is still alive Gen 45:25-28

6Benjamin and Judah went ahead to bring the news about Joseph to Jacob their father. 7And when Jacob heard the voice of Benjamin he rejoiced exceedingly and said, "Blessed is the God of my fathers who has shown me the face of my son in peace." 8And Benjamin said, "Our father Jacob, receive greetings from your beloved Joseph! 9Behold, my father, he is the one who confined Simeon and oppressed my brothers." 10And Benjamin related everything that Joseph did to his brothers, (and) he showed him the royal garments with which Joseph clothed him. 11And the Elders and venerable men from the house of Pharaoh entered and bowed down before Jacob and said to him, "Receive the greetings of your son Joseph, lord of Egypt." 12And when Jacob saw the chariots and wagons that Joseph sent to him he was amazed and wondered and praised God and said, "Glory be to you oh God of my fathers. 13Now I know that God truly loves me and that the dreams of my son Joseph were from God." 14And (Benjamin) brought out the clothing—the magnificent robes that Joseph had sent—and he clothed Jacob, and he divided the clothes between the wives of his brothers and their children. 15And the women rejoiced exceedingly when they heard that Joseph was alive and also had been made a king. 16And Jacob received the Egyptians (**II.25**) with honor. 17And they ate and they drank and enjoyed themselves, and they wondered and were amazed at Jacob's old age and at his stature and at his strength and at his words of wisdom.

Jacob and his household go up to Egypt Gen 46:1, 5-6

49 1And they loaded up their possessions on the wagons and Jacob sat upon the chariot that Joseph sent for him and he went down to Egypt. 2And the Egyptians entered with Judah and they told Joseph about the arrival of his father. 3And Joseph went in to Pharaoh and said to him, "As your majesty commanded my lord, behold my father and his family have come." 4And Pharaoh said to Joseph, "Take all the nobles with you and make ready the four-horse chariot for yourself, and let the children go out with you that they may be delighted in the presence of your father, and go out and receive your father with honor." 5And Joseph commanded, and the chariot was made ready for him, and all the honorable elders of Pharaoh's court, and the freemen and the nobles and eunuchs went out with him; and all Egypt was astir. 6And the Egyptians adorned themselves and their wives and their children with magnificent garments, and they went out with Joseph to greet his father. 7And there was a great celebration in Egypt at the arrival of Jacob, and they were all making merry and leaping for joy in Jacob's presence.

All Egypt rejoices with Joseph and his family Gen 46:28-29

50 1And Joseph commanded his faithful servants, and they opened the food stores and divided (the food) up among all the Egyptians, and they ate and enjoyed themselves: they, their wives and their children. 2Joseph said, "Let all Egypt rejoice with me this day that I see my father." 3And Joseph commanded, and they opened the prison and set free all those who had been confined there. 4And Joseph forgave the wrongdoings of all the offenders. 5And when the brothers of Joseph saw the great multitude that came out from Egypt, and all their chariots and horsemen, they said to Jacob, "Behold, Pharaoh the king and all

Egypt with him have come out to greet you." [6]And they and their children were exceedingly afraid. [7]And behold, Joseph reached them and the great multitude with him. [8]And as they drew near to him, his sons supported Jacob, and he got down from (**II.26**) the chariot, and Joseph also got down on foot to greet his father, and the two of them kissed each other and they wept bitterly, and the Egyptians also wept, and they saw them embracing each other and crying.

Gen 46:30

Jacob talks with Joseph

51 [1]And Jacob said to his son Joseph, "This day in which I saw you is greater than all the days of my youth. [2]My eyes were enlightened at the sight of you, oh my beloved, and the grief and the suffering and the sadness fled from your father. [3]Behold, I had twenty years, my son, of wearing sackcloth upon my flesh because of you, oh beloved of his father. [4]Behold my son, the weeping has not ceased from the eyes of your father for twenty years, and my body has been worn out from mourning and my strength seeped away. [5]And the light of my eyes was darkened. What happened to you, my son Joseph? Who separated you from your father, my beloved and my darling all this time? [6]Who is it who ruined the old age of your father? [7]Who is it who stripped off your coat and bespattered it with blood and came in and spread it out before the eyes of your father? Behold today it is twenty years. [8]Was it your brothers who did this to you with their hands, or perhaps some other men?" [9]Joseph said to his father, "It is not the time to talk about everything that came upon your son Joseph."

[10]And Joseph got up and sat upon the chariot, and the brothers came with their wives and their children and bowed down before Joseph. [11]And they spoke up and said to him, "We have sinned against you, my lord, and acted foolishly. [12]We lack confidence in your presence, and we are men guilty of death and have done a wicked thing the like of which has never been done. [13]Nevertheless, we entreat the power of your majesty; forgive your servants their folly. [14]And we are not worthy to be called your brothers, but let us be as slaves before you." [15]And Joseph was grieved, and he wept and was distressed because of them. [16]And Joseph said to them, "I am subject to God—far be it from me to repay you (**II.27**) for the wicked thing that you did to me. [17]The God of our father Jacob, He will forgive you." [18]And his brothers rejoiced exceedingly, and the Egyptians praised Joseph, for they saw and heard that he forgave their folly.

Gen 47:7-11

Joseph presents Jacob to Pharaoh

52 [1]And Joseph led his father, and they entered before Pharaoh, and Pharaoh stood up from his throne and embraced Jacob and kissed him and asked after his welfare. [2]And Pharaoh said to Jacob, "Blessed is your root, old man, which went forth like a blessed shoot." [3]And all of the brothers of Joseph approached and bowed down before Pharaoh, and Pharaoh said to Jacob, "Are all of these your sons, old man?" [4]Jacob said to him, "Yes my lord, they are the sons that God gave to me." [5]And Jacob blessed Pharaoh and said to him, "The Lord God of my fathers Abraham and Isaac will bless you and make your kingdom great." [6]And Pharaoh said to Jacob, "Is Abraham part of the race of your fathers?" [7]Jacob said to him, "Yes my lord. I am the son of Isaac, the son of Abraham." [8]And Pharaoh rejoiced greatly and said, "I did not know that Joseph was of the race of those righteous men." [9]And Pharaoh said to Jacob, "how many years has your life lasted?" [10]Jacob said, "Today, I am one hundred and thirty years old. [11]The years of my life are very short and unfortunate, and have not yet reached the age of my fathers."

Pharaoh offers Jacob land on which to settle

Gen 47:5-6

[12]And Pharaoh said to Joseph, "Behold, your father and your brothers have come to you. [13]Take care, and settle them in the best of the land, and see if there are any men among your brothers capable of work, and I will appoint them over the affairs of the kingdom." [14]And he commanded and gave magnificent presents to him. [15]And Jacob and his sons settled down in the land of Egypt like kings. And Joseph supported them with every good thing.

The last days of Jacob

Gen 47:28-29; 49:33; 50:1-14

53 [1]And Jacob was honored in the eyes of all Egypt like an angel of God. [2]And Jacob died at the age of one hundred and seventy[a] (**II.28**) years old. [3]And Joseph commanded the doctors, and they embalmed his body, and all Egyptians mourned for him for seventy days. [4]And Joseph went to Pharaoh and said to him, "My father adjured me while dying, saying, 'Go up and bury me with Abraham and Isaac my fathers.'" [5]And Pharaoh said to him, "Go up with honor, and bury your father with his fathers as he adjured you." [6]And the freemen and the nobles of Egypt went up with him, and he buried his father and returned to Egypt.

The brothers fear retribution

Gen 50:15-21

[7]And when Jacob died the brothers of Joseph feared exceedingly, lest perhaps he would turn and requite them for the wicked things that they had done to him. [8]And they all gathered together, and they led Benjamin with them, and went in and bowed down to Joseph. [9]And they petitioned him that he would not remember their folly against them. [10]And Joseph said to them, "Our father Jacob may be dead, but the God of heaven is alive, by whom I bestowed forgiveness on you. [11]And behold, my eyes are upon you for good things all the days of my life." [12]And his brothers bowed down before him and went out rejoicing.

The last days of Joseph

Gen 50:24-26

54 [1]And when the day of Joseph's death approached, he gathered all his brothers to him and said to them, "You know how I am with you and how I have forgiven you your folly. [2]And now my brothers, behold, I will die like all my fathers. [3]But see to the thing that I will commission for you. [4]I know that God will cause you to go up from Egypt, but I adjure you by the God of our father Jacob, that when you go up from Egypt, you will take my bones up there with you. [5]See to it my brothers that you don't go up and leave my bones here in a foreign land." [6]And his brothers swore to Joseph by the God of their fathers that they would take his bones up with them in honor, just as he had taken their father up in honor.

---

a. Reading with B, L, P and T; cf. Gen 47:28.

[7]And Joseph died (**II.29**) at the age of one hundred and twenty[a] years old. [8]And
the doctors embalmed his body and his brothers mourned greatly for him, and
all Egypt with them. [9]And they buried him in a mummy case outside of Egypt.

I have finished, and to Him be true praise, and to the sinful scribe, forgiveness.

Amen.

---

a. Reading with B, L, P and T; cf. Gen 50:26.

Aramaic Levi
A new translation and introduction

by James R. Davila

Aramaic Levi is a work of rewritten scripture from the Second Temple period which recounts the life story of the patriarch Levi, with special attention to his founding of the Levitical priesthood (long before the time of Aaron) and to detailed sacrificial regulations passed down to him by his grandfather Isaac. It is reconstructed from highly fragmentary manuscripts and quotations in Aramaic, Greek and Syriac. It has a close relationship to the book of *Jubilees* and it also served as the main source for the *Testament of Levi* in the Greek *Testaments of the Twelve Patriarchs*.

Contents
This work is presented as a first-person narrative set in the mouth of the biblical patriarch Levi. The beginning of the text is lost, but the surviving fragments from early in the narrative deal with the vengeance wreaked on the Shechemites for the rape of Dinah (cf. Genesis 34); an obscure episode involving Shechem, Levi, and a number of Jacob's other sons; and a prayer and ablutions of Levi, after which he set out to an uncertain location, probably near Abel Mayyin. There he reports that he had a vision. The order of the material involving Shechem in relation to the passage involving the prayer, ablutions, and vision is unclear. Some additional fragmentary material deals either with this vision or a second one.

After the visionary episode(s), we are told that Jacob ordained Levi as his chief priest and tithed to him at Bethel, and Levi made offerings and exchanged blessings with his father and brothers. Then they traveled to the "fortress of Abraham," apparently in the vicinity of Hebron, where Isaac blessed them and instructed Levi concerning the law of the priesthood, giving him warnings against sexual impurity followed by detailed precepts on the proper procedures for offering sacrifices in the sanctuary.

Then Levi recounts briefly the story of his entry into the land of Canaan, his annihilation of the Shechemites, his marriage, the birth of his sons, the entry of the family into Egypt, and the birth of his grandsons. He reports that at age one hundred and eighteen, in the year that Joseph died, he gathered his sons and grandsons and exhorted them at length concerning the benefits and power of wisdom. There may be a reference to Dinah late in this address. The remainder of the document is lost and it is unknown what, if anything, followed Levi's address.

Manuscripts and Versions

Fragments of Aramaic Levi have been recovered from a wide range of manuscripts in Aramaic, Greek, and Syriac.[1] None of these sources is complete, but when their overlapping fragments are combined they allow us to reconstruct a significant portion of the text, although the beginning and ending, both of uncertain length, are lost. The earliest recoverable text is in Jewish Palestinian Aramaic of the Second Temple period and, although it is possible that the Aramaic version is translated from Hebrew, no convincing case for a Hebrew original has been made and it seems likely that the text was composed in Aramaic.

Eight manuscripts survive in Aramaic, one from the Cairo Geniza (a repository of discarded medieval Jewish manuscripts associated with the Ben Ezra Synagogue in the old city of Cairo) and seven from Qumran (the Dead Sea Scrolls). The Qumran manuscripts all seem to date to roughly the first century B.C.E. (perhaps as early as the late second century B.C.E. for 4QLevi[f] ar). All are very poorly preserved, but the sum total of their evidence gives us much important information about the original Aramaic text at a time not long after the composition of the work. Extracts of the work translated into Greek and Syriac also survive. The details of these sources are as follows.

- The first manuscript of *Aramaic Levi* to be discovered in modern times is a late-ninth- or early-tenth-century C.E. Aramaic codex recovered from the Cairo Geniza, of which three damaged leaves (folios) survive. Each folio has writing on both sides and each side originally contained three columns of text with 23 lines per column. One of the folios and part of a second reside in the Cambridge University Library (T-S 16.94); another fragment of the second is among the Gaster Geniza fragments in the manuscript collections of the John Rylands Library in Manchester (P1185); and the third folio is in the Oxford Bodleian Library (Ms Heb c 27 f. 56r.-v.). Given the lateness of the manuscript—it was copied nearly a millennium after the Qumran manuscripts—the surviving text is remarkably well preserved, although in some cases the grammar and spelling have been updated.
- 1Q21 (1QLevi ar) is a late Hasmonean manuscript that survives in sixty small fragments, two or three of which overlap with the Geniza manuscript.
- 4Q213 (4QLevi[a] ar) is a late Hasmonean or early Herodian manuscript that survives in five fragments, the first and largest of which overlaps with §§82-95 of the Geniza text and with material in 4QLevi[e] ar not found in the Geniza text.
- 4Q213a (4QLevi[b] ar) is a late Hasmonean manuscript that survives in six fragments.

---

1. The most recent editions of all the texts are Drawnell, *Aramaic Wisdom Text* and Greenfield, Stone, and Eshel, *Aramaic Levi Document*. Greenfield, Stone, and Eshel include photographs of the Geniza manuscript and Drawnell includes photographs of all the texts. The edition of the Geniza manuscript by Puech, the editions of the Qumran fragments by Stone and Greenfield in DJD 1 and by Barthélemy and Milik in 22, and the edition of the Greek fragments by de Jonge in *The Testaments of the Twelve Patriarchs*, 25 and 46-48, should also be noted. In 2008 Gideon Bohak identified a new fragment of the Aramaic Geniza manuscript (P 1185) in Manchester which had not been included in any of these editions. He very kindly made his publication of the fragment available to me in advance and my translation of it here is based on his transcription. I have not seen a photograph of this fragment. For possible allusions to Aramaic Levi in other works, see the section on Literary Context below. The very poorly preserved Aramaic contents of the Qumran manuscripts 4Q540-541 have sometimes been compared to elements of *Testament of Levi* 17-19, but the parallels are not compelling and these manuscripts do not overlap with any of the surviving text of *Aramaic Levi*. To posit any connection between them is speculative.

The first two of these overlap with the first Greek fragment of the Mt. Athos manuscript.

- 4Q213b (4QLevi[c] ar) is a late Hasmonean manuscript that survives in a single fragment that overlaps with §§6-9 of the Geniza text.
- 4Q214 (4QLevi[d] ar) is a late Hasmonean manuscript that survives in four fragments, one of which overlaps (with variations) with §§25-30 of the Geniza text and another of which may overlap with a variant form of §§20-23 of the same text.
- 4Q214a (4QLevi[e] ar) is a late Hasmonean or early Herodian manuscript that survives in eleven fragments, three of which overlap with (probably) §§24-25 and §§69-71 of the Geniza manuscript. Other fragments have overlaps with material in 4QLevi[a] ar and 4QLevi[f] ar.
- 4Q214b (4QLevi[f] ar) is a Hasmonean manuscript that survives in eight fragments, five of which overlap with §§22-27 of the Geniza text. Some fragments also overlap with 1QLevi ar and 4QLevi[e] ar.
- The Mt. Athos manuscript (manuscript Athos, Monastery of Koutloumous, Codex 39 [catalogue no. 3108]) contains two excerpts of *Aramaic Levi* in a Greek translation which survive in an eleventh century C.E. manuscript of the Greek *Testaments of the Twelve Patriarchs* now located at Mt. Athos in Greece. The first is inserted midway through *T. Levi* 2:3 and is now divided into eighteen verses. It does not overlap with the Geniza manuscript, but its general content along with a substantial overlap with 4QLevi[b] ar frags. 1-2 confirms that it belongs to *Aramaic Levi*. The second excerpt is placed between *T. Levi* 18:2 and 18:3 and overlaps with Bodleian cols. b-c (§§11-32a) and Cambridge col. c (§§66-69a) as well as fragments of 4QLevi[d] ar and 4QLevi[f] ar. A brief third addition is found inserted in *T. Levi* 5:2. It may have come from *Aramaic Levi*, but this is very uncertain, and even if so, its placement is also uncertain. I have not included it in the translation.[2] It is unknown whether the rest of *Aramaic Levi* was translated into Greek or why these particular passages of it were inserted into a manuscript of the Greek *Testament of Levi*.
- The Syriac quotation (B. Add. 17, 193, British Museum, London, catal. no. 861) preserves a brief excerpt corresponding to §§78-81 of the Geniza manuscript, which is introduced as a quotation from Levi's testament. It has been suggested that the Syriac text is a paraphrase of Greek *T. Levi* 12:5-6,[3] but we have no other evidence that the Greek *Testaments of the Twelve Patriarchs* was translated into Syriac and, more importantly, the Syriac text agrees more closely with *Aramaic Levi* than with the Greek *Testament of Levi* and I take it to be an excerpt of the former.

Genre, Structure, Prosody

Earlier editors treated *Aramaic Levi* as a "testament," on obvious analogy with the closely related Greek *Testament of Levi*. Indeed, this identification of genre goes back at least to the excerpter of the Syriac fragment, who tells us that the quotation comes from the "testament" of Levi. But the genre testament is generally agreed to include a pseudonymous deathbed revelation assigned to an ancient worthy, with ethical and perhaps eschatologi-

2. The third addition reads "And He (i.e., God) said to me, 'Levi, to you shall be given the priesthood and to your seed to minister to the Most High in the midst of the land and you are to propitiate for the inadvertent errors of the land.' Then He gave the blessings of priesthood." The passage is inserted into Levi's first vision and if it does come from *Aramaic Levi* it may belong in the lacuna between §xx and §4.

3. Greenfield, Stone, and Eshel, *Aramaic Levi Document*, 199-200.

cal content and, although *Aramaic Levi* contains elements of this genre, it is not clearly a testament. Although in §§82-83 Levi does summon his sons to give them sapiential instructions that seem to act in some sense as his last will and testament, this event seems to be inspired by the death of Joseph rather than Levi's impending death. Indeed Levi lives for nineteen more years. In addition, the only revelation associated with the event is the sapiential poem that follows. It is true that the entire work is presented as a composition by Levi at the end of his life, but we are given no testamentary frame for it in what survives.

In broadest terms, *Aramaic Levi* is an example of rewritten scripture, a retelling of scriptural narrative aimed at solving problems and making the text relevant for its current audience. Other prominent ancient Jewish examples of this genre include the book of *Jubilees*, the *Genesis Apocryphon*, and the *Biblical Antiquities* of Pseudo-Philo. *Aramaic Levi* also has similarities to a genre of fictional autobiography known from Akkadian literature in which the pseudonymous narrator passes on his experiences and wisdom or foretells the future. Examples survive in the names of major figures such as Naram-Sin and Sennacherib, and the *Story of Ahiqar* is an Aramaic composition that is related to this genre.

But on a more detailed level *Aramaic Levi* consists of a skillful collection of material in many different genres, including the retelling of scriptural stories; an individual poetic lament with apotropaic elements aimed at protecting the speaker from malign spiritual forces; a description of one or two heavenly visions with connections to the genre apocalypse; detailed directives regarding the priestly ritual cult; metro-arithmetical directions with roots in Babylonian scribal lore; and a sapiential and didactic poem.[4]

For the most part the structure of the work is clear and requires little additional comment. But two elements remain controversial due to the fragmentary nature of the document: whether Levi had one or two visions and where to place the prayer of Levi in the narrative. The two issues are related. The Greek *Testament of Levi* assigns two visions to Levi: one taking place at Abel-Maoul, in which a single angel guides him through the seven heavens, takes him through the gates of heaven to the throne of God, and then instructs him to take vengeance on Shechem (2:5-5:7), which he does (chapters 6-7); the other happening at Bethel after the Shechem incident (chapter 8), with seven angels investing Levi as a priest. *Aramaic Levi* has Levi departing from Abel Mayyin when he begins to see a vision involving a single angel and the gates of heaven. The text breaks off at this point and an uncertain amount of it is lost, although two Qumran fragments are plausibly assigned to the lacuna. The narrative resumes at the end of a vision involving seven figures who have somehow honored Levi. The geographical location is unclear.

Kugler has argued that there was only one vision in *Aramaic Levi*, which took place after the Shechem incident and which was freely reworked into two visions in the Greek *Testament of Levi*.[5] He points out that the seven-heaven cosmography did not yet exist in the time of the composition of *Aramaic Levi* and that since Levi was departing from Abel Mayyin, he could already have arrived at Bethel at the time of his single vision. His interpretation is possible, but no one has been fully convinced by it, and the reference

4. The most comprehensive discussion of the genre(s) of *Aramaic Levi* is given by Drawnell in *Aramaic Wisdom Text*, 85-96.

5. Kugler, *From Patriarch to Priest*, 45-51. In *Pseudepigrapha of the Old Testament*, 110, 131-34, De Jonge finds Kugler's reconstruction unpersuasive. In *Aramaic Levi Document*, 11-18, Greenfield, Stone, and Eshel remain agnostic as to whether there were one or two visions, but place §§1-3 (their chapters 1-2) before the prayer in agreement with Kugler (see below). In *Aramaic Wisdom Text*, 43-49, Drawnell reconstructs two visions and places §§1-3 in the lacuna between §xx and §4.

to multiple "visions" in §xx (alas, in a broken context) and Levi's comment in §7 that he "concealed this (i.e., vision) also in my heart" (as though he was already concealing a first vision) are difficult to reconcile with it. (Kugler's attempt to translate "this also" as "this very thing" is philologically unconvincing.) I am inclined to think that there were two visions in *Aramaic Levi*, the first of which was freely expanded in the Greek *Testament of Levi*, but dogmatism on the matter is unwarranted.

As for the prayer and the beginning of the vision that followed it, one can argue that they originally went either before or after the incident(s) regarding Dinah and Shechem (§§1-3 plus the Manchester fragment). Kugler's reconstruction of one vision would require that the latter incident(s) came first. The prayer could be taken as a purificatory ablution following the ritual defilements associated with the slaughter of those events or it could be taken as a purification undertaken in preparation for the events in which sexual immorality was to be turned away, lawlessness obliterated from under heaven, and a righteous seed established in the line of Abraham (cf. vii, xiii, and xvi). There is no consensus on this issue. I have placed §§1-3 and the Manchester fragment before the prayer in order to retain Kugler's reconstruction as a possibility, but a good case can also be made for placing this material between §xx and §4.

Date and Provenance

The date of the composition of *Aramaic Levi* is much debated, with proposed dates ranging from the late second century B.C.E. to the fourth century B.C.E. The one uncontroversial datum is that the earliest manuscript, 4QLevi^{f} ar, is written in a "Hasmonean" script that dates from the second half of the second century B.C.E., rendering it virtually certain that the work must have been written before about 100 B.C.E. Representative views about the date are summarized below.

James Kugel argues that *Aramaic Levi* was composed in the last third of the second century B.C.E., and therefore not long before 4QLevi^{f} ar was copied. The document was commissioned by the Hasmoneans—the dynasty of high priests and kings descended from the Maccabees who ruled an independent Jewish state from 142 to 63 B.C.E.—as propaganda presenting Levi as passing down both priestly and royal authority to his line. The writer drew on the book of *Jubilees* and two reconstructed documents that Kugel calls the "Levi Apocalypse" and "Levi's Priestly Initiation."[6] This theory depends on reading the reference to "priests and kings" and "your kingdom" in *Aramaic Levi* §§99-100 as referring to Levi's line, but the passage is badly broken and its exact meaning is uncertain. The theory also depends on *Aramaic Levi* being dependent on *Jubilees* and two hypothetical lost sources, on which more below.

Greenfield, Stone, and Eshel argue for a composition date in the third or early second century B.C.E. They consider *Aramaic Levi* to be a source used by *Jubilees*, and they find elements of the former to fit this period best. These include possible non-polemical allusions to the sectarian solar calendar in §§65-72; possible royal elements attributed to the line of Levi in §§xxiii, 67, and 99-100; stress on the purity of the Levitical line and the long-term transmission of priestly lore; "distinctive" notions about exorcism, demonology, and the doctrine of the two spirits; a paradigmatic role for Joseph as tradent of wisdom; and a lack of sectarian language of the type found in the Qumran literature.[7] Kugler too accepts

6. Kugel, "Levi's Elevation"; *Ladder of Jacob*, 115-68.

7. Greenfield, Stone, and Eshel, *Aramaic Levi Document*, 19-22, 189-90.

a third-century date, although he argues that *Jubilees* and *Aramaic Levi* drew on a common source, the "Levi-apocryphon," rather than one using the other. He also points to the mild dualism of *Aramaic Levi* and its non-polemical advancement of priestly traditions alternative to the biblical Priestly material as evidence for this date.[8]

None of these arguments is compelling. The relationship of *Jubilees* and putative lost Levi sources to *Aramaic Levi* continues to be debated. The royal elements appear only in damaged passages (§xxii and §§99-100), a possibly secondary passage found only in the Greek text (§67), and a possible subtle allusion to Gen 49:10 (§67).

In any case, royal elements can be used to support either a Hasmonean date or an earlier one. The other features advanced are subjective and by no means prove a third-century date.

Drawnell accepts a date in the late fourth or early third century B.C.E. He argues that the Babylonian metrological traditions he finds in *Aramaic Levi* were likely brought to Palestine by the exiles who returned with the priestly and scribal leader Ezra. Ezra took on a political role consonant with the royal and priestly roles found in *Aramaic Levi.* Ezra and Nehemiah introduced priestly marriage reform and Nehemiah introduced tithing reform and in his time priests took an interest in wood procurement, all themes of interest in *Aramaic Levi.* The royal leadership assigned to the Levitical priesthood by the Hellenistic historian Hecataeus of Abdera ca. 300 B.C.E. accords well with the picture of the priesthood in *Aramaic Levi.* In addition, Josephus's account of the events that led to the building of the Samaritan Temple on Mount Gerizim involves the expulsion of a brother of the high priest because of his marriage to the daughter of the governor of Samaria in the late fourth century (*Ant.* 11.302-347), reinforcing Jewish hostility to Samaritans, a theme found implicitly in the retelling of the destruction of the Shechemites (Genesis 34) in *Aramaic Levi.*[9]

Again, none of these arguments is compelling. The evidence indicates that in the fifth through second centuries B.C.E. the Levitical priests were understandably concerned with genealogical purity and the correct and smooth procurement of tithes and undertaking of sacrifices. Not surprisingly, they also took advantage of the vacuum of power from the loss of the monarchy to accumulate for themselves as much royal power as political circumstances allowed. Once Babylonian metrological traditions had been adopted by some or all of the Levitical priesthood, such traditions could have survived for centuries. The story in Genesis 34 is an integral element of the life of Levi and could hardly be ignored in *Aramaic Levi*, whatever the contemporary relationship was with the Samaritans.

Aramaic Levi is usually taken to have been composed in Palestine, although Milik also proposed a Samaritan provenance on the basis of the place names in the work, and Kugler has offered additional support for this view on the basis of a single textual variant in possible agreement with the "Samaritan" text-type; a medieval Samaritan parallel to the strict requirement in *Aramaic Levi* that a priest marry a woman in the priestly line (§17); and the exaltation of Levi as the source of the priesthood and of Joseph as an honored role model associated with wisdom in both *Aramaic Levi* and Samaritan tradition. He even raises the possibility that *Aramaic Levi* was composed by Samaritan exiles in Egypt. But these arguments do not add up to a strong case. When Levi is told by Isaac in §17 to marry within "my clan," the command is more naturally taken as a reference to Jewish rather than specifically priestly endogamy. The place names and role of Levi mostly arise naturally from

8. Kugler, *From Patriarch to Priest*, 131-35.

9. Drawnell, *Aramaic Wisdom Text*, 63-75.

the relevant biblical narratives, and the scribal and sapiential interests of the author suffice to explain the focus on the sapiential elements of the Joseph story.[10]

In short, *Aramaic Levi* could have been composed any time between the fourth century and about 100 B.C.E. and there seems little to be gained by insisting on a more specific date with our current state of knowledge. Given that our earliest manuscripts are of a Palestinian provenance, origin in that region is the natural working hypothesis, although we cannot be certain. The purpose of the work remains opaque. It clearly was written to exalt the Levitical priesthood and transmit some of its cultic and sapiential traditions, but more than this cannot be said with confidence.[11]

Literary Context

Sources, inspirations, and closely related texts

The obvious and fundamental source of the story in *Aramaic Levi* is the Hebrew Bible, especially the book of Genesis. The biblical stories of Abraham, Isaac, Jacob, and Joseph are assumed as background to the narrative. The vengeance taken by the brothers Levi and Simeon on Shechem for the rape of their sister Dinah (Genesis 34) seems to have been retold in the earlier part of *Aramaic Levi* (§§1-2 plus the Manchester fragment, and perhaps §3, although the latter may pertain to the sale of Joseph in Gen 37:25-28 or to the wars of the sons of Jacob; see below). Jacob's vow to tithe to God (Gen 28:20-22) is fulfilled when he consecrates Levi as priest and gives him the tithe (§§9-10). The genealogy of Levi and his line as found in Genesis 46:11, Exodus 6:16-20, Numbers 3:17-20, 26:59, and 1 Chr 6:16-18 forms the narrative scaffolding for Levi's account of his life and descendants in §§62-81. The priestly regulations in the Pentateuch (especially Leviticus) and in a few cases, Ezekiel, lie behind Isaac's instructions on priestly ritual in §§11-61. Kugel has argued that Levi's first vision (§xx, supplemented by *T. Levi* 2:5–5:7) was inspired by exegesis of Mal 2:4-7, which could be interpreted to say that God revealed a covenant of peace to Levi himself (not just his line) and that Levi guarded or kept this knowledge to himself as a special revelation from an "angel of the Lord of Hosts" ("messenger" and "angel" are the same word in Hebrew). Indeed, the consonantal text of 2:5b ("and from before my name he was terrified" according to the Masoretic Text) can be creatively vocalized to mean "and from before my name (or even 'my heavens') did he descend."[12]

There is also a close relationship between *Aramaic Levi* and the book of *Jubilees*, especially 30:1–32:9, although there is disagreement on whether one used the other or both used a common source. Both texts describe the revenge taken by Levi and Simeon on Shechem; the visit of Jacob and his family to Isaac; Isaac's consecration of Levi as priest; Levi's dream vision of being consecrated as priest; and Jacob's tithing to Levi at Bethel. In addition the instructions of Isaac to Levi in *Aramaic Levi* (which Isaac reports that

10. Milik, "Le Testament de Lévi," 403-5; Kugler, *From Patriarch to Priest*, 137-38; idem, "Some Further Evidence." Drawnell critiques the hypothesis of Samaritan origins in *Aramaic Wisdom Text*, 75-76.

11. It has been asserted that the cultic rules in *Aramaic Levi* contradict the parallel rules in the Pentateuch (Kugler, *From Patriarch to Priest*, 109-110). Lawrence Schiffmann ("Sacrificial Halakhah"), however, has argued in detail that these variations from the Pentateuch are no greater than those found in Tannaitic or Qumran halakhah, which does not support Kugler's view of *Aramaic Levi* as a "protest document" against the contemporary priesthood of the author's time. Martha Himmelfarb has taken a similar position, arguing that Aramaic Levi is critical of the priesthood only in the matter of marriage customs and that it builds on the precepts of the Pentateuch rather than altering them ("Earthly Sacrifice").

12. Kugel, "Levi's Elevation," 30-32; *Ladder of Jacob*, 144-48.

he received from Abraham in §57) appear in *Jub.* 21:5-20 as instructions of Abraham to Isaac. It is also possible that the poorly preserved episode figuring in *Aramaic Levi* §3 pertained not to the revenge on the Shechemites, but to the wars of the sons of Jacob, a non-scriptural story that figures in *Jub.* 34:1-9, *T. Jud.* 3-7, the medieval *Midrash Vayissa'u*, and elsewhere.[13]

It is possible that other sources can be detected behind *Aramaic Levi*. The work itself claims to be dependent on a *Book of Noah* that included cultic regulations concerning blood (§57). A *Book of Noah* is also cited in *Jub.* 10:13, 21:10, and *Genesis Apocryphon* v.29, as well as in medieval sources.[14] Kugel argues that the account of Levi's first vision is drawn from a lost "Levi Apocalypse" that was based on the exegesis of Malachi noted above. Kugel also reconstructs a second document, "Levi's Priestly Initiation," which may have once formed a trilogy with the *Testament of Qahat* and the *Visions of Amram*, both known from the Dead Sea Scrolls. This document included Levi's priestly initiation by seven angels in a vision and Isaac's instructions to Levi about sacrificial matters. *Aramaic Levi* adopted this material as Levi's second vision (xxi-xxii, 4-7) and Isaac's instructions (§§11-61), while *Jubilees* only briefly alluded to the vision in 32:1 and transferred the instructions to Abraham in chapter 21.[15] Since most of Levi's vision or visions in *Aramaic Levi* no longer survives, the reconstruction of source material for the vision(s) must depend heavily on *T. Levi* 2-5 and 8 and remains very speculative.

Influence on later texts

The Greek *Testament of Levi*, the third text in the Greek *Testaments of the Twelve Patriarchs*, used *Aramaic Levi* as its primary source, frequently keeping fairly close to its wording, although at other times changing, adapting, and Christianizing the contents freely. The *Testament of Levi* deals with the revenge of Levi and Simeon on the Shechemites (2:2-3, 6:1-7:4; cf. *Aramaic Levi* §§1-2, the Manchester fragment, and possibly 3). It is aware of Levi's prayer in *Aramaic Levi* §§i-xix, alluding to it briefly in 2:4 and drawing on material from it in 4:2-6. The *Testament of Levi* contains two visions (2:5–5:7 and 8:1-19) which correspond at least to some degree to the visionary material ascribed to Levi in *Aramaic Levi* §§xx-xxiii and 4-7. In both documents, Jacob ordains Levi as a priest and tithes to God through him (*T. Levi* 9:1-3; cf. *Aramaic Levi* §§8-10). Isaac's cultic instructions in *Aramaic Levi* §§11-61 are heavily abbreviated in *T. Levi* 9:4-14 but it is clear that the author knew them. The rest of Levi's life story in *Aramaic Levi* §§62-81 is followed closely in *T. Levi* 11:1-12:5a. Levi's sapiential instructions in *Aramaic Levi* §§82-104+ are summarized in *T. Levi* 12:5–13:9, perhaps extending into chapter 14. Expansions with Christian content are found in *T. Levi* 2:11b, 4:4b, 10:1-5, and perhaps 5:2b and 8:14. The remainder of the text of *Aramaic Levi* is lost, so the relationship between it and *Testament of Levi* chapters 14–19 is unknown.

Aramaic Levi may be alluded to or may have directly or indirectly influenced other ancient works as well. The Geniza manuscript of the Damascus Document refers to "the three nets of Belial about which Levi son of Jacob said" and specifies of these nets that "the first is sexual immorality, the second is wealth(?), the third is making the sanctuary impure" (CD iv 15, 17-18). The word translated "wealth" is unintelligible as it stands, but

13. Martha Himmelfarb has published a translation of *Midrash Vayissa'u* in this volume.

14. See also Martha Himmelfarb's contribution "The Book of Noah" in this volume.

15. Kugel, "Levi's Elevation," 52-64; idem, *Ladder of Jacob*, 151-68.

has this meaning if we adopt a simple emendation of a single letter. Jonas Greenfield, however, has proposed a more violent, but still feasible emendation of the word to mean "wantonness." If we adopt this emendation it becomes plausible that the Damascus Document is referring to *Aramaic Levi* §16, in which Isaac tells Levi to guard himself "from all wantonness and impurity and from all sexual immorality." The context (cf. §17b) indicates that the concern is to protect the sanctuary from desecration.[16]

In addition, a Greek letter by a fourth-century Egyptian monk named Ammonas twice quotes otherwise unknown material which he attributes to "Levi." The first quotation reads, "and who knows the sweetness of the spirit except those in whom it dwells?" The second reads, "So when Levi was found worthy of it (i.e., the holy spirit), he thanked God greatly, saying, 'I hymn You, O God, because you have granted to me the spirit whom You gave to Your servants.'" The second passage looks to be the incipit of a hymn similar in structure to those found in the Qumran Hodayot. The first could be a line from the same hymn, perhaps even the second line of that hymn. These quotes are not found in Levi's prayer in *Aramaic Levi* (§§i-xix), but in it Levi does ask God for the holy spirit (§viii) and he refers to himself as one of God's servants (§§xi, xv, xix). Moreover, in general this letter of Ammonas is concerned with the need for purification before receiving the holy spirit and with the understanding of God's mysteries that the spirit brings, themes also present in *Aramaic Levi* (§§viii, xiv, xx). Although Ammonas does not seem to have known a Greek version of *Aramaic Levi* itself, he may have had access to closely related Greek traditions about Levi.[17]

One passage in a late rabbinic text may allude to Levi's (first?) vision in *Aramaic Levi* or to its source. In *Pirqe Rabbi Eliezer* 37 (eighth or ninth century C.E.) we are told that the angel Michael brought Levi to God and introduced him as God's "allotted portion" among created beings. God gave Levi the blessing that his descendents would have an earthly priesthood like the angelic one in heaven and he granted them the right to eat of the holy offerings. This corresponds to the taking of Levi to heaven, apparently by an angel (*Aramaic Levi* §xx; cf. *T. Levi* 2:5-6, 5:1), and to God's granting of the priesthood to Levi in *T. Levi* 5:2).[18]

This Translation

Aramaic Levi is preserved in numerous fragmentary but overlapping manuscripts in three languages, and the contents of these manuscripts have to be combined to recover as much of the document as possible. This raises problems not only for versification of the work, but also for reconstructing it as a smoothly flowing narrative while at the same time indicating the manuscript sources of each passage in the reconstructed text as unobtrusively as possible. I have adopted the versification of Charles for the Geniza fragments[19] and the second Mt. Athos Greek passage, which passage, because of its overlap with the Geniza text, was the only one from the Mt. Athos manuscript which Charles recognized as belonging to *Aramaic Levi*. Greek and Aramaic fragments with no overlap with the Geniza text are versified independently with Roman numerals. The first Mt. Athos Greek passage is numbered as §§i-xix, following Milik's enumeration but with §i beginning slightly

16. Greenfield, "The Words of Levi Son of Jacob."
17. Tromp, "Two References."
18. Kugel, "Levi's Elevation," 34-36; idem, *Ladder of Jacob*, 149-50.
19. For the Manchester fragment see n. 21 below.

earlier to include the single word surviving in the overlapping 4QLevi[b] ar frag. 2.1. The end of the latter fragment is numbered as §xx. (The overlap of the Mt. Athos passage with the Qumran manuscript confirms that the former is part of *Aramaic Levi*.) The order of §§i-xx is secure. Two other Qumran fragments (4QLevi[b] ar frags. 3-4 [which form a unit] and 1QLevi ar frag. 1) seem to belong in the lacuna between §xx and §4 (the beginning of Bodleian col. a). I have numbered them as §§xxi and xxii. Several Qumran fragments may continue the document beyond the last text preserved in the Geniza manuscript. These are 4QLevi[a] ar frag. 3-5 (§§ci-ciii) and 4QLevi[d] ar frag. 3 (§civ). Their order and placement here are plausible but uncertain. Numerous other small fragments survive in the Qumran manuscripts, but their placement is extremely uncertain and I have not included them in this translation, since they add nothing significant to our understanding of the text. I have also not included the third addition to the Mt. Athos manuscript in the translation (see above under Manuscripts and Versions), but I have translated it in n. 2 of this Introduction.

In the translation I have assigned each surviving manuscript a font or a particular emphasis or effect, such as italics or underscoring, as follows.[20]

The Cairo Geniza manuscript—sans serif font
All other material not in the Geniza manuscript — regular serif font
The Greek Mt. Athos manuscript — regular italic. (Note that the Greek text is written in two different fonts: in a regular serif font when on its own and in a sans serif font when the text overlaps with the Geniza manuscript.)
4QLevi[a] ar — dotted underscoring
4QLevi[b] ar — regular underscoring
4QLevi[c] ar — **boldface**
4QLevi[d] ar — ***italic boldface***
4QLevi[e] ar — SMALL CAPITALS
4QLevi[f] ar — thick underscoring
1QLevi ar — wavy underscoring
The Syriac quotation — double underscoring

The following is a concord between the major verse divisions of *Aramaic Levi*.

Davila	**Kugler**	**Drawnell**	**Greenfield et al.**
1-2[21]	1-2	1c-2	1:1-3
3	3	3	2:1
–	–	–	2:2-3 (1QLevi ar frag. 8)
i-ii	s1-s2	1a1-1a2	2:4-5
iii-ixa	s3-s9a	1a3-1a9a	3:1-7
ixb	s9b	1a9b	3:8
x-xix	s10-s19	1a10-1a19	3:9-18
xx	s20-s21	1b	4:1-6

20. The normal convention in this collection is to use italics to indicate verbatim scriptural quotations, but since no such quotations are found in *Aramaic Levi*, italics instead indicate the text of the Greek manuscript from Mt. Athos.

21. The two passages in the Manchester fragment recto and verso come between my 2 and 3 but, following Bohak, I have not assigned them verse numbers.

Davila	Kugler	Drawnell	Greenfield et al.
xxi	s22-s27	3a	unplaced fragment
–	–	3b (4QLevi[a] frag 5)	–
xxii	–	3c	4:7
–	–	–	4:8 (1QLevi ar frag. 7 i)
4-7a	4-7a	4-7a	4:9-12
7b	7b	7b	4:13
8	8	8	5:1
9	9	9	5:2-4
10	10	10	5:5
11-13a	11-13a	11-13a	5:6-8
13b-14	13b-14	13b-14	6:1
15-18	15-18	15-18	6:2-5
19-25a	19-25a	19-25a	7:1-7
25b-31	25b-31	25b-31	8:1-7
32-44	32-43a	32-43a	9:1-12
44-46a	43b-46a	43-46a	9:13-16
46b-47	46b-47	46b-47	9:17-18
48-61	48-61	48-61	10:1-14
62-72	62-72	62-72	11:1-11
73-81	73-81	73-81	12:1-9
82	82	82	13:1
83-84	83-84	83-84	13:2
85-87	85-87	85-87	13:3
88-90a	88-90a	88-90a	13:4-6
90b-91a	90b-91a	90b-91a	13:7
91b	91b	91b	13:8
91c-92	91c-92	91c-92	13:9
93-94	93-94	93-94	13:10
95a	95a	95a	13:11
95b-96a	95b-96a	94b-96a	13:12
96b-97a	96b-97a	96b-97a	13:13
97b	97b	97b	13:14
98	98	98	13:15
99a	99	99a	13:16a
99b-100a	100	99b-100a	13:16b
100b	101	100b	13:16c
ci	102	101	unplaced fragment
cii	103-105	102	unplaced fragment
ciii	106	103	unplaced fragment
civ	–	104	unplaced fragment

Bibliography

Barthélemy, D., and J. T. Milik. "Testament de Lévi." Pages 87-91 and plate xvii in *Qumran Cave I*. DJD 1. Oxford: Clarendon, 1955. (The official edition of 1QLevi ar.)

Bohak, Gideon. "A New Geniza Fragment of the Aramaic Levi Document." *Tarbiz* (Heb.) (forthcoming).

Charles, R. H. *The Greek Versions of the Testaments of the Twelve Patriarchs.* Oxford: Clarendon, 1908. (*Aramaic Levi* is covered on pp. 245-56.)

Drawnell, Henryk. *An Aramaic Wisdom Text from Qumran: A New Interpretation of the Levi Document.* JSJSup 86. Leiden: Brill, 2004. (See here for additional bibliography.)

Greenfield, Jonas C. "The Words of Levi Son of Jacob in Damascus Document IV, 15-19." *RevQ* 13/49-52 (1988): 319-22.

Greenfield, Jonas C., Michael E. Stone, and Esther Eshel. *The Aramaic Levi Document: Edition, Translation, Commentary.* SVTP 19. Leiden: Brill, 2004. (See here for additional bibliography.)

Himmelfarb, Martha. "Earthly Sacrifice and Heavenly Incense: The Law of the Priesthood in *Aramaic Levi* and *Jubilees*." In *Heavenly Realms and Earthly Realities in Late Antique Religions*, 103-22. Edited by Ra'anan S. Boustan and Annette Yoshiko Reed. Cambridge, England: Cambridge University Press, 2004.

__________. *Midrash Vayyisa'u* in this volume, pp. 143-59.

Hollander, H. W., and M. de Jonge. *The Testaments of the Twelve Patriarchs: A Commentary.* SVTP 8. Leiden: Brill, 1985. (*Aramaic Levi* is translated on pp. 457-69.)

Jonge, M. de. *Pseudepigrapha of the Old Testament as Part of Christian Literature: The Case of the Testaments of the Twelve Patriarchs and the Greek Life of Adam and Eve.* SVTP 18. Leiden: Brill, 2003.

__________. *The Testaments of the Twelve Patriarchs: A Study of Their Text, Composition and Origin.* 2nd ed. Theologische Bibliotheek 25. Assen/Amsterdam: Van Gorcum, 1975.

__________ (ed.). *Studies on the Testaments of the Twelve Patriarchs: Text and Interpretation.* SVTP 3. Leiden: Brill, 1975.

Jonge, M. de, et al. *The Testaments of the Twelve Patriarchs: A Critical Edition of the Greek Text.* PVTG 1. Leiden: Brill, 1978.

Kugel, James. *The Ladder of Jacob: Ancient Interpretations of the Biblical Story of Jacob and His Children.* Princeton, N.J.: Princeton University Press, 2006. (See chapter 5, "How Levi Became a Priest," which is a revised version of his article below.)

__________. "Levi's Elevation to the Priesthood in Second Temple Writings." *HTR* 86 (1993): 1-64.

Kugler, Robert A. *From Patriarch to Priest: The Levi-Priestly Tradition from* Aramaic Levi *to* Testament of Levi. SBLEJL 9. Atlanta, Ga.: Scholars Press, 1996.

__________. "Some Further Evidence for the Samaritan Provenance of *Aramaic Levi* (*1QTestLevi; 4QTestLevi*)." *RevQ* 17/65-58 (1996): 351-58.

Milik, J. T. "Le Testament de Lévi in Araméen." *RB* 62 (1955): 398-406.

Puech, Émile. "Le *Testament de Lévi* en Araméen de la Geniza du Caire." *RevQ* 20/80 (2002): 509-56.

Schiffman, Lawrence H. "Sacrificial Halakhah in the Fragments of the *Aramaic Levi Document* from Qumran, the Cairo Geniza, and Mt. Athos Monastery." In *Reworking the Bible: Apocryphal and Related Texts at Qumran*, 177-202. Edited by Esther G. Chazon et al. STDJ 58. Leiden: Brill, 2005.

Stone, M. E., and J. C. Greenfield. "Aramaic Levi Documents." Pages 1-72 and plates i-iv in *Qumran Cave 4 XVII Parabiblical Texts, Part 3*. Ed. George Brooke et al. Oxford: Clarendon, 1996. (The official edition of 4QLevi$^{a\text{-}f}$ ar.)

Tromp, Johannes. "Two References to a Levi Document in an Epistle of Ammonas." *NovT* 39 (1997): 235-47.

Aramaic Levi

Vengeance on the Shechemites

1(Cambridge col. a)[a] ... she has defiled the s[ons of] ... that all ... to do according to the law of al[l] ... Jacob my father and Re[uben my brother ...] and we said to them ... they wish for our daughter and that we all become br[others] and companions. 2Circumcise the foreskin of your flesh and you will appear like us and you will be sealed like us with circumcision of [righteo]usness ... and we will be to you

T. Levi 6:3; Rom 4:11
Gen 34:13-16

(Manchester recto)[b] ... know that they have been made impure [by] their [s]ons ... them(?) and they will not leave them alone until [all of them] perish. [Th]en ... [Ha]mor. And they spoke with words of ... [the m]en of their city ... them to circumcise and to do it ... to be sons-in-law[c] to them ... them and to lead them astray[d] ... foreskin of [their flesh] ... and I reckoned

Jub. 30:4-5
Gen 34:20-23
Jub. 30:3 | *T. Levi* 6:3?

(Manchester verso)[e] ... and I ... in secret and let us kill all the so[ns of] Shechem, for on this day God has given ... and at this time God has consigned all of them into [our] hand to kill them and to make ... s[eed](?) of truth. Then answered ... [Simeon] my brother, very zealous from ... Get up, come in, in [your] wisdom ... and take my sword and yours ... and we will accomplish judgm[ent] ... Shechem and God(?) ...

Gen 34:25
T. Levi 6:3
T. Levi 5:3?
Jub. 30:6

More on Shechem

3(Cambridge col. b)[f] ... my brothers in every time ... who were in Shechem ... my brother(s) and he revealed this[g] ... in Shechem and whatever ...

Gen 37:12-13?; *T. Levi* 2:1-2; 5:3-4?; *Jub.* 34:1-9?

---

a. The first 14 lines (of 23 total) of Cambridge col. a are missing. An indeterminate number of preceding columns are probably also missing.

b. Cambridge col. a ends a column and Manchester recto begins the immediately following column, the first 3 lines of which are virtually entirely lost. The last 10 lines (i.e., nearly half) of this column are also missing.

c. "sons-in-law"; or "bridegrooms"

d. "to lead them astray"; or "to neglect/abandon them"

e. Manchester verso is the reverse side of the Manchester recto fragment and contains the immediately following column, the first 2 lines of which are virtually entirely lost, as are its last 10 lines.

f. Cambridge col. b is the recto side of Cambridge col. a. It contains the column that followed immediately after Manchester verso and its first 14 lines are completely lost.

g. "he revealed this"; or "Dan revealed"

[do]ers of violence. And Judah told them that I and Simeon my brother went to j[oi]n Reuben our brother, who was eas[t of As]her, and Judah leapt forward [to
Gen 37:26? le]ave the sheep.[a]

The Prayer and Ablutions of Levi[b]

[i](4QLevi[b] ar frags. 1.1–2.10) ... this ... (Mt. Athos Greek fragment 1) *Then I*
Zech 3:4-5 *washed my clothes and purified them in pure water* [ii]*and I washed completely in*
Lev 15:13; *T. Levi* 8:5; *running water and I made all my paths straight.* [iii]*Then I raised my eyes and my*
m. Miqw. 1.8 *face to heaven and I opened my mouth and spoke* [iv]*and I spread out the fingers*
Ps 28:2; 134:2; Isa *of my hands and my hands to the truth before the sanctuary.*[c] *And I prayed and*
1:15-17; *Jub.* 25:11; *Sib.* *I said:* [v]*O Lord, You know all hearts, and You alone understand*[d] *all thoughts of*
Or. 4:162-70 | *T. Levi* *insights.* [vi]*And now my children are with me. And give me all the ways of truth.*
2:4; 4:2-6 [vii]*Put far from me, O Lord, the unrighteous spirit and wicked thought*[e] *and turn*
sexual immorality and insolence away from me. [viii]*Let there be revealed to me,*
Master, the holy spirit, and give me counsel and wisdom and knowledge and power
Prov 8:12-14; Isa 11:2 [ix]*to do the things pleasing to You and to find grace*[f] *before You and to praise Your*
words with me, O Lord.[g] [x]*And let no satan dominate me to make me stray from*
Ps 119:133; Rev 12:9 *Your path.* [xi]*And have mercy on me*[h] *and bring me near to be Your slave and to*
minister to You well. [xii]*Let Your peace be a wall around me and let the shade of*
Your power shelter me from all harm. [xiii]*Deliver (me), therefore indeed, and oblit-*
erate lawlessness from under heaven and terminate lawlessness from the face of the
1 En. 10:20 *earth.* [xiv]*Purify my heart, Master, from all impurity and may I myself be raised up*
to You[i] [xv]*and do not turn Your face away from the son of Your servant Jacob. You,*
O Lord, blessed Abraham my father and Sarah my mother, [xvi]*and You promised to*
Gen 12:2-3, 7; 13:15; *give them a righteous seed, blessed forever.* [xvii]*And listen and let the voice of*[j] *Your*
15:18; 17:16; 18:10; *servant Levi be near to You,* [xviii]*and make me and my sons participate in Your*
28:14; Gal 3:16 *words so as to accomplish true judgment to all the eternal generations,* [xix]*and do*
Deut 33:10; Mal 2:4, 6; *not withdraw the son of Your servant from*[k] *Your face for all the days of eternity.*
T. Levi 18:2

Levi's (First?) Vision

T. Levi 2:3, 5-10; 3:1-5; *1 En.* 13:7-9

[xx]*And I became silent while still praying.*[1] ... (4QLevi[b] ar frag. 2.11-18) Then I set out in ... to my father Jacob and whe[n] ... from Abel Mayyin. Then ... I lay down

---

a. Eight columns of 23 lines each are missing between the end of Cambridge col. b and Bodleian col. a.

b. It is possible that the prayer and ablution of Levi and the visionary material in 4QLevi[b] ar frag. 2 should go before Cambridge col. a, with an indeterminate amount of lost material preceding this episode.

c. "*sanctuary*"; or "*holy ones*"

d. "*understand*"; 4QLevi[b] "know"

e. Emending from "*of thoughts of the wicked ones*"

f. "*grace*"; 4QLevi[b] ar "Your grace"

g. "*and to praise ... Lord*"; 4QLevi[b] ar omits this phrase and has a different phrase that included the words "of the fair and of the good before You"

h. "*on me*"; 4QLevi[b] ar adds "O Lord"

i. "*to you*"; 4QLevi[b] ar may have read "to your eyes"

j. "*the voice*"; 4QLevi[b] ar "the prayer"

k. "*from*"; 4QLevi[b] ar adds "b[efore]"

l. Mt. Athos Greek fragment 1 ends here.

and I myself stayed ... Then I was shown a vision ... in a vision of visions, and I saw the hea[vens] ... under me, high until it clung to the heave[ns] ... to me the gates of heaven and a single angel ...

Levi's (Second?) Vision

T. Levi 8:1; *Jub.* 30:5-17?; 32:1 — Lev 21:9

[xxi](4QLevi[b] ar frags. 3-4[a]) ... and now ... men ... a woman, and she profaned her name and the name of her father ... with regret and every [vir]gin ... who corrupted her name and the name of her ancestors and brought shame to all her brothers ... her father. And the name of her shame is not blotted out from all her people forever ... to all generations of eternity and ... holy ones of the people ... tablet(?) ... holy tithe, an offering to God from[b]

[xxii](1QLevi ar frag. 1) ... since they will be three ... the kingdom of the priesthood is greater than the kingdom of [the sword (?)] ...

Exod 19:6; *T. Levi* 8:11?; *T. Jud.* 21:2-4?

4(Bodleian col. a) ... peace and everything desirable of the first fruits of the
entire earth for food, and to the kingdom of the sword belong fighting and
(1QLevi ar) w**ar** and butchery and exertion and shrieking and killing and famine. 5At times it shall eat and at times it shall go hungry, at times **it shall labor**
and at times it shall rest, at times it shall sleep and at times the sleep of the
eye shall flee. 6Now see for yourself (4QLevi[c] ar 1) h**ow we have increased**[c]
you more than all[d] and how we have given you the greatness[e] of **eternal**
peace.
7**And** their seven glided away from me and **I woke from my sleep. Then** I
said, "This was a vision." And so I was astonished that there should be to me[f]
any vision and **I** concealed **this also in my heart and** I did **not** reveal it **to**
anyone.

Num 18:13; *T. Levi* 8:16 — *1 En.* 91:12 — Matt 26:52 — Exod 40:15; *T. Levi* 8:3-4 — *T. Levi* 8:2; *1 En.* 20:1-8 — *T. Levi* 8:18; *Jub.* 32:1-2 — *T. Levi* 8:19; 1QapGen 6.12; Luke 2:19

Jacob Ordains Levi as Priest

8And we went in to my father, Isaac, and he also thus [blessed] me. 9Then
(1QLevi ar frag. 4) wh**en** Ja]**cob** [**my father**] **was tith[ing]** everything that he
had, according to his vow, ... I was first at the head of the [priesth]o**od and**
to me of all[g] **his sons he gave** the sacrificial gift of the tit[he] to God, and
he clothed me with the vestment of the priesthood and ordained me[h] and I
became a priest to the Go**d of eternity**[i]. And I offered all his offerings and I

T. Levi 9:1-3; *Jub.* 31:4-32 — Gen 28:20-22; *T. Levi* 9:4; *Jub.* 27:27; 32:2 — Num 18:21-28 — Lev 8:5-9; *T. Levi* 8:2 — Exod 28:40-41; *T. Levi* 8:10 — *Jub.* 32:1

---

a. The placement of 4QLevi[b] ar frags. 3-4 and 1QLevi ar frag. 1 at this point in the narrative is plausible but conjectural. It is possible that §§1-3 should be placed in this lacuna as well. See the Introduction for discussion. Note also that if the third addition to the Mt. Athos manuscript (translated in n. 2 of the Introduction) is part of *Aramaic Levi*, it may belong at this point in the narrative as well.

b. "to God from"; or, with a different reading of the Aramaic letters, "for teaching"

c. "we have increased"; 4QLevi[c] ar "**I have favored**"

d. "all"; 4QLevi[c] ar adds "**fle[sh]**"

e. "greatness"—This word could also be translated "anointing"

f. "to me"—Emending from "to him"

g. "all" is missing in 4QLevi[c] ar.

h. "ordained me"—Literally "filled my hands"

i. "of eternity"—Probably with 4QLevi[c] ar (the reading is damaged). It appears that this

Lev 9:22 blessed my father in his lifetime and I blessed my brothers. 10Then all of them
blessed me and also (my) father blessed me and I finished (Bodleian col. b)
offering his offerings at Bethel.[a]

Isaac Instructs Levi

Gen 35:27 | *Jub.* 29:19; 11(Mt. Athos Greek frag. 2) *And we went from Bethel and we camped at the for-*
T. Levi 9:5; *Jub.* 33:21 *tress of Abraham our father with Isaac our father. 12And Isaac our father saw*[b] *all*
Jub. 33:23 *of us and he blessed us and he rejoiced. 13And when he knew that I was a priest of*
Gen 14:18-20 God Most High,[c] *Lord of heaven, he began* to instruct me and[d] *teach me the law*
Deut 18:3; *T. Levi* 9:7 *of the priesthood. And he said* to me,[e] 14*Levi, guard yourself,* my son, my son,[f]
Aramaic Levi xiv *from all impurity* and from all sin.[g] *Your law is greater than all flesh. 15And now,*
my son,[h] *I will show you the true law and I will not conceal any matter from you*
to *teach you* the law of the priesthood.[i]

16"First,[j] *guard yourself,* my son,[k] *from all wantonness and impurity and from*
T. Levi 9:8-10 *all sexual immorality. 17And as for you,*[l] *take for yourself* a wife[m] *from* my clan[n]
Gen 24:38 | Gen 28:1; *and do not desecrate your seed with* prostitutes.[o] *Behold, you are*[p] *a holy seed*
Lev 21:7, 14-15 *and your seed is holy,* just like *the holy place,*[q] *since* you are[r] *called a holy priest*
for all the seed of Abraham. 18You are near to [Go]d a[nd] near to all[s] *His holy*
1QSb iv 22-28 *ones.* Now[t] *[be wort]hy in your flesh from all impurity of every man.*

19(Bodleian col. c) *And when you stand to enter the house of God, bathe in*
T. Levi 9:11-14; *water and then put on the priestly vestment. 20And when you are clothed, wash*
Jub. 21:6-18 *your hands and your feet once again before you approach the altar* at all.[u] 21[v]*And*
Exod 30:19-21 *when you take (?) to offer all that is proper to take to the altar, wash your hands*
Jub. 21:16 *and your feet once again, 22and make the offering,*[w] (4QLevi[f] ar frags. 2-5i-6i)

---

reading was written over the reading "**Most High**" (cf. Gen 14:18) as a correction in the Geniza manuscript.

a. The second Mt. Athos Greek fragment begins with §11.
b. "*saw*"—Emending the Geniza Aramaic "he" to read with the Greek
c. "God Most High"; Greek "*the Lord*"
d. "to instruct me and"; Greek omits
e. "to me"; Greek omits
f. "my son, my son"; Greek "*child*." Or perhaps translate the Aramaic as "Be pure, my son."
g. "and from all sin"; Greek omits
h. "my son"; Greek omits
i. "to *teach you* the law of the priesthood"; Greek "*I will teach you*"
j. "First"; Greek omits
k. "my son"; Greek omits
l. "And as for you"; Greek adds "*first*,"
m. "a wife"; Greek omits
n. "my clan"; Greek "*the seed*"
o. "prostitutes"; Greek reads "*many apart from (the) seed*"
p. "*Behold, you are*"; Greek adds "*from*"
q. "just like *the holy place*"; Greek reads "*and the seed of the holy place is yours*"
r. "you are"; Greek "*he is*"
s. "all"; Greek omits
t. "Now"; Greek omits
u. "at all" (the translation of the Aramaic is unclear); Greek "*to offer a holocaust*"
v. 4QLevi[d] ar frag. 1 may preserve a very small amount of a variant text of §§21-25.
w. "*make the offering*"; Greek adds "*first*"

splitting logs, and examine them first for worms.[a] And then lift them up, for — Lev 1:7; *Jub.* 21:13;
like so did I see Abraham my father taking pains. [23]From all[b] *twelve kinds of*[c] — *m. Mid* 2:5
wood, he said to me that it is proper to take of them *to the altar,*[d] *the scent of* — Gen 22:3
whose smoke rises sweetly. [24]*And these are their names: cedar, juniper, almond,* — Lev 1:9
fir, acacia, pine, cypress, fig,[e] *and oleaster, laurel, myrtle,* (4QLevi[e] frag. 1) *and*
asphalathos.[f] [25]*These are* the ones that *he said to me* it is fitting to lift up of them[g]
be[nea]th the *holocaust on the altar*. And when y[ou] li[ft up] any of these woods — *T. Levi* 9:12; *Jub.*
onto[h] the altar[i] *and the fire begins to kindle* (Bodleian col. d) *them,* and behold,[j] — 21:12-14
then you shall begin (4QLevi[d] ar frag. 2) *to sprin**kle** the blood on the sides of the*
altar. [26]*And again, wash your hands and* **your feet of** *the blood and begin to lift* — *Jub.* 21:7 | *Jub.* 21:16
up the salted limbs. [27]*And lift up* **the head**[k] *first and cover it with abdominal* **fat**
— ***and there should not be seen*** on it *the blood* of the freewill offering of the
ox.[l] [28]*And after it, its neck;* ***and after*** *its neck, its* ***forelegs;***[m] *and after its forelegs,*
*the breast with the (rack of) ribs; and aft****er*** this,[n] ***the thighs*** *with*[o] ***the spinal col-***
um*n of the loins; and after the thighs, the back legs was****hed with the entrails;***
[29]***and all of th****em salted with salt such as is proper for th****em****, as* ***much as they***
require*.* [30]***And af****ter this, fine meal mixed with oil.* ***And after* it all,**[p] *libate* ***wine*** — Ezek 43:24; *T. Levi*
and burn incense over them and thus[q] *let* ***your actions***[r] ***be in or****der and all your* — 9:13-14; *Jub.* 21:11; Lev 2:1
offerings [accepta]ble as a soothing odor before God[s] *Most High.* — Num 15:1-9; *Jub.* 21:7

[31]*A[nd everything that] you do, do it in order, d[o it by measure], and by*
weight. You shall not add anything that is not [proper] and you shall not leave — Lev 19:35-36; Ezek
out of reckoning what is proper.[t] *Of the wo[od] proper*[u] *for offering for all that* — 45:10; 1 Chr 23:24, 29

---

a. "worms"; Greek reads "*all defilement*"

b. "And then ... all"; Greek omits

c. "*kinds of*"; 4QLevi[f] ar omits

d. "that it is proper to take of them to the altar"; Greek reads "*Offer (them)* (imperative) *on the altar,*"

e. "*fig*"—The name of the tree in 4QLevi[f] ar is unidentified and perhaps damaged.

f. The identification of some of these trees is uncertain. Only eleven are given in the Greek text.

g. "it is fitting ... of them"; Greek reads "*for you to lift up/offer up*"

h. "onto"; 4QLevi[f] ar "to"

i. "And when ... altar"; Greek omits

j. "and behold"; Greek omits

k. Reading with the Greek. The Geniza Aramaic is corrupt and meaningless. 1QLevi ar frag. 45 may also preserve the words "salted" and "head" in 26-27.

l. "on it ... the ox"; Greek "*the blood on its head.*" Perhaps emend the phrase "freewill offering of the ox" to read "slaughtered ox."

m. "***and after*** *its neck, its* ***forelegs***"; 4QLevi[d] ar "***and after them the forelegs***"

n. "*and after* this"; emended from Aramaic "and after the forelegs"; Greek "*and after these*"; 4QLevi[d] ar "[aft]***er them***"

o. "*with*" Geniza and Greek; 4QLevi[d] ar "***and***"

p. "***it all***" Geniza and 4QLevi[d] ar; Greek "*these things*"

q. "thus"; Greek omits

r. "***actions***"; 4QLevi[d] ar "***action***" (singular)

s. "God"; Greek "*the Lord*"

t. "*what is proper*"—Following this phrase, Greek has three words that seem to be a corruption

u. "proper"—Emending the meaningless Aramaic to read with the Greek

ascends the altar: [32]*for the mature*[a] *bull a talent of wood*[b] *for it by weight. And if the fat is offered by itself, six minas, and if it is a second bull*[c] *that is offered,*[d] *fifty minas; and with reference to its fat only, five minas;* [33]*and for an unblemished calf, forty minas.* [34]*And if a ram of sheep or a he-goat of goats is what is being offered, for this thirty minas and for the fat three minas.* [35]*And if a lamb of sheep or a kid of goats, twenty minas, and for the fat two minas.* [36]*And if a year-old unblemished lamb or kid of goats, fifteen minas, and for the fat, one mina and a half.* [37]*And produce*[e] *salt for the large bull to salt its meat, and offer (it) on the altar. A seah is fitting for the bull; and in a case in which there is a superabundance of salt, salt the skin with it.* [38]*And for the second bull, five-sixths of a seah; and of the calf, two-thirds of a seah;* [39]*and for the ram, half of a seah and the same for the he-goat;* [40]*and for the lamb and the kid, a third of a seah. And fine wheaten flour fitting for them:* [41]*for the mature bull and the second bull and the calf, a seah of fine wheaten flour;* [42]*and for the ram and the he-goat, two parts of a seah; and for the lamb and the kid of goats, the third part of the seah. And the oil:* [43]*and a fourth of a seah for the bull, mixed with this fine wheaten flour;* [44]*and for the ram, a sixth of a seah; and for the lamb, an eighth of a seah; {and of a lamb}*[f] *also wine according to the measure of the oil for the bull and the ram and the kid libate as a drink offering.* [45]*Six shekels of frankincense for the bull and half that much for the ram and a third of it for the kid. And all the mixed fine wheaten flour,* [46]*which you shall offer alone, not on fat, there shall be poured out on it a weight(?) of frankincense of two shekels. A third of a seah is a third of an ephah,* [47]*and two-thirds of a bath, and the weight of a mina is fifty of shekels, and a quarter of a shekel is the*
T. Levi 10:1-5 *weight of four thermoi.*[g] *Let the shekel be about sixteen thermoi and of one weight.* [48]*And now, my child, hear my words and hearken to my commands and do not let these words withdraw from your heart in all your days, for you are a holy priest of the Lord,* [49]*and all your seed shall be priests. And so command your sons that they should do according to this law as I have shown you.* [50]*For so father Abraham commanded me to do and to command my sons.*

[51]*And now, child, I rejoice that you have been chosen for holy priesthood and to offer sacrifice to the Lord Most High, as is fitting to do according to this that*
Deut 21:5; *T. Reub.* 6:8 *has been commanded.* [52]*When you undertake to carry out a sacrifice of any flesh before the Lord, accept thus according to the reckoning of the wood, as I command you, and the salt and the fine wheaten flour and the wine and the frankincense accept also from their hands concerning all flocks.* [53]*And every hour wash (your) hands and feet when you go to the altar. And when you go out of the sanctuary,*

a. The Greek word translated "*mature*" in this passage (in accordance with the Aramaic original) can also mean "*unblemished,*" and the latter meaning seems to fit the context better in §§33 and 36, but not in §41. Unfortunately the Aramaic of the last three passages is lost.

b. "*a talent of wood*"; Greek adds "*is fitting*"

c. "*a second bull*"; reading with the Greek. The Geniza Aramaic reads "an ox of bulls"

d. §§32b-65 is preserved only in the Greek

e. "*produce*"—A conjectural translation of a corrupt word

f. "*and of a lamb*" appears to be a corrupt reading that makes no sense in context.

g. "*thermoi*"—A unit of measure whose identification remains very unclear. Elements of this list of measures seem to be corrupt: there were three seahs to an ephah and a bath was equivalent to an ephah. See Greenfield, Stone, Eshel, *Aramaic Levi Document*, 44.

do not let any of the blood touch your robe; do not lay hold of it[a] *on the same day.* 54 *And wash (your) hands and feet completely of all flesh* 55 *and let there not be seen on you any blood or any life, for the blood is life in the flesh.* 56 *And if in the house you eat some meat for yourself,*[b] *cover its blood with earth first, before you eat any of the meat and do not any longer be eating in proximity to the blood.* 57 *For thus did my father Abraham command me, because he found it so in the writing of the Book of Noah concerning the blood.* 58 *And now as to you, beloved child, I say, you are beloved to your father and a holy one of the Lord Most High and you shall be beloved over all your brothers.* 59 *By your seed shall one be blessed on the earth, and your seed shall be preserved for all the ages in the Book of Remembrance of Life,* 60 *and your name and the name of your seed shall not be erased for the ages.* 61 *And now, child, Levi, blessed shall your seed be on earth for the generations of the ages.*

Jub. 7:30
Lev 17:11, 14; Deut 12:23; *Jub.* 21:17
Lev 17:13; Deut 12:24; *Jub.* 7:30-31
Jub. 10:13; 21:10; 1*QApGen ar* 29
Exod 32:32-33; Ps 69:28; Mal 3:16; Rev 3:5; 20:12
Jub. 30:18; 31:13

Levi Tells the Rest of His Life Story

62 *And when four weeks were fulfilled for me with regard to the years of my life, in the twenty-eighth year*[c] *I took a wife for myself from the kin of Abraham my father: Milcah, daughter of Bethuel, son of Laban, brother of my mother.*[d] 63 *And when she had become pregnant by me, she gave birth to a first son and I called his name Gershon, for I said that my seed shall be a sojourner in the land where I was born; we are sojourners like this one in the land reckoned as ours.* 64 *And concerning the little boy — I myself saw in my vision that he and his seed shall be expelled from the high priesthood <his seed shall be>.*[e] 65 *I was thirty years old in my life when he was born, and he was born in the tenth month at the setting of the sun.* 66 (Cambridge col. c) *[And it came] about according to [the fitting, proper] tim[e of women* that I was with he]r [and *she became pregn]ant again [by me and she bore* to me] another [son].[f] *[And] I*[g] *[called[his name [Qahat*[h] 67 *and]*[i] *I [saw] that the assembly of all [the people] [would b]e his [and that] the great high priesthood [of all Is]rael would be his.*[j] 68 *In the [th]irty-fourth year* of my life[k] *he was born, in the fi[rst] month [on the fi]rst of [the] mon[th], with the rising of [the] sun.*

69 *And I was wi[th her] yet again*[l] *and she bore me a third son and I called his*

T. Levi 11:1; *Jub.* 34:20
Gen 46:11; Exod 6:16; Num 3:17; 1 Chr 6:1, 16
Gen 15:13; *T. Levi* 11:2
Judg 18:30?
Gen 46:11; 49:10; Exod 6:16; Num 3:17; 1 Chr 6:1, 16; *T. Levi* 11:4-6
4Q559 3 2

---

a. "*do not lay hold of it*"—The meaning of the phrase is unclear

b. "*you eat some meat for yourself*"—The text of this phrase seems to be corrupt

c. The MS reads "*years*"

d. According to Genesis, Milcah was the wife of Nahor and mother of Bethuel. Bethuel in turn was the father of Laban and Rebekah (cf. Gen 24:24, 29). *Aramaic Levi* seems to assume that the names were reused by Laban's son and granddaughter.

e. "*his seed shall be*" seems to be a corruption in the Greek

f. "[And it came] about ... another [son]"; Greek "*And becoming pregnant again she gave birth by me according to the fitting, proper time of women.*"

g. "I"; Greek "*she*"

h. or "Kohath"

i. "[Qahat and]"; Greek adds "*when he was born*"

j. "would be his"; Greek adds "*He and his seed shall be ruler of kings, a priesthood of Israel*" (cf. Exod 19:6)

k. "of my life"; Greek omits

l. "yet again"; Greek "*again, and she became pregnant*"

Gen 46:11; Exod 6:16; Num 3:17; 1 Chr 6:1, 16; *T. Levi* 11:7

name Merari, because it was bitter to me concerning him[a] very much, because (4QLevi[e] ar frags. 2-3 i)[b] when he was born he was on the point of death and it was very bitter to me concerning him, inasmuch as he was about to die. And I requested and made supplication concerning him, and it was utter bitterness. 70In the fortieth year of my life she gave birth in the thir[d][c] month. 71And once more I was with her yet again and she became pregnant and she bore me a daughter and I assigned (her) the name Jochebed. [I] sai[d] as she was born to me, "For value she was born to me, for the glory of Israel." 72In the sixty-fourth year of my life she was born, on the first (day) of the seventh month after (Cambridge col. d) [He] br[ought us int]o Egypt.

Exod 6:20; Num 26:59

T. Levi 11:8

73In the sixtee[nth] year we [e]ntered into the land of Egypt and to my sons ... the daughters of my brother at the time corresponding to their ages ... to them sons. 74The name of the sons of Gershon: L[ibni and]Shimi. And the name of the sons of Q[a]h[a]t: [Am]ram, Yizhar, Hebron, and Uzziel. [And the nam]e of the sons of Merari: Mahli and Mushi.

Exod 6:17; Num 3:18; 1 Chr 6:17; *T. Levi* 12:1

Exod 6:18; Num 3:19; 1 Chr 6:18; *T. Levi* 12:2

75And Amram took my daughter Jochebed for himself as wife while I was alive, in the ninety-four[th] year of my life. 76And I called Amram's name "Amram" when he was born, because I said when he was born, "This one shall lead[d] the people from the land of E[g]ypt." [T]hus [his name] is ca[ll]ed the lifted-up [people]. 77On one and the same day, behold, he (and) Jochebed my daughter [were] bor[n].

Exod 6:19; Num 3:20; 1 Chr 6:19; *T. Levi* 12:3

Exod 6:20; Num 26:59; *T. Levi* 12:4

78(Syriac Fragment[e]) At age eighteen[f] years, I was brought into[g] the land of Canaan, and when I was eighteen years old I killed Sh[echem] and I annihilated the doers of violence. 79And at age nineteen years I became a priest and at age twenty-eight years I married me a wife. 80And I was forty-eight years old when we were brought into[h] the land of Egypt and I lived eighty-nine[i] years in Egyp[t]. 81(Cambridge col. e) And all the days of my life[j] are a [hu]ndred th[irty]-seven years. And I have seen th[ird]-(generation) sons and am not yet dead.

Gen 33-34; 49:5; *T. Levi* 12:5

Gen 50:23

Levi Teaches His Sons about Wisdom

82And in the [one-hundred-eig]hteenth y[ear] of my life, the y[ear] (4QLevi[a] ar i 1-20) in which Joseph my brother died, I called to [my] so[ns and] to their

Gen 50:26; *T. Levi* 12:5

---

a. The second Greek fragment from Mt. Athos ends partway through §69.

b. The Aramaic fragment 4QLevi[e] ar 2-3 i seems to have preserved a variant, shorter version of the text of §§69-72.

c. "thir[d]"; 4QLevi[e] ar reads a different number, perhaps either "[fou]rth," [seve]nth," or "[ni]nth."

d. "shall lead"—this word seems to have been written across the word "shall lift up" in the Geniza manuscript.

e. The Syriac fragment is a quotation that is introduced with the following: "Again, some of the life of Levi; the history that he reveals from his Testament. Levi says in his Testament:"

f. "[eig]hteen"; the Syriac and *T. Levi* 12:5 read "eight"

g. "I was brought into"; Syriac "I entered"

h. "we were brought into"; Syriac "I entered"

i. "eighty-nine"; Syriac "ninety"

j. "the days of my life"; Syriac "my years"

sons and I began to tell them my last wishes[a]—everything that was in my heart. [83]I answered and said to my sons, [Hear] the word of Levi your father and heed the last wishes of the one cherished by God. [84]I am telling you my last wishes, my sons, and I am revealing the truth to you, my dear ones. [85]The chiefmost of your works[b] should be the truth, and forev[e]r l[e]t it reside with you. [If] y[ou so]w righteousness and [86]truth, you shall bring in a blessed and good crop. [87]He who sows what is good brings in what is good, and he who sows evil, his seed returns upon him. [88]And now my sons,[c] teach your sons book, tradition, (and) wisdom and let wisdom[d] be with you for eternal honor. [89]He who teaches wisdom, honor is in it, but he who despises wisdom is given over to contempt.[e] [90]See,[f] my sons, Joseph my brother [who] was a teacher of book, tradition, (and) wisdom (Cambridge col. f) [for honor and greatness and to kings ... do not forgo wisdom to teach ...] ... [91]... man who teaches [wisdom all] his [d]ays ... and increased ... to every la[nd] and province into which he [ente]rs[g] a brother ... in it . . . he [is not] a stranger in it, not[h] resemb[ling in it] a stranger and not resembling in it one of mixed ancestry, because all of them give to him honor in it, [bec]ause all want to learn from his wisdom. [92]Hi[s] friends are many and those who seek his welfare are great ones[i] [93]and they enthrone him on a throne of glory in order to hear his words of wisdom. [94]His wisdom is great wealth that is honor[j] and a good treasure to all who acquire it. [95]If powerful kings come, and a multitudinous people and an army and cavalry and many chariots with them, and they remove possessions of land (4QLevi[e] ar frags. 2-3 ii) AND PROVINCE and they despoil all that is in them, they shall not despoil the treasuries of wisdom, NOR SHALL THEY FIND (4QLevi[a] ar frags. 1 ii 1-19 + 2.5-19). [96]its hidden things and they shall not enter its gates and not[... ITS GOOD THINGS ...] shall they be able to overcome its walls ... and not ... they shall see its treasure. Its treasure ... (4QLevi[f] ar frag. 8) and there is [n]o price[k] corresponding to it [97]... he seeks wisdom ... the [wis]dom ... he hides it FROM HIM/HER[l] ... and not la[ck]ing ... all seekers ... truth ... [[98]AND

T. Levi 13:1

Ps 119:160

Job 4:8; Hos 10:12-13; Mark 4:1-20; *T. Levi* 13:5-6; Sir 6:18-19

Prov 15:33; *T. Levi* 13:2; *Jub.* 4:17

Prov 1:7

Gen 41:39-40; Ps 105:20-22; *Jub.* 40:5

T. Levi 13:9

T. Levi 13:3-4; Sir 39:4

T. Levi 13:9; 1 Sam 2:8; Isa 22:23

Matt 13:44-45; Sir 51:21

Ezek 26:7

Job 28:12; Qoh 7:23-24; Matt 7:19-21; Col 2:3; *T. Levi* 13:7; Bar 3:14-15, 29-31

Job 28:15-18

---

a. "last wishes"—The Aramaic word can have this connotation and, although Levi actually lived nearly two more decades, it seems we are to understand that he is here setting his affairs in order, evidently spurred on by the death of his brother Joseph.

b. "your works"; 4QLevi[a] ar "all your works"

c. "my sons,"; 4QLevi[a] ar omits

d. "wisdom"—The references to "wisdom" here and in §89 are paralleled in *T. Levi* 13:2-3 by references to "the Law of God." Either reading is possible, since the passage is arguably assimilating Torah and wisdom (note the references to "book and tradition and wisdom" in 88 and 90), as does, for example, Ben Sira. (I owe this last point to Richard Bauckham in a personal communication.)

e. "to contempt"; 4QLevi[a] ar adds "and to despising"

f. "See"; 4QLevi[a] ar adds "therefore,"

g. "[ente]rs"—The word is badly damaged and may read "[goe]s." 4QLevi[a] reads "proceeds"

h. "not"; 4QLevi[a] ar "but not"

i. "great ones"—The word could also be translated "numerous"

j. "honor"; 4QLevi[a] ar adds "for those who know her"

k. "there is [n]o price" preserved as indicated in 4QLevi[a] ar frag. 2.4 and 4QLevi[f] ar frag. 8.

l. "FROM HIM/HER"—Approximately the four immediately preceding three lines in 4QLevi[a] ar (§97; also apparently originally found in 4QLevi[a] ar) seem to have been missing in 4QLevi[e] ar.

NOW, MY SONS,] BOOK and tradition (and) wisdom … <which> … [I SAW IN A VISION THAT …] you shall inherit them[a] … great … you shall give … [ho]nor [99]…
Jub. 31:15 also in the books … chiefs, and judges … and slaves … [al]so priests and kings …
[100]your kingdom shall be … and there is no end to … shall pass from you until all … with great honor.

T. Levi 14:3; Sir 50:6-7 [101](4QLevi[a] ar frag. 3) [i]… all the peoples [ii]…[mo]on and stars [iii]…from/who [iv]… to the [m]oon

[102](4QLevi[a] ar frag. 4) [i]… so you grow dark … [ii]… did not receive … [iii]… we/us and upon whom shall be the guilt [iv]… is it not against me and against you, my sons? Behold, they know it [v]… [pa]ths of truth you leave and all the roads of
Jn 12:35; 1 Jn 2:11; 1QS xi 10 [vi]… you shall forgo and you shall walk in the dark[ness] of s[a]t[a]n [vii]… that da[rkn]ess shall come upon you and you shall [wa]lk [viii]… now at ti[mes] you shall be abased[b] [ix]…

[103](4QLevi[a] ar frag. 5) [i]… [ii]… your … then … [t]ongues among you [iii]… among you from all …

[104](4QLevi[d] ar frag. 3) [i]***Behold, from honor …*** [ii] ***I that you say to me <that>***
Genesis 34? ***D[inah?]*** … [iii]***more honored than women …***[iv]…

---

a. "you shall inherit them"—Alternate translation: "they are two"

b. "abased"—Another reading of the letters of the word would mean "insightful"

Midrash Vayissa'u
A new translation and introduction

by Martha Himmelfarb

Midrash Vayissa'u is an account of three wars fought by Jacob and his sons, the first against the Ninevites, the second against the Amorites, and the third against Esau and his sons. The Hebrew in which it is written is clearly post-rabbinic, and some scholars have suggested that *Midrash Vayissa'u* is best understood as the Jewish equivalent of Christian stories about knights and Crusaders.[1] But while developments in contemporary Christian culture may account for the composition of the first chapter of the work and for the work's appeal to medieval Jews, the significant points of contact between the narratives of the second and third chapters and the accounts of wars fought by Jacob and his sons in the *Testaments of the Twelve Patriarchs* and the *Book of Jubilees* demonstrate that *Midrash Vayissa'u* preserves ancient traditions. How medieval Jews came into possession of these traditions is by no means clear, however, as will be discussed below.

Content

Each chapter of *Midrash Vayissa'u* offers an account of a series of battles fought by Jacob and his sons to defend themselves against a different enemy who has chosen to make war on them. The work locates the battles in the context of the narrative of Genesis with explicit connection to the biblical text, although in the case of the Ninevites, the enemy of the first chapter, it is a challenge to make the connection. The only mention of Nineveh in Genesis is the report in Genesis 10 of the building of the city by Nimrod (Gen 10:11-12). *Midrash Vayissa'u* relates the Ninevites to the narrative of Genesis by suggesting that their army passed through Canaan on a campaign of world conquest just in time to hear an account of the sack of Shechem by Simeon and Levi; angered by the account, the Ninevites attack our heroes. The enemies of chapter 2, the Amorites, are one of the nations that preceded Israel in the holy land according to the Torah. The narrative of chapter 2 takes place seven years after the sack of Shechem. Jacob and his sons have again settled in the neighborhood, and the Amorite kings, outraged by this return to the scene of the crime, make war against them. Chapter 3 recounts a particularly despicable attack, this one by Esau and his sons, which takes place while Jacob and his family are mourning the death of Leah.

Perhaps needless to say, Jacob and his sons are ultimately triumphant against each of these enemies. But while all the brothers fight heroically, in every chapter it is Judah who plays the most prominent role. Remarkably, it is not one of the brothers but the elderly Jacob who is second to Judah, singlehandedly holding off the Ninevite army (*Midrash*

1. Tamar Alexander and Joseph Dan, "The Complete *Midrash Vayissa'u*" (Heb.), *Folklore Research Center Studies* 3 (1972): 68; Joseph Dan, *The Hebrew Story in the Middle Ages* (Jerusalem: Keter, 1974), 138-40.

Vayissa'u 1:5-6), slaying several Amorite kings with his bow (*Midrash Vayissa'u* 2:6), and fatally wounding his brother Esau, also with his bow (*Midrash Vayissa'u* 3:5).

Manuscripts and Editions

There exist two critical editions of *Midrash Vayissa'u*. The first, by Jacob Lauterbach, was published in 1933;[2] the second, by Tamar Alexander and Joseph Dan, appeared in 1972.[3] Unfortunately, Alexander and Dan were unaware of Lauterbach's work, and only one manuscript is common to the two editions. The translation below is based primarily on Lauterbach's edition, but it takes the Alexander-Dan edition into consideration as well. The paragraph divisions in the translation of chapters 2 and 3 are inherited from earlier translations, but I am responsible for the divisions in chapter 1. I believe that my translation is the first ever undertaken of this chapter.

The evidence of the manuscripts and medieval anthologies indicates that *Midrash Vayissa'u* had a complicated compositional history.[4] The two editions between them make use of five manuscripts that contain chapter 1 alone as well as two manuscripts containing fragments of chapter 1. Only two manuscripts contain all three of the chapters.[5] Another manuscript contains chapters 2 and 3 without chapter 1. *Bereshit Rabbati*, an eleventh-century midrashic collection, includes the opening lines of chapter 2 in relation to Gen 35:5 and a complete version of chapter 3 in relation to Gen 36:6 but lacks chapter 1. The *Chronicles of Yerahme'el*, an eleventh-century anthology of rabbinic and post-rabbinic texts, contains a complete version of chapters 2 and 3, also without chapter 1.[6] So too *Sefer haYashar*, a retelling of biblical stories from the fifteenth or sixteenth century, makes use of only the last two chapters.[7] But *Yalqut Shim'oni*, an anthology of rabbinic exegesis and legend from the thirteenth century, contains all three chapters; it cites chapters 1 and 2 together in relation to the word *vayissa'u*, "they journeyed" (Gen 35:5), while chapter 3 appears later, at "He went to a land" (Gen 36:6). The evidence just surveyed is compatible with the picture of chapter 1 as a later composition based on chapters 2 and 3, a picture for which I shall argue below. It also suggests that chapter 1 was more popular than chapters 2 and 3 or the complete work and that the earlier version of *Midrash Vayissa'u*, consisting of chapters 2 and 3, continued to circulate even after the composition of chapter 1.

Genre

In his commentary to the Torah (to Gen 34:13), Nahmanides (1194-1270) refers to the work as "The Book of the Wars of the Sons of Jacob," a good description of its content.[8] The title "*Midrash Vayissa'u*" appears in the British Museum manuscript that forms the basis

---

2. "*Midrash Vayissa'u*: or, The Book of the Wars of the Sons of Jacob" (Heb.), *Abhandlungen zur Erinnerung an Hirsch Perez Chajes* (Vienna: Alexander Kohut Memorial Foundation, 1933), 205-22.

3. Alexander and Dan, "Complete *Midrash Vayissa'u*," 67-76.

4. What follows is drawn from the introductions to the editions: Lauterbach, "*Midrash Vayissa'u*," 209-11; Alexander and Dan, "Complete *Midrash Vayissa'u*," 68. See the editions for more details.

5. They are London (British Museum) 1076 (27.089), known to both editions, and Hamburg 150, known only to Alexander and Dan, "Complete *Midrash Vayissa'u*."

6. Portions of the *Chronicles of Yerahme'el* come down to us as part of a fourteenth-century anthology *Book of Memory*; for the relationship of the *Chronicles of Yerahme'el* to the *Book of Memory*, see Eli Yassif, *The Book of Memory: That Is, The Chronicles of Jerahme'el: A Critical Edition* (Heb.) (Tel Aviv: The Chaim Rosenberg School of Jewish Studies, Tel Aviv University, 2001), 27-28.

7. For the date, Dan, *Hebrew Story*, 137-38.

8. Lauterbach, "*Midrash Vayissa'u*," 205.

of Lauterbach's edition and in *Yalqut Shim'oni*, where, however, it is used of only the first two chapters.[9] The term *midrash* in the title implies that the text is a rabbinic work with an exegetical relationship to the biblical text; as already noted, *vayissa'u*, "they journeyed," appears in one of the verses (Gen 35:5) to which the work attempts to attach its narrative. While it is true that each chapter of *Midrash Vayissa'u* begins with a verse from Genesis and that the work then proceeds to demonstrate the connection between the verse and the narrative that follows, the establishment of this connection is more or less the extent of the work's exegetical activity. Rather, *Midrash Vayissa'u* consists almost exclusively of narrative with little of the reference to the biblical text that defines the genre of midrash.

Relation to Earlier Literature

While *Midrash Vayissa'u* is clearly a medieval work, chapters 2 and 3 contain striking parallels to two ancient texts, the *Book of Jubilees*, from the second century B.C.E., and the *Testament of Judah*, part of the *Testaments of the Twelve Patriarchs*, probably from the second century C.E. Both works offer accounts of wars against the Amorites and Esau and his sons. In *Jubilees* the account of the war against the Amorites is very brief (*Jub.* 34:1-9) while the account of the war against Esau and his sons is much longer (*Jub.* 37-38); in the *Testament of Judah* the situation is reversed (*T. Jud.* 3-7 [Amorites]; *T. Jud.* 9 [Esau and his sons]).

The points of contact between *Midrash Vayissa'u* and the ancient texts go far beyond the already significant fact of a shared non-biblical tradition about wars fought by Jacob and his sons. Thus, for example, according to the *Testament of Judah* Judah uses a sixty-pound stone to kill the horse of one of the kings of Canaan so that he can engage him in hand-to-hand combat (*T. Jud.* 3:3); in *Midrash Vayissa'u* Judah uses a sixty-*sela* stone to unseat a different Amorite king from his horse so as to engage him in hand-to-hand combat (*Midrash Vayissa'u* 2:2). Both texts describe the king in question as a fearsome warrior capable of throwing weapons both in front of him and behind as he rode on his horse (*T. Jud.* 3:3, *Midrash Vayissa'u* 2:2).

So too both *Midrash Vayissa'u* and *Jubilees* place the war against the sons of Esau just after the death of Leah, when Jacob and his family were mourning her (*Jub.* 37:14, *Midrash Vayissa'u* 3:1). The two texts also describe the defense of the citadel where Jacob and his sons were encamped in strikingly similar terms (*Jub.* 38:4-8, *Midrash Vayissa'u* 3:6). They agree on the division of Jacob's sons into four squads of three men each and on the identity of the men in each squad despite the fact that the groupings are not based on any biblical precedent. In both texts Enoch the son of Reuben takes the place Joseph should have held in the last squad; *Midrash Vayissa'u* explains that Joseph had already been sold at the time of the events in question. The two texts also agree on which side of the citadel each of the squads defended, and they list both the squads and the members of the squads in the same order.

There are also some points at which the earlier texts help to clarify difficult passages in *Midrash Vayissa'u*. The reference in *Midrash Vayissa'u* to the presence of women as the sons of Judah enter the city of Shiloh in victory (*Midrash Vayissa'u* 2:8) is confusing to the reader who has heard nothing about women up to this point. The *Testament of Judah*, however, gives women a role in the battle against the men of Makir (*T. Jud.* 6:4), which follows the battle against the men of Shiloh (*T. Jud.* 6:2). In *Midrash Vayissa'u* the

9. Lauterbach, "*Midrash Vayissa'u*," 209.

existence of the iron tower that Judah, Naphtali, and Gad attack in the course of the war against Esau and his sons (*Midrash Vayissa'u* 3:7) comes as a surprise. But the *Testament of Judah* reports that the sons of Jacob pursued the sons of Esau to their city, which had an iron wall (*T. Jud.* 9:4).

There are, to be sure, many important points of divergence between *Midrash Vayissa'u* and the ancient texts. *Midrash Vayissa'u*'s account of the wars is longer, more elaborate, and bloodier than those of *Jubilees* and the *Testament of Judah*. While the *Testament of Judah* describes battles between small groups with relatively small numbers of casualties, *Midrash Vayissa'u* describes battles between armies, with hundreds of wounded and dead; *Jubilees*' account of the war against Esau and his sons is closer to *Midrash Vayissa'u* in this regard. In addition, the narrative of *Midrash Vayissa'u* includes elements missing in the narratives of the *Testament of Judah* and *Jubilees*, and vice-versa, while some common elements appear at different points in the narratives. Yet the similarities are so numerous and striking that they require explanation.

Jubilees and the *Testament of Judah*

Many scholars believe that the war narratives of *Jubilees* and the *Testament of Judah* should be understood as reflecting battles fought by the Maccabees in which local opponents joined the Seleucid armies.[10] This reading is based to a considerable extent on the identification of place names mentioned in *Jubilees* and the *Testament of Judah* with sites mentioned in 1 and 2 Maccabees. Not all of these identifications are equally persuasive, and they have been subjected to criticism. Thus one scholar has suggested, on the basis of somewhat different identifications of the place names, that the battles described in *Jubilees* and the *Testament of Judah* reflect a war between Judeans and Samaritans from the Persian period,[11] while another scholar has called into question the very enterprise of seeking historical references, arguing that the war narratives serve a function in *Jubilees*' literary and ideological structure and therefore might well have been invented for *Jubilees*' own purpose.[12]

Fortunately for us, the determination of whether the battles of *Jubilees* and the *Testament of Judah* reflect historical events and, if so, which ones, is not of great importance for understanding *Midrash Vayissa'u*. What is important is an understanding of the relationship between the narratives in the two ancient works. If, as I believe, the *Testament of the Twelve Patriarchs* is a Christian composition of the second century C.E., it is theoretically possible to understand the accounts of the wars in the *Testament of Judah* as derived from those in *Jubilees*, which dates to some time in the second century B.C.E. But while the *Testament of Judah*'s account of the war against Esau and his sons could well be an abbreviation of the longer account in *Jubilees* made by an author concerned with the glorious deeds of Judah rather than the family drama *Jubilees* recounts, it is much harder to understand the *Testament of Judah*'s version of the war against the Amorites as an expansion of *Jubilees*' very schematic treatment. Indeed here it looks as if it is *Jubilees*

10. See James C. VanderKam, *Textual and Historical Studies in the Book of Jubilees* (HSM 14; Missoula, Mont.: Scholars Press, 1977), 217-38, and the references there to earlier discussions.

11. Ze'ev Safrai, "*Midrash Vayissa'u*: The War of the Sons of Jacob in Southern Samaria" (Heb.), *Sinai* 100 (1987): 621-25.

12. Robert Doran, "The Non-Dating of Jubilees: Jub 34-38; 23:14-32 in Narrative Context," *JSJ* 20 (1989): 1-11. Unfortunately, he does not address the evidence that suggests that *Jubilees* draws on a source for the wars against the Amorites and Esau and his sons; this evidence clearly has implications for his argument.

that is engaged in abbreviation. Even if the *Testaments of the Twelve Patriarchs* is a Jewish work roughly contemporary with *Jubilees*, as some scholars still believe, it is hard to argue that for one war *Jubilees* abbreviates the account in the *Testament of Judah* while for the other the *Testament of Judah* abbreviates the one in *Jubilees*. It thus seems more likely that the two works drew on a common source that contained full accounts of both wars, but they revised and developed it in different ways. In *Jubilees*, Jacob is the leading figure in both wars; while Judah plays a prominent role in the defeat of Esau and his sons, he is not singled for special notice in the war against the Amorites. But in the *Testament of Judah* the focus of the accounts of both wars is on Judah, with Jacob a distant second and the other brothers mere supporting players.

Midrash Vayissaʿu, *Jubilees* and the *Testament of Judah*

While *Midrash Vayissaʿu* clearly reflects knowledge of the traditions found in *Jubilees* and the *Testament of Judah*, there can be no doubt that *Midrash Vayissaʿu* itself is a medieval work. Its language could not possibly be mistaken for Hebrew of the Second Temple period. Furthermore, its style reflects familiarity with rabbinic literature. It begins each chapter with the citation of a biblical verse (Gen 35:5 in chaps. 1 and 2, Gen 36:6 in chap. 3), and it introduces the narrative that follows with the formula, "Our rabbis said," thus representing the accounts of the wars as rabbinic tradition. It also includes elements of rabbinic lore. Its two alternative explanations for Esau's decision to exile himself from his homeland (*Midrash Vayissaʿu* 3:1) are drawn from *Genesis Rabbah*, a Palestinian midrash completed in the fifth century, while its claim that Esau's son Eliphaz was Jacob's student (*Midrash Vayissaʿu* 3:13) is a variant of the view of several late midrashim that Eliphaz was Isaac's student.[13]

Based on the features of *Midrash Vayissaʿu* just described, one might argue that it represents a medieval retelling of the source on which *Jubilees* and the *Testament of Judah* drew, with the addition of a newly composed war narrative (chapter 1) inspired by those of the source. Yet the relationship between *Midrash Vayissaʿu* and the source is even more complicated, for many of the cities mentioned in *Midrash Vayissaʿu* are called not by their biblical names but by Hebrew names that reflect a Greek form of the biblical name. Thus, for example, in the *Testament of Judah* one of the Amorite cities is called *Asour* (3:1); the name is a Greek version of Hazor (*ḥṣr*/*ḥṣwr*), a city mentioned many times in Joshua 11 and elsewhere in the Bible.[14] But instead of calling the city by its biblical name, *Midrash Vayissaʿu* refers to it as Hasar (*hsr*) (*Midrash Vayissaʿu* 2:5-7), apparently a Hebraization of *Asour*.[15] The impact of Greek on the names of the cities strongly suggests that *Midrash Vayissaʿu*'s source came to it not in Hebrew but in Greek.

Elsewhere in this volume I suggest that the ninth- or tenth-century *Book of Asaph* made use of a work about Noah that was also used by *Jubilees* in the second century B.C.E.; the work has not come down to us, and I deduce its existence from a comparison of *Jubilees* and the *Book of Asaph*. Here I am suggesting something even more surprising: that medieval Jews made use of a source also used by *Jubilees* but that the source reached them in translation. We have no concrete evidence for the existence of this translation; we can do no more than speculate about the circumstances under which it was made and

13. See the translation for references to *Genesis Rabbah* and the late midrashim.

14. The Greek translation of the Book of Joshua uses a slightly different transliteration, *Asōr*.

15. Not surprisingly, the *Chronicle of Yerahme'el* corrects the name to Hazor (*ḥṣr*).

then transmitted. Yet despite our lack of knowledge, it seems to me that such a Greek version of the ancient Hebrew source on which *Jubilees* and the *Testament of Judah* drew offers a more plausible explanation for the contents of *Midrash Vayissa'u* than the use of the Greek versions of both *Jubilees* and the *Testament of Judah*. The *Testaments of the Twelve Patriarchs*, to be sure, circulated widely in the Byzantine Empire. The Greek text of *Jubilees*, however, disappeared quite early, and although there is evidence for the transmission of excerpts from *Jubilees* in the work of the Byzantine chronographers, including the story of the death of Esau at Jacob's hands, I know of no evidence for the transmission of the account of the war of Jacob and his sons against Esau's sons or of the brief description of the war against the Amorites.

But even if we could be confident that the relevant material from *Jubilees* was available in the Byzantine world, the accounts of the wars in *Midrash Vayissa'u* are not simply a combination of the narratives found in *Jubilees* and the *Testament of Judah*. It is striking that *Midrash Vayissa'u*'s account of the war against Esau and his sons, which corresponds largely to the lengthy narrative of *Jubilees*, includes at least one detail, the iron tower discussed above, that is not mentioned in *Jubilees* but is clarified by the iron wall mentioned in the brief and obviously abridged account in the *Testament of Judah*. Altogether, then, it seems more likely that *Midrash Vayissa'u* drew on a source that contained the account that lies behind both *Jubilees and the Testament of Judah*. The assumption that the source was in Greek and thus that its contents had to be translated back into Hebrew explains the post-rabbinic character of the language of *Midrash Vayissa'u*.

The War Against the Ninevites

Chapter one's account of the war against the army from Nineveh drew not on ancient works but on chapters 2 and 3. It follows chapter 2 in placing the war in the aftermath of Simeon and Levi's attack on Shechem, and it links the war to the same biblical passage with which chapter 2 begins, although it must go further afield to supply Jacob and his sons with an enemy. It also follows chapters 2 and 3 in making Jacob and Judah the most eminent of its heroes. But its style differs to a certain extent from that of chapters 2 and 3 in its more extensive use of biblical phrases, a feature of medieval Hebrew narratives.

Tamar Alexander and Joseph Dan have suggested that the impetus for the composition of *Midrash Vayissa'u* was the romance literature of western Europe that recounted the exploits of heroic knights.[16] This suggestion is appealing, but it is implausible for chapters 2 and 3 if I am correct about their Byzantine provenance. There is nothing to suggest a Byzantine provenance for chapter 1, however, which is first attested in *Yalqut Shim'oni*, compiled in Frankfurt in the thirteenth century. Alexander and Dan's theory, then, may help to explain the composition of chapter 1 and the popularity of the work as whole in Western Europe.

Date and Provenance

Only a broad-brush sketch of the context in which *Midrash Vayissa'u* took shape is possible at this stage of our knowledge. The Byzantine Empire seems the most likely location. There Jews would have known Greek well, and we have evidence for the circulation of works or portions of works of the Second Temple period in Greek among Byzantine Christians. It is also worth noting that although *Bereshit Rabbati*, the earliest midrashic

16. Alexander and Dan, "Complete *Midrash Vayissa'u*," 68; Dan, *Hebrew Story*, 138-40.

anthology to make use of *Midrash Vayissa'u*, was compiled in southern France, it is known to have used material of Byzantine provenance. The eleventh-century date of *Bereshit Rabbati* provides the upper limits for dating chapters 2 and 3; although *Bereshit Rabbati* quotes only a single paragraph from the beginning of chapter 2 (*Midrash Vayissa'u* 2:1, starting from "Our rabbis said"), it is virtually certain, given their common dependence on the source used by *Jubilees* and the *Testament of Judah*, that chapters 2 and 3 were composed at the same time. Furthermore, their composition must have taken place early enough to allow them to reach southern France from the Byzantine Empire in time for inclusion in *Bereshit Rabbati*. Chapter 1, as just noted, is first attested in thirteenth-century Frankfurt.

Impact on Later Literature

As discussed above, *Midrash Vayissa'u* or parts of it appear in three medieval anthologies: *Bereshit Rabbati* and the *Chronicles of Yerahme'el* from the eleventh century and *Yalqut Shim'oni* from the thirteenth century. A reworking of chapters 2 and 3 forms part of the retelling of the biblical narrative in *Sefer haYashar*, composed in the fifteenth or sixteenth century.

Bibliography

Alexander, Tamar, and Joseph Dan. "The Complete *Midrash Vayissa'u*" (Heb.). *Folklore Research Center Studies* 3 (1972): 67-76. (Critical edition.)

Dan, Joseph. *The Hebrew Story in the Middle Ages* (Heb.). Jerusalem: Keter, 1974.

Gaster, Moses. Pages 80-87 in *The Chronicles of Jerhameel; or, The Hebrew Bible Historiale*. Prolegomenon by Haim Schwarzbaum. New York: Ktav, 1971. First ed., London: Royal Asiatic Society, 1899.

Hollander, H. W., and M. de Jonge. *The Testaments of the Twelve Patriarchs: A Commentary.* SVTP 8. Leiden: Brill, 1985. (Translation of chapters 2 and 3 of *Midrash Vayissa'u*, 451-56. Based on the translation of Gaster, *Chronicles* [see above], extensively revised by A. van der Heide.)

Lauterbach, Jacob Z. "*Midrash Vayissa'u*: or, The Book of the Wars of the Sons of Jacob" (Heb.). Pages 205-22 in *Abhandlungen zur Erinnerung an Hirsch Perez Chajes*. Vienna: Alexander Kohut Memorial Foundation, 1933. (Critical edition.)

Safrai, Ze'ev. "*Midrash Vayissa'u*: The War of the Sons of Jacob in Southern Samaria" (Heb.). *Sinai* 100 (1987): 613-27.

Yassif, Eli. *The Book of Memory: That Is, The Chronicles of Jerahme'el: A Critical Edition* (Heb.). Tel Aviv: The Chaim Rosenberg School of Jewish Studies, Tel Aviv University, 2001.

Midrash Vayissa'u

Chapter 1

Gen 35:5 [1](*As they journeyed,*) *terror from God came upon* (*the cities around them*). Our
rabbis said: When Simeon and Levi killed the Shechemites, fear and trembling
fell upon all the nations around them. They said, "If the two sons of Jacob could
kill (the inhabitants of) the great city of Shechem, if they all came together
against us, how much more so." What did Jacob do? He gathered his possessions
to go to Isaac his father. When he had gone a journey of eight days, an army met
Gen 22:17, 1 Sam 13:5, him, as great *as the sand on the seashore*. The army had come from Nineveh to
1 Kgs 5:9 [Evv 4:29] take tribute from the whole world and to conquer it. When that army came near
Shechem, it heard the report of what the sons of Jacob had done to Shechem.
The men of Nineveh immediately became angry and came against Jacob to fight
him.

[2]When Jacob became aware of the army, he said to his sons, "Do not be
afraid, my sons. The Holy One, blessed be he, will fight for you against your
enemies. Only *remove the foreign gods in your midst and purify yourselves and*
Gen 35:2 *change your clothes*." And Jacob took his sword in his right hand and his bow
in his left hand and went out against that army. He began to kill two thousand
of the weakest among them. Then his son Judah said, "Father, you have become
Deut 25:18 tired and weary. Allow me to fight against them." Jacob said, "My son, I know
how strong and courageous you are. There is no one in the world as courageous
Gen 31:42 as you are. The Fear of your father will be your help. Go and fight against them."
Gen 49:9 [3]Judah went against them with fierce anger, and his face was the face of a lion.
He fought against them and killed twelve myriads of the army, all warriors of
renown. Then his brother Levi came to help him, and there was fighting around
Judah and his brother Levi on every side. Now Judah's hand was victorious in
war, and he killed five thousand more of the army, all of them with their swords
drawn. Levi came and struck with his right hand, and the army fell before him
as the grain falls before the reapers.

[4]Then the men of Nineveh said to each other, "How long shall we fight
against these destroyers? Let us retreat lest they destroy us so that not one of us
remains." But the king of Nineveh said to them, "Where are the mighty warriors,
the resolute, the glorious, the strong? What came over you to make you say that
you would return to your land? What happened to your courage, you who conquered many lands and many nations, that now you are unable to fight against
twelve men? When the nations and kings whom we conquered, who now pay
us tribute, hear, they will gather together against us as one and abuse us and do

to us as they wish. You gather together, men of *Nineveh, the great city*, and let your glory and your name be great, and do not fall prey to your enemies." When (the men of Nineveh) heard the words of their king, they were willing to fight on. They sent emissaries to all the countries they had conquered, asking them to come to their aid. So men from all the countries came to the aid of the men of Nineveh, and they waged war against the sons of Jacob. Jonah 1:2, 3:2

5Then Jacob said to his sons, "My sons, strengthen yourselves and act like men and fight against your enemies." The sons of Jacob divided up into twelve armies, each at a distance from the next. Jacob their father went before them, his sword in his right hand and his bow in his left. Jacob fought on that day, and there was fighting around him on every side, and he dealt them a very great blow. When two thousand men came against Jacob alone to strike him, he sprang about two thousand cubits in a single leap so that they did not know where he was. Jacob's hand was victorious over the army, and he mowed down about twenty-two myriads, all of them warriors. But at evening, when Jacob wanted to rest, there suddenly came ninety thousand (men). So Jacob arose and stood in the breach and began to kill them as before, but the sword that was in Jacob's hand broke.

6When Jacob saw that the sword that was in his hand had broken, he took some large stones and pulverized them in his hand like plaster. Then he threw it on the soldiers so that they were unable to see because of the plaster and also because evening time had arrived and night was near, for the sun was setting. And Jacob rested that night.

7The next day Judah said to his father, "Look, father, you fought yesterday, and *you are tired and weary*. I shall fight today." Jacob said, "Judah my son, go and succeed." And Judah went and fought on that day. When the men of the army saw that Judah's face was like a lion's face and that his teeth were like lion's teeth, they were very much afraid of him, but they strengthened themselves to fight against him *with a high hand*. Judah was almost overpowered by the fighting, but he leapt and sprang into the midst of the army, going from one to another, striking as he went, as does a flea. And from the morning until the ninth hour of the day, Judah struck 80,496 men, all with swords drawn and bows bent. Deut 25:18 Gen 49:9 Exod 14:8 1 Sam 24:14, 26:20

8But Judah was very tired, and his brother Zebulon[a] came from his left to help him and fight against them. And (Zebulon) mowed down three thousand of them. When Judah had rested, he arose in anger and wrath and gnashed his teeth violently as the heavens thunder in the season of Tammuz.[b] The army heard and fled eighteen *mils*.[c] And Judah rested that night.

9The next day, on the third day, the army came again to fight and to take vengeance. They blew trumpets, and Jacob said to his sons, "My sons, go and fight against your enemies." Issachar and Gad said, "We shall fight against our enemies today." Their father said, "Go and fight, and the rest of your brothers will

a. According to MS Hamburg (Alexander-Dan, "Complete *Midrash Vayissa'u*"), the brother who comes to Judah's aid is Levi.

b. A month in mid-summer.

c. A *mil* is a Roman mile, *mille passus* or *mille passuum*, a thousand paces, estimated at 1618 yards, 142 yards shorter than an English mile. One Roman mile is approximately 1,479 meters.

Deut 25:18 be on the lookout until you become tired and weary so that they can help you." Then Issachar and Gad went out and fought that day. They destroyed 36,000 men of the army, and twelve myriads fled into caves opposite.[a] Issachar and Gad came and took trees from the forest and made a big fire in front of the openings of the caves. When the fire grew strong, the soldiers said to each other, "Why do we stay in this cave to die from the smoke and the heat of the fire? Let us go and fight against them. Perhaps we will survive." They left the cave in every direction by way of the north.[b] Then they waged war against Issachar and Gad, and there was fighting on every side. Dan and Naphtali saw and rushed into the midst of the army and struck to their right and to their left until they came to their brothers. And the four of them did battle, Issachar, Gad, Dan, and Naphtali.

Gen 22:17, 1 Sam 13:5, 1 Kgs 5:9 10 That day a people as many *as the sand on the shore of the sea* came from other lands to help the men of Nineveh. All the sons of Jacob saw this great army, and they all came together as one and stood to strike and kill the soldiers with very great blows without number. Judah's hand was victorious over that great army, and he struck them a very great blow. The entire army fled before him.

11 When the sons of Jacob saw that the army was fleeing, they arose in fierce anger and pursued them. And men of the army said, "Why should we flee before them? Let us fight with them. Perhaps we shall overcome them for they are tired." So they came and fought against them, and the battle was very intense. When Jacob saw that his sons were being overpowered in battle, he arose and sprang into the midst of the army, striking to his right and to his left. They fell before him as grass falls behind the reaper. But the army's hand was victorious, and they separated Judah from his brothers. Jacob saw and gnashed his teeth, and Judah heard and he too gnashed his teeth, and his brothers heard and came to help him.

12 Judah was very tired and thirsty for water, but he had no water. So he thrust his finger hard into the ground and water came up against it. The men of the army saw the water coming out opposite Judah, and they said to each other, "Let
Exod 14:25 me take flight from these destroyers because God fights for them." The entire army fled by way of the forest, but the sons of Jacob pursued them and struck them great blows without number. A few of them fled for[c] their lives, and the sons of Jacob were unable to pursue them. They blew trumpets and returned to their tents. But Joseph was not there. The sons of Jacob were very troubled about their brother Joseph, and they said, "Perhaps they killed him or took him into captivity." They blew the trumpets, and Naphtali their brother ran to search for him. He found him fighting against the army. Naphtali called out, "Is that you, Joseph my brother?" And he said, "It is I." Then Naphtali helped him, and they destroyed soldiers without number. They pursued those who remained and drowned them in the waters of the forest. The soldiers fled before them, and

a. The term translated "opposite" is difficult to construe in this context since it is a preposition rather than an adverb. Perhaps it is a mistake for a closely related term, which differs by only a single letter and has an adverbial sense: "at a distance."

b. The text as it stands does not make sense. The problematic phrases "in every direction by way of the north" are omitted in MS Hamburg.

c. Here I follow MS Hamburg (Alexander-Dan, "Complete *Midrash Vayissa'u*"), *'l*, rather than MS British Museum (Lauterbach, "*Midrash Vayissa'u*"), *'l*, which is difficult to construe.

they stopped pursuing them. About them Solomon said, "*Better are the two than the one.*" And they came to Jacob their father, and he rejoiced. The remaining sons of the kingdom did not pursue them.[a] And (Jacob) went safely to his father Isaac, to Mamre, Qiryat ha-Arba'.

Eccl 4:9

Gen 35:27

Chapter 2

[1]*As they journeyed, terror from God came upon the cities around them, and they did not pursue the sons of Jacob.* For they said, "If two sons of Jacob could do this thing, if they all gather together, they will be able to destroy the world." And the fear of the Holy One, blessed be he, fell upon them. Therefore they did not pursue the sons of Jacob. Our rabbis said: Although they did not pursue them at this time, seven years later they did pursue them. For all the kings of the Amorites came together against the sons of Jacob and sought to kill them in the valley of Shechem because after that Jacob and his sons had returned to Shechem and stayed there. When the kings of the Amorites heard that Jacob and his sons were living in Shechem, they said, "Isn't it enough that they killed all the men of Shechem? But they also take possession of their land." They all gathered together and came against them to kill them.

Gen 35:5

Jub. 34:2

[2]When Judah saw this, he sprang into the midst of the array of troops fighting against them, and he killed first Yishov, king of Tappuah,[b] who was covered from head to toe in iron and bronze. (Yishov) was riding on a horse and throwing javelins with both his hands from upon the horse, in front of him and behind him. He never missed the spot at which he threw because he was a warrior mighty in strength and trained to throw with both his hands. When Judah saw him, he was not afraid of him or his might. He sprang and, as he ran toward him, he took a stone weighing sixty *selas*[c] from the ground and threw it at him. He was at a distance of two parts of a *ris*,[d] which are 177 cubits and a third. (Yishov) came toward Judah, armed with weapons of iron and throwing javelins. But Judah struck him on his shield with that stone and made him fall off his horse to the ground.

Jub. 34:7, *T. Jud.* 3:2

T. Jud. 3:3

T. Jud. 3:3

[3]As he tried to get up, Judah ran to try to kill him before he could get up from the ground. (Yishov) hurried to stand on his feet facing Judah, and he waged war against him, shield to shield. He drew a spear and tried to cut off Judah's head. Judah raised his shield against the spear and took the blow of the spear, which cut the shield in two. What did Judah do? He bent and struck (Yishov) with his

---

a. The conclusion of MS Hamburg is rather different.

b. MS British Museum mentions two kings, the king of Lishah and the king of Tappuah, but does not name either (Lauterbach, *Midrash Vayissa'u*). Much of the evidence in the apparatus as well as MS Hamburg (Alexander-Dan, "Complete *Midrash Vayissa'u*") read "Yishov, king of Tappuah," which fits the pattern of other mentions of kings. According to the *Testament of Judah*, however, Judah killed the king of Hazor before killing the king of Tappuah (*T. Jud.* 3:1). The Book of Joshua lists the king of Tappuah as one of the kings defeated by Joshua during his conquest of the promised land (Josh 12:17).

c. A *sela* is an ancient coin mentioned in rabbinic literature, weighing approximately 14 grams. Thus Judah's stone was not heavy.

d. A *ris* is equivalent to a Greek stadion, about 2/15 of a mile, approximately 266 cubits. Thus the "two parts" of a *ris* above are two-thirds, and Judah is somewhat less than a tenth of a mile from his adversary.

spear and cut both his legs above the ankles. Then (Yishov) fell to the ground, and his spear fell from his hand. Judah sprang up and cut off his head.

4 But before (Judah) had stripped off (Yishov's) armor, nine of (Yishov's) com-
T. Jud. 3:5 panions came against him.[a] Judah took a stone and struck the first of them to
arrive on his head. His shield fell from his hand, and Judah took it and stood
facing the eight. Then his brother Levi arrived and came and stood with him. He
Jub. 34:7 shot an arrow and killed Elon, king of Ga'ash, and Judah killed all eight (com-
Jub. 34:7, *T. Jud.* 3:7 panions). Jacob his father approached and killed Zihori, king of Shiloh. None of
them rose up again against the sons of Jacob, and they no longer had the heart to
stay but only to flee. The sons of Jacob pursued them, and Judah killed a thousand of them that day before the sun set.

5 The rest of the sons of Jacob went out from the hill of Shechem, from the place where they had been standing by his side, and pursued them on the mountain until they came out to the city of Hasar. The battle before the city of Hasar was even heavier than the battle they fought against them in the valley of Shechem.

6 Jacob shot arrows and killed Par'aton, king of Hasar, Susi, king of Sartan,
Jub. 34:7 Laban, king of Kitron, and Shakhir, king of Mahaneh. Judah engaged the battle
T. Jud. 4:2 first. He went up on the wall of Hasar, and four mighty warriors engaged Judah in battle before Naphtali arrived beside him, having followed him up onto
the wall. But before Naphtali came up beside him, Judah had killed those four
mighty warriors, and Naphtali sprang up and came up after him. Judah stood on
the right of the wall, and Naphtali stood on the left of the wall, and they began
to kill them. The rest of the sons of Jacob leapt and came up after them. They
passed before them[b] on that day and captured Hasar, killing all the mighty warriors. They did not leave a single man alive, and they took all the captives.[c]

7 On the second day they went to Sartan, and there too there was a heavy
battle against them. It was a high city on a high hill, and it could crush anyone
who came near. There was no place to come near the wall because the fortifica-
T. Jud. 5:1 tion was strong and very high, and there was no spot from which to seize it. But
that day they went up on the wall and took it. Judah went first, going up from the
east, Gad went up from the west, Simeon and Levi went up from the north, and
T. Jud. 5:2 Reuben and Dan went up from the south. Naphtali and Issachar came near and
T. Jud. 5:5 set fire to the hinges of the gates. There was a heavy battle against them on the
wall until a group of their comrades came up there. They stood against them on
the tower before Judah conquered the tower. Afterwards Judah went up to the
top of the tower and killed two hundred men on the roof of the tower before he
came down from it. Then they captured all the inhabitants of the city and killed
all the gentiles, leaving none of them alive, for the men were strong and fierce in

a. According to the *Testament of Judah*, the companions number eight.

b. The text is difficult here. My translation follows Lauterbach's suggestion for understanding his text (*Midrash Vayissa'u*, 217 n. 2) rather than the reading of MS Hamburg (Alexander-Dan, "Complete *Midrash Vayissa'u*"), which appears to be an attempt to correct the difficult reading.

c. *Jub.* 34:7-9 offers a similarly self-contradictory description of the outcome of the battle against the kings: first Jacob kills the kings and their armies, and then he imposes tribute and makes peace with them.

battle. They took the captives out of there and turned back and went to Tappuah because the men of Tappuah had come out to rescue the captives they had taken from the city of Hasar. They went from there to (Qiryat) Arbaʿ and killed those men who came out to rescue the captives. *T. Jud.* 5:6

[8]On the third day they went to Tappuah at morning time, and as they were gathering the captives together, the inhabitants of Shiloh came to make war against them. Then they girded themselves and went out after them and killed them all before midday. They entered Shiloh after the women[a] and they would not make an agreement with them.[b] On that same day they captured the city and took out all the captives, and a group of their comrades whom they had left in Tappuah came to them with the booty of Tappuah. *T. Jud.* 5:7, 6:2

[9]On the fourth day they passed opposite Mahaneh Shakhir,[c] and they too came out to rescue the captives. Some of them came down into the valley, and (the sons of Jacob) sprang up and went up after them and killed them before they went up the hill. On that same day men came out against them from Mahaneh Shakhir and threw stones on them. On that same day (the sons of Judah) captured them, killing all their mighty warriors. They took out the captives and joined them to those they had with them.

[10]On the fifth day they went to Mt. Gaʿash because a great number of Amorites had gathered there, planning to attack them. Gaʿash was a strong city, one of the cities of the Amorite kings. They went there and made war against the city until midday, and they were unable to capture it because it had three walls, wall inside wall. (The Amorites) began to trouble them and insult them. *T. Jud.* 7:1 *T. Jud.* 7:5

[11]At that moment Judah became angry and a spirit of mighty zeal entered him. He sprang up with all his strength and went up first onto the wall. There Judah would have come to his death if it were not for his father Jacob, who drew his bow and killed (men) to his right and to his left until his brother Dan came up beside him. Judah had to rely on him, for they were throwing stones at him from the right and attacking him from the left and in front of him, all trying to drive him off the wall. When his brother Dan came up, he drove them a little distance from the wall. Then Naphtali came up third after them. And Simeon and Levi captured (it?) and went up from the west. The five of them arrived, and they would not make an agreement with them.[d] They killed so many of them that a river of blood flowed from them. They took the city at the time the sun was setting in the west. They killed all the mighty warriors on that day, and taking out the captives, they went and rested outside the city since they were tired. *T. Jud.* 7:5-6

[12]On the sixth day all the Amorites gathered together and came to them without any weapons of war and bowed before them and sought to make peace

a. Thus most of the MSS, including MS Hamburg (Alexander-Dan, "Complete *Midrash Vayissaʿu*"); Lauterbach seems to prefer this reading (*Midrash Vayissaʿu*, 218 n. 1), but he prints "those who had fled," which is graphically quite similar to "the women." *T. Jud.* 6:5 gives the women of Makir a role in defending their city from within, which lends support to the reading "the women."

b. The text is difficult here.

c. Or: "the camp of Shakhir." Because Shakhir was previously identified as king of Mahaneh, I prefer to take the two words as the full name of the city.

d. The wording is identical to the difficult language about Shiloh (n. b).

T. Jud. 7:7 | *Jub.* 34:9 with them. Then they made peace with (Jacob and his sons) and gave them
Timnah and all the land of Horiah. Then Jacob made peace with them, and they
paid the sons of Jacob for all the flocks that they had taken from them two for
Jub. 34:7 | *Jub.* 34:8 one, and they gave them tribute and returned all the captives to them. And Jacob
Jub. 34:8, *T. Jud.* 7:9 built up Timnah and Judah (built up) Dahabel,[a] and from then on they lived in
peace with the Amorites. And this is the meaning of what Jacob said to his son
Joseph, "*Look, I give you one portion*[b] *more than your brothers, which I took from*
Gen 48:22 *the hand of the Amorites with my sword and my bow.*"[c]

Chapter 3

Gen 36:6 1It is written, "*He went to a land because of Jacob his brother.*" Because of a
promissory note. And some say, because of shame.[d] Our rabbis said: Certainly[e]
though Esau abandoned his weapons because of Jacob and went (away), he did
not remove the hatred from his heart. Rather, "*His anger takes prey forever, and*
Amos 1:11 *his rage remains eternal.*"[f] Even though (Esau) went away at that time, some time
later he attacked (Jacob). It was the year that Leah died. Jacob and his sons were
sitting in mourning, and a few of his sons were comforting him about Leah's
death. (Esau) came upon them with a large force of warriors wearing armor of
iron and bronze, all equipped for war with shields, bows, and spears, four thou-
T. Jud. 9:2, *Jub.* 37:1-13 sand mighty warriors. They surrounded the citadel where Jacob and his sons
were encamped, they and their servants and their children and all that belonged
to them, for they had all gathered together there to comfort Jacob in his mourning for Leah.

2They were sitting peacefully, for it did not occur to them that anyone would
attack them, and they knew nothing of this until the whole force attacked that
Jub. 37:14-16 citadel. Only Jacob and his sons were there, and two hundred of their servants.

3When Jacob saw that Esau had insolently decided to attack and kill them
within the citadel and that he was shooting arrows against them, he stood on the
Deut 2:26, Esth 9:30 wall of the citadel and spoke *words of peace*, friendship, and brotherhood to Esau
Jub. 37:17 | *Jub.* 37:18-23 his brother. But Esau did not accept them.

4At once Judah said to Jacob his father, "How long will you go on speaking
Deut 2:26, Esth 9:30 *words of peace* and love when he comes upon us as an enemy dressed in armor
Jub. 38:1 to kill us?" When Jacob heard this, he drew his bow and killed Adoram the
Jub. 38:3 Edomite.

---

a. MS Hamburg (Alexander-Dan, "Complete *Midrash Vayissa'u*"): Arbael; *T. Jud.* 7:9: Rambael. According to the *Testament of Judah*, it is Judah who builds Timnah (Thamna) while Jacob builds Rambael.

b. The text is difficult here. The word translated "portion" is *shekhem*, the same word as the name of city Shechem.

c. The point of the quotation appears to be that Jacob himself spoke of having defeated the Amorites, not that Joseph received an extra portion, a claim the narrative of *Midrash Vayissa'u* does not support. The reference to Joseph is required by the biblical context of Jacob's words.

d. These alternatives are drawn from *Genesis Rabbah*'s comment to Gen. 36:6 (*Gen. Rab.* 82:13), where the first opinion is attributed to R. Eleazar and the second to R. Joshua b. Levi.

e. Following MSS Hamburg (Alexander-Dan, "Complete *Midrash Vayissa'u*") and Darmstadt and witnesses to *Yalqut Shim'oni* (Lauterbach, *Midrash Vayissa'u*).

f. The verse describes sins for which Edom will be punished; the Bible understands Edom as the nation descended from Esau.

[5]He drew his bow again and struck Esau in his right buttock.[a] Then (Esau) *Jub.* 38:2
became ill from the arrow. His sons lifted him up and placed him on a donkey
foal and he went and died there in Arodin.[b] But there are some who say he did *T. Jud.* 9:3
not die there.

[6]Then Judah went out first with Naphtali and Gad to the south of the citadel, with fifty of the servants of Jacob their father. Levi, Dan, and Asher went out to the east of the citadel with fifty servants. Reuben, Issachar, and Zebulon went out to the north of the citadel with fifty servants. Simeon, Benjamin, and Enoch the son of Reuben went out to the west of the citadel with fifty servants. Joseph *Jub.* 38:4-8
was not with them because he had already been sold. Genesis 37

[7]At that moment Judah made ready for war. He, Naphtali, and Gad went into
the midst of the army and attacked that iron tower.[c] Their shields were hit by *T. Jud.* 9:4
smooth stones that (Esau's men) threw and shot at them. The sun was darkened *T. Jud.* 9:5
because of the throwing of stones and the shooting of arrows and catapults that they threw down on them. Judah went first into the midst of the army and killed six mighty warriors. Naphtali and Gad went with him, one to the right and one to the left, protecting him so that the army could not kill him. They too killed four mighty warriors of the army, each one killing two. Also the fifty servants who were with them helped them. They went out to battle with them, and each one killed his opponent, fifty mighty warriors.

[8]Despite this Judah, Naphtali, and Gad were unable to drive the army from the south of the citadel or to move them from their place. Then (the sons of Jacob) made ready for war, and they all gathered together and fought against them, and each man killed his opponent. But despite this they could not chase them from their place, and the army stood against them, arranged for war in its divisions. Then Judah, his brothers, and their servants strengthened themselves and gathered together and fought against them, each one of them killing two from the (opposing) army.

[9]When Judah saw that the army was standing firm and that they were unable to move it, Judah, Naphtali, and Gad clothed themselves in the spirit of strength and the counsel of mighty warriors and all of them joined together to go into the midst of the warriors and kill them. Judah killed twenty mighty warriors, and Naphtali and Gad killed eight mighty warriors. And when their servants saw that Judah and his brothers had strengthened themselves and gone into the depths of the battle, they too strengthened themselves to stand with them to fight against (the enemy). Judah struck a hundred mighty warriors of the army on his right and on his left. Naphtali and Gad followed after him, killing

a. The passage is difficult. According to almost all of the witnesses, the arrow strikes Esau's right "chair." "Buttock" is my attempt to find an anatomical equivalent of chair. I have been unable to find any other examples of such a use, however. In *Jubilees*' account of the battle, Jacob hits Esau in the right breast (*Jub.* 38:2).

b. This place name does not appear in the Bible. According to *Jubilees* the battle takes place near Hebron, and Esau dies on the spot (*Jub.* 36:20, 38:2), but Jacob buries Esau in Aduram (*Jub.* 38:9). Adora was a major city of the Idumeans, as the Edomites were called during the Second Temple period.

c. At the beginning of the chapter, Jacob and his sons are in the citadel and can apparently shoot down on Esau and his men. The appearance of the iron tower, not previously mentioned, reverses the situation. Now Esau and his men can shoot down on Jacob and his sons.

them until [10]they drove the whole army from the south of the citadel, and (the men of the opposing army) turned their backs to flee. When the whole army saw that those whom Judah encountered had been destroyed before him, they trembled as they gathered together for battle. They waged war against Judah and his brothers, but they all stood their ground, fighting with power and strength. Thus did Levi and those who were with him, Reuben and those who were with him, and Simeon and those who were with him. Thus they stood against them for battle and gave over their souls to fighting them fiercely.

[11]When Judah saw that all (the men of) the army had strengthened themselves and gathered together for battle, unifying themselves[a] to fight against them and standing firm to wage war against them, he raised his eyes to the Holy One, blessed be he, (asking) that he help him and his brothers, for they were exhausted by the pressure of battle and were unable to fight against them any longer.

[12]At that moment the Holy One, blessed be he, accepted their prayer. He looked upon their trouble and came to their aid by bringing a storm wind from his storehouse. It blew against (the army's) faces, and their eyes filled with darkness and deep gloom, and they could not see to fight. But the eyes of Judah and his brothers were illumined because the wind hit them from behind. So Judah and his brothers began to kill (their enemies), and they made the dead fall to the ground as the thresher makes the threshing and bundles of sheaves fall, piling them into heaps, until they had killed the whole army that came against them at the south of the citadel.

[13]Reuben and Simeon and Levi with them stood ready for battle against the army before them. After Judah and his brothers had killed the men of the army before them, they went to their brothers to help them. A storm wind filled the eyes of their enemies with dust in darkness and deep gloom. And Reuben, Simeon, and Levi and all who were with them fell upon them and killed them, making them fall to the ground in heaps, until they had killed all the forces that had come against Judah, Reuben, and Levi. And there fell four hundred mighty warriors of those who did battle against Simeon, and the remaining six
Gen 36:4-5 hundred fled. These are the sons of Esau: Jeush, Jalam, Korah, and Reuel. But
Gen 36:4 Eliphaz did not want to go with them because Jacob our father was his teacher.[b]

[14]The sons of Jacob pursued them to the city of Arodin, so the (sons of Esau) left their father Esau dead, laid out in Arodin, and fled to Mt. Seir at the ascent

---

a. The phrase is difficult, and my translation is a guess. A literal translation would be "they did/made in a single way."

b. Or "rabbi," "master." MS Hamburg (Alexander-Dan, "Complete *Midrash Vayissa'u*") reads, "Eliphaz did not want to go with them because he had become a son to Isaac our father." Several late midrashim claim that Eliphaz became a righteous man despite his ancestry because he was raised by Isaac (*Tanhuma* [Buber] to Gen. 21:2 [*Vayera'* 38], *Deut. Rab.* 2.20, *Midrash haGadol* to Gen 36:6; *Midrash haGadol* notes Eliphaz's unwillingness to make war against Jacob and his sons in relation to this information about his upbringing, but the war in question is the war waged by Eliphaz's son Amalek when the children of Israel left Egypt). Louis Ginzberg, *Legends of the Jews* (Philadelphia, Pa.: Jewish Publication Society, 1925), 5.322 n. 318, suggests emending "Jacob" in the version of *Midrash Vayissa'u* translated above to "Isaac" on the basis of these midrashim. I suspect that the reading of the Hamburg MS is evidence of just such an emendation, but it seems to me far from certain that "Isaac" was the original reading of *Midrash Vayissa'u*.

of Aqrabim.[a] The sons of Jacob entered (Arodin) and rested there that night, and when they found Esau dead and laid out, they buried him out of respect for their father. And some say that (Esau) did not die there but that he left Arodin ill and *Jub.* 38:9
fled with his sons to Mt. Seir. The next day the sons of Jacob girded themselves and pursued (the sons of Esau). They went and caught them at Mt. Seir at the ascent of Aqrabim. The sons of Esau came out, and all of the men who fled, and fell down before the sons of Jacob and prostrated themselves before them and beseeched them until they made peace with them and gave them over to forced labor. *Jub.* 38:10-14

a. This place name appears in Num 34:4, Josh 15:3, and Judg 1:36.

The Testament of Job (Coptic Fragments)
A new translation and introduction

by Gesa Schenke

The Coptic *Testament of Job (T. Job)* forms part of a fragmentary papyrus codex housed in the Cologne papyrus collection. Other texts included in the codex are the *Testament of Adam*, the *Testament of Abraham*, and the *Acts of Peter and Andrew*. The importance of the *Testament of Job* was quickly recognized since no Coptic version of this text had previously been known. Moreover, the Cologne papyrus codex shows all the characteristics of a solid fourth-century manufacture, which makes this Coptic witness the earliest testimony of *T. Job* to date. It has therefore raised high hopes for the advancement of the study of this somewhat altered Jewish legend, considered to be a particularly interesting example of Jewish haggadah.

Contents

Generally assumed to have originally been composed between the late second century B.C.E. and the early second century C.E., this famous "reversal of fortune" story became and remained so popular that it was translated and copied at least until the seventeenth century, as the latest known Slavonic manuscript indicates. While elaborating upon the biblical book of Job, *T. Job* makes Job the king of Egypt and gives the narrative a framing-tale of Job's final days, during which he summons his sons and daughters to tell them the story of his life. While *T. Job* contains all the familiar characters of the book of Job, a much more prominent role is given to Job's first wife Sitios, who cares for and worries about him, as well as to his three daughters, each of whom inherits a magical girdle that enables them to escape earthly sufferings and to witness the ascension of their father's soul.

As the richest of kings in the east, Job is formerly named Jobab and is a worshipper of idols. Through the epiphany of an angel, he learns that his worship is a false one and consequently he desires to destroy the idol's temple. The angel informs him of all that would happen to him if he should carry out his plan, but that in the end he will have a place with God. Not unlike a Christian martyr, Jobab, enlightened after this experience, embraces his destiny with dignity. All earthly tortures—loss of possessions, loss of health, loss of offspring, and loss of status—have no effect on his iron will to live this through. Much unlike a Christian martyr, however, he does not die, but rather receives as a reward the restoration of all his earthly belongings—new wife, new children, twofold his former possessions and thus an even higher status. On his deathbed, he relates the story of his eventful life to his children, and gives them final instructions on how to conduct their lives.

Manuscripts and Versions

T. Job has formerly been known essentially only through three medieval Greek manuscripts, the earliest of which, *P* (Paris, Bibliothèque Nationale gr. 2658, fol. 72r–97r), dates to the eleventh century. Of this manuscript there also exists a sixteenth-century copy, known as P^2 (Paris, Bibliothèque Nationale gr. 938, fol. 172v–192v). The other two are the Vatican manuscript *V* (Rome, Biblioteca Vaticana Vat gr. 1238, fol. 340v–349v), dating to the year 1195, and the manuscript *S* (Sicily, Biblioteca Universitaria San Salvatore in Messina 29, fol. 35v–41v) of the year 1307. In addition to these, at least three Slavonic manuscripts have come to light, dating to the fifteenth and seventeenth century.[1]

All three Greek manuscripts (*P*, *S*, and *V*) of *T. Job* seem to be more or less independent witnesses as they show various small variations among them. Nonetheless, they all seem to belong to the same manuscript family, going back to one and the same original. However, the manuscripts *S* and *V* seem to share more similarities and are believed to stem from a later branch than the manuscript *P*.[2] The most recent editions of these manuscripts are the edition of *P* by Sebastian Brock, produced in 1967,[3] and the edition of *S* and *V* by Robert Kraft in 1974.[4]

The Coptic *T. Job* agrees at times freely with *P*, *S*, and *V*, but also offers unique material that seems to go back to an earlier textual tradition. While the large number of Greek loan words present in the Coptic *T. Job* testifies to the translation from a Greek text, the deviations from the known Greek witnesses seem to point to a much earlier Greek version of *T. Job* as the *Vorlage* for the Coptic translation. The evidence seems to suggest that the Coptic *T. Job* presents a version of the original Greek composition which contained certain poetic parts of which the later Greek witnesses have been cleaned.

Genre and Structure

The text belongs to the genre of testamentary literature: a dying father calling his children to listen to his life story and to receive his final instructions, as well as their inheritance. Within that framework, however, the life story told becomes so vivid, filled with numerous dialogues and long choruses, that the composition has been compared to dramatic poetry.[5] Clearly it is religious literature intended to uplift the spirit of a religious community. Which community exactly, whether Jewish, Christian, or a particular heretic group, is still being debated.[6]

Date and Provenance

The existence of such an early Coptic translation seems only to strengthen the idea of Egypt as the birthplace of the original Greek composition as well as to supply further proof of a distinct Christian interest in the text. The fourth-century date given to the

1. The dates reported for these manuscripts differ slightly, cf. Schaller, *Testament Hiobs*, 316 with n. 133 and 317 with n. 134; R. P. Spittler, "The Testament of Job: A History of Research and Interpretation," in Knibb and van der Horst, *Studies on the Testament of Job*, 9-10; as well as R. A. Kraft, *The Testament of Job according to the SV Text*, 3.

2. Cf. Schaller, *Testament Hiobs*, 317f. For a longer analysis of the relationships between *P*, *S*, and *V* cf. Kraft, *Testament of Job according to the SV Text*, 5-11.

3. Brock, *Testamentum Iobi.*

4. Kraft, *Testament of Job according to the SV Text.*

5. Cf. Schaller, *Testament Hiobs*, 313.

6. See for example Schaller, *Testament Hiobs*, 314, reviewing various suggestions as to the possible audience of this text.

Coptic *T. Job* is based on the evidence from the codex type, as well as on palaeography and language peculiarities. What remains of the Cologne papyrus codex amounts to a total of 40 leaves, i.e., 80 pages. The script gives an overall regular impression. The letters are more or less square and do not display any distinction between thinner and thicker strokes, so that they seem in many respects comparable to other fourth-century hands, like many of the Nag Hammadi Codices, the Berliner Koptisches Buch, or the Schøyen Codex. Some minor corrections to the text are occasionally found over the line, when letters or a whole word have been added or replaced. At other times, small additions seem to have been made later in the lower margins in different ink. But overall the copying of the manuscript appears to have been carried out very carefully.

While, on the whole, the 48 fragmentary pages of the Coptic *T. Job* offer common Sahidic forms, almost every page displays some "oddities" as well. These deviations from the classic Sahidic dialect of the Coptic language fall mainly into five categories, though not all of the same documentary value, and display many peculiarities of the Middle Egyptian dialect *M*. We find variations in the conjugation bases, inconsistencies in assimilation, interchanges of consonants and vowels, as well as additions and omissions of various characters. In a need to combine and evaluate all these synchronizing features it would perhaps be safest to say that the Coptic *T. Job* is an early, not yet fully standardized Sahidic text originating from somewhere in Middle Egypt.

Literary Context

What becomes, however, painfully obvious while looking at the pages of the Coptic *T. Job*, is that not a single line is complete. There is no continuous text, neither from line to line, nor from page to page. Every page lacks at least one side margin, often both, and strangely the top of the page lacks the left, the lower part of the page the right margin, or the other way around. Nonetheless, even in its fragmentary state, the disagreements with the Greek manuscripts are clearly visible. Moreover, the author not only mentions himself, but also explains what he did write and what he did not, and why. Just as in the Greek manuscripts, Nereus, the brother of Job, is present at the scene of transformation when Job's daughters gird themselves and become spiritually removed from this world. But contrary to the Greek manuscripts *S* and *V*, in the Coptic text at chapter 51 Nereus claims to be the author only of the book of Job, not of the three hymns sung by Job's daughters, since they have recorded these "splendours of God" for each other. The text of *S* and *V* is not very clear at this point, which caused editors to propose conjectures to the text,[7] while *P* actually preserves something rather similar to the Coptic manuscript.

So *T. Job* has an explicitly named author, Nereus, writing down the story of his brother's life. The original purpose, one would assume, was not to forget what gifts the Lord holds for as enduring and just a man as Job. The popularity this text received is presumably based on the hopefulness it projects; even in the depth of despair one ought not to turn one's back on God, for there is salvation through his hands.

That this text is grouped with other life and death stories of famous figures, such as the *Testament of Adam*, the *Testament of Abraham* and the *Acts of Peter and Andrew*, in a fourth-century Coptic codex, testifies to its popularity in Christian circles. There appears to have been an early need to provide a translation of that text for the native Egyptian

7. See for example Kraft, *Testament of Job according to the SV Text*, 83 with his note on chap. 51.3.

population. The large number of Greek loan words included in the Coptic translation seems to suggest either a high level of familiarity with many Greek literary words among the Egyptian population, or an educated audience as the recipient of that Coptic translation. Only the word *aphedrōn*, "latrine," seems to the translator to need an explanation, which he duly supplies by adding "that is the place of urinating and the place of producing excrement."

The popularity of the story of Job among Christians in Egypt is attested by numerous Coptic martyr legends referring to his sufferings as an example of steadfastness in overcoming this world and receiving glory through God. Job seems to have been celebrated as the prime martyr; and many of these legends show similarities to *T. Job*,[8] in as much as they treat the martyr's sufferings as a result of turning away from the worship of idols to the true service of God. The martyr's sufferings are seen as a fight between good and evil, between saint and Satan, in which the saint is always victorious for he is indifferent to earthly concerns and sufferings, longing only for the glory of eternal life.[9] In addition, most of the famous Coptic martyr saints, such as St. Coluthus, St. George, St. Menas, or St. Mercurius, come from an affluent background. They thrive on charity towards those in need and distribute their riches among the poor. In the face of tortures and sufferings, they are not to be convinced by family members or public authorities to turn away from God in order to save their life on earth, because through a heavenly messenger they had already been informed of what was to come for them, on earth and in heaven. Thus, they are already one step ahead and not won back by arguments tailored to convince mankind on earth. When arguing with the provincial authorities, the saints often give an account of the rewards awaiting them in the heavenly kingdom, juxtaposing it with the fleeting reign of authorities on earth. "My throne [is in] the supernatural (realm). Its [glory and] its beauty are to the right of the father. [My throne] is eternal. [Its glory and] its beauty is without blemish. [This world will] pass by. Its glory [and those who] rely on it [will perish through] its shame," claims Job in chapter 33 to the rage of his fellow kings who were most concerned with Job's loss of worldly possessions. In many of the martyr legends it is likewise a brother or close friend who claims to have been an eyewitness to the scene and to have written everything down for the memory of the saint.

Differences between the Coptic and the Greek Texts

Besides Nereus as the author of the book, the main differences between the Coptic and the Greek manuscripts are the following: In the Coptic text the fellow king who first questions Job in chapter 31 to ensure his identity is not Elious, but Eliphas. It is also he who laments the loss of Job's riches in a long hymn, juxtaposing Job's past and present situation, which is more elaborately composed than in the Greek versions. In chapter 40, when the fellow kings see Job's children in heaven, the narrative changes from the first to the third person singular. The sacrificial hymn, which Eliphas delivers in chapter 43, after the three fellow kings have been forgiven by the Lord, seems to present a more original and formal pattern with the constant repetition of the main point, that they are forgiven, while Elious

8. Similarities between *T. Job* and the description of the conduct of St. Paese towards the poor in the martyrdom of SS. Paese and Thecla, *Four Martyrdoms from the Pierpont Morgan Coptic Codices* (ed. E. A. E. Reymond and J. W. B. Barns; Oxford: Oxford University Press, 1973), have already been pointed out by Brock and Schaller; cf. the remarks by Schaller, *Testament Hiobs*, 374.

9. Cf. here the list of differences between the Old Testament *Book of Job* and *T. Job*, given by Schaller, *Testament Hiobs*, 315.

is not and thus is eternally doomed. In its preserved Coptic form the hymn matches the previous songs in structure. Finally, the weeping scene at Job's burial in chapter 53 seems to have been slightly more elaborate in the Coptic text, which unfortunately is very fragmentary at that point.

The Translation

In the following translation the chapter and verse numbers are cited according to Brock. The page numbers 1–48 refer to the fragmentary pages of the codex itself, containing the Coptic *T. Job*, rather than corresponding to any original pagination within the codex of which no traces have been preserved. This translation is best read alongside one of the English translations of the complete Greek text by Spittler or Thornhill (see the bibliography).

Bibliography

Begg, Ch. T. "Comparing Characters: The Book of Job and the Testament of Job." Pages 435-445 in *The Book of Job*. Edited by W. A. M. Beuken. Louvain: Leuven University Press, 1994.

Brock, S. P. *Testamentum Iobi*. Pages 1-59 in *Pseudepigrapha Veteris Testamenti Graece* II. Leiden: Brill, 1967.

Garret, S. R. "The 'Weaker Sex' in the Testament of Job." *JBL* 112 (1993): 55-70.

Jacobs, I. "Literary Motifs in the Testament of Job." *JJS* 21 (1970): 1-10.

James, M. R. *The Testament of Job*. Pages 104-137 in *Apocrypha Anecdota* II. Texts and Studies. Contributions to Biblical and Patristic Literature V, 2. Cambridge: Cambridge University Press, 1897.

Kirkegaard, B. A. "Satan in the Testament of Job: A Literary Analysis." Pages 4-19 in *Of Scribes and Sages: Early Jewish Interpretation and Transmission of Scripture II, Later Versions and Traditions*. Edited by C. A. Evans. Library of Second Temple Studies 51. London: T.&T. Clark, 2004.

Knibb, M. A., and P. W. van der Horst (eds.). *Studies on the Testament of Job*. SNTSMS 66. Cambridge: Cambridge University Press, 1989.

Kraft, R. A., *The Testament of Job according to the SV Text*. SBLTT 5. SBL Pseudepigrapha Series 4. Missoula, Mont.: Society of Biblical Literature, 1974.

Kugler, R. A., and R. L. Rohrbaugh. "On Women and Honor in the Testament of Job." *JSP* 14 (2004): 43-62.

Philonenko, M. "Le Testament de Job. Introduction, traduction et notes." *Sem* 18 (1968): 1-75.

Rahnenführer, D. "Das Testament des Hiob und das Neue Testament." *ZNW* 62 (1971): 68-93.

Schaller, B. *Das Testament Hiobs. Unterweisung in lehrhafter Form*, 303-387. *JSHRZ* III,3. Gütersloh: Gerd Mohn, 1979.

__________. "Das Testament Hiobs und die Septuagintaübersetzung des Buches Hiob." *Bib* 61 (1980): 377-406.

Schenke, G. *Der koptische Kölner Papyruskodex 3221, Teil I: Das Testament des Iob*. Abhandlungen der Nordrhein-Westfälischen Akademie der Wissenschaften und der Künste, Sonderreihe Papyrologica Coloniensia 23. Paderborn: Schöningh, 2009.

__________. "Neue Fragmente des Kölner Kodex 3221: Textzuwachs am koptischen Testament des Job." *Zeitschrift für Papyrologie und Epigraphik* 187 (2014): [in print].

Spitta, F. *Das Testament Hiobs und das Neue Testament*, 132-206. *Zur Geschichte und Literatur des Urchristentums* III, 2. Göttingen: Vandenhoeck und Ruprecht, 1907.

Spittler, R. P. "Testament of Job." *OTP*, 1:132-206.

Thornhill, R. "The Testament of Job." *AOT*, 617-48.
Wahl, H.-M. Elihu. "Frevler oder Frommer? Die Auslegung des Hiobbuches (Hi 32-37) durch ein Pseudepigraphon (TestHi 41-43)." *JSJ* 25 (1994): 1-17.
Weber, M. "Addendum zur Übersetzung des Testamentum Hiobs." In M. Philonenko, "Le Testament de Job." *Sem* 18 (1968) (see above): 61-63.

The Testament of Job (Coptic Fragments)

(page 1: Beginning of the text) 1:1The book of] Jobab, that is, the affairs [of Job], [...]

(page 2: Job reports to his children , Chap. 1:6–2:2) [...] in a [bitter] death. [But listen to me] and I will tell you [and reveal] to you the things [that happened to me], who [I have been] and what my [name, by which I had been called, was]. 2:1Before [the Lord called] me Job, [I had been given the name Jobab]. 2:2I lived [...]

(page 3: The light of the Lord speaks with Job, Chap. 4:1–4:4) [...] ... he will cause them to ...[...] to you all the things [that the Lord ordered] me to say to you. [...] obey me!" 4:2[And I said]: "All the things that are [brought over me], I will obey [and do them]." 4:3He said to me: "[All the] things [that the Lord says] are the following: 4:4 'Behold, [if you go forth now] to destroy [the place of Satan, ...']

(page 4: Job embraces his destiny, Chap. 4:10–5:2) [...] ... the crown. [4:11Then you will know] that the Lord is [just." 5:1And] I, [my] children, [replied to him and said]: "I will endure [until my death] and I will [never] turn back." 5:2After he had signed [me, he went] away from me. [...] during the next night, [...] I ran [out to the temple of the] idol [and turned it over to the ground. ...]

(page 5: Satan comes to the door, Chap. 7:3–6) [...] ... [burned] bread [...] ... to cause any [...] ... : "Take it for him [and say to him:] 7:4'You will not eat of [my bread from] this time [onwards], because [...].'" 7:5Then the servant [door keeper ...] the burned bread. She was [ashamed to give it to him] burnt as it was, 7:6[since she did not know] that it was Satan, [...] ... that which [... she gave it] to Satan. [...]

(page 6: Satan utters his threat, Chap. 7:11–12) [...] ... it and he [...] to him. 7:12After Satan [had heard] these things, he [...] to the servant saying: "[...] to Jobab: 'Just as [this bread is completely] burnt, I will destroy [also your body in] this manner. I [...] you ... [... in a short] time ....'" [...] ... [...]

(page 7: Job's animals, Chap. 9:4–6) [...] I had [nine thousand camels]. I divided them [... three] thousand and I commanded [... to do work in] every city. 9:5I used to [load them with goods] and send them [down to the cities] and the villages, saying: "[...] ... and the poor and [...] and anyone who [has need ...] ...." 9:6There were [...] ... [...]

(page 8: Job's charity for the poor, Chap. 10:1–5) [...] to anyone 10:2[...] my twelve [tables ...] came for [...] ... [...]10:3Before they went, [I ..., that which they] needed. 10:4... [...] at my door, while ... [...] fold (of garment?) ... 10:5[...] pair of oxen [...] five hundred [...]

(page 9: Job lends money, Chap. 11:3–6) [...] serve the poor. 11:4[Afterwards, we will] restore to you [all that belongs to you]. 11:5When I [heard this ... great] joy, since they took [from me provision] for the poor. 11:6... [...] to them, that which [...] ... it ... [...] ... [...] ... [...]

(page 10: The riches of Job's cattle, Chap. 12:2–13:2) [...] honoured [...] poor. 12:3Therefore, [...] reward. 12:4I did not use to let [...] ... in [...]. 13:1They used to loathe [...] my cattle herds ... 13:2[...] while butter and [milk ...] on the hills and the [roads ...] namely the hills [...] my animals [...]

(page 11: Job worries about his children, Chap. 15:1–5) [...] ... also their ... 15:2[...] ... [...] and my daughters in their house. 15:3[The] female [servants] who served them [...] 15:4... because of them ... [...] whenever I rose [...] I had offerings there [...] ... three [hundred doves, fifty] kids [...] 15:5... [...] to the poor [...] ... [...]

(page 12: Satan's destruction of Job's animals, Chap. 16:2–7) [... Then] Satan came 16:3and [burned down] the seven thousand sheep [...] to the poor and the three [thousand] female camels and five [hundred female donkeys and five] hundred pair of [oxen. 16:4...] them [...] ... [according to the] authority which had been appointed [to him ...]. 16:5They sought after [...] my animals 16:6[...] them 16:7[...] blasphemy [...]

(page 13: Satan incites a mob to plunder Job's possessions, Chap. 17:4–6) "[... Take for] yourselves his belongings! [...] into his house! Despoil [...]!"17:5But they said: "[He] has [seven] sons and three [daughters]. Will they not depart angrily [to other] countries and destroy [us as] thieves?" 17:6He said: "[Do not be afraid! The greater part] of his animals [...] ... [... a] fire [has] eaten them. [...] ..."

(page 14: Job remembers the promised rewards, Chap. 18:5–7) [... I did] remember the honoured words [concerning] them, which the angel had spoken [...] strength for myself alone. 18:6I [became just like] a man who wishes to go [to a city] in order to see [its] great wealth [...] and who wishes to inherit [a ...] of it, 18:7(a man) who has entered a [ship with] freight ... [...] out to the middle [...] strong [winds] and [...]

(page 15: Satan attacks Job, Chap. 20:2–5) [...] and he brings [...] 20:3The Lord handed me over to him, so that [he might] do with my body as he pleases. (But) he did not gain power over [my] soul. 20:4He [came] to me while I was sitting on my throne grieving. 20:5He was just like a whirlwind. He turned me around and threw the throne upon me. [...] ... I spent three [hours ... under] the throne ... [...] come out from under him [...] ...

(page 16: Job sees his wife working as a servant, Chap. 21:2–4) [...] serve ... [...] and I saw her, as the sorrow was coming to her, for she was drawing water for the house [...] of this city, until they would give [her] bread and she would bring it to me, 21:3and I would be exceedingly grieved by the archons, saying: "Look at the archons of this city, those whom [I could not] value as much as the [dogs of my herds! For] what did they do? They have [...] like a slave [...]" 21:4... and I took ... [...] ... [...]

(page 17: Satan as the bread seller, Chap. 23:5–8) [...] ... if not, [then you shall see!] 23:6But he said to her: "If he had not been worthy of those evils, [they] would not have come over you. 23:7Now then, if you want bread not having any money in your hands, then give me the hair of your head [and I] give you three loaves of bread and you can [live on them for] three days." 23:8And she [said to herself]: "What shall I do with [the hair on my head? My husband] Jobab, he is [...]

(page 18: Sitios' sufferings, Chap. 24:2–7) [... while I am going] from house to house 24:4[working] by day, suffering by night, until I find bread and bring it to you. 24:5[For] they cease to give me the other loaf of bread which [I used to] give to you. My [own] food [for my] body, which is given to me, I have divided it between the two of us. 24:6But he does not grieve because of me, [as I am] saying: "He is [in these afflictions, while being] unfilled with bread. 24:7[And I went] out to the [market place without shame]."

(page 19: The laments about Sitios' losses, Chap. 25:2–5) [...] ... at her door ... [...] into her place. 25:3For bread she [has] sold her hair. 25:4Look at the one whose camels were working down in the lands loaded with goods, which she gave to those [in need]! For [bread she has] sold her hair. 25:5[...] ... while you will not [...] there, and they will not bring [...]

(page 20: Sitios incites Job to curse God, Chap. 25:9–10) [...] ... [...] ... 25:10But rise, [take] these loaves of bread [from my hand], eat and [be satisfied and] speak one word against the Lord, [lie down] and die and quit these sufferings [and] afflictions ... [...] ... [...] because of the pain [...] your heart which [...] in which you are [...]

(page 21: Job's reaction to his wife's suggestion, Chap. 26:4–6) [...] Why [can] you [not remember] those great riches in which we lived earlier? If we have received the goods of fortune from the hand of the Lord, why will we not bear the evil? 26:5[But let us] now remain in [patience], until the Lord [takes pity on] us and shows us mercy. 26:6[Do you not see] the devil [...]

(page 22: Job defies Satan, Chap. 27:1–2) [...] ... [...] But I for myself am ready [... and] to fight with you. 27:2Then Satan [came out] from my wife, and stood right before me. He wept saying [to me]: "Behold [...] from you, [even though] you [are] of the flesh, [while I am of] the spirit. [You ...]"

(page 23: Satan is defeated, Job's fellow kings arrive, Chap. 27:3–28:3) [... to] the ground. [...] the one above [...] every [thing] that comes [over him ...] is great, long-suffering [...] 27:4... the one on the ground with the limbs [...] ... them. He caused [...] 27:5In this manner you too, [Jobab ...] down in [this great suffering]. But [you have been victorious (?) ...] (ca. 4 lines missing) 27:7[... everything] that comes over [you, for patience is stronger than anything.

28:1After twenty years [were completed], while I was in this suffering, 28:2my fellow kings heard about the sufferings that had been [brought] over me. They rose and came to me [from their own countries] in order to pay me a visit [and to give] me (strength for) patience. 28:3[And after they had reached] me, [...]

(page 24: The fellow kings do not recognize him, Chap. 28:3–6) [... tear] his [own garment and they spread dust on] their head. 28:4[They sat by me] for seven days, while [none of] them dared to [speak with] me. 28:5They did not speak [not because] they were long-suffering, [or because] they would have asked: "Why [have you not] spoken?" [But] they did not speak [because they had seen ...] (ca. 3 lines missing)

[... Since when [...] were, and I showed [them] my precious stones, and they clapped [their] hands together, saying: "If we would [bring] all the property of the three kings to a single place, they ... [...] not the precious stones of [your kingdom]." 28:6There was no king [richer than] myself in [the East]. [...]

(page 25: The fellow kings question his identity, Chap. 28:7/8–30:3) ["... the one who rules over all of Egypt?"] 28:9They enquired after my animals [and my property]. They were told about [every] evil. 29:1Then they rose and [came to me]. The people of the [city showed] me [to them]: "This [is Job." 29:2They] said: "No! Behold,] this [is not Job, our fellow king!"] (ca. 4 lines missing)

29:3["Are you] Job, our fellow king?" 29:4And I wept, took dust [from the ground] and threw it on my head. [I] moved my head towards them (saying): "I am." 30:1They fell down onto [the ground]. Their mind was beside themselves 30:2and a great disturbance was [in their] army of soldiers, [after they had seen] the kings falling [down onto the ground]. 30:3After three [hours ...]

(page 26: The fellow kings discuss Job's former riches, Chap. 30:4–31:2) [... They] contended [... and my] animals, while they were [speaking about my possessions], saying: 30:5"Do you not know [... the] wealth, which he used to [send down] to the [surrounding] cities [and] villages for those in need? [... his] house [...] (ca. 3 lines missing)

31:1[... seven] days, while they were speaking about my possessions, [they did not] speak to me at all. And [therefore] Eliphas said to his other fellow kings: "Rise and let us approach him and ask him precisely if he is indeed [Job, or not."] 31:2And they [rose, being half a stade] away from me because of the [stench of my body].

(page 27: Eliphas questions Job and begins his lament, Chap. 31:6–32:4) [... But I answered him] and spoke, [saying]: "I am." 31:7[And] he wept [in a] loud wail and [grief, worthy of] the kingdom, 31:8while the other fellow kings answered him. 32:1Hear [the weeping of Eliphas], as he is telling everyone [about the prosperity] of Job: 32:2"[Are] you [Job, the one of that great] glory? Where is the glory of [your throne?] [The one of those seven thousand] sheep [who clothe the poor? Are] you [Job, the one of that great glory?] Where is the glory of your throne? Are you Job, the one of those three thousand camels who carry goods to the poor? Where is the glory of your throne? 32:3Are you Job, [the one of that] great glory? Where is the glory of your [throne]? 32:4The one of that [golden bed]? Why is he now sitting [in the dust]? Where is [the glory] of your throne [...]?

(page 28: Eliphas' lament, Chap. 32:5–10) [...] [Where is the glory of your] throne? 32:6[Who is it], who dared to [... amidst] your children, [while you were like an apple tree] in fragrance? [... Where is the] glory of your throne? 32:7The owner of those sixty tables [which were destined] for the poor, [now] he is [sitting there] like a [poor man. 32:8Where is the glory of your] throne? [The owner of those many fragrant] incense burners? He (now) lives [in] stench. Where is the glory of your throne? 32:9The one whose oil, which used to anoint him, was an ointment of the frankincense-tree? Where is the glory of your throne? 32:10[The owner of] those golden lamps on those [silver] lamp-stands? But behold, how will he [receive light]? The moon [will shine for him]. [Where is] the glory of [your throne]?

(page 29: Eliphas ends his lament and Job responds, Chap. 32:11–33:3) The one who used to [laugh about the] sinners? Now they laugh [about him. Where] is [the glory] of your throne? 32:12[Sitios], your wife, the one of that [noble] descent, [now] she is a servant. Are you [Job? Where is the glory of your] throne, the glory of [your throne]?"

33:1When [Eliphas] continued to say these things, while [the other] kings and the army [of soldiers] answered [him], so that [there was] a great [disturbance], 33:2I myself cried [out to them right] into their shouting. [I spoke to them], saying: ["Be quiet! Now I] will [tell you about my throne. My] throne [is in the upper realm, the place of] origin of all things(?). Its glory and its beauty are among the saints [of the kingdom]. You enquire [after the kingdom down] on earth. 33:3I will tell [you that my] throne is in [the heavens]. Its glory and its beauty are in [the heavenly kingdom] of the father. My throne [is in] the supernatural (realm). Its [glory and] its beauty are to the right of the father. [My throne] is eternal. [Its glory and] its beauty is without blemish.

(page 30: Job's response and Eliphas's reaction, Chap. 33:4–34:3) [This world will] pass by. Its glory [and those who] rely on it [will perish through] its shame. 33:5My throne [is in a] holy [land]. Its glory [and its beauty are] in the unchanging aeons. 33:6[The rivers] will dry up. [The fish] will perish. The glory of [their wave] will go down to the abyss. 33:7But [my rivers], my land, in [which my throne stands], can never [dry up, but] they remain [eternally. 33:8The kings will] pass away. The [governors will pass by. Their glory] and [their honour] [...33:9But my] kingdom is eternal. Its glory and its honour are in the chariots of the father."

34:1While I was saying these things to them, they remained quiet. 34:2Eliphas was furious and said to the other [two]: "What is the use or what is [the gain] for us to have come here to [him to comfort him] and to have been worried, [we ourselves and] our armies of [soldiers? 34:3It is fitting] to let others do [... and to let them] speak [with him. ...]

(page 31: Eliphas' anger and Baldad's explanation, Chap. 34:4–35:3) He himself is sitting [in] pains, in [worms and stench], and he has also risen [against us], saying: 'The [kings will] pass by, and the governors [will pass away], and my kingdom [will remain] eternal.' "

34:5Eliphas rose [greatly] disturbed. [He turned] away from us with a [great] threat: "I shall go [off]. Behold, we have come so that we would give [him comfort]. He has humiliated us [in the presence] of our soldiers!"

35:1[After that, king Baldad] rose. [He] spoke [to him] saying: "It is not [right to] say [these things to anyone] who is in [great sorrow and pain], but is moreover in great sufferings with sickness and [worms], smelling disrespectfully. 35:2Behold, [we ourselves while being] strong could not [approach] him and endure the stench [which is] about him, unless we [took] perfume [along]. 35:3Remember [the] two days of sickness [you suffered], king Eliphas, so that [...] which you have said [to him].

(page 32: Baldad questions Job's mind, Chap. 35:4–36:3) [We are] people whose mind [(usually) remained stable] and who are (now) unclear. [...] Now then, let us not [be downcast], but let us be patient [with him] and understand exactly [in what (shape) he is]. Perhaps [his mind] has withdrawn? Perhaps he remembers [his] wealth, which was around him? [Perhaps] he has gone crazy and his mind [left] him while he was in this suffering? 35:5For we, although being strong [were] almost [beside ourselves] with great fury, because of [the glory in which he was] earlier. There is no [one who endures this without] hating [it]. 35:6[Now then let me approach him, so that I understand ... and] evaluate him." 36:1Then Baldad rose. Because he had stayed away from [me], he approached me [and said to me]: "Are you Job?" [I said to him]: "I am." 36:2And [he said to me]: "Is [your mind] agreeable to you?" 36:3But I said: "My mind [does not fancy] the things of the world, it does not [have trust in them], for [this world is] unstable together with [those who dwell] on it.

(page 33: Baldad speaks with Job, Chap. 36:3–37:5) My mind does [have trust in] the [heavenly] things, [for there is no disturbance in] heaven." 36:4[But he said to me: "We know that the world is unstable. It changes now and then. Sometimes] it spends time [well] and nobly, other times [it causes evil]. Sometimes it is [pleasing], other times one takes to warfare [also causing] outrage. 36:5Also concerning heaven we know [that what is] in it, is stable. But [if] your mind is stable, I [will ask you] one thing. 36:6[If you give me an intelligent answer] first, [I will ask you a second] time. [If you give] me [an intelligent answer again, I will know] that your [mind is stable." 37:1He said to me]: "In whom do you put your hope?" 37:2[And] I said to him: "It is the [living] God in whom I put my hope." 37:3[And] he said to me: "Who is it, [who has taken] your possessions [presently]? And who is it, who has brought [these numerous] sufferings over you?" 37:4[I said to him]: "It is God." 37:5He said to me: "If you put [your hope in] God and you have trust in him,

(page 34: Job's reaction to Baldad's questions, Chap. 37:5–38:1) [Job, how then do you evaluate] this ill treatment [... these] sufferings [...] 37:6[...] ... [...] ... then let him not [give him anything in the first place]! Job, which king [is it, who would [punish] a soldier who is counted [among his own, knowing] that he has trust in him?" 37:7[I said]: "Who are they, who have not gained [from the Lord] and his wisdom? ... [...] utter words against God." 37:8[...] ... and the [soldier (?) ...] him, Job, [...] ... if you are a [...] [why do we see] the sun daily rising in the east [and moving to (sailing to)] the west. Contrary to this, we rise every morning and we find [it] rising in the east. [Instruct me, if] you are the servant [of God!" 38:1I answered saying: ["Is it fitting] to say this that my mind is stable? [My mind] is stable. Yet to say this [...] while my mouth explains the greatness [of the Lord] in your presence, [...]. It will not attain [...]

(page 35: Job's question to his fellow kings and Sophar's offer, Chap. 38:2-7) [...] ... [... We] are earthly, while [our share is] of dust and [ashes. 38:3In order that] you may know that my mind [is stable], listen to what I will ask you and tell it to me. Your [food] which you eat—tell [me:] Why does this mouth [drink water und] eat bread, while this [throat] is one and the same throat? When [we] come to the latrine—that is the place of [urinating] and the [place] of producing excrement—we will send [them forth separate from one another. Who then is it who has] separated them from one another?"

38:4Baldad said: "I do not know." 38:5I answered and said to him: If you do not know the ways of your body, how they are, [then] how will you understand how the ways of heaven are?

38:6Sophar answered saying: ["We do not wish] to enquire after the things that are difficult [to understand], but we wish to know whether [your mind] is stable or not. We have [understood that] there [was] no change in you [concerning your mind]. 38:7What then is it that you want us [to do for you]? Behold, we have brought all the physicians of the three kingdoms when we came. [If you] want them to treat [you, then perhaps] you are relieved quickly."

(page 36: Sitios arrives at the scene of discussion, Chap. 38:8–39:8) [... I answered] saying: ["My healing] is through the [Lord], the physician who is above [all] physicians."

39:1As I was speaking with them, Sitios, my wife, [came] wearing torn [garments] 39:2as she fled from [her master] to whom [she was] a slave, serving [him], because he would not let her go out at all, so that also my fellow [kings] might not see her and [seize] her on [their own authority].

39:3Immediately after [she came] out, she ran and threw herself down at the feet of my [fellow king]. She wept, saying: 39:4["Remember me], Eliphas, together with your two [fellow kings], how I was [with you and what] kind and glory my riches [were] that I wore. 39:5And behold how I am going around or what I wear!" 39:6Then [they cried] and wept greatly, so that [my wife suffered] even more.

39:7After this, Eliphas took his purple garment and handed it over to [take it apart, and] he put it around her. 39:8[But she continued to] implore them. First [she spoke, saying]: "I entreat [you to command] your army [of soldiers ...]

(page 37: The quest for Job's children, Chap. 39:8–40:3) [...] [bring] them (back) to light.—39:9[For] we were unable to bring them out, because [...] what we have — , and I may look at [the bones of my] children again. 39:10Surely I do not [have] an animal's womb, [have I], which [brought forth the young], so that ten children died [on me, before I could] speak with any of them? [I wish to bury them] and to understand their death."

39:11[As they rose], I called them saying [to them]: 39:12 "You will not find my children, [since] their creator, their king, has taken them up to heaven." 39:13Then they answered saying to me: ["But who] is it who [will] now not [say] that [you are deranged], Job, saying: 'My children have been taken up to heaven.' Now then, tell us, is it [the] truth what you are saying?"

40:1But he said: "Come and [lift me up] so that I stand!" They lifted [him] up, firmly holding] his forearms, one under this (arm), [another under that (arm)], 40:2and he gave praise [to the Lord].

40:3[After] the great prayer, Job [turned around] in his suffering [and] Job [said] to his companions: "Raise [your eyes] towards the side of the east!" [And they] looked up and saw his children

(page 38: Sitios's death, Chap. 40:3–11) [...] up in heaven. 40:4[After] his wife [had seen this herself], she threw herself [down onto the ground] at Job's feet. [Sitios spoke] saying: "Job, [I myself know now] that my remembrance is [with the Lord. Nothing] is destroyed through me [by the Lord, since] this is what I have seen, I have [seen. I shall get up] now and go down [to the city and] lie down for an hour and [rest myself], before the time of duty [comes] and before I rise and serve in slavery."

40:5Sitios, my wife, went into the city. She [entered] the stable [of the] cattle that the archons had seized. 40:6She lay down next to a manger lightheartedly and died peacefully. She did [not] do her service. 40:7Her master rose and searched for [her] until the evening. 40:8When he [came to the stable], the animals stood up, and [he found her lying] in the stable. 40:9[Her] cattle saw her being [dead] and all cried out [in a loud lament] and wept over her. [Their great noise] went out of the city. 40:10[One was amazed about the] animals and thus rose [in order to go] into the stable, so that one might [understand what] was going on. 40:11One found her [dead, while the animals

(page 39: Elious rises against Job, Chap. 40:11/12–41:6) wept over her] ... [... 40:13Also the poor] wept for her, saying: "Look [at her, the one of] all [pride], for she was not worthy [of being buried (properly)]." 40:14The lament that was produced over [her is written] in the Paraleipomena [of Eliphas].

41:1After this, they sat around and got into a big quarrel [in front of me]. They uttered [boasts] to my face, 41:2and so they [rose after] twenty-seven days [to go back to their] countries, 41:3and [Elious] invoked them: "Remain with me, until I tell [...] him, for you have spent all these days, enduring Job saying: 'I am just.' 41:4Whereas I have [...] I will not be able to endure it (any longer). At the beginning I have not [ceased] to cry tears for him and to remember his former kingship, for perhaps [he ...] the four fellow kings [... each] one, and we caused him to be in [...] He also exalted himself [... saying]: 'The glory of [my throne is] in heaven.' 41:5Now then, [listen to me and] I tell you [of what kind] his share is." Then Satan [was set in him who] spoke words of [hard-heartedness] against me. 41:6Behold, they

(page 40: The light of the Lord speaks to the kings, Chap. 41:6–43:5) [are written in the Paraleipomena of Eliphas.

42:1After the] whole [speech, the Lord appeared in a cloud] of light. 42:2He was [furious with Elious], telling him of his [judgment. He told me] that it was not a human, [but a beast] who was speaking (before).

42:3[When the] Lord [spoke] in the cloud of light, also the [four kings heard him] looking up. 42:4After the Lord finished talking [to me, he] spoke also with Eliphas [saying]: 42:5"You have sinned, you and [also] your two [comrades], for you have not spoken truthfully like [my] servant Job. 42:6But rise then and let him [bring] up sacrifice for [you], so that I forgive you your sin. If not for [Job], I would not have mercy on you."

42:7And they brought their sacrifice and the offering equipment, 42:8[and I] offered it for them. The Lord [received it and forgave] them. 43:1But to Elious [he did not consent].

43:2Eliphas was in [the Spirit] and sang a hymn 43:3[and] also his fellow kings [and their] whole army of soldiers [replied] after him [surrounding] the altar, 43:4while he was singing: ["Our] sin has been taken away. Our lawlessness [has been cleansed]. 43:5Elious, that evil one, [was not remembered

(page 41: Eliphas's lament for Elious, Chap. 43:5–11) among the living. 43:6...] [... to] condemnation.

[Our sin has been taken away. Our] lawlessness has been cleansed. [Elious, that evil one], was not remembered [among the living. A child] of darkness is he, [not] of light. [It is not this one], who will inherit the glory.

[Our sin has been taken away.] Our lawlessness has been cleansed. [Elious, that evil one], was not remembered [among the living]. 43:7He loved the beauty of the snake and [the scales of the] dragon. Its bitterness and its [poison too will] be a fodder for him.

Our [sin has been taken away. Our] lawlessness has been cleansed. Elious, that evil one, was not remembered among the living. 43:8[His] reign has passed. His throne has become [rotten. The glory] of his dwelling place will be in the underworld.

Our sin has been taken away. [Our] lawlessness has been [cleansed.] Elious, that evil one, was not [remembered among] the living. 43:9He did not acquire the Lord for himself and did not fear him. He quarreled [with] his honourable [comrades too.

Our] sin has been taken away. Our lawlessness [has been cleansed]. Elious, that evil one, [was not] remembered among the living. 43:10The Lord has [condemned him] eternally. He is continuously forgotten. [The saints] have [left him]. 43:11The wrath is [in vain] for him.

[Our] sin has been taken away. Our lawlessness [has been cleansed]. Elious, that evil one, [was not] remembered among the living.

(page 42: Eliphas' lament for Elious comes to an end, Chap. 43:12–44:4) [...]

[Our sin has been taken away. Our lawlessness] has been cleansed. [Elious, that evil one], was not remembered [among the living]. 43:13The Lord is [just]. Truthful are [his judgments. There are no favours] from him, when he will judge us [at some point].

Our sin has been taken away. Our lawlessness [has been cleansed]. Elious, that evil one, was not [remembered among] the living. 43:14Behold, the Lord has come! Behold, [the saints have] prepared themselves! Behold, the crowns [of justification] draw before him.

Our [sin has been taken away]. Our lawlessness has been cleansed. Elious, [that] evil one, was not remembered among the [living]. 43:15[Let] the saints rejoice and [be jubilant] in their heart, 43:16for they have found [what they had] looked for.

43:17[Our] sin has been taken away. Our lawlessness has been cleansed. Elious, that evil one, was not [remembered] among the living."

44:1After Eliphas finished singing [his] hymn, while they all replied [after him, surrounding] the altar, we [rose and went] into the city. We came into [the house in which we] are now. 44:2[We celebrated festivities in] the Lord and in his joy. I was [seeking to do] good for the poor. 44:3And [they came to me, my] brothers and those who knew [to do] good [deeds]. 44:4They asked me saying: ["What] is it that you want from [us now?" And I

(page 43: Job divides his possessions among his sons, Chap. 44:4–46:5) remembered the poor ...] [...] lambs [...] those naked 44:5[...] gold to the place of [...]. The Lord blessed them greatly. [And that] which was mine before, he [gave to me] twice.

45:1Now, my children, [I will die]. Do not neglect the Lord! 45:2Do [what is good to the] poor! Do not overlook [the weak]! 45:3Do not take a wife from [among strangers]! 45:4Behold, I will divide all [my own] between you, and each one (of you) will be master over what is his, so that if one wishes to do what is good, he shall be his own master and no one [shall hinder] him.

46:1What [was his] was brought forth and put down. He divided it between his seven sons. 46:2He did not give any goods [to their] sisters. His daughters [said] to him: ["Our] lord and our father, are we not [your children] then, that you have not given to us from [what is yours?" 46:3He] answered and said to them: "[Do not be grieved, my] children, that we brought goods [to them! Do not say:] 'This is not our father. He has been negligent.' 46:4For I have left behind for you an [inheritance] far more exquisite than the inheritance [of your] seven brothers." 46:5He called [his daughter] Hemera and said to her: "Take

(page 44: Job's inheritance for his daughters, Chap. 46:5–47:4) [the ring ...] [... and I give you] your inheritance." 46:6[She came and brought] them, just as he had [told her (to do)]. 46:7And he opened them [and produced] three golden bands, while it is not in the [human] power to speak about their likeness. 46:8For they were not [from] this world, but from [heaven. They] threw out sparks of light. 46:9[He gave one band] to each one of his daughters [saying] to them: "Take [this], my children, for yourselves and gird yourselves [with] it around your breast, so that what is good shall be with you all the days of your life."

47:1[Kasia, the other daughter, said] to him: "Is this the inheritance [of which you have] said: 'I have left behind for you [yours, which is] greater than the one of your brothers?' [What is the use] of these ribbons? Shall they be set up for [us? How] will we live off them?"

47:2[Job] spoke, [saying]: "It is not only that you [will live] off them [on earth], 47:3but these ribbons [will lead you] into the great [eternal] life [in] heaven. 47:4Do you [not know the value] of these ribbons with which I have adorned [your body]? These (ribbons) of which the Lord [let me be worthy on the day] on which he wished to [have mercy on me? ...]

(page 45: Job relates the magic power of the three ribbons, Chap. 47:5–49:1) [...] these ribbons [...: 'Rise] and gird yourself [with them] around [... and find] your strength!' 47:6When I [girded myself with the ribbons], at the very moment I had girded myself, [the worms left] my body and the sufferings ceased [from it. 47:7It happened] through great power from [the Lord, as if] I had indeed not suffered at all. 47:8[Also the grief] in my heart I did forget. 47:9[The Lord spoke with] me through his power. He told [me the things that are] and the things that will be. 47:10Now [then, my children], if you gird yourselves with these [ribbons], the enemy will not have power over you. [And also] no evil thought will capture [your] heart. 47:11For [these are] guards of the father. Rise now [and gird] yourselves before I die, [so that] you shall see [those who] are coming after my soul and so that you [marvel] at the creatures of God."

48:1[Hemera] rose immediately and girded herself with the ribbon just as [her father] had told her (to do). 48:2As soon as [she] had [girded herself], her heart withdrew from the things of the world. 48:3She [replied] speaking in the language of the angels [with God] just as the angels sing. The hymns that the [Spirit had produced] are written on her own gravestone.

49:1Kasia too [girded herself] in this [manner].

(page 46: The transformation of Job's daughters and the writing of the book, Chap. 49:1–52:1) [Her heart withdrew from] the things [of the world. 49:2Her mouth spoke in the language] of the authorities, singing [in the manner of those] exalted about the creation [of the exalted place]. 49:3Whoever wishes to know about [the creation of heaven], behold, they are written in the [chant of Kasia.

50:1Then Amaltheias] Keras girded herself in that] manner. 50:2Her heart withdrew from the things of the world. [And her mouth] spoke in the language of the [Cherubs, singing] about the master of excellence, [displaying] his glory. 50:3Whoever then wishes [to know] about a fraction of the glory of the father, [behold], it is written in the unchangeable prayers.

51:1After the daughters finished [singing] their hymns 51:2while the Lord and [the] Holy Spirit were present with them, 51:3I, Nereus, the brother of Job, was sitting [on] Job's bed close to him. I heard [the splendours], since [one (daughter) was] at once writing (them) down for the other. 51:4I [myself wrote] this entire book except for [the three hymns]. I did not write down their signs of [the words from the daughters] of my brother, for they were caused [through the Lord], not having been written down in this book [of Job, since] these are the splendours of God.

52:1[After] three days, while he was lying down for [a while on his] bed, giving the impression of [someone ill, even though he] did not suffer, since no [pain tormented him],

(page 47: Job's death, Chap. 52:2–53:3) [...] 52:3[He] rose and stood [up. He took a lyre] and gave it to Hemera, [his first daughter]. 52:4He gave a vessel of incense to Kasia, [and gave a kettledrum] to Amaltheias Keras, 52:5[so that they would praise in song] the one who came for [him. 52:6When they had received them], they saw the entourage that had [come for his soul]. 52:7They praised and glorified (it) [each one] again [in her] language. 52:8After it, [came this one who] is seated in the great chariot. [He greeted] Job 52:9while (only) his [three] daughters and their father saw him. [But] the others present [were not] seeing him. 52:10He took his [soul and] flew up, [holding] it [in his arms]. He raised it [upon the] chariot and drove [away] to the east.

52:11[But] his body was prepared for burial [and] was carried off. It was taken to the grave, 52:12while [his] three daughters were girded and going before him, praising in song [that] commemoration of the father.

53:1I, [Nereus], together with the sons and the [poor and the] orphans and anyone [powerless] were all weeping, 53:2saying: ["Woe] to us today in a great woe! [A great woe] to them, for today [the strength of the] powerless has been taken away! 53:3The light of [the blind] has been taken away! The father of the orphans [has been taken away]! [The host of] the strangers has been taken away!"

(page 48: Job's burial, epilogue, Chap. 53:3–end) [...] ... [...] his miracles, for [there] never [was any] violence done. 53:4[The entire city] was groaning after Job [and marvelling] at the creatures of God.

53:5[All the people] at the grave spent [three days], the poor, [the widows,] and the orphans weeping for him and [seeking] his body, 53:6while they were not allowed [to enter] the grave.

53:7He lay down [for a] good rest. 53:8His name became [famous] among all mankind on [earth] up until today.

(title) **The Book of [the] story of [Job] with the Testament of [Jobab]**

The Tiburtine Sibyl (Greek)

A new translation and introduction

by Rieuwerd Buitenwerf

The *Tiburtine Sibyl* is one of the apocalyptic writings from the late Roman period. The Greek version that has been the basis for the present translation dates from the beginning of the sixth century. The work is mainly an *ex eventu* description of history, culminating in a prophecy about the hardships of the last days of Jesus Christ and his glorious return.[1] The book derives its name from the opening lines of the Latin version. After citing Varro's list of ten Sibyls (probably borrowed from Lactantius, *Inst.* 1.6.6-14), the book continues: "This Sibyl was a daughter of king Priam, born from a mother called Hecuba. However, in Greek she was called Tiburtina, and in Latin Albunea." Varro was a Roman historian writing in the first century B.C.E. Although Varro's *Antiquitates rerum humanarum et divinarum*, from which the list of ten Sibyls originally stems, has not been preserved, the Tiburtine prophetess must have been part of the original catalog, since the first-century B.C.E. Roman poet Tibullus, who presumably knew Varro's list, mentions the Sibyl from the city of Tibur in 2.5.[2] In the Greek version of the *Tiburtine Sibyl*, the prophecy is not attributed to Albunea, the Tiburtine Sibyl, but simply to "the Sibyl"; the Greek version has sometimes been called *The Oracle of Baalbek*, because of its origin in or near that city. The attribution of the prophecy to the Tiburtine Sibyl appears to be a specific, later feature of the Latin tradition. Nevertheless, we will refer to the book as the *Tiburtine Sibyl*.

Contents

The work is presented as a dream interpretation by the prophetess Sibyl. The setting is the arrival of the Sibyl in Rome. One hundred judges have had an identical dream about nine suns. They understand that it is a prophetic dream that needs explanation, and present it to the Sibyl. She explains to the judges that the nine suns represent the nine generations into which the history of humankind can be divided; during this time span the situation on earth declines. The fourth generation sees the birth of Jesus Christ. The description of the eighth generation is the last to contain historical references; the ninth generation is the period of the eschatological events, during which Enoch and Elijah will return and ending in the victory and reign of Jesus Christ.

---

1. For this introduction to the *Tiburtine Sibyl* I have made frequent use of Paul Julius Alexander, *The Oracle of Baalbek: The Tiburtine Sibyl in Greek Dress* (Dumbarton Oaks Studies 10; Washington, D.C.: Dumbarton Oaks Center for Byzantine Studies, 1967); Rieuwerd Buitenwerf, *Book III of the* Sibylline Oracles *and Its Social Setting: With an Introduction, Translation and Commentary* (SVTP 17; Leiden: Brill, 2003); Anke Holdenried, *The Sibyl and Her Scribes: Manuscripts and Interpretations of the Latin* Sibylla Tiburtina *c. 1050-1500* (Aldershot: Ashgate, 2006); Ernst Sackur, *Sibyllinische Texte und Forschungen* (Halle: M. Niemeyer, 1898), 117-87.

2. Cf. also Horace, *Carmina* 1.7.12.

Manuscripts and Versions

The *Tiburtine Sibyl* exists in three Greek and one hundred and twelve Latin manuscripts.[3] The oldest manuscripts date from the eleventh century, while the most recent are from the fifteenth or sixteenth century. The textual history of the *Tiburtine Sibyl* can be summarized as follows.

Between 378 and 390, during the reign of Theodosius the Great, a new Sibylline prophecy was written in Greek, and this version is the archetype of the *Tiburtine Sibyl* as we know it now (see below for an explanation of this dating). This archetype, now lost, is usually called the "Theodosian Sibyl." The Theodosian Sibyl was translated into Latin, perhaps as early as the fourth century. At some time in the tenth or eleventh century, the names of German and Lombard rulers were included in the text of this Latin archetype, and other editorial changes were made. This new version of the Latin *Tiburtine Sibyl* formed the basis of the four versions represented in the extant Latin manuscripts.[4] One of these versions has been edited by Ernst Sackur.[5] The Greek Theodosian Sibyl itself was reworked by Greek editors in the early sixth century, and all extant Greek manuscripts depend on this version of the text.[6] The translation presented here is based on Paul J. Alexander's reconstruction of that Greek text in his book *The Oracle of Baalbek* (which also contains an English translation of the work). In Alexander's edition, the three manuscripts containing the Greek text are indicated as K, Q and A; they derive from a common archetype.

- K = *Codex Athos* 1527 (*Karakallou* 14), from the twelfth century. It contains some apocalyptic texts, among them the *Tiburtine Sibyl*.
- Q = *Codex Vaticanus Graecus* 1120, from the fourteenth century. Besides theological works this codex contains parts of the Greek *Sibylline Oracles* (books 6, 6/1, 7.218-428, 4 and 11-14) and the Greek version of the *Tiburtine Sibyl*.[7]

3. Besides the Greek and Latin versions, translations in other languages have also been preserved. There are, for instance, Ethiopic and Arabic versions; see J. Schleifer, "Die Erzählung der Sibylle: Ein Apokryph nach den karschunischen, arabischen und äthiopischen Handschriften zu London, Oxford, Paris und Rom," in *Denkschriften der kaiserlichen Akademie der Wissenschaften: Philosophisch-historische Klasse* 53 (Vienna 1910); 1-80; Rifaat Y. Ebied and Michael John Lewis Young, "An Unrecorded Arabic Version of a Sibylline Prophecy," *OCP* 43 (1977): 279-307. There is also an early French version of the prophecy; see Hugh Shields, ed., *Le livre de Sibile, by Philippe da Thaon* (Anglo-Norman Texts 37; London: Anglo-Norman Text Society, 1979). Ingeborg Neske, *Die spätmittelalterliche deutsche Sibyllenweissagung: Untersuchung und Edition* (Göppingen Arbeiten zur Germanistik; Göppingen: Kümmerle, 1985), 18-23, maintains that the medieval German Sibylline prophecies are in part also translations of the *Tiburtine Sibyl*.

4. The 112 Latin manuscripts, which contain 114 copies of the Latin *Tiburtine Sibyl*, have been adequately described and studied by Holdenried, and will not be listed here. See Holdenried, *The Sibyl and Her Scribes*.

5. Sackur, *Sibyllinische Texte*, 177-87. Two other Latin versions have also been published, one by C. Erdmann, "Endkaiserglaube und Kreuzzugsgedanke im 11. Jahrhundert," *ZKG* 51 (1932): 384-414, the other by Bernard McGinn, "Oracular Transformations: The Sibylla Tiburtina in the Middle Ages," in *Sibille e linguaggi oracolari: mito, storia tradizione. Atti del convegno Macerata-Norcia, settembre 1994* (ed. Ileana Chirassi Colombo and Tullio Seppilli; Pisa: Istituti Editoriali e Poligrafici Internazionali, 1998), 603-644.

6. David Flusser rightly argues that this reconstruction should remain hypothetical, and that it is also possible that there was an additional stage in the text development between the archetype and the sixth-century Greek version on the one hand and the Latin versions on the other. See David Flusser, "An Early Jewish-Christian Document in the Tiburtine Sibyl," in A. Benoit et al., eds., *Paganisme, Judaïsme, Christianisme: Influences et affrontements dans le monde antique: Mélanges offerts à Marcel Simon* (Paris: E. de Boccard, 1978), 153-183 (esp. 153-155).

7. See Johannes Geffcken, *Die Oracula Sibyllina* (GCS 8; Leipzig: J. C. Hinrichs, 1902), xxi.

- A = *Codex Atheniensis Bibliothecae Nationalis* 2725 (= Suppl. 725), from the fifteenth or sixteenth century. It contains a number of apocalyptic texts, among them the *Tiburtine Sibyl.*

Genre and Structure

The book of the *Tiburtine Sibyl* belongs to the genre of apocalyptic dream interpretations (compare Daniel, *4 Ezra*, etc.). The Sibyl plays the role of the wise, divinely inspired dream interpreter. Like other books of its genre, the *Tiburtine Sibyl* contains many references to political events, and the genre of the book is loosely related to the other Jewish and Christian Sibylline books. In conformity with pagan Sibylline prophecies, the Jewish and Christian *Sibylline Oracles* are written in Homeric hexameters. Although the *Tiburtine Sibyl* is entirely in prose, there are still some traces of the genre of Sibylline prophecy. The enumeration of emperors and political events, for instance, is a feature well known from the Jewish and Christian Sibylline books. The division of history into generations is also found in the *Sibylline Oracles* (see, for instance, the division into ten generations in *Sibylline Oracles* 1-2). The same can be said of some of the details in the text; a clear example is found in lines 152, 157, 158 and 159, where emperors are indicated by the first letters of their names (compare, e.g., *Sib. Or.* 5:1-51 and books 11-14).

The structure of the *Tiburtine Sibyl* is easy enough to perceive. After an introduction (lines 1-2), the dream of the one hundred judges is presented (3-30). In the following lines the Sibyl begins her interpretation: the nine suns are the nine generations in the history of humankind. The first three generations receive relatively little attention (31-38a), but from line 38b onwards the description of the generations determines the structure of the book: the fourth (38b-75), fifth (76-80), sixth (81-103), seventh (104-135), eighth (136-178a) and ninth generation (178b-227).

Date and Provenance

The archetype, now lost, of the *Tiburtine Sibyl* (called the "Theodosian Sibyl") was written in Greek at the end of the fourth century C.E., probably during the reign of Theodosius the Great (378-395 C.E.). The contents of the original Theodosian Sibyl may be reconstructed by comparing the Latin and Greek texts. Ernst Sackur, whose edition of one of the Latin versions of the text is still widely used, has italicized those parts of the text which he considered medieval additions to the Latin *Vorlage*. However, both the Greek and the Latin versions contain not only additions, but also editorial changes, which makes it difficult to reconstruct the text of the Theodosian Sibyl exactly.

In all versions of the text Constantine the Great is praised as an emperor who was important for Christianity. His death is also presupposed in all variants, which makes 337 C.E. a first *terminus post quem*. Slightly more hypothetical is the reference to the death of emperor Valens in a fire (see lines 96-98 of this translation). Sackur's Latin text does not mention this, but two other Latin text families do; therefore, it probably also belonged to the *Vorlage* of the Latin text families. Valens (364-378 C.E.) is the last emperor to whom the Theodosian Sibyl refers, which makes it probable that the Theodosian Sibyl was written during the reign of Valens' successor, Theodosius the Great.

The *terminus ante quem* depends on the oracle about the rebuilding of the city of Byzantium (see lines 91-95). Again, the Latin text of Sackur does not contain these lines, but the common *Vorlage* of the Latin manuscripts probably did. In lines 94-95, the Sibyl announces that Byzantium will lose its importance after one hundred and eighty years ("three times sixty years"). In the Latin manuscripts, the variant "sixty years" is found. This variant is probably the older version—the Greek reading may be explained as an updated version of an oracle that had not yet come true. Since Byzantium was refounded as Constantinople in 330 C.E., the Sibyl predicted that the city would be ruined in about 390. Therefore, the archetype of the *Tiburtine Sibyl* must have been written between roughly 378 and 390 C.E. Its provenance is difficult to determine; Alexander suggests that because it was in Greek the book was written in the eastern part of the Roman Empire.

The Theodosian Sibyl was written in a period when pagan Sibylline prophecy still existed. In the first quarter of the fifth century the pagan Roman poet Rutilius Namatianus wrote in *De redito suo* 2.41-52 that the Sibylline books had been burnt by the Roman general Stilicho (commander of the Roman army from ca. 393 to 408 C.E.). This seems to prove that in that period there was still an interest in Sibylline oracles among pagans. In the same period, most of the Jewish and Christian Sibylline books preserved in the Sibylline collections (*Sib. Or.* 1-8 and 11-14) already existed and had a function in the church. They served as prophecies of the coming of Jesus Christ that were independent of the Old Testament. Therefore in apologetic literature the *Sibylline Oracles* were widely used as an argument against pagans who denied the importance of Christ. The Theodosian Sibyl was part of that tradition, since it also contained the message of the birth of Jesus allegedly brought to a pagan audience by the Greek prophetess. The conflict between paganism and Christianity plays an important role in the book. In relation to that, the apocalyptic and political functions appear to have been the most important: the history of humankind is described as a story of decline (with some interruptions, such as the birth of Christ and the reign of Constantine). The period in which author and readers live is considered the last period of human history; after that, the eschatological agonies will take place and Christ will rule over the world.

The text of the Theodosian Sibyl was expanded and edited by the Greek editor at the beginning of the sixth century, and that is the text version reconstructed by Alexander in his edition. Both the description of the birth of Christ and the eschatological section have been preserved. The text of the Theodosian Sibyl was supplemented with political events of the fourth and fifth centuries, in order to bring it up to date. The political function of the book appears to have been accentuated even more, although the historical events are again presented as a prelude to the final, glorious coming of Jesus Christ.

The *terminus post quem* of the new Greek version may be determined by the reference to the emperor Anastasius, who reigned from 491 to 518 C.E. (see line 166) and to the Persian war during his reign, in 502 C.E. (see line 170). The *terminus ante quem* may be found by combining a few elements. First, the prediction in line 172 that Anastasius will reign for thirty-one years seems to indicate that the author was not yet aware of Anastasius' death in 518. Second, the ruin of Constantinople is predicted to take place 180 years ("three times sixty years"—see lines 94-95) after its refoundation in 330, i.e., before 510 C.E. Although the figure could be interpreted as symbolic, this *terminus ante quem* is confirmed by the absence of a reference to the victory of the Romans over the Persians and the peace treaty in 505-506. It is, therefore, probable that this Greek version of the *Tiburtine Sibyl* was written between roughly 502 and 510 C.E. The book contains references to the Lebanon and to Heliopolis in Phoenicia (Baalbek) (see lines 78, 79, 87, 111, 115, 205). These appear to have been added to the text by the sixth-century editor. It is, therefore, probable that this new version of the *Tiburtine Sibyl* was made in or near Heliopolis (Baalbek).

The Literary Context

The *Tiburtine Sibyl* was written by a Christian who was at home in various literary traditions. It is clear that he knew some specific characteristics of the prophetess Sibyl. One example is the setting in which the Sibyl presents her dream interpretation: she is sitting on the Capitoline Hill. In antiquity the Sibyl was indeed known to be sitting down when prophesying (see, for example, the inscription found in the Sibylline cave in Erythrae;[8] Plutarch, *Pyth. Orac.* 398C; Pseudo-Justin, *Cohortatio ad Graecos* 37.1-3).[9] The connection between the Sibyl and the Capitoline Hill in Rome was also famous: the official Sibylline books were stored in the temple of Jupiter there.

At first sight, the New Testament appears to have been the most important source for the book, especially for the passage about the birth of Jesus Christ (lines 38b-75). Indeed, many parallels with the New Testament are found, but the details often differ from those in the parallel New Testament texts. A clear example is found in lines 74-75, where the Sibyl describes Jesus' crucifixion. According to John 19:34, a soldier pierced the side of Jesus "with a spear," whereas the *Tiburtine Sibyl* states that Jesus' side was pierced "with a reed." Insignificant as this detail may seem, together with other, similar differences it may indicate that the author did not use the New Testament as a direct source. For this particular detail, for instance, a close parallel is found in *Sib. Or.* 1:373-374 and 8:296 (compare also *Gos. Pet.* 9 and *Acts John* 97). Similar analyses can be made for other references to events described in the New Testament.

Although the genre of the *Tiburtine Sibyl* differs from that of the collection of Jewish and Christian *Sibylline Oracles*, many details from the *Sibylline Oracles* also occur in the *Tiburtine Sibyl* (compare, for instance, line 41 with *Sib. Or.* 8:300-301, line 105 with *Sib. Or.* 3:364 and 8:165, and line 202 with *Sib. Or.* 2:25-26). Since the *Sibylline Oracles* were important and well known in the early church, it is rather probable that the author of the *Tiburtine Sibyl* knew (some of) the Jewish and Christian Sibylline books and used them as a source of inspiration for his own work. Special attention should be paid to the parallels between the *Tiburtine Sibyl* and the Coptic *Apocalypse of Elijah*, a Christian prophetic work dating from the end of the third century C.E. There are some literal correspondences between the *Tiburtine Sibyl* and this work, especially in the eschatological section of the *Tiburtine Sibyl* (lines 178b-227). The most probable explanation for these correspondences is that the fourth-century author of the archetype of the *Tiburtine Sibyl* had access to the *Apocalypse of Elijah* and used it as a source.[10]

The importance of the *Tiburtine Sibyl* is already reflected in the number of manuscripts preserved. The main reason for the Church to cherish the *Sibylline Oracles* was the fact that the books contained prophecies about Jesus Christ. Since the *Tiburtine Sibyl* was written in regular prose instead of poetic lines, it was easier to understand than the Jewish and Christian Sibylline books, and certainly easier to adapt to new situations. The differences between the Latin and Greek versions illustrate the way medieval scribes changed and expanded the book in order to adapt it to their own situation. If one compares these

8. Helmut Engelmann and Reinhold Merkelbach, eds., *Die Inschriften von Erythrai und Klazomenai* (Inschriften griechischer Städte aus Kleinasien 1-2; Bonn: Habelt, 1973), 2:379-383, Inscription 224.

9. For an overview of the Sibylline prophecy in antiquity, see H. W. Parke, *Sibyls and Sibylline Prophecy in Classical Antiquity*, ed. B. C. McGing (London: Routledge, 1988); Buitenwerf, *Book III of the* Sibylline Oracles, 92-123.

10. David Frankfurter, *Elijah in Upper Egypt: The Apocalypse of Elijah and Early Egyptian Christianity* (SAC; Minneapolis, Minn.: Fortress, 1993), 24-25.

versions with the extant Arabic, Ethiopian, and early French translations, the variety becomes even greater. The many shapes the book has taken can all be seen as interesting medieval expressions of popular religion. Its nucleus, however, goes back to the late Roman period in which Sibylline oracles were still an important form of prophecy among both pagans and Christians.

Bibliography

Alexander, Paul Julius. *The Oracle of Baalbek: The Tiburtine Sibyl in Greek Dress*. Dumbarton Oaks Studies 10. Washington D.C.: Dumbarton Oaks Center for Byzantine Studies, 1967.

Buitenwerf, Rieuwerd. *Book III of the* Sibylline Oracles *and Its Social Setting: With an Introduction, Translation and Commentary*. SVTP 17. Leiden: Brill, 2003.

Colpe, Carsten. "Review of P. J. Alexander, *The Oracle of Baalbek*." *JAC* 13 (1970): 89-94.

Ebied, Rifaat Y., and Michael John Lewis Young. "An Unrecorded Arabic Version of a Sibylline Prophecy." *OCP* 43 (1977): 279-307.

Erdmann, Carl. "Endkaiserglaube und Kreuzzugsgedanke im 11. Jahrhundert." *ZKG* 51 (1932): 384-414.

Flusser, David. "An Early Jewish-Christian Document in the Tiburtine Sibyl." Pages 153-83 in *Paganisme, Judaïsme, Christianisme: Influences et affrontements dans le monde antique: Mélanges offerts à Marcel Simon*. Edited by A. Benoit et al. Paris: E. de Boccard, 1978.

Frankfurter, David. *Elijah in Upper Egypt: The Apocalypse of Elijah and Early Egyptian Christianity*. SAC. Minneapolis, Minn.: Fortress, 1993.

Geffcken, Johannes. *Die Oracula Sibyllina*. GCS 8. Leipzig: J. C. Hinrichs, 1902.

Holdenried, Anke. *The Sibyl and Her Scribes: Manuscripts and Interpretations of the Latin* Sibylla Tiburtina *c. 1050-1500*. Aldershot: Ashgate, 2006.

McGinn, Bernard. "Oracular Transformations: The *Sibylla Tiburtina* in the Middle Ages." Pages 603-44 in *Sibille e linguaggi oracolari: mito, storia tradizione. Atti del convegno Macerata-Norcia, settembre 1994*. Edited by Ileana Chirassi Colombo and Tullio Seppilli. Pisa: Istituti Editoriali e Poligrafici Internazionali 1998.

__________. "*Teste David cum Sibylla:* The Significance of the Sibylline Tradition in the Middle Ages." Pages 7-35 in *Women of the Medieval World: Essays in Honor of John H. Mundy*. Edited by Julius Kirshner and Suzanne F. Wemple. Oxford: Blackwell, 1985.

Parke, H. W. *Sibyls and Sibylline Prophecy in Classical Antiquity*. Edited by B. C. McGing. London: Routledge, 1988.

Sackur, Ernst. *Sibyllinische Texte und Forschungen*. Halle: M. Niemeyer, 1898.

Schleifer, J. "Die Erzählung der Sibylle. Ein Apokryph nach den karschunischen, arabischen und äthiopischen Handschriften zu London, Oxford, Paris und Rom." Pages 1-80 in *Denkschriften der kaiserlichen Akademie der Wissenschaften: Philosophisch-historische Klasse* 53. Vienna, 1910.

The Tiburtine Sibyl (Greek)

Title

[1]Heading: By the Sibyl, who received a revelation by which she was able to interpret the vision of [2]one hundred judges of the great city of Rome.

The Dream of the One Hundred Judges

[3]When the Sibyl came to Rome, all people [4]from the city wanted to meet her, from great to small. The one hundred judges also came to meet [5]her, and said: "Your Majesty, your wisdom and knowledge are immense. [6]Now, please interpret the vision we (the hundred judges) have seen today, [7]since we are not able to interpret it [8]or find out its meaning." The Sibyl answered them: "Let us go [9]to the Capitol of the great city of Rome and let a hearing [10]take place." And they did as she commanded them.

[11]She said to them: "Tell me the vision you have seen, and I [12]will explain its meaning to you." The Sibyl was sitting on the [13]Capitol, among the olive trees, and said: "Tell me [14]what you have seen." The one hundred judges answered: [15]"We have seen nine suns shining on the earth." The Sibyl [16]answered: "The nine suns are nine generations." They said: [17]"Let it be so, our lady. We will tell you everything we have seen in [18]the vision." The Sibyl answered: [19]"Let it be so." The judges said: "We will tell you [20]the vision exactly as we have seen it."

The Sibyl asked: "What [21]have you seen?" They said: "This is what we have seen. The first [22]sun was multicoloured; it shone with rays and was huge and [23]very bright. The second sun was even brighter, huge and multicoloured, [24]and also shone with rays. The third sun was blood-red, like Tartarus, [25]huge, a burning fire. The fourth sun was blood-red, like Tartarus. The [26]fifth sun was blood-red and very bright; it flashed forth like [27](lightning) in a thunderstorm. The sixth sun was like mist, like snow and like blood. [28]The seventh sun was like Tartarus and like blood; it was frightening. The eighth sun [29]shone with rays as if it had hands in the middle. The ninth sun was like Tartarus more than the [30]other suns and shone."

The Explanation of the Dream; the First Three Generations

[31]The Sibyl answered: "The nine suns are nine generations. [32]The first sun is the first generation. It consists of innocent people, who are long-lived, [33]free, honest, gentle, reasonable, and who love the truth. The [34]second sun is the second generation. It also consists of truthful people, [35]who are gentle, hospitable, innocent, and who love the (first) generation, (that) of the free people. The [36]third

sun is the third generation. *Kingdom will rise against kingdom,* [37]*people against people.* There will be wars, but not in the city of the Romans; [38]there the people will be hospitable and merciful. Matt 24:6-7; Mark 13:8; Luke 21:10; cf. Mic 4:3; *4 Ezra* 6:24; 13:31; 4Q246 II 2-3

The Fourth Generation

The fourth sun is the fourth generation. [39]The offspring of the deity will appear in the South, since a woman [40]from the Hebrew land called Mary will bear a son. He will be [41]called Jesus. He will annul the Hebrew law and establish [42]his own law. And his law will rule. (*Sib. Or.* 8:300-301) And the heavens [43]will open for him, and he will hear a voice. And armies of angels will [44]carry his throne, and six-winged creatures will worship the [45]imprints of his feet. (Ezek 1:26; 10:1; Isa 6:2; Rev 4:8) He will take men from Galilee, give them his law [46]and say to them: 'Preach the message that you receive [47]from me to the peoples of the seventy-two languages.' "[a]

[48]The priests of the Hebrews said to her: "Most awesome mistress [49]of ours, we would like to pose you a question." The Sibyl answered: [50]"Tell me want you want." This is what they said to her: [51]"From the Gentiles we heard the news that the heavenly God will [52]beget a son. Do you believe that will happen, our lady?" The Sibyl answered: [53]"Do you, priests of the Hebrews, not believe that?" [54]They said: "We do not believe that God will beget a son, [55]because he promised our ancestors that he would not take his hands [56]from us." The Sibyl said: "That law is a thorn [57]for you." They said: "And what do you say about this question, [58]our mistress?"

[59]And the Sibyl answered them: "The heavenly God will [60]beget a son, who will be like his father and who will take the shape of a [61]child. Kings will stand up against him—Alexander, Seleucus, [62]and Herod[b]—but they will not be able to save themselves. (*Sib. Or.* 8:255-256; 12:32-33) They will carry out many [63]persecutions in the Judaean land, and will murder so many children [64]together with their parents, that the (water of the) river Jordan will be mixed with blood. [65]They will, however, not benefit from that. After that, he who will be crucified [66]will perform many healings. And when people sacrifice [...] [67]her altars, they will hear about the signs he offered in the Judaean [68]land. From Phrygia,[c] a king will arise named Augustus [69]and he will reign in Rome. And he will subject the entire [70]inhabited world. The name of that king of the Romans will be [71][Augustus]. The very blessed cross, on which Christ will be [72]stretched out [...] and after that, the Jewish [73]crowds will be gathered, and he who will be nailed to the cross will perform signs and cure [74]many people. They will nail three men to the cross together with him, (Matt 27:38; Mark 15:27; Luke 23:33) and they will [75]spear his side with a reed, but they will not harm him. (John 19:31-37; *Sib. Or.* 1:373-374; 8:296; *Gos. Pet.* 9; *Acts John* 97)

---

a. Cf. Luke 10:1, where Jesus appoints seventy (or, according to some manuscripts, seventy-two) people to go to every town where he wanted to go.

b. These three rulers are probably mentioned here because they were known as persecutors of the Jews (Alexander the Great, 336-323 B.C.E.; Seleucus I, who died in 281 B.C.E.; and Herod the Great, 37-4 B.C.E).

c. According to some traditions Augustus Caesar was a Trojan (see, e.g., Virgil, *Aen.* 1.286-288).

The Fifth Generation

In the fifth generation, three kings will arise—Antiochus, Tiberius and Gaius[a]—and they will carry out many persecutions because of him who was crucified. They will rebuild the temples of Heliopolis and the altars of the Lebanon. The temples of this city will be very large and will look better than any other temple in the world.

The Sixth Generation

In the sixth generation, two kings[b] will arise who will reign for a short period and who will carry out many persecutions against the Christians. And their leaders will judge and destroy the ranks of the senators and they will kill them because of the name of Christ. They will, however, not benefit from that. After that, a king named Constantine[c] will arise, a frightening and powerful warrior. He will destroy all pagan temples, all the altars of the Lebanon and all the sacrifices made there, and he will humiliate the Gentiles. A sign will appear to him in the sky, and his mother Helen will go to the Judaean land and look for the wood of the cross on which Christ was crucified, the Son of the living God.[d] He will rebuild Byzantium, but the name of that city will be changed into Eudocopolis-Constantinopolis, and all the tribes of the seventy-two languages[e] will live there. Do not boast, city of Byzantium, because your reign will certainly not last for three times sixty years!

After that, three kings will arise—Valens, a grandson of Constantius, Valentinian and Jovian[f] —and they will carry out many persecutions. One of them will be consumed by fire.[g] The barbarians will not harm the Roman cities. After that, two kings will arise, Marcian and Theodosius,[h] powerful rulers, warriors and righteous judges, teachers of the faith. They will destroy the abandoned pagan temples, and the temples of the Gentiles will become the tombs of the saints.

---

a. These three emperors disturb the chronological order in the book (it is unclear which Antiochus is meant, but the first Antiochus reigned from 281 to 261 B.C.E., the last (Antiochus XIII) from 69 to 64 B.C.E.; Tiberius, 14-37 C.E.; Caligula, 37-41 C.E.). Alexander, *The Oracle of Baalbek*, 58-59, maintains that lines 76-80 should be considered an interpolation by the sixth-century author/redactor of the Greek text.

b. Perhaps Decius (249-251) and Valerian (253-260) are meant; both reigned for a short period, at a time when a considerable number of senators had become Christians. Both persecuted the Christians, and Valerian is known to have opposed Christianity in the Senate. See Cyprian, *Ep.* 80.839-840.

c. Constantine the Great (306-337 C.E.).

d. Cf. John Chrysostom, *Hom.* 85.1; Ambrose, *Ob. Theo.* 41-49.

e. Cf. line 47.

f. In the manuscripts, the names of these three emperors are corrupted. The most likely reconstruction is Valens, emperor in the East (364-378), Valentian (Valens' brother), emperor in the West (364-375) and Jovian (363-364). Two manuscripts suggest the reading "Julian" (Julian the Apostate, 360-363) instead of Valens.

g. Ammianus Marcellinus 31.13:11-17 relates two stories about the death of Valens. According to one story, he died in a fire.

h. Marcian, emperor in the East (450-457). Marcian is also mentioned in line 128. Probably "Marcian" is a scribal error for Gratian, son of Valentianus, who was the third emperor in the time of Valens and Valentinian, and reigned from 367 to 383. Theodosius I (379-395).

The Seventh Generation

[104]In the seventh generation, when Arcadius and Honorius[a] reign, [105]Rome will
be no more than a street, a city of only one street. In Phrygia, people will be tak- *Sib. Or.* 3:364; 8:165
en captive; [106]Pamphylia will be desolate. After that, two kings will arise, [107]The-
odosius and Valentinian,[b] who will be gentle and reasonable. However, [108]under
their rule, people will wage war after war. Syria will be taken captive, and [109]then
a strong generation of tyrants will arise. They will plunder the [110]Taurus in the
East, the Antitaurus in Armenia and the [111]Lebanon, and the cities in which
they used to live will not be restored. [112]Then the Persians will arise for a mighty
war, [113]but they will be disrupted by the Romans and offer peace for forty years.
[114]A man [...], a warrior, will enter [Hieropolis] and shatter [115]the temples of
the cities and the altars of the Lebanon. Many locusts and [116]their larvae will appear, and they will eat the (fruit of the) labour of Syria and Cappadocia, [117]and
Cappadocia will suffer from famine. However, after that there will be prosperity.

[118]Then parents will reject their children and children their parents. Brothers will [119]give each other up to be killed. Brothers will sleep with their sisters,
fathers will have [120]sexual intercourse with their daughters, and young men will *Sib. Or.* 7:44-45
marry old women. Bishops [121]will be sorcerers, and elders will commit fornication. Blood will be shed [122][in the land and] armies will violate the temples of
the saints. [123]There will be all kinds of adultery, fornication and homosexual
lust, and people will [124]dishonour themselves.[c] They will be greedy, grasping,
avaricious and [125]arrogant charlatans. Everywhere sheep and cows will [126]die. 2 Tim 3:1-5
Thrace will be desolated by barbarians, because the Romans will betray [127]it and *Sib. Or.* 5:466-467
because of its[d] enormous avarice. After that, [128]Marcian[e] will arise, and there
will be wars. From Africa, [129]a tyrant named Gaeseric will arise and capture
Rome,[f] [130]and he will be among the champions until the time of his life will
[131]be fulfilled; his kingdom will last for thirty years. [132]Rome will be humiliated
because of its enormous avarice, and [133]Rome will not reign until its time has
come. All of Dalmatia [134]will sink into the sea; Campania and Calabria will be
taken [135]captive.

The Eighth Generation

[136]In the eighth generation, a king will arise who is named after a wild beast.[g]
[137]The birthpangs of the world will begin in that period, earthquakes, floodings
[138]of cities and countries, and there will be wars and cities will be burned down.
Thrace [139]will be desolated and there will be no one left to control or manage
the Roman Empire. [140]Taurocilicia will lift up its neck, and Scylla will arise, the

a. Arcadius, emperor in the East (395-408), and Honorius, emperor in the West (395-423).

b. Theodosius II, emperor in the East (408-450), and Valentinian III, emperor in the West (425-455).

c. Meaning of Greek uncertain; other options: "they will bring dishonour on their clothes," "they will dishonour their appearance."

d. Literally: "their"; it probably refers to the Thracians and not to the Romans.

e. Marcian, emperor in the East (450-457).

f. In 455, the Vandals under Gaeseric reached Rome.

g. Leo I, emperor in the East (457-474) is meant; his name means "lion."

wife of the [141]wild beast that is king, and she will produce two wombs.[a] From one of them, [142]she will beget a son. He will be called after his father,[b] and will also [143]share the throne with his father who is named after a wild beast, and the way [144]they rule the earth will be identical.[c] During his reign, an Isaurian will appear.[d] [145]He will be worshipped by his father. Then they will speak [146]blasphemous words against the nature of the Son. Because of these words, [147]his father will be removed from his throne by force, but the power [148]and the might of the womb will last for fifty-two years.[e]

[149]After that, an Isaurian will become king,[f] and he will hate the people in [150]his city and he will flee to his country. And another [151]king will arise, whose name is that of the crawling beast. [152]The name of the beast begins with the second letter: [153]Basiliscus.[g] He will blaspheme the Most High God. Because of [154]this blasphemy a woman will bring shame on him, [155]and he and his entire family will be ruined. After that, again an [156]Isaurian will be king, but his kingdom is not given to him [157]by heaven. In Roman letters, his name will begin with [158]the last letter of the alphabet, but when written in Greek with the seventh[h]—[159]his name will be Graeco-Latin. His kingdom [160]will be powerful and pleasing for the entire population. He will love the poor and [161]humiliate the powerful and the rich. After that, another [162]king will rise from the Western city of Epidamnos, in Latin called [163]Dyrrhachium. The name of this king will be unclear for Gentiles; [164]it will be the same as that of the last day.[i] (Originally,) his name will begin with [165]the eighteenth letter, but when he seizes his kingship, [166]he will be called Anastasius.[j] He will be bald, good-looking, his face will look [167]like silver,[k] and he will have a long right arm. He will be noble, fearsome, [168]generous and free, and he will hate all beggars. He will ruin [169]many of the people, lawfully and unlawfully, and he will destroy those who practice [170]idolatry. In those days, the Persians will arise and [171]overturn the cities of Anatolia and most of the soldiers of the [172]Roman Empire by violence. And he (i.e., Anastasius) will be king for thirty-one years.

[173]After that, the people will be grasping and greedy tyrants; [174]they will be barbarians who will hate their mothers. They will behave like [175]barbarians instead of being virtuous and reasonable. They will plunder [176]their own ancestral

---

a. The wife of Leo I was called Verina (here she is called Scylla). She begat two daughters (two "wombs"), Ariadne and Leontia.

b. Leo II (474).

c. "and will also share ... identical" – The text is probably corrupt and the meaning of Greek is uncertain.

d. Zeno, emperor in the East (474-475, 476-491).

e. The reference is to Ariadne, who became the wife of Anastasius I (491 to 518 C.E.) and was probably still queen when the present version of the Tiburtine Sibyl was written.

f. Zeno, emperor in the East (474-475, 476-491). It may be that Zeno is mentioned more than once (here, in 144 and in 155-161) because of the interruption in his reign.

g. Basiliscus (475-476), emperor in the East. A *basiliskos* is a kind of serpent.

h. That is, respectively, *z* and *zeta*, in Latin and Greek the first letter in the name Zeno.

i. The name is Anastasius (see 166); the last day is the day of the resurrection (*anastasis*).

j. Anastasius I (491-518).

k. Cf. *Sib. Or.* 12:164, where Hadrian is called a "silver-headed man."

cities, and there will be no one to resist their deeds and [177]works. They work their land because of their enormous [178]avarice.

The Ninth Generation

In the ninth generation, the years will be shortened as if they were [179]months, the months as if they were weeks, the weeks as if they were days, and the days [180]as if they were hours. Two kings will arise from the East and two [181]from Syria, and the Assyrians will be countless as the sand of the [182]sea, and they will take over many areas in the East, unto Chalcedonia. [183]So much blood will be shed that, mixed together [184]with (the water of) the sea, it will reach the chests
of the horses. [185]The cities will be captured and burned and the East will [186]be Rev 14:20
stripped. After that, another king will arise from the East, [187]whose name will be Olibos. He will take his four predecessors [188]into captivity and kill them. He will grant a public tax [189]exemption and restore the [190]peoples in the entire East and in Palestine. After that, [191]another king will arise who has an altered appearance.[a] He will reign [192]for thirty years and rebuild the altars of Egypt. [193]He will wage war against the king of the East, kill him and [194]his entire army, and seize children aged twelve and older. [195]People will take asps, draw milk from women with newborn babies and [196]take blood (from them), to use that
as poison for arrows, because the wars will be violent. [197]Woe to women who *Apoc. El. (C)* 2:35-36
are pregnant or who suckle their babies in those [198]days! Nothing will be left of Matt 24:19; Mark
the cities in the East but hills. The king [199]will be established by the foul nation 13:17; Luke 21:23; *Sib. Or.* 2:190-192
of the Cappadocians, and he will hiss and say: [200]'Was there ever a city here?' After that, a woman will arise. She [201]will run from the place where the sun sets to the place where it rises and she will not see a man. [202]She will long for
a footprint of a man, but she will not find it. When she finds a vine and [203]an *Sib. Or.* 2:25-26
olive tree, she will say: 'Where is the man who has planted these?' Then she will embrace [204]those trees and die, and the wolves will eat her.

[205]After that, a king will arise from Heliopolis and he will wage [206]war against the king of the East and kill him. He will grant [207]tax exemption to entire countries for three and a half years. The [208]land will yield its fruits, but there will be no one to eat them. Then, the ruler [209]of destruction, he who has
changed, will come and strike out, and he will kill him. [210]He will perform signs Matt 24:24; Mark
and miracles on earth. He will turn the sun into [211]darkness and the moon 13:22; 2 Thess 2:9-10; Rev 13:13-14
into blood. After that, the springs and [212]the rivers will dry up, and the Nile in Rev 6:12
Egypt will be turned into blood. [213]The people that remain will dig wells and Exod 7:17, 20
search for [214]running water,[b] but they will not find it. Then two men will appear
[215]who do not know the experience of death, Enoch and Elijah, and they will 2 Kgs 2:11; Mal 4:5;
wage war [216]against the ruler of destruction. But he will say, 'My time has come,' *1 En.* 90:31
and [217]he will kill them in his anger. And then he who will have been crucified *Apoc. El.* (C) 4:7-14
will come down [218]from heaven like a great and flashing star, and he will raise [219]those two men. And he who will have been nailed to the cross will wage war

a. The description of the battle between this eschatological king and the "king of the East" appears to be repeated in 205-208; probably the "king with an altered appearance" (191), the "king from Heliopolis" (205), "the ruler of destruction" (208-209) and "he who has changed" all refer to one and the same eschatological ruler.

b. Alternative: "water that gives life."

2 Thess 2:8; Rev 19:11-21

against the [220]son of destruction and he will kill him and his entire [221]band. Then the land of Egypt will be burned twelve cubits (deep), and the land [222]will cry out to God, 'Lord, I am a virgin.' Thereupon the Judaean [223]land will be burned eighteen cubits (deep), and the land will cry out to God, [224]'Lord, I am a virgin.' Then the Son of God will come with [225]great power and glory to judge the nine generations. Then [226]Christ, the Son of the Living God, will rule with his holy [227]angels. Amen, let it be so, amen."

The Eighth Book of Moses

A new translation and introduction

by Todd E. Klutz

The *Eighth Book of Moses* (hereafter *Moses VIII*) is important both as a witness to the rich interpenetration of Judaism and paganism in late antiquity, and as one of a small number of complete handbooks of magico-religious ritual that have survived from the same period. Although the text's self-designation as the *Eighth Book* seems to assume the existence of a sixth book and a seventh (in addition to the five books of the Pentateuch), historical evidence of ancient texts circulating under the title of either Moses' sixth or seventh book is lacking. Both *Moses VIII* (*PGM* XIII. 1-734) itself, however, and the textual material directly following it in the same papyrus codex[1] include references to other magico-religious writings associated with the name of Moses: *The Key (of Moses)* is cited six times in *Moses VIII* (lines 21-22, 31, 35-36, 60, 381-82, 431-32), and in the ensuing discourse mention is made of an *Archangelical Book of Moses* (XIII. 970-71), a *Secret Moon Book of Moses* (XIII. 1057), and perhaps (depending on how a single Greek letter is interpreted) also a *Secret Tenth Book of Moses* (XIII. 1077-78). The name "Moses" is also conspicuously conjoined with several of *Moses VIII*'s various self-designations;[2] and in two other passages the text is given titles that lack the name of Moses—*The Only* in XIII. 341, and *The Seven-Zoned* in XIII. 217, 723. The text's rhetoric of Mosaic authorship assumes a high degree of respect for Moses not only within Judaism but also in pagan circles, for the cultural and religious assumptions of the document as a whole are thoroughly hybridized rather than Jewish in any narrow sense. The ancient editors' attribution of the text to Moses in particular is undoubtedly motivated at least in part by a desire to enhance the authority and prestige of its contents.

Contents

The opening lines of *Moses VIII*, including the title, function much like an abstract, indicating that what follows will be concerned with a hierarchy of divine beings (including one that outranks all the others), with certain traditions allegedly associated with Moses, and with the name of the highest and most powerful god in the assumed context. Those concerns and related matters are then presented in the form of a recipe for a complex ritual process consisting of a combination of prescribed actions and formulaic utterances. One version of the recipe, corresponding to lines 1-343 (hereafter "version A") in the papyrus, has as its goal a revelatory encounter with "the god," who can be expected

1. *PGM* XIII. 734-1077 corresponds approximately to the final third of the text preserved in Leiden Papyrus J 395.

2. The variants including "Moses" are "a holy, secret book of Moses called *Eighth* or *Sacred* (XIII. 344-45); the *Only of Moses* (XIII. 724); the *Secret, Eighth of Moses* (XIII. 731); and the *Secret Book of Moses concerning the Great Name* (XIII. 732-33).

to disclose his own powerful name—an adaptable tool useful for everything from fetching a lover to resurrecting dead bodies—and to provide desired information about the initiate. A different version of the recipe, detailed in lines 343-734 (hereafter "version B"), has the same general revelatory aims but also expects the god to disclose details concerning the initiates' fate (e.g., their horoscope, where they will live, and where they will die) and a strategy for persuading the god to improve inauspicious oracles. The following table indicates the correspondences between versions A and B in the order of their occurrence in A.[3]

Version A	Version B	Content
1-4	343-47	Title and preview
4-8	347-49	Setting of initiation ritual
13-29	351-56	The seven types of incense
34-37	381-82	Names and spell in Moses' *Key*
38-60	383-432	Picture on the natron
61-87	568-600	Text on the natron
88-90	600-607	Powerful sounds and invitation
91-114	646-70	Additional materials for use in ritual
114-38	671-99	Ritual speech, sleep, and drink
128-31	360-63	Sacred gustable: beginning and end
138-61	443-71	Panlingual invocation
161-206	471-564	Creation by divine laughter
206-209	700-702	Vocalic imitation of the god
210-12	564-67	The revelatory event
213-24	718-30	Ascertaining the ruler of the moment
227-29	692-93	Recording the revelation
341-43	731-34	Coda

Even a cursory inspection of these parallels shows that the correspondences are substantial and at many points very close. Version B in particular contains little that is not present in version A. The most substantial passages unique to B are XIII. 610-45, detailing what the initiates should say and how they should breathe when the angel Sarapis appears; and XIII. 389-408, where ritual action prescribed in both versions (XIII. 38-44 and XIII. 383-88) is correlated with the cycle of the four seasons and the flooding of the Nile River.

A much larger proportion of version A consists of unique material. Most of that material is concentrated in a lengthy list of wonders (XIII. 230-340) which the text's users are promised they can achieve by following its instructions.

Manuscripts and Versions

The only extant witness to the text of *Moses VIII* is Leiden Papyrus J 395, a fourth-century C.E. codex whose contents are now best known as papyrus XIII in Karl Preisendanz's *Papyri Graecae Magicae*. Consisting of 1,077 lines of Greek text, the codex contains not only

3. The present table reflects the synoptic translation below and differs at several points, for reasons indicated below, from the summary by M. Q. Smith, "The Eighth Book of Moses and How It Grew (Pleid. J 395)," *Atti del XVII congresso internazionale di papirologia* (ed. the International Congress of Papyrology; Naples: Centro internazionale per lo studio dei ercolanesi, 1984), 690-93; and in the form of Smith's annotations in *GMPT*, 182.

the two versions of *Moses VIII* (i.e., lines 1-734) summarised above but also another hybridised magico-religious handbook (lines 734-1,077) that includes a number of Jewish elements and several references to Moses in particular. The manuscript was part of the larger collection of Greco-Egyptian papyri brought together in the first quarter of the nineteenth century by the consular representative of Sweden at the court of Alexandria, a man who called himself Jean d'Anastasi (1780-1857).[4] The manuscript was transcribed in 1830 by the Dutch scholar C. J. C. Reuvens,[5] whose work on the text was soon reviewed and partially translated into German by K. O. Müller.[6] A complete edition, however, was not published until 1885, when both a corrected form of the text and a transcription of Leiden Papyrus J 384 (*PGM* XII) were made available by the Dutch Egyptologist C. Leemans.[7] Thereafter editions of the same two papyri were published by A. Dieterich (1891), K. Preisendanz, and most recently R. Daniel (1991).[8] The work by Daniel provides a photographic plate of each page of the Greek text and, on facing pages, a fresh transcription; it also includes a list of suggestions for improving the text printed in Preisendanz's influential edition, which served as the basis of the English translation by M. Q. Smith in H. D. Betz's *GMPT* (1986). At several points, therefore, Daniel's edition contributes to the *raison d'être* of the present translation.

As for the language of the text, the variety of Greek in several of the so-called "magical papyri" has been compared by A. Deissmann and others to the Koine dialect of the earliest Christian writings.[9] As far as such comparisons go, they illuminate the dialect realised in *Moses VIII* in particular. However, despite the standardisation that characterised the development of the Koine, variation in Greek continued throughout the Hellenistic and Roman periods not only on the basis of differences between particular situations of communication (i.e., register) but also in accordance with more general considerations of geography (i.e., dialect). In that connection, the distinctively Egyptian contribution to the magico-religious synthesis of *Moses VIII* deserves more scholarly attention than it has received thus far;[10] for in addition to its interest to the historian of religion, it is realised largely by terms and phrases that collectively identify the variety of the text's language with late antique Egypt[11] far more closely than generalised talk about the international

4. The history of the manuscript's transmission from antiquity to modern times is shrouded in mystery; but a lively and informed reconstruction is offered by Betz, "Introduction to the Greek Magical Papyri," *GMPT*, xlii-xliii.

5. C. J. C. Reuvens, *Lettres à M. Letronne, sur les Papyrus bilingues et Grecs, et sur quelques autres Monumens Gréco-Egyptiens du Musée d'Antiquités de l'Université de Leide* (Leiden: Luchtmans, 1830).

6. K. O. Müller, untitled piece in *Göttingische gelehrte Anzeigen* 56 (April 9, 1831): 545-54.

7. C. Leemans, *Papyri graeci musei antiquarii publici Lugduni-Batavi. Regis augustissimi jussu edidit, interpretationem latinam, annotationem, indicem et tabulas addidit C. Leemans* (2 vols.; Lugduni Batavorum: Brill, 1843, 1885).

8. A. Dieterich, *Abraxas: Studien zur Religionsgeschichte des spätern Altertums* (Leipzig: B. G. Teubner, 1891); K. Preisendanz and A. Henrichs, eds., *Papyri Graecae Magicae: Die griechischen Zauberpapyri* (3 vols.; rev. 2nd ed.; Munich and Leipzig: Saur, 1973-74); and R. Daniel, ed., *Two Greek Magical Papyri in the National Museum of Antiquities in Leiden: A Photographic Edition of J 384 and J 395 (= PGM XII and XIII)* (Papyrologica Coloniensia 19; Opladen: Westdeutscher Verlag, 1991).

9. See, e.g., A. Deissmann, *Light from the Ancient East* (4th ed.; trans. L. R. M. Strachan; London: Hodder & Stoughton, 1927), 142, 301-7.

10. On the role of indigenous Egyptian religion in the magical papyri generally, see Betz, "Introduction," *GMPT*, xlvi. On its role in *Moses VIII* more specifically, see *GMPT*, 173 nn. 13 and 15; 175 n. 30; 176, n. 34; 183 nn. 83 and 86; 184 n. 91.

11. Consider, e.g., the cumulative effect of the words translated "Egyptian bean" (22), "Manetho" (24),

character of either the Koine or "magic" would suggest. In the present context, however, we can do little more than stress that the language of *Moses VIII*, like that of the Greek magical papyri generally, is sorely in need of fresh description and analysis informed by recent linguistic discussions of dialect and register.[12]

In recent decades, scholarship on Leiden Papyrus J 395 has been unanimous in understanding the text's contents as including more than one version of *Moses VIII*. Precisely how many versions, however, and the degree of specificity with which a tradition history for those versions can be responsibly conjectured, are far from certain. As on a great many issues pertaining to *Moses VIII* so on these two in particular, the scholarly contributions of Morton Smith have special importance and deserve attention here. Most notably, both in the notes accompanying his English translation in *GMPT* and in an article published three years earlier, Smith departed from the mainstream of earlier scholarly opinion by:

- proposing that Leiden Papyrus J 395 includes not just two different versions of *Moses VIII* but three, namely lines 1-343 (labelled "A" by Smith), lines 343-646 (Smith's "B"), and lines 646-734 (Smith's "C");
- constructing a five-stage process of tradition history culminating in the production of our manuscript; and
- postulating the existence of a single basic text of which our extant versions are variants, and whose contents and purpose can be reconstructed.[13]

Smith's views on these issues have strongly influenced the most important study recently published on *Moses VIII*;[14] yet a different understanding is reflected in the translation and accompanying notes below. Because Smith's opinions concerning the tradition history of *Moses VIII* and his implicit theory of translation affect one another at a deep level, the main weaknesses of his position ought to be noted.

Most of the difficulties in Smith's interpretation stem from his controversial judgement that lines 646-734 constitute by themselves a whole distinct version of *Moses VIII* (i.e., Smith's version "C"), rather than forming the end of a much lengthier version that begins in the middle of line 343. Against the existence of Smith's C, and as his very own synopsis of the three hypothetical versions well illustrates, all the parallels to his version "C" except one are found not in "B" (343-646) but rather in "A" (1-343);[15] and since both "A" and "B" (as defined by Smith) individually contain doublets, the negligible amount of material found both in 343-646 and 646-734 can easily be construed as a doublet within 343-734, viewed as a single version.

Furthermore, by interpreting the end of line 646 as the beginning of his version "C," Smith requires his version "B" (i.e., 343-646) to conclude unsatisfactorily, namely with an

---

"Egyptian flail" (34), "falcon-faced crocodile" (41 and passim), "the nine-formed god" (42 and passim), "Achebukrōm" (141 and passim), "Anok" (150 and passim), and "hippopotamus" (309-18). A full study of dialect, of course, would be obligated to consider not only vocabulary but also grammar.

12. See, e.g., R. A. Hudson, *Sociolinguistics* (2nd ed.; Cambridge Textbooks in Linguistics; Cambridge: Cambridge University Press, 1996), 38-50.

13. See Smith, "The Eighth Book of Moses," 683-88.

14. B. J. L. Peerbolte, "The Eighth Book of Moses (PLeid. J 395): Hellenistic Jewish Influence in a Pagan Magical Papyrus," in *A Kind of Magic: Understanding Magic in the New Testament and Its Religious Environment* (ed. M. Labahn and B. J. L. Peerbolte; London: T.&T. Clark, 2007), 189-90.

15. See Smith, "The Eighth Book of Moses," 690-93. Lines 688-92 are parallel in thought both to lines 131-34 and lines 434-37, while lines 704-5 are broadly similar both to lines 210-11 and to lines 564-65.

unremarkable ritual utterance rather than with the dramatic revelatory encounter promised at the beginning of "B" in its abstract (345-47); whereas if, contra Smith, "B" is understood to conclude in line 734 rather than line 646, its ending is just as conventional, functional, and satisfying as the ending of "A" is. Third, the beginning of Smith's version "C" (646 ff.) neither parallels the beginnings of versions "A" and "B" (both of which open with a titular abstract followed by a prescription for ritual purification) nor functions as an abstract or orientation for the putative version as a whole; moreover, the first clause of that same beginning in the Greek text of Smith's "C" includes a connective particle which serves, against Smith's thesis, to link together what precedes (i.e., in "B") and what follows (i.e., in "C"), and immediately afterwards the Greek verb translated "he says" has an unexpressed subject that can only be identified by reading the same clause in the light of the ending of "B," a strategy that should not be necessary if Smith's hypothesis were correct.

Fourth, just as the phrase "as I said before" in lines 114-15 refers to antecedent discourse found in lines 4-8, so also the parallel phrase in line 671 refers to antecedent discourse found in lines 347-50,[16] forming a reference chain that connects part of Smith's version C (line 671) to the beginning of "B" (347-50) and thus undermines the very idea of "C" as a version in its own right.[17] And finally, when lines 345-47 are recognised as an abstract previewing the programme of discourse that follows in the co-text, and thus also as promising that both a ritual pertaining to "the name" and a procedure for facilitating a revelatory "meeting" are to follow, the occurrences of the phrase "When the god enters" both in lines 564-65 and in line 704 can be construed as introducing parallel fulfilments of the prior two-sided promise, with lines 564-65 introducing the disclosure of the name, and line 704 marking the beginning of the revelatory "meeting." The overall effect of this feature is to produce a schematic structure that ties together the abstract of "B" (lines 345-47) and lines 564-65 and 704 into a single, largely coherent macrostructure, an effect that militates strongly against Smith's notion of a third version of *Moses VIII* in Leiden Papyrus J 395.

Thus, instead of following Smith and taking lines 343-734 as consisting of two versions (i.e., "B" and "C"), the present interpretation construes the same lines as belonging to a single version, which for sake of convenience is referred to below as "B."

Genre, Structure, and Prosody

The amount of scholarly attention devoted to *Moses VIII*'s literary genre pales into insignificance by comparison with the volume of discussion given to its sources and tradition history. Indeed, in scholarship published to date on *Moses VIII* no sustained attention has been given to the text's genre. To be sure, summaries have been given of the text's content, and scattered comments have been made on its function as a whole and on the purpose of some of its parts; but the kind of comparative analysis required by careful genre criticism, whereby all of *Moses VIII* would be compared with other documents similar to it and of known literary genre, is still awaited. Until a thorough study of this matter becomes available, little can be done beyond trying to synthesise a recent scholarly attempt to classify a small set of broadly similar texts from late antiquity, a few comparative observations on

16. Cf. W. M. Brashear, "The Greek Magical Papyri: An Introduction and Survey: Annotated Bibliography (1928-1994)," in *ANRW* 18.5: 3539.

17. Indeed, if the phrase "as I said before" in line 671 is not understood as referring (as suggested above) to lines 347-50, it causes that part of Smith's version "C" to be incoherent, a quality which Smith undoubtedly attributed to *Moses VIII* more often than is necessary.

two of those texts in particular, and a proposal concerning the way in which the creation account embedded in both versions of *Moses VIII* (i.e., "A" and "B") might be related to the instructions surrounding them in each case.

In a recent treatment of so-called "magical manuals" from late antiquity, P. S. Alexander has proposed that such texts should be classified as consisting of two broad subtypes, namely "books of recipes" on the one hand and "books of magical theology" on the other hand.[18] The former category Alexander defines as "collections of incantations" presented in the style of master copies, whose blank forms (e.g., "N son of N") would have been personalised when the master was copied onto an amulet for a particular client.[19] These collections are, according to Alexander, more directly pragmatic and less explicitly theoretical than are texts such as *Sefer ha-Razim*, *Harba di-Moshe*, the *Great Magical Papyrus of Paris* (especially the *Mithras Liturgy*), and the *Testament of Solomon*. This latter group of documents, especially *Sefer ha-Razim* and the *Mithras Liturgy*,[20] provides what are probably the closest parallels available for comparative study of *Moses VIII* and could be expanded so as to make room for our text without doing violence to the boundaries of the genre. *Sefer ha-Razim*, in fact, is the only text that scholars have mentioned in connection with the genre of *Moses VIII*;[21] but unfortunately such references have not been developed into anything resembling a sustained comparative analysis of the two texts. In lieu of that sort of treatment, but also as a step in that direction, the following list of resemblances may prove illuminating.

The narrators of both *Moses VIII* and *Sefer ha-Razim* explicitly define themselves by association with a range of earlier traditions and legendary agents of cosmic power, with figures from the history of Israel, and Moses in particular, being named in both.[22] In contrast moreover to both *Harba di-Moshe* and the *Testament of Solomon* (especially chapters 1–18), which are united in general by a prominent interest in the activities of demonic beings, both *Moses VIII* (especially version "A") and *Sefer ha-Razim* transmit ritual procedures and formulaic utterances for performance in a great variety of situations, many of which have nothing to do with evil spirits or the misfortunes they cause.[23] The same two documents also share a strong interest in ritual activities that have revelatory aims.[24] And finally, tabular lists of the names and identities of important cosmic powers are provided in both texts so that users might avail themselves of the knowledge essential to achieving the respective pragmatic goals envisaged in the text.[25] Of course, none of these features is so unusual as to be highly significant by itself for purposes of genre criticism; but consid-

---

18. P. S. Alexander, "Contextualising the Demonology of the *Testament of Solomon*," in *Die Dämonen: Die Dämonologie der alttestamentlich-jüdischen und frühchristlichen Literatur im Kontext ihrer Umwelt* (ed. A. Lange; Tübingen: Mohr Siebeck, 2003), 614-15.

19. Alexander, "Contextualising the Demonology of the *Testament of Solomon*," 614; cf. M. Meyer and R. Smith, eds., *Ancient Christian Magic: Coptic Texts of Ritual Power* (San Francisco: HarperCollins, 1994), 7.

20. The *Testament of Solomon* is excluded from consideration because, as the present writer has argued elsewhere (T. Klutz, *Rewriting the Testament of Solomon* [LSTS 53; London: T.&T. Clark, 2005], 14-19, 68-69), its long forms are too literarily complex to be satisfactorily categorised as an example of a "book of magical theology." Like the *Testament*, moreover, *Harba di-Moshe* differs strikingly not only from *ShR* and the *Mithras Liturgy* but also from *Moses VIII* by virtue of the high prominence it assigns to demonology.

21. See Peerbolte, "The Eighth Book of Moses," 192.

22. E.g., *PGM* XIII. 21, 382-83; and *ShR* preface lines 1-30.

23. E.g., *PGM* XIII. 234-42; and *ShR* 1.84-106.

24. E.g., *PGM* XIII. 38-212, 345-567; *ShR* 4.25-42.

25. E.g., *PGM* XIII. 217-24, 722-30; and *ShR* 1.18-26; 2.12-14; 3.13-16; and passim.

ered collectively, they serve to distinguish *Moses VIII* and *Sefer ha-Razim* from other late antique handbooks of ritual power, including even works such as *Harba di-Moshe* and the *Testament of Solomon*.

However, like most texts consisting of more than a few clauses, *Moses VIII* is an interdiscursive combination of various linguistic registers and literary sub-genres (e.g., ritual prescriptions, prayers, incantations, astrological treatise, creation myths). Both the interplay between these different styles and their dialogical impact on the force of *Moses VIII* as a whole would therefore require close attention in anything resembling a full discourse analysis of the text. In that connection special consideration should probably be devoted to the presence and communicative force of the creation myth embedded roughly in the middle of each of the text's two versions.[26] Sandwiched in each case between a ritual recipe and instruction concerning how to behave when the climactic revelation takes place, the creation story may be intended to suggest that the same kind of power realised in the creation of the cosmos is now to be re-actualised in the context of the user of *Moses VIII* as a result of the power inherent in the story itself. Perhaps because the events of creation were understood to involve no small display of divine power, creation myths had great appeal for adaptation and redeployment by ancient authors of incantation texts and magico-religious handbooks. In modern study of ancient texts of ritual power, instances of this particular type of mythic intertextuality have been grouped together to form a literary sub-genre known as "historiola formulas";[27] historiolas are present in many late antique and medieval incantatory texts, so that suitable material for comparative study of lines 138-206 and 443-564 in *Moses VIII* is not in short supply.[28]

Date and Provenance

Recent scholarship on Leiden Papyrus J 395 is unanimous with regard to the setting within which the text of both versions of *Moses VIII* was inscribed. There is general agreement that the codex as a whole is from the fourth century C.E., and that the hand responsible for all but a few lines of *Moses VIII* is typical of writing from around 350 C.E.[29] From the earliest phase of research to the present, moreover, no challenge has been raised against the notion of a broadly Egyptian provenance for both the extant text itself and the composition assumed to lie behind it;[30] in this latter connection *Moses VIII* is representative of the Greek magical papyri more generally.

The current consensus about the date of the manuscript constitutes a change, albeit a minor one, in scholarly opinion, with research prior to the 1980s having suggested a slightly earlier range of dates (third or fourth century C.E.) than that agreed more re-

26. Lines 138-206, and 443-564. The feature is mentioned briefly by J. Gager, *Moses in Greco-Roman Paganism* (Nashville: Abingdon, 1972), 146, but has never been discussed satisfactorily in terms of its impact on the force of the text as a whole.

27. See, e.g., G. Bohak, *Ancient Jewish Magic: A History* (Cambridge: Cambridge University Press, 2008), 312-14; and D. Frankfurter, "Narrating Power: The Theory and Practice of the Magical *Historiola* in Ritual Spells," in *Ancient Magic and Ritual Power* (ed. M. Meyer and P. Mirecki; Leiden: Brill, 1995), 457-76.

28. See, e.g., Oxyrynchus 1077 (Preizendanz, *PGM*, 2:211); Cairo 10263 (Preizendanz, *PGM*, 2:220-22); Berlin 11858 (Preizendanz, *PGM*, 2:231-32); and *PGM* IV.94-153. English translations of the first three of these are available in Meyer and Smith, eds., *Ancient Christian Magic*, 33-36.

29. See, e.g., Peerbolte, "The Eighth Book of Moses," 190; *GMPT*, 181, 184 n. 92; and Daniel, *Two Greek Magical Papyri*, x-xi.

30. Betz, "Introduction," xlv-l.

cently.[31] This shift in favour of a later dating of the extant text, however, has been accompanied by a tendency to postulate several stages of redaction, or literary "generations," going backward in time four or five generations to a hypothesised *Ur*-text, postulated as originating in the second century C.E. (or perhaps even the first) and assumed to be largely recoverable through processes of source and redaction criticism. Smith, for instance, proposes a multi-stage tradition history largely on the basis of his own thesis that *PGM* XIII. 1-734 consists of not merely two versions of *Moses VIII* but three,[32] a thesis already criticised above as vulnerable on both linguistic and historical grounds. Smith's programme of dating the literary sources of the magical papyri earlier than the evidence requires may be explained, at least in part, by reference to his controversial study *Jesus the Magician* (1978), in which comparison of the magical papyri (and *Moses VIII* in particular) and the New Testament Gospels is casually interpreted as supporting very early datings of the sources embedded in the former.[33]

A more specific example of the same tendency is Smith's suggestion that the original version behind all or part of version B should perhaps be dated to 139 C.E., a date suggested by a possible correspondence between the festival of the "birth of Horus" (alluded to in XIII. 386-94) on the twenty-eighth day of Pharmuthi on the one hand and March 21 on the other hand, the date of the spring equinox in "an ideal year."[34] Although Smith's interpretation of the meteorological discourse in this passage is not implausible, alternative readings that are equally defensible have been offered by others,[35] and his willingness in this connection to assume meteorological competence on the part of the ancient author deviates strikingly from his own lack of "initiative trust"[36] with regard to the text's worldview at so many other points.[37]

One other argument for postulating a very early (first or second century C.E.) original behind the extant versions deserves at least brief attention here. The argument in question focuses on the several items scattered throughout the text that have associations with the religious ideas and institutions of Judaism in particular. More specifically, according to a recent study of *Moses VIII* by B. J. L. Peerbolte, the several references to Moses and ancient writings attributed to him (see above), the occurrence of "magical phonemes" derived from Hebrew words,[38] and the reference to "the temple of Jerusalem" (line 233) have a cumulative effect of making the Jewish aspects of the text more prominent than previous interpreters have allowed.[39] A type of cultural hybridity in which Judaism plays a lively role is therefore understood by Peerbolte as being essential to the implied context, an en-

31. Third or fourth century: Preisendanz, "Die griechischen Zauberpapyri," *Archiv für Papyrusforschung* 8 (1927), 122-23; and Gager, *Moses in Greco-Roman Paganism*, 146.

32. See Smith, "The Eighth Book of Moses," 683-88.

33. See M. Q. Smith, *Jesus the Magician* (New York: Harper & Row, 1978), 136.

34. *GMPT*, 183 n. 81.

35. The German translation of XIII. 389–90 in Preisendanz, *PGM*, 2:107, interprets "the birth of Horus" as the winter solstice ("Winterwende") rather than the spring equinox.

36. The phrase is borrowed from George Steiner (*After Babel: Aspects of Language and Translation* [3rd ed.; Oxford: Oxford University Press, 1998], 312-13), who uses it to denote the first move in every successful act of translation, namely the translator's operative assumption that the source text is coherent, meaningful and, however foreign or strange its assumptions might be, capable of being understood.

37. A particularly striking example is Smith's description of the reference in XIII. 233 to the Jerusalem temple as "pretentious hokum" (*GMPT*, 179 n. 56).

38. E.g., *Adōnaie Basēmmiaō* in XIII. 147.

39. Peerbolte, "The Eighth Book of Moses," 190-91.

vironment characterised by vibrant exchange between Jewish and pagan "magicians," with the magico-religious synthesis of *Moses VIII* in particular being "somehow connected to Judaism" and "perhaps even to the period of the Second Temple."[40] Although Peerbolte does not interpret the reference to the temple in particular as entailing that the temple was still standing when the original of *Moses VIII* was composed, he does understand it as implying a context in which the temple was still held in high esteem and considered spiritually important, a context that in his mind is better suited to a first- or second-century dating than to a third- or fourth-century one.[41] However, what Peerbolte's proposal overlooks is that both the reference to the temple in line 233 and the other Jewish elements just mentioned serve in good measure to enhance the prestige and authority of the text itself, so that the temple reference in particular is better understood as part of a rhetoric of ancient (and thus venerable) origins than as some innocent reflection of the document's historical context or date of composition.[42]

The scholarly consensus in favour of a broadly Egyptian provenance for the composition of *Moses VIII* is reinforced by the comments above concerning the text's dialect. The consensus is therefore accepted without criticism in the present context; however, evidence in favour of a more specific setting within Egypt should not be overlooked. Most notably, a mid-nineteenth-century catalogue of the Anastasi collection indicates that at least a substantial part of the corpus was obtained in Thebes, where only a few years earlier a contemporary of Anastasi's had collected various papyri recovered from local tombs and their immediate environs.[43] If *Moses VIII* in particular was composed in or near Thebes, the reference in lines 394 and 407 to the Nile River simply as "the water" would not have been unintelligible to the text's earliest users but rather would have made sense as an instance of presupposed local knowledge.[44] Of course, this particular feature would cohere not only with a Theban setting but with any settled area near the Nile. Still, taken in conjunction with the nineteenth-century reports that mention Theban tombs, these references to the Nile warrant at least a tentative conjecture that Thebes in particular may have been the place of our text's composition.

Literary Context

Moses VIII is best interpreted as assuming knowledge of a range of other texts and discourses even though most of these are not cited directly or even clearly alluded to. For instance, the combination of Mosaic pseudepigraphy, interest in the power of divine names, and formulaic use of the Hebraism *Adōnaie Basēmmiaō* may be influenced at least indirectly by the biblical portrayal of Moses as experiencing a revelation of the divine name at his calling in Egypt (Exod 3:13-15).[45] The reference in line 233 to the Jerusalem temple, moreover, belongs to a whole set of features that have specifically either Jewish or Christian overtones and are present only in version A. Although the meaning

40. Peerbolte, "The Eighth Book of Moses," 190-91.

41. Peerbolte, "The Eighth Book of Moses," 191-92.

42. As indicated below in the proposed translation of lines 233, an even better interpretation of the temple reference is to construe the preposition *en* + dative noun (*hierō*) in that context not as locative ("in the temple") but rather as instrumental ("by the temple"), a reading which obviates the charge of anachronism whilst preserving the archaising air of the reference.

43. As noted by Betz, "Introduction," *GMPT*, xlii-xlvii, l. n. 12.

44. On "the water" as the Nile, see *GMPT*, 183 n. 83.

45. Peerbolte, "The Eighth Book of Moses," 187.

of those lines is less clear than recent translations suggest, the temple reference is undoubtedly dependent on biblical and related traditions rather than on direct experience. Similarly, the prescribed utterance "I am he on the two cherubim" in lines 254-55 and 334 echoes a motif found in several passages of Jewish Scripture.[46] And the invocation of Christ in line 289, embedded as it is in a formula for effecting "release from chains" (line 288), should perhaps be read as echoing the stories of prison release in the Acts of the Apostles.[47]

Because each of these last three features contributes to the distinctiveness of version A, they might be read collectively as the work of a redactor whose aim was to make traditions such as those in version B more palatable to ordinary Christians, many of whom would have seen magico-ritual performances of cosmic power as essential to their religious practice,[48] and for whom the Jewish biblical motifs just summarised would have possessed positive significance. Version A, after all, has been interpreted generally by Smith as the reworking of an edition very similar to B; and just as earliest Christianity sometimes understood itself as winning people who formerly trafficked in demonic "magic" and books of ritual power,[49] so also dealers in magico-religious handbooks and incantations would have seen the Christ cult as a promising market for their wares. That market would have been especially attractive around the time accepted above as the date of the production of Leiden papyrus J 395, near the middle of the fourth century C.E., when the numerical growth of Christian converts in the immediately preceding decades was so great that nearly half the population of the empire may have been Christian in one sense or another by 350 C.E.[50]

Of course, it should not be overlooked that most of the motifs just discussed are not distinctively Christian but rather Jewish. Those elements in *Moses VIII* cannot be fully explained in terms of Jewish biblical sources but rather presuppose a late antique cultural milieu close to that realised, for instance, in *Sefer ha-Razim* (discussed above), in the Hekhalot texts, and in the numerous incantation bowls and amulets published in recent years by Joseph Naveh, Shaul Shaked, and others.[51] All of those materials are products of a Judaism that has been greatly enriched by its interchange with other varieties of religion and culture in the same environment; yet none of those texts is as overtly hybridised as *Moses VIII*, which as a whole defies classification as either a Christian or a Jewish document.[52]

Accordingly, no discussion of the literary context of *Moses VIII* can afford to neglect the text's several allusions to ancient works whose outlook is less Jewish or Christian than pagan. In that connection special mention should be made of the so-called *Secret Tenth Book of Moses* (hereafter *Moses X*), known only in the form of the Greek text that directly follows the end of version B of *Moses VIII* and constitutes the final unit of discourse in

---

46. E.g., Exod 25:22; Num 7:89; 1 Sam 4:4; 2 Sam 6:2; 2 Kgs 19:15; 1 Chr 13:6; Ps 80:2 [Evv 80:1]; 99:1; Isa 37:16; Ezek 9:3; 10:18-19; Dan 3:55 LXX. See *GMPT*, 179 n. 64.

47. See Acts 5:17-26; 12:1-19; and 16:19-40.

48. See, e.g., the numerous Christian spells of protection, healing, and cursing in Meyer and Smith, eds., *Ancient Christian Magic*, passim.

49. See, e.g., Acts 19:13-20.

50. See, e.g., R. Stark, *The Rise of Christianity: A Sociologist Reconsiders History* (Princeton, N.J.: Princeton University Press, 1996), 4-13.

51. For example, J. Naveh and S. Shaked, *Magic Spells and Formulae: Aramaic Incantations of Late Antiquity* (Jerusalem: Magness, 1993), 17-20; and D. Levene, *A Corpus of Magic Bowls: Incantation Texts in Jewish Aramaic from Late Antiquity* (London: Kegan Paul, 2003), 14-17.

52. Gager, *Moses in Greco-Roman Paganism*, 135-36.

Leiden Papyrus J 395 (*PGM* XIII. 734-1077). Both the abruptness of *Moses X*'s beginning—the opening lines constitute neither an abstract nor anything resembling an orientation—and the presence of linguistic features which tie the beginning of that document to version B of *Moses VIII*,[53] give the impression that the author/editor of *Moses X* knows *Moses VIII* (or at least its ending) and expects his reader to know it too. Although *Moses X* does not substantially replicate material from either version of *Moses VIII*,[54] it resembles both versions of the latter in terms of length and literary genre. There is also a notable resemblance with regard to degrees of religious hybridity, with positive references in *Moses X* to Zeus, Zoroaster, and "Orpheus the revealer," for instance, occurring alongside appeals to Michael, "the great name . . . in Jerusalem," and "Abraham, Isaac, and Jacob."

Despite the striking cultural heterogeneity of *Moses VIII*, a contextually sensitive reading of the text's several references to the *Key of Moses* indicates that the author/editor of *Moses VIII* did not view the figure of Moses as merely another name of cosmic power for some syncretistic cocktail but rather understood it as uniquely holy and honourable. Most notably, the titular collocation of "key" and "Moses" probably derives part of its meaning from the ancient rivalry between Moses and Hermes, the latter being understood in broadly contemporaneous Greco-Egyptian literature as the author of the *Key of Hermes Trismegistus*.[55] The rivalry between Moses and Hermes is attested more explicitly in the apologetic Moses romance *Artapanus* 3.27.6, 9.[56] *Moses VIII* itself yields almost no insight into the specific contents of the *Key*;[57] but because detailed knowledge of select instructions prescribed in the *Key* is presented in lines 31 and 35-36 of *Moses VIII* as essential to success in performing the ritual outlined in that context, the non-existence of such a text is highly improbable. The *Key* almost certainly was circulating in the milieu in which *Moses VIII* was composed and edited.

The sense of rivalry just noted between Moses and Hermes is conveyed more explicitly in lines 14-16. In that context, after acknowledging that the information he is about to disclose regarding the seven secret incenses is given not only in his own text but also in a Hermetic document known simply as *Wing*, the author of *Moses VIII* tries to undermine the Hermetic book's authority by claiming that its author stole his information about the incenses from the text of *Moses VIII*. Clearly, though, this accusation presupposes that, in *Moses VIII*'s implied context of editing, Hermes' *Wing* was already in existence;[58] accordingly, the possibility that *Wing* did not in fact plagiarise *Moses VIII* but instead antedated

53. E.g., the lexical string "child" in lines 719 and 734, and the reference chain effected by "this vision" in lines 734-35, which creates a cohesive tie with the visionary content of lines 704-17.

54. The point is well made by Smith, *GMPT*, 195 n. 146, where the distinctiveness of *PGM* XIII. 734-1077 is cited against the attempt by Gager, *Moses in Greco-Roman Paganism*, 148, to interpret line 1077 as referring to the eighth book rather than to a tenth.

55. Cf. Gager, *Moses in Greco-Roman Paganism*, 149, citing the title of the tenth tractate of the *Corpus Hermeticum*.

56. Peerbolte, "The Eighth Book of Moses," 190.

57. An exception is present in lines 21-24, where the ritual instruction pertaining to the use of "sun vetch" is presented both as derived from the *Key* and as consonant with directions allegedly found in a work by the third-century-B.C.E Egyptian priest and historian Manetho. Like Moses, Manetho was widely esteemed, and various astrological and magico-religious texts were posthumously attributed to him; but from the information in lines 21-24 it is impossible to ascertain which book by Manetho the author of *Moses VIII* had in mind.

58. The point acquires additional significance when one recognises that, as noted by Smith, *GMPT*, 172 n. 6, the existence of *Wing* is not attested in ancient sources other than *Moses VIII*.

it and perhaps even served as a source for the latter, at least with regard to the seven types of incense, should not be dismissed lightly.

A full treatment of the literary environment of *Moses VIII* would deal with texts which our document does not mention by name, but which none the less have conditioned its production and reception in various ways. Examples include the creation narrative in both version A and B (lines 138-206, 443-564), which parallels existing Judaeo-Egyptian accounts such as that in 2 *Enoch* 25–30;[59] the diverse prescriptions in lines 230-340, which are highly formulaic in style and probably derived from other ritual handbooks known to the author; and the astrological table referred to as the "Seven-Zoned" in line 217 (par. 723), whose purpose is to enable its users to identify on any given day which of seven Greek gods rules the day (and by extension which god rules the celestial pole on that same day).[60] But more important for the present study, even the introductory discussion here has been able to highlight the complexity of *Moses VIII*'s literary and socio-cultural context. In that environment, ideas and symbols of Jewish origin could be freely combined with Greco-Egyptian ideas, while Moses' name and related Jewish symbols could be presented in the same discourse as uniquely powerful.

Bibliography

Betz, H. D., ed. *The Greek Magical Papyri in Translation: Including the Demotic Spells*. Chicago: University of Chicago Press, 1986.

Bohak, G. *Ancient Jewish Magic: A History*. Cambridge: Cambridge University Press, 2008.

Brashear, W. M. "The Greek Magical Papyri: An Introduction and Survey: Annotated Bibliography (1928-1994)." *ANRW* 18.5: 3380-3730. Part 2, Principat, 18.1. Edited by H. Temporini and W. Haase. Berlin: de Gruyter, 1986.

Daniel, R. W., ed. *Two Greek Magical Papyri in the National Museum of Antiquities in Leiden: A Photographic Edition of J 384 and J 395 (= PGM XII and XIII)*. Papyrologica Coloniensia 19. Opladen: Westdeutscher Verlag, 1991.

Dieterich, A. *Abraxas: Studien zur Religionsgeschichte des spätern Altertums*. Leipzig: Teubner, 1891.

Gager, J. G. *Moses in Greco-Roman Paganism*. Nashville: Abingdon, 1972.

Leemans, C. *Papyri graeci musei antiquarii publici Lugduni-Batavi. Regis augustissimi jussu edidit, interpretationem latinam, annotationem, indicem et tabulas addidit C. Leemans*. 2 vols. Lugduni Batavorum: Brill, 1843, 1885.

Merkelbach, R., and M. Totti, eds. *Abrasax: Ausgewählte Papyri religiösen und magischen Inhalts*. Abhandlungen der Rheinisch-Westfälischen Akademie der Wissenschaften. Sonderreihe Papirologica Coloniensia 17/1. Opladen, Westdeutscher Verlag, 1990.

Peerbolte, B. J. L. "The Eighth Book of Moses (PLeid. J 395): Hellenistic Jewish Influence in a Pagan Magical Papyrus." Pages 184-94 in *A Kind of Magic: Understanding Magic in the New Testament and Its Religious Environment*. Edited by M. Labahn and B. J. L. Peerbolte. London: T.&T. Clark, 2007.

Preisendanz, K. "Die griechischen Zauberpapyri." *Archiv für Papyrusforschung* 8 (1927): 104-67.

Preisendanz, K., and A. Henrichs, eds. *Papyri Graecae Magicae: Die griechischen Zauberpapyri*. 2nd ed. 3 vols. Munich and Leipzig: Saur, 1973-74.

Reuvens, C. J. C. *Lettres à M. Letronne, sur les Papyrus bilingues et Grecs, et sur quelques autres*

59. Smith, *GMPT*, 176 n. 43.
60. Cf. Smith, *GMPT*, 178 n. 54.

Monumens Gréco-Egyptiens du Musée d'Antiquités de l'Université de Leide. Leiden: Luchtmans, 1830.

Smith, M. Q. "The Eighth Book of Moses and How It Grew (Pleid. J 395)." Pages 683-93 in *Atti del XVII congresso internazionale di papirologia*. Edited by the International Congress of Papyrology. Naples: Centro internazionale per lo studio dei ercolanesi, 1984.

The Eighth Book of Moses — Version A (Lines 1-343)

Title (lines 1-4)

God •gods.[a] •A holy book called *The Only* or *The Eighth of Moses*, •concerning the sacred name. It contains what follows here.

The Right Time and Place for Successful Initiation (lines 4-8)

Stay pure forty-one days, having reckoned[b] them beforehand so that their completion arrives in the lunar conjunction that happens in •Aries.

Have a ground-level dwelling, where no one has died during •the past year. Let the door be placed •looking west.

Essential Materials for the Initiation (lines 8-29)

Now set up in the middle of the dwelling an earthen altar •and cypress wood, ten pinecones on the right,[c] two white roosters undamaged and spotless, and two lamps •filled with good oil and holding in total one fourth of a part. And •pour in no more than that; for when the god enters, their flame •will be intensified.

Let the table be prepared with these following types of incense, •which are congenial to the god—from this book Hermes thieved when he named the seven types of incense in •his own holy book called *Wing*—•to Kronos, styrax, for it is heavy and fragrant; to Zeus, •malabathron;[d] to Ares, kostos; to Hēlios-Sun, frankincense; •to Aphrodite, Indian nard; to Hermes, cassia; to Selēnē-Moon,[e] myrrh. These are the secret incenses. •Now Moses says in the *Key*,[f] "On every •occasion prepare sun vetch," by which he speaks of the Egyp-

---

a. Smith (*GMPT*, 172 n. 1) mentions epigraphic parallels to the occurrence of the plural at the beginning and infers "literary and philosophical pretensions" from the placement of the singular; but in terms of literary structure and coherence, the combination as a whole reliably anticipates the cosmology implied in the rest of the text, namely one in which numerous divine beings speak and act, with one deity in particular understood to be greater than the rest (see, e.g., lines 138-212).

b. Contra Preisendanz, *PGM* II.87-88, and as reflected in *GMPT*, 172, the participle here rendered "reckoned" is not an adjective that qualifies "days," but rather is adverbial and qualifies "Stay."

c. Neither Smith's "ten pinecones full of seed" (*GMPT*, 172) nor Preisendanz's German ("zehn vollsamige Tannenzapfen," *PGM* II.88) does justice to the spatial connotations of the Greek word *dexious*.

d. Possibly a type of cinnamon in oily form.

e. Represented in the manuscript not verbally but rather pictographically, as a crescent-shaped moon.

f. The *Key of Moses* is discussed above in the "Introduction." The combination of present tense *legei* ("says") and the separation of the article from its noun ("Moses") serves to foreground the importance and

The Eighth Book of Moses — Version B (Lines 343-734)

Title and Preview (lines 343-47)

A holy, •secret book of Moses called *Eighth* or *Sacred*. Its subject matter is the effect of the •name that encompasses all things. The book contains instructions by which •you might achieve the effect if you leave out nothing that is required.

First Stage of Ritual Preparations for Initiation (lines 347-49)

Keep yourself pure forty-one days, •having reckoned the day and the hour in which •the moon must undergo eclipse in Aries.

Lines 349-57

Whenever (the eclipse[a]) is expected to take place in Aries, sleep on the ground the previous night and, when you have offered sacrifice, burn •the seven original types of incense in which •the god takes pleasure, for the seven censings of the seven stars. •The incenses are these: malabathron, styrax, nard, kostos, •cassia, frankincense, myrrh; and the seven flowers of the seven stars, which are rose, lotus, narcissus, lily, •Roselle fruit, gilliflower, marjoram.

a. Against Smith (*GMPT*, 182), who understands the unexpressed subject of the verb to be "the moon," considerations of both word order and syntax favour taking the eclipse event as the subject.

tian bean;[a] •and having stolen the same instructions from the *Key*,[b] •Manetho spoke about these things in his own book.[c]

The seven stars correspond to the seven flowers,[d] which are marjoram, 25lily, lotus, roselle fruit,[e] narcissus, •gilliflower, rose. Twenty-one •days before the initiation, grind these flowers into a white •mortar and dry them in the shade and have them ready for •that day.

Connecting with the Gods of the Hours (lines 29-34)

But first, at 30whatever new moon is fortune's favourite, get yourself connected to the •gods of the hours, whom you have in the *Key*. You will be initiated with respect to them as follows: •Make three figures from the finest flour, one bull-faced, one •goat-faced, one ram-faced, each one of them standing •on the pole of the celestial axis and holding Egyptian flails.

Lines 100-102

Also have •a cinnamon hanging down from your neck; for •the deity is pleased by it and granted it power.

Lines 128-131

Have a mixing bowl •lying close at hand and containing 130milk from a black cow and wine without seawater, for this is beginning •and end.

---

abiding relevance of Moses as author of the *Key*, which is described as superior in authenticity and value to the discourse of Manetho mentioned in the ensuing lines.

a. A plant of uncertain identity, but possibly the perennial twining vine *Lablab purpureus*, which produces edible seeds and attaches itself to nearby surfaces for support.

b. Cf. Brashear, "The Greek Magical Papyri," 3539. The clause effects an important correspondence between Hermes in line 14 and Manetho in the present context, both of whom are portrayed as having plagiarised from the *Key of Moses*.

c. In order to convey coherent meaning in English, the translation of lines 23-24 above reverses the clause order of the Greek text.

d. The Greek of this clause is elliptical and impossible to render into intelligible English without inferring the notion of cosmic sympathy—in this instance, more specifically cosmic correspondences between stars and plants—on which see T. Barton, *Ancient Astrology* (London: Routledge, 1994), 103-4.

e. Unattested in other ancient Greek texts, so the translation here is conjectural; but since the text offers no explanation, the flower was most likely well-known in the implied setting, so that the exotic overtones of Smith's transliteration (*erephyllinos*) are probably misleading.

Having ground them into a fine powder, •offer all of it with wine undiluted by seawater.

Lines 358-63

•Also wear cinnamon, for the god has clothed it with special power. •Burn the incenses after the twenty-first day in order to conclude that part of the ritual.

With respect to the gustable,[a] •partake of black cow's milk, wine without seawater, •and Greek natron — it indicates what is beginning •and end.

Instructions concerning the Required Sacrifice (lines 363-82)

Whenever the day has arrived, set out •cypress or balsam wood for the sacrifice so that even without the incenses the sacrifice will give off a good scent, •and also set out five pinecones on the right. Also light two lamps, •each holding half a pint of oil, on this side and that of the altar. The altar •should be made of earth. Having prepared and filled the lamps, •pour no further oil into them later. Sacrifice a white unblemished rooster, and let another go free, and •likewise sacrifice a pigeon (and let another go free), so that the god, when he enters, can take the spirit of whichever he prefers. •A knife also should be laid out, and beside it should be laid out both •the seven incenses and the seven flowers prepared as set forth above, •so that if, when the god enters, he wishes to sacrifice again, he might find everything ready. And the sacrifice should be left lying out on the altar.

•Now the tasting is to be done as follows: Whenever you are •to perform the tasting, sacrifice the rooster so that the god might receive plenty •of spirit. And just when you are about to taste, call upon both the •god of the hour and him of the day in order to be recommended by them. For unless you invoke them, they will not listen to you, treating you as one who is uninitiated.

a. *GMPT*, 182, has simply "food"; but instead of the ordinary term for food, the Greek noun here is a word that connotes the sensory, and more specifically gustatory, aspect of food, one consequence being that the prescribed ritual is an event powerfully affecting the sense not only of smell (e.g., burnt incense) but also of taste.

Lines 34-37

And when you have surrounded them with burning incense, eat them and pronounce the formula for the gods of the hours—this is •in the *Key*—both the spell[a] for coercing them and the names of the gods •appointed over the weeks.[b] And thus you will have been initiated with respect to them.

Picture and Text on the Natron Square (lines 38-90)

•Next, for the standard meeting have a natron square, •into which you will scratch[c] the great name with the seven vowels.

Now instead of the snapping[d] and the hissing sounds, sketch into one part •of the natron a falcon-faced crocodile and, standing on him, •the nine-formed god; for the falcon-faced •crocodile himself greets the god •with snapping at the four turning-points of the year;

for after coming up from the deep to breathe, he snaps his jaws, and •the one who has the nine forms replies to him.

---

a. The Greek noun for "coercion spell" in this context is unusual but is employed with similar meaning in *PGM* IV. 2574.

b. Unlike those of both Smith (*GMPT*, 173) and Preisendanz (*PGM* II.89), the translation above understands "spell" and "the names" not as distinct from "the formula" but rather as its main constituents, a reading that presupposes a cosmology wherein knowledge of the names of higher powers can be used against powers lower in the hierarchy.

c. Because natron is a "soapy substance" (*GMPT*, 173 n. 14), the potential of the Greek text to envision a process of "scratching into" makes better sense than the image of "writing upon" commended by both Smith (*GMPT*, 173) and Preisendanz (*PGM* II.89).

d. Collocationally, it makes more sense in English to say that crocodiles "snap" than to say they "pop"; thus Preisendanz's "Schnalzen" (*PGM* II.89) brings home the meaning better than Smith's "popping noise" (*GMPT*, 173).

•You will find both sets of gods — those presiding over hours and those over days — •along with the spell for coercing them, in the *Key of Moses*; •for Moses himself detached them.[a]

Natron Picture and Ritual Invocation (lines 383-441)

As for the great name, •write all of it on the Greek natron.

And instead of the snapping noise, sketch onto the natron •the falcon-shaped crocodile;

for he greets •the God four times a year: at the •beginning of each of the natural[b] seasons of the gods, at the first turning of the world, •called "increase," then at what they call "the birth of Horus," in his own exaltation, next at the rising of the Dog Star, and after that the elevation of Sothis.

At each •increase and decrease of Hēlios-Sun, •(the falcon-shaped crocodile) makes the snapping noise. The nine-formed •gives him capacity for making the noise at that •time, so that Hēlios-Sun might ascend from the sound of water;

for (the falcon-shaped crocodile) co-appears with him.

Therefore (the falcon-shaped crocodile) acquired •the forms and the power of the nine •gods that rise with Hēlios-Sun.[c] Then, at the •downward turning[d] he sends out the weaker and less powerful •sound; for this is the birth of the world and the sun. Next, at the "increase," when the bright sentinels of the sky •have begun to be exalted, •he sends out the sound more powerfully. And at the •rise of the Dog Star, at the turning to the west, •he sends out the noise even more powerfully, to the extent that he does not have nearby the water naturally associated with the noise, and because this turning •increases his power still more. Finally, because the last turning in the cycle •includes the water's retreat and a lowering of Hēlios-Sun, •it takes away what (the falcon-shaped crocodile) gained in the preceding turn.

•So, with the myrrhed ink, draw both of the two together, that is, the falcon-shaped crocodile •and the nine-formed god standing on him. •For at the four turnings the falcon-faced crocodile •greets the god with snapping. •For after coming up from the deep to breathe, he snaps his jaws, and the one who has the nine forms replies to him.

---

a. Neither the idea that Moses "set out . . . one by one" the names and formulae nor that he "brought them all out of secrecy" (*GMPT*, 182 n. 79), does justice to the meaning of the main verb, which normally signifies a process of tearing, dragging, separating, or detaching. That range of meaning inspires the conjecture that the unexpressed circumstance in the same clause might be best understood as "from his other writings" (i.e., Moses detached these names and formulae from the Pentateuch and included them in the present text).

b. I.e., as opposed to the new moons of the calendars.

c. For purposes of coherence in English, the order of the clauses in lines 395-97 of the present translation diverges from the order of the Greek text more than at most other points.

d. As explained parenthetically in *GMPT*, 183, probably meaning the autumnal equinox.

Therefore, instead of the snapping noise, •sketch the falcon-faced crocodile, •for the snapping noise is the first syllable of the name. The second is a hissing; •but instead of the hissing noise, (sketch) a snake snacking[a] on its tail, so that the two—snapping and hissing—are now •falcon-faced crocodile with nine-formed god standing •on him and, in a ring around them, the snake •and the seven vowels. And there are nine names, before which you must first say those of •the gods of the hours with the prayer on the stele, and those of the gods appointed over the days of the week,[b] and the spell for coercing all of these. •For without these the god will not listen but •will reject you as uninitiated, unless you first shrewdly announce the names of the lord of •the day and of the hour, instruction •which you will find at the end of this book. For without these you will not do even one of the things that you have in my *Key*.[c]

•Now the sacred stele to be written in the natron is:

> •I invoke you, the one greater than all, the one who •created all things, you who are self-begotten, the one who sees all and yet is •not seen; for you gave to Hēlios-Sun the glory and all the power, and to Selēnē-Moon the faculty of increasing and decreasing and •running consistent laps. You took nothing from the earlier-born •darkness, but distributed equal portions of things; •for when you appeared, not only did light appear but also order came into being.
>
> •To you all things are subject, you whose true form none of the gods can see. He who transforms himself •into all things, you are the invisible Age of the Age.[d]

---

a. Neither Preisendanz's German ("die Schlange . . . beisst," *PGM* II.89) nor Smith's English ("snake biting," *GMPT*, 173) does justice to the phonaesthetics of the Greek text, where the terms for "snake" and "bite" conspicuously rhyme. In addition to representing part of the word play, the repetition of the "s" in "snake snacking" reinforces the intended correspondence between the drawing and the sound of hissing.

b. Following Daniel, *Two Greek Magical Papyri*, xxiv, both here (XIII. 54-55) and in lines 425-26, and contra Preisendanz and Dieterich (see *PGM* II.90) who harmonise these passages with lines 735-36 by proposing the insertion of a conjunction and thus have both gods of the days *and* gods of the weeks.

c. I.e., the *Key of Moses*, implied here to be another of the first-person narrator's own treatises. Contra Smith (who, following Preisendanz, reads "the *Key*"), the possessive pronoun is present in the Greek text, as is evident in Daniel's photograph of the Greek (*Two Greek Magical Papyri*, xxiv, 34-35). The same word is absent, however, from the parallel in line 432.

d. Against the renderings in Preizendanz, *PGM*, and *GMPT*, both of which transliterate the Greek (e.g., "Aion of Aions") rather than actually translate it, a rendering into familiar English terms associated with lengthy periods of time comes close to bringing home the meaning.

•Therefore, instead of the snapping noise, •sketch the falcon-faced crocodile, for the snapping noise is the first syllable of the •name. The second is a hissing; but instead of the •hissing noise, (sketch) a snake snacking on its tail, so that the two — snapping •and hissing — are now falcon-faced crocodile •with nine-formed god standing on him and, in a ring around •them, the snake and the seven vowels. And there are •nine names, before which you must first say those of the gods of the hours with the prayer on the stele, and those of the gods •appointed over the days of the week,[a] and the spell for coercing all of these. •For without these the god will not listen •but will reject you as uninitiated, unless •you first shrewdly announce the names of the lord of the day and of the hour, instruction which you will find at the end of this book. •For without these you will not do even one of the things that you have •in the *Key*.

Throw the mash of the seven flowers, •which you have prepared, into the ink, and thus write on the natron. •On both sides write what follows, and lick off the one side, and wash off the other •into the wine and the milk; but first, before you wash it off, sacrifice •the rooster and get everything ready. •And, after sacrificing the rooster, push forward by turns the •other two and the pigeon,[b] which you have already prepared;[c] then invoke the gods of the hours, as prescribed earlier, •and then drink up.[d]

The Text Written on the Natron (lines 568-600)

•Now the sacred stele written on the natron — •that is, the invocation — is given here with complete accuracy and runs as follows:

> I invoke you, •the one who created all things, the one greater than all, •you, the self-begotten god, the one who sees all •and hears all, and yet is not seen; for you gave •to Hēlios-Sun the glory and all the power, and to Selēnē-Moon the faculty of increasing and decreasing and •running consistent laps. You took nothing from the earlier-born •darkness, but instead distributed to them equal portions; •for when you appeared, not only did light appear but also order came into being, •and all things were arranged by you.
>
> Therefore all things are also subject to you, whose •true form none of the gods can see, who changes form •in visions, Age of the Age.

---

a. See note on the parallel in lines 54-55.

b. As noted by Smith (*GMPT*, 184 n. 89), this instruction requires more roosters than are provided according to XIII. 369-75. Despite his helpful note, Smith's translation inexplicably omits this part of the text.

c. In *GMPT*, 184, the word "read" ("having made everything . . . read") is apparently a printing error and should be spelled "ready."

d. Line 442, which is the first of page 11 in the codex, has the same content as the final line (441) of the preceding page.

I invoke you, •Lord, that you might appear to me in a good form; for •under your world-government I serve your angel, **Biathiarbar •Berbirs Chilatour Bouphroumtrōm**, and your terror, **Danouph Chrator Belbali Balbithiaō.** •Through you, the celestial pole and the earth are held together.

I invoke •you, Lord, as do the gods below you in order to have power—**•Echebukrōm** of Hēlios-Sun,[a] whose is the glory, **aaa** ēēē •ōōō iii aaa ōōō Sabaōth, Arbathiaō, **Zagourē**, the god **Arathu Adōnaie**.

I invoke •you, Lord, in birdglyphic: **Arai**; in •hieroglyphic: **Lailam**; in Hebrew: **Anoch •Biathiarbath Berbir Echilatour Bouphroumtrom**; •in Egyptian: **Aldabaeim**; in baboonic: **Abrasax**; in falconic: **chi chi chi chi chi chi chi tiph tiph tiph**; •in hieratic: **•Menephōiphōth cha cha cha cha cha cha cha.**

•Then clap three times, make a loud snapping noise, hiss for •a long time.

"Come to me, Lord, blameless and flawless, who defiles no place; for I have been initiated with respect to your name."

Additional Materials Required for the Initiation (lines 91-114)

•Have a tablet on which you will write what •he says to you, and a double-edged knife of unadulterated iron, so that when •you slay the sacrifices they will be clean of all defilements, and a libation—•a jug of wine and a flask full of honey—so that you may pour it out as a drink offering. Let all these things be at hand[b] ready for you. •And you be in clean linen garments, wreathed in an olive •wreath, having made[c] the canopy as follows:

•Taking a clean sheet of cloth, write around the •edge the names of the 365 gods. Make it a tent under which you are to be initiated. Also have •a cinnamon hanging down from your neck; for •the deity is pleased by it and granted it power. And also have the helpful Apollo, carved •from a root of laurel, next •to which should stand tripod and Pythian serpent. Carve around the Apollo •the great name in Egyptian form; on his •chest the palindrome "**Bainchooochooochniab**," down the back •of the figure this name: "**Ilillou Ilillou Ilillou**"; and around the Pythian serpent and the •tripod: "**Ithor Marmarauge**

a. Represented in the papyrus not by a word but rather as a pictograph.

b. Smith's rendering "Have all these ready nearby you" is grammatically very loose and gives the misleading impression that the imperative is second person when in reality it is third.

c. By ignoring the implications of relative time in the aorist tense participle, and treating it as a command rather than as circumstantial, Smith's rendering in *GMPT* gives the impression that "the canopy" is actually made after the candidate has begun to perform the ritual and has put on the appropriate clothing. Against that interpretation, it makes far better sense to see the canopy as having been already prepared, as indeed is suggested both by the aorist tense form of the participle and by the relationship between writing and initiation implied in lines 111-13.

I invoke •you, Lord, that your true form might become apparent to me; •for under your world-government I serve your angel, **Anag Biathiarbar Berbi •Schilatourbou Phrountōrm**, and your terror, •**Danoup Chrantor Belbali Balbith Iaō**. •Through you, the celestial pole and the earth are held together.

I invoke you, •Lord, as do the gods below you in order to have power — **Achebukrōm**, whose is the glory, **aaa** ēēē •ōōō **iii aaa** ōōō **Saba**ōth, •Arbathiaō, Zagourē, the god **Arath Adōnai**.

•**Basummiaō**, I invoke you, Lord, in birdglyphic: •**Arai**; in hieroglyphic: **Lailam**; in Hebrew: **Anag Biathiarbar Berbi Schilatourbour Phountōrm**; •in Egyptian: **Aldabaeim**; •in baboonic: **Abrasax**; in falconic: **chi chi chi chi chi •chi chi ti ti ti ti ti ti ti**; in hieratic: **Menephōiphōth cha cha cha cha cha cha cha**.

Lines 600-607

Then clap three times, •make a loud snapping noise repeatedly, •hiss a great hiss, that is, for a long time.

•"Come to me, lord, who defiles no place and is blameless, •gracious, without anger; for I invoke you, King of kings, Ruler of rulers, •most glorious of the glorious, Deity of deities, Strongest of the strong, Holiest of the holy. Come •to me eagerly, graciously, without anger."

Lines 646-52

•Have a tablet on which you will write •what he says to you, and a knife •so that you may slay the sacrifices clean of all (defilements), •and a libation so that you may pour it out as a drink offering. Let all these things be at hand[a] ready for you. And you be •in clean linen garments, wreathed in an olive wreath, •having made[b] the canopy as follows:

Instructions concerning the Canopy and Other Ritual Objects (lines 653-70)

•Taking a clean sheet of cloth, write •around the edge the names of the 365 gods. Make it as you would a tent under which you are to be initiated. Also have a cinnamon hanging •down from your neck; •for the deity is pleased by it and •granted it power. •And also have the helpful Apollo, carved from a root of laurel, next to which should stand •tripod and Pythian snake. Carve •around the Apollo the great name in Egyptian •form; on his chest •this palindrome "**Bainchooochooochniab**," down the back of the figure this name: •"**Ilillou Ilillou Ilillou**"; and around the •Pythian serpent and the tripod: •"**Ithor Marmarauge Phōchō Phōbōch**." •This too you should have hanging down from your neck when you perform the initiation, for along with the cinnamon it helps in everything.

a. See note on the parallel in line 95.
b. See note on the parallel in line 97.

Phōchō •Phōbōch." This too you should have hanging down from your neck •when you perform the initiation, for along with the •cinnamon it is helpful in everything.

Ritual Speech, Sleep, and Drink (lines 114-61)

So, as I said before,[a] when you have purified yourself just before the seven days of the moon's disappearing,[b] at •the new moon begin using a pallet of rushes on the ground for your bed. •Rising early, greet Hēlios-Sun daily •for seven days, saying first the •gods of the hours, then those appointed over the weeks. After learning the ruling lord of the day, pester him •by repeatedly saying, "Lord, on such-and-such a day I am invoking the god for the sacred •sacrifices," and continue doing this until the eighth day.

•Then, when you have come to this day, •when there is quiet in the middle of the night at about the fifth hour,[c] kindle the altar fire and have at hand the two roosters and the two lamps, •lit—together the lamps should be a fourth of a part—•to which you will add no more oil than that. Begin to recite the stele •and the mystery of the god, which is the sacred scarab.[d] Have a mixing bowl •lying close at hand and containing milk from a black cow and wine without seawater, for this is beginning •and end. Then, having written the text of •the stele on the two sides of the natron, lick off the one side,[e] and wash off the other by bathing it •in the mixing bowl. Let •both sides of the natron[f] be written on (with ink) from the various kinds of incense and the flowers. But before you drink the milk and the wine, utter •this prayer[g] and, having said it, lie down •on the mat, holding both the tablet and the stylus; •and say, "Hermetic (prayer)."

> In every language and every dialect, I invoke you who •surrounds all things, as he first hymned you who was appointed by you and entrusted with all •the spiritual authorities, Hēlios-Sun **Achebukrōm**, who discloses •the flame and the splendour of the disk, and whose is the glory; **aaa •ēēē ōōō**, for on account of you he was glorified; he who •set up the stars, endowing them likewise[h] with beauty, and who in divine light created the world, **iii aaa ōōō**, in which you separated all kinds of things from each other. **•Sabaōth Arbathiaō Zagourē**—these are •the angels who were the first

a. I.e., in the prescription located in lines 4-7; cf. Brashear, "The Greek Magical Papyri," 3539.

b. I.e., the last seven days of the forty-one-day programme of purification.

c. I.e., eleven o'clock.

d. Beetles of the family *Scarabaeidae* were regarded as divine in certain parts of ancient Egypt and were sometimes represented on amulets and in hieroglyphics as a symbol of the solar deity; s.v. "scarab," in *Collins Dictionary of the English Language* (2nd ed.; London: Collins, 1986).

e. Tasting or consuming sacred text is implied in a range of ancient documents to have magico-religious efficacy—see, e.g., Ezek 2:8–3:15.

f. Because the double-sidedness of the natron is signified clearly in lines 131 and 434, "both" is understood here as qualifying not (as in *GMPT*, 175) the incenses and flowers but rather the two sides of the natron; cf. Brashear, "The Greek Magical Papyri," 3540.

g. The identity of this prayer is not as unclear as Smith (*GMPT*, 175) implies; for the elision of "prayer," following "Hermetic" in the immediately ensuing co-text, probably reflects an assumption that the reader will know to supply the unexpressed noun from the present line. "This prayer," then, is the Hermetic petition which directly follows in the co-text.

h. As noted in *GMPT*, 175 n. 29, the text is corrupt at this point and highly difficult to decipher.

Ritual Speech, Sleep, and Drink (lines 671-99)

•So, as I said before,[a] when you have purified yourself just before the seven days •of the moon's disappearing, at the new moon begin a phase of going to sleep at night on the ground. •Rising early, greet Hēlios-Sun daily •for seven days, saying first the gods of the hours, then those •appointed over the weeks. After learning the ruling lord •of the day, pester him by repeatedly saying, "Lord, •on such-and-such a day I am invoking the god for the sacred sacrifices," and •continue doing this until the eighth day.

Then, when you have come to this day, •when there is quiet in the middle of the night, kindle the altar fire •and have at your side the two roosters •and the two lit lamps, to which you will add no more •oil. Begin to recite the stele and the mystery of the god. Have a mixing bowl lying close at hand •and containing milk from a black cow and wine •without seawater, for this is beginning and end. •Then, having written on one side of the natron the text •whose beginning is "I invoke you who are greater than all," and so on as set forth above, lick that side clean;[b] and the other •side, on which is written the figure drawing, •you should wash by bathing it in the mixing bowl. Let the natron be written •on (with ink) from both the various kinds of incense and the flowers. •But before you drink the milk and the wine, utter this prayer and, having said it, lie down •on the mat, holding the tablet •and the stylus; and say the formula of world-creation, whose beginning is, •"In every language and every dialect, I invoke •you who surround all things," and so on.

Lines 443-71

•In every language and every dialect, •I invoke you who surrounds all things. I hymn you, as he first hymned you who was appointed by you and •entrusted with all the spiritual authorities, Hēlios-Sun **Achebukrōm,** •who discloses the flame and the splendour of the disk, •and whose is the glory; **aaa** ēēē ōōō, for •on account of you he was glorified, he who set up the stars — or, •as in other texts, "endowed them with beauty" — and who in divine light created the world, •in which you separated all kinds of things from each other, **iii aaa ōōō. Sabaōth •Arbathiaō Zagourē** — •these are the

---

a. I.e., in the prescription located in lines 346-48. The reference chain between the present context and lines 346-48 is paralleled very closely by the chain that connects lines 4-7 to lines 114-16 within version A. The present lines, by contributing to both the reference chain and the parallel to version A, tacitly undermine Smith's case for interpreting lines 646-734 as a distinct version of *Moses VIII* (i.e., version C), separate both from version A (1-343) and from Smith's shortened version B (343-646). Brashear, "The Greek Magical Papyri," 3539, briefly notes both the reference chain and the parallelism between the two versions but says nothing about their negative implications for Smith's hypothesis.

b. See note on the parallel in line 132.

to appear—**Arath, Adonaie, Basēmmiaō.**[a] The first •angel calls out in birdglyphic, "**Arai**," who has authority over •punishments. Hēlios-Sun hymns you in hieroglyphic, "**Lailam**," and in Hebrew by the same name.[b] **Anok Biathiarbarberbischilatour •bouphroumtrōm**—thirty-six letters[c]—says •"I precede you, Lord, I who rise on the boat, the solar disk,[d] because of you." •Your powerful[e] name in Egyptian: **Aldabiaeim**[f]—nine letters, below. •He who appears on the boat rising with you is a crafty baboon. In his own language he greets you and says, •"You are the number of the days of the year, **Abrasax**."[g] The falcon on the other •side of the boat greets you in his own dialect and cries out •to receive food: "**chi chi chi chi chi chi chi tip tip tip •tip tip tip tip**." And he of the nine forms greets you in Hieratic: "**Menephōiphōth**." By saying this, he means: "I precede you, •Lord."

The Laughter of the God in the Creation of the World (lines 161-206)

Having said this, he clapped three times, and the God laughed •seven times: "**cha cha cha cha cha cha cha**." The God having laughed, •seven gods were begotten, who encompass the world—see above—•for these are the ones that appeared first.

When he cachinnated the first time,[h] Phōs-Light Radiance appeared and irradiated everything; and •he became god over the world and the fire, **Bessun •Berithen Berio.**

---

a. Both the punctuation and the (rather cryptic) translation by Preisendanz (*PGM* II.94) implies the presence of only three names rather than four, the Hebraism **basēmm iaō** being construed as the single phrase "im Namen Jahwe" ("in the name of Yhwh"). However, as noted by Brashear, "The Greek Magical Papyri," 3541, the immediate context of this construction leads the reader to expect not a prepositional phrase but rather a sequence of names, so that **Basēmm** is best understood as parallel to **Adonaie** and **Iaō**, and thus as the name of one of the first angels to be created. With a name so close to that of the "Gnostic" demiurge occurring nearby (**Aldabiaeim**, line 154), the application here of the names **Adonaie** and **Iaō** to created angels invites comparison to the biblical demiurgical myth elaborated in several tractates of the Nag Hammadi library; see, e.g., *Ap. John* II 23, 35.

b. Preisendanz's interpretation of the pronoun as adjectival (i.e., "gleichen," "same") is preferable to Smith's rendering of it as the demonstrative "own" (*GMPT*, 176); yet both of them err by imagining the thirty-six-letter name to be what the author understands as the Hebrew equivalent of "**Lailam**." Far better is the option of understanding "in Hebrew by the same name" as the end of one sentence, with the thirty-six-letter name being the beginning and grammatical subject of another.

c. Notwithstanding the suspicion of Smith (*GMPT*, 176 n. 37), the numerical gloss by the ancient copyist can be accepted as an accurate count of the Greek letters in the name when proper notice is taken of the deletion dot over the final occurrence of the letter rho in **Berbir** (thus **Berbi**), the shorter form corresponding precisely to the parallel in line 459. See Daniel, *Two Greek Magical Papyri*, xxiv.

d. Against Smith (*GMPT*, 176 n. 38), who sees the phrase for "solar disk" as "an uncertain expansion of an abbreviation otherwise unknown," the construction should be taken as an instance of an independent or hanging clause, which here as in certain other contexts serves to highlight the item to which it is most closely linked in the co-text (in this instance, "the boat").

e. The Greek adjective is *physikon*, which conveys overtones of great effectiveness and has none of the potentially negative overtones of Smith's suggestion, "magical."

f. It is perhaps no coincidence that the name corresponds to that applied to the demiurge Yaldabaoth in a number of the tractates from Nag Hammadi (note especially "**Aldabaoth**" in *Ap. John* II 23, 35), whose examples of hybridised Christian discourse from late antique Egypt are comparable at many points to the discursive world of *Moses VIII* and other texts in the Greek magical papyri.

g. As Smith notes, the numerical values of the Greek letters in "**Abrasax**" add up to 365.

h. Despite the infrequency of its usage in English, the unusual term "cachinnate" (meaning "to laugh loudly," and probably onomatopoeic in character) is employed here both in order to signal that the Greek

angels who were the first to appear—**Araga Arath Adonaie, Basēmmiaō.** The first angel calls out to you in birdglyphic, •"**Arai**," which is "woe to my enemy," and you appointed •him over punishments. Hēlios-Sun hymns you •in hieroglyphic, "**Lailam**," and in Hebrew by the same name. **Anag •Biathiarbar Berbi Schila Tourbouphroumtrōm** says, "I precede you, Lord, I who rise on the boat, the solar disk, because of you." Your powerful name •in Egyptian: "**Aldabaeim**" — this means the boat •on which he ascends when he rises over the world. He who appears •on the boat rising with you is a crafty baboon. •In his own language he greets you and says, "You are the number of the days of the year, **Abrasax**."[a] The •falcon on the other side of the boat greets •you in his own dialect and cries out •to receive food: "**chi chi chi chi chi chi chi •ti ti ti ti ti ti ti**." And he of the nine forms greets you in Hieratic: "**Menephōiphōth,**" meaning •"I precede you, Lord."

The Laughter of the God in the Creation of the World (lines 471-564)

Having said this, he clapped three times, and •the God laughed seven times: "**cha cha cha cha cha cha cha**." •When he laughed, seven gods were begotten, •who encompass all things, for these are the ones that appeared first.

When he cachinnated the first time,[b] •Phōs-Light Radiance appeared and divided everything into separate groups; •and he became god over the world and the fire, **•Besen Bereithen Berio.**

a. See note on parallel in line 156.

b. See note on the parallel in lines 164.

He cachinnated a second time. All was water. •Gē-Earth, hearing the sound, cried out and arose into a heap, and the water became •tripartite. A god appeared; he was given charge of the abyss, for without him moisture neither increases nor decreases. •And his name is **Eschakleō**, for you are Ōēaieiōn •Bethelle.

When he was pleased to laugh the third time, Nous-Mind or Thought, •understanding as he does the heart, •appeared because of the god's harshness. He was called Hermes; he was called **Semesilam**.

The god cachinnated the fourth time, and Genna-Fertility appeared, •having control over sowing. She was called **Badētophōth •Zōthaxathōz**.

He laughed the fifth time and, after laughing, became gloomy; •and Moira-Destiny appeared and was holding scales, indicating that •in herself[a] justice is to be found. But Hermes contended with her, saying, "In me[b] is justice to be found."

While they were fighting, •God said, "By both of you will justice be made apparent,[c] •but all things in the world will be subject to you (Moira-Destiny)." She was the first •to receive the scepter of the world—she whose name in palindromic form •is great and holy and glorious. It is this: **Thoriobrititamma Ōrraggadōiōdaggarrōammatitir Boiroth**—forty-nine letters.

He cachinnated the sixth time and was made very happy. •And Kairos-Time appeared and was holding a scepter, indicating kingship, •and he gave over the scepter to the first-created god.[d] •Receiving it, the first-created god said, "You, because you enveloped yourself in the glory of Phōs-Light, will be with me."

---

verb in this context differs from that rendered "laugh" in lines 162-63 and in order to do justice to the paronomasia in the relationship between "**cha cha cha** … " and the verb *kachazō* (cachinnate).

a. Preisendanz ("in ihr sei die Gerechtigkeit"; see *PGM* II.96) captures the emphasis of Moira's interchange with Hermes better than does Smith ("justice was in her province"; see *GMPT*, 177), who ignores the emphatic position of the prepositional phrase.

b. Appropriately, in Greek the word order of Hermes' response highlights his own counter-claim to honour.

c. Because the word order in Greek puts special emphasis at this point on the new information (i.e., that justice will be the responsibility of neither deity on its own but rather of "both" Moira and Hermes), Smith's rendering in *GMPT* ("What *seems to be just* will depend on both"; emphasis mine) is a muddle—the idea that the highest god has doubts about what is just has no support in this context.

d. I.e., Phōs-Light; see lines 164-65.

He cachinnated •a second time. All was water; but Gē-Earth, hearing the sound and seeing Radiance, was alarmed and arose into a heap, •and the water became tripartite. •A god appeared and was given charge of the abyss, and thus •without him moisture neither increases nor decreases. •And his name is **Promsacha Aleeiō**, for you are Ōēai Bethe.

When he was pleased •to laugh the third time, •Nous-Mind, also known as Thought, understanding as he does the heart, appeared because of the god's harshness; and •he was called Hermes, for through him have come all things hermeneutical.[a] •He is also in charge of the faculties of thought, through which everything is managed. And he is also known as **Semesilamps**.

•The god cachinnated the fourth time, and Genna-Fertility appeared, •having control over the sowing of all things, and through whom all things were sown.[b] •She was called **Badētophōth Zōthaxathōzō**.

He laughed the fifth time and, after laughing, became gloomy; and Moira-Destiny appeared[c] •and was holding scales, indicating that in herself justice is •to be found. But Hermes contended with her, saying, "In •me is justice to be found."

While they were fighting, •God said to them, "By both of you will justice be made apparent, but all things in the world will be subject to you (Moira-Destiny)." •She was the first to receive the scepter of the world, •and she was called by a holy, palindromic name, •fearful and frightful. It is this: **Thoriobriti** and so on. •Her name in palindromic form is great and holy and glorious. And this is of great merit, a mighty name: **Thoriobriti•ta mmaōrraggadōiōdaggarrōammati•tirboiroth** — forty-nine letters.

He cachinnated •the sixth time[d] and was made very happy. And Kairos-Time appeared and was holding a scepter, •indicating kingship, and he gave over the scepter to the first-created god.[e] Receiving it, the first-created god said, "You, because you enveloped yourself in the •glory of Phōs-Light, will be with me, because you were the first •to give me a scepter. All things will be under your control, things •past and things yet to be. In you •will be all power." When Kairos-Time enveloped himself in the glory of Phōs-Light, the manner of the light underwent a certain change of course.[f] •The god[g] then said to

---

a. Despite its association in English with modern epistemology and theories of understanding, the word "hermeneutical" is commended here as preferable to previous suggestions (e.g., *GMPT*, 185: "... have been interpreted"; and Preizendanz, *PGM* II.111: "verdolmetscht") because of its ability to articulate the word-play effected in Greek by *Hermēs* and *methermēneustai*.

b. Both *GMPT* and Preisendanz's German obscure the morphological correspondence between the Greek terms for "sowing" and "were sown," a correspondence that contributes to redundancy and inelegance in the Greek text.

c. Like several other lines earlier in the text, this one is written twice by accident, occurring both as the last line (494) on one page and the first (495) on the next.

d. Contra *GMPT*, 185 n. 95, the Greek noun for "time" in the ensuing sentence is not used in this clause.

e. As in the parallel at line 187 so also here, Phōs-Light; see lines 475-76.

f. Smith's literal rendering ("the character of the light produced a certain effluence"; see *GMPT*, 185) is nearly unintelligible and exemplifies, at least at this point, a translation practice that treats meaning as resident in individual words rather than in clauses and sentences.

g. Probably the most high god whose seven cachinnations are narrated in the present section.

Anoch Biathiar Barberbir Silatourbou Phroumtrōm •—thirty-six letters.

When the god cachinnated a seventh time, •Psychē-Soul came into being, and after cachinnating the god wept. On seeing Psychē-Soul, •(the god) hissed, and the earth heaved and gave birth to Pythian serpent, •who foreknew all things. The god called him **Ilillou Ilillou Ilillou Ilillou Ithōrmarmaraugēphōchō •Phōbōch**.

On seeing the serpent, the god was terrified and began to make a clicking noise. •While the god clicked, an armed man appeared who is called •**Danoupchrator Berbalibarbith**. On seeing him, •the god was terrified again, like one who has seen someone stronger, for fear that the earth had cast up a god.

Looking down at the earth, •he said, "**Iaō**." From the echo a god was begotten who is •lord of all.

The preceding man contended with him, saying, •"I am stronger than this god." The (first) god said to the strong man, •"You happen to come from the clicking noise, and this god from an echo. Both of you will be put in charge of every need." The pair was then called **Danoup •Chratorberbalibalbith Iaō**.

the queen,[a] "Having enveloped yourself in the flux •of Phōs-Light, you will be with him, encompassing all things. •You will increase by the light you receive from him and again •you will fall back because of him. With you all things will increase and decrease." The name is great and marvelous — •**Anag Biathiarbar Berbischila Tour Bouphrountōrm** — thirty-six letters.

•He cachinnated the seventh time, panting, and both •Psychē-Soul and all kinds of things came into being.[b] So the god said, •"You will move all things; and with Hermes guiding you, all will be heartened." When the god said this, all things •were put in motion and inspirited like mad.

The •god, seeing this, made the snapping noise, and all things were terrified; and •because of the snapping noise, Phobos-Fear appeared, armed to the teeth. •He is called **Danoup Chratōr Berbali Balbithi** — twenty-six letters.

Then, turning •toward the earth, the god made a loud hissing noise; and the earth was opened up when it received •the echo.

It gave birth to its own creature, the •Pythian serpent, which foreknew all things •through the utterance of the god. Its name is great and holy, **Ililloui Ililloui Ililloui Ithōr•marmaraugē Phōchō Phōbōch**.

When the serpent •appeared, the earth arose into a heap and was lifted up exceedingly high. •But the celestial pole remained stable, so that the earth was about to collide with it. •But the god said, "**Iaō**," with the result that everything came to a stop. Then a very great and mighty god appeared, who established the things that are now already past •in the cosmos and also the things yet to be. Thereafter, •none of the aerial bodies ever moved from its prescribed place.

Phobos-Fear, however, on seeing •someone mightier than himself, opposed him and uttered the boast, •"I am superior to you."

To which the other (**Iaō**) replied, "But I established all things in their places."

So the (highest) god intervened: "You, O serpent, are from an echo, but the god **Iaō** is from •the very utterance itself. The utterance, truly, is better than the echo. •None the less, **Iaō**, the power of you who appeared last will derive not from yourself alone but rather from the both of you, •so that all things might indeed be established in their places." And •from that time he was called by the great and marvelous name **Danoup Chratōr Berbali Balbith Iaō**.

And wanting •to give a grant of honour to his helper •since he had appeared together

---

a. Perhaps, as suggested in *GMPT*, 185 n. 98, Selēnē-Moon; but stronger support is given by the immediate co-text for one of the feminine deities explicitly mentioned in lines 479-505, namely Gē-Earth, Genna-Fertility, and Moira-Destiny.

b. Smith's rendering "came into being and all things were moved" corresponds very literally to what is in the manuscript; but it also creates temporal dissonance with the god's ensuing pronouncement, "You will move all things," and it ignores evidence of scribal error in lines 523-24 where the verb for "were put in motion" has been prematurely copied twice from line 526. See Daniel, *Two Greek Magical Papyri*, xxv-xxvi.

The Initiate Imitates the God (lines 206-209)

"Lord, I imitate (you by pronouncing) •the seven vowels. Enter and hear me, **a ee ēēē •iiii ooooo uuuuuu ōōōōōōō, Abrōch Braōch •Chrammaōth Proarbathō Iaō Ouaeēiouō.**"

The Revelatory Event (lines 210-12)

When the god enters, look down and write what is said •and whatever name they might give you for him; and do not go out •of your tent until he has also told you accurately the things concerning you.

Lines 61-90

•Now the sacred stele to be written in the natron is:

> •I invoke you, the one greater than all, the one who •created all things, you who are self-begotten, the one who sees all and yet is •not seen; for you gave to Hēlios-Sun the glory and all the power, and to Selēnē-Moon the faculty of increasing and decreasing and •running consistent laps. You took nothing from the earlier-born •darkness, but distributed equal portions of things; •for when you appeared, not only did light appear but also order came into being. •To you all things are subject, you whose true form none of the gods can see. He who transforms himself •into all things, you are the invisible Age of the Age.[a]
>
> I invoke you, •Lord, that you might appear to me in a good form; for •under your world-government I serve your angel, **Biathiarbar •Berbirs Chilatour Bouphroumtrōm**, and your terror, **Danouph Chrator Belbali Balbithiaō.** •Through you, the celestial pole and the earth are held together.
>
> I invoke •you, Lord, as do the gods below you in order to have power—**•Echebukrōm** of Hēlios-Sun,[b] whose is the glory, **aaa** ēēē •ōōō iii aaa ōōō Sabaōth, Arbathiaō, **Zagourē**, the god **Arathu Adōnaie**.
>
> I invoke •you, Lord, in birdglyphic: **Arai**; in •hieroglyphic: **Lailam**; in Hebrew: **Anoch •Biathiarbath Berbir Echilatour Bouphroumtrom**; •in Egyptian: **Aldabaeim**; in baboonic: **Abrasax**; in falconic: **chi chi chi chi chi chi chi tiph tiph tiph**; •in hieratic: **•Menephōiphōth cha cha cha cha cha cha cha.**

---

a. Against the renderings in Preizendanz, *PGM*, and *GMPT*, both of which transliterate the Greek (e.g., "Aion of Aions") rather than actually translate it, a rendering into familiar English terms associated with lengthy periods of time comes close to bringing home the meaning.

b. Represented in the papyrus not by a word but rather as a pictograph.

with him, the highest god gave him both leadership of the nine •gods and possession of •power and glory equal to theirs. And he was called by a name derived from the nine gods by taking away, along with the power, •also select letters from their names, **•Bosbeadii**, and from the seven planets, **aeēiouō •eēiouō ēiouō iouō ouō uō ō ōyoiēea •yoiēea oiēea iēea ēea ea a** — great and marvelous when written out as a palindrome! But •his greatest name, which follows, is really great and holy: **•Abōrch Braōch Chrammaōth Prōarbathō •Iaō**. Alternatively: **Abrōch Braōch Chrammaōth Prōarbathō •Iaō Ou Aeēiouō** — twenty-seven letters.

Lines 700-702

"Lord, I imitate you •with regard to the seven vowels; enter and hear me." •Then cite the name of the twenty-seven letters.

The Revelatory Event (564-67; cf. 704-717)

So, when the god enters, look down and write what is said and whatever •name they might give you for him; and do not go out of •your tent until he has also told you the things concerning you.

The Text Written on the Natron (lines 568-600)

•Now the sacred stele to be written on the natron — •that is, the invocation — is given here with complete accuracy and runs as follows:

> I invoke you, •the one who created all things, the one greater than all, •you, the self-begotten god, the one who sees all •and hears all, and yet is not seen; for you gave •to Hēlios-Sun the glory and all the power, and to Selēnē-moon the faculty of increasing and decreasing and •running consistent laps. You took nothing from the earlier-born •darkness, but instead distributed to them equal portions; •for when you appeared, not only did light appear but also order came into being, •and all things were arranged by you. Therefore all things are also subject to you, whose •true form none of the gods can see, who changes form •in visions, Age of the Age.[a]
>
> I invoke •you, Lord, that your true form might become apparent to me; •for under your world-government I serve your angel, **Anag Biathiarbar Berbi •Schilatourbou Phrountōrm**, and your terror, **•Danoup Chrantor Belbali Balbith Iaō**. •Through you, the celestial pole and the earth are held together.
>
> I invoke you, •Lord, as do the gods below you in order to have power — **Achebukrōm**, whose is the glory, **aaa** ēēē •ōōō **iii aaa** ōōō **Saba**ōth, •Arbathiaō, Zagourē, the god **Arath Adōnai**.
>
> **•Basummiaō**, I invoke you, Lord, in birdglyphic: **•Arai**; in hieroglyphic: **Lailam**; in Hebrew: **Anag Biathiarbar Berbi Schilatourbour Phountōrm**; •in Egyptian: **Aldabaeim**; •in baboonic: **Abrasax**; •in falconic: **chi chi chi chi chi •chi chi ti ti ti ti ti ti ti**; in hieratic: **Menephōiphōth cha cha cha cha cha cha cha**.

a. See note on the parallel in line 71.

•Then clap three times, make a loud snapping noise, hiss for •a long time. "Come to me, Lord, blameless and flawless, who defiles no place; for I have been initiated with respect to your name."

Additional Materials Required for the Initiation (lines 91-114)

•Have a tablet on which you will write what •he says to you, and a double-edged knife of unadulterated iron, so that when •you slay the sacrifices they will be clean of all defilements, and a libation—•a jug of wine and a flask full of honey—so that you may pour it out as a drink offering. Let all these things be at hand[a] ready for you. •And you be in clean linen garments, wreathed in an olive •wreath, having made[b] the canopy as follows:

---

a. Smith's rendering "Have all these ready nearby you" is grammatically very loose and gives the misleading impression that the imperative is second person when in reality it is third.

b. By ignoring the implications of relative time in the aorist tense participle, and treating it as a command rather than as circumstantial, Smith's rendering in *GMPT* gives the impression that "the canopy" is actually made after the candidate has begun to perform the ritual and has put on the appropriate clothing. Against that interpretation, it makes far better sense to see the canopy as having been already prepared, as indeed is suggested both by the aorist tense form of the participle and by the temporal relationship between writing and initiation implied in lines 112-14.

Additional Performative Gestures and Invocation (lines 600-609)

Then clap three times, •make a loud snapping noise repeatedly, •hiss a great hiss, that is, for a long time. •"Come to me, lord, who defiles no place and is blameless, •gracious, without anger; for I invoke you, King of kings, Ruler of rulers, •most glorious of the glorious, Deity of deities, •Strongest of the strong, Holiest of the holy. Come •to me eagerly, graciously, without anger."

Prescription for Initiatory Encounter (lines 610-52)

•An angel will enter, and you should say to the angel, "Greetings, Lord. Initiate me into these matters, •present me (to the god), and let the secret meanings •of my time of birth be revealed to me." And if he says anything •inauspicious, say, "Wipe off from me the •misfortunes decreed by fate; do not hold back from me, but reveal to me everything, by night and day and in every hour of the month, •to me NN son of NN. Let your auspicious •form become apparent, for under your world-government I serve your angel, •**Anag Biathi.**" The formula:

> Lord, I invoke you, holy, •much hymned, greatly honoured, ruler of the world, Sarapis: look upon the time of my birth and do not turn me away, •me, NN whom NN bore, who knows your •true and authoritative name, Ōaōēō Ōeoē •Iaō Iiiaaō Thēthouthē Aathō Athērouōramiathar •Migarna Chphouri Iueuēoōaeē a ee ēēē **iiii ooooo uuuuuu ōōōōōōō Semesilammps •Aeēiouō Ēōoue Linoucha Noucha Arsamosi •Isnorsam Othamarmim Achuch Chammō.**
>
> •I invoke you, lord; I hymn your •holy might with a melodic hymn, **aeēiouōōō.**

Then burn incense while saying, •"ēiouō uiyō ouō uō ō a ee ēēē iiii •ooooo uuuuuu ōōōōōōō ōēōaōaō •ooouo iiiiiaō iiuuuoaēauo. Safeguard me •against all my own star-fixed destiny; annul my stinking fate; apportion to me good things from my time of birth; •increase both my longevity and my material prosperity. •For I am your slave and petitioner, and I have hymned your •authoritative and holy name, lord, glorious one, ruler of the world, •measureless one,[a] greatest, provider, apportioner, Sarapis."

Having taken a deep breath with the aid of all your •senses, pronounce the first name in one breath •to the east, the second to the south, the third to the north, the fourth to the •west. And having knelt once to the left on your right knee, pronounce once to the earth and once •to the moon,[b] once to water, once to heaven, "ōaōē ōō eoēiaō **iii aōō thē thou thē aathō athērouō**" — thirty-six letters.

•Have a tablet on which you will write •what he says to you, also a knife •so that you may slay the sacrifices clean of all (defilements), •and a libation so that you may pour it out as a drink offering. Let all these things be at hand[c] ready for you. And you be •in clean linen garments, wreathed in an olive wreath, •having made[d] the canopy as follows:

---

a. Neither the sequence of letters in the manuscript nor Preisendanz's emendation (see *PGM* II.116) corresponds to a word attested elsewhere in Greek, and Smith's conjecture ("of ten thousand names"; see *GMPT*, 188) lacks support. The translation offered here is based on the undisputed presence of the Greek stem known in various words signifying boundlessness, infinity, etc.

b. Represented not verbally but pictographically at this point in the papyrus.

c. See note on parallel in line 95.

d. See note on the parallel in line 97.

•Taking a clean sheet of cloth, write around the •edge the names of the 365 gods. Make it a tent under which you are to be initiated. Also have •a cinnamon hanging down from your neck; for •the deity is pleased by it and has granted it power. And also have the helpful Apollo, carved •from a root of laurel, next •to which should stand tripod and Pythian serpent. Carve around the Apollo •the great name in Egyptian form; on his •chest the palindrome •"**Bainchooochooochniab**," down the back •of the figure this name: "**Ilillou Ilillou Ilillou**"; and around the Pythian serpent and the •tripod: "**Ithor Marmarauge Phōchō •Phōbōch**." This too you should have hanging down from your neck •when you perform the initiation, for along with the •cinnamon it is helpful in everything.

Ritual Speech, Sleep, and Drink (lines 114-61)

So, as I said before,[a] when you have purified yourself just before the seven days of the moon's disappearing,[b] at •the new moon begin using a pallet of rushes on the ground for your bed. •Rising early, greet Hēlios-Sun daily •for seven days, saying first the •gods of the hours, then those appointed over the weeks. After learning the ruling lord of the day, pester him •by repeatedly saying, "Lord, on such-and-such a day I am invoking the god for the sacred •sacrifices," and continue doing this until the eighth day.

•Then, when you have come to this day, •when there is quiet in the middle of the night at about the fifth hour,[c] kindle the altar fire and have at hand the two roosters and the two lamps, •lit—together the lamps should be a fourth of a part—•to which you will add no more oil than that. Begin to recite the stele •and the mystery of the god, which is the sacred scarab.[d] Have a mixing bowl •lying close at hand and containing milk from a black cow and wine without seawater, for this is beginning •and end. Then, having written the text of •the stele on the two sides of the natron, lick off the one side, and wash off the other by bathing it •in the mixing bowl. Let •both sides of the natron[e] be written on (with ink) from the various kinds of incense and the flowers. But before you drink the milk and the wine, utter •this prayer[f] and, having said it, lie down •on the mat, holding both the tablet and the stylus; •and say, "Hermetic (prayer)."

> In every language and every dialect, I invoke you who •surrounds all things, as he first hymned you who was appointed by you and entrusted with all •the spiritual authorities, Hēlios-Sun **Achebukrōm**, who discloses •the flame and the splendour

---

a. I.e., in the prescription located in lines 4-7; cf. Brashear, "The Greek Magical Papyri," 3539.

b. I.e., the last seven days of the 41-day programme of purification.

c. I.e., eleven o'clock.

d. Beetles of the family *Scarabaeidae* were regarded as divine in certain parts of ancient Egypt and were sometimes represented on amulets and in hieroglyphics as a symbol of the solar deity; s.v. "scarab," in *Collins Dictionary of the English Language* (2nd ed.; London: Collins, 1986).

e. Because the double-sidedness of the natron is signified clearly in lines 132 and 434, "both" is understood here as qualifying not (as in *GMPT*, 175) the incenses and flowers but rather the two sides of the natron; cf. Brashear, "The Greek Magical Papyri," 3540.

f. The identity of this prayer is not as unclear as Smith (*GMPT*, 175) implies; for the elision of "prayer," following "Hermetic" in the immediately ensuing co-text, probably reflects an assumption that the reader will know to supply the unexpressed noun from the present line. "This prayer," then, is the Hermetic petition which directly follows in the co-text.

Instructions concerning the Canopy and Other Ritual Objects (653-70)

•Taking a clean sheet of cloth, write •around the edge the names of the 365 gods. Make it as you would a tent under which you are to be initiated. Also have a cinnamon hanging •down from your neck; •for the deity is pleased by it and •has granted it power. •And also have the helpful Apollo, carved from a root of laurel, next to which should stand •tripod and Pythian serpent. Carve •around the Apollo the great name in Egyptian •form; on his chest •this palindrome: "**Bainchooochooochniab**"; down the back of the figure this name: •"**Ilillou Ilillou Ilillou**"; and around the •Pythian serpent and the tripod: •"**Ithor Marmarauge Phōchō Phōbōch**." •This too you should have hanging down from your neck when you perform the initiation, for along with the cinnamon it helps in every way.

Ritual Speech, Sleep, and Drink (lines 671-704)

•So, as I said before,[a] when you have purified yourself just before the seven days •of the moon's disappearing,[b] at the new moon begin a phase of going to sleep at night on the ground. •Rising early, greet the Hēlios-Sun daily •for seven days, saying first the gods of the hours, then those •appointed over the weeks. After learning the ruling lord •of the day, pester him by repeatedly saying, "Lord, •on such-and-such a day I am invoking the god for the sacred sacrifices," and •continue doing this until the eighth day.

Then, when you have come to this day, •when there is quiet in the middle of the night, kindle the altar fire •and have at your side the two roosters •and the two lit lamps, to which you will add no more •oil. Begin to recite the stele and the mystery of the god. Have a mixing bowl lying close at hand •and containing milk from a black cow and wine •without seawater, for this is beginning and end. •Then, having written on one side of the natron the text •whose beginning is "I invoke you who are greater than all," and so on as set forth above, lick that side clean;[c] and the other •side, on which is written the figure drawing, •you should wash by bathing it in the mixing bowl. Let the natron be written •on (with ink) from both the various kinds of incense and the flowers. •But before you drink the milk and the wine, utter this prayer and, having said it, lie down •on the mat, holding the tablet •and the stylus; and say the formula of world-creation, whose beginning is,

> •"In every language and every dialect, I invoke •you who surrounds all things," and so on. And when you come to the vowels, say, "Lord, I imitate you •with regard to the seven vowels; enter and hear me." •Then cite the name of the twenty-seven letters. Be reclined •on a pallet of rushes, spread under you •as sleeping mats.

---

a. I.e., in the prescription located in lines 346-49. The reference chain between the present context and lines 346-49 is paralleled very closely by the chain that connects lines 4-8 to lines 114-16 within version A. The present lines, by contributing to both the reference chain and the parallel to version A, tacitly undermine Smith's case for interpreting lines 646-734 as a distinct version of *Moses VIII* (i.e., version C), separate both from version A (1-343) and from Smith's shortened version B (343-646). Brashear, "The Greek Magical Papyri," 3539, briefly notes both the reference chain and the parallelism between the two versions but says nothing about their negative implications for Smith's hypothesis.

b. See note on the parallel in line 115.

c. Tasting or consuming sacred text is implied in a range of ancient documents to have magico-religious efficacy; see, e.g., Ezek 2:8–3:15.

of the disk, and whose is the glory; **aaa** •ēēē ōōō, for on account of you he was glorified; he who •set up the stars, endowing them likewise[a] with beauty, and who in divine light created the world, **iii aaa ōōō**, in which you separated all kinds of things from each other. •**Sabaōth Arbathiaō Zagourē**—these are •the angels who were the first to appear—**Arath, Adonaie, Basēmmiaō.**

The first •angel calls out in birdglyphic, "**Arai**," who has authority over •punishments. Hēlios-Sun hymns you in hieroglyphic, "**Lailam**," and in Hebrew by the same name. **Anok Biathiarbarberbischilatour•bouphroumtrōm**—thirty-six letters[b]—says •"I precede you, Lord, I who rise on the boat, the solar disk, because of you." •Your powerful[c] name in Egyptian: **Aldabiaeim**[d]—nine letters, below.

•He who appears on the boat rising with you is a crafty baboon. In his own language he greets you and says, •"You are the number of the days of the year, **Abrasax**."[e] The falcon on the other •side of the boat greets you in his own dialect and cries out •to receive food: "**chi chi chi chi chi chi chi tip tip tip •tip tip tip tip**." And he of the nine forms greets you in Hieratic: "**Menephōiphōth**." By saying this, he means: "I precede you, •Lord."

The Revelatory Event (lines 210-12; cf. lines 564-67)

When the god enters, look down and write what is said •and whatever name they might give you for him; and do not go out •of your tent until he has also told you accurately the things concerning you.

Ascertaining the Ruler of the Celestial Pole (lines 213-26)

•The way to determine who is ruling the celestial pole at a given moment involves the following: •Learn, child, whose day it is in the Greek reckoning.[f] Coming to the seven-zoned, count from the bottom up[g] and you will discover who it is. For if the day belongs

a. As noted in *GMPT*, 175 n. 29, the text is corrupt at this point and highly difficult to decipher.

b. Notwithstanding the suspicion of Smith (*GMPT*, 176 n. 37), the numerical gloss by the ancient copyist can be accepted as an accurate count of the Greek letters in the name when proper notice is taken of the deletion dot over the final occurrence of the letter rho in **Berbir** (thus **Berbi**), the shorter form corresponding precisely to the parallel in line 459. See Daniel, *Two Greek Magical Papyri*, xxiv.

c. The Greek adjective is *physikon*, which conveys overtones of great effectiveness and has none of the potentially negative overtones of Smith's suggestion, "magical."

d. It is perhaps no coincidence that the name corresponds to that applied to the demiurge Yaldabaoth in a number of the tractates from Nag Hammadi (note especially "**Aldabaoth**" in *Ap. John* II 23, 35), whose examples of hybridised Christian discourse from late antique Egypt are comparable at many points to the discursive world of *Moses VIII* and other texts in the Greek magical papyri.

e. As Smith notes, the numerical values of the Greek letters in "**Abrasax**" add up to 365.

f. Apparently, as suggested parenthetically in *GMPT*, 178, counting from the top down.

g. As suggested by the order of the table, counting from the bottom up the same number that was counted from the top down.

Instructions concerning the Meeting with the God (lines 704-717)

Now when the god enters, do not stare at his face, but look at his feet while beseeching, •as set forth above, and giving thanks that he did not treat you with disdain; •that you were counted worthy of the things to be said to you for the correction of •your life. Next you make your inquiry: •"Master, what is fated for me?" And he will answer you in terms of your star and what sort of daimon you have and your •ascendant decan[a] and where you will live and where you will die. •Should you hear something bad, do not yawp, do not yawl,[b] •but instead request that he cancel[c] or avert it; •for this god is able to do anything. Thus, before you begin to inquire, give him thanks for hearing you •and not disregarding you. This will always be the way in which you should perform the rite •and offer pious regards to the god; for this is how he is persuaded to hear you.

Ascertaining the Ruler of the Celestial Pole (lines 718-30)

•The way to determine who is ruling the celestial pole at a given moment involves the following: •Learn, child, whose day it is in the Greek reckoning.[d] Coming to the seven-zoned, count from the bottom up[e] •and you will discover who it is. For if the day belongs

a. By merely transliterating the Greek term, Smith's use of "horoscope" evades the real interpretive problem of translation and gives a sense which is both too general and more domesticating than necessary. The "ascendant decan" would be the particular ten-degree segment of the zodiacal circle that happened to be emerging in the East at the moment of the child's birth; see Barton, *Ancient Astrology*, 18, 20; and Brashear, "The Greek Magical Papyri," 3543.

b. The Greek verb phrases (*mē kraxēs* and *mē krausēs*) evince a wordplay that neither the English of *GMPT* ("do not cry out or weep") nor the German in Preizendanz, *PGM* II.119 ("brich nicht in Schreien, nicht in Weinen aus") tries to approximate.

c. Smith's rendering "wash it off" (*GMPT*, 189) ignores better alternatives within the semantic range of the Greek verb and also effects a misleading correspondence to different terminology used in the antecedent co-text (XIII. 689-91) where it is precisely various types of washing that is envisaged.

d. See note on the parallel in line 214.

e. See note on the parallel in line 215.

•to Hēlios-Sun[a] in the Greek reckoning, Selēnē-Moon rules the pole, and so also the rest as mentioned here:

•**The Greek**	**The Seven-Zoned**
• Hēlios-Sun	Kronos-Time
• Selēnē-Moon	Zeus
Ares	Ares
•Hermes	Hēlios-Sun
•Zeus	Aphrodite
•Aphrodite	Hermes
•Kronos-Time	Selēnē-Moon

The inexhaustible and godly solution of these things I have declared •to you, child, a solution which not even kings had power to comprehend.

Recording the Revelation on the Natron (lines 227-29)

•Now you should write[b] on the natron with the ink from the flowers of the •seven stars and types of aromatic spices. In a similar way you should also make the vetch mixture,[c] which I spoke about allegorically •in my *Key*, from the flowers and the types of incense.

Various Ritual Uses of the Revealed Name (lines 230-340)

The initiation known as *The Monad* has been declared to you fully, child. •Now I shall append for you, child, the uses of this sacred book, the things that all •the masters accomplished by means of this sacred and blessed •book. As I made you swear, child, by the temple[d] of Jerusalem, •when you have been filled with the divine knowledge put the book in a place where it cannot be found.

First, then, is the marvellous invisibility. Taking the egg of a falcon, gild half of it •and smear the other half with cinnabar. Wearing this, •you will be invisible when you say the name.

•For a love charm, say the name three times to the sun. It charms woman for man •and man for woman in a way that will make you marvel.[e]

If you want someone to be repulsive—either a woman to a man or a man to a woman—take •a dog's feces and put it in the socket of their door while saying •the name three times, and then saying, "I separate NN from NN."

---

a. Represented in the papyrus not by word but rather as a pictograph.

b. As hinted in lines 38-39, what is to be written on the natron depends on what name is revealed during the initiatory encounter.

c. Neither Smith's use of "bean" (*GMPT*, 178) nor Preisendanz's "Erbse" (pea) is warranted by the Greek vocabulary used in this context, though the referent of "vetch" here should most probably be understood as the same as that of "the Egyptian bean" mentioned in lines 21-22.

d. Smith (*GMPT*, 179 n. 56), interprets this occurrence of preposition *en* with the dative as locative ("*in* the temple of Jerusalem"), the consequent anachronism apparently justifying his famous evaluation of the formula as "pretentious hokum"; but *en* with the dative can just as easily communicate an instrumental nuance, which in fact is more suitable in a context of magico-ritual utterance or oath-making (cf. Acts 16:18) and in this context obviates any sense of anachronism.

e. Cf. *ShR* 2.30-37.

to Hēlios-Sun in the Greek reckoning, • Selēnē-Moon rules the pole, and so also the rest as mentioned here:

The Greek		**•The Seven-Zoned**
• Hēlios-Sun	*The Only of Moses*, which is also a treatise called "The Seven-Zoned."	Kronos-Time
Selēnē-Moon		Zeus
•Ares		Ares
•Hermes		Hēlios-Sun
•Zeus		Aphrodite
•Aphrodite		Hermes
Kronos-Time		Selēnē-Moon

Lines 692-93

692b Let the natron be written •on (with ink) from both the various kinds of incense and the flowers.

•If you say the name to a demoniac while putting brimstone and asphalt to his nose, •he will speak immediately and the demon will go away.[a]

If you say it over inflamed skin, having smeared the skin with crocodile feces, it will be removed from them immediately.

•If you say the name three times over a sprain or a fracture, •having smeared the area with earth and vinegar, you will remove it.

If you say it •over any bird, into its ear, it will die.

•If you see a cobra and want to make it stay in its place, say "Stay!" while turning yourself to and fro. The four names[b] are said, and it will stay.

To restrain anger: Enter the presence of a king •or other man of high rank, and •say the name of the sun disk while keeping your hands inside your wrap or cloak and tying a knot. You will marvel!

•If you want deliverance from spells: Having written the name on a piece of hieratic papyrus, •wear it.

To call up the sun: Say toward the east, "I am he upon the two cherubim, between the two natures, heaven and •earth, sun and moon, light and darkness, night and day, •rivers and sea. Appear to me, O archangel of those under the natural order, •Lord Hēlios-Sun, the one assigned a position of authority by the One and Only Himself. •The Eternal and Only commands you."[c] Say the name. And if his appearance is marked by sullenness, say, "Give me a day, give an hour, give a month, give •a year,[d] Lord of life." Say the name.

If you want •to kill a snake, say "Stay, for you are Aphyphis."[e] And taking a •fresh palm branch and laying hold of its heart, split it •into two and say the name seven times. Immediately the snake will be split or will burst.

Foreknowledge comes through the operation already mentioned above, •that with the natron. And you will be spoken of as a god,[f] for •on many occasions I have performed the operation when you yourself were present.

---

a. The sense of smell plays a similar role in the broadly exorcistic ritual mentioned in Tob 6:16-17; 8:2-3. See also Josephus, *Ant.* 8.47.

b. The plural here is discordant with the literary co-text; and as noted by Smith (*GMPT*, 179 n. 60), the discordance may be due to the use of a source uninterested in the immediately preceding rites, whose performance involves the invocation of only one name rather than several. However, since a Greek letter *delta*, signifying the number 4, should probably be read instead of the *alpha* proposed by Preisendanz (*PGM*, 2:100, followed by *GMPT*) directly after the symbol for "name," the phrase here can be interpreted more specifically—and coherently—as a reference to the four names mentioned in *PGM* XIII. 746-47: namely "that of nine letters and that of fourteen letters and that of twenty-six letters and that of Zeus." Daniel, *Two Greek Magical Papyri*, xxiv-xxv.

c. Cf. lines 335-40. As noted by Brashear, "The Greek Magical Papyri," 3540, the initiate is assumed in this context to have internalised a culture of spirit possession and, in order to call up Hēlios-Sun, must externalise such beliefs by identifying in the ritual performance with the highest deity in the cosmic order.

d. For three different possible meanings of the verb rendered "give" in this context, see *GMPT*, 179 n. 65; and Preisendanz's parenthetical expansion (*PGM* II.100).

e. The name "Aphyphis" is enigmatic; but whatever the assumed background, the name contributes to an instance of wordplay, with *Aphyphis* (lit. "from a snake") being formally related to the noun used for "snake" (*ophis*) in the same context.

f. Against Preizendanz, *PGM* II.101 (followed by *GMPT*: "the god will talk with you . . . "), the photographic plate of the Greek text indicates that the main verb is not third-person but rather second, with the implied addressee (i.e., "you") rather than "god" being the grammatical subject. The process of acquiring foreknowledge is thus represented as a positive experience of divine spirit possession, the same type of experience promoted for a different ritual purpose in lines 254-60. Cf. Daniel, *Two Greek Magical Papyri*, xxv, 44-45.

Invisibility? As follows: •"Come to me, primordial darkness, and hide me, NN, •by order of him who is self-begotten in heaven." Say the name.

Alternatively: "I invoke you alone, the only one in the cosmos who puts •gods and men in their places, who changes himself •into holy forms and makes both existence out of non-existence and •non-existence out of existence, holy Thayth, the •true vision of whose face none of the gods can bear to see. In the eyes of all creatures make me look like a wolf, dog, lion, •fire, tree, vulture, wall, water, or whatever you want; for you are able." •Say the name.

Resurrection of a dead body: •"I put you under oath, spirit wandering about in the air, enter, inspire, •empower, resurrect this body by the power of the eternal god, and let it walk about in this •place; for I am he who acts by the power •of Thayth." Say the name.

If you want •to cross over a river on a crocodile, sit down and say, "Hear me, you who •pass your time in the water. I am he who has leisure in heaven and wanders about in water and in fire and in air •and earth. Return the favour done for you on that day when •I created you and you made your request. You will carry me over to •the other side, for I am NN." Say the name.

Release from chains: Say, •"Hear me, O Chrēstos,[a] in torments; help me in distress, O merciful in times of violence, able to do much in the world, •who created distress and retribution and torment." •Say it twelve times by day after hissing thrice eight times. Say the whole name of Hēlios-Sun beginning from **Achebykrōm**.[b] •"Let every chain be loosed, every •violent force, let every fetter be broken, every rope or every strap, every knot, let every bond be cut open, •and let no one subdue me by violence, for I am"—say the name.

•To quench fire: "Hear, fire, not a mere word but a deed, a deed[c] of divine advantage, •glory of the honoured luminary, be quenched, turn into snow, for the one speaking to you is the eternal one who puts on fire as if •it were asbestos. Let every flame be repelled from me, •every physical element of power, by order of Him who exists forever. •By no means shall you touch me, fire, by no means shall you harm my flesh, •for I am"—say the name.

To make a fire last: "I put you under oath, •fire, divinity of holy love, he who is both invisible and manifold, both unitary and in all places, to last long in •this lamp at this time, shining brightly •and not dying out, •by order of NN"—say the name.

Sending of dreams: •Make a hippopotamus of red wax—it should be hollow—and

---

a. Chiefly because the first vowel of the name in the papyrus is not an iota but rather an ēta (thus not *Christos* but rather *Chrēstos*), the name is understood by Daniel, *Two Greek Magical Papyri*, xxv, as conveying no specifically Christian overtones in this context. However, if (as seems likely) this particular formula was added either by the copyist or by a recent editor, and thus close to the middle of the fourth century C.E., one must wonder what cosmic power other than Christ would have been associated with this name. Reference to Christ is supported both by consideration of the name's spelling (*Chrestus*) in Suetonius, *Claudius* 25; and by the possibility of echoes of Acts 16:19-40 in this same formula of release. On the relationship more generally between *Christos* and *Chrēstos*, see BDF §24.

b. The name is spelled variously in XIII. 78-79, 141-47, 446-47, and 590-92, and joined by "Hēlios" in every case except the last.

c. Contra Preizendanz, *PGM* II.102 (followed by *GMPT*), the second occurrence of "deed" (*ergon*) in this line of the manuscript is not in the plural but rather in the singular; see Daniel, *Two Greek Magical Papyri*, xxv, 44-45.

put into the belly of this beast[a] •both gold and silver and the •so-called castings[b] of the Jews;[c] and dress •him in pure linen and put him in a pure window and, taking a hieratic papyrus leaf, write on it with myrrh-ink and baboon's blood •what dreams one wishes to send. Having rolled it tightly into a wick and •used it to light a new, pure lamp, put •the foot of the hippopotamus on the lamp and say the name, and he sends the dreams.

•A drinkable love-charm: Take lion-wasps that are in a spider's web and, having ground them to a powder over a drink, give it to the chosen victim to drink.

If you want your wife not to be had •by another man, take some soil, •mix ink and myrrh with it, shape it into a crocodile, and put it into a lead funerary urn[d] •and inscribe on the urn the great name and that of your wife and •"Let NN not become sexually intimate with any man except me, NN." The name to be written on the feet of the figure is: **Bibiou Ouēr Apsabara •Kasonnaka Nesebach Sphē Sphē Chphouris.**

•Opening doors by means of the name: "Open, open, four regions of the world, for •the lord of the inhabited world is going out. Archangels •of decans, of angels, rejoice! For the Age of the Age himself, the only and preeminent, is going through the place unseen. Open yourself, •door; listen, bolt; break in half, bar. By the name **Aia Ainruchath**, toss up, Gē-Earth, all things for the master, as much as you have in yourself; •for he is the sender of storms and owner of the nether abyss, ruler •of fire. Open; **Achebukrōm** is speaking to you." Say **Achebukrōm** eight times; it is a name of Hēlios-Sun.[e]

•The spell for Hēlios-Sun by another route: "I am he upon the two cherubim, at the center of the cosmos, of heaven and earth, of light and darkness, of night and day, •of rivers and sea. Appear to me, archangel •of God, placed in authority by the One and Only Himself." With this •spell perform the rites for winning favour, love charms, sending dreams, •requesting dreams, making Hēlios-Sun appear, charms for success, charms for victory, and absolutely everything.

Concluding Claims about the Book Itself (lines 341-43)

•You now possess in full, o child, the holy and fortune-bringing •book *The Only*, which no one hitherto was able to translate or put into practice. •Farewell, child.

---

a. Contra *GMPT*, 181 n. 70, it is not the preceding word rendered "hippopotamus" that is uncertain but rather the word here rendered "beast," whose interpretation in both *GMPT* and Preizendanz, *PGM* II.103 as not merely co-referential but synonymous with "hippopotamus" lacks support.

b. As noted by Smith (*GMPT*, 181 n. 71), the word used here is not attested elsewhere. Its formal resemblance to the verbal part of the biblical phrase for "casting lots" (e.g., LXX 1 Chr 25:8; 26:13) suggests that it might be either an unfamiliar or garbled term for objects used in lot casting.

c. The existence of only four lines rather than the expected five in the present translation of lines 310-14 is the result of dittography in lines 312-13; see Daniel, *Two Greek Magical Papyri*, 46.

d. Contra *GMPT*, 181, an urn rather than a coffin is suggested, both by use of the diminutive variant of the noun and perhaps also by the substance.

e. The last clause of line 333 in the manuscript is a pictograph.

Titular Colophon (lines 731-34)

•*The Secret, Eighth of Moses.* In another manuscript that I found was written, •*The Secret Book of Moses concerning the Great* •*Name*; or, *Concerning Everything to Which Pertains the Name of Him Who Governs* •*All Things.*

The Balaam Text from Tell Deir 'Allā
A new translation and introduction

by Edward M. Cook

The Balaam Text from Tell Deir 'Allā was discovered during the course of the excavation of the tell, east of the Jordan River, in 1967 under the direction of H. J. Franken of Leiden University, and was fully published in 1976. It is not an Old Testament pseudepigraphon in the sense of its main character, Balaam, being based on or secondary to the Balaam whose story is told in Numbers 22-24. Rather, the biblical and the epigraphic texts are independent narratives based on a common tradition of the Trans-Jordanian seer Balaam, son of Beor. But this text is published in this collection on the grounds that it is a (presumably) fictional work attributed to a character who appears in the Hebrew Bible and it is set in the biblical period, but it is not included in any Jewish or Christian scriptural canon. In addition, the identity of the name and similarity of setting are of importance, since this is the only extra-biblical document from the pre-exilic period that mentions a figure from the Pentateuch.

Contents

The Balaam Text from Deir 'Allā, as reconstructed by its first editor, J. Hoftijzer,[1] is preserved in two main parts, Combination I and II. (Numerous unplaced fragments have been compiled as Combinations III-XII, but their interpretation is difficult and there is no consensus on how to fit them in.) Combination I, as reconstructed, tells how Balaam, the seer, saw a troubling vision that caused him to weep. He tells his concerned people that he saw the gods sitting in session, and that they decreed darkness over the earth to hide from sight a world where everything is topsy-turvy. The natural order, where birds of prey have themselves become prey, is in a state of chaos, and so is the social order, where the leaders of society find themselves in a state of subservience, and the lower orders are on top. Combination II presents a picture of death and the underworld, where all is desolation, and this, it seems, is the threatened fate of those Balaam is addressing. The ending of the text is preserved only in fragments that are very small and in part illegible.

Manuscripts and Versions

The Balaam text from Deir 'Allā exists in only one exemplar, a collection of plaster fragments discovered in 1967 during the excavation of Tell Deir 'Allā, located in the Jordan River valley, east of the river, near the head of the River Jabbok. One of the 20 levels of the mound, Level IX, was dated to the Middle Iron Age, and in this level the plaster fragments were found.

One set of fragments, now referred to as Combination I, was found in a pit in one

1. J. Hoftijzer and G. van der Kooij, *Aramaic Texts from Deir 'Allā* (Leiden: Brill, 1976).

room; another set of fragments, Combination II, was found in an adjoining room. Smaller single fragments were scattered between both loci. Archaeologists determined that the text was painted in ink on plaster applied to the wall that separated the two rooms; the plaster was dislodged from the wall and broken during the earthquake that destroyed the buildings from level IX. All of the plaster fragments are now in the Archaeological Museum in Amman, Jordan.

Date, Language, and Provenance

Despite attempts to assign the text to the late eighth or early seventh centuries B.C.E.,[2] the archaeological context and analysis of the letter forms (palaeography) both point to the first half of the eighth century B.C.E. as the time when the text was copied onto plaster.[3] The composition of the text may be earlier, but how much earlier it is difficult to determine. It has been suggested that the earthquake that shattered the wall on which the text was painted was the same earthquake mentioned by the biblical prophet Amos (Amos 1:1), which would place the destruction around 760 B.C.E.; but this area of the Jordan Valley is frequently troubled by earthquakes, so it is impossible to say which one was responsible.

The language of the text is an otherwise unattested Northwest Semitic dialect. The nature of the dialect has eluded precise linguistic definition, since it has some Aramaic traits and some Hebrew (or, more broadly, Canaanite) traits, and it lacks some diagnostic traits altogether (e.g., the definite article and the relative pronoun). Some specialists strongly assert that it is Hebrew or a related dialect; others, with equal force, argue that it belongs in the Aramaic family. In fact, the dialect of the texts may belong to a period before Aramaic and Hebrew had evolved to a point of clear differentiation; this suggests a date of composition some centuries before the date of copying, possibly the ninth or tenth centuries B.C.E. or even earlier, since both Hebrew and Aramaic were certainly separate languages by the time the text was copied onto plaster. But the debate about linguistic classification may have assumed a share of attention that is out of proportion to its importance, since few interpretive decisions depend on which language the text is assigned to.

The provenance of the find is not in doubt, since the fragments were discovered *in situ*. The identification of Tell Deir ʿAllā with any site known from the Hebrew Bible is more uncertain. The most popular hypothesis is that the tell is to be identified with Succoth. The general location fits, but the guess is based on a passage from the Jerusalem Talmud which states that Succoth was, at the time of the Talmud, called "Tarʾelah" or "Darʾelah," i.e., Deir ʿAllā.[4] No documentary evidence has been found at the site itself to confirm or refute this identification. André Lemaire suggests that the site is to be identified with biblical Penuel.[5]

Whatever ancient location Tell Deir ʿAllā may have been, it does not seem to have been

2. E.g., J. Hackett, "Deir ʿAllā, Tell: Texts," *ABD* 2:129.

3. M. M. Ibrahim & G. van der Kooij, "The Archaeology of Deir ʿAllā Phase IX," in *The Balaam Text from Deir ʿAlla Re-Evaluated,* (ed. J. Hoftijzer and G. van der Kooij; Leiden: Brill, 1991), 28. See also André Lemaire, "Deir ʿAllā Inscriptions," *OEANE* 2:139.

4. The identification dates from the nineteenth century; see George Adam Smith, *The Historical Geography of the Holy Land* (rev. ed., 1931; repr. New York: Harper Torchbook, 1966), 392 n. 2. The Talmudic passage itself is from the first half of the first millennium C.E. The name Deir ʿAllā is Arabic and means "high monastery." See also Jo Ann H. Seely, "Succoth (2)," *ABD* 6:217-218.

5. A. Lemaire, "Fragments from the Book of Balaam Found at Deir Alla," *BAR* 11.5 (Sep/Oct 1985): 26-39.

Israelite. The material remains of the site are Ammonite,[6] as is the palaeography of the inscription itself (if not the actual language). The content of the text, with its mention of "the gods," "Shaddayin," "El," and possibly "Shamash," but none of "Yahweh," also suggests an origin outside of the Israelite cultural sphere. The biblical Balaam is said to have come from "Pethor, which is by the Euphrates" (Num 22:5), or from "Aram Naharaim" (Deut 23:4), but the home of the Deir 'Allā Balaam is not specified in the text, and he probably was considered an indigenous soothsayer. In fact, there is no good reason to think that the provenance of the original text is outside Trans-Jordan.

Genre and Function

The fragmentary state of the text has impeded a definite assignment of literary genre. Obviously, the mention of "Balaam son of Beor" suggests a connection of some kind to the Balaam stories in the Hebrew Bible (Num 22-24), which themselves incorporate different genres—fable (the tale of the talking donkey, Num 22:22-35), poetic oracle (Num 23:7-10, 18-24; 24:3-9, 15-24), and prophet story (Num 22:2-21, 22:36–23:7, 11-18, 23:25–24:3, 10-14). The plaster text is likewise in the broadest sense a story, and Combination I, at least, contains the report of a vision of the gods conveyed in poetic form like the oracles of the prophets of Israel. Combination II, as understood here, preserves a further vision of destruction and death that climaxes with a pronouncement of judgment. In general, though, the Balaam text does not align itself with any of the genres of prophetic speech that form-critics have identified. Although it contains a message of judgment (if the translation of II.17 is correct), it preserves no reason for the judgment, and therefore is not a "judgment oracle" in the form-critical sense. Balaam, in fact, is not commissioned as a messenger to the people at all. He is a seer, not a prophet, and this is consistent with his presentation in the Hebrew Bible.

The Deir 'Allā text has some tantalizing similarities to the kind of pseudo-prophecy that is known from the Egyptian Prophecy of Nefer-rohu (or Neferti).[7] In that work, dating from the early second millennium B.C.E., the lector-priest Nefer-rohu (or Neferti) prophesies in the presence of King Snefru that in the future the land will be in chaos: "The sun disc is covered over. It will not shine (so that) people may see. . . . I show thee the land topsy-turvy. The weak of arm is (now) the possessor of an arm. Men salute (respectfully) him who (formerly) saluted. I show thee the undermost on top." But the chaos is ended by the coming of a king, Ameni, who will restore justice and eliminate wrongdoing.[8] The reference is to Amen-em-het I of the Twelfth Dynasty. The work is therefore a "prophecy after the fact" (*vaticinium ex eventu*), justifying the reign of Amen-em-het.

Since the Balaam text is fragmentary, and it is not known how it may have ended, or how long it may originally have been, it may or may not have had an ending like that of the Egyptian prophecy, as well as a similar purpose: to justify or support the reign of a new ruler. If the Balaam text did serve such a purpose, it is still difficult to discern which ruler's authority might have been supported by such a document. Since the date of the original composition is unknown, almost any change of dynasty between the Late Bronze Age to the Middle Iron Age might be suggested. Of course, since that period saw the appearance

6. H. J. Franken, "Deir 'Alla Revisited," in *The Balaam Text Re-Evaluated*, 12.

7. For this hypothesis, see Jo Ann Hackett, *The Balaam Text from Deir 'Alla* (Chico, Calif.: Scholars Press, 1984), 75-76.

8. "The Prophecy of Nefer-rohu," trans. J. A. Wilson, *ANET*, 444-46, from which the translation is taken.

of Israel in the area, as well as the beginning of its monarchy, it is possible that the original text might have had in view the rise of Israelite hegemony in Trans-Jordan or even the establishment of the monarchy of Saul or David in the region of Gilead, where Tell Deir ʿAllā was located. In this respect, it would have been very much like the biblical story of Balaam, whose oracles climax with a prediction of an Israelite conquest of the Trans-Jordan (Num 24:17-19). The Deir ʿAllā text would continue to have relevance throughout the eighth century B.C.E., when Gilead changed hands among the rulers of Israel, Aram, and Moab.[9] But this idea, though plausible, is only a guess, and in the absence of further evidence, must remain so.

The function of the inscription in its archaeological context remains obscure. Although initial interpretations assumed that the place where the fragments were found was a temple or sanctuary, there is no evidence other than the text itself that the room was used for cultic activity.[10] It has been proposed that the room was "a meeting place of a group of prophets ... where the visions and deeds of that Balaam were remembered,"[11] but this can be no more than a conjecture. It is also possible that the room was the meeting place of a *marzeah*, a cultic association that held luxurious feasts either to honor dead ancestors or to worship a particular deity. The plaster text might have had relevance for such an organization.[12]

Literary Context

As noted above, there is no reason to posit any direct connection between the Deir ʿAllā text and the Balaam pericope in Numbers 22-24. It is clear, however, that both texts drew on common existing traditions about Balaam. In the Deir ʿAllā text, he is described as a "seer of the gods," a messenger of the "Shaddayin," who receives the "oracle of El"; likewise, in the biblical passages, he is portrayed as a foreign soothsayer "who hears the utterances of El, sees the vision of Shaddai" (Num 24:4). In both texts, he is the medium of oracles unfavorable to his auditors in the narrative; but in the biblical story, the message, although unfavorable for the Moabites who employed him, is actually favorable for the real auditors of the story, the Israelites. The same might or might not have been true for the Deir ʿAllā inscription.

Nevertheless, the biblical Balaam was remembered as an enemy of Israel, one who lured the Israelites into idolatry (Num 31:16) and who was killed by them (Num 31:8). In

9. Baruch Levine hypothesizes a more exact historical connection; he avers that the biblical Balaam poems "celebrate Israelite power in Moab during the reign of Omri and his successors before the middle of the ninth century B.C.E.," while the plaster text "may memorialize the sparing of Gilead from Mesha's reconquest, begun in the early forties of the ninth century" (Baruch Levine, *Numbers 21-36* [AB 4; Garden City, N.Y.: Doubleday, 2000), 232. For Omri and Mesha, see 1 Kgs 16:16-22 and 2 Kings 3.

10. M. M. Ibrahim & G. van der Kooij, "The Archaeology of Deir ʿAlla Phase IX," in *The Balaam Text Re-Evaluated,* 20.

11. R. Wenning and E. Zenger, "Heiligtum ohne Stadt — Stadt ohne Heiligtum? Anmerkungen zum archäologischen Befund des Tell Der ʿAlla," *ZAH* 4 (1991): 189, cited by Martin Rösel, "Inscriptional Evidence and the Question of Genre," in *The Changing Face of Form Criticism for the Twenty-First Century* (ed. M. Sweeney and Ehud Ben Zvi; Grand Rapids, Mich.: Eerdmans, 2003), 117-18.

12. From a much later period, there are hints that Balaam was connected with the *marzeah*. *Tg. Ps.-J.* Num 25:2 and *Sifre Numbers* 131 state that Israel ate food offered to idols in the *marzeahs* of the Moabites (Num. 25:2) at Baal Peor, an apostasy attributed to the influence of Balaam (Num. 31:16). The connection is remote, however, and the putative location of Baal Peor, opposite Jericho, is not in the vicinity of Tell Deir ʿAllā.

the rabbinic literature of late antiquity, the figure of Balaam developed into an arch-villain who, when he found that God would not allow him to curse Israel, came up with a plan to use the Moabite women to tempt the Israelites into eating illicit sacrifices.[13] Although the Balaam of the Deir 'Allā text, from the standpoint of strict Yahwism, was a messenger of "the gods" and "the Shaddayin,"[14] and therefore an idolater, there is nothing in the text that leads us to suspect any connection between his behavior in this story and the development of later traditions about Balaam within Judaism.[15]

Bibliography

A comprehensive bibliography to 1992 is found in J. A. Fitzmyer and S. A. Kaufman, *An Aramaic Bibliography, Part I: Old, Official, and Biblical Aramaic.* Baltimore, Md.: Johns Hopkins Univ. Press, 1992, section B. 1. 19.

High-resolution photographs of the inscription are available to scholars at the West Semitic Research Project's Inscriptifact website (www. inscriptifact.com).

Dijkstra, M. "Is Balaam Also among the Prophets?" *JBL* 114 (1995): 43-64.

Franken, H. J. "Deir 'Alla, Tell." *OEANE* 2:137-38.

Hackett, Jo Ann. *The Balaam Text from Deir 'Allā.* HSM 31. Chico, Calif.: Scholars Press, 1984.

__________. "Deir 'Alla, Tell: Texts." *ABD* 2:129-30.

Hoftijzer, Jean, and G. van der Kooij. *Aramaic Texts from Deir 'Allā.* Documenta et monumenta orientis antiqui 19. Leiden: Brill, 1976.

Hoftijzer, Jean, and G. van der Kooij (eds.). *The Balaam Text from Deir 'Allā Re-Evaluated: Proceedings of the International Symposium Held at Leiden 21-24 August 1989.* Leiden: Brill, 1991.

Lemaire, André. "Deir 'Alla Inscriptions." *OEANE* 2:138-40.

__________. "Fragments from the Book of Balaam Found at Deir Alla." *Biblical Archaeology Review*, Sept./Oct. 1985, n.p. *Biblical Archaeology Review: The Archive 1975-2003*, Version 1.0 CD-ROM, 2004.

Levine, B. A. "Comment 5: The Balaam Inscriptions from Deir 'Alla." Pages 241-75 in *Numbers 21-36.* AB 4. Garden City, N.Y.: Doubleday, 2000.

Lipinski, Eduard. "The Plaster Inscription from Deir 'Allā." Pages 103-70 in *Studies in Aramaic Inscriptions and Onomastics II.* OLA 57. Leuven: Peeters, 1994.

Milgrom, Jacob. "Excursus 60: Balaam and the Deir 'Alla Inscription." Pages 473-76 in *Numbers [Ba-Midbar]: The Traditional Hebrew Text with the New JPS Translation.* The JPS Torah Commentary. Philadelphia, Pa.: Jewish Publication Society, 1990.

---

13. For the later development of the Balaam legend in Judaism and Christianity, see James Kugel, *The Bible As It Was* (Cambridge, Mass.: Harvard University Press, 1997), 482-94.

14. The plural "Shaddayin" is evidently connected in some way with the name "Shaddai," which is used as an epithet of the God of Israel in the Bible (e.g., Gen 17:1), although it is also often found in the mouths of foreigners such as Job and his friends (Job 6:4 and frequently) and Balaam (Num 24:4, 16). In the plaster text, "Shaddayin" is used as a synonym of "gods."

15. Jacob Milgrom conjectures that the function of the plaster text was to record the story of Balaam's founding of a fertility cult, which might have provided the kernel of the story of the apostasy at Baal Peor (Milgrom, *Numbers [Ba-Midbar]: The Traditional Hebrew Text with the New JPS Translation* [Philadelphia, Pa.: Jewish Publication Society, 1990], 473-46). However, this construal of the text is not common.

The Balaam Text from Tell Deir 'Allā

Due to the difficulty of reconstructing and reading the plaster fragments, the existing publications and translations of the Balaam text often differ greatly in significant details. Although I have checked the photographs of the fragments available at the West Semitic Research Project's Inscriptifact website (www.inscriptifact.com) to confirm particular readings, I have not introduced many new ones into the following translation, which is based, with some exceptions, on the readings of the fragments as published by Jo Ann Hackett, *Balaam Text*, and the numbering of the lines also follows hers. The translation is, of course, my own.

Combination I

1. The book of [Balaam son of Be]or; he was a seer of the gods. And the gods came to him at night and he saw a vision
2. like an oracle of El. And they said to [Bala]am son of Beor, Thus shall do [...] afterwards. [...]
3. So Balaam rose the next day [.........] and he could not [eat or drink anything] but
4. wept instead. Then his people came to him [and said to] him, Balaam son of Beor, why are you fasting and weeping? And he
5. said to them, Sit, I shall tell you what the Shad[dayin have done;] and come, see the deeds of the gods: The gods met together,
6. and the Shaddayin stood up in session, and they said, O Sh[amash (?)[a] ...] annul,[b] close up the heavens with your cloud, put there darkness and not
7. the light of strength (?)[c]; and put a se[al] on your lock [...] darkness and do not remove it for ever. For the swift
8. taunts the eagle; the song of the vultures is heard[d]; the st[ork ...] the young of the hawk (?), and maims the chicks of the cormorant; the swallow tears
9. the dove, and the sparrow [......] the staff follows[e] sheep, the rod leads hares, the [...] have eaten
10. [...] low born[f] [...........] drink wine, hyenas hear instruction; the cubs of [....]

a. Or possibly, "O Sh[agar . . .]."

b. Or: "sew up."

c. Hackett reads the word as "perpetual," but this is palaeographically unlikely.

d. Literally, "the voice of the vultures sings out."

e. Cf. Job 23:11.

f. The translation is based on an Akkadian cognate meaning "of low status." Others translate "free born."

11. [........................] mock the wise, and the poor woman mixes myrrh;[a] and the priestess
12. [..........................] to wear a belt of threads; the esteemed esteems, and the esteemer is es[teemed].[b]
13. [..] and the deaf hear from afar.
14. [...] the lowly see offspring and fertility[c]
15. [..] the pig puts the panther to flight, the son of
16. [...the nobles] fasten shoes,[d] and the eye of [

Combination II

1-3 [...]
4. his strong man drinks from breasts[e] [...]
5. why is it desolate (?),[f] and the soil is as without moisture [...............................Unless]
6. El gives (him) to drink, he will pass to the house of eternity,[g] the house of [............................]
7. not a house a traveler enters, nor does the groom enter this house[h] [...................]
8. and the worm from the tomb;[i] far from the lusts of mankind and from the drink of[j] [.....................]
9. [...] Behold, as for counsel, no one will take counsel with you; or, as for advice, none will seek advice (from you). He who sits[k] [......................]
10. [............] you will wear a single garment;[l] whether you hate, O man, or whether you [love[m] ....]

---

a. Myrrh is usually the possession of the rich.

b. Or, "consider all things and again consider" (M. Dijkstra, "Is Balaam Also Among the Prophets?" *JBL* 114 [1995]: 49).

c. "Offspring and fertility": Some commentators see here the name of a fertility goddess with a double name, Shagar-and-Ashtar (Dijkstra, "Balaam," 49; Levine, *Numbers*, 246). The words are used as names for the offspring of livestock in biblical Hebrew (Deut 7:13; 28:4, 18, 51), and are so taken here. See Hackett, *Balaam Text*, 41.

d. The fastening of the master's shoes was one of the lowliest acts of a slave.

e. Or, "his boy, full of love" or "young woman, drink your fill of love" (Hackett, *Balaam Text*, 56); cf. Dijkstra, "Balaam," 49. I take the phrase to be still presenting the chaos of the social order: the strong warrior suckles milk like an infant.

f. The meaning of the difficult word translated here "desolate" or "desolation" (II. 5, 12, 14) is taken from an Akkadian cognate meaning "to take apart or disassemble." Other suggestions include "blinded one" (Hoftijzer), "sprout/scion" (Hackett), "corpse" (Levine).

g. "House of eternity" is a widely used expression in Hebrew and Aramaic for the grave.

h. In other words, the "house of eternity" is not a temporary refuge for the traveler, nor a home for the family.

i. The word translated "tomb" also appears in Job 21:32.

j. Or, "far from the genitals of man and far from the thighs of [woman]." Construed in this way, the text means that the grave is a place where sexual activity has ceased. For a cognate of the word translated "genitals," see *Tg. Onq.* Lev 21:20. See also J. Milgrom, *Numbers*, 473.

k. Following Levine, *Numbers*, 257. Another possible translation is, "As for counsel, is it not you with whom he will take counsel; or for advice, will he not ask advice from one residing ..." (Hackett, *Balaam Text*, 30).

l. In other words, in the grave only one garment is necessary. Others translate "you will cover him with one garment" (Hackett, *Balaam Text*, 30; similarly Dijkstra, "Balaam," 49). A different reading yields "they cover themselves with a wrap" (Levine, *Numbers*, 257).

m. Similarly, Dijkstra, "Balaam," 49. Hackett takes the same letters to mean "if you are unkind to him, he will falter; if you ..." (Hackett, *Balaam Text*, 30; similarly Levine, *Numbers*, 257).

11. guilt [...........] under your head; you will lie on your eternal bed for a portion [and inheritance ....]
12. [..........................] in your heart sighing (and) desolation (?), in his heart sighing [(and) desolation (?) ....]
13. a wasteland of horror kings shall behold[a] [............] for their habitation. Death takes the suckling of the womb and for [........]
14. [.................................] death of horror [............] shall be firm; the heart of the desolate grows faint[b] for it has come to [...........]
15. to its end [.......] and adorns[c] a plastered wall [......] the request of the king is worms[d] and the re[qu]e[st .....]
16. [....................................] vision far-off[e] [.............] your request for [............For those not able to]
17. understand writing,[f] a word for his people was on (his) tongue:[g] For you is the judgment and the punishment, he said, [...................................]
18. and for my oath[h] and for [my] counsel [..][i]

---

a. A Hebrew cognate of the word translated "wasteland" is found in Isa 5:6. Hackett does not translate this phrase. See also Hoftijzer and van der Kooij, *Aramaic Texts*, 240.

b. The translation "grows faint" is based on an Aramaic cognate. Dijkstra translates "the heart of the blinded will be struck dumb" ("Balaam," 50), Levine "the heart of the corpse is desolate" (*Numbers*, 258).

c. The translation "adorns" is based on an Aramaic cognate, but the reading of the word is uncertain. The following reference to a "plastered wall" is intriguing, in view of the nature of the text, but the context is not clear.

d. That is, in the grave the desires of even the king come to nothing. The translation "worms" is based on an Aramaic cognate. Similarly, Levine translates "the quest of a king is moth rot" (*Numbers*, 258).

e. At this point, the recitation of the vision is at an end, and Balaam apparently begins to explain it. Because of the gaps in the text, we do not know if Balaam says that the vision is "far," that is, for the distant future (compare Num 24:17a), or, perhaps, "not far off," about to be fulfilled.

f. The same expression "to understand writing" is found in Isa 29:12.

g. Or "he spoke to his people with the tongue [i.e., orally]."

h. The translation "oath" is a guess based on a similar word in the Hadad inscription (ll. 28, 29) and an Akkadian cognate. See J. C. L. Gibson, *Textbook of Syrian Semitic Inscriptions*, Vol. 2: *Aramaic Inscriptions* (Oxford: Clarendon, 1975), 68-69.

i. There are numerous other pieces of plaster containing text, but they are very fragmentary and often illegible, and are not translated here. For details on these fragments, see Hoftijzer and van der Kooij, *Aramaic Texts*, 248-67.

Eldad and Modad

A new translation and introduction

by Richard Bauckham

Attestation and Contents

According to the biblical narrative in Numbers 11, the Lord told Moses to bring seventy elders of the people to the tabernacle, where he would "take some of the spirit that is on you and put it on them" (11:17). When this occurred, the seventy elders prophesied, though this is said not to have been something they continued to do (11:25). Presumably it was a sign of their reception of the Spirit. Two elders named Eldad and Medad (Modad is the LXX form of his name) did not go out of the camp to the tabernacle with the others, but remained in the camp. They too prophesied. When Moses and Joshua heard of this, Joshua asked Moses to stop them, but Moses said, "Are you jealous for my sake? Would that all the LORD's people were prophets, and that the LORD would put his spirit on them!" (Num 11:26-30).

This is the only reference to Eldad and Medad in the Bible. But the fact that nothing is said about the content of their prophecy was taken by later Jewish exegetes as an invitation to supply it by deducing from Scripture in some way what it was that the two elders prophesied. Exegetical traditions in the Targums and rabbinic literature offer three topics about which they were supposed to have spoken (see below).

There was a book called *Eldad and Modad*. It is listed among apocrypha of the Old Testament in the list of Sixty Books, the synopsis of Pseudo-Athanasius, and the stichometry of Nicephorus. The stichometry gives it 400 lines (*stichoi*), indicating a relatively short work, longer than Ephesians (312 lines) but shorter than 2 Corinthians (590 lines).[1] We can be reasonably sure that it contained prophecies of Eldad and Medad, but in all the extant literature it is only once explicitly quoted, and this quotation consists of only four Greek words. The brevity of the book may partly account for the lack of other explicit allusions to it in patristic literature.

The sole quotation is in the *Shepherd* of Hermas (*Vis.* 2:3:4), the Roman Christian prophet of the second century C.E. Curiously, within Hermas's long book, this is the only quotation from or allusion to a named book. Hermas was a prophet and did not need to bolster his authority with references to scripture. The explanation for this singular exception may be that it is part of a personal message that Hermas, in a prophetic revelation, was instructed to give to a Roman Christian named Maximus, who had evidently denied his faith in circumstances of persecution. Maximus is warned that another time of trial is coming, in which he may, if he chooses, deny again. But, in order to encourage him to return to faithful discipleship, Hermas is to quote to him the words of Eldad and Modad: "The Lord is near to those who return to him." This occurs in the second of Hermas's

1. James, *The Lost Apocrypha*, 38.

visions, when his own authority as a prophet may not have been sufficiently established for his own prophetic words to carry sufficient weight with Maximus. That *Eldad and Modad* would carry weight indicates that it must have been respected as a work of prophecy within, if not the Roman church as a whole, at least the circles in which Hermas and Maximus moved.

Is it possible to know anything more about the contents of this lost work? It has been argued that traditions about Eldad and Medad in the Targums and rabbinic literature may derive from the book, and there are also a number of quotations from unknown sources that scholars have conjectured may be from the book of *Eldad and Modad*. We shall consider the Jewish traditions first.

Jewish traditions about Eldad and Medad

There are six main items of tradition about Eldad and Medad in extant Jewish literature:

(1) Family relationships:

Tg. Ps.-J. Num 11:26.

> *But two men remained behind in the camp. The name of one was Eldad, and the name of the second was Medad*, the sons of Elisaphan bar Parnak. Yokebed, daughter of Levi, gave birth to them for him at the time when Amram her husband divorced her and to whom she was married before she gave birth to Moses.[2]

(2) Prophecy about Moses and Joshua:

Pseudo-Philo, *L.A.B.* 20:5a.

> The people said to him [Joshua], "Behold, we see today what Eldad and Modad prophesied in the days of Moses, saying, 'After Moses' death, the leadership of Moses will be given to Joshua the son of Nun.' Moses was not jealous but rejoiced when he heard them."[3]

Tg. Ps.-J. Num 11:26.

> *And the* prophetic *spirit rested upon them*. Eldad was prophesying and said: "Behold Moses shall be gathered from the world, and Joshua bar Nun shall be standing in his place and leading the people of the house of Israel and bringing them to the land of the Canaanites and giving them possession of it."[4]

Tg. Neof.1. Num 11:26.

> *And two men remained in the camp; the name of one was Eldad and the name of the second was Medad, and the* holy *spirit rested upon them....* And Medad prophesied

2. Translation by Ernest G. Clarke from Martin McNamara and Ernest G. Clarke, *Targum Neofiti: Numbers; Targum Pseudo-Jonathan: Numbers* (ArBib 4; Edinburgh: Clark, 1995), 220. There is a similar tradition in Pseudo-Jerome, *Qu. hebr.1 Par.* 4.17 (PL 23.1372). In these quotations, italicized words are translations of the biblical text.

3. Translation from Howard Jacobson, *A Commentary on Pseudo-Philo's* Liber Antiquitatum Biblicarum (2 vols.; Leiden: Brill, 1996), 1:124.

4. Translation by Ernest G. Clarke from McNamara and Clarke, *Targum*, 220.

and said: "Behold, Moses the prophet is taken up from the midst of the camp, and Joshua bar Nun exercises his leadership in his stead."[5]

b. Sanh. 17a.
[R. Simeon says,] "And what was the prophecy that they delivered? They said, 'Moses is going to die and Joshua will bring Israel into the Land.' "[6]

This tradition doubtless arose as an attempt to explain Numbers 11:28, where Joshua asks Moses to stop Eldad and Medad from prophesying. This request has been understood as due to Joshua's modesty when he heard that they were prophesying that he would succeed Moses.

(3) Prophecy about the quails:

Tg. Ps.-J. Num 11:26.
Medad was prophesying and said: "Behold, quail came up from the sea and were covering the entire camp of Israel and shall become a stumbling-block to the people."[7]

Tg. Neof.1. Num 11:26.
Eldad *prophesied* and said: "Behold, quail come up from the sea and shall become a stumbling block for Israel."[8]

b. Sanh. 17a.
Abba Hanin says in the name of R. Eliezer, "They prophesied concerning the matter of the quail: 'Arise, quail, arise, quail.' "[9]

The biblical account of Eldad and Medad is embedded in a narrative about the quail (Num 11:18-23, 31-35) and so their prophecy is, according to this tradition, related to it.

(4) Prophecy about Gog and Magog:

Tg. Ps.-J. Num 11:26.
But the two prophesied as one and said: "Behold a king shall arise from the land of Magog at the end of days. He shall gather kings crowned with crowns, and prefects attired in silken clothing, and all the nations shall obey him. They shall prepare for war in the land of Israel against the sons of the exile. However, the Lord is near them at the hour of distress, and all of them will be killed by a burning breath in a consuming fire that comes from beneath the throne of Glory; and their corpses will fall on the mountains of the land of Israel. Then all the wild animals and birds of heaven

---

5. Translation by Martin McNamara from McNamara and Clarke, *Targum*, 73-74.

6. Translation from Jacob Neusner, *The Talmud of Babylonia: XXIIIA: Tractate Sanhedrin Chapters 1-3* (BJS 81; Chico, Calif.: Scholars Press, 1984), 107. The word "prophesy" has been corrected to "prophecy." This tradition is also in *Sifre* to Numbers 95.

7. Translation by Clarke from McNamara and Clarke, *Targum*, 220.

8. Translation by McNamara from McNamara and Clarke, *Targum*, 73-74.

9. Translation from Neusner, *The Talmud*, 107.

shall come and consume their bodies.[10] And after this all the dead of Israel shall live [again][11] and shall delight themselves with the good which was hidden for them from the beginning. Then they shall receive the reward of their labors."[12]

Tg. Neof.1. Num 11:26.

And both of them prophesied together, saying: "At the very end of the days Gog and Magog ascend on Jerusalem, and they fall at the hands of King Messiah, and for seven years the children of Israel shall kindle fires from their weapons; and they will not have to go out to the forest."[13]

b. Sanh. 17a.

R. Nahman says, "They prophesied concerning Gog and Magog, as it is said, 'So says the Lord God, Are you [Gog] he of whom I spoke in olden time by my servants, the prophets of Israel, that prophesied in those days for many years that I would bring you against them? [Ezek 38:17; instead of "years" (*shanim*) read "two" (*shenaim*).' And who are the two prophets who prophesied the same message in the same prophecy? You have to say it was Eldad and Medad."[14]

The last of these passages, from *b. Sanh.* 17a, explains how the idea that Eldad and Medad prophesied against Gog and Magog was derived exegetically from Ezek 38:17. There God says that his prophets had prophesied in the distant past that he would bring God against Israel. Who were these prophets who together prophesied the same message in a time long before Ezekiel? Eldad and Modad, who Numbers says prophesied but to whom it attributes no specific prophecy, were the obvious candidates. A prophecy lacking prophets (Ezek 38:17) was matched with prophets lacking a prophecy (Num 11:26-27). That the prophets in the former passage prophesied "for many years" is evaded by R. Nahman, who proposes to vocalize the text differently, but it may also have helped originate the tradition that Eldad and Medad did indeed continue to prophesy for many years (see (6) below).

(5) Their humility:

Tg. Ps.-J. Num 11:26.

And they belonged to the elders whose (names) were found inscribed on the registers. They had not gone to the tent but they hid themselves in order to escape the honor (which awaited them). *They were prophesying in the camp.*[15]

10. The passage alludes to Ezek 38:2, 4-7, 15-16; 39:4-6, 17-20.

11. Cf. Ezek 37:1-14.

12. Translation by Clarke from McNamara and Clarke, *Targum,* 220-221.

13. Translation by McNamara from McNamara and Clarke, *Targum,* 74. The passage alludes to Ezek 39:9-10.

14. Translation from Neusner, *The Talmud,* 107-108. The word "prophesy" has been corrected to "prophecy."

15. Translation by Clarke from McNamara and Clarke, *Targum,* 221.

Tg. Neof.1. Num 11:26.

And these were from the seventy wise men who were set apart. *And the seventy wise men did not leave* the camp while Eldad and Medad *were prophesying in the camp.*[16]

b. Sanh. 17a.

R. Simeon says, "They remained in the camp. When the Holy One blessed be he said to Moses, 'Gather for me seventy men' [Num 11:16], Eldad and Medad said, 'We are not worthy of that high position.' Said the Holy One, blessed be he, 'Since you diminished yourselves, lo, I shall add greatness to your greatness.'"[17]

(6) They prophesied until they died:

b. Sanh. 17a.

[R. Simeon says,] "What is the greatness that he added to them? It was that all the others prophesied and then ceased to prophesy, but they prophesied and did not cease to prophesy."[18]

Sifre to Numbers 95:

[R. Simeon said:] "Of the seventy elders, Scripture says, '*And when the spirit rested upon them, they prophesied, but they did so no more*' [Num 11:25]. So they prophesied for a moment and then stopped. But of Eldad and Modad it says, '*So they prophesied in the camp*' [Num 11:26]. For they prophesied to the day of their death."[19]

The Jewish Traditions and the Book of Eldad and Modad

Could the book of *Eldad and Modad* have been a source of these Jewish traditions or some of them? Or is it at least likely to have contained some of these same traditions? An important point to observe about the traditions in the Targums and the rabbinic literature concerns the three topics said to have been the content of Eldad and Medad's prophecy: Moses and Joshua, the quails, and Gog and Magog. In the Babylonian Talmud these are attributed to different rabbis and treated as various answers to the question what it was the two prophesied. In the Targums all three topics are affirmed: one is attributed to Eldad, one to Medad, and one (as Ezek 38:17 requires) to them both. It seems clear that this passage in the Targums must be dependent on the collection of three different opinions in the Talmud. So the set of three topics as such cannot be an older tradition.

However, Pseudo-Philo, *L.A.B.* 20:5, is good evidence that, already in the late first century C.E., there was a view that Eldad and Medad prophesied the death of Moses and Joshua's succession to the leadership of Israel. Either or both of the other two traditions about the topic of the prophecies could also be as early, but there is no evidence for this, unless perhaps it is to be found in Hermas's quotation from their book.

Several scholars have noted the resemblance between Hermas's quotation from *Eldad*

---

16. Translation by McNamara from McNamara and Clarke, *Targum*, 74.

17. Translation from Neusner, *The Talmud*, 107. This tradition is also in *Sifre* to Numbers 95 and *Num. Rab.* 15.19.

18. Translation from Neusner, *The Talmud*, 107.

19. Translation from Jacob Neusner, *Sifré to Numbers* (2 vols.; BJS 119; Atlanta, Ga.: Scholars Press, 1986), 2:107.

and Modad and a clause in *Targum Pseudo-Jonathan*'s account of their prophecy about Gog:[20]

> Hermas: "The Lord is near to those who return (to him)."
> *Tg. Ps.-J.* Num 11:26: "the Lord is near them at the hour of distress."

But the resemblance is not so close as may at first appear:

(1) It is remarkable that of five words in the clause in the Targum no less than three are Greek loanwords. (Geza Vermes speaks of "an extraordinary Greco-Aramaic glossolalia"![21]) But only one of these corresponds to the Greek of Hermas's quotation:

> Hermas: "The Lord (*kurios*) is near (*engus*) to those who turn (to him)."
> *Tg. Ps.-J.* Num 11:26: "the Lord (*qiris* = *kurios*) is near (*'itimos* =*hetoimos*) them at the hour of distress (*'anikin* = *anankē*)."

Hermas does speak just before this of "tribulation," but the word is *thlipsis*, not *anankē*. The two passages in English translation look closer than they really are, because *'itimos* has been translated as "near," whereas *hetoimos* in Greek means "ready." It is not easy to find a suitable English equivalent, but presumably the sense is "ready to help." The use of the three Greek loanwords might suggest that the Targum is here dependent on a Greek source, but in that case the source can hardly be the Greek quoted by Hermas. Translating Greek words with *different* Greek loanwords seems an unlikely translation procedure.

(2) The meaning of the two statements is also less similar than may at first appear. It is true that both concern the eschatological tribulation of the people of God.[22] But Hermas is speaking of those who turn back to God after denying him, whereas the Targum refers simply to the situation of the people under attack by the invading nations without suggesting that they need to turn back to God (though it is not impossible that in a longer version of the tradition this was the case).

The conclusion must be that, while it is intrinsically likely that the traditions about Eldad and Medad in the Targums and rabbinic literature are in some way related to the contents of the *Eldad and Modad* pseudepigraphon, we lack the evidence to show that the latter included any one of those traditions in particular. We turn now to consider whether there are quotations in early Christian literature from unnamed sources that could be identified as *Eldad and Modad*.

Other Quotations: James 4:5?

Although there have been attempts to read James 4:5 differently, most scholars agree that it gives a quotation from an apparently unknown work. But the translation of the quotation is a difficult and debated issue. Elsewhere I have provided a critical review of all the proposed translations, and proposed one that seems to me the most satisfactory: "The Spirit he [God] made to dwell in us loathes envy." This entails supposing that the original text of the apocryphal work quoted was in Hebrew, that the translator has treated the two Hebrew roots *t'b* ("to long for") and *t'b* ("to abhor, to loathe") as one, and used the Greek

20. E.g. Marshall, "Eldad"; Martin, "Eldad," 464.

21. Geza Vermes, *Jesus the Jew* (London: Collins, Fontana edition, 1976), 113.

22. Marshall, "Eldad."

word *epipothein* as though it had the same range of meaning. Hence *epipothein*, which does mean "to long for," is here used to mean "to loathe." This provides an excellent sense in the context. Not only does it follow on well from 3:13–4:3, where envy is the theme, but also from 4:4, which correlates friendship with the world and enmity with God. The quotation provides the basis for this by pointing out God's enmity towards envy.[23]

I have suggested that the quotation may well come from *Eldad and Modad*. The story in Num 11:25-30 is one of the few passages in the Hebrew Bible that could be understood as a warning against envy (cf. 11:29, and Pseudo-Philo, *L.A.B.* 20:5), while the reference in James's quotation to "the Spirit he [God] made to dwell in us" could easily reflect the biblical statements that God made "the spirit rest on" the seventy elders and then on Eldad and Medad (Num 11:25, 26).

Supporting this proposal are two links with Hermas. First, the verb *katoikizein*, "to make to dwell," occurs in Christian literature before Justin only here in James's apocryphal quotation and twice in Hermas (*Mand.* 3:1; *Sim.* 5:6:5), in both cases with reference to the Spirit that God makes to dwell in the flesh (either of Christians or of Jesus). Hermas may have learned this phrase from *Eldad and Modad*. Secondly, in the immediate context of his apocryphal quotation James has the closest extant parallel to the one sentence that Hermas quotes from *Eldad and Modad*. James advises those who have forsaken God's way: "draw near to God and he will draw near to you" (4:8). This is a recasting, in measure-for-measure form, of: "The Lord is near to those who return to him."

Other Quotations: 1 Clem. 23:3-4 and 2 Clem. 11:2-4?

It is clear that these are independent quotations from the same apocryphal source, called "Scripture" in *1 Clement* and "the prophetic word" in *2 Clement*. Lightfoot may have been the first to suggest that this was *Eldad and Modad*,[24] and several other scholars have followed him.[25] In favour of this identification is the association of Hermas and *1 Clement* (and perhaps *2 Clement* also)[26] with the church in Rome, as well as the term "prophetic word," used in *2 Clement*, which would well suit prophecies attributed to Eldad and Modad. M. R. James dissented from Lightfoot's view, preferring to assign these quotations to the apocryphal Ezekiel. His reason was that he could not see how the people addressed in the quotation could be contemporaries of Eldad and Modad,[27] but it could be that the two prophets were represented as addressing, not their contemporaries, but the people in the last days about which they prophesied.

Of special interest is the fact that this quotation, in *1 Clement* and *2 Clement*, uses the word "double-minded" (*dipsychos*). Curiously, this word and its cognates, the verb *dipsychein* ("to be in two minds") and the noun *dipsychia* ("double-mindedness"), are almost confined to the four early Christian writings we have been considering: James, Hermas, *1* and *2 Clement*. James uses *dipsychos* twice (1:8: 4:8), on the second occasion in close

23. Bauckham, "The Spirit."

24. J. B. Lightfoot, *The Apostolic Fathers:* Part I: *S. Clement of Rome* (revised edition; London: Macmillan, 1890), 2:80-81, 235.

25. Donald A. Hagner, *The Use of the Old and New Testaments in Clement of Rome* (NovTSup 34; Leiden: Brill, 1973), 87-88; Richard Bauckham, *Jude, 2 Peter* (WBC 50: Waco, Texas: Word Books, 1983), 284-85; Seitz, "Afterthoughts," 332-34. For other suggestions, see Denis, *Introduction*, 482-83, 1246-47.

26. The association of *2 Clement* with Rome is very debatable.

27. James, *The Lost Apocrypha*, 40. Alfred Resch, *Agrapha: aussercanonische Schriftfragmente* (TU 15/2; Leipzig: J. C. Hinrichs, 1906), 325, also attributed the quotation to the apocryphal Ezekiel.

proximity to the apocryphal quotation we have suggested is from *Eldad and Modad*. Hermas uses it 19 times, and also uses *dipsychein* 20 times and *dipsychia* 16 times. Several of these references are not far from his own quotation from *Eldad and Modad* (*Vis*. 2:2:4, 7; 3:2:2; 3:3:4; 3:7:1; 3:10:9; 3:11:2). In *1 Clement dipsychos* occurs once (11:2) in addition to its appearance in the apocryphal quotation (23:3), and the verb *dipsychein* in the exhortation that leads to the apocryphal quotation (23:2). In *2 Clement dipsychos* occurs in the apocryphal quotation (11:2), the verb *dipsychein* in the exhortation that drives home the message of the quotation (11:5) and the noun *dipsychia* once elsewhere (19:2). Otherwise, the only attestation of words of this group before Clement of Alexandria (who uses it only in quoting Hermas: *Str.* 1.29.181.1) is the use of the verb in the "Two Ways" section that is shared by the *Didache* (4:4) and *Barnabas* (19:5),[28] and which many scholars believe draws on a pre-Christian Jewish source. After the second century the word group is very rare.[29] It is clear that the apocryphal quotation in *1* and *2 Clement* must be in some way connected to the discourse shared by James, *1* and *2 Clement*, and Hermas.

At some point the word *dipsychos* and its cognates must have been coined by a Jewish or Christian author as a translation of the Hebrew expression *belēb wĕ-belēb* (literally: "with a heart and a heart": 1 Chr 12:34 [Evv 12:33]; Ps 12:2 [Evv 12:3]; 1QH[a] XII, 14). Stanley Porter[30] has argued that this was James, whose use of *dipsychos* he claims is the earliest attested. But, quite apart from the issue of whether the other Christian writers in question knew the letter of James, this hypothesis entails supposing that the apocryphal writing quoted by *1* and *2 Clement* was dependent on James.[31] The hypothesis that James, Hermas, *1* and *2 Clement* all derived their use of this word group from *Eldad and Modad* is at least as plausible, and has the advantage of explaining the other links we have noticed between James and Hermas at the same time. That the author of *Eldad and Modad* himself actually coined *dipsychos* and its cognates is more doubtful because of their use in *Didache* 4:4 and *Barnabas* 19:5.

Oscar Seitz goes further and speculates that the book of *Eldad and Modad* was actually the "little book" that Hermas describes in his second vision, and that Hermas himself was instrumental in its publication.[32] Less speculatively, it would seem that *Eldad and Modad* was especially influential in the Roman Christian circles represented by Hermas, *1 Clement* and perhaps *2 Clement*, and with which the letter of James may also be connected by virtue of the close links between the Christian communities of Jerusalem and Rome. The resemblance between the quotation in *1* and *2 Clement* and 2 Peter 3:3-4 suggests that 2 Peter, probably another product of the church of Rome, may also have been influenced by *Eldad and Modad*.[33]

28. Other versions of the same material also use *dipsychein* (*Canons of the Apostles* 13.2) or *dipsychos* (*Ap. Const.* 7.11).

29. Stanley E. Porter, "Is *dipsuchos* (James 1,8; 4,8) a 'Christian' Word?," *Bib* 71 (1990): 469-498, here 494-496. Albert Paretsky, "The Two Ways and *Dipsuchia* in Early Christian Literature: An Interesting Dead End in Moral Discourse," *Ang* 74 (1997): 305-34, explains this as due to a changing Christian anthropology that abandoned Jewish ethical dualism.

30. Porter, "Is *dipsuchos*."

31. Porter, "Is *dipsuchos*," 476, seems quite evasive on this point.

32. Seitz, "Afterthoughts," 332-34.

33. Bauckham, *Jude*, 284-85.

Other Quotations in 1 Clement?

If *1 Clem.* 23:3-4 is a quotation from *Eldad and Modad,* then it is possible that other apocryphal quotations from unnamed sources in *1 Clement* are from the same source. Lightfoot suggested this in the case of 17:6, where Moses is quoted as saying, "I am smoke from a pot."[34] Since Moses would have appeared in *Eldad and Modad,* this is possible, but the *Testament of Moses* and the *Assumption of Moses* are also possibilities.[35]

There is perhaps more to be said for *1 Clement* 46:2: "Cleave to the holy ones, for those who cleave to them will be made holy."[36] Hermas twice uses the phrase "to cleave to the holy ones" (*Vis.* 3:6:2; *Sim.* 8:8:1), and also uses several variations: "to cleave to the servants of God" (*Sim.* 9:20:2; 9:26:3), "to cleave to the righteous" (*Sim.* 8:9:1), "to cleave to the double-minded and empty" (*Mand.* 11:13).[37] It is plausible that he is echoing the saying quoted in *1 Clement* 46:2. We should note that Clement himself varies the phrase in the same way when he echoes the saying soon after quoting it: "let us then cleave to the innocent and righteous" (46:4). If we have here an apocryphal saying from a source known to both Clement and Hermas, then *Eldad and Modad* is a strong possibility. (In that case, it begins to look as though Hermas's ways of speaking may quite often derive from *Eldad and Modad.*)

A third possible quotation from *Eldad and Modad* is *1 Clem.* 8:3:

> Repent of your iniquity, house of Israel. Say to the sons and daughters of my people: "Though your sins reach from the earth to heaven, and though they be redder than scarlet and blacker than sackcloth, and yet you return to me with your whole heart and say, 'Father,' I will listen to you as a holy people."

This has often been assigned to the apocryphal Ezekiel or to an interpolated text of canonical Ezekiel, since it immediately follows a quotation from canonical Ezekiel (8:2) and since Clement of Alexandria attributes it to Ezekiel (*Paed.* 1.91.2).[38] But Clement of Alexandria may be dependent on *1 Clement* (as he certainly is some instances) and may simply have inferred from the latter that the quotation is from Ezekiel. A case could be made for *Eldad and Modad,* since the theme of this quotation resembles that of the one explicit quotation from that book that is extant (Hermas, *Vis.* 2:3:4). The same word is used for returning to God in repentance (*epistrephein*), while the phrase "with your whole heart" is the positive opposite of being "double-minded." Moreover, Hermas might be echoing this passage in *Mand.* 9:2 ("return to the Lord with your whole heart"), but the phrase is biblical (Deut 30:2; Jer 24:7; Joel 2:12).

Clement is likely to have known other apocryphal literature that is no longer extant, and so we cannot regard the derivation of these three quotations from *Eldad and Modad* as more than possibilities.

---

34. Lightfoot, *The Apostolic Fathers,* 64-65.

35. Hagner, *The Use,* 72-73.

36. On this quotation, see Lightfoot, *The Apostolic Fathers,* 2:139-140; Hagner, *The Use,* 89-90. Neither suggests *Eldad and Modad* as the source. The saying is quoted from *1 Clement* by Clement of Alexandria, *Str.* 5.52.3.

37. Cf. also Hermas, *Mand.* 11:4; *1 Clem.* 15:1; 30:3; *Barn.* 10:3, 4, 5; 19:2, 6. The phrase "to cleave to the good" (Rom 12:9; *Did.* 5:2; *Barn.* 20:2) is not plausibly derived from this saying.

38. Lightfoot, *The Apostolic Fathers,* 2:39-41; James, *The Lost Apocrypha,* 68; Hagner, *The Use,* 71, 90-91.

Other Suggestions

M. R. James, arguing that there must have been a description of the "Lost Tribes" of Israel to which the *Story of Zosimus*, the Ethiopic *Conflict of Matthew*, and the Latin poet Commodian were all indebted, suggested, "if a conjecture is to be hazarded," that this source was the book of *Eldad and Modad*.[39] In the ninth century a Jewish adventurer who called himself Eldad the Danite (though some sources call him Elhanan son of Joseph) claimed to have visited the Ten Tribes in the distant land of their exile,[40] but the name Eldad is hardly sufficient to establish a connexion with the book of *Eldad and Modad*. (The sections of Commodian and related sources are discussed elsewhere in this volume.)

Among the traditional critical marks in manuscripts of the Torah, two dots ("inverted *nuns*") are placed either side of the passage Num 10:35-36. According to the *Midrash on Proverbs*, Rabbi Judah the Prince explained the marks as indicating that these verses formed an independent book.[41] Two medieval Jewish sources understood this to mean that these verses were not by Moses, but taken from the prophecy of Eldad and Medad. Saul Lieberman concluded that Rabbi was alluding to the book of *Eldad and Modad* that is known from Christian sources,[42] but Lieman has contested this interpretation of the Midrash, concluding that a connexion between Numbers 10:35-36 and Eldad and Medad was not made before the Middle Ages.[43] There seems no reason to suppose that any of these texts had any knowledge of the actual book of *Eldad and Modad*.

Date and Provenance

The date of the *Shepherd* of Hermas is not certain because the indications of date do not all seem to fit the same time, but it has become widely accepted that at least *Visions* 1-4 date from around the end of the first century C.E., though the rest of the work may have been written over an extended period.[44] Hermas's reference to *Eldad and Modad* (*Vis.* 2:3:4) would in that case provide a *terminus ad quem* of the end of the first century, and *1 Clement*, usually dated in the 90s, would confirm that date, if it does indeed quote from *Eldad and Modad*. If James 4:5 is a quotation from *Eldad and Modad*, this might well provide an earlier *terminus ad quem*, but the date of the letter of James is contested. There is no way, on present evidence, of determining a *terminus a quo*.

If my argument about James 4:5 is accepted, *Eldad and Modad* originated in Hebrew, but was current in a Greek translation. This would strongly suggest a non-Christian Jewish provenance, without entirely ruling out a Christian Jewish provenance. The latter would also be improbable if the letter of James is an authentic work of James the brother of Jesus and one of the earliest of Christian writings, as I and others have argued.[45] If James

39. Montague Rhodes James, *Apocrypha Anecdota* (TS 2/3; Cambridge: Cambridge University Press, 1893), 93 n. 1; cf. Denis, *Introduction*, 485.

40. For the literature, see Denis, *Introduction*, 480 n. 10.

41. See Burton L. Vikotzky, *The Midrash on Proverbs* (New Haven: Yale University Press, 1992), 109, whose translation reflects the interpretation of Saul Lieberman and others, which is strongly contested by Leiman, "The Inverted *Nuns*," whose argument I have followed here.

42. Saul Lieberman, *Hellenism in Jewish Palestine* (2nd ed.; New York: Jewish Theological Seminary, 1962), 41 n. 28.

43. Leiman, "The Inverted *Nuns*."

44. See, e.g., Carolyn Osiek, *Shepherd of Hermas* (Hermeneia; Minneapolis, Minn.: Fortress, 1999), 18-20.

45. Richard Bauckham, *James: Wisdom of James, Disciple of Jesus the Sage* (London/New York: Routledge, 1999), 11-25.

4:5 is not a quotation from *Eldad and Modad*, then it might be possible to see the latter as a Christian composition from the same Christian milieu as the circles to which Hermas and Clement belonged. But the authority it evidently had in those circles would be more easily intelligible if it were an already respected work. Since we know so little of the contents of the work, this is all we can tell about its provenance.

Bibliography

EDITIONS AND TRANSLATIONS (HERMAS)

Holmes, Michael W., and translated by Michael W. Holmes after the earlier work of J. B. Lightfoot and J. R. Harmer (eds.). Pages 466-67 in *The Apostolic Fathers in English: Greek Texts and English Translations*. 3rd ed. Grand Rapids, Mich.: Baker Academic, 2007.

Joly, Robert. Pages 94-95 in *Hermas: Le Pasteur.* SC 53. Paris: Editions du Cerf, 1958. (critical edition of the text and French translation)

Whittaker, Molly. Pages 6-7 in *Die Apostolischen Väter: I: Der Hirt des Hermas.* GCS. Berlin: Akademie-Verlag, 1967. (critical edition of the text)

STUDIES

Bauckham, Richard. "The Spirit of God in Us Loathes Envy (James 4:5)." Pages 270-81 in Graham N. Stanton, Bruce W. Longenecker and Stephen C. Barton, eds., *The Holy Spirit and Christian Origins: Essays in Honor of James D. G. Dunn.* Grand Rapids, Mich.: Eerdmans, 2004. Reprinted: pages 421-32 in Richard Bauckham, *The Jewish World around the New Testament: Collected Essays I.* WUNT 233. Tübingen: Mohr Siebeck, 2008.

Denis, Albert-Marie. *Introduction à la littérature religieuse judéo-hellénistique.* 2 volumes. Turnhout: Brepols, 2000. 1:477-89.

James, Montague Rhodes. Pages 38-40 in *The Lost Apocrypha of the Old Testament.* London: SPCK, 1920.

Lieman, Sid Z. "The Inverted *Nuns* at Numbers 10:35-36 and the Book of Eldad and Medad." *JBL* 93 (1974): 348-55.

Marshall, J. T. "Eldad and Modad, Book of." In James Hastings, ed., *A Dictionary of the Bible,* 4 vols. Edinburgh: T.&T. Clark, 1898-1902. 1:676.

Martin, E. G. "Eldad and Modad." *OTP* 2:463-65.

Seitz, Oscar J. F. "Afterthoughts on the Term 'Dipsychos.'" *NTS* 4 (1958): 327-34.

———. "The Relationship of the Shepherd of Hermas to the Epistle of James." *JBL* 63 (1944): 131-40.

Eldad and Modad

Blessed are all those who practice righteousness. They will never perish. But say to Maximus, "Look, tribulation is coming. If it seems right to you, deny again. **'The Lord is near to those who return to him,' as it is written in the book of Eldad and Modat,**[a] **who prophesied to the people in the wilderness."** Ps 34:19 [Evv 34:18]

Hermas, *Vis.* 2:3:3-4 (Hermas 7:3-4)

Additional texts not certainly known to belong to *Eldad and Modad*

Adulterers! Do you not know that friendship with the world is enmity with God? Or do you think it is for nothing that **the scripture says: "The Spirit that he has made to dwell in us loathes envy"**? But he gives all the more grace, and so it says: *God opposes the proud, but gives grace to the lowly.* Submit yourselves therefore to God. Resist the devil and he will flee from you. Draw near to God and he will draw near to you. Cleanse your hands, you sinners, and purify your hearts, you double-minded. Prov 3:34

James 4:4-8

So let us not be in two minds, nor let our soul entertain false notions about his [God's] excellent and glorious gifts. **Let this scripture be far from us, where he says: "Miserable are the double-minded, those who doubt in their soul and say, 'We heard these things even in the days of our fathers, and, look, we have grown old, and none of these things has happened to us.' You fools, compare yourselves with a plant: take a vine. First it sheds its leaves, then it begins to bud, then a leaf appears, then a flower, and after those a sour grape, and then a full ripe bunch."** Notice that in a brief time the fruit of the plant reaches ripeness. 2 Pet 3:4; Mark 13:28

1 Clem. 23:2-4

So let us serve God with a pure heart, and we shall be righteous. But if we do not serve him because we do not believe the promise of God, we shall be miserable. **For the prophetic word also says: "Miserable are the double-minded, those**

---

a. This unusual form of the name is the reading of Codex Sinaiticus and is preferred by most editors. A variant has the form Modad, as in Num 11:26-27 LXX. Manuscripts of *L.A.B.* 20:5 have Modat, Medat and Meldat.

who doubt in their heart and say, 'We heard all these things even in the days
2 Pet 3:4 **of our fathers, but we have waited day after day and have seen none of them.'**
Fools, compare yourselves with a plant: take a vine. First it sheds its leaves,
then it begins to bud, and after those a sour grape, then the full ripe bunch.
Mark 13:28 **In the same way my people have had tumults and tribulations; afterwards**
they will receive the good things." So, my brothers and sisters, let us not be in two minds, but let us patiently endure in hope, so that we too may receive the reward.

2 Clem. 11:1-5

Songs of David

A new translation and introduction

by G. W. Lorein and E. van Staalduine-Sulman[1]

The Songs of David probably belonged to a long series of liturgical psalms, written in Hebrew, but only four survive. The introductions to the songs suggest that the collection contained psalms for each day of the year. The songs mention King David (I, 15) in our opinion as the name of the Lord's servant (I, 6, 8, 14), which is to be identified with the "I" of the songs (II, 1, 8, 24, etc.). Hence the songs can be called a Jewish[2] pseudepigraphic writing.

Contents

The four extant psalms speak about God's election of David as his servant and his justice spread over the entire world through the great David, first rejected but now head of the nations (first song); God's salvation for his people, his mercy for the world through his servant David, and the praise of God for his Word (second song); God ruling the earth by humbling and exalting (third song); and God's justice and faithfulness (fourth song). All four speak about God separating the wicked oppressors and the humble believers.

The songs are Israel-centred, but have a universalistic flavor. God's actions are meant to clean and save his people (I, 5). The nations will, however, learn from God through his servant David (II, 14-16; III, 19). They will abandon their idols and turn to God (II, 18; III, 18). In the end, David will be king over all the nations (I, 23).

Manuscripts and Versions

The Songs of David are preserved in one manuscript, found in the Cairo Genizah. It is now kept in the Russian National Library in St Petersburg as number B 798 of the Antonin Collection (= Evr III).[3] The Hebrew handwriting resembles Egyptian square script of the tenth century at the latest.[4] There is no indication that Hebrew would not be the original language.

---

1. Parts of the introduction and the translation were published in G. W. Lorein and E. van Staalduine-Sulman, "A Song of David for Each Day. The Provenance of the *Songs of David*," *RevQ* 22/85 (2005): 33-59; and G. W. Lorein and E. van Staalduine-Sulman, "CšD II, 4 – IV, 9. A Song of David for Each Day," *Hen* 31 (2009): 387-410.

2. D. Flusser and S. Safrai, "The Apocryphal 'Songs of David'" (Heb.), in *Bible Studies, Y.M. Grintz in Memoriam* (ed. B. Uffenheimer; Tel Aviv: Tel Aviv University Press, 1982), 83-105, esp. 96-98, emphasize that the absence of any reference to Jesus in connection with the Messianic expectations surrounding the figure of King David leads to the conclusion that the songs are Jewish and not Christian.

3. The Antonin Collection is described by A. J. Katsh, "The Antonin Genizah in the Saltykov-Schedrin Public Library in Leningrad," in *The Leo Jung Jubilee Volume. Essays in His Honor on the Occasion of His Seventieth Birthday* (ed. M. M. Kasher et al.; New York: The Jewish Center, 1962), 115-31.

4. See the examples in A. Yardeni, *The Book of Hebrew Script. History, Palaeography, Script Styles, Cal-*

Genre, Structure and Prosody

The songs are introduced as prayers, following a vision which is not described in the song. Each song ends with a benediction, taken from the endings of the second and fourth books of the Biblical Psalms. The structure of the songs is very similar to that of the prayers from the Qumran Community, as described by Nitzan: they are part of a series and contain numerous variations on Biblical materials. These elements also occur during the rabbinic period.[5] However, the typical elements of the morning prayers of later times are barely present here: the songs do offer insight in the Law and contain prayers for mercy, but there is no attention to demons, self-deprecation and forgiveness. Moreover, the rebuilding of Jerusalem receives little mention.[6]

Although the songs are introduced as prayers, they are not all directed to God. Especially the third song speaks about Him in the third person. Therefore, it is best to classify these poems as psalms, the more so since they abundantly cite the Biblical Psalm book.[7]

The four remaining songs were given the dates of the first four days of the month Iyyar. On the one hand, there is no need to assume the existence of exactly 364 songs. The Qumran Community, for example, had daily prayers,[8] but worked with cycles in order to limit the total number.[9] On the other hand, there is no indication that the series was restricted.[10] Daily prayers may be intended as a substitute for the daily Temple service, which is not mentioned in the songs at all. At least, this is how rabbinic Judaism understood them.[11]

The first extant song is an alphabetical acrostic, of which the introduction and at least the two first lines are missing. Each verse starts with a letter of the Hebrew alphabet and consists of two lines, indicated by the manuscript itself. The letters that are used twice are the letters that have a final position variant.[12] The last five lines are a separate acrostic, which can be understood as "not in the alphabet." Harkavy interprets these letters as the name of the poet, i.e., "by Aba Baruch," whereby Baruch is the first word of the last line.[13] Philonenko and Marx suggest that verses I, 27 – II, 1 actually formed the start of this first

---

ligraphy and Design (Jerusalem: Carta, 1997), 80-83.

5. B. Nitzan, *Qumran Prayer and Religious Poetry* (STDJ 12; Leiden: Brill, 1994), 7, 20-23, 71-72, 75.

6. See J. Maier, "Zu Kult und Liturgie der Qumrangemeinde," *RevQ* 14 (1990): 543-86, esp. pp. 556; cf. M. Weinfeld, "The Morning Prayers (Birkhoth hashachar) in Qumran and in the Conventional Liturgy," *RevQ* 13 (1988): 481-94.

7. So also D. Flusser, "Psalms, Hymns and Prayers," in *Jewish Writings of the Second Temple Period* (ed. M. E. Stone; CRINT II/2; Assen: Van Gorcum, 1984), 551-77, esp. pp. 568-69.

8. Maier, "Zu Kult und Liturgie," 544, 552.

9. See F. García Martínez and A. S. van der Woude, *De Rollen van de Dode Zee II. Liturgische teksten, eschatologische teksten, exegetische literatuur, para-bijbelse literatuur en overige geschriften* (Kampen: Kok, 1995), 20-21; B. Nitzan, "The Dead Sea Scrolls and the Jewish Liturgy," in *The Dead Sea Scrolls as Background to Postbiblical Judaism and Early Christianity* (ed. J. R. Davila; STDJ 46; Leiden: Brill, 2003), 195-219, esp. p. 215 n. 67.

10. The Essenes wanted to have more than one Psalm for each day, hence 11QPs; see R. T. Beckwith, *Calendar and Chronology, Jewish and Christian: Biblical, Intertestamental and Patristic Studies* (Leiden: Brill, 1996), 149.

11. See *Tg. Isa* 1:13 and *Tg. Hos* 14:3.

12. That is, final *kaf, mem, nun, pe,* and *tsade.*

13. A. E. Harkavy, "Prayers in the Style of the Songs of the Psalms by an Anonymous Person" (Heb.), *Ha-Goren. Abhandlungen über die Wissenschaft des Judenthums* 3 (1902): 82-85, esp. p. 82.

song.[14] It is safer to say that what is left of our manuscript just starts in the third verse of what was probably not the first song of the original collection.

In most of the verses, internal parallelism can be distinguished, either through formal similarities (e.g., three times "between" in I, 4), or through parallel meanings (e.g., "You drove out all sons of the aliens from among Your nation" and "You cleansed Your flock of unclean animals" in I, 5). The fact that this song contains so much parallelism and verbal repetition, and does not have the poetical features of the *piyyutim*, such as alliteration, rhyme and rhythm or other such figures of speech,[15] is reminiscent of the prayers from Qumran[16] and the poetical compositions in the Targum.[17]

Date and Provenance

Establishing the date and place of origin of the Songs of David is a rather hypothetical enterprise. The extant manuscript might be from the tenth century or so, but most features of the songs such as philology, genre and theology point to an earlier date of origin. Apart from Harkavy, who discussed these psalms long before the Qumran findings, all earlier authors connect the songs' provenance with the Qumran Community, although there is no definite proof for such an origin.

According to Tov, the use of the five final letters can be dated back to the Persian period, although it was not applied consistently: several early Qumran manuscripts do not contain all the final letters, but they do all occur in *PNash* (150 B.C.E.) and 4QXII[a] (150-125 B.C.E.).[18] The use of the *khet* instead of the *he* (I, 3) occurs more frequently in Targum and in Qumran writings and does not exclude an early date.[19] Kasher claims this is a typical Palestinian phenomenon,[20] which points to an origin in the Holy Land. The references to Midian (I, 24) and Kedar (I, 25) may concur with that.

The general impression of the Hebrew used is that of Classical Hebrew. However, there are several characteristics that resemble Qumran Hebrew and even Mishnaic Hebrew. There are no consecutive tenses. The alternate use of the perfect and the imperfect has to be explained theologically: God will do again what He has done in the past. However,

---

14. M. Philonenko and A. Marx, "Quatre « chants » pseudo-davidiques trouvés dans la gueniza du Caire et d'origine esséno-qoumrânienne," *RHPR* 77 (1997): 385-406, esp. p. 386.

15. Cf. W. J. van Bekkum, "Language and Theme in the Piyyut – *ṭqs* and Its Derivations," in *Proceedings of the Ninth World Congress of Jewish Studies. Division C. Jewish Thought and Literature* (ed. D. Assaf; Jerusalem: WUJS, 1986), 63-68.

16. Nitzan, *Qumran Prayer*, 20-21.

17. See S. Segert, "Rendering of Parallelistic Structures in the Targum of Neofiti: The Songs of Moses (Deuteronomy 32:1-43)," in *Salvación en la Palabra: Targum – Derash – Berith* (ed. D. Muñoz Léon; Mem. A. Díez Macho; Madrid: Christiandad, 1986), 515-32; E. van Staalduine-Sulman, *The Targum of Samuel* (SAIS 1; Leiden: Brill, 2002) 639-64 on *Tg. 2 Sam* 22 and 664-686 on *Tg. 2 Sam* 23:1-8; J. W. Wesselius, "Biblical Poetry through Targumic Eyes: Onkelos' Treatment of Genesis 49:8-12," in *Give Ear to My Words: Psalms and Other Poetry in and around the Hebrew Bible* (ed. J. Dyk; Fs. N. A. van Uchelen; Amsterdam: Societas Hebraica Amstelodamensis, 1996), 131-45.

18. E. Tov, *Textual Criticism of the Hebrew Bible* (Minneapolis, Minn.: Fortress; Assen: Van Gorcum, 1992), 210. See F. M. Cross, "The Development of the Jewish Script," in *The Bible and the Ancient Near East* (ed. G. E. Wright; Fs. W. F. Albright; London: Routledge, 1961), 133-202, esp. pp. 148-49. Even the Biblical verse Zeph. 3:8 contains all the Hebrew letters including the *litterae finales* (A. S. van der Woude, *Habakuk Zefanja* [POut; Nijkerk: Callenbach, 1978], 131), but that could be by chance.

19. For Targum, see Van Staalduine-Sulman, *Targum of Samuel*, 365. For Qumran, see E. Qimron, *The Hebrew of the Dead Sea Scrolls* (HSS 29; Atlanta, Ga.: Scholars Press, 1986), §200.11.

20. R. Kasher, *Targumic Toseftot to the Prophets* (Heb.) (Jerusalem: WUJS, 1996), 111.

the system of our text largely matches that of the Wisdom Text from Cairo,[21] which can certainly be described as Rabbinic Hebrew.

The fact that a psalm was intended for each day as well as the presence of strings of Biblical quotations make the songs parallel to Qumran compositions. The many verses of praise to God point to what a prayer must be according to the Targum: there the Hebrew word "to sing" is usually translated with the Aramaic "to praise."[22] It is not surprising that the songs also have some prophetic elements. Both the Targumim and rabbinic Judaism attribute prophetic value to songs and prayers.[23] At Qumran, the Psalms are considered as prophetic.[24] The important role played by songs in general is strongly emphasized. David is portrayed as a writer (I, 22) and the righteous as singers (I, 8). This emphasis on the song is also comparable with Qumran writings[25] and the Targum.[26]

What may speak against a Qumranic origin is the meaning of the word *ʿôlām* in I, 4, 17, II, 8 and III, 20. We translated it with "world," since the alternative translation ("You divided *eternity* into darkness and light") is improbable. This translation deviates from the way the word is used in the Old Testament and most of the times at Qumran. The meaning "world" occurs more frequently in later Hebrew, probably under the influence of *ha-ʿôlām habâ*, "the world to come."[27] The meaning "world" is therefore usual in rabbinic Hebrew.[28] Brin, however, remarks that the word is regularly used as a kind of superlative in the Qumran writings and he suspects that the shift towards the meaning of "world" had already started at Qumran.[29] We may conclude that the use of this word in this meaning does not narrow down the possible time of origin of the Songs of David very much.

One area in which a link with Qumran seems possible is that of the dualism in I, 4, which is actually toned down in the same line: even though light and darkness are opposites, God remains the Initiator. It is common knowledge that the Qumran Community was of the same view. For instance, we see two opposites in the global struggle between light and darkness in 1QS III, 20 – IV, 16, but also the qualification that eventually everything comes from God in 1QS III, 15-18, 22. However, strong parallels can also be found in rabbinic texts, such as *Gen. Rab.* 3:8.

The first song seems to be quite particularistic (e.g., I, 5). Also I, 21 seems to point to particularism, but this depends on the interpretation of the Hebrew word *ʾerets*, which we translated with "earth" elsewhere (I, 9, 16). Salvation is connected to Israel and the righteous to the Holy Land. The other three extant psalms have a more explicit interest in the world. The first Psalm mainly speaks concerning the past in which God divided the

21. G. W. Nebe, *Text und Sprache der hebräischen Weisheitsschrift aus der Kairoer Geniza* (Heidelberger orientalistische Studien 25; Frankfurt am Main: Lang, 1993), 233.

22. Van Staalduine-Sulman, *Targum of Samuel*, 180.

23. See the interpretation of the songs of Hannah, David and Solomon in *Tg. 1 Sam* 2:1-10; *2 Sam* 22; 23:1-8; *1 Kgs* 5:12-13.

24. S. Berrin, "Qumran Pesharim," in *Biblical Interpretation at Qumran* (ed. M. Henze; Grand Rapids: Eerdmans, 2005), 110-33, esp. p. 121; G. J. Brooke, "Thematic Commentaries on Prophetic Scriptures," in *ibid.*, 134-157, esp. p. 135.

25. See 1QS X, 9; 4Q511 1 3-5; 10 7-9.

26. See *Tg. 1 Kgs* 5:12.

27. Qimron, *Hebrew of the Dead Sea Scrolls*, §500.1.

28. M. Pérez Fernández, *An Introductory Grammar of Rabbinic Hebrew* (trans. J. Elwolde; Leiden: Brill, 1997), 24, 83, 173. Also in the Wisdom Text from the Cairo Geniza, see Nebe, *Text und Sprache*, 310-13.

29. G. Brin, *The Concept of Time in the Bible and the Dead Sea Scrolls* (STDJ 39; Leiden: Brill, 2001), 286-89 (as superlative), 289-93 (shift of meaning).

darkness from the light, both physically and ethically. The three other Psalms principally concern the future, in which God presents a messianic king. The division between darkness and light is not abolished, for the nations will turn away from their religious darkness and turn to the light of God's Torah, through David his servant. Dating this kind of theology has its difficulties. The particularistic parts strongly resemble Qumranic ideas. The Targum is also quite particularistic, but not fully.[30] It should be noted that (proto-)Pharisaic literature (Judith, *Psalms of Solomon*) contains obviously universalistic tendencies, in contrast with (proto-)Essene literature (not only Qumran but also *Jubilees*).[31]

There is one peculiarity in the description of King David: the expression of his gratitude concerning his exaltation (III, 12-16). The image of David's exaltation above all nations is complemented in I, 19 and 23 by a reference to his kingship over all nations. Of course David was king of Israel, but the concept of kingship over all nations has eschatological connotations, which are made even more explicit with the words "for ever." This idea occurs only rarely in the intertestamental and the rabbinic periods. The passages in the Qumran writings that match this most closely are actually descriptions of David's *descendants*.[32] The idea that David's offspring shall reign forever also occurs in *Pss. Sol.* 17:4. There are references to David's eschatological kingship, in a Messianic context, but less often than one would expect. The Songs of David seem therefore closer to the Targum[33] and the early rabbinic writings[34] than to the Qumran Community, although in the latest period of the Qumran Community the members of the community showed a great interest in a royal, Davidic Messiah.[35] A growth of this kind of text after the turn of the era is seen by several scholars.[36]

The emphasis on David as the deliverer of God's Word and the Servant of the Lord does not fit the Qaraite theology (although the manuscript was found in their genizah),

---

30. See *Tg. Ob* 21 (a universalistic interpretation which the MT does not require); *Zech* 2:15; 14:9 (Targum does not attempt to interpret a universalistic text as more restrictive). E. Levine, *The Aramaic Version of the Bible: Contents and Context* (BZAW 174; Berlin: De Gruyter, 1988), 184-85 points out the contempt for the pagans, which does however make space for proselytes.

31. Cf. R. T. Beckwith, "The Pre-History and Relationships of the Pharisees, Sadducees and Essenes: A Tentative Reconstruction," *RevQ* 11 (1982): 3-46, esp. pp. 29, 33-34.

32. See 4Q174 1 I, 11-13; 4Q252 V, 3-4; 4Q161 III, 18-22. These texts are related to our text, but they are speaking about "the shoot of David," and this expression cannot mean David himself.

33. See *Tg. 2 Sam* 23:5; this can however also be interpreted as referring to his dynasty. The phenomenon of David's eschatological rule is actually biblical; see Ps 89:28; Jer 30:9; Ezek 34:23; 37:24.

34. See *Gen. Rab.* 96 (New Version), based on Ezek 37:25, and *y. Ber.* 2.3. Cf. J. Klausner, "The Source and Beginnings of the Messianic Idea," in *Messianism in the Talmudic Era* (ed. L. Landman; New York: Ktav, 1979), 25-37, esp. p. 21; and his "The Name and Personality of the Messiah" in the same book, 215-26, esp. p. 219.

35. G. J. Brooke, "Kingship and Messianism in the Dead Sea Scrolls," in *King and Messiah in Israel and the Ancient Near East* (ed. J. Day; JSOTSup 270; Sheffield: Sheffield Academic Press, 1998), 434-55, esp. pp. 447-48, 451, 453-55; K. E. Pomykala, *The Davidic Dynasty Tradition in Early Judaism: Its History and Significance for Messianism* (SBLEJL 7; Atlanta, Ga.: Scholars Press, 1995), 214-15; K. R. Atkinson, "On the Use of Scripture in the Development of Militant Davidic Messianism at Qumran: New Light from *Psalms of Solomon* 17," in *The Interpretation of Scripture in Early Judaism and Christianity: Studies in Language and Tradition* (ed. C. A. Evans; JSPSup 33; Sheffield: Sheffield Academic Press, 2000), 106-23 (*passim*).

36. E.g. J. Zimmermann, *Messianische Texte aus Qumran: Königliche, priesterliche und prophetische Messiasvorstellungen in den Schriftfunden von Qumran* (WUNT 2.104; Tübingen: Mohr Siebeck, 1998), 448-52; E. Puech, *La croyance des Esséniens en la vie future: immortalité, résurrection, vie éternelle? Histoire d'une croyance dans le judaïsme ancien* (EB NS 22; Paris: Gabalda, 1993), 772.

which gives more attention to the person of Moses.[37] This emphasis seems to indicate progressive revelation rather than a strong emphasis on the Law of Moses.

Angels are mentioned in passing in I, 23. They do feature, but not prominently. This corresponds with what is usual in Qumran writings[38] and in the "official" Targums.[39]

Interesting in the first psalm is that the end is said to be imminent: "I have brought nigh the end and You will no longer delay it" (I, 14). The most striking element of I, 14 is the use of the past tense: at the time of writing the end has already come near and cannot be delayed. This imminence is also found in Qumran writings, where the sense of a pre-eschatological situation can be observed.[40] This is more or less unknown in the Targum.[41]

Looking back, we can say that the Songs of David, found in the Cairo Genizah of the Qaraite community, have several characteristics of writings from the Second Temple period or early rabbinic times. Many of these features concur with the writings of the Qumran Community, but several others speak against this connection.[42] The same applies to connections with the Targum, the apocrypha and the official rabbinic writings. These characteristics deny a later Qaraite origin, the more so since the emphasis on David as Messiah and Law-giver is not attested in their theology. Therefore, an origin during the latter period of the Qumran Community seems a valid option.

The question that remains is how the text arrived in Cairo. A Syriac letter from 800 seems to indicate that a number of manuscripts were found at Qumran around the year 790, which ended up with the Qaraites in Cairo via Jerusalem.[43]

Literary Context

The Songs of David stand in a literary tradition of psalms and prayers, especially those of the Old Testament Psalter and the idea of daily psalms. The community of Qumran assumed that King David himself had composed liturgical Psalms, one for each day. This assumption is expressed in 11Q5. The last phase of the Qumran Community is known for its large number of liturgical manuscripts. It is our hypothesis that 11Q5 (or similar ideas in other Jewish communities) gave rise to the making of these compositions, a series of Psalms for every day of the year.[44]

---

37. J. Alobaidi, *Le commentaire des Psaumes par le qaraïte Salmon Ben Yeruham. Psaumes 1-10. Introduction, édition, traduction* (La Bible dans l'histoire 1; Bern: Lang, 1996), 101-102.

38. See 1QM and 4/11QŠŠ, but also 4Q511 2 I, 8; 4Q185 1-2 II, 6; 4Q418 55 8; 4Q504 1-2 VII, 6. Similar angelology in *1 Enoch* and *Jubilees*. Apparently the Qumran writings in question are mostly early, but 1QM is relatively recent.

39. The official Targums avoid them, the Palestinian Targums on the Pentateuch do not; *Tg. Ps* does not either, but it is less enthusiastic than the Apocrypha: Levine, *Aramaic Version*, 66, 71.

40. Cf. the discussion of CD in G. W. Lorein, *The Antichrist Theme in the Intertestamental Period* (JSPSup 44; London and New York: T.&T. Clark, 2003), 163-79.

41. Levine, *Aramaic Version*, 220-21.

42. Especially the universalism, although this could be caused by a larger Pharisaic influence: cf. J. Murphy-O'Connor, "La genèse littéraire de la *Règle de la Communauté*," *RevB* 76 (1969): 528-49, esp. p. 548; Lorein, *Antichrist Theme*, 196.

43. O. Braun, "Ein Brief des Katholikos Timotheos I. über biblische Studien des 9. Jahrhunderts," *Oriens Christianus* 1 (1901) : 299-313, esp. pp. 304-307.

44. See also "énoncées par, ou découlant de [!] la col. XXVII 9-10 du rouleau 11QPs[a]" in E. Puech, "Les deux derniers Psaumes davidiques du rituel d'exorcisme, 11QPsAp[a] IV 4 – V 14," in *The Dead Sea Scrolls: Forty Years of Research* (ed. D. Dimant and U. Rappaport; STDJ 10; Jerusalem: Magnes; Leiden: Brill, 1992), 64-89, esp. p. 78. Cf. Philonenko and Marx, "Quatre « chants » pseudo-davidiques," 387: "une date de composition plus tardive que celle des psaumes pseudo-davidiques de la grotte XI."

Bibliography

Elwolde, J. F. "Developments in Hebrew Vocabulary." Pages 17-55 in *The Hebrew of the Dead Sea Scrolls and Ben Sira*. Edited by T. Muraoka and J. F. Elwolde. STDJ 26. Leiden: Brill, 1997.

Fleischer, E. "Medieval Hebrew Poems in Biblical Style" (Heb.). Pages 201-248 in *Studies in Judaica*. Edited by M. A. Friedman. Te'uda 7. Tel-Aviv: University Publishing Projects, 1991.

Flusser, D. "Psalms, Hymns and Prayers." Pages 551-577 in *Jewish Writings of the Second Temple Period*. Edited by M. E. Stone. CRINT II 2. Assen: Van Gorcum, 1984.

Flusser, D., and S. Safrai. "The Apocryphal 'Songs of David'" (Heb.). Pages 83-105 in *Bible Studies, Y.M. Grintz in Memoriam*. Edited by B. Uffenheimer. Tel Aviv: Tel Aviv University Press, 1982. Translated as: "The Apocryphal Psalms of David." Pages 258-282 in *Judaism of the Second Temple Period I. Qumran and Apocalypticism*. Translated by A. Yadin. Grand Rapids: Eerdmans; Jerusalem: Magnes; and Jerusalem: Perspective, 2007.

Harkavy, A. E. "Prayers in the Style of the Songs of the Psalms by an Anonymous Person" (Heb.). *Ha-Goren. Abhandlungen über die Wissenschaft des Judenthums* 3 (1902): 82-85.

Lorein, G. W., and E. van Staalduine-Sulman. "CšD II, 4–IV, 9. A Song of David for Each Day." *Hen* 31 (2009): 387-410.

__________."A Song of David for Each Day. The Provenance of the *Songs of David*." *RevQ* 22/85 (2005): 33-59.

Philonenko, M., and A. Marx. "Quatre « chants » pseudo-davidiques trouvés dans la gueniza du Caire et d'origine esséno-qoumrânienne." *RHPR* 77 (1997): 385-406.

Stec, D. M. *The Genizah Psalms. A Study of MS 798 of the Antonin Collection*. Ètudes sur le Judaïsme Médiéval 57. Leiden: Brill, 2013. (This publication came to our attention too late to be taken into account.)

Songs of David

First Song (CšD I, 1–II, 4a; first two verses missing)

Ezek 21:8-9 [Evv 21:3-4]; CD XX, 20-21; 1QH^a XII, 39 [*olim* IV, 38]

. . .
I, 1 Revealed before Your face[a] are the righteous and the wicked
and You do not seek human testimonies about them.

I, 7, II, 9, IV, 12, 19, 24; *Pss. Sol.* 17:10; 1QS XI, 14-15; *Tg. Onq., Ps-J.* Gen 18:25

2 Judging generations and ruling in righteousness,
He makes known on the ways of every living one.[b]
3 You desired righteousness and rejected wrong-doing

Ps 5:6a [Evv 5:5a]

and the foolish shall not (be able to) stand before Your glory.
4 And You divided the world between darkness and light,
and between the unclean and the clean and between righteousness and deceit.
5 You drove all sons of aliens out from among Your nation
and You cleansed Your flock of unclean animals.
6 You gave Your powerful wisdom to Your servant,[c]

III, 1a, 4b; CD III, 15

for (You) gave insight in everything according to the wishes of Your will.
7 You have planted righteous deeds in a faithful land,
and You have multiplied justice in eternities.
8 All those who serve Your Name will learn[d] a song,
those who believe the words of Your servant.
9 As great as all the earth they will increase their righteousness,
and their good deeds, which they loved in their hearts.
10 You guided their paths according to Your command
and You judged their strength in accordance with all Your wondrous works.
11 For ever, (yes) for ever they will serve Your Name
and for ever and always they will extol Your Name.

12 Who is like Your deeds and who is like Your works?

IV, 8; Isa 40:25

And who is as You as regards the greatness of all Your deeds?
13 You have pardoned and forgiven all our sins
and in love You have covered all our transgressions.

---

a. As in the Targum, anthropomorphisms are not suppressed, but are often used to create a buffer between God and mankind: the extant text is more reverential than "Revealed before You." Also below in II, 11a, 12b, 15a, 25a, III, 3b, 22 (= Job 12:10), IV, 26a.

b. Conjecture: "knowing the ways of every living one." For the last part of this expression, cf. 1QH^a VII, 35 (*olim* XV, 22).

c. David.

d. Or: "teach."

14 You prophesied by Your spirit through the mouth of Your servant,[a]
for I[b] have brought nigh the end and You will no longer delay it.
Isa 60:22; Sir 36:8a (Heb.); 4Q385 3; *Pss. Sol.* 17:45; *4 Ezra* 4:26; *2 Bar.* 83:1; *Barn.* 4:3
15 From the beginning You swore to David Your servant
and You anointed Jesse's root[c] with Your mercy.
Ps 89:4b [Evv 89:3b]
16 You sustained his arm with Your holiness,
for he established Your praise up to the ends of the earth.
17 You established his name as a pillar of the world,
and as a repairer of a breach and as a re-builder of ruins.
Exod. Rab. 15.7; *b. Yoma* 38b; *b. Sanh.* 26b; *Tg. Cant* 5:15
18 The rejected cornerstone, which the builders rejected,
Isa 58:12
rose[d] to be the head of all nations.[e]
Ps 118:22
19 You made him inherit turban[f] and crown with joy
and You called out his name to be praised among all nations.[g]
20 Righteousness and justice You have multiplied in his days
and well-being and blessings without number.
21 All the righteous chosen ones shout for joy before Your face,
for they rejoice in the <de>sirable la<nd>.
22 By his mouth You sanctified the great Name,
and all day long he recites[h] Your powerful songs.[i]
23 You made his greatness (as) the great number of all angels[j]
and You appointed him king of all nations for ever.

24 Before his face You broke all the kings of Midian[k]
and caused all those who hated his soul to sink into the depths.[l]
25 You firmly pressed his right hand against his sword
and You strengthened his arm against all the heroes of Kedar.[m]
26 His foot does not stumble, for he trusted Your Name,
and his strength does not falter, for You helped him in love.
27 Blessed is the man who trusts Your word,
Ps 40:5a [Evv 40:4a]

---

a. Cf. 11Q5 XXVII, 11; Flavius Josephus, *A.J.* VI 166; *Tg.* 2 Sam 23:2; *Tg.* Ps 45:3 about David speaking by s/Spirit of prophecy of divine origin; cf. *Tg.* Ps 49:16; 51:13; 103:1. See also CD V, 2, however, as a statement that David had not received special revelation.

b. Conjecture: "You."

c. David (see 1 Sam 16:1); interpreted messianically in Isa 11:1-10.

d. Conjecture: "did You raise."

e. This image is based on Ps 118:22. In the New Testament it is applied to Jesus Christ: see Mark 12:10-12; Acts 4:11; 1 Pet 2:7. The Targum applies it to David: see *Tg. Ps* 118:22 (possibly as Messiah; cf. *Tg. Zech* 10:4).

f. Honourable headdress, e.g., for priests.

g. The *Songs of David* are exceptional in attributing the eschatological kingship to David himself (rather than to one of his descendants, as in *Pss. Sol.* 17:4; 4Q174 1 I, 10-13; 4Q252 V, 2, 4; 4QpIsa[a] III, 18-22)—it does, however, perhaps occur in *Tg. 2 Sam* 23:5. See also below, IV, 4. For the historical David, cf. 1 Sam 16:12; *Pss. Sol.* 17:4.

h. This translation to be preferred over "counts" and "writes."

i. Cf. 1QS X, 9 for the importance of singing.

j. The occurrence of angels corresponds with what is usual at Qumran and in the official Targums: they do feature, but not prominently.

k. Group of tribes east of the Gulf of Aqabah.

l. For God slaying David's enemies, cf. 1QM XI, 1-2.

m. Tribe in the Syro-Arabic desert; cf. Isa 21:17.

for ever, (yes) for ever his face will not be ashamed.
Ps 27:7b II, 1 My soul trusts in You; *be merciful to me and answer me.*
Blessed are You, LORD,[a] the God who answers His servant during the entire
Ps 118:5 time of his calling.[b]
2 God of mercy, have mercy on us.
Blessed be the majestic name of His kingship, forever and always.
Ps 72:19a | *1 En.* 39:13 3 *Blessed be His majestic name for ever* and always.
Blessed be the LORD, the God of Israel, from everlasting to everlasting.
Ps 106:48 4 *And all the people say: "Amen."*[c]

Second Song (CšD II, 4b–III, 9)

II, 4b In the month Iyyar,[d] on the second (day) of the month, I surveyed in a vision and (in) all His prophecies,[e] 5 and I prayed before the face of the LORD and I said:

6 Your mercy, O LORD our God, be on the slaughtered cattle,
Ezek 34:2-3, 23-24; Zech 11:5; *1 En.* 89:65, 69 which the shepherds slaughtered and did not spare.
7 Bind up the battered bones in Your mercy
IV, 1b and heal in love the fractures of Your heritage,
8 for You made me for the well-being of the world before Your face
Isa 42:6; 49:6; Luke 2:31-32; Acts 13:47 and You made me a light for the nations by Your power.
9 All the peoples shall declare Your glory,
for they shall see Your righteousness at the side of the one who is faithful to You.[f]
10 Governors shall gather and all the kings of the earth,
dignitaries of the world and rulers of mankind,
11 to see the heroic deeds of Your right hand
and to understand the aim of Your holy words.
12 And they all will know Your strength,
Isa 45:7b for Your hand, *O LORD, is doing all these things.*[g]
13 The righteous one rejoices, for he sees it
and he exalts with songs and hymns before Your face.
14 All the inhabitants of the world will learn from me
and they will return to Your way and serve You with faithfulness,

---

a. In contrast to the general tendency in literature of the Second Temple Period, in this text the name of God occurs in its normal form. Also below in II, 5, 6, 12, 16; III, 9, 11, 18, 19, 20; IV, 15, 17.

b. Cf. Kh. Al As'ad and M. Gawlikowski, *The Inscriptions in the Museum of Palmyra* (Palmyra and Warsaw: s.n., 1997), nos. 9, 14 and 16 (250-252 C.E.).

c. Same ending in III, 8-9 and in IV, 14-15; this points to a liturgical use. It cannot be by chance that the endings of the Second Book and the Fourth Book of the Psalms have been chosen: in this way the poet gives added weight to his own poems. The verse following Ps 72:19 (i.e., 72:20) will also have been in the mind of the poet!

d. April/May, no festival. The use of the name of a month is rare in Qumran, but not unknown: cf. 4Q318 2 II, 1.

e. God gives visions and prophecies to David: cf. I, 14.

f. Or: "Your confidant."

g. The "hand" is added in Isa. 66:2; for the idea, cf. *Tg. 1 Sam* 2:6.

15 and they will come before Your face with thanksgiving,
with melodies and with songs and hymns. Ps 95:2
16 They will magnify Your glory in the midst of their camps
and they will know that You, O LORD, created them.
17 All the servants of an image will be ashamed,
for they are wise in their statues.
18 They will no longer serve idols
and they will no longer kneel down before the works of their hands *T. Levi* 18:9a
19 *and the idols will disappear altogether,*[a] Isa 2:18
their desirable things will vanish forever,
20 but You will be magnified and sanctified from the mouth of all Your works,
from now on and until eternity.
21 For Your servant tells Your wonders
in accordance with his strength and the spirit of his words.
22 For there is no joy with me in any word
but in Your words and the appearance of Your glory.[b]
23 Do not hide Yourself from me in Your mercy for the many,
and do not let me die for the sake of (Your) love for them.[c]
24 For *I love to stay in Your house,* Ps 26:8a
more than in all the royal palaces.
25 The instruction of Your mouth is better to me
than a thousand thousands of talents of gold.
26 The sanctification of Your word is better to me
than all the precious vessels.[d]
27 The commandments of Your will are better to me than all the gems
and precious pearls of kings.[e]
III, 1 Blessed is the one who finds glory in the wishes of Your will
and for Your sake I will ask so from Your face.
2 And this is my wish concerning all my requests:
that I may continually be before Your face. Ps 27:4
3 And I make go[f] in Your righteousness without sin[g] and I follow

---

a. Cf.—besides Isa 2:18—*1 En.* 91:9 (about the idols); Tob 14:6; Wis 14:11; *T. Mos.* 10:7. That evil in general will disappear is often attested: 1QH[a] VI 26-27 (*olim* XIV, 15-16), 1Q27 1 I, 5-7, *1 En.* 10:16-22; 107:1; *4 Ezra* 6:27-28; *2 Bar.* 73:4.

b. Cf. the idea of *śimḥat hattôrâh*, "the rejoicing in the law."

c. Philonenko and Marx (p. 397) give a smoother, but grammatically more difficult interpretation: "Do not hide from me Your many mercies, and do not let me die, on the grounds of love for (Your mercies)."

d. Obviously, the author of this text did not know the practice of calling the Torah scrolls "precious vessels," e.g., in a *Tosefta Targum* to 1 Sam 10:22 and in *y. Taan.* 2:1 (65a).

e. The words for "gems" and "pearls" occur elsewhere with this meaning only from rabbinic times.

f. Conjecture: "I will go."

g. The sinlessness of the Messiah is mentioned in *Pss. Sol.* 17:36-38. Abraham, Isaac and Jacob are called sinless in Pr Man 8. David more or less fits in this category (11Q5 XXVII, 3, although the word used there (*tāmîm*; cf. below on IV 23) cannot be translated as "perfect, sinless"). Human sinlessness is generally denied (cf., e.g., 1QS III, 21-25, 1QH[a] XII, 30-32 (*olim* IV, 29-31); and David's sinlessness in particular is denied in Sir 47:11, mentioning the forgiveness of his sins, while *Tg. Ps* 51 does not attempt to let the reader think otherwise.

in Your faithfulness every day, according to what is right in Your eyes.
4 Do not refuse me my petition
11Q5 XXIV, 4-5 (5 and grant my request according to the wishes of Your will.
Apoc. Syr. Pss. 155:3-4) 5 I will stand on them forever
to know all Your righteous ways.
6 Blessed be God Who is doing all this,
blessed be the One Who works out all these things.
Pss. Sol. 17:4 7 Blessed be He Who has chosen His servant
2 Sam 23:5 and will fulfil all the wishes of my heart.
8 Blessed be the majestic Name of His kingship forever,
Ps 72:19a *blessed be His majestic Name for ever* and always.
9 *Blessed be the* Lord, *the God of Israel, from everlasting to everlasting.*
Ps 106:48 *And all the people say: "Amen."*

Third Song (CšD III, 10–IV, 15)

10 On the third (day) of the month Iyyar I surveyed in a vision and (in) all His prophecies, 11 and I prayed before the face of the Lord and I said:

12 Blessed be the One Who makes inherit and makes rich
1 Sam 2:7 and blessed the One Who humbles and exalts,
13 Who raises the weak from the dust
1 Sam 2:8a and lifts the afflicted from the ash heap,
1 Sam 2:8a; *1 En.* 45:3; 14 and Who makes his[a] throne great above all princes
51:3; 62:5 and magnifies his strength above all rulers
1 Sam 2:10b 15 and Who gives him every desire of kings,
the elite of nations and the treasures of kings,
16 daughters of kings to his honour
2 Sam 5:13 and daughters of Jerusalem for his majestic beauty.[bc]
Luke 1:48 17 All the ages will call him blessed
III, 22; 2 Sam 22:44-45 and before his face, all resisting powers of the earth shall bow
Joel 2:21 18 and they will trust in the Lord, *for He accomplished great things,*
Acts 17:30 and they will no longer wander in confusion and inattention,
19 for they will all know the Lord,
Jer 31:34; Heb 8:11; from the greatest of humanity to the least of mankind.
L.A.B. 51:4 20 For the Lord judges the entire world,
humiliating the one and exalting the other.[d]
21 According to His will, He gives,

---

a. In the light of III, 13, this concerns the throne of the *humble*.

b. It is peculiar that this text mentions David's polygamy without any comment; cf., contrarily, CD IV, 20–V, 6.

The beauty of David is described in 1 Sam 16:18 and 17:42. The beauty of the Messiah is a later theme, cf., e.g., *Tg. Ps* 45:3 and perhaps *Tg. 1 Sam* 17:42-43 (tosefta).

c. The expression of David's gratitude concerning his exaltation (III, 12-16) deviates from the general Jewish attitude (2 Sam 7:18; 11Q5 XIX [= 11Q6]; *Tg. 2 Sam* 7:18 ["I am not worthy"]): he gives thanks for the exaltation rather than supplicating on account of his humbleness. It does, however, concur with Psalm 151 (adopted in 11Q5 XXVIII), Sir. 47:2-11.

d. As with lines 12-14, 19, a reminder of the line of thought in Hannah's Prayer. God judging the world is not specifically mentioned in the canonical version, but is added in *Tg. 1 Sam* 2:8-9.

and to the needy of mankind[a] He arranges a heritage.
22 For *the soul of all the living ones is in His hand*
and the spirit of all flesh kneels before Him.[b] Job 12:10
23 *Sing to Him, sing for Him a psalm,*
consider all His miracles. Ps 105:2 = 1 Chr 16:9
24 Sing at all times to His Name,
for beauty and strength are fitting to Him,
25 Who saves from anguish the soul of the one who loves Him,
and the spirit of the one who is loyal to Him, from the hand of those who cause harm. Jer 20:13
26 For he trusted in His Name and in the glory of a vision[c]
and in His holy words and on all the paths of life.
27 We will serve His Name forever
and report His strength for ever and always.
IV, 1 *For He heals the brokenhearted*
and He binds up the bones of the oppressed Ps 147:3
2 and He turned his[d] mourning into gladness, Jer 31:13b
trembling and fear into great forms of trust. 1QH[a] XII, 34 [*olim* IV, 33]
3 *For the earth is His, and everything in it,*
the world, and all who live in it. Ps 24:1; cf. Ps 89:12 [Evv 89:11]; 1 Sam 2:8b
4 For from before His face He commanded concerning His servant
his royal majesty and glory and magnificence,
5 The One Who wants the good for His people
and sent the healer and healed their flesh. Ps. 107:20a
6 And He consolidated His instruction through the mouth of His servant
and the commandments of His word through the hands of the one who trusts Him.
7 He multiplied wisdom and insight in his heart
and the greatness of his holiness without number.
8 Who is like Him and who is His equal?
He does not forget the outcry of the needy Ps 9:13b [Evv 9:12b]
9 and remembers His mercy over the afflicted and the weak
and also (over) me, for I have thought about the strength and the power
of His reign and the beauty of His vigour.
10 Night and day I stand before His face
and I praise His remembrance of all His works.[e]
11 You are praised and exalted, O Lord of all generations,

a. Cf., e.g., 1QpHab XII, 3 and 4QpPs[a] II, 10 (with the word "to inherit" in l. 9), where "the needy" is clearly a self-designation of the group. The idea of "the needy" as "group of believers" is already present in the Hebrew Bible (Isa 29:19; Ps 37:14; 40:18 [Evv 40:17] about David!; 69:34 [Evv 69:33]; 109:31) and also in other writings (*Pss. Sol.* 15:1; *T. Jud.* 25:4; Matt 5:3 [cf. v. 5, for the combination with "to inherit"]).

b. Cf. 1QH[a] IX, 29-30 (*olim* I, 27-28), where, however, God is recognized as Creator.

c. Conjecture: "and in the glory of His appearance."

d. Singular (strange after the pl. in IV, 1): probably refers to the loyal one in III, 25-26.

e. The text means: "I praise Him because He remembers His creatures." Cf. Ps 145:9 for this construction.

You are sanctified and have shown Yourself glorious as ruler over all His[a] works.
12 You will be confessed as the Only One,[b] O my King, from the mouth of all who serve You,
5 Apoc. Syr. Pss. 155:7 ruling in righteousness and judging in truth.
13 Blessed be You, O Lord God, please! In His mercy may He remain mindful
Ps 89:29 [Evv 89:28]; Isa 55:3; Acts 13:34 of the covenant of His servant forever.
14 Blessed be the majestic Name of His kingship for ever and always;
Ps 72:19a *blessed be His majestic Name for ever* and always.
15 *Blessed be the Lord, the God of Israel, from everlasting to everlasting.*
Ps 106:48 *And all the people say: "Amen."*

Fourth Song (CšD IV, 16-27; end missing)

16 On the fourth (day) of the month Iyyar I surveyed in the spirit in a holy vision and (in) all His prophecies and I prayed before the face of the 17 Lord and I said:[c]

18 Blessed (be He) for He has broken the wicked,
1 Sam 2:1, 4, 10 but He has made the horn of the righteous stand firm.
19 And His knowledge and His wisdom are in all my heart,[d]
for You are the One Who is ruling in righteousness,
20 for no deceitful right emanates from before Your face,
but only truth and faithfulness.
21 You give to man according to his ways,
and according to the fruit of his deeds, You repay him.[e]
22 There is no deceit in all Your deeds
and there is no lie in all Your word.
23 Your work is all in one piece[f]
and injustice is not found in what You do.

---

a. The sudden alternation of 2 m.s. and 3 m.s. is not uncommon in prayers.

b. Difficult text. Flusser and Safrai (p. 91) interpreted as "The servants of God set apart the Name in their prayers." Elwolde (p. 26 n. 38) as "may you, O my king, be the object of special address from the mouth of all your ministers." Philonenko and Marx (p. 388; in French): "May it be said that You are one." This last translation points to an anti-trinitarian view, but it is only one possible translation.

c. Although these lines can be compared with the introductions to the other Songs (II, 4b-5 and III, 10-11), the parallel with rabbinic data on seeing in the Holy Spirit (*Lev. Rab.* 21:8; 37:3) is very strong here.

d. Cf. 4Q511 18 II, 8 (cf. 28+29 3) for the knowledge in the heart. The fact that these hymns are numbered (see 4Q511 8 4 and 42 4) makes this text a parallel to our Songs, although there are no clues that their subject might be identified with David. For David's wisdom, cf. 11Q5 XXVII, 2; compare, however, CD V, 2-5, where David's wisdom is minimized.

e. For the theme of individual repayment, cf. 1QS X, 18; *Tg. Ps* 10:14; *Jub.* 5:15-16; *b. Sanh.* 27b; *b. Ber.* 7a. This theme is not necessarily in contradiction to predestination, which was alluded to in the First Song, I, 21: cf. 1QH[a] XIII, 7-8 (*olim* V, 5-6).

f. This line can be connected with the theme of "not being double, integrity" (*haplotēs*) in Hellenistic Jewish literature, especially in the *Testament of Issachar*, although the Hebrew word which is used here (*tāmîm*; cf. above on III, 3) is normally connected with "purposefulness" (*teleiotēs*). The two themes, however, are closely interrelated.

24 You have multiplied Your justice like a growing stream,
and You made Your righteousness bud as blessed seed.
25 Blessed is the one who is pure according to Your holiness:
he recounts Your glory the entire day.
26 My help (comes) from before Your majestic face, Ps 121:2a
to eat forever and to stand in Your will.
27 For You ...[a] the day.
Blessed are they who observe Your commandments.

a. The text is illegible here and cannot be reconstructed for lack of a sequel. Perhaps: "For You <circumcise my heart> today" (cf. Deut 10:16; 30:6; 1QpHab xi 13; 4Q504 4 11; and *Tg. Josh* 5:2-8 in MS T.-S. B13,12 from the same Cairo Genizah, about circumcising [the foreskin of] the heart).

The Aramaic Song of the Lamb (The Dialogue between David and Goliath)

A new translation and introduction

by C. T. R. Hayward

The Aramaic Song of the Lamb was discovered in 1993 by Johannes C. de Moor and Eveline van Staalduine-Sulman, following their observation that a *Tosefta Targum* attached to 1 Sam 17:43 represented an acrostic poetic composition describing David as a lamb who defeats the bear Goliath. Further research led them to conclude that this *Tosefta Targum* had once been part of a larger work, much of which is now lost; but sufficient evidence was forthcoming, they argued, to indicate that a fragment of *Tosefta Targum* attached to 1 Sam 17:8 (another acrostic), along with Targum of 2 Sam 23:8, had also belonged to a *Song of the Lamb*. These several part-texts, they maintained, might be identified as the surviving remains of the poem of that name, mentioned at Rev 15:3 in tandem with the Song of Moses. This *Aramaic Song of the Lamb* appears to reflect material dating from around the time of the Book of Revelation, since it presents some striking affinities with traditions preserved in the late-first-century or early-second-century-C.E. work *Liber Antiquitatum Biblicarum* falsely ascribed to Philo (hereafter *L.A.B.*).[1]

Contents

The *Tosefta Targum* of 1 Sam 17:43 expands Goliath's question to David, "Am I a dog, that you come to me with sticks?" into a dialogue beginning with an urgent plea from Goliath: David, described as a lamb who is very beautiful, should depart and avoid a battle with an offspring of lions. Goliath reminds David that he is not yet married, is possessed of good looks, and stands to inherit a kingdom: he will lose all these advantages if he fights with the bear Goliath. Goliath's words suggest that he is physically attracted to David; and he begs him to return to his former state, and to recognize the impossibility of defeating Goliath. David replies that God will save the lamb from the bear's mouth, and contrasts his reliance on God with Goliath's idolatry (see also 1 Sam 17:45). In addition, David refers to Saul, whose humility Goliath has reviled, as an element in the giant's forthcoming defeat. Goliath's reply repeats his earlier remarks about David's beauty and graceful appearance, with the implication that it would be tragic were he to become a Philistine slave.

Five stones chosen by David to hurl at Goliath now vie with one another for precedence. Each stone is inscribed with a name: one is ascribed to Abraham, the others severally to Isaac, Jacob, Moses, and Aaron. Abraham's stone speaks, and demands the privilege of being the first to be cast at Goliath, when David has a vision of the angels consulting about Goliath, and the Lord chooses the stone with Aaron's name to be hurled at the giant,

1. de Moor and van Staalduine-Sulman, "The Aramaic Song of the Lamb," 266-79; van Staalduine-Sulman, "The Aramaic Song of the Lamb," 256-292; *Targum of Samuel*, 350-54, 364-83, 682-86. On *L.A.B.*, see Harrington, "Pseudo-Philo" in *OTP*, 2:297-303.

since Aaron pursues peace. The collapse of Goliath is then recorded in language recalling the fate of Belshazzar, king of Babylon (Dan 5:6), and the composition ends with a brief expression of hope for the future.

The *Tosefta Targum* of 1 Sam 17:8 amplifies Goliath's challenge to Israel's armies. The giant introduces himself as the one who had killed Eli's two sons and carried off the Ark of the Covenant to the house of Dagon, where it stayed for seven months. He insists that the Lord did not defeat him; and that in every war undertaken by the Philistines he had led their armies and had been victorious. Even so, the Philistines had not made him a captain. Israel, however, had appointed as king the nonentity Saul, a man without a military record of any kind. Goliath ends by challenging Saul to battle if he be a heroic man; otherwise, he urges Israel to select another man to fight with him.

Targum Jonathan of 2 Sam 23:8 expounds a verse, whose original Hebrew is mightily obscure and seems to catalogue the names of persons otherwise unknown, with special reference to David as a military man surrounded by prophets and elders. He is anointed, nobly born, and handsome. He possesses wisdom, intelligence, and strength. He is victorious in battle; and his prowess extends to his ability to dispatch eight hundred men at one time.

Manuscripts and Printed Editions

A critical printed edition of the Aramaic texts making up *Song of the Lamb* was published in 1959 by Alexander Sperber.[2] This edition, however, was unable to take into account witnesses to the Babylonian Targum tradition, an omission rectified in 1987 by E. Martínez Borobio.[3] The researches of Eveline van Staalduine-Sulman have further increased the volume of textual material available.[4] The translation given here is based on Sperber's edition, with reference to significant manuscript readings noted by van Staalduine-Sulman.

(A) Sperber records two witnesses to the *Tosefta Targum* of 1 Sam 17:43. The first, Ms. p.116 of the Montefiore Library, Jews' College, London, he designated by the *siglum* c; the second, the printed edition of the Former Prophets published in Leiria in 1494, by the *siglum* d. The readings of d appear to agree with c; but d's text is much shorter than c, extending only to the words "the form of your face" at the beginning of Goliath's second speech. van Staalduine-Sulman reported the presence of this *Tosefta Targum* also in Ms 1 of the University of Salamanca, a text written by Alfonso de Zamora in 1532: this divides the text of the *Tosefta Targum* between 1 Sam 17, verses 42 and 43.[5] This witness is referred to here as Ms.Sal. 1.This Tosefta has been studied in detail by Kasher, who records its appearance also in Codex Munich 5 attached to 1 Sam 17:42, there provided with an introductory link to what precedes.[6]

(B) *Tosefta Targum* 1 Sam 17:8 begins in the middle of *Targum Jonathan*'s translation of the verse, at the words "Am I not the Philistine?" Sperber records its presence in Ms. Or. 1471 of the British Library, first marginal note (*siglum* w_1); Ms. Add. 26879 of the British Library (*siglum* a); *Biblia Rabbinica* of Bomberg, Venice 1515/17 (*siglum* b); Ms. p. 116 of the Montefiore Library, Jews' College (*siglum* c); the printed edition of the Former Prophets published at Leiria in 1494 (*siglum* d); and the printed edition of R. David Kimhi's

2. Sperber, *The Bible in Aramaic,* 2:127, 130-31, 207.

3. Martínez Borobio, *Targum Jonatán de los Profetas Primeros.*

4. van Staalduine-Sulman, *Targum of Samuel,* 49-58.

5. van Staalduine-Sulman, "The Aramaic Song," 267; *Targum of Samuel,* 364-365.

6. Kasher, *Toseftot,* 109-110.

Commentary by Soncino, 1485 (*siglum* K). To Sperber's list we should add Ms. Sal. 1, and Ms. Kennicott 5 [85] of the Bodleian Library, Oxford. These witnesses sometimes display significant differences from one another, which are catalogued in our translation. The differences may in part be explained by the transmission of this *Tosefta Targum* by different Jewish communities. Thus a c Ms. Sal 1 and Ms. Kennicott 5 [85] represent a Sephardic version of the Targum, whereas other witnesses preserve an Ashkenazi tradition.[7]

A second *Tosefta Targum* differing from, but related to, that given by the other witnesses, is preserved in the margin of Codex Reuchlinianus, preceded by an abbreviation indicating a *Targum Jerushalmi*, which Sperber designates with siglum f_6. A separate translation of this Targum is given below.[8]

(C) *Targum Jonathan* of 2 Sam 23:8 is represented in Sperber's edition by Ms. Or. 2210 of the British Library (his base text), to which he gives the *siglum* p. He records variant readings in his other witnesses listed in sections (A) and (B) above, along with readings of the Antwerp Polyglot 1569/1573, *siglum* o; and Ms. Or. 2371 of the British Library, *siglum* y.

Genre, Structure, Prosody

The *Song of the Lamb* is preserved in the Aramaic version of the Bible known as Targum, a succinct and accurate genre definition of which is given by Samely as "an Aramaic narrative paraphrase of the Biblical text in exegetical dependence on its wording."[9] Certain biblical texts engendered more than one Targum; some, indeed, attracted *Tosefta Targum*, that is, additional Targum, which could be quite elaborate in character.[10] Sometimes, *Tosefta Targum* presents lengthy poetic compositions, some of which make use of acrostics: van Staalduine-Sulman has been able to identify a poetic structure in *Tosefta Targum* 1 Sam 17:43, based on the order of the letters of the Hebrew alphabet, each new strophe beginning with the next letter in sequence. This alphabetic acrostic, however, is not complete. Strophes beginning with letters *he*, *qoph*, and *tav* are unrepresented; so van Staalduine-Sulman restores letter *he* by a simple textual emendation; notes that letter *qoph* appears in its correct place in the text of Ms. Sal. 1; and discovers letter *tav* concealed in two strophes which, she suggests, interrupt the final stages of the acrostic.[11] These restorations, however, may not be necessary. The Bible itself yields an example of a poem with "broken acrostic" structure at Pss. 9-10, where the letters *dalet*, *mem*, *nun*, and *samekh* are unrepresented, and letters *'ayin* and *pe* appear in reverse order. Significantly, the Aramaic Targum of Ps. 9:6 explicitly relates this Psalm to the contest between David and Goliath. Consequently, the composer of *Tosefta Targum* 1 Sam. 17:43 may have felt that a "broken acrostic" was especially appropriate for this topic. Either way, the status of this *Tosefta Targum* as an acrostic composition of a kind which recalls the composition of some biblical psalms, and of Aramaic poetry familiar from other Targumim, seems secure.

Tosefta Targum of 1 Sam 17:8, by contrast, presents difficulties. The witnesses to this text differ from one another quite considerably; and what may be a second *Tosefta Targum* is preserved in the margin of Codex Reuchlinianus. A separate translation of this text is

7. van Staalduine-Sulman, *Targum of Samuel*, 349-45; Kasher, "Is there a Single Source?", 1-2.

8. van Staalduine-Sulman, *Targum of Samuel*, 348-49 comments on this Targum.

9. Samely, *Interpretation of Speech*, 180.

10. Alexander, "Targum, Targumim," 324-25. For an alphabetic acrostic poem in Aramaic Targum of Exod 12:2, see Klein, *Genizah Manuscripts* I, 191.

11. van Staalduine-Sulman, *Targum of Samuel*, 368 for letter *he*; "The Aramaic Song," 267-68 for letters *qoph* and *tav*.

given here. Two witnesses also contain the *Tosefta Targum* of 1 Sam 17:43; and it is the text of these two witnesses which van Staalduine-Sulman believes to be the original version of *Tosefta Targum* 1 Sam 17:8. This, too, she suggests, contains an acrostic, now incomplete, but capable of restoration. It originally spelled out the Aramaic *hww kwkby'*, "they became stars," alluding to Dan 12:3 and *Targum Jonathan* of 2 Sam 23:4, thus giving the text an eschatological flavor, and linking it with eschatological material set out in *Targum Jonathan* of 2 Sam 23:1-9. An acrostic structure in this *Tosefta Targum*, it must be said, is not immediately apparent from the witnesses to this text; and we have not here followed van Staalduine-Sulman's admittedly speculative reconstruction of it.[12] Nonetheless, a close relationship between the *Tosefta Targums* of 1 Sam 17:8 and 1 Sam 17:43 seems indicated by the fact that both texts make a special point of emphasizing Goliath's contempt for Saul, and both have an affinity with extra-biblical traditions brought together in the *Liber Antiquitatum Biblicarum* chapter 61.

The final component segment of the Song has survived as an integral part of *Targum Jonathan* of the Prophets, whose version of 2 Sam 23:8 seeks to offer an explanation in Aramaic of an original Hebrew text where the sense is obscure. It may therefore be classified generically simply as Targum. This Targumic verse, van Staalduine-Sulman argues, is directly related to the preceding verses 2 Sam 23:1-7, which *Targum Jonathan* interprets with respect to the coming of the messianic age and last judgment. She then suggests that the Targum of 2 Sam 23:8 must also deal with the final judgment, over which a *David redivivus* is depicted as president,[13] and further considers the likely presence of another acrostic in this verse, yielding the word *mšḥ*, "anoint."[14] The Targumic verse certainly alludes to conflict between David and Goliath; but it presents massive difficulties, all of which need to be considered carefully. What seems very clear, however, is that the Targum is attempting to do exegetical justice to a Scriptural verse which is replete with obscurities and rare words which, in the Targumist's opinion, offer an inventory of David's qualities as military leader and pious Jew.

Date and Provenance

It will be most convenient to begin by considering the date of *Targum Jonathan* of 2 Sam 23:8, since *Targum Jonathan* of the Former Prophets is quoted in the Babylonian Talmud, and was therefore almost certainly in existence before the Talmud's final redaction. The quotations are presented not as "*Targum Jonathan*," but in the name of Rab Joseph, the head of the academy at Pumbeditha who flourished in the fourth century C.E. A list of such quotations was drawn up by Pinkhos Churgin, who demonstrated that Rab Joseph himself was not their author.[15] Study of *Targum Jonathan*'s Aramaic likewise suggests that the Targum very probably received its final redaction in Babylon.[16] Churgin also noted that *Targum Jonathan* of 2 Sam 23:8 reflects two comments on the meaning of the verse by R. Abbahu, a Palestinian Amora and head of the school at Caesarea, who died probably in 309 C.E. He explained, first, that the opening of the verse referred to David sitting at the session of the scholars; he then went on to consider the obscure Hebrew words 'Adino the

12. Her case is set out in detail in van Staalduine-Sulman, "The Aramaic Song of the Lamb," 279-80.

13. van Staalduine-Sulman, "The Song of the Lamb", 283; "Reward and Punishment," 273-96.

14. van Staalduine-Sulman, *Targum of Samuel*, 682-83; at 683-85 she discusses Targum of 1 Chr 11:11, which is exegetically very similar to *Targum Jonathan* 2 Sam 23:8.

15. Churgin, *Targum Jonathan*, 11-15, 146-151.

16. Kuty, "Determination," 197-201.

'Eznite, often taken to be a name, as again referring to David: "when he was sitting and engaged in the Torah, he was twisting himself around like a worm; but when he went out to war, he was hardening himself like a lance."[17] A not dissimilar approach to 2 Sam 23:1-8 may be discerned in Josephus, who lists the heroes of David's armies, and then describes David as a composer of hymns and provider of instruments for the Levites to praise God on Sabbath and festivals.[18] While proof is not forthcoming, it seems that 2 Sam 23:8 could have been expounded already in Josephus's days as a summary of David's character and exploits.

Josephus may help to provide a possible date for some component parts of *Tosefta Targum* 1 Sam 17:43. Smolar and Aberbach suggested that the dialogue between Goliath and David might reflect the circumstances and tensions which led to the First Jewish Revolt against Rome in 66 C.E.[19] In this, Goliath would represent Rome, and David those Jews who sought freedom: their Targumic debate would amount to a propaganda war between the two opposing parties. Smolar and Aberbach note that Goliath plays a sympathetic role, warning David of the consequences of opposition while emphasizing the lad's youth. They cite Josephus's accounts of closely argued speeches, especially those of Agrippa II, which sought to turn the Jewish people back from a disastrous collision with the Roman authorities.[20] They note the crucial part played by young men in starting and fostering the revolt.[21] They point out that the words of David's parents reported in the Targum echo the appeal of Agrippa II to the young revolutionaries; and they draw attention to the Targum's emphasis on peace: Aaron, the pursuer of peace, is the name on the stone which, somewhat paradoxically perhaps, kills Goliath. In support of Smolar and Aberbach, we might note the theme of dishonour and shame, present in the Bible, but heavily stressed in the *Tosefta Targums* of 1 Sam 17:43 and 1 Sam 17:8 with regard to Saul. David announces Saul's humility, which Goliath has reviled, and which will be responsible for the giant's downfall. A similar account of Goliath's scorn for Saul is found in the late-first-century or early-second-century-C.E. writing *Liber Antiquitatum Biblicarum* (*The Book of Biblical Antiquities*).[22] This writing not only has a particular interest in Israel's leaders and their legitimacy,[23] but also agrees with the Targum on points of detail, including Goliath's claim to have captured the Ark and killed Israel's priests;[24] the inscription of the Patriarch's names on the stones which David selected for his sling;[25] and the tradition that Goliath was descended from Orpah.[26]

These observations lend support to the view that some of the material preserved in the Aramaic texts which de Moor and van Staalduine-Sulman have presented as *The Song of the Lamb* was at home in a late-first–early-second-century-C.E. setting among Jews in the Land of Israel. At the same time, the texts contain traditions which may derive from a later

---

17. *b. Mo'ed Qat.* 16b. Very similar is Jerome's Vulgate of 2 Sam 23:8, which also describes David as "most delicate": *Targum Jonathan* calls him *mpnq*, "delicately reared."

18. Josephus *Ant.* 7.301-306; compare Sir 47:7-10.

19. Smolar and Aberbach, *Studies in Targum Jonathan*, 72-74.

20. Josephus *War* 2.345-404; 5.361-419; 6.93-110.

21. Josephus *War* 2.267, 290, 303, 346, 409; 4.128; also Goodman, *The Ruling Class*, 210-14.

22. *L.A.B.* 61:2. For the date of *Liber Antiquitatum Biblicarum*, see Harrington, "Pseudo-Philo," 299; Schürer, *The History of the Jewish People*, III.1, 328-29.

23. Mendels, "Pseudo-Philo's Biblical Antiquities," 261-75.

24. *L.A.B.* 61:2 and *Tosefta Targum* 1 Sam. 17:8.

25. *L.A.B.* 61:5 and *Tosefta Targum* 1 Sam. 17:43.

26. *L.A.B.* 61:6 and *Tosefta Targum* 1 Sam. 17:4.

period, or material whose nature makes it difficult to date in any precise way. For example, the description of Aaron as a pursuer of peace is not attested earlier than the Mishnah, which was probably redacted at the beginning of the third century C.E., with *m. ʾAbot* perhaps as late as ca. 300 C.E.[27] *Tosefta Targum* 1 Sam 17:43 may also present David as the putative son of a slave-girl, a tradition not attested before mediaeval times.[28] Any final verdict on the date of the present state of the texts must take these things into account, and be prepared to envisage many layers of tradition whose dates range from the first century C.E. to the Talmudic period or later. The most likely place for the origin of these Targumic traditions is Palestine, although, as we have seen, the Babylonian academies will have played a part in the final redaction of *Targum Jonathan* in particular.

Literary Context—Sources, Inspirations, and Closely Related Texts

Targum's relationship to its parent Hebrew text is crucial for proper appreciation of its contents, and that relationship will be examined first. Since the Septuagint version conveys some of the most ancient Jewish exegesis of the Hebrew Bible it, too, deserves close attention, along with the other ancient versions where relevant. We shall treat each section of Targum in the order in which van Staalduine-Sulman sets them out as constituting *The Song of the Lamb*, beginning with *Tosefta Targum* of 1 Sam 17:43.

The Hebrew of 1 Sam 17:43 may be translated: "And the Philistine said to David: 'Am I a dog, that you are coming to me with sticks?' And the Philistine cursed David by his gods." The repetition of the names "Philistine" and "David" in a short verse might have suggested to ancient interpreters that a conversation had taken place between the two, especially since the Philistine asks a question. David is said to be equipped with sticks, *maqlôt*, even though an earlier verse (1 Sam 17:40) had noted that David had taken just his one stick, *maqlô*. This apparent inconsistency in the Hebrew text may have prompted exegetes to take seriously the fact that *maqlô* and *maqlôt* are similar in sound to the Philistine's act of cursing, Hebrew *wayᵉqallel*, a word which may also be translated "and he made light of."[29] Thus it might be perceived that David had come to the Philistines with *maqlôt*, understood as things which made light of, or expressed contempt for, his enemy; and that the Philistine had responded in kind, which is indeed what Scripture reports (1 Sam 17:45-47). Scripture itself, then, might be taken to imply an extended dialogue of the sort the *Tosefta Targum* later supplied.

Those who translated 1 Sam 17:43 into Greek actually provided such a dialogue. Their interpretation of the verse runs: "And the foreigner said to David: 'Am I like a dog, that you should come to me with a staff and stones?' And David said: 'No, but worse than a dog!' And the foreigner cursed David by his gods." This explicit introduction of dialogue, albeit brief, between the two men may be dated to some time before the end of the second century B.C.E., since Ben Sira's prologue to his translation of his grandfather's Wisdom book indicates that a Greek version of the books of the Prophets was already in existence. It is possible, then, that the LXX of 1 Sam 17:43 is witness to an early stage in a process which culminated in the full-scale dialogue set out in the *Tosefta Targum* of that verse. It should also be noted that LXX alludes to stones, one of which will dispatch Goliath: this detail

---

27. *m. ʾAbot* 1:12; *ARNb* 24.

28. *Yalqut Makhiri* II.124, 214; although in private communication Dr. Alison Salvesen suggests that this notion may have been developed earlier through exegesis of Pss. 86:16; 116:16.

29. In 17:43 Symmachus has *eloidorei*, "he reviled, railed against, abused."

is absent from the Masoretic Hebrew Text, but was either present in the Hebrew *Vorlage* translated by the LXX, or was included here by the translators deliberately to heighten the importance of the stone which was to kill Goliath. In either case, the significance of the stone is underlined, and would later be further developed by the *Tosefta Targum*.

Targum Jonathan of 1 Sam 17:43 offers the following interpretation: "And the Philistine said to David: 'Am I a mad dog, that you are coming to me with a stick?' And the Philistine cursed David by his idol." The Targum insists that the Philistine's gods are idols, using an Aramaic word which means literally "errors," the conventional Targumic term for referring to deities other than the God of Israel. The *Tosefta Targum* of this verse makes David point out explicitly that Goliath acted in the name of his idol.

Although fully exploiting the possibilities for dialogue between David and Goliath afforded by the materials recorded in the Hebrew and Greek forms of the biblical text, *Tosefta Targum* of 1 Sam 17:43 omits other items which are prominent in the material we have examined. Thus *Tosefta Targum* has no reference to the dog, the staff, or to Goliath's cursing. Instead, the *Tosefta Targum* introduces details found in 1 Sam 17:34-37, describing David's exploits as a shepherd, when he killed a lion and a bear, reworking them to support the symbolism of the lamb who routs the bear in combat.[30] Similarly, the account of David's physical beauty found in 1 Sam 16:12 provided biblical support for the *Tosefta Targum*'s extended disquisition on David's impressive appearance. Thus the immediate source for the imagery of lamb, lion, and bear may be discovered in the Hebrew of 1 Sam 16-17. The description of Goliath as "an offspring of lions" and "a bear" may, however, find its source in Daniel's account of the first two beasts which appeared in his vision of the four world empires (Dan 7:4-5), and hint at the ultimate overthrow of tyrants by Israel's divinely chosen leader.[31]

Daniel's book, however, does not depict the opponent of the fourth world empire as a lamb; and the moderate, almost irenic language of the bear Goliath in the *Tosefta Targum* is unexpected in the mouth of a beast perceived by Dan 7:5 as crunching ribs between its teeth and being under orders to gorge itself on flesh. Even so, the *Tosefta Targum* does envisage Goliath as a threat to David; and its description of the giant's fall is reminiscent of Daniel's account of king Belshazzar's feast. Confronted with writing inscribed by no human hand, "the king's countenance changed...and the joints of his loins were loosed, and his knees smote one against the other" before his kingdom fell to Darius the Mede (Dan 5:6). *Tosefta Targum*'s direct allusion to these events is no accident; for Belshazzar's feast had desecrated sacred vessels plundered from the Jerusalem Temple (Dan 5:2-4); and Goliath, according to *Tosefta Targum* of 1 Sam 17:8, had desecrated the Ark by removing it from the sanctuary and putting it in his idol-house, killing Israel's priests. And just as Belshazzar's doom was sealed with words mysteriously inscribed on his palace wall (Dan 5:5), so Goliath was felled by a stone inscribed with a name doubtless unknown to him. The collapse of Belshazzar's realm paved the way for the return of sacred vessels to Jerusalem and the rebuilding of the Temple. *Tosefta Targum* 1 Sam 17:43 therefore invites the reader to perceive in Goliath's demise at David's hand the first stage of a future restoration of the desecrated Ark to a rebuilt sanctuary, and the reversal of Israel's humiliation. Certainly the plea that God act in the future as He had done in the past, which closes this *Tosefta Targum*, is consonant with a hope for Israel's future, confident in divine help.

---

30. van Staalduine-Sulman, "The Aramaic Song," 278.

31. van Staalduine-Sulman, "The Aramaic Song," 287-88.

The Hebrew text of 1 Sam 17:8 gives details of Goliath's challenge to Israel: "And he stood and called to the ranks of Israel, and said to them, 'Why do you not go out to arrange war? Am I not the Philistine, while you are servants of Saul? Choose [someone] for yourselves, and let him go down to me.'" The principal difficulty in this verse lies in the word translated "choose," where the Hebrew has *b^erû*, a word found nowhere else in the Hebrew Bible. No unease seems to have been felt about this, however: as we shall see, both LXX and *Targum Jonathan* took the word to mean "choose."[32] The Greek translation of this verse carefully chooses words to suggest the self-regard and overweening confidence of Goliath: "And he stood and shouted out aloud to the battle array of Israel, and said to them, 'Why are you going forth to set up the army in array for war against us? Am I myself not the foreigner, while you are the Hebrews of Saul? Choose for yourselves a man, and let him go down to me.'" Where the Hebrew spoke of Saul's servants, LXX have put "Hebrews of Saul": only one consonant differentiates these two words in an unvocalized Hebrew text, "servants" being *'bdym*, while "Hebrews" would be *'brym*, and the letters *dalet* and *resh* are graphically nearly identical in all periods. Either the LXX translators had before them a Hebrew *Vorlage* which read *'brym*; or they sought to explain Saul's servants as Hebrews in the light of 1 Sam 14:11, where the word could easily be taken as a derogatory expression on the lips of non-Israelites. Goliath's contempt for David, so marked in the Targum, may thus find some outlet also in this LXX verse. *Targum Jonathan* has a most interesting introduction to Goliath's words: "And he stood and roared against the ranks of Israel and said to them, 'Why should you go out to set war in order? Am I not the Philistine, and you servants of Saul? Choose for yourselves a man and let him go down to me.'" The Targum has *w'kly*, "and he roared": the verb may mean "call," "give a signal," but is also used of lions roaring and of loud noises among animals. It coheres with Goliath's self-description as "an offspring of lions" in *Tosefta Targum* of 1 Sam 17:43.

The Hebrew of 2 Sam 23:8 informs us: "These are the names of the mighty men whom David had: Josheb-basshebeth, a Tahchemonite, the head of the Three—he is 'Adino the 'Eznite (who was) against eight hundred slain at once." Difficulties abound. The name Josheb-basshebeth occurs nowhere else. It may also not be a name, but a phrase "sitting upon the seat," describing David, and such is *Targum Jonathan*'s understanding of it. The gentilic Tahchemonite is also *hapax legomenon*: its individual consonants include *ḥkm*, "be wise" in both Hebrew and Aramaic, which *Targum Jonathan* would take to indicate David's wisdom and to create a picture of him as Torah scholar surrounded by prophets and elders, seated in judgment.[33] It also contains the consonants *mny*, Aramaic "appoint, ordain," which indicated to the Targumist that David was an anointed king. The enigmatic phrase "the Three" was understood by *Targum Jonathan* in light of Exod 15:4, where a related term describes a warrior or military officer of Pharaoh. 'Adino the 'Eznite is also unique to this verse; *Targum Jonathan* selected from its Hebrew consonants the stem *'dn*, representing daintiness and luxury, to describe David as delicately reared or nobly born. The Targum also focused on the consonants *'ts*, meaning "tree, wood," which suggested the wooden shaft of a weapon. The consonants *'dn* could also be understood to refer to beauty or order, and intimate that David had been ordered or suitably adorned with weap-

32. van Staalduine-Sulman, *Targum of Samuel*, 348, suggests that the Targumists perceived here the root *brr*, "select"; cf. 1 Chr 7:40.

33. For David as Torah scholar, see also *b. Shabb.* 30a-30b; *Lam. Rab.* 2:22; *Midrash Tehillim* on Ps. 119:97.

ons.[34] These, Targum says, he used *against* 800 men to kill them, being aided in this interpretation by 2 Sam 23:18, which speaks clearly of a *spear* being wielded *against* large numbers of men to kill them.

The influence of 2 Sam 23:18 on *Targum Jonathan* of 2 Sam 23:8 may also help to explain a difficult phrase in the latter, which van Staalduine-Sulman has highlighted. The former verse speaks of the warrior as *ʿôrēr*, "brandishing" his spear; and *Targum Jonathan* understood this Hebrew word in its fundamental root sense of "shouting, rousing up" with his spear. It is this "shouting" or "rousing up" which probably led the translator to state in the Targum of 2 Sam 23:8 that David went out "at the mouth of the voice," a phrase representing the literal translation of the Aramaic *bpwm ql'*: van Staalduine-Sulman describes its difficulties, and notes how students of this verse have tended to view the words as concealing a foreign loan word. She herself suggests that the words are best explained with reference to Babylonian *pungullu*, meaning "very strong"; thus, she maintains, David went out as a champion fighter.[35] This explanation, however, may not be needed if we understand that David went forth to battle accompanied by a voice—either the voice of God or, more probably, the sound of one of his own poetic compositions. It will be recalled that the Targum of Psalm 9 relates that poem to David's fight with Goliath; and the first of two Targums to Ps 9:1 preserved in Ms. Paris Bibliothèque Nationale Héb. 110 as *targum aher* reads: "To the singer, concerning the sweetness of the youthful voices, *qlpwnyn*, of the praise offered by the son. A psalm of David."[36] David's military exploits and his music were also set side by side by Josephus (*Ant.* 7.301-306) and Ben Sira (47:5-10). Quite possibly *Targum Jonathan* of 2 Sam 23:8 also evokes this juxtaposition.

Targum Jonathan of 2 Sam 23:8 follows a segment of poetic text (2 Sam. 23:1-7) which the Hebrew Bible describes as being the last words of David. The Targum interpreted this segment explicitly as constituting a prophecy about the world to come (*Targum Jonathan* 2 Sam 23:1-2). Consequently, it is possible that the Targum of 2 Sam 23:8 forms the concluding verse of this eschatological prophecy, as van Staalduine-Sulman has suggested.[37]

Apart from the Hebrew Bible and its ancient versions, the Targumic texts which compose the Song of the Lamb are related, to a greater or lesser extent, to a number of extra-biblical Jewish writings. We have already remarked on the writings of Ben Sira and Josephus which juxtapose David's military and musical expertise: this is developed further by poets of the late first or early second century C.E. who imitated the biblical Psalter and composed extra Davidic psalms.[38] The Syriac Psalm 151 A and B (5 *Apoc. Syr. Ps.* 1 a) is headed: "By David, when he alone fought against Goliath." It describes how David made instruments and fashioned lyres, and celebrates his attack on the Philistine who cursed David by his idols, but whose head David cut off, removing Israel's shame.[39] The heading of 5 *Apoc. Syr. Ps.* 4 locates this poem after David's fight with lion and wolf: it speaks of killers who confronted David, symbolically depicted as "the lion." These killers seek not only the sheep, but David himself. He describes himself as "the elect one," and prays for deliverance. 5 *Apoc. Syr. Ps.* 5 records his thanksgiving after killing a lion and a wolf.[40]

34. Field, *Origenis Hexaplorum*, 1:585 records *alia exempla* of LXX with a similar interpretation.
35. van Staalduine-Sulman, "The Aramaic Song," 280-81; *Targum of Samuel*, 351-52.
36. Stec, *Targum of Psalms*, 38.
37. van Staalduine-Sulman, "The Aramaic Song," 283, 287; *Targum of Samuel*, 682-86.
38. Charlesworth and Sanders, "More Psalms," 609-24.
39. 5 *Apoc Syr Ps.* 1 b; Charlesworth and Sanders, "More Psalms," 614-15.
40. Charlesworth and Sanders, "More Psalms," 616-17.

The *Liber Antiquitatum Biblicarum* prefaces its version of David's encounter with Goliath by recording David's slaughter of 15,000 Midianites (*L.A.B.* 61:1). It tells how Goliath set himself against Saul and Israel, boasting that they fled when he had captured the Ark and killed the priests. Goliath demands that Saul behave like a king, and fight with him. Should Saul refuse to do this, Goliath promises to capture him and make Israel serve Philistine gods (*L.A.B.* 61:2). Traditions very closely related to these are found in *Tosefta Targum* of 1 Sam 17:8. We also hear in *L.A.B.* 61:2 how Saul and Israel were afraid of Goliath, who took it upon himself to reproach Israel for the same length of time, namely forty days, as they had spent receiving the Torah, and then he would fight them.[41] After these forty days, *L.A.B.* 61:3 informs us, David came to see the battle and decided that this was the time for the fulfilment of a divine promise made to him earlier (*L.A.B.* 59:6), that God, through David's actions, would deliver Israel by means of stones. This is not, however, represented in *The Song of the Lamb*; nonetheless, it serves to underline the significance of stones both for the Targum and the compiler of the *L.A.B.* Indeed, from *L.A.B.* 61:5 we learn that David chose seven stones (not five, as recorded in *Tosefta Targum* of 1 Sam 17:43): he inscribed on them the names of Abraham, Isaac, Jacob, Moses, Aaron, his own name, and the Name of the Most Mighty.[42] This same passage of *L.A.B.* also states that God sent to David the angel Zervihel, who is in charge of strength, a detail lacking in Targum.

L.A.B. 61:6 includes a lengthy speech addressed to Goliath by David, who recalls that the two men have family ties: Goliath's mother was Orpah, a tradition found also in a *Tosefta Targum* of 1 Sam 17:4, while David's "mother" (that is ancestress) was Ruth. Orpah chose foreign deities and went after them, whereas Ruth "chose for herself the ways of the Most High and walked in them." Thus the two men represent polytheism on the one hand and the Jewish worship of the Unique God on the other. Goliath and his three brothers, David declares, have arisen "to swallow up Israel"—similar imagery occurs in *Tosefta Targum* of 1 Sam 17:43—but all will die by David's hand, and their mother will be told of their death. *L.A.B.* 61:7 then tells how David's stone struck Goliath, who asks David to kill him swiftly; but David orders him (*L.A.B.* 61:8) to open his eyes to see his killer who has killed him. At this point Goliath sees the angel, and acknowledges that not alone had David brought about his death, "but he who was with you, whose appearance is not as of a man." The section ends (*L.A.B.* 61:9) with the note that the angel lifted up David's face so that no one, not even Saul, recognized him.

While some of the details recorded in the *L.A.B.* tally almost exactly with the Targumim, others, van Staalduine-Sulman points out, "are used in a reverse way."[43] Thus Goliath's mother is to be told of the death of her children, so it will not be David's mother who is to lament, as Goliath suggests in *Tosefta Targum* of 1 Sam 17:43. According to that same Targum, David saw angels; but in *L.A.B.* 61:8 it is Goliath who sees the angel Zervihel as David's helper. *Tosefta Targum* of 1 Sam 17:43 brings its *Song of the Lamb* to a climax by reporting that Goliath's face was changed through human weakness; whereas *L.A.B.* 61:9 portrays the victorious David's face as transformed and unrecognized even by those who know him well. One possible explanation of this state of affairs might be that both *L.A.B.*

41. A similar tradition is recorded in *Tanhuma Wayyigaš* 8.

42. For further information on these stones, see Kasher, *Toseftot*, 111.

43. van Staalduine-Sulman, "The Aramaic Song," 285.

and the Targum have drawn on traditions which are older than both of them, and have molded them to suit their own particular purposes.

This Translation

The part-texts which de Moor and van Staalduine-Sulman have identified as belonging to *The Aramaic Song of the Lamb* are here translated from Alexander Sperber's critical edition of the Targum of the Former Prophets. This edition of the primary sources is readily available, and most students of Targum continue to make use of it in their researches. This translation therefore has used Sperber's text as its base, but has taken careful note of the manuscript evidence, unavailable to Sperber, which van Staalduine-Sulman has assembled in her studies of *The Song of the Lamb* in particular and of the *Targum of Samuel* in general. The textual notes appended to the translation draw special attention to, and catalogue the readings of the various witnesses known to Sperber, and list details of significant manuscript readings discovered by van Staalduine-Sulman, particularly the evidence of Ms. Sal. 1.

Bibliography

Alexander, P. S. "Targum, Targumim." *ABD*, 6:320-31.

Charlesworth, J. H., and J. A. Sanders. "More Psalms of David." In *OTP*, 2:609-24.

Churgin, P. *Targum Jonathan to the Prophets*. New York and Baltimore, Md.: Ktav, and Baltimore: Hebrew College, 1983.

Field, F. *Origenis Hexaplorum Quae Supersunt*, vol. 1. Oxford: Clarendon, 1875.

Goodman, M. *The Ruling Class of Judaea. The Origins of the Jewish Revolt against Rome A.D. 66-70*. Cambridge: Cambridge University Press, 1987.

Harrington, D. J. "Pseudo-Philo." In *OTP*, 2:297-337.

Kasher, R. "Is There a Single Source for Toseftot Targum of the Prophets?" *AJSR* 22 (1997): 1-21 (Heb.).

___________. *Toseftot of Targum to the Prophets*. Sources for the Study of Jewish Culture 11. Jerusalem: The World Union of Jewish Studies, 1996 (Heb.).

Klein, M. L. *Genizah Manuscripts of Palestinian Targum to the Pentateuch I*. Cincinnati: Hebrew Union College Press, 1986.

Kuty, R. "Determination in Targum Jonathan to Samuel." *Aramaic Studies* 3 (2005): 187-201.

Martínez Borobio, E. *Targum Jonatán de los Profetas Primeros en tradición Babilónica, I-II Samuel*. Madrid: Consejo Superior de Investigaciones Científicas, 1987.

Mendels, D. "Pseudo-Philo's *Biblical Antiquities*, the 'Fourth Philosophy,' and the Political Messianism of the First Century C.E." Pages 261-75 in *The Messiah: Developments in Earliest Judaism and Christianity*. Edited by J. H. Charlesworth. Minneapolis, Minn.: Fortress, 1992.

Moor, J. C. de, and E. van Staalduine-Sulman. "The Aramaic Song of the Lamb." *JSJ* 24 (1993): 266-279.

Samely, A. *The Interpretation of Speech in the Pentateuchal Targums*. Tübingen: Mohr Siebeck, 1992.

Schürer, E. *The History of the Jewish People in the Age of Jesus Christ*, III.1. Revised and edited by G. Vermes, F. Millar and M. Goodman. Edinburgh: T.&T. Clark, 1986.

Smolar, L., and M. Aberbach. *Studies in Targum Jonathan to the Prophets*. New York and Baltimore: Hebrew College, 1983.

Sperber, A. *The Bible in Aramaic*. Vol. 2: *The Former Prophets According to Targum Jonathan*. Leiden: Brill, 1959.

Stec, D. *The Targum of Psalms*. The Aramaic Bible 16. London: T.&T. Clark, 2004.

van Staalduine-Sulman, E. "The Aramaic Song of the Lamb." Pages 265-92 in *Verse in Ancient Near Eastern Prose*. Edited by J. C. de Moor and W. G. E. Watson. AOAT 42. Neukirchen: Neukirchener-Verlag, 1993.

__________. *The Targum of Samuel*. Studies in Aramaic Interpretation of Scripture 1. Leiden: Brill, 2002.

The Aramaic Song of the Lamb (The Dialogue between David and Goliath)

(***Tosefta Targum* of 1 Sam 17:43**) And he said to him] + And he said to him, (*'Aleph*) "Go! Have compassion on your youth. Why do you engage in battle with an offspring of lions? (*Bet*) You are chosen, O lamb,[a] and exceeding beautiful!"

(*Gimel*) Goliath said to David: "Your father has not [yet] spread out the wedding canopy above you: be mindful of your wedding, and return to your former state. (*Dalet*) Your splendour is like the splendour of my king[b]; and I have confidence in you[c], that you have inherited a kingdom. Alas[d] for you, O lamb! because your slavery has straitened you.[e] Alas for your youth! because you have sought to be slain. (*Vav*) Woe to you, O lamb! because you are engaging in battle with a bear; and there is no lamb that can stand up against a bear. (*Zayin*) You are small, but your heart is strong. Woe to you! because you are engaging in battle with one who is stronger than you. (*Het*) Your looks and your flesh I shall give to the birds of the heavens, if you do not go and pasture your sheep. (*Tet*) It will be good for you, O lamb, if you go from my presence, lest I spit upon you and drown you in my spittle. (*Yod*) The day you went out into was an evil day. Your father cried aloud, and your mother lamented: Woe! Woe! (*Kaph*) Incline your head, and return to your former state, lest my sword, which is sharp[f], should have dominion over you. (*Lamed*) As for your heart which has been lifted up—the Lord will bring it low."

David said to Goliath: (*Mem*) "The Word[g] of my God who has come with me, he will save me from the mouth of the bear. (*Nun*) Repose is what belongs to me: but wrath belongs to you. You (act) in the name of the idol, but I in the Name of the Lord of hosts. (*Samekh*) As for your sword, which is sharp, I will cut off your head with it."

---

a. "Lamb" represents Aramaic *tly'*, and may also signify "boy" or "child": it yields a play on words with "your youth," Aramaic *tlywtk*.

b. Or "kings," if the word be understood as an East Aramaic plural form.

c. Ms. Sal. 1 reads "for I love you" instead of "and I have confidence in you": for its possible homosexual implications, see Kasher, *Toseftot*, 110-11; and van Staalduine-Sulman, "The Aramaic Song," 278; *Targum of Samuel*, 373.

d. This word, Aramaic *hbl*, begins with the letter *het*: the acrostic seems to require a word beginning with the letter *he*. Accordingly, van Staalduine-Sulman, "The Aramaic Song," 277-278; *Targum of Samuel*, 368, suggests we read *hbl*, "wasting (on you)," noting Kasher's comment, *Toseftot*, 11, that *het* may have been pronounced as *he* in Palestine.

e. Aramaic *dgmdk msrk*, which van Staalduine-Sulman, "The Aramaic Song," 277-78; *Targum of Samuel*, 368, regards as a Hebraism "for your shortness will be your undoing," referring to David's youth. But the Aramaic may also have the sense given here, and refer to a tradition that David was thought by some to be a slave girl's son, *Yalqut Makhiri* II. 124, 214: see Ginzberg, *Legends*, vol. IV, 82; vol VI, 246.

f. "Sharp" is Aramaic *hryp*, whose root in the *Pa'el* conjugation means "blaspheme," and suggests Goliath's contempt for God.

g. Aramaic *memra'*.

David said to Goliath: (*'Ayin*) "The humility of Saul, the son of Kish, whom you have reviled, will eat you up to the bone and make your stature to fall. (*Pe*) I open my mouth, and swallow you up."

Goliath said to David: (*Tsade*) "The form of your face is beautiful and ruddy, and you are [so] handsome in looks and graceful in appearance that you should not[a] be subservient to the Philistines, that the lamb should fight with the bear."

(*Resh*) There was a great commotion among the five stones, for one said to the other: "I shall go up first." (*Shin*) The name of Abraham the righteous was written on the first; that of Isaac the bound was written on the second; that of Jacob the unblemished was written on the third; on the fourth and on the fifth were written the names of Moses and Aaron the prophets.

The name of Abraham said: "Let me go up into the sling in the first place, and I shall smite this uncircumcised Philistine upon his foreskin, and remove the shame from those of the House of Israel." At that moment David lifted his eyes to the height, and saw angels who were taking counsel about Goliath the Philistine. At that moment there was good pleasure from before the Lord which [came] upon the stone of Aaron, and it went up into the sling, because he was one who pursues peace; and it smote the Philistine on his forehead, to make peace dwell by his agency in the border of Israel. At that moment the splendour of his face was changed, and his knees knocked together, and his sword fell, and the shaft of his lance was shattered.

And what He did with that generation, may He do with us, for ever.

Goliath's Contempt for Saul

(*Tosefta Targum* of 1 Sam 17:8) Am I not Goliath[b] the Philistine from Gath, who killed the two sons of Eli the priest,[c] Hophni and Phineas? And I carried off the ark of the covenant of the Lord, and brought it to the house of Dagon, my idol. And it was there, in the cities of the Philistines,[d] for seven[e] months; and the Lord your creator did not prevail against me.[f] Moreover,[g] [in] every war which the Philistines had,[h] I myself was going out at the head of the army,[i] and was victorious in the war; and I was throwing up the slain ones like the dust of the earth; but until now the Philistines have not permitted me to be even the captain of a thousand men. And as for you, O men of the house of Israel[j]—what mighty deed has Saul the son of Kish who is from Gibeah achieved for you, that you have

a. We read *dl'* as in Sperber's edition of the text. There appears to be no line beginning with letter *qoph*; but van Staalduine-Sulman, "The Aramaic Song," 267, notes that Ms. Sal. 1 reads *ql'*, "voice, rumour," instead of *dl'*. She adopts this reading, but is then required further to emend the Aramaic to yield her preferred sense, "a rumour was heard among the Philistines."

b. K omits "Goliath."

c. b c d omit "the priest."

d. c d omit "in the cities of the Philistines."

e. See 1 Sam. 6:1. c d "six"; K "three."

f. w_1 a b K omit "and the Lord…me." For "the Lord your creator, *qwnykwn*," Ms. Sal. 1 has "the Lord of your covenant, *qymykwn*": see van Staalduine-Sulman, *Targum of Samuel*, 349, 351.

g. c d read "and concerning"; K "and if."

h. K reads: "which you had with the Philistines."

i. For "at the head of the army," c d read *lpm ql'*, literally, "at the mouth of the voice": see above.

j. w_1 reads: "O sons of Israel."

appointed[a] him as king over you? Now say to him:[b] "If he is a heroic[c] man, let him go down and make war with me. But if he is a weak man, choose for yourselves a man and let him go down to me."

(***Targum Jerushalmi*** **of 1 Sam 17:8 in marginal note to Codex Reuchlinianus, Sperber siglum f_6**) Am I not Goliath the Philistine, who made war with you at Aphek? And I was victorious over you, and I took from your hands the ark of the Lord. But you are servants of Saul. And if you say: "We are trusting in the Word of the Lord, the Master of victories in wars"—call to Him, and let him go down to me.

The Virtues of David

(***Targum Jonathan*** **of 2 Sam 23:8**) These[d] are the names of the men who were with David the mighty man,[e] the head[f] of the military camp, sitting[g] upon thrones of judgment and all the prophets and the elders surrounding him,[h] anointed with holy oil, chosen and nobly born, beautiful in appearance and comely in looks, wise in wisdom and intelligent in counsel, mighty in strength, head of the mighty men is he; ordered in weapons of armour he goes out[i] to war at the sound of "the mouth of the voice" and is victorious in war; and he cuts down by means of his lance eight hundred men slain at one time.[j]

---

a. From "but until now..." up to this point, c d read: "all this I did for them, and they have not appointed me over them, neither as king, nor as general; and this Saul, who is from Gibeah of Benjamin, what has he done for you, that you should appoint?" The word translated "general" is a loan word from the Greek, *stratēgos*.

b. K b w_1 omit "now say to him."

c. c d read "mighty."

d. b c o read "and these."

e. w reads: "the mighty men"; y b "his mighty men."

f. y b read "the heads."

g. c reads "and sitting."

h. o omits "and all the prophets and the elders surrounding him"; for "the elders," Ms. T.-S. BS 2 reads "the scribes": see van Staalduine-Sulman, *Targum of Samuel*, 680. note 1472.

i. K a c d f o read "and he goes out."

j. Ms. T.-S. BS 2 adds "helping the humble and frightening the wicked": see van Staalduine-Sulman, *Targum of Samuel*, 681, note 1477.

Exorcistic Psalms of David and Solomon

A new translation and introduction

by Gideon Bohak

The composition and recitation of exorcistic spells and hymns was an extremely common Jewish practice both in the Second Temple period and in late antiquity, and their attribution to David or Solomon was common enough in both periods. This may be seen from Josephus' description of a Jewish exorcist who carried out a "Solomonic" exorcism ritual, from a Qumran list of "Davidic" compositions which includes "four hymns to be recited over the demoniacs," and from the testimony of Origen (or Pseudo-Origen), who insists that "Solomonic" exorcisms were still in circulation and use in his own time.[1] But it is especially clear from the exorcistic psalms that are attributed to David or Solomon in several different ancient sources, all of which are the subject of the present survey. Their importance lies in the fact that they testify both to the ongoing Jewish practice of exorcism and to the survival of some pseudepigraphic compositions, or, at least, of the "pseudepigraphic habit" itself, among some Jews well into the fifth and sixth centuries C.E., and perhaps even later.

Contents

The six texts that are translated below do not belong to a single composition, and probably stem from different times and places. They are currently found in textual sources that are as far apart as Qumran of the first century C.E., Babylonia and Egypt of the fifth or sixth centuries, and the medieval monasteries where the Latin version of the *Book of Biblical Antiquities* was being copied. What unites them is their focus on exorcism—by which we refer both to driving demons out of a human being and to driving them out of a certain physical location—and their attribution to David or to Solomon.

The search for such ancient Jewish compositions must take into consideration two important factors. The first is that the attribution of hymns and psalms to David and Solomon was extremely common already in the Hebrew Bible (e.g., Psalms 3-9, 11-32, etc.), and remained common at least throughout the Second Temple period.[2] What separates the psalms studied below from all other "Davidic" and "Solomonic" compositions is their exorcistic aim, which gives them a very practical flavor. They were meant not only to be recited, but also to be effective. In a society where the belief in the dangers of demons was pervasive, and where numerous illnesses and aberrant behaviors were attributed to their malicious ef-

1. See Josephus, *Ant.* 8.42-49; 11Q5 = 11QPs[a], col. XXVII, lines 4-10; Origen, *In Matthaeum Commentariorum Series* 111 (PG 13.1757) (=GCS 57, 229-30).

2. And note, for example, the apocryphal psalms of David which are usually numbered Psalm 151-55 (for which see J. H. Charlesworth and J. A. Sanders in *OTP*, 2:609-624); note also the list in 11Q5 (see n. 1), which includes 4,050 Davidic compositions, only four of which have anything to do with demons, as well as Josephus' description of David's poetic compositions in *Ant.* 7.305.

fect, such hymns were seen as one major way of fighting back, and of driving demons away and averting their evil effects.[3] But the pervasive belief in demons led to the composition of numerous anti-demonic hymns, spells, and adjurations, and a second feature that sets the hymns below apart from other ancient Jewish exorcistic formulae is their specific attribution to David or Solomon.[4] This feature is due not only to the general tendency to father hymnic compositions upon these two composers, but also to the famous biblical story of how the young David drove the "evil spirit" out of King Saul (1 Sam 16:14-23), a story that was commonly interpreted as the account of a successful exorcism.[5] Similarly, the biblical stories of Solomon's great wisdom (e.g., 1 Kgs 5:9-14 [Evv 4:29-34]) and numerous compositions (1 Kgs 5:12-13[4:32-33]) soon developed to a full-fledged tradition regarding Solomon and his magical expertise.[6] Thus, whenever a Jewish exorcist composed a new exorcistic psalm, the temptation was great to father it upon David, and even to identify the new composition as the very psalm used by David when he exorcized King Saul, as we shall see below, or to attribute it to Solomon, along with so much other magic lore.[7] However, the fact that any exorcistic composition, regardless of its real provenance or contents, could be attributed to these two by merely adding the words "To David / Solomon" (or a similar formula of attribution and identification) in the first line or as a title also means that a few additional anti-demonic hymns that have come down to us may belong in the present corpus, but as they are badly preserved it is far from certain whether they originally contained such an attribution.[8] In the following translation, we have included one such hymn, whose attribution to David seems extremely likely, but have omitted others, which *may* also have been attributed to David, but the attribution is no longer extant.[9]

While the compositions translated below stem from widely divergent contexts, their attributions to David and Solomon and their exorcistic agenda make for a general similarity of form and contents. Among their formal features, we may note that they were all composed in Hebrew (except, perhaps, the last one, which may have been written in Greek), they are all quite short, and they were all meant to be recited orally, even if they ended up embedded in larger, written texts, such as metal-plate or papyrus amulets or a clay incantation bowl. And as for their contents, the texts below seem to share several basic techniques that are used to scare demons away. These include the praise, or descrip-

3. For other methods of fighting demons in ancient Jewish society see G. Bohak, *Ancient Jewish Magic: A History* (Cambridge: Cambridge University Press, 2008), esp. pp. 88-114.

4. For exorcistic hymns which definitely were not attributed to David or to Solomon see, e.g., 4Q510-511 (=4QSongs of the Sage), which are the first-person recitations of the Qumran *maskil*. Note also the endless stream of anti-demonic texts in most of the Babylonian incantation bowls, which normally contain no attribution to any specific author.

5. See, e.g., Josephus, *Ant.* 6.166-68.

6. See Torijano, *Solomon the Esoteric King.*

7. Solomon also was seen as the author of a "Book of Remedies," suppressed by King Hezekiah, but it does not seem to have contained exorcistic psalms—see Halperin, "The Book of Remedies."

8. The situation is further complicated by the tendency of the Greco-Egyptian magical literature to attribute magical texts to very unlikely authors. Thus, PGM IV. 3007-3086, which clearly began its textual life as a Jewish exorcism, is attributed to the Egyptian "Pibechis," whereas the text identified as "The Falling Down of Solomon" (PGM IV. 850-929) seems entirely non-Jewish in origin. For a fuller analysis of this phenomenon, see also LiDonnici, "'According to the Jews': Identified (and Identifying) 'Jewish' Elements in the *Greek Magical Papyri*," with further bibliography.

9. This includes not only all the other hymns in 11Q11, but also such texts as the Greek exorcistic composition published by Benoit, "Fragments d'une prière contre les esprits impurs?" and analyzed by van der Horst and Newman, *Early Jewish Prayers in Greek*, 125-133, which may have been attributed to a specific author.

tion, of God's great powers, at which the demon(s) should shudder and flee, the citation of, or allusion to, potent biblical verses, and the direct second-person appeal to the demon, with threats and taunts intended to scare it away, and with rhetorical questions intended to remind it of its lowly origins and marginal status. While the first two features are common to many ancient Jewish texts, the third is unique to the exorcistic texts, and often gives them their special flavor.

Manuscripts and Versions

The texts translated below stem from a variety of textual sources, which include a scroll from Qumran, a para-biblical narrative that is extant in several Latin manuscripts, a metal-plate amulet apparently found in Egypt, a clay incantation bowl from Sassanian Iraq, and a Christian amulet written on papyrus. They may be listed as follows:

- 11Q11 = 11QApocryphal Psalms: A leather scroll, ca. 9.5 cm high and 71 cm wide, which originally contained six columns of Hebrew text, and which is usually dated to ca. 50-70 C.E.[10] It is badly mutilated, and only the last two columns are reasonably well preserved. The penultimate column contains an exorcistic psalm that is attributed to David, and the last column contains a version of Psalm 91, a Psalm whose exorcistic use was extremely common in Jewish circles, and later in Christian ones too.[11] This psalm may have been attributed here to David (unfortunately, there is a lacuna in this part of the text), an attribution that also is found in the Septuagint version thereof, hence its inclusion below. The extant parts of the earlier columns clearly show that the entire scroll consisted of exorcistic hymns, and in one place Solomon too is mentioned, but it is not clear whether they were all attributed to David or to Solomon, or perhaps they were attributed to other biblical figures, or were transmitted anonymously.[12]

  One interesting feature of this scroll is that the exorcistic psalm of David found in its penultimate column, or at least one of its central components—the direct rebuke of the demon and the description of his lowly origin and disturbing appearance—finds parallels both in several Babylonian incantation bowls and in one Genizah fragment, as shall be noted in the comments to the translation.[13] While in the later sources this refrain is nowhere identified as coming from a larger composition, or as originally being attributed to King David, the survival of such formulae within the Jewish magical tradition is quite remarkable.
- Pseudo-Philo, *Book of Biblical Antiquities* (*Liber Antiquitatum Biblicarum*; *L.A.B.*): This apocryphon retells the history of Israel from Adam to the death of Saul, adding many stories not found in the original biblical narratives.[14] It is extant only in a Latin version, which probably is a translation of a Greek text, which probably was translated from a Hebrew original, perhaps written in the first century B.C.E. or C.E. The passage that interests us is found in chapter 60, embedded in the stories about David, his rise to power (ch. 59), his fight with Goliath (ch. 61), and his friendship with Jonathan (ch.

10. For the text, see García Martínez et al., "11. 11Qapocryphal Psalms"; for a fuller discussion and further bibliography, see Bohak, *Ancient Jewish Magic*, 108-111.

11. See Kraus, "Septuaginta-Psalm 90 in apotropäischer Verwendung."

12. For the reference to Solomon, see col. II, line 2.

13. For a detailed study of these parallels, see Bohak, "From Qumran to Cairo."

14. For the *Liber Antiquitatum Biblicarum*, see esp. Jacobson, *A Commentary on Pseudo-Philo's* Liber Antiquitatum Biblicarum.

62). That the author of this narrative chose to devote a lengthy passage to the exorcistic psalm with which David cured Saul is hardly surprising, given his apparent interest in various magical practices and practitioners, and in David's psalms.[15] Unfortunately, the psalm he cites seems quite corrupt, and the many attempts to elucidate its obscure parts have not yet met with complete success, as may be seen from our translation of this difficult text.[16]

- A trilingual amulet (Ashmolean Museum, 1921.1121): A silver lamella, ca. 6 cm high and 12 cm wide, containing 38 lines of text, in Greek, Aramaic, and Hebrew, and dated by its editors to the fifth century C.E.[17] It is said to have come from Tell el-Amarna, and has been in the Ashmolean Museum, Oxford, from 1921. It contains an interesting mixture of magic words, signs and formulae, including the exorcistic psalm of David that is cited in lines 21-25.[18] Many features of this complex amulet show that it was copied from a written *Vorlage*, presumably a book of Jewish magical recipes of the kind that is well known from later copies, especially from the Cairo Genizah onwards.[19]
- A Babylonian incantation bowl, currently in the Moussaieff collection (M117): A clay bowl, 17.6 in diameter and 4.7 cm high, inscribed on its inside with 7 lines of text, in Aramaic and Hebrew.[20] It comes from an unknown location in present-day Iraq, and probably dates to the fifth or sixth century C.E. It contains the exorcistic psalm of David, followed by anti-demonic adjurations in Aramaic.
- A Christian amulet (*PGM* XVII = *P. land.* 6, Inv. 14): A Greek amulet, written on the verso of a papyrus sheet measuring 15.5 cm high and 30 cm wide and probably dating to the fifth or sixth century C.E. It comes from an uncertain location in Egypt (probably el-Ashmunein, i.e., Hermopolis), and contains several Christian passages (including an almost complete Pater Noster) and a "Solomonic" exorcism. Unfortunately, the scribe seems to have miscopied his *Vorlage*, which must have been written in several different columns, but was mistakenly copied as if it were one continuous text. In our translation, we follow the reconstruction of the text offered by Kuhlmann, which differs from that of Preisendanz in the *PGM* edition.[21]

Genre, Structure, and Prosody

As noted above, the exorcistic psalms are a distinct sub-genre of the wider genre of psalms and hymns, and are characterized by their very practical and very specific aims. Originally, they were meant to be recited in the presence of the demon(s)—either in a demon-infested environment or in the presence of a demoniac whom the exorcist was trying to cure. They therefore tended to be quite short, and to alternate between direct address of the demon(s) and more general descriptions of God's glory. And at least in some cases,

15. For other magic-related passages, see *L.A.B.* 34 (Aod, the Midianite magician) and 44 (Micah's magic idols). For another Davidic psalm, see *L.A.B.* 59.

16. For previous studies of *L.A.B.* 60, see esp. Bogaert, "Les *Antiquités Bibliques* du Pseudo-Philon"; Jackson, "Echoes and Demons"; and Jacobson, *A Commentary*, 82, 187-88, 1173-81.

17. See Kotansky, Naveh and Shaked, "A Greek-Aramaic Silver Amulet."

18. There is another reference to David's words spoken over King Saul in line 18a, but the words themselves are either lost in a lacuna, or were not quoted at all.

19. For a detailed discussion of this amulet, see Bohak, *Ancient Jewish Magic*, 232-34, 301-302.

20. See Levene, *A Corpus of Magic Bowls*, 77-82.

21. See Kuhlmann, *Die Gießener literarischen Papyri*, 170-83, esp. p. 176; for a translation which follows Preisendanz, see Meyer and Smith, *Ancient Christian Magic*, 45-46 (no. 21).

they may have been accompanied by music—this, at least, is how all our sources reconstructed the exorcism of Saul by David, in which David's words, accompanied by the playing of his lyre (cf. 1 Sam 16:23), are what drove the evil spirit away from King Saul.

Date and Provenance

As noted above, our psalms diverge widely when it comes to date and provenance. The two psalms from 11Q11 certainly stem from Second Temple period Palestine, and probably were composed in the first century B.C.E. or C.E. Unlike some of the other exorcistic hymns found at Qumran, they seem to be non-sectarian in origin, and they probably enjoyed quite a wide circulation in the Second Temple period, and perhaps even in later periods too, as can be seen from the echoes thereof among the Babylonian incantation bowls and a Genizah magical text. Similarly, the psalm now found in chapter 60 of the *Book of Biblical Antiquities* clearly stems from the Second Temple period, probably from Palestine, but it is not clear whether it first circulated as an exorcistic hymn and was then incorporated into the *Book of Biblical Antiquities*, or perhaps it was composed by the book's author as a kind of a literary exercise, in light of what he knew about contemporary Jewish exorcisms. In later periods, and in Christian hands, it clearly enjoyed a separate existence, and was transmitted both as a part of the *Book of Biblical Antiquities* and as an independent piece, the "Song of King David against Saul's Demon."[22]

When we turn to the last three psalms in our collection, the situation becomes much more complex. The trilingual Jewish amulet, the Moussaieff bowl, and the Greek Christian amulet were all written in the fifth or sixth centuries C.E., and they clearly do not preserve any Second Temple Jewish exorcistic psalms in their original state. However, in all three cases it is not clear whether the sections attributed to David and Solomon—within larger magical texts that have nothing to do with them or with their compositions—point to the survival, even if in garbled form, of older "Davidic" or "Solomonic" compositions, or to the composition, in late antiquity, of new exorcistic hymns and their attribution to these biblical figures. In the former case (which seems to the present writer far more likely), we would have sound evidence of the ongoing circulation of some of the exorcistic psalms of the Second Temple period in late-antique Egypt, Palestine(?), and Babylonia.[23] In the latter, we would have even sounder evidence that new "biblical" exorcistic hymns were being produced in late antiquity as well, and that the "pseudepigraphic habit" was still alive among some Jews at a time when it is often is assumed that Jews were no longer producing pseudepigraphic literature.

Literary context

One final question that needs addressing is the issue of the different literary contexts and social *Sitze im Leben* of these exorcistic psalms, and their relations to other ancient Jewish texts. As far as we currently know, Jews did not write on amulets, and certainly did not on incantation bowls, in the Second Temple period, and at that time the main use of magical psalms and spells was their recitation. This certainly is true of chapter 60 of the *Book of Biblical Antiquities*, which is identified as the psalm that David used to *recite*

22. See James, "Citharismus regis David contra demonium Saulis," 164-65, 183-85.

23. For the provenance of the Tell el-Amarna amulet, note that its Aramaic section begins with the words "this amulet is from Jerusalem" (Kotansky, Naveh, and Shaked, 8, line 7)—a claim which must, of course, be taken with more than a grain of salt.

before King Saul to drive the evil spirit away, and is likely to be true of 11Q11 as well—a collection of exorcistic psalms that probably were intended to be recited. But with our last three psalms, we move to late antiquity, to a time when Jews (and Christians) began to develop a more scribal form of magic, and to write down spells, hymns and adjurations on different writing surfaces as a part of the ritual process.[24] Thus, while the production of both the el-Amarna amulet and the Moussaieff bowl may have involved the oral recitation of the "Davidic" exorcistic psalms (and this certainly is true of the Christian amulet, with its Pater Noster and "Solomonic" exorcism), the main use of these exorcistic psalms now was scribal rather than oral, and they were incorporated into larger textual units and written down on a silver lamella, a clay bowl, or a piece of papyrus. How many exorcistic psalms supposedly composed by David and Solomon continued to be recited orally, or were written on organic writing materials that usually perished within a few centuries, are questions that are likely to remain open for many years to come.

The psalms' textual contexts are closely associated with their social *Sitze im Leben*. Being practical and technical, they seem to have circulated mainly among professional exorcists, or among groups with a great interest in demons and their evil powers, such as the Dead Sea sect. Thus, while they may have been accessible to anyone with an interest in Jewish magical practices (such as the author of the *Book of Biblical Antiquities*), in most cases they probably were transmitted from one exorcist to another in professional networks, and often suffered from the regular processes of textual entropy, including both errors in transmission and deliberate transformations and adaptations. As even a cursory reading of our translations would surely demonstrate, what we have today are merely the tattered remains of what once was a flourishing industry of "Davidic" and "Solomonic" exorcisms.

Bibliography

Benoit, Pierre. "Fragments d'une prière contre les esprits impurs?" *RB* 58 (1951): 549-65.

Bogaert, P.-M. "Les *Antiquités Bibliques* du Pseudo-Philon à la Lumière des Découvertes de Qumrân." Pages 313-31 in *Qumrân: Sa Piété, sa Théologie, et son Milieu*. Edited by M. Delcor. Paris: Duculot, 1978.

Bohak, G. *Ancient Jewish Magic: A History*. Cambridge: Cambridge University Press, 2008.

__________. "From Qumran to Cairo: The Lives and Times of a Jewish Exorcistic Formula (with an Appendix by Shaul Shaked)." Pages 31-52 in *Ritual Healing: Magic, Ritual and Medical Therapy from Antiquity until the Early Modern Period*. Edited by Ildikó Csepregi and Charles Burnett. Florence: SISMEL Edizioni del Galluzzo, 2012.

García Martínez, F., et al. "11. 11Qapocryphal Psalms." Pages 181-205 in *Qumran Cave 11 / II*. DJD 23. Oxford: Clarendon, 1998.

Halperin, David J. "The Book of Remedies, the Canonization of the Solomonic Writings, and the Riddle of Pseudo-Eusebius." *JQR* 72 (1982): 269-92.

Horst, Pieter Willem van der, and Judith H. Newman. *Early Jewish Prayers in Greek*. Commentaries on Early Jewish Literature. Berlin: Walter de Gruyter, 2008.

Jackson, H. M. "Echoes and Demons in the Pseudo-Philonic *Liber Antiquitatum Biblicarum*." *JSJ* 27 (1996): 1-20.

24. For the scribalization of the Jewish magical tradition, see Swartz, "Scribal Magic and Its Rhetoric"; Bohak, *Ancient Jewish Magic*, 281-85.

Jacobson, Howard. *A Commentary on Pseudo-Philo's* Liber Antiquitatum Biblicarum. AGJU 31. 2 vols. Leiden: Brill, 1996.

James, M. R. "Citharismus regis David contra demonium Saulis." Pages 164-65, 183-85 in *Apocrypha Anecdota*. Texts and Studies II/3. Cambridge: Cambridge University Press, 1893.

Kotansky, R., J. Naveh, and S. Shaked. "A Greek-Aramaic Silver Amulet from Egypt in the Ashmolean Museum." *Mus* 105 (1992): 5-26.

Kraus, Thomas J. "Septuaginta-Psalm 90 in apotropäischer Verwendung: Vorüberlegungen für eine kritische Edition und (bisheriges) Datenmaterial." *BN* 125 (2005): 39-73.

Kuhlmann, Peter Alois. *Die Gießener literarischen Papyri und die Caracalla-Erlasse: Edition, Übersetzung und Kommentar*. Berichte und Arbeiten aus der Universitätsbibliothek und dem Universitätsarchiv Giessen, 46. Gießen: Universitätsbibliothek, 1994.

Levene, Dan. *A Corpus of Magic Bowls: Incantation Texts in Jewish Aramaic from Late Antiquity*. The Kegan Paul Library of Jewish Studies. London: Kegan Paul, 2003.

LiDonnici, Lynn R. "'According to the Jews': Identified (and Identifying) 'Jewish' Elements in the *Greek Magical Papyri*." Pages 87-108 in *Heavenly Tablets: Interpretation, Identity and Tradition in Ancient Judaism*. Edited by Lynn LiDonnici and Andrea Lieber. JSJSup 119. Leiden: Brill, 2007.

Meyer, Marvin, and Richard Smith. *Ancient Christian Magic: Coptic Texts of Ritual Power*. San Francisco: HarperSanFrancisco, 1994.

Swartz, Michael D. "Scribal Magic and Its Rhetoric: Formal Patterns in Hebrew and Aramaic Incantation Texts from the Cairo Genizah." *HTR* 83 (1990): 163-180.

Torijano, Pablo A. *Solomon the Esoteric King: From King to Magus, Development of a Tradition*. JSJSup 73. Leiden: Brill, 2002.

Exorcistic Psalms of David and Solomon

1) 11Q11 col. V l. 4–col. VI, l. 3

Of David, [.. a whi]sper in the Name of the Lord [..] time to heaven.
1 [If] it comes to you by ni[ght[a] s]ay to it:
Who are you, (born) [from the seed] of man and from the seed of the ho[ly on]es?[b]
2 Your face is the face of [nothingne]ss,
and your horns are the horns of [a dre]am;[c]
3 You are darkness and not light,
[injusti?]ce and not righteousness.
4 The chief of the army, the Lord [shall send you down] to the depth of
Luke 8:31 [Sheo]l,
[and shall shut the ga]tes of bronze,
[... n]o light, and the sun, which [shines for the] righteous,
shall not [shine for you?].[d]
5 [..] and you shall say...[e]

Psalm 91 2) 11Q11 col. VI, ll. 3-14[f]

1 [Of David. Whoever dwells] in the shelter [of the Most High],
[and resides in the shadow] of the Almighty,

---

a. This reconstruction is supported by the Genizah parallel (see note c) and by the reference in *L.A.B.* 60 (our No. 3) to exorcism by night.

b. For the demons' origins from the miscegenation of the Fallen Angels and the daughters of man (Gen 6:1-4), see *1 Enoch* 6-9.

c. A Genizah fragment of the eleventh century (T-S K 1.123) contains the following Hebrew formula, in the midst of an Aramaic spell: "...and it c[omes] up[o]n you, whether by day or by night, and it shall say to you (or, perhaps, 'it shall be said to it'), Who are you, whether from the seed of man or from the seed of cattle? your face is the face of old age(?) and your horns(?) are (like) a water-current." For the demons' horns, see also *b. Pesah* 111b, and the horned demons depicted on some of the Babylonian incantation bowls.

d. Two Babylonian incantation bowls, Martin Schøyen 2053/7 and 2053/236, contain the following Hebrew formula, embedded in much longer Aramaic texts: "Your (sg.) face is the face of a lowly creature, your horn is the horn of animate beings. May God smite you and put an end to you, for you shall die if you come near and if you touch (the client's name)." Similiar expressions appear in two other bowls, Moussaieff 123 and 138, published by Levene, *A Corpus*, 83-91.

e. The text continues for 5 more lines, which are too mutilated to support a coherent translation.

f. While this psalm is badly mutilated, its strong similarity to Psalm 91 increases the likelihood of the accuracy of the reconstructed lacunae.

2 Who says [to the Lord, my God is my haven] and my fortress,
a stronghold in which [I shall trust].
3 [For h]e will save you fr[om the fowler's tra]p,
from a troub[lesome] pestilence.
4 He shall cover [you wi]th his pinions,
and under his [wing]s you shall abide.
5 His mercy is upon you as a protection,
and his truth is a shield, Selah.
6 You shall not fear the terror by night,
or the arrow that flies by day,
or the scourge that rages at [n]oon,
or the pestilence that walks in [the da]rk.
7 A thousand will fall on your (left) side,
a myr[iad on] your [r]ight,
(but) it shall [no]t touch [you].
8 Only look with your eyes,
[and you shall s]ee the recompense of the wicked.
9 [You have invo]ked [your ha]ven,
[..] his delight.
10 [You sha]ll see no [evil],
and no affliction [shall touch your te]nt.
11 For He shall comman[d his angels]
to protect you on your way.
12 They [shall carry] you in their hands,
lest your foot [stumble upon a st]one.
13 You shall tread upon a snake and [a viper?],
and trampl[e a lion] and a serpent.
14 You desired [the Lord] and [He shall save you],
and [exalt you and sh]ow you his salva[tion, Selah].

3) Pseudo-Philo, L.A.B. 60

And at that time the Spirit of the Lord was removed from Saul, and an evil spirit
tormented him. And Saul sent for and brought David, and David played on his
lyre a psalm by night. And this is the psalm that David played for Saul in order 1 Sam 16:14-23
that the unjust spirit would depart from him:

1 Darkness and Silence existed before the world came into being;
and Silence spoke, and Darkness appeared.
2 Then your name was created in the fastening together (?) of what had been spread out,
of which the upper part was called Heaven and the lower one was called Earth.
3 And the upper part was commanded to bring down rain according to its season,
and the lower part was commanded to produce food for all creatures.
4 And after that was the tribe of your spirits created.
5 And now, do not be troublesome, since you are a secondary creation.

6 Otherwise, remember Tartarus wherein you walk.[a]
7 Or is it not enough for you to hear that by means of what resounds before you, I play the psalm to many?
8 Or don't you remember that your creation was from an echo in the abyss?[b]
9 But the new womb, from which I was born, will rebuke you, from which in time one will be born from my loins and will rule over you.[c]

And as David sang this hymn, the spirit spared Saul.

4) The Tel el-Amarna Amulet

These are the words of David, the singing songs that he would recite over King [Saul]:
1 Redeem me, Lord, and save me from all the evil demons and all the evil spirits that [...].
2 Recite a song of praises to the glorious King [..] and mighty,
the God who created the spirits. [...] Hallelujah.
Zech 3:2; Jude 9 3 May the Lord rebuke you, He who rebukes the Satan,
he who rules all [...] of the eye, who dwells in Jerusalem in holiness.[d]
4 Harbiel is on my right, Azriel is on my left,
above me is God's Shekh[ina], before me are two camps (*Mahanayim*),
as it is said "And Jacob said when he saw them,
Gen 32:3 [Evv 32:2] This is a camp of God."

5) The Moussaieff Bowl

2 Sam 23:1; 1 Chr 29:29 These are th[e words of David], the first, the last, {the last}, which he is playing
before King Saul:
1 In the name of the Lord of Hosts,
the God of Israel,
who sits upon the Cherubim,
2 against all the afflictions,
against all the demons,
against every spirit,
against every fever and shivering,
against every (evil) eye.
3 And give glory to the Name of Glory,
and may they go away from the place of dwelling of, {which is before} (client's name).
4 Blessed are you, Lord, the God of David, who heals the sick.

---

a. Cf. the reference in 11Q11 (our No. 1) to the demons' banishment to the depth of Sheol.

b. For the creation of a demon out of an echo (derived from a Hebrew pun on *hed* and *shed*?), see also *T. Sol.* 4.8.

c. This might be a Christian interpolation, but might also be a rather cryptic allusion to Solomon and his war on demons.

d. The original psalm may have ended here, but as the next sentence is still in Hebrew, it may have been considered a part of the Hebrew psalm.

6) PGM XVII

An exorcism of Solomon against every impure spirit, (which?) God has granted:

1 *You shall tread upon a snake and a viper,*
and trample a lion and a serpent. Ps 90:13 LXX
2 [... God?] is invincible and [..],
by whose side stand myriads of myriads of angels,
and thousands of th[ousands]. Dan 7:10
3 [...] which govern the [...]
the demon of noon or of night, Ps 91:6
of shivering [...] by day or by night,[a]
or the blind,
dumb,
speechless,
toothless demons.[b]
4 [... I adjure] you, by the arm of the immortal [God,
and by] his right hand,
and by his fearful and holy Name.[c]
[Drive witch]craft and every illness and evil (demonic) encounter away from the wearer (of this amulet).

a. For this formula, cf. the Genizah parallel adduced above, p. 294, n. c.

b. This list probably is intended as a taunt hurled at the demons, stressing their powerlessness and ugly appearance.

c. The "Exorcism of Solomon" probably ended here, but even this is uncertain.

The Selenodromion of David and Solomon

A new translation and introduction

by Pablo A. Torijano

The *Selenodromion of David and Solomon* is an example of the esoteric writings that were popular during late antiquity in Jewish, Christian, and pagan environments. The present title of this text appears in one of the manuscripts that preserve it (*Atheniensis* 10), although it can have other attributions such as to Aristotle or Ezra or no attribution at all. This title makes reference to a particular astrological genre that was linked to the lunar month.

Contents

The text mentions each day of a lunar month, describing who was born or what happened in that day, whether it is lucky or not, whether a sick person will recover or not, what sort of child is born in that day, whether the fugitive and the lost thing will be found or not, whether a dream will come true or not. The nature of each day depends on the Biblical character or situation that supposedly occurred in it. There is no mention of specific types of magic as we find in other similar genres such as the so-called *apotelesmata* of the moon (i.e., effects of the moon).

Manuscripts

The work is preserved in the following Greek manuscripts:

1. *Codex Atheniensis 10*, f. 22-26. An eighteenth-century manuscript that lacks the first four days of the month and the thirteenth day. It is the text edited by Delatte and the basis for the present translation. It is named "Selenodromion of David and Solomon."

2. *Codex Mediolanensis 16*, f. 39v-46. A thirteenth-century manuscript whose text is very similar to that of the *Selenodromion*. In the present translation, it supplies the first five days that *Atheniensis* lacks and some additional material from days eleven, thirteen, and sixteen. It expands in various ways the actions that could or could not be undertaken on each day and preserves some allusions to the pagan gods and other entities. Each day is referred to both a pagan god and an OT character or situation. The work is called "Selenodromion or prophetic oracle of the moon."

3. *Codex Parisinus Graecus 1884*, f. 150v-153. A sixteenth-century manuscript whose text seems to be a parallel tradition to the *Selenodromion*, since it distributes the days of the month according to their suitability to certain actions. The work is attributed to Melampodus, "sacred scribe," and is divided into two books, the second one being the *Selendromion*-like text. It shares with the *Codex parisinus Graecus 1148* (see below) the mention of Heliopolis as the supposed place of origin of the work. The actions to be performed or avoided follow closely the structure of the *Selenodromion of David and Solomon*. There is no mention of OT characters or situations. It is named "Selenodromion."

4. *Codex 2280 Bibliothecae Universitatis* f. 333v-334. A sixteenth-century manuscript whose text is related to that of *Cod. Med 16*, but without the allusion to pagan divinities. The work is called "Selenodromion of every day, good and bad."

5. *Codex Berolinensis 173*, f. 150-152; f. 177v-180. A fifteenth-century manuscript that preserves two works similar to *Codex Mediolanensis 16*. The first one is called "Diagnostic of the thirty days of the moon." The second one is called "Selenodromion of the Thirty Days." It lacks the mentions of the pagan gods.

6. *Codex Dredensis 33*. A sixteenth-century manuscript that is similar to *Mediolanensis 16*, but which has been abbreviated. It has no title.

7. *Codex Parisinus Graecus 1191*, f. 59v-64 v. A fifteenth-century manuscript related to *Mediolanensis 16* and *Atheniensis 10*. The work is called "About the moon. Prognostic of the days that God revealed to the Prophet Ezra."

8. *Codex Parisinus Graecus 2149*, f. 1166v. A fifteenth-century manuscript related to *Codices Mediolanensis 16* and *Atheniensis 10*. The work is called "Explication of all the days of the moon, the good and the bad ones. Doctrine of Aristotle."

9. *Codex Parisinus Graecus 1148,* f. 189-1195. The work begins as follows: "Book found at Heliopolis of Egypt, in the Temple's sanctuary, written in sacred characters during the reign of Psamilos."

These manuscripts are dated from the thirteenth to the eighteenth centuries. Most of them are similar in contents, but show some variety in their distribution of the material and their exact wording. The fact that the work was copied during a long period indicates its popularity. The original language of the work is Koine Greek.

Genre, Structure, and Literary Context

The work fits perfectly in the so-called selenodromion or lunarium genre. The oldest examples of this type of astrological texts have parallels in Akkadian literature and are well documented from the second century C.E. in the Greco-Roman Mediterranean world. They were known and used in Jewish circles as well, as 4Q318 (*4QZodiology and Brontology ar*) indicates. These texts suggest the actions to be undertaken for a determined day according to the course of the moon. In some of them, each day was linked with the birth of a god. In the *Selenodromion of David and Solomon* the pagan allusions are replaced by biblical material, referring in most cases to well-known characters or biblical situations; these "quotations" are taken mainly from the creation narrative and the stories of the patriarchs, with only three references to the book of Exodus (Exod 2, 15, 16), one to the Jews entering the Promised Land (Josh 3:17) and one to the birth of Samuel (1 Sam 1). As it has been said above, part of the manuscript tradition has a double day-attribution (to both a pagan god and a biblical character), and the *Selenodromion* mentions Apollo in the eighth day. This suggests that the final stage of the *Selenodromion* tradition resulted from the reworking of previous pagan models. The title of the work has little to do with its actual contents; its ascription to David and Solomon was made on the basis of the ancient esoteric traditions that were linked with both kings in Jewish and Christian contexts. It reinforces the pseudepigraphic fiction that would otherwise be quite weak.

Date and Provenance

The text does not offer direct data about its origin and dates of composition and redaction. However, the Koine Greek in which it is written could be dated roughly around the sixth or seventh century C.E. It is clear that it is a pagan text that was reworked; the absence of Christian themes and the use of the OT motifs seem to point to a Jewish setting. It is interesting to note that the calendar of the *Selenodromion* does not follow the Jewish lunar calendar of 354 days nor the solar one of 364 but assumes a 360-day year that is the calendar used in the traditional Mesopotamian astrology. As that calendar underlies the calendar of *1 Enoch* and 4Q318, it seems to strengthen the Jewish provenance of the text, since that calendar was known and used in earlier Jewish texts of similar contents.

The actions and situations that are described in each day point clearly to an urban setting with a significant presence of servants and slaves. The *Selenodromion* insists on telling whether a fugitive will be found or not on a determined day, which could refer to a social phenomenon called *anachōrēsis* ("withdrawal, departure, flight") which is well documented mainly in Roman and Byzantine Egypt. The *anachōrēsis* was a sort of civil resistance by which the poor and the servants that were linked to the field fled from the overburden of official taxes. This last aspect could be alluded to in the text by the use of the Greek verb *anachōrein* ("to retire") at least in the twenty-fifth day. This evidence points to the text having been written in Roman-Byzantine Egypt by the end of late antiquity, around the fifth or sixth century of our era.

Bibliography

Cumont, F., H. Boll, et al. *Catalogus Codicum Astrologorum Graecorum.* 12 vols. Brussels: H. Lamertin, 1898-1956.

__________. "Les Présages lunaires de Virgile et les Selenodromia." *L'Antiquité Classique* 2 (1933): 259–70.

García Martínez, Florentino. "Magic in the Dead Sea Scrolls." Pages 13-34 in *The Metamorphosis of Magic from Late Antiquity to the Early Modern Period.* Edited by Jan N. Bremmer and Jan R. Veenstra. Groningen Studies in Cultural Change 1. Leuven: Peeters, 2002.

Goodenough, E. R. *Jewish Symbols in the Greco-Roman Period.* Bollingen Series, vol. 37. 13 vols. New York: Pantheon, 1953-68.

Greenfield, J. C. "4QZodiology and Brontology Ar." Pages 259-74 in *Qumran Cave 4.XXVI: Cryptic Texts and Miscellanea.* Edited by P. Alexander et al. DJD 36. Oxford: Clarendon, 2000.

Nau, F. "Analyse de deux opuscules astrologiques attribués au prophete Esdras et d'un calendrier lunaire de l'Ancient Testament attribué à Esdras, aux Egyptiens et même à Aristote." *Révue de l'Orient Chrétien* 12 (1907): 14-21.

Reiner, Erica. *Astral Magic in Babylonia.* TAPS 85. Philadelphia, Pa.: American Philosophical Society, 1995.

Torijano, Pablo A. *Solomon the Esoteric King: From King to Magus, Development of a Tradition.* JSJSup 73. Leiden: Brill, 2002. An earlier version of the translation published below was published in this volume on pp. 300-315.

Principle of the Selenodromion of David the Prophet and His Son Solomon

1. On the first day of the moon, Adam, the first formed, was created. This day is good and beautiful for any action: to buy, to sell, to sail, to travel, to make testaments, to buy bodies. The fugitive and the lost thing will be found. The ones born will be lively, lucky, and successful. The one who begins to be sick in this day will be soon healed. If someone sees a dream, it is revealed on the same day. The one who will go to feast, if he sees himself sleeping, understand that you will conquer all your enemies. Gen 1:27; 2:7

2. On the second day, the morning star was created. Eve was formed from Adam's side. This day is good for everything and favorable for marriages, it is good to spread oil and grain, to speak with the powerful, to do business. The fugitive servant and the lost thing will be found, the one who begins to be sick, after suffering greatly, will stand up again. If someone sees a dream, it will turn out true after three days. The one who is born on this day will be wise if he is male Gen 2:21-22

3. On the third day, the winds and the spirits were created. Cain was born. This day is terrible among all and dangerous; no sowing, no reaping, no going to the big road, nor planting vineyards. The fugitive and the lost thing will not be found. The one who begins to be sick will die. The ones who are born on this day will be evil, forsworn, mad, abuser, intractable, sullen. If someone sees a dream, it will turn out true in the same day, especially if it is difficult. Gen 4:1

4. On the fourth day, Abel was born. This day is good and beautiful to offer sacrifices and make prayers to god and the holy ones, to try any action, especially to work in the field, to buy slaves and cattle, and to do any business. The fugitive and the lost thing will not be found. The ones born will be sick and short-lived. The one who begins to be sick will die. If one sees a dream, it will turn out true after three days, especially if it hurts. Gen 4:2

5. On the fifth day, Cain made sacrifices to God, but he was not recognized. This day should be observed without offering sacrifices or going to the big road. The begotten male (is) forsworn and reckless. If she is female, she will be reckless with her own parents. The fugitive will be found with difficulty. The person who has begun to be sick dies. Your dream, if you see it, do not disclose. Gen 4:3-5

6. Day six. On the same (day), Cain was killed and Nimrod was born. And it will Gen 10:8

be good for carrying out any procedure, learning techniques, buying animals and beasts, hunt, fish, making marriages, sowing, (and) harvesting. The newborn will be troublesome and ill educated. If a girl is born, (she will be) rebellious and prone to run away. The sick heals and the fugitive after {...} days will be found. And the dream will turn out true quickly.

7. Day seven. On the same day Abel was killed by his brother Cain and Apollo
Gen 4:8 was born. The same day is good to sow, harvest, collect medicinal plants, and make petitions, to intercede for someone, (and) cut off one's hair in mourning. The newborn will be skilled in everything, wise and strong; he is short-lived, excellent in selling and buying; he will have a sign on his right foot. If female, she will be a midwife. The fugitive will be saved, the sick person dies quickly.

Gen 5:21-22 **8**. Day eight. On the same (day) Methuselah was born. The same (day) is good to sell and buy anything you want. The newborn (is) useful and will live seventy-five years. The fugitive will be found. The sick person heals quickly.

Gen 5:32 **9**. Day nine. On the same (day), Ham was born. The same (day) is transitional, neither good nor bad. In the same (day), if you want something, do it with care. The fugitive will be brought back tied. The one who begins to be sick worsens. What has been taken will be hidden away; and the dream will become true in nine days.

Gen 5:28-29 **10**. On the tenth day, Noah was born. The same (day) is good to plough the fields, buy animals, (and) educate children. Whoever is born will be fortunate and long-lived. The fugitive will be found. What has been destroyed will be hidden. The one who begins to be sick dies, and your dream will quickly become true.

Gen 5:32 **11**. On the eleventh day, Shem was born. This day is good and beautiful for every action, to buy, to sell, to sow, to harvest fruits, and to pour wines; if you want something, do it; do not be afraid of sailing, making marriages, engaging in business, digging foundations, selling, (or) buying. The fugitive will be found quickly. The one who is sick will heal quickly; but if he worsens in his sickness, he will die.

Gen 8:20 **12**. On the twelfth (day) of the Moon, Noah offered sacrifice to God. The same (day) is good to make sacrifices, sow, (and) harvest. Do not buy slaves, because they will flee and die. Those who are born (will be) ill educated. If they hurry to the prime of life they will encounter many good things. The one who begins to be sick will die quickly.

13. On the thirteenth (day), the vineyard was planted by Noah **(cf. Gen 9:20)**. This day is good and beautiful for planting vineyards, to prune, (and) to plant trees. It is bad to hunt and to go on the road. The drunk fugitive will be captured. The ones born are drunk and mad and abusive. The one who begins to be sick will die. If someone sees a dream, it will turn out true in two or four days. He has quarrels and fights, however he does not prevail.

14. On the fourteenth (day), Noah blessed Shem. The same (day) is good for anything you may do: All who are in court will be slowly destroyed; they will make friendship in battle; (it is good) to make marriages (and) to be engaged in business. The ones born will be fortunate and long-lived. The fugitive will be found. The sick person will heal; and the dream will come true quickly. Gen 9:26-27

15. On the fifteenth (day), the languages of the builders of the tower changed into many. This day is good and nice to prepare the furnace, clear thorns from the field, forge iron tools, build houses, to devote oneself to learning, to weave, to buy, (and) to sell. The one born will be knavish, with ability in all the skills and talkative. The tied fugitive will be found quickly. Gen 11:6-9

16. On the sixteenth (day), Nahor was born and suffered pain to be born. This is good to give oneself to the learning of music and instruments, to sow, harvest, buy fields, (and) lay foundations. The one born will be great but intemperate, both in his youth and his old age. He will have a sign on his head. The ones born will be drunk and abusive. The one who begins to be sick will recover quickly. If a person sees a dream, it will come true in the same day. Gen 11:22

17. On the seventeenth (day), Sodom and Gomorrah came to ruin. This day is good for harvesting (and) to have one's hair and one's beard cut. Do not go out walking or to the court of justice, and do not become surety for another. The ones born are short-lived. The one who begins to be sick will be in danger, and from the peril will die. And the dream will come true quickly. Gen 19:24-25

18. On the eighteenth (day), Isaac was born. In the same day (it is good) to water the gardens and dig wells. The children born are prescient. The sick will recover and the dream will be good and beautiful. Gen 21:2-3

19. On the nineteenth (day), Jacob was born. This day is good to make money. Those born then are long-lived. If he is a male, he will live long. The feeble heals. And the dream will turn out true in a good manner. Gen 25:26

20. On the twentieth (day), Isaac blessed Jacob. On the same day it is good to repay a vow, cast seed, water the fields, pour wine and dissolve wine and honey, sell, buy and associate with many. The fugitive will be found in the mill. Those born are fortunate and long-lived. And the sick will recover. Gen 27:27-29

21. On the twenty-first (day), Esau was honored by Isaac. This day is useful for nothing but for castrating young pigs, rams, bulls, and horses. The children born will be hateful. The fugitive and the lost will be hidden. The person who is very sick is in danger. The one born will be libertine, full of curses, and tricky. Gen 27:39-40

22. On the twenty-second (day), the very handsome Joseph was born. On the same (day) it is good to sell and buy, to take care of the house, to pay the workers. The ones born thrive like young plants. The fugitive and what is lost will appear as hateful. The sick heals; and the dream will quickly come true. Gen 30:24-25

Gen 35:16-18 **23**. On the twenty-third (day), Benjamin was born. This day is good for any practical procedure, and for taking care of the house. The fugitive will reach supplication. The sick heals. The children born will be short-lived. What is lost will be found, and the dream will turn out true.

24. On the twenty-fourth (day), Joshua son of Nun was born. [...] and the child born will be whole to his parents and will live to eighty-eight years. The soldier who is away from home in the war will be back in good health. The one who has been engaged in business, will have profit. The sick will die quickly. What is lost will be found quickly. And her dream will come true.

Gen 40:20 **25**. On the twenty-fifth (day), Pharaoh was born. Avoid any activity: no selling or buying, no sailing, no going out to the road or buying slaves. The child born dies by iron. The slave who fled into the wilderness will be found. The sick person heals with difficulty. The robber will not be found. And the dream manifests itself in seven days.

Exod 2:2 **26**. On the twenty-sixth (day), Moses the prophet was born. This (day) is good for any action, to sell, buy, sow, harvest, sail and hunt, (and) dedicate (oneself) to learning a technique. What is born then will be sick and in all kind of danger. The fugitive, the lost thing, and the one who steals will not be found. The sick heals and the dream will come true.

Exod 15:17-26 **27**. On the twenty-seventh (day), the children of Israel went out from Egypt. This (day) is good for any deed, to sell, to buy, for marriage. The newborn is short-lived if it is male; if it is female, (it will be) full of life. And whoever may be sick, quickly heals. And the dream will come true.

Exod 16:13 **28**. On the twenty-eighth (day), God showered quail upon the children of Israel. The same (day) is good for anything, to take care of the fields, to speak with the powerful, to educate the children. The slave who has fled to the wilderness will be found. The sick heals; and what is lost will be found; and the dream will turn out true.

Gen 11:26 **29**. On the twenty-ninth (day), Abraham was born and the Jews entered into
Josh 3:17 the land of promise. The same (day) is productive for anything: to take care of the fields, to do business, to make a will. The sick heals, and what is born will be disobedient. What is lost will not be found. And her dream is not true.

1 Sam 1:20 **30**. On the thirtieth (day), Samuel the prophet was born. This (day) is good; whatever you want, do it: going on a journey, taking care of birds, bees, and pruning raw silk. The one born will be a great man, a ruler of high repute, but a fornicator. If he is male, he will be very shameless and evil and will do bad actions. The fugitive will be found after some time. What is lost will be hidden. The sick heals. And the dream will turn out true in ten days.

End of the Selenodromion of David the prophet and his son Solomon.

The Hygromancy of Solomon

A new translation and introduction

by Pablo A. Torijano

The *Hygromancy of Solomon* is part of the corpus of esoteric writings that were frequent in both Judaism and Christianity during late antiquity and that were still used and copied until the modern era. The title is due to Heeg, editor of one of the manuscripts that preserve it; it has been called the *Epistle to Rehoboam* as well, on the basis of the dialogue between Solomon and his son Rehoboam which structures its contents. Two of the surviving manuscripts present different titles, "Interpretation of Solomon to his son Rehoboam" and "Beginning of the astrological treatise of the congregation and addition of the spirits" respectively; they seem to be more introductory headers than titles, so it is better to maintain the modern denomination of the work for the sake of clarity.

Contents

The *Hygromancy* deals with astrology and several magical procedures, and its text varies greatly, depending on the manuscript. In the version that is presented in these pages, Solomon purportedly teaches his son Rehoboam the technique of divination through water (hygromancy—"divination by means of moisture") although in fact such a technique is not explained; it is shown how this way of divination is linked with the exact knowledge of the planets, zodiacal signs, and the times when each of them gives its power. The text begins with a brief dialogue between Solomon and Rehoboam, which will constitute the literary frame for the astrological techniques necessary for securing power, wealth, and love. Afterwards, the text presents a hierarchy of planetary gods, angels and demons and furnishes a detailed account of the actions to be undertaken in every hour of each day of the week, depending on what planet (Helios, Aphrodite, Hermes, Kronos, Zeus, Ares) rules it. The week begins with the day of Helios, Sunday, and ends in Saturday, following the Jewish chronological sequence of days; the deeds and actions refer mainly to everyday situations (business, love, work, networking, and public relations) and in many occasions only indicate that the day is lucky or unlucky without mentioning a determined activity. After this weekly calendar, Solomon gives further instructions to Rehoboam, indicating for each of the twenty-four hours of each day a demon and an angel who rule in that hour. The text goes on to describe the prayers that should be addressed to the planets to gain their favor, the symbols (*charactēres*) of each and every planet and the way to prepare them and, finally, the plants that correspond to each zodiacal sign and planet; this last unit of the text constitutes a small tractate of astrological medicine dealing with the properties and effects of the plants of the planets in various situations.

Manuscripts and Original Language

The textual history of the *Hygromanteia* is complex. The work has been preserved in eighteen manuscripts, dated from the fifteenth to the eighteenth centuries C.E. They are the following:

1. *Codex Monacensis Graecus 70*. A sixteenth-century manuscript that presents a fairly continuous text written in a Greek that sometimes is difficult to understand. This is the text edited by Heeg, which is the basis for the present translation.

2. *Codex Taurinensis C VII* 15. A fifteenth-century manuscript formed with fragments of several codices written by different hands in the fifteenth century. The title's work is "Interpretation." It was lost in a fire, so we have only the beginning of the work and a brief description of its general content.

3. *Codex Parisinus Graecus 2419*. A fifteenth-century manuscript that seems to be a handbook of magic, astrology, and similar matters. It preserves only the beginning of the text and it is written in a cryptographic alphabet.

4. *Codex 1265 of the National Library of Athens*. A sixteenth-century manuscript that contains, among other materials, a magical treatise attributed to Solomon which is clearly linked with the *Hygromancy*.

5. *Manuscript 115 of the Historic and Ethnographic Society of Athens*. An eighteenth-century manuscript; besides diverse magical material, it preserves a different version of the same magical treatise of *Codex 1265*. Both this manuscript and *Codex 1265* seem to be a later version of the text of the *Hygromancy* as appears in *Monacensis 70*, and provide supplementary materials that shed light on the inner working of the textual tradition.

6. *Codex Harleainus 5596, British Museum*. An important manuscript of the fifteenth century. It is a handbook of magic and astrology, containing fragments of two recensions of the *Testament of Solomon*. The *Hygromancy* is called here "astrological treatise of the congregation and addition of the spirits."

7. *Codex Petropolitanus 3 (Cod. Academicus Musaei Palaeographi)*. A seventeenth-century manuscript; it contains, among other materials, the beginning of the *Hygromancy* that is entitled here "Interpretation."

8. *Codex Petropolitanus 4 (Cod. Bibl. Publicae 575)*. A seventeenth-century manuscript that preserves a fragment of the *Hygromancy*. The two Petropolitani codices show a striking interest in both the *Hygromancy* and the *decans* of the *Testament of Solomon*. The work is called "Technique."

9. *Codex Petropolitanus 5 (Cod. Bibl. Publicae 646)*. A eighteenth-century manuscript, the work is called "technique." There is not direct mention of Solomon but it is related to *Cod. Petr. 3* and *4*.

10. *Codex Mount Athos Dionys. Mon. 282*. A manuscript of the sixteenth century which contains an incomplete version of the *Hygromancy*. The title is "Little key of the complete technique of the Hygromancy found by different creators, and compiled by Solomon."

11. *Codex Atheniensis 30 (=cod. 167)*. A manuscript from the beginning of the eighteenth century; one of the works it contains is entitled "Prayer and exorcism of the prophet Solomon." It lists the names of the angels and demons who preside each hour of the day of the week. The text is incomplete.

12. *Manuscript U of Testament of Solomon* (=cod. 1030 Library Ambrosiana). It is a manuscript of the sixteenth century; besides other materials, it contains several incomplete fragments of the *Testament of Solomon* and two pages of the *Hygromancy*.

13. *Manuscript Bononiensis 3632*. A fifteenth-century manuscript; the work is called

"Astrological treatise for the congregation of spirits." Part of the manuscript is written in a cryptographic system.

14. *Manuscript Mediolanensis H 2 infer.* A sixteenth-century manuscript; the work is called "Hygromancy: The small key of the whole art of the hygromancy found by several creators and by the holy prophet Solomon."

15. *Manuscript Mediolanensis E 37 sup.* A sixteenth-century manuscript; it has the same title as that of the previous manuscript.

16. *Neapolitanus II C 33.* A fifteenth-century manuscript; the work appears without title and in an abridged version. The disposition of the material is different from that of *Monacensis 70.*

17. *Manuscript Vindobonensis ph. gr. 108.* A fifteenth-century manuscript; it is written in two different cryptographic systems that appear in the *Codex Parisiensis Graecus 2419* and in *Manuscript Bononiensis 3632.*

18. *Manuscript Gennadianus 45.* A sixteenth-century manuscript that preserves several parts of the *Hygromancy* of Solomon, but in a different order. The botanical treatise differs slightly from *Monacensis 70.*

Although it is likely that this list of manuscripts is not complete due to the transmission peculiarities of the texts of ritual power, it gives us an idea of the importance and popularity of the *Hygromancy*. The earliest manuscript can be dated in the fifteenth century and the latest one at the beginning of the eighteenth, so the work was still used in modern times. It is written in Koine Greek, and there are no hints of a previous Semitic version either in Hebrew or Aramaic; the use of the suffix *-el* as part of the angelic names is recurrent in magical text of various provenances and does not imply any concrete filiation. The quality of the language of each manuscript varies greatly; the version that is being translated in these pages (*Monacensis Graecus 70*) presents a fairly good Greek. The other witnesses oscillate between Koine Greek of poor quality and Medieval Greek. On linguistic and philological grounds they seem to go back to Byzantine copies. Their geographic origin is also very diverse, which adds to the popularity of the work. It is noteworthy that three of the manuscripts (numbers 3, 6, 12), which show a clear inner relation between them, seem to have been copied in Southern Italy.

Genre and Structure

It is difficult to classify the *Hygromanteia* with regard to its literary genre. The pseudepigraphic fiction of the dialogue between Solomon and Rehoboam has a didactic finality; however its setting is very crude. It begins without any introduction or background such as we do find, for example, in other genres (testaments, apocalypses, etc.). The main asset of that literary pattern is the presence of Solomon as anchor of the astrological material present in the text. Strictly speaking, the *Hygromancy* is a technical compendium of astrological and demonological material; it fits well in the category of literary handbooks of esoteric knowledge much in the line of the Jewish *Sefer ha-Razim* and *Harba di-Moshe*, or the *Testament of Solomon.*

If it is difficult to define the literary genre, we tackle the same problem when analyzing its structure. In the majority of the manuscripts, the work is clearly divided in two parts. The first one, which we have called the *Hygromancy*, composed mainly of astrological instructions and in which the different units that form it are structured around the dialogue between Solomon and Rehoboam, shows no hints of Christianization and for the most part it is written in Koine Greek. The second part, which appears in at least nine of the more complete manuscripts, is formed by a treatise composed of a collection of magical practices and recipes (hygromancy, lecanomancy, catoptromancy, exorcisms). In its present state, this treatise is later than the first part or Hygromancy, since it is written in Byzantine Greek; however, many of the practices it describes are either directly linked with or are Christian reworkings of the ones that appear in magical papyri of late antiquity. Its relationship with the first part is weak since the pseudepigraphic fiction of the dialogue between Solomon and Rehoboam, which constitutes the structural backbone of the *Hygromancy*, is kept only in part of the textual tradition and in a partial way. Its exact contents vary greatly in each single manuscript following the fluid transmission of the ancient magical texts.

As it stands, the *Hygromancy* constitutes the textual core to which the rest of the materials were appended. It is organized around the direct instruction of Solomon to his son Rehoboam, who acts as a sort of "vicarious" student to be instructed; this structure acts as a "macroform" that configures the work. Several "microforms" hang from it with a great variability regarding their order.

Date and Provenance

The determination of a date and a provenance for the *Hygromancy* entails several difficulties due to its composite structure. It is not mentioned directly in other literary works that could allow us to posit a *terminus ante quem* or *post quem* and a likely provenance; this could be due to the dubious and specialized character of much of its content. In the same way, the text does not hint at any historical event or geographical connection, which means that the identification of its provenance and its date must lie exclusively on internal data of the text and would be, therefore, quite hypothetical.

From a linguistic point of view, the text in its present state can be dated around the fifth or sixth century C.E.; the main characteristics of its late Koine Greek fit in that temporal frame at least for some of the manuscripts (e.g., *Monacensis 70*). It shows no medieval influences in the syntax or the vocabulary, excepting some botanical terms that seem to be medieval. However, it has to be noted that the names of the plants correspond in the majority of cases with the classical denominations that are in Dioscorides' *Materia Medica* (first century C.E.), rather than with their Byzantine equivalents.

The contents of the work give some clues about its date and provenance. Generally speaking, most of the actions that appear to be performed or to be avoided depending on the hour (going into court, fights, problems with great lords, business ventures, speaking in public) fit clearly in any urbanized setting of late antiquity. There are no Christian overtones whatsoever, with the possible exception of the denomination of Sunday as the "day of the Lord," but this epithet was used also in pagan ambiances since it was the day consecrated to Helios. The chronological sequence of the week (Sunday as first day and Saturday as the last, the ordinal numerals as names of the days) as well as the denomination of Friday as day of Preparation point clearly to a Jewish background. Besides, the prayers of the planets seem to be an adaptation of a pagan model to monotheist traits that would fit well in a Jewish setting. Finally we may add two further details. First, the mention of an "androgynous" demonic entity is surely strange, but it is less so when considering the importance that androgyny had both in some Greek texts of late antiquity and in the rabbinic literature. Although the text has demonized the androgynous, we find a similar narrative in Gnostic literature. Second, the unit about the symbols (*charactēres*) of the planets is better understood when considering the importance of such drawings in the Jewish magical tradition.

Summing up, it seems that the work in its actual form originated at the end of late antiquity, very likely around the fifth or sixth centuries C.E., in an urbanized milieu and quite likely within a Jewish environment, which was highly syncretized and whose main language was Greek. The weight of the astrological material in the whole of the work could point to Egypt as the ultimate origin of the work. However, the individual units could be earlier than the fourth century C.E.

Literary Context

To speak of the literary context of the work is out of place with this kind of text, since the *Hygromancy* is not a literary text but rather a working copy or handbook, prone to be adapted and modified should the necessity arise. The work does not allude to or quote Scripture except for the references to Solomon and his son Rehoboam, which have more to do with the esoteric Solomonic traditions than with Scripture (cf. 1 Kgs 5:9-14 [Evv 4:29-34]). There are no direct quotations of the *Hygromancy*, but there are allusions and parallel traditions that relate to the Solomonic astrological and magical traditions that were widespread and very popular in late antiquity and which reached modern times. It is possible that the *Hygromancy* was referred to in the Syriac *Zosimus*, some fragments of the Mandean *Ginzah*, and the Gnostic tractate *On the Origin of the World*, but although these texts show certain affinities with the *Hygromancy*, linking Solomon with astrological material and demonology, they neither quote the *Hygromancy* nor do they offer direct textual parallels. However, in the *Testament of Adam*, we find that a list of hours with the actions that can be undertaken in them shows certain similarities ("the names of the hours of the day and the night"). The so-called "angelology" also shows the angelic host and gives the names of the different classes of angels. In part of the textual tradition of the *Testament of Adam*, the "hours" is included within a larger astrological and magical work, called the *Apotelesmata*, and attributed to the legendary first-century philosopher Apollonius of Tyana. Although the *Testament* is dated by its editor between the second and the fifth centuries C.E., and no direct relation with the *Hygromancy* can be proposed, both texts share similar textual units.

Finally, in the manuscripts that preserve the *Hygromancy*, it appears frequently alongside the *Testament of Solomon*, so the texts and traditions of both works seem to be related. Parts of them went to constitute the most important grimoire of the Middle Ages, the so-called *Clavicula Solomonis*, which was translated from the original Latin into most of the European languages and which has a Hebrew counterpart as well.

Bibliography

Bohak, Gideon. *Ancient Jewish Magic: A History*. Cambridge: Cambridge University Press, 2008.

__________. "Hebrew, Hebrew Everywhere? Notes on the Interpretation of Voces Magicae." In *Prayer, Magic, and the Stars in the Ancient and Late Antique World*, 69-82. Edited by Scott Noegel and Joel Walker. University Park, Pa.: Pennsylvania State University Press, 2003.

Carroll, Scott. "A Preliminary Analysis of the Epistle to Rehoboam." *JSP* 4 (1989): 91-103.

Cumont, F., H. Boll, et al. *Catalogus Codicum Astrologorum Graecorum*. 12 vols. Brussels: H. Lamertin, 1898-1956.

Delatte, A. *Anecdota Atheniensia*. Bibliothèque de la Faculté de Philosophie et Lettres de l'Université de Liège, vol. 36. Liège; Paris, 1927.

__________. "Un nouveau témoin de la littérature Solomonique, le codex Gennadianus 45 d'Athènes." *Bulletin de la Académie Royale de Belgique, Classe des Lettres et des Sciences Morales et Politiques* 45, 5th ser. (1959): 280-321.

Heeg, J. "Excerptum ex Codice Monacensi Graeco 70: Hygromantia Salomonis." Pages 139-76 in *Catalogus Codicum Astrologorum Graecorum* VIII:2. Edited by C. A. Ruelle. Brussels: H. Lamertin, 1911.

Johnston, Sara Iles. "The *Testament of Solomon* from Late Antiquity to the Renaissance." Pages 35-50 in *The Metamorphosis of Magic from Late Antiquity to the Early Modern Period*. Edited by Jan N. Bremmer and Jan R. Veenstra. Leuven: Peeters, 2002.

McCown, C. C. *The Testament of Solomon, Edited from Manuscripts at Mount Athos, Bologna, Holkham Hall, Jerusalem, London, Milan, Paris and Vienna*. Leipzig: Hinrichs'sche Buchhandlung, 1922.

Muñoz Delgado, Luis. *Léxico de magia y religión en los papiros mágicos griegos*. Diccionario Griego-Español. Madrid: CSIC, 2001.

Reitzenstein, R. *Poimandres: Studien zur griechisch-ägyptischen und frühchristlichen Literatur*. 1904. Darmstadt: Wissenschaftliche Buchgesellschaft, 1966.

Robinson, Stephen E. *The Testament of Adam: An Examination of the Syriac and Greek Traditions*. SBLDS 52. Atlanta, Ga.: Scholars Press, 1982.

Schäfer, Peter. "Tradition and Redaction in Hekhalot Literature." *JSJ* 14 (1983): 172-81.

Stone, Michael E. *Armenian Apocrypha: Relating to the Patriarchs and Prophets*. Jerusalem: The Israel Academy of Sciences and Humanities, 1982.

__________. *A History of the Literature of Adam and Eve*. SBLEJL 3. Atlanta, Ga.: Scholars Press, 1992.

Torijano, Pablo A. *Solomon the Esoteric King: From King to Magus, Development of a Tradition*. JSJSup 73. Leiden: Brill, 2002. An earlier version of the translation published below was published in this volume on pp. 231-53.

The Hygromancy of Solomon

Title

THE LITTLE KEY OF THE WHOLE ART OF DIVINATION THROUGH WATER, DISCOVERED BY SEVERAL CRAFTSMEN AND THE HOLY PROPHET SOLOMON, IN WHICH HE SEEMS TO WRITE TO HIS SON REHOBOAM

Introduction

1 [1]Pay attention, my very dear son Rehoboam, to the exactness of my—your father Solomon's—art, to the procedures in which the whole matter of divination through water lies, because it is necessary before anything [...] to master the observations of the planets and the signs of the Zodiac and to follow them and perform them according to your will.
[2]Rehoboam says to his father Solomon:
Father, where does the force of the acts lie?
[3]Solomon responds:
The entire art, grace, and force of what is sought remains in plants, words, and stones. First of all, know the positions of the seven planets; because the seven planets lead the seven days of the week; let us begin from the week's first day, that is, from the Sun's day. And in the first period we assume that the Sun rules, and, in the same way, we will explain the others which follow.

The Days and the Planets

2 Inquiry.
[1]Inquiry about the seven planets and about what it is necessary to do in the periods when they rule the seven days of the week.
On the lord's day the Sun rules.
On the first day, the sun rules, first hour [...].
On the second, Aphrodite: (it is a good hour) for getting the love of those who have full power, great men and tyrants.
At the third hour, Hermes: they favor the fortune of those who have absolute power.
At the fourth hour, the Moon: (a good hour) for you to associate with the all-powerful.
At the fifth hour, Kronos: (a good hour) for you to reject fortune.
At the sixth hour, Zeus: (a good hour) for you to be established in front of the powerful ones.
At the seventh hour, Ares: take care to do nothing.
At the eighth hour, Helios: labor, because you lack wealth.
At the ninth hour, Aphrodite: and the lords likewise.
At the tenth hour, Hermes: (an hour) for you to make a report.

At the eleventh hour, the Moon: (a good hour) for you to begin a conversation.
At the twelfth hour, Kronos: you will not do anything at all.
At the thirteenth hour, Zeus: speak in aid of friends.
At the fourteenth hour, Ares: you will thwart a deed.
At the fifteenth hour, Helios: you will dream of a king.
At the sixteenth hour, Aphrodite: (a good hour) for you to dream of a princess.
At the seventeenth hour, Hermes: you will not do anything at all.
At the eighteenth hour, the Moon: a good hour for business.
At the nineteenth hour, Kronos: take care not to do anything.
At the twentieth hour, Zeus: make friendships among the all-powerful.
At the twenty-first hour, Ares: make difficulties.
At the twenty-second hour, Helios: (a good hour) for being introduced to the king.
At the twenty-third hour, Aphrodite: present yourself to the princess.
At the twenty-fourth hour, Hermes: rest.

[2]On the second day, the Moon rules.
At the first hour, the moon rules and it is good for writing a contract for selling and for the market-place.
At the second hour, Kronos: a bad hour.
At the third hour, Zeus: a good hour for you to open workshops.
At the fourth hour, Ares: (a good hour) for you to avoid workshops.
At the fifth hour, Helios: (a good hour) for you to begin selling.
At the sixth hour, Aphrodite: (a good hour) for dealings.
At the seventh hour, Hermes: (a good hour) for you to go on a journey.
At the eighth hour, the Moon: (a good hour) for you to buy something in the market.
At the ninth hour, Kronos: (a good hour) for you to thwart (something).
At the tenth hour, Zeus: try to set up a business.
At the eleventh hour, Ares: (a good hour) for you to satisfy your fortune.
At the twelfth hour, Helios: set up a business.
At the thirteenth hour, Aphrodite: rest yourself.
At the fourteenth hour, Hermes: act for the profit of life.
At the fifteenth hour, the Moon: worry about the businesses.
At the sixteenth hour, Kronos: do not worry at all.
At the seventeenth hour, Zeus: write and speak as well.
At the eighteenth hour, Ares: he is an impediment and he goes against (you).
At the nineteenth hour, Helios: begin all legal procedure.
At the twentieth hour, Aphrodite: rest and worry.
At the twenty-first hour, Hermes: set the thing in motion and stir it.
At the twenty-second hour, the Moon: vote the disposition.
At the twenty-third hour, Kronos: do not worry about anything.
At the twenty-fourth hour, Zeus: open your workshop.

[3]On the third day, Ares rules.
At the first hour of the third day, Ares rules. It is good for you to work with paper and you will win the war and other things.
At the second hour, Helios: (a good hour) for you to earn money.
At the third hour, Aphrodite: (a good hour) for you to make a demonstration.

At the fourth hour, Hermes: (a good hour) for you to march to battle.
At the fifth hour, the Moon: (a good hour); you will march and escape.
At the sixth hour, Kronos: be aware of your enemy.
At the seventh hour, Zeus: (a good hour) to become visible to your enemies.
At the eighth hour, Ares: help yourself.
At the ninth hour, Helios: you take the money from the fortress.
At the tenth hour, Aphrodite: (a good hour) for domination.
At the eleventh hour, Hermes: (a good hour) for protesting.
At the twelfth hour, the Moon: the hour of spoiling.
At the thirteenth hour, Kronos: be careful of everything.
At the fourteenth hour, Zeus: (a good hour) to suffer calumny.
At the fifteenth hour, Ares: (a good hour) to act for salvation.
At the sixteenth hour, Helios: no gain at all.
At the seventeenth hour, Aphrodite: jealousy manifests itself.
At the eighteenth hour, Hermes: (a good hour) for escaping.
At the nineteenth hour, the Moon: (a good hour) for overcoming the adversary in a lawsuit.
At the twentieth hour, Kronos: (a good hour) for attacking the enemy.
At the twenty-first hour, Zeus: (a good hour) for keeping concealed.
At the twenty-second hour, Ares: pray to the god.
At the twenty-third hour, Helios: manifest yourself in battle.
At the twenty-fourth hour, Aphrodite: an enviable hour.

[4]On the fourth day, Hermes rules.
At the first hour of the fourth day, Hermes rules: it is good for making things disappear and suchlike and for teaching a child.
At the second hour, the Moon: (a good hour) for resting and being of good cheer.
At the third hour, Kronos: a useless hour.
At the fourth hour, Zeus: (a good hour) for practicing alchemy.
At the fifth hour, Ares: (a good hour) for proclaiming concealed things.
At the sixth hour, Helios: (an hour) for despising the ravager.
At the seventh hour, Aphrodite: (a good hour) for influencing a woman.
At the eighth hour, Hermes: (an hour) for making a tribunal.
At the ninth hour, the Moon: (a good hour) for going out with a woman.
At the tenth hour, Kronos: be careful!
At the eleventh hour, Zeus: begin the path concerning that which you desire.
At the twelfth hour, Ares: do not do anything.
At the thirteenth hour, Helios: begin the above instruction.
At the fourteenth hour, Aphrodite: begin the prayer.
At the fifteenth hour, Hermes: (a good hour) for dreaming.
At the sixteenth hour, the Moon: (a good hour) for making wands.
At the seventeenth hour, Kronos: a useless hour.
At the eighteenth hour, Zeus: (a good hour) for punishing certain people.
At the nineteenth hour, Ares: (a good hour) for taking retribution.
At the twentieth hour, Helios: hour useful to all.
At the twenty-first hour, Aphrodite: (a good hour) for dreams.
At the twenty-second hour, Hermes: (a good hour) for the learning of letters.

At the twenty-third hour, the Moon: an hour of the payment.
At the twenty-fourth hour, Kronos: a useless hour.

[5]On the fifth day, Zeus rules.
At the first hour of the fifth day, Zeus rules. And it is good for performing cures on men and beasts.
At the second hour, Ares: a useless hour.
At the third hour, Helios: (a good hour) for appearing in front of kings.
At the fourth hour, Aphrodite: (a good hour) for appearing in front of queens.
At the fifth hour, Hermes: (a good hour) for the learning of rhetoric.
At the sixth hour, the Moon: (a good hour) for suspicions.
At the seventh hour, Kronos: in this hour, keep watch!
At the eighth hour, Zeus: good and blessed hour.
At the ninth hour, Ares: an hour to make people jealous.
At the tenth hour, Helios: (a good hour) for doing good to the body.
At the eleventh hour, Aphrodite: (a good hour) for healing a woman.
At the twelfth hour, Hermes: (a good hour) for being very far away from home.
At the thirteenth hour, the Moon: (a good hour) for making a fortune.
At the fourteenth hour, Kronos: a useless hour.
At the fifteenth hour, Zeus: an hour for any healing.
At the sixteenth hour, Ares: (a good hour) for making an incision.
At the seventeenth hour, Helios: (a good hour) for the king's service.
At the eighteenth hour, Aphrodite: (a good hour) for serving the princess.
At the nineteenth hour, Hermes: (a good hour) for not being afraid of robbers.
At the twentieth hour, the Moon: a useful hour.
At the twenty-first hour, Kronos: a useless hour.
At the twenty-second hour, Zeus: in this useful hour, do what you want.
At the twenty-third hour, Ares: (a good hour) for throwing (yourself) into battle.
At the twenty-fourth hour, Helios: do (things) concerning the very rich and powerful.

[6]On the day of preparation Aphrodite rules.
At the first hour of the day of preparation, Aphrodite rules: thus, do things concerning love and affection.
At the second hour, Hermes: (a good hour) for indications of public recognition.
At the third hour, the Moon: good for anything.
At the fourth hour, Kronos: obstacle to love.
At the fifth hour, Zeus: (a good hour) for gifts and good relations.
At the sixth hour, Ares: (a good hour) for producing the jealousy of love.
At the seventh hour, Helios: good and lovable hour.
At the eighth hour, Aphrodite: good hour to make love.
At the ninth hour, Hermes: an hour for indication of courtship.
At the tenth hour, the Moon: a beautiful hour if you want to do something.
At the eleventh hour, Kronos: it is a useless hour.
At the twelfth hour, Zeus: (a good hour) for making a covenant.
At the thirteenth hour, Ares: in this hour, begin the courtship.
At the fourteenth hour, Helios: (a good hour) for binding the androgynous (demon).
At the fifteenth hour, Aphrodite: (a good hour) for making bonds of love.

At the sixteenth hour, Hermes: (a good hour) for having dreams of love.
At the seventeenth hour, the Moon: a good hour.
At the eighteenth hour, Kronos: (a good hour) to have dreams of love.
At the nineteenth hour, Zeus: (a good hour) for acting in favor of any good disposition.
At the twentieth hour, Ares: do not do anything at all.
At the twenty-first hour, Helios: good hour.
At the twenty-second hour, Aphrodite: hour of love.
At the twenty-third hour, Hermes: hour for alchemy.
At the twenty-fourth hour, the Moon: (a good hour) for being in need.

[7]On the Sabbath day, Kronos rules.
At the first hour of the Sabbath, Kronos rules and it is an hour for you to harm your enemy, that is, for you to make the man ill.
At the second hour, Zeus: (a good hour) for you to produce the shipwreck of someone.
At the third hour, Ares: (a good hour) for you to set up enchantments.
At the fourth hour, Helios: (a good hour) for you to attack those who have power.
At the fifth hour, Aphrodite: (a good hour) for you to cause the androgynous one to be hated.
At the sixth hour, Hermes: (a good hour) for finding a useful treasure.
At the seventh hour, the Moon: (a good hour) for speaking with demons.
At the eighth hour, Kronos: (a good hour) for performing divination through dishes.
At the tenth hour, Ares: (an hour) for people to be drowned at the sea.
At the eleventh hour, Helios: (a good hour) for you to provoke the wrath of adversaries in a lawsuit.
At the twelfth hour, Aphrodite: (a good hour) for you to produce fear and enmity.
At the thirteenth hour, Hermes: (a good hour) for the useful finding of secrets.
At the fourteenth hour, the Moon: (a good hour) for seeing the ones who have died a long time ago.
At the fifteenth hour, Kronos: (a good hour) for seeing by divination through water.
At the sixteenth hour, Zeus: (an hour) useful for education.
At the seventeenth hour, Ares: (an hour) that is very hurtful.
At the eighteenth hour, Helios: a useless hour.
At the nineteenth hour, Aphrodite: (a good hour) for getting profit from dice.
At the twentieth hour, Hermes: (a good hour) for hindering any beautiful thing.
At the twenty-first hour, the Moon: a useless hour.
At the twenty-second hour, Kronos: (a good hour) for having visions.
At the twenty-third hour, Zeus: (an hour) useful for enjoyment.
At the twenty-fourth hour, Ares: an hour of war and enmity.

The Angels and Demons of Each Hour

3 [1]Know, my very dear son Rehoboam, that one good angel and one evil demon rule at each hour. If you want to do a good deed, adjure the good angel, so that he may be an ally to you; if you want to do any other, bad, deed, adjure the demon, so that he may be your ally; and you will do so, if you want something. It starts easily in this way.

Angels and demons on the Lord's Day

At the first hour	angel Michaēl	demon Asmodai.
At the second hour	angel Argphnaēl	demon Ornai.
At the third hour	angel Perouēl	demon Pērrath.
At the fourth hour	angel Iōraēl	demon Silēdon.
At the fifth hour	angel Piel	demon Sitros.
At the sixth hour	angel Iōchth	demon Zephar.
At the seventh hour	angel Pel	demon Manier.
At the eighth hour	angel Ioran	demon Osmie.
At the ninth hour	angel Kataēl	demon Pnix.
At the tenth hour	angel Bidouēl	demon Gērat.
At the eleventh hour	angel Ēdiēl	demon Nēsta.
At the twelfth hour	angel Sanaēl	demon Peliōr.
At the thirteenth hour	angel Opsiēl	demon Ho Istos.
At the fourteenth hour	angel Teraēl	demon Apios.
At the fifteenth hour	angel Lysiel	demon Nēgmos.
At the sixteenth hour	angel Nalouēl	demon Arax.
At the seventeenth hour	angel Orkiēl	demon Nēstriaph.
At the eighteenth hour	angel Periēl	demon Askatos.
At the nineteenth hour	angel Iarēl	demon Kinopigos.
At the twentieth hour	angel Inhouēl	demon Araps.
At the twenty-first hour	angel Thamaniēl	demon Tartarouēl.
At the twenty-second hour	angel Bradaēl	demon Melmeth.
At the twenty-third hour	angel Klinos	demon Mēthridanou.
At the twenty-fourth hour	angel Iōn	demon Phrodatos.

2 *Angels and demons of the second day*

At the first hour	angel Gabriēl	demon Mamonas.
At the second hour	angel Pharsaphaēl	demon Skoliōn.
At the third hour	angel Pindōēl	demon Thetidōph.
At the fourth hour	angel Kopiēl	demon Arban.
At the fifth hour	angel Kelekiel	demon Azan.
At the sixth hour	angel Tariēl	demon Memachth.
At the seventh hour	angel Mniēl	demon Skamidinos.
At the eighth hour	angel Ezekiēl	demon Stirphan.
At the ninth hour	angel Iōēl	demon Giram.
At the tenth hour	angel Sinaēl	demon Menaktinos.
At the eleventh hour	angel Menaēl	demon Menaktinos.
At the twelfth hour	angel Rochaēl	demon Mexiphon.
At the thirteenth hour	angel Arēsiēl	demon Outolōch.
At the fourteenth hour	angel Traphēdoēl	demon Nyktidōn.
At the fifteenth hour	angel Akinatiēl	demon Ouistos.
At the sixteenth hour	angel Organiēl	demon Kasierōph.
At the seventeenth hour	angel Rōmatiēl	demon Kēsiepopos.
At the eighteenth hour	angel Selpidōn	demon Androphai.
At the nineteenth hour	angel Outitōm	demon Niōech.
At the twentieth hour	angel Metabiēl	demon Entauros.

At the twenty-first hour	angel Akbaēl	demon Syritōr Phlinaphe.
At the twenty-second hour	angel Eikoniēl	demon Kyknit.
At the twenty-third hour	angel Genekiēl	demon Kēnops.
At the twenty-fourth hour	angel Krotiēl	demon Sarkidōn.

3 *Angels and demons of the third day*

At the first hour	angel Samouēl	demon Kakistōn.
At the second hour	angel Isamēl	demon Lithridōn.
At the third hour	angel Phrereēl	demon Mailōth.
At the fourth hour	angel Eudēl	demon Sarapidie.
At the fifth hour	angel Piktōēl	demon Tartarouēl.
At the sixth hour	angel Okaēl	demon Kerinoudalos.
At the seventh hour	angel Gnathaēl	demon Klinotios.
At the eighth hour	angel Perganiēl	demon Tyrrytōr.
At the ninth hour	angel Gestiēl	demon Plēlatan.
At the tenth hour	angel Legmiel	demon Sythlos.
At the eleventh hour	angel Nachōēl	demon Osthridie.
At the twelfth hour	angel Oknan	demon Omimot.
At the thirteenth hour	angel Gorphil	demon Aprox.
At the fourteenth hour	angel Patiēl	demon Skōēn.
At the fifteenth hour	angel Partan	demon Prophai.
At the sixteenth hour	angel Saltiēl	demon Achlitōl.
At the seventeenth hour	angel Abaēl	demon Ornan.
At the eighteenth hour	angel Stragiēl	demon Chalmōth.
At the nineteenth hour	angel Opadouēl	demon Touddedēn.
At the twentieth hour	angel Marniēl	demon Tephra.
At the twenty-first hour	angel Methniēl	demon Niran.
At the twenty-second hour	angel Stirōel	demon Rakirō.
At the twenty-third hour	angel Ismatiēl	demon Irgotie.
At the twenty-fourth hour	angel Triziōēl	demon Gegaōr.

4 *Angels and demons of the fourth day*

At the first hour	angel Ouriēl	demon Loutzipher.
At the second hour	angel Arakēl	demon Goukoumōr.
At the third hour	angel Miemphiēl	demon Eispniryx.
At the fourth hour	angel Trōsiel	demon Midōkēt.
At the fifth hour	angel Chartisiel	demon Ntadadiph.
At the sixth hour	angel Sphykinoēl	demon Skintogēr.
At the seventh hour	angel Oulōdias	demon Phnidōtas.
At the eighth hour	angel Kalbagiel	demon Karatan.
At the ninth hour	angel Skitamiēl	demon Miag.
At the tenth hour	angel Tirōēl	demon Gatzar.
At the eleventh hour	angel Miel	demon Pnidōr.
At the twelfth hour	angel Charakiēl	demon Toiblas.
At the thirteenth hour	angel Ydrōēl	demon Taxipōn.
At the fourteenth hour	angel Sidrēl	demon Ophitan.
At the fifteenth hour	angel Parapiēl	demon Abluchos.

At the sixteenth hour	angel Mourouēl	demon Malakis.
At the seventeenth hour	angel Kourtaēl	demon Bleminch.
At the eighteenth hour	angel Koupeēl	demon Cheirōn.
At the nineteenth hour	angel Peraniēl	demon Ephippas.
At the twentieth hour	angel Santaēl	demon Orkistaph.
At the twenty-first hour	angel Katziēl	demon Loginaph.
At the twenty-second hour	angel Louliēl	demon Pharōs.
At the twenty-third hour	angel Saltaēl	demon Roktat.
At the twenty-fourth hour	angel Gabtel	demon Opnax.

[5]*Angels and demons of the fifth day*

At the first hour	angel Raphaēl	demon Meltiphrōn.
At the second hour	angel Perniphel	demon Ochlos.
At the third hour	angel Kisphaēl	demon Ouēros.
At the fourth hour	angel Kaliēl	demon Thaphōt.
At the fifth hour	angel Glōstas	demon Tzippat.
At the sixth hour	angel Mnimeēl	demon Amōr.
At the seventh hour	angel Chalriēl	demon Orphōr.
At the eighth hour	angel Skiaēl	demon Outaēt.
At the ninth hour	angel Misoēl	demon Ergōtas.
At the tenth hour	angel Dalbōth	demon Azouboul.
At the eleventh hour	angel Chartōēl	demon Aplēx.
At the twelfth hour	angel Kiphar	demon Sigōs.
At the thirteenth hour	angel Sitioēl	demon Asmōdas.
At the fourteenth hour	angel Bokiel	demon Ouōch.
At the fifteenth hour	angel Senoēl	demon Nikokep.
At the sixteenth hour	angel Oriator	demon Kopinos.
At the seventeenth hour	angel Chumeriēl	demon Kaēte.
At the eighteenth hour	angel Orphniēl	demon Lastōr.
At the nineteenth hour	angel Kidouēl	demon Epiē.
At the twentieth hour	angel Goth	demon Organ.
At the twenty-first hour	angel Phisnael	demon Nierier.
At the twenty-second hour	angel Karaaēl	demon Oualielos.
At the twenty-third hour	angel Kōndar	demon Galielōr.
At the twenty-fourth hour	angel Kispōl	demon Choukan.

[6]*Angels and demons of the day of Preparation*

At the first hour	angel Agathouēl	demon Gouliōn.
At the second hour	angel Nidouēl	demon Bizēk.
At the third hour	angel Amphiloēl	demon Zorzorath.
At the fourth hour	angel Kanikel	demon Raphiōph.
At the fifth hour	angel Seliniel	demon Ermag.
At the sixth hour	angel Karkanpher	demon Kerinoudalos.
At the seventh hour	angel Aniel	demon Tabaltalis.
At the eighth hour	angel Mouriēl	demon Thapnix.
At the ninth hour	angel Tophatiēl	demon Eliasem.
At the tenth hour	angel Skirtouēl	demon Amich.

At the eleventh hour	angel Armōēl	demon Galgidōn.
At the twelfth hour	angel Otraēl	demon Ephirit.
At the thirteenth hour	angel Talkidonios	demon Staget.
At the fourteenth hour	angel Roudiēl	demon Anthēros.
At the fifteenth hour	angel Thēkiel	demon Pēzētos.
At the sixteenth hour	angel Glukidōl	demon Aprich.
At the seventeenth hour	angel Psalmatios	demon Niphōn.
At the eighteenth hour	angel Stauphnēl	demon Otrichos.
At the nineteenth hour	angel Deaukōn	demon Chimeri.
At the twentieth hour	angel Asphodoēl	demon Melu.
At the twenty-first hour	angel Petilōl	demon Kapnithel.
At the twenty-second hour	angel Gorgiel	demon Tachman.
At the twenty-third hour	angel Bataaniēl	demon Oukisem.
At the twenty-fourth hour	angel Poliōn	demon Ouniphrēr.

[7]***Angels and demons of the Sabbath***

At the first hour	angel Sabapiel	demon Klēndatōr.
At the second hour	angel Salōēl	demon Cheirim.
At the third hour	angel Besaēl	demon Spindōr.
At the fourth hour	angel Abaēl	demon Keriak.
At the fifth hour	angel Gielmōn	demon Nikem.
At the sixth hour	angel Retaēl	demon Mōriēl.
At the seventh hour	angel Pelaphiēl	demon Suniberōm.
At the eighth hour	angel Samōsan	demon Aphios.
At the ninth hour	angel Pletanix	demon Thorios.
At the tenth hour	angel Marmichaēl	demon Stelpha.
At the eleventh hour	angel Ntecharinx	demon Kupōs.
At the twelfth hour	angel Arkiēl	demon Skar.
At the thirteenth hour	angel Geabiēl	demon Tēchar.
At the fourteenth hour	angel Pitriel	demon Akrōk.
At the fifteenth hour	angel Golgoēl	demon Argitan.
At the sixteenth hour	angel Sanipiēl	demon Atomeos.
At the seventeenth hour	angel Belaraēl	demon Gnōtas.
At the eighteenth hour	angel Opiael	demon Merkou.
At the nineteenth hour	angel Ophniēl	demon Enaritar.
At the twentieth hour	angel Patriēl	demon Niouchan.
At the twenty-first hour	angel Ianiēl	demon Amphou.
At the twenty-second hour	angel Kondiēnēl	demon Mankōs.
At the twenty-third hour	angel Ouxounouēl	demon Moigrōn.
At the twenty-fourth hour	angel Thanaēl	demon Nigrisph.

The Prayers of the Planets

4 [1]I impress upon you a method so that you, Rehoboam, may know the precise procedures, because it is completely necessary to know the hour in which you want to accomplish your will: first, utter the prayer of the planet that is found in that hour; afterwards, adjure the angel and the servant, that is, the demon. The prayer of Kronos is the following:

Prayer of Kronos

Eternal God, ungovernable power, you who regulate all for our salvation, give us grace so that I may subdue the terrible planet to my will. I adjure you, Planet Kronos, by your path and your plant, by your inheritance and your heaven, by your shining and your power, and by these names of yours, Gasial, Agounsael, Atasser, Beltoliel, Mentzatzia, to give me grace, force and power in the hour in which you rule.

2**Prayer of Zeus**

Lord and God, all-powerful father, creator of the visible and invisible, king of those who rule and lord of those who are lords, give us the power of your grace, so that Zeus may be subject to us, because all is possible for you, Lord. I adjure you, Zeus, by your wisdom and your knowledge, by your curative force and your heavenly course in which you orbit and by these names, Anōph, Orsita, Atnox, Onigeui, Atziniel, Ankanitei, Tyneos, Genier, Kaniptza, to incline your grace in subjection to me in this deed that I am doing.

3**Prayer of Ares**

Fearful God, indescribable God, invisible God, whom no one among humans saw or can see, whom the abysses saw and they shuddered, and the animals were killed. Show grace to us, so that we may subject the planet Ares. I adjure you, fiery Ares, by the god who has created the sensible essences and the whole fiery army; I adjure you by your forces and your course, and by your shining and by these names, Outat, Nouēt, Chorēzē, Tiniaē, Dachli, Ampira, Noliem, Siat, Adichaēl, Tzanas, Plēsym, to give me your grace because of this service.

4**Prayer of Helios**

King of those who rule and Lord of those who are lords, the origin that is prior to the beginnings, ever-flowing power, inconceivable light, boundless light, the only provider of wealth, the dispenser of mercy, observe us through your grace and kindness so that we may be able to subdue Helios, the planet now present and to hold fast his force. I adjure you, untouched, inextinguishable, splendor of the day, Helios, by your temporal cycle, by your four seasons, and by your course, by your rays, by your wings, by your powers and by these your names: Glibiōd, Antikon, Lithetioud, Touldōrag, Ēnōan; by these names I adjure you; do not disobey me but through your grace, assist me in this service.

5**Prayer of Aphrodite**

Unique good god, warder of the evil by love of men, you who infinitely possess an inscrutable sea of goodness, besides which is the good heart of friendship, I prostrate myself in front of your love of men, so that you may give us power and grace, so that you may give me useful and practicable effectiveness (and) this planet, so that I may do these things; I adjure you, very beautiful and sweet Aphrodite, by your grace and your course and your power and your sweetness and by these names, Ēreth, Labm, Suar, Satēr, Touid, Toutimar, Pesphodōn, Sirōph, Kakem, Setiap. By these (names) I adjure you not to disobey me but at least to give me your grace, in order that I may be able to do such-and-such a thing.

6**Prayer of Hermes**

Almighty lord, searcher of wisdom and knowledge, craftsman of heavenly things and of those that are above the heavens, all-seeing and powerful, give us your grace, such as that of the planet Hermes, which you left behind so that we could do such and such. I adjure you, all-wise, very learned and intelligent, easily-detected and very wakeful Hermes, by your wisdom and your eloquence and by the sphere in which you walk about, and by these names: Nēphan, Piout, Nomēn, Selak, Merepōn, Stemēnos, Kazētok, Miōt, to incline your grace and power in subjection to me for this deed I want to accomplish.

[7]***Prayer of the Moon***

Lady, mistress, you who are mistress of the living and the dead, you who created man with wisdom so that he might be master of the creatures that came into being through you, with piety and understanding, attend to me, so that I, your slave, may be able to receive the grace and subject the planet Moon and perform the deed I am set upon. I adjure you, Moon, very ripe purple adornment of the sky and relief of the night. I adjure you by your course, and by your renewal and by your immeasurable steps in which you come down, and by these names, Sabaēl, Boaēl, Ōnitzēr, Sparou, Sōtrērcha, Gabēd, Outoupōn, Kaipolēs, Gōmedēn, Marēbat. By these (names) I adjure you, Moon, to incline your grace and power in this deed that I am undertaking.

[8]***Prayer of the angels***

When you want to adjure an angel or demon in the hour that they rule, adjure them in this way:

I adjure you, Angel so-and-so, you who rule over this hour and are appointed for the provision and the service of the human race, (angel) so-and-so, ready on any occasion, powerful, courageous, keen, I adjure you by God, who ordered you to watch this hour, to be my attendant together with the demon so-and-so, submissive to you, who was appointed beforehand to be a servant in this hour, that he might be my attendant and perform this service because it is fitting, good and true.

The Symbols (*charactēres*) of the Planets

5 [1]Know, my very dear son Rehoboam, that, when you want to prepare a deed, you must make sure that you know the planet and the hour. First pronounce the prayers, then adjure the angel and the demon of that hour, so that he might be your attendant in what you want to accomplish. Finally make the planet's symbols *(charactēres)* with black ink and incense of each kind. And the one who has power, the lord of the hour, grants it to you.

The symbols of Kronos

Make the symbols of Kronos with the dross of lead and with vinegar and fumigate the sulphurium with them [...]. Write them on parchment made from a he-goat.

[2]***The symbols of Zeus***

Make the symbols of Zeus with silver dross and with extract of roses prepared with honey and smoke them with myrrh and write them on parchment made from an unborn ox.

[3]***The symbols of Ares***

Write the symbols of Ares with pure vermilion and with extract of roses prepared with honey and fumigate them with dried human blood and write at the top on the skin of a vulture or seal and the one who holds power grants it to you.

[4]***The symbols of Helios***
Write the symbols of Helios either with gold or with yellow orpiment mixed with water: fumigate them with the nut of a twig and write them either on parchment made with human skin or on a horse's skin.

[5]***The symbols of Aphrodite***
The symbols of Aphrodite are {...} and write them either with bat's blood or with genuine lapis lazuli and with extract of roses prepared with honey on the skin of a dog or on an unborn deer's hide and fumigate them with mastic and gum-laudanum.

[6]***[The symbols of Hermes]***
The symbols of Hermes are written with the blood of bull, ass or cattle or with blood and water on virgin parchment; smoke them with a hare's hide and frankincense.

[...]

The Plants of the Astrological Signs

6 [1]The plant of Aries is the water milfoil; its sauce, mixed with essence of roses, has extraordinary power when the same zodiac sign rules and it will restore to health in three days the mortal blow from a sword. If it is put on the body, the evil spirits are useful to the one who has it. It also does good to the one who has it. The root, being put around the right arm, gives the one who wears it extreme grace and all grief will be chased away from the one who wears it.

[2]The plant of Taurus is the trefoil; gather it, when the same zodiac sign—that is the Bull—rules. It has these powers: throw its fruit on an unborn bull's hide and wear it when you come into the presence of kings, powerful lords and rulers; you (will) have honor. Their leaves, put on the body [...]. Its sauce heals the eyes and any ocular sickness. Its root, when it is worn, chases away demons and demonesses.

[3]The plant of Gemini is the corn-flag: when the same zodiac sign rules, gather its flowers and throw them on the bed of a newborn child, then wear them and you will be loved by the lowly and the great. The leaves, when they are worn, will heal the one possessed by a demon. Give the upper root to humans or to beasts to eat and they will love you, the lower root and they[a] will be hated.

[4]The plant of Cancer is the mandrake; gather it when the same zodiac sign—the Crab—rules. The flowers, when the ears are anointed, heal all kinds of headache. Give its root to a barren woman to eat, two wheat grains from the first day of the purification till the fourteenth day and she will conceive; she also has to wear some of the plant.

[5]The plant of Leo is called black horehound; gather it on the day when its zodiac sign rules, and, after taking the juice, anoint a crushed kernel of stone pine and tie (it). And they will be extraordinarily solid. Wear the root and you will catch a lot of fish. If you mix the juice from the leaves with oil, it will be (used) instead of a special balsam.

[6]The plant of Virgo is thorn apple; gather it at the hour and on the day in which Virgo rules. And gather its leaves and fruits, mix them with enough hard fat, anoint those who suffer from a flux and they will be healed. And gather the plant's branches, make a crown and bring it to a young woman and if she laughs, she has been ruined and is not a virgin.

---

a. Perhaps emend to "you."

But if she has a gloomy look or weeps, then she is a virgin. If you put its root together with a wolf's hide and you wear it, you will be unconquerable, prevailing over all.

[7]The plant of Libra is the *belonikē*. Gather it when Libra rules. Indeed it has great powers. Its fruit, if drunk, heals those possessed by demons, epileptics, those who look like stone, and colics of intestines. Its leaves, if eaten, are amazingly curative of any illness suffered by the one who eats it. The root, if fumigated, heals angina, catarrh and charms. Again tie it around a fox hide, wear it on your right arm and you will not fear marauders or demons.

[8]The plant of Scorpio is the "dog tongue." Gather it when Scorpio rules. It has an extraordinary and awful power. Pick the seed up and hang it around black hellebore while you desist from any evil deed and you will appear fearful and of high repute. And what you may say as false, they will believe you like a god. After having kneaded the leaves, take the juice and mix it with oil from a white lily, anoint any wound and it will be incredibly healed. Put the root in your hand and dogs will not struggle with you. Again, after having kneaded the entire plant, make an ointment with sufficient fat and anoint those who suffer from a flux, and in three days they will be healed. If you give some of the root to any wild animal to eat, it will be tamed. It has other powers; whatever the attempt will be, it will make them evident.

[9]The plant of Sagittarius is the *anakardios*: gather it when the zodiac sign—the archer—rules. After having rolled up its entire root with a fox hide, wear it on your head and you will conquer any teacher, judge, umpire, king, and ruler. After having kneaded the leaves, make a wax and put it on any inflammation and ailment of the kidneys and it will be healed, so contrary to expectation that all will marvel. Its root has another power: being put in a house it brings success and good luck to that house. Do not marvel at the good luck of the plant but at the god who gives the favors.

[10]The plant of Capricorn is the so-called stinking tutsan. Gather this when its zodiac sign rules. If you give some of the plant to a woman to drink, she will live a few days. If you wear its leaves, all wild beasts will flee from you. Still more, if anyone wears the plant and a great number of beasts and lions surround him, they will approach him as to a god and will not hurt him and will not touch him; neither will they harm him, if they were dreamed of as well. Give the root to an epileptic to eat, he will be healed in three weeks and will be fearless in whatever place he finds himself, during the day and at night, in any moment and in any place. If he wears it as an amulet, prophetic grace will come suddenly upon him from the god.

[11]The plant of Aquarius is the so-called ranunculus.[a] After having kneaded the leaves and having kept the juice, give it to someone, if you long for someone, so that it will make the person suffer convulsions and die. Gather its root and throw it on a fish skin, when Aquarius rules, and throw it on a vessel and it will suffer shipwreck, in the place from which it departed. The one who wears the flowers is healed. The same plant has other powers. If you knead the leaves and mix them with wheat flour and put it on putrefactions and warts of wounds, in three hours it removes them.

[12]The plant of Pisces is the *aristolochia*.[b] When the same zodiac sign rules, gather it. It has great virtues. Its fruit, drunk with wine and honey, chases away all sickness from the body. The root, when fumigated and worn, drives away any demon and mist and chases

a. Hairy crow-foot.

b. A plant that promotes childbirth.

away all sickness and plagues from the one who eats it. It is the antidote against all venomous animals. If any man bitten and polluted by any snake or poison carries out these procedures and puts it on, he will be healed without delay.

The Plants of the Planets

7 [1]There are as well the plants of the seven planets, my very dear son Rehoboam, and when you want to plant them, toss them out at the hour when the planet rules in succession in its hour. And pronounce the names and the prayers and after them you will do wonders that no man can utter with his tongue.

[2]The plant of Zeus is the golden thorn. Gather it at the hour in which Zeus rules and name the angels and also say the prayers and you will have fearful and awful cures. Give the root to eat for three mornings; it will heal epileptics. If you give the root together with frankincense to an epileptic to wear it, the demon will go away. Give the root to drink together with indigo to those who suffer from the sickness and foaming; it will heal them straightaway. After having kneaded some of the leaves, take the juice and anoint cuts, sword blows and wounds; and in fourteen hours you will treat it. If you give the plant's head to be worn, no man will fear to be attacked with magical arts. If there is a man who suffers from drinking poison, give him the plant's head to drink with water and honey and he will be healed.

[3]The plant of Ares is the petasites. Gather it in the hour of Ares and wear it on your weapons, wrapped in a wolf's hide, and if a thousand enemies encircle you, they will not be able to harm you, but you will be delivered from them unharmed. After having kneaded and drained the leaves completely, give them to drink together with wine to any man or woman suffering from hemorrhage, and the person will be healed so wonderfully that all will wonder at the plant's power. Take the root to any war and any line of battle and you will win and be saved unharmed so that you will marvel at the divine power. The one who wears the plant's flower will be deemed fortunate by all human beings and he will be admired and mighty in power.

[4]The plant of Kronos is the heliotrope. Gather it at the hour at which Kronos rules. Gather it and say the prayer and summon the angels who rule. And the plant has this power; if you give some of the flower to someone to eat in secret, chills and cold will enter into him. If you give two flowers, he will have it two days; if three, three days; if four, four days and so on. If you throw its leaves on the pillow of someone in secret, he will not wake up, unless you take it from his pillow. If you give him some to eat, he will go in sickness until death all the moments of his life and he will not wake up until you give him some of the plant of Zeus to eat. Wear its root yourself as an amulet against demonesses.

[5]The plant of Helios is called sunflower, among the Italians *tzirasolem*. When the sun is there, it turns aside its head; because of this it is called sunflower. Gather this plant in the hour in which Helios rules; after the prayers, throw the flowers as well as its fruit on an eagle's hide and carry it with you. And wherever there is a treasure, it will be disclosed straightaway as in the twinkling of an eye. And you will see that gold or silver and again the earth will close itself at once. After having marked for yourself the place, dig it up and you will find what you saw. After kneading the leaves and mixing it with extract of roses prepared with honey, anoint your face and walk. And any wild man or marauder will worship you like a god and will honor you. Wear the root tied to the hide of a donkey. You will pacify angry lords and kings. If you put on a seal's hide and wear it, you will be

admired and honored by kings, princes and powerful ones. The plant has these virtues without hindrance.

[6]The plant of Aphrodite is called man orchid. Gather it in the hour when Aphrodite rules, after prayer and the angels. And take the flowers and the fruit and after having wrapped it up in a deer's hide, wear it on your right arm and you will be loved by all women. After kneading its leaves, throw extract of roses prepared with honey and anoint your face and walk. You will be successful in beginning any marriage. If you say something, it will be believed; if you take the fresh part of the root and give it to any woman you long for, it will be loved and an agreement will be unanimously approved by both man and woman. If you give the dried root to those who love each other, together with an invocation and the hours of Kronos, at once they will hate each other and fight.

[7]The plant of Hermes is the cinquefoil. Gather it in the hour when Hermes rules, after the prayer and the names. And gather the flowers and the fruit, wrapping them in the heart of a cat and wear it on yourself, you will be invisible. And if you do so one[a] will not be despised. After drying its leaves, making them like dust and mixing them with oil, anoint any bruise of the eye, darkening, mist, cloud-like opacity and bird-like blindness, and immediately you will heal it. If you wear some of the fingers of the root, you will heal any ailment of hands and fingers. If you eat some of the root's fingers, you will have a good memory and be skilled in making speeches. And if you hear something, it will not be forgotten. And after wrapping the root up again in a dog's hide, wear it, and no dogs will kick you. And wrapping the root up in fish skin, wear it and you will catch fish, as many as you want. And after wrapping the root up in purple silk and unmixed fat, walk and you will hunt down animals and wild herds. This plant has these virtues and many more without discussion. But the root, if eaten completely, chases away any sickness of the body and leads toward the improvement of life. Wear the root with medical frankincense; and you will be guarded against any magic or meddling of evil men.

[8]The Moon's plant is the peony, called "*Lunaria*" among the Italians. Gather this in its hour with the prayer, the names of the angels, the hour, the month, the wind and special zodiacal sign of its house, which is Cancer. It has these powers: if you throw its heads together with a cock's comb, all the things you approach will be done at once, and all the services you undertake, you will bring to success, as well as any business, presiding over gain in trade. When the moon waxes, if you mix its fresh leaves with money, gold, silver or other coin and with all the earnings you may have in business, then your treasure will increase after a short time and you will become the possessor of many riches. If you mix its fresh leaves with the money of your enemy, it will disappear. Equally, if you give a man some of these leaves, he will have good luck. If you eat the same leaves, then the things will improve again. If you coat the plant's shoot and the root with the same metal, covering them completely in a smelting-furnace, you will find pure, very bright and excellent silver. The plant has many other powers and virtues.

The end. Amen.

---

a. Perhaps emend to "you."

Questions of the Queen of Sheba and Answers by King Solomon

Introduction and a new translation of the Armenian version

by Vahan S. Hovhanessian

with a translation of the Syriac version by Sebastian P. Brock

The biblical story of the Queen of Sheba's visit to King Solomon, inquiring about his wisdom, is found in 1 Kings 10 and 2 Chronicles 9. The Bible, however, does not record the dialogue between the two monarchs. The reader, therefore, is left wondering about the text or nature of the Queen's questions and Solomon's answers. The Bible's silence on this matter sparked the imagination of later generations to expand the story. Consequently, later apocryphal documents picked up the narrative and wove an interesting dialogue between the two monarchs, which produced the apocryphal *Questions of the Queen of Sheba and Answers by King Solomon* (henceforth, *The Questions*).

Contents

This apocryphon is presented as a dialogue between the Queen of Sheba and King Solomon in his palace in Israel. It includes a list of questions attributed to the Queen. Each of the questions is followed by an answer by Solomon. In some traditions, a final riddle attributed to Solomon is inserted at the end of the list and remains unanswered. The number and content of the questions vary in the different traditions. Some questions are numbered in some manuscripts, while others are not.

A remark by the Queen praising Solomon's wisdom is inserted in this apocryphon. In some traditions this remark is found in the middle of the list and in others at the end. Introductory and concluding paragraphs are also found in some Armenian manuscripts of *The Questions*.

Manuscripts and Versions

Various versions of *The Questions* are preserved in Judaic and Christian traditions. Although the focus of this introduction is the Armenian version, it is helpful to offer a brief review of the other versions of *The Questions*. The post-biblical Judaic rendering of *The Questions* is found in the following four Hebrew documents:

- *Midrash Mishle*[1] is a haggadic exegetical interpretation of, and a commentary on, the Book of Proverbs. In its discussion of Prov 1:1, *Midrash Mishle* records four of the Queen's questions, two riddles and two tests. This version includes only the text of the questions and Solomon's answers. Nothing is mentioned about the visit and the encounter of the two monarchs.[2]

1. For a discussion of *Midrash Mishle* as one of the sources of the Hebrew text of *The Questions*, see Lassner, *Demonizing the Queen of Sheba*, 11-13.

2. Toy, "The Queen of Sheba," 208-209.

- *Targum Sheni* to Esther,[3] which is a fourth century or later commentary on the Book of Esther,[4] includes only three of the Queen's riddles.[5] This version includes an embellished introduction to the story of the visit of the Queen, followed by her three riddles.[6]
- *Midrash haHefes* or *Midrash Hachephez*[7] is a medieval Yemenite midrash on the Pentateuch,[8] which contains nineteen riddles attributed to the Queen. The text of the introduction and the first four riddles of this version are similar to those found in *Midrash Mishle* with minor differences.[9]
- Four riddles attributed to the Queen are preserved in an early-eighteenth-century Yemenite story known as *Ma'aseh Malkat Sh'ba* (The Tale of the Queen of Sheba).[10] The first three riddles in this version correspond to the first three riddles in *Midrash Mishle*. The fourth riddle is a modification of the first riddle in *Targum Sheni*.[11]

In post-biblical Judaic traditions the Hebrew text of *The Questions* is found as a section within either a targum, an Aramaic paraphrase of a biblical book, or a midrash, a commentary on a biblical book. *The Questions* is inserted into an embellished version of the story of the Queen's visit. The four documents that preserve the Hebrew text of *The Questions* differ in the number of questions each contains. However, they agree in that the questions asked by the Queen are all in the form of riddles.

In Christian traditions, *The Questions* evolved in a different context and with different theological emphases than those in rabbinic literature. The apocryphon is found in Syriac and Armenian manuscripts. The Syriac traditions, dating back to the fourteenth century, are found in the following three West Syrian manuscripts:[12]

- "Cambridge Add. 2012," which Sebastian P. Brock identifies as (A), contains a collection of apocryphal and ecclesiastical writings such as *Didascalia Apostolorum*, the *First Epistle of Clement to the Corinthians*, the *Epistle of Jacob of Jerusalem to Quadratus*, the *Letters of Herod and Pilate*, and others.[13] Folios 157b-158a of this manuscript contain

3. *Targum Sheni* (Hebrew for "Second Targum") is an Aramaic translation that includes insertions of considerable new apocryphal material into the biblical text. For a discussion of *Targum Sheni* as one of the sources for the Hebrew text of *The Questions*, see Lassner, *Demonizing the Queen of Sheba*, 14-17.

4. The dating of this targum is debatable. See Bernard Grossfeld, *The Targum Sheni to the Book of Esther* (New York: Sepher-Hermon, 1994) and Yehuda Komlosh, "Targum Sheni" in *EncJud* 15:811-813.

5. Toy, "The Queen of Sheba," 209-10. See also Lassner, *Demonizing the Queen of Sheba*, 14-17.

6. According to this version, the Queen receives a letter from King Solomon ordering her to appear before him. This happens because of a story told by a bird as an excuse for being absent from Solomon's feast which, in addition to the neighboring kings and princes, all the beasts and demons had been ordered to attend. Toy, "The Queen of Sheba," 207-12.

7. Schechter, "The Riddles of Solomon," 349-58. The English translation is found on 354-56. See also Lassner, *Demonizing the Queen of Sheba*, 13-14.

8. Neil Danzig, "The First Discovered Leaves of Sefer Hefes," *JQR*, N.S. 82 (1991): 96-97.

9. Schechter, "The Riddles of Solomon," 351. The introductory verse refers to a much later rabbi as the editor of the document than the one referred to in *Midrash Mishle*.

10. Aviad, "The Matter of the Queen of Sheba."

11. Lou H. Silberman, "The Queen of Sheba in Judaic Tradition" in James B. Pritchard, *Solomon and Sheba* (London: Phaidon, 1974), 75-76.

12. A fourth Syriac manuscript containing *The Questions*, Syriac 8, exists in Yale University's Beinecke Rare Book and Manuscript Library collection. It is a miscellany of which folios 1v-2v contain *The Questions*, identified as "Questions by Queen Sheba to King Solomon." I did not have access to this manuscript.

13. Goshen-Gottestein, *Syriac Manuscripts in the Harvard College Library*, 78. See also, Vööbus, *Handschriftliche*, 112.

only two of the Queen's questions. The title of the text in this manuscript reads, "The questions which the Queen of Sheba asked Solomon."

- "Mingana Syr. 480," which Brock identifies as (B),[14] was copied in Mardin in 1712-1713 C.E. It contains a collection of various documents including the longest Syriac text of *The Questions*. Folios 398[a-b] of this manuscript contain thirteen questions attributed to the Queen. This represents the largest number of questions in the Syriac traditions. The first seven questions are numbered, followed by six unnumbered questions. The final question in the list is attributed to Solomon. Questions 1 and 3 in this manuscript correspond to the two questions in (A). The unnumbered six questions differ from the earlier seven questions in that they are more like riddles than inquiries. The title of the text in this manuscript reads, "The Seven Questions which the Queen of Sheba asked Solomon."
- "Harvard Syr. 99," which Brock identifies as (C), was copied in 1899 C.E. It comprises a collection of various documents including the *Book of the Dove*, extracts from *Teghrāthā* of Barhebraeus, prayers and creeds.[15] Folios 171[a]-172[a] and 175[b]-176[a] of this manuscript contain seven questions which are the same as the first seven questions found in (B). However, questions 1 to 5 are separated from questions 6 to 7 by two folios. The title of the text of *The Questions* in this manuscript reads, "The Seven Questions which the Queen of Sheba asked King Solomon."

The Syriac text, based on the B manuscript, was translated into English and published by Sebastian P. Brock.[16] He indicates in the footnotes of his article the variations between the text of B and those of A and C. The Syriac text of *The Questions*, concluded Brock, must be based on a Greek original. He based his conclusion on several syntactic structures in the Syriac.[17] The phrase "he was in himself," for example, in Solomon's answer to Question 3—*hu le beh* —is found as a common Syriac rendering of the Greek *heauton*, in translation literature, especially of the seventh century.[18] The phrase "(All kinds of wisdom) which are beautiful"—*d-šappira'it 'it lhen*—in Solomon's answer to Question 6, is another example of a syntactic structure found only in seventh-century Syriac translations of Greek texts.[19] These observations help the reader conclude that the Syriac text can be traced to a seventh-century Greek original.

The Queen's questions in the Syriac traditions, unlike in rabbinic literature, were circulated and transmitted independently. No embellished or expanded version of the biblical story is found in the Syriac manuscripts of *The Questions*. Furthermore, the questions in the Syriac tradition end with a riddle told by King Solomon, not found in the Hebrew manuscripts. This riddle, which is identified as question 13, remains unanswered. Following Solomon's riddle, the Queen concludes the dialogue and the entire apocryphon,

14. For a review of the Mingana manuscripts, see Sebastian P. Brock, "Notes on Some Texts in the Mingana Collection," *JSS* 14 (1969): 205-26.

15. Wright, *A Catalogue of the Syriac Manuscripts*, 534.

16. Brock, "The Queen of Sheba's Questions to Solomon," 331-45. The Syriac text is found on 336-41, and its English translation on 341-45. His English translation of the Syriac is also reprinted in this chapter after the translation of the Armenian version.

17. Brock, "The Queen of Sheba's Questions to Solomon," 334-35.

18. Sebastian P. Brock, *The Syriac Version of the Pseudo Mythological Scholia* (Cambridge, 1971), 37-38.

19. Brock, "The Queen of Sheba's Questions to Solomon," 334-35.

saying, "May your Kingdom be for ever in that you have rejoiced the world with your wisdom."

Another Christian tradition that preserved and transmitted *The Questions* is that of the Armenian Church. Armenian manuscripts containing *The Questions* can be classified into two groups based on key textual and contextual variations. The first Armenian version (henceforth, ARM) is found in a group of manuscripts containing the text of *The Questions* independent of any context, story or narrative. It is preserved in manuscripts that are copies of a miscellany or a collection of independent writings, such as hagiographies and sermons. This version includes thirteen questions, with a paragraph narrating the Queen's praise of Solomon's wisdom, inserted after the eighth question. The questions are not numbered in this version. This version was published by the Mekhitarist priest Sargis Yovsēpeanc based on two manuscripts in the Mekhitarist Monastery of San Lazzaro, Venice.[20] The following is a partial list of the manuscripts of this group:

- Venice (San Lazzaro) 264 (old numbering 423), copied in 1366 C.E. This is a miscellany, which contains *The Questions* in folios 97[a]-98[b];
- Venice 266 (old numbering 394), is a thirteenth-century miscellany which contains *The Questions* in folios 222[b]-225[a];
- Vienna (Mekhitarist Monastery) 324 (old numbering 101), a miscellany copied in 1305 C.E., folios 231[a]-231[b];
- Matenadaran 75, a miscellany copied in 1631, folios 58[b]-60[b];
- Matenadaran 341, *Vardaṇ Arewelc'i - Answers from the Holy Scriptures,* copied in 1365 C.E., folios 138[a]-141[a];
- Matenadaran 573, a fifteenth-century miscellany;
- Matenadaran 750, a fourteenth-century miscellany;
- Matenadaran 1114, a miscellany copied in 1425 C.E., folios 106[a]-107[b];
- Matenadaran 1770, a miscellany copied in 1589 C.E., folios 157[a];
- Matenadaran 1784, a seventeenth-century miscellany;
- Matenadaran 2080, an eighteenth-century miscellany;
- Matenadaran 2335, a miscellany copied in 1476 C.E.;
- Matenadaran 4246, a fifteenth-century miscellany.

The second Armenian version of *The Questions* (henceforth, MA) is found as part of *The Chronicle by Michael the Great.* This twelfth-century document (henceforth, *The Chronicle*) is a well-known historical narrative attributed to the Jacobite Patriarch Michael the Syrian. Its Armenian translation was also popular among the Armenians.[21] Scholars have noticed that the Armenian version of *The Chronicle* is not an exact translation of the Syriac original.[22] In fact, the Armenian translation contains material not found

20. Yovsēpeanc, *The Uncanonical Books*, 229-32.

21. *Tearn Mixayēli Patriarki Asorwoy Žamanakagrutiwn,* i.

22. Armenian manuscripts preserve two versions of *The Chronicle.* One of them is considered an older version which does not include *The Questions.* The other includes, among several other insertions, *The Questions.* See Barsegh Sarghissian, "Syriac Chronology" [Armenian], *Bazmavep* 47 (1889): 319-21; Felix Haase, "Die armenische Rezension der syrischen Chronik Michael des Grosen," *OrChr* N.S. 13 (1915): 60-82 and 271-83; Andrea B. Schmidt, "Warum schreibt Petrus der Iberer an die Armenier? Ein pseudonymer Brief und die Armenisierung der syrischen Plerophorien," in *Horizonte der Christenheit. Festschrift für*

in the Syriac version of *The Chronicle*, including *The Questions*.[23] This version includes twelve questions, with an expanded version of the paragraph narrating the Queen's praise of Solomon's wisdom inserted at the end of the questions. Only the first six questions of this version are numbered. The following are the manuscripts that preserve the MA version of *The Questions*:

- Venice (San Lazzaro) 882 (old numbering 1153), which is an Armenian translation of *The Chronicle* dated to the fourteenth century. This manuscript is labeled as the *11th Book of History of the Armenians*, of which the first section contains *The Chronicle*, including *The Questions*.
- Venice (San Lazzaro) 892 (old numbering 662), which is an Armenian translation of *The Chronicle* completed in 1610 C.E. This manuscript is labeled as the *21st Book of History of the Armenians*, of which the first section contains *The Chronicle*, including *The Questions*.
- Venice 898 (old numbering 1023), copied in 1656 C.E., the *27th Book of History of the Armenians*, of which the second part contains *The Chronicle*, including *The Questions*.
- Venice (old numbering 1152), dated to the late fifteenth century, contains *The Chronicle* with *The Questions*.
- Bibliothèque Nationale de France 199 (ancien fonds arménien 90), which is a collection of historical books and sermons including *The Questions*, copied in 1721 C.E.

Compared to the first seven questions in the Syriac, both Armenian versions (ARM and MA) have the same first six questions, and do not include the seventh Syriac question. The second question in MA is identical to that in the Syriac tradition. In ARM, however, the second question is divided into two parts: 2 and 2a. The second part is simply the interrogative pronoun "how." Because of this, the third question in MA and the Syriac version is equivalent to the fourth question in ARM. Likewise, while the numbering of questions 3 to 7 differs between the Syriac and ARM, the eighth question is the same in both versions. The eighth question in the Syriac tradition is inserted after the initial six numbered questions in MA, making it the seventh question of this version (Table 1).

The sequence of the questions in the Armenian versions (ARM and MA) is the same as that in the Syriac version. As in the Syriac, the Armenian questions can be divided into two groups based on their content and intent: 1 to 7 in ARM—counting 2a as the third question—which corresponds to questions 1 to 6 in MA; and the remaining six questions in ARM and MA. The content of the first group of questions reflects a genuine interest in knowledge and a desire to gain wisdom. They inquire about subjects such as theology, metaphysics, biology, astrology and the earth. The questions in the second group, as in the Syriac, are riddles similar to the ones preserved in rabbinic literature.[24]

The two Armenian versions differ in that the Queen's praise of Solomon, inserted after Solomon's answer to the eighth question in the ARM and Syriac versions, is shifted to the end of the list of questions in MA, after Solomon's riddle. The Queen's praise in MA includes an expansion describing the glory of the temple, Solomon's palace and his servants,

F. Heyer (ed. Michael Kohlbacher and Markus Lesinsky; Erlangen: Lehrstuhl für Geschichte und Theologie des christlichen Ostens, 1994), 250-67.

23. Chabot, *Chronique de Michel le Syrien*, 60-61.

24. Brock, "The Queen of Sheba's Questions to Solomon," 334.

which is found neither in ARM nor in the Syriac version. Finally, a concluding blessing attributed to the Queen is inserted at the end of *The Questions* in the Syriac version; it is not found in any of the Armenian versions.

None of the questions in ARM is numbered, while only the first six questions in MA are numbered. Furthermore, each of the Queen's remaining six questions in MA, unlike the earlier ones, is introduced by the Armenian term *aṙak* meaning "fable" or "riddle." Solomon's corresponding answers to the same questions are introduced by the Armenian word *lucumn* meaning "the solution." Neither term is found in any of the questions in ARM.

Through the centuries, the list of questions must have been subjected to a complicated process of redaction. The following observations help us conclude that the first seven questions must have circulated independently: the title of the Syriac manuscript C; the contents and genre of the first seven questions compared to the remaining riddles; and the numbering and introduction of the first seven questions and answers in Syriac, and their corresponding ones in MA. Furthermore, the shifting of the Queen's praise of Solomon from the eighth question in ARM and the Syriac version to the end of the list in MA indicates a later editorial process in order to combine the two groups of questions into one document (see Table 1).

As in the Syriac, the final question in the two Armenian versions is a riddle attributed to King Solomon. This riddle remains unanswered in the two Armenian versions, as in the Syriac. In one Armenian manuscript, the following statement is inserted after Solomon's riddle, "And she found no answer to this word."[25] However, the Armenian versions differ from the Syriac in that they do not have the Queen's concluding comment after the final riddle found in B.

TABLE 1 NUMBER AND SEQUENCE OF QUESTIONS IN THE SYRIAC AND ARMENIAN MANUSCRIPTS

Question	A	B	C	ARM	MA
Q1	X	X	X	X	X
Q2		X	X	X	X
Q2a				X	
Q3	X	X	X	X	X
Q4		X	X	X	X
Q5		X	X	X	X
Q6		X	X	X	X
Q7		X	X		
Q8		X		X	X
Queen's Praise		X		X	
Q9		X		X	X
Q10		X		X	X
Q11		X		X	X
Q12		X		X	X

25. See manuscript Venice 264, folio 87[b].

Question	A	B	C	ARM	MA
Q13		X		X	X
Queen's Praise					Expanded Version
Concluding Remark		X			
Total number of Questions	2	13	7	13	12

The fact that the Syriac version of *The Chronicle* does not include *The Questions* confirms that MA is a later insertion into the Armenian translation of *The Chronicle*. This is further supported by the fact that the Armenian manuscripts preserve two versions of *The Chronicle*. Only one of the two Armenian versions of *The Chronicle* includes *The Questions*. Having carefully read the Armenian version of *The Chronicle*, Barsegh Sarghissian, a priest of the Mekhitarist Order in Venice, Italy, concluded that the Armenian text of *The Questions* is independent of the original text of *The Chronicle*.[26] Therefore, *The Questions* must be an insertion in the Armenian translation of *The Chronicle* by the translator or by a later editor.

Internal textual and contextual evidence demonstrate that ARM preserves an older version of *The Questions* than does MA. First and foremost, as stated earlier, the fact that the questions are not found in the Syriac and some Armenian manuscripts of *The Chronicle* argues for a later insertion of MA into *The Chronicle*. The introduction and conclusion before and after *The Questions*, which are found only in MA, clearly serve as seams inserted later into the text to incorporate the otherwise independently circulating *Questions* into the narrative of *The Chronicle*. These two paragraphs incorporate material reflecting documents from the seventh century and later, such as the identification of the Queen's kingdom in the south as the land "where women ruled."[27] Furthermore, the phrase "a few of which we present here," in the introductory paragraph found in MA only, clearly indicates that the editor who inserted these questions into MA was aware of the existence of other traditions of longer lists of questions.[28] As mentioned earlier, the placement of the Queen's praise of Solomon after the final riddle further supports our argument that MA's version of *The Questions* represents a later edition. Thus, ARM must be an older version of *The Questions* than MA. Issaverdens reaches the same conclusion in the brief introductory remarks to his English translation.[29] The present study will focus on the text of ARM, unless otherwise indicated. References will be made to textual variations whenever it is important to understand the meaning of the text.

A careful reading of ARM and comparing its text with that of the Syriac version indicate a Syriac origin for the Armenian version. For example, comparing the word order and sentence structure in ARM with the Syriac text demonstrates that ARM is a literal translation of the Syriac. This is also demonstrated by syntactic and stylistic elements in the ARM version, including the obvious Syriac transliteration in Solomon's answer to question 2a in ARM (question 2 in MA and the Syriac), where the Syriac word *sahr* is written in Armenian and then translated as "moon." There is no doubt that the Armenian

26. Sarghissian, *Studies on the Apocryphal Books*, 453ff.
27. See, for example, Qur'an 27:23.
28. *Tearn Mixayēli*, 63.
29. Issaverdens, 206.

versions are translations of a Syriac version. The latter, in turn, as discussed earlier, is a translation of a lost Greek original.

A French translation of MA preceded the publication of its Armenian text. In 1868 Victor Langlois published his French translation of MA utilizing three Armenian manuscripts of *The Chronicle*. These included two manuscripts from the collection of the Mekhitarist fathers in San Lazzaro, Venice, and one manuscript from the Bibliothèque impériale de Paris (Bibliothèque Nationale de France).[30] The first Armenian version of MA was published as part of *The Chronicle* in Jerusalem in 1870. This text was based mainly on one manuscript dated to 1480. The editor of this volume, however, compared the Armenian text in this manuscript with the texts in nine other manuscripts.[31] The very insignificant differences between the main and other nine manuscripts are indicated in its footnotes. One year later, in 1871, a version of *The Chronicle* known as the "old copy" was published in Jerusalem.[32] This Armenian version did not include *The Questions*.

In 1901, the first and, as of yet, only English translation of the Armenian Questions was published by Issaverdens.[33] This translation, however, was the result of comparing the texts of MA with ARM and included elements from both versions.[34] In his English translation, Issaverdens unfortunately does not indicate the elements from MA that he incorporated into the text of ARM. Brock translates very few Armenian sentences in the footnotes of his article whenever comparing the Armenian version with the Syriac text. No other translation of ARM or MA into English or any other language is available. The translation following this introduction is based on the ARM version. All the variations found in MA and the three Syriac manuscripts are indicated in the footnotes.

Genre, Structure and Prosody

This apocryphon in the ARM version is simply a list of questions (first to seventh) and riddles (eighth to thirteenth), with no introduction or conclusion. The questions are not numbered but listed consecutively.[35] Each question is introduced by the Armenian word for "The Queen" followed by Solomon's answer introduced by the word "Solomon." The only exception to this format is the ninth question which is introduced by the phrase "The Queen says." A short paragraph attributed to the Queen, in the first person plural, praising Solomon's wisdom, is inserted after the eighth question.

Date and Provenance

The oldest Armenian manuscript that includes the text of ARM is dated to the thirteenth century (Venice 266). However, as indicated in the colophons of this manuscript, its text is a copy of an earlier version. Thus, a copy of ARM must have existed and circulated before the thirteenth century. In fact, the abundance of Armenian manuscripts of ARM from the thirteenth century and later attests to the popularity of this apocryphon among the Armenians during that time.

A careful examination of the Armenian text in ARM and its comparison with the Syr-

30. Langlois, *Michel le Grand*, 15.

31. *Tearn Mixayēli Patriarki Asorwoy Žamanakagrutiwn*, i.

32. Ibid., and Chabot, *Chronique de Michel le Syrien*, LIII.

33. Issaverdens, *The Uncanonical Writings*, 211-15.

34. Ibid., 206.

35. For convenience of reference, the Armenian questions have been assigned the same numbers as the corresponding Syriac questions in Brock's translation.

iac, including its word-order and syntax, lead the reader to conclude that ARM is a literal but not slavish translation of the Syriac. Linguists date this style of Armenian translation of Syriac documents, as a rule, to the period of the fifth to the seventh centuries.[36] Furthermore, the remarkable clarity and richness of the Armenian language in ARM and its refined style support the dating of this Armenian text to no later than the seventh century. Issaverdens agreed with Sarghissian, who published the English translation of *The Questions*, in suggesting the seventh century as the date of the translation of *The Questions* into Armenian.[37]

Literary Context

The biblical story of the Queen's visit to Solomon is the context against which *The Questions* were created. The Bible records this story in two passages representing two stages in the development of the biblical text. It is the story as preserved in the Deuteronomistic History (1 Kgs 10:1-13)[38] and its modification by the Chronicler (2 Chr 9:1-12).[39]

In the overall structure of 1 Kings, the story of the Queen's visit belongs in the first part of the book (chapters 1-11) which is dedicated to King Solomon. It is in this part of 1 Kings that we are told about Solomon's leadership, wisdom, achievements and his worldwide prestige and fame.[40] The international aspect of Solomon's prestige, for example, is indicated by the location of the kingdom of Sheba or Saba from which the Queen came to visit Solomon.[41] The scholarly consensus today is that Sheba was a kingdom on the southwestern tilt of the Arabian Peninsula, modern-day Yemen, which controlled some of the coastal regions of today's Ethiopia and Eritrea.[42]

36. Ter Petrosian, *Ancient Armenian Translations*, 5-6.

37. Issaverdens, *The Uncanonical Writings*, 205-207 and 211-15; and Yovsēpeanc, 229-32.

38. The story of the Queen's visit to Solomon, narrated in 1 Kgs 10:1-13, is part of the Bible known in Jewish traditions as the "Former Prophets." This is a collection of works that provides a prophetic interpretation of Israel's history from the conquest of Canaan to the end of the monarchy. Modern scholars call this biblical corpus the "Deuteronomistic History" because the narratives share common vocabulary, literary style and theological perspectives that are heavily influenced by the book of Deuteronomy, which many scholars regard as the introduction to the corpus.

39. For a review of the Deuteronomistic History and the scholarly research associated with it, see Arnold Nicolaas Radjawane, "Das deuteronomistische Geschichtswerk," *Theologische Rundschau* 38 (1974): 177-216; Werner H. Schmidt, *Old Testament Introduction* (New York: Crossroad, 1990), 136-159; and Hans W. Wolff, "The Kerygma of the Deuteronomistic Historical Work," in Walter Brueggemann and Hans W. Wolff, *The Vitality of Old Testament Traditions* (Atlanta, Ga.: John Knox, 1975), 83-100.

40. For a review of scholarly publications concerning Solomon in the Deuteronomistic History, see Gary N. Knoppers, *Two Nations Under God: The Deuteronomistic History of Solomon and the Dual Monarchies.* Volume 1: *The Reign of Solomon and the Rise of Jeroboam* (HSM 52; Atlanta, Ga.: Scholars Press, 1993), 1-56; Schmidt, *Old Testament Introduction*, 160-170; and Marvin A. Sweeny, "The Critique of Solomon in the Josianic Edition of the Deuteronomistic History," *JBL* 114 (1995): 607-22.

41. In the Bible, Sheba is the name of one of the sons of Yoktan (Joktan), son of Eber, son of Shelah, son of Arphaxad, son of Shem, one of the three sons of Noah (Gen 10:28).

42. The Old Testament associates the kingdom of Sheba with wealth and prosperity (Isa 60:6, Jer 6:20 and Ezek 27:22). The New Testament books identify Sheba as a land in the southern reaches of the world (Mt 12:42, Lk 11:31). Flavius Josephus in *Ant.* 8.165-75 calls the visiting monarch "the Queen of Egypt and Ethiopia." Later traditions identify her as an Ethiopian queen. For a detailed examination of the location of this kingdom, see Gus W. van Beek, "The Land of Sheba" in Pritchard, *Solomon and Sheba*, 40-63. See also Muhammad A. Bafaqih, *L'unification du Yémen antique* (Paris: Librairie orientaliste P. Geuthner, 1990); Richard LeBaron Bowen and Frank P. Albright, *Archeological Discoveries in South Arabia* (Baltimore, Md.: Johns Hopkins, 1958); Ray L. Cleveland, *An Ancient South Arabian Necropolis* (Baltimore, Md.: Johns Hopkins, 1965); Albert Jamme, *Sabean Inscriptions from Mahram Bilqis (Marib)* (Baltimore, Md.: Johns Hop-

The narrative in 1 Kgs 10:1-13 describes a visit by the Queen of Sheba to Jerusalem. Having "heard of the fame of Solomon," the Queen came to Jerusalem to test Solomon "with hard questions" (v. 1). She came accompanied "with camels bearing spices, and very much gold, and precious stones" as gifts to the King (v. 2). When the two monarchs met, the Queen asked him "all that was on her mind." Solomon in turn answered all her questions so that "there was nothing hidden from the king which he could not explain to her" (v. 3). At the end of the visit the Queen was so impressed by Solomon's brilliance, wisdom, intelligence, wealth and luxury that she was left "with no more spirit in her" (v. 5). In other words, the King's wisdom demonstrated through his answers to her questions left her breathless.

Scholars agree that the Queen's visit, as narrated in 1 Kings, was motivated by political and economic reasons, which necessitated this historic trade mission. The Queen journeyed all the way to Jerusalem with the likely hopes of discussing and clarifying difficult diplomatic issues raised by the changing world economy, and Israel's expanding role in the region.[43] This perhaps was the reason for the phrase "hard questions" in verse 1.

According to the conclusion of the biblical story, the Queen was successful in her mission to visit King Solomon in Jerusalem and negotiate trade issues with him (1 Kgs 10:13). However, despite the original reasons for this historic visit and what its outcome might have been, it is obvious that the Deuteronomistic editor in the Bible is depicting the story as another expression of Solomon's international triumphs and universal fame. This interpretation remains the main theme of the retelling—and of the later versions—of this story in Judaic circles throughout the centuries.

The Deuteronomistic narration of the story in 1 Kgs 10:1 is incorporated into the later retelling of the story of Israel's kings edited by the post-exilic Chronicler.[44] The story, found in 2 Chr 9:1-12, echoes the same elements of 1 Kgs 10:1-13, with minor modifications expressing the Chronicler's theological emphases. The theocratic viewpoint of the Chronicler, for example, is strikingly evident in verse 8, where the phrase "set you on his throne as king for the Lord your God" contrasts with the parallel in 1 Kgs 10:9 which simply states "set you on the throne of Israel." For the Chronicler, Solomon is not simply a local prince of a small kingdom. He is the ruler over God's kingdom.

Centuries after its origin in the Bible, and development from 1 Kings 10 to 2 Chronicles 9, the story of the visit of the Queen of Sheba to King Solomon continued circulating and being edited and expanded beyond the biblical parameters. The story entered the circles of the early rabbinic, Christian and Islamic communities in the East. Today we have many

kins, 1962) and Jacques Ryckmans, *Textes du Yémen Antique inscrits sur bois* (Louvail-la-Neuve: Université catholique de Louvain, Institut orientaliste, 1994).

43. For a scholarly review of the political and economical status of Israel during the times of Solomon, see Benjamin Mazar, "The Era of David and Solomon," *JNES* 48 (1989): 38-39; and Juan Alberto Soggin, "The Davidic-Solomonic Kingdom" in *Israelite and Judean History* (ed. John H. Hayes and J. Maxwell Miller; Philadelphia, Pa.: Westminster, 1977), 332-80.

44. For a review of the scholarly research in the Chronicler's history, see Ernst Jenni, "Aus der Literatur zur chronistischen Geschichtsschreibung," *Theologische Literaturzeitung* 45 (1980): 97-108; Rudolf Mosis, *Untersuchungen zur Theologie des chronistischen Geschichtswerkes* (Freiburger theologische Studien 92; Vienna: Herder, 1973); and Hugh G. M. Williamson, *Israel in the Books of Chronicles* (Cambridge: Cambridge University Press, 1977).

manuscripts in Armenian, Arabic,[45] Ethiopian,[46] Hebrew, and Syriac which preserve diverse versions of the story of the visit. The story, as mentioned earlier, served as the source which gave birth to the apocryphal questions of the Queen and the Answers of Solomon. Although all the versions of this apocryphon assume the biblical story of the Queen's visit to Solomon, not all of them mention the visit and its details.

The Syriac and ARM versions of *The Questions* circulated independent of any context. They are simply a list of the questions and their answers. They have no introduction or a conclusion. No mention is made in these two versions of the Queen's visit to Solomon and the exchange of gifts between the two monarchs. This version starts with the first question asked by the Queen, immediately following the title of the apocryphon. It ends with the last question in the series, which is the only question asked by Solomon and which remains unanswered.

The MA version, however, has its own context. The questions are inserted in the Armenian translation of The Chronicle in the part of the narrative following the story of the rebellion of Hadad the Edomite against Solomon (1 Kgs 11:14-22). The questions are incorporated into chapter four of The Chronicle, titled "Concerning the Coming of the Queen to Solomon."[47] A paragraph introducing the questions is found immediately after a brief narrative retelling the prophecy of the prophet Ahi'ja the Selonite concerning the division of the kingdom because of Solomon's association with foreign women (1 Kgs 11:30-31).[48] The questions are introduced by a paragraph that is not found in the ARM version. In this paragraph we read about the visit of a queen from the south who is introduced as a descendant of Noah. The queen comes from a country whose leaders have always been women. The final two sentences in this paragraph, which is followed by the text of The Questions, read, "(the Queen) came because of the fame of his wisdom, and tested him with words through questions of fables, of which we present a few here. First she questioned concerning God, saying...." This is followed by the text of the questions.

Bibliography

Aviad, Yeshayahu. "The Matter of the Queen of Sheba" (Heb.). In *Sefer Asaf.* Edited by M. D. Cassuto et al. (Festschrift in honour of Simha Asaf). Jerusalem: Mossad HaRav Kook, 1953.

Brock, Sebastian P. "Notes on Some Texts in the Mingana Collection." *JSS* 14 (1969): 205-26.

45. The Arabic version of the story is preserved in the Qur'an and its later commentaries. Like the Bible, the Qur'an preserves a version which does not mention the name of the Queen of Sheba. Later Arabic commentaries name her Bilqis. According to the Qur'anic narrative, *Sura* 27:16-44, King Solomon hears about a prosperous kingdom ruled by a queen who worships the sun (22-26). He sends a message to the queen, first ordering her to visit him (28-31), and when she hesitates to do so, he threatens to invade her country (36-37). She eventually agrees and travels to Jerusalem. Following the visit, and after the exchange of gifts, the Queen converts to monotheism (44). The Qur'anic version does not include the text of the questions asked by the Queen, nor the answers by Solomon.

46. The Ethiopian version of the visit of the Queen of Sheba to Solomon is preserved in a medieval Ethiopian national saga known as *Kebra Nagast* (Glory of the Kings). The objective of this story is to prove that Ethiopia was the lawful successor of Israel as the chosen people of God. See, Edward Ullendorff, "The Queen of Sheba in Ethiopian Tradition," in James B. Pritchard, *Solomon and Sheba*, 104-14. The Ethiopian sources give the queen the name Makeda. The Ethiopian embellishments of the story do not include the questions of the Queen nor Solomon's answers.

47. *Tearn Mixayēli Patriarki Asorwoy Žamanakagrutiwn*, 63-69.

48. Ibid., 57-58.

__________. "The Queen of Sheba's Questions to Solomon – A Syriac Version." *Mus* 92 (1979): 331-45.

Chabot, Jean-Baptiste. *Chronique de Michel le Syrien, Patriarche Jacobite d'Antioche (1166-1199).* Paris: Ernest Leroux, 1899.

Goshen-Gottestein, Moshe H. *Syriac Manuscripts in the Harvard College Library – A Catalogue.* Ann Arbor, Mich.: Scholars Press, 1979.

Issaverdens, Jacob. *The Uncanonical Writings of the Old Testament Found in the Armenian Manuscripts of the Library of St. Lazarus.* Venice: Armenian Monastery of St. Lazarus, 1900.

Langlois, Victor. *Chronique de Michel le Grand, patriarche des Syriens jacobites.* Venice: Typ. de l'Académie de Saint-Lazare, 1868.

Lassner, Jacob. *Demonizing the Queen of Sheba: Boundaries of Gender and Culture in Postbiblical Judaism and Medieval Islam.* Chicago Studies in the History of Judaism. Chicago: University of Chicago Press, 1993.

Pennacchietti, Fabrizio Angelo. *Three Mirrors of Two Biblical Ladies.* Piscataway, Ill.: Gorgias, 2006.

Sarghissian, Barsegh. *Studies on the Apocryphal Books of the Old Testament* (Armenian). Venice: S. Ghazar, 1898.

Schechter, Solomon. "The Riddles of Solomon in Rabbinic Literature." *Folklore* 1 (1890): 349-358.

Stone, Michael. "The Apocryphal Literature in the Armenian Tradition." PIASH 4 (1971): 59-77.

__________. *Selected Studies in Pseudepigrapha and Apocrypha.* Leiden: Brill, 1991.

Ter Petrosian, Levon. *Ancient Armenian Translations.* New York: St. Vartan Press, 1992.

Toy, Crawford. H. "The Queen of Sheba." *Journal of American Folklore* 20/78 (1907): 208-209.

Tearn Mixayeli Patriarki Asorwoy Žamanakagrutiwn (The Chronicle of Lord Michael the Assyrian Patriarch) [Armenian]. Jerusalem: St. James, 1870.

Vööbus, Arthur. *Handschriftliche Überlieferung der Memre Dichtung des Jacob von Serug.* Louvain: Secrétariat du CSCO, 1973.

Wright, William. *A Catalogue of the Syriac Manuscripts Preserved in the Library of the University of Cambridge.* Cambridge: Cambridge University Press, 1901.

Yovsēpeanc, Sargis. *The Uncanonical Books of the Old Testament* (Armenian). Venice: Mekhitarist Press, 1896.

Questions[a] of the Queen[b] and Answers by[c] Solomon the Son of David[d]

Armenian version translated by Vahan S. Hovhanessian

(1) The Queen says[e]—What is your God, whom is he like and what is his form?

Exod 3:14 LXX Solomon[f]—My[g] God is He who is.[h] Every being is from him, and he is superior to all beings.[i] He does not resemble anything, because everything is subject to change and has its opposite. My Lord, however, is unchangeable and has no opposite.[j]

(2) The Queen[k]—How does the[l] sphere move versus the heavens,[m] to the right or to the left? And in its rotation does it revolve completely or partially?[n]

Solomon—It has the two norms of rotation.[o]

---

a. + "The Seven" B and C. The title in MA reads, "Concerning the Queen's Coming to Solomon."

b. + "of Sheba" A, B and C.

c. + "King" C.

d. Omit "Son of David" Syriac and MA. Following the title, MA includes the following paragraph which is not found in ARM: "The Queen of the South, who they say is the daughter of Noah from Esther's descendants, where the practice is to have women rulers since the days of Patriarch Noah until today, came to him (Solomon). The name of the Queen is Noa, who came because of the fame of his wisdom, and tested him with words through questions of fables, of which we present a few here."

e. The Syriac does not have the verb "says." Instead it reads, "First Question." MA adds: "First she asked concerning God." The remaining questions in the Armenian start with the word that translates as "The Queen" and the answers with "Solomon."

f. A, B and C replace "Solomon" by the word "Answer." The same is true for Questions 1 to 7 in the Syriac tradition. MA: "Solomon says."

g. Cf. Brock, 341 n. 83.

h. The phrase "He who is" is the translation of the seventh letter of the Armenian alphabet appearing here in the sentence, which is also the third person singular conjunction of the present tense of the verb "to be."

i. Omit "Every being is from him" MA.

j. The sentence "my Lord, however, is unchangeable and has no opposite" is not in the Syriac.

k. MA does not have "The Queen." Instead the question begins with the second character of the Armenian alphabet identifying it as the second question. The same applies for questions 3 through 6, using the third to the sixth characters of the Armenian alphabet.

l. + "this" B.

m. Omit "versus the heavens" B and C.

n. The second part of this question in the Syriac text reads as follows, "And when the whole of it revolves, does it revolve equally or part of it in one way, part of it another?"

o. Syriac: "The sphere has a double revolution." See Brock, 342 and the translation below. In

(2a) The Queen—How?[a]

Solomon—The circle of the firmament is from the east with a movement to the right, southward toward the west, coming back northward to the same place. Thus, moving rapidly by force of command in a day and a night, it completes one round. But the luminous things which are called planets, turn from the west to the left, toward the east. And each of them, according to its high and low positions and according to the broadness or the narrowness of the orbits, completes its turn within thirty years to thirty days, beginning from *Kronos* proceeding to *Sahr*,[b] which is from Saturn to the Moon.[c]

(3) The Queen—Before the[d] existence of everything,[e] where was the Creator of all?[f] And after the destruction of all, in what place shall the Immovable dwell?[g]

Solomon—Before the formation of beings, the Creator dwelt by Himself,[h] and was complete in His essential nature,[i] and rejoiced in unlimited goodness. And when the creation shall be no more, He in like manner shall dwell in His immutability.[j] Now all are in Him, but then the souls of the pure shall be in Him and He in them. He will glorify and be glorified immutably and in the like manner.[k] John 6:56

(4) The Queen—What is the reason that an Indian woman[l] no longer gets pregnant after eating a pomegranate?

Solomon—The pomegranate is cool and moist,[m] while India is hot and dry, but a woman is moist and cold.[n] Consequently, mixing the nature of the woman

---

the Syriac and MA Solomon's answer continues, without the Queen's question "How?" as is the case in ARM.

a. Omit B, C and MA. This question is part of question 2 in the Syriac and MA.

b. The word *sahr* is an Armenian transliteration of the Syriac word *sahra* meaning moon.

c. Omit "beginning from *Kronos* proceeding to *Sahr*, which is from Saturn to the Moon" B and C. MA reads: "from *Kronos*, which is Saturn to *Sahr*, which is the Moon."

d. + "all this" B and C.

e. Omit "the existence of everything" B and C.

f. Omit "of all" B, C and MA.

g. The second part of the question in the Syriac manuscripts reads, "and after it, where will he be?" See Brock, 342 and the translation below.

h. + "that is, he existed" B and C; and "The Being always existed in himself" MA.

i. Omit "and was complete in His essential nature" B and C.

j. Omit "And when the creation shall be no more, He in like manner shall dwell in His immutability" AM.

k. The rest of this paragraph is totally different in the Syriac tradition. It reads, "And after he has undone everything that he has established for the honour of his creative ability, he will dwell at the banquet of the just and in the hearts of those who please him, remaining endlessly in his kingdom. As far as change is concerned, there is no alteration for him from one place to another."

l. Syriac: "How is it possible that a woman who eats pomegranates in the land of the Indians does not become pregnant?" See Brock, 342 and the translation below.

m. MA reads: "The pomegranate is for the cold and moist."

n. Omit "but a woman is moist and cold" B and C.

with that of the pomegranate against the nature of the country does not produce pregnancy.[a]

(5) The Queen—Why is it that an Indian man who drinks wine is unproductive in sperm?[b]

Solomon—The nature of wine increases sleepiness, and even more among the Indians, and is hot and dry.[c] Combining wine and the country together makes [a man] unproductive.[d]

(6) The Queen—Is wisdom general or partial?[e] Is it natural or a gift?[f]

Solomon—It is general and partial,[g] general in its kind and partial in its type. And it is through nature and a gift. As natural it is common especially to animated beings. That which is gifted is not common but particular. And the choice is up to the giver and belongs to him by nature.[h]

(8) The Queen[i]—The plant tied a tiara, but not by nature;[j] and rays of flame were fixed as hair; and it wove a crown of glory for the unworthy sons.[k]

---

a. The Syriac reads, "...women who eat them do not become pregnant because they are of the same composition as a woman."

b. MA replaces this question with the following statement: "A drunken Indian man is unproductive in sperm." The question in the Syriac reads, "When a man drinks wine in the land of the Indians, how is it that (his) intercourse does not result in conception?" See Brock, 342 and the translation below.

c. + MA: "Likewise is the nature of man."

d. The Syriac text of the answer is much longer than that in the Armenian manuscripts with textual variations between B and C. See Brock, 342 and the translation below. MA, however, reads: "And frequenting in the opposite, the man becomes unproductive."

e. The Syriac reads, "Is our wisdom and yours, and everyone's, one and the same?"

f. The Syriac reads, "How was it given, and from whom does it come? Or does the donor who gives it divide it up and give it to everyone according to his need?" MA: "Is wisdom general or partial? And is it by nature, or learning or a gift?"

g. The answers in the Syriac and MA versions are completely different from one another and from ARM and are much longer than the text in ARM. See Brock, 343 and the translation below, and *Žamanakagrutiwn*, 63-64.

h. This question in the Syriac version is followed by question 7, which is not found in the ARM and MA versions. Following Solomon's answer to question 7 we read the following subtitle found only in the Syriac version, "Further questions that the Queen of Sheba asked Solomon." See Brock, 343 and the translation below.

i. With this question and through the remaining ones, the Queen's questions are introduced in MA with the Armenian word *ar̄ak* meaning "riddle" or "fable."

j. Syriac: "A plant has woven an unusual and unnatural crown."

k. MA: "And crowns were woven for unworthy sons." The Syriac text of this part of the statement is different and much longer than ARM and MA. See Brock's translation below.

Solomon[a]—You have heard that God appeared to Moses through the burning bush,[b] and from that vision came forth questions and variations of words.[c]

The Queen[d]—We had heard about your wisdom,[e] but did not think that you were a seer of hidden mysteries.[f] And now I believe that your God is the true God, the God of things visible and invisible.[g]

(9) The Queen says[h]—Foreign mother and foreign sons;[i] murderess and fosterer of lawless (people); revealed theft and living thief, fostered kings by disgrace.[j]

Solomon[k]—Are you insulting my father and myself?[l] For Tamar, the suspected murderess of husbands,[m] by stealing from Judah fostered our fathers.[n] Genesis 38

(10) The Queen[o]—What is that filthy thing which, being transformed, fosters kings and, honored by clouds, proceeds to the fields with excrement?[p]

Solomon[q]—From the wombs of women changed into the breasts of the clouds, kings and the poor are fostered.[r]

---

a. Solomon's answers to this and the remaining questions in the Syriac version are introduced with the word "solution." In MA the Armenian word *lucumn* meaning "resolution," "analysis" or "solution" is used.

b. The Syriac text does not include the name "Moses" in this phrase. It inserts it in a statement at the end of the answer, which is not in the Armenian.

c. This part of the answer is expanded in the Syriac to read, "And flowers shone out on its branches in its flames of glory, while its leaves did not scorch up in the burning. Now we say that he is the God of Moses, and we worship that eternal being who begat utterances from a thorny plant." MA: "and from that revelation questions and variations of answers were made."

d. This paragraph is moved to the end of the questions in MA. The Syriac version introduces this comment with the phrase, "She says to him."

e. Syriac: "I had heard that you were wise."

f. Syriac: "But I did not realize that you sought out the thoughts of the heart."

g. The Syriac text of this part of the statement is completely different: "In truth it is God, your God, who makes wise your reasoning."

h. Syriac: "Question"; MA: "Riddle."

i. Syriac: "Native sons"; MA: "sons of defilement."

j. MA: "revealed theft and living kings with stain."

k. Syriac: "Solomon said to her."

l. This phrase is not a question in the Syriac. It reads, "You insult my ancestors with your questions." MA: "You insult my fathers and me."

m. The Armenian word for "husband" can also be translated as "man."

n. The second part of Solomon's answer in the Syriac reads, "For Phares son of Judah, by the cunning and the theft of Tamar, who was considered to be the murderer of her husbands, produced the king David in his line." The final phrase in MA reads: "fostered my fathers."

o. Syriac: "The Queen of Sheba says." The same is repeated in the following question.

p. The Syriac text is not a question. It reads, "An unclean thing that brings up kings and that is softened; it is honored in clouds, and is sprinkled with change, and is sent like excrement on the paths of the fields."

q. Syriac: "Solution: Solomon says:".

r. The Syriac version offers an expansion that reads, "In the menstruation which becomes milk, in the excretion on the breast, are kings and lowly nourished. This is what you say, set out in a delightful way."

(11) The Queen—The head-cook of the king multiplies the cooks, and in order to create various tastes he labors and makes others labor,[a] yet the taste is one.

Solomon[b]—If you have an excellent cook from your country, add him to our thousands. However, as you say, the taste is one. Nevertheless the wicked is bitter and far from my Lord, and remains in judgment.[c]

(12) The Queen—The bridegroom does not appear (show up), the wedding cannot be changed, and the chamber remains spotless; and the enraged bride is embarrassed.

Solomon[d]—Do not insult our people who are eternally married to God through the ineffable word.[e] We do not fornicate with foreign gods. For if we are ashamed then you also be ashamed of the worship of the bird Trane.[f]

(13) Solomon—But, from us to you a fable. He says, a strong tower and a vessel of injury;[g] a triangular temple whose bricks are joy and whose foundation is love and building is water. Its foundation is tenderness and its ceilings are dances. Its pillar is happiness and its invention is foreign. Its inhabitants have not persons. Its follower ("attendant" or "imitator") is according to the location and not fixed.[h] And its battlements[i] are from it and in it. Its windows are private and individual. Its laborers are against its building and its protectors are invisible.[j]

---

a. Syriac: "and through labor he changes fine food."

b. Syriac: "Solution: Then Solomon laughed (and) said to her."

c. The Syriac answer is totally different and does not make sense. Brock suggests that it must be corrupt.

d. Syriac: "Solution: Solomon said."

e. The Syriac is in the form of a question.

f. MA offers the following variant reading, "And you, who worship the bird Trane which is the Phoenix, ought to be ashamed."

g. The Syriac is in a question form.

h. Syriac: "Its leader wandering and without foundation." MA: "And its followers are according to the location."

i. MA: "monuments."

j. Following Solomon's riddle, MA inserts the following expanded version of the Queen's response found after the seventh question in the Syriac and ARM versions. "And the Queen says, we had heard about you, a wiseman, but did not think that you were a seer of hidden things. And now I believe that your God is alone the God of things visible and invisible. The Queen praised also the construction of the temple, the servants of the temple who according to the months worshipped before the Lord, twelve classes, twenty-four thousand in a class, and six thousand judges, four thousand lyric-poets, and four thousand door-keepers, which David his father had established. And the dimension of the temple was sixty feet, with twenty in length and a hundred-twenty feet in height, with ten golden tables and ten golden candlesticks, with two external pillars of thirty-seven feet on the right and the left, whose names are Bsogh and Yakum, who are called power and straightness. And the Holy of Holies is twenty feet wide and twenty feet long, concerning which the Queen was astonished. And she departed from him with many profits." See *Žamanakagrutiwn*, 68-69.

The Queen of Sheba's Questions to Solomon

Syriac version translated by Sebastian Brock[a]

The seven questions that the Queen of Sheba asked Solomon

1 *First Question*

What is your God, and what does he resemble, or to what is he likened?

Answer: My God is something from which everything else derives, and (who) is exalted above everything; and he has no comparison, and there is nothing that is like him, because everything (else) is changeable and subject to opposition.

2 *Second Question*

How does this sphere revolve, to the right or to the left? And when the whole of it revolves, does it all revolve equally (in the same direction), or part of it one way, part of it another?

Answer: The sphere has a double revolution: its firm part revolves westwards, to the right, and turns rapidly, each night and day completing the movement of its course. But the planets, which ride above it, revolve eastwards, to the left; and each of them completes the revolution of its journey in accordance with the measure of its altitude, ranging from every thirty years to every thirty days.

3 *Third Question*

Before all this where was the Creator, and after it, where will he be?

Answer: Before the Creator made all this he was in himself; that is, he existed, and took pleasure and dwelt in the contemplation of his goodness alone. And after he has undone everything that he has established for the honour of his creative ability, he will dwell at the banquet of the just and in the hearts of those who please him, remaining endlessly in his kingdom. As far as change (of abode) is concerned, there is no alteration for him from one place to another.

4 *Fourth Question*

How is it possible that a woman who eats pomegranates in the land of the Indians does not become pregnant?

---

a. Published originally in "The Queen of Sheba's Questions to Solomon – A Syriac Version." *Mus* 92 (1979): 331-45. The editors are grateful to Dr. Brock and to Brill Academic Publishers for permission to republish his translation of the Syriac text here.

Answer: Pomegranates are cold and moist, while India is hot and dry, and so, when they are eaten there as opposites, women who eat them do not become pregnant because they are of the same composition as a woman.

5 *Fifth Question*
When a man drinks wine in the land of the Indians, how is it that (his) intercourse does not result in conception?

Answer: The wine in the land of the Indians induces a heavy sleep, and because it is hot and dry by nature, and of the same composition as that region, it prevents cohabitation, being of the same composition as intercourse, and causes desire to become confused in a disrupting manner, not allowing nature to flow in accordance with the norm of procreation.

6 *Sixth Question*
Is our wisdom and yours, and everyone's, one and the same? How was it given (in the first place), and from whom does it (come)? Or does the donor who gives it divide it up and give it to everyone according to his need?

Answer: All (kinds) of wisdom, which are beautiful and well thought of, and have no cunning or snares, derive from the gifts of God. They are not to be found in equal measure, but every one has it in accordance with the worth of (his) mind, and in so far as he can contain it. As for cunning, craftiness, devices and the machinations of worldly knowledge, in so far as someone is pure in the thoughts of (his) soul, he is rich in them (*sc.* the gifts of God).

7 *Seventh Question*
Is all this everlasting in its nature, or is there something with a different existence that is more eternal?

Answer: There is nothing eternal save the Creator alone, —he who has no "when," or time or beginning; who has no superior, or care, no (set) course for (his) rule, so that it would be possible to achieve, by a small breath, saying that he was not. But these created things derive from and through him, even though one may precede another by some period or time: nevertheless they have a time when they were not. But when they came into being, they were brought (into being) at the beginning of each of their (existences), because the Creator is eternal, while they are creatures and subject to time.

Further question(s) that the Queen of Sheba asked Solomon.

8 A *plant* has woven an unusual and unnatural crown which has manifested fire (as its) splendid flowers; and the Hebrews weave crowns of glory for the Son, (consisting) of bitter branches.

Solution: Solomon said to her: You have indeed heard that the Lord appeared in a thorn bush, and flowers shone out on its branches in its flames of glory, while its leaves did not scorch up in the burning. Now we say that he is the God of Moses, and we worship that eternal being who begat utterances from a thorny plant.

She says to him: I had heard that you were wise, but I did not realize that you sought out the thoughts of the heart. In truth it is God, your God, who makes wise your reasoning.

9 *Question*
A foreign mother of native sons, a murderess who brought up lawless men; the theft prospered, and in cunning bore as fruit a king.

Solution: Solomon said to her: You insult my ancestors with your questions, for Phares son of Judah, by the cunning and the theft of Tamar, who was considered to be the murderer of her husbands, produced the king David in his line.

10 *Question*
The Queen of Sheba says: An unclean thing that brings up kings and that is softened; it is honoured in clouds, and is sprinkled with change, and is sent like excrement on the paths of the fields.

Solution: Solomon says: In the menstruation which becomes milk, in the excretion (<<clouds>>) on the breast, are kings and lowly nourished. This is what you say, set out in a delightful way.

11 *Question*
The Queen of Sheba says: A king's cook who excels with many bakers so as to vary the taste of the foods, and through labour he changes fine food, yet the tastes are the same.

Solution: Then Solomon laughed (and) said to her: If you have from your own country the fine food of your parable, then add our cook, that he may be filled with a thousand women, for in truth the species is the same.

12 *Question*
The bridegroom is invisible and the wedding cannot be changed, and the bridal chamber is not (yet) used; the bride is raging and put to shame.

Solution: Solomon said: will you insult (our) congregation *(or* synagogue) which is betrothed to God in an unutterable betrothal, so as not to play the harlot with the idols of the nations? <...> because you too honour the bird Trane.

13 *But do you accept from us a question:* What is a strong tower and a stone of stumbling, a four-gated temple, its stones (are) exulting, its foundation love, its buildings water, its coping stone an embrace, dancing its roof, and leaping its pillars, its presence (Shekhina) strange, its pillars without stature, its leader wandering and without foundation, its battlements both in it and of it, the windows of its entirety separated in isolation, the instrument(s) contrary to the building, and the guard who guards the house is not seen by the people of the country?

The Queen of Sheba says to him: May your kingdom be for ever, in that you have rejoiced the world with your wisdom.

The Nine and a Half Tribes

A new translation and introduction

by Richard Bauckham

The Latin Christian poet Commodian, in his long poem known as the *Apologetic Poem* (*Carmen apologeticum*) or the *Poem on the Two Peoples* (*Carmen de duobus populis*), devotes part of his narrative of eschatological events to the exiled tribes of northern Israel (whom he counts as nine and a half tribes) and their return to the land of Israel (lines 941-990). He says that they are at present hidden, in an unknown, distant land in the east, where they observe the law of Moses faithfully, as well as a vegetarian diet, and are therefore protected from untimely death and from any bodily illnesses. In the last days, in order to fulfil his promises, God will dry up the river that bounds their dwelling place, so that they can cross it and return to Judaea. As they travel, led by the angel of God, nature makes miraculous provision for them. Because God is with them, they defeat every nation that opposes them and plunder all their cities. When the tyrant in Jerusalem (the Antichrist figure whom Commodian has described earlier) hears that they are coming, he flees north to raise an army, but when he launches an attack on the returning tribes, angels intervene to defeat him. He and the false prophet are consigned to the lake of fire, while the other leaders become slaves to the Israelites, who now inherit the promises of God for eternity.

In another poetic work, the *Instructions* (*Instructiones*), Commodian has a slightly shorter version of the same material (1.42).[1] One significant difference is that this version speaks of Christ where the version in the *Poem* speaks of God. Other differences of detail include the statement in the *Instructions* that the nine and a half tribes number many thousands and the explicit statement that their intention is to liberate Jerusalem from the tyrant.[2]

It has been suggested that in these passages Commodian is dependent on an apocryphal work that is no longer extant.[3] It is certain that Commodian did make use of apocryphal literature, and, in fact, he refers to such an apocryphal source shortly before the passage about the nine and a half tribes in the *Poem*: "But on this subject I am adding (or: suggesting) a few secret things that I have read" (line 936). This statement appears to refer back to the preceding account of the king from the east (the second of the two Antichrist figures in Commodian's narrative), but it is possible that the following narrative of the nine and a half tribes is dependent on the same apocryphal source.

1. It is not known in which order the two works were written, though Poinsotte, *Commodien: Instructions*, xix-xx, proposes an argument for the priority of the *Poem*.

2. The correspondences between the two passages are set out in tabular form in Poinsotte, *Commodien: Instructions*, 313-14.

3. James, *The Lost Apocrypha*, 103-106; Charlesworth, *The Pseudepigrapha and Modern Research*, 147-49; Salvatore, *Commodiano: Carme Apologetico*, 213-21; Daniélou, *The Origins*, 118-19.

An Apocryphal Source in Commodian

The case for an apocryphal source that is no longer extant depends on the relationship between Commodian's account of the nine and a half tribes and other such accounts of the exiled northern tribes (numbered either as nine and a half or as ten) in Jewish and Christian literature. That these tribes would one day return from exile to be reunited in the land of Israel with the southern tribes (Judah and Benjamin) is predicted in several passages in the biblical prophets (Isa 11:11-16; 27:12-13; Jer 31:1-22; Ezek 37:15-23; 47:13–48:29; cf. Bar 5:5-9). But traditions about their whereabouts in the meantime and about their return (sometimes based on other scriptural passages, such as Isa 35:1-10; 49:8-12, that were held to apply to them) developed in early Judaism and were also taken up in some early Christian literature.[4] We shall consider a series of passages in which there are close parallels to Commodian.

Sibylline Oracles 2

> Dreadful wrath shall fall on them,[5]
> when from the east the people of ten tribes
> come seeking the people the Assyrian shoot destroyed,
> their fellow Hebrews.[6] Nations shall fall to them.
> Later the elect, faithful Hebrews[7]
> shall rule those mighty men, making them
> slaves, as of old; their power will never wane. (*Sib. Or.* 2:170-176)[8]

As well as the coming of the tribes (ten here, nine and a half in Commodian) from the east, this passage has in common with Commodian:

1. they are called "elect" (Commodian, *Instr.* 1.42.22);
2. they overcome nations (Commodian, *Carm.* 975);
3. the mighty men become their slaves (Commodian, *Carm.* 987-988; *Instr.* 1.42.43).

4 Ezra

> And as for you seeing him gather to himself another multitude that was peaceable, [40]these are the nine and one half[9] tribes which were led away from their own land into captivity in the days of King Hoshea, whom Shalmaneser the king of the Assyrians led captive; he took them across the river, and they were taken into another land.

4. Besides the texts discussed below, see also *5 Ezra* 1:38, which Bergen, "The 'People,'" argues takes up the Jewish tradition of the ten tribes returning from the east but substitutes the Christian people for the Israelite tribes.

5. The antecedents are probably Beliar and the false prophets (lines 165-67).

6. Presumably this refers to the southern tribes (Judah and Benjamin), whose city and state (not the people themselves) Nebuchadnezzar destroyed. (He was in fact Babylonian, not Assyrian; but cf. *Sib. Or.* 5:336 where "Assyrians" means Persians.) The term "Hebrews" is typical of *Sibylline Oracles* 1-2.

7. It is not clear whether these are the ten tribes or all Israel.

8. Translation adapted from J. L. Lightfoot, *The Sibylline Oracles: With Introduction, Translation, and Commentary on the First and Second Books* (Oxford: Oxford University Press, 2007), 317.

9. The versions and manuscripts vary between "ten," "nine and a half," and "nine." Michael Edward Stone, *Fourth Ezra* (Hermeneia; Minneapolis, Minn.: Fortress, 1990), 393, 404, rightly prefers "nine and a half" as the more unusual figure, which would understandably have been corrected to "ten" in many of the Latin manuscripts.

> [41]But they formed this plan for themselves, that they would leave the multitude of the nations and go to a more distant region, where no human race had ever lived, [42]that there at least they might keep their statutes which they had not kept in their own land. [43]And they went in by the narrow passages of the Euphrates river. [44]For at that time the Most High performed wonders for them, and stopped the springs of the river until they had passed over. [45]To that region there was a long way to go, a journey of a year and a half; and that country is called Arzareth. [46]Then they dwelt there until the last time; and now, when they are about to come again, [47]the Most High will stop the springs of the river again, so that they may be able to pass over. Therefore you saw the multitude gathered together in peace. And it will be when he destroys the multitude of the nations that are gathered together, he will defend the people who remain. (*4 Ezra* 13:39-49)[10]

This passage is part of the interpretation of a symbolic vision Ezra has seen, most of which described the destruction of the enemy nations by God. But in the last part of the vision Ezra saw the Messiah "call to himself another multitude that was peaceable" (13:12). Our passage explains who this multitude was.

The following details correspond to Commodian's accounts:[11]

1. the tribes are reckoned as nine and a half;
2. there is reference to their captivity (*4 Ezra* 13:40; Commodian, *Carm.* 945);
3. they dwell beyond a river (*4 Ezra* 13:43: "the narrow passages of the Euphrates"; Commodian, *Carm.* 943: "a river beyond Persia");[12]
4. God dries up the river for them on their way to the distant land (*4 Ezra* 13:44): Commodian alludes to this when he says that, on their way back, God dries up the river "as before" (*Instr.* 1.42.30);
5. their land is distant (*4 Ezra* 13:41; Commodian, *Instr.* 1.42.1);
6. they observe the law faithfully (*4 Ezra* 13:42; Commodian, *Carm.* 956; *Instr.*1.42.5);
7. they remain there until the last times (*4 Ezra* 13:46; Commodian, *Carm.* 944; *Instr.* 1.42.16);
8. God dries up the river again, for them to return (*4 Ezra* 13:47; Commodian, *Carm.* 960; *Instr.* 1.42.30).

There is one wide-ranging difference between Commodian and *4 Ezra*. In Commodian the role of the returning tribes in the events of the last days is military. They are "God's army." This feature is more prominent in the *Poem*, where, with divine aid, they defeat all who oppose them as they march to the holy land in order to liberate Jerusalem from the Antichrist figure who has it in his power. They defeat the Antichrist when he returns to Jerusalem with all the forces he can muster. Admittedly this victory occurs through miraculous aid: the opponents "are thrown to the ground by the angels" (line 984). In the

10. Translation from Stone, *Fourth Ezra*, 393-94.

11. I attach no importance to the fact that God is entitled "the Most High" in both cases, since this is generally characteristic of *4 Ezra* and Commodian, not confined to these passages.

12. Not until the medieval period was this river identified with the fabulous river Sambation: see Elena Loewenthal, "La storia del fiumi Sambaṭion: Alcune nota sulla tradizione ebraica antica e medievale," in *Biblische und Judaistische Studien* (ed. Angelo Vivian; Frankfurt am Main: Peter Lang, 1990), 651-63; Zvi Ben-Dor Benite, *The Ten Lost Tribes: A World History* (New York: Oxford University Press, 2009), 77-82.

Instructions, they "are struck down by heavenly terror" (1.42.40). The combination of an army and miraculous intervention resembles some of the narratives of holy war in the Hebrew Bible (Joshua 6; 2 Chr 20:1-30). In *4 Ezra,* however, a military role is explicitly denied to the returning tribes. It is emphasized that they are "peaceable" (13:12, 39, 47). They do not arrive at Jerusalem until the Messiah has already, single-handedly, destroyed the "innumerable multitude" of Gentile enemies who have gathered to oppose him.

To understand this difference we must appreciate the role of the nine and a half tribes in *4 Ezra.*[13] It seems very probable that, in the wake of the catastrophe of 70 C.E., this author wishes to avoid any element of messianic militarism. Even the Messiah does not fight with weapons (13:9), but defeats the enemies by pronouncing judicial sentence against them (13:10-11, 37-38, with allusion to Isa 11:4). He certainly does not need an Israelite army to assist him, and so the returning tribes are explicitly not cast in such a role.[14] The role they do play is not readily apparent in this passage considered alone, but it relates to the central problem with which Ezra throughout the book has been wrestling. He has had to accept that only the righteous few within his people can be saved, but this seems to contradict flagrantly the promise of God that Abraham would have innumerable offspring. The nine and a half tribes are the solution to this conundrum. In their remote abode, isolated from contact with sinful nations, they have been able to keep the law (13:42) and so qualify for eschatological salvation, as most of Ezra's people do not. As we shall see, the idea that the northern tribes fulfil the promise of innumerable descendants for Abraham is not unique to *4 Ezra*, but it is given here a particular role in the argument of the book.

It seems likely that *4 Ezra*'s emphasis on the peaceableness of the returning tribes presupposes a tradition in which they were expected (as in *Sibylline Oracles* 2 and Commodian) to play a military role in the events of the last days. *4 Ezra* does not want them in that role, but does need them in a different role. This explains why their story is given considerable space and emphasis, especially in the interpretation of the vision, while at the same time their peaceableness is stressed. It would follow that in this respect Commodian's accounts reflect a version of the tradition already known to and deliberately corrected by the author of *4 Ezra*.

Ethiopic Acts of Matthew

At the beginning of this work the apostle Matthew meets Peter and Andrew, and tells them he has come from a city where Jesus Christ himself takes part in the worship of the community.

> And I said unto them, "How did ye make yourselves worthy of the great honour of our Lord Jesus Christ keeping the festival with you?" And they said unto me, "Hast thou not heard the story concerning the nine tribes and the half tribe whom God Almighty brought into the land of inheritance? We are they! ... As for gold and silver we desire it not in our country; we eat not flesh and we drink not wine in our country, for our

13. See Richard Bauckham, "Apocalypses," in *Justification and Variegated Nomism;* Volume 1; *The Complexities of Second Temple Judaism* (ed. Donald A. Carson, Peter T. O'Brien and Mark. A. Seifrid; Tübingen: Mohr Siebeck/Grand Rapids, Mich.: Baker, 2001), 135-87, here 165-69; reprinted as "Covenant, Law and Salvation in the Jewish Apocalypses," in Richard Bauckham, *The Jewish World around the New Testament: Collected Essays I* (WUNT 233; Tübingen: Mohr Siebeck, 2008), 269-323, here 301-304.

14. Perhaps the failure of the eastern diaspora to support the Jewish war against Rome was also a factor in the background.

> food is honey and our drink is the dew. And we do not look upon the face of women with sinful desire, and our firstborn children do we offer as a gift unto God and they may minister in the church and in the sanctuary all the days of their life until they be thirty years [of age]. The water which we drink [floweth] not from cisterns which have been hewn by the hand of man, but [we drink] of the water which floweth from Paradise. We do not array ourselves in apparel which hath been made by the hand of man, but our raiment is made of the leaves of trees. No word of lying hear we in our land, and no man knoweth another who speaketh that which is false. No man taketh to wife two women in our country, and the son dieth not before his father, and the young man speaketh not in the presence of the aged, the lions dwell with us, but they do no harm unto us, and we do no harm unto them. When the winds are lifted up we smell the scent of Paradise, and in our country there is neither spring, nor cold, nor ice; but there are winds and they are [always] pleasant."[15]

This passage has nothing to say about the return of the tribes, but in its description of their life it has a few close parallels with Commodian's account of this:

1. the tribes are reckoned as nine and a half;
2. they do not eat meat (Commodian, *Carm.* 951);
3. there is no deceit (Commodian, *Carm.* 947);
4. sons do not die before their fathers (Commodian, *Carm.* 948; *Instr.* 1.42.25).

The Ethiopic *Acts of Matthew* probably derives, via Arabic and Coptic translations, from a Greek *Vorlage*, but we do not know whether this particular passage originated in Greek or in one of the subsequent versions. Although the resemblances between this passage and Commodian could be explained by dependence of the former on the latter, this seems unlikely because Commodian's work is not known in any language other than Latin. So M. R. James was probably right to state: "That Commodian and the *Acts of Matthew* draw ultimately from a common source seems clear."[16]

One important general difference between this passage in the *Acts of Matthew* and Commodian's work is that the *Acts of Matthew* describes paradisal conditions, whereas Commodian only describes the way the tribes live and the consequences for their own physical life (no untimely death; no illness). They do not live in a paradise resembling Eden. The *Acts of Matthew*, whether dependent on Commodian or his source, has greatly elaborated the description we find in Commodian, mainly by assimilating the place where the tribes live to paradise.[17]

---

15. Translation from E. A. Wallis Budge, *The Contendings of the Apostles* (London: Oxford University Press, 1935), 94-95. On this passage see also Montague Rhodes James, *Apocrypha Anecdota* (TS 2/3; Cambridge: Cambridge University Press, 1893), 92-93.

16. James, *The Lost Apocrypha*, 105.

17. James, *Apocrypha Anecdota*, 93-94 (cf. also idem, *Lost Apocrypha*, 105-106), sees resemblances, in both Commodian and the *Acts of Matthew*, to the account of the abode of the Blessed Ones (the Rechabites) in the *Story of Zosimus*, but these resemblances are very general and do not require any literary relationship.

Josephus

> Then he [Ezra] read the letter [from Xerxes, permitting Jewish exiles to return to Jerusalem] in Babylon to the Jews who were there, and, while he kept the letter itself, sent a copy of it to his countrymen who were in Media. When they learned of the king's orders... they were all greatly pleased, and many of them, taking along their possessions also, came to Babylon out of longing to return to Jerusalem. But the Israelite nation as a whole remained in the country. In this way it has come about that there are two tribes in Asia and Europe subject to the Romans, while until now there have been ten tribes beyond the Euphrates – countless myriads whose number cannot be ascertained. (Josephus, *Ant.* 11.131-133).[18]

Josephus here seems to locate the ten tribes in Media and other areas beyond the Euphrates where they were settled when first taken into exile (2 Kgs 17:6; 18:11). (In *Ant.* 9.279 Josephus says they were taken to Media and Persia.)[19] He clearly is not thinking of a much more distant place, such as *4 Ezra* envisages as the present abode of the nine and a half tribes, or as Commodian implies when he says that they are hidden in a distant and unknown land (*Carm.* 942; *Instr.* 1.42.1-2). His statement that two tribes dwell within the Roman Empire and the ten tribes beyond the Euphrates is somewhat puzzling, but he must mean that the greater part of the eastern diaspora consisted of the ten tribes. The reason that he thinks this is his impression of the vast numbers belonging to these tribes in the east. At this point his account becomes more than simply factual. He is evoking God's promise to the patriarchs that their descendants would be innumerable (Gen 13:16; 15:5; 32:12; Hos 1:10).[20] He evidently agrees with *4 Ezra* in thinking that this promise was fulfilled, not so much by the two tribes, but by the stupendous degree to which the ten tribes were thought to have multiplied in the east. The same idea is perhaps to be found in *Testament of Moses* 4:9, if the corrupt text is amended to give the sense: "the ten tribes will grow and become [many] among the nations in the time of tribulations."[21]

While Josephus differs from Commodian in other respects, his allusion to the promise to the patriarchs illuminates the significance of one statement of Commodian: that the ten tribes "have become so many thousands" (*milia tot facti*: *Instr.* 1.42.24).

The Signs of the Messiah

> *The tenth sign.* Michael will blow a loud blast (on the shofar), and the Holy One, blessed be He, will lead forth all the tribes located beyond the river of Gozan and from Halah and from Habor and from the cities of Media (cf. 2 Kgs 17:6). They will

---

18. Translation by Ralph Marcus (LCL).

19. Probably this, rather than the scenario in *4 Ezra*, is envisaged in *2 Baruch*, when Baruch sends a letter to the nine and a half tribes in exile, commanding the eagle who carries it not to "sit on any tree until you have flown over the breadth of the many waters of the river Euphrates and have come to the people that live there" (77:22).

20. Note also the description of the returning exiles of Israel as "a great company" in Jer 31:8.

21. Since it accords with what Josephus says about the ten tribes, this rendering seems to me much more likely than Tromp's: "the ten tribes will be more and more absorbed among the nations in a time of tribulations" (see Johannes Tromp, *The Assumption of Moses* [SVTP 10; Leiden: Brill, 1993], 13, 183-84). The idea that the ten tribes disappeared through assimilation to the Gentiles is not found in ancient Jewish (or Christian) literature.

> come together with the "people of Moses,"[22] (a large group) impossible to number or to measure. "The land before them will be like the garden of Eden, and behind them a flame will burn" (cf. Joel 2:3; note Ezek 36:35), and nothing will remain alive among the nations of the world. At the time that the tribes depart, clouds of glory will encompass them, and the Holy One, blessed be He, will march before them, as scripture states: "the breaker will go up before them" (Mic 2:13). The Holy One, Blessed be He, will open for them springs connected with the Tree of Life in order to supply them with water on the way, as it says in Isaiah: "I will open rivers on the high places and fountains in the midst of the plains; I will turn the wilderness into a pool of water and the dry land into springs of water" (Isa 41:18), and it is written "they will not be hungry or thirsty; heat and sun will not afflict them, [for the One showing them mercy will lead them and He will guide them by springs of water]" (Isa 49:10).[23]

The following parallels with Commodian are noteworthy:

1. luxuriant vegetation grows ahead of the returning tribes (Commodian, *Carm.* 963);
2. the nations of the world will be destroyed, though in this text it is not clear whether this occurs through miraculous divine action or the tribes themselves defeat the nations, as they do in Commodian (*Carm.* 975);
3. fountains of water spring up (Commodian, *Carm.* 965; *Instr.* 1.42.34);
4. they will be protected from the sun (Commodian, *Carm.* 967);
5. God himself will lead them (Commodian, *Instr.* 1.42.33);[24]
6. they will be very numerous (Commodian, *Instr.* 1.42.24).

We should notice also that this text quotes scriptural passages that are likely to have been behind the account in Commodian. It is typical of later apocalypses, both Jewish and Christian, that they often explicitly quote scripture, whereas earlier apocalypses only allude.

Interestingly, there are two points at which this text is closer to Josephus than to Commodian: (1) the tribes are in the places to which they were originally exiled, not in an unknown, distant land; (2) the comment on the size of the company ("impossible to number or measure") alludes, like Josephus ("countless myriads whose number cannot be ascertained"), to the patriarchal promise more clearly than does Commodian ("so many thousands").

The one feature of this passage that shows it to be no earlier than the eighth century C.E. is the reference to "the people of Moses" (*bene Mosheh*) accompanying the tribes. This notion of a group of very strictly law-observant Levites who live with the exiled northern tribes seems to have originated with Eldad ha-Dani (Eldad the Danite) in the eighth or ninth century.[25] The parallels with Commodian show that, in most other re-

---

22. Literally "the sons of Moses."

23. Translated by John C. Reeves, *Trajectories in Near Eastern Apocalyptic: A Postrabbinic Jewish Apocalypse Reader* (Resources for Biblical Study 45; Atlanta, Ga.: Society of Biblical Literature, 2005), 128-29. The parenthetical notes are his.

24. In *Carm.* 969-70, the angel of the Lord leads them.

25. See Reeves, *Trajectories,* 200-24; Adolf Neubauer, "Where Are the Ten Tribes?," *JQR* 1 (1889): 14-28, 95-114, 185-201, 408-23; here 95-114 (he thinks the idea older than Eldad). It is based on Exod 32:10, where God speaks of making Moses into a great people, and is found in *Tg. Ps.-Jon.* 34:10. On Eldad, see also

spects, this passage embodies very much older ideas about the return of the northern tribes from exile. The medieval Jewish apocalypses frequently preserve traditional material alongside material of more recent composition.

Finally, it is worth considering the parallels to Commodian's unusual numbering of the northern tribes as nine and a half and the southern tribes as two and a half. In most Jewish and Christian literature of the ancient and medieval periods, the northern tribes who were taken into exile in Assyria and Media were reckoned as ten, while the southern tribes were reckoned as two (Judah and Benjamin) (e.g., *T. Mos.* 2:3; 3:4-6; 4:8-9; *2 Bar.* 1:2-3;[26] Josephus, *Ant.* 11.133; *Sib. Or.* 2:171; *m. Sanh.* 10:3; *t. Sanh.* 13:12; *b. Sanh.* 110b; *Gen. Rab.* 73:6).[27] But Commodian follows a minority tradition in which the northern tribes were reckoned as nine and a half and the southern tribes as two and a half (*4 Ezra* 13:40;[28] *2 Bar.* 62:5; 63:3; 64:5; 77:17; 78:1; *Ascen. Isa.* 3:2;[29] Ethiopic *Acts of Matthew* [as cited above]).[30] Bogaert suggested that this numbering results from a confusion with the distinction the book of Joshua makes between nine and a half tribes who settled west of the Jordan and two and a half (Reuben, Gad and half the tribe of Manasseh) who settled east of the Jordan.[31] But there is a better explanation. The Hebrew Bible poses for its readers a problem about the numbering of the tribes. Israel is always said to consist of twelve tribes, descended from the twelve sons of Jacob, but in fact there were thirteen tribes, because the two tribes descended from the two sons of Joseph—Ephraim and Manasseh—were usually regarded as tribes in their own right. Another complication is that the tribe of Levi was not, like the other tribes, assigned a territory in which to settle, but lived, without land of its own, scattered over the territories of the other tribes. Therefore, when the book of Joshua distinguishes the tribes settled on each side of the Jordan, Levi is left out of account and it is the rest of the tribes that are divided into nine and a half and two and a half. Similarly, when the tribes are distinguished as ten northern and two southern, we should probably suppose that Levi is not being counted. In the minority tradition, however, Levi is included.[32] Half of the tribe of Levi went into exile with Judah and Benjamin (cf. Ezra 1:5), making two and a half southern tribes, while the other half of Levi went into exile

---

David J. Wasserstein, "Eldad ha-Dani and Prester John" in Charles F. Beckingham and Bernard Hamilton eds., *Prester John, the Mongols and the Ten Lost Tribes* (Aldershot, Hampshire: Variorum [Ashgate], 1996), 213-36; Ben-Dor Benite, *The Ten Lost Tribes*, 86-100. It is notable that one feature of the life of the nine and a half tribes as Commodian describes it—no son dies before his father—becomes a regular feature of the descriptions of the life of "the people of Moses": Reeves, *Trajectories*, 209, 213, 217, 221.

26. Because this is inconsistent with the division into nine and a half and two and a half that occurs elsewhere in *2 Baruch*, Pierre M. Bogaert, *Apocalypse de Baruch* (SC 144-145; Paris: Cerf, 1969), 1:348, considers that 1:2-3 has been secondarily altered to conform to the more usual way of numbering the tribes.

27. For the ten tribes in medieval Christian literature, see Andrew Runni Anderson, *Alexander's Gate, Gog and Magog, and the Inclosed Nations* (Monographs of the Mediaeval Academy of America 5; Cambridge, Mass.: Mediaeval Academy of America, 1932), 62-78. The Bible refers to "the ten tribes" only at 1 Kgs 11:31, 35, where, surprisingly, their southern counterpart is only one tribe (Judah) (11:32, 36).

28. The textual witnesses are divided here: (1) most of the Latin manuscripts have "ten"; (2) Syriac, Arabic and two Ethiopic manuscripts have "nine and a half"; (3) most Ethiopic manuscripts and a few Latin have "nine." Since (1) is the usual number, (2) is an unusual but attested number, and (3) is explicable as a corruption of (2), (2) is most likely the original reading. A further consideration in favour of this reading is that *2 Baruch* also refers to nine and a half tribes. *4 Ezra* and *2 Baruch* have many affinities.

29. Greek and Latin have "nine and a half," Ethiopic "nine."

30. In *T. Jos.* 19:2, the tribes are divided into nine and three (Judah, Benjamin, Levi); cf, also 1QM 1:2.

31. Bogaert, *Apocalypse de Baruch*, 1:348-52.

32. Cf. Stone, *Fourth Ezra*, 404.

with the northern tribes and will return with them. In order to avoid a total count of thirteen, the northern tribes without Levi's half-tribe have to be reckoned as nine rather than ten, no doubt by treating Ephraim and Manasseh as a single tribe, Joseph.

Thus the tradition of numbering the tribes that Commodian follows is not confused, but a quite logical alternative to the more usual division into ten and two, and arguably it is more satisfactory because it does not discount the tribe of Levi as the more usual division has to do.

From the parallels with other literature it is clear that Commodian's accounts of the nine and a half tribes preserve traditional material from an earlier date and most probably from an apocryphal work that is no longer extant.

Date and Provenance

There has been much debate as to the period in which Commodian lived and wrote, but several recent scholars place him in the middle of the third century C.E.[33] Any attempt to date more precisely the putative source of his account of the nine and a half tribes must obviously be very tentative, since the source itself is not extant. However, we may note that the parallel passages that show most affinity with Commodian's material are *4 Ezra*, the Ethiopic *Acts of Matthew* and the *Signs of the Messiah*. Since the latter two are much later in date than Commodian, only *4 Ezra* may assist with the dating of his source. If our argument that the author of *4 Ezra* deliberately corrects the account of the nine and a half tribes that he knew by depriving them of a military role, whereas Commodian in this respect preserves the older tradition, is convincing, then it is certainly possible that Commodian knew an apocryphal work that was also known to *4 Ezra* and which must therefore date from the first century C.E. at the latest. In favour of such an early date we can also cite Commodian's numbering of the tribes as nine and a half. This unusual number is otherwise found only in *4 Ezra*, *2 Baruch*, the *Ascension of Isaiah* and the Ethiopic *Acts of Matthew*. *2 Baruch*, like *4 Ezra*, dates from around the end of the first century C.E., while the *Ascension of Isaiah* may well date from the late first century and is certainly no later than the middle of the second.[34] While having due regard for the limitations of our evidence, this would also seem to point to a relatively early date for Commodian's source, and certainly coheres with the suggestion that it was known to the author of *4 Ezra*. At least there is a strong case for claiming that the traditions known to Commodian from his source were already current by the end of the first century C.E., whether or not the source itself dates from that period. These considerations also suggest a non-Christian Jewish context of origin at least for these traditions. But the arguments of Schmidt[35] and Salvatore[36] for associating Commodian's source with the Qumran community seem to me tenuous.

There is no reason to suppose that Commodian's source was limited to an account of the nine and a half tribes. The possibility that it was also his source for his account of the king from the east, which he explicitly ascribes to an apocryphal source (*Carm.* 936), de-

33. See especially Salvatore, *Commodiano: Carme Apologetico*, 5-31; Daniélou, *The Origins*, 99-101, 286-87.

34. Richard Bauckham, "The Ascension of Isaiah: Genre, Unity and Date," in Richard Bauckham, *The Fate of the Dead: Studies on the Jewish and Christian Apocalypses* (NovTSup 93; Leiden: Brill, 1998), 363-90, here 381-90.

35. Schmidt, "Une source essénienne," 22-25.

36. Salvatore, *Commodiano: Carme Apologetico*, 217-221.

serves further investigation (which would require a study of the parallels to that material). While it is possible that Commodian's source was one of the apocryphal works whose names we know but which are no longer extant, except in some cases in small fragments, there seems to be no real basis for suggesting any of these in particular.[37]

Bibliography

EDITIONS AND TRANSLATIONS

(My English translations of Commodian are based on the editions listed here, by Martin, Poinsotte and Salvatore.)

Martin, Joseph. *Commodiani Carmina.* CCSL 128. Turnhout: Brepols, 1960. (Critical edition of the text of all works of Commodian)

Poinsotte, Jean-Michel. *Commodien: Instructions.* Collection des Universités de France. Paris: Les Belles Lettres, 2009.

(Critical edition of the text of the *Instructions*, French translation, and commentary)

Roberts, Alexander, and James Donaldson (eds.). *Tertullian, Part Fourth; Minucius Felix; Commodian; Origen, Parts First and Second.* ANF 4. Peabody, Mass.: Hendrickson, 1995 (reprint of 1885 edition). (Pages 203-18: English translation of the *Instructions* by Robert Ernest Wallis.)

Salvatore, Antonio. *Commodiano: Carme Apologetico.* Corona Patrum 5. Turin: Società Editrice Internazionale, 1977.

(Critical edition of the text of the *Poem on the Two Peoples*, Italian translation, and commentary)

STUDIES

Bergen, Theodore A. "The 'People Coming from the East' in 5 Ezra 1:38." *JBL* 108 (1989): 675-83.

Charlesworth, James H. Pages 147-49 in *The Pseudepigrapha and Modern Research with a Supplement.* SBLSCS 7S. Chico, Calif.: Scholars Press, 1981.

Daniélou, Jean. Pages 116-119 in *The Origins of Latin Christianity.* (*A History of Early Christianity before the Council of Nicaea,* vol. 3.) Ed. John Austin Baker. Trans. David Smith and John Austin Baker. London: Darton, Longman & Todd/ Philadelphia, Pa.: Westminster, 1977.

James, Montague Rhodes. Pages 103-106 in *The Lost Apocrypha of the Old Testament.* London: SPCK, 1920.

Schmidt, Francis. "Une source essénienne chez Commodien." Pages 11-25 in *Pseudépigraphes de l'Ancien Testament et Manuscrits de la Mer Morte 1.* Cahiers de la Revue d'Histoire et de Philosophie Religieuses 41. Ed. Marc Philonenko, Jean-Claude Picard, Jean-Marc Rosenstiehl and Francis Schmidt. Paris: Presses Universitaires de France, 1967.

37. James, *Apocrypha Anecdota*, 93 n. 1, ventured: "If a conjecture is to be hazarded, I would suggest that the *Prophecy of Eldad and Modad* may have dealt with this matter.... If this were so, we might be able to see a reason for the assumption of the name Eldad by the famous imposter [Eldad ha-Dani] who in the ninth century pretended to have visited the Ten Tribes in their distant dwelling place." Since James's conjectures had a habit of proving correct, I would not dismiss this one entirely.

The Nine and a Half Tribes

Commodian, *Poem on the Two Peoples* (*Carmen de duobus populis*) or *Apologetic Poem* (*Carmen apologeticum*) 937-90:

However, eventually even the Jews themselves become dissatisfied,
and complain among themselves of having been deceived with a trick.[a]
Together they will cry to heaven, weeping aloud,
for the true God to come to their aid from on high.[b]

Then almighty God, in order to bring to fulfilment all that he has said,
will bring forth a people that has been hidden for a long time.
4 Ezra 13:43 They are the Jews who are confined by a river beyond Persia,
who God decreed should remain there until the end.
4 Ezra 13:40 Captivity constrained them to be in that place;
of the twelve tribes nine and a half dwelled there.
In that place there is neither deceit nor hatred;
Hos 9:12 therefore a son does not die before his parents,
nor do they mourn or lament for the dead as we do,
because they are expecting resurrection in the future.
Among their foodstuffs they eat no animal,
but only vegetables, in order to avoid the shedding of blood.
Full of righteousness, they live with bodies unimpaired,
And in them no unholy procreation[c] exercises influence.
No fevers or severe chills come near them,
4 Ezra 13:42 since they observe with sincerity the whole law.
We ourselves would attain the same if we lived purely.
Only death and labour are there, the other burdens absent.
4 Ezra 13:46-47; Such were the people who are now kept in a place beyond.
Isa 11:15-16 When the river is dried up, they will return to the land of Judaea.
Bar 5:9 With them will God also come, to fulfil his promises;
Bar 5:5 and throughout the journey they exult in the presence of God.

---

a. The Jews have been deceived by the king from the east.

b. These four lines conclude the previous section of Commodian's account, about the two Antichrists (lines 805-940), but they also provide a transition to the following account of the nine and a half tribes. God, it is implied, hears the cry of the Jews and brings the nine and a half tribes to their aid (see lines 979-88).

c. The meaning of *genesis* here is uncertain.

Everything grows green before them, everything rejoices. Isa 35:1-2
Creation itself delights to receive the holy ones.
In every place fountains spring up to make provision, Isa 35:6-7; 41:18
where the people of the Most High proceed with heavenly terror.
Clouds make shade for them, so that they should not be troubled by
the sun, Isa 4:5-6; 49:10
and, lest they should grow tired, the mountains subside, Isa 40:4; 49:11; Bar 5:7
for the angel of the High One is sent ahead of them,
and he provides peaceable guidance for them on their journey.
They proceed on their way easily, without effort, Jer 31:9
and wherever they pass, like lions they lay everything waste. Mic 5:8
No legion will be able to stand against them;
should it wage war, God himself is with them.
They overcome nations and bring down cities; *Sib. Or.* 2:173
with God's permission they plunder every land; Isa 11:14
they acquire a vast booty of gold and silver,
and, thus adorned, they sing hymns together. Jer 31:12
But soon they make haste to reach the holy city of their ancestors,
for the fearsome tyrant[a] becomes afraid,
and flees with great haste to the kings of the north,
and from there brings an army, in order to resist attack.
But when the rebels make haste to encounter God's army
and battle is joined, they are thrown to the ground by the angels. 2 Macc 3:24-28
The Adulterer[b] is captured, along with the false prophet, Rev 19:20
and they are sent alive into a lake to suffer fiery punishments.[c] Rev 19:20
Their leading men, whether prefects or legates,
are reduced to slaves of the holy ones, in return for their wickedness. *Sib. Or.* 2:173-176
Meanwhile the holy ones enter the holy land
in order to receive the promises of God with never-ending joy.

Commodian, *Instructions* (*Instructiones*) 1.42:

About the hidden, holy people of the omnipotent Christ, the living God[d]

There remains the hidden, distant, holy people.
Where they abide is unknown to us.
They consist of nine and a half tribes,

---

a. This is the king from the east described in *Carm.* 892-935, the second Antichrist, who has captured Jerusalem and deceived the Jews with signs.

b. At *Carm.* 179, this term refers to the devil, but must here be the king in the preceding lines.

c. In these two lines Commodian is clearly dependent on Revelation, as he is elsewhere in the eschatological part of the *Poem.*

d. The poem is an acrostic. The letters of the Latin title (*De populo absconso sancto omnipotentis Christi Dei vivi*) are used to begin each line of the poem. The editions divide the poem into eight stanzas, corresponding to the eight words of the title, but since the stanzas do not relate to the sense but only to the acrostic form, I have not retained them in this translation.

leaving aside the two and a half tribes who are here with us.
Christ commanded them of old to live by the law.
So let us all live now according to the teaching of the new law,
as the law itself teaches. I point it out to you more clearly.
Two and a half tribes have been left. Why
the additional half tribe? So that they might be martyrs,
when he would bring war on his elect ones on the earth,
5 Ezra 1:39-40 or rather when the choir of holy prophets
would rise up together over that people and put a check on them,
those whom the abominable horses have slaughtered by kicking.
To obtain peace at any time would not have been in their power.[a]
These tribes[b] have been scattered so that the mysteries of Christ
may all be fulfilled through them up to the end of the age.
Gen 34:13-31; 49:5-7 They[c] were born out of the crime of two brothers,[d]
under whose guidance they have pursued evil-doing.
Were not such blood-thirsty people deservedly scattered?
They assemble again in camp on account of the mysteries.
Then the things written in the law hasten to be fulfilled.
The omnipotent Christ descends to his elect ones,
Jer 31:8; *T. Mos.* 4:9; Josephus, *Ant.* 11.133; Rev 7:4 who for so long have been hidden from us,
and have become so many thousands: this is the true heavenly people.
Hos 9:12 There no son dies before his father; they feel
no pain in their bodies, no tumour grows.
Isa 65:20; *2 Bar.* 73:3 They depart in old age, at rest on their beds,
4 Ezra 13:42 fulfilling all requirements of the law, and so protected.
They are commanded to cross over from those parts to the Lord,
4 Ezra 13:44, 47; Isa 11:15-16 and he dries up the river, as before, so that they may cross.
The Lord himself even goes forth with them.
He has crossed to our lands; they come with the heavenly king.
Isa 41:10; Bar 5:9 How can I describe how God leads them on their journey?
Isa 35:6; 40:4; 41:18; Bar 5:7 | Isa 35:1-2 Mountains will subside before them and fountains spring up.
Creation rejoices to see the holy people.
Isa 52:2; *4 Ezra* 10:7; Gal 4:26 But they hasten to go to the defence of their captive mother.[e]
Dan 11:44 The wicked king who holds her in his power, when he hears of them,

---

a. Lines 9-14 are very obscure: see especially the discussion in Poinsotte, *Commodien*, 317-320. I have largely followed Poinsotte's interpretation, and have accepted his emendations in line 14 (*fuerit* for *ruerit, tenere* for *temere*). He is probably right in thinking that these lines, whatever precisely they mean, are Commodian's attempt to explain why not just two, but two and a half tribes remain, when the nine and a half are scattered. The additional half apparently consists of Jewish Christian martyrs.

b. These must be the nine and a half tribes. Commodian picks up his account of them, following his parenthetical explanation of the two and half tribes in lines 8-14.

c. The nine and a half tribes (*contra* Poinsotte, *Commodien*, 320).

d. Probably Simeon and Levi, the sons of Jacob, condemned, as in Gen 49:5-7, for their treacherous slaughter of the people of Shechem (Gen 34:13-31). Commodian supposes that the northern Israelite tribes continued the kind of violent behaviour for which these two patriarchs set the example.

e. Jerusalem.

flees to the lands of the north and assembles all his people. Ezek 38:15
But when the tyrant comes up against the army of God,
his soldiers are struck down by heavenly terror,
and he himself is seized along with the unspeakable false prophet. Rev 19:20
By the decree of the Lord they are handed over alive to Gehenna. Rev 19:20
His chiefs and his leaders are required to be slaves.
Then the holy ones will enter the ancient bosom of their mother.
So that those whom the evil one has persuaded may also be refreshed,[a]
he will torment them with various punishments so that they may believe in him.[b]
Then comes in the end the time for temptations to be removed from the world.
The Lord will begin to give judgment by fire.

---

a. *refrigerent.* In Christian Latin the terms *refrigerare* and *refrigerium* regularly refer to the future life of the saved.

b. The meaning seems to be that Christ will inflict purgatorial punishments on the Jews who had been deceived by Antichrist, so that they come to believe in Christ and share in the blessings of the new age along with the nine and a half tribes.

The Heartless Rich Man and the Precious Stone

A new translation and introduction

by William Adler

Sources and Contents

The story of the heartless rich man and the precious stone survives in virtually identical form in two Greek chronicles of Byzantium: the *Chronicon* of George the Monk (ninth century), and the *Compendium historiarum* of George Cedrenus (eleventh century).[1] Conscience-stricken after reading Prov 19:17 ("He who is merciful to the poor lends to God"), the man is left destitute after distributing almost everything he owns to the poor. While traveling to Jerusalem to arraign God for having deceived him, he meets up with two men struggling over a stone, which he purchases from them for the two remaining coins in his possession. A goldsmith in Jerusalem later reveals to him that the stone, a gem of great value, had been lost for three years. He instructs the man to return the stone to the high priest, in exchange for which he would become wealthy. In the meantime, an angel of the Lord appears to the Jerusalem high priest and tells him about the discovery of the precious stone, which once belonged to the robe of Aaron. When the stone is restored to the Jerusalem temple, the high priest, in accordance with the angel's instructions, pays the man a handsome sum, and reproves him for lacking faith: the riches that he received far exceeded the amount he had "loaned" to God, and would be even greater in the world to come. With his trust in God restored, the man gives thanks to God and leaves all of his newly-found wealth behind in the temple.

Genre and Provenance

M. R. James rightly characterized this succinct and self-contained story as a "parabolic narrative."[2] The events recounted take place in some indeterminate time in the biblical past. The figures of the story, including the protagonist, are anonymous, identified only by their office or position in society. Details in the narrative serve a single purpose: to demonstrate God's faithfulness to his promises, even when his actions are mysterious and human beings waver in their own faith in him. Because God initially does not repay the "loan" that the rich man makes to him in the form of charity to the poor, he faces a crisis of confidence in God and the truth of his scriptures. As the narrative unfolds, God's faithful dealings with the rich man gradually become clearer. From the very outset, the reader is given hints that God is secretly orchestrating affairs in the man's life. The scroll of Proverbs that he unrolls immediately opens to the life-changing verse. His subsequent

1. *Georgii Monachi chronicon*, ed. C. de Boor (2 vols.; Leipzig: Teubner, 1904), 1.216.24–218.8 (hereafter George Mon.); *Georgius Cedrenus. Compendium historiarum*, ed. I. Bekker (2 vols., Bonn: CSHB, 1838-39), 1.193.3–194.11. The Greek text is reproduced in M.-R. Denis, ed., *Fragmenta pseudepigraphorum quae supersunt Graeca* (PVTG 3; Leiden: Brill, 1970), 232-33 (frg. g).

2. M. R. James, "The Apocryphal Ezekiel," *JTS* 15 (1914): 241.

hardships, and the contempt with which others treat him, are described as a test from God. The seemingly chance encounter with two men fighting over the stone and the conversation with the goldsmith about its value further suggest to the reader that God is guiding events to a satisfactory resolution. When the angel appears to the high priest in Jerusalem, all the pieces finally fall into place. Through the high priest, who, at the bidding of the angel, buys back the stone, God ultimately makes good on the loan with interest. In showing his faithfulness, God also restores the faith of the rich man. One sign of his faith is his decision to return his payment to the temple. His renewed trust in God and holy scripture, and, along with it, a confidence that he will receive even greater riches in the age to come are reward enough for him.

Although neither of the Greek witnesses sheds much light on its date or provenance, James offered the guarded conjecture that the story at one time formed part of the *Apocryphon of Ezekiel,* a fragmentarily preserved Jewish work dating no later than the first century C.E.[3] But the resemblances that James discerned with the parable of the blind man and lame man ascribed by Epiphanius to the *Apocryphon of Ezekiel* are hardly probative. The possibility that the story is rooted in an older Jewish source or tradition cannot be precluded. Para-biblical traditions about biblical figures and events, some of which draw at least indirectly on older Jewish sources, are plentiful in both chronicles. But the story's interpretation of Prov 19:17, its promise of heavenly rewards in exchange for charity to the poor, and its emphasis on renunciation of the things of this world as a demonstration of faith, point to monastic circles in the Christian East.[4]

Literary History and Parallel Versions

The absence of historical and chronological markers in the story suggests that it was integrated into works of universal history only at a later stage in its transmission. This is also implied by the differing ways in which the two Greek witnesses have woven the story into their respective narratives. In Cedrenus' chronicle, it occurs during the reign of king Hezekiah and follows a summary of the book of Tobit (191.15–193.2). James' inference from this that the story came to Cedrenus with "some sort of Biblical sanction" is not entirely warranted.[5] The older version found in George the Monk sets the story during the reign of king Joash, without drawing any connection with Tobit. Since Cedrenus' treatment of biblical history elsewhere depends upon George the Monk for source material, the col-

3. James, "Apocryphal Ezekiel," 241-42; idem, *The Lost Apocrypha of the Old Testament, Their Titles and Fragments* (London: SPCK; New York: Macmillan, 1920), 85-86; cf. A.-M Denis, *Introduction aux pseudepigraphes grecs d'Ancien Testament* (SVTP 1; Leiden: Brill, 1970), 188. See also Benjamin G. Wright III, "Apocryphon of Ezekiel," in this volume.

4. For additional evidence of its date and provenance, see the Syriac witness to the story described below. For a similar understanding of Prov 19:17, see also the legend of the conversion of Evagrius by Synesius, the early-fifth-century bishop of Cyrene. First attested in the *Pratum spirituale* of the sixth-century Syrian monk John Moschus (195 [PG 87.3077]), the story also appears in the same two Byzantine chronicles that preserve our story of the rich man and the precious stone (George Mon. 676.12–678.15; Ced. 1.673.1–674.11). Initially, Evagrius, a rich pagan philosopher, rebuffed Synesius' efforts to convert him; among other things, he scoffed at the belief that those who give to the poor lend to God, who will then reward them a hundredfold in heaven (cf. Mark 10:29-30). He finally did convert, however, and gave a large sum of money to the poor. He also asked Synesius for a voucher, to ensure that Christ would honor the debt in the next life. When Evagrius died, he was buried with the receipt in his hand. Synesius, acting in response to a vision, subsequently opened his tomb, and found Evagrius clutching the receipt, which contained a codicil written in Evagrius' hand certifying that Christ had repaid his debt in full.

5. M. R. James, "The Apocryphal Ezekiel," *JTS* 15 (1914): 242.

location with Tobit may simply have been a personal editorial decision, and not part of a received tradition. In either case, however, an editor at some stage in their transmission must have recognized a connection between the two stories. In both instances, an angel gives instructions and guidance and explains the inscrutable workings of God in the affairs of the two men. The language of Cedrenus' own account is tailored to draw a sharp contrast between the "rich and merciless man" and his contemporary Tobit, the latter a "merciful man" who risked his life to attend to those who had died during the Assyrian captivity. But despite the vast differences in their character, God cared equally for the welfare of both of them, working behind the scenes to restore the eyesight of the one and the faith of the other.

Of the several parallel versions that circulated in the Christian East, the one with the closest similarities to the Greek version survives in a Syriac collection of sayings attributed to the Egyptian desert fathers of the third and fourth centuries C.E.[6] This witness offers additional clues about the story's origins and literary history. Its inclusion in a compilation made by the seventh-century Syrian monk Enanisho proves that it is substantially older than the two Greek witnesses. The Syriac version, placed in the mouth of one of the monks associated with Abbâ Arêâ, also confirms its monastic provenance and raises the likelihood of an oral stage in its history. In this telling of the story, the rich man, even before he opens to the convicting verse from Proverbs, is already repentant for his avarice and oppression of the poor. And the providential role of God in the rich man's life is far less prominent than in the Greek account: his teacher guides him to the book of Proverbs, and there is no mention of his suffering as a test from God. Two other notable variations from the Greek version appear at the conclusion of the story. When the priest, acting on the angel's instructions, scolds the man for his faithlessness, he further charges him with lending to God in the wrong spirit; his conduct, says the priest, does not comport with that of a "believer and a true man." One noteworthy omission is the man's decision to return the reward to the temple.

A more developed retelling of the story, set in a completely different context, is found in the Ethiopic *Maṣhafa Gadla Ḥawâryât* (*Contendings of the Apostles*).[7] In this version, the protagonist is not an anonymous figure, but rather Kewestôs, a wealthy Roman prefect and the father of Clement of Rome. The inspiration behind Kewestôs' decision to distribute his wealth to the poor is not a verse from Proverbs, but rather a teaching of the apostle Peter. Kewestôs happens to be on hand when Peter is teaching in Rome and hears him bless those "who give to the poor, for unto them shall God give in return." Kewestôs subsequently comes to regret his decision to follow this teaching. When the Emperor summons him for counsel, he realizes that he lacks the means to offer him a gift. His wife 'Akrôsyâ rejects his plan to hide himself from view and have her pretend to the Emperor's agents that he has gone mad; and his brother angrily refuses his appeals for aid. With two coins that 'Akrôsyâ managed to find in the house, he journeys to Jerusalem to petition God for aid. On the journey, he settles an argument between two men by purchasing a stone that was the source of their contention. After a goldsmith in Jerusalem informs him about the source and value of the stone, he takes it to Dêmâs, the Jerusalem priest, who tells him

---

6. E. A. W. Budge, trans., *The Paradise or Garden of the Holy Fathers* (2 vols.; London: Chatto and Windus, 1907), 2.241-42 (#423).

7. Ethiopic text and English translation in E.A.W. Budge, ed., *Contendings of the Apostles* (2 vols.; London: OUP, 1901; rpr. Amsterdam, 1976). English translation of the episode of the precious stone in 2:11-14.

that the stone had been missing from the time of the Babylonian captivity. Now that the lost stone, which completed the number of the 12 tribes of Israel, is restored, Dêmâs is able once again to offer incense to God. With money raised from the populace, the priest rewards Kewestôs with double the amount he had previously distributed to the poor.

The Ethiopic version probably represents a later stage in the story's literary history. The setting is clearly Christian, and there are more characters, some of whom are identified by name. Side-stories about Kewestôs' relationship with his wife, his brother, and the emperor make the plot more diffuse. The crisis created by Kewestôs' distribution of his fortune is now woven into a more elaborate narrative about his decision to conduct his life according to all of Peter's teachings. Peter's blessing on those who give to the poor is only one of several blessings that Kewestôs hears from him in Rome. Included among Peter's other beatitudes are blessings on peace-makers and those who renounce sexual relations with their wives. As the story unfolds, we see Kewestôs acting on all three beatitudes. Before disbursing his wealth, he forswears, with his wife's consent, sexual relations with her. And his purchase of the precious stone from the two men is more than a reward for his donations to the poor. By settling a conflict between them, he realizes Peter's blessing on the peace-makers, that they "shall be called and become the children of God."

The underlying themes of the Ethiopic version are also different. In the Greek version, a personal crisis facing a callous man of wealth leads to both a renewal of his faith and a change in his attitudes towards worldly prosperity. These elements are far less prominent in the Ethiopic story. Kewestôs does not experience the inner turmoil and loss of faith in God recounted in the Greek version. His crisis is more practical: he fears what will happen to him when he is unable to offer a gift to the Emperor. Nor do we hear much about his moral reformation. The story does not describe Kewestôs' unfeeling disregard for the poor before hearing Peter's teachings. And it does not conclude with his decision to return to the temple the money given to him by the high priest. Richer than he was before, Kewestôs is now able to visit with the Emperor without fear.

The story is thus oriented more to the blessings of prosperity that Kewestôs receives from God than to the restoration of his faith and moral character through self-renunciation and almsgiving. The same observation also applies to another retelling, found in Gaselee's *Stories from the Christian East.*[8] In this story, set in the Syrian city of Nisibis, a pagan man and his Christian wife decide to "invest" their savings with the God of the Christians, in the hope of getting a good return on their money. They do so by giving their money to beggars sitting outside the great church of the city. After three months, they are reduced to utter poverty. On the advice of his wife, the man returns to the church and is discouraged to find there no one but beggars. As he is about to return home, he spots lying on the ground one of the coins that he had given to the beggars. With this money, he purchases wine and food, including a fish. In the course of preparing the fish, his wife finds inside a dazzling stone. Unaware of its great value, she gives it to her husband and asks him to find a buyer. When the man offers it to a jeweler and money-changer, he senses from his interested reaction that the stone may be worth something. After prolonged haggling, he finally bids the price up to six times the value of the couple's original holdings. Now con-

8. Stephen Gaselee, *Stories from the Christian East* (London: Sidgwick, 1918), 41-46. Regrettably, Gaselee provides no information about the story's origin, except to say that he translated it into English from the Latin.

vinced of the reality of the God of the Christians, he agrees to be baptized. Both he and his wife live to a good age.

Bibliography

Bekker, I., ed. *Georgius Cedrenus. Compendium historiarum.* 2 vols. Bonn: CSHB, 1838-9.
de Boor, C., ed. *Georgii Monachi chronicon.* 2 vols. Leipzig: Teubner, 1904.
Budge, E. A. W., ed. and trans. *Contendings of the Apostles.* 2 vols. London: Oxford, 1901; reprint Amsterdam, 1976.
__________, trans. *The Paradise or Garden of the Holy Fathers.* 2 vols. London: Chatto and Windus, 1907.
Denis, A.-M., ed. *Fragmenta pseudepigraphorum quae supersunt Graeca* (PVTG 3). Leiden: Brill, 1970.
__________. *Introduction aux pseudepigraphes grecs d'Ancien Testament* (SVTP 1). Leiden: Brill, 1970.
Gaselee, S. *Stories from the Christian East,* 41-46. London: Sidgwick, 1918.
James, M. R. "The Apocryphal Ezekiel." *JTS* 15 (1914): 236-243.
__________. *The Lost Apocrypha of the Old Testament, Their Titles and Fragments.* London: SPCK; New York: Macmillan, 1920.

The Heartless Rich Man and the Precious Stone

1 [1]There was a man in Israel who was both rich and without mercy.[a] [2]He went to
one of his teachers and after unrolling a scroll of the *Wisdom of Solomon*, immediately found the words: "He who is merciful to the poor lends to God."[b] [3]Keep- Prov 19:17
ing to himself and moved to contrition, he left, sold everything and distributed
his money to the poor, leaving nothing for himself except for two coins. [4]He
became extremely poor. And because he was being tested by God, he received
mercy from no one. [5]Faint of heart, he then said to himself, "I will go out to Jerusalem and bring my case before my God, because he misled me into dispersing
my possessions."

2 [1]As he was on his way, he saw two men fighting with each other over a
precious stone that they had found. [2]He said to them, "Why are you fighting,
brethren? Give it to me and accept two coins in return." [3]They happily handed
it over to him (for they were unaware of the stone's high value), and he departed
for Jerusalem, taking the stone with him. [4]As soon as he showed the stone to a
goldsmith, the goldsmith got up and made obeisance to God. [5]Taken aback, he
asked him, "Where did you find this most precious and holy stone? [6]Look, for
three years to this day, Jerusalem has been in disarray and confusion over this
renowned stone. [7]Now be off and give it to the high priest, and you will become
exceedingly wealthy."

3 [1]As he was leaving, an angel of the Lord said to the high priest, "A man will
presently come to you having in his possession the celebrated lost stone from
the robe of Aaron the high priest. [2]Take it from him and in exchange give gold Exod 28:21
and silver in abundance to the man who has brought it to you. [3]And give him
a mild slap and tell him, 'Do not waver in your heart or lose faith in God over
the words of Scripture, "he who is merciful to the poor lends to God." [4]For look,
in the present age I have enriched you many times more than the amount you
loaned to me. [5]And if you believe, you will also receive unsurpassed riches in
the age to come.'"

---

a. George Cedrenus: "At this time (the time of Tobit and the reign of Hezekiah), a man was becoming known in Israel, who was both rich and without mercy." In the version of George Mon., the story is set during the reign of Joash, king of Judah. See the Introduction.

b. Referring here to Proverbs, and not to the deuterocanonical/apocryphal Greek work also known as the *Wisdom of Solomon*. Greek Christian authors sometimes refer to Proverbs as "Wisdom" or the "Wisdom of Solomon (*Sophia Solomōntos*)," instead of the more traditional "Proverbs of Solomon (*Paroimiai Solomōntos*)"; see Justin Mart. *Dial.* 129.3; Eus. *Hist. Eccl.* 4.22.9; Gregory of Nyssa, *Life of Moses* 2.303.

4 [1]The high priest did all the things that he was instructed to tell the man.
[2]When the man heard these words, he started to tremble, and left everything
in the temple. [3]And he went away giving thanks and trusting in the Lord and
everything that was declared in Holy Scripture.

Jeremiah's Prophecy to Pashhur

A new translation and introduction

by Darrell D. Hannah

This pseudepigraphon, consisting in its present form of a single paragraph, contains the prophecy quoted in Matt 27:9-10 concerning the thirty pieces of silver which were given to Judas Iscariot for his betrayal of Jesus and subsequently used, by the Jewish chief priests, to purchase the field of the potter:

> Then was fulfilled what had been spoken through the prophet Jeremiah, "And they took the thirty pieces of silver, the price of the one on whom a price had been set, on whom some of the sons of Israel had set a price, and they[1] gave them for the potter's field, as the Lord commanded me."[2]

The words "cited" by Matthew appear nowhere in the canonical Book of Jeremiah. The most probable explanation for the quotation is that Matthew here combined words, phrases and themes from Jeremiah (18:1-12; 19:1-2, 6, 11; 32:6-15) and Zechariah (11:13), but attributed the whole to the more famous of the two prophets. Such conflated prophetic citations are encountered elsewhere in early Christianity (e.g., Matt 21:5; Mark 1:2; Rom 9:27; *1 Clem.* 34:6).[3] The *Prophecy to Pashhur* offers a "solution" to the difficulty of Matthew's "misquotation" of Jeremiah by placing on the prophet's lips this same combination of canonical Jeremiah and Zechariah in a rebuke addressed to a certain Pashhur, a priest, temple official and false prophet mentioned in Jeremiah 20:1-6.[4]

Jeremiah's Prophecy to Pashhur is today found only in medieval and early modern manuscripts which stem from Coptic, Ethiopian and Arabic Christianity. It is still read in the Coptic and Ethiopian Churches as an authentic prophecy of Jeremiah. Nonetheless, there is good reason to conclude it was not composed in any of these Eastern branches of Christianity, but in all probability is a product of early Jewish Christianity and reaches back to a time before the emergence of Coptic, Ethiopian or Arabic Christian traditions. It is not to be confused with the *Legend of Jeremiah* which also appears in some Ethiopian

1. Some MSS read, "I gave them."

2. Adapting the NRSV.

3. Cf. W. D. Davies and Dale C. Allison, *The Gospel according to Saint Matthew* (ICC; Edinburgh: T.&T. Clark, 1997), 3:568-69, and Raymond E. Brown, *The Death of the Messiah: From Gethsemane to the Grave: A Commentary on the Passion Narratives in the Four Gospels* (London: Geoffrey Chapman, 1994), 1:647-52.

4. The Pashhur of Jer 20:1-6 is "the son of Immer." At 21:1 and 38:1 MT another Pashhur, the "son of Malchiah" is also mentioned. In addition, 38:1 also speaks of a "Gedaliah son of Pashhur." There is, however, no reason to think that either of these two Pashhurs should be identified with the "Pashhur son of Immer" of 20:1-6 or that any ancient exegete ever made such an identification.

biblical manuscripts and in fact is the Jeremiah chapter from the *Lives of the Prophets* (see *OTP*, 2:379-99).

Manuscripts and Versions

To this day *Jeremiah's Prophecy to Pashhur* serves as one of the readings in Coptic lectionaries for Good Friday.[5] Three manuscripts have been consulted for the translation here presented, although many more are probably in existence. Two of the manuscripts are in Sahidic and the third is in Bohairic. Each of the Sahidic manuscripts has been published at least once. The Bohairic manuscript, however, has to my knowledge never been published, although Henry Tattam published the text of a similar manuscript over a century ago.

> Sa^{O}: Oxford, Bodleian Coptic XX (= Huntington 5). A fragmentary codex written on paper of which only 37 folia survive. A Lectionary for Holy Week, with readings from both Testaments. *Jeremiah's Prophecy to Pashhur* is found on fol. 17v-17r, that is, the 273rd and 274th pages of the once complete codex. Given the fragmentary nature of the MS, it is impossible to be certain for which day and office our text was appointed to be read. The manuscript has been dated to the twelfth (so Horner) or twelfth-thirteenth (Feder) centuries.[6] The text of the *Prophecy to Pashhur* from this manuscript was published by Adolf Erman.[7]

> Sa^{R}: Rome, Borgian. 109, N. xcix. A reasonably complete Sahidic-Arabic lectionary for Holy Week, with readings from both Testaments in Coptic and, in the margins, prayers, liturgies, Trisagioi and hymns in Arabic. The *Prophecy to Pashhur* occurs at fol. 134v-135r, i.e., pages 212-13, and is the fourth reading for the first daylight Office for Good Friday. (The days of Holy Week are divided into five night offices and five day offices.) This paper manuscript has been variously dated to the twelfth-thirteenth (Hynernat), the thirteenth (Horner) or the thirteenth-fourteenth (Balestri) centuries.[8] Our text from this manuscript has been published twice, in 1810 by George Zoega and then in 1889 by P. Agostino Ciasca.[9]

> Bo: London, British Library, Add. 5997 (= Crum 1247).[10] A Bohairic and Arabic manuscript, from Nitria, written in 1274 C.E. and described by Crum as "a Lectionary for Palm Sunday, Holy Week and Easter." The manuscript is written on paper and the *Prophecy to Pashhur* is found on fol. 213a-213b, which corresponds to pages 431 and

---

5. Similarly, the noncanonical 2 Esdras (*5 Ezra*) 2:42-48 is still a possible reading for All Saints' Day in the lectionary of the Church of England.

6. See Frank Feder, *Biblia Sahidica: Ieremias, Lamentationes (Threni), Epistula Ieremiae et Baruch* (TU 147; Berlin: De Gruyter, 2002), 41-42.

7. Adolf Erman, *Bruchstücke der oberaegyptischen Übersetzung des alten Testamentes* (Göttingen: Dieterich'sche Verlags, 1880), 34.

8. See Karlheinz Schüssler, *Biblia Coptica: Die koptischen Bibeltexte*, Vol. 1.4 (Wiesbaden: Harrassowitz, 2000), 49-69, and Feder, *Biblia Sahidica: Ieremias*, 42-43.

9. George Zoega, *Catalogus codicum copticorum manuscriptorum qui in Museo Borgiano* (Rome: Sacra Congregatio de Propaganda Fide, 1810), 216, and P. Agostino Ciasca, *Sacrorum Bibliorum fragmenta copto-sahidica Musei Borgiani* (Rome: Sacra Congregatio de Propaganda Fide, 1889), 2:260.

10. W. E. Crum, *Catalogue of the Coptic Manuscripts in the British Library* (London: Gilbert and Rivington, 1905), 513-14.

432 of the original manuscript. Here also it is the fourth reading for the first daylight office of Good Friday. The Bohairic text of the *Prophecy to Pashhur* was published by Henry Tattam from another manuscript and included in the preface to his critical edition of the Bohairic text of the Major Prophets.[11] Tattam's manuscript is very closely related to, but not identical with BL Add. 5997. Where they differ, I designate Tattam's text as Bo^T and the British Library manuscript as Bo^L.

Jeremiah's Prophecy to Pashhur is also found in numerous Ethiopic manuscripts. Indeed, most but not all Ethiopic manuscripts that contain the Septuagint corpus of Jeremian texts—Baruch, Lamentations, and the Epistle of Jeremiah— add to them the *Prophecy to Pashhur* and the *Paralipomena Jeremiae* or *4 Baruch*. Because the *Prophecy to Pashhur* was often copied in biblical manuscripts of the Old Testament prophets, literally dozens of manuscripts are known which include it. I list only a few of the most important and a number of others which I was able to consult in the British Library.[12]

Ambāssal, Ethiopia, Private Library, fol. 117b; fifteenth-sixteenth cent. (= EMML 2080)[13]
London, British Library Or. 496, fol. 121b; seventeenth cent. (= Wright's 20; Heider's M)
London, British Library Add. 24991, fol. 35a; seventeenth cent. (= Wright's 14; Heider's K)
Paris, Abbadie 35, fol. 176r; seventeenth cent. (= Heider's A)
Paris, BN Eth. 9 (Zotenberg 6), fol. 63a; seventeenth cent. (= Heider's P)
Berlin, Or. Quart. 986, fol. 112; seventeenth to eighteenth cent. (= Hammerschmidt & Six's 106)
London, British Library Or. 484, fol. 118b; eighteenth cent. (= Wright's 7; Heider's G)
London, British Library Or. 486, fol. 158b; eighteenth cent. (= Wright's 8; Heider's H)
London, British Library Or. 489, fol. 57b; 1730 C.E. (= Wright's 11; Heider's I)
London, British Library Or. 492, fol. 117b; eighteenth cent. (= Wright's 16; Heider's L)
London, British Library Or. 502, fol. 59a; eighteenth cent. (= Wright's 26; Heider's N)

All of these manuscripts witness to a text of *Jeremiah's Prophecy to Pashhur* which is reasonably near to that found in Sa^O and Bo (and Ar, see below). Another Ethiopic form

---

11. Henry Tattam, *Prophetae majores in dialecto linguae aegyptiacae memphiticae seu copticae* (Oxford: Clarendon, 1852), 1:v-vi.

In his preface, Tattam asserted that *Jeremiah's Prophecy to Pashhur* is to be found "in many manuscript copies of the Coptic Church prayer books," but he only mentions two specific manuscripts: one in his own possession "for the seven days of holy Pascha," which he transcribed, and a "Manuscript of the British Museum, numbered 5997." The designation "numbered 5997" is not particularly helpful, but I have been able to identify it with BL Add. 5997 (= Crum 1247). I have not been able to trace the second MS mentioned by Tattam, the one which belonged to him and which he transcribed.

12. For descriptions of the following manuscripts, see William Wright, *Catalogue of the Ethiopic Manuscripts in the British Museum Acquired since the Year 1847* (London: Gilbert & Rivington, 1877), 8-16; August Heider, *Die aethiopische Bibelübersetzung* (Halle: Zahn & Baendel, 1902), 21-23; Getatchew Haile and William F. Macomber, *A Catalogue of Ethiopian Manuscripts Microfilmed for the Hill Monastic Manuscript Library* (Collegeville: St. John's Abbey and University, 1982), 6:147-49; and Ernst Hammerschmidt and Veronika Six, *Äthiopische Handschriften Preussicher Kulturbesitz* (Wiesbaden: Franz Steiner, 1983), 200-204.

13. Photographs of this manuscript were supplied by Hill Museum & Manuscript Library, Saint John's Abbey and University, Collegeville, Minnesota.

of the *Prophecy to Pashhur*, however, is known. This other version is decidedly longer, about twice the length, and is to be found in a single manuscript: Frankfurt Or. Rüpp. II, 5; seventeenth century (= Heider's F). This long recension (Eth^{LR}) differs from the short recension (Eth^{SR}) of the majority of manuscripts in another respect as well. Unlike the majority text, it does not appear as a discrete work in a corpus of Jeremian writings, but as an interpolation between the third and fourth verses of the second chapter of canonical Jeremiah. This long recension shows itself, in a number of respects, to be a secondary expansion of the short recension. The long recension was edited by August Heider,[14] while an edition of the short recension was prepared by August Dillmann.[15]

An Arabic translation of *Jeremiah's Prophecy to Pashhur* is also in existence. The Arabic translation of the Old Testament prophets made in the ninth century by a certain Pethion ibn Ayyub al-Sahhar includes our text immediately following Jer 20:3. Alberto Vaccari, S.J., prepared a critical edition of this Arabic version as part of his larger study of the Arabic versions of the Old Testament prophets.[16] Vaccari concluded that the Syriac Peshitta serves as examplar for Pethion's translation of the Prophets and that it was none other than Pethion himself who translated our pseudepigraphon into Arabic and interpolated it into his translation of Jeremiah. However, as Pethion occasionally drew on Greek texts, as well as the insight of commentators, we cannot be certain from where he obtained our brief pseudepigraphon or from what language he translated it. The four manuscripts which Vaccari used are the following:

A: Milan, Ambrosiana C 58; 1226 C.E.
C: Rome, Casanatense 169; seventeenth cent.
L: London, British Library Or. 5918; 1618-19 C.E.
V: Rome, Vatican Library Arab. 503; 1361 C.E.[17]

As the notes to the translation make clear, Sa^{O}, Bo, Ar and, to a lesser degree, Eth^{SR} often agree and are probably to be regarded as the most reliable witnesses to the original text of *Jeremiah's Prophecy to Pashhur*. Both Eth^{LR} and Sa^{R} have clearly been revised, the former by considerable expansion, the latter by the addition of an ending which harmonizes the text with Jer 20:6. Nonetheless, all our witnesses are late and there are occasions when either Sa^{R} or Eth^{LR} will agree with one or more of the other witnesses in support of the best reading. The translation, therefore, represents an eclectic text which draws on the best from each of our six text-types.

If Vaccari is correct, the *Prophecy to Pashhur* first entered into an Arabic translation of the Bible in the latter half of the ninth century, when Pethion's translation was produced. It is significant, however, that our text does not seem to have had a wider currency in Arabic bib-

14. Heider, *Aethiopische Bibelübersetzung*, 46-48.

15. August Dillmann, *Chrestomathia Aethiopica* (Leipzig: Weigel, 1866), viii-ix, and republished in August Dillmann and Johannes Bachmann, *Anthologia Aethiopica* (Hildesheim: Georg Olms, 1988), viii-ix, n. 2.

16. A. Vaccari, "Le versioni arabe dei Profeti," *Bib* 3 (1922): 401-23. See also Vaccari's previous installments under the same title and in the same journal: 1 (1920): 266-68, and 2 (1921): 401-23. I am grateful to Wieland Willker who called my attention to these articles and to the Arabic version, of which I was unaware.

17. Arabic is not a language I read. Vaccari, however, provides a literal Italian translation (421). James R. Davila also made a literal English translation for me; I here record my thanks and indebtedness to Prof. Davila.

lical translations. Just when the *Prophecy to Pashhur* entered the Coptic lectionary tradition and the Ethiopic biblical manuscript tradition is uncertain. It must have entered the former before the twelfth or thirteenth centuries and the latter before the fifteenth or sixteenth, the date of our earliest manuscripts of each, respectively. Moreover, the *Prophecy* must have been translated into Coptic considerably earlier than the twelfth or thirteenth century for it to have established a place in the liturgy on as important a day as Good Friday. Concerning Ethiopic, it is probably significant that some of our earliest Ethiopic manuscripts of the Jeremian corpus (e.g., Berlin Peterm. Nach. 42, fourteenth-fifteenth cent. [= Heider B]; Ambāssal, Ḥayq Esṭifānos, late fifteenth cent. [= EMML 1768]; Paris, Abbadie 55, fifteenth-sixteenth; Cambridge, UL Add. 1570, 1588 C.E. [= Heider C]) do not include the *Prophecy to Pashhur*, even though many of them do have the *Paralipomena Jeremiae* or *4 Baruch*. This suggests that *Jeremiah's Prophecy to Pashhur* entered the Ethiopic tradition rather late,[18] perhaps not before the Ethiopian cultural renaissance of the thirteenth century. If this is correct, then the Ethiopic text is in all probability a translation of an Arabic *Vorlage*. The numerous agreements between Ar and Eth, especially Eth^{SR}, lend support to this conclusion. Given the history of the document detailed below, a Greek version almost certainly once stood behind the Coptic and Arabic versions. However, it is an open question whether either was translated directly from the Greek or the Coptic depends on the Arabic, as Vaccari supposed,[19] or vice versa. In other words, I do not think we can decide, given our current knowledge, on the priority of the Coptic or Arabic version, but both in all probability descend, directly or via the other, from a now lost Greek version.

The textual witnesses for the *Prophecy to Pashhur* can be set out as follows:

Sa^{O}: Sahidic Coptic; Oxford, Bodleian Library, Cod. XX (Huntington 5); twelfth-thirteenth cents.
Sa^{R}: Sahidic Coptic; Rome Borgian. 109, N. xcix; twelfth-fourteenth cents.
Sa: The agreement of the two Sahidic witnesses.
Bo^{L}: Bohairic Coptic; London, British Library, Add. 5997; 1274 C.E.
Bo^{T}: Tattam's manuscript.
Bo: The agreement of the two Bohairic witnesses.
Copt: The agreement of the three Coptic versions.
Eth^{SR}: Short recension of Ethiopic.
Eth^{LR}: Long recension of Ethiopic.
Eth: The agreement of the two Ethiopic versions.
Ar^{A}: Arabic; Milan, Ambrosiana C 58; 1226 C.E.
Ar^{C}: Arabic; Rome, Casanatense 169; seventeenth cent.
Ar^{L}: Arabic; London, British Library Or. 5918; 1618-19 C.E.
Ar^{V}: Rome, Vatican Library Arab. 503; 1361 C.E.
Ar: The Arabic version.

18. A gloss in the margin of EMML 2080 opposite the end of Lamentations and the beginning of the *Prophecy to Pashhur* reads: "Here is the end of the Hebrew Book [of Jeremiah]." A similar gloss in British Library Or. 489 opposite the end of the Epistle of Jeremiah and the beginning of the *Prophecy to Pashhur* reads: "Here is completed the Bo[ok] of Jer[emiah] which was written in Hebrew." In other words, these two scribes recognized that the *Prophecy to Pashhur* and the *Paralipomena Jeremiae*, which follow, did not belong to the original Hebrew of the Book of Jeremiah, although they thought that Baruch and Lamentations (so EMML 2080) or Baruch, Lamentations and the Epistle of Jeremiah (so BL Or. 489) did.

19. Vaccari, "Versioni arabe," 420-21.

Matt 27:9-10 in the Early Church and Early Attestation of Prophecy to Pashhur

The fact that the quotation of "Jeremiah" cited at Matthew 27:9-10 does not appear on the pages of canonical Jeremiah exercised some of the Church's earliest exegetes. Some scribes, for example, solved the difficulty by simply omitting the name "Jeremiah."[20] Others substituted the name "Zechariah,"[21] and at least one added "Zechariah" to "Jeremiah."[22]

Origen, in his commentary on Matthew, admitted that the passage was not to be found either in the version of Jeremiah read in the Church, i.e., the Septuagint, nor in that read by the Jews, i.e., the Hebrew original. Origen supposed that "Jeremiah" might be a copyist's error for "Zechariah" or that the passage was to be found in an apocryphal writing under the name of Jeremiah. In defense of this latter suggestion, Origen reminds his readers that Paul quoted an apocryphal Elijah at 1 Cor 2:9, as well as the *Book of Jannes and Jambres* at 2 Tim 3:8 (*Comm. Matt. ser.* 117). Origen clearly knows an apocryphal Elijah which contained the saying Paul quotes in 1 Cor 2:9 and an apocryphon about the two Egyptian magicians, Jannes and Jambres, to which allusion is made in the Second Epistle to Timothy, but it is not at all clear that he actually knows of an apocryphal Jeremiah. Origen's words can be understood one of two ways. First, he is indulging in pure speculation: He knows the two apocrypha he mentions and on the basis of such hazards the guess that a Jeremiah apocryphon was also in existence. Second, Origen is vaguely aware of or half-remembers such an apocryphon attributed to Jeremiah, which he had heard about or, perhaps, read long before. The first option takes us nowhere for Origen's pure speculations are no better than ours. The second possibility, *if* it is correct, offers evidence for the existence of such an apocryphon in the middle of the third century.

The witness of Jerome suggests that the latter option may in fact be correct. In his commentary on the Gospel of Matthew, when he arrives at Matthew's quotation of "Jeremiah," Jerome informs us that "I recently have read in a certain Hebrew book, an apocryphon of Jeremiah, which a Hebrew of the Nazoraean sect showed me, in which I found this, word for word" (*Comm. in Matt.* on 27:9-10). Jerome claims to have read, in Hebrew, a work attributed to Jeremiah, but not identical with canonical Jeremiah, and which contained the prophecy that Matthew cites. While Jerome is not the most trustworthy authority, in this case his testimony should probably be credited, for he harboured a strong suspicion of Jewish apocrypha and, unlike Origen, would not have regarded an appeal to such an apocryphon an adequate solution to a problem text.[23] Since Jerome's commentary on Matthew was dashed off in a few weeks in March of 398,[24] we may conclude that this Hebrew Jeremiah apocryphon was current among the Jewish-Christian sect of Nazoraeans around the end of the fourth century.[25] If this is the same work as the Jeremian work

---

20. Including the scribes of Greek (Φ 33), Latin (it^{a,b}) and Syriac (Syr^{s,p}) witnesses.

21. So a late Greek manuscript (22) and a marginal note in one Syriac version (Syr^{h}).

22. So a manuscript in Middle Egyptian Coptic (Copt^{mae}).

23. Jerome had a more positive attitude toward *the* Apocrypha (i.e., the Jewish works included in the Septuagint but not in the Hebrew canon) than toward other apocrypha. Even so his view of all such writings was not positive and seems to have hardened as he grew older. Cf. e.g., *Ep.* 107.12, written in 401 or 402, in which he gives the following advice for the education of a young girl: "Let her avoid all the apocryphal books..." or his exegesis of Ps 10:3: "...the devil lies in wait in the apocrypha" (*Comm. Isa.* 17).

Cf. also James, *The Lost Apocrypha,* 63: "[Jerome] is oftener contemptuous and angry when apocryphal writings come into his ken."

24. Cf. J. N. D. Kelly, *Jerome: His Life, Writings and Controversies* (London: Duckworth, 1975), 222-23.

25. Jerome dealt with the problem of Matt 27:9-10 on one other occasion, in a letter to Pammachius (*Ep.* 57.7) which was written in 395. Since on that occasion Jerome does not mention the Nazoraean Jeremian

which Origen half-remembered—if that is the correct interpretation of his words—then Origen's discussion would replace Jerome as our earliest attestation of the work. All this, of course, carries real significance for dating *Jeremiah's Prophecy to Pashhur* (see below). A note of caution must, however, be sounded. It is possible that *Jeremiah's Prophecy to Pashhur* is entirely unrelated to Jerome's Hebrew Jeremiah apocryphon, to say nothing of Origen's speculation. For, as we have seen, the problems raised by the "Jeremiah" quotation in Matt 27:9-10 were widely felt in early Christianity and they could well have inspired more than one such Jeremiah apocryphon. While this cannot be entirely ruled out of consideration, it nonetheless seems more probable than not that there is some connection between Jerome's text and the apocryphon here translated. The match is simply too close to be ignored.

Original Form of Jeremiah's Prophecy to Pashhur

Jerome speaks of a passage which he had read "in a certain Hebrew book," and the text here translated can easily be read as an excerpt from a longer work. Note the "again" at the beginning of Jeremiah's words to Pashhur; this alone implies a larger context. In other words, it seems the Coptic, Arabic and Ethiopic manuscripts transmit a pericope taken from a larger work and one which Jerome had read in Hebrew. Jerome's description, brief as it is, offers a few clues as to the nature of this work. Clearly it was attributed to Jeremiah and, since he describes it as an apocryphon (*apocryphum*), could not have been merely an interpolated version of canonical Jeremiah. Further, since Jerome received it from a member of the Jewish-Christian sect of the Nazoraeans and given the content of the *Prophecy to Pashhur* (e.g., "the one who heals diseases, and forgives sin"), it must have been a Jewish-Christian composition or, perhaps, a Jewish-Christian adaptation of an earlier Jewish work.[26] Moreover, the work shown to Jerome was in Hebrew.

We know of at least one other Jeremian work which circulated among Christians during the early centuries, the *Paraleipomena Jeremiae* or *4 Baruch*, and it is possible that others also reach back into this period (e.g., the Coptic *Apocryphon of Jeremiah*, the Jeremiah portion of the *Lives of the Prophets*). Moreover, a number of Jeremiah apocrypha existed in pre-Christian Judaism: 2 Macc 2:1-8; the Epistle of Jeremiah; and the Qumran Jeremiah texts provisionally entitled *Apocryphon of Jeremiah A* (4Q383), *Apocryphon of Jeremiah B* (4Q384), and *Apocryphon of Jeremiah C* (4Q385a, 387-390). All of this suggests that it would not be greatly surprising if another Jeremian work had been composed by the Nazoraeans. To be sure, it may be that this Nazoraean work was not a composition from whole cloth, but a Jewish-Christian revision of an already existing Jewish work. For example, it is possible that a Jewish-Christian took a Jeremiah apocryphon like one of those preserved at Qumran, and christianized it by adding passages like the excerpt here

---

work, it is possible that when Jerome says in 398 that he had only "recently" become acquainted with this work he means it: He had only been shown the work sometime between 395 and 398.

26. Cf. the similar conclusion of Georg Strecker, *Der Weg der Gerechtigkeit: Untersuchung zur Theologie des Matthäus* (Göttingen: Vandenhoeck & Ruprecht, 1962), 80-81. Although he makes no mention of *Jeremiah's Prophecy to Pashhur*, Strecker argued that Matthew quoted a pre-Christian Jeremiah apocryphon at 27:9-10. He makes a few strong points, but most scholars have not been convinced. Even if Strecker were correct, the clear Christian elements in *Jeremiah's Prophecy to Pashhur* (the persecution of the one who heals disease and forgives sins, the obstinacy and condemnation of the Jews, the allusion to Matt 27:25) make it obvious that it is a Christian work and not a pre-Christian Jewish one.

translated. Something similar may have taken place in the case of the Coptic *Apocryphon of Jeremiah*.[27]

Original Language, Date and Provenance

If Jerome's Jeremiah apocryphon originally included *Jeremiah's Prophecy to Pashhur*, then it follows that the original language of our text was Hebrew, that it was composed sometime in the early Christian centuries and that it was probably written in Palestine or, perhaps, Syria. Each of these statements can be expanded upon. First, regarding original language, Jerome clearly did not read Aramaic or at least did not read it well (as he admits in his prologue to his Latin translation of the Book of Tobit). Thus, when he claimed that this Jeremiah apocryphon was in Hebrew, he meant Hebrew and was not using "Hebrew" for "Aramaic." Further, Jerome at first claimed that the Nazoraeans used a gospel written in Hebrew (*Vir. ill.* 2-3; *Comm. Matt.* 12.13), but later was of the opinion that this gospel was written in "the Chaldean (i.e., Aramaic) and Syriac language but with Hebrew letters" (*Pelag.* 3.2). His latter opinion would seem to be the better informed of the two, and probably reveals that Jerome at first only knew about the gospel indirectly, most probably having read about it in Origen, and only later came into direct contact with it.[28] In any case, on the basis of the Aramaic gospel which Jerome knew, we may conclude that it is entirely plausible that the Nazoraeans preserved writings in Semitic languages, either Hebrew or Aramaic; that they had a Jeremiah apocryphon in Hebrew presents no great difficulty. Secondly, regarding date, Jerome's testimony offers us a firm *terminus ad quem*: The work must have been written sometime before March 398 when Jerome wrote his *Commentary on Matthew*. A *terminus a quo* is provided by the composition of the Gospel of Matthew itself, probably sometime in the 80s-90s. In other words, the Jeremiah apocryphon must have been composed sometime during the three-hundred-year period between ca. 90 and ca. 390. Attempting to arrive at a narrower time period for the apocryphon's composition is fraught with difficulties, but a few suggestions can be made. It would have taken some years for Matthew's gospel to have established itself as a work of some authority and for the problem of the Jeremiah attribution in Matt 27:9-10 to have been noticed. In other words, it is unlikely that Jerome's Jeremiah apocryphon was composed before the first half of the second century. Origen's half-remembered testimony—if it is that and not pure speculation—would take the latest possible date of composition back into the first-half of the third century. These considerations tentatively allow us to narrow the date of the work to the century between ca. 150 and ca. 250. Thirdly, regarding provenance, the use of Hebrew suggests Palestine. Jerome, however, informs us that he encountered Nazoraeans in Beroea in Syria, modern day Aleppo (*Vir. ill.* 3). Origen could support the former possibility, for his Matthean commentary was written during his Caesarean period. I regard Palestine as the more probable possibility, but Syria cannot be ruled out. In any case, there is no reason to place the Jeremiah apocryphon with its prophecy against Pashhur anywhere other than the Eastern end of the Mediterranean world.

---

27. A translation of the Coptic *Apocryphon of Jeremiah* is to be published in volume two of this collection.

28. So A. F. J. Klijn, *Jewish-Christian Gospel Tradition* (VCSup 17; Leiden: Brill, 1992), 16-19.

Other Passages from Apocryphal Jeremiah?

A number of other texts, canonical and noncanonical, were assigned to Jeremiah apocrypha in antiquity.[29] For example, the hymnic fragment cited in Eph 5:14 was attributed to an apocryphal Jeremiah by George Syncellus in his *Chronography*[30] and in the Euthalian Apparatus found in many NT manuscripts (PG 85.721C).[31] However, Hippolytus once attributed this hymn to Isaiah (*Comm. Dan.* 4.55.4) and once to "the prophet" (*Christ and Antichrist* 65), while Epiphanius says that Paul derived it from "Elijah" (*Pan.* 42.12.3). A prophecy of Christ's descent to the realm of the dead is quoted as scripture by both Justin and Irenaeus.[32] Justin asserts that Jewish scribes had removed the words from their copies of the Book of Jeremiah. Irenaeus, who cites this "scripture" five times, twice credits it to Jeremiah (*Haer.* 4.22.1; *Dem.* 78), once to Isaiah (*Haer.* 3.20.4), once to "the prophet" (5.31.1) and once to "other (prophets)" (4.33.12). The *Passion of James Son of Zebedee*, which has come down to us as Book 4 of Pseudo-Abdias' *History of the Struggles of the Apostles*,[33] records in a speech of the apostle James a prophecy of Jeremiah concerning the advent of the Messiah who will open the eyes of the blind, restore hearing to the deaf and raise the dead. It is possible that any or all of these were once found in Jerome's Nazoraean Jeremiah apocryphon, from which the *Prophecy to Pashhur* probably derives. It is more probable, however, that none of them do. The hymnic fragment of Ephesians is accredited to so many different sources that one suspects that they are all nothing more than guesses. The prophetic "scripture" quoted by Justin and Irenaeus is probably best explained as a Christian interpolation in the canonical Book of Jeremiah (or Isaiah). And the witness of Pseudo-Abdias is so late and so uncertain that it would be hazardous to place much weight on it. In the end we simply do not know what the apocryphal Jeremiah contained beyond its probable inclusion of the *Prophecy to Pashhur*.

Literary Context

The author of *Jeremiah's Prophecy to Pashhur* was clearly dependent on at least two canonical writings. The very purpose of the passage is to remove the difficulty which arises from Matthew's attribution of his mixed citation to the prophet Jeremiah. The author of the *Prophecy to Pashhur* clearly wrote this passage to defend Matthew's authority. In addition, the final line of Jeremiah's words to Pashhur about the eternal judgment which will come on "the sons of Israel and their children because they condemned" to death

---

29. For the following, cf. the discussions in Albert-Marie Denis et al., *Introduction à la Littérature religieuse judéo-hellénistique (Pseudépigraphes de l'Ancien Testament)* (Turnhout: Brepols, 2000), 1:713-18; and James, *Lost Apocrypha*, 62-64.

30. See Alden A. Mosshammer, ed., *Georgii Syncelli Ecloga Chronographica* (Leipzig: Teubner, 1984), 27, lines 16-18. Cf. also the English translation of William Adler and Paul Tuffin, *The Chronography of George Synkellos: A Byzantine Chronicle of Universal History from the Creation* (Oxford: Oxford University Press, 2002), 36.

31. Similarly, the Euthalian Apparatus attributes 1 Cor 2:9 to an Elijah apocryphon, Gal 6:15 to an apocryphal Moses text, 1 Cor 15:33 to Menander, Tit 1:12 to an oracle of the Cretan soothsayer Epimenides, Jude 9 to the *Assumption of Moses*, Jude 14-15 to the *Book of Enoch*, and identifies 1 Cor 15:32 as an ancient laconic proverb.

32. "The Lord God, the Holy One of Israel, remembered his dead that slept in (the) earth of (the) grave, and he descended to preach to them his salvation" (*Dial.* 72.4).

33. Ps.-Abdias' *History*, compiled no earlier than the end of the sixth century, brings together legends about the missions and deaths of individual apostles. It purports to be the work of Abdias, one of the Seventy and the first bishop of Babylon, who wrote in Hebrew. The collection is manifestly a late Latin production.

"innocent blood," recalls the statement of the crowd to Pilate, "His blood be upon us and our children" (Matt 27:25). It follows, from both these facts, that the author of the *Prophecy to Pashhur* must have known the Gospel of Matthew with more than a passing familiarity. The author also knew well the Book of the Prophet Jeremiah. For he has chosen to build this passage on the basis of a rather minor character who appears only once in the whole of the longest prophetic book in the Hebrew Scriptures (20:1-6).[34] Why Pashhur was chosen and not, say, one of the troika of 38:1—Shephatiah, Gedaliah and Jucal—is not altogether clear. If we had more of the context from which this excerpt comes, the choice of Pashhur might be obvious. As it is, the context of Jer. 20:1-6, the only mention of Pashhur in the Book of Jeremiah, offers a possible clue. Pashhur is described as a false prophet (20:6) as well as a priest, a potent combination. It is noticeable that "the chief priests" figure as major *dramatis personae* in Matt 27:3-10. Moreover, prophecy—true prophecy—is a major theme of Matthew's gospel and one which figures significantly in Matt 27:3-10. The selection of Pashhur, then, may rest on a penetrating intertextual reading of Jer 20:1-6 and the Gospel of Matthew. It may be possible to go even further. The *Prophecy to Pashhur* quite clearly condemns Pashhur's descendants as those who will "receive thirty (pieces) of silver (as) the price" of the one betrayed. Since Pashhur is not only a priest, but is even described as "chief officer in the house of the LORD" (Jer 20:1), it is possible that the author of the *Prophecy* found in Pashhur an ancestor of the high priest, or at least the high priestly family, of Jesus' day.[35] Those who condemned Jesus were true sons of him who persecuted the prophet Jeremiah. One further possible connection with the Book of Jeremiah could perhaps be suggested. The sons or children of Pashhur, who follow him and whose deeds of lawlessness surpass his, could be construed as the mirror image of the Rechabites of Jeremiah 35: The children of Pashhur are "faithful" to the example of their father, just as the Rechabites were faithful to the commands and example of their father.

There are no obvious connections between the *Prophecy to Pashhur* and any of the apocryphal books other than the very general connection which our text has with Jeremiah apocrypha like the text(s) preserved in 4Q383, 4Q384, 4Q385b and 4Q389a, the *Paraleipomena Jeremiae* or *4 Baruch* and the Coptic *Jeremiah Apocryphon*, all of which are peopled with characters from the canonical Book of Jeremiah. It should be noted, however, that in no Jeremiah apocrypha, other than the text here translated, do we encounter Pashhur. Obviously, if we possessed more of the apocryphon of which the *Prophecy to Pashhur* is but an excerpt, we might well find a number of other parallels and connections to canonical and noncanonical literature.

If *Jeremiah's Prophecy to Pashhur* is indeed an excerpt from the Jeremiah apocryphon in Hebrew which Jerome had read, then it becomes an important piece of evidence for Jewish Christianity in general and the Nazoraeans in particular, a piece of evidence which until now has been largely neglected in scholarship. The Jewish Christianity of the early Christian centuries, including its Nazoraean manifestation, is a movement for which we have little information and for which we must be grateful for every fragment which survives. Further, if the *Prophecy to Pashhur* was composed in the period ca. 150 to ca. 250, which I tentatively suggested above, then it must be regarded as an important witness

---

34. At 21,835 words, Jeremiah is the longest of the three so-called major prophets. Ezekiel follows with 18,730 words and Isaiah with 16,932. So J. R. Lunbom, *Jeremiah 1-20* (AB 21A; Garden City, N.Y.: Doubleday, 1999), 57.

35. I owe this suggestion to Richard Bauckham.

to the early development of the New Testament canon and reflects one of the earliest attempts to wrestle with the difficulty of an authoritative and apostolic writing seemingly containing an obvious error and, in particular, with the problem of Matt 27:9-10. Of course, if it was written a century later, then its importance in this regard is lessened. Finally, the picture, here depicted, of the Jewish rejection of the claims made for Jesus of Nazareth by Christians and the prophecy of a "judgment of eternal destruction" which is to come on the Jews, reminds us of the unfortunate history of Christian anti-Semitism. *Jeremiah's Prophecy to Pashhur* is the kind of text which has been used to justify ghettos, pogroms and gas chambers. It does not take a great deal of imagination to suppose that it may have been appealed to numerous times through the centuries by anti-Semitic Christians just as Matt 27:24-25, 1 Thess 2:14-16, and John 8:44-45 have been.[36]

Bibliography

COPTIC TEXTS

Ciasca, P. Agostino. Vol. 2:260 in *Sacrorum Bibliorum fragmenta copto-sahidica Musei Borgiani.* Rome: Sacra Congregatio de Propaganda Fide, 1889.

Erman, Adolf. Page 34 in *Bruchstücke der oberaegyptischen Übersetzung des alten Testamentes.* Göttingen: Dieterich'sche Verlags, 1880.

Tattam, Henry. Vol. 1:v-vi in *Prophetae majores in dialecto linguae aegyptiacae memphiticae seu copticae.* Oxford: Clarendon, 1852.

Zoega, George. *Catalogus codicum copticorum manuscriptorum qui in Museo Borgiano,* 216. Rome: Sacra Congregatio de Propaganda Fide, 1810.

ARABIC TEXTS

Vaccari, Alberto. "Le versioni arabe dei Profeti." *Bib* 3 (1922): 401-423.

ETHIOPIC TEXTS

Dillmann, August. Pages viii-ix in *Chrestomathia Aethiopica.* Leipzig: Weigel, 1866. Republished in August Dillmann and J. Bachmann, *Anthologia Aethiopica,* viii-ix n. 2. Hildesheim: Georg Olms, 1988.

Heider, August. Pages 46-48 in *Die aethiopische Bibelübersetzung.* Halle: Zahn & Baendel, 1902.

GENERAL

Denis, Albert-Marie et al. Pages 713-18 in *Introduction à la Littérature religieuse judéo-hellénistique.* Vol. 1: *Pseudépigraphes de l'Ancien Testament.* Turnhout: Brepols, 2000.

James, Montague Rhodes. Pages 62-64 in *The Lost Apocrypha of the Old Testament: Their Titles and Fragments.* London: SPCK, 1920.

Strecker, Georg. Pages 80-81 in *Der Weg der Gerechtigkeit: Untersuchung zur Theologie des Matthäus.* Göttingen: Vandenhoeck & Ruprecht, 1962.

36. Nonetheless, one must also remember the likely Nazoraean origin of *Jeremiah's Prophecy to Pashhur.* Its author, in his historical context, was no more anti-Semitic than the author of the *War Scroll,* although both said very hard things about Jews who did not belong to their particular form of Judaism. Historical criticism demands that we must always make careful distinction between the purpose for which a text was originally written and the use to which it has been put in subsequent history.

Jeremiah's Prophecy to Pashhur

Jeremiah said again[a] to Pashhur,[b] "You (plur.) and your ancestors always oppose[c] the truth.[d] And your children, who come after you, they will commit lawlessness which surpasses yours.[e] They will sell[f] the one for whom there is no price. And they will injure[g] the one who heals diseases, and (who) forgives sin.[h] And they are bound to receive thirty (pieces) of silver[i] (as) the price of one whom[j] the

Melito, *On the Passover* 73

a. So Sa^{O} Bo Ar. Sa^{R} Eth omit "again"; the Arabic word could be rendered "also." It is difficult to imagine why a scribe would add this, but not at all difficult to understand why a scribe copying a lectionary might find it superfluous.

b. So Sa Bo^{L} Ar and Eth^{SR} (although with various spellings of "Pashhur"). Bo^{T} reads "Lafachshour" (evidence that the Bohairic is dependent upon Arabic syntax). Eth^{LR} omits the whole phrase, doubtless as part of the process of conforming the passage to the text of Jer 2:3-4.

c. So Sa^{R} Eth^{SR}. Sa^{O} reads "will at that time be opposed to the truth," while Bo Eth^{LR} have "from of old you have opposed the truth" and Ar "(were) resisters of the truth."

d. Both the Coptic and the Ethiopic terms for "truth" also carry the connotation of "justice, righteousness."

e. So Sa^{O} Bo Eth^{Mss} (Ar: "vile error"). Sa^{R} and Eth^{Mss}: "they have committed lawlessness...."

f. So Sa^{O} Bo Eth (Ar: "will set a price on") Sa^{R}. "They have sold...."

g. Sa^{O} Bo have or presuppose the future tense, while Sa^{R} reads the present. The imperfect tense of the Eth and Ar could support either translation.

h. So Copt. and Ar^{ACL}. Ar^{V} reads "forgives sinners and sin." The Ethiopic versions both expand the text. Eth^{SR} merely adds "and will condemn the one" before "who forgives sin." Eth^{LR}, however, replaces this sentence with "And they will deny the one who restores the sick and heals the ill. And they will reject [lit. dismiss] the one who forgives [lit. dismisses] transgression and sin and iniquity. And they disdain the one who will cause the blind to see and the deaf to hear and the mute to speak and the leprous to be clean, the one who will expel unclean spirits from men, the one who will cause the lame and (those with) broken (limbs) to run about, the one who will walk on the sea as one walks on dry land, the one who reproves the wave(s) of the sea and the flood and the winds and they will obey him, and they will deny and reject the one who does all these things among [lit. to] them."

i. Sa^{O} and Sa^{R}, utilizing the emphatic Coptic third future, could be translated as "they are bound to receive..." or "they must inevitably receive...." Eth^{LR} effectively agrees with this: "they will eagerly receive...." Ar and Eth^{SR} have simply "they will receive." Bo appears to have a scribal error here, but apparently agrees with the reading of the Sahidic Mss and Eth^{LR}.

j. So Sa^{O} Bo Ar and Eth^{LR}. Sa^{R} and Eth^{SR} insert after "the price" and before "whom the children of Israel" the phrase "of one who is honored." The latter agrees more closely with the text of Matt 27:9 and so is suspect.

children of Israel will hand over.[a] They gave the price[b] for the field of the potter, just as the Lord commanded.[c] And thus it will be said,[d] 'A judgment[e] of eternal destruction will come down upon them and upon their children, because they condemned innocent blood.'"[f]

Matt 27:9-10

2 Thess 1:9

Jer 7:6; 22:3; Matt 27:4, 25; Melito, *On the Passover* 74

a. So Sa^{O} Bo. Ar Eth read "whom the children of Israel *will sell*," but otherwise agree with Sa^{O} and Bo. Sa^{R} once again goes its own direction: "This is (the price) fixed for him by the children of Israel." Again this is closer to the text of Matt 27:9 and, one suspects, has been revised toward it.

b. So Sa^{R} (Ar) Eth^{SR}. Sa^{O} Bo Eth^{LR} all leave the object implied.

c. So Sa^{O} Bo. Sa^{R} Ar (Eth), probably under the influence of the text of Matthew, add "me." Eth^{LR} replaces "commanded me" with "told me." To the phrase, most MSS of Eth^{SR} add "so I will speak," while some have "so I will say and speak and do."

d. So Sa^{O} Bo (Ar). Eth^{SR}: "Therefore,...." Eth^{LR}: "Therefore, just as he said so he will cause...." Sa^{R}: "Thus, these are the things which the Lord said...."

e. The word the Arabic uses here can mean either "judgment" or "the final judgment."

f. So Sa^{O} Ar Bo (Eth^{SR}). Eth^{LR} is similar but intensifies the text replacing the "judgment of eternal destruction" with "a condemnation of affliction ... which will never end" and "innocent blood" with "innocent blood and righteous blood." Sa^{R} is very different: "Thus, these are the things which the Lord said, 'Behold, I will bring about your death, and (that of) all your children [so Zoega; Ciasca: "your companions"]. They will fall by the sword of their enemies. Your [sing.] eyes will see, and you [sing.] and all Judah I will send to the Kingdom of Babylon and they will be removed (there), they will be slaughtered by the sword.'" The influence of Jer 20:4 on Sa^{R} is obvious.

The Apocryphon of Ezekiel
A new translation and introduction

by Benjamin G. Wright III

The *Apocryphon of Ezekiel* was most likely an ancient Jewish work transmitted in the name of the biblical prophet Ezekiel. Only small portions of the work have survived, most notably five "fragments" that somewhere in their tradition history bear an attribution to the prophet. That such an apocryphon did exist is confirmed through references to it by the Jewish historian Josephus (*Ant.* 10.5.1 [10.79]; first century C.E.), by the church father Epiphanius of Salamis (*Panarion* 64.70.5; fourth century C.E.) and in the *Stichometry of Nicephorus* (eighth–ninth century C.E.), together with part of a manuscript copy (Papyrus Chester Beatty 185; fourth century C.E.). From the evidence that has survived, the major themes of the work seem to have been repentance, judgment, and the hope for resurrection. Several of the fragments have similarities to biblical prophets, notably Isaiah, Jeremiah, and Ezekiel.

Contents

Traditionally, scholars have recognized only five fragments of the apocryphon, but several other apocryphal citations in the Christian church fathers might have come from this work as well. Fragment 1 takes the form of an illustrative story in which a lame man and a blind man steal and eat the fruit in a king's orchard. The lame man rides upon the back of the blind man so that they can procure the fruit. When the king finds out, he judges them together. This story is taken as evidence that God judges body and soul together for their misdeeds. Fragment 2 is a short saying about repentance in which God speaks in the first person to Israel. Fragment 3 is a one-line saying about a heifer that gives birth and does not give birth. Fragment 4, also attributed to Jesus by Justin Martyr, is a single sentence about judgment. Fragment 5 compares God to a shepherd who will return his wandering flock to a good pasture and who will be near to his sheep.

Versions and Manuscripts

Fragment 1[1]

Epiphanius of Salamis attributes the story of the lame and blind men to Ezekiel—in fact he claims to have found it "in his own apocryphon" (*Panarion* 64.70.5). The moral of the story is somewhat confusing in Epiphanius. He begins by claiming that it concerns

1. Since the different fragments have multiple witnesses, almost all of which come from a range of sources, I have not listed here the editions from which the original texts have been taken. For the original languages and editions of those texts translated here, see Michael E. Stone, Benjamin G. Wright, and David Satran, eds., *The Apocryphal Ezekiel* (Atlanta, Ga.: Society of Biblical Literature, 2000), 8-33, 46-49; and James R. Mueller, *The Five Fragments of the Apocryphon of Ezekiel: A Critical Study* (Sheffield: Sheffield Academic Press, 1994), chap. 3.

resurrection, but by the end he concludes that the story shows how God will judge body and soul together, not separately. As Epiphanius tells the story, the lame and blind men become angry when they are the only two in the kingdom not invited to the wedding banquet of the king's son. They thus plot vengefully to enter the king's orchard and steal the fruit. Their plot is revealed when wedding revelers find their tracks in the orchard, tracks that differ from everyone else's because they are the only two civilians in the kingdom. Everyone else is in the military. The situation presumes that soldiers would wear a shoe/ sandal different from that of a civilian.[2] Epiphanius later in the *Panarion* (64.71.6–13) returns to similar themes, and he alludes to the story on at least two occasions, once citing an identical clause from the story and once referring to the "parable" (Gk. *parabolē*).

We also find this story in several rabbinic versions, the most important being *b. Sanh.* 91ab; *Lev. Rab.* 4.5; *Mekhilta of Rabbi Simeon bar Yochai to Exodus* 15.1; *Midrash Tanhuma* on Lev 4:1, reported as an "illustration" (Heb. *māšāl*) of the same idea, that God judges body and soul together.[3] Although the rabbinic versions have slightly variant forms, they all differ from Epiphanius's version in that they lack the wedding banquet motif. In the rabbinic story the king sets the two men as guards over his orchard, because he thinks that they will not be able to eat the beautiful fruit growing there. The two men, however, desire the fruit and concoct a plan to eat it. The rabbinic versions of the blind and lame also lack the soldier/civilian distinction. This motif appears in another rabbinic story found in the *Yelammedenu* midrash and in *Tanhuma*. In this *Tanhuma-Yelammedenu* tradition, a king judges a commoner (Heb. *pagan*) and a soldier (Heb. *polēah*), the same distinction found in Epiphanius's version.[4]

Fragment 2

1 Clement 8:3 (late first century C.E.) offers the earliest citation of this saying, although Clement does not attribute it to Ezekiel. The passage is reminiscent of Ezek 18:30–32 and Isa 1:18. Because this citation differs significantly from these biblical passages and since Clement cites Isa 1:16–18 immediately afterwards, most scholars are convinced that Clement was citing an apocryphal Ezekiel text and not some variant biblical text.

A Coptic version of the saying came to light in the *Exegesis on the Soul* (late second-third century C.E.) discovered among the Nag Hammadi texts (Codex II; fourth century C.E.). In this case, attribution is made to an unnamed prophet. This form of the saying is very close to that in *1 Clement*. We find only two major differences: (1) The first clause, "Repent, O house of Israel," is lacking, and (2) rather than the first-person singular address of the *1 Clement* citation, the initial verb is in the imperative, which frames the entire saying as something that God instructs the prophet to say to the people.

Clement of Alexandria (late second century C.E.) knows four of the five fragments traditionally thought to come from the apocryphon. For this saying, he reports the shortest version, but he alone attributes it to Ezekiel. His citation begins with "If you turn" and runs to the end of the saying as we have it in *1 Clement*. In his tractate *What Rich Man Will Be Saved?* Clement cites a passage that might also reflect this same saying, although

2. See Stone et al., *Apocryphal Ezekiel*, 14-15 n. 28, in which Esther Chazon suggests the story has in mind the nail-studded sandals of Roman soldiers.

3. An abbreviated reference to this story is also found in the *Mekhilta of Rabbi Ishmael to Exodus* 15.1 immediately following a section explicating this biblical verse. See Mueller, *Five Fragments*, 90-91.

4. For this tradition, see M. Bregman, "The Parable of the Lame and the Blind," *JTS* 42 (1991): 125-38.

it is more likely a composite citation depending on Isa 1:16–20, Ezek 33:11, and the Ezekiel apocryphon.[5]

Fragment 3

This fragment is transmitted in two separate forms: a longer version, which mentions a "heifer" that has and has not given birth, and a short version that lacks any reference to the heifer. Tertullian (late second–third century C.E.), Epiphanius of Salamis, and Ps.-Gregory of Nyssa (fifth century C.E.?) all cite the longer version. The shorter version is found in Tertullian, who attributes it to "the Academics," the *Acts of Peter* (the *Vercelli Acts*),[6] and Clement of Alexandria. Clement of Alexandria and Epiphanius cite the fragment as scripture, Clement employing his standard formula, "scripture says" (*phēsin hē graphē*). Tertullian, the earliest witness to the fragment, attributes the long version to Ezekiel and cites both versions in the same passage in which he argues with those who would question that Mary conceived Christ as a virgin.

The two versions probably derived from the same saying originally with the longer version most likely being original. Since the fragment is used in connection with Christian arguments about the virginity of Mary, one might easily see the reference to the heifer being removed due to discomfort with comparing Mary to a cow. Epiphanius, Ps.-Gregory, and the *Acts of Peter*, either explicitly or implicitly, seem to connect the fragment with Isa 7:14, a passage commonly invoked as a proof text of the virgin birth.

Fragment 4

This fragment is a saying about judgment that has the broadest and longest attestation of all of the apocryphal Ezekiel fragments. It appears in a dizzying number of sources, in languages such as Greek, Latin, Syriac, Armenian, Old French, and Middle English, dating from the second century through the late Middle Ages, and it can be found in two different forms. The first form, found in the earliest witnesses, Justin Martyr (mid-second century C.E.) and Clement of Alexandria, has the pronouns in the plural, has the Greek particle *an* in the first clause, and has no object for the verb "judge." The second form uses the singular throughout, lacks *an*, and gives an object for the verb.

In addition to the broad attestation of this fragment, the sources also give multiple attributions. Justin Martyr alone explicitly attributes the saying to Jesus, and Clement offers "God" as the one who said it. Other sources refer to God "through a prophet" or to God "through the prophets." Only two sources, Evagrius in his Latin translation of Athanasius's *Life of St. Anthony* (fourth century C.E.) and John Climacus (c. 600 C.E.), explicitly attribute the quote to Ezekiel. This situation creates a confusing picture of the transmission history of the saying. The most reasonable explanation for the attributions is that the saying originally began with something like "Therefore also the Lord says." Cyprian (mid-third century C.E.) and the Syriac *Liber Graduum* (date uncertain) preserve the attribution "Lord," but understand it to mean Jesus. The saying was read alternatively as from God and subsequently God through a prophet or prophets, and in this way became attributed to Ezekiel in Evagrius and John Climacus.[7] It is thus possible that some sources encountered this fragment as a

5. Stone et al., *Apocryphal Ezekiel*, 21.

6. The Latin translation of the *Acts* is only found in one sixth/seventh-century manuscript, codex Vercellensus CLVIII.

7. This suggestion was made by A. J. Bellinzoni in *The Sayings of Jesus in the Writings of Justin Martyr* (SNT 17; Leiden: Brill, 1967), 131-34.

free saying, but some might have found it as part of an Ezekiel apocryphon (see below for a discussion of the larger questions about transmission of the apocryphon).

Fragment 5

This fragment was known for a long time only through its citation and attribution to Ezekiel in Clement of Alexandria, *Paedagogus* I.[9.]84.2–4. In 1940, however, Campbell Bonner published the text of Papyrus Chester Beatty 185, which contained a fragmentary text that overlaps with Clement's and which almost certainly is part of a manuscript copy of the *Apocryphon of Ezekiel*. These papyrus fragments were originally part of a larger book that also included the final chapters of *1 Enoch* and the *Paschal Homily* of the second century Christian writer Melito of Sardis. The manuscript itself dates to the fourth century.

Chester Beatty 185 is fragmentary, and only the verso of the largest fragment bears any resemblance to Clement of Alexandria. The recto side contains a number of words and phrases, and one could conclude that it, too, was part of the apocryphon. Two other fragments that go with this largest fragment could also have been part of the Ezekiel apocryphon, but this is not at all certain. In the interest of completeness, I have given all three fragments in the translation below.

Chester Beatty 185 and Clement of Alexandria represent important independent witnesses to this portion of the apocryphon. Certainly Chester Beatty 185 is not a copy of Clement of Alexandria, since Clement inserts homiletical comments in between his citations of the apocryphon. Chester Beatty 185, although the text has the same order and structure as Clement's citations of the apocryphon, does not have room for any of Clement's sermonic additions. Thus, in Chester Beatty 185 we have an important and early witness, in fact our only manuscript witness, which confirms the existence of an *Apocryphon of Ezekiel*.

The text itself has reminiscences of Ezekiel 34 and shares the biblical text's major metaphor, in which God condemns Israel's leaders, referred to as shepherds, for not protecting and caring for God's sheep. As a result, God tells the prophet that he will do precisely those things that Israel's leaders have neglected to do. The Chester Beatty papyrus preserves some material before the place where Clement's citation begins. This earlier section contains God's indictment of Israel's leaders, addressed in the second person plural, and it leads up to the transition to what God will do, which begins with "And I will bind up the lame"—the place where Clement's citation starts.

Possible Unattributed Fragments

Outside of the five fragments that bear attributions to Ezekiel, a number of unattributed citations in early Christian sources might have claim to be part of the apocryphon. Of this number I translate the two that represent the best possibilities and that illustrate the issues at stake in such cases.[8]

1 Clement 8:2

This unattributed citation resembles Ezek 18:23 and 33:11, although the differences between Clement's version and the biblical texts are great. In general, when Clement cites

---

8. For a complete list and discussion of passages for which one might argue, see Stone et al., *Apocryphal Ezekiel*, 46-54. This list does not include the 4QPseudo-Ezekiel fragments. For a discussion of this work, see below.

biblical texts, he stays close to their wording. This passage, if it were a biblical citation, would be the one exception. In addition, the passage ends with "He also added a virtuous declaration," a clause that connects this citation with 8:3, one of the fragments of the apocryphon. Thus, its similarity to Ezekiel combined with the connection to 8:3 has persuaded some scholars that this citation might have originated in the *Apocryphon of Ezekiel*.

1 Clement 50:4

Clement cites this passage with the formula "For it is written," indicating that he thought it to be scripture. The first clause has verbal parallels to Isa 26:20, and the third resembles Ezek 37:12. The middle clause has no identifiable biblical parallel. Clement clearly regards this passage as a single saying, and it is clearly not a "biblical" quotation. Furthermore, Isa 26:19-20 appears in other contexts in connection with material from Ezekiel, most notably in Epiphanius's introduction to the story of the blind man and the lame man and in 4Q385 3, part of a text from Qumran called Pseudo-Ezekiel.[9] All these considerations lend support to the possible inclusion of this passage among the fragments of the apocryphon.

Genre and Structure

Since such a small amount of material of the *Apocryphon of Ezekiel* survives, only some tentative observations are possible. Four of the five apocryphal Ezekiel fragments have the character of prophetic utterances. Even Fragment 3, the heifer who has and has not given birth, could fit well into a prophetic framework. The story of the lame and the blind is different. In its rabbinic forms, it is given as a *māšāl*, an illustrative story. Epiphanius's label "parable" (Gk. *parabolē*) also comports with this description. Whether this story could have been included in the same work as the other fragments is a different question, and with such sparse evidence, it is impossible to say anything about the overall structure or literary character of the work. Even though these fragments have similarities to biblical prophetic texts, they cannot really be called an example of "rewritten scripture," since we have no knowledge of what the scope of the apocryphon was or how it employed the prophetic texts that it seems to have used. Perhaps the best way to characterize them is by the term "parascriptural" or even more specifically "paraprophetic."[10] Without further evidence, all of these questions must remain open and unanswered.

Date, Provenance, and Original Language

As with questions of genre and structure, answers to questions of date, provenance, and original language are hard to come by for this work, but some synthetic conclusions are possible. At the very beginning, however, we must admit that any conclusions will be very tentative, and we have to begin by asking the extent to which the evidence allows us to think about the *Apocryphon of Ezekiel* as *a single work having literary integrity that was transmitted over the course of numerous centuries*. While there seems little doubt that an *Apocryphon of Ezekiel* existed, as the testimony of Josephus, Epiphanius, and the *Stichometry of Nicephorus* attest, was its text perhaps somewhat fluid, with traditions being introduced into it or excerpted from it at different times in the course of its long transmission

9. Devorah Dimant, the editor of 4Q385, renumbered all the fragments in her DJD edition. What I refer to here as fragment 3, used to be 4Q385 12.

10. For the term "parascriptural" and its implications, see Robert A. Kraft, "Para-mania: Beside, Before, and Beyond Biblical Studies," *JBL* 126 (2007): 5-27.

in Christian sources? What did the apocryphon look like at different points in its transmission history? Perhaps its contents changed over the course of time and transmission. So, for example, Fragment 4 is only attributed to Ezekiel in the fourth century and later, even though earlier authors knew the citation but did not report Ezekiel as its author. Did this saying about judgment receive its attribution to Ezekiel at a later time and, as a result, find its way into the apocryphon at some point significantly after its composition/redaction? Was Fragment 4 ever part of what we are calling the *Apocryphon of Ezekiel*, despite its attribution to the prophet? Does the fact that Clement of Alexandria, who cites four of the five fragments (two as coming from Ezekiel and two as from scripture), cites the fragment provide any support that it would have belonged to the work? These questions remain difficult to answer in the face of the available evidence.

A second important consideration must precede any discussion of date, provenance, or original language—the existence of another non-biblical Ezekiel work, 4QPseudo-Ezekiel from Qumran. What possible relationship(s) might it have had to the *Apocryphon of Ezekiel*? Several scholars have argued that some passages in Christian sources might have derived from the Qumran work, suggesting that it circulated more widely than at Qumran and that it was translated from Hebrew into Greek.[11] If there was a relationship between the Qumran Pseudo-Ezekiel and the *Apocryphon of Ezekiel*, that would push conclusions about date, provenance and language in a very particular direction. At this juncture, however, scholars are not agreed about how to assess any connection between the two works, and so I only note the possibility here.

With these caveats in mind, we can venture some remarks about the *Apocryphon of Ezekiel*. Whereas the Qumran work certainly originated in Hebrew, most likely in Palestine in the second century B.C.E., we cannot be certain of the original language, date, or provenance of the *Apocryphon of Ezekiel*. Clement of Alexandria in the late second century provides the earliest attribution of a fragment to Ezekiel, and so it certainly predates 200 C.E. If we begin from the earliest citation of a fragment of the apocryphon, however, the work could date from earlier than the end of the first century, since *1 Clement* knows at least one fragment of it. The surviving sources suggest Greek as the major language of its transmission, but the story of the blind and the lame men circulated in Hebrew (in rabbinic sources), although how it moved between its Greek and Hebrew forms is not at all clear. The apocryphon's provenance cannot be identified with certainty either, especially in light of the wide geographical range of the witnesses to it. The earliest witness, *1 Clement*, originated in Rome, but Clement of Alexandria, who has the most extensive knowledge of the apocryphon, wrote in Egypt.

One of the crucial questions is whether the apocryphon was Jewish or Christian originally. If we only take into consideration the five traditional fragments, then the most that we can say is that they are preserved almost exclusively in Christian sources (with the exception of the story of the lame and blind men). Does the fact that both *1 Clement* and Clement of Alexandria consider fragments of the apocryphon to be from scripture, presumably from their "Old Testament," have any bearing on whether the apocryphon was

11. The passages are *Barnabas* 12:1 [see Menahem Kister, "Barnabas 12:1; 4:3 and 4Q Second Ezekiel," *RB* 97 (1990): 63-67]; *Apocalypse of Peter* 7:4-9 [see Richard Bauckham, "A Quotation from *4Q Second Ezekiel* in *The Apocalypse of Peter*," *RevQ* 15/59 (1992): 438-45]; and *1 Clement* 50:4 [see Benjamin G. Wright, "Qumran Pseudepigrapha and Early Christianity: Is 1 Clement 50:4 a Citation of 4QPseudo-Ezekiel (4Q385 12)?" in *Pseudepigraphic Perspectives: The Apocrypha and Pseudepigrapha in Light of the Dead Sea Scrolls*, edited by Michael E. Stone and Esther G. Chazon, 183-93. STDJ 31. Leiden: Brill, 1999].

Jewish or not? Josephus's testimony to a second Ezekiel book would probably indicate that it was a Jewish composition, as would its inclusion in the *Stichometry of Nicephorus*'s category of "pseudepigrapha" that also includes Baruch, Habakkuk, and Daniel.

Thus, we might tentatively conclude that the *Apocryphon of Ezekiel* was originally a Jewish composition, composed or redacted in Greek (without ruling out a possible Hebrew original) sometime before the end of the first century C.E. Its place of origin must remain uncertain, although it has strong early attestation in Egypt (Clement of Alexandria and Chester Beatty 185). Given the available evidence for this work, however, we might just as easily hypothesize that apocryphal Ezekiel material was collected and transmitted in multiple ways. One could envision this material circulating in more than one form—in an apocryphal book or books, in florilegia or testimonia, or as free floating sayings. Thus, there might have never been a single and original *Apocryphon of Ezekiel* that contained all of these fragments, and thus not a single *original* date, language or provenance that applies to them collectively. This apocryphon, if that is what we ultimately choose to call it, illustrates the variety of possibilities confronting scholars as they try to trace the paths of material such as *the Apocryphon of Ezekiel* through the centuries of their transmission.

Bibliography

Bauckham, Richard. "The Parable of the Royal Wedding Feast (Matthew 22:1-14) and the Parable of the Lame Man and the Blind Man *(Apocryphon of Ezekiel).*" *JBL* 115 (1996): 447-64.

Bonner, Campbell. *The Homily on the Passion by Melito of Sardis and Some Fragments of the Apocryphal Ezekiel.* SD XII. Philadelphia, Pa.: University of Pennsylvania, 1940. (Treats Chester Beatty 185 on pp. 183-202)

Bregman, M. "The Parable of the Lame and the Blind." *JTS* 42 (1991): 125-38.

Dimant, Devorah. *Qumran Cave 4 • XXI: Parabiblical Texts, Part 4: Pseudo-Prophetic Texts.* DJD 30. Oxford: Clarendon, 2001. (Official edition of five of the six Qumran 4QPseudo-Ezekiel texts [pp. 7-88 and plates i-iii])

Eckart, K.-G. "Das Apocryphen Ezechiel." Pages 45-56 in *Jüdische Schriften aus hellenistisch-römischer Zeit.* Vol. 5.1, edited by H. G. Kümmel and H. Lichtenberger. Gütersloh: Gütersloher Verlagshaus, 1974.

James, M. R. "The Apocryphal Ezekiel." *JTS* 15 (1914): 236-43.

Kraft, Robert A. "Para-mania: Beside, Before, and Beyond Biblical Studies." *JBL* 126 (2007): 5-27.

Mueller, James R. *The Five Fragments of the Apocryphon of Ezekiel: A Critical Study.* JSPSup 5. Sheffield: Sheffield Academic Press, 1994. (See here for additional bibliography.)

Mueller, James R., and S. E. Robinson. "*Apocryphon of Ezekiel.*" *OTP*, 1:487-95.

Smith, Mark. "Pseudo-Ezekiel." Pages 153–93 and plates xvii-xxv in *Qumran Cave 4 • XIV: Parabiblical Texts Part 2.* DJD 19. Edited by Magen Broshi et al. Oxford: Clarendon, 1995. (Official edition of the sixth copy of 4QPseudo-Ezekiel)

Stone, Michael E., Benjamin G. Wright, and David Satran. *The Apocryphal Ezekiel.* SBLEJL 18. Atlanta, Ga.: Society of Biblical Literature, 2000. (The *Apocryphon* is treated on pp. 7-68, including 4QPseudo-Ezekiel. See here for additional bibliography.)

Wright, Benjamin G. "Talking with God and Losing His Head: Extra-Biblical Traditions about the Prophet Ezekiel." Pages 290-315 in *Biblical Figures Outside the Bible.* Edited by Michael E. Stone and Theodore A. Bergren. Harrisburg, Pa.: Trinity, 1998.

The Apocryphon of Ezekiel

Fragment 1

a. Epiphanius, Panarion 64.70.5-17

Introduction

§5 *For the dead will be raised and those in tombs will be lifted up*, says the prophet. Isa 26:19
But so that I also do not pass over in silence those things said by the prophet Ezekiel in his own apocryphon concerning resurrection, I will cite them here as well.

The crime of the lame man and the blind man

§6 For narrating in riddles, he speaks of the just judgment in which both soul and body share. "A certain king had everyone in his kingdom in military service, and there were no civilians, except for two only, one lame man and one blind man, and each of them sat separately and dwelt separately. §7 And when the king made a wedding for his own son,[a] he invited everyone in his kingdom, but he treated the two civilians with contempt, both the lame man and the blind man. And they were very angry among themselves, and they purposed to carry out a plot against the king. §8 Now the king had an orchard,[b] and the blind man spoke to the lame man from far away saying, 'How much more would our morsel of bread have been with the crowds of those invited to the merry-making? Come now, just as he did to us, let us pay him back.' §9 But the other asked, 'In what way?' And he said, 'Let us be off into his orchard, and we will steal the things there in the orchard.' But he said, 'How can I, since I am lame and unable to walk?' And the blind man said, 'What am I myself able to do, not seeing where I am going? But let us figure out a way.' §10 When he had plucked grass that was close by and had plaited a rope, he threw it to the blind man and said, 'Grab hold, and come along the rope to me.' And doing what he had urged, when he arrived, he said, 'Come, become feet for me and carry me, and I will become eyes for you, guiding you from above, to the right and the left.' §11 When they had done this, they went down into the orchard. For the rest, whether they did wrong or they did not do wrong, all the same, their tracks were apparent in the orchard. §12 But

a. Although not the same story, the motif of a king giving a wedding banquet is also found in the New Testament in Matt 22:2-14.

b. The Greek term *paradeisos* can also mean an enclosed garden. The emphasis on fruit as the object of the blind and lame men indicates that the translation "orchard" is best suited to the context. The same is true for the Hebrew *pardēs*, which is used in the rabbinic versions of the story.

when the merry-makers left the wedding and went down into the orchard, they were astonished, having found the tracks in the orchard, and they reported these things to the king, saying, 'Everyone in your kingdom is in military service, and there are no civilians. How then are there tracks of civilians in the orchard?' §13 And he was amazed."

Epiphanius's interpretive remark

And the parable in the apocryphon speaks quite clearly as to a human being since it speaks in riddles, but God is ignorant of nothing. But the narrative says:

The king's judgment

"Then he sent for the lame man and the blind man, and he asked the blind man, 'Did you not go down into the orchard?' And he said, 'Oh, Lord! You see our disability, knowing that I do not see where I am going.' §14 Then coming to the lame man, he asked him as well, 'You went down into my orchard?' He answered and said, 'O Lord, do you want to embitter my soul due to my disability.' Furthermore, the case is at an impasse. §15 What does the just judge do? Realizing the manner in which both were joined, he places the lame man upon the blind man, and he imposes whips on both, and they are unable to deny it.[a] §16 Each one accuses the other. The lame man says to the blind man, 'Did you not lift me and carry me?' And the blind man says to the lame man, 'Did not you yourself become my eyes?'"

God judges body and soul together

§17 Thus, the body is joined to the soul, and the soul to the body for the conviction of their common deed. And the final judgment will be for both, body and soul, of the works that were done, both good and worthless.

b. Sanhedrin 91ab

Introduction

Antoninus said to Rabbi, "Body and soul are able to exempt themselves from the judgment. In what manner? The body says, 'The soul sinned, since from the day that it separated from me, I have been lying like a silent stone in a tomb.' And the soul says, 'The body sinned, since from the day that I separated from it, behold I have been flying in the air like a bird.'" And he (i.e., Rabbi) said to him, "I will give you an illustration. To what may the matter be compared?

The illustration of the lame man and the blind man

To a flesh and blood king who had a beautiful orchard and in it there were beautiful early fruits, and he placed in it two guards—one lame and one blind—and the lame man said to the blind man, 'Beautiful early fruits I see in the orchard. Come, and let me ride, and we will procure them in order to eat them.' And the lame man rode upon the shoulders of the blind man, and they procured them

---

a. This sentence seems to be a combination of Epiphanius's own comment and the continuation of the story. Note that the rabbinic form of the story also has the king set the one on the other.

and they ate them. A few days later the owner of the orchard came. He said to them, 'Where are those beautiful early fruits?' The lame man said to him, 'Do I have feet that I am able to walk?' The blind man said to him, 'Do I have eyes that I am able to see?' What did he (i.e., the king) do? He made the lame man ride upon the shoulders of the blind man, and he judged them as one."

God judges body and soul together

Thus, the Holy One, blessed be He, brings the soul, and casting it into the body,
he judges them as one. As it is said, *He will call to the heavens above and to the*
earth in order to judge his people. "He will call to the heavens above"—this is the Ps 50:4
soul—"and to the earth in order to judge his people"[a]—this is the body.

Fragment 2

1 Clement 8:3

"Repent, O house of Israel, from your lawlessness," I said to the children of my Ezek 18:30-32
people. "If your sins be from the earth up to the heaven and if they be redder
than scarlet and blacker than sackcloth and you turn to me with a whole heart Isa 1:18
and say, 'Father,' I will listen to you as a holy people." Jer 3:19

Clement of Alexandria, Paedagogus I.[10.]91.2

For he (or: it) says through Ezekiel, "If you turn with your whole heart and you say, 'Father,' I will listen to you just like a holy people."

Exegesis on the Soul (NHC II, 6:135.30–136.4)

Therefore, [30]he said through the Spirit to the pro[32]ph[e]t, "Say to the children of the people, [32]'[If your] sins extend [[33]from the earth to] heaven and if they become [34][red] like scarlet and [35]blacker than [sackcloth and if] **136** [1]you turn to me with your whole [2]soul and you say to me, [3]'My Father,' I will listen to you as a [4]holy people."

Fragment 3

Tertullian, De Carne Christi 23

We recognize, then, the sign to be spoken against, the conception and parturition of the virgin Mary, concerning which the Academics say, "She has given birth and not given birth; she is a virgin and not a virgin," ...[Here ensues a long discussion about how Mary conceived as a virgin.]... We read in Ezekiel of a heifer that has given birth and not given birth, but it seems more likely that by this expression the Holy Spirit, even then having you in mind, censured those who would argue about the womb of Mary.

Ps.-Gregory of Nyssa, Adversus Judaeos 3

And again, "Behold, the heifer has given birth and has not given birth."

---

a. The unpointed Hebrew here could read *ʿammō* (his people) or *ʿimmō* (with it). If we read with the latter pointing, as do some scholars, the phrase would be "and to the earth to go to trial with it." That is, body and soul are judged together.

Epiphanius, Panarion 30.30.3

And again in another place it says, "And the heifer will give birth, and they say she has not given birth."[a]

Clement of Alexandria, Stromateis 7.94

"She has given birth and not given birth," says scripture.

Acts of Peter 24

And again he says, "She has given birth and not given birth."[b]

Fragment 4

Group 1

Justin Martyr, *Dialogue with Trypho* 47.5

Therefore also our Lord, Jesus Christ, said, "In those things in which I discover you, in (or: by) those things I will judge."

Ezek 18:24, 26, 30; 33:20

Clement of Alexandria, *Quis dives salvetur* 40.2

"For in whatever things I find you," it (or: he) says, "in those things will I also judge."

Group 2

John Climacus, *Scala Paradisi* 7

"Woe is me, woe is me." Where then was the voice of Ezekiel, so that he might say to them, "In that which I find you, in it also I will judge you."

Athanasius, *Life of St. Anthony* 15 (Evagrius's Latin translation)

In this way it is right for us to obey the divine precepts, knowing that he who is just, in whatever he finds him, he will be judged in it, which is witnessed by the prophetic word through Ezekiel.

Other citations belonging to this second group are: A. (earlier than the seventh century) Cyprian, *De Mortalitate* 17; Basil, *Ad Chilonem*; Jerome, *Commentary on Ezekiel* 18.20 and *Epistle 122 to Rusticus*; Augustine, *Epistle* 199.2; Amphilocius, *De Poenitentia*; *Liber Graduum*, Sermon 3.3; Pseudo-Athanasius, *Quaestio ad Antiochum* 36; *Consultationes Zacchaei et Apolonii*; *Testamentum XL Mart.* (Lambeccius) and B. (later than the seventh century) Armenian *Questions of Ezra* B.4; Sahdona *Matyrius*; *Nilus ap. Anastasium Sinait. Quaest* 3; Theodore the Studite, *Catecheticorum sermo* 36; *Vita S. Johannici*; Theodorus Balsamo, *In canones XIII Concilii Neocaesariensis*; Joannis Geometrae Paradisus, *Epigrammata tetrastiche*; Elias Cretensis, *Jus Graeco-Romanum Lib. V Responsorium I*; Gennadius Scholarius, *Epist. de paedestinatione*; *'La vision de Kaioumos et le sort eternal de Philentlos Olympion'*; Alcuin, *De Confessione Peccatorum*; Paulinus,

a. In this same section Epiphanius cites what looks like the shorter version found in Tertullian. He says, "Since certain of the Manichaeans and the Marcionites say, 'She shall give birth, and they say she has not given birth.'"

b. This citation comes amidst several that the author clearly connects with the prophet Isaiah, including Isa 7:14.

Liber Exhortationis; *Roman de Rou* (Old French); An Anonymous Middle English Sermon.[a]

Fragment 5
Clement of Alexandria, Paedagogus I.[9.]84.2–4

He (or: it) says, therefore, through Ezekiel, being extended to the elders and
delivering to them a certain saving pattern of reasonable thought, "And I will
bind up the lame, and I will heal the troubled, and what has wandered, I will turn
back, and I will feed them on my holy mountain." These are the promises of the Ezek 34:14-16
good shepherd. Feed us, the infants, as sheep. Yes, master, fill us with your pasture, that is, righteousness. Yes, pedagogue, shepherd us on your holy mountain,
toward the church, which is lifted up above the clouds, touching heaven. "And I
will be," he (or: it) says, *their shepherd, and I will be near to them as the garment* Ezek 34:11
of their skin. He desires to save my flesh, clothing (it with) the tunic of immortal- Jer 13:11
ity, and he has anointed (it). "They will call me," he (or: it) says, "and I will say, 'Behold I am here.'" You heard sooner than I expected, Lord. "And if they cross, they will not slip," says the Lord. For we who are crossing into immortality will not fall into destruction, because he clings to us. For he has spoken, and he has desired it.

Papyrus Chester Beatty 185
Fragment 1, recto

[1][…]of the Egyptians, [I will] rejoice [2][in] them. If they sa[y ..[3]..] it will be [.],
and they will be [.. [4]in the la]nd of life. O Jerusalem, s[ay … [5]do n]ot punish me
i[n your anger [6]nor] chasten me in [your wrath.] [7]I am [.] up to [my] kid[neys.] Ps 6:1 | Jer 11:20; 17:10;
[8]I am [.] unto [my] stomach. [Grant [9]me] your mercy dai[ly as you had mercy on Ps 7:10; 25:2
[10]A]braam [ou]r father [and on [11]Isaac an]d on Jacob. But you, the Lord [12][ou]r
[God] we have known, and [...[13]..] and he begat [... [14]si]tting apart[..[15]..] we were Ezek 4:16-17, 22
loathsome [...[16]...] the name [...[17]...] for the one who(?)[...[18]...] street [...]

Fragment 1, verso

[1][..]did not tu[rn b]ack [.[2]..] did not he[al.[3]...] my people wand[er .[4]...] good and
proceed[.[5]..a]nd thorns instead of p[asture [6]..]you [.] my com[mandment [7]...] Ezek 34:4-6
from you ope[n .. [8]...] for food for t[hem. [9].. bu]t see, I will judg[e ram [10]against
ram] and bull against bul[l, and [11]the lam]e I will bind up, and the troub[led] Ezek 34:17, 22 | Ezek
[12]I will [hea]l, and the one that wande[rs I will [13]turn back, a]nd I will shepherd 34:16
the[m, and [14]I will give them rest u]pon [my] holy mountain, [and [15]I will be to Ezek 34:14
th]em a shepherd. A[nd I will be near [16]to them as the g]arment of [their] sk[in Ezek 34:11
. And] [17]they [will call upon] me [and I will say, "Behold, I am here." [18]If] they Jer 13:11
[cross over, they will] not [slip, [19]says the Lord ...]

Fragment 2, recto

[[1]... [2]...]of fire(?) [... [3]...] polluti[ng... [4]...] still(?) they approached the(?)[... [5]...ol]d men who were incapab[le... [6]...u]pon the heights and [... [7]...]because of the guide

a. This list is compiled from several different scholarly sources. See Stone et al., *Apocryphal Ezekiel*, 26-28 and Mueller, *Five Fragments*, 142-46.

did not[... [8]...] are those who [.] the voice [... [9]...] but I looked up [... [10]...] of the one hung[... [11]...] who flew do[wn... [12]...] and sai[d...]

Fragment 2, verso

[[1]... [2]...] since the [... [3]... [4]..] is for the one who has been enslaved [.. [5]...] pure heat an[d.. [6]...] upon the Lord, the God[.. [7]...] you and he(?) sto[od .. [8]..] the things that are shattered[.. [9]..] after everything that(?)[.. [10]..w]as laid waste by[... [11]...]he will be[... [12]...]and[... [13]...]

Fragment 3, recto

[[1]...] now yo[u(?)... [2] ...] from the [... [3]...wre]tched and[...]

Fragment 3, verso

[[1]...] country [... [2]...] hide/hidden [... [3]...]

Origen, Homilies on Jeremiah 18.9

And it is promised through the prophets, saying, "I will be nearer to them than the tunic of their skin."

Manichaean Psalmbook 239.5–6

He is not far from us, my brethren, as he said when he preached, "I am near to you, like the garment of your skin."

Possible Unattributed Fragments of the *Apocryphon of Ezekiel*

1 Clement 8:2

And the master of everything himself spoke about repentance with an oath, "For as I live," says the Lord, "I do not desire the death of the sinner as much as repen-
Ezek 18:23; 33:11 tance." He also added a virtuous declaration.

1 Clement 50:4

For it is written, "Enter into your chambers[a] for a little while until the time when
Isa 26:19 my wrath and anger pass away, and I will remember a good day, and I will raise
Ezek 37:12 you up out of your graves."

a. The Greek term *tameia* may well be a technical term referring to the treasury of the souls.

The Treatise of the Vessels (*Massekhet Kelim*)

A new translation and introduction

by James R. Davila

The *Treatise of the Vessels* (*Massekhet Kelim*) is a legendary account of the hiding of the treasures of Solomon's Temple before its destruction by the Babylonians. It is not to be confused with the Mishnaic tractate of the same name. This work is written in Hebrew and survives only in two very late sources that preserve substantially different recensions of it. Its date of composition is very uncertain and may be quite late. Its provenance is unknown. Nevertheless, it is worthy of inclusion in this collection because it has many interesting connections with much more ancient legends about the Temple treasures.

Contents

The *Treatise of the Vessels* purports to reveal some of the places where the treasures of Solomon's Temple were hidden before that Temple's destruction. The treasures were concealed by a number of Levites and prophets, who wrote a list of them on a tablet or tablets of bronze. The *Treatise* offers vastly exaggerated lists of the treasures, including the Tabernacle; the Ark of the Covenant; the golden table of the bread of the Presence; the silver trumpets; enormous caches of vessels, implements, and musical instruments of gold, silver, and bronze, often decorated with precious stones; the vestments of the high priest, along with thousands of vestments of the regular priests; and fantastic implements and ornaments made of gold from the Garden of Eden and gems from the celestial pavement. Some of these were hidden in various locations in the Land of Israel and in Babylonia, while others were delivered into the hands of the angels Shamshiel, Michael, Gabriel, and perhaps Sariel, and the treasures will not be revealed again until the coming of the Messiah.[1]

Manuscripts

Two recensions survive of the text of the *Treatise of the Vessels*. The first is found in the edition of Adolph Jellinek in *Bet ha-Midrasch*, a collection of minor midrashim published originally in 1876. Jellinek reports that he took the Hebrew text from a book called *The Valley of the King*, which was published in Vilna in 1802. He adds that it is a pseudepigraphic adaptation of a work called *The Baraita* (i.e., *External Tractate*) *of the Workmanship of the Tabernacle*, which described the construction of the Tabernacle and which was first published in Venice in 1602. Neither of these earlier books is available to me, although I have located a printing of this recension of the *Treatise of the Vessels* published by R. Naf-

1. This text has never before been translated into English, but it was summarized by Ginzberg in *Legends of the Jews*, 4:321.

tali Hertz Bachrach in *Emek Halachah*, published in Amsterdam in 1648, pp. 14a-14b. It is virtually identical to Jellinek's text.[2]

The second source for the text is a remarkable manuscript indeed. In 1959 J. T. Milik published an article of notes on Palestinian epigraphy and topography.[3] In it he reports that "a good number of years ago" his Reverence Jean Starcky was shown in a house in Beirut a collection of marble plaques inscribed in relief with the full text of the Book of Ezekiel, followed on the last two plaques by the Hebrew text of §§I-IX of the *Treatise of the Vessels* with an additional prologue that precedes the one in Jellinek's text. Milik writes that "it seems that they were intended for a synagogue of Syria or of Lebanon."[4] Starcky photographed the next-to-last plaque and transcribed the first three and last three lines of the final plaque. In this article Milik published Starcky's photograph, which is of poor quality, and republished Jellinek's text, giving the variants of the available text of the Beirut plaques in footnotes. The plaques containing the book of Ezekiel are now on display at the Yad Ben Zvi Institute in Jerusalem but the two plaques that bear the last verse and a half of Ezekiel, followed by the *Treatise of the Vessels*, are not with them and I have not been able to trace their whereabouts.[5] A recent article in the *Jerusalem Post* reports that the Ezekiel plaques were removed over a century ago from the traditional tomb of the prophet Ezekiel in Kifl, Iraq, about fifty miles south of Baghdad. The plaques had been built into the interior wall(s) of the shrine sometime before that with the inscribed side facing inward. They were taken to Lebanon and then, in 1953, to Israel. The date when the plaques were inscribed remains to be determined.[6]

As far as I can ascertain, no other independent manuscript of the work survives.[7]

My translation is of the combined text of Jellinek's edition (J) and the Beirut plaques (B). Variants that affect the translation are given in the notes. I have usually followed the reading of J in the text, which is frequently longer than that of B. Although textual critics normally prefer the shorter reading, the difficulty of inscribing the text in stone may have led to the text of B being abbreviated. The manuscript evidence is far too narrow for us to hope to reconstruct the original text with any confidence, and the substantial differences in what is included in the two surviving sources indicate that the text has been transmitted with considerable freedom. Jellinek's paragraph numbers are given as roman numerals. The line numbers of the Beirut plaques are given as superscript Arabic numerals, with the beginning of each of the two plaques indicated with a superscript roman numeral. The prologue of B is given the siglum "oB" and that of J (also found in B after oB) is "oJ."

2. I am grateful to Eli Gurevich for drawing this edition to my attention.

3. Milik, "Notes d'épigraphie et de topographie palestiniennes."

4. Ibid., 567-68: "Il semble qu'elles étaient destinées à une synagogue de Syrie ou du Liban."

5. I am grateful to Robert R. Smith for alerting me to the location of the Ezekiel plaques and to Michael Glatzer, the Academic Secretary of the Institute, for verifying their presence.

6. David Parsons and Florence Back, "Dating the Ezekiel Plates," *Jerusalem Post*, 1 May 2011. Accessed online on 2 May 2011 at http://www.jpost.com/ChristianInIsrael/Features/Article.aspx?id=218495.

7. A search of the catalogue of the Department of Manuscripts and the Institute of Microfilmed Hebrew Manuscripts of the Jewish National and University Library yielded only one manuscript of the *Treatise of the Vessels* (NY JTS 5962) which was copied from the book that was used by Jellinek. I have not seen this manuscript. I am grateful to the Acting Head of the Department and Institute, Yael Okun, for help with negotiating the catalogue.

Genre and Structure

There is no clear structure to the *Treatise of the Vessels*. The version of the Beirut plaques begins with an unidentified speaker transmitting the traditions from another unidentified person, whether a human being, an angel, or God.[8] Jellinek's version opens by attributing the traditions in it to the five great righteous men who catalogued and hid the treasures. Each subsequent paragraph passes on a tradition about the fate of some of the treasures, with some treasures appearing more than once (e.g., trumpets appear in §I 8 and §IV 16; the table(s) of gold in §I 9 and §V 18; and the high priestly vestments in §I 9 and §VIII). The Beirut plaques conclude at the end of §IX with a suitable statement about the return of the treasures when the Messiah comes. Jellinek's text concludes with §XII, also with a suitable ending that predicts the revelation of the treasures in the messianic age. The document thus shows signs of being a loose compilation of traditions about the Temple treasure whose structure has received very minimal attention.

The genre of the work is therefore difficult to pin down. It has affinities with the genre apocalypse in that it contains esoteric revelations involving angels. The opening line of B could even be understood as defining the text as a revelation from a divine being to a human being, although this is not made explicit. The unusual combination of elements (a fictional list of hidden temple treasures) is difficult to parallel. The folkloric motif of Aladdin's cave comes to mind, which contained the magic lamp and fruit trees that bore gems and which could only be entered and harvested by the right person at the right time.[9] More concretely, Crossan has established a typology of world treasure tales which is built upon the bipolar categories hiding/not hiding, seeking/not seeking, finding/not finding, obtaining/not obtaining, securing/not securing, using/not using, each category of which follows from the previous one. In other words, in folklore a treasure can be hidden or not hidden, then either actively sought by a character or not, then whether sought or not it may be found or not found, and having been found or not, it may or may not be obtained. Even after being obtained, the treasure must be secured or it could be lost and, even once secured, all too often a curse or the like robs the owner of its use.[10] The treasure in Aladdin's cave was hidden underground, then it was sought by the Moorish sorcerer who posed as Aladdin's uncle, but not by Aladdin himself. Nevertheless Aladdin found the treasure and obtained it both because his destiny favored his success and because he followed the correct taboos, whereas the sorcerer, although he found the treasure by proxy through Aladdin, failed to obtain it due to his own evil nature. Aladdin did obtain the treasure (the gems and, especially, the magic lamp) and used it to create his own vast fortune and to secure his marriage to the Sultan's daughter. But he failed to secure it and so the sorcerer was able to steal the lamp, the fortune, and his wife, robbing Aladdin of their use. Nevertheless, he was able to foil the sorcerer by means of the Moor's own magic ring and in the end Aladdin both secured and had use of the treasure.

But as Crossan notes, this typology of world treasure tales is of limited use when ap-

8. In a personal communication, Richard Bauckham has made the plausible suggestion that the Beirut plaques be read in the context of the immediately preceding Book of Ezekiel. If so, the "me" of the opening line is the prophet Ezekiel (and the work is thereby transformed into a pseudepigraphon) and the agent of revelation is presumably the angel of Ezek 40:1-4, who reveals the contents of chapters 40–48 to the prophet. But we have no way of knowing whether the association with the Book of Ezekiel was in the mind of the original author. I can see no internal indications in the work that this was the case.

9. Dawood, "Aladdin."

10. Crossan, *Finding Is the First Act*, 11-51.

plied to the *Treatise of the Vessels*.[11] The treasure is hidden in various places, usually underground. There is no interest in anyone seeking it, since it is destined by God not to be found until the coming of the Messiah, at which time (and not before) it shall be revealed and the reconstituted nation of Israel shall obtain it. The focus of the narrative is on the wonders of the treasure and the details of its hiding, with its future revelation and obtaining coming almost as an afterthought. The common plot developments that revolve around heroes and villains who seek or do not seek the treasure and find or fail to find it, after which they obtain it or not, are entirely absent.

Perhaps the closest literary parallel surviving from antiquity is the Lindian Temple Chronicle, a long stone inscription erected in 99 B.C.E. Much of the stele is now badly damaged but it listed a catalogue of some 45 votive offerings given to the Temple of Athena at Lindos in Rhodes over many centuries, most of them fictional and derived from legendary literary sources. It also included four accounts of divine epiphanies of the goddess Athena when her help was needed by the inhabitants of Lindos. The Chronicle was commissioned by the Lindian city council and seems to have served the purpose of testifying to the fame and antiquity of the sanctuary of Athena in Lindos.[12] Both the Lindian Temple Chronicle and the *Treatise of the Vessels* describe lost and imaginary treasures derived from literary legend; both include epiphanies of divine beings; and both were written to glorify the memory of a particular sanctuary that had been destroyed by fire and rebuilt. The fact that both at least at one stage in transmission became stone inscriptions is perhaps coincidental, but it may be worth noting that the *Treatise of the Vessels* also claims that the Temple treasures were listed on a tablet of bronze (II 11, J) or tablets of unspecified material (B).

Thus as a preliminary attempt to locate the genre of the *Treatise of the Vessels*, I propose that it is a fictional inventory of lost temple offerings and divine epiphanies, written to glorify the sanctuary in question, and that this basic genre has been influenced by folkloric themes about the recovery of lost treasures and by Jewish apocalyptic eschatological themes involving the restoration of Israel in the messianic era.

Date and Provenance

The date and provenance of the *Treatise of the Vessels* are very uncertain. It is written in an unremarkable literary Hebrew that gives no obvious clue to its date. It shows awareness in a general way of Talmudic and earlier traditions but I have not been able to identify clear knowledge of any sources later than the Talmud (see below).[13] It is possible that the geographical name Bagdat in §IV 16 refers to Baghdad, in which case the text may have been written after this city was founded by the Abbasid Caliph al-Masur in 762 C.E. But the name Bagdat also appears in the Babylonian Talmud as the place of origin of one R. Hana (e.g., *b. Ket.* 7b; *b. Zeb.* 9a). The place name Bagda' mentioned in *b. Qidd.* 71b may also be related. Thus the appearance of the name in the *Treatise of the Vessels* is not a conclusive indicator of the date of composition. Given our current knowledge, we can say nothing more than that the *Treatise of the Vessels* must have been composed sometime between

11. Crossan cites Ginzberg's summary of the *Treatise of the Vessels* in this connection on p. 54.

12. For a summary of the contents of the Lindian Temple Chronicle, reflections on its function, and bibliography, see Shaya, "The Greek Temple as Museum." For a discussion of the genre of the Chronicle, see Higbie, *The Lindian Chronicle*, 258-88.

13. That said, I do not have access to the *Baraita of the Workmanship of the Tabernacle*, which, as noted above, seems to be considered by Jellinek to be a source of the *Treatise of the Vessels*.

late antiquity and the seventeenth century. It could have been composed anywhere someone well versed in Jewish traditions could have written a work in Hebrew. If the reported Iraqi provenance of the marble plaques containing the work proves to be correct, this may point in the direction of an origin for the work in the Iraqi Jewish community. It is to be hoped that further research may help us to narrow this wide range of possible dates and provenances.

Literary Context

The most basic literary source for the *Treatise of the Vessels* is the Hebrew Bible. The descriptions of the Temple treasures are based on the accounts of the building of the Tabernacle in Exodus 25–40; the building of the Jerusalem Temple by Solomon in 1 Kings 6–7 and 2 Chronicles 3–4; and the plans and materials for the Temple passed down from David to Solomon according to 1 Chronicles 28–29. Most of the characters in the story are known from the Bible. These include Moses; Aaron the high priest; Kings David, Solomon, Hezekiah, Zedekiah, and Nebuchadnezzar; the prophets Haggai and Zechariah; Baruch the scribe and Ezra the priest-scribe; and the angels Michael and Gabriel. Shimmur the Levite, his son Heleq, Hilkiah the scribe, and the angels Shamshiel and Sariel are not, or at least not obviously, scriptural figures. Some of the hiding places for the treasures are locations mentioned in or inspired by scripture, such as the Tower of Babel and the willow on which the Jewish exiles hung their lyres in Babylon according to Psalm 137:1-2.[14]

The fate of the treasures of Solomon's Temple has been a subject of fascination from antiquity to the present. The Bible itself gives little information. It tells us in 2 Kgs 25:1-17 that the Chaldeans (i.e., the Babylonians) looted the bronze pillars, the gold and silver vessels, and the bronze sea and its stands at the time of the destruction of the Temple and, according to 2 Chr 36:18, all of the vessels and treasures of the Temple were taken to Babylon at that time. Reportedly, many of the gold and silver vessels were returned to the Jewish community after the Exile by Cyrus the Great (Ezra 1:7-11). The fate of the Ark of the Covenant goes unreported, although the prophet Jeremiah promises that in the future it will neither be missed nor made again, implying it was lost when the Temple was destroyed (Jer 3:16).

The missing information was willingly supplied in postbiblical legend. According to 2 Maccabees 1:18-36 (first century B.C.E.), the priests of the Temple preserved some of the Temple fire as naphtha, which was recovered by Nehemiah and used to relight the fire in the new Temple. This book also reports that Jeremiah hid the Tabernacle, the Ark of the Covenant, and the incense altar in a cave whose location would not be recoverable until the eschaton (2:4-8).[15]

According to 2 *Baruch* 6-7 (c. 100 C.E.), when the Chaldean army had surrounded Jerusalem, angels rescued the curtain, the ephod, the tablets containing the Ten Commandments, the priestly vestments, the incense altar, forty-eight stones associated in some way with the priestly vestments (a corruption of the twelve stones of the high priest's breastpiece?), and all the vessels of the Tabernacle. These were swallowed up by the earth until the eschaton. The city was then destroyed. Variant versions of this legend are developed

14. The exegesis of scripture in the *Treatise of the Vessels* is sophisticated and I have treated it in more detail in "Scriptural Exegesis in the *Treatise of the Vessels*."

15. Versions of both stories in 2 Maccabees also appear in the medieval compilation *Josippon* (*Yosifon*) 7, with Ezra rather than Nehemiah as the main player in the first story.

in the closely related texts the *Paraleipomena of Jeremiah* (*4 Baruch*) and the *Coptic Jeremiah Apocryphon* (both of uncertain date, but perhaps composed in the early centuries C.E). According to *4 Bar* 3:6-11, 18-20, Jeremiah and Baruch, at the command of God, delivered the vessels of the Temple service to the earth, which swallowed them up "until the coming of the Beloved." Then in the morning Jeremiah threw the keys of the Temple up to the sun until such a time as God asked for them back (4:1-5).[16] The *Coptic Jeremiah Apocryphon* 28 reports that Jeremiah delivered the vestment of the high priest to the cornerstone of the Temple, which opened to receive the vestment and then closed to preserve it. Then Jeremiah took the golden plate on which is inscribed the divine name and threw it up to the sun, telling the sun to keep it until Jeremiah should request it back.[17] The rest of the Temple vessels were taken to Babylon by Nebuchadnezzar. There is also a cryptic reference to the hiding and future restoration of Temple vessels and precious stones in Pseudo-Philo, *L.A.B.* 26:12-13. Likewise the *Lives of the Prophets* (a work surviving in many forms and produced sometime between the first and fifth centuries C.E.) reports that the prophet Habakkuk predicted that at the time of the destruction of the Temple angels would carry away the capitals of the two pillars and that these would reappear at the time of the end (12:12-13).

The rabbinic literature also preserves legends about the fate of the Temple treasures. The Mishnah (third century C.E.) reports that prostration was made opposite the woodstore in the Second Temple because there was a tradition that the Ark was hidden there, and that a hapless priest who noticed that a block of the pavement there was different from the surrounding area promptly died, confirming that this was the hiding place of the Ark (*m. Sheqal.* 6.1-2).[18] According to the Tosefta (third to fourth century C.E.) in *t. Sotah* 13:1, King Josiah ordered the Levites to hide the Ark in the Temple. Stored inside the Ark were the jar of manna, the jar of anointing oil, Aaron's rod with its bud and flowers, the chest given to the Israelites when they returned the Ark, and the tablets containing the Ten Commandments (cf. *t. Yoma* 2:15). This account is repeated and expanded upon in the Babylonian Talmud (seventh century C.E.) in *b. Yoma* 52b, *b. Hor.* 12a, and *b. Ker.* 5b. According to *b. Sotah* 9a and *Num. Rab.* 15.13, the gates of the Temple were hidden in the earth to protect them from destruction.

The *Treatise of the Vessels* shows awareness of a number of these traditions and other traditions about the Temple treasures, although it is difficult in most cases to demonstrate a direct literary connection with these sources. The common elements may also come from shared oral traditions, independent exegesis of scriptural passages, and the deployment of obvious folkloric motifs about hidden treasure. The list of treasures in the *Treatise of the Vessels* is nearly comprehensive and includes everything given in the other sources and more, apart from the keys to the Temple, the capitals of the two pillars, and the chest of the Philistines. The notion that the Levites were involved with the hiding of the treasures appears often in the *Treatise of the Vessels* (e.g., in §§oJ and IV 14) and is paralleled

16. This is according to the versification by S. E. Robinson in "4 Baruch," *OTP* 2:418-19. The same passages are given as 3:6-8, 14 and 4:1-4 by Jens Herzer in *4 Baruch (Paraleipomena Jeremiou)* (Writings from the Greco-Roman World 22; Atlanta, Ga.: Society of Biblical Literature, 2005), 7-11.

17. Rabbinic variants of this legend of someone throwing the keys of the Temple into the sky appear in *'Abot R. Nat.* §1 (the chief priests) and *Lev. Rab.* 19.6 (King Jeconiah [i.e., Jehoiachin]).

18. On a related note, according to *m. Mid.* 1.6, the stones of the altar in the Second Temple which had been defiled during the persecution associated with the Maccabean revolt of 167-165 B.C.E. were hidden in one of the rooms in the Temple's Chamber of the Hearth (cf. 1 Macc 4:44-46).

in the rabbinic texts. We find the idea that the earth took some of the treasures in §III 12, paralleled in *2 Baruch*, *4 Baruch*, the *Coptic Jeremiah Apocryphon*, and rabbinic texts. The *Treatise of the Vessels* also reports with *2 Baruch* that angels were involved in the hiding of the treasures (§§VI, XII). Like a number of the other texts, the *Treatise* says that the treasures will not be revealed again until the messianic age (§§oJ, IX, XII).

The *Treatise of the Vessels* also alludes to other traditions about the Temple treasures which are not associated with their hiding. The first-century C.E. Jewish historian Flavius Josephus tells us that Solomon made ten thousand golden lampstands (*Ant.* 8.90) and the *Treatise* increases this number by a factor of ten in §IV 17, but the biblical text refers to only one (Exod 37:17-24). In general, the vast number of gold and silver furnishings and vessels, as well as priestly vestments, mentioned in the *Treatise of the Vessels* is paralleled by Josephus when he claims these items numbered in the tens of thousands (*Ant.* 8.89, 91-94). And the claim in the *Treatise* XII that the twelve stones on the breastpiece of the high priest used to shine is similar to the claim of Josephus that these stones and two sardonyx stones that held the breastpiece together shone at times to give oracular revelations (*Ant.* 3.214-18).[19] A very fragmentary Dead Sea Scroll similarly reports that stones associated with the priestly vestment were lit with tongues of fire (1Q29; 4Q376).

The reference to "the trees of the gold of Parvaim" in *Treatise* §VII is ultimately derived from 2 Chr 3:6, which says that Solomon used "gold of Parvaim" in the Temple. Related to this is the reference in the *Treatise* to "sycamore trees of gold on which all kinds of dainties hang" (§X). The rabbinic literature also takes an interest in gold of Parvaim, describing it as one of seven types of gold and reporting traditions that it was as red as blood and that it yielded fruit (*Num. Rab.* 12.4; 13.18; *y. Yoma* 4,41d). There is also a tradition in *b. Yoma* 39b that the biblical House of the Forest of Lebanon (1 Kgs 7:2; 10:17, 21//2 Chr 9:16, 20) was Solomon's garden of fruit-bearing golden trees. And the traditions about numerous precious stones and pearls decorating the Temple treasures in *Treatise* §§IV, V, VI, VII, XI are paralleled in a general way by traditions about the adornment of Jerusalem and the borders of Israel with precious stones and the giant pearl set aside for a gate of the Temple at the time of the end (*Pesiq. Rab Kah.* 18.4-6; *Midr. Psalms* 87.2-3).

The power of King Solomon over demons and spirits is also mentioned briefly in Treatise §IX. These powers are well known in Jewish and Christian traditions going back to antiquity (e.g., Wis 7:17, 20; Josephus, *Ant.* 8.45-49; the *Testament of Solomon*; *b. Git.* 68a-68b). But I am unaware of any other text that associates Solomon with soothsayers or that claims that the demons brought him musical instruments.

The Copper Scroll

Another ancient document, an exceedingly mysterious one, is of potential relevance for our understanding of the *Treatise of the Vessels*. This is the Copper Scroll (3Q15), a twelve-column Hebrew document incised on copper sheets and discovered in Qumran Cave 3 in 1952.[20] Its script dates it to sometime between the mid-first century and the early second century C.E. The Copper Scroll is a list of sixty or more treasures hidden in the vicinity of Jerusalem, Qumran, and elsewhere, and it contains a number of striking parallels to

---

19. Although the *Josippon* (*Yosifon*) includes material from Josephus, I can find none of these details in it.

20. The most comprehensive technical treatment of the Copper Scroll is Lefkovits, *The Copper Scroll*. For a brief nontechnical introduction and translation see Wolters, *The Copper Scroll*.

the *Treatise of the Vessels. Treatise* §II 11 reports that those who hid the Temple treasures "wrote them on a tablet (or with B, 'tablets') of bronze (only J)," bringing to mind the Copper Scroll itself.[21] Likewise, the Copper Scroll mentions both "books" (3Q15 vi 5; viii 3) and perhaps "writings" (3Q15 v 7; xi 1, 4, 11, 15; xii 11), the latter apparently written accounts of specific treasures, in turn bringing to mind the *Treatise of the Vessels* and its claim that Ezra wrote down the traditions in it in Babylon (§III 14). Like the *Treatise of the Vessels*, the Copper Scroll refers frequently to "vessels" or "implements" (the word is the same in Hebrew) (3Q15 ii 6, 8; iii 9; viii 3; x 11; xi 1, 4, 10, 14; xii 8), including vessels or implements of gold or silver (3Q15 iii 2-3). The name Kohlit (vocalization uncertain) is associated with several locations in the Copper Scroll (3Q15 i 9; ii 13; iv 1?, 11-12; xii 11-12). The B prologue (0B 3) mentions the similar name, Ein Kohel, the name of a spring that it seems to place in the vicinity of Mount Carmel. The name Ein Kotel ("Spring of the Wall"?) also appears in J §X, and this may be a copyist's error for Ein Kohel.[22] Both texts list libation-jars (3Q15 iii 4 and *Treatise* §I 8) and (priestly?) vestments and clothing (3Q15 iii 9; xi 4, 10 and *Treatise* §§I 9; VIII). Both texts list large amounts of gold and silver, some identified as vessels and other items and some not. The amounts in the *Treatise* are truly vast and the amounts in the Copper Scroll have generally been interpreted as being on a similar scale, but Lefkovits has proposed that a key abbreviation in the Scroll which has been taken to refer to "talents" (weighing approximately 75 pounds) actually refers to "silver *karsh*," a unit of weight only 1/300th that of a talent. If so, the hoards of treasure in the Copper Scroll amount to much less than had been thought.

The purpose of the Copper Scroll remains stridently debated. For some decades after its discovery it was widely accepted to be a collection of legends and folklore, in part due to Milik's comparison with the *Treatise of the Vessels*. More recently the dry factual nature of the document and the inscribing of it on durable metal sheets, along with elements of the contents, has convinced virtually all scholars that it describes a real treasure. But which treasure? The collected resources of the quasi-monastic (Essene?) community at Qumran? The treasures of the Jerusalem Temple, hidden at the time of the Roman siege of Jerusalem? Contributions meant for the Temple but which were not delivered before its destruction? Treasures collected during the Bar Kokhba Revolt of 132-135 C.E.? All these possibilities have been argued. If the Copper Scroll is a record of hidden Temple treasures, it does constitute a remarkable parallel to the *Treatise of the Vessels*, and the *Treatise* can be

---

21. Weitzman notes that in the first century C.E., Pausanius (*Descr.* 4.20.4; 4.26.3-8) tells a legend of a tin scroll of sacred mysteries hidden in a bronze jar and buried by the southern Greek Messenians in a time of crisis. The preservation of the scroll led the gods to bring the Messenians back to their territory from exile and to reveal the location of the buried jar so that it could be recovered. Weitzman takes this not as evidence that the treasures of the Copper Scroll are legendary (see below), but that the genuine treasures recorded in it were freighted with a mythic significance associated with divine preservation and return from exile.

22. It is difficult to know what to make of the similarity in the names Kohlit and Ein Kohel. Milik proposes that Ein Kohel should be identified with a site known as Wadi Ein es-Siah, which seems to fit the geographical description ("Le roleau de cuivre de Qumrân [3Q 15]," 355-56). The Babylonian Talmud mentions a "Kohlit that is in the wilderness" (*b. Qid.* 66a). This may be related to the place(s) mentioned in the Copper Scroll and/or in the *Treatise*. There was also a type of hyssop plant that was known as "Kohlit" (*m. Neg.* 14.6; *m. Parah* 11.7; *Sifre Num* 129; *b. Hull.* 62b; *b. Suk.* 13a), and one could imagine some connection between it and those places. But the Hebrew root of both names means a color used in women's eye makeup (cf. Ezek 23:40), related to the word "kohl," and such a color designation ("blue" in modern Hebrew) might appear in any number of place names.

understood as a wildly imaginative collection of legends which are embodied in a fictional listing of Temple treasures that shares essentially the same genre as the Copper Scroll. Nevertheless, there are great differences between the documents. First, the unadorned documentary style of the Copper Scroll contrasts strongly with the legendary tone of the *Treatise of the Vessels*. Second, the Copper Scroll refers to the treasures of the Second Temple, not the First, and so does not include the Ark of the Covenant or the two golden cherubim that shared its place in the Holy of Holies in the Temple, presumably because they were lost to the Babylonians when Solomon's Temple was sacked. Moreover, the Copper Scroll makes no mention of the golden lampstand, the golden table for the display of the bread of the presence, or the silver trumpets, key treasures which were borne off by the Romans and which are portrayed in the visual representation of the triumphal procession of Vespasian which now survives on the Arch of Titus in Rome and of which procession we have an eyewitness description from Josephus in *J. W.* 7.120-62. There is no evidence to indicate that the *Treatise of the Vessels* has any direct connection with the Copper Scroll.

The Fate of the Temple Treasures

Interest in the fate of the Temple treasures continues to the present. Besides entertaining fiction such as *Raiders of the Lost Ark*, a scholarly case has recently been argued that the furnishings from the Second Temple mentioned above which were looted by the Romans (the golden lampstand, the golden table, and the silver trumpets) may have survived even to the present. Archaeologist Sean Kingsley has traced the references to these objects in the ancient literature.[23] Josephus tells us that the golden lampstand and the golden table were deposited in the Temple of Peace, which Vespasian built in Rome after his Triumph (*J. W.* 7.148-62). Rome was sacked by the Vandals in 455 C.E. and the Byzantine historian Theophanes the Confessor (c. 760-817) reports in his *Chronographia* that king Gaiseric brought back with him to Carthage the Jewish vessels that Titus had taken to Rome. One might reasonably doubt this claim, written well over three centuries after the fact, but the sixth-century historian Procopius provides us with eyewitness confirmation that when the Vandals had been conquered in turn by Belisarius, the general of the Emperor Justinian, the Jewish treasures brought to Rome by Titus and others were displayed in the Triumph of Belisarius in 534 (*Wars* 4.9.4-6). But, superstitious about the doom that followed all those who kept these treasures, Justinian had them sent to "the sanctuaries of the Christians in Jerusalem" rather than keeping them in Constantinople. The late-seventh-century *Khuzistan Chronicle* places the treasures in the Church of the Holy Sepulcher, but also reports that the Sassanian invaders who sacked Jerusalem in 614, although they supposedly found the casket of Joseph of Arimathea, failed to find the Temple treasures. Kingsley speculates that Modestus, the contemporary acting Patriarch of Jerusalem, had hidden the treasures at the Monastery of St. Theodosius at Deir Dosi, where he had been the superior, and that perhaps they are still buried there on what is today the territory of the West Bank. But even if we accept the claims of all these various historians, who may have had their own reasons to exaggerate and augment the facts in the interest of the reputations of their patrons, we have no evidence for what happened to the Temple treasures after they came to Jerusalem in the 500s.

23. Kingsley, *God's Gold*.

Bibliography

Bachrach, R. Naftali Hertz. *Emek Halachah.* Amsterdam, 1648.

Crossan, John Dominic. *Finding Is the First Act: Trove Folktales and Jesus' Treasure Parable.* SBL Semeia Supplements 9. Philadelphia, Pa.: Fortress/Missoula, Mont.: Scholars Press, 1979.

Davila, James R. "Scriptural Exegesis in the *Treatise of the Vessels*, A Legendary Account of the Lost Temple Treasures." Pages 45-61 in *With Letters of Light: Studies in the Dead Sea Scrolls, Early Jewish Apocalypticism, Magic, and Mysticism in Honor of Rachel Elior.* Edited by Daphna V. Arbel and Andrei A. Orlov. Ekstasis: Religious Experience from Antiquity to the Middle Ages 2. Berlin: De Gruyter, 2010.

Dawood, N. J. "Aladdin and the Enchanted Lamp." Pages 165-236 in *Tales from the Thousand and One Nights.* Rev. ed. London: Penguin, 1973.

Flusser, David. *Sefer Yosifon.* 2 vols. Jerusalem: Bialik Institute, 1980-81.

Ginzberg, Louis. *The Legends of the Jews.* 7 vols. Philadelphia, Pa.: Jewish Publication Society of America, 1936-47.

Grelot, P. "Parwaïm: des Chroniques à l'Apocryphe de la Genèse." *VT* 11 (1961): 30-38, esp. pp. 37-38.

Higbie, Carolyn. *The Lindian Chronicle and the Greek Creation of Their Past.* Oxford: Oxford University Press, 2003.

Jellinek, Adolph. "Tractat von den Tempelgeräten." *BHM*, 2:xxvi-xxvii, 88-91.

Kingsley, Sean. *God's Gold: The Quest for the Lost Temple Treasure of Jerusalem.* London: John Murray, 2006.

Lefkovits, Judah K. *The Copper Scroll—4Q315: A Reevaluation.* STDJ 25. Leiden: Brill, 2000.

Milik, J. T. "Notes d'épigraphie et de topographie palestiniennes." *RB* 66 (1959): 550-75, esp. pp. 567-75.

__________. "Le roleau de cuivre de Qumrân (3Q 15): traduction et commentaire topographique." *RB* 66 (1959): 321-57, esp. pp. 355-56.

Shaya, Josephine. "The Greek Temple as Museum: The Case of the Legendary Treasure of Athena from Lindos." *American Journal of Archaeology* 109 (2005): 423-42.

Weitzman, Steven P. "Myth, History, and Mystery in the Copper Scroll." Pages 239-55 in *The Idea of Biblical Interpretation. Essays in Honor of James L. Kugel.* Edited by Hindy Najman and Judith H. Newman. JSJSup 83. Leiden: Brill, 2004.

Wolters, Al. *The Copper Scroll: Overview, Text and Translation.* Sheffield, England: Sheffield Academic Press, 1996.

The Treatise of the Vessels (*Massekhet Kelim*)

The hiding of the Temple treasures on Mount Carmel

(oB) And he said to me:
2 *Write this as a memorial* for the children of Israel, for Exod 17:14
it has been written fourfold in holiness and purity, written
once on the skin of a ram that is pure. And he[a] commanded Exod 25:5
the children of Israel when they went to 3 my sanctuary and
they hid them on Mount Carmel. For he set them apart[b] in Amos 9:3
the year three thousand, three hundred, and thirty-one of
creation. Josephus, *Ant.* 8.61; *S. 'Olam Rab.* 15, 27
Ein Kohel[c] is a very great and deep valley. 4 And in it is 3Q15 i 9; ii 13; iv 1, 11-12; xii 11-12; *m. Neg.* 14.6; *b. Qidd.* 66a
a spring of good water and it is called by the name Ein Ko-
hel because there (on) its east is a very high, exalted, slop-
ing mountain and on its top is hewn a stopped-up gate. And
they say that 5 hidden there are the vessels[d] of the sanctuary Dan 1:2
in order to appear to the sons of Israel who seek the glory of
our God to sigh (over) our being steeped[e] (in) our iniquities. Prov 25:2

The men who hid the treasures

(oJ) Five 6 great righteous men wrote these recited traditions.
And they are Shimmur the Levite, Hezekiah, Zedekiah, 2 Kgs 20:13//Isa 39:2; *b. Pesah.* 56a | *b. 'Erub.* 61b
Haggai the prophet, and Zechariah son of Iddo the proph- Ezra 5:1; 6:14; Hag 1:1; 2:6-9; Zech 1:1; 11:13
et. And they hid the vessels of the sanctuary and the riches
of the 7 treasuries which were in Jerusalem. And they shall

---

a. The "he" of this sentence and the next appears to be God. If so, it may be that "my sanctuary" in this sentence should be emended to (the graphically similar) "his sanctuary." If the revealing agent in this paragraph is meant to be the angel of Ezekiel 40-48 (see Introduction), it would be unusual for an angel to refer to "my sanctuary."

b. The word translated "set apart" in this document normally means to "sanctify" or "make holy." But often in this text the sense is clearly that the objects are being set aside for their protection (cf. 2 Sam 8:11 and 1 Chr 26:26-28).

c. See the Introduction for a discussion of this place name.

d. The same Hebrew word is translated "vessels" and "implements" throughout as context requires.

e. The meaning of this word is unclear.

not be revealed[a] until the day of the coming of the Messiah son of David—swiftly, in our days, amen,[b] and so may it be favorable![c]

The hidden implements

2 Macc 2:4-8; 2 *Bar.* 6:7; *m. Ta'an.* 4.6 | Exod 25:9

Exod 36:35; 2 Chr 3:14 | Exod 37:17-24; Num 8:1-4; 2 Chr 4:7 | Exod 37:1-6; *m. Sheqal.* 6.1-2

Exod 39:30; *Cop. Jer. Apoc.* 28 | Exod 39:30; Exod 39:8-21 | Num 10:1-10 | Exod 37:7-9

Exod 38:1-7; 40:6, 29; Lev 4:7; 1 Kgs 7:48

Exod 38:3; Num 4:14; 2 Chr 4:16 | Exod 37:16; Num 4:7; 1 Chr 28:17; 3Q15 iii 4 | Exod 37:10-16; 1 Kgs 7:48; 2 Chr 29:18 | Exod 38:18

Exod 38:30; 1 Kgs 8:64; 2 Chr 4:1; Ezek 9:2

Exod 39:1-31; Lev 16:1-34; 23:26-32; 25:9; 3Q15 iii 9; xi 4, 10; Josephus, *Ant.* 3.159-78; *m. Yoma* 7.5; *Cop. Jer. Apoc.* 28

Exod 39:25-26

Exod 4:17; Num 17:10 [26]; *m. 'Abot* 5.6; *b. Yoma* 52b | Exod 16:33-34

(I) These are the implements that were set apart and[d] hidden when the sanctuary was destroyed[e]: the tabernacle; the curtain; the holy lampstand; the Ark of [8]the Testimony; the plate of gold and the holy crown of Aaron the priest; the breastpiece of judgment; the silver trumpets; the cherubim; the holocaust altar; the curtain of the Tent of Meeting; the forks[f]; the libation-jars[g]; [9]the table[h]; the screen of the gate; the bronze altar; the holy[i] clothes for Aaron[j] which were the vestment of the High Priest on the Day of Atonement; the bells and the pomegranates[k] that were on the skirts of the robe; the holy [10]vessels that Moses made on Mount Sinai by the holy commandments[l]; the rod; and the jar of manna.

The recording of the hidden treasures on a tablet

(II) These are the holy vessels and the vessels of the sanctuary that were[m] in Jerusalem and in every (other) [11]place. Shimmur the Levite and his companions[n] wrote them on a tablet[o] of bronze[p], along with all the vessels of the most holy sanctu-

---

a. "shall not be revealed" J; "shall not be redeemed" B

b. This phrase alludes to a passage in the Jewish liturgical prayer the Kaddish:

"May he establish his kingdom
[and make his redemption blossom
and bring near the destined time of his Messiah]
in your lifetime and in your days
and in the lifetime of the whole house of Israel
in haste and at a near time. And say, Amen."

(The bracketed lines are not found in all versions.) I am grateful to Richard Bauckham for the reference.

c. "—swiftly ... favorable!" J; omit B

d. "the implements that were set apart and" J; "the implements of the sanctuary that were" B

e. "when the sanctuary was destroyed" J; omit B

f. "the forks" J; the text of B is unreadable

g. "the libation-jars" J; omit B

h. "the table" J; + "and its implements" B

i. "holy" J; omit B

j. "for Aaron" J; omit B

k. "and the pomegranates" J; omit B

l. "by the holy commandments" J; "according to the holy word/order" B

m. "that were" J; omit B

n. "companions" J; "companion" B

o. "a tablet" J; "tablets" B

p. "of bronze" J; omit B

ary which Solomon the son of David made. And in the place of Shimmur there were with him Hezekiah, [12]Zedekiah, Haggai the prophet, and Zechariah the son of Berechiah son of Iddo the prophet.

1 Kings 6-7; 2 Chronicles 3-4

The implements the earth took

(III) These are the implements[a] the earth took: the holy bars and pegs and the rings; and the pillars of [13]the courtyard. These are the vessels: one hundred twenty myriad silver basins; five myriad basins of fine[b] gold; sixty myriad (basins) of fine gold; and one hundred twenty [14]myriad and five of silver. These (men) and the rest of the prophets who were with them and Ezra the priest-scribe wrote these recited traditions in Babylon.

4 Bar. 3:6-11, 18-20; *Cop. Jer. Apoc.* 28; *Num. Rab.* 15.13; *b. Sotah* 9a

Exod 36:31-34; 38:20 | Exod 38:9-20

3Q15 iii 2-3; xii 6-7; Josephus, *Ant.* 8.89, 91

Num 7:84-85

Ezra 7:11

The treasures hidden by the Levites in Babylon

(IV) One hundred and thirty of the Levites were killed and a hundred escaped with Shimmur the Levite and his companions.[c] They hid fifty [15]myriad platters of fine gold and a hundred and twenty myriad of silver; fifty myriad libation-jars of fine gold and one hundred twenty myriad of silver; and on every single libation-jar were five pearls[d] (and) the like of fine stones. And the value of every single fine stone was a hundred talents[e] of gold. The whole value of [16]the pearls was two hundred thousand talents of gold. Forty-six trumpets of gold. All these things they concealed and hid in a tower in the land of Babylon in a city and its name is Bagdat[f]. [17]Ten myriad lampstands of fine gold and seven lamps on every single one; twenty-six fine stones were on every single lampstand. As for each one of the pearls, its value was unknown. [18]And between every single stone were two hundred stones; likewise their value was unknown.

Exod 37:16

Num 7:84-85

Exod 37:16; Num 4:7; 1 Chr 28:17; Josephus, *Ant.* 8.89

Let. Aris. 73-77

Gen 11:4-5; *b. Sanh.* 109a | *b. Ber.* 54b?; *b. Ket.* 7b; *b. Qidd.* 71b

Exod 37:17-24; Josephus, *Ant.* 8.90

The gold and silver of Solomon and David hidden in a cistern

(V) Seventy-seven tables of gold, and their gold was from the walls of the Garden of Eden that was revealed to Solomon,[g] and they radiated like the [19]radiance of the sun and moon, which radiate at the height of the world. And as for all the sil-

2 Chr 4:8, 19; Josephus, *Ant.* 8.89

Gen 2:8; Ezek 28:13, 16

---

a. "the implements" J; "implements of implements" B

b. "fine" J; omit B

c. "One hundred ... companions" J; omit B

d. "pearls" J; omit B

e. "talents" J; "talent" B

f. "and ... Bagdat" J; omit B. See the Introduction for a discussion of this name.

g. "Solomon" J; the meaning in B is unclear

Gen 1:1-31 ver and gold that was in the world in the six[a] days of creation
2 Kgs 24:18 until the day that Zedekiah became king[b], they [*sic*] were not
equal to the valuation [20]of the gold that was overlaid[c] on the
1 Kgs 6:20-22; Josephus, *Ant.* 8.68, 75; *m. Mid.* 4.1 Temple of the House inside and outside. There was no reckoning and no measure and no limit and no weight to this gold that was overlaid on the Temple and on the surface of [21]the Temple. And also seven[d] thousand talents of gold. All these they concealed[e] and hid in the treasure of the cistern.

The temple stones hidden from before Nebuchadnezzar

And fine stone in which the Temple was built, and three
courses of costly [22]stones and one course of almug-wood
1 Kgs 7:9-12; 10:11-12//2 Chr 9:10-11 and the three courses were of fine stones. And the length of
one fine stone was seven[f] cubits and its width was five cubits
m. Kelim 17.9? [23]that David established. And the length of one pearl was ten
cubits. All these David prepared for the great House for Solo-
1 Chr 29:1-5 mon[g] his son.

(VI) The number of stones was forty-six thousand and the number of pearls was the II [1]same.[h] With all these the Temple was built: three courses and one course of almug-wood, and they were overlaid with fine [2]gold and set in the building. All these the worthy who were in Israel concealed
from before Nebuchadnezzar, and the almug-wood [3]radiated
Dan 12:3 like the radiance of the firmament.

The pearls and precious metals of David and Solomon hidden in Borsif

(VII) The fine stones and pearls and silver and gold[i] that King David set aside for the great House were a thousand thousand talents of silver and a hundred thousand talents of gold. And (there were) the trees of the gold of Parvaim which
used to produce fruit of six hundred and sixty-six myriad tal-
1 Kgs 10:14 ents of fine gold that was underneath the Tree of Life in the
Gen 2:8-9; Ezek 28:13; 31:8-9, 16, 18; 2 Chr 3:6; Holy Garden. All these were revealed to Hilkiah the scribe,
Num. Rab. 12.4; 13.18; *y. Yoma* 4,41d; *b. Yoma* 39b and he transmitted them to Shamshiel the angel, who shall

a. "in the six" J; "from the six" B

b. "king" B; "king and" B

c. "overlaid" J; omit B

d. "seven" J; the reading of B is incomprehensible but is perhaps a corruption of "seventy-seven"

e. "they concealed" B; the reading of J is corrupt

f. "seven" J; "seventy" B

g. "for Solomon" J; "for completion by" B

h. Plaque I of B ends here. The first three lines of plaque II are from Starcky's transcription.

i. Starcky's transcription of B col. II ceases here and recommences in §IX.

keep them until the King, David, shall arise, and he shall transmit into his hand the silver and the gold, with the gold that Solomon volunteered, and with them talents of gold and fine stones that are without price. All these were hidden and made secret and kept from before the army of the Chaldeans in the place that is called Borsif[a].

2 Chr 4:19-22

Gen. Rab. 38.11; *b. Shab.* 36a; *b. Sukkah* 34a; *b. Qidd.* 72a; *b. Sanh.* 109a

The curtains and vestments hidden by the worthy

(VIII) The seven curtains of gold in which was [*sic*] collected twelve thousand talents of gold and the vestments of the Levites and their belts—twelve thousand vestments, and the ephod of the High Priest who used to minister in them, and his robe, apart from the seventy thousand vestments of the priests and their belts and their turbans and their drawers—all these that David made for them for Israel's benefit. And the worthy took them in secret, for there was revealed to them all this usage to be theirs for the future for Israel's benefit.

Exod 39:27-29; 3Q15 iii 9; xi 4, 10

Exod 39:2-7; Josephus, *Ant.* 8.93; *m. Yoma* 7.5

Exod 39:22-26

Ezek 44:17-18; Josephus, *Ant.* 3.151-58; *m. Yoma* 7.5

David's lyres and lutes hidden at the Spring of Zedekiah

(IX) A thousand lyres that David made and seven thousand lutes for Israel's benefit; cymbals for song and for praisesongs and for thanksgivings and for psalmody to the God of Israel which were given to Moses from Sinai. And inscribed upon them from beneath the feet of the throne of glory is a sapphire stone (in the) likeness of a throne. And the lyres were of almug-wood overlaid with fine gold; and five stones were upon every single lyre which the soothsayers, the satyr-demons, and the spirits who were subject to Solomon used to bring. And on every single lyre was a bell of burnished bronze from before the throne of glory and one fine stone, precious and outstanding, which Moses hewed out at Mount Sinai from beneath the throne of glory that was on the sapphire stone. Everything was treasured up and hidden at the Spring of Zedekiah, for the worthy knew in council that they could fall—heaven forbid!—into the hands of a foe who would hate Israel,[b] for they did not make use of these vessels except for Israel's benefit. And Baruch and Zedekiah hid them so that the Chaldeans could not make use of them—heaven forbid!—and they stored them up until the day that Israel returns to their former state. And they shall receive glory and

1 Chr 15:16; 25:1; Josephus, *Ant.* 8.94; *m. Sukkah* 5.4; *m. Mid.* 2.6

Jer 17:12 | Exod 24:10; Ezek 1:26; 10:1

1 Kgs 10:11-12//2 Chr 9:10-11

Lev 17:7; Isa 2:6; 13:21; 34:14; Jer 27:9; 2 Chr 11:15; Wis 7:17, 20; *b. Git.* 68a-68b

Exod 24:10

2 Kgs 25:7

Jer 32:12-14; 45:1-5

a. That is "Borsippa," an ancient Mesopotamian city southwest of Babylon on the east bank of the Euphrates River.

b. The text of Starcky's copy of B recommences in the midst of the word "Israel." These are the last three lines of B, but the line numbers are not indicated in Milik's edition.

the preciousness of (the) world when there is found for them
Ezek 34:23 a man—David son of David is his name—and there shall be
revealed to him the silver and the gold when all Israel shall be
gathered together[a] and they shall make a complete pilgrim-
Isa 66:20 age to Jerusalem. Amen.

The metal objects hidden in Ein Kotel

(X) And these are the weights of the silver that was hidden
in Ein Kotel[b] by the hands of Baruch and Zedekiah: one
hundred twenty myriad talents of silver; and one hundred
sixty myriad of fine silver; two hundred myriad vessels of
Exod 38:3; 1 Kgs 7:45; 2 Chr 4:11 bronze (and) pots of fine bronze; one hundred ten myriad
Ezek 40:43 of iron; hooks that do not contain cast metal and things cast
2 Chr 4:9? of bronze surrounding the gate of bronze; cherubim that are
Exod 37:7-9?; 1 Kgs 7:29?; Ezek 41:17-20, 25? | beyond weighing; lavers of bronze that are beyond weighing;
Exod 38:8; 1 Kgs 7:38; 2 Chr 4:6; *m. Mid.* 3.6 three thousand griddles of fine gold; seventy tables of fine
Lev 2:5 gold from beneath the Tree of Life that stands in the Garden
2 Chr 4:8 of Holiness, upon which was the bread of the Presence —
Lev 24:5-9 there is no valuation of their price; sycamore trees of gold on
which all kinds of dainties hang, and they are of refined gold
1 Chr 28:11-19 that David, King of Israel, refined. Zedekiah hid all these.

The treasures of gold and silver hidden in Babylon

(XI) And the treasuries of gold and silver from the days of
David and until Zedekiah and until when Israel were exiled
to Babylon: a myriad myriads of shields of gold and of silver
1 Kgs 10:17//2 Chr 9:15-16 beyond measure; 1,353 thousand pearls and fine stones, all
Jer 51:12, 44, 58 these treasured up and hidden in the wall of Babylon and at
Tel Baruq underneath the great willow that is in Babylon on
Ps 137:2 whose (branches) they used to hang their lyres; and from the
1 Kgs 7:2; 10:17, 21//2 Chr 9:16, 20 House of the Forest of Lebanon they took gold to the measure of 1,009 thousand kors.[c] And all the prophets and the
sages and the scribes could not calculate the wealth and the
glory that used to be in Jerusalem.

The twelve stones hidden by Heleq

(XII) And in addition twelve fine stones were transmitted by
the hand of[d] Heleq son of Shimmur the Levite, by his hand
to preserve them and to return them to the tribes, those on
Exod 39:10-14 which the names of the tribes were engraved, which used to
1Q29; 4Q376; Josephus, *Ant.* 3.214-18 shine over the heads of the tribes, increasingly outstanding

a. The text of B ends here.

b. Milik emends to Ein Kohel, based on the place name in oB. See the Introduction for discussion.

c. A kor is a measure of capacity rather than weight and is roughly equivalent to 6.5 bushels.

d. "by the hand of"; emending the corrupt text of J

and precious in their value, vying with one another. And no king or prophet or man knew in which place these were hidden, except Heleq son of Shimmur the Levite.

The future revelation of the treasures

And as for the rest of the riches and the glory that was [*sic*] in Jerusalem, Shamshiel the angel took it. And Shimmur and Heleq and their companions the Levites showed it again to Michael. And Gabriel and Sariel[a] concealed the vessels until a righteous king should arise for Israel, and there is nothing more except that both groups swore a great oath that the vessels should not be revealed until David son of David should arise, and they shall deliver into his hands all silver, gold, and pearls that they treasured up in the hour that the exiled of Israel are gathered from the four winds of the world and they shall ascend in greatness and great ascent up to the Land of Israel. And at that time a great river shall go forth from the most holy House, whose name is Gihon. And it shall flow as far as *the great and fearsome desert* and shall mingle with the Euphrates River and at once all the vessels shall ascend and reveal themselves.

Dan 10:13, 21; 12:1 | Dan 8:16; 9:21 | 1 En. 9:1

Judg 21:5

Ezek 37:9; Matt 24:31//Mk 13:27

Gen 2:13; Ezek 47:1; Joel 4:18 [Evv 3:18]; Zech 14:8; Rev 22:1-2; *m. Mid.* 2.6

Deut 8:15

a. "Sariel"; emending with Milik, J reads "all Israel"

The Seventh Vision of Daniel
A new translation and introduction

by Sergio La Porta

The *Seventh Vision of Daniel* (henceforth, *7Dan*) is a lengthy vision composed in the late fifth century which predicts the destruction of the Roman Empire, the coming of the Antichrist, and the end of the world. The work is preserved only in Armenian and is known from five manuscripts. Although the work was originally written in Greek, the title was attached to the text in its Armenian version. As the biblical book of Daniel frequently appears divided into six visions in Armenian Bibles, this extra-biblical vision was considered the seventh.[1] The early date of the original composition of this text renders it important for our understanding of the development of the Daniel *apocalyptica*.[2]

Contents[3]

7Dan begins with a brief account of the circumstances of Daniel's vision. It asserts that three years after all the other visions had been granted to Daniel, the Lord sent the angel Gabriel to reveal the following vision to Daniel. The initial vision foretells disasters that will befall various cities and provinces in the eastern Empire as well as Rome. Following this prophecy, the text presents an overview of Byzantine history from the city's founding up until the reign of Zeno. Although the identity of many of the emperors and a number of the enigmatic historical references have been deciphered, many allusions remain obscure. The author explicitly mentions the Emperors Theodosius II and Marcian, and refers to Theodosius I through a pun on his name.

The author depicts the reign of Theodosius II as a time of prosperity for the Empire, but asserts that the first problems will originate at this time. The "groanings" mentioned are a likely reference to the beginnings of the Christological controversies, to which the author refers more explicitly during the reign of Marcian. From his comments, it is clear that the author of *7Dan* was a supporter of the decision at Chalcedon.

The historical narrative is presented in greater detail beginning with the reign of Leo I to whom the text refers as "the beast." Leo I himself is praised as a strong ruler, but the text predicts that many catastrophes will befall Byzantium during his reign. The author describes the wars between both parts of the Empire and the Goths and Huns in allegorical terms of beasts, dogs, pups, lions, and dragons. He may refer to Gaiseric's attack on Rome in 455 and his defeat of Imperial forces in 468. The author devotes much time to the

---

1. Kalemkiar, "Die siebente Vision," 111; Macler, "L'apocalypse arménienne," 289; DiTommaso, *The Book of Daniel*, 101 and citations in n. 48.

2. On the term *apocalyptica*, see DiTommaso, "The Early Christian Daniel Apocalyptica."

3. See also the summary in DiTommaso, *The Book of Daniel*, 102-3.

intrigues of Aspar the Alan, Leo I's *magister militum*, and Leo I's eventual defeat of this powerful personage.

While relating these events, the author also first introduces the reader to Zeno and Basiliscus. The focus of the text then turns to the rise of Zeno and his accession to the throne. Subsequently, the text details the revolts of Basiliscus and Illus that the Emperor Zeno faced during his reign.

At this point, the author shifts from history to prophecy and predicts what will happen to the Empire before the arrival of the Antichrist. The text evokes natural disasters and the breakdown of society, but then returns to the historical figures of Verina and Zeno. The author, however, incorrectly predicts Zeno's murder at the hands of a certain Plakitas. Following the death of Zeno, there will be a time of great violence and warfare during the reign of the fictional ruler Orloghios who should be identified with the king Olibos in the *Oracle of Baalbek*.[4] *7Dan* specifically mentions the destruction of Bithynia and Nicomedia during this period preceding the coming of the Antichrist, suggesting that this may have been the locus of the text's original composition.[5]

The author then briefly describes the return of an Arian emperor or of an emperor named Arianos during whose reign Constantinople will mourn for itself. After the Arian Emperor, the Empire will be beset by violence and the uprisings of barbarians. Constantinople will be spared this violence, but it will suffer from a war that was allotted for it alone and a fiery column will appear stretching from heaven to earth. These events will introduce the coming of the Antichrist, whose physiognomy and character are described in detail. In particular, the author stresses that the Antichrist will imitate the actions of Christ himself, although in an illusory fashion. He will deceive many who will suffer from a devastating famine. They will try to flee but will be unable. God's chosen, however, who have been hiding in the hills and in caves will be able to flee. Nevertheless, the end will come only after the righteous suffer torments and the seven-hilled city is destroyed. To describe the aftermath of the destruction, the author evokes the image of a woman looking for fruit and embracing an olive-tree as found in the *Tiburtine Sibyl*.

The final paragraph of the vision provides a description of the destruction of the world and the last judgment. This portion of the text is finely constructed around a series of biblical quotes and allusions. It concludes with a short intercessory prayer that will be spoken by the righteous and is inspired by the Lord's Prayer and the Prayer of Manasseh.

Manuscripts and Versions

The Armenian version of *7Dan* is preserved in five known manuscripts. Three manuscripts were used by G. Kalemkiar for his *editio princeps* and German translation of the text. These are:[6]

- A. Lambeth Archiepiscopal Library, London, cod. arm. 1209. This manuscript is an Old Testament, written on paper by a priest Yovhannēs (John). Kalemkiar dates the

4. Cf. Paul Alexander's comments on the name, *Oracle of Baalbek*, 112 n. 50. *The Oracle of Baalbek* is translated in the current volume by Rieuwerd Buitenwerf under the title the *Tiburtine Sibyl* and the latter name for the document is used here from this point on.

5. See also DiTommaso, *The Book of Daniel*, 107.

6. The manuscript denotations are those of Kalemkiar, "Die siebente Vision," 112-13. Macler, "L'apocalypse arménienne," based his French translation of *7Dan* on Kalemkiar's edition.

manuscript to the twelfth century.[7] *7Dan* appears between 2 Esdras and Jeremiah. Kalemkiar judged this manuscript to preserve the best text-form of the vision.

- B. Vienna Mxit'arist Library, cod. 39. The manuscript is written on paper and was copied by the priest Margarē in 1337 for his brother, Lazar. The manuscript contains: 1. Proverbs; 2. Ecclesiastes; 3. Song of Songs; 4. Wisdom; 5. Job; 6. Twelve prophets; 7. Daniel, which is divided into 6 visions followed by *7Dan*, entitled *The Seventh Vision of Daniel about the end of the world.*
- C. Vienna Mxit'arist Library, cod. 14. This manuscript is a Bible with miniatures written by Yovhannēs, bishop of Ani, in 1375 for the Archbishop Manuel. The book of Daniel is divided into six visions, although the attribution of the fifth vision is not given. At the end of the book of Daniel is written, "End of the prophecy of Daniel"; it is immediately followed by *7Dan* bearing the ascription "Again, a vision on the end of the world."
- In addition to these three manuscripts, S. Yovsēp'eanc' published an additional two manuscripts in 1896.[8] These manuscripts have been identified with codices 1635 [D] and 935 [E] of the Venice Mxit'arist Library.[9]
- D was dated to the fifteenth century by Yovsēp'eanc' based on paleographic evidence. According to Yovsēp'eanc', this text is a copy of that found in the Bible housed at Lambeth Palace [A]. The text of D is damaged in parts. In the notes to the translation, I have placed the corresponding material missing in D in square brackets.
- E was included in a Bible dated to 1341. It nearly always agrees with BC, particularly with C. Yovsēp'eanc' has proposed emendations of the text of E in places; these have been noted.

J. Issaverdens based his English translation of *7Dan* on the versions published by Yovsēp'eanc'; he relied primarily on the text of D, but he also took the variants of E into account.[10]

I have investigated several other manuscripts that contain works attributed to Daniel in the National Institute of Ancient Manuscripts (Matenadaran) in Erevan, Armenia, but did not find any further copies of the text.

The original language of *7Dan* was unquestionably Greek.[11] This can be demonstrated on both contextual as well as linguistic grounds. The concerns of the text all revolve around the Roman Empire and, particularly, Constantinople and its environs; neither Armenia nor Armenians have any role in the text. The Armenian version contains at least one scribal error that could only occur at the Greek level of transmission;[12] two calques on

---

7. Kalemkiar mistakenly notes that the famous Armenian scholar, Yovhannēs Imastasēr Sarkawag (Deacon), mentioned by the copyist in the foreword to the Psalms lived in the thirteenth century; Yovhannēs died in 1129.

8. Yovsēp'eanc', *Uncanonical Books*, 237-50, 387-99.

9. Sargisean, *Studies*, 134-35. See also, Issaverdens, *The Uncanonical Writings*, 235; DiTommaso, *The Book of Daniel*, 101-102. I have assigned the designations D and E to these manuscripts.

10. Issaverdens, *Uncanonical Writings*, 249-65.

11. This judgment is also shared by, amongst others, Kalemkiar, "Die siebente Vision," 113-14; Macler, "L'apocalypse arménienne," 290; Brandes, "Apokalyptische Literatur," 308; DiTommaso, *The Book of Daniel*, 101.

12. The appearance of Carthage in the list of cities and provinces strikes one as odd as does its association with the Persians in *7Dan* 15; however, Paul Alexander has observed that Carthage and Chalcedon were often confused in Greek manuscripts (*Oracle*, p. 112 n. 48). He further remarks that in later texts,

Greek terms;[13] and a pun on the name of the Emperor Theodosius that is impossible in Armenian in *7Dan* 22. We may observe that exact textual parallels with the *Tiburtine Sibyl* also exist.[14] These are significant, as no known Armenian version of this text exists and so the shared material must derive from a Greek textual milieu.

Genre, Structure, and Prosody

The overall genre of *7Dan* conforms to that of a historical apocalypse that contains an *ex eventu* prophecy without an otherworldly journey and without personal eschatology.[15] The author, however, employs several other genres within the composition of the text.

We may note the introductory paragraph or preamble that calls the prophet to his vision. This invocation of Daniel to his vision by the angel Gabriel is common to a number of other texts; the closest parallel is the opening of the Slavonic version of *The Vision and Revelation of the Prophet Daniel.*[16]

It is clear that the prophecy of the cities and provinces (*7Dan* 2-17) comprises a discrete unit. This list of prophetic disasters of cities resembles those that occur in the *Sibylline Oracles.*[17] It is possible that a similar block of material had circulated independently prior to the composition of *7Dan* which the author of *7Dan* reworked within his text. The original oracular material may have included prophecies concerning the subjugation of the East by Rome and the subsequent transfer of its wealth to the West.[18] It is uncertain whether the preamble that includes the attribution to Daniel was originally part of this oracular material or whether the author of *7Dan* added it; the latter is more probable.

Within the "historical narrative" (*7Dan* 18-28), we can identify two general motifs: the first is the rise of horns and scepters, prominent in 18-26; the second, the wars of the beasts in 26-28. The portrayal of the historical tribulations of the Byzantine Empire in terms of a succession of scepters followed by series of battles between dogs, beasts, pups, lions, dragons, etc. is common to the Daniel *apocalyptica*. We may note that while the scepters return within the eschatological portion of the text—in 29-31 and 36-37—the beasts do not.

Chalcedon was considered the limit of Assyria. Thus, it is likely that "Carthage" in *7Dan* should be taken as Chalcedon, a confusion that could only have occurred in Greek; also noted by Pertusi, *Fine di Bisanzio*, 62-63 n. 183. We may further note that if we understand Carthage as Chalcedon, then all the cities and provinces mentioned in the list with the exception of Rome belong in the Eastern Empire.

13. These are: 1) "seven-hilled" (e.g., 3:1, 8:1, 18:1, etc.), *eawtʻnblur*, a calque on Gk. *heptalophos*. The *New Dictionary of the Armenian Language* does not have an entry for the word. The first recorded instance of its occurrence in Armenian is in a work by Aṙakʻel Bałišecʻi (c.1380-1454), *Middle Armenian Dictionary*, 1:205. The designation, however, appears in *Sibylline Oracles* 2 and 13 as well as in nearly all of the Byzantine Daniel *apocalyptica*; cf. the remark of DiTommaso, *The Book of Daniel*, 169 n. 337. 2) "having many seats," "polyhedrous" (17:4), *bazmanist*; a hapax in Arm., but cf. Gk. *polyedros*.

14. These have been noted in the footnotes to the translation; see, in particular, *7Dan* 38.

15. See Collins, "Introduction: Towards the Morphology of a Genre," 14.

16. In addition to biblical Dan 8:16, Gabriel addresses the prophet in the Slavonic version of *The Vision of the Prophet Daniel on the Emperors* and *The Vision of Daniel by the River Kebar* (Heb.). The angel Gabriel also plays a minor interpretative role in *The Apocalypse of Daniel on the Events after al-Muʻtamid* (Arabic); see Cook, "An Early Muslim Daniel Apocalypse," 88-91; see also DiTommaso, *The Book of Daniel*, 171.

17. For example, 3.162-95, 295-349, 401-88; 4.130-51; 5.52-92, 111-36, 286-327, 333-60; 7.40-63, 96-117; cf. also the remarks of Macler, "L'apocalypse arménienne," 291 n. 2.

18. In the *Sibylline Oracles*, Rome is often depicted as having taken the East's wealth which it will have to repay two-fold in the future; see, for example, 4.145-48 and 8.126-30. The prophecy in *7Dan* 3 refers in a general sense to the conquest of Asia by Rome, here, seven-hilled Babylon; *7Dan* 6 speaks of the many people who will flee Galatia to Rome; *7Dan* 7 apparently alludes to the capture of Karpathos by the Romans in 42 B.C.E.

In *7Dan* 28, 30, 32, 35, and particularly in 37, the author interweaves a series of "woes." In 37, we may also detect the motif of the "description of the Antichrist." The final paragraph includes an intercessory prayer modeled on the Lord's Prayer in Matthew 6 and, possibly, the Prayer of Manasseh.

The author of *7Dan* has often connected these different textual forms with transitional paragraphs or sentences using the technique of interlocking. The invocation flows naturally into the prophecy of the cities (*7Dan* 2); the motif of horns and scepters also fairly seamlessly transforms into the struggle between the beasts in 26. Similarly, the transition from "historical narrative" to eschatological prediction (29) is well constructed. Although these two paragraphs seemingly break up the narrative of the historical account, they cleverly add greater "authenticity" to the following prophecy. By inserting the prophetic material in this paragraph about the destruction of civil society between the "historical" account of Zeno's reign and the semi-historical/semi-prophetic prediction of his assassination at the hands of a certain Plakitas, the author of *7Dan* has fused history with prophecy. The reader may have felt certain at the beginning of 29 that he or she had entered the realm of prophecy, but the return of the historical figures of "the widow" and the "Salamander" in 30 clearly disrupt that sense and leave one wondering whether this paragraph is prophecy or history.

Date and Provenance

Scholars have dated *7Dan* anywhere from the fifth to the seventh centuries. Macler[19] and DiTommaso[20] proposed a fifth-century date of composition. Alexander suggested "about 500 AD" without providing his reasons;[21] he was followed by Brandes.[22] Kalemkiar[23] thought he could detect references to the reign of Heraclius and dated both the text and translation to the middle of the seventh century.[24] Zahn had already doubted this hypothesis, but also dated the text to the seventh century.[25] Bousset noted that "the history of Leo I, of Zeno and of the usurper Basiliscus is still clearly related," and acknowledged Zahn's hesitations about Kalemkiar's proposition, but still concluded that "the author of the Armenian Apocalypse of Daniel probably expected the end to come in the time of Heraclius."[26]

The original composition of *7Dan* is almost certainly to be dated to the reign of Zeno.[27] The figure of the Salamander who slays the dragon is to be identified with Zeno who defeated his mother-in-law's brother, the general Basiliscus.[28] The author predicts (*7Dan* 30) that the Salamander will face a revolt and will unsuccessfully try to flee. Zeno had faced several revolts during his reign and had fled for a time, thus such a prediction was not completely baseless. The author notes that the Salamander will then be killed by a certain

19. Macler, "L'apocalypse arménienne," 289.
20. DiTommaso, *The Book of Daniel*, 103.
21. Alexander, "Medieval Apocalypses," 1002.
22. Brandes, "Apocalyptische Literatur," 310.
23. Kalemkiar, "Die siebente Vision," 113-14.
24. Denis, *Introduction*, 312, cites both the opinion of Kalemkiar and Macler.
25. Zahn, "Paralipomena 4," 115-18.
26. Bousset, *The Antichrist Legend*, 68 and 78.
27. Although there is a possible reference to the Islamic invasions of the seventh century in *7Dan* 22, this should be considered a later interpolation. Cf. Macler, "L'apocalypse arménienne," 296 n. 1.
28. As witnessed in texts such as the *Physiologus*, salamanders were the legendary destroyers of basilisks and, hence, an appropriate designation for the Emperor.

Plakitas. As Zeno was not assassinated, this fact must be considered the author's own prophetic claim. This mistaken prophecy about Zeno's assassination provides a *terminus ante quem* of 491, the year of his death.

The *terminus post quem* may be established from the events noted in the reign of Zeno as between 484 and 488. The author refers to the defeat of Basiliscus which occurred in 477; he also alludes to the fall of the "youth" who helped Zeno/Salamander achieve victory and the death of the "widow." The "widow" is to be identified with Verina, Zeno's mother-in-law, who died in 484. The "youth" is likely to be identified with the general Illus who defected to Zeno's party. Illus himself, however, revolted in 483 or 484 and was finally defeated by Zeno and executed in 488. The prophecy is not specific to the youth's defeat and it is possible that the final blow to the revolt had not yet been dealt. *7Dan* was therefore composed in the last years of Zeno's reign between 484 or 488 and 491.

The text was composed in the Eastern Empire and possibly in Nicomedia or Bithynia more generally. The author was Christian as was his intended audience; and, as noted above, he was also a supporter of the Council of Chalcedon.

The date of the translation into Armenian is much more difficult to surmise. The manuscript evidence is not helpful as all the witnesses are rather late. Likewise, citations or references to the text are also late; at present, our earliest reference to the text in Armenian occurs in Mxit'ar Ayrivanec'i's list of apocryphal books (ca. 1285).[29] Our primary evidence for dating the translation, then, rests on an analysis of the language. Kalemkiar had posited a seventh-century date for the translation, but he did not give his reasons for such a dating. As he had also dated the original composition to the seventh century, he seems to have attributed a roughly contemporaneous date to the translation. If we accept the late fifth century as the date of the original composition, there is nothing to exclude a sixth-century date for the translation.

While the language of the translation is often obscure and may not attain to the standard of the "Golden Age" of Armenian composition and translation in the fifth century, there are also no certain indicators that would definitely suggest a much later date. A style of translation known as the Hellenizing style or school flourished in Armenia between approximately between 570 and 730 that aimed at achieving greater precision than their predecessors in the reproduction of Greek vocabulary and syntax.[30] Despite the presence of calques and the awkward syntax of *7Dan*, the translation does not reflect translation techniques consistent with those found among the translations of the Hellenizing style. Obviously, it does not necessarily follow that the text was translated prior to the development of the style—the translation may have been executed by someone not associated or unfamiliar with the development. Nevertheless, the conspicuous lack of influence of the Hellenizing style does lend some support to the speculation that the translation was completed earlier rather than later. It may be suggested that the translation occurred during

29. Zahn, "Paralipomena 4," 115-16. The list was more recently published and discussed by M. Stone, "Armenian Canon Lists III." Although Stone has demonstrated that the list itself is based on non-Armenian sources—most probably Greek—he suggests that the inclusion of *7Dan*, cited according to that title, may imply that the text was known to the compiler in its Armenian version (p. 292). *7Dan* was not included, however, in the earlier list compiled by Yovhannēs Imastasēr Sarkawag (d. 1129), published by Stone in the same article, 293-95.

30. See Terian, "The Hellenizing School."

the reign of Justinian (527-565), a period when apocalyptic expectations and speculation were particularly acute.[31]

We may further observe that the translator was able to identify the biblical allusions in the text. He usually has not rendered these literally, but has employed the corresponding Armenian version. This suggests that the translator recognized the biblical allusion in Greek and was aware of how it was translated into Armenian. The translator's knowledge of the Greek Bible may allow us to suggest tentatively that he may have been an Armenian who resided in the Byzantine Empire (possibly in the environs of Constantinople) and was learned in both versions of the Bible. The translation would have been executed for other Armenians living within the borders of the Empire. This would also help explain why the text is unattested in Armenian sources until the Middle Ages. It is uncertain whether the translation was executed by and for Chalcedonian or non-Chalcedonian Armenians;[32] however, if the translation was executed during the reign of Justinian, who reversed the tolerant policy of the Emperors Zeno and Anastasius towards non-Chalcedonians, a text that predicted the end of the Empire may have been welcome among a non-Chalcedonian community.[33]

I have already noted that in *7Dan* 22 there occurs a possible reference to the Islamic invasions of Byzantium in the seventh century. It is very likely that this remark represents an interpolation, as it disrupts the flow of the narrative. The question remains, however, at what point this insertion was made. On the one hand, if this material was already present in the Greek *Vorlage* of the Armenian version or if it was inserted by the Armenian translator himself, then the translation could only have been executed in the middle of the seventh century at the earliest. On the other hand, if it was inserted by an Armenian scribe who copied the text, it is possible that the scribe "updated" the prophecy in order to take the Islamic invasions into account. This would support a sixth-century date for the translation. In sum, a sixth-century date of translation would not be inconsistent with the evidence but, for the moment, this solution must remain speculative.

Literary Context

Sources, Inspirations, and Closely Related Texts

Although it is difficult to detect many of the likely sources that the author of *7Dan* drew upon, it is clear that the Bible and sibylline oracular literature constitute two of the most important.

The impact of Scripture on *7Dan* is especially felt in the introductory and eschatological portions of the text. Particularly prominent are allusions to the biblical books of Daniel, the "Synoptic Apocalypse" (Mt 24:1-36; Mk 13; Lk 21:5-36), and the Book of Revelation; echoes of Isaiah, Joel, and the Psalms are also found. As noted, the final paragraph closes with an intercessory prayer modeled on the Lord's Prayer in Mt 6:13 and possibly on the Prayer of Manasseh. The Woe form used throughout the work, too, ultimately reflects the prophetic books, although the author of *7Dan* may have been influenced by other oracular or prophetic literature that also employ this form.

---

31. See, for example, Magdalino, "The History of the Future."

32. While the activity of Chalcedonian Armenians in the Byzantine Empire has been well documented (cf. Garitte, *Narratio*), that of Armenian non-Chalcedonian communities residing in Byzantine territory has been the focus of less scholarly attention. There is evidence, however, that Greek texts purged of their Chalcedonian elements were available to Armenians who traveled to Byzantium at the beginning of the eighth century; see La Porta, "Purging John of Scythopolis."

33. This, of course, assumes that the translator did not recognize the positive references to the Council of Chalcedon.

7Dan shares the greatest textual affinity with the *Tiburtine Sibyl.* The two texts share not only *topoi,* but also identical phrases and depictions; these have been identified in the notes to the translation. We may observe that all of these examples derive from those sections of the text that Alexander has designated as belonging to the fourth-century "Theodosian Sibyl," and not to those that he ascribes to the sixth-century composer of the *Tiburtine Sibyl.*[34] It therefore does not seem imprudent to conclude that the author of *7Dan* was aware of some form of the "Theodosian Sibyl."

As noted, the influence of the *Sibylline Oracles*—or of an oracular text similar in nature to them—is felt in a general manner in the "prophecies of the cities" section of the text. It is possible that *7Dan* 2-17 preserves an independent oracle on the destruction of these cities and provinces. The use of the term "seven-hilled" may witness the influence of the Sibylline material, as may the description of Rome's becoming a "three-street town" (17).

Influence on Later Texts

If a fifth-century date of composition is accepted for *7Dan,* then it is one of the oldest, and possibly the oldest, Byzantine apocalypse ascribed to Daniel.[35] It has long been recognized that some of the *topoi* and motifs in *7Dan* appear in the later Daniel *apocalyptica.*[36] Given the early date of *7Dan,* it is likely that this text played an instrumental role in creating an associational complex[37] between these *topoi* and the figure of Daniel. Among these later texts, *7Dan* shares the greatest affinity with the *Vision and Revelation of the Prophet Daniel.* The author of the latter possibly abridged the prophecies of the destruction of the cities and provinces found at the beginning of *7Dan.*[38]

That said, several later motifs present in the Daniel *apocalyptica* are completely absent from *7Dan. 7Dan* makes no mention of the coming of the Blond Race, of Gog and Magog, of the barbarian nations enclosed in the north, or of Enoch and Elijah; nor does the author designate a special role for "the last Roman Emperor." Many of these motifs may be traced back to the *Apocalypse of Ps.-Methodius,* with which *7Dan* shares very little

34. The one exception is the reference to Rome's being a "three-street town." The similar though not identical description of Rome's being "a (mere) street" occurs in l.105 which Alexander ascribes to the later stage of redaction. However, the expression—which is a pun in Greek—is already present in the *Sibylline Oracles;* it is likely that both the author of *7Dan* and the redactor of the *Tiburtine Sibyl* employed the expression independently of each other's work and possibly under the influence of the *Sibylline Oracles.*

35. DiTommaso, *The Book of Daniel,* 99-100, based partially on an analysis by Schmoldt, has tentatively assigned early dates to two of the Daniel *apocalyptica, The Vision of Daniel on the Island of Cyprus* (fourth cent.) and *The Vision of Daniel on the Blond Race* (fifth cent.). However, as DiTommaso admits, both these texts could be much later and the evidence for their dating is poor; both texts merit further study.

36. Many correspondences have also been treated in the works of Alexander, *Byzantine Apocalyptic;* Pertusi, *Fine di Bisanzio;* and Berger, *Daniel-Diegese.* The relationship between these texts is complex. Older scholarship tended to posit a common tradition or Urtext that rested behind the shared material; see, for example, Zahn, "Paralipomena 4," 120; Bousset, *Antichrist Legend,* 66-72; Denis, *Introduction,* 312. More recent scholarship has questioned this approach; see, K. Berger, *Die Griechische Daniel-Diegese,* 1-2; Henze, *The Syriac Apocalypse of Daniel,* 7; DiTommaso, *The Book of Daniel,* 224-30; see also now DiTommaso, "The Armenian *Seventh Vision.*"

37. I borrow the phrase "associational complex" from Stone, *Features of the Eschatolgy of IV Ezra.* This is particularly so for those elements which occur in *7Dan* but are not present in the *Apocalypse of Ps.-Methodius.*

38. See the Italian translation by E. Falco of the Slavonic version of this text with Pertusi's comments in Pertusi, *Fine di Bisanzio,* 81-90. Cf. the remarks of DiTommaso, *The Book of Daniel,* 142. It is possible that the author of the *Vision and Revelation* knew another form of this oracular material.

common material.[39] This is not surprising given that the narrative and the purpose of the two texts differ markedly. It is noteworthy, however, given the incredible impact the *Apocalypse of Ps.-Methodius* had on subsequent Daniel *apocalyptica*. *7Dan*'s independence from the *Apocalypse of Ps.-Methodius* further lends support, albeit *e silentio*, to an early date for *7Dan*.

7Dan did not exert a significant influence in Armenian tradition. Mxit'ar of Ayrivank', although he cited the text in his list of apocryphal books, did not include it in his compilation of biblical texts which contains a number of other apocryphal works.[40] As of yet, no earlier reference to *7Dan* has been identified in Armenian literature. Further research may yet yield a greater awareness of this text in medieval Armenian literature.

This Translation

The English translation presented below is based on Kalemkiar's edition unless otherwise noted. None of the published editions of the text provide chapter, paragraph, or verse numbers. The paragraph numbers adopted for this translation are those used by Macler in his French translation. I have added the more general section titles as well as the versification. While I have striven to render my translation as readable as possible, I have also tried to provide some sense of the Armenian version of the text. I have indicated those instances in which I have diverged noticeably from a literal translation.

Bibliography

Alexander, P. *The Byzantine Apocalyptic Tradition.* Los Angeles: University of California Press, 1985.

__________. "Medieval Apocalypses as Historical Sources." *American Historical Review* 73 (1968): 997-1018.

__________. *The Oracle of Baalbek: The Tiburtine Sibyl in Greek Dress.* Washington, D.C.: Dumbarton Oaks Center for Byzantine Studies, 1967.

Berger, K. *Die Griechische Daniel-Diegese. Eine Altkirchliche Apokalypse.* Leiden: Brill, 1976.

Bousset, W. *The Antichrist Legend. A Chapter in Jewish and Christian Folklore.* Trans. A. H. Keane. London: Hutchinson, 1896.

Brandes, W. "Die apokalyptische Literatur." Pages 304-22 in *Quellen zur Geschichte des frühen Byzanz (4.-9. Jahrhundert). Bestand und Probleme.* Edited by F. Winkelmann and W. Brandes. Berliner byzantinistiche Arbeiten 55. Amsterdam: Gieben, 1990.

Collins, J. J. "Introduction: Towards the Morphology of a Genre." *Semeia* 14 (1979): 1-20.

Cook, D. "An Early Muslim Daniel Apocalypse." *Arabica* 49 (2002): 53-96.

Cox, C. "The 'Songs of Zion' in Armenian." Pages 33-59 in *The Armenians in Jerusalem and the Holy Land.* Edited by M. Stone and R. Ervine. Hebrew University Armenian Studies 4. Leuven: Peeters, 2002.

Denis, A.-M. *Introduction aux pseudépigraphes grecs d'Ancien Testament.* Leiden: Brill, 1970.

DiTommaso, L. "The *Seventh Vision of Daniel* and the Historical *Apocalyptica* of Late Antiquity." In *The Armenian Apocalyptic Tradition: A Comparative Perspective.* Edited by K. B. Bardakjian and S. La Porta. SVTP. Leiden: Brill, forthcoming.

39. A possible exception is the legend of Byzas as the founder of Byzantium, which the *Apocalypse of Ps.-Methodius* also invokes, but his role in that text is much more developed than it is in *7Dan*. Byzas also appears in the *Discourses of John Chrysostom Concerning the Vision of Daniel*, whose source is the *Apocalypse of Ps.-Methodius*.

40. See Stone, "Armenian Canon Lists III," 292.

———. *A Bibliography of Pseudepigrapha Research, 1850-1999*, pp. 333-35. JSPSup 39. Sheffield: Sheffield Academic Press, 2001.

———. *The Book of Daniel and the Apocryphal Daniel Literature*, pp. 100-108 and bibliography on pp. 499-502. SVTP 20. Leiden: Brill, 2005.

———. "The Early Christian Daniel Apocalyptica." Pages 269-86 in *Apocalyptic Thought in Early Christianity*. Edited by Robert J. Daly. *Holy Cross Studies in Patristic Theology and History*. Grand Rapids, Mich.: Baker Academic Press, 2009.

Garitte, G. *La Narratio de Rebus Armeniae*. CSCO 132, *Subsidia series*, vol. 4. Louvain: Peeters, 1952.

Henze, M. *The Syriac Apocalypse of Daniel*. Studien und Texte zu Antike und Christentum 11. Tübingen: Mohr Siebeck, 2001.

Issaverdens, J. "Seventh Vision of Daniel." Pages 219-34 in idem, *The Uncanonical Writings of the Old Testament found in the Armenian mss. of the Library of St. Lazarus*. 2nd edition. Venice, 1934 (first edition, Venice, 1901, 1907). (English translation based on Yovsēpʻeancʻʼs edition of the text)

Kalemkiar, G. "Die siebente Vision Daniels." *WZKM* 6 (1892): 109-36; 227-40. (Armenian edition and German translation)

La Porta, S. "Purging John of Scythopolis: A Miaphysite Redaction of the Scholia on the Corpus Dionysiacum and Its Armenian Version." *Le Muséon* 126 (2013): 45-82.

Macler, F. "Les apocalypses apocryphes de Daniel. IV. L'apocalypse arménienne de Daniel." *RHR* 33 (1896): 288-309. (French translation based on Kalemkiar's edition of the text)

Magdalino, P. "The History of the Future and Its Uses: Prophecy, Policy and Propaganda." Pages 3-34 in *The Making of Byzantine History. Studies Dedicated to Donald M. Nicol on His Seventieth Birthday*. Edited by R. Beaton and C. Roueché. Aldershot, 1993.

Middle Armenian Dictionary (Mijin Hayerēn Baṙaran). Erevan, 1987.

New Dictionary of the Armenian Language (*Nor Baṙgirkʻ Haykazean Lezui*). Venice 1836, repr. Erevan, 1978.

Pertusi, A. *Fine di Bisanzio e fine del mondo. Significato e ruolo storico delle profezie sulla caduta di Constantinopoli in Oriente e in Occidente*. Roma: Istituto storico Italiano per medio evo, 1988.

Sargisean, B. *Studies on the Apocryphal Writings of the Old Testament (Usumnasirutʻiwnkʻ hin ktakarani anvawer grocʻ vray)*. Venice, 1898.

Stone, M. E. "The Armenian Apocryphal Literature: Translation and Creation." *Il Caucaso: Cerniera fra Culture dal Mediterraneo alla Persia (secoli IV-XI)*. 2 vols. Spoleto: *Centro Italiano di Studi sull' Alto Medioevo*, 1996. 2:611-46.

———. "Armenian Canon Lists III – The Lists of Mechitar of Ayrivankʻ (c. 1285 C.E.)." *HTR* 69 (1976): 289-300.

———. *Features of the Eschatology of IV Ezra*. HSS 35. Atlanta, Ga.: Scholars Press, 1989.

Terian, A. "The Hellenizing School: Its Time, Place, and Scope of Activities Reconsidered." Pages 175-86 in *East of Byzantium: Syria and Armenia in the Formative Period*. Edited by N. Garsoian, T. Mathews, and R. Thomson. Washington, D.C.: Dumbarton Oaks, 1982.

Voicu, S. J. "Gli apocrifi armeni." *Augustin* 23 (1983): 161-80.

Yovsēpʻeancʻ, S. *Uncanonical Books of the Old Testament* (*Ankanon girkʻ Hin Ktakaranacʻ*), pp. 237-50, 387-99. Venice, 1896. (Armenian edition based on two manuscripts of the text)

Zahn, T. "Paralipomena 4. Über einige armenische Verzeichnisse kanonischer und apokrypher Bücher." Pages 109-57 in *Forschungen zur Geschichte des neutestamentlichen Kanons und der altkirchlichen Literatur V*. Edited by T. Zahn. Leipzig, 1893.

The Seventh Vision of Daniel

The calling of the prophet

1 [1]In the third year,[a] after all the revelation(s)[b] that had been given to the prophet[c]
Dan 8:16; 9:21 Daniel, the angel Gabriel, having been sent to him before, was sent by the Lord,[d]
Dan 9:23; 10:11, 19 and he said[e] to him: [2]"Daniel, *desirable man*, I was sent by the Lord to you[f] to tell you things and to show you the end of days, which will occur after the coming of the Word, who will be announced[g] by me.[h]

2 [1]There will be a virgin in Israel,[i] and she will receive the Word from the Word, and he will become man[j] for the sake of the world and he will save many within Israel.[k]

Prophecy of the cities and provinces

[2]And put to heart[l] and listen to the impending events at the end of days in all the cities and provinces on account of the iniquity of humanity." [3]And I, Daniel, said:[m] "Speak, my Lord." [4]And he spoke to me,[n] after fulfilling[o] all the prophetical sayings,[p] concerning all cities and provinces: Asia, Pontus, Phrygia, Galatia,

---

a. "In the third year"; omit A; "[In the third ye]ar" D; "After the third year" CE.

b. All MSS read "revelation."

c. "the prophet"; omit AD.

d. "by the Lord"; omit BCE.

e. "said": "says" BCE, in the present tense; AD read, "said," in the aorist.

f. "to you" omit CE.

g. "will be announced"; "is announced" BCE.

h. Cf. *The Vision and Revelation of the Prophet Daniel* [*VisRevDan*], lines 1-7. All references to this text are to the translation of E. Falco in Pertusi, *Fine di Bizansio*, 81-89, and follow the lineation provided there.

i. "in Israel"; "from Israel" BCE.

j. "He will become man"; "He will be prophesied" BCE.

k. "he will save many within Israel"; lit., "he will make many within Israel alive." Cf. *VisRev-Dan*, lines 7-8.

l. "put to heart": "pay attention" AD, but cf. *VisRevDan* line 8.

m. "I, Daniel, said"; "you, Daniel, will say" C; "And say, Daniel" E; Yovsēp'eanc' emends E in accordance with C.

n. "'Speak, my Lord.' And he spoke to me"; "Lord, speak to me" BE, "the Lord said to me" C. Yovsēp'eanc' emends E in accordance with C.

o. "After fulfilling"; "I, after fulfilling" B; "I will fulfill" CE.

p. "all the prophetical sayings"; "all my prophetical sayings" BCE.

Cappadocia, Karpath<os>,[a] Smyrna, Antioch, Alexandria, Egypt, Nicaea, Nicomedia, <Chalcedon>,[b] Byzantium, and Babylon, Rome.[c]

3 1Tears[d] of sons, and an increase of famine will destroy the productive earth;[e] your princes will become children of groanings and your possessions which surround you will come into ruin, and they will be removed from you to seven-hilled[f] Babylon.

4 1The prince of Pontus will fall and a sword will devour his children; his forces
will fall by the edge of a sword; they will transfer many to Byzantium and there — Lk 21:24 [Gk]; cf. Josh
they will bury them.[g] — 6:21; 10:37, 39 [Arm]

5 1The children of the Phrygians will be devoured by a famine of bread, and its
earth will be rent by water, and they will be turned into food for birds. 2And
many of them will flee to <Chalcedon>.[h]

6 1In Galatia fire will appear from heaven and thunder and lightning will devour
it. 2And the thrones of its princes will be razed to the ground, and its southern
part will be burned in blood and fire, and many will flee at that time to Rome.

7 1In Cappadocia Minor, their children will slaughter each other and imprison each other, and their princes[i] will be defeated, and they who may dwell around it will be in affliction and in lamentation in Babylonia Minor.

8 1In Karpath<os>, their sons will be in affliction, they will see conflagrations and will not believe it; there will be a rending (of the earth); everyone will arrive at[j] hell; many will flee to the seven-hilled (city).[k]

9 1In Smyrna, anger will be increased; it will be filled like a cup with blood, and there will be a fall from the heights. Your princes will be removed and your nobles will fall, for the day of the anger of the Lord will be for you. — Isa 13:9; Ezek 7:19; Zeph 1:18, 2:2

10 1The children of Antioch will be destroyed and its constructed buildings will
turn to ruin, and its princes will not enjoy (them). 2An earthquake will befall
you, and the abundance of your wealthy will destroy you.

---

a. Karpath<os>; lit., "Karpathias"; but cf. Macler, "L'apocalypse arménienne," 291 n. 3.

b. All manuscripts read Carthage, but see the introduction on the confusion between Carthage and Chalcedon in Greek.

c. Cf. *VisRevDan*, lines 10-13.

d. "Tears"; "mourning" BCE. Macler, "L'apocalypse arménienne," 291 n. 2, justly perceives that this paragraph refers to Asia.

e. Cf. *VisRevDan*, lines 13-14.

f. On the designation "seven-hilled," see Introduction.

g. "them": omit AD; "him" C.

h. All manuscripts: "Carthage," see Introduction.

i. "imprison each other, and their princes"; omit BCE.

j. "arrive at"; "descend into" BCE.

k. Karpathos fell to Rome in 42 B.C.E.

11 [1]In Alexandria there will be many tumults of war and the neck of its rebellion (will reach) the bowstrings[a] of its walls. [2]Its princes will be chased out.

12 [1]The children of the Egyptians will flee, struck by famine;[b] your possessions will turn to nothing, and the Nile will become dry land, and your princes will be destroyed.

13 [1]The daughters of the Nicaeans will be in mourning and grief on account of the captivity of their relatives and husbands by powerful men, and your princes will serve them whom they will not know.

14 [1]Woe unto you, O Nicomedia, who have lifted up your horn and ate the bodies of your saints who were in you; you will be destroyed by the blood of righteous men who will recompense you in kind—you will be cast down into hell.[c] [2]Cry and lament, O miserable one, for you will be exterminated with your sons. [3]Your princes (will be) princes of groanings, and your priests (will be) lovers of gold and silver, and the beauty of your radiance will be engulfed.

15 [1]<Chalcedon> and the nation of the Persians[d]—you do not know what will happen to you at the end of days and how much your time will be at the end of ages after all the cities and provinces. [2]You, O city, fattened by gold and silver, and (you), O nation, prettified and adorned, will be destroyed by famine. [3]Many debaucheries will be for you, and your sons will play with gold and then be destroyed by famine.

16 [1]The land of Byzantium and of Babylon will be engulfed, and it will be seized by powerful ones and its foundations will be destroyed, and its power will fall.

17 [1]There will no longer be a prince of Rome at that time, but its sword[e] will be sharpened and its arrow hardened and its deception thickened. [2]Many times a prince will arise and again fall. [3]It will become a three-street town.[f] [4]And many will fear you on account of the radiance of your princes that have many seats[g] and on account of your proud neck and your excessive wealth.[h]

---

a. "bowstrings"; "ballistae" BCE.

b. "by famine"; "by the sword" C.

c. A possible allusion to Maximinus' massacre of 20,000 Christians in Nicomedia in 311-12; Macler, "L'apocalypse arménienne," 292 n. 4.

d. See Introduction.

e. "sword"; "weapon" AD.

f. "It will become a three-street town"; cf. *Tiburtine Sibyl,* line 105 and Alexander's comments on 87 and 124; also *Sib. Or.* 3:364, 8:165.

g. See Introduction.

h. "wealth"; "pride" CE.

History of Byzantium from its founding until Marcian

18 [1]The sons of Byzantium will become[a] a miracle, for a Byzantine man will go from that one to the named[b] seven-hilled (city), and he will establish its foundations.[c] [2]Its name will spread[d] throughout all the inhabitants of the world until the division of tongues.[e] [3]And a wonder-working man[f] born of a famous woman[g] will rebuild it.[h] [4]And in his time the desire of his heart[i] will be completed, and he will find the wood of life. [5]And his scepter will become great and he will find the nails which belonged to the Cross, and he will put it in his bridle for the sake of victory in strenuous wars.[jk] [6]And his horn (will be) high and mighty, and his name (will be famous) in every tongue, and an eternal memory will be bequeathed to the city.

19 [1]And after him the <second>[l] scepter will arise, who will shed the blood of righteous men. [2]And he will read the commandments but will not know God and he will handle the holy scriptures with a blinded heart.[m]

20 [1]And after him will come a philosopher for you, O seven-hilled Babylon, and he will erect an image in you, on account of which you will not be taken by force.[n]

21 [1]And after all this, elevated horns and very great scepters will arise, and they will be empowered over you, and their memory will be very great.[o]

22 [1]And yet another scepter will be high;[p] he will be miraculously empowered and elevated on account of the name and revelation[q] of the Lord, since a "gift"

---

a. "will become"; "will appear" BCE.

b. "named"; omit BCE.

c. This is likely a reference to the legend of Byzas of Megara, who, according to Philostratus, founded a Greek colony on the European side of the Bosporus in 657 B.C.E. following a prophecy delivered by the oracle at Delphi. Byzas receives fuller treatment in the *Apocalypse of Ps.-Methodius* and subsequently in the *Discourses of John Chrysostom Concerning the Vision of Daniel*; Alexander, *Byzantine Apocalyptic*, 19, 23, 72.

d. "Its name will spread"; omit AD; "will spread"; lit., "will be."

e. Cf. *Tiburtine Sibyl*, lines 93-4.

f. Constantine.

g. Helena. "of a famous woman"; omit BCE.

h. "will rebuild"; lit. "will build again"; cf. *anoikodomēsei* ("he will rebuild"), *Tiburtine Sibyl*, line 91, in reference to Constantine's rebuilding of Byzantium. Byzantium had been severely destroyed during the campaign of Septimus Severus. "will build" omit BCE.

i. "heart"; omit BCE.

j. "strenuous wars"; "wars of salvation" BCE.

k. John Chrysostom is the first to mention this detail in his "Homily on the Death of Theodosius," delivered in 395; Macler, "L'apocalypse arménienne," 293 n. 7.

l. "second" DE; "third" ABC. The two are easily confused in Armenian.

m. Constantine's son, Constantius I (337-61), who was an Arian.

n. A reference to Jovian (363-64); Macler, "L'apocalypse arménienne," 294 n. 2.

o. Valentinian (364-75), Gratian (367-83), and Valens (364-78); Macler, "L'apocalypse arménienne," 294 n. 3.

p. "high"; omit BCE.

q. "and revelation"; omit BCE.

from God was in him.[a] [2]Through him life will be great and from his joy all mankind will rejoice; they will be gathered from the cities and provinces in you, and they will reach you, O seven-hilled (city), and each one will do his own work. [3]And the scepter of the kingdom will be empowered until it will be ended.

23 [1]And two scepters will go forth from the one scepter,[b] and your one scepter will become a wild beast,[c] and your second scepter will become an animal[d] in both streets in the seven-hilled (city). [2]From Rome[e] an abatement of anger[f] will reach you and you will have a full bosom and cup. [3]First, the song of the city will be a philosophy of chants; and second, your wealth will be a gushing spring for everyone. [4]You will appear adorned like a bride and like a widow.[g] [5]Your[h] productive grapes which existed at some point will be diminished, and your great glory will be divided and fall.

24 [1]The kingdom which is in you will raise up another scepter,[i] who is called Theodosius[j] by name, being in holiness, and his name being dedicated to you, O seven-hilled (city). [2]And at his birth your sons will be happy, and each and everyone will do that which he may contemplate. [3]Every city and province will serve you, and there will be much rejoicing in your fullness on the earth. [4]And the Nile of the Egyptians will give you drink, and you will be a bulwark for churches.[k] [5]There will greatly be fear and trembling in your scepter, and this is the beginning of groanings in your kingdom.[l] [6]And the time of his scepter (will be) long and very great. [7]And his scepter will possess (everything) until the ends of the entire earth, from the east and from the west, from the north and from the south. [8]And his neck (will be) solid; and his right hand, powerful; and his years, many, as was never for any other king. [9]And after all this he will turn his face towards his father,[m] and the reckoning of his years will be many; and his name will be awesome, and his kingdom will be radiant.

25 [1]And yet a third king will be under you in Rome, O seven-hilled (city). [2]"Seven-hilled" you were called because all the nations of the Persians entered you, O

---

a. A play on the name Theodosius (379-95).

b. Honorius (395-423) and Arcadius (395-408).

c. "and your one scepter will become a wild beast"; "and there will be one old scepter" BCE.

d. "and your second scepter will become an animal"; "a third scepter, an animal scepter" BCE.

e. "in both streets in the seven-hilled (city). [2]From"; "of both in these streets from the seven-hilled Rome" BCE.

f. "anger"; "elevation" CE.

g. "You will appear adorned like a bride and like a widow"; "it will appear adorned and like a brave (man)" BCE

h. "Your"; omit BCE.

i. "and your great glory...another scepter"; "its kingdom in you will fall, and another scepter will arise" BCE.

j. Theodosius II (408-50).

k. "for churches"; "for the church" BCE.

l. A reference to the beginning of the Christological controversies.

m. A possible reference to the installation of Valentinian III (425-55) as the Emperor of the western Roman Empire.

Rome; they shall not reign until the completion of eternity.[a] [3]And an old man shall reign over you as second, and his name (will be) Marcian, and his scepter will be of lesser duration than the first scepter with his very formidable reign.[b] [4]And that time will be good for some and evil for some. [5]And his reign will be for times and for hours and for half an hour,[c] and the builder having given you, O seven-hilled (city), to him, he will raise it to himself with a letter of faith.[d] [6]And there will be a great schism in his kingdom:[e] priests will fall from their thrones, there will be a fall of many priests, and there will be many vicissitudes for men, but your rejoicing, O seven-hilled (city), and your extent will not diminish. [7]And after all this he too will come to an end with his fathers.

The reign of Leo I

26 [1]And another scepter will reign in you, and he will be a beast,[f] and he will accept the first scepter which will at one point be struck by a dog.[g] [2]And this beast will be like the first great scepter and powerful in words and wisdom, and he will not be held in contempt by his nobles. [3]And his neck will be like the neck of an ox,[h] and his eyes like the eyes of a lion; he will call out terribly and all cities and provinces will be afraid of his horns. [4]And in his time a rainbow will appear in heaven, as will various signs in heaven and earth. [5]The sound of thunder and the fall of many cities will be heard, and the earth will be rent and buildings will be razed to their foundations. [6]Its streets will be fiery and there will be wars in it and in you, O seven-hilled (city).[i] [7]And then the buildings[j] of your beauty will be burned by fire, and your elevation will be overthrown to the earth. [8]And your sons will lament in you and your great joy will be turned to mourning, and your sons will drag the bodies of the nobles over the earth. [9]And suddenly a whirlwind will fall from heaven and cover the earth; and nations in the form of

---

a. This sentence does not reflect any historical situation between the reign of Theodosius II and that of Marcian when Pulcheria ruled; cf. Macler, "L'apocalypse arménienne," 296 n. 1. It is likely a reference to the Islamic invasions added by a later scribe.

b. The reference to the first scepter is obscure. In 26:1, the first scepter appears to refer to the western Emperor. Here, Marcian's reign is said to be shorter than that of the first scepter. The reign of Marcian's western contemporaries, Petronius Maximus (455) and Avitus (455-56), were certainly not longer, nor was that of Majorian (457-61). It is possible that the first scepter should be understood as Valentinian III (425-55).

c. "for times and for hours and for half an hour"; Macler, "L'apocalypse arménienne," 296 n. 2, understands this to mean times (2 years), hours (1 year) and half an hour (half a year) (cf. Dan 7:25; 12:7). Marcian ruled alone after the death of Pulcheria from 453 until 457, or approximately three and a half years. "for times and half a time" BCE.

d. A reference to the decree of the council of Chalcedon.

e. I.e., the schism between the churches following Chalcedon.

f. "The beast" is Leo I (457-74); cf. *Tiburtine Sibyl*, line 136.

g. Possible reference to Leo I's support of Anthemius (467-72) as the western Emperor (first scepter) and the attacks on the western Empire by the Vandals.

h. "ox"; "soldier" BCE.

i. Cf. *Tiburtine Sibyl*, lines 137-38. This work, however, has nothing positive to say about Leo such as *7Dan* does. Macler, "L'apocalypse arménienne," 297 n. 4, notes that Antioch was destroyed by an earthquake in 458. There was also a fire in Constantinople that lasted four days in 469.

j. "buildings"; "environs" AD.

dragons will appear on the earth and many will become impoverished and many indigent will become rich, and there will be great confusion in you.[a]

10Cry out, O forces bearing arms and swords, in Thrace and in Cilicia.[b] 11And at that time the beast will send his sword[c] to the East, and he will not be able to conquer, and a certain man in the shape of a dragon[d] in the middle and on top will disdain him; and he will send with him a second[e] sword to the west, and he will not be strong[f] enough to conquer it,[g] and the dragon will be disdained by the dog.[h] 12With many presents and gold and with many things[i] the beast will be vexed by the dog,[j] and the dog will rise up against the beast[k] and he will raise up his cubs over the thrones and scepters of the beast, and the beast will be destroyed and his den seized by the dog.[l] 13And the dogs will remove the beast and all men will know that a dog had chased out a lion.[m] 14And thence the lion will return and kill the dog and his cub, and the lion will call out with a very great roar, and his roar will be heard in every city and region.[n] 15And there will be fear of him in his den, and men will be confused by each other on account of the roar of the lion and the death of the dog.

27 1And the second dog,[o] while changing its tongue to another form, will pursue (him) as far as the den of the lion, and he will depart from that one as he will not be able to overpower him. 2And the pup of the dog will lie hidden for times and a time and an hour, and in his time he will reign, and his name will be "pup of the dog," which translated means "scepter[p] of nations."[q] 3And the beast[r] will erase

a. A possible allusion to the attack on Rome in 455 by Gaiseric.

b. According to Macler, "L'apocalypse arménienne," 298 n. 2, these are the Goths from Thrace and the Isaurians from Cilicia.

c. I.e., Tarasicodissa, later Emperor Zeno the Isaurian.

d. I.e., the general Basiliscus, brother-in-law of Leo I.

e. "second"; "third" BCE.

f. "strong"; "patient" BCE.

g. A reference to Gaiseric's defeat of the combined forces of the eastern and western Empire under the command of Basiliscus in 468.

h. The dog here must be Aspar the Alan, the *magister militum* of the eastern Empire, whose prominence at court rose again after the defeat of Basiliscus.

i. "and with many things"; omit BCE.

j. Aspar is alleged to have bribed Leo's soldiers against him. "by the dog": "by the sign (cross)" C.

k. "and the dog will rise up against the beast"; omit BCE.

l. In 469, Aspar's son, Patricius, received the title of Caesar and was betrothed to Leo's second daughter, Leontia.

m. The "lion" must also refer to Leo.

n. In 471, Aspar and his son Ardabur were assassinated in the palace by eunuchs; Patricius was wounded, but escaped. He was divorced from Leontia and stripped of the rank of Caesar.

o. Macler, "L'apocalypse arménienne," 299 n. 1, suggests that the second dog may be Ostrogothic king Theodemir, father of Theodoric the Great.

p. "scepter"; "king" BCE.

q. If the "second dog" is to be identified with Theodemir, then the "pup of the dog" is Theodoric.

r. "beast"; "scepter" BCE.

the memory of the dog.[a] [4]Knowing (this) beforehand, they will slander him,[b] and in his city they will erase his image. [5]And many in the den[c] of the beast will contemplate killing him and they will not overpower[d] him, and those who share the scepter with him will die in another city by the sword, and they will know well the prayers of the priest on behalf of unknown (things).

The rise of Zeno

[6]And someone among the nobles, a youth from the forces of the beast, will bind many by hand and foot and send them to the beast. [7]And then when the beast will receive many slaves from various nations, calling (them) to himself as lord, another man will stand before him and he will receive him into his bosom.[e] [8]And he will persecute military men, and he himself will be persecuted by them.[f] [9]And he will flee from them[g] on foot, and no one will reach him, because he is fleet of foot[h] and he will flee to the beast and he, who (is) in his bosom, will also present himself to him.[i] [10]And the little beast[j] will go out and be courageous, and the big beast will seat him on his throne, and will make him a sharer of his scepter and throne in his place; two beasts[k] will dwell in one cave.[l] [11]The pup will be emboldened[m] to an act of war, and the big beast will return to his land whence he came.[n] [12]And the little beast will hold[o] his place until a time, having not been crowned by anyone, but by his own violence he will come to the dens[p] of the kingdom, and the little beast will turn towards the big beast, and, forsaking the dens of which he himself was the creator,[q] he will reign in you, O seven-hilled (city), and he will hold you in affliction.[r] [13]His joy will be great, he

---

a. The text seems to return to events concerning Aspar and his family.

b. "they will slander him"; lit., "they will sing slander about him."

c. "in the den"; "at the door" BCE.

d. "overpower"; "endure" BCE.

e. This is probably a reference to Zeno, who in 466 or 467 was married to Leo's eldest daughter, Ariadne.

f. Leo created a new imperial guard of 300 men called the Excubitors. It probably consisted of Isaurians of whom Zeno was chieftain; it was intended to combat the influence of Aspar.

g. "he will flee from them"; "they will flee from him" BCE.

h. During his campaign against the Huns in Thrace, some of Zeno's soldiers, allegedly bribed by Aspar, attempted to assassinate Zeno. The latter discovered the plot and fled to Sardica. We may also note that, according to the author of the second part of the *Excerpta Valesiana* (Ammianus Marcellinus, *Roman History* III, LCL 331, 1939), Zeno was an exceptionally fast runner: 9.40.

i. Upon his return, Zeno was made *magister militum* of the East.

j. "beast"; "scepter" AD.

k. "beasts"; "scepters" AD.

l. This sentence and the rest of the paragraph continue to recount Zeno's early career and rise. The "big beast" refers Leo I; the "little beast," to Zeno.

m. "will be emboldened"; "will embolden" AD.

n. This is probably a reference to Theodoric Strabo who launched a revolt in Thrace and finally exacted terms from Leo in 473; Leo was born in Thrace. It is possible that the author confused Theodoric the Great, called the pup above, with Theodoric Strabo.

o. "hold"; "receive" BCE.

p. "dens"; "judgment" BCE.

q. "dens of which he himself was the creator"; lit., "dens for his creator."

r. Zeno's son Leo II was proclaimed Emperor after the death of Leo I in 474. As Leo II was

will play and will be loved by the nobles, and hated by many, he will give life and fullness, and the dragon[a] will play with him, and he will lead him along by the hunting scepter of the beast.[b]

The reign of Zeno

28 [1]Woe[c] to you at that time, O seven-hilled Babylon, when a widow will reign and the dragon[d] will pursue the stranger, and the stranger, who is called Salamander,[e] will turn in flight having turned his face to the islands, (taking) gold and silver and precious stones and a crown of scepters.[f] [2]And no one among men will persecute him who is in the bosom of the beast, tripled by the nation of the Persians from <Chalcedon>,[g] on account of love for the dragon and that great radiance which was in you. [3]And he will be moved from land to land and will be vexed by strangers. [4]And forced (by the strangers) from nourishment and from ways, he will sigh to the Creator with his innocent ones. [5]And the hunting scepter, which was from the beast, will be allied with the dog,[h] and the dragon will hold the place of affliction and ceremony and will be attended by vain thrones.[i] [6]And he will persecute the place of holiness, and <the dragon will heap rebuke>[j] with his tongue on holy men and holy relics. [7]And he will obstruct the leadership of the patriarchs,[k] and he will hold captive the churches of holiness.[l] [8]And they who may be dwelling in the caverns and caves and hollows of the earth, they will become wanderers in the desert (and) will come to you, O seven-hilled (city), forced by the dragon. [9]And after all this, they will shake off the dust of their feet in you, and be martyred in you.[m] [10]Then the beauty of your splendor will be burned by a fire.[n] [11]And a certain youth (will) escape under the pretext of bringing[o] with his hunting scepter the first scepter that is called

---

a minor, his father was proclaimed co-Emperor. Leo II died in the same year, possibly having been poisoned by his own family, and Zeno was proclaimed sole Emperor.

a. Basiliscus, the brother of Zeno's mother-in-law.

b. This refers to the Isaurian general, Illus, who, at first, had joined Basiliscus in his overthrow of Zeno.

c. "Woe"; "he gives" E.

d. The "widow" is Verina, the widow of Leo I and the mother-in-law of Zeno. The "dragon" is Basiliscus, her brother-in-law, who ousted Zeno in 476-77.

e. Zeno is called Salamander because he eventually killed the dragon (basilisk), Basiliscus.

f. At the outset of the rebellion, Zeno sailed to Chalcedon and then headed to his homeland, Isauria. He took with him a tremendous amount of wealth.

g. See Introduction.

h. The "hunting scepter" is again Illus; the "dog" likely refers to Theodoric Strabo who, as an enemy of Zeno, was supportive of Basiliscus' coup.

i. "to the islands...vain thrones"; omit BCE.

j. "he will rebuke the dragon" AD; "he will slaughter the dragon" BCE.

k. "patriarchs"; "chiliarchs" BE; "legitimate ones" C.

l. Basiliscus was an opponent of the council of Chalcedon and favored the Alexandrian Patriarch Timothy Aelurus; he is supposed to have removed the Asiatic sees from the jurisdiction of the bishop of Constantinople.

m. The monks seemed to have played a particularly important role in forcing Basiliscus to change his mind. "in you, and be martyred in you": "in you, testified by him" AD.

n. During the reign of Basiliscus, a tremendous fire damaged Constantinople and, in particular, the Basilica, the library founded by Julian.

o. "bringing"; "capturing" C.

Salamander.[a] 12 And then at that time the dragon will be persecuted and will be seized by his successors[b] and will be bound by those at his left, and no one will receive him since he shed the blood of saints in the cities and provinces. 13 And he will flee into the holy temple that he had formerly taken captive, and no one will receive him as there will be heavenly scourges upon him. 14 And the youth will reach Salamander, and he will <urge on>[c] the stranger against the dragon, and the dragon, seeing[d] (that), will flee from him. 15 And the stranger will not kill the dragon; he will take away his honor.[e] 16 And the youth will fall with a mighty[f] fall, and the widow will not survive.[g] 17 And they will show[h] the stranger and the sharer of his throne to him, and they[i] will become tributary in his tent that he created. 18 And the blood of his father will be sought on his throne. 19 And the stranger will become great for a short period, and[j] there will be fullness in you, O seven-hilled (city), as well as the death of many men who had gathered in you from the cities and provinces.

Predictions of disaster

29 1 Then there will be earthquakes in various places and they will hear the voice of many and they will not believe.[k] 2 And your wealth and your glory saddened you in your becoming proud and arrogant, and your love of glory humbled you; but your abundance and beauty will become much in you. 3 The end of time will reach you, and the hunting scepter, which is from the beast, will go out from you, and will go[l] to the places of strangers. 4 And your daughters will adorn themselves for (being) a stumbling block for youths to corrupt many, and your nobles will fall, there will be much affliction and agitation.

5 At that time the angel of death[m] will strike you with all the cities and provinces, and violent deaths will be sent from heaven. 6 Suddenly it[n] will be angry at the earth, the earth will be moved and temples will fall, and *their houses will*

---

a. Basiliscus had dispatched Illus to capture Zeno, but Illus, encouraged by certain ministers at court, changed sides and allied himself with Zeno. "Salamander"; "Theodosius" BCE.

b. "successors"; "leaders" BCE.

c. "he will urge on"; I propose this emendation against all MSS which read, "he will teach previously."

d. "the dragon, seeing"; omit BCE.

e. "will take away his honor"; lit. "will separate him from his face." Basiliscus, however, was sent to Cappadocia and beheaded.

f. "mighty"; omit BCE.

g. Illus himself eventually became estranged from Zeno. He was sent as *magister militum* of the East in 481-82 and subsequently revolted against the Emperor. Illus supported the Patrician Leontius as Emperor. Verina, his old opponent, also joined his cause and crowned Leontius Emperor in Antioch. Verina died in 484 (see below) after the defeat of Illus' forces. Illus managed to persevere until 488 when he and Leontius were captured and executed.

h. "they will show"; "he shows" BCE.

i. "they"; "he" BCE.

j. "for a short period, and"; "in his time" BCE.

k. Earthquakes afflicted Constantinople in 480 and eastern Anatolia in 488.

l. "will go"; "they will go" AD.

m. "angel of death"; lit., "the death-bearing angel."

n. I.e., heaven.

Ps 49:11 [48:11 Arm] *become tombs,*[a] and the sea will bring the waves up to a boil and will cover mankind, and whoever they may be[b] will flee and will live.[c] 7Then there will be a
crowd of angels, and they will stand in front of and pray before the throne.
8Then, O seven-hilled Babylon, you will weep over your sons, while donning
the sack-cloth and spreading ashes over (your) head,[d] and seeing humanity fall
on account of sins and transgressions. 9Men will be destroyed with sons and
women with suckling babes for the anger of the Lord is upon (them). 10Your
walls will be rent and your tabernacles will be razed to the ground.[e] 11Children
will beseech God[f] with their mouths burned[g] at the breast, and your priests,
scraping, will mourn your scepters. 12Your nobles will cry and your citizens
will be very grieved, and your travelers will be straitened, and your bunches of
grapes will fall and your vineyards will be depleted. 13The earth will be rent by
agitation and will destroy men both young and old.[h] 14But the Lord[i] will not destroy you completely, O seven-hilled[j] (city), as the time of your destruction has
not yet arrived; although (He is prepared) to cover humanity in an abyss, He will
not cover (them), since your time has not yet arrived. 15Torments are prepared
for you, for you have committed every iniquity in you, taking the earth in your
bosom.[k] 16People's thoughts will be greatly agitated until the Lord will command
from above to destroy humanity; but the Lord's plan will be evident, whence the
punishment[l] will come to be. 17And those who have taken refuge in you will
receive torments; the people who hoped in you and the hunting scepter will destroy you.[m] 18And cub will put cub to flight seeking the blood of his fathers, and
he will willingly deliver himself to strangers, to dogs and to his friends; and he
will raise languages and peoples and he will rule over many nations. 19And two[n]
dogs will fight with each other[o] and they will destroy each other.

Prophecy concerning the death of Zeno

30 1Woe, when the widow will reign, and she will move with deception[p] against
the strangers, and the other stranger will seek her destruction and through deception he will eradicate her.[q] 2And these days will be cruel and evil. 3Sons of

a. "and *their houses will become tombs*"; omit AD.
b. "whoever they may be"; "in four" BC; "in valleys" E.
c. "they will also live"; omit BCE.
d. "head"; "heads" BC.
e. "to the ground"; omit BCE.
f. "God"; "Lord" BCE.
g. "burned"; "pacified" AD; "unhappy" B.
h. "both young and old"; lit., "up to suckling babes and old."
i. "the Lord"; "God" BCE.
j. "O seven-hilled"; omit BCE.
k. "bosom"; "work" AD.
l. "punishment"; "occurrence" BCE.
m. "and the hunting scepter will destroy you"; omit BCE.
n. "two"; "second" AD.
o. "each other"; "similars" AD.
p. "with deception"; "with affliction" BCE.
q. Verina first plotted against Illus but then, possibly under duress, sided with him in support of Leontius against Zeno. The forces of Illus, Verina, and Leontius were defeated by Zeno's army in 484. Verina fled to the security of the fortress Cherris and died a few days later.

the scepters will be in dispute and battle with each other, and then humanity will (suffer) much affliction and evil such as has never been. 4And the prince, having believed, will not have confidence in Salamander, since he is a stranger; and they will receive from his people[a] that which they did not ask. 5And Salamander will want to flee and he will not be able, and Plakitas[b] will reach him[c] and will kill him.

31 1And another scepter will rule in you, O seven-hilled (city), and there will be many labors. 2A poor man who will not know gratitude will arise—arrogant, proud, avaricious, loving war—and his name will be Orloghios,[d] and his throne (will be) few in days, and (he will be) easily angered. 3And his nobles will hate him, and his citizens will be vexed by him. 4There will be heavenly anger in his[e] days; many times it will trouble Babylon. 5In the time of his reign, voices of lamentation will reach you, and forces of barbarians will trouble you and they will not be fought. 6And another violent[f] king will arise, and he will battle and persecute him openly;[g] and he will slay him with great sorrow and groaning. 7And this one, having been made king, will hold the scepter[h] which is in you, O seven-hilled (city), and he will be great among very great and radiant thrones, and that man (will be) skillful from the right and from the left. 8And in his time, there will be a great famine and not small, and the earth will be destroyed by humanity and torrents of water will pour out,[i] and black air will be agitated,[j] and your vineyards will become few, and your splendors will be constrained, and the days will become less and the day will be six hours.

32 1Woe to people who will be at that time, and the king will turn his face to the West. 2Then woe to you, O seven-hilled (city), when your king (will be) a youth. 3At that time you will suffer great affliction. 4A man who[k] will have his brother's wife; a son, his mother; and daughter will ascend to her father's bed; brother (will have) his sister; and blasphemies, homicides, oaths, slanders, mendacities, filth, pains,[l] depredations, sibling hatred, turmoils, the shedding of blood of the holy servants in the temple will increase. 5And kings (will rise up) against kings, princes against princes; the powerful from the poor will rise up, and the rich and the poor will fall.

33 1And Bithynia, which is on the seashore, will be razed to the ground by an

---

a. "his people"; "his peoples" AD; "strangers" C.

b. This Plakitas is clearly not a historical figure, although the name is found among the Coptic Papyri.

c. "him"; omit BCE.

d. "Orloghios"; "Lucius" BCE; cf. Olibos in the *Tiburtine Sibyl*, line 187.

e. "his"; "those" BCE.

f. "violent"; "rational" A; omit E.

g. "openly"; "against him" BCE.

h. "this one, having been made king, will hold the scepter"; omit BCE.

i. "will pour out"; "will reach" BCE.

j. "black air will be agitated"; "black airs will be mixed" BCE.

k. "who"; "when" BCE.

l. "pains"; omit BCE.

earthquake, and the waves of the sea will rise up and will surge and will cover the foundations of Bithynia as far as the junior town of Nicomedia.

34 [1]And then again another king will arise, and his time (will be) brief in days, evil and utterly terrible; and thenceforth there will no longer be good times, but evil. [2]And his son will battle against him and he will consume him with the sword.

35 [1]And another king will arise from another cult,[a] who is Arianos; he will draw everyone to himself.[b] [2]Woe to you at that time, O seven-hilled (city), for more than everyone you will mourn for yourself[c] and for your borders.

36 [1]And then kings and princes and leaders and champions will arise against cities and provinces and places, and people will be agitated and confused. [2]And a nation of barbarians will arise against cities and provinces,[d] and the earth will sink seventy-three cubits from the multitude of people. [3]And you will not be troubled by them at that time, O seven-hilled (city), but a special war will torment[e] you, and the splendor of the earth will be diminished in you. [4]Heavenly[f] anger and a great blow will be upon you; and a fiery column will be apparent, (stretching) from heaven to earth. [5]And[g] then your[h] kingdom will be changed, and you, having remained corrupted by sin, will also be in famine.[i] [6]Then in this way, the second scepter will be rent[j] and brought[k] to the other city by a nothing prince, and fiery arrows will rain from heaven; there will be many *signs*
Mt 24:24, Mk 13:22, Jn 4:48 *and wonders.*

The coming of the Antichrist

37 [1]At that time the Antichrist will reign and people will be led away from the worship of God to disbelief from the coming (of him) whom they were not seeking, and were not expecting, that one in whom they did not believe, who was contrary to everything. [2]This one whom they were not seeking[l] will be conceived[m] and born from a defiled virgin.[n] [3]And the scepter of deception will seize the human race; for three times and half a time he will lead the souls of many

a. "from another cult"; "from strangers" AD.

b. "he will draw everyone to himself"; "he [will draw every]one [to himself]" D; "to draw everyone to himself" E.

c. "you will mourn for yourself"; omit AD.

d. "and places…and provinces"; omit BCE.

e. "will torment"; "will be in torment" BCE.

f. "Heavenly"; "But heavenly" BCE.

g. "And"; omit BCE.

h. "your"; "[your]" D.

i. "by sin, will also be in famine"; "[by sin, will also be in famine]" D; "by sin"; "eternal" E.

j. "the second scepter will be rent"; "[the second scepter will be rent]" D.

k. "brought"; lit. "will bring."

l. "whom they were not seeking"; omit BCE.

m. "will be conceived"; "will be" AD.

n. Cf. *Apoc. Dan.* 9:8-11, although there the virgin is impregnated by a fish, see Berger, *Daniel Diegese*, 104-14.

to perdition;[a] to be co-inheritors of everlasting Gehenna. 4 Then the angels will
be agitated when they see the signs that <he showed>[b] previously. 5 And those
people who love God[c] will understand this, recognizing and seeing the one
contrary to everyone who is human, of which these are the signs:[d] bound and
unable to bend at the knee, crippled in eye,[e] smooth-browed, hook-fingered,
pointy-headed, graceful, a braggart, wise, with a sweet laugh, a seer, prudent,
quick, meek, calm, working miracles, having the souls of the damned near him,
taking bread from stones, giving sight to the blind, making the lame walk, and
he will move mountains from place to place.[f] 6 He will do all this illusorily[g] and
many will believe in him. 7 Woe unto those who will believe in him and[h] receive
his mark. 8 Their right hand[i] will be bound so that one will not return to him in Rev 13:17; 19:20
whom they had previously hoped. 9 Then there will be a very[j] great famine, the
heavens will not grant rain,[k] and the earth will not sprout forth verdure; all fruits
will be dried up and then all the cities and provinces will lament for themselves.
10 They will flee, and they will not (be able to) flee[l] from east to west nor from
west to east; but they who will dwell in mountains and caverns and caves and
hollows of the earth, they alone will be able to flee until the second coming (of
him) who was born from the virgin. 11 Then his chosen will be revealed when
they see the eternal coming of the Lord. 12 He[m] will come forth and many will
be judged. 13 There will be troubles from heaven and then there will be terrible
agitation over the universe. 14 *Woe to pregnant women and to those who suckle in*
the last *days!*[n] 15 Woe unto the impatient who believed in the adversary! 16 Woe Mt 24:19; Mk 13:17; Lk 21:23
unto those who worshipped him and were revealed on account of his coming!

38 1 And after all this happens and (after) righteous people, inspired by God,[o]
who had been afflicted by necessity and by violence,[p] bear tortures, then the
end will arrive. 2 And some people having been shown a sign will recognize[q] the
seven-hilled (city) and will say: "Indeed had this been a city?"[r] 3 And a woman
will tread the land in the East, in the West, in the North and in the South, and
she will not find fruit, but she will only find an olive-tree, and embracing the

---

a. "for three times and half a time he will lead the souls of many to perdition"; omit BCE.
b. This is Kalemkiar's emendation; all MSS read: "he caused to go."
c. "who love God"; "who love Christ" AD.
d. "of which these are the signs"; lit. "of which this sign is."
e. "in eye"; "in soul" BCE.
f. The Antichrist's imitation of the acts of Christ is common to many texts; cf., e.g, *Apoc. Dan.* 13; *Apoc. El. (C)* 3:5-10; *Gk. Apoc. Ezra* 4:27.
g. "illusorily"; lit., "to the eyes."
h. "many will believe in him. Woe unto those who will believe in him and"; "which" BCE.
i. "hand"; "eye" BCE.
j. "very"; omit BCE.
k. "will not grant rain"; "will not rule to give rain" AD.
l. "10 They will flee, and they will not (be able to) flee"; "They will flee" BCE.
m. "He"; "They" BCE.
n. "in the last days" AD; "in those days" BCE (with Mt 24:19; Mk 13:17; Lk 21:23).
o. "inspired by God"; "God" BCE.
p. "and by violence"; omit BCE.
q. "having been shown a sign will recognize"; "will show a sign having recognized" BCE.
r. Cf. *Tiburtine Sibyl*, line 200, and *Oracle of Baalbek*, p. 114 n. 59.

olive-tree, she will give up her spirit and will say: "Blessed is that one who has planted this olive-tree."[a] 4And her soul will go up from her thence in that place.

Jl 2:31; Acts 2:20; **39** 1Then *the sun will be turned to darkness and the moon to blood*, the stars will
Rev 6:12 fall like leaves, and the heavens will be rolled up like a scroll, and the sea will boil
Isa 34:4; Rev 6:13-14 (and) come up from its depths to cover men,[b] and everything will be burned[c]
and desiccated by the airs. 2Fiery angels will descend from heaven, and a fire
will flare up through the universe. 3There will be mice[d] in the form of fire and
bronze,[e] and that which is like them, and beasts that eat corpses will come out
of the mountains. 4And he[f] will not fear that one whom they were not seeking
and he will destroy the land of the impious. 5And the righteous will be carried
Dan 9:23 away to the Father, for *a command came forth* from the Lord. 6Thrones will fall[g]
Rev 20:12 and *books will be opened*, and judgments will be written up; angels will sound
Rev 8:7-13; 9:1, 13; 11:15 a trumpet, and the righteous will dance; they will offer up praise to the Father
and they will be judged each according to his deeds;[h] but only the Lord (is) a
Rev 20:13 righteous judge. 7And all his works and all peoples will open their mouths be-
seeching and saying: "Lord, Lord, *do not lead us into temptation, but deliver us*
Mt 6:13 *from evil*,[i] for you, Lord, know and recognize that we are not able to persevere,
for we are corporeal,[j] but like a beneficent and philanthropic[k] father have pity
PrMan 15; Mt 6:13 on us, for yours[l] is the glory, now and for ever, and unto ages from ages. Amen.

---

a. Cf. *Tiburtine Sibyl*, lines 200-204 and *Oracle of Baalbek*, p.115 n. 60.

b. "(and) come up from its depths to cover men"; "and having come up and covered the earth" BCE.

c. "will be burned"; "to destroy" A; "having been destroyed" D.

d. "mice"; "children" BCE.

e. "and bronze"; omit BCE.

f. "he"; "they" BCE.

g. "will fall"; "are set up" BCE.

h. E ends here.

i. "evil"; "evils" B.

j. "corporeal"; lit., "a body."

k. "and philanthropic"; omit BC.

l. "have pity on us, for yours"; "may you have pity on us, and may you have mercy on us, for you created us and yours" BC.

A Danielic Pseudepigraphon Paraphrased by Papias

A new translation and introduction

by Basil Lourié

Papias, bishop of Hierapolis (after 69 C.E.–middle of the second cent. C.E.), in his lost work *Interpretations of the Sayings of the Lord* (written about 100 C.E. according to the scholarly consensus) quoted many ancient Christian and Jewish pre-Christian traditions which are now partially accessible through the preserved fragments.[1] One such tradition goes back to a Jewish source standing at odds with almost the whole corpus of pseudepigraphic testimonies on the Watchers and relying on the authority of the prophet Daniel.

According to this peculiar tradition, the Watchers are the warriors of Michael who were helpful to humanity and, in particular, transmitted to it the Law and the prophetic knowledge.

Papias gives us no information about his literary source. It is easy to see, however, that this source had nothing to do with either the canonical Book of Daniel or any other known Danielic pseudepigraphon.[2]

Manuscripts and Versions

The testimony of Papias subsists within the series of the fragments of his *Interpretations of the Sayings of the Lord* in the *Commentary on the Apocalypse [of John]* by Andrew, bishop of Caesarea (563-637), written in the seventh century.[3] Both Papias and Andrew were writing in Greek.

Andrew of Caesarea's text is the most popular commentary on the Apocalypse in the Eastern Church, and so it is preserved in many Greek manuscripts and in Armenian, Georgian, and Church Slavonic versions.[4] Among these versions, the Armenian one is of special interest (the Slavonic one being an exact rendering of the known Greek text and the Georgian one being so far unpublished and unstudied).[5] It contains, in the part dedicated to Rev 12:9, two paragraphs (according to its *editio princeps* of Jerusalem, 1855), almost completely lost in the known Greek recension and its Slavonic version. This part

1. On Papias, see, e.g., W. R. Schoedel, "Papias," in: *ANRW* 27.1, 235-70.

2. Lorenzo DiTommaso, *The Book of Daniel and the Apocryphal Daniel Literature* (SVTP 20; Leiden: Brill, 2005).

3. This commentary on the Apocalypse is preceded in the Byzantine tradition by that of Oecumenius (ca. 600 C.E.) to whom Andrew of Caesarea owes very much. Critical edition and study: M. de Groote, *Oecumenii Commentarius in Apocalypsin* (Traditio exegetica graeca 8; Louvain: Peeters, 1999).

4. Critical edition of the Greek text with a study taking into account, more or less, all other versions, especially the Slavonic one: J. Schmid, *Studien zur Geschichte des griechischen Apokalypse-Textes.* I. *Der Apokalypse-Kommentar des Andreas von Kaisareia.* Vol. 1. *Text*; Vol. 1a. *Einleitung* (Münchener theologische Studien. I. Historische Abteilung. 1. Ergänzungsband; Munich, 1955, 1956).

5. The Georgian version is dated to 978 and belongs to a great Georgian scholar and translator Euthymius of Athos. The quotes from Papias in this version must be studied in the future.

was republished in 1981 by Fölker Siegert who added two Vienna manuscripts to the three of Jerusalem already used by the Armenian editors.[6] Among the earliest manuscripts, one is dated to 1306, another one is datable to the late thirteenth or early fourteenth century. All five manuscripts are identical in the part relevant to our Papias quote.

The quality of the Armenian version is excellent. It was prepared in about 1179 during the short period when the Armenian Church was on the edge of the union with that of Byzantium. The translator is Constantine, bishop of Hierapolis, who was acting on demand of the Catholicos (the head of the Armenian Church) Nerses of Lambron. Therefore, this translation itself was an act of the high Church politics. This is important to know because this is an argument for evaluating the quality of the manuscript of the Greek original. The quality of such a manuscript must be high.

In a paper dedicated to the differences between the Greek and the Armenian texts of Andrew of Caesarea, I reached the conclusion that the known Greek recension is secondary in comparison with the lost Greek original of the Armenian one. Two paragraphs of the original text of Andrew representing an archaic and hardly understandable tradition for late Byzantium exegesis were excluded from the Greek but preserved in Armenian. Among these two paragraphs only the first contains a quote from Papias, while the second one is an original text of Andrew himself.[7] Therefore, it is only the first paragraph that will be dealt with below.

There is one phrase within the Papias quote which is preserved also in Greek, while in the known Greek recension of Andrew of Caesarea it would be impossible to determine that its source is Papias rather than Andrew himself. However, this phrase, attested in both Greek and Armenian, does not belong to the Danielic pseudepigraphon we are interested in.

Contents

We shall limit ourselves to an analysis of the Danielic tradition only, without its framework in Papias.

Although the intercession of the angels in the revelation of the Law to Moses at Sinai is a well-known early Christian tradition going back to a pre-Christian Jewish milieu, any specific role of Michael in this process is almost unknown (we shall survey exceptions). As to the Watchers, their intercession at Sinai is not only at odds with the mainstream Jewish and Christian traditions, but goes against the well-established and prevailing tradition in both Jewish and Christian worlds identifying them as the begetters of the Giants by mortal women and revealers of forbidden arts to humanity. This tradition starting from *1 Enoch* (the Book of the Watchers [cf. the Book of Giants], both perhaps as early as the third cent. B.C.E.) and going through the Qumranic texts, ends with the Middle Age Byzantine historiographers, thus becoming a part of the trivial medieval knowledge.[8] By the

---

6. Fölker Siegert, "Unbeachtete Papiaszitate bei Armenischen Schriftstellern," *NTS* 27 (1981): 605-14, esp. 606-607 (text in transliteration, German tr.), 611 n. 10.

7. B. Lourié, "A Quote from Papias within the Armenian Version of the *Commentary on Apocalypse* of St Andrew of Caesarea: Translation and Study in the History of the Exegesis," *Writings of the Apostolic Fathers* (ed. Alexey G. Dunaev; Moscow: Editorial Council of the Russian Orthodox Church, 2002; rpt. 2008), 511-32 (in Russian), quoted below as Lourié, "Papias." The same conclusion but without a detailed analysis and formulated as the most probable guess in Enrico Norelli, *Papia di Hierapolis. Esposizione degli oracoli del Signore, i frammenti* (Milan: Paoline, 2005) 406-7, quoted below as Norelli, *Papia*.

8. See the references in Lourié, "Papias," and also in Lourié, "An Unknown Danielic Pseudepigraphon from an Armenian Fragment of Papias," *JSP* 21 (2012): 243-59.

way, this is, in my opinion, the reason why our fragment was cut off from the Greek text of Andrew's *Commentary*.

No doubt there were in Second Temple Judaism some movements where the Watchers were not painted only in black. For instance, in *Jub.* 4:15 they came down to earth in order "to do justice," in contrast to *1 Enoch* where they taught humanity to do bad things. Nevertheless, in *Jub.* 7:21 the standard story of their fall with the women took place, and this "place" is before the Flood, that is, long before Moses. Moreover, in *2 Enoch* 18, some unfallen Watchers are depicted as inhabitants of the fifth heaven; however, they are quite passive and are instructed themselves by Enoch.[9]

In our Papias fragment the image of the Watchers is not only absolutely positive, with no connection to Giants, but even crucial for the Old Testament as a whole—because the Watchers, together with Michael, become the intercessors in the revelation of the Law to Moses. This is an independent tradition that should be traced.

Literary Context

There are two early Christian texts, both in Greek, that certainly represent the same tradition. Beside this, there is a third Greek Christian text, not so early (fifth cent.), that has to be read in the light of two previous sources and could in turn shed some light on them both.

The first *testimonium* belongs to Origen (ca. 185–ca. 254), fragment 109 of his *Commentary on Lamentations* preserved in the catenae. The author explains the only place in the *Christian* Greek Bible (that is, *not* in Aquila or Symmachus) where the term "Watchers" (*egrēgoroi*) occurs, Lam 4:14 LXX: "Her watchers were shaken in the exits, they were defiled with blood. Since they could not help it, they touch their garments."[10] The relevant part of the commentary runs as follows: "*Watchers* the Scripture calls angels, as (it is) in Daniel. And they were those by whom probably the Law has been given to Moses, according to *for if the Law spoken by angels*... (Heb 2:2)."[11]

Origen mentions the Watchers in the situation of the reception of the Law by Moses and refers to Daniel. He refers here to the Epistle to the Hebrews, namely, to the theology of angelic intercession that the author of Hebrews was trying to complete by his own concept of the priesthood according to the order of Melchizedek.

Our second source is the Greek title of a pseudepigraphic work called *Apocalypse of Moses* or *Life of Adam and Eve*. This title, lacking from all the Oriental and Latin versions of the work, has no internal relation to the text and is considered as a later addition peculiar to the Greek recension.[12] However, for us it is an independent source representing some ancient tradition, regardless of its own date. The title in question is: "Story and

9. I am grateful to Richard Bauckham for drawing my attention to this parallel.

10. Tr. by Peter J. Gentry in *A New English Translation of the Septuagint* (ed. A. Pietersma and B. G. Wright; Oxford: Oxford University Press, 2007), 941.

11. Origen, *Fragmenta in Lamentationes (in catenis)*, fr. 109, l. 3–5, in *Origenes Werke* (ed. E. Klostermann; GCS 6; Leipzig: Hinrichs, 1901), 3:235–78 (quoted according to *TLG* 2042.011). In all the MSS of Heb 2:2 there is "word" (*logos*) here instead of "law" (*nomos*); on this variant reading, which is not very strange in the early patristic context, and on its possible Jewish background cf. Lourié, "Papias," 520, note, and J. Daniélou, *The Theology of Jewish Christianity* (London: Darton, Longman, & Todd, 1964), 164.

12. Critical edition: D. A. Bertrand, *La vie grecque d'Adam et Ève. Introduction, texte, traduction et commentaire* (Recherches intertestamentaires 1; Paris: A. Maisonneuve, 1987). The work is certainly a pre-Christian Jewish one, even if the attempts at its precise localization within its Jewish context failed (cf. J. R. Levison, *Portraits of Adam in Early Judaism. From Sirach to 2 Baruch* [JSPSup 1; Sheffield: Sheffield Academic Press, 1988), 163-190 (chap. 10. Apocalypsis of Moses and *Vita Adae et Evae*).

Life of Adam and Eve the first-created, revealed by God to Moses his servant, when he received from the hand of the Lord the tablets of the Law of the Covenant,[13] being taught by archangel Michael."

There is no mention of the Watchers or Daniel, but in this case Michael is mentioned as a intercessor between Moses and God at Sinai.

Finally, Michael, Daniel, and even the angels and the citation of Heb 2:2 are gathered together around the figure of Moses at Sinai in the commentary of Theodoret of Cyrrhus (ca. 393-466) on Gal 3:19 (where the Law is said to be "ordained by angels"). This text is especially informative if checked against its more archaic background which is clearly the same as that in the above-quoted commentary by Origen.

After having quoted Heb 2:2, Theodoret continues: "Because the God of all established Michael for them, and this is what blessed Daniel taught us. And to great Moses He [*scil.*, God] promised to send together [with him] to the people an angel (Exodus 32:34)."[14]

Let us compare this quote with our first *testimonium* from Origen. An angelic intercession at Sinai is explained with the same double reference to Heb 2:2 (quoted explicitly in both cases) and to a "Daniel" (not quoted *verbatim*, in both cases as well). This is a distinctive mark of a common exegetical tradition. So, if we are still in the same exegetical vein, we have to identify "Michael" and the "angel" of Theodoret with the "Watchers" of Origen — taking into account that, according to our Papias, these "Watchers" are the guard of the same Michael! "Watcher" is replaced by "angel." Such a replacement is an example of the so-called concealment (of one notion by another), a phenomenon which affected very much the whole tradition under study.

It is most probably that Theodoret in the fifth century was the last Father (Andrew of Caesarea taken aside) who referred to an obscure Danielic source attributing to Michael and his angels-Watchers an intercessory role in the revelation of the Law at Sinai.

Now we can reconstruct the skeleton of our source as the following scheme:

1. claiming the authority of Daniel, it
2. describes the revelation of the Law to Moses at Sinai, when
3. Michael and
4. his angelic warriors—Watchers—
5. are the intercessors, and where
6. the Watchers are the helpers of humanity, with no connection to the fallen giants.

Biblical Connection: Dan 4:14 MT

Despite the fact that our Danielic source could not be identified with any part of any recension of the canonical Book of Daniel, it has some connection with this book, and especially with one verse, Dan 4:14 MT (Evv 4:17), the relevant part of which is lacking from the Septuagint (cf. its corresponding verse Dan 4:17 LXX), although translated into Greek by Aquila and Symmachus, as well as by Pseudo-Theodotion.

---

13. On the very peculiar phrase "the Law of the Covenant" known so far only from the Latin and Georgian versions of the *Epistles* attributed to St. Anthony the Great and also recovered with a great certitude in one place of a Tura papyrus of Didymus the Blind (this is the only case, besides the above, where it is available directly in its Greek original), cf. Lourié, "Papias," 521, note, and Lourié, "An Unknown Danielic Pseudepigraphon"; cf. also G. Couilleau, "'L' alliance' aux origines du monachisme égyptien," *Collectanea Cisterciensia* 39 (1977): 170-93.

14. Theodoret of Cyrrhus, *In Gal.* 3:19; PG 82, col. 481.

In its Aramaic original, Dan 4:14 MT runs as follows: "The sentence is rendered by decree of the Watchers, the decision is given by order of the holy ones, in order that all who live may know that the Most High is sovereign over the kingdom of mortals; he gives it to whom he will and sets over it the lowliest of human beings" (NRSV). Aramaic *ʿīrīn* "watchers" is rendered as *egrēgoroi* by Aquila and Symmachus, transliterated as *ir* by Pseudo-Theodotion and reinterpreted as *angelos* in the Septuagint in two neighbouring verses Dan 4:13, 23 LXX (= 4:10, 20 MT [Evv 4:13, 23]).

Although Dan 4:14 does not mention Moses or the Law revealed at Sinai, its topic is very close: "the sentence" of the Watchers and "the decision" of the holy ones, both on behalf of the Most High.

Indeed, the Book of Daniel is one of the most widely distributed books of the Bible, and so it is difficult to evaluate to what extent our pseudepigraphon was close to the Persian-era Jewish traditions crystallized here.

"Watchers" vs. "The Blind Ones"

We have already noticed that our source where the Watchers are good angelic beings contradicts the mainstream tradition where they fathered the fallen giants. But this is not all.

When comparing above a *testimonium* from Theodoret with another one from Origen we have seen an elimination of the term "Watcher" replaced by the neutral term "angel." We have seen as well the same policy in the Septuagint translation of Dan 4. But the ultimate roots of this policy are most probably within the Hebrew Bible — at least, such a hypothesis was put forward by Robert Murray.[15]

There is a need to recollect some points from Murray's article. He is working in a well-known field, although with new tools. As it is known, the mentions of (quasi-)divine beings were often excluded, by one means or another, from the Hebrew Bible: for example, Deut 32:43 where the "sons of God"—preserved in LXX and confirmed by Qumran—are deleted from MT. Sometimes, such names—as it was supposed by quite a few scholars—are not deleted, but simply distorted to obtain another meaning with a minimal alteration of the pronunciation. It is possible that the phenomenon of Aramaic-Hebrew bilingualism interfered here. The processes like these affected very much the history of the Aramaic term for "Watcher."

According to Murray, there was, in ancient Hebrew, a word *ʿ*yr* [pronounced as *ʿār* / *ʿēr* (pl. *ʿārîm* / *ʿērîm*)] having the etymological meaning "protect" and designating some protecting deities. As it is especially important, "*ʿār* / *ʿēr* could denote benevolent beings, and so be applied to good angels, obedient to God" (p. 315) — not to the fallen giants, let us add. Then, "like *malʾāk*, *ʿār* / *ʿēr* was adopted in Aramaic, where we find it vocalized *ʿîr* and soon understood as 'one who keeps awake' [that is, etymologized as a genuine Aramaic word]" (ibid.). During the process of suppression of the names of the pagan deities, this word became a subject of different changes. Sometimes it was replaced by its (consonantal) homograph "city" (e.g., Mic 5:13 [Evv. 5:14]), other times it was replaced by somewhat similar words with similar meaning relating to angelic/divine beings, e.g., *ṣîr* ("messenger" or maybe "intercessor"—as in Isa 63:9, where it is rendered by LXX as *presbys* in a verse very remarkable for us: "It was no ambassador or angel but the Lord himself that saved them").[16]

15. R. Murray, "The Origin of Aramaic *ʿir*, Angel," *Or* 53 (1984): 303-17.

16. Tr. by Moisés Silva in *A New English Translation of the Septuagint and the Other Greek Translations*

Finally, and this is the most original part of Murray's argument, sometimes the concealment was controlled by the purposes of the satire—"to help laugh them [polytheistic deities] out of people's hearts." So, a "mocking substitute" of *'ārîm* / *'ērîm* appears: it is *'iwrîm* "blind ones." "This would be the origin of the satirical sequence 'they have eyes and see not', etc. (Ps 115:5-7, 135:16-18). Perhaps it was 'Second Isaiah' who began the game" (cf. Isa 42:7, 16-19, 43:8, and 44:18) (pp. 312-13). The case of *'iwrîm* turned out to be analogous to that of other protecting divinities, *psḥ* (another root with the meaning "protect"), as it is especially evident in 2 Sam 5:6: "...the *'iwrîm* and *pisḥîm* which the Jebusites said would defend them... both refer to protecting deities" (p. 312).

But the textbook case is Lam 4:14, on which, as we have seen, Origen comments: "They have wandered *as* blind *men* in the streets" (NRSV), where the MT is "rendered" here as "Her watchers were shaken in the exits" by LXX (pp. 312-13). The only explanation of this fact is that the Hebrew original of LXX had "watchers" instead of "blind ones."

Two important points emerge from this review of Murray's study. First, our term *'îr* turns out to be somewhat akin to the term *ṣîr*, "messenger," "intercessor"; sometimes they are even used as synonyms, as in Isa 63:9. This corresponds to the intercessory role of the Watchers in our Danielic source. Even if suppressed and "concealed," this role is familiar to the biblical literature.

Second, in satirical contexts blindness could be a fitting mocking term for the Watchers who are, by definition, never sleeping and must be always clairvoyant.

The idea that some deities must be punished by blindness is certainly older than its "satirical" applications. What is especially significant to us is that it is already connected to the name of Daniel in Ugarit. Thus, in a prayer of Daniel (Dan'el) against 'Anatu (*CTA* 19.167-168), we find *'wr. yštk. b'l. lht. w'lmh*: "let Ba'al make thee blind from now and forever."

Bibliography

Lightfoot, J. B., and J. R. Harmer (editors and translators) and Michael W. Holmes (editor and reviser). Pages 589-90 in *The Apostolic Fathers: Greek Texts and English Translations of Their Writings.* 2nd edition. Grand Rapids, Mich.: Baker, 1992; 3rd edition, 2007, 763. (English translation, reviewed for publication by Joseph Alexanian)

Lourié, B. "A Quote from Papias within the Armenian Version of the *Commentary on Apocalypse* of St Andrew of Caesarea: Translation and Study in the History of the Exegesis." Pages 511-32 in *Writings of the Apostolic Fathers.* Edited by Alexey G. Dunaev. Moscow: Editorial Council of the Russian Orthodox Church, 2002 (rpt. 2008). (in Russian; contains a reprint of Siegert's edition and a Russian translation)

__________. "An Unknown Danielic Pseudepigraphon from an Armenian Fragment of Papias." *JSP* 21 (2012): 243-59. (English translation)

Norelli, Enrico. *Papia di Hierapolis. Esposizione degli oracoli del Signore, i frammenti*, pages 394-411. Milan: Paoline, 2005 (reprint of Siegert's edition, Italian translation by Valentina Calzolari, short study and commentaries based on this translation).

Siegert, Fölker. "Unbeachtete Papiaszitate bei Armenischen Schriftstellern." *NTS* 27 (1981): 605-14. (critical edition and German translation)

Traditionally Included under That Title (ed. A. Pietersma and B. G. Wright; Oxford: Oxford University Press, 2007), 872.

A Danielic Pseudepigraphon Paraphrased by Papias[a]

And Papias in his sermon (said) as follows: "The heaven did not bear his (the Dragon's) earthly thoughts, because it is impossible for the light to have communion with darkness. *He* (the Dragon) *was cast out into the earth* to live here, and when humanity came where he was, he did not allow (them) to behave according to the natural needs,[b] but led them astray into many evils. But Michael and his warriors who are the Watchers of the universe helped humanity, as Daniel taught, by giving the Law and by making the prophets wise."

2 Cor 6:14 | Rev 12:9

---

a. The whole Armenian fragment republished by F. Siegert was translated into German by him and into Russian by me (Lourié, "Papias"). It was translated into English in J. B. Lightfoot and J. R. Harmer (editors and translators) and Michael W. Holmes (editor and reviser), *The Apostolic Fathers: Greek Texts and English Translations of Their Writings* (3rd ed.; Grand Rapids, Mich: Baker, 1992), 763, but this translation is somewhat vague and contains some mistakes which make this translation unsuitable for any research purpose (e.g., in the part of the text quoted below he translates "treatises" [instead of "treatise/sermon"] and "laws" [instead of "Law"] despite the fact that the corresponding Armenian plural forms have normally the meaning of singular). In all the three previous translations, including my own Russian one, there was an important mistake corrected in Lourié, "An Unknown Danielic Pseudepigraphon."

b. Papias uses here a Stoic term "natural needs" unrecognised by the previous students of the fragment. See the full discussion in Lourié, "An Unknown Danielic Pseudepigraphon."

The Relics of Zechariah and the Boy Buried at His Feet

A new translation and introduction

by William Adler

The conclusion of the ninth book of the *Ecclesiastical History* of Salaminius Hermias Sozomenus (ca. 400-450 C.E.; hereafter Sozomen) recounts the discovery of the relics of the prophet Zechariah during the reign of Theodosius II, Roman emperor of the East from 408 to 450.[1] In the Palestinian village of Caphar-Zechariah near Eleutheropolis, Zechariah appeared to a tenant farmer named Calemerus and told him to dig up a double-coffin buried in a garden that he pointed out to him.[2] When Calemerus did so, he found two corpses. One, the body of the prophet, was dressed in the white raiment of a priest; despite the passage of time, his remains were in remarkably good condition. The other, clad in royal attire and lying outside the coffin at the prophet's feet, was that of a small boy, the identity of whom confounded the local priests and scholars. When Zacharias, the superior of the monastery of Gerara, consulted a Hebrew book, he learned that the young son of King Joash had died seven days after the king's assassination of Zechariah.[3] Interpreting the boy's death as a sign of divine displeasure over the murder of the prophet, Joash atoned for his act by burying his son at the feet of the prophet.

Provenance and Literary History

Sozomen's history contains numerous accounts of the finding of relics of prophets, saints and martyrs.[4] Eleutheropolis, in southwest Palestine, was a major site of their discovery. According to Sozomen, the remains of Micah and Habakkuk had previously been discovered there during the reign of Theodosius I.[5] For Sozomen, the discovery of findings

1. Sozomen, *Ecclesiastical History*, 9.16.3-17.6, ed. J. Bidez and G. C. Hansen (GCS 50; Berlin, 1960). For a later version of the same story, see Nicephorus Callistus Xanthopoulos, *Ecclesiastical History*, 14.8 (PG 146.1080-81).

2. Eleutheropolis (Beit Jibrin) was a Roman city of southwest Palestine. On the Madaba map, the village of Caphar-Zechariah is called Beth Zachar, and the tomb of Zechariah is shown next to it. For discussion of the contested location of the village, see J. Wilkinson, *Jerusalem Pilgrims before the Crusades* (Warminster: Aris and Phillips, 1977), 154 (according to Wilkinson, modern Horbat Bet Dikhrin, not Tel Zakariya). For various and competing Christian traditions about the burial site of Zechariah ben Jehoiada, see J. Jeremias, *Heiligengräber in Jesu Umwelt* (Göttingen: Vandenhoeck and Ruprecht, 1958), 67-72, 73 n. 3.

3. Gerara is Biblical Gerar (Gen 20:1), a city in the Negev; see Eusebius, *Onomasticon*, 60.7, who situates it twenty-five Roman miles south of Eleutheropolis. According to Sozomen, *Eccl. Hist.* 6.32.8, Zacharias succeeded Silvanus, a Palestinian monk who founded the monastery at Gerara. For discussion, see D. J. Chitty, *The Desert a City* (Crestwood, N.Y.: St. Vladimir's Press, 1995), 72-73.

4. Sozomen, *Eccl. Hist.* 7.21 (on the discovery of the head of John the Baptist); 9.2 (on the discovery of the remains of the 40 martyrs of Sebaste), following a dream of empress Pulcheria; see also the following note. On Sozomen's interest in relics, see R. Greer, *The Fear of Freedom* (University Park, Pa.: Penn State University Press, 1989), 99-100.

5. Sozomen, *Eccl. Hist.* 7.29.

like these were tokens of divine favor. Although Theodosius II had acceded to rule of the eastern empire at a very young age, his reign, Sozomen writes, was marked by unexpected peace and prosperity, and the discovery of the relics of many ancient people of piety. As proof that all of these things were orchestrated by God, he promises to describe in detail the miraculous discoveries of the remains of both the prophet Zechariah and Saint Stephen. But book nine of the work, the last book of the *Ecclesiastical History,* ends prematurely, with a brief description of the well-preserved state of Zechariah's corpse, and nothing said about the equally sensational finding of Stephen's remains.[6]

In his narrative of the discovery of the remains of Zechariah, Sozomen identifies the prophet Zechariah with Zechariah ben Jehoiada, a priest who was stoned to death in the Temple by agents of king Joash for accusing the king of transgressing divine commandments (2 Chr 24:20-22). Uncertainty over the meaning of Jesus' words in the Gospel according to Matthew was partly responsible for the conflation of the two figures. In Matthew's Gospel, Jesus refers at one point to the "blood of Zechariah, the son of Barachiah, whom you murdered between the sanctuary and the altar" (Matt 23:35). Zechariah ben Berechiah, the prophet and author of the biblical book in his name, lived at a time when the rebuilding of the Jerusalem temple was still underway; nor is there any corroborating biblical evidence about his martyrdom.[7] For these reasons, some Christian interpreters supposed that Jesus was referring here to the martyrdom of the priest Zechariah at the hands of King Joash. According to Jerome, the text of Jesus' words in the *Gospel of the Nazarenes* reinforced this identification by reading Zechariah, "son of Jehoiada" instead of "son of Barachiah." One of the recensions of the *Vitae Prophetarum* actually combined the lives of the two Zechariahs into a single biography.[8] Known to both Jerome and John Chrysostom, the fusion of the two figures must have been fairly widespread by the late fourth century. Sozomen's own report of the discovery of the relics of Zechariah, which describes him as both priest and prophet, presupposes the same identification.[9]

In the account in Chronicles, Zechariah's call upon God to avenge his death came to pass when Joash's army was subsequently delivered into the hands of a much smaller Syrian force. Wounded in battle, Joash himself was murdered in his bed by his servants and then denied a burial in the tombs of the kings (2 Chr 24:23-25). Later Jewish and Christian writers, evidently dissatisfied with this act of divine retribution for the slaying of a priest and prophet in God's own sanctuary, enlarged both the enormity of the crimes against

6. On Sozomen's failure to complete the ninth book, see D. Rohrbacher, *The Historians of Late Antiquity* (London: Routledge, 2002), 121-22. Nicephorus' reprise of Sozomen's story appends an account of the findings of Stephen's relics (*Eccl. Hist.* 14.9); see also *Epistola Luciani* (PL 41.807-818), which locates his tomb in Caphar-Gamala, a village 20 miles to the north of Jerusalem. For discussion see D. Hunt, *Holy Land Pilgrimage in the later Roman Empire* (Oxford: Clarendon, 1982), 212-16.

7. See W. D. Davies and D. Allison, *A Critical and Exegetical Commentary on the Gospel according to Saint Matthew* (ICC; Edinburgh: T.&T. Clark, 1997), 3:318-19.

8. Jerome, *Comm. in Matt.* 23:35-36, ed. E. Bonnard (SC 259; Éditions du Cerf, Paris, 1979), 180.297–182.1; C. C. Torrey, ed. and trans., *Lives of the Prophets*, 31 n. 76 (recension E1 of the *Vitae Prophetarum*).

9. John Chrysostom, *Hom. 74.2 in Matt.* (PG 58.681); Jerome, *Comm. in Matt.* 23.35-36. Some other interpreters suggested the possibility that Jesus was referring to the martyrdom of Zechariah, the father of John the Baptist; see Origen, *Comment. ser.* 25 (on Matt 23:29-36), ed. E. Klostermann (GCS 38.2; Leipzig: Teubner, 1933), 42.14-42. For discussion of the tradition, see G. H. W. Lampe, "Martyrdom and Inspiration," in W. Horbury and B. McNeil, eds., *Suffering and Martyrdom in the New Testament* (Cambridge: Cambridge University Press, 1981), 127-28; H. von Campenhausen, "Das Martyrium des Zacharias," in idem, *Aus der Frühzeit des Christentums* (Tübingen: J. C. B. Mohr, 1963), 302-7; H. J. Schoeps, "Die jüdische Prophetenmorde," in idem, *Aus frühchristlicher Zeit* (Tübingen: Mohr, 1950), 138-41.

Zechariah and the punishments visited upon the king and the people of Israel. According to the *Vitae Prophetarum*, Zechariah was buried in the temple next to his father, after which all revelations in the Temple came to an end.[10] Rabbinic accounts implicate all of Israel in the crime, and extend the number of crimes committed against him from one to seven. One well-attested Jewish legend describes how the spilt blood of Zechariah was later avenged by the Babylonian general Nebuzaradan. After finding Zechariah's blood still boiling in the Jerusalem temple 250 years after his murder, Nebuzaradan tried to atone for his death by slaughtering 80,000 young Jewish priests.[11] The sequence of events recorded in the anonymous "Hebrew book" consulted by Zacharias implicitly contests the rabbinic legend about Zechariah's unavenged blood. The untimely death of Joash's young son, "who was very dear to him," the king's penitence, and his act of atonement expiated the king's crime against the priest and prophet (4.4).

Apart from his comment that the Hebrew book did not circulate in the churches (4.1), Sozomen says little else about the work, even failing to provide it with a title.[12] There are also some unexpected turns in his account of events leading up to and following the discovery of Zechariah's tomb. At the beginning of his narrative, Sozomen describes in some detail the character and background of Calemerus, the tenant farmer to whom Zachariah appeared. The description of Calemerus' moral failings—most notably his cruelty and dishonesty to the local peasants—invites the initial impression that the story will conclude with an account of his moral reformation. But after the discovery of the relics, Calemerus abruptly departs from the scene. From that point, the tale turns into a suspense story about the identity of the mysterious young boy buried at the prophet's feet and the role of the superior of a nearby monastery in helping to solve the puzzle. Zacharias not only finds the little-known Hebrew book; he possesses the learning to understand its contents.

Text and Translation

The GCS edition of Sozomen's *Ecclesiastical History* by J. Bidez and G. C. Hansen supplied the Greek text for this translation. A recently published volume of books 7-9 of the *Ecclesiastical History* in *Sources Chrétiennes* contains a French translation of the discovery of Zechariah's remains.[13] An older English translation of Sozomen can also be found in the *Nicene and Post-Nicene Fathers*.[14]

Bibliography

Berendts, A. *Studien über Zacharias-Apokryphen und Zacharias-Legenden*. Leipzig: Deichert, 1895.

10. Torrey, *Lives of the Prophets*, 31-32.

11. *b. Git.* 57b. A variant version of the legend (*b. Sanh.* 96b) sets the number of deaths at 940,000. For an enumeration of the several crimes committed against Zechariah, see, for example, *Eccl. Rab.* 3.16. For discussion of the rabbinic witnesses, see S. H. Blank, "The Death of Zachariah in Rabbinic Literature," *HUCA* 12-13 (1937-38): 338-46; B. H. Amaru, "The Killing of the Prophets," *HUCA* 54 (1983): 166-70.

12. For discussion of this book in relationship to other apocryphal books circulating in the name of Zechariah, see A. Berendts, *Studien über Zacharias-Apokryphen und Zacharias-Legenden* (Leipzig: Deichert, 1895), 13-19; also A. Denis, *Introduction aux pseudepigraphes grecs d'Ancien Testament* (SVTP 1; Leiden: Brill, 1970), 302-3, who raises the possibility that the book circulated in the name of Zechariah.

13. A. J. Festugière and B. Grillet, trans., *Sozomène. Histoire Ecclésiastique* (SC 516; Paris: Éditions du Cerf, 2008). For their translation, Festugière and Grillet used the Greek text of the Bidez-Hansen edition.

14. P. Schaff and H. Wace, eds., *A Select Library of Nicene and Post-Nicene Fathers of the Early Church*, Second Series, Vol. 2, *Socrates, Sozomenus: Church Histories* (New York, 1890), 179-427.

Bidez, J., and G. C. Hansen, eds. *Sozomenus. Kirchengeschichte* (GCS 50). Berlin: Akademie-Verlag, 1960.

Blank, S. "The Death of Zechariah in Rabbinic Literature." *HUCA* 12-13 (1937-38): 327-46.

Denis, A.-M. *Introduction aux pseudepigraphes grecs d'Ancien Testament* (SVTP 1). Leiden: Brill, 1970.

Festugière, A.-J. and B. Grillet, trans. *Sozomène, Histoire Ecclésiastique, Livres VII-IX* (Sources Chrétiennes 516). Paris: Éditions du Cerf, 2008.

Lampe, G. W. H. "Martyrdom and Inspiration." Pages 118-35 in *Suffering and Martyrdom in the New Testament*. Edited by W. Horbury and B. McNeil. Cambridge: Cambridge University Press, 1981.

The Relics of Zechariah and the Boy Buried at His Feet

1 [1]He (Constantius III) did not live much longer, and died, leaving two children, Valentinian,[a] who succeeded Honorius, and Honoria. [2]At this time, the part of the empire to the east was free of its enemies, and the management of affairs there was very orderly. This was contrary to everyone's expectation, because the emperor was still young.[b] [3]God, it seemed, was obviously pleased with this reign, not only by unexpectedly arranging military matters in this way, but by bringing to light the holy bodies of many people of old who were highly esteemed for piety. [4]This is in fact what happened at that time in the case of
Acts 6:5 Zechariah the ancient prophet and Stephen the deacon ordained by the apostles.
[5]Because the discovery of each one of them was both miraculous and divine, it is necessary to describe how it happened.[c]

2 [1]I shall begin with the prophet. Caphar-Zacharia is a village of the territory of Eleutheropolis in Palestine.[d] [2]The manager of this village was someone named Calemerus, who was a tenant farmer on the land. [3]He was congenial to the owner, but harsh, ill-tempered, and unfair towards the neighboring peasants. [4]Although he was a man of such character, the prophet appeared to him while he was awake, and revealed who he was. [5]He pointed out a garden and said, "Go and dig there at a measured distance of two cubits from the wall to the garden, along the road leading to the village of Beththerebis. [6]You will find a double coffin, the interior one made of wood enclosed inside a lead one on the outside. [7]Around the coffin, you will find a glass vessel full of water and two serpents of moderate size, docile and innocuous, so as to be seemingly tame."[e]

3 [1]In accordance with the instruction of the prophet, Calemerus arrived at the place he had indicated, and wasted no time in getting to work. [2]When, thanks to the aforementioned markers, the sacred chest was revealed, the divine prophet was discovered inside, outfitted in a tunic and white raiment; hence,

---

a. Valentinian III (419-455), the Roman emperor in the West from 425 to 455.

b. The emperor in the East at the time was Theodosius II (408-50), who was seven years of age at the time of his accession to the throne.

c. Sozomen fails to follow through on his promise to describe the discovery of Stephen's relics; see the Introduction.

d. On the locations of these places, see the Introduction.

e. For snakes as symbols of the dead, see J. M. C. Toynbee, *Death and Burial in the Roman World* (Baltimore, Md.: Johns Hopkins, 1996), 14, 256 For the understanding of a pair of docile snakes as portents and guardian spirits in Roman religion, see G. K. Boyce, "Significance of the Serpents on Pompeian House Shrines," *AJA* 46 (1992): 13-22

I suppose he was a priest. [3]At his feet, outside of the chest lay a child who had been honored with a royal burial. [4]He was wearing a golden crown on his head, golden sandals, and a costly robe.

4 [1]Because the priests and sages of that time were at a loss about this child—
who he was, where he came from, and why he was attired this way—, it is said
that Zacharias, the superior of a monastic community in Gerara,[a] came upon an
ancient Hebrew book, not used in the churches. [2]It explained how, when Joash,
king of Judea, had executed Zachariah, he experienced a short time thereafter a
terrible calamity that befell his household. [3]On the seventh day after the death of 2 Chr 24:20-22
the prophet, his son, who was very dear to him, suddenly died. [4]After concluding that he had suffered this misfortune through the wrath of God, he buried the
youngster at his feet, thereby making satisfaction for the wrong he had done to
him. This is what I have learned.[b] [5]As for the prophet, although he had been in
the ground for a great many generations, he had a well-preserved appearance,
his hair shorn, nose straight, with a beard moderately grown, and a rather small
head, eyes slightly sunken and covered by his eyebrows.[c]

a. Biblical Gerar (Gen 20:1). On Zacharias and the monastery of Gerara, see n. 3 in the Introduction.

b. Cf. Nicephorus: "And this was determined in the following way." Nicephorus apparently understood the intact preservation of Zechariah's body as evidence that God had absolved Joash of his transgression.

c. See Festugière and Grillet, *Sozomène*, 3449 (n. 5 to *Eccl. Hist.* 9176), who point to a similarity between Sozomen's physical description of Zechariah's remains and the representation of Christian saints and church fathers in Byzantine iconography.

Sefer Zerubbabel: The Prophetic Vision of Zerubbabel ben Shealtiel

A new translation and introduction

by John C. Reeves

Sefer Zerubbabel, or the "Book of Zerubbabel," is the rubric most commonly applied to an influential post-talmudic assemblage of Jewish apocalyptic traditions depicting the elusive postexilic biblical leader Zerubbabel as the recipient of a set of revelatory visions which outline a succession of personages and events that are to be associated with the restoration of Israel at the End of Days. Extant in a number of manuscript and print editions, almost all of which vary from one another in significant ways, the textual cluster(s) signaled by this title are a prime example of what has been termed the "anthological model" of documentary composition, an authorial process whereby smaller relatively integral thematic units "were viewed by their literary handlers as elements in a larger kaleidoscope of tradition perceived as an authentic communal possession ... a kind of freeze-frame of that tradition, temporarily stilled by the intervention of the compilational activity itself."[1] There are in fact a multitude of *Sefer Zerubbabels*, each one of which reflects the time, place, and concerns of its compilers.[2] Those who work with the materials comprising this text must recognize that its various extant forms weave together traditions which emanate from a variety of textual environments: given the present state of the witnesses, the preparation of a critical edition or even the editorial attainment of an *Urtext* or "original edition" of *Sefer Zerubbabel* would appear to be an impossible task.

Contents

Sefer Zerubbabel's importance for the history of medieval apocalypticism cannot be overstated. It repeatedly demonstrates how a written text—in its case, the Jewish Bible—has achieved an almost unsurpassed authority in the invention and construction of a special kind of discourse that thanks to the political and social turbulence of the times was enjoying widespread popularity among a variety of religious communities in the Near East dur-

1. Martin S. Jaffee, "Rabbinic Authorship as a Collective Enterprise," in *The Cambridge Companion to the Talmud and Rabbinic Literature* (ed. Charlotte Elisheva Fonrobert and Martin S. Jaffee; Cambridge: Cambridge University Press, 2007), 17-37, at p. 33. See especially the discussions found in *The Anthology in Jewish Literature* (ed. David Stern; Oxford: Oxford University Press, 2004).

2. With regard to the way texts like *Sefer Zerubbabel* were "authored" and transmitted, see Malachi Beit-Arié, "Publication and Reproduction of Literary Texts in Medieval Jewish Civilization: Jewish Scribality and Its Impact on the Texts Transmitted," in *Transmitting Jewish Traditions: Orality, Textuality, and Cultural Diffusion* (ed. Yaakov Elman and Israel Gershoni; New Haven: Yale University Press, 2000), 225-47.

This is an abbreviated and revised version of my previously published introduction to and translation of *Sefer Zerubbabel* in John C. Reeves, *Trajectories in Near Eastern Apocalyptic: A Postrabbinic Jewish Apocalypse Reader* (Atlanta and Leiden: Society of Biblical Literature and Brill, 2005), 40-66. I am grateful to those publishers for granting me permission to reutilize some of that material here.

ing the second half of the first Christian millennium. Many of the structural elements in *Sefer Zerubbabel* possess intriguing reflections or echoes within a number of roughly contemporary Christian, Muslim, Zoroastrian, and gnostic apocalypses that were produced within the Islamicate world. It either initiates or significantly enhances several motifs that attain popularity in certain strands of medieval Jewish literature, such as an eschatological role for the figure of Zerubbabel,[3] a linear redemptive scheme that involves the participation of two named messianic heroes (the messiah of the lineage of Joseph [Nehemiah ben Ḥushiel] and the messiah of the lineage of David [Menaḥem b. 'Amiel]), the performance of marvels through the recovery of wonder-working prophetic relics (e.g., the rod of Moses/Aaron), and the ominous advent, hubristic tyranny, and eventual suppression of the monstrous supernaturally-sired opponent known as Armilos, a name which also occurs in two seventh-century Christian texts.[4] *Sefer Zerubbabel* also has curious features which are employed in no other Jewish work, such as the martial exploits associated with the mother of the Davidic messiah, a heroine who bears the curious name Hephṣibah.[5]

Editions and Manuscripts

The first printed edition of *Sefer Zerubbabel* appeared in Constantinople in 1519[6] within an anthology of similarly revelatory and didactic midrashim.[7] This edition of the work was reprinted together with brief annotations in 1807 as *Sefer Zerubbabel we-neḥemot Ṣiyyon* (i.e., *Sefer Zerubbabel and the Consolation of Zion*). This annotated edition was reprinted again, together with a so-called *(Sefer) Malkiel*, in Vilna in 1819,[8] and then reprinted once more by S. A. Wertheimer in his *Leqeṭ Midrashim* in 1903 in Jerusalem. Wertheimer had

3. For details, see Reeves, *Trajectories*, 41-47.

4. N. Bonwetsch, ed., *Doctrina Iacobi nuper baptizati* (Abhandlungen der königlichen Gesellschaft der Wissenschaften zu Göttingen, phil.-hist. klass., n.f., bd. 12, nr. 3; Berlin: Weidmannsche Buchhandlung, 1910), 60, 74, 86; G. J. Reinink (ed.), *Die syrische Apokalypse des Pseudo-Methodius* (CSCO 540, script. syri 220; Louvain: Peeters, 1993), 18. The designation "Armilos" is most often compared to that of the founder of Rome "Romulus," but it probably derives instead from the Greek *Erēmolaos* "destroyer of a people" which is consonant with the folk etymology for the name "Balaam" supplied in *b. Sanh.* 105a ("destroyer of a people"). See Israel Lévi, "L'Apocalypse de Zorobabel et le roi de Perse Siroès," *REJ* 68 (1914): 152 n. 6; Reeves, *Trajectories*, 19-20; and especially the persuasive arguments of David Berger, "Three Typological Themes in Early Jewish Messianism: Messiah Son of Joseph, Rabbinic Calculations, and the Figure of Armilus," *AJSR* 10 (1985): 158-62.

5. According to 2 Kgs 21:1, this was the name of the mother of Manasseh. However, the same name is used figuratively (meaning "my delight is in her") for Zion in Isa 62:4. Many scholars view her as a Jewish foil to the Christian image of the Virgin Mary as mother of Jesus.

6. Zunz-Albeck, *Haderashot*, 311 n. 89; Even-Shmuel, *Midreshey Ge'ullah*, 67-70. Graetz identified the anthology as a volume entitled *Liqquṭim Shonim* (idem, *Geschichte*[3], 6:53 n. 4), an identification that was repeated by Moses Buttenwieser, *Outline of the Neo-Hebraic Apocalyptic Literature* (Cincinnati: Jennings & Pye, 1901), 23, 33. Contrast however Marvin J. Heller, *The Sixteenth Century Hebrew Book: An Abridged Thesaurus* (2 vols.; Leiden: Brill, 2004), 1:127, who places its first printing within a collection called *Haliqquṭim we-ha-ḥibburim* (Constantinople: Astruq de Toulon, 1519), 60a-62b; also see Lévi ("L'Apocalypse," 130), who claims that its first printing was in a volume now "introuvable" ("unfindable") bearing the title *Sefer Ben Sira*. These latter two works are in fact the same; see Eli Yassif, *Sippurey Ben Sira be-yemey ha-benayim* (Jerusalem: Magness, 1984), 196.

7. *Ma'asiyōt* (Constantinople: Astruq de Toulon, 1519), 74a-76b. For its contents and a listing of the various editions of *Sefer Zerubbabel*, see Moritz Steinschneider, *Catalogus librorum hebraeorum in bibliotheca Bodleiana* (3 vols.; Berlin: Ad. Friedlaender, 1852-60), 203, 208.

8. Hezekiah (Chiskia) ben Abraham, *Malkiel* (Vilna and Grodno: [Romm?], 1819), 25a-28a (the latter leaf misprinted as 27), to which are appended the Sabbatian chapters from *Hekhalot Rabbati* (28a-29a) and excerpts from *Pesiqta Rabbati* (29a-29b) and *Yalquṭ Šimoni* (29b-30b).

previously uncovered and published two manuscript fragments of the work stemming from the Cairo Genizah and Oxford Ms. Heb. f. 27 (2642) respectively, the latter of which he placed under the artificial rubric "Aggadat yemot ha-mašiaḥ" ("Narrative about the Messianic Age").[9] The revised and enlarged edition of Wertheimer's separate midrash anthologies prepared by his grandson presents a lightly annotated version of the Constantinople *editio princeps* together with five brief fragments culled from the aforementioned "Aggadat yemot ha-mašiaḥ."[10] Another shorter recension of the work based on two manuscripts contained in the municipal library at Leipzig was published by Adolph Jellinek in the mid-nineteenth century.[11] The fullest edition of the work, prepared by Israel Lévi, is based on a lengthy rendition that was incorporated within Oxford Ms. Heb. d. 11 (2797), the *Sefer ha-Zikronot* or the so-called *Chronicles of Yeraḥmeel*.[12] Lévi also drew attention to Oxford Ms. Opp. 236a, a version in an Ashkenazi cursive script which varies from both the *editio princeps* and the briefer recension published by Jellinek,[13] and Paris Ms. 326, a compilation which "contient une paraphrase partielle de notre libelle."[14] Lévi's edition also features a critical apparatus wherein he reproduces a number (although not all) of the variant readings found in the aforementioned manuscript and print editions. Even-Shmuel's *Midreshey Ge'ullah* presents that editor's highly idiosyncratic conflate version of the work. It contains many speculative emendations and questionable reconstructions, but also is accompanied by a comprehensive discussion which includes many valuable annotations. He also separately reproduces the printed editions of Constantinople, Jellinek, and Lévi.[15] Finally, there are some manuscript fragments which have not been employed in the standard printed editions of the work. Oxford Ms. Opp. 603 contains a brief version of *Sefer Zerubbabel* (fols. 32b-34b).[16] Alexander Marx called attention to some further examples of *Zerubbabel* materials.[17] Simon Hopkins in his published anthology of literary texts has reproduced the photographs of several fragments of *Sefer Zerubbabel* which have been recovered from the Cairo Genizah.[18]

---

9. S. A. Wertheimer, *Batey Midrashot* (4 vols. in 3; Jerusalem: M. Lilyanthal, 1893-97), 2:29.

10. Wertheimer, *Batey Midrashot* (ed. A. J. Wertheimer), 2:497-505.

11. Jellinek, *BHM*, 2:xxi-xxii, 54-57. The text published by Jellinek was reprinted by J. D. Eisenstein, *Ozar Midrashim: A Library of Two Hundred Minor Midrashim* (2 vols.; New York: J. D. Eisenstein, 1915), 1:158-61.

12. Lévi, "L'Apocalypse," 131-44. That manuscript has recently been transcribed and published by Eli Yassif, *Sefer ha-Zikronot hu' Divrey ha-Yamim le-Yeraḥme'el* (Tel Aviv: Tel Aviv University, 2001); see pp. 427-35 for *Sefer Zerubbabel*.

13. Fols. 13a-15b. Cf. Adolf Neubauer, *Catalogue of the Hebrew Manuscripts in the Bodleian Library* ... (Oxford: Clarendon, 1886), 26-27; also Malachi Beit-Arié, *Catalogue of the Hebrew Manuscripts in the Bodleian Library: Supplement of Addenda and Corrigenda to Volume I (A. Neubauer's Catalogue)* (Oxford: Clarendon, 1994), 22.

14. Lévi, "L'Apocalypse," 130. See Alexander Marx, "Studies in Gaonic History and Literature," *JQR* n.s. 1 (1910-11): 61-104, at p. 77, where a lengthy passage from this manuscript is transcribed. Marx dates the manuscript "between 1160 and 1180."

15. Even-Shmuel, *Midreshey Ge'ullah*, 71-88. Cf. ibid. 379-82 (Constantinople); 383-85 (Jellinek); 385-89 (Lévi).

16. Beit-Arié, *Catalogue*, 440: "with variations from the printed editions and shorter towards the end." This is followed (35a-36b) by a piece entitled "The King Messiah," and fols. 41b-42a of the same manuscript feature a short presentation entitled "(On) the Subject of the River Sambatyon," a work related to the Eldad ha-Dani legends.

17. See Marx, "Studies," 77-78 n. 35; idem, "Additions et rectifications," *REJ* 71 (1920): 222.

18. T-S A45.5, 45.7, 45.19, and 45.22; published in Simon Hopkins, *A Miscellany of Literary Pieces from the Cambridge Genizah Collections: A Catalogue and Selection of Texts in the Taylor-Schechter Collection, Old Series, Box A45* (Cambridge: Cambridge University Library, 1978), 10, 15, 64-65, 72-73.

The present translation is based primarily on the text of the Oxford manuscript first published by Lévi and a comparison of its text with the new transcription of Yassif. In addition, I have also consulted the printed editions supplied by Jellinek, Wertheimer, and Even-Shmuel, and have made occasional use of the Genizah fragments published in Hopkins. Other manuscript versions of this work which I have examined for this translation and which sometimes figure in the notes include Oxford Ms. Opp. 236a fols. 13a-15b; Oxford Ms. Opp. 603 fols. 32b-34; and Oxford Ms. Heb. f. 27 (2642) fols. 42-43.[19]

Date, Provenance, and Literary Context

Issues pertaining to the date and provenance of *Sefer Zerubbabel* are problematic. Allusions to Islam or the suzerainty of Arab rulers are minimal at best.[20] The repetitious calculations pertaining to a lapsed number of years or dynastic successions of kings probably reflect later attempts to update the book's information in the light of more recent history. Although Adolph Jellinek considered the work "sehr alt,"[21] a number of late-nineteenth-century interpreters followed the influential historian Heinrich Graetz in placing the work in the middle of the eleventh century.[22] Most modern scholars accept the persuasive arguments advanced by Israel Lévi for locating the work during the first quarter of the seventh century in Palestine within the context of the fierce struggles of Persia and Rome for control of the Holy Land.[23] Joseph Dan has recently argued against this seventh-century setting, preferring instead to place it indeterminately "within the range of the third to the sixth centuries."[24] A number of scholars, however, have sought to use the enigmatic references to the passage of "990 years" after the destruction of the Temple as a clue for dating *Sefer Zerubbabel* later than the seventh century.[25] Moshe Gil has for example stated: "It is

19. With regard to this last manuscript, see Adolf Neubauer and A. E. Cowley, *Catalogue of the Hebrew Manuscripts in the Bodleian Library Volume Two* (Oxford: Clarendon, 1906), 37.

20. Cairo Geniza fragments 2 and 4 published in S. A. Wertheimer, *Batey Midrashot* (ed. A. J. Wertheimer; 2 vols.; 2nd ed.; Jerusalem, 1948-53; repr., Jerusalem: Ktav wa-Sefer, 1980), 2:497-505, at 503-505; also in various fragments from the Geniza recently identified and published by Moshe Gil, "The Apocalypse of Zerubbabel in Judaeo-Arabic," *REJ* 165 (2006): 1-98.

21. Jellinek, *BHM*, 2:xxii.

22. H[einrich]. Graetz, *Geschichte der Juden von ältesten Zeiten bis auf die Gegenwart* (3d ed.; 11 vols. in 13; Leipzig: Oskar Leiner, 1890-1908), 6:53-55. For references to other scholars who followed Graetz, see Israel Lévi, "L'Apocalypse de Zorobabel et le roi de Perse Siroès: (Suite)," *REJ* 69 (1914): 108-111. Graetz also opined that it was composed in Italy and was probably unknown in Palestine, neither of which conclusions seems likely now. Renewed support for Graetz's dating has been recently voiced by Gil, "Apocalypse of Zerubbabel," 9-10.

23. See Lévi, "L'Apocalypse (Suite)," 108-15. Note also Joseph Dan, *Ha-Sippur ha-'ivri be-yemey ha-benayim: 'Iyyunim be-toldotav* (Jerusalem: Keter, 1974), 36-37, 43; Salo W. Baron, *A Social and Religious History of the Jews* (18 vols.; 2nd ed.; Philadelphia, Pa., and New York: Jewish Publication Society and Columbia University Press, 1952-83), 5:354 n. 3; Brannon M. Wheeler, "Imagining the Sasanian Capture of Jerusalem," *OCP* 57 (1991): 73; Walter E. Kaegi, *Byzantium and the Early Islamic Conquests* (Cambridge: Cambridge University Press, 1992), 207; David Biale, "Counter-History and Jewish Polemics Against Christianity: The *Sefer toldot yeshu* and the *Sefer zerubavel*," *Jewish Social Studies* n.s. 6 (1999): 137; Hagith Sivan, *Palestine in Late Antiquity* (Oxford: Oxford University Press, 2008), 241-42, 351-52. Wheeler departs from a general consensus that the work is Palestinian in provenance by suggesting that *Sefer Zerubbabel* was authored in Edessa after the arrival of Heraclius in Jerusalem in 630.

24. Joseph Dan, "Armilus: The Jewish Antichrist and the Origins and Dating of the *Sefer Zerubbavel*," in *Toward the Millennium: Messianic Expectations from the Bible to Waco* (ed. Peter Schäfer and Mark Cohen; Leiden: Brill, 1998), 73-104, at 98.

25. See Lévi, "L'Apocalypse (Suite)," 109 n. 1.

quite likely that the hardship and stress of these years [the mid-eleventh century] were the major factors contributing to predictions of the imminent end of the world in 1058 ('when 990 years from the destruction of Jerusalem are completed')."[26] Yet it is also observable that the number "990" possesses millenarian and even astronomical/astrological significance within multiple apocalyptic contexts.[27] Even-Shmuel has suggested that the book's reference to the passage of "990 years" need not begin its count with the destruction of the Temple in 68 C.E., but may be keyed to its reconstruction in the sixth century B.C.E. If so, then by using the rabbinic calculation of the duration of the Second Temple as 420 years and subtracting that sum from 990, the work may aim at 570 + 68 or 638 C.E. as the anticipated time of the End.[28]

References to or explicit acknowledgement of *Sefer Zerubbabel* among medieval Jewish sources do not clarify these questions to any great extent. The *Zohar* (III, 173b) is cognizant of the legend of Hephṣibah, the mother of the Davidic messiah: as observed above, her name and role are unique to *Sefer Zerubbabel* and its derivative literature.[29] R. Eleazar b. Judah of Worms (1165-1230) refers to the book in his *Sefer Roqeaḥ* under the rubric "Baraitha de-Zerubbabel."[30] In his commentary to Exod 2:22, Abraham Ibn Ezra (1089-1164) criticizes *Sefer Zerubbabel* as "unreliable."[31] Some editions of the commentary to *'Abot* contained in *Maḥzor Vitry*, supposedly the work of Rashi (1040-1105), refer to *Sefer Zerubbabel* for the identification of Aaron's rod (*m. 'Abot* 5.6).[32] It seems likely that both R. Saadya Gaon (882-942) and R. Ḥai ben Sherira Gaon (939-1038) knew it, although neither refers to it by name.[33] Nevertheless firm evidence for the existence of *Sefer Zerubbabel* prior to the tenth century remains elusive. The partial inclusion and expansion of some sections of *Sefer Zerubbabel* found in the final portion of some editions of *Hekhalot Rabbati* are not indigenous to that work, but stem from the seventeenth-century mes-

---

26. Moshe Gil, *A History of Palestine, 634-1099* (Cambridge: Cambridge University Press, 1992), 401-402.

27. See Manetho, frag. 64 (*apud* W. G. Waddell, *Manetho with an English Translation* [LCL 350; Cambridge, Mass.: Harvard University Press, 1940], 164-65), together with the comments of Ludwig Koenen, "Manichaean Apocalypticism at the Crossroads of Iranian, Egyptian, Jewish and Christian Thought," in *Codex Manichaicus Coloniensis: Atti del Simposio Internazionale (Rende-Amantea 3-7 settembre 1984)* (ed. Luigi Cirillo and Amneris Roselli; Cosenza: Marra Editore, 1986), 315-16 nn. 90-91; and especially Moritz Steinschneider, "Apokalypsen mit polemischer Tendenz," *ZDMG* 28 (1874): 629-34. The "revelation of Akatriel to R. Ishmael" mentioned by the latter scholar (p. 631) refers to the so-called *'Aggadat R. Ishmael*; see Yehudah Even-Shmuel, *Midreshey Ge'ullah* (2nd ed.; Jerusalem: Mosad Bialik, 1954), 144-52, 399-400.

28. Even-Shmuel, *Midreshey Ge'ullah*, lix-lx, 61-63.

29. For some recent discussions of this figure, see Biale, "Counter-History," 139-42; Peter Schäfer, *Mirror of His Beauty: Feminine Images of God from the Bible to the Early Kabbalah* (Princeton, N.J.: Princeton University Press, 2002), 213-16; Martha Himmelfarb, "The Mother of the Messiah in the Talmud Yerushalmi and Sefer Zerubbabel," in *The Talmud Yerushalmi and Graeco-Roman Culture, III* (ed. Peter Schäfer; TSAJ 93; Tübingen: Mohr Siebeck, 2002), 369-89; Sivan, *Palestine*, 236-43.

30. Alexander Marx, "Studies in Gaonic History and Literature," *JQR* n.s. 1 (1910-11): 76.

31. "Any book not authored by a prophet or a Sage reliant upon tradition is unreliable ... such as *Sefer Zerubbabel*...." Passage translated from the edition prepared by Asher Weiser, ed., *Perushey ha-Torah le-Rabbenu Abraham Ibn Ezra* (3 vols.; Jerusalem: Mosad Harav Kook, 1977), 2:20. See also Graetz, *Geschichte*[3], 6:53-54 n. 4; Leopold Zunz and Ḥanokh Albeck, *Haderashot be-Yisrael* (2nd ed.; Jerusalem: Mosad Bialik, 1954), 311 n. 88.

32. Other editions however read "Chronicles of Moses" here instead.

33. Even-Shmuel, *Midreshey Ge'ullah*, 66. Jellinek (*BHM*, 2:xxii) points out that Saadya already knows the Armilos legend. See also Gil, "Apocalypse of Zerubbabel," 3-5.

sianic movement of Shabbatai Ṣevi.[34] Some have pointed to the eschatological poetry of Eleazar ha-Qallir as evidence for the work's existence, especially a *piyyut* known by the title *'Oto ha-yom* prepared for recitation on Tish'a be-Av, the fast-day commemorating the destruction of the First and Second Temples.[35] Joseph Yahalom has published a more complete version of this *piyyut* based upon at least seven recensions that have been recovered from the Cairo Genizah,[36] all of which (he argues) should be dated prior to the extant "prose versions" of *Sefer Zerubbabel*.[37] It is of course possible that *Sefer Zerubbabel* takes its inspiration from the *payyetan*,[38] whose precise *floruit* at any rate is much disputed. Further study would seem to be required before more definitive results in the comparative dating of the "prose" and alleged "poetic" versions can be achieved.[39]

Several targumic passages are also reminiscent of the book's distinctive contents. *Tg.* Cant 7:13-8:14 weaves a rich eschatological tapestry which intersects at key points with motifs from *Sefer Zerubbabel*.[40] Some manuscripts and printed editions of *Tg.* Isa 11:4 interpret that biblical verse's statement about how the wicked will be slain "with the breath of his mouth" as an allusion to the Davidide messiah's future dispatch of Armilos.[41] *Tg. Ps.-J.* Deut 34:1-3 exploits the toponyms found in those verses to depict a visionary scene which invokes several of the characters and events found in *Sefer Zerubbabel*.[42] Finally, *Tg.*

34. Gershom Scholem, *Sabbatai Ṣevi: The Mystical Messiah, 1626-1676* (Princeton, N.J.: Princeton University Press, 1973), 738 n. 135; Ithamar Gruenwald, *Apocalyptic and Merkavah Mysticism* (AGJU 14; Leiden: Brill, 1980), 150 n. 2.

35. For an edition of the *piyyut* and bibliographical notices, see Even-Shmuel, *Midreshey Ge'ullah*, 154-60. Note also Bernard Lewis, "On That Day: A Jewish Apocalyptic Poem on the Arab Conquests," in *Mélanges d'Islamologie: Volume dédié à la mémoire de Armand Abel* (ed. Pierre Salmon; Leiden: Brill, 1974), 197-200; Robert G. Hoyland, *Seeing Islam As Others Saw It* (Studies in Late Antiquity and Early Islam 13; Princeton, N.J.: Darwin, 1997), 319-20.

36. Joseph Yahalom, "On the Value of Literary Works as Sources to Elucidate Historical Questions," *Cathedra* 11 (1979): 125-33 (Heb.). See also Louis Ginzberg, *Ginze Schechter* (3 vols.; New York: Jewish Theological Seminary of America, 1928-29), 1:310-12.

37. Joseph Yahalom, "The Temple and the City in Liturgical Hebrew Poetry," in *The History of Jerusalem: The Early Muslim Period, 638-1099* (ed. Joshua Prawer and Haggai Ben-Shammai; Jerusalem and New York: Yad Izhak Ben-Zvi and New York University Press, 1996), 278-80.

38. See, e.g., Baron, *History*, 5:152; Ezra Fleischer, "Haduta – Hadutahu – Chedweta: Solving an Old Riddle," *Tarbiz* 53 (1983-84): 71-96 (Heb.); idem, "Solving the Qiliri Riddle," *Tarbiz* 54 (1984-85): 383-427 (Heb.); Gilbert Dagron and Vincent Déroche, "Juifs et Chrétiens dans l'Orient du VIIe siècle," *Travaux et mémoires* 11 (1991): 17-274, at 26-28.

39. Note especially the evaluative remarks by Gil, "Apocalypse of Zerubbabel," 9-11; also Hagith Sivan, "From Byzantine to Persian Jerusalem: Jewish Perspectives and Jewish/Christian Polemics," *GRBS* 41 (2000): 277-306; Günter Stemberger, "Christians and Jews in Byzantine Palestine," in *Christians and Christianity in the Holy Land: From the Origins to the Latin Kingdoms* (ed. Ora Limor and Guy G. Stroumsa; Turnhout: Brepols, 2006), 293-319, at 315-16.

40. I am indebted to Philip S. Alexander for calling my attention to this passage. An edition of *Tg.* Cant 7:13-8:5 is available in Gustav Dalman, *Aramäische Dialektproben* (2nd ed.; Leipzig: J. C. Hinrichs, 1927; repr., Darmstadt: Wissenschaftliche Buchgesellschaft, 1960), 12-14.

41. Alexander Sperber, ed., *The Bible in Aramaic: Based on Old Manuscripts and Printed Texts* (5 vols.; Leiden, 1959-73; repr., Leiden: Brill, 1992), 3:25 and the critical apparatus. Many scholars consider this a later addition to the targumic text; see Zunz-Albeck, *Haderashot*, 252 n. 9; 430 n. 31.

42. See David Rieder (ed.), *Targum Yonatan ben 'Uziel on the Pentateuch* (Jerusalem: Salomon, 1974), 308; Even-Shmuel, *Midreshey Ge'ullah*, 91-92. A translation of this targumic passage is available in Reeves, *Trajectories*, 50.

Tos. Zech 12:10[43] reads that biblical verse as a cryptic reference to the fate of the Ephraimite messiah;[44] i.e., the messiah of the lineage of Joseph.

Bibliography

Even-Shmuel, Yehudah. "Sefer Zerubbavel." Pages 55-88, 379-89 in idem, *Midreshey Ge'ullah.* 2nd ed. Jerusalem: Mosad Bialik, 1954.

Gil, Moshe. "The Apocalypse of Zerubbabel in Judaeo-Arabic." *REJ* 165 (2006): 1-98, 523.

Himmelfarb, Martha. "Sefer Zerubbabel." Pages 67-90 in *Rabbinic Fantasies: Imaginative Narratives from Classical Hebrew Literature.* Edited by David Stern and Mark Jay Mirsky. Philadelphia, Pa.: Jewish Publication Society, 1990.

Hopkins, Simon. *A Miscellany of Literary Pieces from the Cambridge Genizah Collections: A Catalogue and Selection of Texts in the Taylor-Schechter Collection, Old Series, Box A45.* Cambridge: Cambridge University Library, 1978.

Jellinek, Adolph. "Das Buch Serubabel." *BHM,* 2:xxi-xxii, 54-57.

Lévi, Israel. "L'Apocalypse de Zorobabel et le roi de Perse Siroès." *REJ* 68 (1914): 129-60; 69 (1914): 108-21; 71 (1920): 57-65. Reprinted in idem, *Le ravissement du Messie à sa naissance et autres essais* (ed. Evelyne Patlagean; Paris: Peeters, 1994).

Reeves, John C. "Sefer Zerubbabel." Pages 40-66 in idem, *Trajectories in Near Eastern Apocalyptic: A Postrabbinic Jewish Apocalypse Reader.* Resources for Biblical Study 45. Leiden/Atlanta, Ga.: Brill/Society of Biblical Literature, 2005.

Wertheimer, S. A. "Sefer Zerubbavel." Pages 495-505 in vol. 2 of idem, *Batey Midrashot.* 2 vols. 2nd ed. Edited by A. J. Wertheimer. Jerusalem, 1948-53; repr., Jerusalem: Ktav wa-Sefer, 1980.

Yassif, Eli. "Ḥazon Zerubbavel." Pages 427-35 in idem, *Sefer ha-Zikronot hu' Divrey ha-Yamim le-Yeraḥme'el.* Tel Aviv: Tel Aviv University, 2001.

43. A marginal note in the targumic manuscript known as Codex Reuchlinianus, cited from the critical apparatus of Sperber, *Bible in Aramaic,* 3:495.

44. See also Dalman, *Aramäische Dialektproben,* 12; Even-Shmuel, *Midreshey Ge'ullah,* 92 n. 16. For a translation, see Reeves, *Trajectories,* 50.

Sefer Zerubbabel: The Prophetic Vision of Zerubbabel ben Shealtiel

Initial visionary experience

(This is) the word which came to Zerubbabel the son of Shealtiel, (future) *governor* Jer 7:1; 11:1; 18:1; 21:1; 30:1; 32:1; 34:1, 8; 35:1; 40:1; 44:1
of Judah. On the twenty-fourth day of the seventh month, the Lord showed me Hag 1:1, 14; 2:2
this spectacle there while I was prostrate in prayer before the Lord my God, Neh 9:1; 8:14
experiencing a visionary spectacle which I saw by the river Kebar.[a] And as I was Ezek 3:23; 10:22; 43:3
reciting[b] (the passage of the *'Amidah* which ends) "Blessed are You, O Lord, the
One Who resuscitates the dead!" my heart groaned within me, thinking "[How
will][c] the form of the Temple[d] come into existence?" He answered me from the
doors of heaven and said to me, "Are you *Zerubbabel ben Shealtiel, governor of*
Judah?" I responded, "I am your servant." He answered me and conversed with Hag 1:1, 14; 2:2
me just as a person would speak to their friend. I could hear His voice, but I Exod 33:11
could not see His appearance. I continued to lie prostrate as before, and I completed my prayer. Then I went to my house.

Subsequent encounter and a visionary journey to Rome

On the eleventh[e] day of the month Adar He was speaking with me (again) there,
and He said to me, "Are you my servant Zerubbabel?" I responded, "*I am your* Hag 2:23
servant." He said to me, "Come to me! Ask (anything) and I will tell you!" I an- Ps 116:16; 143:12
swered and said, "What might I ask? That my appointed lifespan be short and
my days fulfilled?" He said to me: "I will make you live (a long life)." He repeated, Gen 29:21
"May you live (a long time)!"[f]

A wind lifted me up between heaven and earth and carried me to the great Ezek 8:3
city Nineveh, city of blood, and I thought "Woe is me, for my attitude has been Jonah 1:2; 3:2; 4:11
contentious[g] and (now) my life is at great risk!" So I arose in distress in order Nah 3:1
to pray and entreat the favor of the name[h] of the Lord God of Israel. I confessed
all my transgressions and my sins, for my attitude had been contentious, and I

a. Following Jellinek.

b. Following Lévi's emendation.

c. Supplied from Jellinek.

d. Literally "eternal House," an early rabbinic circumlocution for the Temple.

e. Oxford Ms. Opp. 236a reads: "twenty-first."

f. Counteracting Zerubbabel's sarcastic wish to die prematurely?

g. Both Lévi and Yassif emend, but T-S A45.19 (Hopkins, *Miscellany*, 64.3) confirms that the *Yeraḥmeel* text is correct. For the idiom, see Hos 10:2 and its interpretation in early rabbinic sources.

h. Jellinek's text follows the wording of Zech 7:2; 8:21-22.

said: "Ah Lord! I have acted wrongly, I have transgressed, I have sinned,[a] for my attitude has been contentious. You are the Lord God, the One Who made everything by a command[b] from Your mouth, and (Who) with a word from Your lips will revivify the dead!"

He said to me, "Go to the 'house of filth'[c] near the market-district,"[d] and I went just as He had commanded me. He said to me, "Turn this way," and so I turned. He touched me, and then I saw a man (who was) despicable, broken
Isa 53:3 down and in pain.

Zerubbabel's interview with the Messiah

That despicable man said to me: "Zerubbabel!? What business do you have here? Who has brought you here?" I responded and said: "A wind from the Lord lifted me up and carried me to this place." He said to me: "Do not be afraid, *for you*
Ezek 40:4 *have been brought here in order to show you....*"[e] When I heard his words, I was consoled and regained my self-composure.[f] I asked him, "Sir, what is the name of this place?" He said to me, "This is mighty Rome, wherein I am imprisoned."[g] I said to him, "Who then are you? What is your name? What do you seek here? What are you doing in this place?" He said to me, "I am the Messiah of the Lord,
Dan 8:17; 11:35, 40; the son of Hezekiah,[h] confined in prison until the time of the End." When I
12:4, 9 heard this, I was silent, and I hid my face from him. His anger burned within him,[i] and when I looked at him (again), I became frightened.

He said to me, "Come nearer to me," and as he spoke to me my limbs quaked, and he reached out his hand and steadied me. "Don't be frightened," he said, "and let your mind show no fear." He encouraged me, and said: "Why did you become silent and hide your face from me?" I said to him: "Because you said, 'I
2 Sam 21:17 am the servant of the Lord, His Messiah, and the light of Israel.'" Suddenly he appeared like a strong young man, handsome and adorned.

---

a. Quoting the beginning of the high priest's confession from *m. Yoma* 3.8; 4.2; *Sifra*, §*'Aḥarey Mot* 2.4 (ed. Weiss, 80b) and their parallels.

b. T-S A45.19 (Hopkins, *Miscellany*, 64.5) and Jellinek are closer to Ps 33:6 with "by the breath of Your mouth."

c. Jellinek has the correct reading (in place of the manuscript's "winter-palace"). As Yassif points out, the former is a term in medieval Jewish literature for a Christian church or cathedral.

d. There is no need to posit a corruption here as Lévi has suggested. Rome/Constantinople contained more than one Christian sanctuary.

e. And to continue the biblical lemma: "Report everything that I show you to the House of Israel."

f. T-S A45.19 (Hopkins, *Miscellany*, 64.8) reads instead: "and he spoke with me clearly, and when I heard (this) I was astonished and as[ked...]"

g. Not Capitoline Rome but Constantinople, the imperial Christian capital of the eastern Roman empire. Byzantine and Islamicate Jewish, Christian, and Muslim texts all refer to the latter city as "Rome."

h. According to Lévi, these words have been erased. They do not occur in any of the other extant manuscripts or printed editions probably because the different name "Menaḥem b. 'Amiel" is provided below for this figure.

i. Manuscript reads "and my anger burned within me." I have followed the reading in T-S A45.19 (Hopkins, *Miscellany*, 64.10) which continues "his face reddened and [his garmen]ts changed [...]."

Michael's intervention

I asked him: "When will the light of Israel come?"[a] And as I was speaking to him, behold, a man with two wings approached me and said to me, "Zerubbabel! What are you asking the Messiah of the Lord?" I answered him and said, "I asked when the appointed time for deliverance is supposed to come." "Ask me," he replied, "and I will tell you."

I said to him, "Sir, who are you?" He answered and said, "I am Michael,[b]
the one who delivered good news to Sarah.[c] I am the leader of the host of the
Lord God of Israel, the one who battled with Sennacherib and smote 180,000
men.[d] I am the prince of Israel, the one who fought battles against the kings Dan 12:1
of Canaan. In the time to come, I will fight the battles of the Lord alongside Josh 5:14-15
the Messiah of the Lord—he who sits before you—with the *king strong of face* Dan 8:23; cf. Deut 28:50
and with Armīlōs, the son of Satan, the spawn of the stone statue.[e] The Lord
has appointed me to be the commanding officer over his people and over Dan 10:21
those who love Him in order to do battle against the leaders of the nations."

Michael is Metatron[f]

Michael, who is (also) Metatron, answered me[g] saying: "I am the angel who
guided Abraham throughout all the land of Canaan. I blessed him in the name
of the Lord. I am the one who redeemed Isaac and [wept][h] for him. I am the one Gen 22:11-13
who wrestled with Jacob at the crossing of the Jabbok.[i] I am the one who guided Gen 32:25-31 [Evv 32:24-30]
Israel in the wilderness for forty years in the name of the Lord.[j] I am the one Exod 23:20-23
who appeared to Joshua at Gilgal,[k] and I am the one who rained down brimstone Josh 5:13-15
and fire on Sodom and Gomorrah.[l] He placed His name within me: Metatron in Exod 23:21
gematria is the equivalent of Shadday.[m] As for you, Zerubbabel son of Shealtiel,
whose name is Jeconiah, ask me and I will tell you what will happen at the End 1 Chr 3:17-19
of Days." Gen 49:1

---

a. Jellinek: "When will the lamp of Israel shine?"

b. T-S A45 19 (Hopkins, *Miscellany*, 64.17): "I am Metatron-Michael, leader of the host of the Lord." For the epithet, see Josh 5:14-15.

c. Gen 18:10. See *b. B. Meṣiʿa* 86b: "Michael (is) the one who delivered good news to Sarah."

d. Cf. 2 Kgs 19:35-36; Isa 37:36-37; 2 Chr 32:21-22. The first two sources total the number of the slain as 185,000. *Exod. Rab.* 18.5 identifies the anonymous biblical angel as Michael.

e. This conjunctive pairing suggests that "the king strong of face" and "Armilos" are two separate entities, as they are in, e.g., the later *Secrets of R. Šimʿōn ben Yoḥai*. By contrast, the still later *Midrash Wa-yoshaʿ* conflates them into one figure.

f. Apparently a variant doublet of the preceding paragraph.

g. The manuscript literally reads "Michael answered Metatron and said to me." I have followed the reading suggested by Lévi, "L'Apocalypse," 133 n. 17.

h. An emendation proposed by Lévi and now confirmed by T-S A45.19 (Hopkins, *Miscellany*, 64.19).

i. See, e.g., *Midr. Tanḥ.* (ed. Buber), *Wayishlaḥ* §7.

j. See Rashi *ad* Exod 23:21; cf. *b. Sanh.* 38b.

k. See Ramban *ad* Exod 23:20.

l. Lévi points out that *b. B. Meṣiʿa* 86b accords this role to Gabriel, not Michael.

m. The proper names "Metatron" and "Shadday" both have the numerical value 314. For the role of Metatron in eschatological literature, see Moshe Idel, *Messianic Mystics* (New Haven and London: Yale University Press, 1998), 46-47; Reeves, *Trajectories*, 179-86.

Occultation of the Messiah

Then he (i.e., Michael/Metatron) said to me: "This is the Messiah of the Lord:
(he has) been hidden in this place until the appointed time (for his manifestation). This is the Messiah of the lineage of David, and his name is Menaḥem ben
ʿAmiel.[a] He was born during the reign of David, king of Israel,[b] and a wind bore
Dan 11:35; 12:4, 9 him up and concealed him in this place, waiting for the time of the end."

Hephṣibah, the mother of the Messiah

Then I, Zerubbabel, posed a question to Metatron, *the leader of the host of the*
Josh 5:14, 15 *Lord.*[c] He said to me: "The Lord will give a rod (for accomplishing) these salvific
acts to Hephṣibah, the mother of Menaḥem ben ʿAmiel.[d] A great star will shine[e]
Num 24:17 before her, and all the stars will wander aimlessly from their paths.

Hephṣibah, the mother of Menaḥem ben ʿAmiel, will go forth and kill two
kings, both of whom are determined to do evil. The name(s) of the two rulers
(whom she will slay): Nōph, king of Teman, (so named) because *he will shake*
Isa 11:15 *(henīph) his hand toward* Jerusalem, (is the first one), and the name of the second is ʾĪsrīnan,[f] king of Antioch. This conflict and these signs will take place
during the festival of Shavuʿot in the third month.[g]

Oracle about the Temple's destruction and a final deliverance[h]

Dan 10:1; 2 Chr 9:5 *The word is true.* Four hundred and twenty years after the city and Temple have
been rebuilt, they will be destroyed a second time.[i] Twenty years after the <con-
quest> of the city of Rome,[j] after seventy kings corresponding to the seventy

---

a. The name "Menaḥem" for the Messiah derives from Lam 1:16: "for a comforter (Hebrew *menaḥem*)—the one who would restore my life—remains far away from me." The numerical value of that name's letters (138) is also equal to that of the letters of the ancient messianic epithet "Branch"; see Jer 23:5, 33:15; Zech 3:8 with Ibn Ezra *ad loc.*, 6:12; *y. Ber.* 2.4, 5a; *Lam. Rab.* 1.51; *Midr. Tanḥ.*, *Qoraḥ* §12; *Pirqe R. El.* §48 (Luria, 116a). The name Menaḥem b. ʿAmiel for the future Davidic messiah is also used in uncensored versions of *Pirqe R. El.* §19 (e.g., HUC Ms. 75 fol. 25b: note that this manuscript inverts the order of §§18 and 19!), whereas standard printed editions of *Pirqe R. El.* attest an anomalous form "Menaḥem b. ʿAmiel b. Joseph (!)" (e.g., see Luria, 45b).

b. Some texts read "born within the family of David, king of Israel." According to the version of the text published by Wertheimer, he was born "at the time Nebuchadnezzar entered Jerusalem." Cf. *y. Ber.* 2.4, 5a: "for on the day he (i.e., the Messiah) was born the Temple was destroyed."

c. The question however is lacking in the *Yeraḥmeel* manuscript. Wertheimer's edition supplies here: "What are the signs which this Menaḥem ben ʿAmiel will realize?" See Yassif, *Sefer ha-Zikronot*, 429 n. 18; also T-S A45.19 (Hopkins, *Miscellany*, 65.5): "what are the signs which Menaḥem ʿAmiel will realize?"

d. See the introduction.

e. Emending the text to read with T-S A45.19 (Hopkins, *Miscellany*, 65.7).

f. Referred to later in this same manuscript as ʾEsrōgan. Alternate spellings in the other manuscripts and printed editions are *ʾbrtn*, *ʾṭrs*, and *ʾsrnw*.

g. The *Yeraḥmeel* manuscript lacks the year. See T-S A45.19 (Hopkins, *Miscellany*, 65.10-11): "in the sixth year during the third month which [...] the festival of Shavuʿot." Presumably this is the penultimate year of a final sabbatical period of years.

h. This paragraph is out of place in its present context.

i. According to rabbinic chronography, 420 years was the duration of the Second Temple. See *b. Yoma* 9a.

j. Emending the *Yeraḥmeel* manuscript's *lkšybnh* to *lkb(w)šh*. Cf. Jellinek: "twenty years nations have ruled in it, when ten kings have finished their reigns, the tenth king will come.[a] He will destroy the sanctuary, stop the daily offering, the *saintly people* will be dispersed, and he will hand them over to destruction, despoiling, and panic. Many of them will perish due to their faithfulness to Torah, but (others) will abandon the Torah of the Lord and worship their (i.e., Rome's) idols. *When they stumble, a little help will provide assistance.* From the time that the daily offering ceases and the wicked ones install the one whose name is 'abomination' in the Temple, at the end of nine hundred and ninety years, the deliverance of the Lord will take place—*when the power of the holy people is shattered*—to redeem them and to gather them by means of the Lord's Messiah.[b]

Dan 11:31
Dan 8:24
Dan 11:34
Dan 11:31; 12:11
Dan 12:7

The recovery of the wonder-working rod

The rod which the Lord will give to Hephṣibah, the mother of Menaḥem [ben] 'Amiel, is made of almond-wood; it is hidden in Raqqat, a city in (the territory of) Naphtali. It is the same rod which the Lord previously gave to Adam, Moses, Aaron, Joshua, and King David.[c] It is the same rod which sprouted buds and flowered in the Tent (of Meeting) for the sake of Aaron.[d] Elijah ben Eleazar[e] concealed it in Raqqat, a city of Naphtali, which is Tiberias.[f] Concealed there as well is a man whose name is Nehemiah ben Ḥushiel ben Ephraim ben Joseph."[g]

Josh 19:32-39
Num 17:16-26 (Evv 17:1-11)

The Messiah of the lineage of Joseph

Zerubbabel spoke up and said to Metatron and to Michael (*sic*) the prince: "My lord, I want you to tell me when the Messiah of the Lord will come and what will happen after all this!" He said to me, "The Lord's Messiah—Nehemiah ben Ḥushiel—will come five years after[h] Hephṣibah. He will collect all Israel together

---

after the subjection of Rome...."

a. Titus is the tenth Roman emperor.

b. A number of scholars have sought to use this number in order to posit a late date for *Sefer Zerubbabel*. See the introduction.

c. T-S A45.19 (Hopkins, *Miscellany*, 65.14-15) provides an expanded list of worthies: "which the Lord gave to Seth, Noah, Abraham, Is[aac...], Judah, Peretz, Moses the servant of the Lord, Joshua, David, and Elijah." See also Wertheimer, *Batey Midrashot*, 2:499 for a slightly variant roster.

d. T-S A45.19 (Hopkins, *Miscellany*, 65.16) reads: "'it had budded and flowered and etc. (Num 17:23 [Evv 17:8]).' I spoke up and said—I Zerubbabel—to Met[atron...]."

e. I.e., Pinḥas ben Eleazar, grandson of Aaron (cf. Num 25:7). This text attests the popular exegetical assimilation of Pinḥas with the prophet Elijah; see *L.A.B.* 48.1; *Tg. Ps-J.* Num 25:12; *Pirqe R. El.* §29 and §47; Robert Hayward, "Phineas—the Same is Elijah: The Origins of a Rabbinic Tradition," *JJS* 29 (1978): 22-34. His role here in the concealment of Aaron's rod coheres with his final position in the list of the rod's custodians in some other versions (see above) of the book. The identity of Pinḥas as the one who conceals the staff is also known to the thirteenth-century Christian *Book of the Bee*; see Ernest A. Wallis Budge, ed., *The Book of the Bee* (Anecdota Oxoniensia Semitic Series 1.2; Oxford: Clarendon, 1886), 52.9-10: "Pinḥas hid the staff in the desert, beneath the dirt at the gate of Jerusalem, and it remained there until Our Lord the Messiah was born."

f. For the identification of Raqqat with Tiberias, see *y. Meg.* 1.1, 70a; *b. Meg.* 5b-6a.

g. The messiah of the lineage of Joseph. For his Galilean association, see also *'Aggadat Mašiaḥ* (Jellinek, *BHM*, 3:141); Even-Shmuel, *Midreshey Ge'ullah*, 49; Reeves, *Trajectories*, 145.

h. *Sic* in the base text and Jellinek. Wertheimer and T-S A45.19 (Hopkins, *Miscellany*, 65.18) have "before," a reading which in context makes better sense.

as one entity and they will remain for <four>[a] years in Jerusalem, (where) the
Mal 3:4 children of Israel will offer sacrifice, and it will be pleasing to the Lord.[b] He will
inscribe Israel in the genealogical lists according to their families. But in the fifth
Deut 33:3 year of Nehemiah and the gathering together of the holy ones,[c] Šērōy the king
of Persia[d] will attack Nehemiah ben Ḥushiel and Israel,[e] and there will be great
suffering in Israel. Hephṣibah—the wife of Nathan the prophet[f] (and) mother
of Menaḥem ben ʿAmiel—will go out with the rod which the Lord God of Israel
Isa 19:14 will give to her, and the Lord will place *a spirit of dizziness* upon them (i.e., the
Persian army), and they will kill one another, each (slaying) his companion or
his countryman. There the wicked one (Šērōy) will die."

Meaning of Isa 27:10

When I heard (this), I fell upon my face and said, "O Lord! Tell me what Isaiah
the prophet (meant) when he said: *There the calf will graze, and there it will*
Isa 27:10 *crouch down and finish its branches*?" He answered me, "This calf is Nineveh, the
Nah 3:1 city of blood, which represents mighty Rome."

Advent of Armīlōs

Dan 9:25; 11:22 I continued asking there about the prince of the holy covenant. He held me close and they (*sic*) brought me to the "house of filth" [and scorn].[g] There he showed me a marble stone in the shape of a maiden:[h] her features and form were lovely and indeed very beautiful to behold. Then he said to me, "This statue is the [wife][i] of Belial. Satan will come and have intercourse with it, and a son named Armīlōs will emerge from it, (whose name in Greek means) 'he will destroy a nation.'[j] He will rule over all (peoples), and his dominion will extend from one end of the earth to the other, and ten letters will be in his hand. He will engage in the worship of foreign gods and speak lies. No one will be able to withstand him, and anyone who does not believe in him he will kill with the sword: many

---

a. In spite of the unanimous extant textual evidence, read "four" in place of "forty."

b. Some historians read this notice as evidence for the brief restoration of a Jewish sacrificial cultus on the Temple Mount following the Persian capture of Jerusalem in 614; for references, see Reeves, *Trajectories*, 57-58 n. 126. This interpretation is dismissed by Peter Schäfer, *The History of the Jews in Antiquity: The Jews of Palestine from Alexander the Great to the Arab Conquest* (n.p.: Harwood Academic Publishers, 1995), 191.

c. The "holy ones" or "saints" are Israel; see Deut 33:3 and *Tg. Onq.* to that verse.

d. Šērōy, who used the regnal name Kavād II, assumed the Sasanian throne in 628 C.E. and reigned for less than one year, falling victim to illness rather than military debacle.

e. Oxford Ms. Heb. f. 27 (2642) fols. 42-43 adds at this point: "and he will kill Nehemiah in Jerusalem, and all Israel will mourn him and complain about this with embittered grief."

f. A curious designation, since it cannot refer to David's prophet or to David's son. Perhaps it is an interpolation referring to Nathan of Gaza, a major theorist and the prophetic voice announcing the seventeenth-century messianic movement of Shabbatai Ṣevi.

g. Correcting in accordance with the varying manuscript evidence assembled by Lévi, "L'Apocalypse," 136 n. 4.

h. A statue of the Virgin Mary?

i. Note Wertheimer, *Batey Midrashot*, 2:500: "this stone is the wife of Belial."

j. The phrase is corrupt in all witnesses, but it is clear that an etymology is offered here for the name "Armilos," one that is moreover dependent not upon Hebrew but upon Greek *Erēmolaos* "destroyer of a people."

among them will he kill. He will come against the holy people of the Most High, and with him there will be ten kings wielding great power and force, and he will do battle with the holy ones. He will prevail over them[a] and will kill the Messiah of the lineage of Joseph, Nehemiah b. Ḥushiel,[b] and will also kill sixteen righteous ones alongside him. Then they will banish Israel to the desert in three groups.[c]

Israel's response to Armīlōs

But Hephṣibah, the mother of Menaḥem b. ʿAmiel, will remain stationed at the
eastern gate, and that wicked one will not enter there, thereby confirming what
was written: *but the remainder of the people will not be cut off from the city*. This Zech 14:2
battle will take place during the month of Av.[d] Israel will experience distress such
as there never was before. They will flee into towers, among mountains, and into
caves, but they will be unable to hide from him. All the nations of the earth will 1 Sam 13:6
go astray after him except for Israel, who will not believe in him. All Israel shall
mourn Nehemiah b. Ḥushiel for forty-one days. His thoroughly crushed corpse
will be thrown down before the gates of Jerusalem, but no animal, bird, or beast
will touch it. Due to the intensity of the oppression and the great distress, the Rev 11:8-10
children of Israel will then cry out to the Lord, and the Lord will answer them."

Metatron's response to Zerubbabel's distress

As I listened to the content of the prophecy of the Lord to me, I became very
agitated and got up and went to the canal. There I cried out to the Lord God
of Israel, *the God of all flesh*, and He sent His angel to me while the prayer was Jer 32:27
still in my mouth <before I had finished (it)>.[e] The Lord sent His angel to me,
and when I saw (him) I knew that he was the angel who had spoken with me
regarding all the previous matters. I knelt and bowed before him, and he again
touched me as he had the first time. He said to me, "What's the matter with you,
O Zerubbabel?" I answered him, "Sir, my spirit remains depressed." Job 32:18

Metatron responded by saying to me: "Ask me (questions) and I will provide
you with answers before I depart from you." So I again asked him and said to
him, "My lord Metatron, when will the *Light of Israel* come?"[f] He answered and Isa 10:17
said to me, "By the Lord Who has sent me and Who has appointed me over
Israel, I solemnly swear to reveal to you the Lord's doing(s), for the Holy God
previously commanded me, 'Go to My servant Zerubbabel, and tell him (the answers to) whatever he may ask of you.'" Then Michael, who is (also) Metatron,[g]

a. Oxford Ms. Opp. 236a adds: "and a multitude will fall."

b. Armilos is the usual slayer of the Messiah of the lineage of Joseph. Note, however, that according to the version of *Sefer Zerubbabel* found in Oxford Ms. Heb. f. 27 (2642) fols. 42-43 (cited above) and an intriguing seventh-century *piyyut* first published by Ezra Fleischer, it is the Persians who are responsible for executing the community leader who temporarily restored the sacrificial service in Jerusalem. See Sivan, "From Byzantine to Persian Jerusalem," 288.

c. A reference to the expulsion of Jews from Jerusalem by Heraclius upon its recapture from the Persians in 629.

d. Oxford Ms. Opp. 236a states the war will last "the entire month."

e. Slightly emending the printed text.

f. Resuming a line of inquiry which began above.

g. An attempt to simplify the identity of Zerubbabel's angelic interlocutor.

said to me, "Come closer and pay careful attention to everything which I shall
Dan 10:1 tell you, for *the word* which I am speaking to you *is true*; it was one spoken by
the Living God."

First month of the year of redemption: Advent of the Messiah of the lineage of David

Mal 3:1 He said to me: "Menaḥem b. ʿAmiel will suddenly come on the fourteenth day
of the first month; i.e., of the month Nisan. He will wait by the Valley of ʾArbʾel[a]
(at a tract) which belonged to Joshua b. Jehoṣadaq the priest,[b] and all the surviving sages of Israel—only a few will remain due to the attack and pillage of Gog
and Armīlōs and the plunderers[c] who despoiled them—will come out to him.
Menaḥem b. ʿAmiel will say to the elders and the sages: 'I am the Lord's Messiah: the Lord has sent me to encourage you and to deliver you from the power
of these adversaries!' The elders will scrutinize him and will despise him, for
they will see that despicable man garbed in rags, and they will despise him just
as you previously did. But then his anger will burn within him, *and he will don*
Isa 59:17 *garments of vengeance (as his) clothing and will put on*[d] *a cloak of zealousness*,
and he will journey to the gates of Jerusalem. Hephṣibah, the mother of the
Messiah, will come and give him the rod by which the signs were performed. All
the elders and children of Israel will come and see that Nehemiah (b. Ḥushiel)
is alive and standing unassisted, (and) immediately they will believe in the Messiah." Thus did Metatron, the leader of the host of the Lord, swear to me: "This
Zech 6:13 matter will truly come to pass, for there will be full cooperation between them[e]
in accordance with the prophecy of Isaiah, *Ephraim will not envy Judah, nor will*
Isa 11:13 *Judah antagonize Ephraim*.

On the twenty-first day of the first month, nine hundred and ninety years
after the destruction of the Temple, the deliverance of the Lord will take place
for Israel. Menaḥem b. ʿAmiel, Nehemiah b. Ḥushiel, and Elijah the prophet will
come and stand by the Mediterranean Sea and read the prophecy of the Lord.
All the bodies of those Israelites who had thrown themselves into the sea while
fleeing from their enemies will emerge: a sea-wave will rise up, spread them out,
Joel 4:2, 12, 18 [Evv 3:2, 12, 18] and deposit them alive within the valley of Jehoshaphat near the Wadi Shiṭṭim,
for there judgment will transpire upon the nations.

---

a. A locale in Galilee associated with the "dawning" of eschatological redemption. See *y. Ber.* 1.1, 2c; *Yoma* 3.2, 40b; *Cant. Rab.* 6.16 (*ad* Cant 6:10). For a fascinating discussion of this location's many significances, see Elchanan Reiner, "From Joshua to Jesus: The Transformation of a Biblical Story to a Local Myth: A Chapter in the Religious Life of the Galilean Jew," in *Sharing the Sacred: Religious Contacts and Conflicts in the Holy Land, First–Fifteenth Centuries CE* (ed. Arieh Kofsky and Guy G. Stroumsa; Jerusalem: Yad Izhak Ben Zvi, 1998), 223-71.

b. Some manuscripts read this name as "Joshua b. Saraf/Nisraf," a priestly figure associated with this locale. For a convincing explanation for this unusual epithet ("the burned one"), see Reiner, "From Joshua to Jesus," 244-46.

c. Read thus in place of the printed text's "the horses."

d. Slightly emending the printed text.

e. See the commentary of Radaq *ad loc.*; note too the commentary of Rashi to Isa 11:13.

The second month

In the second month; i.e., Iyyar, the congregation of Qoraḥ will reemerge[a] upon Num 16:1-11, 16-24, 26-33
the plains of Jericho near the Wadi Shiṭṭim. They will come to Moses (*sic*!).[b] Asaph (the biblical choirmaster) was a member of the cohort of the Qoraḥites.

On the eighteenth day of it (the second month) the mountains and hills will quake, and the earth and everything on it will shake, as well as the sea and its contents.[c]

The third month

On the first day of the third month those who died in the desert[d] will revive and will come with their families to the Wadi Shiṭṭim.[e] On the eighteenth day of the month of Sivan (i.e., the third month), there will be a mighty earthquake
in Eretz Israel.[f] Ezek 38:19

The fourth month

In Tammuz, the fourth month, the Lord God of Israel will descend upon the
Mount of Olives, and the Mount of Olives will split open at His rebuke. He Zech 14:4
will blow a great trumpet, and every foreign deity and mosque[g] will crumple Isa 27:13; Zech 9:14
to the ground, and every wall and steep place will collapse. The Lord will kill Ezek 38:20
all their plunderers,[h] and He will battle those nations *like a warrior fired with*
zeal. The Lord's Messiah—Menaḥem b. ʿAmiel—will come and breathe in the Isa 42:13
face of Armīlōs and thereby slay him. The Lord will place each man's sword on Isa 11:4
the neck of his companion and their dead bodies shall fall there. The *saintly* Ezek 38:21
people will come out to witness the Lord's deliverance: all of Israel will actually Dan 8:24
see Him (equipped) like a warrior with *the helmet of deliverance on His head* and
clad in armor. He will fight the battle of Gog ha-Magog and against the army of Isa 59:17
Armīlōs, and all of them will fall dead in the Valley of ʾArbʾel. All of Israel will

a. In *m. Sanh.* 10.3, R. Akiva and R. Eliezer disagree as to whether the congregation of Qoraḥ will play a role in the World to Come, with the latter Sage citing 1 Sam 2:6 ("the Lord kills and revitalizes; He sends down to Sheol and brings back up...") in support of his opinion that they could potentially "reemerge" at that time.

b. A corruption of "Messiah"?

c. A date traditionally associated with the death of Joshua b. Nun, which was reportedly marked by an earthquake. See the references accumulated by Reiner, "From Joshua to Jesus," 229-30 n. 13; 248-55.

d. I.e., the generation who died during Israel's forty-year wandering in the wilderness prior to the conquest of Canaan (Num 14:35). See again *m. Sanh.* 10.3 for a similar dispute about this group's final fate.

e. Wertheimer, *Batey Midrashot*, 2:500-501: "On the first day of the third month, those who died in the desert will come and rejoin their brethren at the Wadi Shiṭṭim."

f. Wertheimer, *Batey Midrashot*, 2:501: "an earthquake will shake the houses, walls, and towers, and the land and its inhabitants will quiver. Menaḥem b. ʿAmiel, Nehemiah b. Ḥushiel, Elijah the prophet, all Israel from both near and far, and those revivified ones whom the Lord will resurrect will come up to Jerusalem."

g. Literally 'decorated shrine' (*bet masqīt*). However, the Hebrew word *masqīt* may here serve as an oral pun on Arabic *masjid* "mosque." Compare also *Tg. Onq.* Num 33:52 for another possible instance of this same paronomasia.

h. As above, read "their plunderers" in place of "their horses."

then issue forth and *[despoil]*[a] *their despoilers, looting those who previously plun-*
Ezek 39:10 | Ezek 39:10-14 *dered them* for seven months.

The fifth month

Josh 18:28 However, some survivors will escape and they will all regroup at Ṣela' ha-Elef:[b] five hundred men, and (another) one hundred thousand wearing armor. (Opposing them will be) five hundred from Israel with Nehemiah and Elijah, and you, O Zerubbabel, will be their leader. They (*sic*) will kill all of them: one man
Josh 23:10 will pursue a thousand.

This will be the third battle, for three battles will take place in the land of Israel. One will be waged by Hephṣibah with Šērōy the king of Persia,[c] one will be fought by the Lord God of Israel and Menaḥem b. 'Amiel with Armīlōs, the ten kings who are with him, and Gog and Magog, and the third will be at Ṣela' ha-Elef, where Nehemiah b. Ḥushiel and Zerubbabel will see action. The third battle will take place in the month of Av.

Resurrection of the dead and the restoration of Zion

After all this (has taken place), Menaḥem b. 'Amiel will come, accompanied by Nehemiah b. Ḥushiel and all Israel. All of the dead will resurrect, and Elijah the prophet will be with them. They will come up to Jerusalem. In the month of Av, during which they formerly mourned for Nehemiah (and) for the destruction of Jerusalem, Israel will hold a great celebration and bring an offering to the Lord, which the Lord will accept on their behalf. The offering of Israel will be pleasing
Mal 3:4 to the Lord as it was formerly during her past history. The Lord will discern the
Ezek 20:41 pleasant aroma of His people Israel and greatly rejoice. Then the Lord will lower the celestial Temple which had been previously built to earth,[d] and a column of fire and a cloud of smoke will rise to heaven. The Messiah and all of Israel will follow them to the gates of Jerusalem.

Zech 14:4 The holy God will stand on the Mount of Olives. Dread at and reverence for Him will be[e] upon the heavens and the uppermost heavens, the entire earth and its deepest levels, and every wall and structure to their foundations. No one will be able to catch their breath when the Lord God reveals Himself before every-
Zech 14:4-5 one on the Mount of Olives. The Mount of Olives will crack open beneath Him, and the exiles from Jerusalem will come up to the Mount of Olives. Zion and Jerusalem will behold (these things) and ask: '*Who bore these to us? … Where*
Isa 49:21 *have these been?*' Nehemiah and Zerubbabel will then come up to Jerusalem and

---

a. Slightly emending the printed text.

b. It is particularly interesting that Ṣela' ha-Elef was the name borne by the Karaite quarter of medieval Jerusalem. See Gil, *History*, 651-53; idem, "Apocalypse of Zerubbabel," 8 n. 15.

c. Obviously typological, since Šērōy never left Persia after usurping the throne from his father and he died after a reign of only seven months. See Walter E. Kaegi, *Heraclius: Emperor of Byzantium* (Cambridge: Cambridge University Press, 2003), 174-81.

d. For a parallel descent of a celestial Temple, see *Midrash 'Aseret ha-Dibbarot* (*apud* Jellinek, *BHM*, 1:64): "then the Holy One, blessed be He, will lower the Temple which is (located) in (the heaven named) Zevul to the terrestrial Jerusalem." For a conceptually cognate descent of a "celestial Jerusalem" *sans* Temple, see Rev 21:9-27. A new Temple may be constructed in Jerusalem by God in *1 En.* 90:29.

e. Oxford Ms. Opp. 236a: "dread at Him will weigh upon…."

say to her: 'Behold, (they are) your children whom you bore who went into exile from you. *Rejoice greatly, O daughter of Zion!*'" Ezek 16:20 Zech 9:9

Marvelous future dimensions of Zion

Again I started to question Metatron, leader of the host of the Lord: "Sir, show me how far and how wide Jerusalem will extend, along with its architecture." He showed me the walls which surrounded Jerusalem—walls of fire—extending from the Great Desert unto the Mediterranean Sea and unto the Euphrates River. Deut 11:24; Josh 1:4 Then he showed me the Temple and the structure. The Temple was built on the peaks of five mountains which the Lord had chosen[a] to support His sanctuary: Lebanon, Mount Moriah, Tabor, Carmel, and Hermon.[b] Isa 2:2 Michael spoke and said to me, "At the completion of nine hundred and ninety years for the ruins of Jerusalem is the appointed time for the deliverance of Israel." He also continued to interpret for me the message and the vision in accordance with what he had first said to me: *"If you wish to know, ask! Keep coming back!"* Isa 21:12

An alternative sabbatical denouement[c]

In the fifth (year) of the week[d] Nehemiah b. Ḥushiel will come and gather together all Israel. In the sixth (year) of the week Hephṣibah, the wife of Nathan the prophet, she who was born in Hebron, will come[e] and slay the two kings Nōph and 'Esrōgan.[f] That same year the *shoot of Jesse*, Menaḥem b. 'Amiel, will spring up. Isa 11:10

A decade of gentile rulers

Ten kings from among the nations shall also arise, but they will not supply enough (rulers) to rule for a week (of years) and a half-week (of years), each one (ruling) for a year. These are the ten kings who will arise over the nations for the (final) week of years: these are their names correlated with their cities and their places. The first king is Sīlqōm and the name of his city is Seferad, which is Aspamya, a distant country. The second king is Hartōmōs, and the name of his city is Gītanya. The third king is Flē'vōs (Flavius?), and the name of his city is Flō'yas. The fourth king is Glū'as (Julius?), and the name of his city is Galya (Gaul?). The fifth king is Ramōshdīs, and the name of his city is Mōdīṭīka. The sixth king is Mōqlanōs, and the name of his city is Italya. The seventh king is 'Ōktīnōs, and

---

a. Slightly emending the printed text.

b. Based on Isa 2:2 as interpreted in *Midr. Teh.* 68.9, although the latter source names only four peaks (Tabor, Carmel, Sinai, and Zion). Note *Pesiq. Rab Kah.* 21.4 (ed. Mandelbaum, 1:321), and see the further references cited by Louis Ginzberg, *The Legends of the Jews* (7 vols.; Philadelphia, Pa.: The Jewish Publication Society, 1909-38), 6:31 n. 184; Avraham Grossman, "Jerusalem in Jewish Apocalyptic Literature," in Prawer and Ben-Shammai, *The History of Jerusalem* (New York: New York University Press, 1996), 299-300 n. 13.

c. This appears to provide an alternative description of the sequence of events and personalities associated with the eschatological redemption of Israel.

d. I.e., the sabbatical cycle during which the advent of the Davidic Messiah is scheduled. See *b. Sanh.* 97a; Reeves, *Trajectories*, 107-108.

e. Read with Oxford Ms. Opp. 236a.

f. Above this latter king was named 'Īsrīnan.

the name of his city is Dōrmīs. The eighth king is 'Aplōstōs from Mesopotamia. The ninth king is Šērōy, the king of Persia.

Tenth king is Armīlōs

The tenth king is Armīlōs, the son of Satan who emerged from the sculpted
stone. He will gain sovereignty over all of them. He will come along with the rul-
Jer 49:28 ers of Qedar and the inhabitants of the East[a] and provoke a battle in the Valley
of 'Arb'el, and they will take possession of the kingdom. He will ascend with his
force and subdue the entire world. From there in Riblah, which is Antioch,[b] he
will begin to erect all the idols of the nations on the face of the earth and to serve
their gods, those whom the Lord hates. During those days there will be reward
Zech 8:10 for neither human nor beast. He will construct four altars,[c] and he will anger the
Lord with his wicked deeds. There will be a very terrible and harsh famine upon
the surface of the whole land for forty days—their food will stem from the salt-
Job 30:4 plant; leaves plucked from shrubbery and broom to sustain them. On that day
Joel 4:18 (Evv 3:18) *a fountain will flow forth from the Temple of the Lord and fill the Wadi Shiṭṭim.*

Now this Armīlōs will take his mother—(the statue) from whom he was spawned—from the "house of filth"[d] of the scornful ones, and from every place and from every nation they will come and worship that stone, burn offerings to her, and pour out libations to her. No one will be able to view her face due to her beauty. Anyone who refuses to worship her will die in agony (like?) animals.

This is the mark of Armīlōs: the color of the hair of his head is similar to
gold, and (he is) green, even the soles of his feet. His face is one span in width,
his eyes are deep-set, and he has two heads. He will arise and rule over 'Īmīs (?),
the province of Satan, the father of Belial.[e] All who see him will tremble before
him. Menaḥem will come up from the Wadi Shiṭṭim and breathe in the face of
Armīlōs and thereby slay him, just as it is written: *he will slay the wicked one with*
Isa 11:4 *the breath of his mouth.* Israel will take possession of the kingdom; *the holy ones*
Dan 7:18 *of the Most High will receive sovereign power.*

Epilogue

These were the words which Metatron spoke to *Zerubbabel the son of Shealtiel,*
Hag 1:1, 14; 2:2 (future) *governor of Judah,* while he was still living in exile during the time of the
Persian empire. Zechariah ben 'Anan and Elijah recorded them when the period
of exile was completed.[f]

---

a. Literally "the children of Qedem," a generic term for the nomadic tribes living east of Eretz Israel. See Gen 29:1; Judg 6:3; Job 1:3. "Qedar" and "the children of Qedem" appear together in Jer 49:28.

b. See *b. Sanh.* 96b.

c. Oxford Ms. Opp. 236a reads "seven" instead of "four." Armilos's construction of "seven altars" would establish a parallel with the wicked schemes of Balaam and Balaq (see Num 23:1); see Berger, "Three Typological Themes," 160.

d. See above, p. 456 n. c.

e. This clause is an Aramaic phrase.

f. Oxford Ms. Opp. 236a reads: "Zechariah ben 'Iddo and Elijah wrote them down."

Fifth Ezra
A new translation and introduction

by Theodore A. Bergren

Fifth Ezra (2 Esdras chapters 1-2) is a short, early Christian tractate written in Latin or Greek in the late second or third centuries in an unknown locale. Adopting an oracular style similar to that found in the biblical prophets, it is pseudepigraphically ascribed to an "Ezra the son of Chusi" (1:4). *Fifth Ezra* presents Ezra as a prophet who excoriates the Jewish people for their sins, predicts the advent of a new people (the Christians) who will take their place, and describes the eschatological delights that will devolve upon this new people.

Fifth Ezra is significant as an example of early Christian "Adversus Ioudaios" literature, writings devoted to criticism of the Jewish people. Also noteworthy are the book's pseudepigraphic character; its status as an example of early Christian literary prophecy; its almost complete lack of explicitly Christian themes and language; its "supersessionist" theology; the "Exodus review" in 1:4-23; and the evocation of "mother Church" in 2:15-32.

Fifth Ezra survives today associated with (but technically not part of) the "Apocrypha," comprising the first two chapters of the composite work 2 Esdras. (Second Esdras 3-14 constitutes the Jewish apocalypse *4 Ezra*; 2 Esdras 15-16 make up the Christian writing *6 Ezra*.)

Contents

Fifth Ezra may be divided into six main text units. In the first, 1:4-24, the author launches into a scathing indictment of the behavior of God's people, Israel, during the Exodus. Speaking through the prophet Ezra, God enumerates the benevolent acts he has performed for the people, punctuating his review with caustic comments and rhetorical questions documenting the people's disobedience. Finally, God announces the decision to "go over to another nation and . . . give it [God's] name" (1:24).

The second section (1:25-34) continues in the same vein, citing further examples of Israel's disobedience and heinous actions. Evidence of this behavior is now drawn largely from the prophetic and sapiential books of the Hebrew Bible. The third section of *5 Ezra* constitutes a sympathetic and laudatory description of the people who will inherit Israel's patrimony (the Christians). The narrative continues with Ezra's vision of a "people coming from the east" (1:38), and the section closes with a list of figures who will lead the westward-bound procession (1:39-40).

In the fourth section (2:1-14), *5 Ezra* switches again to a negative mode. Drawing on the apocryphal book of 1 Baruch, the narrative depicts the "mother" of the old people, a character readily recognizable as Jerusalem, bemoaning her fate as a "widow" abandoned by her children (cf. Bar 4:8-20). God, speaking through Ezra, consigns the mother to "plunder" and the disobedient offspring to a childless existence, scattered among the nations.

Fifth Ezra's fifth section (2:15-32) again changes tone. God now addresses the "mother" of the *new* people, comforting her and encouraging her to remain steadfast in the face of adversity.

The book's sixth and final section (2:33-48) begins with Ezra's "receiv[ing] an injunction from the Lord on Mount Horeb" (2:33), an injunction that (the old) Israel predictably rejects. The remainder of the book constitutes a passionate parenetic discourse directed to the new people of God, exhorting them to embrace the celestial, eschatological delights that await them. The section concludes with Ezra's vision on Mount Zion of the "son of God" handing out crowns and palms to a surrounding multitude.

Manuscripts, Versions, Languages, and Tradition History

The text of *5 Ezra* is extant in a significant form only in Latin. The Latin text is attested in nine primary manuscripts that are known not to depend exclusively on any other known manuscript of the work. They date from the ninth to the thirteenth centuries.[1]

Eight of these manuscripts are complete manuscripts that also contain complete texts of *4* and *6 Ezra*. They are:

S- Sangermanensis: Paris, Bibliothèque Nationale latin (11504-)11505; 821/22 C.E., from St. Riquier, later at St. Germain des Prés.

A- Ambianensis: Amiens, Bibliothèque Communale 10; ninth cent., from Corbie.

C- Complutensis 1: Madrid, Biblioteca de la Universidad Central 31; ninth–tenth cent., from Toledo or southern Spain, then at Alcalá de Heñares.

M- Mazarinaeus: Paris, Bibliothèque Mazarine (3-)4; eleventh-twelfth cent., from les Cordeliers (Paris).

N- Bruxellensis: Brussels, Bibliothèque Royale 1er Série (9107-)9109(-9110); twelfth cent., origin unknown.

E- Epternacensis: Luxemburg, Bibliothèque Nationale 264; 1051-1081 C.E., from Echternach.

V- Abulensis: Madrid, Biblioteca Nacional vitr. 15-1; twelfth-thirteenth cent., from Avila.

L- Legionensis 2: León, Real Colegiata de San Isidoro I,3; 1162 C.E., from León.

The ninth significant manuscript is a partial manuscript that contains *5 Ezra* 1:1–2:20, and nothing of *4* or *6 Ezra*:

K- Victorensis: Paris, Bibliothèque Nationale latin 14233; thirteenth cent., probably from Chesnay (Nièvres).

Transmission History

The nine significant Latin manuscripts of *5 Ezra* manifest two distinct textual recensions, usually labelled the "Spanish" and the "French." Seven manuscripts (MSS CMNEVLK) feature the so-called "Spanish" text of *4-6 Ezra*, while MSS S and A have the "French" text. All eight complete manuscripts are complete Bibles except for the Amiens manuscript, which is a collection of five writings of Ezra.

1. For further details on the manuscript situation for *5 Ezra*, see Theodore A. Bergren, *Fifth Ezra: The Text, Origin and Early History* (SBLSCS 25; Atlanta, Ga.: Scholars Press, 1990), 39-58; Michael Wolter, *5. Esra-Buch, 6. Esra-Buch* (JSHRZ 3,7; Gütersloh: Gütersloher, 2001), 768-73.

The relationship between the two recensions is discussed in detail in Bergren's 1990 textual study.[2] It is maintained there first that the French and Spanish text forms probably derive from inner-Latin development, rather than depending independently on a *Vorlage(n)* in some other language. Secondly it is argued that, in virtually every case where there exist criteria by which to judge the relative merits of the recensions, the Spanish reading seems superior. It is concluded that the Spanish version on the whole represents the more original form of the text, and that its readings are to be accepted in every case where the French reading is not clearly preferable. The French text is judged to represent a deliberate and thorough-going editorial recension of an earlier text, made on the basis of stylistic, grammatical and theological factors.

The Latin text of *5 Ezra* is first attested by primary evidence in the mid-fifth century. The fifth-century sources that quote *5 Ezra* are discussed below. Although none of these sources also quotes *4* or *6 Ezra*, it is my opinion that by that time *4* and *5 Ezra* were already literarily connected with one another. This opinion is based on the fact that one of the fifth-century sources referred to above, the *Acta Silvestri*, quotes *5 Ezra* as an authoritative work, giving it the same status as other Jewish and Christian scriptural writings. In my judgment, this status probably accrued to *5 Ezra* only in its association with *4 Ezra*.

A Latin form of *6 Ezra* was probably appended to the end of the Latin text of *4 Ezra* at some time before 400 C.E. This would have occurred before *5 Ezra* was appended to the end of the *4/6 Ezra* corpus. Thus, *5 Ezra* was probably connected to a corpus that already consisted of *4/6 Ezra* by 450 C.E. This original sequence of *4/6/5 Ezra* is preserved in the "Spanish" manuscripts.[3]

Fifth Ezra seems to have had little impact in its own time, and might well have faded from view were it not for its attachment to the end of the *4/6 Ezra* corpus. *Fifth Ezra* was subsequently moved to the head of the corpus, resulting in the order preserved in the "French" manuscripts (*5/4/6 Ezra*). It is this sequence that is preserved today in editions of "2 Esdras" in the Apocrypha.

The first source known to me that places material deriving from *5 Ezra* in the same context as material from *4 Ezra* is the *Inventiones Nominum*, a medieval writing of uncertain date and provenance that is first attested in eighth-century manuscripts (see further discussion below).

The first firm and extensive evidence for an association of the Latin texts of *4*, *5* and *6 Ezra* coincides with the first attestation in Latin of the complete texts of each of the three books. This is in MS S, a two-volume Bible manuscript dated to 821/2 C.E.

Original Language[4]

Fifth Ezra was almost certainly written either in Greek or in Latin. The strongest indications of a Greek *Vorlage* are the possible confusions between *periblepsai* and *patēr blepsai* in 1:38 (Latin *pater aspice*) and between *egō* and *erō* in 1:30 (Latin *dicam*). However, neither of these cases is decisive, since intra-Latin explanations can be advanced for both.

Lexical, grammatical and stylistic considerations yield no firm evidence for a Greek or Semitic text of *5 Ezra* underlying the Latin. Although the book contains several "Semi-

2. See Bergren, *Fifth Ezra*, chap. 4.

3. See Theodore A. Bergren, "Christian Influence on the Transmission History of 4, 5, and 6 Ezra." In *The Jewish Apocalyptic Heritage in Early Christianity* (ed. J. C. VanderKam and W. Adler; CRINT 3.4; Assen: Van Gorcum; Minneapolis, Minn.: Fortress, 1996), 102-27.

4. For fuller discussion, see Bergren, *Fifth Ezra*, chap. 7; Wolter, *5. Esra-Buch, 6. Esra-Buch*, 784-85.

tisms," these could be products of a Latin or Greek author writing in a Semitic style. A Semitic original for the entire text is rendered less likely by the apparently Christian origin of the present form of the book.

Thus, in my opinion, the original language of 5 *Ezra* remains an open question. Greek and Latin are the likeliest possibilities. The argument for composition in Latin is strengthened by the theme of the Christian church as "mother" apparent in 2:15-32. This issue is discussed further below, under "Date of Composition."

Genre and Structure

Genre

Especially in its initial sections (1:4–2:14), 5 *Ezra* is most properly described as a "prophetic" or "oracular" writing. 5 *Ezra* is clearly introduced as a "prophetic" work in 1:4, and most of the book consists of prophetic oracles spoken either by God, through the mouthpiece of Ezra, or by the prophet himself. As in the classical biblical prophets, most of these oracles either inveigh against the sins of the people of Israel or anticipate a time when the people will conform more closely to God's will.

However, the book, especially in its latter sections (2:15-48), also contains much material of a visionary and eschatological nature. In this regard it reflects the development and evolution of the "prophetic" genre that occurred generally in both Jewish and Christian literature during the Second Temple period. 5 *Ezra* 2:42-48 constitutes an "apocalypse" in the formal sense of the word.

Structure

It can plausibly be argued that 5 *Ezra* originated as a revisionist, Christian supersessionist reading of the apocryphal book of Baruch (1 Baruch). The author of 5 *Ezra* seems to have drawn overarching structural frameworks for his book from both 1 Baruch and Galatians 4:21-31, skillfully integrating these two distinct sets of structural principles into an integrated literary product.

In terms of 5 *Ezra*'s affinities with 1 Baruch, the author of 5 *Ezra* seems to have discerned in 1 Baruch a sequential outline or schema of (Christian) salvation history which the author then adopted as a template for his or her own work. As a result, the six major text units of 5 *Ezra* outlined above can be seen roughly to coincide with six main thematic sections of 1 Baruch, as follows:

The first salvation-historical stage discerned in 1 Baruch by the author of 5 *Ezra* is the early period of God's original people, Israel. This period, described in the Torah and in the historical books of the Hebrew Bible, is dominated by the people's sin and ingratitude to God, exemplified during the Exodus. This period is documented in Bar 1:15–2:29; 3:1-8, Baruch's prayer of national confession of sins. It is represented in 5 *Ezra* 1:5-24, the so-called "Exodus review."

The second salvation-historical stage discerned in 1 Baruch by the author of 5 *Ezra* is the period of Israel represented in the prophetic and sapiential books of the Hebrew canon. This, again, is a period of the people's disobedience and indifference toward God, leading eventually to their punishment in the form of exile. This stage is represented in Bar 3:9–4:4, a paean to Wisdom. It is reprised in 5 *Ezra* 1:25-34, which uses prophetic and sapiential material to continue the polemic against the Jewish people.

The third salvation-historical stage is the initial rise of the Christians. The author of 5 *Ezra* sees this event reflected in Bar 2:30-35, which actually lionizes the moral qualities of the Jewish exiles in Babylon. This salvation-historical stage is set out in a cursory, almost proleptic fashion in *5 Ezra* 1:24, and is fleshed out in *5 Ezra* 1:35-40. Both of these passages describe the ideal qualities of the "new" people (Christians) whom God has chosen to receive God's patrimony.

The fourth stage is the desolation and destruction of the "mother" of God's original people, the city of Jerusalem, and the dispersion of the Jewish people. These events are discerned by *5 Ezra*'s author in Bar 4:5-20. This period of salvation history is documented in *5 Ezra* 2:1-7.

The fifth salvation-historical stage in *5 Ezra*'s schema is the rise of the Christian church, "mother Church." *5 Ezra*'s author interprets Bar 4:21-35, which now comforts and encourages the "mother" of the Jewish people, as describing this period. This salvation-historical phase finds its correlate in *5 Ezra* 2:15-32, which idealizes and exhorts the "mother" of the new people, the Christian church.

Finally, *5 Ezra*'s author seems to read Bar 4:36-5:9, a glorious, idealized portrait of Jewish exiles returning from Babylon, as a description of the future, eschatological glorification of God's newly chosen people, the Christians. This stage, characterized by the resurrection and eschatological rewards to be received by righteous Christians, is reprised in *5 Ezra* 2:33-48.

In terms of its dependence on Gal 4:21-31, *5 Ezra* can be interpreted as manifesting sequentially three major pairs of opposites that derive from Paul's argumentation in Gal 4:21-31. In this passage Paul presents an "allegory" based on the two wives and two sons of Abraham: Hagar (the "slave") and her son Ishmael, and Sarah (the "free woman") and her son Isaac. The two women, Paul writes, represent two "covenants."

Fifth Ezra expresses in sequence three pairs of opposites that stem from Paul's argumentation in this passage. One pair is the "children" of the slave woman vs. the "children" of the free woman. The author of *5 Ezra*, following Paul's lead, interprets this pair as the "old" people (Israel) vs. the "new" people (Christians). A second is the "mother" of the slave children, or old people (Hagar, or the earthly Jerusalem) vs. the "mother" of the free children, or new people (Sarah, or the heavenly Jerusalem). The author of *5 Ezra* interprets this pair as Jerusalem vs. the Christian church. A third pair of opposites, this one implicit in Gal 4:21-31, is the mountain associated with the "old" covenant (Sinai, or Horeb) vs. the mountain associated with the "new" covenant (Zion).

The text of *5 Ezra* reflects these three pairs of antithetical opposites in sequential fashion. *5 Ezra* chapter 1 sets out an oppositional contrast between the "old" and "new" peoples, Jews and Christians. Here Ezra reviews the events of the Exodus and condemns the Israelites of that generation for their hardness of heart. At the end of the Exodus review, in 1:24, God expresses his frustration with the old people and announces his intention to "give [God's] name" to "another nation." *5 Ezra* 1:25-34 continues God's polemic against the "old" people.

In 1:35, God initiates a description of the "new" people. Although they have not been provided with the traditional signs and benefits of God's presence, they immediately accept the new teaching. In 1:38-40 God summons Ezra to witness the coming of this new people.

The second set of paired opposites constitutes the two "mothers" of the two peoples: Hagar (the "mother" of the slave children) vs. Sarah (the "mother" of the free children). *Fifth Ezra* 2:1-32 contrasts these two "mothers," interpreted by him respectively as Jerusalem and the Christian church. In 2:1-7, the author first uses imagery and wording from

Baruch 4 to evoke pity for Jerusalem, "mother" of the Jewish people, and then has God pronounce destruction on her and her offspring for their disregard for God's "covenant." This section is balanced by 2:15-32, which invokes the "mother" of the new people, namely, the Christian church. This mother is exhorted to comfort and encourage her offspring.

The third set of paired opposites constitutes the two mountains, Sinai and Zion, where the old and new peoples respectively have received divine revelation. On Sinai the "old" people "spurned" the revelation that they received from God (2:33). The remainder of the book (2:34-48) is concerned with Mount Zion. First, the new people are instructed to prepare themselves for the rewards that await them (2:34-39); then Mount Zion herself is exhorted to "complete [the] number" of the holy people (2:40-41). In the book's climax (2:42-48), Ezra witnesses the "son of God" standing on Mount Zion distributing crowns and palms to a surrounding multitude.

Religious Affiliation, Date and Provenance

Religious Affiliation[5]

The attribution of 5 *Ezra* to an "Ezra" who lived "in the days of King Nebuchadnezzar" (1:4) is universally regarded as false. The late date of the book's attestation, its primary survival only in Latin, its apparent use of literary works such as 1 Baruch, and its general thematic and literary affinities with writings of a relatively later period all contribute to this judgment.

Determination of the book's actual origin, however, is more difficult. First, the work contains few internal indications as to authorship or date or place of composition. Likewise, there is little external or historical evidence that helps to resolve these questions.

It can probably be assumed that 5 *Ezra* was written by a Jew or a Christian: this much is suggested by the book's ideology and mode of argumentation, and by the author's obvious familiarity with the Jewish scriptures.

In the opinion of most commentators, 5 *Ezra* is almost certainly Christian in its present form. This judgment is based on several factors. One is the book's uncompromising rejection of parties or individuals bearing traditional marks or labels of Jewish self-identification (e.g., Israel in 2:10 and Jacob and Judah in 1:24), and the lack of application of such labels to the "coming people" that is to inherit Israel's patrimony. Another is the close affinities that exist between textual material grouped in 5 *Ezra* 1:30-33 and Matt 23:34-38. These affinities are best explained by hypothesizing dependence of 5 *Ezra* on Matthew or a related Christian document.

These two factors, when considered in concert with the fact that 5 *Ezra* seems to quote or allude to a wide range of other Christian writings, make the argument for a Christian origin for the work almost certain. Thus, while most of the individual ideas, themes and other textual data in 5 *Ezra* are admissible in a Jewish setting, the particular constellation of these phenomena in 5 *Ezra* indicates a Christian origin.

Date of Composition[6]

An initial *terminus a quo* for the work can be set at the time of the book of Revelation, which 5 *Ezra* probably cites (see esp. 5 *Ezra* 2:42). Revelation is usually dated around 95 C.E. With regard to its *terminus ad quem*, 5 *Ezra* is cited as authoritative by a variety

5. For fuller discussion, see Bergren, *Fifth Ezra*, chap. 8; Wolter, *5. Esra-Buch, 6. Esra-Buch*, 786-89.
6. For fuller discussion, see Bergren, *Fifth Ezra*, 24-26; Wolter, *5. Esra-Buch, 6. Esra-Buch*, 789-90.

of fifth-century Christian sources in Latin that come from a wide range of geographical locales. Also, one of the fifth-century witnesses to *5 Ezra*, the *Acta Silvestri*, quotes a part of the text that is attested in only one of the manuscript substreams (viz., the secondary "interpolation" between 1:32 and 1:33 in manuscripts MNE).[7] This suggests that the textual history of the book was already well developed by the fifth century, again indicating a relatively earlier origin. Thus, the book can probably be assumed to have been written before 300 C.E.

In theory, then, *5 Ezra* could have been written at almost any time between 95 and 300 C.E. With regard to the *terminus a quo*, however, it seems clear that *5 Ezra* 2:15-32, which idealizes and exhorts the "mother" of the new people, is actually a paean to the Christian church. The characterization of the church as "mother Church," or *mater ecclesia*, is a theologoumenon that developed first in the late second century, and that is not widely attested until the third century. Furthermore, the particular language and imagery used to describe the church in 2:15-32 find their closest parallels in the writings of Tertullian and Cyprian, the "fathers" of Latin Christianity. Indeed, both Tertullian and Cyprian wrote in Latin, in northern Africa, during the period 200-260. Thus there is reason to argue that *5 Ezra* was written in Latin, in northern Africa, during this period. This supposition is bolstered by the thematic affinities between *5 Ezra* and the ps.-Cyprianic treatise *Adversus Ioudaios*, also a product of the same literary milieu.

On the basis of these factors, I would suggest a date for *5 Ezra* in the late second or third centuries, perhaps specifically between 180 and 300 C.E.

Provenance[8]

It is my opinion that none of the arguments previously advanced for a particular provenance for *5 Ezra* is definitive, and that the contents of the book offer no certain grounds for determining its place of origin. Also the extant attestation for the book's text, in the form of manuscripts and quotations, is so late and widespread that it cannot contribute significantly to this question. Thus, the provenance of *5 Ezra* remains, for now, uncertain.

If, however, the points made above (under "Date of Composition") concerning the ideological affinities between *5 Ezra* 2:15-32 and the theme of "mother Church" as expressed by Tertullian and Cyprian are accepted, the argument for an origin in northern Africa is strengthened.

Literary Context

Textual Sources Influencing 5 Ezra

Each of the six major text units of *5 Ezra* shows substantial influence from a variety of Jewish and Christian biblical and "apocryphal" sources.

In *5 Ezra* 1:4-24, the main structural influence seems to have been Psalm 78, a classical "Exodus review."[9] Other important biblical Exodus reviews that might have played a

---

7. Further details on the *Acta Silvestri* are provided below, under "Literary Context."

8. For fuller discussion, see Bergren, *Fifth Ezra*, 26.

9. See Theodore A. Bergren, "5 Ezra, Dayyenu and Improperia: The Tradition History of the Exodus-Review in 5 Ezra 1," in *A Multiform Heritage: Studies on Early Judaism and Christianity in Honor of Robert A. Kraft* (ed. B. G. Wright; SPHS 24; Atlanta, Ga.: Scholars Press, 1999), 109-122. This study is revised and expanded in "The Tradition History of the Exodus-Review in 5 Ezra 1," in *Of Scribes and Sages: Early Jewish Interpretation and Transmission of Scripture. Vol. 2: Later Versions and Traditions* (ed. C. A. Evans; London: T.&T. Clark, 2004), 34-50.

role are Psalms 105 and 106, and Nehemiah 9. In terms of its content, *5 Ezra* 1:4-24 covers the narrative material presented in, and borrows heavily from, the Exodus narratives in Exodus 13–17 and Numbers 11–14; 20–21.

Fifth Ezra 1:25-34 shows influence from Matt 23:29-39//Luke 11:49-51; 13:34-35; Jeremiah 7; Proverbs 1; Isa 1:11-15; 59:1-7, and a variety of other Hebrew biblical sources.

In *5 Ezra* 1:35-40 the author quotes or paraphrases 1 Pet 1:8-12; Heb 2:3-4; 4:2-3; and Bar 4:36-37; 5:5.[10]

Fifth Ezra 2:1-14 evidences direct quotation of Bar 4:8-23, and alludes to Zeph 2:13–3:5 and a variety of passages from the NT gospels.

The strongest influence in *5 Ezra* 2:15-32 comes from 2-3 Isaiah and from parallel material in Baruch 4–5. This section also manifests quotations from or allusions to Ezek 37:12; Isa 26:19-20; and *1 Enoch* 24–25.

Finally, in *5 Ezra* 2:33-48, the strongest textual influences are the book of Revelation (esp. chaps. 7, 21–22) and 1 and 2 Corinthians (viz., 1 Cor 15:53-54; 2 Cor 5:2-4).

Influence of 5 Ezra on Later Christian Literature[11]

The text of *5 Ezra* is attested in a relatively small number of subsequent early Christian writings:

(1) What seem to be the earliest datable references to the text of *5 Ezra* occur in the anonymous *De altercatione ecclesiae et synagogae*. The consensus of scholarly opinion places the *De altercatione* in the fifth century, perhaps between 438 and 476. The *De altercatione* twice quotes logia of "Esdras" that seem to derive from *5 Ezra*: one from *5 Ezra* 1:24 and the other from 2:2.

(2) *5 Ezra* also seems to be quoted in another fifth-century Christian writing, the so-called *Acta* (*Actus, Vita*) *Silvestri*. This anonymous work contains a series of stories about Silvester, the pope/bishop of Rome between 314 and 335 C.E. In one of these, Silvester quotes a logion, ascribed by him to *Hesdras*, that is paralleled in a section of *5 Ezra* that is unique to the manuscript family MNE. This section of text, located between 1:32 and 1:33 of the standard text, is an interpolation in a common ancestor of MNE. The *Acta Silvestri* is generally regarded as having been composed in Latin in the second half of the fifth century at Rome.

(3) The most extensive parallels to the text of *5 Ezra* in any outside sources occur in the Mozarabic and Roman ecclesiastical liturgies. Although the early histories of these corpora are unclear, both seem to go back in their earliest form at least to the fifth or sixth century. A number of antiphons, responses and other formulae in these corpora show influence from *5 Ezra*.

Numerous parallels with *5 Ezra* appear in the Mozarabic liturgical corpus. This material is most evident in a tenth-century Visigothic Mozarabic antiphonary from León, Spain.[12] Chants from this antiphonary show influence from *5 Ezra* 2:10-12, 18; 2:13-14; 2:17, 19; 2:23, 31, 35; 2:36-37; and 2:45.

The liturgy of the Roman church in areas outside Spain also features several parallels

10. See Theodore A. Bergren, "The 'People Coming from the East' in 5 Ezra 1:38" (*JBL* 108 [1989]: 675-83); *idem*, "The List of Leaders in 5 Ezra 1:39-40" (*JBL* 120 [2001]: 313-27).

11. For further discussion of all of these sources, see Bergren, *Fifth Ezra*, 58-78, 128-45.

12. See Louis Brou, "Le 4e Livre d'Esdras dans la Liturgie Hispanique et le Graduel Romain 'Locus iste' de la Messe de la Dédicace" (*Sacris Erudiri* 9 [1957]: 75-109).

to 5 *Ezra*. Most of these passages also appear in the Mozarabic liturgical material already cited. The Roman liturgy shows influence from 5 *Ezra* 2:34-35; 2:36-37; 2:39; and 2:45.

Also, the "Improperia" ("Reproaches") that form part of the Roman Mass on Good Friday find close parallels in 5 *Ezra* 1:7-23 and may have been inspired by that text.[13]

(4) A Latin Christian composition of uncertain date entitled the *Inventiones Nominum* ("Findings of Names") appears to show a knowledge of 5 *Ezra* in connection with *4 Ezra*. This work is a collection of short pericopes that first cite names that belonged to more than one person in ancient Jewish-Christian tradition, and then go on to list the individuals who possessed that name. The work exists in two recensions, both attested in manuscripts of the eighth century. One of these manuscripts is, however, judged by E. A. Lowe on paleographic grounds to derive from "an exemplar of high antiquity."[14]

Bibliography

Bensly, Robert L. *The Fourth Book of Ezra*. Introduction by M. R. James. Texts and Studies 3,2. Cambridge: Cambridge University Press, 1895.

Bergren, Theodore A. "Christian Influence on the Transmission History of 4, 5, and 6 Ezra." Pages 102-27 in *The Jewish Apocalyptic Heritage in Early Christianity*. Edited by J. C. VanderKam and W. Adler. CRINT 3.4. Assen: Van Gorcum; Minneapolis, Minn.: Fortress, 1996.

__________. *Fifth Ezra: The Text, Origin and Early History*. SBLSCS 25. Atlanta, Ga.: Scholars Press, 1990. (Further bibliography may be found here.)

__________. "5 Ezra, Dayyenu and Improperia: The Tradition History of the Exodus-Review in 5 Ezra 1." Pages 109-122 in *A Multiform Heritage: Studies on Early Judaism and Christianity in Honor of Robert A. Kraft*. Edited by B. G. Wright. SPHS 24. Atlanta, Ga.: Scholars Press, 1999. Reprinted in slightly expanded form in: "The Tradition History of the Exodus-Review in 5 Ezra 1." Pages 34-50 in *Of Scribes and Sages: Early Jewish Interpretation and Transmission of Scripture*. Vol. 2: *Later Versions and Traditions*. Edited by C. A. Evans. London: T.&T. Clark, 2004.

__________. "The List of Leaders in 5 Ezra 1:39-40." *JBL* 120 (2001): 313-27.

__________. "The 'People Coming from the East' in 5 Ezra 1:38." *JBL* 108 (1989): 675-83.

__________. "The Structure and Composition of 5 Ezra." *VC* 64 (2010): 115-39.

Brou, Louis. "Le 4e Livre d'Esdras dans la Liturgie Hispanique et le Graduel Romain 'Locus iste' de la Messe de la Dédicace." *Sacris Erudiri* 9 (1957): 75-109.

Daniélou, Jean. "Le 5e Esdras et le judéo-christianisme latin au second siècle." Vol. 1:162-71 in *Ex orbe religionum* (G. Widengren Festschrift). 2 vols. Studies in the History of Religions 21. Leiden: Brill, 1972. Reprinted in English translation: "5 Esdras." Pages 17-31 in *The Origins of Latin Christianity. A History of Early Christian Doctrine before the Council of Nicea*. Vol. 3. Translated by D. Smith and J. A. Baker. Philadelphia, Pa.: Westminster, 1977.

Duensing, Hugo, and Aurelio de Santos Otero. "The Fifth and Sixth Books of Ezra." Vol. 2:641-652 in *The New Testament Apocrypha*. 2 vols. Ed. Edgar Hennecke and Wilhelm Schneemelcher. Louisville: Westminster/John Knox Press, 1992 = "Das fünfte und sechste Buch Esra." Vol. 2:581-590 in *Neutestamentliche Apokryphen*. 2 vols. 5th ed. Ed. Wilhelm Schneemelcher. Tübingen: Mohr Siebeck, 1987-89.

13. See Bergren, "5 Ezra, Dayyenu and Improperia," 109-22.

14. E. A. Lowe, *Codices Latini Antiquiores* 7 (Oxford: Clarendon, 1934-1966), no. 911.

Geoltrain, Pierre. "Remarques sur la diversité des pratiques discursives apocryphes. L'example de 5 Esdras." *Apocrypha* 2 (1991): 17-30.

Knibb, Michael A. "The Second Book of Esdras." Pages 76-307 in R. J. Coggins and Michael A. Knibb, *The First and Second Books of Esdras*. Cambridge Bible Commentary. Cambridge: Cambridge University Press, 1979.

Kraft, Robert A. "Towards Assessing the Latin Text of '5 Ezra': the 'Christian' Connection." Pages 158-69 in *Christians Among Jews and Gentiles* (K. Stendahl Festschrift). Edited by G. W. E. Nickelsburg and G. W. MacRae. Philadelphia, Pa.: Fortress, 1986. Also in *HTR* 79 (1986): 158-69.

Myers, Jacob M. *1 and 2 Esdras*. AB 42. Garden City, N.Y.: Doubleday, 1974.

Stanton, Graham N. "5 Ezra and Matthean Christianity in the Second Century." *JTS* N.S. 28 (1977): 67-83.

Strickert, Frederick. "2 Esdras 1.11 and the Destruction of Bethsaida." *JSP* 16 (1997): 111-22.

Wolter, Michael. *5. Esra-Buch, 6. Esra-Buch*. JSHRZ 3,7. Gütersloh: Gütersloher, 2001. (Further bibliography may be found here.)

Fifth Ezra

Ezra inveighs against Israel for her sins during the Exodus

1 4[a]The word of the Lord that came to Ezra, the son of Chusi,
in the days of King Nebuchadnezzar saying, 5"Go, announce Zeph 1:1
to my people their sins, and to their children the iniquities
that they have committed against me. And let their children Isa 58:1
announce to their children's children 6that their fathers' sins Joel 1:2-3
have increased in the children, because they have forgotten Jer 7:26
me and sacrificed to foreign gods. 7Didn't I lead them out of Deut 32:17-18
the land of Egypt and out of the house of slavery? Why have Exod 13:3, 14
they provoked me and rejected my counsels?
8"Thus says the Lord: Shake the hair of your head and
shake out all these evils upon them, because they have not
obeyed my law. Foolish people! 9How long shall I, who con- Neh 5:13; Jer 7:28-30 | Isa 26:11 (LXX)
ferred such benefits on them, endure them?[b] 10I overthrew Num 14:11, 26-27
many kings because of them. I sank Pharaoh, with his servants, and his entire army in the sea! Exod 14:8, 23, 27-28
11"Didn't I overthrow the town of Bethsaida because of
you, and to the south burn two cities, Tyre and Sidon, with
fire, and kill those who hated you? 13[c]Didn't I lead you across Matt 11:21-24; Luke 10:12-15
the sea, and make walls on the right and the left? I gave you Exod 14:22, 29
Moses and Aaron as leaders. 14I gave you light in a pillar of Ps 77:20; Num 33:1
fire. These are my great wonders that I have done for you, but Exod 14:24
you have forgotten me, says the Lord. Ps 78:11-12
15"Thus says the Lord: The quails were a sign for you. I Exod 16:1-13; Num 11:4-34
gave you a camp for your protection, and there you com-
plained. 16I sank your pursuer with his army in the sea, but Exod 17:1-3

---

a. The superior "Spanish" recension lacks verses 1-3. In v. 4, the author abandons the "traditional" genealogy of Ezra found in Ezra 7:1-5 and 1 Esdr 8:1-2 in favor of one similar to that of Zephaniah in Zeph 1:1.

b. Or "How long shall I endure them, on whom I conferred such benefits?"

c. The superior "Spanish" recension lacks verse 12. In v. 11, the author unexpectedly introduces material from the synoptic gospels (Matt 11:21-24; Luke 10:12-15).

still the people themselves complain about their own de-
Num 14:26-27 struction! 17Where are my benefits that I gave you?
"Also, in the desert, when you were hungry and thirsty,
you cried out to me 18and said: 'Why have you led us into this
desert for us to die? It would have been better for us to serve
Exod 14:10-12; 17:1-3; Num 20:1-5 the Egyptians than to die in this wilderness!' 19Because of
this, I felt sorry at your groaning and gave you manna to eat,
Exodus 16 and you ate. 20When you were thirsty, I split the rock, and
Exod 17:1-7; Num 20:1-13 water flowed abundantly. And because of the heat, I made
Bar 5:8 trees covered with leaves for you.
Neh 9:35 21"I gave you fertile lands. I drove out the Canaanites, the
Hittites, the Perizzites, and their children from your pres-
Exod 34:11 | Isa 5:4 ence. What more will I do for you? 22Thus says the Lord:
When you were in the desert at the bitter stream, thirsty and
cursing my name, 23I did not become angry, but I cast a tree
Exod 15:22-25 into the water and made the stream sweet for you.
24"What will I do for you, Jacob? You were[a] unwilling to
Hos 6:4 obey me, Judah! I will go over to another nation and will give
Matt 21:43 | Deut 6:17 it my name, and they will certainly keep my statutes.

Castigation of the "old" people (Israel) continues

25When those who have abandoned me seek mercy, I will not
Prov 1:28; Jer 11:11, 14 pity them. 26When they call on me, I will not listen to them,
for they have stained their souls, and they have hands that are
Isa 1:11-15 stained with blood.
Isa 59:1-3, 7; Prov 1:16 "Your feet are not slow to commit murder.[b] 27It is not be-
Jer 2:17; 7:19 cause you have forsaken me, says the Lord, but yourselves!
28"Thus says the Lord: Didn't I ask you, as a father his
son, and as a mother her daughter, and as a nurse who loves
her child, 29that you be my people and I your God, that you
Jer 7:23; 2 Sam 7:14; 2 Cor 6:16-18 be my children and I your father? 30I gathered you as a hen
Matt 23:37b; Luke 13:34b (gathers) her chicks under her wings. But now, what will I
Hos 11:8 do to you?
5 Ezra 1:33b; Jer 7:15 "I will cast you forth from my presence![c] 31When you of-
Isa 1:11, 15; Amos 5:21-22; Mal 1:13 fer sacrifices to me, I will turn my eyes from you, for I did not
command you (to observe) feast days, new moons, sabbaths
Jer 7:22; Isa 1:11-15 and circumcisions. 32I sent my servants the prophets to you,
but you took them and killed them, and tore to pieces the
Matt 23:34; Luke 11:49 bodies of the apostles.[d] I will require their souls and blood,
Matt 23:35-36; Luke 11:50-51 says the Lord.
Matt 23:38; Luke 13:35 33"Thus says the Lord Almighty: Your house is desolate! I
5 Ezra 1:30c; Isa 17:13; Jer 7:10-15 will drive you out as the wind drives straw. 34And your chil-

---

a. The "Spanish" recension reads "He was."
b. The "Spanish" recension reads "to shed blood."
c. The "Spanish" recension reads "I will say, I will cast you forth . . ."
d. Or "emissaries."

dren will not have offspring, because they have neglected my *5 Ezra* 2:6b
commandment and have done evil in my presence.

Ezra predicts the advent of a “new” people (the Christians)

35“I will hand over your houses to a people coming from far
away, and those who have not known me[a] will believe me,[b] Deut 28:49-50; Jer 5:15; 6:12, 22; Ezek 7:24; Hab
and those to whom I have not shown signs will do what I 1:6, 8
have said. 36They have not seen prophets, but are mindful of Num 14:11; Isa 52:15-53:1; 55:5; 65:1
the antiquity of the prophets.[c] 37The apostles[d] bear witness 1 Pet 1:8-12
to the coming people with joy. Although they do not see me Heb 2:3-4; 1 Pet 1:12
with bodily eyes, they believe with the spirit, and they have John 20:29; 1 Pet 1:8-12
heard the things that I have said, and believe me. Heb 4:2-3
38“Now, father, look with glory and see the people coming
from the east. 39I will lead them, (I) together with Abraham, Isa 49:18; 60:4; Bar 4:36-37; 5:5 | Isa 42:16; 43:5-7;
Isaac, and Jacob, Elijah and Enoch, Zechariah and Hosea, Bar 5:9
Amos, Joel, Micah, Obadiah, Zephaniah, 40Nahum, Jonah,
Malachi,[e] Habakkuk, and twelve angels with flowers. Matt 8:11-12; Luke 13:28-29; Rev 21:12-14; Sir 49:10

The “mother” of Israel (Jerusalem) is consigned to destruction

2 1“Thus says the Lord: I led out a people to whom I gave
commandments, which they were not willing to obey, but
they made my counsels vain. 2The mother who bore them Ezek 20:13, 16, 24; Prov 1:25
says[f] to them: ‘Go, children, because I am a widow and for- Isa 49:21
saken. 3I brought you up with gladness, I will send you away
with mourning[g] and sadness,[h] because you sinned before the
Lord God and did iniquity in his presence. 4But now, what
will I do for you? For I am a widow and forsaken by my children. Go, children, seek mercy from the Lord, 5for I am desolate.’” Bar 4:8-23
“I invoke you, father, over the mother of those who were
unwilling to keep your covenant, 6that you might give confusion to them and (bring) their mother to plunder.”
“Let them never have offspring, 7let them be scattered *5 Ezra* 1:34
among the nations, and let their name be blotted out from
the earth, because they have spurned my covenant. Lev 26:33; Deut 4:27; Ps 44:12 [Evv 44:11]; Jer 9:16
8“Woe to you, Assyria, who hide sinners in your midst.

a. The “Spanish” recension reads “you.”
b. The “Spanish” recension reads “you.”
c. Lat.: “of them.”
d. Or “emissaries.”
e. The “Spanish” recension reads “Mattathias.”
f. The “Spanish” recension reads “They begot for themselves a mother who says.”
g. The “Spanish” recension reads “weeping.”
h. The “Spanish” recension reads “mourning.”

Evil city! Remember what I did to Sodom and Gomorrah, [9]whose land sinks to hell. I will do the same to those who have not obeyed me!"

Zeph 2:13-3:5; Matt 11:23-24; Luke 10:12, 15

[10]Thus says the Lord to Ezra: "Tell my people that I have prepared for them to eat, and I will give them the kingdom of Jerusalem, which I was going to give to Israel. [11]And I will take for them the glory of Israel,[a] and I will give to them the eternal dwelling places that I had prepared for Israel.[b] [12]The tree of life will be an aroma of ointment for them, and they will neither labor nor become tired.[c]

Matt 8:11; 22:1-14//Luke 13:28-29; 14:15

Matt 21:43

Luke 16:9; John 14:2-3; 2 Cor 5:1, 4; Rev 21:3

Gen 2:9; 3:17-19, 22; *1 En.* 24:4–25:7

[13]"Seek and you will receive. Ask for yourselves few days, so that your days may be lessened; for already my kingdom is ready to come. Be watchful in spirit! [14]I call to witness heaven and earth: I have set aside evil and created good, because I live, says the Lord.

Matt 7:7-8//Luke 11:9-10; John 16:24

Matt 24:22//Mark 13:20

Matt 25:34 | Mark 13:33-37; 14:34-38//Matt 24:42; 25:13; 26:38-41//Luke 21:36

The "mother" of the new people (the Christian church) is exhorted

[15]"Good mother, embrace your children. Give them happiness like the dove that rears her children, and strengthen their feet, because I have chosen you, says the Lord. [16]And I will raise the dead from their places and from their graves, because I have recognized my name in them.

Ps 18:34 [Evv 18:33]; Cant 2:13-14; Isa 49:7; 60:8; Hab 3:19

Ezek 37:12; Isa 26:19

Rev 3:12; 14:1; 22:4

[17]"Do not be afraid, mother of the children; I have chosen you, says the Lord. [18]I am sending to you for assistance my servants Jeremiah, Isaiah and Daniel, according to whose counsel I sanctified you. And I will prepare for you twelve trees with various kinds of fruits, [19]and seven fountains flowing milk and honey, and immense mountains that have roses and lilies, which I have prepared for you and your children. I have filled your children with joy!

5 Ezra 2:15; Isa 43:1; 44:2; Zeph 3:16-20

Rev 22:2

1 En. 18:6; 24-25; 32:1; 48:1; Hermas *Sim.* 9

Job 21:11

[20]"Treat the widow rightly; secure justice for the orphan; give to the needy; protect the fatherless; clothe the naked; [21]care for the injured and weak. Do not ridicule the lame person, but protect (him). Admit the blind to the vision of my splendor. [22]Gather the old and young within your walls. Watch over your infants. Let your servants and free men be joyful, and your whole company will be happy.

Isa 58:6-10; Matt 25:35-45; Hermas *Mand.* 8.10 | Joel 2:16

[23]"When I find your dead, I will raise them; I will watch for signs, and I will give your dead[d] the place of honor in my resurrection. [24]Wait a little; your rest will come.

Ezek 39:15; Sir 38:16; Matt 20:23 | Isa 26:19-20; Dan 12:13; Rev 6:11

[25]"Good nurse, nourish your children. Strengthen those

---

a. Lat.: "them."

b. Lat.: "them."

c. The "Spanish" recension reads ". . . that I had prepared for Israel in an aroma of ointment. They will neither labor . . . ."

d. Lat.: "them."

whom you bore and strengthen their feet, 26because none of those whom I gave you will die. I will require them from your number. 27Do not worry; strengthen them. Days of tribulation and distress will come. Others will lament and be sad, but you will be happy and have abundance. 28All the nations will envy you, but they will not be able to do anything against you, says the Lord. 29All things tremble at me; my eyes see Gehenna.

30"Rejoice, mother, with your children, and I will save you, says the Lord. 31I will remember your children who sleep, because I will seek them out from the breadth of the earth. And be strengthened in the greatness of your glory, and perform mercy, because I am merciful, says the Lord. 32Embrace your children until I come, and to the others, show mercy, because my fountains will overflow and my grace will not fail."

5 Ezra 2:15; Num 11:12; Zech 10:9

Isa 34:16; John 10:28; 17:12; 18:9

Isa 51:7

Exod 22:27; Dan 12:2

5 Ezra 2:15; Isa 49:10; 51:6, 8; Jer 2:13; 3:12

Final instructions to God's "new" people; Ezra's vision

33I, Ezra, received an injunction from the Lord on Mount Horeb[a] for Israel, but they spurned this commandment. 34I say to you who hear and understand: "Await your shepherd. I will give you the restfulness of your eternity, because the end of the age and the diminution of mankind are near. 35Be prepared for the rewards of the kingdom. Perpetual light will shine upon you, and eternity of times has been prepared for you. 36Flee from the shadow of this age, the captivity of your glory. I testify that my savior has been commanded by the Lord.

37"As for you, receive the joy of your glory, giving thanks to the one who called you to heavenly kingdoms. 38Rise, and stand, and see in the banquet the number of the sealed, 39who have borne themselves from the shadow of the world and have received splendid garments from the Lord.

40"Mount Zion, receive your number. Bring to completion your people clothed in white, who serve you with obedience, because they have fulfilled the law of the Lord. 41Since formerly you wished your children to come, complete their number. Ask the authority of the Lord that the people may be sanctified, because they were called from the beginning."

42I, Ezra, saw on Mount Zion a great crowd that I could not count;[b] all of them were praising the Lord with songs. 43And in the middle of them was a tall young man who stood out above all of them. And he was placing crowns on

Jer 6:19; Mal 4:4; Acts 13:46; *4 Ezra* 14:1-4, 30, 37-38

Matt 13:13-23; 15:10//Mark 4:12-20; 7:14; 8:17-21 | Matt 25:32

Matt 11:28-30

Isa 6:9-10; 14:3, 7; Matthew 24; Luke 10:11; 21:31; 1 Pet 5:4

Isa 9:2; 60:19-20; Rev 21:23-25; 22:5

Col 2:17; Eph 6:12; Heb 8:5; 10:1; Jas 1:17; 2 Pet 1:4

Bar 4:36-37; 1 Thess 2:12; 1 Pet 5:10

Bar 5:5; Matt 8:11//Luke 13:28-29; Matt 22:1-14; Luke 14:15; Rev 7:4; 19:9; *1 En.* 62:15-16

5 Ezra 2:36; Isa 52:1-2; 61:3, 10; Bar 5:1-3; Rev 3:4-5; *1 En.* 62:15-16

Rom 11:25; Rev 3:4; 6:11; 7:4, 14; *1 Clem.* 2:4; 59:2

Bar 4:37; 5:5

Rom 8:28-30; 2 Thess 2:13-14; *4 Ezra* 4:36-37

1 Pet 2:9

Heb 12:20-22; Rev 7:9-17; *4 Ezra* 13:5, 12, 35; *2 Bar.* 40 | Rev 14:1-5; 15:2-4

Rev 14:1; *4 Ezra* 13:5, 35; Hermas *Sim.* 9.6.1; *Gos. Pet.* 40

a. The "Spanish" recension reads "Chobar."

b. The "Spanish" recension reads "that no one could count."

2 Tim 4:8; 1 Pet 5:4; Rev 2:10; 3:11

the heads of each of them, and they were becoming more
exalted.[a]

Rev 17:6-7; *4 Ezra* 13:11

Zechariah 1, 4-5; Rev 7:13-14

I began to look with amazement. 44 And I asked an angel
and said, "Who are these people?" 45 And he responded and
said to me, "They are those who have laid aside the mortal
clothing and donned the immortal, and confessed the name

1 Cor 15:53-54; 2 Cor 5:2-4; Col 3:9-10; Eph 4:22-24 | John 12:13; Rev 7:9

of God. Now they are being crowned and receive palms."

46 And I said to the angel, "Who is that young man who
gives them crowns and palms?" 47 And he answered me and
said, "He is the son of God, whom they confessed in the mor-

4 Ezra 7:28-29; 13:32, 37, 52; 14:9

tal world."

Then I began to praise and glorify the Lord. 48 And the
angel said to me, "Go, and tell his people how many wonders

5 Ezra 1:5, 14; *4 Ezra* 13:50; Exod 10:2; Luke 19:37; 1 Pet 2:9

you have seen from the Lord God!"

a. Or "taller."

Sixth Ezra
A new translation and introduction

by Theodore A. Bergren

Sixth Ezra (2 Esdras 15–16) is a short, oracular Christian writing that was composed in the eastern Mediterranean region at some time during the second or third centuries. It reflects a situation of severe socio-religious crisis in the community or communities in which it originated. The book is cast as the words of God mediated through an unnamed prophet. The main part of the work sets forth predictions of impending doom for the world at large and for certain specific sections of it, conveying this message with eschatological language and imagery. In this regard *6 Ezra* is reminiscent of, and stands in the tradition of, Jewish and Christian prophetic writings of the Hebrew Bible and elsewhere. *6 Ezra* is also concerned to exhort a group of God's "chosen" people to remain faithful and resist sin in order to escape the imminent calamities.

6 Ezra survives today associated with (but technically not part of) the Apocrypha as the final two chapters of the composite writing 2 Esdras (2 Esdras 1–2 = *5 Ezra*; 2 Esdras 3–14 = *4 Ezra*; 2 Esdras 15–16 = *6 Ezra*).

Contents

Sixth Ezra can be divided into two major sections. The first, 15:1–16:34, describes destruction and calamities that will soon take place in the world as punishment for human sin. In the initial part of this section (15:5–16:1), attention focuses successively on four specific regions: Egypt, Assyria, Rome ("Babylon"), and Asia Minor. The latter part (16:2-34) is more generally directed. The second major section, 16:35-78, exhorts God's chosen people to withdraw from worldly activity and to abstain from sin if they wish to be saved.

In 15:1-4, God commissions the unnamed prophet who is to deliver the oracles in the book. 15:5-19 predicts world-wide catastrophes that will result from the iniquity prevalent on the earth, while 15:20-27 condemns the sinners whose actions have precipitated these calamities. In 15:28-45 the seer describes two symbolic visions, one of a fierce battle in the east between the "Arabians" and the "Carmonians" (see below under "Date of Composition"), and the other of storm clouds that destroy "Babylon," almost certainly to be identified with Rome (cf. *4 Ezra* 3:28-36; Rev 14:8; 18:2-3).

In 15:46-63, "Asia" is singled out for special condemnation due to her collaboration with the hateful "Babylon." 16:1-17 emphasizes the inevitability and finality of God's judgment, while 16:18-34 sketches some details of the catastrophe and desolation that will soon prevail on the earth in the wake of God's judgment.

In the second major section (16:35-78) the book's emphasis shifts from prediction of destruction to parenesis of God's chosen people. In 16:35-52, the people of God are warned of impending doom and counseled to be "like strangers on the earth" (16:40) during the tribulations. 16:53-67 contains warnings to sinners and a recitation of God's mighty acts of creation. In 16:68-73, the seer envisions a time of persecution of God's elect, while in 16:74-78 he promises God's people that they will be saved if they guard carefully against sin.

Manuscripts, Versions, Languages, and Tradition History

The primary textual base for *6 Ezra* consists of eight complete Latin manuscripts that are known not to depend exclusively on any other known manuscript of the work. These are the same as the eight complete significant Latin manuscripts of *4* and *5 Ezra*; they are described in the introduction to *5 Ezra* in this volume. Thus, in the tradition of significant Latin manuscripts, *6 Ezra* occurs only in its complete form, and only in conjunction with complete forms of *4* and *5 Ezra*. All of these manuscripts are Bibles (MSS SCMNEVL) or collections of biblical materials (MS A).[1]

To these eight Latin manuscript witnesses must be added the fourth-century Greek vellum fragment of 15:57-59 found at Oxyrhynchus (fragment 1010). This fragment provides a *terminus ante quem* for *6 Ezra*.[2]

One other datum pertinent to the early textual history of *6 Ezra* is the issue of the book's recensions. The Latin text of *6 Ezra*—like those of *4* and *5 Ezra*—survives in two distinct recensions. One, normally labelled the "French," is attested in two manuscripts (S and A); the other, the "Spanish," is present in six (CMNEVL). The recensional situation is analyzed in detail in Bergren's 1998 textual study.[3] There it is argued that the two texts arose on the basis of intra-Latin recension, rather than being independent translations of a Greek *Vorlage*. In almost every case, examination of the recensional variations strongly suggests the superiority, or temporal priority, of the French text. It seems most likely that the "French" recension represents the earliest recoverable Latin text of *6 Ezra*, and that the "Spanish" recension is a revision of this text made on stylistic and grammatical grounds.

All of the complete manuscripts of 2 Esdras that follow the Spanish recension have the order *4/6/5 Ezra*. Both manuscripts of the French recension, however, have the order *5/4/6* Ezra. It seems most likely that *6 Ezra* at some point in time became attached to the end of *4 Ezra*, and that *5 Ezra* was later appended to the *4/6 Ezra* corpus. At a later date, *5 Ezra* was moved to the head of the corpus, resulting in the form of 2 Esdras preserved today in the Apocrypha (*5/4/6 Ezra*).[4]

Sixth Ezra, which in its present form is anonymous, does not seem to have been widely known in its time, and might well have been lost were it not for its having been appended to the end of *4 Ezra* at some time before 400 C.E. Although it is sometimes surmised that this association occurred in the Greek tradition, or even that *6 Ezra* was composed as an appendix to the Greek version of *4 Ezra*, these possibilities are discounted by two considerations. First, no other daughter version of the Greek text of *4 Ezra* besides the Latin includes *6 Ezra*. Second, a study of the Oxyrhynchus Greek fragment of *6 Ezra* 15:57-59 by A. S. Hunt indicates that, given the pagination of the fragment, it is improbable that

1. For further details on the manuscript situation for *6 Ezra*, see Theodore A. Bergren, *Sixth Ezra: The Text and Origin* (New York: Oxford University, 1998), 28-37; Michael Wolter, *5. Esra-Buch, 6. Esra-Buch* (JSHRZ 3,7; Gütersloh: Gütersloher, 2001), 768-73.

2. A full discussion of the Oxyrhynchus fragment may be found in A. S. Hunt, ed., *The Oxyrhynchus Papyri*, vol. 7 (London: Egyptian Exploration Fund, 1910), 11-15.

3. See Bergren, *Sixth Ezra*, chap. 4.

4. See Theodore A. Bergren, "Christian Influence on the Transmission History of 4, 5, and 6 Ezra." In *The Jewish Apocalyptic Heritage in Early Christianity* (ed. J. C. VanderKam and W. Adler; CRINT 3.4; Assen: Van Gorcum; Minneapolis, Minn.: Fortress, 1996), 102-27.

the copy of *6 Ezra* to which the fragment belonged was preceded by a work as long as *4 Ezra*.[5] Thus it seems most likely that *6 Ezra* was an independent composition, that it was translated into Latin before the year 400, and that the textual connection between *4* and *6 Ezra* occurred in the Latin tradition.

The manuscript tradition suggests that the Latin text of *6 Ezra* was first simply placed after *4 Ezra*, retaining its separate identity. Later, in some manuscript streams, the two works actually became textually conjoined, as they are in modern editions of 2 Esdras.[6]

The rationale and date for the association of *4* and *6 Ezra* are difficult to ascertain. As noted above, *6 Ezra* in its present form is anonymous, and nowhere mentions the name Ezra. This would imply that the connection was not made on the basis of a common attribution. There are, however, reasons to believe that both the end of *4 Ezra* and the beginning of *6 Ezra* might have been textually modified when or after the two works became connected. First, virtually every language version of *4 Ezra* besides the Latin features an ending to the book which describes Ezra's assumption to heaven, his transcription of *4 Ezra*, and his continuing function as a heavenly scribe. The Latin version lacks all of this, ending with Ezra still on the earth. Presuming that the original Latin translation of the Greek text had the longer ending, it seems reasonable to postulate that it was excised when *6 Ezra* became connected to the end of *4 Ezra*, in order to allow the seer to continue to prophesy in an earthly setting.

Also, it is often observed that the present text of *6 Ezra* begins rather abruptly, without the name of a prophet or a context for prophecy ever being given. It seems possible that part of the original beginning of *6 Ezra*, which might have included these elements, was removed when it was connected to *4 Ezra*, perhaps to afford a smoother transition between the two works. Indeed, when the two are read together, *4 Ezra* provides both the name of the seer and a prophetic context.

In the mid-sixth century, the Latin text of *6 Ezra* is quoted by Gildas, a historian of Britain. There are also two early liturgical citations of *6 Ezra*, a response in the ancient Mozarabic (Hispanic) liturgy and an antiphon in the Roman liturgy. These are discussed below. Since the Roman liturgy includes material from *4*, *5* and *6 Ezra*, it can probably be assumed that these three works were textually connected by the mid-sixth century. At some point before 821, a secondary recension (the "Spanish" recension) of *6 Ezra* was made on stylistic and grammatical grounds. The first appearance of *4*, *5* and *6 Ezra* in full, in Latin, is in the St. Germain manuscript (MS S), dated 821/22.

Original Language[7]

The fragment of a Greek text of *6 Ezra* 15:57-59 found at Oxyrhynchus strongly suggests that the surviving Latin version was based on a Greek *Vorlage*. That is, there is no evidence, nor any reason to speculate, that the Greek version preserved at Oxyrhynchus was translated from the Latin. This is indicated both by the early date of the Oxyrhynchus fragment (fourth century C.E.) and by the fact that, in the first centuries of the common era, translation of Jewish and Christian literature from Greek to Latin was far more common than that in the opposite direction.

---

5. Hunt, ed., *The Oxyrhynchus Papyri*, 7.11-15.

6. For further details on the manuscripts of *6 Ezra*, see Bergren, *Sixth Ezra*, 28-37; Wolter, *5. Esra-Buch, 6. Esra-Buch*, 768-73.

7. For fuller discussion, see Bergren, *Sixth Ezra*, 17-18; Wolter, *5. Esra-Buch, 6. Esra-Buch*, 828-29.

Another equally compelling factor indicating that the Latin text of *6 Ezra* was translated from Greek lies in the vocabulary and character of the Latin text itself. The Latin *6 Ezra* abounds both in Greek calques and in highly distinctive Latin lexical elements that are best explained as translations from Greek. The nature and quantity of these elements make it almost certain that the Latin text was translated from a Greek *Vorlage*.

There is no reason to believe that a version of *6 Ezra* in Hebrew or Aramaic underlay the Greek version.

Genre, Structure, Form-Critical Categories[8]

The most important point to be made about the genre or literary form of *6 Ezra* is the extent to which this work is, through and through, a writing in the classical, biblical prophetic style. In virtually every aspect—its language, style, ideology, types of discourse, contents, morality, modes of expression, use of imagery, ways in which the audience is envisioned and addressed, use of rhetoric and rhetorical devices, mix between general postulates and specific incidents, admixture of the personal element, use of visual and visionary elements, and balance between threat of condemnation and consolation or parenesis—this work evokes the biblical prophets. The fact that *6 Ezra* seems to have been written at a relatively late date (second to third centuries C.E.) suggests that it stands self-consciously within these traditions and was influenced by them.

Eschatology

Sixth Ezra can be characterized more specifically as "eschatological prophecy," since it is concerned mainly with calamitous events that will precede the end of the present, sinful world (see esp. 16:15, 52, 74).

The eschatology of *6 Ezra* is rather simple and primitive in form. There is no complex eschatological timetable or elaborate apocalyptic scenario. Simply put, God will, in the near future, bring a variety of "evils" on the world and its inhabitants—warfare, famine, civic unrest, bloodshed, death, destruction, pestilence and poverty. These evils are intended as punishment for the iniquity that has generally overtaken humankind and as recompense for the persecution of the just, both of which elements have reached a breaking point. It is due to an accumulation of human sinfulness and unrighteous deeds that God will strike the earth in anger.

Sixth Ezra does not specify any one particular agency or event through which God's eschatological wrath will be unleashed. Rather the book's form, a series of smaller vignettes, leads to the expression of a number of different eschatological devices and scenarios. The eschatological "evils" will manifest variously as civic disorder (15:16-19), as divine fire devouring the earth's foundations and sinners (15:23), as conflict in remote areas of the world (15:28-33), as terrible storm-clouds that will rain down fire, hail, floods, and general destruction (15:34-45, 60-63), as earthquakes, thunder, and cosmic turmoil (16:3-20), and as conquest by foreign peoples (16:40-48). Warfare and famine are the two main avenues through which God wreaks consternation, terror, havoc and destruction among the earth's inhabitants.

---

8. For fuller discussion, see Theodore A. Bergren, "Prophetic Rhetoric in 6 Ezra," in *For a Later Generation: The Transformation of Tradition in Israel, Early Judaism, and Early Christianity* (G. W. E. Nickelsburg Festschrift; ed. R. A. Argall, B. A. Bow and R. A. Werline; Harrisburg, Pa.: Trinity, 2000), 25-32.

Religious Affiliation, Date and Provenance

The Religious Affiliation of the Author[9]

The contents and style of *6 Ezra* make it almost certain that the book was written by a Jew or Christian. Deciding between these two, however, is more difficult.

Two factors suggest strongly that *6 Ezra* was written by a Christian. The first is the striking linguistic and thematic parallels between *6 Ezra* and the book of Revelation, specifically between *6 Ezra* 15:43–16:1 and Revelation 14:8; 16:19–19:3. Both documents discuss in detail a city called "Babylon," and both describe the city's characteristics and fate in a remarkably similar way. Both label Babylon with certain negative features associated with femininity. In *6 Ezra* many of the negative points connected with Babylon are extended also to "Asia." Both books attribute to Babylon (or Asia) the persecution and murder of God's elect, and both describe Babylon's cataclysmic overthrow and the subsequent mourning of those around her.

The parallels between these documents in this regard are, in fact, so close that dependence of one upon the other, or of both upon a common source, seems almost certain. Of these three options, by far the most historically plausible is that the author of *6 Ezra* knew and used Revelation. Such dependence would suggest that the author of *6 Ezra* was a Christian.

A second factor indicating Christian authorship of *6 Ezra* lies in the book's descriptions of an impending persecution of God's "elect" in 16:68-74. These descriptions are so vivid and concrete that they seem to reflect an actual setting in life in the community of *6 Ezra*. *6 Ezra* was probably written in the second or third centuries C.E., in either Asia Minor or Egypt. A survey of Jewish history in these places during this period reveals little, if any, incidence of violent pagan persecution of Judaism of the type that seems to be envisioned in *6 Ezra*.

An examination of Christian history in the same locales and period, however, reveals numerous situations that are remarkably close to that apparently reflected in *6 Ezra* 16:68-74. These situations arose in the context of Roman persecution of Christianity as an illegal and dangerous cult. Indeed, each aspect of the persecution envisioned in *6 Ezra* 16:68-74—the outbreaks of mob violence against "God's elect," the destruction of their property, their forced eating of sacrificial meat, and the mockery of those who acceded to this demand—is graphically documented in historical accounts of Roman persecution of Christians in the second and third centuries. The striking parallels between documented historical evidence of Christian persecution in the Roman empire and the literary record of *6 Ezra* 16:68-74, in conjunction with the almost total lack of evidence for persecution of Jews in the same period, strongly suggest that *6 Ezra* is a Christian document.

Date of Composition[10]

To start with the broadest possible limits, it is fairly certain that *6 Ezra* was composed between 95 and 313 C.E. The *terminus post quem* is set by the apparent date of the book of Revelation, which *6 Ezra* almost certainly knows (see above). The *terminus ante quem* is suggested by the fact that *6 Ezra* seems to be a Christian work and to reflect a situation in which persecution of Christians is a live issue; such persecution had effectively ceased by

9. For fuller discussion, see Bergren, *Sixth Ezra*, chap. 6; Wolter, *5. Esra-Buch, 6. Esra-Buch*, 835-37.

10. For fuller discussion, see Bergren, *Sixth Ezra*, chap. 7; Wolter, *5. Esra-Buch, 6. Esra-Buch*, 829-33.

the year 313. Also, a *terminus ante quem* in the fourth century is provided by a small vellum Greek fragment of *6 Ezra* 15:57-59 that was found at Oxyrhynchus.

Although these are the closest firm boundaries that can be set, it is possible to narrow the limits somewhat based on other internal indications in the text.

A. von Gutschmid's determination in 1860 that *6 Ezra* was written precisely in the year 263,[11] a theory that in its broad outlines has decisively influenced virtually all subsequent commentary on the book—despite its erudition and the many cogent points that it advances—is overly optimistic, depends on outmoded views regarding the nature and methods of apocalyptic eschatology, and furthermore is based on several faulty historical assumptions. Consequently, it seems advisable to adopt a more flexible position on the book's dating.

One of von Gutschmid's most compelling arguments is that *6 Ezra* 15:28-33 refers historically to conflicts between the Palmyrene ruler Odaenathus, fighting in cooperation with the Romans, and the Persian king Shapur I that took place in 262-267 C.E. on the frontiers between the Roman and Persian empires.[12] If this pericope does in fact refer in principle to concrete events locatable in history, von Gutschmid's identification of it would seem by far the most plausible choice. This would place the composition of *6 Ezra* between ca. 262 and 313. Furthermore, several additional factors suggest a date toward the beginning of this period.

There are, however, various considerations indicating that 15:28-33 may not in fact refer to locatable historical events. First, certain details within the pericope suggest that it possesses a more "mythological" or paradigmatic eschatological than a "historical" frame of reference; and second, the details of the pericope do not fit particularly well with what little is known from independent historical sources about the Persian-Palmyrene wars and their socio-historical context. If, then, 15:28-33 is not intended to refer to the specific historical events of the Persian-Palmyrene wars, then *6 Ezra* could indeed have been written at almost any time between 95 and 313 C.E.

Although it is impossible to resolve this issue with certainty, it seems more likely that 15:28-33 does in fact refer to the Persian-Palmyrene wars, and that *6 Ezra* is therefore to be dated betweem 262 and 313 C.E., probably in the earlier part of this period. Nevertheless, as historians we are well advised to tread a path of methodological caution, and to acknowledge that, in principle, *6 Ezra* could have been written at almost any time during the second or third centuries C.E.

Provenance[13]

There are no direct, certain internal or external indicators as to the provenance of *6 Ezra*. There are, however, several factors both within and outside the text that allow reasonable conjectures as to its place of origin.

The most obvious indicators are (1) the probable original language of the book (Greek) and (2) geographical references within the text. The first factor indicates that *6 Ezra* origi-

11. Alfred von Gutschmid, "Die Apokalypse des Esra und ihre spätern Bearbeitungen," *ZWT* 3 (1860): 1-81.

12. See A. F. J. Klijn, "*6 Ezra* 15,28-33 and the Historical Events in the Middle of the Third Century." In *All Those Nations* (ed. H. L. J. Vanstiphout et al.; Han Drijvers Festschrift; Groningen: STYX Publications, 1999), 95-100.

13. For fuller discussion, see Bergren, *Sixth Ezra*, 18-21; Wolter, *5. Esra-Buch, 6. Esra-Buch*, 833-34.

nated in a Greek-speaking milieu; this, however, could be virtually anywhere in the Mediterranean world.

More useful are the extensive geographical notices within the text of *6 Ezra*. As noted above, the first part of *6 Ezra* (15:5-63) focuses successively on four distinct locales: Egypt (15:10-13); Assyria (15:28-33); Rome (figuratively called "Babylon") (15:43-45); and Asia (15:46-63). *6 Ezra* 16:1, the verse immediately following this section, recapitulates these geographical loci in reverse order: "Woe to you, Babylon and Asia! Woe to you, Egypt and Syria!" These four locales, of course, constitute a ring around the northern and eastern Mediterranean from Italy to Egypt (excluding Greece).

The contents and character of the geographical references in chapter 15 (mostly "threat-" or "woe-discourses") suggest that *6 Ezra* was written in one of the locales mentioned there. Of the four places alluded to, "Asia" seems, on internal grounds, to be the most likely possibility. Not only is the section devoted to Asia in *6 Ezra* the most extensive of the four locales (eighteen verses, as opposed to three to six verses for the other places), but the contents of that section are highly direct, vivid, and personal, in contrast to the more stylized treatments given the other places. This feature is evidenced most strongly in passages like *6 Ezra* 15:46-63. This passage and others like it impart the distinct impression that Asia, and its transgressions, represent immediate and pressing concerns for the author.

Further indication of a provenance in Asia is provided by the compelling and imaginative way in which the language and imagery used in the book of Revelation for "Babylon" are apparently taken over in *6 Ezra* and reapplied to "Asia." Also, the apparent references to persecution of the book's audience (God's "elect") in 16:68-78 accord well with what is known about persecution of Christians in Asia Minor in the second and third centuries C.E.

It is sometimes argued that the early date of the Oxyrhynchus fragment suggests a place of composition in Egypt. However, the internal textual indicators discussed above regarding *6 Ezra*'s provenance seem to me to outweigh the factor of the early date of the Oxyrhynchus fragment.

Literary Context

Texts Influencing 6 Ezra

Sixth Ezra displays numerous parallels to early Jewish and Christian writings, especially those of minatory prophetic and of eschatological nature. The closest similarities are with the prophetic writings of the Hebrew Bible. There are also noteworthy parallels to *4 Ezra*, the *Sibylline Oracles*, and various early Christian writings.

The calamities that are forecast as precursors to the eschaton in 15:5-19 find parallels in *4 Ezra* 5:1-13; 6:17-24; 13:30-31 and in the "synoptic apocalypse" in Mark 13 and parallels. The vision in 15:28-33 is close to *Sib. Or.* 13:147-171. The apparent use of "Babylon" as a symbol for Rome in 15:43–16:1 is paralleled in *4 Ezra* 3:28-36 and Rev 14:8; 17:3-5; and 18:2-3. There are also important thematic parallels between *6 Ezra* 15:43-55 and Rev 14:8; 17:1-6; 17:16–18:10; and 18:23–19:3.

The series of rhetorical questions in 16:3-11 is similar to Amos 3:3-8. The descriptions of desolation in 16:28-32 find parallels in Amos 5:3; Isa 7:23-25 and 17:6; Matt 24:40-41; and *Sib. Or.* 8:223.

The image of child-birth in 16:38-39 is similar to *4 Ezra* 4:40-42 and 1 Thess 5:3. To the exhortations in 16:41-47, compare Deut 28:30-33, 38-42 and 1 Cor 7:29-31. The recital of God's mighty creative acts in 16:55-62 is paralleled in Job 38, Sirach 43, and *Sib. Or.* 8:361-377.

Influence of 6 Ezra on Later Christian Literature[14]

Sixth Ezra leaves only a few traces of literary influence after its composition in the second or third century.

(1) In the mid-sixth century, Gildas, a historian of Britain, in his "De excidio Britanniae" (ca. 540), quotes (in succession) *6 Ezra* 15:21-27 and 16:3-12.

(2) There are also two known Christian liturgical citations of *6 Ezra*. One is a response in the ancient Mozarabic (Hispanic) liturgy that quotes 15:8-9. This response is attested in a tenth-century Visigothic antiphonary from León, Spain. The other is in an antiphon in the Roman liturgy (antiphon no. 3, from the *Ad laudes* in the *In Vigilia nativitatis Domini*; 24 December) that seems to reflect 16:52. Although these liturgical sources cannot be dated precisely, both the Roman and Hispanic types are thought to go back in their earliest forms to at least the fifth to sixth centuries.

Bibliography

Bergren, Theodore A. "Christian Influence on the Transmission History of 4, 5, and 6 Ezra." Pages 102-27 in *The Jewish Apocalyptic Heritage in Early Christianity*. Edited by J. C. VanderKam and W. Adler. CRINT 3.4. Assen: Van Gorcum; Minneapolis, Minn.: Fortress, 1996.

__________. "Prophetic Rhetoric in 6 Ezra." Pages 25-32 in *For a Later Generation: The Transformation of Tradition in Israel, Early Judaism, and Early Christianity* (G. W. E. Nickelsburg Festschrift). Edited by R. A. Argall, B. A. Bow, and R. A. Werline. Harrisburg, Pa.: Trinity, 2000.

__________. *Sixth Ezra: The Text and Origin*. New York: Oxford University, 1998. (Further bibliography may be found here.)

Duensing, Hugo, and Aurelio de Santos Otero. "The Fifth and Sixth Books of Ezra." Vol. 2:641-652 in *The New Testament Apocrypha*. 2 vols. Edited by Edgar Hennecke and Wilhelm Schneemelcher. Louisville: Westminster/John Knox Press, 1992 = "Das fünfte und sechste Buch Esra." Vol. 2:581-590 in *Neutestamentliche Apokryphen*. 2 vols. 5th ed. Edited by Wilhelm Schneemelcher. Tübingen: Mohr Siebeck, 1987-89.

Gutschmid, Alfred von. "Die Apokalypse des Esra und ihre spätern Bearbeitungen." *ZWT* 3 (1860): 1-81.

Hunt, A. S., ed. *The Oxyrhynchus Papyri*. Vol. 7. London: Egyptian Exploration Fund, 1910.

Klijn, A. F. J. "*6 Ezra* 15,28-33 and the Historical Events in the Middle of the Third Century." Pages 95-100 in *All Those Nations* (Han Drijvers Festschrift). Edited by H. L. J. Vanstiphout et al. Groningen: STYX Publications, 1999.

Knibb, Michael A. "The Second Book of Esdras." Pages 76-307 in *The First and Second Books of Esdras*. Edited by R. J. Coggins and Michael A. Knibb. Cambridge Bible Commentary. Cambridge: Cambridge University Press, 1979.

Myers, Jacob M. *1 and 2 Esdras*. AB 42. Garden City, N.Y.: Doubleday, 1974.

Wolter, Michael. *5. Esra-Buch, 6. Esra-Buch*. JSHRZ 3,7. Gütersloh: Gütersloher, 2001. (Further bibliography may be found here.)

---

14. For further details on all of these sources, see Bergren, *Sixth Ezra*, 37-42, 59-61.

Sixth Ezra

Prophetic commission

15 [1]Behold, speak in the ears of my people the words of the prophecy that I will
put into your mouth, says the Lord, [2]and cause them to be written (down) on Jer 1:7-9; 26:2; Hab 2:2
paper, because they are reliable and true. [3]Do not fear the plots against you, and Rev 21:5; 22:6
do not let the unbelief of those spreading rumors disturb you, [4]because every Jer 18:20-23
unbeliever will die in his unbelief.

Initial summary of main themes: prediction of world-wide catastrophes

[5]Behold, says the Lord, I am bringing evils upon the world—the sword, and
famine, and death, and destruction— [6]because iniquity has overwhelmed the
whole earth, and their evil deeds have reached the limit. [7]Therefore, says the
Lord, [8]I will no longer be silent about their impieties which they sacrilegiously
commit, nor will I tolerate the things that they do unjustly. Behold, innocent and
just blood cries out to me, and the souls of the just cry out continuously. [9]Surely I Gen 4:10; Rev 6:9-10
will vindicate them, says the Lord, and I will take back all of the innocent blood
from them to me. Deut 32:43

[10]Behold, my people is led like a flock to the slaughter. I will no longer allow
them to live in the land of Egypt, [11]but I will lead them out with a strong hand
and an upraised arm, and I will strike Egypt with a blow[a] as before, and I will
destroy its whole land. Deut 4:34; 26:8; Ps 44:23 (Evv 44:22); Isa 53:7; Jer 51:40

[12]Let Egypt and its foundations mourn because of the blow[b] of beating and
lashing that the Lord will bring about. [13]Let the farmers who work the earth
mourn, because their seeds will fail and their trees will be destroyed by blight
and hail and by a terrible storm. [14]Woe to the earth and those who live in it, Joel 1:11
[15]because the sword has drawn near, and their destruction, and nation will rise
up against nation in battle, and the sword (will be) in their hands. Mark 13:8

[16]For there will be turmoil among some people; others, growing very strong,
will not respect their king and the chief of their[c] nobles in their power. [17]For
a person will wish to go into a city and will not be able, [18]for because of their 2 Chr 15:5-6
pride, cities will be thrown into confusion, houses will be destroyed, people will
be afraid. [19]A person will not pity his neighbor enough to let their houses alone, Luke 21:26

---

a. The Latin *plaga* can also mean "plague."
b. The Latin *plaga* can also mean "plague."
c. Some manuscripts read "his."

but will pillage their property with a sword because of hunger for bread and
great tribulation.

[20]Behold, says God, I call together all the kings of the earth, to provoke them,
who are from the north and from the south and from the east and from the
Ps 72:11 west, to turn themselves and to return what they have given to them. [21]Just as
they have done until this day to my elect, so I will do, and I will repay into their
Isa 65:6 bosom.[a] Thus says the Lord God. [22]My right hand will not spare the sinners,
nor will the sword desist from those who pour out innocent blood on the earth.
[23]And fire has gone forth from his wrath, and it has devoured the foundations
Jer 4:4 of the earth and the sinners like straw that is burned up. [24]Woe to those who
sin and do not keep my commandments, says the Lord: [25]I will not spare them.

Depart, faithless children; do not defile my holiness. [26]God knows those who
sin against him; therefore he will hand them over to death and slaughter. [27]For
now evils have come over the earth,[b] and you will remain in them. For God will
not deliver you, because you have sinned against him.

Two major visions witnessed by the seer: (1) Clash of the "Arabians" and "Carmonians"

[28]Behold, a terrible vision and its appearance from the east, [29]and the nations of
the Arabian serpents will come out in many chariots, and their hissing is borne
over the earth from the day of (their) march, so that all who hear them will
also be afraid and tremble. [30]The Carmonians, raging in wrath, will go out of
the woods[c] and (they) will arrive in great strength and will stand in battle with
them, and (they) will destroy a portion of the land of the Assyrians with their
teeth.

[31]And after these things the serpent, remembering its origin, will become
still stronger, and if they turn back,[d] agreeing in great strength to pursue them,
[32]those[e] also will be thrown into turmoil and will be silent because of their
strength, and they will turn their feet in flight. [33]And from the territory of the
Assyrians, an ambusher will lie in ambush for them, and will destroy one of
them, and there will be fear and trembling in their army and turmoil in their
Sib. Or. 13:147-171 kingdom.

(2) Vision of storm clouds that destroy "Babylon" (i.e., Rome) and "Asia"

[34]Behold, clouds from the east and from the north across to the south, and their
appearance (is) extremely frightful, full of wrath and tempest. [35]And they will
clash together, one against another, and pour out a huge storm over the earth,
and their storm, and there will be blood from the sword up to the belly of a
Rev 14:20 horse, [36]and the thigh of a human, and the hock of a camel. And there will be
great fear and trembling upon the earth. [37]And those who see that wrath will be
terrified, and trembling will seize them.

---

a. The text of Gildas' first quotation begins here.
b. The text of Gildas' first quotation ends here.
c. MSS SMNE here add "like wild boars."
d. The Latin *converterint se* can also mean "flee."
e. Or "the former."

38And after these things, huge clouds will be set in motion from the south
and north, and another part from the west, 39and winds will swell up from the
east; and they will drive away[a] it[b] and the cloud which it stirred up in wrath;
and the storm that sprang up to cause destruction from the east {and it}[c] will be
driven violently west.[d]

40And great and powerful clouds, full of wrath and storm, will be raised up,
in order to destroy the whole earth and those living in it, and they will pour
out over every high and lofty (place) a terrible storm, 41fire and hail and flying
swords and many waters, so that even all the plains and all the rivers are filled
up with the abundance of those waters. 42And they will destroy cities and walls
and mountains and hills and trees of the forests and grasses of the meadows and
their grain, 43and they will go steadily across to Babylon and will destroy her.
44They will converge on her and surround her, and pour out a storm and every
wrath upon her, and the dust[e] and smoke will rise up to the sky, and everyone
around will mourn her. 45And those who remain behind will serve those who Rev 18:9-10, 15; 19:3
destroyed her.

46And you, Asia, consort in the beauty of Babylon and the glory of her person: 47woe to you, miserable one, because you have made yourself like her. You
have adorned your daughters in fornication in order to please and glory in your
lovers, who have always wanted you to fornicate. 48You have imitated that hateful one in all her deeds and designs. Ezek 16:33; Rev 14:8;
Therefore, says God, 49I will unleash evils upon you—want, poverty, and 17:2-5; 18:3
famine, and the sword, and pestilence—in order to destroy your houses for injury and death. 50And the glory of your strength will be dried up like a flower, Rev 18:7-8
when the heat that has been sent upon you rises up. 51And you will be weakened Rev 17:16
and (made) poor by a blow and beaten from (the) wounds, so that it is impossible for you to receive powerful ones and lovers. Jer 3:1; Rev 18:9-10

52Would I have acted so zealously against you, says the Lord, 53if you had not
killed my elect, always exulting with clapping of hands and talking about their
death when you were drunk? 54Make up the beauty of your face! 55The wages of Rev 17:6; 18:24
a whore (are) in your bosom; therefore, you'll get your recompense!

56Just as you will do to my elect, says the Lord, so God will do to you, and he
will hand you over into evils. 57And your children[f] will perish with hunger, and Rev 19:2
you will fall by the sword, and your cities will be destroyed, and all of you who
are in the plains will fall by the sword, 58and those who are in the mountains and Jer 18:21
highlands will perish with hunger, and eat their own flesh and drink their own

a. Or "lay open; uncover."

b. The antecedent is unclear.

c. These words do not make sense here and may be an error.

d. Or "and a storm for causing destruction from the east will be driven violently north and west."

e. Or "ashes."

f. The text of the Oxyrhynchus Greek fragment begins here.

blood from hunger for bread and thirst for water. [59][a]At first you will come suffering, and again, a second time,[b] you will receive evils.
[60]And in passing they will strike the hateful city and destroy her, some part
Rev 18:21 of your glory and your land, while they are returning from Babylon. [61]You will
be destroyed by them like straw, and they will be fire to you. [62]All of them will
devour you and your cities and your land and mountains, and all of your forests
and fruit-bearing trees they will consume with fire. [63]And they will take your
Rev 18:14 children captive, and despoil your honor, and take away the glory of your face.

Rhetorical evocation of God's power

16 [1]Woe to you, Babylon and Asia! Woe to you, Egypt and Syria! [2]Gird yourselves with sackcloth, wail for your sons,[c] and grieve for them, because your
dismay has drawn near. [3][d]The sword has been sent against you, and who is there
Amos 3:3-8 who can turn it away? [4]Fire has been sent upon you, and who is there who can
put it out? [5]Evils have been sent upon you, and who is there who will repel them?
[6]Will anyone (be able to) repel a hungry lion in the woods, or put out a fire when
the straw has been kindled, [7]or repel an arrow shot by a strong archer?
[8]The Lord God sends evils, and who will repel them? [9]And fire will go forth
Jer 4:4 from his wrath, and who is there who can put it out? [10]He will quake, and who
will not be afraid? He will thunder, and who will not tremble? [11]The Lord threatens, and who is not terrified at his appearance? [12]The earth and its foundations
will quake; the sea is shaken from the depth,[e] and its waves and fish will be
thrown into turmoil at the appearance of the Lord and the glory of his strength.
[13]Because strong in glory (is) the one who stretches the arrow—and its point (is)
sharp—which has been shot by him; it will not fall short, having been shot over
2 Sam 22:8, 15-16// Ps 18:8, 15-16 (Evv 18:7, 14-15); Ps 7:14 (Evv 7:13); Isa 51:15; Sir 16:19 the ends of the earth.
[14]Behold, evils are sent out, and they will not return until they come over the
earth. [15]And fire will be kindled, and it will not be put out until it consumes the
foundations[f] of the earth. [16]Just as an arrow shot by a strong archer does not
Jer 30:23-24 return, so the evils that will be sent out over the earth will not return. [17]Woe to
Deut 32:22; 2 Pet 3:10 me, woe to me! Who will save me in those days?
[18]The beginning of groaning, and much sighing; the beginning of famine,
and many will perish; the beginning of war, and those in power will be afraid;
the beginning of evils, and they will tremble[g] at them. What will they do when
the evils come? [19]Behold, a plague[h] of famine has been sent out, and its affliction
(is) like a scourge, a punishment as discipline. [20]And despite all of these things,

---

a. From this point to 16:31 the text of MS S switches from the "French" to the "Spanish" recension.

b. The text of the Oxyrhynchus Greek fragment ends here.

c. Or "children."

d. The second quotation from Gildas begins here.

e. The second quotation from Gildas ends here.

f. The "French" manuscripts here read "grain" (*frumenta*) for *fundamenta*.

g. The standard Latin text of *6 Ezra* begins 16:19 here. From this point to the end of (English) 16:77, the numeration of the Latin text is one verse higher than that of the standard English text. This translation employs the standard English numbering.

h. The Latin *plaga* can also mean "blow."

they will not turn themselves from their sins, nor despite these plagues[a] are they ever mindful.

Hag 2:17; Rev 9:20-21

Graphic description of the eschatological scenario

[21]Behold, in a short time produce will be cheap on the earth, so that they think that peace is assured for them;[b] then evils will break out over the earth, the sword and famine, [22]and life will be under duress[c] on the earth, and the sword will scatter[d] those who survive the famine. [23]And the dead will be thrown out like dung, and they do not have anyone to comfort them, and the earth will be left deserted, and its cities will be demolished. [24]There will be no farmer left to till the earth or sow it.

Jer 9:22

[25]The trees will bear fruit, and who will gather from them? [26]And the vine will be ready for[e] vintage, and who will bind it? For indeed, places will be completely deserted. [27]For a person will long to see a(nother) person, or even to hear his voice. [28]For ten will be left from a city, and two from a field, who have hidden themselves in the forest and in the clefts of rocks.

Amos 5:3

[29]Just as three or four olives will be left behind in an olive grove, [30]or as in a vineyard which is being harvested, a cluster of grapes (may) even remain behind, exposed by those who carefully search through the harvest, [31]so[f] three or four will be left behind in those days by those who search through their houses with the sword. [32]And the land will be left deserted, and its fields have grown old,[gh] and its roads and all of (its) paths will grow thorn bushes, so that sheep will not wander through it.

Isa 17:6

Isa 7:23-25; *Sib. Or.* 8:223

[33]Young women will mourn because they do not have grooms; women will mourn because they do not have husbands; their daughters will mourn because they do not have a helper. [34]Their grooms will be killed in war, and their husbands will perish with hunger.

Joel 1:8

Instructions to and encouragement of God's "elect"

[35]Indeed, listen to these things, and understand them, servants of the Lord. [36]Behold, the word of the Lord: receive it! Do not disbelieve the things that the Lord says!

[37]Behold, evils draw near, and they are not delayed. [38]Just as a woman pregnant (with) her child in the ninth month, when the hour of her delivery draws near, groans for two or three hours beforehand (with) the pains around her womb,[i] and when the baby comes out of the womb, it will not delay for one moment, [39]so the evils will not delay in coming forth over the earth, and the world will groan, and pains encompass it.

4 Ezra 4:40-42; 1 Thess 5:3

---

a. The Latin *plagas* can also mean "blows."
b. Or "so that they think to themselves that peace is assured."
c. Lit.: "and they are uncertain (about) life."
d. Lit.: "has scattered."
e. Lit.: "will present itself for."
f. At this point the text of MS S rejoins the "French" recension.
g. That is, with non-use.
h. "Spanish" recension: "and its fields will be full of (lit.: in) briars."
i. Lit.: "the pains around her womb groaning for two or three hours beforehand."

[40]Hear the word, my people; prepare yourselves for battle. In the evils, be like strangers on[a] the earth: [41]the one who sells, like one who will flee; and the one who buys, like one who is going to lose; [42]the one who does business, like one who will not make a profit; and the one who builds, like one who is not going to inhabit; [43]the one who sows, like one who is not going to reap; and the one who prunes, like one who is not going to harvest; [44]those who marry, like ones who will not have children, and those who do not marry, like ones bereaved; [45]because those who labor, labor in vain.

[46]For strangers will gather their fruits and seize their property and destroy (their) houses and take their children captive, because they beget their children in captivity and famine. [47]And those who do business, do business to be plundered.[b]

Lev 26:16; Deut 28:33

Deut 28:30-33, 38-42; 1 Cor 7:29-31

Polemic against sin and sinners

For as long as they adorn their cities and houses and possessions and their own persons, [48]so much more will I strive zealously against them, because of (their) sins, says the Lord. [49]Just as a whore strives very zealously against a dignified and good woman, [50]so righteousness will strive zealously against iniquity, when she adorns herself, and accuses her to her face, when the one comes who will defend the one seeking out every sin on the earth.

[51]Therefore, do not imitate her or her actions! [52]Because behold, a little while longer and iniquity will be taken away from the earth, and righteousness will rule over us. [53] Let the sinner not say that he has not sinned, because coals of fire will burn on the head of the one who says, "I have not sinned before God and his glory."

Prov 25:22

[54]Behold, the Lord knows all the actions of a person, and their designs and their intention and their hearts. [55]He (is the one) who said, "Let there be earth," and it appeared; "Let there be sky," and it appeared. [56]And by his word the stars were set up, and he knows the number of the stars.

Ps 33:15; Sir 15:18-19; 39:19

Gen 1:6, 9

Job 38; Ps 147:4; Sir. 43; *Sib. Or.* 8:361-377

[57]He (is the one) who searches out the abyss and their storehouses, who has measured the sea and its capacity, [58]who has enclosed the sea in the middle of the waters and suspended the earth over the water by his word, [59]who stretched out the sky like a vault and established it over the waters, [60]who put springs of water in the desert and, on the tops of the mountains, lakes, to send forth streams from the height so that the earth might drink; [61]who formed a human being, and put a heart in the middle of (his) body, and sent to him spirit and life and understanding [62]and the breath of almighty God, who made all things and searches out hidden things in hidden places. Surely [63]he knows your intention and the things that you think in your hearts!

Isa 40:22; 44:24; Ps 104:2; 136:6; Prov 8:29

Ps 107:35; Isa 41:18

Job 32:8; 33:4; Rev 2:23

Woe to sinners and those who wish to hide their sins! [64]Because the Lord has surely examined all of their deeds, and he will show up all of you. [65]And you will be confounded when your sins come out in front of people, and it will be (your) iniquities that will stand as (your) accusers in that day! [66]What will you do, or how will you hide your sins before the Lord and his glory? [67]Behold, God

a. Lit.: "of."

b. Lit.: "in plunder."

is the judge! Fear him, and give up your sins and forget your iniquities, ever to
do them again, and God will deliver you and free (you) from every tribulation.

Prediction of persecution and final exhortation of God's elect

68 For behold, the burning (wrath) of a great crowd will be kindled over you,
and they will seize certain of you, and will feed (them) what was killed for idols. Exod 34:15; Acts 15:20, 29; 1 Cor 8:1-13; 10:14-22; Rev 2:14, 20; 4 Macc 5:2
69 And those who consent to them will be held by them in derision and disgrace
and will be trampled under foot.

70 For there will be in (various) places[a] and in neighboring cities a great[b] in-
surrection against those who fear the Lord. 71 For people pressed by their own
evils will be like madmen, sparing no one, in order to pillage and destroy those
who still fear the Lord. 72 For they will destroy and pillage their property, and
will drive them out of their house(s). 73 Then the proving of my elect will become
manifest, like gold that is proven by fire. Zech 13:9; 1 Pet 1:7

74 Listen, my elect, says the Lord. Behold, (the) days of tribulation are here,
and I will deliver you from them. 75 Do not be afraid or hesitate, because God is Dan 12:1
your leader. 76 And the one who keeps my commandments and rules, says the
Lord God: do not let your sins weigh you down or your iniquities mount up.

77 Woe to those who are choked by their sins and covered over by their iniquities, as a field is choked by the forest and its path covered over by thorn bushes,
so that no one (can) traverse it; 78[c] and it is shut off and relegated to a devouring Prov 5:22; Mk 4:7, 18-19 par.
by[d] fire. 2 Sam 23:6-7; Heb 6:8

---

a. Or "in Lociis/Locii/Lociae."

b. Or "many an."

c. At this point the standard Latin numeration of the text rejoins the standard English numbering.

d. Lit.: "of."

The Latin Vision of Ezra
A new translation and introduction

by Richard Bauckham

The *Latin Vision of Ezra*[1] is one of a number of Ezra pseudepigrapha that stem from the influence of *4 Ezra*. Previous English translations and introductions[2] were written before the existence of a much longer form of the text became generally known. This longer recension requires a fresh evaluation of the work, which is offered here along with the first English translation of the whole text.

Contents

The work can be divided into three parts. In the first part (vv. 1-59f) Ezra, whom this work considers a prophet (cf. vv. 88, 92, 117), is conducted by angels on a tour of hell (Tartarus) and paradise. Descending ever deeper into the underworld he sees a series of thirteen different punishments being inflicted on various categories of the wicked after death. He also sees four ordeals, through which both the righteous and the wicked dead pass, the former without harm, the latter with suffering (vv. 3-11, 23-33, 36a-36e, 58). In most cases, Ezra's response to seeing the punishments is to pray to God to have mercy on the sinners. Before completing his tour of the punishments, Ezra is shown the abode of the righteous in paradise, which is much more briefly described (v. 59-59e).

In the second part of the work (vv. 60-92) Ezra is taken up to the seventh heaven, where he pleads the cause of sinners, not only asking God to spare them the punishments of hell, but also arguing with God about whether the damnation of sinners is in accordance with the divine righteousness and mercy. Finally, Ezra offers his own life in exchange for the world, and in response God grants the wicked in hell a weekly period of respite from punishment for two nights and one day (v. 90). Within this debate with God there is also a passage in which God predicts the coming of the day of judgment, in which the heavens and the earth will perish (vv. 69-70), and also gives a prophecy of the career, appearance and fate of Antichrist (vv. 71-79).

The third part of the work (vv. 93-116) narrates the death of Ezra. When the Lord sends Michael to fetch Ezra's soul, Ezra refuses to surrender it. Each part of the body through which the soul might be extracted Ezra claims is inappropriate because of the special way it has been related to God. When Michael fails to recover Ezra's soul, the Lord himself descends to earth to fetch it. Already Ezra has secured God's promise of blessing for everyone who buys or copies his book (vv. 95-96); now he secures blessing for those who

1. For the titles in the MSS, see the first note to the translation below.

2. Notably Mueller and Robbins, "Vision of Ezra"; Shutt, "The Vision of Esdras." Nuvolone, "Vision d'Esdras," provides a French translation that is the first translation of MS B into any modern language.

preserve it and use it to commemorate his death (v. 108). Finally he dies. The conclusion (v. 117) promises salvation to all who celebrate Ezra's memory on his feast day.

Manuscripts

The *Latin Vision of Ezra* is extant in nine manuscripts, whose text can be classified in four recensions:[3]

long: MS B: Vatican, Barberinus lat. 2318, f. 106ʳ-110ʳ, end of fifteenth cent.
intermediate: MS L: Linz, Bibliothek des Priesterseminars, A I/6, f. 14ʳ-17ᵛ, tenth-eleventh cent.
short: 6 MSS:
H: Heiligenkreuz, Stiftsbibliothek, 11, f. 272ᵛ-273ʳ, twelfth cent.;
K: Klosterneuberg, Stiftsbibliothek, 714, f. 139ᵛ-141ᵛ, twelfth cent.;
Lf: Lilienfeld, Stiftsbibliothek, 145, f. 70ʳ-70ᵛ, thirteenth cent.;
M: Melk, Stiftsbibliothek, 310.F.8, f. 208ᵛ-209ᵛ, thirteenth cent.;
Z: Lilienfeld, Stiftsbibliothek, 134, f. 109ʳ-110ʳ, thirteenth cent.;
Augsburg, Stadtbibliothek, Ms. 4° Cod. 3, f. 26ʳ-28ᵛ, fifteenth cent.
very short: MS V: Vatican, lat. 3838, fol. 59ʳ-61ʳ, twelfth cent.

Although the presence of a copy of the *Latin Vision of Ezra* in MS Barberinus lat. 2318 (MS B) was indicated in a catalogue of MSS in the Vatican library published in 1910,[4] scholars working on the *Latin Vision of Ezra* were unaware of this copy—and therefore of the long recension—until an edition was published by Bogaert in 1984.[5] Previously scholars had been divided between the view that the shortest recension (MS V) was the most original, while the longer recensions (MSS H and L) incorporated later interpolations,[6] and the view that the longer recensions (MSS H and L) were closest to the original form of the text, which had been abbreviated in the shortest recension (MS V).[7] But the discovery of the long recension in MS B puts this question in quite a new light. Only the first half of this text (vv. 1-65) corresponds to the content of the other recensions, and here it has parallels to the material that is found in MSS L and H but not in MS V[8] and to most of the material found in MS L but not in MSS H or V.[9] But the second half of the text in MS B (vv. 67-117) is entirely additional, corresponding to nothing in the other recensions.

Despite the fact that MS B is the latest manuscript, there are good reasons for thinking

3. This classification of manuscripts into four recensions is made by Nuvolone, "Vision d'Esdras," 601. I have retained the sigla given to eight of the mss by Wahl, *Apocalypsis Esdrae*, and "Vier neue Textezeugen." The Augsburg MS, listed by Nuvolone, was not known to Wahl, and is not given a siglum of its own by Nuvolone. For one or two references to manuscripts now lost, see Denis, *Introduction*, 867.

4. Albert Poncelet, *Catalogus Codicum Hagiographicum Latinorum Bibliothecae Vaticanae* (Subsidia Hagiographica 11; Brussels: Bollandists, 1910), 477: "Legenda B. Exdrae propheta." For descriptions of the MS, see Bogaert, "Une version longue"; Nuvolone, "Valeur ajoutée," 182-83.

5. Bogaert, "Une version longue."

6. So Mueller and Robbins, "Vision of Ezra." Shutt, "The Vision of Esdras," also chose to translate MS V, noting the additional material in L and H in footnotes, but did not present an argument for the greater originality of V.

7. So Wahl, "Vier neue Textzeugen."

8. B has vv. 36a-36e, 57a-57b, 59a-59e, all missing in V.

9. B has the longer text of vv. 3, 34, 36a, 56, 59b, 59d, 60, agreeing with L against H and V. On the other hand B lacks material in vv. 45, 59e, that L has but H and V do not.

that it best preserves the content of the original work, and that the other recensions represent progressive abbreviations of the text. Of crucial importance is the relationship with the *Greek Apocalypse of Ezra*. Scholars have long recognized that there is a close relationship between this work and the *Latin Vision of Ezra*. The major parallels are as follows:

Vis. Ezra	*Gk. Apoc. Ezra*
11	5:6
19-20	4:22
29	4:14
34	4:21
37-39	4:9-12
53a-54	5:2-3
57b	5:25
62	1:22
65-66	1:13-14
67	2:8
70	4:40-41
75-76	4:28-31
81	2:3
89	2:10
89	1:11
93-107	6:3-17
108-109	7:8-13
110	7:1-3
115	6:17
116	7:14

The table shows that the parallels are spread throughout the *Latin Vision of Ezra*, and that many of them are in the section extant only in MS B (vv. 67-117). The parallel passages occur in a quite different order in the two works. In the *Latin Vision* they belong to a coherent narrative sequence, but in the *Greek Apocalypse* they are scattered through a much more disjointed and episodic text. It looks as though the *Greek Apocalypse* has borrowed the parallel material from a work very much like the *Latin Vision* in its long recension (MS B).

An especially revealing phenomenon is the variation between first-person and third-person narration in the various texts. In MS B, following the initial reference to Ezra in the third person, the whole of the text from v. 1 to v. 64 is narrated by Ezra in the first person. Following a section (vv. 65-69) that in the extant text lacks any indications of first- or third-person narration, the rest of the work (vv. 70-117) refers throughout to Ezra in the third person. The *Greek Apocalypse of Ezra* frequently moves back and forth between first- and third-person narration, but it is very striking that in almost every case where material is parallel to the *Latin Vision* it agrees with the latter in this matter of first- or third-person narration. (The only exception is 6:3, but the text moves immediately into the third person, corresponding with the *Latin Vision*, in the following verse.) This confirms the view that the order of material in the *Latin Vision* is the original sequence, and shows that the use of first- and third-person narration in MS B was the same in the version of the work that was used by the author of the *Greek Apocalypse*.

In the other recensions of the *Latin Vision* the text does not extend beyond the point at which MS B switches from first- to third-person narration. MS L uses mostly the first person, but switches inconsistently[10] into the third person from time to time (vv. 8a, 11, 15, 30, 36, 38-39, 41, 65). The other recensions use the third person throughout. The use of the third person in all these recensions seems to be a secondary development.

It is curious that the long recension (MS B) switches from first- to third-person narration just where the other recensions end. It might be suggested that the change of person in the long recension results from the combination of two sources, and that the other recensions are based on the first of these two sources alone. Such a hypothesis would have to suppose that the two sources were already combined in a Greek text, since the *Greek Apocalypse of Ezra* reflects the whole of the content of MS B, and therefore that MS L is based on the first of the two sources in Greek, independently of the long Latin recension. But this is not plausible because there is far too much close verbal agreement between MS B and MS L for them to represent independent Latin translations of a common Greek original. It must be that the long Latin text of MS B was deliberately cut by a scribe to the short form found in the other recensions.

The transition from first- to third-person narration in MS B corresponds roughly to a transition from vision, in the first part of the work, to dialogue, in the second. Making Ezra himself narrate what he saw in hell and paradise adds vividness and authenticity to the account, but in the second half of the work, where Ezra does not see but only speaks, that function would be less appropriate. Moreover, a transition from first- to third-person narration was required at some point in this long recension, because otherwise Ezra would have to narrate his own death.

It is not, in fact, difficult to see why a scribe/editor should have wished to abbreviate the work, omitting its second half and reducing it to Ezra's vision of hell and paradise.[11] This was the material that was of most interest to medieval readers, as can be seen in the fact that the medieval Latin redactions of the *Apocalypse of Paul* similarly reduce it to the account of hell and paradise or even to the account of hell alone. Moreover, Ezra's unwillingness to die and refusal to surrender his soul could well have been thought unedifying.

While MS B has preserved the full scope of the work, its readings are not necessarily always to be preferred to variants in the other manuscripts, though frequently they are. The manuscripts of the short and very short recensions, as well as tending to abbreviate the text, also show a tendency to improve it (e.g., by changing the first person to the third, or by substituting the classical Latin *viri* for the medieval Latin *barones* in v. 19) and to omit obscure material (e.g., v. 23). They often omit numbers, perhaps because these are often uncertain through careless transmission. By comparison with MS B, the other recensions (including L) have a tendency to add explicitly Christian details (see vv. 10, 26, 36, 36d, 45-46, 64). The variations of vocabulary between the manuscripts, where the sense is scarcely different, are probably not to be explained as variant translations of a common Greek original, as Mueller argued,[12] but as due to attempts by scribes to improve the Latin text.

The translation provided below is of MS B, corrected by reference to the other manu-

10. It is not the case, as Bogaert, "Une version longue," 55, supposes, that L *consistently* uses the third person to introduce dialogue (*Esdras dixit*).

11. Cf. Nuvolone, "Apocalypse d'Esdras," 105-106.

12. Mueller and Robbins, "Vision of Ezra," 582-83.

scripts only when it is very clearly corrupt. All major variants that make a difference to the translation are noted in the footnotes.

Genre and Structure

The *Latin Vision of Ezra* is an apocalypse, a genre with a long history, used by Jewish and Christian authors from the second century B.C.E. until at least the late middle ages. Typically, an apocalypse is pseudepigraphal, attributed to a prominent character in the Old or New Testament (though there are a few exceptions, such as the *Apocalypse of John* in the NT, which was written by the author in his own name). This pseudonymous seer is given revelations of heavenly secrets that are otherwise inaccessible, often, but not always, eschatological in nature. The revealer is a heavenly being, such as an angel, and often serves as a guide who interprets what the seer sees in visions. The work takes the form of a narrative account of the seer's visionary experience, written either in the first person (as though by the seer) or in the third person (about the seer). Revelation may be given in visions of the other world or in symbolic visions or in discourse by God or the revealer figure.

The *Latin Vision of Ezra* clearly falls within this generic tradition, but it also belongs to a more specific category of apocalypse. This kind of apocalypse is a revelation of the fate of the dead in hell and paradise.[13] The visionary (often in an out-of-the-body experience) is taken on a tour of the places of the dead by the heavenly guide. In some cases the seer sees the places which the wicked and the righteous will inhabit after the last judgment (e.g., *2 Enoch*), but in most cases, including the *Latin Vision of Ezra,* the seer sees the wicked already suffering punishment in hell and the righteous already enjoying the rewards of paradise. This kind of tour of hell and paradise is only possible when the intermediate state is envisaged, not merely as a state of waiting for the judgment, but as a present experience of punishment in hell or joy in paradise, already, before the last judgment. In the Jewish tradition this view of the intermediate state seems to have been emerging, alongside the older view, during the first century C.E. The oldest of such tour apocalypses that we know about may have been the Greek *Apocalypse of Elijah,* of which only fragments have survived.[14] Others include the *Apocalypse of Zephaniah*, the *Apocalypse of Paul*, the *Greek Apocalypse of the Virgin Mary*, and the *Gedulat Moshe*.[15] One feature of such apocalypses is that the seer sees a whole series of different types of sinners suffering a variety of punishments in hell, each appropriate to a specific sin. Another common feature is that the sight of sinners suffering in hell moves the seer to pray God to have mercy on them. Both features are found in the *Latin Vision of Ezra*. It also resembles other examples of the genre in that the account of hell is much longer and more detailed than the account of paradise. (In some of the later Latin redactions of the *Apocalypse of Paul* and in the *Greek Apocalypse of the Virgin Mary*, paradise is omitted altogether and only the punishments in hell are described.)

In the medieval West, the *Apocalypse of Paul* was extremely popular in a series of Latin redactions and in many vernacular versions. It was valued, no doubt, for its detailed accounts of the fate of the dead in the other world, which Scripture did not provide. But the medieval West also produced its own works of this type, probably inspired especially by

---

13. See Bauckham, *The Fate*, especially chapters 2-3; Himmelfarb, *Tours*.

14. See Richard Bauckham, "The Greek Apocalypse of Elijah," in the second volume of this collection.

15. The *Gedulat Moshe* ("The Greatness of Moses") is translated by Helen Spurling in "Hebrew Visions of Hell and Paradise" in this volume.

the *Apocalypse of Paul*. These works, generally known as "visions" (*visiones*), were written over a period of more than eight centuries, from the end of the sixth century to the fifteenth century.[16] One difference from the apocalypses is that these visions are not attributed to biblical characters, but to contemporaries or people of the recent past, mostly otherwise unknown persons. In some cases the visionary himself or herself narrates their own vision; others are third-person narratives. Quite frequently it is during an experience of temporary death that the visionary sees the other world, a feature found among the apocalypses only in the *Apocalypse of Zephaniah*.

In many cases the accounts of hell and paradise are broadly similar to those in the apocalypses, and there are also many resemblances in detail, but another respect in which the medieval visions differ is that the development of ideas of purgatory can be traced in them.[17] Some form of purgatorial punishment is described in most of them. Another thematic difference is that the motif of the seer's pleas to God for mercy for those who suffer the pains of hell, which is found in most of the tour apocalypses, does not occur in the medieval visions.

A particular generic feature which is characteristic of the apocalypses, but is absent from the medieval visions, is the "demonstrative explanations."[18] During his tour of hell, the seer asks his angelic guide who each category of sinner is, using the form, "Who are these...?", and the guide explains, "These are the ones who...." In the medieval visions, although the visionaries do sometimes ask their guide (an angel or a saint) questions and the guide frequently explains to the visionary what he or she is seeing, the demonstrative explanation in the form found in all the apocalypses seems to occur hardly at all.[19] In the tour of hell in the *Latin Vision of Ezra*, however, there are sixteen demonstrative explanations.

In all these respects in which the medieval visions differ from the apocalyptic tours of hell and paradise the *Latin Vision of Ezra* resembles the apocalypses rather than the medieval visions. It is not surprising that the scribes gave the work the Latin title *Visio Esdrae* or *Visio Beati Esdrae*, just as they gave the name *Visio Sancti Pauli* to the *Apocalypse of Paul*. The two terms *visio* and *revelatio* (the Latin translation of *apokalypsis*) were used

16. English translations of many of them appear in Eileen Gardiner, *Visions of Heaven and Hell before Dante* (New York: Italica, 1989), which also provides a list of other visions not included in the volume. For an even fuller survey of the various texts, see Alison Morgan, *Dante and the Medieval Other World* (Cambridge Studies in Medieval Literature 8; Cambridge: Cambridge University Press, 1990), 211-33. See also Claude Carozzi, *Le Voyage de l'Âme dans l'Au-delà d'après la Littérature Latine (Ve-XIIIe siècle)* (Collection de l'École Française de Rome 189; Rome: École Française de Rome, 1994); Carol Zaleski, *Otherworld Journeys: Accounts of Near-Death Experience in Medieval and Modern Times* (Oxford: Oxford University Press, 1987); Howard Rollin Patch, *The Other World according to Descriptions in Medieval Literature* (Cambridge, Mass.: Harvard University Press, 1950); Jean-Michel Picard and Yolande de Pontfarcy, *The Vision of Tnugdal* (Dublin: Four Courts, 1989).

17. See Jacques Le Goff, *The Birth of Purgatory* (trans. Arthur Goldhammer; London: Scolar, 1984); Morgan, *Dante*, chapter 5; Carozzi, *Le Voyage*, 249-79.

18. See especially Himmelfarb, *Tours*, chapter 2. The form appears in all the apocalyptic tours of hell studied by Himmelfarb except the *Gedulat Moshe*.

19. To my knowledge, the closest parallel is in the *Vision of Tnugdal (Tundale)* 3, where Tnugdal asks the angel, "I beg you please to tell me what sort of evil those souls ever did to have been judged worthy of such torments?", and the angel replies: "These are the homicides, parricides and fratricides" (Picard and de Pontfarcy, *The Vision*, 117; see also 119). But I have not searched all the medieval visions for this form.

synonymously, probably because of the occurrence of both terms in the Vulgate version of 2 Corinthians 12:1.[20]

It is primarily the first half of the *Latin Vision of Ezra* (vv. 1-59f) that aligns it generically with the apocalypses that feature a visionary's tour of hell and paradise. Prominent among the contents of the second half of the work (vv. 60-116) is the following series of events: Ezra, brought into God's presence, prays for mercy for the damned; he enlists the inhabitants of the heavens in this prayer; he supports his prayer by debating the justice of hell with God; and God grants the damned a respite from their suffering. This material, including the debate, finds parallels, among the tour apocalypses, in the *Apocalypse of Paul*, the *Greek Apocalypse of the Virgin Mary*, and to some extent the *Apocalypse of Peter*, as well as in the *Questions of Ezra* and the two apocalypses that are closely related to the *Latin Vision of Ezra*: the *Greek Apocalypse of Ezra* and the *Apocalypse of Sedrach*. This last work has no tour of hell or paradise, but features the same kind of debate with God about the justice of hell. The motif of the seer's debate with God, as well as some of the arguments used, has entered this tradition of apocalyptic works from *4 Ezra*, a very different kind of apocalypse, in which Ezra prays for God's mercy for sinners and debates with God the justice of his judgment of sinners, but in which Ezra's prayers are refused and he is finally reconciled to God's purposes. Again this theme of debate with God connects the *Latin Vision of Ezra* with various apocalypses, but is not found in the medieval visions.

The passage of eschatological prophecy (vv. 69-78), a revelation of events of the last days given by God to Ezra, is, of course, quite appropriate to the genre of apocalypse, but the last section of the work (vv. 93-116) is unusual among apocalypses, which do not usually end by narrating the death of the seer. (The *Greek Apocalypse of Ezra* and the *Apocalypse of Sedrach* end with accounts of Ezra's death related to that in the *Latin Vision of Ezra*.) However, *4 Ezra* seems to have ended with the reference to Ezra's assumption to heaven (which in *4 Ezra* is the substitute for death in his case, as in Enoch's) that is found in all the versions except the Latin (*4 Ezra* 14:50),[21] while the main narrative of *2 Enoch* ends with an account of Enoch's assumption (vv. 67-68). A narrative of the seer's death is therefore an unusual, but coherent and appropriate way to end an apocalypse.

The structure of the *Latin Vision of Ezra* is relatively clear. Ezra's tour of the punishments in hell (vv. 1-58) is followed by the visit to paradise (vv. 59a-59e), but it is odd that after seeing paradise he continues the tour of hell in order to see just one more punishment (v. 59f). (The omission of v. 59f by all MSS except B is therefore easily understandable, but is secondary.) Ezra then ascends through the heavens to the seventh where he stands in the presence of God. His plea for mercy for sinners and his debate with God (vv. 61-68, 80-92) seem awkwardly interrupted by the prophecy of the last judgment and Antichrist

20. See Carozzi, *Le Voyage*, 105, 144-45; Peter Dinzelbacher, *Vision und Visionliteratur im Mittelalter* (Monographien zur Geschichte des Mittelalter 23; Stuttgart: Hiersemann, 1981), 45-50.

21. The account of Ezra's death found in the *Latin Vision of Ezra*, the *Greek Apocalypse of Ezra*, and the *Apocalypse of Sedrach* of course contradicts the tradition of his assumption to heaven without dying that is found in *4 Ezra*. Since all three works are indebted to *4 Ezra*, the original author of the Greek *Vorlage* of the *Latin Vision of Ezra*, who adapted an account of the death of Moses by telling the same story about Ezra, must have been aware of this difference and probably wished to restrict assumption to its two biblical instances (Enoch and Elijah). Such an objection to the idea of Ezra's assumption may partly account for the omission of 14:49-50 in the Latin version of *4 Ezra*, though this also serves to facilitate the addition of chapters 15 and 16 (*6 Ezra*).

(vv. 69-79), though this is loosely connected to the reference to the last judgment in v. 68. The final section concerns his death.

Date and Provenance

Our earliest direct evidence of the existence of the *Latin Vision of Ezra* is MS L, which was written in the tenth or eleventh century. But, as we have seen, this is an abbreviated version of the text, and the text of the long recension, though now extant only in the fifteenth-century MS B, must have existed before MS L.

The relationship with the *Greek Apocalypse of Ezra* is crucial for establishing the original language and date of the *Latin Vision of Ezra*. That there is a literary relationship is clear. Some scholars have postulated a common Greek source, which may also have been a source for the *Apocalypse of Sedrach*[22] and explain the latter's parallels to the *Greek Apocalypse of Ezra*. However, now that we know the long recension of the *Latin Vision of Ezra* in MS B, it seems very probable that the common source was simply the Greek *Vorlage* of the latter. As we have seen, the many parallels between the *Latin Vision of Ezra* and the *Greek Apocalypse of Ezra* occur in a quite different order in the two works, but the former has a largely coherent narrative sequence that is likely to be original. This is confirmed by the distribution of first- and third-person narration in the two works. Flavio Nuvolone has proposed that the *Greek Apocalypse of Ezra* is "an exercise of sacred rhetoric," composed by an editor who wished to produce a new work out of dismembered elements of older works (the Greek *Vorlage* of the *Latin Vision of Ezra* being his principal, but not his only source).[23]

Certainly, the Latin text of MS B has suffered, like the other recensions, from both careless transmission and deliberate redaction. In detailed studies of several of the parallel passages, Nuvolone has shown both that the Latin text is often more original than the Greek, and that there are also passages where the text of the *Greek Apocalypse of Ezra* can be used to restore a more original form of the Latin (or perhaps only of its Greek *Vorlage*).[24] He has also argued that *Greek Apocalypse of Ezra* 1:1-5 is an introduction to the original Greek work that has been omitted in our texts of the *Latin Vision*.[25] There might be other material within the *Greek Apocalypse of Ezra* that derives from the same original work but has been omitted from the text in the tradition that produced the Latin text we have in MS B. Probably we have no way of identifying such material. But it does seem very probable that this text has preserved to a very large extent the content of the Greek work that was also used by the author of the *Greek Apocalypse of Ezra*. (Quite how the *Apocalypse of Sedrach* is related to these works is difficult to tell, but is unimportant for our present concerns.[26])

Although both the *Latin Vision of Ezra* (76) and the *Greek Apocalypse of Ezra* (4:29-

22. E.g. Himmelfarb, *Tours*, 167; Stone, "An Introduction," 309.

23. Nuvolone, "Apocalypse d'Esdras," 89; idem, "Valeur ajoutée," 183-84.

24. Nuvolone, "Apocalypse d'Esdras"; idem, "Valeur ajoutée."

25. Nuvolone, "L'initiation prophétique."

26. Almost all parallels between the *Latin Vision of Ezra* and the *Apocalypse of Sedrach* are also parallels between the latter and the *Greek Apocalypse of Ezra*, and can be explained as due to dependence by the *Apocalypse of Sedrach* on the *Greek Apocalypse of Ezra*. But there is one agreement between the *Latin Vision of Ezra* and the *Apocalypse of Sedrach* independently of the *Greek Apocalypse of Ezra*. In the *Latin Vision of Ezra* both Michael and the Lord say to Ezra, "Give (me) your soul" (vv. 94, 97, 107), while in *Apoc. Sedr.* 9:5, Christ says to Ezra, "Give me your most desired soul." These words are not used in the *Greek Apocalypse of Ezra* (cf. 6:3, 17), but they are such natural words in the context that the agreement can be regarded as

33) have descriptions of Antichrist, the descriptions have very little in common.[27] The description in the *Greek Apocalypse of Ezra*, however, corresponds almost verbatim to the description of Antichrist in chapter 7 of the *Apocryphal Apocalypse of John*[28] (called the *Second Apocalypse of John* by John Court in his edition and translation).[29] Nuvolone argues that the *Greek Apocalypse* has borrowed the description from the *Apocryphal Apocalypse of John*,[30] which Alice Whealey has proposed was written between 720 and 843 C.E.[31] This would mean that the *Greek Apocalypse of Ezra* would date from the second half of the ninth century at the earliest. But it is also possible that the dependence is the other way around.[32] Thus the *Greek Apocalypse of Ezra* does not help very much in establishing a *terminus ad quem* for the Greek original of the *Latin Vision*.

Comparison with other apocalypses that contain tours of heaven and hell may provide more help. We have already observed that, in terms of its literary genre, it is with these apocalypses, rather than with the visions of heaven and hell that were composed in the medieval West, that the *Latin Vision of Ezra* belongs. Of these apocalypses much the most popular and influential in Christian contexts was the *Apocalypse of Paul*, which was composed in Greek around 400 C.E.,[33] but translated not only into Latin, but also into Armenian, Coptic, Slavonic, and Syriac. In its various Latin forms it was hugely influential in the medieval West. In the Greek East it fell out of favour only because its function of providing information about the afterlife was taken over by the *Greek Apocalypse of the Virgin Mary*, which was itself dependent on the *Apocalypse of Paul*. It is significant that neither the *Latin Vision of Ezra* nor the *Greek Apocalypse of Ezra* seems to be dependent on the *Apocalypse of Paul*. There are general resemblances that show that they all belong to the same literary tradition of tours of hell, but nothing sufficiently close to require a direct literary relationship. In view of the great popularity of *Apocalypse of Paul*, this suggests that the Greek *Vorlage* of the *Latin Vision of Ezra* was written before the *Apocalypse of Paul*. This is close to Martha Himmelfarb's judgment that both the *Greek Apocalypse of*

---

coincidental. In that case the *Apocalypse of Sedrach* could be dependent on the *Greek Apocalypse of Ezra*, without access to the Greek *Vorlage* of the *Latin Vision*.

27. On descriptions of Antichrist, see Jean-Marc Rosenstiehl, "Le Portrait de l'Antichrist," in Marc Philonenko, Jean-Claude Picard, Jean-Marc Rosenstiehl, and Francis Schmidt, *Pseudépigraphes de l'Ancient Testament et Manuscrits de la Mer Morte* (*Cahiers de la Revue d'Histoire et de Philosophie Religieuses* 41; Paris: Presses Universitaires de France, 1967), 45-60. Rosenstiehl was not aware of MS B of the *Latin Vision of Ezra* and therefore did not include its portrait of Antichrist in his analysis. But it is notable that it shares very few features with the portraits he assembles.

28. See the table in Nuvolone, "Apocalypse d'Esdras," 91. Some words appear to have been lost from the text of the *Greek Apocalypse of Ezra* in this verse, but otherwise the correspondence is very close.

29. John Court, *The Book of Revelation and the Johannine Apocalyptic Tradition* (JSNTSup 190; Sheffield: Sheffield Academic Press, 2000), chapter 3.

30. Nuvolone, "Apocalypse d'Esdras," 90-93.

31. Alice Whealey, "The Apocryphal Apocalypse of John: A Byzantine Apocalypse from the Early Islamic Period," *JTS* 53 (2002): 533-40. She argues against Court's dating of the work to the late fourth century.

32. Nuvolone's argument from the alternation of first-person and third-person narration in *Gk. Apoc. Ezra* 4:25-29 is not convincing. Comparison of the forms of the prophet's question about Antichrist that precedes the description in the three texts (*Vis. Ezra* 75; *Gk. Apoc. Ezra* 4:28; *Apocr. Apoc. Jn.* 6) suggests that the relationship is best explained by the order: *Apocryphal Apocalypse of John* depends on *Greek Apocalypse of Ezra* which depends on the Greek *Vorlage* of the *Latin Vision of Ezra*. The relationship between these forms of the question makes the hypothesis of a common source behind the *Greek Apocalypse of Ezra* and the *Apocryphal Apocalypse of John* (Stone, "An Introduction," 308) less plausible.

33. For the date see Pierluigi Piovanelli, "Les origines de l'*Apocalypse de Paul* reconsiderée," *Apocrypha* 4 (1993): 25-64.

Ezra and the *Latin Vision of Ezra* "derive from a Christian tour of hell written relatively early in the development of the genre, before the dominance of the Apocalypse of Paul had been established."[34] She thought that a few elements of the tour in the *Latin Vision of Ezra* that are not found in the *Greek Apocalypse of Ezra* derive from the *Apocalypse of Paul* or, more specifically, from the sixth of its medieval Latin redactions.[35] It is certainly possible that the Latin transmission of the *Latin Vision of Ezra* was influenced by redactions of the *Apocalypse of Paul*, but it is, of course, possible that Redaction VI of the *Apocalypse of Paul* was influenced by the *Latin Vision of Ezra*. In any case, the resemblances are too general and slight to require a close relationship.

All the tours of hell specify many different sins for which sinners suffer punishment. We can compare the sins that feature in the *Latin Vision of Ezra* with those in the three major Christian tours of hell: the *Apocalypse of Peter* (early second century C.E.), the *Apocalypse of Paul* (c. 400 C.E.), and the *Greek Apocalypse of the Virgin Mary* (later than 400 C.E.). Allowing some flexibility in the precise definition of the sin, there are seven categories of sin common to the Latin *Vision of Ezra* and the *Apocalypse of Peter*, six common to the *Latin Vision of Ezra* and the *Apocalypse of Paul*, three common to the *Latin Vision of Ezra* and the *Greek Apocalypse of the Virgin Mary*. Only four sins are common to all four tours: adultery, abortion/infanticide, and usury. Two more are common to all except the *Greek Apocalypse of the Virgin Mary*: despising God's commandments, and losing virginity before marriage (where the sinners are women). When we remember that the *Latin Vision* distinguishes thirteen categories of sinner and that all of the others list more, it is clear that the categories of sin vary considerably in each work and that the selection found in the *Latin Vision of Ezra* has no particular resemblance to any of the others.[36]

If we make broader comparisons, we can observe that the *Apocalypse of Peter* gives particular prominence to sins that relate to a situation of persecution and martyrdom: apostasy, betrayal, giving false testimony that leads to martyrs' deaths, persecution. The *Vision of Ezra* has nothing of this except for the case of Herod, "who killed many children on account of the Lord" (v. 38). Sins of this kind are entirely absent from the *Apocalypse of Paul* and the *Greek Apocalypse of the Virgin Mary.* We might therefore suppose that, like these latter two apocalypses, the *Latin Vision of Ezra* originated in a post-Constantinian context. The *Apocalypse of Peter* also includes the making of idols and idolatrous worship, whereas the *Vision of Ezra* makes no such references to false religious practices. The *Apocalypse of Paul* is concerned with false religion, but the focus has shifted from idolatry to heresy (*Apoc. Paul* 41-42). In the *Greek Apocalypse of the Virgin Mary* it is the unbelieving Jews who are condemned. Again, the differences between the *Apocalypse of Peter* and the others suggest a post-Constantinian context for the latter.

The *Apocalypse of Paul* gives prominence to what we might call ecclesiastical sins (sins that are the more heinous because they are committed in or after church worship [*Apoc. Paul* 31]) and sins committed by ecclesiastics (bishops, priests, deacons, readers). Such sins are absent from the *Apocalypse of Peter* and from the *Latin Vision of Ezra*, with only one exception common to all the recensions (v. 10). This distinguishes the *Latin Vision* sharply from the *Apocalypse of Paul*, but also from the *Greek Apocalypse of the Virgin Mary*, where a majority of sins fall into these ecclesiastical categories, as well as from most

34. Himmelfarb, *Tours*, 167.

35. Himmelfarb, *Tours*, 163-65.

36. If we compare the punishments as well as the sins, the variation is even greater.

of the visions of the other world in the medieval West, where sins of religious practice and the sins of clergy and monks are routinely prominent.[37] In the variant readings of the manuscripts of the *Latin Vision of Ezra*, we can see the tendency of the scribes/editors to introduce ecclesiastical aspects of the sins (vv. 26 VH, 36 VH, 46 LVH, 50 B), in line with other such visions that they knew.

The absence of ecclesiastical sins is one of the strongest indications that the Greek *Vorlage* of the *Latin Vision of Ezra* was composed before the *Apocalypse of Paul*. If we also take into account the indications we have noticed of a post-Constantinian date, we could tentatively date the work to the second half of the fourth century.[38] However, these arguments about the date assume that the work belongs to the Christian tradition. The differences and resemblances between the *Latin Vision* and the other three apocalypses (all clearly Christian) are also consistent with the hypothesis that the account was originally non-Christian Jewish and in that case would not be arguments for dating the work. At this point we must turn from considerations of date to the question of provenance. Although the work has been preserved in the Christian tradition, are there features that could be better explained by an originally Jewish provenance?

Another, very distinctive feature of the categories of sin in the *Latin Vision of Ezra* is the extent to which they are based on the laws in the Pentateuch. Of course, this is the case with sins that appear also in one or more of the other three tours: adultery, homosexual intercourse, rebellion against parents, usury, loss of a woman's virginity before marriage, blasphemy, slander. Others not explicitly specified in the law of Moses were regarded by Jews and Christians as forbidden by implication: abortion, infanticide, lack of hospitality to strangers. But it is notable that several sins unique to the *Latin Vision of Ezra* among these four tours of hell are taken from the Mosaic laws: incest (v. 21), misdirecting travellers (v. 41), defrauding servants of their wages (v. 50a) and altering a boundary mark (v. 57b). Of these, the first is rare in the tours of hell in general,[39] while the other three are unique to the *Latin Vision of Ezra* (apart from the parallel to the last in *Gk. Apoc. Ezra* 5:25).

The *Latin Vision of Ezra* condemns incest, not in general, but specifically with parents,[40] and referring apparently not to sexual abuse of children by parents, since it is the children who are condemned. The reason is perhaps that incest with father and mother heads the list of forbidden sexual relationships in Leviticus 18 (18:7). As such, this most heinous form of incest may, in the *Latin Vision*, stand representatively for all the others listed in that chapter of the law. Defrauding servants of their just wages (v. 50a) may well reflect Deuteronomy 24:14-15. Altering a boundary mark (v. 57b) certainly reflects Deuteronomy 27:17 (cf. also Deut 19:14; Prov 23:10-11).[41]

The most interesting of these cases is that of directing travellers to the wrong paths (v 41). This is based on Deuteronomy 27:18: "Cursed be anyone who misleads a blind

37. The *Vision of Tnugdal* is unusual in this respect, though even here there is a special category of fornication by ecclesiastical persons (chap. 9).

38. A specific motif that is relevant to the date of the work but also very problematic in that regard is the bridge (vv. 36a-36e). On this see Culiano, "'Pons subtilis'"; Bauckham, "Hell in the Latin *Vision of Ezra*."

39. Himmelfarb, *Tours*, 70, lists, besides the *Latin Vision of Ezra* and the *Greek Apocalypse of Ezra*, only the *Ethiopic Apocalypse of Mary*, the *Ethiopic Apocalypse of Baruch*, and the *Gedulat Moshe*.

40. The scribes may not have realized the sin is incest, but this is clear from the parallel in *Gk. Apoc. Ezra* 4:22-24.

41. As Himmelfarb, *Tours*, 162, notes, the Greek of *Gk. Apoc. Ezra* 5:25 is close to the LXX of Deut 27:17.

person on the road." The application has been extended from blind people to anyone who needs help in finding the way.[42] Just such a broadening of the scope of the commandment is found in Jewish sources. In *Targum Pseudo-Jonathan to Deuteronomy*, this curse in 27:18 has the form: "Cursed be he who misdirects the stranger on the way, who is like a blind man!"[43] The same interpretation is found in *Sipre Deut.* 223. Moreover, just such an extension of the commandment is already attested by Josephus, who, in summarizing the requirements of the Mosaic law, writes: "People should show the roads to those who do not know them, and not, hunting for something to laugh at, hinder another person's need by deception" (*Ant.* 4.276; cf., more briefly, *C. Ap.* 2.211, also in a summary of the Mosaic commandments).[44] By contrast, in the writings of the Church Fathers in the pre-Constantinian period there is no such interpretation of Deuteronomy 27:18.[45]

In this light we may also consider *Latin Vision of Ezra* 46 in MS B: "These are the ones who mocked the law and corrupted (or: destroyed) it." In other manuscripts this has been expanded: "These are teachers of the law who confused baptism and the law of the Lord, because they taught with words but did not fulfil [their words] with deeds" (VH, cf. L). This expansion has created a reference to religious teachers, in line with the medieval tendency to feature ecclesiastical persons in tours of hell, and has added an allusion to Matthew 23:3. The probability that B preserves the more original reading is supported by *Apocalypse of Peter* 9:7, which refers to people who neglected charity to the needy "and thus despised the commandment of God," and by *Apocalypse of Paul* 37: "They are those who reviled the Word of God in church, paying no attention to it, but counting God and his angels as nothing." This last text is evidently a more Christianized version of the category of sinners in *Latin Vision of Ezra* 46, and suggests that we should perhaps take *corruptores* in *Latin Vision of Ezra* 46 in the sense of "destroyers," meaning that these people count the law as nothing by not heeding it.[46] In any case, the B text of *Latin Vision of Ezra* 46 refers to the Torah and is thus closely coherent with the extent to which the categories of sinners in this tour of hell reflect the commandments of the Torah, with a particular emphasis on the curses of Deuteronomy 27:15-26.

Since the biblical Ezra was an interpreter of the Torah and since in this and other pseudepigrapha he is portrayed as a second Moses (see the next section), it is, of course, very appropriate that the sins in this tour of hell should so largely reflect the commandments of the Mosaic law. We might imagine a Christian author, a reader of *4 Ezra*, composing a work that would be appropriate for the pre-Christian Jewish figure of Ezra. We should have to suppose that this author also had access to Jewish halakhic traditions from

---

42. I am not convinced by Nuvolone, "Vision d'Esdras," 614, that the reference is to those who are figuratively blind, i.e., going astray religiously.

43. The same reference to a stranger, who is like a blind man, is found in the *Fragmentary Targum* to Lev 19:14. In the ancient world, of course, where travellers relied heavily on asking local people for directions, this was a very serious matter.

44. See especially the discussion in Louis H. Feldman, *Flavius Josephus: Judean Antiquities 1-4* (Leiden: Brill, 2004), 445-46. He argues that Josephus' statement of this law "would seem to be a direct refutation of the charge of such a bitter satirist as his contemporary, Juvenal, who declares (*Sat.* 14.103) that Jews do not point out the road except to those who practise the same rites."

45. Agnete Siquans, *Der Deuteronomium-kommentar de Theodoret von Kyros* (Österreichische Biblische Studien 19; Frankfurt am Main: Peter Lang, 2002), lists all patristic comments on Deuteronomy up to the early fourth century. The only comments on Deut 27:18 are in Theodoret, *Quaestiones in Deuteronomium* 34 (251/3-4) and Origen, *Adnot. Deut.* 27:18. Both read the verse figuratively as referring to religious error.

46. Cf. Nuvolone, "Vision," 615, referring to *4 Ezra* 7:20-24; *2 Bar.* 51:4-6.

which he or she drew the extension of Deuteronomy 27:18 into a command not to misdirect travellers. However, we should also note that the present form of the text contains also some material which, when placed in the time of Ezra, is grossly anachronistic, such as the punishment of Herod (vv. 37-38) and Ezra's address to "apostles, martyrs, confessors and virgins" (v. 113). A Christian author who was carefully writing a text appropriate to Ezra in his pre-Christian context would not have included such gross anachronisms.

Most of the explicitly Christian features in the first half of the *Latin Vision of Ezra* (where we have more MSS than B) are actually missing from one or more of the recensions and can be fairly confidently regarded as scribal additions to the text.[47] This could well be true also of minor Christian features of the second half of the work, which is extant only in MS B.[48] But such observations leave us with two substantial passages of indubitably Christian origin: the punishment of Herod (vv. 37-39) and the account of Antichrist (vv. 71-79). Both passages are represented also in the *Greek Apocalypse of Ezra* (4:9-12, 25-35), and so they were present in the Greek *Vorlage* of the *Latin Vision* on which the *Greek Apocalypse* is dependent. There are, however, indications that they are secondary additions. The episode in which Ezra sees Herod being punished in hell is the only occasion on which he voices approval of God's judgment and does not pray for mercy for the sinner. The account of Antichrist is awkwardly placed in its context, unconnected with the theme of the work or the course of the narrative, attached to its context solely by its eschatological nature.

An original text without explicitly Christian features could have been written by a Christian. We could explain v. 41 by postulating a Christian author of the early period, familiar with Jewish halakah. But it may be easier to postulate an originally non-Christian Jewish work. In either case, the dependence of the work on *4 Ezra* (c. 100 C.E.) provides a *terminus a quo,* while if the work was originally Christian it probably dates from the second half of the fourth century.[49] An originally Jewish work could be considerably earlier.

Literary Context

The *Latin Vision of Ezra* is one of a number of pseudepigraphal works attributed to Ezra. These works owe little, if anything, to the biblical portrayal of Ezra, the scribe of the Torah, but instead are indebted, directly or indirectly, to the oldest and most popular of Ezra pseudepigrapha: *4 Ezra.*[50] The Ezra of *4 Ezra* is a prophet and visionary, who debates with God about the fate of sinners, asks God to be merciful to them and spare them from judgment, receives prophecies and visions of the end times, and, like a new Moses, is inspired by God to write both the books of the Hebrew scriptures and other, esoteric revelations. Various aspects of this work inspired the various themes and events that are associated

47. This is true of vv. 1, 26, 36, 46, 50, 60, 64. Only the Christian features of vv. 10 and 37-38 are found in all MSS.

48. See vv. 83-84, 90 (the period of time), 108, 110-111, 113, 114, 115. 117.

49. Nuvolone's view that the work originated in a second-century Christian community in which Christian prophets were the leaders ("Vision d'Esdras," 600) seems to me too dependent on the phrase "prophets of the churches" (v. 60), which occurs only in B. The word *ecclesiarum* looks like the same kind of anachronistic Christian gloss that occurs here and there in the various recensions. Without it, the reference here, as in vv. 88 and 92, is much more naturally understood as to the Old Testament prophets, whom Ezra could, without anachronism, have seen in heaven.

50. On the Ezra pseudepigrapha and the figure of Ezra, see Stone, "An Introduction"; "The Metamorphosis"; Robert A. Kraft, "'Ezra' Materials in Judaism and Christianity," *ANRW* 2.19.1 (1979): 119-36.

with Ezra in the other Ezra pseudepigrapha.[51] None of them attains anything like the literary or the theological excellence of *4 Ezra* itself.

Of all these writings, the *Latin Vision of Ezra* and the *Greek Apocalypse of Ezra* have the most varied range of contents. The *Latin Vision* includes (a) Ezra's tour of hell and paradise; (b) his prayer to God to spare sinners from judgment; (c) God's response giving a respite from punishment; (d) a debate with God about his judgment of sinners; (e) eschatological prophecy; (f) Ezra's struggle to avoid surrendering his soul in death; (g) his securing of God's blessing on those who copy or preserve his book. Of these elements, (b), (d) and (e) are all prominent in *4 Ezra*. The tour of hell and paradise could be seen as a substitute for 7:75-101, an account of what happens to souls after death, or *4 Ezra* 4:8 ("I never went down into the deep, nor as yet to Hades") might have been taken as a hint that Ezra did descend to the underworld at a later date. But the tour of hell and paradise was a form of apocalypse that almost certainly already existed. Element (f) actually contradicts *4 Ezra* 14, which states that Ezra ascended to heaven without dying (14:9), but it is also coherent with that chapter in that, as we shall see, it treats Ezra as a new Moses. In *4 Ezra* there is nothing like (c). On the contrary, Ezra's prayers for mercy are rejected by God, who remains implacably severe in judging sinners. This is the point at which the authors, not only of the *Latin Vision of Ezra*, but also of other apocalypses, found Ezra's prayers in *4 Ezra* more congenial than God's response.[52]

The *Greek Apocalypse of Ezra*, which seems to be directly dependent on *4 Ezra* as well as on the Greek *Vorlage* of the *Latin Vision of Ezra*, includes all seven elements, but has much more emphasis on (d), less on (a) and much less on (c). The *Apocalypse of Sedrach* (where "Sedrach" is probably a corruption of "Ezra"),[53] the third of this closely related group of writings, lacks (a) and (e), while developing especially elements (d) and (f) and a different form of (c). It too appears to be independently indebted to *4 Ezra*. A fourth apocalypse, the Armenian *Questions of Ezra*, probably has no literary relationship with the three already discussed, but is inspired by *4 Ezra* in a rather similar way. It has elements (b) and (d), but in place of (a) there is an account of what happens to souls after death that is rather more like *4 Ezra* 7:75-101, while its equivalent to (c) concerns the efficacy of prayers for the dead. But it is notable that here too there is an attempt to mollify the unyielding harshness of God towards sinners in *4 Ezra*.[54]

The notion of Ezra as a new Moses, presumably inspired by his biblical role of reintroducing the Torah to the people after the exile (Ezra 7:10, 25; Neh 8:1-8; 1 Esd 8:7, 23; 9:37-48), is found also, though in a milder form, in rabbinic literature (*t. Sanh.* 4:7; *b. Sanh.* 21b; *Sifre Deut.* 48), and so presumably did not originate with *4 Ezra*. The three main forms in which it appears in the *Latin Vision of Ezra* are not derived from *4 Ezra*. First, Ezra's pleas for God to have mercy on the sinners condemned to hell reach their climax in his request to perish in place of them (v. 89). It is this that secures the weekly respite from punishment that God concedes (v. 90). Ezra's request is modelled on that of Moses, who offered

51. The eschatological prophecies and the prophetic visions are the features of *4 Ezra* that inspired *5 Ezra*, the *Syriac Apocalypse of Ezra*, the *Falasha Apocalypse of Ezra*, and perhaps, though in a much more general way, the calendrical prognostications ascribed to Ezra. Ezra figures as a prophet also in *Coptic Jeremiah Apocryphon* 34.

52. Bauckham, *The Fate*, 136-42.

53. In Greek the names are quite close: Sedrach and Esdras or Esdram (the latter is used in the *Greek Apocalypse of Ezra*).

54. The same concern can be seen in the Armenian redaction of *4 Ezra*.

himself to God as atonement for the sin of Israel at Sinai (Exod 32:30-32). Secondly, most of the sins for which the damned are punished are either explicitly forbidden in the Torah or regarded in Jewish tradition as forbidden by implication. Thirdly, the story of Ezra's refusal to surrender his soul in death (vv. 93-116) has been transferred from Moses to Ezra.[55]

The story of Moses' struggle for his soul is found in various sources and the relationship between them is a complex issue. But the fully developed form that includes the discussion of the parts of Moses' body through which his soul could be extracted (paralleled, with reference to Ezra, in *Vis. Ezra* 97-104; *Gk. Apoc. Ezra* 6:3-15; cf. *Apoc. Sedr.* 10-11) occurs in some versions of the Hebrew *Petirat Moshe*,[56] in the Armenian *Death of Moses*,[57] and in the Arabic *Death of Moses*.[58] Late as these texts are in the form we have them, the very close parallels show that they must derive from some common source known also to the author of the Greek *Vorlage* of the *Latin Vision*.[59] The version in the *Greek Apocalypse of Ezra* retains some signs of its original application to Moses (Ezra "spoke mouth to mouth with God" [cf. Num 12:8] and "walked with Moses on the mountain") which are not in the Latin text, while the latter has one that is not in the *Greek Apocalypse* (Aaron anointed the crown of his head), and both have perhaps the most distinctively Mosaic feature: that Ezra's eyes saw the back of God (cf. Exod 33:23). (The *Latin Vision* makes this true of Ezra by having Ezra see God's back in v. 60.) We have to assume that the Greek original of the *Latin Vision* had more Mosaic features that have been reduced in transmission to make the dialogue more appropriate to Ezra.

The *Greek Apocalypse of Ezra* has something of all three Mosaic features of the *Latin Vision*, but the significance of the first two is greatly reduced by rearrangement and revision of the material (cf. 1:10-11; 5:10; 4:24; 5:1-3). The only other apocalyptic seer who prays for mercy for the damned as consistently and persistently as Ezra does, and similarly offers to suffer instead of them,[60] is the Virgin Mary in the *Greek Apocalypse of the Virgin*. In this respect this *Apocalypse of the Virgin* must be dependent on the Greek original of the *Latin Vision of Ezra*. It is interesting to find that the figure of Ezra contributed in this way to the image of the Theotokos in the Orthodox churches as the merciful and effective intercessor for sinners.[61]

Ezra's bold and intelligent debate with God about his judgment of sinners is a highly distinctive feature of *4 Ezra*. In later apocalypses it finds significant echoes only in other Ezra apocalypses: the *Latin Vision of Ezra*, the *Greek Apocalypse of Ezra*, the *Apocalypse*

55. Chazon, "Moses' Struggle," was written before MS B of the Latin Vision of Ezra was known, but she shows the relationship between the version of Ezra's struggle for his soul in the *Greek Apocalypse of Ezra* and that of Moses in various sources. See also Nuvolone, "Apocalypse d'Esdras," 93-98.

56. E.g. MS Parma 327/37ff. 135b-138a, translated in Rella Kusbelevsky, *Moses and the Angel of Death* (Studies on Themes and Motifs in Literature 4; New York: Peter Lang, 1995), 261-78.

57. Michael E. Stone, *Armenian Apocrypha Relating to the Patriarchs and Prophets* (Jerusalem: Israel Academy of Sciences and Humanities, 1982), 154-55.

58. Gustav Weil, *The Bible, the Koran, and the Talmud; or Biblical Legends of the Mussulmans* (London: Brown, Green, and Longmans, 1846), 140-43; Edward Ullendorf, "The 'Death of Moses' in the Literature of the Falashas," *BSOAS* 24 (1961): 419-43, here 441.

59. *T. Abr.* A 15-20 is also indebted to a version of the story of the struggle of Moses for his soul but does not include the discussion of the parts of the body.

60. The motif is adapted in that Mary offers to be punished instead of the Christians, but explicitly not for the Jews. Mary's request is not found in all versions of the *Greek Apocalypse of the Virgin*.

61. She also prays for the damned, with varying results, in the other three apocalypses of the Virgin: see Bauckham, *The Fate*, chapter 13.

of Sedrach, and the *Questions of Ezra*. In other apocalyptic tours of hell—the *Apocalypse of Peter*, the *Apocalypse of Paul*, and the *Greek Apocalypse of the Virgin Mary*—it occurs, but only in very brief and muted forms (*Ap. Pet.* 3:4-6; *Ap. Paul* 33, 42; *Apoc. Vir.* 26-28). It may have been thought too challenging and irreverent to be attributed to seers other than Ezra. But behind all these works there is evidently the sense that God would not rebuff the prayers of a saintly person for mercy for sinners as uncompromisingly as he does in *4 Ezra*.

The influence of the *Latin Vision of Ezra* on the medieval visions of paradise and hell is a subject that requires further study. The *Vision of Alberic* (c. 1130) is certainly dependent on it,[62] and a case can be made for its influence on the *Vision of Adamnán* (tenth or eleventh century), Latin Redaction IV of the *Apocalypse of Paul*, and *St Patrick's Purgatory* (c. 1180). Whether it influenced the iconography of paradise and hell remains to be investigated.

Bibliography

EDITIONS AND TRANSLATIONS

Bogaert, Pierre-Maurice. "Une version longue inédité de la 'Visio Beati Esdrae' dans le légendier de Teano (Barberini Lat. 2318)." *RBén* 94 (1984): 50-70. *Editio princeps* of MS B.

Mueller, James R., and Gregory Allen Robbins. "Vision of Ezra." *OTP*, 1:581-90. (English translation based on MS V)

Nuvolone, Flavio G. "Apocalittica cristiana extra-canonica: Il profeta Esdra querela Dio." *Parola & parole* 4 (2008): 65-87. (Italian translation corresponding to Nuvolone's French translation [next item]).

__________. "Vision d'Esdras." Pages 595-632 in vol. 1 of *Écrits apocryphes chrétiens*. Edited by François Bovon and Pierre Geoltrain. 2 vols. Paris: Gallimard, 1997, 2005. (French translation based primarily on MS B)

Shutt, R. J. H. "The Vision of Esdras." *APOT*, 943-51. English translation based on MS V.

Wahl, Otto (ed.). *Apocalypsis Esdrae; Apocalypsis Sedrach; Visio Beati Esdrae*. PVTG 4. Leiden: Brill, 1977. (The edition [pp. 49-61] presents the text of MS L alongside that of MSS V and H.)

Wahl, Otto. "Vier neue Textzeugen der Visio beati Esdrae." *Salesianum* 40 (1978): 583-89. (Records variants from MS H in MSS K, M, Z and Lf.)

STUDIES

Bauckham, Richard. *The Fate of the Dead: Studies on the Jewish and Christian Apocalypses*. NovTSup 93. Leiden: Brill, 1998.

__________. "Hell in the Latin *Vision of Ezra*." Pages 323-42 in *Other Worlds and Their Relation to This World: Early Jewish and Ancient Christian Traditions*. Edited by Tobias Nicklas, Joseph Verheyden, Erik M. M. Eynikel, and Florentino García Martínez. JSJSup 143. Leiden: Brill, 2010.

Chazon, E. Glickler. "Moses' Struggle for His Soul: A Prototype for the *Testament of Abraham*, the Greek *Apocalypse of Ezra*, and the *Apocalypse of Sedrach*." *SecCent* 5 (1985): 151-64.

Culiano, Ioan P. "'Pons subtilis': Storia e Significato di un Simbolo." *Aev* 2 (1979): 301-12.

Denis, Albert-Marie. Pages 865-70 in vol. 1 of *Introduction à la littérature religieuse judéo-hellénistique*. Turnhout: Brepols, 2000.

62. Dinzelbacher, "Die Vision Alberichs."

Dinzelbacher, Peter. "Die Vision Alberichs und die Esdras-Apokryphe." *Studien und Mitteilungen zur Geschichte der Bayerischen Benediktinerakademie* 87 (1976): 433-42.

Himmelfarb, Martha. *Tours of Hell: An Apocalyptic Form in Jewish and Christian Literature.* Philadelphia, Pa.: University of Pennsylvania Press, 1983.

Nuvolone, Flavio G. "Apocalypse d'Esdras grecque et latine, rapports et rhétorique." *Apocrypha* 7 (1996): 81-108.

__________. "L'initiation prophétique dans l'Apocalypse grecque d'Esdras." *Freiburger Zeitschrift für Philosophie und Theologie* 44 (1997): 408-41.

__________. "Valeur ajoutée pour investissements bibliographiques 'apocryphes' (*Visio Esdrae B*, § 95-96)." Pages 181-90 in *Mélanges de langue, de littérature et de civilisation latines offerts au professeur André Schneider.* Edited by Denis Knoepfler. Neuchâtel/Geneva: Librarie Droz, 1997.

Stone, Michael E. "An Introduction to the Esdras Writings." Pages 305-20 in vol. 1 of *Apocrypha, Pseudepigrapha and Armenian Studies.* OLA 144. Leuven: Peeters, 2006.

__________. "The Metamorphosis of Ezra: Jewish Apocalypse and Medieval Vision." *JTS* 33 (1982): 1-18.

The Latin Vision of Ezra[a]

Ezra sees the judgments of sinners in hell

[1]When Ezra had prayed to the Lord Jesus Christ, he said,[b] "Give me faith, Lord,
so that I may not fear when I see the judgments of the sinners."

[2]And there were granted[c] to me[d] seven angels who had charge of Tartarus[e]
and they lifted[f] me[g] down six thousand and seven hundred[h] steps into hell. *Gk. Apoc. Ezra* 4:6

[3]And I[i] saw there a fiery gate and through it was spurting a very strong flame
for seventy-two feet, and outside the gates were lying dragons and lions and Ps 90:13 LXX (Evv 91:13)
black dogs[j] from whose mouth and ear[k] and eyes was spurting a very strong
flame.[l]

[4]Righteous[m] men were coming[n] and going through[o] with joy.[p] [5]And I asked
the angel who was guiding me,[q] "Lord,[r] who are these who proceed with such

---

a. The title in B is: "The reading (*legenda*) about the blessed Ezra the prophet"; L: "The vision of Ezra"; VH: "The vision of the blessed Ezra."

b. VH: "Ezra prayed to the Lord, saying." B's reading (but without "Jesus Christ") is probably preferable, reflecting a now lost introductory section of the work in which Ezra had already prayed (as in *Gk. Apoc. Ezra* 1:2-7). See Nuvolone, "Apocalypse," 88-89.

c. A "divine passive," meaning "God granted"

d. VH: "him"

e. Angels "in charge of Tartarus" (Greek *tartarouchos*, Latin *tartarucus*) appear in several visions of the punishments in hell (*Apoc. Pet.* 13:5; *Apoc. Paul* 16; *Apoc. Seven Heavens* 7, 11; *Thom. Cont.* 142:41).

f. VH: "carried"

g. VH: "him"

h. "six thousand and seven hundred"; LVH: "seventy"

i. VH: "he"

j. "through it was spurting a very strong flame for seventy-two feet, and outside the gates were lying dragons and lions and black dogs"; L: "he was going in through its flame, and seventy-two feet outside the gates (I saw) two (animals) like lions lying"; VH: "in these gates he saw two lions lying"

k. L: "ears"; VH: "nostrils"

l. L: "(something) like a flame"

m. L: "great"; VH: "very powerful"

n. L adds "through it"

o. L adds "its flame"; VH add "the flame"

p. "with joy"—L: "and it was not touching them"; Lf: "did not harm them" (cf. Isa 43:2)

q. "I asked the angel who was guiding me"; L: "I asked the angels who were guiding me"; VH: "Ezra said"

r. LVH omit "Lord"

great joy?"[a] [6]He[b] said to me,[c] "These are[d] the holy and God-fearing men[e] whose
Acts 10:4 almsgiving[f] has been raised up to heaven; [7]these are the ones who have given
alms plentifully, who have clothed[g] the naked, who have fed the hungry, who
Job 22:7; Isa 58:7; Tob 4:16; Matt 25:31-46 have given drink to the thirsty.[h]

[8]And sinners[i] were coming in order to enter through the same gate.[j] The dragons and the dogs[k] were striking them[l] and the fire was burning them.[m] [8a]They were saying, "Lord, have mercy," but he was not having mercy.[n]

[9]And I asked the angel who was guiding me,[o] "Lord,[p] who are these who have been placed[q] in such a great punishment?"[r] And he[s] said to me,[t] [10]"These are the ones who have denied the Lord, and have spent the night[u] with women on the Lord's day,[v] and for this reason they are in torments."[w]

Gk. Apoc. Ezra 5:6 [11][I said,][x] "Lord, spare the sinners."

---

a. "with such great joy"; VH: "so safely"

b. LVH: "the angels"

c. VH: "him"

d. Demonstrative questions and answers ("Who are these who…?," "These are the ones who …"), exchanged between the visionary and the interpreting angel, are characteristic of the tours of hell in apocalypses.

e. "holy and God-fearing men"; LV: "righteous (people)"

f. LVH: "fame"

g. L adds "and put shoes on"

h. "who have fed the hungry, who have given drink to the thirsty"; LVH: "who have desired a good desire." The latter is the harder reading and probably more original. Cf. the comparable expression, "to desire an evil desire," in vv. 17, 21, 32. These expressions are not the same as the biblical phrase in Num 11:4; Ps 106:14; Luke 22:15, which simply means "to desire intensely." But they are an example of the cognate accusative, a Semitism that is found in the Greek of the LXX and NT. Other examples are in v. 39 (paralleled in John 7:24) and v. 87.

i. L: "other men"; VH: "others"

j. "through the same gate "; LVH: "the gates"

k. "the dragons and the dogs" ; LVH: "dogs"

l. LVH: "were ripping them apart"; Lf: "they were being torn apart by the dogs"

m. "the fire was burning them"; L omits; VH: "the fire was consuming them"; Lf: "they were being consumed by the fire"

n. For v. 8a, L has: "And the blessed Ezra was saying to the Lord, 'Lord, spare the sinners.' But he was having no mercy." VH have: "And Ezra said, 'Lord, spare the sinners.' But he did not have mercy." These readings conform the statement to later passages in which Ezra prays, "Lord, spare the sinners" (vv. 11, 18, 22, 33, 42, 47, 55, 61), but B's text is paralleled in vv. 28, 36e.

o. "I asked the angel who was guiding me"; L: "I asked the angels who were guiding me"; V: "Ezra said"

p. LVH omit "Lord"

q. LVH: "who are"

r. L adds: "and in such great torments"; VH add: "and in such great torment"

s. LVH: "the angels"

t. VH omits "to me"

u. VH: "have sinned"

v. LH add "before mass." The meaning of B is clarified by the *Vision of Alberic* 5 (which is dependent on *Vis. Ezra*): "On the Lord's days or saints' festivals or principal fast days they did not at all strive to restrain themselves from carnal pleasure and from their wives."

w. "and for this reason they are in torments"; L: "and for this reason they are in such a great torment"; VH: omit

x. This phrase is missing in B. L has: "The blessed Ezra said"; VH have: "And Ezra said"

12 And they brought[a] me down and plunged me seven hundred[b] steps into
hell. And I saw there people tied by the hands, (hanging head) downwards.[c] *Apoc. Pet.* 7:5-8
13 Some devils[d] were administering fire,[e] others were striking them with a club[f]
of fire. 14 And the earth was interjecting,[g] saying, "Beat them and do not spare
them, because they have done many wicked deeds on me."

15 And I asked the angel,[h] "Lord,[i] who are these who are placed[j] in such a
great punishment?"[k] 16 And he[l] said to me,[m] "These are the ones who have fornicated[n] with married women. 17 These are wives who adorned themselves, not for *Apoc. Paul* 38
their husbands, but to please others, desiring with an evil desire."[o] *Apoc. Pet.* 7:6

18 And I said,[p] "Lord, spare the sinners."

19 And they brought me down and placed me[q] in the south. And I saw there
people[r] hanging by their eyelids[s] over fire, women and men, and four devils in *Apoc. Paul* 39
charge of Tartarus[t] were striking them with a fiery club.[u]

20 And I said to the angel,[v] "Who are these who are placed in such great
evils?"[w] 21 He[x] said to me,[y] "These are the ones who have done evil to their father
and their mother[z] and always[aa] wished[ab] with an evil desire." *Gk. Apoc. Ezra* 4:22-24

22 And I said,[ac] "Lord, spare the sinners."

---

a. VH: "led"

b. "seven hundred" ; L omits; VH: "fifty"; Lf: "forty"

c. "I saw there people tied by the hands, (hanging head) downwards"; L: "I saw (people) hanging downwards"; VH: "he saw there people standing in punishments"

d. LH: "angels." This reading is doubtless original (cf. v. 2). In earlier Jewish and Christian literature, those who punish the wicked in hell were angels serving God by carrying out his judgments. In later medieval literature, devils take their place.

e. VH: "were pushing fire at their face"

f. L: "bars"; VH: "whips"

g. VH: "was crying out"

h. L: "And the blessed Ezra asked the angels"; VH: "And Ezra said"

i. LVH omit "Lord"

j. "are placed"; LVH: "are daily"

k. VH: "in such great punishments"

l. L: "they"; VH: "the angels"

m. VH omit "to me"

n. LVH: "have spent the night"

o. So LVH. B omits v. 17.

p. So L. B omits; VH: "Ezra said"

q. So BL. VH: "And again they placed him"

r. LVH: "poor people"

s. "by their eyelids"; LVH omit

t. "devils in charge of Tartarus"; LVH: "angels." See note on v. 13.

u. "with a fiery club"; L omits; VH: "with fiery clubs"

v. "I said to the angel"; L: "I said"; V: "Ezra said, 'Lord, spare the sinners!'"

w. "who are placed in such great evils"; LVH omit

x. L: "they"; VH: "the angels"

y. VH omit "to me"

z. "who have done evil to their father and their mother"; LVH: "have spent the night with their mother." The reference is certainly to incest.

aa. LVH omit "always"

ab. L: "have desired"; VH: "desiring"

ac. So L. B omits this phrase; VH: "And Ezra said"

[23]And they took me down two thousand[a] five hundred steps[b] into hell.[c] And
I saw there a cauldron (which means a not large cooking pot);[d] its width was
twelve cubits.[e] There they saw sulphur of pitch and resin,[f] and it was seen twelve
cubits higher[g] like a wave of the sea.

[24]And righteous people came and entered walking[h] through the middle of it
on waves of fire, praising the Lord,[i] as if they walked on dew and cool water.[j]

[25]And I asked the angel and said,[k] "Lord,[l] who are these who proceed with
such great joy?"[m] [He said,][n] [26]"These are the ones who gave alms plentifully,
who clothed the naked, and put shoes on them."[o]

[27]And sinners came, and angels of Satan were placing them in fire and were
pressing fiery fork-shaped yokes[p] onto their necks.[q] [28]And they were crying,[r]
"Lord, have mercy[s] on me," but he was not having mercy.[t] [29]Their[u] voice was
Gk. Apoc. Ezra 4:14 heard, but their[v] body could not be seen on account of the fire and torments.[w]

[30]And I said to the angel,[x] "Who are these?" [He said,][y] [31]"The ones who

---

a. L omits "thousand"

b. "two thousand five hundred steps"; VH omit

c. L omits "into hell"

d. "a cauldron (which means a not large cooking pot);"; L: "a cooking pot and basins"; VH: " a cooking pot." B explains the meaning of the unusual Latin word *lebes* (a loanword from Greek), "cauldron." All MSS except B have dropped the unfamiliar word *lebes* altogether.

e. L: "its height two hundred cubits"; VH omit

f. "there they saw sulphur of pitch and resin"; LVH: "in which sulphur and bitumen were burning"

g. "it was seen twelve cubits higher"; L: "it was overflowing"; VH: "it was rising and falling." These readings may be attempts to correct the obscure text of B.

h. "entered walking"; LVH: "were walking"

i. "the Lord"; LVH: "the name of the Lord"

j. "on dew and cold water"; L: "on dew"; V: "on dews or cold water." Perhaps *frigidam* ("cold") here means "frozen."

k. "I asked the angel and said"; L: "I asked the angels"; VH: "Ezra said"

l. LVH omit "Lord"

m. "who proceed with such great joy"; VH omit

n. B omits; L: "they"; VH: "the angels"

o. L omits "and put shoes on them" (cf. v. 7, where B lacks it and L has it). In VH the whole verse reads: "These are the ones who make progress daily by practising confession before God and the holy priests, by distributing alms (and) by resisting sins."

p. Latin *furca* refers to a Roman punishment in the form of a yoke in the shape of a two-pronged fork that was placed on the culprit's neck, while his or her hands were fastened to the two ends of the fork.

q. L: "And sinners came, and they were placing them in the basins, so that those who did not wish to go down should go down. They were pressing onto their necks with fiery fork-shaped yokes." VH: "And sinners came, wishing to cross over, and angels of Tartarus came and submerged them in burning fire."

r. LVH: "from the fire they were crying out, saying"

s. L: "spare"

t. L: "will not have mercy on them"; H: "did not have mercy on them"

u. LVH omit "their"

v. LVH omit "their"

w. LVH: "torment"

x. L: "the blessed Ezra said to the angels"; VH: "Ezra said"

y. B lacks this phrase; L: "they said to me"; VH: "the angels said"

were[a] greedy [lustful?], thieves, covetous[b] all the days of their life, who did not Lev 25:35-36; Job
receive the poor[c] and the stranger into their house,[d] 32 and they and all their 31:32; Isa 58:7; Matt
wealth have perished."[e] 25:35; Heb 13:2; *Apoc. Paul* 40

33 [I said,][f] "Lord, spare the sinners."

34 And I walked in a dark place and saw there incalculable worms; their length *Gk. Apoc. Ezra* 4:20;
and height cannot be reckoned; their length is said to be seven hundred cubits.[g] Isa 66:24; Mark 9:48;
35 And in front of its mouth stood many souls of sinners,[h] and whenever they[i] *Apoc. Paul* 42
drew breath, twelve thousand souls went into it like flies, and whenever they[j]
breathed out, they all came out, at different degrees of heat.[k]

36 And I said to the angel,[l] "Lord,[m] who are these?" And he said to me,[n] "These
are the ones who were filled with every kind of evil." [o]

36a And I walked further and saw there[p] a fiery river and there was a great
bridge over it. Its width was such that forty pairs of oxen could cross.[q] 36b And
when the righteous came they were crossing it with joy and happiness.[r] 36c And
the sinners in turn[s] were coming and crossing it as far as the middle,[t] and it
reduced itself to the narrowness of a thread. 36d And they were plunging into
the river and many snakes and scorpions that were lying there were receiving Deut 8:15; Luke 10:19

a. LVH: "These were"

b. "thieves, covetous"; L: "and thieves"; VH: "and slanderers"

c. LVH: "aliens"

d. LVH omit "into their house" and add "and did not give any alms"; K adds: "and had an evil desire"

e. "and they and all their wealth have perished"; L: "and for this reason they have been plunged into torments and they took other people's things for themselves. They desired an evil desire."; VH: "they unjustly took other people's things for themselves, they had an evil desire, and for this reason they are in torments"

f. BL omit this phrase; VH: "And Ezra said"

g. L: "And I walked and saw in a dark place the inextinguishable worm; its length and height I could not reckon, of which (?) it had seventy cubits." VH: "And he walked further and saw in a dark place the immortal (H: inextinguishable) worm, whose magnitude he was not (H: no one was) able to reckon." The singular worm is probably original, as in *Gk. Apoc. Ezra* 4:20 ("the unsleeping worm") and many other visions of hell (Himmelfarb, *Tours*, 118-119). In fact, even in B the worms are reduced to one in v. 35a. The idea of a single worm in hell results from a literal reading of Isa 66:24; Mark 9:48. In these texts it is the fire that is never extinguished, while the worm does not die. B has chosen an adjective related to the following statement that the size cannot be reckoned.

h. L: "many thousands of sinners"; VH: "many sinners"

i. LVH: "it"

j. LVH: "it"

k. LVH: "a different colour"

l. L: "the blessed Ezra said to the angels"; H: "Ezra said to the angels"; V: "Ezra said"

m. LVH omit "Lord"

n. L: "they said to me"; VH: "they said"

o. "every kind of evil" may be a scribe's substitution for an unintelligible text. VH add: "and crossed over without confession and penance"

p. LVH omit "there"

q. L: "its width was such that it could accommodate seventy pairs of oxen"; H omits

r. LH: "they crossed with joy and exultation"

s. L: "in truth"

t. LH omit "and crossing it as far as the middle"

the souls of widows and men.[a] 36e They were asking for mercy,[b] but no one was
having mercy on them.[c]

37 And I[d] walked further and saw a man[e] sitting on a fiery chair, and angels
of Satan[f] were administering fire on all sides and his counsellors were standing
around him.[g]

Gk. Apoc. Ezra 4:9-11; 38 And I said to the angel,[h] "Lord,[i] who is this?"[j] And he said to me, "This is
Apoc. Paul 26; Matt 2:16 king Herod[k] who killed many children[l] on account of the Lord." 39 And I[m] said,
John 7:24 "Lord, you have judged a right judgment!"

40 And I[n] walked further[o] and saw there people who were bound and angels in
charge of Tartarus were piercing their eyes with thorns. 41 And I asked the angel[p]
who these were.[q] And he said,[r] "These are the ones who showed wrong paths to
Deut 27:18 travellers."[s]

42 And I[t] said, "Lord, spare the sinners."[u]

43 And I[v] saw there[w] girls coming, with fiery[x] collars[y] weighing five hundred
pounds, crying out, towards the Ocean.[z]

And I said to the angel,[aa] "Lord,[ab] who are these?" 44 And he said to me,[ac] "These
Apoc. Pet. 11:7 are the ones who violated their virginity before marriage."

---

a. LH: "They were falling into that river, confessing their sins and saying, 'We have done every kind of evil, and for this reason we have been handed over to this punishment.'" This may be a scribe's attempt (following v. 36) to supply the lack, in B's text, of any indication of how these people had sinned.

b. L omits "for mercy"

c. H: "none was given to them." V omits the whole of vv. 36a-36e.

d. VH: "he"

e. L: "good man"

f. LVH: "they." On B's reading, cf. note on v. 13.

g. VH add "in fire," no doubt a scribal addition to avoid the impression that the counsellors were not being punished.

h. L: "the blessed Ezra asked"; VH: "Ezra said"

i. LVH omit "Lord"

j. L: "who are these"

k. L: "This one, was a king for a long time, Herod"; VH: "This man was king for a long time, by name Herod"

l. LVH: "who in Bethlehem of Judea killed children"

m. L: "the blessed Ezra"; VH: "Ezra"

n. VH: "he"

o. VH omit "further"

p. L: "I asked the angels"; V: "Ezra said"

q. LVH: "'Who are these?'"

r. L: "they said to me"; VH: "the angels said"

s. LVH: "to people who were straying"

t. VH: "Ezra"

u. So LVH. B omits this verse.

v. VH: "he"

w. LVH omit "there"

x. LVH omit "fiery"

y. L: "goatskins"

z. LVH: "to the West"

aa. L: "I said to the angel"; V: "Ezra said"

ab. LVH omit "Lord"

ac. L: "the angels said to me"; VH: "the angels said"

45 And I walked further and I saw there many people and over them many
thousands of [pieces of] molten iron and lead.[a] And I asked the angel[b] what this
was.[c] 46 And he said to me,[d] "These are the ones who mocked the law and cor- *4 Ezra* 7:24
rupted it[e] and for this reason they are judged." *Apoc. Paul* 37
47 [I said,][f] "Lord, spare the sinners."
48 And I walked further towards where the sun sets. And I saw there a smelting-furnace of burning fire, into which kings and princes were being dispatched,[g] *Apoc. Seven Heavens* 2
49 and poor people[h] standing there and interjecting,[i] "Lord,[j] these are the ones
who deprived us of all our power."[k]
50 Then I saw there another furnace and there sulphur of pitch was burning,
and other [pieces of] wood that had been brought there on the Lord's day.[l] And Num 15:32
there children who had lifted their hand against[m] their parents were being dis- Exod 21:15
patched (into it),[n] 50a and those who denied their Lord[o] and those who defrauded *Apoc. Pet.* 11:8
their servants of their just wages[p] were similarly being thrown in. Deut 24:14-15; Jas 5:4
51 And I[q] saw in a dark[r] place another[s] furnace, and women who were there[t] *Gk. Apoc. Ezra* 5:4

---

a. L: "I went out and saw a baptismal pool, in front of the baptismal pool a multitude lying down, and they were pouring many thousands of [pieces of] molten and iron and lead were being poured over them"; VH: "and he saw a multitude of old men lying down and molten iron and lead was being poured over them"

b. L: "I asked the angels"; VH: "and he said"

c. LVH: "'Who are these?'"

d. L: "they said to me"; VH: "the angels said"

e. L: "these are the doctors of the law and the corruptors of God, who confused baptism"; VH: "these are the doctors of the law, who confused baptism and the law of the Lord, because they taught with words but did not fulfil with deeds" (cf. Matt 23:2-3). These readings are probably attempts to explain the more original text in B.

f. B omits this phrase. L: "and I said"; VH: "and Ezra said"

g. "a furnace of burning fire, into which kings and princes were being dispatched"; of these words B has only "kings and princes"; the rest has to be supplied from LVH. The whole verse in these recensions reads: L: "And I walked further towards the place where the sun sets, (and) I saw men descending into a furnace of burning fire, where kings and princes were being dispatched"; VH: "And he saw, over against the place where the sun sets, a furnace of wondrous size burning with fire, into which many kings and princes of this world were being dispatched"

h. LVH: "many thousands of poor people"

i. "standing there and interjecting"; L: "standing and interjecting and saying"; VH: "accusing them and saying"

j. LVH omit "Lord"

k. LVH: "who through their power did harm to us and forced free people into slavery"

l. L: "and I saw there another furnace, and pitch and sulphur and bitumen were burning"; VH: "and he saw another furnace burning with pitch and sulphur"

m. L: "spent the night with"

n. LVH add "and did injuries to them with their mouth"

o. L: "their Lord"; H: "God." Probably the reference was originally to slaves who disobeyed their masters, balancing the following reference to masters who treated their slaves unjustly.

p. LH: "who did not give servants their just wages" (L omits "wages"). V omits v. 50a.

q. VH: "he"

r. LVH: "very dark"

s. VH add "burning"

t. L: "many (people)"; VH: "many women"

Gk. Apoc. Ezra 5:3; *Apoc. Pet.* 8:2; *Apoc. Paul* 40 were being dispatched into it. And I said to the angel,[a] "Lord,[b] who are they?"[c]
52[He said,][d] "These are the ones who had their children from adultery[e] and rejected them."[f]

53And the infants themselves were interjecting, saying, "Lord, the soul that
Apoc. Pet. 8:6 you gave us they have taken from us."[g]

Gk. Apoc. Mary 20; *Apoc. El. (C)* 2:35 53aAnd in the same place[h] I saw other women hanging by the hairs of their heads[i] and snakes around their necks were drinking from their breasts.[j]

54I said,[k] "Lord,[l] who are they?"[m] [He said,] "These are the ones who did not
Gk. Apoc. Ezra 5:2-3 offer their breasts to infants and orphans."[n]

55[I said,][o] "Lord, spare the sinners."[p]

56Then[q] Michael and Gabriel came and said to me, "Ezra,[r] come up to heaven so that we may celebrate the Pasch."[s]

57And I said,[t] "As the Lord[u] lives, I will not come until I have seen all[v] the judgments of sinners."

57aAnd I walked further and saw people tearing their clothes,[w] 57band I[x] said,
Gk. Apoc. Ezra 5:25; Deut 27:17; Prov 23:10-11 | Exod 20:16; Deut 5:20 "Who are these?" And the angel said,[y] "These are the ones who altered a boundary-mark[z] and who gave false testimony."[aa]

58And they placed me[ab] down four thousand nine hundred[ac] steps in hell. I[ad]

---

a. L: "the blessed Ezra asked the angels"; VH: "he said"

b. LVH omit "Lord"

c. L: "who are these" (masculine); VH: "Who are these" (feminine)

d. B omits this phrase. L: "they said"; VH: "the angels said"

e. VH: "in adultery"

f. LVH: "killed them"

g. LVH omit "from us"

h. LVH omit "in the same place"

i. "hanging by the hairs of their heads"; L: "through fire"; VH: "in fire"

j. LVH: "and snakes sucking their breasts"

k. L: "I said to the angels"; VH: "he said"

l. LVH omit "Lord"

m. LVH: "who are these"

n. LVH: "who killed their infants (VH: children) and did not give their breasts to other orphans"

o. B omits this phrase. L: "I said"; V: "Ezra said"; H: "the blessed Ezra said"

p. L adds "but he was not having mercy on them"

q. L adds "the angels"

r. LVH omit "Ezra"

s. VH omit "so that we may celebrate the Pasch"

t. VH: "Ezra said"

u. Lf: "God"

v. So LVH. B omits "all"

w. L: "people whom animals were tearing apart." The whole of v. 57a in H: "He saw, in addition, people whom animals were tearing apart." This punishment occurs in *Apoc. Paul* 40.

x. H: "he"

y. L: "the angels said to me"; H: "the angels were saying"

z. LH: "boundary-marks"

aa. V omits vv. 57a-57b

ab. VH: "led him"

ac. L: "fourteen"; VH: "more than fourteen"

ad. VH: "he"

saw lions and little dogs[a] lying around the fiery flames, and righteous people were coming through them and crossing over into paradise.[b]

Ezra sees paradise

[59]And I[c] saw there many people[d] and their dwelling-place was shining bright.[e]
And at all times [59a]there was light there. They had joy and happiness[f] [59b]because
they did many good deeds on earth, and there was no sadness in them.[g] They
enjoyed the heavenly manna,[h] because they had given much charity and[i] many
gifts of alms.[j]

cf. *2 En.* 42:5; *5 Ezra* 2:35-36
Rev 2:17; *2 Bar.* 29:8; *Sib. Or.* 7:149; *b. Hag.* 12b

[59c]But there were (people)[k] who had not done well[l] because they had not the
means to do so. There appeared to them people who were also in distress, [59d]
(and) they said a word of consolation (to them).[m] They are strengthened in light
just like those who had done many good deeds, [59e]and they praise the Lord, who
has[n] loved righteousness.[o]

T. Zeb. 7:3

Ezra completes his tour of the punishments

[59f]I walked further and saw a pit that was a thousand five hundred feet deep and a large quantity of bushels of food[p] were burning there like wax, and sinners were being set on fire there.

And I said, "Lord, who are these?" And the angel said, "These are the ones who received usury and had no compassion for those people."[q]

Lev 25:36-37; Deut 23:19; *Apoc Pet.* 10:1; *Apoc. Paul* 37

---

a. So V. LH: "camels"

b. B omits the second sentence of v. 58.

c. VH: "he"

d. LVH: "many thousands of righteous"

e. VH: "shining very bright"

f. L: "There (there is) light, and joy and happiness and health"; H: "there there is light, joy and health"

g. L: "For those who had done good deeds on earth there was no sadness"; H omits

h. L: "and heavenly manna nourishes them"; H: "and daily they have manna from heaven"

i. LH omit "much charity and"

j. H adds "on earth"

k. LH: "many." H adds: "there"

l. LH omit "well." In these recensions "gifts of alms" (v 59b) is the understood object of "had not done." Probably B has added "well" to make up the sense.

m. L: "they suffered in the face of impoverished circumstances (?). [59d]Being in want (?), because they did not have the means to give (alms), they said a good word"; H omits. The general meaning of B and L is that people who did not have the means to give alms to those in distress gave them what they could give: a word of consolation.

n. "they praise the Lord who has"; these words are not in B, but they occur in L and H (see next note) and should probably be supplied in B.

o. L: "they were stronger in piety than others who did many good deeds. They praise the Lord, who has loved righteousness. For generous almsgiving, which will be around him (?), is acceptable (to him)." H: "But they have a similar rest (to the others) on account of the good will that they had. And so they praise the Lord our God, who has loved righteousness." V omits vv. 59a-59e.

p. The text is somewhat obscure, but probably this is a measure-for-measure punishment. The usurers are punished by means of the large quantity of produce they have amassed by charging interest in kind.

q. This verse (59f) is only in B.

Ezra ascends to heaven and pleads the cause of sinners with God

60 And when they[a] had seen all the judgments of hell that were around them,[b] the angels[c] Michael, Gabriel and Raphael[d] came, and placed me on a cloud of flame and took me up onto one heaven, and not onto the seventh. And hosts[e] of angels came and asked me what the judgments of sinners were.[f] I said, "Bow down and[g] pray[h] for the sinners."

And they brought me up to another heaven, and the prophets of the churches came to me, asking me similarly, and I said, "Bow down and pray for the sinners."[i]

And they brought me up to the seventh heaven, to the back of the Lord.[j] I was not worthy to see anything further.[k, l]

61 And I[m] said, "Lord, spare the sinners."[n]

And he said,[o] "Ezra, I will give to you according to your works.[p] But [the sinners] receive according to their works.[q]"

And I said,[r] 62 "Lord, the animals who feed on grass you have made better than humans,[s] since they do not render you praise,[t] they die and they do not have sin, whereas we are wretched when alive and tortured when dead."[u]

63 And the Lord said to me,[v] "Ezra, I made the man and the woman[w] in my own image, and commanded them not to sin, and they sinned, and for this reason they are in torments. 64 And there are others who asked me but did not carry out my commands, and similarly they are not elect in my kingdom."[x]

Gk. Apoc. Ezra 5:7
Apoc. Sedr. 14:1
Exod 33:23
Gk. Apoc. Ezra 1:10; 2:23
Ps 62:13 (Evv 62:12); Prov 24:12; Matt 16:27; Rom 2:6; 1 Pet 1:17; Rev 20:13
Gk. Apoc. Ezra 1:22; *4 Ezra* 7:65-69; *Ques. Ezra* A5; B3
4 Ezra 7:70-72; *Apoc. Sedr.* 4:4-5
Gk. Apoc. Ezra 5:19 | Matt 7:21

---

a. In B probably an error for "I."
b. L: "and I saw all the judgments of sinners"
c. L omits "the angels"
d. L: "Uriel." Probably all four archangels were in the original text.
e. L: "many thousands"
f. L: "because I had seen the judgments of sinners"
g. L omits "and I said, 'Bow down and'"
h. L: "intercede with the Lord"
i. L omits this sentence.
j. L: "to the entrance of the Lord my God"
k. L: "to see any other heaven." B means that Ezra, like Moses (Exod 33:23), was not permitted to see more of God than God's back (so also v. 100). L has turned the statement into an explanation for the fact that Ezra has seen only one lower heaven and the seventh. In B he sees two lower heavens, but perhaps in the original text he visited all six of the lower heavens and called on their various inhabitants to intercede for the sinners in hell.
l. The whole of v. 60 in VH: "And after he had seen these things, he was taken up to heaven, and a multitude of angels came and were saying to him, 'Pray to the Lord for sinners.' And they placed him in the sight of God."
m. VH: "he"
n. B omits this sentence.
o. L: "and the Lord said to me"; VH: "and the Lord said"
p. LVH omit "I have given to you according to your works"
q. L: "But they receive according to their works"; VH: "they will receive according to their works"
r. L omits this phrase; VH: "and Ezra said"
s. VH: "you have been kinder to the animals that feed on grass than to us"
t. "since they do not render you praise"; LVH: "and they do not render your praises"
u. LVH: "whereas us you torture when alive and when dead"
v. L omits this phrase; VH: "and the Lord said"
w. L: "I formed humans"; VH: "I formed the human being"
x. L: "and others are elect, in rest, through penance and prayer and confession and generos-

65 [And I said,][a] "Lord, what have the righteous done, that they do not receive condemnation?"[b]

Gk. Apoc. Ezra 1:13

66 The Lord said,[c] "The servant who has served his master well receives[d] his freedom; so it is with the righteous in the kingdom of heaven."[e]

Gk. Apoc. Ezra 1:13-14

67 [And I said,][f] "Since you are righteous, since you are almighty, since you are merciful, <spare> (sinners)."[g]

Gk. Apoc. Ezra 1:15; *4 Ezra* 7:132-140; 8:32, 36

68 [And the Lord said,][h] "Ezra, there are <those whose evil deeds will reproach>[i] them on the last day."

Wis 4:20; *Apoc. Pet.* 6:3; *6 Ezra* 16:65

On the day of judgment and Antichrist

Ezek 32:7-8; Joel 2:10 | Matt 24:29

69 "And the sun <will turn to blood, fall to the ground and lie down>,[j] and shadows will come, and the stars will fall onto the earth, and it will burn [to a depth of] seventy cubits."

Gk. Apoc. Ezra 4:39; *Apoc. El. (C)* 5:23; *2 Apoc. Jn.* 14

70 And Ezra said, "In what way has the heaven sinned?"

Gk. Apoc. Ezra 4:40

And the Lord said, "This heaven sees the evil ways of humans.[k]

T. Levi 3:2

71 In a little while Antichrist will be released, with grief and temptation for the people, and he will say that he preaches in my name.

2 Thess 2:6-8; Matt 24:5

72 And one Christian will go out and say that he is contending for the human race and will say, 'If you are the Christ, the Son of God, move this mountain!' And he has the ability to do it but will not be able to recover it.[l]

Matt 17:20; 21:21; 1 Cor 13:2

73 And he will say again, 'Make a storm so that rain comes.' But it did not come.

1 Sam 12:17-18

'From a serpent make a fish, from a stone bread, from sand water.'

Matt 4:3; 7:9-10; *Gk. Apoc. Ezra* 4:27

74 And the one who believes in him will be always hungry and thirsty and will never be satisfied."

John 6:35

75 And Ezra said, "What appearance has this Antichrist?—so that I may make it known to the children of humans?"

Gk. Apoc. Ezra 4:28

---

ity in giving alms"; VH: "and those who are elect go into everlasting rest through confession and penance and generosity in giving alms"

a. L: "and the blessed Ezra asked"; VH: "and Ezra said"

b. This is the text of L. VH: "Lord, what do the righteous do, that they do not appear for judgment?" B omits v.65.

c. VH add "to him"

d. V: "will receive"

e. LVH add "Amen." These recensions end at this point. B omits v.66.

f. B omits this phrase.

g. I have emended *decore* to *parce.* A different emendation, reading *quoque* for *quoniam,* would give the sense: "<How> are you righteous, <how> are you almighty, <how> are you beautifully merciful?"

h. B omits this phrase.

i. I have emended *qui malis operibus corripuit* to *quorum mala opera corripient.*

j. Something may have fallen out of the text at the beginning of this verse, perhaps indicating that the moon, rather than the sun, will turn to blood (Joel 2:31; Acts 2:20; Rev 6:12). In order to make reasonable sense of the text of B, I have emended *in sanguinem eius corruet, convertetur* to *in sanguinem convertetur corruet.*

k. Something like *Gk. Apoc. Ezra* 4:42-43 seems to have fallen out of the text here: "And Ezra said, 'In what way has the earth sinned?' And God said, 'Since the enemy, when he has heard my terrible threat, will hide (in it), and for that reason I will make the earth melt and with it the rebel of the human race.'"

l. This sentence may be corrupt.

Isa 14:12 | Isa 14:15
Gk. Apoc. Ezra 4:29-31

76 And the Lord said, "His forehead is very high, his head is long, he will have joined eyebrows, his eyes will be like Lucifer, his nose will be (like) the abyss, his upper lip will be thinner, he will have no knees.

77 And one Christian will say, 'If you are the Christ, the Son of God, bend your knee and pray.' But he is unable to kneel.

Hos 10:8; Luke 23:30; Rev 6:16

78 But when he comes to the day of judgment, one Christian who has believed in him will go to mount Sinai and say, 'Mountain and rock, I adjure you by the precious name of the Lord to fall on me and cover me.' 79 But the mountain, hearing the name of the Lord, will dissolve and pour over him, and he will remain on the hard ground."

Ezra obtains a weekly respite for sinners in hell

Ps 139:7-10

80 And he (Ezra) said, "Lord, where shall I flee? If I go down to hell, will I find rest there? If I go down to the ocean of the sea, you are there. I cannot flee from you, because my sins hand me over before your face.

4 Ezra 3:4; 4:38 etc.
Gk. Apoc. Ezra 2:4, 26

81 But, I beseech you, sovereign Lord, rise up from your throne,[a] and let us pronounce judgment."

82 And the Lord said, "Who will hear us?"

83 Ezra replied, "Your son hears us."

Ps 2:7; Matt 3:17; John 1:1-11

84 [The Lord said,] "My son, who was born from my voice, how would he not hear us?"

85 And Ezra said, "Let your priest hear us."

86 And the Lord said, "Go and summon my priest. He can pronounce judgment with me."

Gk. Apoc. Ezra 2:7

87 And Ezra said, "As the Lord lives, I judge judgment[b] against you on behalf of all the people who have no place."[c]

4 Ezra 8:52-54

88 [The Lord said,] "You will be chosen along with my prophets."

Gk. Apoc. Ezra 2:10

89 And Ezra said, "Who formed the sinners?"

And the Lord replied, "I (did)."

Gk. Apoc. Ezra 1:11; Exod 32:32; *Gk. Apoc. Mary* 26; John 11:50
Gk Apoc. Ezra 5:10; *Apoc. Paul* 44; *Gk. Apoc. Mary* 29

And Ezra said, "If you created both the sinners and me, it is better for me to perish than for the whole world (to perish)."

90 And the Lord replied, "The sinners from the ninth hour of the Sabbath until the second day of the week[d] are at rest, but on the other days they do penance because of their sins (?)."

91 And Ezra said, "Let it be as you decree."

4 Ezra 14:9

92 And the Lord said, "Ezra, go in peace and walk with my prophets. Where the righteous are, there also you will be."

Ezra resists surrendering his soul in death

Apoc. Sedr. 9:1

93 And the Lord said to Michael, "Go and recall the soul of Ezra my beloved."

Apoc. Sedr. 9:5

94 And Michael said, "Ezra, give (me) your soul."

95 And Ezra replied, "I beseech you that whoever buys my book or has it cop-

---

a. God stands to pronounce judgment (Ps 76:9; Isa 3:13).

b. For the cognate accusative, see note on v. 7.

c. "no place" probably means "no place among the elect."

d. The original text may have read "until the first hour of the second day of the week," as in *Apoc. Paul* Latin redactions III, IV.

ied, for every denarius he gives in payment for my book, may he have as many
golden books by way of profit, as well as consolation and eternal life." *Apoc. Sedr.* 16:3-4

96 And the Spirit came and said, "Ezra, your prayer has been heard as you
asked, and everything has been granted you."

97 The angel came to Ezra and said, "Give (me) your soul." *Apoc. Sedr.* 9:5

98 And Ezra said, "From which place will my soul go out?" *Gk. Apoc. Ezra* 6:4; *Apoc. Sedr.* 10:1

99 And the angel said, "Through your mouth." *Gk. Apoc. Ezra* 6:5

Ezra replied, "My mouth has proclaimed the praise of the Lord. I am not giv- Exod 15:1; Ezra 7:27; Neh 8:6; *Gk. Apoc. Ezra* 6:6
ing back my soul through my mouth."

100 And the angel said, "Through your eye." *Gk. Apoc. Ezra* 6:9

[And Ezra said,] "My eyes have seen the back of the Lord. I am not giving *Gk. Apoc. Ezra* 6:10; Exod 33:23
back my soul through my eyes."

101 [And the angel said,] "Through your nostrils." *Gk. Apoc. Ezra* 6:7

[And Ezra said,] "My nostrils have smelt the fragrant spices of the Lord. I am
not giving back my soul through my nostrils." *Gk. Apoc. Ezra* 6:8

102 [And the angel said,] "Through the crown of your head."

[And Ezra said,] "Aaron, the holy one of the Lord, anointed the crown of my
head with the consecrated oil. My soul will not go out through the crown of my Ezra 7:5
head."

103 [And the angel said,] "Through your hands."

[And Ezra said,] "My hands have held the psaltery of the Lord. My soul will Neh 12:27-36
not go out through my hands."

104 [And the angel said,] "Through your feet." *Gk. Apoc. Ezra* 6:12

[And Ezra said,] "My feet have stood before the Lord. I will not give back my Exod 33:21; *4 Ezra* 5:15; 6:13
soul through my feet." *Gk. Apoc. Ezra* 6:12, 14

105 Michael came to the Lord and reported to him all he had seen.

106 And the Lord said, "I will descend with my angels and bring back his soul." *Gk. Apoc. Ezra* 6:16

107 And the Lord descended and said, "Ezra, give (me) your soul." *Apoc. Sedr.* 9:5

108 And Ezra said, "*Lord, hear my prayer and let my cry come to you.*[a] Lord Ps 102:1
God almighty, I beseech you: The one who [preserves my book and][b] makes
a memorial of my passion[c]—may no sin cast him down but all (his sins) be *Gk. Apoc. Ezra* 7:9-11; *Apoc. Sedr.* 16:3-4
remitted."

109 And the Lord said, "I agree to all that you have asked, but only give me *Gk. Apoc. Ezra* 7:13; *Apoc. Sedr.* 9:5
your soul."

110 And Ezra said, "Lord, I am afraid of death."

And the Lord said, "I was dead and crucified and I rose and now sit at the
right hand and do not fear death." *Gk. Apoc. Ezra* 7:1-2

---

a. In this quotation the Latin corresponds almost exactly to the Vulgate text of Ps 101:2 (English versions 102:1). Nuvolone, "Valeur ajoutée," 187, suggests that the quotation has been taken from the liturgy of the dead.

b. Nuvolone, "Valeur ajoutée," 187, argues that the words *meum servaverit et* have fallen out of the text here.

c. This refers to a liturgical act of remembrance (cf. v. 117). Ezra's "passion" may allude to v. 89, where Ezra's willingness to suffer himself in place of the world becomes the basis for the respite for sinners in hell that God grants him.

Matt 26:38; Mark 14:34

[111]Ezra replied, "If you did not fear death, why did you say, '*My soul is sad to the point of death*'?"[a]

Gk. Apoc. Ezra 7:3; 4 Ezra 7:78

[112]The Lord replied, "You have already said much. Give (me) your soul, for you will not die. The body goes whence it came; the soul returns to the Father who gave it."

Gk. Apoc. Ezra 6:25-26

[113]And Ezra again addressed the angels: "Mourn for me, good angels and archangels, prophets, apostles, martyrs, confessors and virgins, and afterwards bury me."

[114]And again Ezra said, "Lord Jesus Christ, do not abandon me when my soul leaves my body; do not let the angels of Satan[b] encounter me and do not let them do me any harm."

Gk. Apoc. Ezra 6:3, 17, 21

[115]And the angel Michael said, "[Give me] what my Father has entrusted to you."

Deut 32:49-50; 34:1 | John 19:30; *L.A.B.* 40:3; *L.A.E.* 45:3; 50:3 *Gk. Apoc. Ezra* 7:14

[116]The mountain quaked, and [Ezra] gave back the spirit on the ninth day of the month of July.

Conclusion

[117]But whoever celebrates the feast and the memory of the blessed Ezra, the prophet, has a part with my Lord Jesus Christ and with the blessed mother of God Mary and with the blessed Michael your archangel. Amen.

Here ends the reading[c] about the blessed Ezra the prophet.

---

a. In this quotation the Latin corresponds exactly to the Vulgate text of Matt 26:38 and Mark 14:34.

b. Here the angels are evil angels (cf. *Apoc. Paul* 14).

c. Latin *legenda* refers to a text for liturgical reading on a saint's day.

II. Thematic Texts

The Cave of Treasures

A new translation and introduction

by Alexander Toepel

Among Old Testament Pseudepigrapha, the Syriac *Book of the Cave of Treasures*[1] stands, as it were, at the cross-road between older legendary expansions of the Hebrew Bible and those medieval texts which are treating biblical history as merely a prolegomenon to contemporary historical and political events. In this regard *Cave of Treasures* functions very much like a concave mirror: It collects a wealth of older apocryphal lore and transmits it in condensed form to later authors of both oriental and western provenance.[2] Apart from that, under closer scrutiny the text reveals itself to be a carefully structured work with a clear theological purpose and marked Christian character.[3]

Contents

Cave of Treasures essentially takes its name from a cave near paradise in which Adam is said to have deposited a number of items taken from paradise. These are called "treasures" and later on will be carried by the magi to Bethlehem in order to be presented to the newborn Christ. This basic plot serves the author to construct a panoramic view of Christian salvation history spanning from creation to Pentecost. The narration therefore starts in the same way as the first book of the Bible, describing the creation-week in tabular form (*SpTh* 1:1-25), and then passes on to a lengthy account of Adam and Eve's creation and stay in paradise, their temptation, fall, expulsion and settlement at the outskirts of paradise, where the Cave of Treasures is introduced for the first time (*SpTh* 2:1–5:17). On occasion of their first sexual act Adam and Eve deposit within the cave gold, myrrh and incense, that is, those items which were presented to Christ by the magi according to the Gospel narrative (*SpTh* 5:17-18). Later on Adam will be embalmed and buried in the Cave of Treasures (*SpTh* 7:22). The narrative continues with the story of Cain and Abel (*SpTh* 5:19-32). Great emphasis is put upon Seth and his progeny, who are said to have lived apart from the offspring of Cain, and are pictured as a quasi-monastic community dwelling near paradise and praising God in unison with the angels (*SpTh* 6:1–10:16). Cain's descendants, however,

1. Henceforth abbreviated as *SpTh*, standing for Latin *Spelunca Thesaurorum*, i.e., "Cave of Treasures." The *Cave of Treasures* shows a chapter and verse division which does not belong to the original text but was introduced in the German translation of Paul Riessler in 1928 (*Altjüdisches Schrifttum außerhalb der Bibel* [tr. Paul Riessler; Augsburg: Filser, 1928], 942-1013).

2. Cf. the seminal article of Albrecht Götze, "Die Nachwirkung der Schatzhöhle," in *ZS* 2 (1923): 51-94 and *ZS* 3 (1924): 53-71, 153-77.

3. Cf. Renate Knippenberg, "Schatzhöhle," in *Biblisch-historisches Handwörterbuch* (ed. Bo Reicke and Leonhard Rost; 4 vols.; Göttingen: Vandenhoeck & Ruprecht, 1966), 3:1687; Clemens Leonhard, "Observations on the Date of the Syriac *Cave of Treasures*," in *Studies in Language and Literature in Honour of Paul-Eugène Dion* (ed. P. M. Michèle Daviau, John W. Wevers and Michael Weigl; vol. 3 of *The World of the Aramaeans*; JSOTSup 326; Sheffield: Sheffield Academic Press, 2001), 261-62.

lead a life of depravity in the plain where Cain slew his brother Abel, and eventually succeed in luring the Sethites away from paradise into their lodgings, so that in the end only Noah and his family remain in the vicinity of paradise (*SpTh* 11:1–15:8). The deluge is brought about on account of the Cainites' misdeeds, the Sethites being interpreted as the "sons of God" mentioned in Gen 6:1-4 (*SpTh* 15:1-8).

The story continues with Noah and his family being described in accordance with biblical narrative (*SpTh* 16:1–20:12), albeit in considerably expanded form. A central element in this regard is the transference of Adam's body into the ark together with the "treasures" gold, myrrh and incense (*SpTh* 17:6, 21). The cursing of Canaan by Noah (cf. Gen 9:20-27) is treated at some length (*SpTh* 21:1-28), Canaan being presented as renewing the Cainites' evil practices. Then follows a central passage relating Adam's burial "in the centre of the earth," that is, Golgotha, by Noah's son Shem and the installation of Melchizedek as priest at the very spot of Adam's tomb upon Golgotha (*SpTh* 22:1–23:25). The narrative proceeds with a number of genealogical tables, interspersed with anecdotes, which lead over to the story of Abraham (*SpTh* 24:1–27:23).

Abraham's life is likewise presented in accordance with the Bible (*SpTh* 28:1–31:4) and develops into a history of the patriarchs and kings of Israel which in the end merely copies out of the biblical books of Kings (*SpTh* 31:5–41:22). In connection with the fall of Jerusalem the loss of the ancient Jewish writings and their restoration by Ezra the scribe are treated in some depth (*SpTh* 42:1–43:5). There follow more genealogical tables which eventually lead to the birth of Mary, mother of Christ, thus proving her (and Christ's) descent from David (*SpTh* 43:6–44:57).

The remaining chapters (*SpTh* 45:1–54:17) treat the life of Jesus with special emphasis being put upon the magi's visit in Bethlehem and their delivery of the "treasures" gold, myrrh and incense (it is not said where these have been kept since the deluge, but merely that the magi took them from the "entranceways to the east"; cf. *SpTh* 45:12). A central theme is the passion of Christ, which is shown to stand in typological relation to Adam's creation (*SpTh* 48:11-30), and the baptism of Adam's body, which lies buried upon Golgotha underneath the cross of Christ, by the blood of Christ. The account ends with Christ's ascension and the founding of the Church at Pentecost.

Manuscripts and Versions

Besides the Syriac version, which is commonly taken as the original one and upon which the present translation is based, *Cave of Treasures* is extant in two Arabic, an Ethiopian, a Coptic and a Georgian version.[4] The Syriac text today survives in 34 manuscripts, the oldest ones having been written in the sixteenth century C.E. Su-Min Ri's authoritative edition of the Syriac text from 1987 is based upon nineteen of the extant manuscripts.[5] Ri furthermore discovered that there exist two different recensions of the Syriac text, which at times differ considerably but nevertheless must be derived from a single source. Since the Syriac versions correspond to the manuscripts' West-Syrian (i.e., Syrian-Orthodox) or

4. The following two paragraphs are based upon my *Die Adam- und Sethlegenden im Syrischen* Buch der Schatzhöhle (CSCO 618; Subsidia 119; Louvain: Peeters, 2006), 8-24.

5. *La Caverne des Trésors: Les deux recensions syriaques* (ed. Su-Min Ri; CSCO 486; Scriptores Syri 207; Louvain: Peeters, 1987). The first edition of Carl Bezold (*Die Schatzhöhle: Aus dem syrischen Texte dreier unedierter Handschriften* [Leipzig: Hinrichs, 1883] 1; *Die Schatzhöhle: Nach dem syrischen Texte der Handschriften zu Berlin, London und Rom nebst einer arabischen Version nach den Handschriften zu Paris, Rom und Oxford* [Leipzig: Hinrichs, 1888] 2) thereby was rendered obsolete.

East-Syrian (i.e. Nestorian) provenance, they likely owe their existence to separate textual traditions within the two Syriac denominations. While thus none of the recensions can be said to represent the original text of *Cave of Treasures*, there are in both traditions some manuscripts which reveal an effort to merge the different textual trajectories, most notably the West-Syrian manuscript *Harvard College Library, Syr. 39*, written in 1846 C.E., and the East-Syrian *British Museum Add. 25875*, written in 1709 C.E. It has, however, to be kept in mind that these, being mergers of both textual traditions, are in this regard secondary to the older Syriac manuscripts.

The Arabic translation of *Cave of Treasures* is extant in two independent versions, the older one having been translated in Egypt around 750 C.E. and being part of a larger Arabic work attributed to Clement of Rome. Presently 46 manuscripts of this work are known, which have been neither edited nor translated so far. Compared with the Syriac text this Arabic version shows considerable additions and is especially characterized by replacing chapter 6:10-15 of the Syriac text with another, independent unit called *Testament of Adam*. Apart from that there is another and considerably later Arabic version which renders the Syriac text pure and simple and is extant in a single manuscript written in Arabic with Syriac characters.[6] The Ethiopic version is part of a translation of the Arabic work attributed to Clement of Rome, and therefore cannot be earlier than 750; most likely it came into being during the thirteenth to fourteenth century C.E. The Ethiopic *Cave of Treasures* likewise has been neither translated nor edited. Its text shows similar additions as the older Arabic translation. A Coptic version of *Cave of Treasures* survives in two fragments containing chapters 2-6, 44:1-31 and 47:3–48:6 of the Syriac text. They obviously have been part of a—now lost—Coptic homily on Mary Magdalene attributed to Cyril of Jerusalem, which incorporated parts or the whole of *Cave of Treasures*. The surviving Coptic fragments correspond closely to the extant Syriac text. Since there seem to be hints that the translator of the earlier Arabic version knew this homily, it might have been written before 750.[7] Apart from that, the Coptic text shows traces of Greek linguistic influence which would suggest that the Syriac original reached Coptic through a Greek version of *Cave of Treasures*—perhaps as part of a larger homiletical text — of which, however, no other traces have yet been found.[8] Finally there is a Georgian version of the *Cave of Treasures* which corresponds closely to the Syriac text and perhaps was translated in the eighth century C.E.[9] For this version an Arabic original has been proposed on account of the fact that several names in it seem to reflect Arabic rather than Syriac forms and that the Georgian version, too, has *Testament of Adam* instead of *SpTh* 6:10-15.[10] But since the Georgian version corresponds closely to the Syriac text and—except for *Testament of Adam*—does not show the additions of the older Arabic version, this would point to another, more literal Arabic text of *Cave of Treasures* akin to the late Arabic version mentioned above.

---

6. Ms. *Mingana Syr. 32* at John Rylands Library in Manchester; cf. on this Su-Min Ri, *Commentaire de la Caverne des Trésors* (CSCO 581; Subsidia 103; Louvain: Peeters, 2000), 57-61.

7. Cf. Toepel, *Adam- und Sethlegenden*, 16-17.

8. Cf. René-Georges Coquin and Gérard Godron, "Un encomion copte sur Marie-Madeleine attribué à Cyrille de Jérusalem," in *Bulletin de l'Institut français d'archéologie orientale* 90 (1990): 169.

9. The Georgian *Cave of Treasures* has been edited by Ciala Kourcikidzé: *La Caverne des Trésors: Version géorgienne* (CSCO 526; Scriptores Iberici 23; Louvain: Peeters, 1993).

10. Cf. *La Caverne des Trésors: Version géorgienne* (tr. Jean-Pierre Mahé; CSCO 527; Scriptores Iberici 24; Louvain: Peeters, 1992), XXIII-XXVI.

As to the original version, there is little doubt that *Cave of Treasures* was composed in Syriac. Not only does *Cave of Treasures* show itself to be heavily dependent upon Syriac theology, but in *SpTh* 24:11 Syriac is actually said to be the most ancient language of the world. Furthermore, *Cave of Treasures* is first made use of in the *Revelations of Pseudo-Methodius*, a Syriac text written in Eastern Mesopotamia around the middle of the seventh century C.E., all of which presupposes a Syriac environment for *Cave of Treasures*. This, however, does not answer the question of how the two Syriac recensions extant today are related and which one represents the original text. A comparison of the surviving Syriac manuscripts with the older Arabic, Coptic and Georgian translations shows that these versions witness to a text more or less similar to those Syriac versions which try to fuse the characteristics of both Syriac recensions.[11] As these translations (although not the manuscripts) are of much earlier date than the oldest surviving Syriac manuscripts, this would indicate that the original Syriac text of *Cave of Treasures* was indeed more comprehensive than both the West and East Syrian recension and that those Syriac manuscripts which attempt to merge both textual strands come—intentionally or not—close to the original form. In light of this it seems justified to base a translation of *Cave of Treasures* not on either one of the Syriac recensions but upon those manuscripts which merge the two versions and in this regard can be considered as coming close to the Syriac original, even though they have to be considered secondary in terms of Syriac manuscript tradition.

First and foremost among those is the manuscript *British Museum Add. 25875*, which was written in Eastern Iraq in 1709 and is today in the possession of the British Museum in London. This manuscript does not, to be sure, represent the original Syriac text, but in the light of its close textual correspondence to the ancient versions it can be taken as being more true to the original Syriac than any one of the two Syriac recensions. For this reason the present translation is based upon manuscript *British Museum Add. 25875*.[12]

Genre and Structure

As can be seen from the outline of its contents, *Cave of Treasures* in literary genre is most akin to texts which purport to recount biblical history under a preconceived perspective, such as *Liber Antiquitatum Biblicarum*, *Book of Jubilees* or Josephus' *Jewish Antiquities*, and which today are generally labelled as "rewritten Bible." Among these texts *Cave of Treasures* stands out by its marked Christian character, which is manifest not only in the strong parallelism between Adam and Christ, but also by a millennial framework dividing history into seven millennia and putting Christ's second coming at the end of the sixth millennium.[13]

---

11. Cf. Albrecht Götze, *Die Schatzhöhle: Überlieferung und Quellen* (Sitzungsberichte der Heidelberger Akademie der Wissenschaften; Philosophisch-historische Klasse 4 [1922]; Heidelberg: Winter, 1922), 32; Coquin/Godron, in *Bulletin de l'Institut français d'archéologie orientale* 90 (1990): 212; Kourcikidzé (ed.), *Caverne des Trésors*, VI, VIII-XII, XIV.

12. Incidentally this is the same manuscript that was used by Ernest Alfred W. Budge in his first English translation of *Cave of Treasures* (*The Book of the Cave of Treasures* [London: The Religious Tract Society, 1927]).

13. Cf. Witold Witakowski, "The Idea of *Septimana Mundi* and the Millenarian Typology of Creation Week in Syriac Tradition," in *V Symposium Syriacum 1988* (ed. René Lavenant; OCA 236; Rome: Pontificium Institutum Studiorum Orientalium, 1990), 93-109. The *Cave of Treasures* refers to this framework in *SpTh* 10:16; 17:22; 24:27; 34:12; 42:22; 44:53-54 and 48:6-7.

Date and Provenance

In the heading of some Syriac manuscripts—among them *British Museum Add. 25875*, upon which the present translation is based—*Cave of Treasures* is attributed to Ephrem the Syrian (ca. 306-373 C.E.), but this seems out of the question in the light of historical research. Since *Cave of Treasures* is first quoted in the so-called *Revelations of Pseudo-Methodius*, an apocalyptic text written around the middle of the seventh century C.E., and furthermore does not show any knowledge of Muslim conquest, it seems safe to assume that it was written before 630 C.E. The name "Parwezdad" in *SpTh* 45:19 most likely is a reference to the late Sasanian king Xusro II Parvez who ruled from 590 until 628.[14] The *Cave of Treasures* in its present form can therefore safely be dated to this time, most probably to the early years of Xusro Parvez' reign, when there were rumours about this Persian ruler's baptism. The millenarian outlook of *Cave of Treasures* as well as its polemical and apologetic stance against Jews fits in with this, since at the beginning of the seventh century there were widespread hopes for the universal spread of Christianity which was thought to inaugurate Christ's second coming and would imply the conversion of Jews to Christianity.[15]

While the final redaction of *Cave of Treasures* thus can be dated with reasonable safety there has been controversy as to the sources. So far three hypotheses have been put forward, two of which regard the text as a combination of older sources while the third one purports its overall unity. Albrecht Götze as well as Su-Min Ri regard *Cave of Treasures* as an amalgam of older texts, while differing about the scope and content of these sources. Götze claimed that the book in its present form is a reworking of a much older text, which he dated into the fourth century C.E. and claimed to be of Jewish-Christian provenance. This in turn he regarded as a compilation of three independent sources comprising the legends concerning Adam and Seth (*SpTh* chapters 1-7), the genealogy of Mary (chapter 44) and the sections concerning the life of Christ (chapters 45-48), which he thought to be of Gnostic origin. This text would have been edited by a Syriac Nestorian writer who added the biblical material and theological interpolations in chapters 8-43 as well as the book's conclusion in chapters 49-54.[16] Ri, however, identifies chapters 44-54 as the oldest element, which he dates back to the third century C.E. The *Cave of Treasures* in its present form would then be the result of subsequent additions to this basis.[17] Over against this Clemens Leonhard upholds the general unity of *Cave of Treasures*.[18] He convincingly argues that the text is structured by the Adam-Christ typology which serves as an inclusion and to a large extent determines the array of biblical and apocryphal lore within the book. In this context he would even regard chapters 44-54, which stand out by their epistolary form and abrupt mention of an addressee in *SpTh* 45:1, as part of an original composition. While this is disputable it does not detract from Leonhard's overall argumentation since

14. This is based upon unpublished work of Alexander Schilling (*Die Anbetung der Magier und die Taufe der Sasaniden* [unpubl. Ph.D. thesis; Tübingen, 2005], 146-49). Cf. also Toepel, *Adam- und Sethlegenden*, 5 with n. 13.

15. Cf. Schilling, *Anbetung der Magier*, 218-19, 260-61.

16. Cf. the summary of his results in: Götze, *Schatzhöhle: Überlieferung und Quellen*, 90-91.

17. Cf. Su-Min Ri, "La Caverne des Trésors: Problèmes d'analyse littéraire" in *IV Symposium Syriacum 1984* (ed. Han J. W. Drijvers, René Lavenant, Corrie Molenberg and Gerrit Reinink; OCA 224; Rome: Pont. Institutum Studiorum Orientalium, 1987), 183-90.

18. Cf. his "Observations on the Date of the Syriac *Cave of Treasures*," in *Studies in Language and Literature in Honour of Paul-Eugène Dion*, 255-93. I follow Leonhard's argumentation in my *Adam- und Sethlegenden*, 22-23.

the portions in question fit well with the overall outlook of the whole text. Most likely chapters 1-43 form an introduction to an earlier work—perhaps by the same author—and venture on expanding a typological framework and historical perspective contained *in nuce* in *SpTh* 44-54.

The *Cave of Treasures* thus appears to be an original work of the late sixth or early seventh century, proposing a Christian view of salvation history with a strong polemical bias against Judaism.This viewpoint is offensive to modern readers, but the work is a product of its own time and its faults should not prevent us from appreciating it as an important historical source for understanding early Syriac Christianity, flawed as it was. Given its emphasis on Syriac language and theology in combination with traces of a Persian environment it most likely was written within an East Syriac context, that is to say, by a Syriac-speaking Christian living in the Sasanian empire under the rule of Xusro II Parvez.

Literary Context

Accepting the work's originality and Christian provenance, however, is not tantamount to saying that its author did not make use of various sources, some of which might be of Christian heterodox, Jewish or even Iranian provenance. An analysis of chapters 1-7, which are especially rich in apocryphal lore, has shown that there are indeed present a number of motifs which can easily be traced to Jewish sources.[19] One striking example is *SpTh* 15:1-8, where the "sons of God" in Gen 6:1-4 are interpreted as sons of Seth. This motif, which stands in contrast to older legends concerning the fallen angels, has parallels in rabbinical literature.[20] Closer scrutiny, however, reveals that the author of *Cave of Treasures* took this motif from Ephrem the Syrian's *Commentary on Genesis* 6:1-4, and the same holds true for a number of other cases where apparently Jewish traditions in reality reached *Cave of Treasures* through Christian intermediaries. While a thorough examination of the whole book has still to be done,[21] it thus appears reasonably safe to assume that its author most likely had only limited access to rabbinical sources and certainly did not incorporate Jewish writings into *Cave of Treasures*.

The same can be said regarding allegedly Gnostic elements in the book. For instance *SpTh* 4:13 ("she [Eve] saw her own image [in the Snake]") seems to imply an essential kinship between Eve and the Snake, i.e., Satan, which is well known from Gnostic texts such as *Hypostasis of the Archons*. Similar traditions, however, can be found in midrash *Genesis Rabba* §20, Ephrem's hymn *De Ieiunio* 3:4, and the homilies on Genesis 1:247-248 by the East Syrian theologian Narsaï, from where the author of *Cave of Treasures* most likely took over the motif in question. Likewise a number of other purportedly Gnostic elements can safely be dismissed as going back to a common stock of midrashic lore which was used by Gnostics as well as Jews and mainstream Christians.

An important element in *Cave of Treasures*, which serves to establish a direct link between Adam and Christ, is the motif of treasures taken from paradise, and the cave in which these treasures are deposited.[22] While the cave can be traced back to rabbinical

19. Cf. Toepel, *Adam- und Sethlegenden*, 241-48.

20. E.g. in *Midr. Gen. Rab.* 26:5; cf. Toepel, *Adam- und Sethlegenden*, 212 n. 11.

21. Su-Min Ri's *Commentaire de la Caverne des Trésors* (CSCO 581; Subsidia 103; Louvain: Peeters, 2000) presents a wealth of material in this regard.

22. Cf. on this Gerrit Reinink, "Das Problem des Ursprungs des Testamentes Adams," in *Symposium Syriacum 1972* (ed. Ignacio Ortiz de Urbina; Rome: Pontificium Institutum Studiorum Orientalium, 1974), 387-99.

traditions concerning the burial-place of Adam and the patriarchs,[23] the "treasures" correspond to similar items, which Adam is said to have received or taken from paradise in the Greek *Apoc. Mos.* 29:6.[24] Connected with this is the notion of a "Testament of Adam" not in the sense of a written text but as an annunciation of Christ's birth to Adam by God (cf. *SpTh* 5:12-13), which Adam passes on in somewhat cryptic form to his son Seth in *SpTh* 6:13. It is in this context that the theological rationale of *Cave of Treasures*, as well as its anti-Jewish attitude become most visible: Primeval history does not find its fulfilment in the establishment of priestly order at Sinai, as the *Book of Jubilees* holds, nor does it serve as an introduction for the history of the Jews as a nation, as is Josephus' aim in his *Jewish Antiquities*. Instead the Christian author takes pains to show that Adam's expulsion from paradise is resolved only by Christ. The whole historical display of *Cave of Treasures* is subjected to this aim, which explains the book's emphasis upon apocryphal lore concerning Adam's burial-place in Jerusalem, the transmission of the treasures from paradise to Bethlehem and the genealogical tables, which are meant to prove Christ's linear descent from Adam and the fulfilment of God's promise mentioned in chapter 5:12-13. A key-passage in this regard is *SpTh* 5:17-18 which follows immediately upon the announcement of Christ's birth and states that Adam deposited the "treasures" within the cave on the occasion of the consummation of his marriage with Eve, thus linking the token of salvation with the beginning of its fulfillment in the creation of progeny from which ultimately Christ will be born. This emphasis upon Christ as the restorer of paradise completely supersedes the giving of Torah at Sinai and the installation of temple-service, which figure so prominently in *Jubilees* and rabbinical literature: Moses receives only little attention in *Cave of Treasures*; the giving of the law at Sinai is not mentioned at all.

Besides this, *Cave of Treasures* makes ample use of the classical writers of Syriac theology, especially Ephrem and Aphrahat. The close, at times verbal, correspondences with these authors have been taken as proof of an extremely early date, which would render *Cave of Treasures* as the source, rather than recipient, of these elements. But in this case, too, an early date of the book or portions of it is ruled out by the way in which the said traditions are handled. The author quotes pseudo-Ephremical texts as well as the original ones, misrepresents Ephrem's figurative speech in a literal way and furthermore does not show any interest in the ascetical elements which are so dominant in early Syriac theology.[25]

As has been noted in connection with the literary genre of *Cave of Treasures*, there is a marked—albeit formal—influence of older Jewish rewritten Bible-texts like *Book of Jubilees* and Josephus' *Jewish Antiquities*. These texts, however, have been used more in the sense of a model or blue-print; the book's actual content to a large degree seems to have been derived from earlier Greek and Syrian theologians in combination with thoroughly Christian apocrypha such as the *Pseudo-Clementine Homilies*, the *Protevangelium Jacobi* and the *Gospel according to Bartholomew*.[26] In this regard the regrettable anti-Jewish stance of the book deserves further attention. It is present throughout the book, at times surfacing in invectives against "older" or "Jewish" authors, whose books *Cave of Treasures* seeks to replace to the extent of doubting the authenticity of the Hebrew Bible (cf. *SpTh*

23. Cf. *Midr. Gen. Rab.* 58.4; *Pirqe R. El.* 20.

24. This in turn is part of a rich apocryphal tradition concerning the reversal of Adam and Eve's expulsion from paradise; cf. generally Esther C. Quinn, *The Quest of Seth for the Oil of Life* (2nd ed.; Chicago: University of Chicago, 1962).

25. Cf. Toepel, *Adam- und Sethlegenden*, 32, 113-14, 122 with n. 52.

26. Cf. Toepel, *Adam- und Sethlegenden*, 241-48.

42:6-7). This tendency is especially violent in the portions on Christ's crucifixion where the author is concerned with showing that the Jews have forfeited the divine covenant (which has presumably gone over to the Christians), a motif common in anti-Jewish polemics from Justin Martyr's *Dialogue with Trypho* onwards.

The *Cave of Treasures* thus seems to be an attempt to replace older rewritten Bible-texts of Jewish provenance by a Christian work, and its reception-history shows that the book was perceived as such.[27] The earliest work depending upon *Cave of Treasures* is the apocalyptic *Revelations of Pseudo-Methodius* which was written in Eastern Iraq in the middle of the seventh century C.E. under the impact of the Muslim conquest and makes ample use of the legendary traditions preserved in *Cave of Treasures*. Since the *Revelations* was enormously popular not only in Western Europe but likewise in Byzantium, Syria, Armenia and the Slavic countries, *Cave of Treasures* can in this regard be seen as an important precursor of medieval popular Bibles which in turn were instrumental in spreading apocryphal lore to later authors like Dante Alighieri and John Milton.[28]Apart from this truly transcultural, albeit indirect, reception of *Cave of Treasures*, the book exerted a lesser but not altogether negligible influence upon the literary production of Eastern Christianity. Traces of it can be seen in the Ethiopic tradition, where it gave rise to a legendary life of Adam, and in Syriac historiography, where it makes its appearance in the chronicles of Pseudo-Dionysius of Tell-Mahre (ca. 775 C.E.), Michael the Syrian (end of twelfth century C.E.) and Barhebraeus (thirteenth century C.E.), as well as in Solomon of Basra's *Book of the Bee* (ca. 1222 C.E.).[29] Traces of *Cave of Treasures* are also to be found in Arabic tradition: Eutychius of Alexandria (876-940 C.E.), Melchite (i.e., Greek-Orthodox) patriarch of Alexandria makes ample use of *Cave of Treasures* in his Arabic world-history, as did the Muslim polygraphs al-Jaqubi (late ninth century C.E.) and Tabari (ninth/tenth century C.E.).[30] Last but not least the Georgian version of *Cave of Treasures* is among the sources of Leont'i Mroveli's *Mokcevay Kartlisay* ("Conversion of the Georgian"; eighth century C.E.) and is furthermore prefixed in at least one manuscript to the Georgian world-chronicle *Kartlis Cxovrebay*, where it serves as an introduction to the history of the Georgian nation.[31] All these authors purport to write history *a principio mundi* and invariably use *Cave of Treasures* as a source covering the time between creation and the beginning of their own communities, which highlights once more the book's position at a pivotal point, transforming biblical lore into primeval history.

Bibliography

EDITIONS AND TRANSLATIONS

Budge, Ernest Alfred W. *The Book of the Cave of Treasures*. London: The Religious Tract Society, 1927.

27. Cf. Götze's investigation mentioned above in n. 2 and Rudolf Strothmann's review of Götze's *Schatzhöhle: Überlieferung und Quellen* in *Islam* 13 (1923): 304-7 on *Cave of Treasures* within Islamic tradition.

28. Cf. Götze, in *ZS* 2 (1923): 55-56.

29. Cf. Götze, in *ZS* 2 (1923): 56-94; Götze, in *ZS* 3 (1924): 53-60, 175-77.

30. Cf. Götze, in *ZS* 3 (1924): 60-71, 153-75.

31. Cf. Kourcikidzé (ed.), *Caverne des Trésors* VI; Michael Tarchnišvili and Julius Assfalg, *Geschichte der kirchlichen georgischen Literatur* (Studi e testi 185; Vatican City: Biblioteca Apostolica Vaticana, 1955), 91-94.

Coquin, René-Georges and Gérard Godron. "Un encomion copte sur Marie-Madeleine attribué à Cyrille de Jérusalem." *BIFAO* 90 (1990): 169-212.

Kourcikidzé, Ciala. *La Caverne des Trésors: Version géorgienne.* CSCO 526. Scriptores Iberici 23. Louvain: Peeters, 1993.

Ri, Su-Min. *La Caverne des Trésors: Les deux recensions syriaques.* CSCO 486. Scriptores Syri 207. Louvain: Peeters, 1987.

__________. *La Caverne des Trésors: Les deux recensions syriaques.* CSCO 487. Scriptores Syri 208. Louvain: Peeters, 1987.

Riessler, Paul. *Altjüdisches Schrifttum außerhalb der Bibel,* pages 942-1013. Augsburg: Filser, 1928.

STUDIES

Götze, Albrecht. "Die Nachwirkung der Schatzhöhle." *ZS* 2 (1923): 51-94 and *ZS* 3 (1924): 53-71, 153-77.

__________. *Die Schatzhöhle: Überlieferung und Quellen.* Sitzungsberichte der Heidelberger Akademie der Wissenschaften; Philosophisch-historische Klasse 4. Heidelberg: Winter 1922.

Leonhard, Clemens. "Observations on the Date of the Syriac *Cave of Treasures.*" Pages 261-62 in *Studies in Language and Literature in Honour of Paul-Eugène Dion.* Ed. P. M. Michèle Daviau, John W. Wevers and Michael Weigl. Vol. 3 of *The World of the Aramaeans.* JSOTSup 326. Sheffield: Sheffield Academic Press, 2001.

Ri, Su-Min. "La Caverne des Trésors: Problèmes d'analyse littéraire." Pages 183-90 in *IV Symposium Syriacum 1984.* Ed. Han J. W. Drijvers, René Lavenant, Corrie Molenberg and Gerrit Reinink. OCA 224. Rome: Pontificium Institutum Studiorum Orientalium, 1987.

__________. *Commentaire de la Caverne de Trésors.* CSCO 581. Subsidia 103. Louvain: Peeters, 2000.

Toepel, Alexander. *Die Adam- und Sethlegenden im Syrischen* Buch der Schatzhöhle. CSCO 618. Subsidia 119. Louvain: Peeters, 2006. (Extensive bibliography)

Witakowski, Witold. "The Idea of *Septimana Mundi* and the Millenarian Typology of Creation Week in Syriac Tradition." Pages 93-109 in *V Symposium Syriacum 1988.* Ed. René Lavenant. OCA 236. Rome: Pontificium Institutum Studiorum Orientalium, 1990.

The Cave of Treasures

1 [1]With the help of our Lord Jesus Christ we begin to write the book concerning
the sequence of generations, that is, "The Cave of Treasures," which has been
authored by the holy Mar Ephrem. [2]Lord, help me in your mercy. Amen.

The seven days of creation

[3]In the beginning, on the first day, that is, the holy Sunday, chief and firstborn of
Gen 1:1 all days, the Lord made heaven and earth, water, air, fire and the invisible pow-
Col 1:16 ers, that is, the angels, archangels, *thrones, authorities, powers, rulers*, cherubs
and seraphs, and all the ranks and spiritual armies, darkness, light, nights and
days, winds and storms—all those were created on the first day. [4]On this Sunday
Gen 1:2 the Holy Spirit, one of the persons of the Trinity, was hovering over the waters
[5]and through this hovering upon the surface of the waters they were blessed
and became fertile. [6]The very essence of the waters was heated and inflamed,
and the leaven of creation was united within them: [7]Just as a bird is warming
its offspring by the overshadowing hovering of its wings, and through the fiery
heat therefrom the young are fashioned within the eggs, likewise the Spirit, the
Paraclete, too, by hovering over the waters united the spiritual leaven within
them through the working of the Holy Spirit.

Gen 1:6-8 [8]On the second day God created the lower heaven and called it "firmament"
in order to show that it does not have the nature of the upper heaven and is different in appearance from the one above it, for the upper heaven consists of fire
[9]and the second one of light. Because the lower, second one has the liquid nature
of water it is called "firmament." [10]On the second day God made a separation
Gen 1:7 between the waters, that is, between the upper and the lower waters. [11]The ascent of those waters above the heavens took place on the second day: They went
up like the clouds' moist assembly and behold! they take their stand above the
firmament and neither spill nor swerve to any side.

[12]On the third day God commanded those waters underneath the firmament
Gen 1:9 to gather at one place so that the dry land might show itself. [13]When the veil
of the waters was withdrawn from the face of the earth it showed itself to be
unstable and not firmly founded, that is, wet and of soft nature. [14]The waters
gathered within the seas underneath the earth, inside of it, and upon it. [15]Within
the earth God made passages from below, pipes and drains as passageways for
the waters and winds which ascend from inside the earth through those pipes
and passages, (that is,) heat and cold for the earth's benefit. [16]For underneath
the earth is made like a sponge, because it rests upon the waters. [17]On this third

day God also commanded the earth to bring forth herbs from below, [18]and it
conceived trees, seeds, plants and fruits within it. Gen 1:11-12
[19]On the fourth day God made the sun, moon and stars. [20]The sun's heat Gen 1:14-18
spread at once upon the face of the earth, and its softness hardened, because the
humidity and wet were removed. [21]When the dust of the earth burned it brought
forth all kinds of trees, plants, seeds and fruits which had been conceived within
it on the third day.
[22]On the fifth day God commanded the waters and they brought forth various species of manifold appearances which move, swarm and crawl in the waters; whales, Leviathan and Behemoth of frightful appearance, and birds of the
air and water. [23]On this day God made out of earth all the animals, creatures, Gen 1:20-21
and reptiles which crawl upon the earth.
[24]On the sixth day, that is, Friday, God made Adam from dust and Eve from
his side. Gen 2:7, 21-22
[25]On the seventh day God rested from his work and called it Sabbath. Gen 2:2-3

The creation of Adam

2 [1]Adam's making, building and foundation was thus: [2]On the sixth day, that
is, Friday of the first week, when silence lay upon all the ranks of powers, God
spoke: [3]"*Let us make man in our image, according to our likeness,*" thus indicating Gen 1:26
the blessed persons (of the Trinity). [4]When the angels heard this heavenly voice
they said in fear and trembling to each other: [5]"A great miracle is being shown to
us today, the image of our God and maker." [6]They beheld the right hand of God
stretching forth and spreading out upon the whole world, and all creatures were
gathered within the palm of his hand. [7]Then they beheld him taking from the Isa 40:12
whole earth one grain of dust, from the whole essence of the waters one drop of
water, from the whole air above one breeze of wind and from the whole nature
of fire a little flame of heat. [8]The angels beheld these four elements being put
together within the palm of his right hand, that is, cold and heat, moisture and
dryness, [9]and God formed Adam. [10]For what reason did God make him from Gen 2:7
these four elements if not in order that everything within the world might thus
serve him? [11]He took one grain of earth so that all the beings consisting of dust
might be subservient unto him; one drop of water so that everything within the
seas and rivers might be his; one whiff of air so that all the species of birds in the
air might belong to him; one flame of fire so that all the fiery beings and powers
might be for his help. [12]God formed Adam with his holy hand in his image according to his likeness. [13]When the angels beheld his glorious appearance they Gen 2:7; 1:26
were agitated from the first sight [14]because they saw the appearance of his face
flashing with glorious beauty like the fiery orb, the light of his eyes like the sun,
and the figure of his body like shining crystal. [15]When he stretched himself and
rose in the middle of the earth [16]he put his feet on that place where the cross
of our savior would be erected, because Adam was created in Jerusalem. [17]At
that place he wore the gown of kingship, and the crown of glory was put upon
his head; [18]there he was made king, priest and prophet, and there God made
him sit upon the throne of his glory. [19]There God also put all creatures under
his dominion: [20]All the wild animals, cattle and birds gathered before Adam, Gen 1:28
and while they passed by he named them and they bowed their heads. [21]All be- Gen 2:20

ings worshipped him and submitted themselves before him. 22 Then the angels heard God's voice speaking to him: 23 "Adam, behold, I made you king, priest and prophet, lord, chief and leader, so that everything made and created may be subservient unto you and belong to you. 24 To you I give dominion over every created thing." 25 When the angels heard this heavenly voice[a] they all bent their knees and worshipped him.

The fall of Satan

3 1 When the chief of that lowest rank saw what greatness had been bestowed
upon Adam he envied him from this day on. He did not want to worship him
and spoke to his army: 2 "Let us not worship and glorify him together with the
angels. It is meet that he worships me who am fire and spirit and not that I wor-
L.A.E. 12:1-16:1; *Gosp.* ship dust formed from dirt." 3 As soon as the rebel conceived this and was dis-
Bart. 4:54-56; Qur'an, obedient as regards the wish of his soul and volition he separated himself from
Sura 7:11-13; 38:72-78 God. 4 He was cast down and fell, he and his whole rank, on Friday, the sixth day,
and their fall from heaven lasted for three hours. 5 The garments of their glory
were taken from them 6 and he was called "Satan" because he set himself apart,[b]
and "Sheda" because his glory had been shed[c] and he had forfeited the garment
of his glory. 7 Behold, since that day until now they are naked and bare and of
despicable look, he and all his hosts.

The formation of Eve

8 When Satan had been cast down from heaven Adam was lifted up and ascended
to paradise in a fiery chariot. Adam went up to paradise with praises, the angels
Isa 6:2-3 glorifying him while the seraphs sang the Trisagion[d] before him and blessed
him. 9 Immediately after he had gone up he was commanded not to eat from
Gen 2:17 the tree. 10 His ascent to paradise took place in the third hour of Friday. 11 Then
Gen 2:21 (God) brought a sleep upon him and he slept. 12 He took one of his shorter ribs
Gen 2:21-22 from his right side and made Eve out of it. 13 When Adam woke up and saw Eve
he was exceedingly glad about her. 14 Adam and Eve stayed in paradise wearing
the garments of glory and shining in splendour for three hours.

15 This paradise is in the heights, it is thirty cubits higher than all the mountains and hills according to the measure of the spirit of air, and it surrounds
Ephrem, *De parad.* the whole earth. 16 Now the prophet Moses speaks thus: "God planted paradise
1:8; 2:6 within Eden and put Adam there." 17 But Eden in truth is the holy Church, and
Gen 2:8 the Church is God's mercy which he is going to bestow upon all humankind.
18 Because in his foreknowledge God knew what Satan planned against Adam,
out of his bottomless mercy he prepared (the Church) in advance for him as the
blessed David sings: "*Lord, you are a place of rest for us from generation to gen-*
Ps 90:1 *eration,*" that is, you make us rest in your mercy. 19 And praying to God for the
salvation of humankind, he says: "Remember your Church which you ransomed
Ps 74:2 from of old," 20 that is, your mercy which you are going to bestow upon our weak

a. Syr. *bat qala* "daughter of a voice."

b. Syr. *seta*. Cf. Justin, *Dial. cum Tryph.* 103:5.

c. Syr. *sheda.*

d. The "Trisagion" ("triple-holy") refers to the song sung by the seraphim in Isa 6:3, which begins "Holy, holy, holy ..."

race. [21]Eden is the holy Church, and paradise within it (signifies) the place of rest and inheritance of life which God prepared for all the holy ones.

The fall of Adam and Eve

4 [1]Because Adam was priest, king and prophet, God brought him into paradise in order to minister in Eden like a priest of the holy Church as testifies the
blessed Moses concerning him: "*That he may tend it,*" that is, for God through (Gen 2:15)
priestly ministry in glory, "*and keep it,*" that is, the commandment which had (Gen 2:15)
been entrusted to him by God's mercy. [2]Then God planted the tree of life in the (*Tg. Ps. J.* Gen 2:15; *Midr. Gen. Rab.* 16.5-6; *Pirqe R. El.* 12)
middle of paradise. [3]It is a true word heralding our salvation that this tree of life
in the middle of paradise signifies our saviour's cross, and this is the one which (Gen 2:8-9)
has been fastened in the middle of the earth.

[4]When Satan saw Adam and Eve rejoicing in paradise the rebel was inflamed
and tormented by envy. [5]He went and took residence within the snake, lifted it (*Ap. Mos.* 16:4)
up and made it fly through the air to the outer fringes of paradise. [6]For what
reason did he enter the snake to hide himself? [7]Because he knew that his appearance was hideous, and if Eve had seen his shape she would have fled from
him at once. [8]Just as when someone teaching Greek to a bird produces a large mirror and, putting it between him and it, starts talking to it, the bird who hears his voice will at once turn around, behold its own image in that mirror and immediately rejoice, thinking it is its companion talking to him, [10]will thus quietly lend its ear, [11]listen to those words that are being spoken to it and eagerly learn
to talk, [12]likewise Satan entered the snake, took residence within it, waited for (Ephrem, *De fide* 31:6; Gregory Nazianzen, *Carm. mor.* 2:620-626)
the moment when he saw her alone and called her by her name. [13]When she
turned toward him she saw her own image.[a] He spoke to her and deceived her with his crafty words, because women's nature is soft, and she believed him.
[14]As soon as she heard from him about the tree and its fruits, she went in a rush because he had flattered and persuaded her, plucked from the tree the fruit of disobedience concerning which (God) had given a strict commandment of certain death, and ate. [15]At once she was stripped bare, [16]and perceiving the shame of her nakedness she ran away naked, hid herself in another tree, and covered her nakedness with the foliage of that tree. [17]Then she called Adam and he came toward her. She gave him that fruit from which she had eaten, [18]he also ate from it and was stripped bare, too. [19]So they made for themselves loincloths out of
fig-leaves, [20]wearing these loincloths of disgrace for three hours. [21]In the middle (Gen 3:7)
of the day (Adam) received judgment. [22]God made for them garments of skin (Gen 3:21)
taken from the trees, that is, trees' bark, because the trees of paradise have soft bark, softer than fine linen and the tunics of kings, [23]weak (clothing) spread over the hurting body.

The expulsion from Eden

5 [1]During three hours they were going up to paradise, three hours they enjoyed its blessings, three hours they remained being stripped naked, and in the ninth hour their descent from paradise took place. [2]When they left it in grief God spoke with Adam, comforted him and told him: [3]"Do not grieve, Adam, because

a. Word-play on Aram. *hiwya* "snake" and *Hawwah* "Eve"; cf. *Midr. Gen. Rab.* 20.11.

I will return your inheritance to you. Behold, I love you so much [4]that I cursed
the whole earth on your account and excepted you from the curse. [5]I closed the
Tg. Ps. J. Gen 3:14; snake's legs up inside its belly and gave it the dust of the earth for food, and I
Ant. 1:50; *Ap. Mos.* subdued Eve under the yoke of servitude. [6]Leave now, because you transgressed
26:2; *Midr. Gen. Rab.* my commandments, but do not grieve, [7]for after the completion of the time
20.5; *Pirqe R. El.* 14 declared for you to spend in exile upon the cursed earth I shall send my son.
Gen 3:14, 17 [8]He will descend for your salvation, dwell within a virgin and put on a body.
[9]Through him your salvation and return will be wrought. [10]But command your
children and tell them to embalm your body after your death with myrrh, cassia
and stacte, and put you down within that cave in which I will let you dwell today
until the time when their descent from the environs of paradise to that outer
world will take place. [11]Whoever will be left in those days shall take your body,
carry it and put it down where I am going to show him, in the middle of the
earth, [12]because there salvation will be wrought for you and all your offspring."
[13]Then God revealed to Adam all that the Son was going to suffer on his behalf.

[14]When Adam and Eve went down to the mountain of paradise on the stair-
case of wind, they found a cave upon the mountain's peak, [16]went in and hid
themselves within it. [17]Since Adam and Eve were virginal and Adam wished
to know his wife Eve, he brought gold, myrrh and incense from the fringes of
paradise, and by placing them inside the cave he blessed and sanctified it so that
it might be a house of prayer for him and his children, calling it "Cave of Treasures." [18]Then Adam and Eve descended from the holy mountain to its fringes
below and there Adam knew his wife Eve. [19]She conceived and gave birth to
Gen 4:1 Cain and together with him to his sister Levudah. [20]Then she conceived again
Gen 4:2 | *b. Yebam.* 62a; *Midr. Gen. Rab.* 22.7; *Pirqe R. El.* 21 and gave birth to Abel and Kalimath, his sister within the same womb.

The transgressions of Cain

[21]When the children had grown up, Adam spoke to Eve: "Cain shall marry Kalimath who has been born together with Abel, and Abel marry Levudah who
has been born together with Cain." [22]But Cain told his mother Eve: "I want to
take my sister as wife, and Abel may marry his sister," for Levudah was beautiful.
[23]When Adam heard these words, he was exceedingly angry and spoke: [24]"It is a
transgression of the commandment that you want to marry your sister who has
been born with you. [25]Now take from the fruits of the trees and the young of the
Gen 4:3-4 flock, go up to the top of this holy mountain and enter the Cave of Treasures,
make your offerings there, pray before God [26]and then unite with your wives."

[27]When the first priest Adam ascended to the mountain-top together with
his sons Cain and Abel it happened that Satan entered Cain so that he would slay
his brother for Levudah's sake, and (also) on account of his offering being re-
Gen 4:4-5 jected and not accepted in front of God while Abel's offering was accepted. [28]So
Cain's envy against his brother grew once more, [29]and when they went down to
Gen 4:8 the plain Cain rose against his brother Abel and slew him with a piece of rock.
[30]At once he received the judgment of death: [31]He became trembling and restless
Gen 4:12 all the days of his life and God drove him away into exile towards the forest of
Nod. [32]Then he married his sister and lived there with her.

From the birth of Seth to the death of Adam

6 [1]Adam and Eve mourned Abel for 100 years. [2]Then Adam knew Eve again
and she gave birth to Seth, a handsome man and a giant, perfect like Adam. Gen 4:25, 5:3
[3]He became father of the giants before the deluge. [4]Unto Seth was born Enosh,
[5]Enosh begat Kenan and Kenan begat Mahalalel. These are the patriarchs who Gen 5:6-12
were born during Adam's lifetime. [6]When Adam had lived for 930 years, that is, Gen 5:5
until the thirty-fifth year of Mahalalel, [7]the day of his death arrived. [8]His son
Seth, Enosh, Kenan and Mahalalel gathered and came to him, were blessed by
him, and he prayed over them. [9]Then he commanded his son Seth and told him:
"Give heed, my son Seth, to what I command you today, [10]and command and
tell it to Enosh on the day of your death, (likewise) Enosh to Kenan, and Kenan
to Mahalalel, so that it may be a tradition through all your generations. [11]When
I die embalm me with myrrh, cassia and stacte and put my body down in the
Cave of Treasures. [12]Whoever will be left of all your offspring in that time when
your descent from this place in the environs of paradise will take place shall take
my body, carry it and deposit it in the middle of the earth. [13]For it is there that
salvation will be wrought for me and all my offspring. [14]And you, my son Seth,
be a leader for your children with you, guide them in purity and saintliness with
all fear of God, and separate your generations from the generations of Cain the
murderer." [15]When it was heard that Adam would die, the progeny of his son
Seth gathered and came to him: Enosh, Kenan, Mahalalel, their wives, sons and
daughters, [16]and he blessed them and prayed for them. [17]In the 930th year since
creation Adam's departure from this world took place, on the fourteenth, the day
of the full moon of the month Nisan, on the ninth hour of Friday. [18]In the same
hour in which the Son of man gave his soul back to the Father upon the cross
our father Adam gave his soul back to his maker and departed from this world.

The burial of Adam and the separation of the Sethites from the Cainites

[19]After Adam had died his son Seth embalmed him with myrrh, cassia and
stacte, [20]and because he was the first dead upon the earth his mourning was
very great. [20]They mourned his death for 140 days; then they brought his body to
the mountain-top and buried it in the Cave of Treasures. [22]After Adam's burial
the families and generations of Seth's children separated themselves from the
children of Cain the murderer. [23]At that time Seth took his first-born Enosh,
Kenan, Mahalalel, their wives and children, led them and made them ascend
the glorious mountain where Adam lay buried. [24]But Cain and all his offspring
remained in the plain below where Cain had slain Abel.

The Sons of God on the holy mountain

7 [1]Seth became leader of his children with him and guided them in purity and
saintliness. [2]Because of their purity they received a name which is greater than
every other name, for they were called "Sons of God," they themselves, their
wives and their children. [3]Thus they stayed upon the mountain in all purity,
saintliness and fear of God. [4]They ascended instead of Sheda's rank, which had
fallen from heaven, in order to glorify and praise in the environs of paradise.
[5]They were in peace, rest and quietness and did not have to care about any other

work or labour than to praise and glorify God together with the angels because they continuously heard the voice of the angels who glorify in paradise, [6]those being not higher above them than only thirty cubits according to the measure of the spirit. [7]There was no affliction or labour for them, neither sowing nor reaping; rather they fed on those various and pleasant fruits of the glorious trees which are scented by that sweet scent and perfume of the wind coming down from paradise. [8]They were holy and saintly, their wives and sons were pure and their daughters chaste and undefiled. [9-10a] Among their wives, sons, and daughters there was no impure desire or lewdness, [11]nor were there heard among them curses or lies, for their whole oath consisted in "by the blood of Abel." [12]They themselves, their wives and children went out early, ascended to the mountaintop and prayed there in front of God. [13-14b] Then they received blessings from the body of their father Adam and lifted up their eyes towards paradise.

From the death of Seth to the death of Cain

Gen 5:8 [15]Seth lived 913 years;[c] then he became ill unto death. [16]Then his son Enosh,
Kenan, Mahalalel, Jared and Enoch gathered together with their wives and children. [17]When they had been blessed by him and he had prayed for them, he commanded them, made them take an oath and spoke: [18]"I adjure you by Abel's innocent blood that none of you go down from this holy mountain to the children of Cain the murderer, for you know what enmity there is between us and them since the day he slew Abel." [19]Then he blessed his son Enosh and commanded him concerning Adam's body. [20]He made him the leader of his children with him so that he might lead them in purity and saintliness, and minister diligently before Adam's body.

Gen 5:8 [21]Seth died (at the age of) 913 years, on the twenty-seventh of the blessed
month Ab, in the third hour, in the twentieth year of Enoch. [22]His first-born son Enosh embalmed the body of his father Seth with myrrh, cassia and stacte, and buried him in the Cave of Treasures in front of his father Adam. [23]Then they mourned him for forty days.

8 [1]Afterwards Enosh rose to minister in front of God in the Cave of Treasures. He was leader of his children with him and observed all the commandments that his father Seth had given in purity and saintliness by exhorting everyone to remain faithful in prayer. [2]In the days of Enosh, in his 920th year, Lamech the
Midr. Tanḥ. Ber. 11 blind killed the murderer Cain in the forest of Nod. [3]Thus he killed him: Lamech
would lean upon his little son, who guided his arm toward the game as he saw it. [4]He heard the voice of Cain roaming within the forest, because Cain could find neither rest nor repose at any place. [5]Now Lamech thought him to be an animal

a. All the MSS of the Western and some of the Eastern versions insert an additional sentence here: *"There was among them neither envy, hate and strife nor enmity."*

b. All the MSS of the Western and some of the Eastern versions insert an additional sentence here: *"Thus they did all the days of their lives."*

c. The chronological information given for the antediluvian patriarchs differs from that given in the Masoretic and Peshitta (Syriac) texts of Genesis. It loosely corresponds to the data found in the Septuagint which in 17:22 (see below) is explicitly mentioned as source of the chronology.

that had been stirred up within the forest. [6]He lifted up his arm, aimed, drew
his bow and shot in that direction. [7]He hit Cain between the eyes so that he fell
down and died. [8]Lamech thought that he had hit some game and told the lad:
"Go, see the game we have hit." [9]When he had gone and seen, the lad who used
to guide him spoke: "Alas, sir, you have killed Cain." [10]At this he raised his hands
so as to clap them, hit the lad and killed him.

[11]When Enosh had lived for 905 years he fell ill unto death. [12]Then all the Gen 5:11
patriarchs gathered and came unto him: his first-born son Kenan, Mahalalel,
Jared, Enoch and Methuselah, together with their wives and children. [13]When
they had been blessed by him and he had prayed for them he commanded them
and said: "I adjure you by the innocent blood of Abel that nobody of you go
down from this mountain to the plain into the camp of the children of Cain the
murderer and that you do not mingle with them. [14]Beware of this; you know
what enmity there is between us and them since the day he slew Abel." [15]Then
he blessed his son Kenan and commanded him concerning Adam's body that
he minister in front of it all the days of his life and lead his children with him in
purity and saintliness. [16]Then Enosh died at the age of 905 years, on the third of Gen 5:11
Tishri I, a Sabbath, in Methuselah's fifty-third year of life. [17]His first-born Kenan
embalmed and buried him in the Cave of Treasures in front of Adam and his
father Seth. [18]Then they mourned him for forty days.

From Kenan to Mahalalel

9 [1]After this Kenan rose to minister in the Cave of Treasures in front of God.
[2]He was an honourable and pure man, led his children with him in all fear of
God, and kept all the commandments of his father Enosh. [3]When Kenan had
lived for 920 years and fallen ill unto death, [4]all the patriarchs gathered and Gen 5:14
came unto him: his son Mahalalel, Jared, Enoch, Methuselah and Lamech together with their wives and children. [5]After they had been blessed by him, and
he had prayed for them he commanded and told them: "I adjure you by Abel's
innocent blood that none of you go down from this mountain toward the camp
of the children of Cain the murderer. [6]All of you know what enmity there is
between us and them since the day he slew Abel." [7]Then he blessed his son Mahalalel, reminded and commanded him concerning Adam's body, and spoke to
him: "Take heed, my son Mahalalel, that you minister in purity and saintliness in
front of God in the Cave of Treasures. Do not leave the body of our father Adam
all the days of your life. Be the leader of your children with you and lead them
in purity and saintliness." [9]Then Kenan died at the age of 920 years, on the thir- Gen 5:14
teenth of Haziran, at Friday noon, in Lamech the father of Noah's sixty-fifth year
of life. [10]His son Mahalalel embalmed and buried him in the Cave of Treasures.

10 [1]Afterwards Mahalalel rose in order to minister in front of God instead of
his father Kenan. [2]He was steadfast in prayer day and night and exhorted his
children with him once more to observe saintliness and purity and to remain
faithful in prayer. [3]When Mahalalel had lived for 895 years the day of his decease Gen 5:17
drew near and he fell ill unto death. [4]All the patriarchs gathered and came to
him: his first-born Jared, Enoch, Methuselah, Lamech and Noah together with
their wives and children. [5]After they had been blessed by him and he had prayed

for them he commanded and told them: [6]"I adjure you by Abel's innocent blood
that not one of you go down from this holy mountain and that you do not allow any of your offspring to go down to the plain, to the children of Cain the
murderer. [7]All of you know what enmity there is between us and them since the
day he slew Abel." [8]Then he blessed his first-born Jared, commanded him concerning the body of Adam, revealed to him where it was destined to go, made
him take an oath, and spoke to him: "Do not depart from Adam's body all the
days of your life. May you be the guide of your children with you and lead them
Gen 5:17 in purity and saintliness." [9]Then Mahalalel died at the age of 895 years, on the
second of Nisan, a Sunday, at the third hour, in Noah's thirty-fourth year of life.
[10]His first-born Jared embalmed and buried him in the Cave of Treasures [11]and
they mourned him for forty days.

Jared and the descent of Seth's children

[12]After this, his first-born, Jared, rose in order to minister in front of God. He
was an honourable man, perfect in all goodness, and he remained day and night
exceedingly faithful in prayer. [13]Because of his good guidance he lived longer
than all his children with him. [14]In the days of Jared,[a] in his 500th year, the children of Seth broke the oath their forefathers had made them swear and began to
descend from the holy mountain to the villainous camp of Cain the murderer's
children. [15]The descent of Seth's children was thus: [16]In Jared's fortieth year, at
the end of the first millennium (which lasted) from Adam until Jared,

11 [1]in these years there appeared those craftsmen of sin and disciples of Satan,
for it was he who was their teacher. [2]Into them went, took residence and spread
the error-producing spirit by which took place the fall of Seth's children. [3]Jubal
and Tubal-Cain, those two brothers, sons of Lamech the blind who had killed
Cain, were the ones with whom appeared the art and craft of forging, hammer,
Gen 4:22 pincers and anvil. From those two it was passed on to Shelah, from Shelah to
Eber, from Eber to Peleg, from Peleg to Reu, from Reu to Serug, from Serug to
Nahor, from Nahor to Terah, from Terah to Abraham, from Abraham to Isaac,
from Isaac to Jacob, from Jacob to Judah, from Judah to Perez, from Perez to
Hezron, from Hezron to Ram, from Ram to Amminadab, from Amminadab
1 Chr 1:24-28; to Nahshon, from Nahshon to Salmon, from Salmon to Shelah, from Shelah to
Matt 1:1-5 Boaz. From the beginning it was spoken about and prophesied by the Holy Spirit
that until the Jewish ordinances cease, and until Christ's crucifixion, they would
compose and make all kinds of music, from Adam to Seth, from Seth to Enosh,
from Enosh to Kenan, from Kenan to Mahalalel, from Mahalalel to Jared, from
Jared to Enoch, from Enoch to Methuselah, from Methuselah to Lamech, from
Lamech to Noah, from Noah to Shem, from Shem to Arphaxad and from Ar-
Luke 3:36-38 | Gen 4:21 phaxad (onward). [4]Jubal made flutes, zithers and pipes [5]and the demons entered
them and dwelt within them. [6]Whenever they blew them, the demons made mu-
sic from within the flutes. Tubal-Cain made cymbals, rattles, and tambourines.
[8]When lewdness and debauchery had waxed great among the children of Cain,
and when they had no other goal than only debauchery, [9]they did not compel

---

a. The name "Jared" means "descent" in Hebrew.

(anybody) to work nor did they have a chief or guide. [10]Rather (there were) eating, drinking, gluttony, drunkenness, music, dance, diabolical jesting, laughter which is pleasurable to the demons, and the lewd voices of men braying after women. [11]When Satan found himself an occasion through this wrongdoing he was exceedingly glad that thereby he could make descend and bring down the children of Seth from the holy mountain, [12]for they had been made a replacement by God for that rank which had fallen and were called an angelic people and sons of God as the blessed David sings concerning them: "*I have called you gods and sons of the Most High, all of you.*"

Ephrem, *Comm. in Gen.* 6:3
Ps 82:6

12 [1]Since debauchery ruled among the children of Cain women shamelessly ran after men. [2]They mingled with one another like a flock in agitation, (and thus) they openly fornicated in front of each other without shame. [3]Two or three men fell upon one woman and likewise the women ran after the men. [4]Abominable spirits entered into the women so that they were even more furious in their impurity than their daughters. [5]Fathers and sons committed abominations with their mothers and sisters, and neither did the sons know their fathers nor could the fathers distinguish their sons, [6]for Satan had been made chief and guide of their camp. [7]When they raved in diabolical merrymaking they played flutes at the highest pitch and plucked the zithers with demonic skill and strength. Then the sound of tambourines and rattles, which they beat with evil spirits' skill, [8]and the noise of laughter was heard high in the air and went up to the holy mountain. [9]When the children of Seth heard this noisy uproar and laughter in the camp of Cain's children, about 100 valiant men of them gathered and set their mind upon going down to the camp of the children of Cain. [10]When Jared heard and began to know their words, (he said:) [11]"I implore you by Abel's innocent blood: Do not go down from this holy mountain! [12]Remember and think of the oaths which our fathers Seth, Enosh, Kenan and Mahalalel made us swear." [13]Enoch also told them: "Listen, children of Seth, whoever breaks the commandment of Jared and his fathers' oaths and goes down from this mountain, can never come up again." [14]But they did not wish to listen to Jared's advice and the words of Enoch. They became bold, broke the commandment, [15]and 100 valiant men went down. [16]When they saw that the daughters of Cain were beautiful to behold and exposed themselves without shame, [17]the sons of Seth were inflamed by the fire of passion. (Likewise) when Cain's daughters saw the beauty of the sons of Seth they rushed on them like wild animals and soiled their bodies. Thus Seth's sons destroyed themselves by fornication with the daughters of Cain. [18]But when they wanted to ascend the holy mountain from which they had fallen, [19]the stones of this holy mountain appeared to them like fire. [20]God did not allow them to ascend to the place (on top of) the holy mountain because they had soiled themselves by the filth of fornication. [21]After them a multitude of others became bold, too, went down and also fell.

13 [1]When Jared had lived for 960 years and the day of his death approached, drew near and arrived, [2]all the patriarchs gathered and came to him: his first- Gen 5:20
born Enoch, Methuselah, Lamech and Noah together with their wives and children. [3]They were blessed by him, he prayed over them and then told them: "I

adjure you by the innocent blood of Abel that you do not go down from this
holy mountain, [4]for I know that God will not permit you to be numerous in this
holy place anymore. [5]Since you transgressed your father's commandment you
certainly will be cast down to the outer earth and will not dwell at the fringes of
paradise. [6]But take heed that that one of you who will go down from this holy
place take with him the body of our father Adam and those offerings which are
in the Cave of Treasures. He shall carry it and put it down wherever it is commanded by God. [7]And you, my son Enoch, do not leave Adam's body but minister in front of God purely and in holiness all the days of your life." [8]Then Jared
Gen 5:20 died at the age of 960 years, on the thirteenth of the month Iyyar, on a Friday at
sunset, in Noah's 366th year of life. [9]His son Enoch embalmed and buried him
in the Cave of Treasures. [10]They mourned him for forty days, [11]and then Enoch
rose to minister in front of God in the Cave of Treasures.

Enoch is taken away

[12]After this Seth's children went astray [13]and wished to go down, so that they
grieved about them. [14]When Enoch had ministered for fifty years in front of
God, in Noah's 305th year of life, [15]and when he knew that God would take
Gen 5:24 him away, he called Methuselah, Lamech and <Noah>[a] and spoke to them: "I
know that God is wroth with this generation, and a merciless judgment has been
declared against them. [16]You are the chiefs of this generation and its remnant.
[17]There will not be born anyone else on this mountain anymore who might be
the chief of his children with him. [18]Now take heed and minister thus in front
of God in purity and saintliness." [19]After Enoch had commanded these things
to them God took him away to the place of life and the beautiful lodgings in the
Gen 5:24 environs of paradise, to that place which is above death.

Noah and the Ark

14 [1]Of all the children of Seth only Methuselah, Lamech and Noah, those three
patriarchs, remained upon the glorious mountain, for the rest had turned away
towards the camp of the children of Cain. [2]When Noah saw that sin had waxed
Aphrahat, *Dem.* 13:5-6 great in his generation he kept himself in celibacy for 500 years. [3]Then God
spoke to him and said: "Take for yourself as wife Haykal,[b] the daughter of Namos[c] daughter of Enoch, Methuselah's brother." [4]Then God showed him concerning the deluge which he had destined to bring about. [5]God spoke to him and
told him: "130 years from now I will bring about a deluge. [6]Now make yourself an
Gen 6:13-14 ark in order to save the members of your family. [7]Construct it down in the camp
of the children of Cain, but its wood shall be taken from this mountain. [8]Thus it
shall be: Its length (shall be) 300 cubits according to your cubit, [9]its breadth fifty
cubits, its height thirty cubits and it shall be finished to a cubit above. Also make
three decks within it: the lower one for the wild animals and cattle, the middle
Gen 6:15-16 one for the birds and the upper one for you and your family members. [10]Make
water-tanks and storerooms for food within it. [11]Furthermore, make yourself

a. The Syriac text has *Enoch*.

b. Lit. "temple."

c. Lit. "law."

a simandrum[a] out of box-wood which does not rot. Its length (shall be) three
cubits and its width one and a half. The clapper (should be made) out of the
same (material). [12]Strike it three times a day: once in the morning so that the
craftsmen may gather for work on the ark, once at noon for their meal, and once
at sunset so that they may rest. [13]When they hear the simandrum's sound as you
strike it and say to you: 'Why are you doing this?' then tell them: 'God is going to
bring about a deluge of water.'" [14]Noah did as God had commanded him. Gen 6:22

[15]Within a century there were born unto him three sons: Shem, Ham and
Japheth. For them he took wives from among the daughters of Methuselah. Gen 5:32; 6:10
[16]When Lamech had lived for 770 years he died during the lifetime of his father
Methuselah, forty years before the deluge, on the eleventh of Elul, a Thursday, in Gen 5:31
Shem the first-born of Noah's sixty-eighth year of life. [17]His first-born son Noah
embalmed him, and his father Methuselah enshrouded and buried him in the
Cave of Treasures. They mourned him for forty days.

The Sons of God were not angels

15 [1]Methuselah and Noah spent their lives alone upon the mountain, because all
the children of Seth had gone down from the fringes of paradise toward the plain
to the children of Cain. [2]The manly sons of Seth mingled with Cain's daughters,
[3]and there were conceived and borne by them valiant men, the sons of giants
in the likeness of towers. [4]The former authors erred concerning this when they Gen 6:4
wrote that angels came down from heaven and mingled with the daughters of
humankind, and that from them were born those famous heroes. [5]It is not true,
for they are saying this without knowledge. [6]Look, my fellow-readers, and understand that this does not lie within the nature of spiritual beings, [7]nor in the
nature of demons who are impure, evil-doers and lovers of adultery, because
among them there is neither male nor female, and not a single one has been
added to their number since they fell. [8]If the devils could mingle with women
they would not leave a single virgin in the whole human race whom they would
not violate. Eznik of Kołb, *De Deo* 126

Methuselah instructs Noah

16 [1]When Methuselah had lived for 969 years and fallen ill unto death, [2]there Gen 5:27
gathered and came unto him Noah, Shem, Ham and Japheth together with their
wives, [3]since there was nobody from all the generations of Seth, Enosh, Kenan,
Mahalalel, Jared, Enoch, Methuselah and Lamech who did not go down, except
only those four souls: Noah, Shem, Ham and Japheth together with their wives, for
no children had been born unto them before the flood. [4]When those had gathered
with Methuselah and received blessings from him, he embraced them in grief,
weeping over the fall of Seth's children. [5]Then he prayed over them and told them:
"This remnant of souls is left over from all the families and tribes of our fathers.
The Lord, God of our fathers, bless you! [6]God, who solely created our ancestors
Adam and Eve, they being fruitful and multiplying so that the whole blessed earth
around paradise was filled by them, may he make you fruitful and multiply you

a. A wooden board which resounds when struck and is used instead of a bell in Near Eastern churches.

so that the whole earth will be filled by you, may he preserve you from the terrible punishment which has been declared against this stubborn generation, may
he be with you and guard you. 7May the gift which has been bestowed upon our
father Adam go forth from this holy place together with you. 8Those three seals of
blessing which God has given to your father Adam shall be the ferment kneaded
into your seed and the seed of your children, namely, kingship, priesthood and
prophecy. 9Listen, Noah, blessed one of the Lord, and behold, I will leave this
world like all my ancestors, 10and only you, your sons and their wives will be left.
11Do everything which I command you today! God will bring about a deluge.
12As soon as I am dead bury me in the Cave of Treasures together with my fathers.
13Then take your wife, your sons and the wives of your sons and go down from
this holy mountain. 14Take our father Adam's body and those three offerings, gold,
myrrh and incense, with you. Put Adam's body down in the middle of the ark and
those offerings at its upper side. 15You and your sons shall stay on the ark's eastern
side and your wife and your sons' wives on the western (side). 16Your wives must
not come over to your side and you do not go to them. 17Neither eat nor drink
nor unite with them until you go out from the ark, 18because this generation has
angered God so that he did not allow them to be near paradise and to sing praises
together with the angels. 19When the waters of the deluge withdraw from the earth
and you go forth from the ark in order to dwell in this land, you, Noah, blessed
one of the Lord, shall not leave the ark and the body of our father Adam. 20Rather
minister in front of God inside the ark in purity and saintliness all the days of your
life. 21Those gifts (then) shall be put on its eastern (side). 22Also command your
first-born Shem that after your death he take up the body of our father Adam,
carry it and put it down in the middle of the earth. 23Then he shall make dwell
there one man from his progeny in order to be a minister there 24and a Nazirite all
the days of his life, and he must not take a wife. 25He shall not offer there offerings
of wild animals and birds; rather bread and wine shall be the offering for God,
26for it is there that salvation will be wrought for Adam and all his offspring. 27The
angel of the Lord will walk in front of him and will show him the place which is
the middle of the earth. 28The clothes of him who stands there in order to minister
in front of our father Adam's body will be hides of wild animals; he shall not cut
the hair of his head nor clip his fingernails and shall be single for he is a priest of
the highest God."

The death of Methuselah and the departure of Noah and his family

17 1When Methuselah had commanded Noah all these things he died with tears
Gen 5:27 in his eyes and grief in his heart. 2He was 969 years old when he died on the fourteenth of the month Adar, a Sunday, in the seventy-ninth year of the life of Shem,
son of Noah. 3His grandson Noah embalmed Methuselah's body with myrrh,
cassia and stacte, and he and his sons buried him in the Cave of Treasures. 4Then
they mourned him together with their wives for forty days. 5When the days of
mourning were over Noah went into the Cave of Treasures and embraced and
kissed those holy bodies of Seth, Enosh, Kenan, Mahalalel, Jared, Methuselah
and his father Lamech, his tears flowing on account of the great suffering. 6Then
Noah took the bodies of our ancestors Adam and Eve, his first-born Shem took
gold, Ham held myrrh, and Japheth incense, and they left the Cave of Treasures.

7When they went down from the holy mountain, they wept and groaned abundantly because they were driven away from that holy place and habitation of their fathers. 8They lifted up their eyes toward paradise, wept in great and bitter suffering, wailed in grief, were filled with sadness and said: "Rest in peace, holy paradise, habitation of our father Adam who left you naked and ashamed. 9Behold, even in death he is driven away from your environs and sent into exile together with his offspring to this accursed earth where they are going to suffer weeping, illness, toil, weariness and exhaustion. Rest in peace, holy Cave of Treasures! 10Rest in peace, habitation and inheritance of the ancestors! 11Rest in peace, fathers and patriarchs, and pray for us, you who are sleeping in the dust, beloved friends of the living God! 12Pray for the remnant which is left over from your whole progeny, and make supplication for them by your prayers, you reconcilers of God. 13Rest in peace, Enosh, leader of righteousness! 14Rest in peace, Kenan and Mahalalel, Jared and Methuselah, Lamech and Enoch, you ministers of the Lord, cry out in pain because of us! 15Rest in peace, harbour and resting-place of the angels! 16Cry out in pain, our fathers, because of us, for today you are being taken from us! 17We, too, will be in pain because we are being driven to the barren earth so that we will have to live with wild animals. 18As we go down from this holy mountain we kiss its rocks and embrace its trees."

19Thus they went down weeping with great pain and bitter tears. 20When they had come down in sadness, Noah went into the ark, put Adam's body down in the middle of the ark and those offerings at its upper side. 21In that hour when Noah went into the ark, the second millennium came to an end, from Adam's creation until the deluge as those seventy wise authors[a] have delivered unto us.

The Flood

18 1Noah's entrance into the ark took place on a Friday in the blessed month
Iyyar, 2on the seventeenth, a Friday. In the morning the wild animals and cattle Gen 7:11
entered into the lower deck, at noon the birds and all reptiles entered into the
middle deck, and at sunset Noah and all his sons entered the eastern side of the
ark, while his wife and his sons' wives (entered) the ark's western side. 3Adam's Gen 7:7, 13-14
body was put down in the middle of the ark, for all the mysteries of the Church
are foreshadowed in it. 4Inside church women stay on the western side and men
on the eastern side so that the men cannot see the women's faces nor do the
women see the faces of the men.[b] 5Thus also in the ark the women were on the
western side and the men on the eastern side. 6(Adam's) body, however, was
put in the middle like the Bema,[c] 7and just as there is silence between men and
women in church so there was peace inside the ark between animals, birds, and
reptiles. 8Just as kings, judges, rich men and paupers, lords, wretches and beggars are equal to one another, that is, in peaceful agreement, thus there were Jas 2:1-7
inside the ark lions, leopards, and harmful animals in tranquil silence with one
another, the strong ones with the weak and contemptible, the lion with the bull,
the wolf with the lamb, the lion-cubs with the heifer, the snake with the dove,

a. I.e., the translators of the Septuagint.

b. Since the altar is located in the east, women are standing behind the men.

c. Lectern in the center of Near Eastern churches.

Is 11:6-8 and the hawk with the song-birds. [9]When Noah, his sons, his wife and the wives
of his sons had entered into the ark at sunset on the seventeenth of the month
Iyyar the doors of the ark were shut and Noah remained with his sons in sad se-
clusion. [10]After the doors of the ark had been shut, the floodgates of heaven were
Gen 7:11 opened, the depths of the earth burst forth and (likewise) the spring tides of the
ocean, that great sea which surrounds the whole earth. [11]When the floodgates of
heaven were opened, the depths of the earth burst forth, the storehouses of the
winds were unfastened, storms broke loose, and the ocean roared and flushed,
[12]the children of Seth hurried towards the ark beseeching Noah to open the ark's
door for them. [13]As they saw the water-floods surrounding and encircling them
on every side they were in great anguish and tried to ascend paradise-mountain,
but were not able (to do it). [14]The ark was closed and sealed and the angel of the
Lord stood on top of it as its helmsman. [15]When the flood of waters grew strong
and they began to drown in the horribly roaring waves, there was fulfilled in
them what David says: "*I have said: You are gods and sons of the Most High all of*
Ps 82:6 *you.* Since you did this and loved the fornication of the daughters of Cain you
Ephrem, *Comm. in Gen.* 6:3 will perish and die in the same way as they."

Gen 7:17 **19** [1]The ark was lifted up from the earth by the great power of the waters, while
Gen 7:21 all the people, beasts, birds, cattle, reptiles, and everything upon earth drowned.
Gen 7:20 [2]The waters rose fifteen cubits above every mountain-top according to the
Gen 7:17 spirit's measure. [3]The flood swell and the waters made the ark ascend until it
reached the fringes of paradise. [4]Having received blessings from paradise the
flood bowed down, kissed the heels of paradise and turned back in order to
Ephrem, *De parad.* 1:4 destroy the whole earth. [5]The ark, however, flew on the wings of the wind upon
the water from east to west and from north to south, thus tracing a cross upon
the water. [6]The ark flew upon the water for 150 days and came to rest in the sev-
Gen 8:3-4 Peshitta enth month, that is, Tishri I, on the seventeenth, upon the mountains of Qardu.
Gen 1:7 [7]Then God commanded the waters to separate and the upper waters ascended to
their places above heaven from where they had come down, while those waters
which had come up from underneath the earth went back to the lower depths,
and those from the ocean returned into their bed. [8]Thus there remained upon
the face of the earth only those waters which from the beginning had been given
to its use by divine decree, decreasing little by little until the tenth month, that is,
Gen 8:5 Shebat. [9]Suddenly the high mountain-tops became visible and after forty days,
in the month Adar, Noah opened the ark's eastern window and released a ra-
Gen 8:6-7 ven. [10]It went forth and did not return. [11]After the water had withdrawn a little
(more) from the earth Noah sent forth a dove. It did not find a resting place and
returned to Noah within the ark. [12]After seven days he sent forth another dove
Gen 8:8-11 and it came back to him carrying an olive-twig in its beak. [13]These doves typify
for us the two testaments: In the first one the Spirit which has spoken through
the prophets did not find rest among that stubborn people, but in the second one
(the Spirit) came to rest upon the heathen by the water of baptism.

The exit from the Ark

20 [1]In Noah's 601st year of life, on the first of Nisan, the water had dried upon
Gen 8:13 the face of the whole earth. [2]In that (same) second month, that is, Iyyar, in which

Noah had entered the ark, on the twenty-seventh which is a holy Sunday, took
place their exit from the ark. 3 He and his wife went forth together with his sons Gen 8:14
and their wives, 4whereas Noah and his sons, his wife and their sons' wives had Gen 8:18
gone in separately when they were entering the ark, 5and the husbands had not
known their wives until they went forth from the ark. 6On this day also went
forth all the animals and cattle, birds and reptiles, 7and after they had left Noah
began to till the earth. 8They built a city and called it Temanun after the eight[a] 8:18-19
souls which had come forth from the ark. 9Then Noah built an altar and offered
upon it a pure offering from the clean cattle and birds, and God was pleased by
Noah's offering. 10He established an eternal covenant with him and and swore "I
will not again bring about a deluge." 11This was the covenant he established with Gen 8:20-21
him: He removed the arrow of wrath from the bow in the clouds and took away
from it the string of anger in order to spread it in the clouds, 12because before, Gen 9:12-16
when it was stretched out upon the firmament in front of the progeny of Cain
the murderer, they beheld the arrow of wrath being put upon the bow-string of
anger, but after the deluge neither arrow nor string was seen.

Noah becomes intoxicated

21 1When they went out of the ark they sowed seeds, planted vines and pressed
new wine. 2Noah came by and as soon as he drank from it he became intoxicated. 3As he slept his nakedness was uncovered, and when Ham saw his father's
nakedness he did not cover it but laughed and mocked at it. 4Then he hurried
to call his brothers that they also might mock at their father. 5When Shem and
Japheth heard this they were greatly distressed. They rose, took a cloak and went
backwards so as not to see their father's nakedness by turning around. Thus
they threw the coat upon him and covered him. 6When Noah woke up from his
wine-induced sleep his wife told him everything which had happened so that he
himself too came to know everything which had occurred to him. 7Thus Noah
became very wroth with his son Ham and said: "May Canaan be cursed and
may he be a slave of the slaves of his brothers!" 8For what reason did he curse Gen 9:20-27
Canaan while everything had been Ham's foolishness, 9if not because when the
child had grown up and reached the age of knowledge Satan had entered him,
been a teacher of sin for him and renewed within him the deeds of the tribe of
Cain the murderer, so that he went and made flutes and lyres 11into which the
demons entered and dwelt within them, and as soon as air was being blown
through them the devils were singing within them and gave them a powerful
sound, 12while ringing out with these lyres the demons used to twist within
them. 13When Noah had heard what Canaan had done it grieved him much
because that error's transgression had been renewed through which the fall of
the children of Seth had occurred. 14For it had been by music, jesting and the
folly of Cain's children that Satan had made the manly sons of Seth fall into fornication, 15and through music, flutes and lyres sin had waxed great among the
former generation so that God had been enraged and brought about the deluge.
16Because Canaan had been shameless enough to do this he was cursed and his
seed would become slaves of slaves. They are the Cushites, Indians, and (other)

---

a. Syr. *temanya.*

abominable ones. [17]Because Ham had been shameless and mocked at his father
he was called "the lewd one" all the days of his life.

[18]But Noah in his drunken sleep when he had drunk wine typified the cross
of Christ, as the blessed David sings concerning him, saying: "*The Lord has risen*
Ps. 78:65 *from sleep like a man overwhelmed by wine.*" [19]May the heretics be silent who say
that God has been crucified.[a] Here he is called "Lord" as the apostle Peter says:
Acts 2:36 "*God made him Lord and Christ, this Jesus whom you crucified.*" [20]He does not
say "God" but "Lord," thus hinting at the union of the two hypostases which are
united within a single sonship. [21]When Noah woke up from his drunkenness
he cursed Canaan, brought his seed into serfdom and scattered it among the
nations. [22](Likewise) when our Lord rose from the place of the dead he cursed
the Jews and scattered their seed among the nations. [23]The seed of Canaan are,
as I have said, the Egyptians, and behold, they are scattered upon the whole
earth and have been made the slaves of slaves. [24]What is the slavery of slavery?
[25]Behold, the Egyptians are roaming upon the whole earth [26]carrying (loads)
on their necks, whereas those who have not been brought under the yoke of
serfdom do not have to go by foot and carry loads when they are being sent
on errands by their masters; rather they are riding upon beasts with the same
honour as their masters. [27]Ham's seed are the Egyptians who carry (loads) and
are being sent on errands, their necks breaking from carrying, while they are
roaming at the doors of their brother's children. [28]This punishment was brought
about because of Ham's foolishness so that they have to be even slaves of slaves.

The death of Noah

Gen 9:28 **22** [1]After he had come out of the ark Noah lived for 350 years. When he fell
ill unto death, [2]Shem, Ham, Japheth, Arphaxad and Shelah gathered with him.
[3]Then Noah called his first-born Shem and spoke to him secretly: "Take heed,
my son Shem, of what I command you today. As soon as I am dead go into the
ark by which you have been rescued and take the body of our father Adam out
from it when nobody notices you. [4]Bring with you from here bread and wine
for food on the way and take along Melchizedek, the son of Malah, [5]for God
chose him from all your offspring that he may minister in front of him above the
body of our father Adam. [6]Go up, put him down in the middle of the earth and
make Melchizedek dwell there. [7]Behold, the angel of the Lord will go in front of
you and show you the way you have to take. He (will) also (show) you the place
where you shall lay down Adam's body, for this is the middle of the earth. [8]There
the four points of the compass embrace one another, for when God made the
earth his power ran ahead and the earth ran after it from the four points of the
compass like the winds and little breezes, and there his power stood still and
Basil, *Hex.* 1:9-10 rested. [9]There salvation will be wrought for Adam and all his offspring. [10]From
Adam unto us this story has been delivered throughout all generations. [11]Adam
commanded Seth, Seth commanded Enosh, Enosh Kenan, Kenan Mahalalel,
Mahalalel Jared, Jared Enoch, Enoch Methuselah, Methuselah Lamech, Lamech
me and behold, I command you today: [12]Take heed not to tell this story to any-

---

a. Reference to the Monophysites.

one from your offspring, but go up, transport and put him down secretly where
God will show you, until the day of our salvation."

[13]After Noah had commanded this to his son Shem he died at the age of
950 years, on the second of the month Iyyar, a Sunday, in the third hour. His Gen 9:29
son Shem embalmed him and buried him in the city that he had built and they
mourned him for forty days.

Shem invests Melchizedek as priest at Golgotha

23 [1]After Noah's death Shem did as his father had commanded him. [2]At night
he went into the ark, brought Adam's body out of it and sealed it with his father's
seal while nobody noticed it. [3]Then he called Ham and Japheth and said to his
brothers: "My father commanded me to go up and walk on the earth as far as
the sea so that I may see how the earth and rivers are and then return to you.
[4]Behold, my wife and my children, my family (will remain) with you; may you
keep an eye upon them." [5]His brothers said to him: "Take with you a band of our
men, for the earth is desolate, deprived of inhabitants, and there are wild beasts
upon it." [6]Shem told them: "The angel of the Lord will go with me and keep me
from every evil." [7]Now his brothers spoke to him: "Go in peace! The Lord, God
of our fathers, be with you!"

[8]Then Shem spoke to Malah, son of Arphaxad, the father of Melchizedek, and
to his mother Yozdaq: [9]"Give me Melchizedek that he may come and go up with
me and be a companion for me on the way." [10]His father Malah and his mother
Yozdaq told him: "Take him and go in peace." [11]Shem also commanded his brothers and said to them: "My brothers, when my father died he made me swear that
neither I nor anybody else enter the ark, and he sealed it with his seal." [12]He also
told them: "May nobody even come near to the ark!" [13]Then Shem took Adam's
body and Melchizedek, and went forth from his people at night. [14]And behold,
they saw an angel of God going ahead of them, and their journey was very easy
because the angel of the Lord strengthened them until they reached that place.
[15]When they reached Golgotha—for this is the middle of the earth—the angel
showed Shem the exact place. [16]When Shem put Adam's body down upon that
spot the four points of the compass went apart and the earth was opened in the
shape of a cross. Shem and Melchizedek put Adam's body there, and as soon as
they had put it down there [17]the four sides hastened to embrace the body of our
father Adam and the gate of the world was closed at once. [18]This place is called
"place of the skull" because there lies the head of all humankind, and Golgotha Luke 23:33
because it is paved with stones, for there was broken the head of the cruel snake,
that is, Satan, and Gabbatha because all the nations will be gathered there. [19]Then John 19:13
Shem said to Melchizedek: "Be a priest of the Most High God, for God chose you Gen 14:18
alone in order to serve in front of him at this place. [20]Dwell here steadfastly and do
not leave this place all the days of your life. [21]Do not take a wife, do not shave, do
not spill blood at this place, and do not offer here beasts or birds; rather offer bread
and wine continuously, [22]and do not erect a building here. [23]Behold, the angel of
the Lord will always be at your side." [23]Then Shem embraced and kissed Melchizedek, blessed him, and then returned to his brothers. [25]Melchizedek's father Malah
and his mother Yozdaq asked him: "Where is the boy?" Shem told them: "He died
on the way and I buried him there," and they mourned him much.

From Shem to Peleg

Gen 11:10-11 **24** [1]When Shem had lived for 600 years he died, and his brother Arphaxad
together with his sons Shelah and Eber buried him. [2]Arphaxad had begotten
Gen 11:12-13 Shelah at the age of thirty-five. The days of his life were altogether 400 years.
[3]Then he died and his son Shelah (along with) Eber and Peleg buried him in the
city of Arphaxerat which he had built upon his name. [4]At the age of thirty Shelah
Gen 11:14-15 begot Eber. The days of his life were altogether 433 years. [5]Then he died and his
son Eber (along with) Peleg and Reu buried him in the city of Shelahion which
he had built upon his name. [6]At the age of thirty-four Eber begot Peleg. All the
Gen 11:16-17 days of his life were 436 years. [7]Then he died and his son Peleg (along with) Reu
and Serug buried him in the city of Eberin which he had built upon his name.
[8]At the age of thirty Peleg begot Reu. All the days of his life were 239 years; then
Gen 11:18-19 he died. [9]In the days of Peleg all the tribes and generations of Noah and his children gathered, went up from the east and found a plain in the country of Shinar.
Gen 11:1-2 There they lived, all of them having one tongue and one language. [10]From Adam
until then they all spoke that language which is Syriac, that is, Aramaic, for this
language is sovereign of all languages. [11]The earlier writers err in this regard saying that Hebrew is the first, and thus without knowledge they mingle errors into
their writings, for all the languages of the world are derived from Syriac and the
words of every book are mingled with it. In the (direction) of the Syrians' script
the left stretches the right[a] so that all the children of the left reach God's right
hand, but in the Greek, Latin and Hebrew (scripts) the right stretches the left.[b]

The Tower of Babel and the dispersion of the nations

[12]In Peleg's days the tower of Babylon was built, and then the languages were
Gen 11:3-7 confounded and spread from there upon the face of the whole earth. [13]Because
Gen 11:9 the languages were confounded there this place is called "Babylon."[c] [14]After the
division of languages Peleg died in great sadness, with tears in his eyes and grief
Gen 10:25 in his heart, because in his days the earth had been divided. [15]Then his son Reu,
Serug and Nahor buried him in the city of Pelegin which he had built upon his
name.

[16]There were upon the earth seventy-two languages and seventy-two chiefs
of tribes and they made for themselves one chief as king for each tribe and
tongue. [17]From Japheth's seed there were thirty-seven nations and kingdoms:
Gen 10:2 Gomer, Javan, Madai, Tubal, Meshech, Tiras, and all the kingdoms of the Alans;
those are the children of Japheth. [18]Ham's children are: Cush, Egypt, Canaan,
Gen 10:6 and all their children. [19]The children of Shem are: Elam, Assur, Arphaxad, Lud
Gen 10:21 and Aram, and all their children. [20]Japheth's children inhabit the far east from
the mountains of Nod and the outer fringes of the east to the Tigris, and from
the northern fringes of Bactria to Gadryon. [21]The children of Shem live from
eastern Persia to the Adriatic sea in the west; the middle of the earth is theirs

---

a. I.e., the Syriac script runs from right to left.

b. I.e., those scripts run (allegedly) from left to right. Hebrew actually runs right to left, like Syriac.

c. Syr. *balbel* "to confound."

and they are holding kingship and dominion. [22]Ham's children inhabit all the
southern regions and a few of the western ones.
[23]Reu lived for thirty-two years and then begat Serug. [24]In Reu's days, in his Gen 11:20
130th year, the hero Nimrod reigned as first king upon the earth. He ruled for
sixty-nine years and the capital of his kingdom was Babylon. [25]Once he saw Gen 10:8, 10
something like a crown in the sky and then called the weaver Sisan who wove
a similar one for him and put it upon his head. [26]Because of this it is said that
this crown came down from heaven. [27]In the days of Reu the third millennium
ended.

From Reu to Terah

25 [1]In his days the Misreans, that is, the Egyptians, made themselves a king for
the first time. His name was Puntos and he ruled over them for sixty-eight years.
[2]In Reu's lifetime a monarch ruled in Saba, Ophir, and Havila. [3]In Saba (reigned)
one of the daughters of Saba for sixty-seven (years) and Saba remained for many
years under the rule of women, until the reign of Solomon, son of David. [4]The
children of Ophir were ruled by king Poron who built Ophir with golden stones,
for all the stones in Ophir consist of gold. [5]Havila's children were ruled by Havil,
who built Havila. [6]Reu died at the age of 239 years, and his son Serug (along Gen 11:21
with) Nahor and Terah buried him in the city of Reuyin which he had built upon
his name. [7]Serug lived for thirty years and then begot Nahor. All the days of his
life were 230 years. [8]In Serug's days idol-veneration rose in the world and in his Gen 11:22-23
time humankind began to make images for themselves. [9]The rise of idols in the
world came about because humankind was scattered upon the whole earth having neither teachers nor lawgivers nor someone to show them the way of truth
that they might walk upon it. [10]For this reason they erred grossly. [11]In their error
some of them worshipped the sky, others the sun and stars, the earth, animals,
birds and reptiles, trees and rocks, shadows, waters and winds. [12]Now Satan had
blinded their eyes so that they walked in the darkness of error, for they had
no hope of resurrection. [13]When someone of them died they made for him an
image in his likeness and put it upon his grave so that his memory would not
pass away from their eyes. [14]When error had been sown upon the whole earth it
became full of all kinds of idols in the likeness of men and women.
[15]Then Serug died at the age of 230 years. His children Nahor, Terah, and Gen 11:23
Abraham buried him in the city of Serugin which he had built upon his name.
[16]Nahor begat Terah at the age of twenty-nine. [17]In the days of Nahor, in his Gen 11:24
seventieth year, when God saw that humankind was worshipping idols, there
occurred a great earthquake and all their buildings crumbled and fell down.
They, however, did not understand in their minds but increased their wickedness. [18]Nahor died at the age of 147 years, and his son Terah and Abraham buried Gen 11:25
him. [19]Terah had begotten Abraham at the age of seventy-five years. Gen 11:26

The origin of human sacrifice

26 [1]In the days of Terah, in his ninetieth year, sorcery appeared in the land of
Ur, in the city which Harran, son of Eber, had built. [2]There was in it a man who
was very rich and had died at that time. [3]His son made himself an image of gold,
put it upon his grave and made a servant stay there in order to guard it. [4]Then

Satan went and dwelt within this image. [5]And Satan spoke with the boy in the
likeness of his father. [6]Then thieves came and took everything the young man
had collected, so that he went out to his father's grave weeping. [7]Satan spoke
with him and told him: "Do not cry in front of me but go, bring your little son
and sacrifice him for me. Then everything which has been lost will immediately
be returned to you." [8]At once he did as Satan had told him, sacrificed his son and
Gregory Nazianzen, *Orat.* 4:70 — bathed in his blood. [9]Immediately Satan came out from that image, entered into
the young man, and taught him magic, incantations, divination, Chaldaean arts,
fortune-telling, augury, and omens. [10]Behold, from then on humankind began
to sacrifice their children to the demons and to worship idols, for the devils entered into them and dwelt within all the images.

[11]In the 100th year of Nahor, when God saw that humankind was sacrificing
their children to the demons and worshipped idols, God opened the storehouses
of storms, so that great winds went forth upon the whole earth, destroyed the
images and temples of the demons, drove away those idols, images and pacts,
and made great mounds around them (which are there) to the present day.
Jub. 10:26; *Sib. Or.* 3:101-103; *Ant.* 1:118 — [12]This wind-storm has been called "deluge of wind" by the scholars. [13]Now there
are people who chatter and say that these mounds are from the time of the deluge. But in truth those who are saying this err. [14]Before the deluge there were
no idols upon the earth and the deluge did not take place because of idols but
because of the fornication of Cain's daughters, [15]nor were there people upon
earth at that time; rather it was waste and desolate, and our fathers were sent to
it like into exile because they were not worthy to remain neighbours of paradise.
Gen 8:4 Peshitta — [16]From the ark they were cast upon the mountains of Qardu and from there they
spread over the whole earth. [17]Those mounds are there because of the idols,
and all the idols from that time are hidden within them. [18]Likewise those devils
which are said to have been within them are in those (mounds) and there is not
a single mound in which there are not devils.

Nimrod and his learning

27 [1]In the days of Nimrod the hero a fire appeared which had come from the
earth. [2]So Nimrod went down in order to see and to worship it. He installed
Ps.-Clem. Rec. 1:30:7 — priests there in order to minister to it continuously and throw incense into it.
[3]From that time onward the Persians began to worship fire until the present
Xenophon, *Cyr.* 8:3:12 — day. [4]King Sisan found a well of water in Drugin,[a] made a white horse and put
it above it, and those taking a bath worshipped the horse. [5]From then on the
Persians began to worship this horse.

[6]Nimrod went to Yuqdura in (the country of) Nod. [7]When he reached the sea
Otros[b] he found Yonton, the son of Noah, there. [8]He went down and bathed in
that sea. Then he drew near and worshipped Yonton. [9]Yonton said to him: "You
are a king and worship me?" [10]Nimrod told him: "It is because of you that I came
down here." [11]He stayed with him for three years and Yonton taught Nimrod
wisdom and the book of oracles. Then he told him: "Do not come back to me
again." [12]After he had come up from the east he began to use this oracle (so that)

---

a. Perhaps a misspelling of *adorbigan*, i.e., Azerbaijan.

b. Most likely a distortion of *okeanos* "Ocean."

many were amazed by it. [13]When the priest Idashir, who was ministering to that fire which had come from the earth, saw that Nimrod was studying the celestial courses, he prayed to those demons which he had seen around the fire that they might teach him the wisdom of Nimrod. [14]Since it is the demons' habit to corrupt by sin those near to them, the demon spoke to that priest: "Nobody can be priest and magus if he does not first mingle with his mother, daughter and sister." [15]The priest Idashir did thus, [16]and behold, from then on the priests and magi of the Persians began to marry their mothers. [17]Behold, it was this magus Idashir who first began to use horoscopes, omens, augury, auspicious times and similar things, all the Chaldaean arts. [18]Now all this is a doctrine of devilish deceit and those who practice it will receive punishment together with the devils on judgment day. [19]But of the orthodox teachers no one rejects Nimrod's learning because Yonton taught it to him and this is also why they study it. [20]The Persians call it "oracle," the Romans "astronomy." [21]But that which the magi have is astrology, that is, sorcery and deceitful learning. [22]There are those who say that there really are omens, portentous signs and auspicious times but they err.

[23]Now Nimrod built strong cities in the east: Babylon, Nineveh, Resen, Seleucia, Ctesiphon, and Azerbaijan, and he constructed three fortified towns.

Abraham

28 [1]Abraham's father Terah lived for 250 years; then he died [2]and Abraham and
Lot buried him in Harran. [3]God spoke with Abraham there and told him: "Leave Gen 11:32
your country and your relatives and go to the land which I will show you." [4]Then Gen 12:1
Abraham took his family, his wife Sara and his nephew Lot, and went up to the
country of the Amorites. [5]He was seventy-five years old when he crossed the Gen 12:5
Euphrates to the west. [6]He was eighty years old when he pursued the kings and Gen 12:4
freed his nephew Lot. [7]At that time he did not have a son because Sara was bar- Gen 14:14-16
ren. [8]After he had returned from the war with the kings he made a covenant
with God and passed over to the mountain of Jebus. [9]Then Melchizedek, king
of Shalem and priest of the highest God, went out to meet him. [10]When he saw
Melchizedek, Abraham hurried, fell upon his face and worshipped him. Then
he stood up from the ground, embraced and kissed him, and received blessings
from him. [11]Melchizedek blessed Abraham by making him partake in the holy
mysteries, the bread of offering and the wine of salvation. [12]After Melchizedek Gen 14:18-20
had blessed him and made him partake in the holy mysteries God spoke with
Abraham and told him: [13]"Because Melchizedek has blessed you and made you
partake in bread and wine, your benefit will be very great. I, too, will bless you
and multiply your seed exceedingly." Gen 12:2

[14]When Abraham was eighty-six years old Ishmael was born unto him by
Hagar the Egyptian. [15]Hagar had been given by Pharaoh to Sara as a servant. Gen 16:15-16
[16]Sara was Abraham's sister on his paternal side, for Terah had taken two wives. *Ant.* 1:151; *b. Meg.* 14*a*;
[17]After Abraham's mother Yona had died, Terah took a wife whose name was Ephrem, *Comm. in*
Nahrit, and from her Sara was born. [18]Because of that he said: "She is my sister, *Gen.* 9:1
the daughter of my father but not of my mother." Gen 20:12

29 [1]Abraham was ninety-nine years old when God visited his house and gave
Sara a son, [2]and he was 100 years old when Isaac was born unto him. [3]Isaac Gen 18:1-15 | Gen 21:5

was twelve years old when his father took him and went up to the mountain of
Gen 22:1-14 Jebus toward Melchizedek, priest of the highest God. 4The mountain of Jebus
is the mountain of the Amorites and the very place where the cross of Christ
was fastened. 5There also grew that tree which held the ram that saved Isaac.
6This place is the middle of the earth, Adam's tomb, the altar of Melchizedek,
Golgotha, place of the skull, and Gabbatha. 7There David saw an angel holding
1 Chr 21:16 a sword of fire. 8There Abraham made Isaac ascend upon the altar and saw the
cross, Christ, and our father Adam's salvation. 9This was a sign of the cross of
our Lord Christ. The ram in its branches signifies the undivided Logos's human
nature. 10Paul proclaims and says: "*If they had {not} known the Lord of Glory*
1 Cor 2:8 *they would <not> have crucified him.*" May the heretics' mouths be shut who in
their madness attribute suffering to the (divine) nature.[a] 11Rather, when Christ
was eight days old, Joseph, the betrothed of Mary, rose in order to have the child
Luke 2:21 circumcised according to the law, and circumcised him according to the law.
12Thus also Abraham made his son ascend upon the altar, signifying thereby
Christ's crucifixion. 13Through this he openly announced Christ in front of the
synagogue of the Jews, for "your father Abraham wished to see the days, he saw
John 8:56 (them) and rejoiced." 14There the day of Adam's salvation was shown to Abraham, he saw (it) and rejoiced, for Christ had revealed to him that he was going
to suffer in Adam's behalf.

Melchizedek

30 1In that same year in which Abraham made ascend his son upon the altar,
Jerusalem was built. 2The beginning of its building was thus: When Melchizedek had appeared and shown himself to humankind, the kings of the nations
heard about him. These kings gathered and came to him: Abimelech king of
Gen 20:2 Gadar, Amraphel king of Shinar, Arioch king of Dalasar, Kedor-Laomer king of
Elam, Tarel king of the Geleans, Bera king of Sodom, Birsha king of the Amo-
Gen 14:1-2 rites, Shinat king of Admah, Shunair king of Zeboim, Salah king of Bela, Tabiq
king of Damascus, and Baqtor king of the desert. 3These twelve kings gathered
and came toward Melchizedek, king of Shalem (and) priest of the highest God.
4When they saw his appearance and heard his words they asked him to come
with them. 5But he told them: "I do not wish to leave this place." 6So they took
counsel with one another to build a city for him, telling each other that in truth
he was king of the whole earth and father of all kings. 7They built him a city
and made Melchizedek king within it. 8Melchizedek called its name "Jerusalem."
Sib. Or. 3:319 9When Magog, king of the south, heard (about it) he came to him, beheld his
appearance, spoke with him and gave him offerings and gifts. 10Thus Melchizedek was honoured by all and called "father of kings." 11This is what the apostle
Heb 7:3 says: "*His days have no beginning and his life (has) no end.*" 12It is thought by the
simpletons that he was not a human being, and in their error they say that he
was God—far be it!—, 13because his days have no beginning and his life no end.
14For when Shem, son of Noah, separated him from his parents, not a word is
said about how old he was when he went up from the east nor in which age did
his departure from this world take place. 15Because he was the son of Melek, son

a. An invective against the Monophysites.

of Arphaxad son of Shem, and not the son of one of those (other) patriarchs, the apostle wants to say that none of his parents' family was ministering at the altar. [16]His father's name is not written down in the family registers because the evangelists Matthew and Luke were recording only the patriarchs. Because of this neither his father's name nor the name of his mother is known. [17]Thus the apostle did not wish to say that he is without parents but only that they are not recorded by Matthew and Luke in the family registers.

From Abraham to Isaac

[18]In the 100th year of Abraham there was a king in the east whose name was Kumros. He built Samosata upon the name of his son Samsatu, Klaudia upon the name of his daughter Kalod, and Piron upon the name of his son Poron. [19]In Reu's fiftieth year Nimrod went up and built Nisibis, Edessa and Harran. [20]Harranit, the wife of Sin,[a] priest of the mountain, surrounded it with ramparts. [21]Then the Harranians made an image of her and worshipped it. [22]Baltin[b] was given to Tammuz,[c] but because Baal-Shamin[d] loved her, Tammuz flew from her, and she kindled a fire in order to burn Harran.

31 [1]When Sara, Abraham's wife, had died, Abraham took Keturah, the daugh- Gen 25:1
ter of Baqtor king of the desert. [2]By her were born Zimran, Yoqshan, Medan,
Midian, Ishbak, and Shuah, and from them the Arabs (are descended). [3]When Gen 25:2
Isaac was forty years old, Eleasar came down to Abraham's family and brought
Rebecca from the east, and Isaac married her. [4]After Abraham had died, Isaac Gen 24:1-67
buried him next to Sara. [5]When Isaac was sixty years old Rebecca conceived Gen 25:7-10
Esau and Jacob. [6]When she was afflicted she went to Melchizedek. He prayed Gen 25:21
over her and told her: "Two nations are within your belly and two peoples are
being separated in it, that is, will come forth from your womb. Nation will vanquish nation and the greater one will be subjugated by the lesser, that is, Esau
will be subservient to Jacob." Gen 25:22-23

[7]In Isaac's sixty-seventh year Jericho was built by seven kings, by the king of
the Hittites, the king of the Amorites, the king of the Girgashites, the king of the
Jebusites, the king of the Canaanites, the king of the Hivites, and the king of the
Perizzites. [8]Each one of them surrounded it with a rampart. [9]The city of Jericho Gen 15:20-21; Deut 7:1
itself, however, was at first built by the son of Misraim, king of the Egyptians.
[10]Ishmael fabricated hand-mills in the desert, hand-mills of slavery.

Jacob

[11]In his 103rd year Isaac blessed Jacob who was forty years old. [12]After having Gen 27:5-29
received his father's blessing he went down to the east. [13]He walked for one day Gen 28:1-5
in the desert of Beer-sheba and then slept there taking a stone for a pillow when
he went to sleep. [14]In a dream he saw—behold!—a ladder put upon the ground Gen 28:10-11
and its top in heaven, while the angels of God were ascending and descending

a. Name of the Harranian moon-god.

b. Lit. "Our Lady," referring to the goddess Ishtar and the planet Venus.

c. Babylonian deity.

d. Syro-phoenician deity.

Gen 28:12-13 upon it and the Lord standing on top of it. [15]Then Jacob woke up from his sleep
Gen 28:16-17 and spoke: "This truly is the house of God!" [16]He took the stone which he had
used as a pillow, made an altar out of it, anointed it with oil, made a vow and
Gen 28:18-22 said: "I will put the tithe of everything I have upon this stone."

[17]For those who have understanding it is obvious: The ladder which Jacob saw depicts the cross of our salvation; the angels which were ascending and descending upon it are the ministers of the gospel toward Zechariah, Mary, the magi and shepherds. [18]The Lord standing at its upper end is to be understood as Christ who stood at the upper end of the cross in order to descend into Sheol
Aphrahat, *Dem.* 4:5-6 and save us.

[19]When God had shown the cross of Christ to blessed Jacob by the ladder, and (by) the angels, Christ's descent for our salvation, the Church (by) the house of God, the altar by the stone, the offering by the tithe, and unction by the oil, Jacob again went down to the east so that God might show him baptism there. [20]Jacob watched and saw—behold!—three flocks of sheep lying at
Gen 29:2 a well. [21]A big stone was put upon its opening, so Jacob drew near, rolled the
stone away from its opening, and made the sheep of his maternal uncle drink.
Gen 29:2-3, 10-11 [22]Having made the sheep drink he took hold of Rachel and kissed her. [23]The
well is called "baptism" which was being awaited by the generations and tribes. [24]The blessed Jacob and the three flocks of sheep which were lying around it depict for us a symbol of the three orders in baptism, that is, men, women, and
Hippolytus, *Trad. apost.* 16:4-5 children. [25]For Jacob saw Rachel who had come with the sheep, but did not
embrace and kiss her until he had rolled away the stone from the well, and she had made the sheep drink, in correspondence to the law of the Church's children not to embrace and kiss the lambs of Christ until the baptismal font has been opened, and going down they put on the power of Christ. Only then do
Hippolytus, *Trad. apost.* 46:7-8 the children of the Church embrace and kiss them. [26]And just as Jacob worked
seven years for Laban without being given the one he loved, so likewise the
Gen 29:20 Jews when they worked in bondage for Pharaoh, the king of Egypt, were not
given the Testament of the Church, Christ's betrothed, but that one which is old, worn out and corrupted. [27]For the first one whom Jacob married had hate-
Gen 29:17; Justin, *Dial. cum Tryph.* 134:3 ful eyes, whereas Rachel had beautiful eyes and a radiant countenance. [28]The
first Testament has a veil upon its face so that the children of Israel cannot see
2 Cor 3:15 its beauty, but the second one is all light.

32 [1]Jacob was seventy-seven years old when he received his father Isaac's bless-
Gen 29:32 ing. [2]In his eighty-ninth year he begot with Leah his first-born Reuben. [3]These
Gen 29:33-35; 30:17-20 are the sons of Jacob: Reuben, Simeon, Levi, Judah, Issachar and Zebulun; those
Gen 30:23-34; 35:18 are Leah's sons. [4](Furthermore) Joseph and Benjamin, the sons of Rachel; Gad
Gen 30:9-13 and Asher (who were born) from Leah's maid Zilpah; and Naphtali and Dan
Gen 30:3-8 (who were born) from Rachel's maid Bilhah. [5]After twenty years Jacob returned
Gen 35:27 to his father Isaac.

Gen 35:28 [6]All the days of Isaac's life were 180 years. (He lived) until Levi's thirty-first
year and died in Jacob's 120th year of life. [7]Twenty-three years after Jacob went
up from Harran, during Isaac's lifetime, Joseph was sold to the Midianites and
Gen 37:28-36 (Jacob) grieved about it. [8]When Isaac had died his sons Jacob and Esau buried
Gen 35:29 him next to Abraham and Sara. [9]Seven years later Rebecca died and was buried

together with Abraham, Isaac and Sara. Rachel died, too, and was buried beside
them. [10]After Leah had died she was likewise buried beside them. Gen 49:31

[11]Jacob's son Judah took as a wife the Canaanitess Shuah, but it grieved his Gen 38:2
father that he had taken for himself a wife from the seed of Canaan. [12]Jacob
told Judah: "May the God of our fathers Abraham and Isaac not allow Canaan's
seed to mingle with my family!" [13]There were born unto Judah from Shuah the
Canaanitess Er, Onan, and Shelah. [14]For his first-born Er, Judah took as a wife Gen 38:4-5
Tamar, but he had sodomitical relations with her, and God let him die. [15]So Gen 38:6-7
Judah gave Tamar to his second son Onan. But as soon as his seed grew heated
so that he could pour it into Tamar, he corrupted it outside, and God let him
die, too. [16]Thus God did not allow Canaan's seed to be mingled with the seed of Gen 38:9-10
Jacob, just as Jacob had prayed, so that the seed of evil Canaan, Ham's first-born,
might not to the least mingle with the tribes of the patriarchs' offspring. [17]God
brought Tamar out to the wayside and Judah slept with her in depraved desire;
she conceived from him and gave birth to Perez and Zerah. Gen 38:13-19, 29-30

[18]Then Jacob and all his progeny went down to Egypt, to Joseph, and they
stayed in Egypt for seventeen years. [19]Jacob died at the age of 147 years, Joseph Gen 46:1-7; 47:28
being fifty-six years old when his father died, in Kohath's twelfth year. [20]Pha- Gen 47:28; 49:33
raoh's wise physicians embalmed him and Joseph brought him back in order to
bury him together with Abraham and his father Isaac. Gen 50:1-3, 4-14

The sacred blood-lines

33 [1]There are authors who say that since Jacob's death the tribes propagated and
mixed with one another, but they do not do so in the light of knowledge. [2]Now
two genealogies are being put forward: One of the tribes, and one of the children
of Israel, [3]concerning how they went out from Egypt; and in those registers it is
recorded how they mingled with one another. Judah begot Perez, Perez begot
Hezron, Hezron begot Ram, Ram begot Amminadab, Amminadab begot Nah-
shon who was prince in Judah. [4]Amminadab gave his daughter, Nahshon's sister, 1 Chr 2:4-5, 9-10
to Eleazar, son of Aaron the priest. From her was born the high-priest Phinehas
who stopped a plague by praying. Exod 6:23, 25; Num 25:7-8

[5]Behold, I have shown you that through Amminadab and Nahshon's sister
priesthood was bestowed upon the children of Israel, and through her brother
Nahshon kingship. [6]Look now, (both) priesthood and kingship were given to the
children of Israel through Judah. [7]Nahshon begot Salmon and Salmon begot Boaz. 1 Chr 2:11; Matt 1:4; Luke 3:32-33
[8]Look now, from Boaz and the Moabitess Ruth kingship went forth. Old Boaz
married Ruth so that Abraham's nephew Lot might participate in the transmission Ruth 4:19-20; Gen 19:36-38; Deut 2:9, 19; Aphrahat, *Dem.* 23:16
of kingship. [9]Thus God did not refuse to Lot the just his labours' wages, for he
had worn himself out in exile with Abraham and received God's angels in peace. 2 Pet 2:7; Gen 13:1; 19:1-11
[10]Therefore Lot the just was not cursed for having slept with his daughter. [11]God
granted that from the seed of those two might derive the royal blood-line and from Gen 19:33-36
the seed of Lot and Abraham Christ would be born. [12]There was born from the Aphrahat, *Dem.* 23:17
Moabitess Ruth, Obed, from Obed, Jesse, from Jesse, David and from David, Solomon. Those are descended from the Moabitess Ruth, Lot's daughter. [13]From the Matt 1:4-6
Ammonitess Naema, another daughter of Lot whom Solomon had married, there
was born Rehoboam who became king after Solomon. [14]Solomon married many 1 Kgs 14:21; 2 Chr 12:13
women, 700 free ones and 300 concubines, and from the 1000 women whom he

Aphrahat, *Dem.* 23:16 took he did not have a son except from Naema the Ammonitess, [15]so that the
evil seed of the Canaanites, Jebusites, Hittites, Amorites and those (other) nations
whom God hates, may not be mingled with the birth-line of Christ.

From Moses to Solomon

34 [1]The genealogy of the children of Israel: Levi, Amram, Moses, Joshua son of
Exod 6:20; 1 Chr 23:13 Nun, and Caleb, Jephunneh's son; these were being born in Egypt. [2]When Moses
Exod 2:3 had been born he was thrown into the river. [3]The Egyptian Shipor, Pharaoh's
Exod 2:5; Acts 7:23 daughter, pulled him out, and he stayed for forty years in the palace of Pharaoh.
Exod 2:12; Acts 7:23 [4]Then he killed the Egyptian Patkom, chief of Pharaoh's bakers. [5]When this be-
came known in Pharaoh's palace, and also on account of Pharaoh's daughter
Mekri who was called Shipor of Egypt, Moses' wet-nurse, he grew afraid and
Exod 2:15; Acts 7:29 fled to Midian, to the Cushite Reuel, priest of Midian. [6]He took for himself as
wife Zipporah the Cushitess, the priest's daughter, and there were born by her
Exod 2:21; 18:3-4 two sons, Gershom and Eliezer. [7]In Moses' fifty-third year of life Joshua, the
son of Nun, was born in Egypt. [8]Moses was eighty years old when God spoke
to him from within the bush and his tongue began to stammer out of fear, as he
says to God: "Behold, Lord, since the day on which you spoke to me I (am) a
Exod 3:1–4:17, esp. 4:10 stammerer." [9]He spent forty years in Egypt, forty years in the priest's house and
forty years in the leadership of the nation. [10]He died at the age of 120 years upon
Deut 34:5-7 the mountain of Nebo. [11]Then Joshua son of Nun became guide of the children
of Israel for twenty-seven years. [12]After the death of Joshua son of Nun, Cushan
Judg 3:8 the villainous rose over the children of Israel for eighty years, [13]and Othniel son
Judg 3:9-11 of Kenaz, the brother of Caleb son of Jephunneh, rose over Israel for forty years.
Judg 3:14 [14]Then the children of Israel were enslaved by the Moabites for eighteen years.
Judg 3:15-30 [15]Ehur son of Gera led the children of Israel for eighty years, [16]and in his twenty-
sixth year the fourth millennium ended.

35 [1]Then Nabin the lame who was paralyzed led for twenty years, and Debo-
Judg 4:2-5:31 rah and Barak for forty. [2]The children of Israel were enslaved by the Midianites
for seven years until God delivered them through Gideon who ruled them for
Judg 6:1; 8:28 forty years, [3]and his son Abimelech after him for three years; Tola son of Puah
Judg 9:22; 10:1-3 for twenty-three years, and Jair the Gileadite for twenty-two years. [4]The Israel-
ites were again enslaved by the Ammonites for eighteen years. God saved them
Judg 10:7-8; 11:34-40; 12:7 through Jephthah, who sacrificed his daughter, and he led them for six years,
[5]and Ibzan, who is Nahshon, led them for seven years, Elon from Zebulon for
ten years, and Abdon for eight years. [6]The children of Israel were enslaved by the
Judg 12:8-15 Philistines for forty years. God saved them through Samson, the son of Mano-
Judg 13:1; 16:31 ah, who led them for twenty years. [7]Then the children of Israel were without
a leader for eighteen years until the priest Eli rose over them and led them for
1 Sam 4:18 | 1 Sam 7:15 forty years. [8]Samuel rose over them and led them for twenty years. [9]In Samuel's
days the Israelites angered God who had delivered them from the Egyptians'
1 Sam 8:8 slavery. [10]They made Saul, the son of Kish, king for themselves, and he ruled
1 Sam 8:19–10:27; 13:1 over them for forty years. [11]In Saul's days there lived Goliath, the Philistine hero.
He drew near, mocked Israel and blasphemed against God. [12]David, the son of
Jesse, killed him. [13]Then David was glorified and praised by the daughters of
1 Sam 17:4–18:9 Israel and Saul persecuted him. [14]The Philistines could kill Saul because he had

forsaken God and taken refuge with the demons. [15]David ruled over the chil- 1 Sam 28:8-19; 31:2-7
dren of Israel for forty years and after him his son Solomon ruled for forty years. 1 Kgs 2:11; 11:42

The Reign of Solomon

[16]Solomon made great marvels. He also sent to Ophir in order to fetch gold from
the golden mountains, and the ships cruised for thirty-six months upon the sea;
thus they went forth. [17]He built Tadmor within the desert and made great mar- 1 Kgs 9:28; 2 Chr 8:18
vels within it. [18]When Solomon passed by the foothills of the mountain which is 2 Chr 8:4
called Seïr he found an altar there which Piorzani, Pirozaki and Nasnador had
built, [19]those whom the hero Nimrod had sent to Bileam, priest of the mountain
of Seïr, because he had heard that (Bileam) was using horoscopes. [20]When they
passed by the foothills of Seïr they built an altar there to the sun. [21]When Solomon saw it he built a city there and named it "Heliopolis," that is, "City of the
Sun." [22]Then he built Arvad amidst the sea. Ezek 27:8, 11

[23]Solomon rose and was glorified until the news of his wisdom went forth
to all the ends of the created world. [24]The queen of Saba went and came forth 1 Kgs 10:1-13; 2 Chr
in order to meet him. [25]Solomon loved Hiram, the king of Tyre, much. [26]Hiram 9:1-12 | 1 Kgs 5:1-12; 2 Chr 2:3-16
ruled for 500 years in Tyre, from the days of David's reign until the reign of Zed- *Midr. Gen. Rab.* 84:8;
ekiah, so that all the kings of the children of Israel erred, for he was a man who Aphrahat, *Dem.* 5:7; Jerome, *Comm. in Ez.*
blasphemed and said: [27]"*I am God, I sit upon God's throne within the heart of the* 28:11-19
sea!" [28]King Nebuchadnezzar killed him. Ezek 28:2 | *Midr. Lev. Rab.* 18.2

36 [1]In the days of Hiram purple made its appearance as a garment for kings. [2]A
dog was passing along the sea-shore and saw a purple-murex which had come Iulius Pollux, *Onomasticon* 1:45; Achilles
out of the sea. [3]He bit it, and his muzzle was filled at once with the blood of the Tatius, *Leucippe and*
murex. [4]When a shepherd saw this he took wool and wiped the dog's muzzle. *Clitophon* 2:11; Cassio-
[5]Out of this wool he made himself a crown and put it upon his head. [6]When he dorus, *Variae* 1:2:7
was walking around in the sunlight those who saw him thought that flashes of
fire were issuing from his head. [7]When king Hiram heard about it he sent after
him and seeing the wool marvelled at it and was amazed. [8]All the dyers gathered
and were overwhelmed by it; they went out in order to investigate this thing,
gathered some of these murexes, and were exceedingly glad.

[9]Solomon waxed very great. [10]The food on his table consisted every day of
forty oxen, 100 sheep, thirty cors of fine flour, sixty (cors of) meal, and 300
pitchers of wine, regardless of deer, gazelles, antelopes, and game of the field.
[11]Then he became bold, transgressed the law, and did not hearken to his father's 1 Kgs 4:22-23
commandments. [12]He took for himself 1000 women from all the nations God 1 Kgs 11:6
hates. [13]In his old age he gave his soul to the women who played with it. He 1 Kgs 11:3
listened to their words, did as they wished, and forsook the God of his father David. [14]He built altars to the devils, sacrificed to idols and statues, and worshipped 1 Kgs 11:4
the work of human hands. [15]Therefore God turned away his face from him and 1 Kgs 11:5
he died. [16]He had reigned in Jerusalem for forty-one years and after him his son
Rehoboam ruled. 1 Kgs 11:42; 2 Chr 9:30

From Rehoboam to the Babylonian Exile

37 [1]He was forty-one years old when he began to reign, [2]and he soiled Jerusalem 1 Kgs 14:21-24;
with debauchery, altars of devils and the stink of impiety. [3]Then David's king- 2 Chr 12:13

ship was split apart. [4]In the fifth year of his reign king Shishak of Egypt went
up to Jerusalem and took the whole treasure of the temple-service, the whole
treasure of David's kingdom, and Solomon's (treasure), too—the vessels of gold
and silver—while he exalted himself and said: "I do not take what belongs to
1 Kgs 14:25-26; 2 Chr 12:2, 9 you but the riches which your ancestors brought up from Egypt!" [5]Rehoboam
died in the impiety of his father Solomon and his son Abijah reigned after him.
1 Kgs 14:31; 2 Chr 12:16 [6]He corrupted Jerusalem with debauchery and impiety, for Absalom's daughter
1 Kgs 15:2 Maacah was his mother. [7]Then he died in the impiety of his father. [8]After him
1 Kgs 15:10 his son Asa reigned in Jerusalem for forty years. [9]He did what is good in front
of the Lord, removed debauchery from Jerusalem, made impiety cease among
his people, and observed the commandments of God. [10]He expelled her[a] from
his kingdom, mocking her in front of the whole people on account of the altar
1 Kgs 15:13; 2 Chr 15:16 of idols. [11]Zerah went up against Judah, but God humiliated him in front of Asa.
2 Chr 14:9-15 [12]Thus Asa died in righteousness as his father David.

1 Kgs 15:24; 2 Chr 17:1 [13]After him his son Jehoshaphat reigned. [14]He walked in the way of his father
1 Kgs 22:43; 2 Chr 20:32 Asa and did what is good in front of the Lord. [15]However, God was wroth with
him because he loved the house of Ahab and on that account God did not allow
(him) to fetch gold from Ophir. [16]He had made ships in order to send them out
1 Kgs 22:48-49; 2 Chr 20:35-37 but they vanished in Ezion Geber. [17]He was thirty-two years old when he began
1 Kgs 22:42; 2 Chr 20:31 to reign and his mother's name was Azuba, the daughter of Shilhi. [18]Jehoshaphat
died in righteousness and his son Joram reigned after him. [19]He was thirty-two
1 Kgs 22:50; 2 Chr 21:1 years old when he began to rule and he reigned for eight years in Jerusalem,
2 Kgs 8:16-18; 2 Chr 21:5-6 but he did not do what is good in front of the Lord. [20]He sacrificed upon the
devils' altars and died in impiety. [21]His son Ahaziah reigned after him. He was
twenty-two years old when he began to reign and stayed in Jerusalem for one
2 Kgs 8:24-26; 2 Chr 22:2 year. [22]During this year he did bad things in front of the Lord, [23]and on account
of the iniquity and godlessness he committed, God delivered him into the hands
2 Kgs 8:27; 2 Chr 22:4 of his enemies who killed him.

[24]After he had died his mother killed all the princes of David's house because she intended to destroy the kingdom of the Jews. [25]She left no one of the
royal house, whom she did not kill, except only Joash, whom Joram's daughter
2 Kgs 11:1-3; 2 Chr 22:10-12 Jehosheba secretly hid within her house. [26]Ahab's sister reigned for seven years
in Jerusalem. She corrupted it with debauchery because she commanded that
the women fornicate openly and without fear, and the men commit adultery
with one another's wives without being blamed. [27]Thus she committed all the
debauchery of Jezebel and the impiety of Ahab's house in Jerusalem.

38 [1]Seven years later the inhabitants of Jerusalem wondered whom they should
make king. [2]When Jehoiada the priest heard (about this), he gathered them in
the house of the Lord, the temple which Solomon had built. [3]After all the commanders of thousands and commanders of hundreds had gathered, Jehoiada the
priest spoke to them: "Who do you say should be king and sit upon the throne
of David, if not a king and son of a king?" [4]When he showed them (Joash) they
were exceedingly glad. The commanders of thousands and commanders of hundreds went up [5](together with) the runners and messengers, and led the king

a. That is, Maacah.

down to the house of the Lord, while the army surrounded him and guarded
him on all sides. [6]Then Jehoiada the priest made him sit upon the throne of his
father David. [7]He was seven years old when he began to reign [8]and he ruled for
forty years in Jerusalem. His mother's name was Zibiah of Beer-sheba, whereas
Athaliah was killed. [9]Joash, however, was ungrateful for the favours which Jehoiada the priest had bestowed upon him, and after his death he spilled the
innocent blood of (Jehoiada's) sons. Then Joash died.

2 Kgs 11:4–12:1; 2 Chr 23:1–24:1

2 Chr 24:22

[10]After him Amaziah reigned. [11]He was twenty-five years old when he began
to rule and he reigned for twenty-nine years in Jerusalem. His mother's name
was Jehoaddan. [12]Then Amaziah died and his son Uzziah reigned after him.
[13]He was sixteen years old when he began to reign. He ruled fifty years in Jerusalem, and his mother's name was Jecoliah. [14]He did what is good in front of the
Lord. [15]Then he became bold, went to the holy of holies, took a censer from the
priest, and burned incense in the temple of the Lord. [16]Because he had done this,
leprosy spread upon his face, [17]and since the prophet Isaiah had not admonished
him, prophecy was taken from him until Uzziah died.

2 Kgs 12:21; 2 Chr 24:27

2 Kgs 14:2; 2 Chr 25:1

2 Kgs 15:1-5; 2 Chr 26:1-5, 16-21

[18]After him his son Jotham reigned. He was twenty-five years old when
he began to rule, and he reigned for sixteen years in Jerusalem. His mother's
name was Jerusha, daughter of Zadok. He did what is good before the Lord
God. [19]Then Jotham died and his son Ahaz ruled after him. He was twenty years
old when he began to reign. [20]He ruled for sixteen years in Jerusalem and his
mother's name was Aphin, daughter of Levi. [21]He did what is evil before the
Lord and sacrificed to the devils. [22]When Tiglath-Pileser, king of Assur, went up
against him, [23]Ahaz wrote (to him) that he was his slave, and thus the Assyrian
enslaved him. [24]He sent gold and silver from the house of the Lord to the king of
Assur. During his reign the children of Israel were led away captive. [25]Then the
king sent for people to come from Babylon that they might live in this country
alongside the children of Israel, but because lions were killing them, [26]the king
of Assur sent the priest Uri to them, who taught them the laws.

2 Kgs 15:7, 32-34; 2 Chr 26:23–27:2

2 Kgs 16:1-4; 2 Chr 28:1-4

2 Kgs 16:7-8; 2 Chr 28:16-21

2 Kgs 17:23-28

39 [1]Then Ahaz died and his son Hezekiah ruled after him. [2]Hezekiah was
twenty-five years old when he began to reign, and he ruled for twenty-nine
years in Jerusalem. His mother's name was Abi, the daughter of Zechariah.
[3]He did what is good before the Lord: He demolished the altars and took away
the bronze-snake which Moses had made in the desert, for the children of
Israel were worshipping it, and thus he removed impiety from Jerusalem. [4]In
his fourth year Shalmaneser, king of Assur, went up, led the rest of Israel away
captive and sent them to Media beyond Babylon. [5]In Hezekiah's twentieth year
Sennacherib, the king of Assur, went up and led away captive all the cities and
villages of Judah, but Jerusalem was saved through Hezekiah's prayer. [6]When
he fell ill unto death it grieved him and he wept. [7]Now there are people who
blame him, but they do not take pains to know why it grieved him. [8]Hezekiah's
grief was that, when he fell ill unto death, he did not have a son to reign after
him. [9]When he beheld with his inner eye and perceived that he did not have
a son to rule after him, he was afflicted, wept and spoke: [10]"Woe unto me that
I die without children, that this blessing which has been granted for forty-six
generations is taken from me today, (that) I am the one who causes David's

2 Kgs 18:1-4; 2 Chr 28:27–29:2

2 Kgs 18:9, 11

2 Kgs 18:13; 19:14-37; Isa 37:14-38; 2 Chr 32:1, 20-22

2 Kgs 20:1, 3; 2 Chr 32:24; Isa 38:1

Aphrahat, *Dem.* 23:18

kingship to cease, so that the succession of the kings of Judah is taken from me today!" [11]This was Hezekiah's grief.

[12]After he had recovered from his illness he remained (upon the throne) for fourteen years, and Manasseh was born unto him. [13]Then Hezekiah died in great consolation, leaving a son to sit upon the throne of his father David.

40 [1]Manasseh was twelve years old when he began to reign, and he ruled in
Jerusalem for fifty-five years. His mother's name was Hephzibah. [2]He was more
wicked and villainous than all those who had been before him. He built altars
to the devils and sacrificed to the idols, thus filling Jerusalem with iniquity and
2 Kgs 21:1-9; angering God. [3]When Isaiah the prophet blamed him, he threatened him and
2 Chr 33:1-9 sent two villainous men, [4]who sawed the prophet Isaiah apart with a saw inside
Mart. Isa. 5:1-15; a piece of wood, from his head to his feet below. [5]He was 120 years old when they
y. Sanh. 10:2; *b. Yebam.* 49b sawed him apart, and he had been a prophet of God for ninety years. [6]After he
had killed Isaiah, Manasseh repented: He wore sackcloth upon his body, decreed
a fast upon himself, and ate his bread with tears all the days of his life, for he
had committed a crime. [7]Then Manasseh died and his son Amon reigned after
him. [8]He was twenty-two years old when he began to reign, and he ruled for
two years in Jerusalem. His mother's name was Meshullemeth. [9]Amon did what
2 Kgs 21:18-20; is evil before the Lord: He made his son pass through the fire. [10]Then he died
2 Chr 33:20-22 and his son Josiah reigned after him. [11]He was eight years old when he began to
rule, and he reigned in Jerusalem for thirty-one years. His mother's name was
Jedidah, the daughter of Adaiah from Bozkath. [12]He did what is good in front
of the Lord, and did everything just as his father David had, swaying neither to
2 Kgs 21:26–22:2; the right nor to the left. [13]Pharaoh the lame killed him, [14]he died, and his son
2 Chr 34:1-2 Jehoahaz ruled after him.

[15]Jehoahaz was twenty-three years old when he began to rule, and he reigned in Jerusalem for three months. His mother's name was Hamutal, the daughter of Jeremiah from Libnah. [16]He did what is evil before the Lord just as Manasseh had done. [17]Pharaoh the lame, the king of Egypt, took him captive in Riblah, in the land of Hemath, while he (still) reigned in Jerusalem, and exacted a tribute upon the country, 100 talents of silver and ten talents of gold. [18]Pharaoh the lame made Eliakim, son of Josiah, king instead of his father Josiah and changed his name into Jehoiakim. [19]Jehoahaz he led away captive, and thus he came to Egypt and died there. [20]Jehoiakim gave silver and gold to Pharaoh, but exacted the silver and gold from the land according to Pharaoh's command; everybody of the country-folk brought silver and gold as they could, according to the command of Pharaoh the lame.

41 [1]Jehoiakim was twenty-five years old when he began to reign, and he ruled for eleven years in Jerusalem. His mother's name was Zebidah, the daughter of Pedaiah from Ramta. [2]He did what is evil in front of the Lord just as his fathers had done. [3]In his days Nebuchadnezzar, the king of Babylon, went up against Jerusalem. [4]Jehoiakim was his servant for three years; then he changed his mind and rebelled against him, but the Lord incited armies against him on account of his sins. [5]After this Jehoiakim rested with his fathers, and his son Jehoiachin ruled after him. [6]The king of Egypt did not again go forth from his country because the king of Babylon had taken everything which belonged to the king of Egypt, from the brook of Egypt to the river Euphrates. [7]Jehoiachin was seven years old when he began to reign, and he ruled for three months in Jerusalem. His mother's name was Nehushta, the daughter of Elnathan from Jerusalem. [8]He did what is evil in front of the Lord just as his fathers had done. [9]At that time Nebuchadnezzar, the king of Babylon, went up against Jerusalem. [10]The king of Babylon led away (Jehoiachin's) people captive in the eighth year of his reign, and he took away from there the whole treasure of the house of the Lord and the treasure of the king's palace. [11]He exiled to Babylon all Jerusalem, the king, his mother, his wives and noblemen, and led all the men away into exile in Babylon as prisoners of war. [12]Then he made (Jehoiachin's) paternal uncle Mattaniah king in his stead and gave him the name Zedekiah.

[13]Zedekiah was twenty years old when he began to reign, and he ruled for eleven years in Jerusalem. His mother's name was Hamutal, the daughter of Jeremiah from Libna. [14]He did what is evil in front of the Lord just as Jehoiachin had done. [15]Then the wrath of the Lord came upon Jerusalem: [16]Zedekiah rebelled against the king of Babylon. [17]In the ninth year of his reign Nebuchadnezzar, king of Babylon, went against Jerusalem. [18]The city was besieged until king Zedekiah's eleventh year; [19]then it was opened and all the warriors fled from the city at night by the valley-path. [20]The Chaldean army pursued the king and seized him in the plain of Jericho. [21]His whole army was scattered away from him; they took Zedekiah and brought him up to the king of Babylon who pronounced judgment on him. [22]The king of Babylon massacred king Zedekiah's sons in front of his eyes, put out Zedekiah's eyes, bound him with chains and brought him to Babylon.

2 Kgs 23:36–25:7; 2 Chr 36:5-13

The Exile and Return

42 [1]Because the high-priest Simeon had freedom of speech in front of the captain of the guards, he made supplication to him [2]that (the captain) might give him all the books and not burn them. [3]Simeon the high-priest gathered them and put them inside a well. [4]Then Jerusalem was devastated and laid waste, so that no one remained there except the prophet Jeremiah who sat and made lamentations for twenty years. [5]After that Jeremiah the prophet died in Samaria, and the priest Uri buried him in Jerusalem, as Jeremiah had made him swear. [6]Until Jerusalem's first devastation the Hebrew, Greek and Syriac authors are in possession of the truth and can show the genealogies of the tribes and nations. [7]From the destruction of Jerusalem onwards, however, there is no truth in their writings, rather (they list) only the patriarchs, while they do not show the origins of the priests' genealogy.

[8]Jehoiachin stayed bound in prison for thirty-seven years. After he left prison he took for himself as wife Gulit, the daughter of Eliakim, and begot with her in Babylon Shealtiel. [9]Then Jehoiachin died in Babel. Shealtiel took for himself as wife Hetbat, the daughter of Elkana, and begot with her Zerubbabel. [10]Zerubbabel took for himself as wife Malkat, the daughter of Ezra the scribe, but there was not born unto him by her a son in Babylon. [11]As in the days of Zerubbabel, chief of the Jews, the Persian Cyrus ruled in Babylon, [12]Cyrus took as wife the daughter of Shealtiel, Zerubbabel's sister. He married her according to Persian

Ezra 3:2; Neh 12:1; Hag 1:1; Matt 1:12; Luke 3:27

law and made her queen. [13]She, however, begged Cyrus to bring about the return of the children of Israel, [14]and since Zerubbabel was her brother she was
Eph 5:28 concerned about the return from exile. [15]Cyrus loved his wife as himself and fulfilled her wishes. [16]He sent messengers into the whole land of Babylon in order
to gather all the children of Israel. [17]After they had been gathered Cyrus spoke to
Zerubbabel, his wife's brother: "Rise, lead all the children of your nation! Go up
Ezra 1:1-4 in peace to Jerusalem, rebuild the city of your ancestors, dwell and reign in it!"

[18]Because Cyrus brought about the return of the children of Israel, God
Isa 45:1 spoke: *"I hold my servant Cyrus by his right hand."* [19]Cyrus is called "my shep-
Isa 44:28 | Isa 45:1 herd" and "the Lord's anointed," because his seed was united with David's seed
through Meshinat, Zerubbabel's sister, whom he had married. [20]Then the children of Israel went up from Babylon, Zerubbabel having been made king over
Ezra 3:2 them, while Joshua, son of Jozadak son of Aaron, was high-priest, [21]just as the
angel had shown to the prophet Zechariah, telling him: "These are the sons of
Zech 4:14 anointing." [22]When the exile took place the fifth millennium ended.

From the Return to the rebuilding of the Temple

43 [1]When they went up they had neither scribes nor prophets. [2]Ezra the scribe
went down into that well and found a censer filled with fire, while fragrant incense was coming out of it. [3]He took three times from the ashes of those books
and put it inside his mouth. [4]At once God let the spirit of prophecy dwell with-
4 Ezra 14:37-48 in him, so that he renewed all the prophetic books. [5]That fire which had been
2 Mac 1:19-36 found within the well was holy fire from the house of the Lord.

[6]Zerubbabel reigned in Jerusalem, Joshua (was) high-priest, and Ezra wrote
the Law and the Prophets. [7]When they had come up from Babylon, the children of Israel celebrated the Passover. [8]Those three Passovers did the children
of Israel celebrate in all their life: One in Egypt in the days of Moses, the other
one during Josiah's reign, and the third when they had come up from the land
Justin, *Dial. cum Tryph.* 40:2 of Babylon. [9]Then Passover was taken away from them forever. [10]From the first
pillage of Jerusalem, during which Daniel went down into captivity, until the
beginning of Cyrus the Persian's reign there were seventy years according to the
Jer 25:11; 29:10; Dan 9:2 prophecy of Jeremiah. [11]The children of Israel began building the temple in the
days of Zerubbabel, Joshua son of Jozadak, and Ezra the scribe. [12]Its construc-
John 2:20 tion was finished after forty-six years as is written in the Holy Gospel.

Genealogies of Mary, Mother of Jesus

[13]And once more the genealogy of the tribes has been lost to the authors, and
they cannot show us from where the patriarchs took their wives, and where
they came from. [14]I, however, have the true genealogies and will reveal them
truthfully to everybody. [15]When the children of Israel went up from Babylon
Zerubbabel begot together with Malkat, the daughter of Ezra the scribe, Abiud.
[16]Abiud married Zekit, the daughter of Joshua son of the priest Jozadak, and
begot together with her Eliakim. [17]Eliakim married Durnib and begot together
with her Azor. [18]Azor married Yalpat, the daughter of Hazor, and begot together
with her Zadok. [19]Zadok married Qeltin, the daughter of Durnim, and begot
together with her Achim. [20]Achim married Haskat, the daughter of Taël and begot together with her Eliud. [21]Eliud married Bashtin, the daughter of Hasol, and

begot together with her Eleazar. [22]Eleazar married Dihat, the daughter of Tolah, and begot together with her Matthan. [23]Matthan married Sabrat, the daughter of Phinehas, and begot together with her two sons within one womb, Jacob and Jonakir. [24]Jacob married Hadbit, the daughter of Eleazar, and begot together with her Joseph, [25]and Jonakir married Dina, the daughter of Peqor, and begot Matt 1:13-16
together with her Mary, from whom Christ was born. Aphrahat, *Dem.* 23:20

44 [1]Since none of the earlier authors found this genealogy of their ancestors' generations, the Jews are pressing hard the children of the Church to show them the ancestors of blessed Mary within the genealogy of their tribes. [2]On account of their urging the children of the Church to search the genealogies of their ancestors' tribes and show them the truth [3]they call Mary an adulteress. [4]Thus *Toledot Yeshu*
will be shut the mouth of the Jews and they shall believe that Mary is from the seed of the house of David and Abraham. [5]The Jews do not have the genealogy which shows them the truth about the tribes of their ancestors, for their books were burned three times by fire: [6]First in the days of Antiochus who incited them to apostasy, soiled the temple of the Lord, and forced them to sacrifice to idols; [7]second and third in the days of Herod, when Jerusalem was destroyed. [8]Because of this the Jews are greatly worried, for they do not possess the true genealogy of their ancestors. [9]They hurry and make haste to establish the truth but they cannot. [10]They have many writers, and each one of them writes what he wants. [11]They do not agree with one another because they cannot stand upon this foundation of truth. [12]But also our writers, the children of the Church, were not able to show us accurately and with the power of truth from where Adam's body was brought up to Golgotha, from where Melchizedek's ancestors came, and (who are) the ancestors of blessed Mary. [13]When the children of Israel were pressed by the Church and could not find the truth, they grew bold and wrote according to their fanciful errors. But those four (evangelists) have set before us this genealogy of sixty-three generations, from Adam to Christ. [14]Neither the Greek nor the Hebrew or Syriac writers, however, could show from where each one of them took his wife and whose daughter she was. [15]Since (until now) each one of the Syriac divines established true doctrines within the Church and gave faith an armour by which to fight and vanquish her enemies, [16]so the goodness of Christ granted to us, too, that which was impossible for them, so that we might increase the (Church's) rich treasure-house.

[17]This we wished to do with earnest zeal, as it is desired by our brother victorious in Christ and true friend Namosaya. [18]Since I was hindered by my negligence whereas you do not cease in your love of learning—and this on account of your friendship for me, I also will take care not to hold back that which you asked from me, but rather declare it to you. [19]Take heed, my brother Namosaya, of this genealogy which I write down for you. None of all the scholars was able to find it. [20]In those sixty-three generations, through which Christ's bodily substance has been transmitted, it is handed down thus: [21]Adam begot Aphrahat, *Dem.* 23:21
Seth. [22]Seth took for himself as a wife Kalimath, who had been born with Abel, and begot together with her Enosh. [23]Enosh took for himself as wife Hanna, the daughter of Yubal daughter of Huh daughter of Seth, and begot together with her Kenan. [24]Kenan took for himself as wife Perit, the daughter of Kutim

daughter of Yarbel, and begot together with her Mahalalel. [25]Mahalalel married
Zahtepar, the daughter of Enosh, and begot together with her Jared. [26]Jared married Zebida, the daughter of Kuhlon daughter of Kenan, and begot together with
her Enoch. [27]Enoch married Zadqin, the daughter of Tupih daughter of Mahalalel, and begot together with her Methuselah. [28]Methuselah married Sakot,
the daughter of Sukin, and begot together with her Lamech. [29]Lamech married
Kipar, the daughter of Tutab, and begot together with her Noah. [30]Noah married
Haykal, the daughter of Namos, and begot together with her Shem, Ham and
Japheth. [31]Shem begot Arphaxad, Arphaxad begot Shelah, Shelah begot Eber,
Eber begot Peleg, Peleg begot Reu, Reu begot Serug. Serug married Kehal, the
daughter of Peleg, and begot Nahor. Nahor married Naposh, the daughter of
Reu, and begot Terah. [32]Terah took two wives, Yona and Selmut. Together with
Yona he begot Abraham, and together with Selmut Sara. [33]Abraham married
Sara and begot Isaac. [34]Isaac married Rebecca and begot Jacob. [35]Jacob married
Leah and begot Judah. [36]Judah begot Perez together with Tamar. [37]Perez took
as wife Yahbat, the daughter of Levi, and begot together with her Hezron. [38]He-
zron begot Ram, and Ram begot Amminadab. [39]Amminadab begot Nahshon,
Nahshon begot Salmon, and Salmon begot together with Rahab Boaz. [40]Boaz
married Ruth, the daughter of Lot, and begot Obed. [41]Obed begot Jesse, and
Jesse begot king David. [42]David married Bathsheba and begot together with her
Solomon. [43]Solomon begot Rehoboam, Rehoboam begot Abijah, Abijah begot
Asa, Asa begot Jehoshaphat, Jehoshaphat begot Joram, Joram begot Ahaziah,
Ahaziah begot Joash. [44]Joash begot Amaziah, Amaziah begot Jotham, Jotham
begot Ahaz, Ahaz begot Hezekiah, Hezekiah begot Manasseh, Manasseh begot
Amon, Amon begot Josiah, Josiah begot Jehoiakim, Jehoiakim begot Jehoiachin,
Jehoiachin begot Shealtiel. [45]Shealtiel begot Zerubbabel, Zerubbabel begot Abi-
ud, Abiud begot Eliakim, Eliakim begot Azor, Azor begot Zadok, Zadok begot
Achim, Achim begot Eliud, Eliud begot Eleazar, Eleazar begot Matthan. Matthan married Sabrat, the daughter of Phinehas, and begot Jacob and Jonakir.
[46]Jacob married Hadbit, the daughter of Eleazar, and begot Joseph, the betrothed
Matt 1:1-16; of Mary. [47]Jonakir married Dina, who is Anna, the daughter of Peqor, and two
Luke 3:23-38 years after he had married her she gave birth to Mary by whom Jesus was born
who is called "Christ." [48]Because Joseph was Mary's cousin according to God's
foreknowledge, who knew that Mary would be harassed by the Jews, she was
given to her cousin Joseph, in order to guard her. [49]Look, my brother Namosaya, that the ancestors of blessed Mary are from David's progeny. [50]Behold, I
make you stand upon the fundament of truth, upon which none of the (other)
writers could rely. [51]Perceive how these sixty-three generations succeeded one
another from Adam until the birth of Christ. [52]For the Jews likewise it must be
a pleasure to find the generations of their ancestors' tribes. [53]Look, my brother
Namosaya, the fifth millennium ended in the days of Cyrus. [54]From the millennium of Cyrus until the passion of our redeemer it is an era of 500 years in
accordance with the true prophecy of Daniel, who prophesied and spoke: "*After*
Dan 9:26 *sixty-two weeks the Messiah will be killed*" which amounts to 1500 years. [55]Behold
how the mouth of the Jews is shut by this. [56]Because they were bold enough to
say that the Messiah did not yet come, they must needs do one of two things:
either to accept Daniel's prophecy or to admit that they do not accept it, [57]for the

prophecy has been fulfilled, the weeks have passed by, Christ was killed and the holy city was destroyed by Vespasian.

The Magi and the birth of Christ

45 [1]Look now, lover of doctrine, our brother Namosaya: In the forty-second
year of Augustus' reign Christ was born in Bethlehem in Judah, as it is written
in the Holy Gospel. [2]Two years before Christ was born, a star was seen by the
Luke 2:1-7
magi. They saw a star in the heavenly firmament which shone with a brighter
light than all the other stars, [3]and a girl within it holding a child, while a crown
Prot. Jas. 21:2
was being put upon her head. [4]According to their custom the kings of old and
Ephrem, *De nativ.* 24:5
Chaldaean magi studied all the movements of the constellations. [5]When they
saw the star they were agitated, frightened and fearful, and the whole country
of Persia was troubled. [6]The kings, magi, and wise men of Persia were stupe-
fied. They were greatly terrified by the sign which they had seen and said:
[7]"Maybe the king of the Greeks decided to make war against Nimrod's country." [8]Therefore the magi and Chaldaeans hurried and recited from the books
of their wisdom, and by the wisdom of their books they understood, learned,
and made their stand upon the power of truth. [9]Now this thing was truthfully
found out by the Chaldaean magi, who were able by the course of those stars
which they call signs of the Zodiac to know the foreboding of things before
they happen. [10]This knowledge is also given to those who navigate on the sea.
Even before there is an uproar of wind, or a storm awakens against them, the
course of the stars reveals to them what kind of danger is rising against them.
[11]Thus also those magi, when they recited from the revelations of Nimrod,
found within them that a king was going to be born in Judah, and Christ's
whole life was revealed to them. [12]They left the east at once according to the
tradition which they had received from their ancestors, went up to the mountains of Nod, which are on this side of the entranceways to the east, at their
northern foothills, and took from there gold, myrrh, and incense. [13]May you
understand from this, my brother Namosaya, that they knew the whole ministry of our saviour's life by those three offerings which they brought: [14]gold for
the king, myrrh for the physician, and incense for the priest. [15]They perceived
Ephrem, *Comm. in Diat.* 2:25
and knew that he was king, physician, and priest. [16]For when the king of Saba
was a little boy, his father took him to a rabbi who taught him the Hebrew
books more than to his comrades and his (own) sons with him. [17]Then (the
king) told his servants: "It is written in all the books of genealogies, too, that a
king will be born in Bethlehem!" [18]These are the ones who brought gifts to the
Matt 2:5-6; Mic 5:1 [Evv 5:2]
king; (they are) kings and sons of kings: [19]Hormizdad of Makozdi, the king of
Persia, who is called king of kings and dwells in lower Azerbaijan; Yazdgerd,
king of Saba; and Parwezdad, king of Sheba in the east.

[20]When they prepared themselves to go up, the kingdom of giants was agitated and troubled, even though they had a strong army. Likewise all the cities
of the east were frightened on account of them. [21]Jerusalem and Herod were
trembling before them, too, when they approached him. He commanded and
told them: "Go in peace and inquire diligently about the child. [22]When you have
found it come to me that I also may go and worship it." [23]Thus he offered wor-
Matt 2:8
ship with his mouth, while deceit lay hidden within his heart.

46 1When the magi were going up there was great turmoil in Judah on account
of an edict of emperor Augustus which commanded that everybody had to be
Matt 2:3; Luke 2:1 registered in the place and city of his ancestors. 2Herod was very frightened because of this and told the magi: "You should go and inquire about him, for I am a
friend of Caesar." 3They are called magi on account of the magi's regalia worn by
the pagan kings, for when they are sacrificing and make offerings to their gods
they wear two vestments: on the inside the royal one, and the one of the magi
on the outside. 4Likewise also those who were going up to Christ had donned
two vestments in order to bring their offerings. 5When they left Jerusalem and
Herod, the star which guided them on the way appeared to them, so that they
were exceedingly glad. 6The star went ahead of them until it entered into a cave,
Matt 2:9-10; Luke 2:12; and they saw the child wrapped in swaddling-clothes and lying in a manger.
Prot. Jas. 21:3 7While they were on their way they said to one another that once they arrived
they would see great marvels as is befitting the arrangement and order within a
royal mansion. 8As soon as the king was born—thus they thought—they would
find in the land of Israel a kingly palace, golden beds arranged upon carpets, a
king and prince wrapped in purple, rank and file of the king's soldiers standing
in awe, the kingdom's noblemen honouring him with presents, royal dining-
tables being prepared with dainties arranged (upon them), and servants and
maids attending in fear. 9This the magi expected to see, but they did not. Instead
they beheld greater marvels than this. When they entered into the cave, 10they
saw Joseph sitting in wonder and Mary in admiration. 11No bed was arranged
for him, no table prepared, and no royal ceremonial observed. 12When they saw
all this misery and poverty, they did not doubt in their hearts, but drew near in
fear, reverently worshipped him, and produced their offerings: gold, myrrh, and
Matt 2:11-12 incense. 13Mary and Joseph were exceedingly grieved because they did not have
anything to offer them, but the magi fed on their provisions. 14Christ was eight
days old, when the magi brought him gifts. 15At the time when Joseph circumcised Christ, Mary received the offerings. 16Joseph in truth circumcised him ac-
Luke 2:21-24 cording to the law, 17but he performed circumcision without anything being cut
off from (Jesus). 18Like iron which passes and cuts a flame of fire without cutting
anything off from it, in that way also Christ was circumcised, while nothing was
taken away from him.

19While the magi stayed with him for three days, they saw the host of heaven
going up and down towards Christ, and they heard the angels' glorious voice
Luke 2:13 praising and singing: 20"*Holy, holy, holy, Lord God Almighty, heaven and earth are*
Isa 6:3 *full of his glory!*" 21They were in great fear, truly believed in Christ, and said: "He
is the king who came down from heaven and was made man." 22Then Parwez-
dad spoke and told them: "Now I know that Isaiah's prophecy is true, because
when I attended the Hebrew school I read Isaiah and found this: '*For a child is*
born unto us and a son is given to us; his name is called Miraculous, Counsellor,
Isa 9:5 [Evv 9:6] *God, Eternal Hero.*' 23At another place it is written: '*Behold, the virgin will con-*
ceive and give birth to a son; his name will be called Immanuel, which translates
Isa 7:14; Matt 1:23 as "God with us."'"

24Because he was a man and (at the same time) angels came down from heav-
en to him, he was in truth Lord of angels and men. 25All the magi believed and
said: "In truth this king is God, for there were born unto us many kings, heroes,

and sons of heroes, but it has not been heard that angels came down to them."
[26]Then all of them at once rose and worshipped him as lord and king of the
whole earth. (After that) they prepared provisions for themselves and went back
to their country by way of the desert. Matt 2:12

Herod's slaughter of the infants at Bethlehem and his death

47 [1]There are people who quarrel about this and say: "Where was Christ when
the infants were killed?" [2]For it is written that he was not found in the land of Judah. [3]He fled to Egypt in order that there might be fulfilled what is written: "*Out
of Egypt I called my son.*" [4]Know that, when Christ entered Egypt, all the idols Hos 11:1, Matt 2:14-15
within it were cast down, fell upon the ground, and broke, so that there might be Eusebius, *Dem. evang.*
fulfilled what is written: "*Behold, the Lord rides upon the swift clouds and enters* 6:20; 9:2; *Ps.-Mt.* 24; *arab. Inf. Gos.* 10
Egypt, while Egypt's idols tremble before him." [5]He stayed there until Herod had Isa 19:1
died, and his son Archelaus reigned after him. Matt 2:19, 22

[6]Know, my brother Namosaya, that everybody under Herod's rule had to take
part in the census during fifty days. [7]Unless the census had been finished and Luke 2:1-3
closed, and (unless) Herod had ended it and sent (its results) to Augustus in
Rome, Christ would not have fled from Herod, nor were the infants killed until
then. [8]Rather Christ was born during the disturbance of this census. [9]After his
birth, when forty days were finished, he entered the temple of the Lord, and old
Simeon, son of Joshua son of Jozadak, who had come up from Babylon during
the time of exile, embraced him. He was 500 years old when he held Christ upon Luke 2:25
his arms. [10]Then the angel immediately told Joseph: "*Rise, take the child and his
mother and flee to Egypt!*" [11]When the census was finished, and the Jews were Matt 2:13
about to go back each one to his place and village, [12]Herod began to search for
the magi and was told that they had returned to their place. [13]He grew very
angry, sent at once, and had all the children of Bethlehem and the surrounding villages killed. [14]When he passed through the little ones and John, the son Matt 2:16
of Zechariah, was not found among them, he said: [15]"It indeed must be his son
who will rule over Israel!" for he had heard what was said to Zechariah by the
angel when he was expecting (the birth of) John. [16]Then he sent to Zechariah
and told him: "Bring John to me!" [17]Zechariah said: "I am a priest and minister
in the temple. I do not know where are the child and his mother." [18]On account
of this he was slain between the sanctuary and the altar. [19]Elisabeth took John Matt 23:35; Luke 11:51; *Prot. Jas.* 23:1-3
and went out to the desert.

[20]Herod immediately received a merciless judgment of death and fell ill.
[21]His teeth rotted and his body crawled with maggots, and thus he was exceedingly tormented by pain until people were not able to approach him because of
the fetid smell. [22]In this bitter pain his soul went away to utter darkness. [23]How-
ever, even in death he ruined many, for he spoke to his son Archelaus and his
sister Salome: [24]"As soon as I die kill those who have been imprisoned by me!"
[25]For in each family there had been imprisoned by him one soul, and he said:
"I know that my death will be a great joy for the Jews, so in order that they shall
not rejoice and be glad while you are sad and weeping, kill those who have been
imprisoned by me, so that they have to mourn me on account of the death of *Ant.* 17:6:5 [168-178];
those, even though they do not want it." [26]They did as he had commanded them *B.J.* 1:56-59; Aphrahat, *Dem.* 5:20; Eusebius,
[27]and when this happened there was not one family in all Judah which did not *Hist. eccl.* 1:8:5-8

mourn, just as (happened in) the mourning which took place in Egypt in the days of Moses.

Chronological notes

48 [1]When Herod had died and his death came to Joseph's knowledge, he re-
Matt 2:19-22 turned to Galilee. [2]Being thirty years old, Christ was being baptized by John,
the son of Zechariah. [3]John had spent his whole life in the desert and fed on a
Matt 3:1, 4; Mark 1:4-6; Luke 3:2 root which is called Qamuts, that is, honey of the field. [4]In the twelfth year of Tiberius' reign Christ suffered. [5]Understand and see, my brother Namosaya, that
in Jared's days, in his fortieth year, the first millennium ended. [6]In the 600th year
of Noah the second millennium ended, in Reu's seventy-fourth year the third
millennium ended, in Ehud's twenty-sixth year the fourth millennium ended,
[7]in the second year of Cyrus the fifth millennium ended, and in the 500th year of
the sixth millennium Christ suffered according to his human nature.

Christ and Adam

[8]Know also this, that Christ dwelled within Mary in Nazareth, was born in Bethlehem, put into a manger, held by Simeon in the temple of Solomon, raised in Galilee, and anointed by Mary Magdalene. [9]He ate the Passover in the house of Nicodemus, the brother of Joseph from Rama. He was imprisoned in Annas' house and beaten with a stick in the house of Caiaphas. [10]He had to embrace the pillar and was scourged with a whip in the Praetorium of Pilate. [11]On a Friday in Nisan, the fourteenth day of the full moon, our saviour suffered for us. [12]In the first hour of Friday God made Adam from dust, and in the first hour of Friday Christ received spittle from Adam's children. [13]In the second hour of Friday the beasts, cattle, and birds gathered with Adam, and he named them while they bowed their heads in front of him. [14]In the second hour of Friday the Jews gathered against Christ gnashing their teeth at him according to what blessed
Ps 22:13 [Evv 22:12] David says: *"Many bulls encircled me, calves of Bashan surrounded me."* [15]In the
third hour of Friday the crown of honour was put upon Adam's head, and in the third hour of Friday a crown of thorns was put upon the head of Christ. [16]Three hours Adam remained in paradise shining with glory, and three hours Christ stayed in the law-court being scourged by those born of dust. [17]In the sixth hour Eve climbed upon the tree of transgressing the commandment, and in the sixth hour Christ climbed the cross, the tree of life. [18]In the sixth hour Eve gave Adam the fruit of bitter death, and in the sixth hour the accursed synagogue gave vinegar and gall to Christ. [19]Adam stayed three hours stripped bare underneath the tree, and Christ stayed three hours naked upon the wood of the cross. [20]Eve, the mother of mortal children, came forth from Adam's right side, and from the right side of Christ came forth baptism, the mother of immortal children. [21]On a Friday Adam and Eve sinned, and on a Friday their sin was removed. [22]On a Friday Adam and Eve died and on a Friday they were made alive. [23]On a Friday death began to rule over them, and on a Friday they were freed from its rule. [24]On a Friday Adam and Eve left paradise, and on a Friday our Lord went into the tomb. [25]On a Friday Adam and Eve were stripped naked, and on a Friday Christ bared himself in order to clothe them. [26]On a Friday Satan stripped them bare, and on a Friday Christ stripped bare Satan and all his hosts, and openly put

them to shame. [27]Adam left paradise and its door was closed, and on a Friday it was opened for a multitude to go in. [28]On a Friday the sharp sword was given to the cherub, and on a Friday Christ was struck and broke the sword's blade. [29]On a Friday priesthood, prophecy, and kingship were given to Adam and on a Friday kingship, priesthood, and prophecy were taken away from the Jews. [30]In the ninth hour of Friday Adam went down from the height of paradise to the lower earth, and on a Friday Christ went down in the ninth hour from the height of the cross to the lower parts of earth, to those who sleep in the dust.

Aphrahat, *Dem.* 23:20, 46

49 [1]Know that Christ resembled Adam in everything, as it is written. [2]At the same place where Melchizedek ministered as priest and Abraham made his son Isaac ascend upon the altar, the wood of the cross was fastened. [3]This place is the middle of the earth, where the four points of the compass embrace one another. [4]When God created the earth his great power ran in front of him and the earth ran after it from the four points of the compass. [5]There in Golgotha God's power stood still and rested, and there the four directions of the earth were joined together. [6]When Shem brought Adam's body up, this place was the earth's entrance. It opened, [7]and when Shem and Melchizedek had put Adam's body into the middle of the earth, the four points of the compass hurried to embrace Adam. [8]Then this entrance immediately was closed so that none of Adam's children could open it. [9]When the cross of Christ, the redeemer of Adam and his children, was put above it, the entrance of this place opened at Adam's face. [10]When the wood was fastened above it and Christ was struck by the lance, there came forth from his side blood and water. They went down into Adam's mouth and were baptism for him, so that he was baptized by them.

Heb 4:15

Basil, *Hex.* 1:9-10

[11]When the Jews crucified Christ upon the wood of the cross, they divided his garments among them underneath the cross as it is written. [12]Now his purple tunic was a royal garment, [13]and when they took off this royal garment, Pilate did not allow the Jews to dress him in an ordinary garment but in (another) royal garment of purple or scarlet colour. [14]By those two (garments) it shall be known that he was a king, [15]for no one else may wear purple except only a king. [16]Now one of the evangelists says that they dressed him in a purple chlamys, and this word is true and very reliable. [17]The other one says "of scarlet" and he likewise proclaims the truth. [18]"Of scarlet" signifies for us the blood and "of purple" the water—the one on account of its blood-like redness and the other one on account of purple's water-like greenish shade. [19]"Of scarlet" proclaims for us (Christ's) serene immortal nature; "of purple" his sad and mortal human one. [20]Understand therefore, my brother Namosaya, that scarlet proclaims life. [21]For the spies told Rahab the prostitute to tie a scarlet thread to the window, which was the one by which they went down after having been aided by her. [22]This is the typology depicted concerning her: The window is the side of our Lord Christ, and the scarlet thread his life-giving blood.

Matt 27:35; John 19:24

Matt 27:28

Mark 15:17

Josh 2:18

Justin, *Dial. cum Tryph.* 111:4; *1 Clem.* 12:7; Ephrem, *De nativ.* 1:33

The crucifixion of Christ

50 [1]Now they wove a crown of thorns and bristles, and put it upon his head. Behold, thus they clothed him in royal garments without knowing what they were doing. [2]They kneeled down, worshipped him, and idly spoke with their

Matt 27:28-29; Luke 23:34

Matt 27:29 mouths. 3Behold, my brothers, not even in death was anything taken away from
his kingship. 4When the Jews, the soldiers, and the servants of Herod and Pilate
were struggling to tear Christ's tunic apart and divide it among them, all of them
Matt 27:27-28; Mark 15:16-20; Luke 23:34; John 19:1-13, 23-24 being attracted by the beauty of its appearance, 5the centurion who was guarding
the cross also spoke, witnessed, and proclaimed in front of the whole synagogue:
Matt 27:54; Mark 15:39 "Truly, this man was the Son of God." 6He furthermore told them this: "The
sovereign's law does not allow me to cut royal garments apart. Rather cast lots to
whom it shall belong." 7When the Jews and servants of the king cast lots for it, it
fell to one of the soldiers who was a soldier of Pilate.

John 19:23 8The tunic of our Lord was seamless and woven through and through.
9Whenever there was a lack of rain at the place where it was kept and guarded,
the tunic was brought out, and as soon as it was held up to the sky, rain came
down abundantly. 10He also who had received it by lot used to bring it out whenever the seed was in need of rain, and then this miracle took place. 11Pilate took
it from him by violence and sent it to the emperor Tiberius. 12For us this tunic
signifies the true faith which none of the nations can tear apart.

13Three glorious gifts, which they did not honour, were at first given to the
Jews: kingship, priesthood, and prophecy. 14Prophecy through Moses, priesthood through Aaron, and kingship through David. 15These three gifts which
had been made use of through the generations, lines, and ages of the children of
Aphrahat, *Dem.* 23:20, 46 Israel, were taken from them in one day, so that they were stripped naked. 16The
loss of the three (gifts) took place thus: Prophecy (was lost) on account of the
cross, priesthood on account of the tunic's division, and kingship on account of
the crown of thorns. 17Likewise the spirit of holiness who was dwelling in the
holy of holies within the temple, left and went away, while the curtain at the
Matt 27:51 entrance to the holy of holies was torn apart.

18The Passover also fled and left them, for they did not celebrate another
Justin, *Dial. cum Tryph.* 40:2 Passover. 19Know, my brothers, that when Pilate urged them to enter the law-
court they told him: "We cannot enter the Praetorium because we did not yet
eat the Passover." 20When our Lord received the sentence of death by Pilate,
they hurried to enter the temple, brought out the biers of the ark, and made out
of them the cross of Christ. 21It was truly appropriate for them that those timbers by which the covenant was carried should carry the Lord of the covenant.
22The cross of Christ consisted of two timbers of equal height, depth, length,
and breadth. 23Accordingly Paul the apostle was exceedingly eager to make
known to the nations what the power of the cross is like, which was holding
Eph 3:18 the height, depth, length, and breadth of the earth. 24When they made Christ,
a shining lamp for the whole earth, ascend and put him upon the candelabra
of the cross, the sun's light was eclipsed and a veil of darkness was spread upon
Matt 27:45; Mark 15:33; Luke 23:44 the whole earth. 25Three nails penetrated our saviour's body: two in his hands
and one in his two feet. 26There were two robbers: one at his right side and the
Matt 27:38; Mark 15:27; Luke 23:33; John 19:18 other at his left.

Matt 27:48; Mark 15:36; Luke 23:36; John 19:29 **51** 1They gave him vinegar and gall in a sponge. 2By the vinegar which they gave
him it was made manifest that they had changed their mind and turned from
uprightness to evil, 3and by gall (was made manifest) the cruel snake's venom
within them. 4Thus they reveal that they, too, belonged to him who is the good

vine, from whom prophets, kings, and priests drank gladdening wine. [5]But because they were evil heirs they did not wish to cultivate the "vine of my beloved." [6]Instead of grapes they brought forth wild grapes, and the wine pressed from those wild grapes was sour. [7]When they crucified the heir upon the wood they proffered to him the dregs of their bad wine and made him drink of the wine from the heathens' vine, but he did not want to. [8](Rather:) "Give me from that vine which my father brought out of Egypt!" [9]Christ knew that there was to be fulfilled in him the prophecy of Moses, who had prophesied concerning them, saying: [10]"*Their grapes are bitter grapes, and their clusters vinegar for them, their venom is the venom of dragons and their chief moreover is the evil asp*. This you are giving back to the Lord." [11]Look, my brother Namosaya, how blessed Moses saw with the spirit's eye beforehand what they were going to do to Christ: "This you are giving back to the Lord." [12]The vine was rotten, (that is), the synagogue of the crucifiers. Its daughters are bitter grapes and its sons sour clusters. [13]Their chief Caiaphas is the evil asp, they are all evil snakes and full of Satan's venom who is the wicked dragon. [14]For water of the rock which he gave them to drink in the desert they made him drink vinegar, for manna and quails gall. [15]Not in a cup, however, they gave him to drink, but in a sponge, thus revealing that their ancestor's blessings had been denied to them. [16]It is made manifest insofar as, when a vessel is empty and about to be removed, it is cleaned and washed with a sponge. [17]Likewise also the Jews when they crucified Christ: with a sponge he washed away and took from them kingship, priesthood, prophecy, and anointing, and gave it to Christ, so that (only) the devastated and empty vessels of their bodies remained. [18]When the Law and the Prophets were about to be fulfilled and Adam, being naked, would see the well of living water which had been sent down from above for his salvation, Christ was wounded by the spear so that water and blood flowed from his side [19]without being mingled with one another. [20]For what reason did the blood come forth before the water? [21]For two reasons: first, because by the blood life was given to Adam, and only after life and resurrection (also) the water of baptism; second, because through blood he showed that he is immortal, and through water that he is mortal and capable of suffering. [22]Water and blood went down into Adam's mouth, and at that time Adam was saved and could wear the garment of glory. [23]Christ with his body's blood wrote an edict of return and put it into the hands of the robber.

Isa 5:1; Matt 21:33-41; Mark 12:1-9; Luke 20:9-16

Isa 5:2, 4

Ps 80:9 Peshitta

Deut 32:32-33

John 19:28-29

John 19:34

Ephrem, *Comm. in Diat.* 21:10-11

The cessation of the Jewish ordinances

52 [1]When everything was about to be fulfilled, a letter of divorce was written for the synagogue, she was expelled and stripped of the garments, as David had said about her from the first through the holy spirit, prophesying that "*until the horns of the altar*," until there the Jewish ordinance would be transmitted. [2]"Until the horns of the altar" means: until the cross of Christ. [3]From Adam to Seth, from Seth to Enosh, from Enosh to Kenan, from Kenan to Mahalalel, from Mahalalel to Jared, from Jared to Enoch, from Enoch to Methuselah, [4]from Methuselah to Lamech, from Lamech to Noah, from Noah to Shem, from Shem to Arphaxad, from Arphaxad to Shelah, from Shelah to Eber, from Eber to Peleg, from Peleg to Reu, from Reu to Serug, [5]from Serug to Nahor, from Nahor to Terah, from Terah to Abraham, from Abraham to Isaac, from Isaac to Jacob, from Jacob to

Ps 118:27

Justin, *Dial. cum Tryph.* 91:1-2; Tertullian, *Adv. Marc.* 3:18

Judah, from Judah to Perez, from Perez to Hezron, [6]from Hezron to Ram, from Ram to Amminadab, from Amminadab to Nahshon, from Nahshon to Salmon, from Salmon to Boaz, from Boaz to Obed, from Obed to Jesse, from Jesse to David, [7]from David to Solomon, from Solomon to Rehoboam, from Rehoboam to Abijah, from Abijah to Asa, from Asa to Jehoshaphat, from Jehoshaphat to Joram, from Joram to Ahaziah, from Ahaziah to Joash, [8]from Joash to Amaziah, from Amaziah to Uzziah, from Uzziah to Jotham, from Jotham to Ahaz, from Ahaz to Hezekiah, from Hezekiah to Manasseh, from Manasseh to Amon, from Amon to Josiah, [9]from Josiah to Jehoahaz, from Jehoahaz to Jehoiakim, from Jehoiakim to Jehoiachin, from Jehoiachin to Shealtiel, from Shealtiel to Zerubbabel, from Zerubbabel to Abiud, from Abiud to Eliakim, [10]from Eliakim to Azor, from Azor to Zadok, from Zadok to Achim, from Achim to Eliud, from Eliud to Eleazar, from Eleazar to Matthan, from Matthan to Jacob and Jonakir. [11]From Jonakir to Mary, from Mary to the manger, from the manger to circumcision, from circumcision to the temple, from the temple to Egypt, [12]from Egypt to Galilee, from Galilee to Jerusalem, from Jerusalem to the Jordan, from the Jordan to the desert, from the desert to Judah, from Judah to preaching, [13]from preaching to the upper chamber, from the upper chamber to Passover, from Passover to the law-court, from the law-court to the cross, from the cross to the tomb, from the tomb to the upper chamber, from the upper chamber to heaven, and from heaven to the throne at the right hand of the Father.

Matt 1:2-16; Luke 3:23-38; Aphrahat, *Dem.* 23:21

[14]Behold, my brother Namosaya, how the generations and tribes were transmitted from Adam to the Jews, and from the Jews again one upon another until the cross of Christ. [15]From then onwards the Jewish ordinances ceased, as blessed David says concerning them: "*The ordinances are being bound in a chain until the horns of the altar.*" [16]The chain signifies the generations being connected to one another, and the altar is the cross of Christ. [17]Until the cross of Christ the Jewish ordinances were transmitted through priesthood, kingship, prophecy and Passover. [18]But from the cross of Christ onwards everything has been taken away from the Jews, and there is not anymore found among them king or priest or prophet or Passover, as Daniel had prophesied concerning them: [19]"*After sixty-two weeks the Messiah will be killed and the holy city be destroyed until the punishment is fulfilled,*" that is, for ever and ever.

Ps 118:27

Justin, *Dial. cum Tryph.* 91:1-2; Tertullian, *Adv. Marc.* 3:1

Aphrahat, *Dem.* 23:20, 46

Dan 9:26

53 [1]When the whole of the law and prophets was fulfilled and Christ hung upon the cross, Joseph, the brother of Nicodemus and Cleophas, went to Pilate, for he bore Pilate's seal—he was his councillor—and had great freedom of speech with him. [2]He asked for our saviour's body, and (Pilate) commanded that it be given to him. [3]When he had taken his body Pilate immediately commanded that also the garden might be given to him, wherein was the tomb of our saviour, [4] (even though) it belonged to Joseph and had been given to him as an inheritance by the Levite Phinehas, Joseph's cousin. [5]Joseph, too, was from Jerusalem, but he had been made councillor in Arimathea, and all the letters written during Pilate's whole reign had been sealed with the seal Joseph was bearing. [6]When he had taken down our Lord's body from the cross, the Jews hastened, took the cross and brought it into the temple, because it had been made of the ark's biers. [7]Nicodemus furthermore embalmed the body of our Lord (and put it) into pure

Eusebius, *Hist. eccl.* 3:11

Matt 27:57-58; Mark 15:42-45; Luke 23:50-52; John 19:38

and new linen shrouds, whereas Joseph wrapped him up and buried him in a new tomb which had been made for Joshua, son of Nun, to be buried within it. [8]Because he had seen with the spirit's eye, and the way of Divine Economy concerning Christ had been revealed to him, he took the stone which had been travelling with the children of Israel in the desert and put it at the tomb's entrance, and for this reason he was not buried in it. [9]When Joseph, Nicodemus, and Cleophas buried Christ they put this stone at the tomb's entrance. [10]Then the high-priests together with Pilate's retinue went out and put a seal upon the tomb and stone.

Matt 27:59-60; Mark 15:46; Luke 23:53

Ephrem, *Comm. in Gen.* 43:10

Matt 27:60; Mark 15:46

[11]Now, my brother Namosaya, marvel and praise God, because he joined all the beams upon which Christ had been stretched out, to the biers of the ark of divine ministry and the veil of the holy of holies. [12]This is what God commanded to Moses, who should make a belt of justice and peace: a belt of justice for the Jews who crucified him, and one of peace for the nations who believe in him. [13]His cross (consisted) of wood from the temple, and his tomb was a new tomb which had been prepared for Joshua son of Nun's death. [14]This stone, which is Christ, gave life to 600,000 people while in the desert and is now an altar giving life to all nations. [15]The apostle's word is true and indeed trustworthy: "*The stone is Christ.*" [16]Joseph was a councillor in Arimathea, Nicodemus was a teacher of the law in Jerusalem, and Cleophas was a Hebrew scribe in Emmaus. [17]Nicodemus prepared everything which was needed for Passover in the upper chamber. [18]Joseph wrapped (Jesus' body) up and buried him within his inheritance, and Cleophas received him into his house. [19]When he had risen from the dead those were like brothers unto him in holiness and truth. [20]When Joseph was taking him down from the cross, he also took the writing which had been fixed above his head, that is, on top of the cross, because it was written by Pilate's hand in Greek, Latin and Hebrew. [21]For which reason did Pilate not write in Syriac: because the Syrians did not share in (the spilling of) Christ's blood. [22]Pilate was a wise man and loved truth. [23]He did not wish to write a lie as villainous judges would have done but rather had it drawn up in the languages of Christ's murderers, as is written in the law of Moses: *"Those who condemn the innocent* [24] *first raised their hand against him there."* [25]Thus Pilate wrote it in the language of Christ's murderers, fixing it above him: Herod the Greek, Caiaphas the Jew, and Pilate the Roman. [26]But the Syrians did not participate in his killing, as witnesses king Abgar of Edessa, [27]who wished to go up and destroy Jerusalem because the Jews had crucified Christ.

Exod 28:15 Peshitta

Exod 12:37; 17:6

1 Cor 10:4

Mark 15:43; Luke 24:18, 50; John 3:1, 10

John 19:20

Deut 17:7

Ephrem, *Serm. in hebd. sanc.* 6:1113-1143

Eusebius, *Hist. eccl.* 1:13:15

From Christ's descent to Sheol to the coming of the Spirit at Pentecost

54 [1]Now Christ's descent to Sheol was not in vain, but rather the cause of great benefits to our race. [2]For by his descent to the lower parts of the earth he ousted death from its rule, proclaimed resurrection to those sleeping in the dust, and brought forgiveness to those who sinned without law. [3]He laid waste Sheol, killed sin, put Satan to shame, saddened the demons, abrogated sacrifices and altars, wrought return for Adam, and abolished the Jewish ordinances. When he rose from the tomb on the third day he appeared to Peter and John. [4]While Christ was in the tomb and guardians sat around the tomb, Peter wanted to make the guardians drink wine so that they get drunk and fall asleep. Then he would rise

in order to open the tomb and bring out Christ's body without breaking the
Matt 27:64 tomb's seal so that the Jews might not say: "His disciples stole him." 5When the
guardians had eaten and drunk Christ rose and appeared to Peter who was thus
entrusted with the truth and believed that he was the Christ, Lord of heaven and
earth. 6Peter did not come near to the tomb. 7After that (Jesus) showed himself openly and went in to his disciples who kept watch in the upper chamber,
John 20:19, 27 | Thomas touching him. 8Then he appeared to them at the sea-shore. 9Whereas
John 21:1 Peter had denied him three times in front of the Jews, he now acknowledged
him three times in front of his disciples. 10He entrusted and confided to him
the whole flock, telling him in front of the disciples: "Feed my sheep, my rams,
John 21:15-17 | and my lambs!" These are the men, women, and children. 11Forty days after
Aphrahat, *Dem.* 10:4 his resurrection he bestowed (the gift of) priestly ordination on his disciples.
Mark 16:15-19; Luke Then he went up to heaven and took his seat at the right hand of his father.
24:50-51 12The apostles gathered and went up to the upper room together with Mary, the
holy virgin. 13Simon Peter baptised Mary, and John the chaste took care of her.
Acts 1:13-14 14Then they declared a fast until they would receive the Spirit, the Paraclete, at
Acts 2:1 Pentecost. 15They were given tongues in order for each one of them to go and
instruct that nation which had been allotted to him, so that there might not be a
schism among them in all eternity.

16Finished is the writing down of this book concerning the sequence of the
generations' descent from Adam to Christ, which is called "The Cave of Treasures." 17To God be glory world without end. Amen.

Palaea Historica ("The Old Testament History")
A new translation and introduction

By William Adler

Composed no earlier than the ninth century C.E., the *Palaea Historica* (hereafter *Palaea*) is an anonymous work written in Greek and treating Old Testament history from the Creation to Daniel.[1] For students of Old Testament pseudepigrapha, the particular interest of the *Palaea* lies in the copious body of extra-biblical tradition about various biblical personalities, most notably Lamech, Noah, Abraham, Lot, Melchizedek, Ephron, Moses and Balaam.

The Greek Text and Translation of the *Palaea*

A new edition of the *Palaea* is badly needed. The Greek text underlying the present translation is mainly based on A. Vasiliev's 1893 edition.[2] In the introduction to his edition of the Greek text, Vasiliev noted the existence of three manuscripts that he was unable to examine for his edition.[3] For his edition of the Greek text, Vasiliev consulted two manuscripts. The base manuscript (= V.), which dates to the sixteenth century, belongs to the National Library of Vienna (= Cod. Vindobonensis theol. gr. 247 [Lambec. 210], fol 34r-84). The text of this manuscript is marked by numerous, mostly small, lacunae. Vasiliev supplemented this manuscript with a second manuscript, dating to the fifteenth century (Cod. Otthobonianus 205 = MS O). While a fuller text than V, the manuscript is lacunose at the end. Although we have not made a fresh collation of unpublished manuscripts, the section of the *Palaea* dealing with Abraham and Melchizedek includes readings from a third manuscript (= Paris BNF, gr. 37). These readings are based on J. Dochhorn's recent collation of the manuscript with Vasiliev's edition.[4]

Vasiliev used square brackets to indicate places where he supplemented MS V with readings from MS O. These brackets are retained in the present translation. Page numbers from Vasiliev's edition are enclosed in parentheses. For ease of use, we have inserted chapter and verse divisions. For the most part, the translation has regularized biblical names according to NRSV spelling. In a few remarkable cases (e.g., "Zan" for "Uzzah" and "Bit" for "Tobit"), however, the translation has retained the *Palaea* spelling. Cases in which the

---

1. For Greek text, date and provenance of the work, see the next section.

2. Vasiliev, *Anecdota*, 188-292.

3. Vasiliev, *Anecdota*, L-LI.

4. J. Dochhorn, "Die Historia de Melchisedech (Hist Melch)," 33-40. Codex Vatopedinus 659 (fourteenth century), discovered by Marcel Richard in one of the monasteries of Athos, also contains unedited Greek material from the *Palaea* (58v-62v; 74v-89v); for description, see J. Paramelle, *Philon d'Alexandrie: Questions sur la Genèse II 1-7* (Cahiers d'Orientalisme 3; Geneva: Cramer, 1984), 22-24. For other Greek witnesses to the work, see K. Krumbacher, *Geschichte der byzantinischen Litteratur von Justinian bis zum Ende des oströmischen Reiches (527-1453)* (2nd ed.; Munich: Beck, 1897), 398, 1139.

Greek text is either corrupt or too obscure to translate literally are identified in the footnotes. The notes also indicate places where we have accepted Vasiliev's emendations. To help clarify ambiguities or corruptions in the Greek text, we have occasionally consulted Popov's edition of the Slavonic version. For guidance here, we gratefully acknowledge the assistance of Prof. Andrei Orlov and Dr. Alexander Panayotov.

Abbreviation and Sigla[5]

[...]: Text supplied from "O."
{...}: Textual lacuna.
(text). Words added by the translator to improve clarity.
<text>: Correction made by the translator.
Lit.: Literal meaning.
O.: Codex Otthobonianus 205.
P.: Paris, Bibl. Nat., gr. 37.
Slav.: Slavonic version.
V.: Cod. Vindobonensis theol. gr. 247.
Vas.: Variant reading supplied by Vasiliev.

Genre, Date and Provenance

Greek manuscripts refer to the *Palaea* variously as "Passages from the Old Testament" (O.), "History of the Old Testament" (V.), or simply "to Palaion," the same term used by Byzantine writers to describe the Old Testament. In Slavonic manuscripts, it is called "Book of the Genesis of Heaven and Earth" or "Eyes of the Old Testament of Master Theodore."[6] The commonly-used title "*Palaea Historica*" is meant to distinguish it from another work, also preserved in Slavonic translation, known as the "*Palaea Interpretata*" ("Explanatory Palaea"). While the two works contain overlapping material, they differ both in character and purpose. The *Palaea Interpretata*, a more theological and polemical work, interprets scripture from an avowedly Christian perspective.[7] Although the *Palaea Historica* is itself not devoid of theology and polemic,[8] the overall approach of the work is for the most part more narrative and "historical."

Modern attempts to find western counterparts to the *Palaea* have likened it to the twelfth century *Historia Scholastica* of Peter Comestor[9] and the *Biblia Pauperum*, an illustrated book of biblical stories popular in the late Middle Ages.[10] Characterizations of the work as a "rewritten Bible," a "compendium of scriptural stories," and an "expansion and commentary on the Old Testament" do not adequately represent the composition and contents of the work. The author of the *Palaea* was far more than a mechanical compiler of older traditions. Nor is the work a "commentary" on the Old Testament in the usual sense

5. Note also that references to the Psalms are given according to the LXX numbering, with the Psalm number according to the MT following immediately in parentheses, followed, if relevant, by the verse number, e.g., Ps 87 (88):6.

6. See N. K. Kudzy, *History of Early Russian Literature*, tr. W. Jones (New York: Macmillan, 1949), 183.

7. See Vasiliev, *Anecdota*, XLIV-XLVI.

8. For typological interpretation in the *Palaea*, see, for example, 67.6-12; 103.11; 141.13-15. For polemic, see the Introduction.

9. See M. R. James, *Apocrypha Anecdota*, 2.157.

10. See Vasiliev, *Anecdota*, XLVI; F. H. Marshall, *Old Testament Legends from a Greek Poem on Genesis and Exodus by Georgios Chumnos* (Cambridge: University Press, 1925), xxiii.

of that word. For one thing, the *Palaea*'s treatment of biblical history is remarkably uneven. While virtually silent about the post-Davidic monarchy, for example, it discourses at length about relatively marginal, or even unknown, figures in the biblical narrative. Because so much scriptural material is embedded into the narrative of the *Palaea* without attribution, a reader unfamiliar with the biblical text would be generally unable to distinguish between biblical and extra-biblical material. With the exception of the Psalms, we have little sense that the author drew a clear distinction in his own mind between the biblical text and his own expansions upon it. If the term "commentary" is at all descriptive of the work, it would apply mainly to the author's handling of the Psalms and the *Great Canon* of Andrew of Crete. In these two cases, the author does self-consciously play the role of an expositor.[11]

Evidence scattered throughout the text makes it possible to piece together a fragmentary picture of the authorship, date and provenance of this anonymous and undated work. Discussion of Syriac etymologies (27.6; 30.2; 58.19) suggests some acquaintance, however minimal, with the Syriac language.[12] The author, who is familiar with biblical legends either originating in or circulating in Byzantine Palestine, shows an interest in the locations of biblical sites; at one point, he provides the precise distance (twenty-four miles) between the site of Lot's tree and the Jordan River. The *Palaea*'s identification of the two tributaries of the Jordan as the "Jor" and the "Dan" (123.6-7) continued to be repeated by travelers to Palestine as late as the eighteenth century.[13] Palestine is also the geographic and religious center of the universe. After surveying the world, the astrologer Nimrod discovered that Palestine was at its midpoint (25.2). Abraham later tells Ephron that God had come to dwell there (29.7). While this evidence is hardly probative, it does at least raise the possibility of a connection to monastic circles of Byzantine Palestine.

The creedal statement at the beginning of the work (1-2) and citations from well-known figures of the Christian East establish the work firmly within the orthodox Eastern tradition. Although religious invective is rare, the author is sharply critical of opposing views about the fall of Lucifer (3.8) and the nature of the tree of life (5.1-2). A strongly worded condemnation of the claim that Cain was born of intercourse between Eve and Satan identifies the group propagating this interpretation as the "Phundaitae" (7.5), a dualist heresy with large concentrations of adherents in Bulgaria, the Balkans and Western Asia Minor, and often associated with the Bogomils.[14]

A vigorous defense of the privileges of priesthood offers further insight into the author's religious affiliations. The work takes pains to record the dire penalties imposed on those found guilty of flouting ritual law and priestly prerogatives. God destroyed the entire assembly of Dathan and Abiram for demanding the right to burn incense in the ark, a privilege reserved for the line of Aaron (100). Even violations done innocently were

---

11. See the Introduction.

12. Flusser, "Palaea," 78; but cf. Lieberman, "Zenihin," 52-54, who questions the *Palaea*'s knowledge of Syriac.

13. For the earliest attestation of this tradition, see Jerome, *Comm. in Matt.* 16.19, ed. D. Hurst and M. Adriaen (CCL 77; Turnhout, 1969). See further Flusser, "Palaea," 74 n. 99.

14. For general background on the Phundaitae, also known as the "Phundagiagitae," see D. Obolensky, *The Bogomils: A Study in Balkan Neo-Manichaeism* (Cambridge: University Press, 1948), 177-83; G. Ficker, *Die Phundagiagiten* (Leipzig: Barth, 1908). For the birth of Cain from Satan's (Satanael's) seduction of Eve in dualist movements of the Middle Ages, see M. Loos, *Dualist Heresy in the Middle Ages* (Prague: Akademia, 1974), 86, 93 n. 24, 137.

subject to extreme penalties. When "Zan" (= "Uzzah") attempted to steady the ox pulling the cart bearing the ark, God caused his hand to wither (cf. 2 Sam 6:7; 1 Chr 13:10); this was because "there was no provision in the law for the unholy to make contact with the ark" (107.6). God later killed the five sons of the priest Eli for partaking of the sacrificial offerings before the priest had blessed them (140). In places, the elevation and justification of the priesthood has the ring of partisanship. From the perspective of the *Palaea*, Aaron, the first high priest, shared no complicity in the making of the golden calf. If he could be held guilty of anything at all, it was in failing to appreciate the depths of the Israelites' gluttony (93.2-5). When Aaron asked them to surrender their jewelry to be smelted into an idol, he assumed that they would be reluctant to part with the goods that the Israelites had taken from Egypt. That was a miscalculation. The gluttony of some of them exceeded even their attachment to gold and silver.

Assertion of the rights of the priesthood even leads the author to a much-contested subject in Byzantine political ideology: the relationship between priesthood and kingship. The *Palaea* has a grandiose conception of the role of the Aaronid high-priesthood. When God gives Moses instructions about the building of the tabernacle, he tells him that Aaron will "make atonement for ... the air and the storms and kings and rulers and the people and the whole world" (98.8). The leaves that subsequently sprout from Aaron's rod after the other Israelite tribes complain about being barred from the tabernacle ratify the divine origins of his high priesthood (99). Kingship, however, enjoyed no such status. For the *Palaea*, Saul's coronation was a "*parergon*," an accident of history (147-48). Byzantine emperors who liked to appeal to Melchizedek as the prototype of the king as priest would find no support in the Melchizedek of the *Palaea*; the solitary hermit on Mount Tabor is anything but a king.[15] It is telling that the only episode that the *Palaea* records for the period of the kings after David concerns king Uzziah's violations of priestly prerogatives (162). In this story, the king insists that his office affords him the right to burn incense: "Am I not a priest? [Do I not wear the purple?]" While the high priest acknowledges his kingship, he insists that this in no way grants him the right to burn incense. As punishment for the king's insistence upon burning incense anyway, God afflicted him with leprosy. Out of respect for Uzziah's office, the people failed to remove the leprous king from the city, thereby only compounding the wrong. In response, God refused to communicate with them until Uzziah had died.[16]

In the broadest terms, we can trace the work's composition between the ninth and twelfth centuries. The *terminus post quem* of the *Palaea* can be established from a reference in the work to the Byzantine monk and theologian Theodore the Studite (ca. 759-826), chronologically the latest author cited in the work (53.9). According to Vasiliev, the earliest known manuscript of the *Palaea* dates to the twelfth or thirteenth century.[17] The twelfth century was also the date of the translation of the *Palaea* into Slavonic. Certain other clues have allowed scholars to further narrow the time-frame of the composition

15. See below, p. 592. For Melchizedek as the exemplar of the Byzantine emperor/priest, see G. Dagron, *Emperor and Priest: The Imperial Office in Byzantium* (Cambridge: Cambridge University Press, 2003), 173-91. Against Gen 14:18, which calls Melchizedek priest and king, the *Palaea* describes him only as "priest of God, the Most High" (36.8).

16. For Uzziah's transgression against the Temple in Byzantine disputes about the priestly role of the emperor, see Dagron, *Emperor and Priest*, 164-66.

17. Vasiliev, *Anecdota*, L (Cod. 501, class. II from the library of San Marco in Venice).

of the work. Most notably, stories described in the *Palaea* are, already in the early tenth century, represented in visual form in Byzantine paintings and manuscript miniatures.[18]

Extra-biblical Traditions in the *Palaea*

As David Flusser has shown in a thorough summary and analysis of the work, portions of the *Palaea*'s exposition of biblical history are rooted in the literature and traditions of Second Temple Judaism.[19] One of these sources is the *Book of Jubilees*, a work originally composed in Hebrew probably in the second century B.C.E. The *Palaea* knows the *Jubilees*-based equation of the twenty-two acts of creation with the twenty-two letters of the Hebrew alphabet (3.13; cf. *Jub.* 2.1-23). It reports the story, first recorded in *Jubilees*, about how the Canaanites, descendants of Ham, seized Palestine, thereby violating an oath sworn by the three sons of Noah after the habitable earth was divided among them (23.13-14; 27.9-13; cf. *Jubilees* 8). The *Palaea*'s account of Abraham's repudiation of his ancestral religion reproduces the celebrated story in *Jubilees* about Abraham's burning of the temple in Ur housing idols built by his father Terah, an act leading to the death of his brother Haran when he rushed into the temple to retrieve them (26.7-9; cf. *Jub.* 12.1-5).

By the ninth century, excerpts and traditions from *Jubilees* circulated widely and in various adaptations in Byzantine chronicles and biblical commentaries.[20] The *Palaea*'s preservation of legends first attested in *Jubilees* thus need not presuppose direct use of that work. The same can be said of the *Palaea*'s knowledge of Josephus. Neither of the work's two explicit references to Josephus can be verified.[21] While unattributed legends about the young Moses do reveal striking resemblances with stories first found in Josephus's *Antiquities,* variants in the *Palaea*'s version betray the signs of a secondary layer of tradition. According to Josephus (*Ant.* 2.233-36), Moses, while still an infant, taxed the Pharaoh's patience by hurling his crown to the ground after the Egyptian king had set it on his head. When an Egyptian scribe, interpreting this as a bad omen, advised the Pharaoh to kill him, his daughter Thermuthis rescued Moses before her father was able to act on the scribe's advice. The version of this legend in the *Palaea* (69) is more elaborate, weaving together, not altogether adroitly, parts of this story with other stories about Moses' provocations. In the *Palaea*'s version, Moses angered members of Pharaoh's court by casting off

---

18. See, for example, R. Stichel, "Außerkanonische Elemente in byzantinischen Illustrationen des Alten Testaments," *Römische Quartalschrift* 69 (1974): 166-68. Stichel draws attention to a painting of the sacrifice of Isaac from a church in Cappadocia, dating between the years 922 and 930. The inscription accompanying the painting contains the same variant reading of Gen 22:12 attested in the *Palaea* (58.16). For the dating of the *Palaea,* see also A. Giannouli, "*Apocryphon Loth (CAVT*, Nr. 93). Zur Entstehung und Entwicklung einer Legende," in M. Hinterberger and E. Schiffer, eds., *Byzantinische Sprachkunst: Studien zur byzantinischen Literatur gewidmet Wolfram Hörander zum 65. Geburstag* (Byzantinisches Archiv 20; Berlin: de Gruyter, 2007), 88-103. Giannouli (95) maintains that the reference in the *Palaea* to the "Phundaitae" (7.5; see also above, p. 587) establishes the late tenth century as its *terminus post quem.*

19. D. Flusser, "Palaea Historica—An Unknown Source of Biblical Legends," *Studies in Aggadah and Folk-Literature,* in J. Heinemann and D. Noy, eds., *Scripta Hierosolymitana* 22 (Jerusalem: Magness, 1971), 48-79. For discussion of Jewish sources and traditions preserved in the *Palaea,* see also A. Vasiliev, *Anecdota Graeco-Byzantina* (Moscow, 1893), XLV-XLVII; S. Lieberman, "Zenihin" (Heb.), *Tarbiz* 42 (1972-73): 42-54.

20. For the sources, see notes *ad loc.*

21. At 16.3, the *Palaea* cites Josephus as the source for its report about Adam's sixty sons and thirty androgynes. The other citation (23.14) credits Josephus with the *Jubilees*' story about Noah's division of the earth.

his crown and then tugging at his beard. Thanks to a court sage, who proves by a series of tests that he did all of this innocently, Moses barely manages to escape death.[22]

Josephus's *Antiquities* also credits the young Moses with devising an ingenious stratagem to defeat the Ethiopians (*Ant.* 2.243-48). Ibises that his advancing army kept in wicker baskets destroyed venomous snakes blocking their entrance into Ethiopia. While the basic story line in the *Palaea* is much the same, the details are quite different (70). Here the birds are storks, not ibises; and the country he invades is India, not Ethiopia. Given the numerous versions of Moses' youthful exploits in later Jewish, Christian and Muslim tradition, reworkings like these should hardly surprise us.[23]

In its cycle of legends about Moses, the *Palaea* preserves two older Jewish traditions absent from the Old Testament, but known to New Testament authors. At 75.5-10, it describes at some length the contest pitting Moses against Jannes and Jambres, the latter two magicians in Pharaoh's court. Although lacking in the Exodus account (cf. Exod 7:10-12), the same names appear in 2 Tim 3:8. The *Palaea* also recounts the story, first recorded in Jude 1:9, about a struggle between the archangel Michael and Satan over the body of Moses (121.6-8). From as early as the time of Origen (third century C.E.), Christian biblical commentators claimed that the authors of 2 Timothy and Jude acquired these traditions from Jewish pseudepigrapha.[24] One of the many unresolved questions in the study of the *Palaea* is whether and how the author might have received these stories independently of the New Testament references to them.[25]

Duplicated Traditions in the *Palaea*

A notable feature of the *Palaea* is its habit of crediting a character from the Old Testament with accomplishments resembling those elsewhere ascribed to some other biblical figure. One such doublet recalls how Deborah rescued the city of Jerusalem from destruction first by intoxicating the Persian king Artasyris with her beauty and strong drink and then beheading him (145-46).[26] While this story of Deborah's exploits against the Persians has no parallel in the Judges narrative about her (cf. Judges 4–5), an attentive reader would have little difficulty recognizing the similarities between her triumph and Judith's victory over Holophernes, the commander of Nebuchadnezzar's army (cf. Judith 11–13).

The *Palaea*'s account of monuments erected by Enoch for later generations (20.3-5) is another example of the same phenomenon.[27] The most widely-known story about pre-

22. See notes to text at 69.

23. On the Josephus legend and later variants on it, see T. Rajak, "Moses in Ethiopia: Legend and Literature," *JJS* 29 (1978): 111-22.

24. Cf. Origen's *De Principiis* 3.2.1, ed. P. Koetschau (GCS 22: Leipzig, 1913), which attributes the story of the fight over Moses' body to the *Ascension* (or *Assumption*) *of Moses.* In his *Commentary on Matthew*, 250.6-12 (on Matt 27:3), ed. E. Klostermann (GCS 38; Leipzig, 1933), Origen claims that 2 Timothy learned the names of Jannes and Jambres from the *Book of Jannes and Jambres.* For edition, translation and commentary, see A. Pietersma, *The Apocryphon of Jannes and Jambres the Magicians* (Leiden: Brill, 1994).

25. For discussion of the sources of the *Palaea*'s story about the contest over Moses' body, see Flusser, "Palaea," 72-74; K. Berger, "Der Streit des guten und des bösen Engels um die Seele," *JSJ* 4 (1973): 13-14; R. Bauckham, *Jude and the Relatives of Jesus* (Edinburgh: T&T Clark, 1990), 249-52; J. Tromp, *The Assumption of Moses* (Leiden: Brill, 1993), 281-82; J. Davila, *The Provenance of the Pseudepigrapha: Jewish, Christian, or Other?* (Leiden: Brill, 2005), 151.

26. See Flusser, "Palaea," 76.

27. For discussion of this passage in the *Palaea*, see A. Orlov, "Overshadowed by Enoch's Greatness: 'Two Tablets' Traditions from the *Book of Giants* to *Palaea Historica*," *JSJ* 32 (2001): 137-58, esp. pp. 149-51.

flood monuments originates in Josephus's *Antiquities* (1.68-71). According to Josephus, Seth and his descendants, after receiving a warning about a coming flood either of fire or water, erected two sets of monuments, one of brick (in case of a fiery cataclysm), the other of stone (in case of a flood of water). The *Palaea*'s own version of the motif points to a later adaptation. Even though it no longer makes much sense in the work's context, the author retains the older tradition about monuments of stone and brick erected in anticipation of an impending catastrophe.[28] But now Enoch is the hero of the story: He (not Adam) issues the warning about an impending catastrophe, and he alone constructs the monuments. The *Palaea* also changes the description of the learning inscribed upon them. While earlier sources describe it as astronomical and/or esoteric knowledge, the *Palaea* has replaced this with a more religiously edifying variant, and one better suited to the overall aims of the work.[29] On the eve of the flood, the *Palaea* states, Enoch exhorted the sinning giants to repent and glorify God, warning them that the world would be destroyed either by water or fire. In preparation for the calamity, Enoch did nothing else but record the mighty acts of God on these stelae, presumably as a warning for later generations (20.4-6).

Perhaps the most striking example of the reattribution of traditions concerns the *Palaea*'s account of Lot's quest for wood from Paradise (54-55). Among the many ancient and medieval Jewish and Christian stories about the quest for some saving artifact from Paradise, probably the best-known involved the figure of Seth. Developing an older Jewish legend about Seth's foiled quest for oil from the tree of Life, one Christian adaptation of the story describes how the angel guarding Paradise, while denying Seth's request for the oil, does give him seeds or twigs from three trees: the cedar, cypress and pine. Wood that sprouts forth from them was said to have found its way to Solomon's temple and ultimately to the Cross.[30]

The *Palaea* also has a story about a journey to Paradise for three pieces of wood; only in this case, Abraham commissions Lot with the task. After Lot's transgression with his daughters, Abraham sends him to retrieve three fire-brands from Paradise. He did so in the belief that Lot's death in transit would earn him divine forgiveness for an otherwise unforgivable sin. Against all expectations, Lot, with divine protection, does succeed, returning to Abraham with wood from the cypress, pine and cedar trees. After he and Abraham plant the wood in the shape of a triangle, each a cubit from the other, Lot regularly traveled to the Jordan to fetch water for the wood. The three pieces of wood soon sprouted leaves and grew together into a single trunk. The *Palaea*'s narrative breaks off abruptly here, stating only that the tree remained standing until the time of Solomon, and promising to explain the meaning of the tree at a future time (55.7). But a tree with a single trunk and the roots of three different trees—a barely concealed symbol of the Trinity—leaves the reader in little doubt about the future course of events. Abraham drives home the point by telling Lot that the tree will be the "abolition of sin" (55.5). Other versions of the story provide a more fitting resolution of the story. From them, we learn that Lot's tree was cut

28. The fact that God had already told Noah that the catastrophe would be a flood of water would seem to make Enoch's work superfluous (19.5-20.2). For discussion, see Orlov, "Enoch's Greatness," 151.

29. On the theme of sin and repentance in the *Palaea*, see the Introduction.

30. For recent discussion of the sources, see B. Baert, *A Heritage of Holy Wood* (Leiden: Brill, 2005), 317-22; on this motif, see also E. Quinn, *The Quest of Seth for the Oil of Life* (Chicago: University of Chicago Press, 1962), 2-12, 55, 71.

down for use in Solomon's temple, but was never actually used for this purpose. Only later did the tree realize its true purpose: as the wood for the cross. [31]

Developed Legends with No Parallels in Earlier Sources

While some of the legends in the *Palaea* are well-documented in the literature and iconography of the Christian East, their older roots, if any, lie hidden from view. One such case is the *Palaea*'s account of Abraham's meeting with the mysterious figure of Melchizedek, king of Salem (cf. Gen 14:18-20). Earlier Jewish and Christian representations of Melchizedek as a royal and priestly figure provide little insight into the *Palaea*'s depiction of him as a wild-looking ascetic and hermit, with hair and beard extending down to his feet, and nails a cubit in length (36.7).

The author displays great ingenuity in explaining how Melchizedek came to look this way. Even before his historic encounter with Abraham, the *Palaea* links together the lives of the two men by patterning the narrative of Melchizedek's early life and conversion according to its previous account of Abraham's years in Chaldea. Like Abraham, Melchi (later Melchizedek) was the son of an idolater, Josedek, king of the city of Salem, and devotee of the god Cronus. On the eve of a planned sacrifice to Cronus, Melchi stayed up late observing the heavens. As he contemplated the orderly motion of the stars, he recognized, as Abraham had done before him, that a single god must be the author of all of this. But when he informs his father about his discovery, his father, outraged and fearful that his son had angered the gods, decides that the only way to right the wrong is for all the inhabitants of the city to sacrifice their male offspring. Melchi flees from the city and takes up the life of a hermit on Mount Tabor. The circumstances of his flight from his ancestral home thus explain how the epistle to the Hebrews could describe Melchizedek as "without genealogy, without father and mother" (Heb 7:3). After God had destroyed the city of his birth and its inhabitants in an earthquake, Melchi was left an orphan, living alone on Mount Tabor and surviving solely on water and wild plants (36.4).

For the author of the *Palaea*, the meeting between Abraham and Melchizedek was no chance encounter, but rather the outworking of a divine plan. Even before Melchizedek appears on the scene, the author describes a terrifying night-time encounter between Ephron the Hittite king and an angel threatening him with a sword. To propitiate God, Ephron pays Abraham a tithe, which Abraham, only recently arrived from Ur, offers up as a sacrifice (28-29). The *Palaea* then describes how Abraham subsequently received a revelation from an angel of God telling him to take costly raiment, bread, wine and a razor, ascend to Mount Tabor, and shout three times, "Man of God!" (31.4-8). In compliance with the divine decree, Abraham cuts his nails and shaves his head and beard, after which they make an offering to God and partake of the meal of bread and wine that Abraham had brought with him (37.6-9; cf. Gen 14:18).[32] Just as Abraham had received a tithe from Ephron, he then pays a tithe to Melchizedek—thus explaining the meaning of Heb 7:9: "Receiving tithes, he paid tithes."

The closest literary parallel with the *Palaea*'s account, versions of which survive in

---

31. See note to 55.7. For detailed study of the legend of Lot and its origins, see Giannouli, "*Apocryphon Loth*," 88-103.

32. S. E. Robinson proposes that Abraham's shaving of the unkempt Melchizedek was meant to support institutional forms of monasticism against more extreme forms of ascetic practice ("The Apocryphal Story of Melchizedek," *JSJ* 18 [1987]: 26-39, esp. pp. 36-37).

Greek, Syriac, Coptic and Arabic, is found in ps.-Athanasius's *Historia de Melchisedech.*[33] But although the story of Melchizedek's meeting with Abraham on Mount Tabor was widely circulated by the ninth century, the process by which Melchizedek was transformed from priest/king into an orphaned hermit remains obscure.

The *Palaea*'s Non-Literary Sources

Despite suggestive parallels with earlier Jewish/Christian pseudepigrapha, the *Palaea* mentions none of these sources by name. In addition to the well-regarded Josephus, the other named authorities are familiar figures in Byzantine Christianity: Gregory of Nazianzus (7.3-4), Theodore the Studite (53.9), John Chrysostom (53.10), and Andrew of Crete.[34] Unverifiable quotations from even these highly-regarded writers hardly inspire confidence in the author's direct knowledge of or access to older Jewish pseudepigrapha. Any attempt to reconstruct the sources of the *Palaea*'s para-biblical narrative is thus bound to remain highly speculative. Specifically, how much of this material originated in written works, how much in non-literary sources (local legend, liturgy and religious art), and how much was simply a creation of the author's own imagination?

In an environment in which sources were at least as much visual and auditory as they were written, it is hardly surprising that Byzantine art and oral tradition provide some of the closest parallels to the stories preserved in the *Palaea.* The *Palaea*'s account of Abraham's meeting with the hirsute Melchizedek on Mount Tabor turns up in Coptic art and wall paintings in Palestinian monasteries, and in illustrated Byzantine manuscripts.[35] The sequence of events associated with Lot's journey to Paradise, including Lot's watering of the three-rooted tree, is probably most famous from a series of paintings found at the Monastery of the Cross near Jerusalem.[36] Representations of the *Palaea*'s account of an angel's sword threatening David and his kingdom appear in Psalter manuscript miniatures from as early as the ninth century.[37] There is no reason to assume that the *Palaea* was in all cases the literary source of these images; the flow of influence need not have been uni-directional. We might just as easily imagine that a theme found in a religious image inspired the author to represent it in narrative form.

Oral traditions connected with holy places in Byzantine Palestine could also have supplied the author with material for his narrative about Lot's tree, Melchizedek's solitary

---

33. For English translations of the ps.-Athanasius text (in *PG* 28.525-29), see Robinson, "Story of Melchizedek," 26-39 and Pierluigi Piovanelli's translation of *The Story of Melchizedek* in this volume. For discussion of the various versions of the legend, see also J. Dochhorn, "Die Historia de Melchisedech (Hist Melch): Einführung, editorischer Vorbericht und Editiones praeliminares," *Le Muséon* 117.1-2 (2004): 7-48.

34. For the citations from Andrew of Crete, see the Introduction. At various places, the *Palaea* also cites an unknown authority described only as a "wise man" (21.10; 22.11; 97.8; 103.11; 114.16; 115.5; 119.5; 161.16), or "author of hymns" (5.3; 52.9; 67.11; 99.10).

35. See E. S. Bolman, *Monastic Visions* (New Haven: Yale, 2002), 68-69; G. J. M. van Loon, "Priester van God de Allerhoogste: Iconografische en iconologische aspecten van de Ontmoeting van Abraham en Melchisedek en de Apostelcommunie in koptisch Egypte," *Periodical of the Institute of Eastern Christian Studies at Nijmegen* 53 (2001): 5-29; idem, "The Meeting of Abraham and Melchizedek and the Communion of the Apostles," in M. Immerzeel and J. van der Vliet, eds., *Coptic Studies on the Threshold of a New Millennium* (OLA 133; Leuven: Peeters, 2004), 1373-92; P. van Moorsel, "A Different Melchizedek? Some Iconographic Remarks," in M. Krause and S. Schaten (eds.), *Themelia: Spätantike und koptologische Studien: Peter Grossmann zum 65. Geburtstag* (Wiesbaden: Reichert, 1998), 329-36.

36. See V. Tzaferis, "The Monastery of the Cross," *BAR* 27:6 (Nov/Dec 2001): 38-39.

37. See L. Brubaker, *Vision and Meaning in Ninth-Century Byzantium* (Cambridge: Cambridge University Press, 1999), 352-56.

home on Mount Tabor, and Habakkuk and the field where he fed his reapers.[38] According to the ecclesiastical historian Nicephorus Callistus (fourteenth century), Helen, the mother of Constantine, erected a church on Mount Tabor where Melchizedek was said to have blessed Abraham.[39] In the early twelfth century, a Russian pilgrim, Abbot Daniel, describes visiting a cave on Mount Tabor, the supposed home of Melchizedek. His version of their meeting, which includes the story of how Abraham called out for Melchizedek three times, shows striking resemblances with the *Palaea*'s.[40] At the Monastery of the Cross (founded in the seventh century), a site behind the altar of the main church is said to be the place where Lot planted the wood that sprouted into the tree of the cross. The story of Lot's tree was also a widely-circulated piece of native folklore. A traveler to Palestine in the Middle Ages reports having heard a story about how Satan, disguised as an exhausted Russian pilgrim, tried to thwart Lot's efforts by drinking the water that he was carrying from the Jordan.[41] This raises the possibility that the *Palaea*'s story of Lot's quest originated in a tradition of Palestinian provenance co-existing and competing with rival traditions about the origins of the wood of the cross.[42]

Liturgical Influences on the *Palaea*'s Shaping of Biblical History

The way that a Christian of the Byzantine East might learn about biblical history was often through hearing homilies, and the recitation of prayers, hymns and psalms. While this point may seem obvious, it needs to be borne in mind when considering the composition and sources of the *Palaea*. Although otherwise lax in quoting sources, the author knows liturgical texts very well. Those parts of the biblical text that the author cites with any degree of consistency and literalness were likely to be known by heart through repeated recitation. Quotations, for example, from the song of Moses (119.8), the song of the Sea (125.10), and the prayer of Hannah (138.6) make up part of the nine canticles of Byzantine hymnody. By far the most frequently quoted work of the Old Testament in the *Palaea* is the Psalms.[43] Parts of the *Palaea*'s narrative are intended to clarify verses from the Psalter; it has also played a decisive role in shaping the *Palaea*'s rendition of biblical history.

In a few cases, an apparent misunderstanding of the Psalms has stirred the author's story-telling imagination. In the *Palaea*'s rendering of the story of Absalom, for example, the author describes how Absalom listened to the counsel of Hushai "and his son Emene" (159.5). Emene, a figure unknown to 2 Samuel, must have originated from a peculiar reading (or hearing) of the Greek text of Ps 7:1. The heading of the psalm reads: a "psalm of David" which he sang to the Lord because of "the words of Hushai, son of Iemeni." Pre-

38. On Habakkuk's field, see n. to 168.5.

39. *Historia Ecclesiastica*, in *PG* 146.113C.

40. "In this small cave lived the holy Melchizedek, and Abraham came to him here and called him thrice, saying 'Man of God.' Melchizedek came out and brought bread and wine, and having made a sacrificial altar in the cave, offered up the bread and wine in sacrifice and this sacrifice was immediately taken up to God in heaven; and here Melchizedek blessed Abraham and Abraham cut his hair and nails, for Melchizedek was hairy" (tr. J. Wilkinson, *Jerusalem Pilgrimage, 1099-1185* [London: Hakluyt Society, 1988], 162).

41. See J. E. Hanauer, *Folklore of the Holy Land* (London: Sheldon, 1907), 34-36. Satan's attempt to thwart Lot is also depicted in one of the panels of the Monastery of the Cross; see Tzaferis, "The Monastery of the Cross," 39. The *Palaea*'s reference to Lot's "struggles" (55.4) is probably an allusion to the same event.

42. On this, see Baert, *Holy Wood*, 319 n. 121.

43. For citations from the Psalms, see 16.14, 45.6, 46.5, 100.10, 103.6, 105.15, 106.3, 5, 116.10-11, 117.5, 119.7, 125.8, 130.4, 156.14.

sumably, the author understood the words "*Chousi huiou Iemeni*" (= Heb. "Hushai the Benjaminite") to mean "Emene (= Iemeni) son of Hushai."

Out of a creative misunderstanding of a single preposition in a verse of a psalm, the *Palaea* has in one instance created both a new biblical character and a whole legend to go along with him. In its treatment of the rule of the judges, the *Palaea* describes how an Israelite named "Endor" assassinated the Persian king (128-29). According to the *Palaea,* the Jews, under the domination of the Persians, appointed Endor as their leader. After offering gifts to the Persian king "Got," Endor arranged a private meeting with the king, in the course of which he stabbed the king to death. He then plundered the Persians' wealth and returned home in triumph. Although Judges knows no such figure, the quotation from Ps 82 (83):10 that concludes the story explains how the *Palaea* came up with this name: "they were utterly destroyed at (Greek *en*) Endor" (129.13). The *Palaea,* as it does elsewhere, understood *en* to mean "by," thus imagining that a fictional character named "Endor" was responsible for the destruction of the Persians.

With the exception of the Psalms, the most cited work in the *Palaea* is the *Great Canon* of Andrew of Crete (ca. 660-740), the center-piece of Byzantine penitential hymnody.[44] The author must have assumed that his audience knew the work intimately. In the numerous references to his *Canon,* the *Palaea* refers to its author variously as "Andrew," "the Cretan," or simply the "wise man."[45] Occasionally, the *Palaea* quotes only a few words from his hymn (136.8; 144.17; 160.10), presumably on the assumption that the hearer would know the rest.

As with the Psalms, characters in the *Palaea* that are unknown to the Old Testament sometimes owe their origins to a misunderstanding of something the author had heard in the hymn. Andrew's *Canon* states in one place that "Hannah's child, the great Samuel, was reckoned among the judges, and *Arimathea raised him* in the House of the Lord." From these words, the author assumed, mistakenly, that Arimathea was the woman who raised Samuel, and not the place of his birth (139.2, 5; cf. 1 Sam 1:1, 19 [LXX]). The *Palaea*'s rendering of the biblical name "Uzzah" as "Zan" misinterprets another biblical name mentioned in Andrew's hymn. The *Canon* states that "when the Ark was being carried on a wagon, and when one of the oxen slipped, Ozan (= Uzzah) only touched it and experienced the wrath of God." In referring to him as "Zan" (107.3 ,7, 9, 11), the *Palaea* apparently confused the *omicron* in the name "Ozan" with the masculine definite article.[46]

The author knew the contents of Andrew's hymn in fine detail. A single word or phrase in Andrew's *Canon* could completely reshape the *Palaea*'s narration of a biblical episode. One such retelling concerns the brutal assault on the wife of the Levite by the residents of Gibeah (142-144). According to the Judges account (Judges 19), the Levite had come to Bethlehem to recover his concubine, who had fled to her parents. Under constant urging from the girl's father, the Levite delayed his departure for several days. Because it was

44. A point already noted by M. R. James, *Apocrypha Anecdota*, 157.

45. See 8.2; 9.3; 14.4; 16.12; 144.18 (Andrew); 138.8; 139.5 (the "Cretan"); 127.10, 12; 130.22; 133.9; 136.8; 140.21; 141.14; 144.17; 148.9; 160.10 (the "wise man"). For the influence of the *Great Canon* on the Byzantine commentary tradition, see most recently A. Giannouli, *Die beiden byzantinischen Kommentare zum Großen Kanon des Andreas von Kreta* (Wiener Byzantinistische Studien 26; Vienna, 2007), esp. pp. 41-45; eadem, "Die Kommentartradition zum Grossen Kanon des Andreas von Kreta—einige Anmerkungen," *JÖB* 49 (1999): 143-59.

46. At 163-166, the author's identification of "Tobit" as "Bit" could also reflect a confusion of the first syllable in Tobit's name with the definite article "*to*."

almost evening when he finally did leave for home, he chose to spend the night in the Benjaminite city of Gibeah in order to avoid contact with the Jebusites. The *Palaea* has a rather different version of events, ascribing much of the blame for what happened to the Levite himself. The Levite's inattentiveness to the time, not pressure from his in-laws, caused him to delay his departure; for that reason, he had no choice but to spend the night in the hostile city of the Benjaminites. The citation from Andrew of Crete at the end of the episode explains why the *Palaea* chose to make the Levite responsible for the outrage committed against his wife: "The Levite among the judges, *by negligence* (*ameleias*), divided his wife among the twelve tribes, my soul, in order to proclaim lawless outrage of Benjamin" (144.17).

Close attention to the wording of the *Great Canon* also underlies the *Palaea*'s unique account of King Saul's rise to power. In its account of the circumstances preceding Samuel's anointing of Saul (1 Sam 9), 1 Samuel states that Kish, a man of great wealth, dispatched his son Saul and a servant to recover the lost asses. When they arrived at Samuel's city, young maidens drawing water instructed him and his servant to find Samuel. Because God had previously told Samuel about meeting a man who would save the people of Israel, he immediately recognized Saul as the future king of Israel and treated him accordingly. The sequence of events in the *Palaea* is quite different (147-48). In response to the demands of the people, God, with seeming indifference, tells Samuel to anoint as king whomever he finds at the gate of the city. By chance, it turns out to be Saul, a poor manual laborer who had fallen asleep at the city gates following a hapless and disorganized attempt to recover the sheep that he had lost. When Samuel finds him, he unceremoniously anoints him and presents him to the people as king. It is not difficult to discover the creative impulse driving this narrative of events. At the end of the story, the author confirms his account with the words from Andrew of Crete: "When Saul once lost his father's asses, my soul, he *incidentally* found a kingdom" (148.9). Here, the single word "incidentally" (*parergon*) inspired the author to tell a story emphasizing the fortuitous, almost random, nature of Saul's rise from poverty to power.

Recurring Themes in the *Palaea*

The *Palaea* concludes somewhat abruptly with a challenge to the Jews to explain how they can now obtain remission for sins, seeing that the means for atonement provided for in the Old Testament are no longer available to them (169). Because this critique is rather muted, and because the work is otherwise devoid of overt invective against Judaism, Flusser viewed the conclusion to the work as more or less a pro-forma exercise, an obligatory ending to a "book dedicated to the biblical history of the Jews."[47] That judgment may not be entirely warranted. The author's challenge to the Jews is in fact very much in keeping with the overall character of the work. For the *Palaea*, biblical history is largely a record of acts of propitiation, penitence and atonement for sins.

The *Palaea* assigns all manner of transgressions to Old Testament figures, some of them not immediately evident from the biblical text itself. In all, Cain is said to have committed seven sins, hinted at in Gen 4:15 (11.1). Reminders to readers about the dangers of laziness, drunkenness and gluttony permeate the work. Scripture, the author says, "everywhere" reproaches Lot's carelessness in becoming drunk and committing an unthinkable act with his daughters (53.11). Gluttony was behind the manufacture of the golden calf

47. Flusser, "Palaea," 77.

(93.4) and Esau's loss of his birthright (62.9). Laxity and drunkenness led to the downfall of the Nazirite Samson (136.4-7). Negligence was also to blame for the death of the Levite's wife (142-44).

In the *Palaea*, biblical personalities are transformed into agents and exemplars of confession, penitence and atonement. Enoch is an ante-diluvian prophet of repentance to the sinning giants of old (20.1-7). Abraham sends Lot to Paradise in the belief that his death in transit would atone for his sexual transgressions (54.5). For the *Palaea*, Lamech's mysterious words in Gen 4:23 (LXX)—"I have killed a man for my wounding, and a young man to my own hurt"—were the confession of a repentant sinner. On one of his hunting expeditions, Lamech, an archer blind from birth, inadvertently killed Cain with an arrow, mistaking him for a wild animal. When he discovered what he had done, he then struck and killed his young guide in despair. Versions of the story of Lamech's blindness and double-homicide circulated widely in Jewish and Christian tradition.[48] But here the *Palaea* uses the story to examine the nature of sin and repentance. Andrew of Crete, the *Palaea* reminds us, draws our attention to the enormity of Lamech's transgression. By acknowledging his sin, however, Lamech was reconciled to God: "Lamech was the first to become a type of confession and received forgiveness from God because he, of his own free will, pronounced judgment on himself" (14.5).

Sin and repentance are also the themes underlying much of the *Palaea*'s lengthy account of David's flawed reign (150-161). Here the author has organized his narration of David's reign around two penitential texts: a) David's abject appeal for God's forgiveness in Psalm 50 (51), the most commonly recited penitential psalm of the Byzantine liturgy, and b) a citation from an unidentified "wise man," describing how the king's penitence averted the sword of an angel threatening both him and his kingdom. In amplifying on these two passages, the *Palaea* recounts how, after David arranged for the murder of Uriah, God instructed a reluctant Nathan to rebuke the king. Nathan need not fear retribution from the king; if he resisted Nathan's admonitions, the angel would slay him with his sword. While the king's repentance and appeal for God's forgiveness recorded in Psalm 50 turned the angel's sword away, the angel pronounced judgment on his kingdom with the words: a "sword shall not leave your house." The angel and his sword reappear in the *Palaea*'s account of David's illegal census, when the angel turns away his wrath only after David showed penitence. All of these events, the author writes, confirm the "wise man's" summary of David's reign: "To David your prophet, how you stopped your angel smiting the people with the sword" (161.16).

One of the author's aims in treating biblical history as a record of human failing and penitence is to provide a historical explanation of central features of the penitential system and ascetic discipline of the Byzantine church. We have already noted the author's various interpretations of the penitential hymn of Andrew of Crete, a work that was recited in its entirety during the forty-day fast preceding Easter. Observance of the Great Fast probably also underlies the author's remarkable interpretation of the incident of the golden calf. For the *Palaea*, this episode is less a story of idolatry than about the consequences of breaking the fast. While Moses was away on Mount Sinai, the Israelites were unable to observe the forty-day fast that he had enjoined upon them. But in order to break the fast, they had first

48. See J. Kugel, "Why Was Lamech Blind?," *HAR* 12 (1990): 91-103; V. Aptowitzer, *Kain und Abel in der Agada* (Vienna: R. Lowit Verlag, 1922), 59-68.

to make an offering to God: hence, their pleadings with Aaron to make a visible image of God to which they could present their offering (92.4–93.1).

The *Palaea*'s account of Noah's offering after the flood beautifully illustrates how the work uses an event from biblical history to explain another aspect of Byzantine ritual practice, in this case the eucharistic prayer of the Divine Liturgy of Basil the Great. According to Genesis, Noah's first act after disembarking from the ark was to build an altar and make an offering to God. Pleased with Noah's act, God promises never to destroy the world again (Gen 8:20-22). In its own retelling of this event, the *Palaea* includes Noah's actual entreaty as he made the offering: "The offerings are not ours, but rather that part of your possessions that was saved by your command we offer to you, O Lord." His sons then say in response: "We sing of you, we bless you, we give thanks to you, Lord, and we pray to you, our God" (23.3-5). The words of their entreaty would have been immediately recognized by readers familiar with the Divine Liturgy. In the *Palaea*, Noah is made to utter the words of the priest as he raises the bread and wine; his sons recite the words of the congregation. Putting the climactic words of the eucharistic prayer into the mouths of the "priest" Noah and his sons allowed his readers to participate in events occurring in the distant past. By inserting a few explanatory comments of his own, the author also seized upon Noah's offering to explain this most solemn event of the Byzantine liturgical year.[49]

Later Influence

The translation of the *Palaea* into Slavonic, and subsequent extracts and condensations of the work in that language, assured its continued popularity in Russia and south Slavic countries; it continued to be read and used well after the Old Testament first became available in a complete Slavonic translation in the late fifteenth century.[50] Stichel has thoroughly documented the appearance of themes from the *Palaea* in Byzantine painting and manuscript illustrations.[51] One striking example of the influence of the *Palaea* appears in an illustrated Greek poem on Genesis and Exodus, composed by Georgios Chumnos around the year 1500. In the introduction to his English translation of the poem, F. H. Marshall demonstrated that for both the contents and the arrangement of extra-biblical material, the author was deeply indebted to the *Palaea*.[52]

Bibliography

N.b.: The translator was unable to consult Russian scholarship treating the Slavonic version of the *Palaea*. See, for example, R. Curkan, *Slavjanskij perevod Biblii* (Saint Petersburg: Kolo, 2001), 177-81.

---

49. See further Paramelle, *Philon d'Alexandrie*, 30-31.

50. For the Slavonic version, see A. Popov, *Kniga bytia nebesi i semli* (Moscow, 1881). Popov's edition was based on two copies of the work from the Synodal Library of Moscow, dating to the sixteenth and seventeenth centuries. For discussion of the Palaea's transmission among the Slavs and Rumanians, see E. Turdeanu, "La 'Palaea' byzantine chez les Slaves du Sud et chez les Roumains," *Revue des Études Slaves* 40 (1964): 195-206; reprinted in idem, *Apocryphes Slaves et Roumains de L'Ancien Testament* (SVTP 5; Leiden: Brill, 1981), 392-403.

51. R. Stichel, "Außerkanonische Elemente," 163-81.

52. F. H. Marshall, *Old Testament Legends from a Greek Poem on Genesis and Exodus by Georgios Chumnos* (Cambridge: Cambridge University Press, 1925). For further discussion of the influence of the *Palaea*, see Giannouli, "*Apocryphon Loth*," 96-97.

Böttrich, G. "Palaea / Paleja. Ein byzantinisch-slavischer Beitrag zu den europäischen Historienbibeln." Pages 304-13 in *Fragmentarisches Wörterbuch: Beiträge zur biblischen Exegese und christlichen Theologie: Horst Balz zum 70. Geburtstag.* Edited by K. Schiffner, K. Wengst, and W. Zager. Stuttgart: Kohlhammer, 2007. (Discussion of the contents, transmission and translation of the *Palaea Historica* and the *Palaea Interpretata*)

Dochhorn, J. "Die Historia de Melchisedech (Hist Melch): Einführung, editorischer Vorbericht und Editiones praeliminares." *Mus* 117.1-2 (2004): 7-48. (Includes a new Greek edition of the *Palaea*'s account of Melchizedek, incorporating variant readings from Paris, BNF, gr. 37, 67v-73v)

Flusser, D. "Palaea Historica—An Unknown Source of Biblical Legends." Pages 48-79 in *Studies in Aggadah and Folk-Literature.* Edited by J. Heinemann and D. Noy. ScrHier 22. Jerusalem: Magness Press, 1971. (Summary and analysis of the *Palaea*, with emphasis on its preservation of older Jewish traditions)

Giannouli, A. "*Apocryphon Loth (CAVT*, Nr. 93). Zur Entstehung und Entwicklung einer Legende." Pages 88-103 in *Byzantinische Sprachkunst: Studien zur byzantinischen Literatur gewidmet Wolfram Hörander zum 65. Geburstag.* Edited by M. Hinterberger and E. Schiffer. Byzantinisches Archiv 20. Berlin: de Gruyter, 2007. (Detailed study of the *Palaea*'s story of Lot's quest for wood from Eden [54-55])

James, M. R. (ed.). *Apocrypha Anecdota* 2, pages 156-57. Cambridge: Cambridge University Press, 1897. (Brief, but useful, summary of the work)

Kugel, J. *Traditions of the Bible*, pages 344, 557. Cambridge, Mass.: Harvard University Press, 1998. (Discussion and English translations of parts of the *Palaea*, mainly based on the Slavonic version)

Lieberman, S. "Zenihin." *Tarbiz* 42 (1972-73): 42-54 (Heb.). (Close study of a few episodes described in the *Palaea*, with an appendix on Syriac etymologies in the work)

Popov, A. *Kniga Bytiya Nebesi i Zemli: Paleia Istoricheskaya s Prilozheniem Sokrashtennoj Palei Russkoj Redakcii.* Chteniya Obshtestva Istorii I Drevnosti Rossijskih 1. Moscow, 1881. (Edition of Slavonic translation of the *Palaea*)

Robinson, S. E. "The Apocryphal Story of Melchizedek." *JSJ* 18 (1987): 26-39. (Includes analysis of the Melchizedek legend preserved in the *Palaea* and other witnesses)

Stichel, R. "Außerkanonische Elemente in byzantinischen Illustrationen des Alten Testaments." *Römische Quartalschrift* 69 (1974): 159-81. (Detailed study of the influence of the *Palaea* on Byzantine art)

Turdeanu, E. "La '*Palaea*' byzantine chez les Slaves du Sud et chez les Roumains." *Revue des Études Slaves* 40 (1964): 195-206. Reprinted in idem, *Apocryphes Slaves et Roumains de L'Ancien Testament*, 392-403. SVTP 5. Leiden: Brill, 1981. (Very thorough discussion of the transmission of the *Palaea* in Slavonic translation)

Vasiliev, A. *Anecdota Graeco-Byzantina*, XLII-XVI, 188-292. Moscow: Imperial University Press, 1893. (Greek edition of the *Palaea*, with introduction)

Palaea Historica ("The Old Testament History")

1 [1]Before all things and with all things [and] through all things, the true Christian should get to know who God is, in how many ways, [and in what way he is called God]. [2]God is the Father, the one who is eternal, infinite, [unbounded, unbegotten, unlimited, incomprehensible,] encompassing and defining all things [and defined by nothing.] [3]God is the Son, begotten by the Father immutably [before] eternity, [but] in the final times made incarnate through the divine economy from the virgin mother, unmoved, unlimited [according to the Father, but limited] according to the flesh. [4]God is the Holy Spirit, consubstantial with the Father and the Son, at work in all things, controlling, managing and maintaining them. [5]In accordance with both[a] in the Trinity, it is not incomplete, [but] there is rather one kingdom, one will, one essence, one light from three suns, [two natures], I mean a divine nature and a human nature.

2 [1][First of all,] I believe in one God, that is, the Father without beginning, [and] the Son who is likewise unoriginate, [and] the Holy Spirit who is [coeternal and] consubstantial. [2]I believe that the Father is unbegotten, that the Son is begotten, and that [the] Holy Spirit is [co-eternal and] consubstantial. [3]I believe that the Father is infinite, that the Son is bodily finite,[b] and that the Holy Spirit is beyond measure, active in all the purposes of the Father [and] Son. (p. 189)

3 [1]How many works did God create on the six days of creation? [2]On the first day, God created the light, that is to say the day and the night. [3]On the second day, the heaven and the earth. [4]On the third day, the seas, springs and rivers, and in general everything that is of a watery nature. [5]On the fourth day, he created the sun and the moon and the stars, clouds and the rain. [6]On the same day, the one who once brought the dawn, but who is now darkened, saw heaven set in orderly array and, puffed up in his mind, said [to] himself, "I will place my throne on the clouds of heaven and be equal to the Most High." [7]By the command of God, he was hurled down from the order of the angels and deprived
Isa 14:12-15 of his heavenly robe, and instead of light became darkened blackness. [8]Some say that because he did not make obeisance to the man after being formed by God, he was cast out. An anathema on those who speak such nonsense. [9]For the man was formed on the sixth day, but the adversary fell on the fourth day.[c] [10]In

---

a. Text: *kat' ampho*. The meaning is uncertain.

b. Presumably in relation to Christ's corporeal nature.

c. For arguments very similar to those put forth in the *Palaea*, see ps.-Athanasius, *Quaestiones ad Antiochum ducem* (PG 28.604C; 688A). For the tradition that Satan was cast down

like manner, God on the fifth day created the plants and all the [four-footed] animals and reptiles and wild animals. [11]On the sixth day, he formed the man, by taking up dust from the earth. [12]Accordingly, when all these works that come into existence from God in six days are numbered, there are twenty-two works, [identified as the following: 1) light; 2) heaven; 3) earth; 4) the waters; 5) the fish; 6) the reptiles and wild animals; 7) fire; 8) snow; 9) rain; 10) seas; 11) clouds; 12) sun; 13) moon; 14) stars; 15) angels; 16) plants; 17) herbs; 18) winged birds; 19) mountains and hills; 20) crawling things; 21) mist; 22) man. [13]These twenty-two works God created in six days,] and for this reason there are in fact [also] twenty-two Hebrew letters.[a]

4 [1]*Concerning Adam*: After he was formed by God, the man and his companion Eve were set up by God to live sumptuously in Paradise. (p. 190) [2]But the adversary, seized by jealousy, [and] assuming the shape of the serpent, met up with Eve; at which point, [as if] unaware, he asked out of a desire to learn what instructions they had received from God. [3]The woman replied, "Only of
the tree of life shall we not touch, but all the others we have at our disposal."[b] Gen 3:3-4
[4]Whereupon the adversary offered her these words of advice: "If only you touch
the tree, you will become as gods knowing good and evil." [5]Upon beholding Gen 3:5
the beauty of the tree, the woman was carried away by the idea of equality with God, and passed on to her husband the advice of the serpent. [6]Adam, also seduced by her advice,[c] said, "It would be good for us to become gods." [7]As soon as they reached agreement about this, the two found themselves stripped of their divinely-woven raiment. [8]They thus knew from their nakedness that not only had they fallen from their divine nature, but were also separated from the love of God.

5 [1]Many have been distracted with certain disagreements about the tree [of life], and some, supposedly explaining the type [of the tree], say that it was an actual [tree], and regarding the type of its seeds, some say it was the fig, whereas others the grape.[d] [2]But both stray from the correct view. That they say these things in error, the divine scriptures are witness, which say the following: "They
were cast out of Paradise because they strove to be equal with God." [3]And the Gen 3:22-24
author of the hymns also witnesses to my statement when he says, "The serpent crawled out from Eden and by my desire for deification deceived me and threw

---

from heaven because of his refusal to make obeisance to Adam, see, for example, *Life of Adam and Eve*, 13-16.

a. For the twenty-two acts of creation, see *Jub.* 2:1-23, which likens these twenty-two works to the twenty-two biblical patriarchs from Adam to Jacob. Later witnesses also cite *Jubilees* as the source of the tradition identifying the works of creation with the twenty-two letters of the Hebrew alphabet and the twenty-two books of the Hebrew Bible; see, for example, George Syncellus, *Ecloga Chronographica* 3.14-17, ed. A. A. Mosshammer (Leipzig: Teubner, 1984). See also Epiphanius, *On Weights and Measures*, 635-717, ed. E. Moutsoulas (Göttingen: Dieterich, 1877).

b. The author does not appear to distinguish between the tree of life and the tree of the knowledge of good and evil.

c. Vas.: "by the serpent's advice."

d. For discussion of various identifications of the tree of knowledge (identified here as the tree of life), see J. Kugel, *Traditions of the Bible* (Cambridge, Mass.: Harvard University Press, 1998), 125; L. Ginzberg, *The Legends of the Jews* (Philadelphia, Pa.: Jewish Publication Society, 1925), 5.97 n. 70.

me to earth."[a] [4]He attests that they were expelled from Paradise for no other
reason than through striving for equality with God. For in desiring divinity, they
fell. [5]The tree of life is in fact nothing other than Christ himself and the Holy
Spirit, which appeared to Adam like a towering tree reaching as far as the heavens, the vision of which was more beautiful than everything in existence.

6 [1]From this it is (p. 191) plain to see that the very glory of God, which
is clearly the Holy Spirit, was set up in the middle of Paradise, warming it.[b]
[2]Therefore, the devil told Eve, "If you should touch it, you will become won-
Gen 3:4-6 drous beings," for he who touches the divine glory will be glorified. [3]This is why
Gen 2:17 God gave them the command, "If you should touch it, you will die."[c] [4]Do not
be surprised that this was said, for in that place where there is a manifestation
of God, a prohibition is decreed against drawing near. [5]Thus later on, he says
to Moses in Sinai that whenever the glory of God appears on the mountain [in
Exod 19:12 Sinai], "*Everyone who touches* it[d] *will surely die.*" [6]It was accordingly said concerning the glory of God neither to touch it nor to make an attempt to do so.
[7]That is why he also commanded Adam, "As for the tree of life in the middle
Gen 2:17 of Paradise, you shall not touch it." [8]In the book of Genesis, it is thus ordained
to eat [from] every tree in Paradise, that is from trees suitable for eating, but
Gen 2:16-17 not to eat from the tree of knowing good and evil. [9]Clearly, then, it was not an
edible tree, as some claim, but rather the glory of God growing in Paradise,
which Adam was ordered not to touch. [10]But because he disobeyed and desired
to touch it, he was found naked; hence it is clear that they fell because of their
Gen 2:25 aspiration for equality with God.

7 [1]An anathema on those who say that there was intercourse between Adam
and Eve when they were in Paradise. [These people speak a falsehood out of
ignorance of the truth.][e] [2]For Adam after leaving Paradise spent thirty years
grieving and in this way had intercourse with Eve. [3]Hence, Gregory the Theologian, in his work *Yesterday on the Illustrious Day of the Holy Lights,* said, "Jesus
was baptized at age thirty because of the sin of Adam at thirty years." [4]He also
provides this testimony: "From the time he departed from Paradise, he spent
thirty years and in this way he had intercourse with Eve."[f] [5]To those abominable
Phundaitae[g] who say that the adversary had intercourse with Eve and [from

a. The source of this quotation is unknown.

b. The translation is a loose rendering of an apparently corrupt Greek text.

c. The quoted text of Genesis uses the word "eat" instead of "touch." The author has assimilated the Genesis text to the words of Exod 19:12 quoted in 6.5.

d. Exod 19:12 reads "the mountain" instead of "it."

e. For Jewish and Christian sources on Adam and Eve's celibacy in Paradise, see H. S. Benjamins, "Keeping Marriage out of Paradise: The Creation of Man and Woman in Patristic Literature," in *The Creation of Man and Woman: Interpretations of the Biblical Narratives in Jewish and Christian Traditions* (ed. G. Luttikhuisen; Leiden: Brill, 2000), 93-106; Gary Anderson, "Celibacy or Consummation in the Garden? Reflections on Early Jewish and Christian Interpretations of the Garden of Eden," *HTR* 82 (1989): 121-48.

f. The words "yesterday on the illustrious day of the holy lights" come from the first line of Gregory of Nazianzus's *In sanctum baptisma* (orat. 40). Although this work describes Jesus' baptism at age 30 (PG 36: 352A, 400C), it does not refer to Adam's age when he first had intercourse with Eve.

g. On the Phundaitae, see the Introduction. For Cain as the son of Satan, see Kugel, *Traditions,* 157.

him] she gave birth to Cain—anathema. [6]For Adam knew his wife Eve and, after
becoming pregnant, she gave birth to Cain. (p. 192) Gen 4:1

8 [1]*Concerning Cain:* Cain became completely defiled and a rebel against God. He acquired for himself every evil deed.[a] [2]Andrew of Crete attests to my words when he states, "Cain and we ourselves, O wretched soul, have offered to the creator of the universe filthy deeds and a blameworthy offering and a useless life. Therefore we too have been condemned."[b] [3]He testifies, then, that the life of Cain was entirely defiled; not only did he offer a blameworthy offering, but he also possessed every wicked deed of evil.

9 [1]A son was subsequently born to Adam, whom he named Abel; this name
means "sorrow," whereas Cain means "jealousy."[c] [2]*Abel brought an offering to the*
Lord God from his first-born cattle [and from its fat]. [3]Andrew of Crete attests to Gen 4:4
what I say, with the following words: "I am not like the righteousness of Abel, Jesus, for I have never brought acceptable gifts to you, not deeds full of God or a pure offering or a blameless life."[d]

10 [1]*Concerning Abel*: Abel was so devout that he lived in fear of God [and] in
righteousness. [2]God therefore accepted his offerings, while spurning Cain's offering in disgust. [3]Because of this, Cain was jealous of his brother Abel and said
to him, "*Let us go out into the field,*" as if for enjoyment. [4]When they reached the Gen 4:8
field, *Cain rose up against Abel his brother and slew him. The Lord [God] asked*
Cain, "Where is Abel your brother?" [5]*Cain replied, and said to the Lord, "Am I my*
brother's keeper?" [6]*The Lord said to him, "Why have you done this? The voice of*
your brother's blood cries out to me from the ground; as for you, now you are cursed
on the earth, which has opened its mouth to receive the blood of your brother from
your hand." [7]Cain said to the Lord, "*If you cast me out today from the face of the* Gen 4:8-11
earth [and from your face, and I will be hidden] (p. 193) *[from your face, then*
anyone who finds me will kill me." [8]*And the Lord said to Cain, "Not so. Anyone* Gen 4:14
who kills Cain will suffer seven-fold retributions, and Cain will be groaning and
trembling on the earth." [9]Cain was thus cast out from the face of the earth,] and Gen 4:15
there was no one who would dare to kill Cain, lest he become liable to seven-fold retributions. [10]They were called "retributions" because the one who commits this act is not able to flee the pain of death, but such a transgression suffers retribution from God. [11]For this reason they were called "retributions," because they receive retribution from God.

11 [1]These are the evil [deeds] that Cain did:[e] First, he angered God. Second, he brought grief to his father. Third, he killed his brother. Fourth, he perpe-

a. The author's claim that Cain "acquired" every work of evil assumes an etymological connection between the name Cain and the Hebrew word for "acquire (*qanah*)." For "acquisition" (Gr. *ktēsis*) as the meaning of the name Cain, see, for example, Jos., *Ant.* 1.52; Philo, *Cher.* 52; *Sacr.* 1.2.

b. Andrew of Crete, *Canon* (PG 97.1332B).

c. On "jealousy" (Gr. *zēlos* = Heb. *qinah*) as the meaning of the name Cain, see Eus., *Praep. Evang.* 11.6.23; George Mon., *Chronicon*, 369.7 (ed. C. de Boor; Leipzig: Teubner, 1904); ps.-Clement, *Hom.* 3.42.7. On Abel as "sorrow" (= Hebrew *hbl*), see Philo, *Migr.* 74; Eus., *Praep. Evang.* 11.6.24; ps.-Clement, *Hom.* 3.26.1; 3.42.7; George Mon. 369.8.

d. Andrew of Crete, *Canon* (PG 97.1332B).

e. The tradition about Cain's seven sins arose from the enigmatic verse in Gen 4:15: "Any one who slays Cain, vengeance shall be taken on him sevenfold." For a list of Cain's seven sins

trated a lie. Fifth, he committed murder. Sixth, he defiled the earth. Seventh,
he renewed Hades,[a] [and engaged in repudiation of God]. [2]For when asked by
God, "*Where is your brother Abel?*" he repudiated him, saying, *"Am I my brother's*
Gen 4:9 *keeper?"* [3]As a result, the condemnation he received from God was to groan and
Gen 4:14 tremble on the earth, and that anyone finding him would not dare to kill him,
in order that [those] who subsequently saw him might learn how to restrain
themselves from committing murder. [4]Cain was going around groaning and
trembling on the earth. [5]He fathered sons and daughters, and suffered punish-
ment up to the second millennium. [6]Cain had a son and called him Enosh.[b]
Irad[c] was born to Enosh, [and] Irad fathered Mahujael,[d] and Mahujael fathered
Gen 4:18 Mathushael,[e] and Mathushael fathered Lamech.

12 [1]*Concerning Lamech:*[f] Lamech was born blind from his mother's womb.
[2][But] he received as a gift from the Lord God the ability to shoot an arrow
with perfect aim. [3]Although blind, he killed all kinds of animals with the arrow, including elephants, lions, bears, deer, and not only among the four-footed
animals, but also among the birds: eagles, vultures and any other kind [of bird]
it was possible to point out. (p. 194) [4]For he had someone to guide him, and
the guide simply directed his hand, pointing it [at] that place where he saw the
animal or the bird. [5]In this way he fixed the arrow, wounded whatever animal it
was that he saw, killed it, and survived by his hunting. [6]Lamech, the blind man,
Gen 4:19 had two wives, the first one named Adah and the second named Zillah. [7]Each
day, Lamech would take his guide, go out, hunt for animals, and provide for his
wives.

13 [1]*Concerning the death of Cain:* [At that time,] Cain, vexed by his deeply anguished life of groaning and trembling, gave himself over to trackless regions [and impassable woodlands]. [2]He said to himself, "How will I not be devoured by a beast or eaten by a bird?" And no one killed Cain. [3]It came to pass that one day Lamech, the blind man, went out to hunt, and the young man was with him acting as his guide. [4]When they came into a woodland, [the young man guiding him] said to Lamech, "I see reeds rustling in the woods, and I suspect that there is an animal." [5]Lamech said to him, "Direct my hand to where you think you see the animal." [6]The young man guided Lamech's hand and [directed it to what he suspected was the animal. [7]Lamech extended his bow,] struck Cain with the arrow, and killed him, unaware that it was Cain. [8]But when the arrow shot from his hand made impact, [Lamech] knew that he had struck a human

---

virtually identical to the *Palaea*'s, see ps.-Athanasius, *Quaestiones in scripturam sacram* (PG 28.737BC).

a. Cf. ps.-Athanasius, *Quaestiones* (PG 28.737C): "he consecrated Hades." The list in ps.-Athanasius does not refer to Cain's repudiation of God.

b. Cf. Gen 4:18 (Enoch).

c. Text: Gaidad (= LXX).

d. Text: Maleleel (= LXX).

e. Text: Methuselah (= LXX).

f. Cf. Gen 4:23 (LXX): "I (Lamech) have slain a man to my wounding and a young man to my grief." The *Palaea* interprets these words as Lamech's confession to a double homicide. The "man" whom Lamech slew was his forefather Cain; the "young man" was his hunting guide. For discussion of the story that follows, see the Introduction.

being. [9]Cain, then, let out an intense groan and expired.[a] This is how Lamech knew that he had slain Cain. [10]He was [extremely] downcast and struck the young man with his hand and killed him. And Lamech was in grief. [11]Some people found him, took him by the hand, and led him to his house; and he wailed mightily. (p. 195)

14 [1]When his wives came upon him, they began to wail with him, asking him about the reason for his grief. [2]Lamech let out a great and bitter groan and said, *"Adah and Zillah, hear my voice, wives of Lamech, listen to my words: I have killed a man,* [he says], *for my wounding and a youth to my own hurt; because Cain's retribution is seven-fold, Lamech's retribution is seventy-seven-fold."* [3]Why Gen 4:23-24
does he say this? It means: "Seven punishments were imposed for Cain's killing, but seventy-seven will be imposed on me by God, and I will be tested more severely than Cain." [4]The admirable Andrew of Crete attests to my words, when he writes, "'I have killed a man,' he says, 'for my wounding and a young man to my own hurt.' And Lamech in his grief cried out to his wives, and are you not trembling, my soul?"[b] [5]Brethren, this Lamech was the first to become a type of confession and received forgiveness from God, because he, of his free will, passed judgment on himself.[c]

15 [1]*Concerning the death of Abel*: Adam beheld the murdered Abel, and unfamiliar with the essence of death, sat by Abel's body for three days. [2]An angel of the Lord came to him and said, "Why are you sitting next to a corpse? Abel will be mute and unmoving from this day on. [3]This is, then, what you have heard, *'You are earth and you will return to earth.'*" [4]When Adam heard these words Gen 3:19
from the angel, he began to wail vehemently. [5]After finding a rock formed like a cave, he placed Abel's body under it. [6]Each day he would return to it and gaze on Abel's body. [7]As he saw it decay little by little, he grieved more [because] he too was going to drink from the bitter cup of death.[d]

16 [1][Adam fathered a son and named him Seth. [2]He instructed his sons and Gen 4:25
daughters in piety.] [3]Adam fathered sixty sons, as Josephus writes, who also became thirty androgynes.[e] (p. 196) [4]Cain's descendants became wicked and inclined to certain ignoble acts of impiety. [5]By acting with complete impiety and doing everything wicked,[f] they were separated from God. [6]After abandoning God, they turned to their own will and began carrying out the wishes of the wicked [and] destructive devil. [7]And there was no memory of God in them. [8]The Lord was exceedingly wroth with them and wanted to wipe them off the face of all the earth. [9]*[The] sons of God saw the daughters of* Cain *that*

---

a. Cf. *Jub.* 4:32, according to which Cain died when his house fell on him.

b. Andrew of Crete, *Canon* (PG 97.1339C).

c. On Lamech's confession as the source of God's forgiveness, see also ps.-Athanasius, *Quaestiones* (PG 28.740A): "He escaped punishment through the confession of the transgression, and by imposing the judgment on himself averted the judgment of God."

d. According to *Jub.* 4:29, Adam was the "first to be buried under the earth." This tradition may lie behind the tradition that Abel was buried in a cave, and not in the ground. For discussion of the witnesses to this tradition, see M. Eldridge, *Dying Adam with His Multiethnic Family: Understanding the Greek Life of Adam and Eve* (SVTP 16; Leiden: Brill, 2002), 66-70.

e. Cf. Jos., *Ant.* 1.68, which states only that Adam had many other children in addition to those mentioned in Genesis.

f. The text is corrupt.

they [were] beautiful and took for themselves wives from all those whom they
Gen 6:2 *chose.*[a] [10]They learned from them to abandon the Lord God and go by the
individual desires of their will. [11]Concerning this line, Christ makes mention
in the gospels, saying, *"Just as they were in the days before the flood eating and*
Matt 24:38 *drinking, marrying and giving in marriage."* [12]Similarly, Kyr Andrew of Crete
in his hymns says, "I have imitated those who behaved licentiously at the time
of Noah, Savior."[b] [13]And all Scripture, both the Old and the New, laments their
lawlessness. [14]The psalmist also makes mention of them, saying, "*Like the slain*
lying in the grave who are no longer remembered, and they have been cut off from
Ps 87[88]:6 *your hand.*"

17 [1]Seth was born to Adam, and Enosh was born to Seth, and Enosh fathered
Kenan, and Kenan fathered Mahalelel. Mahalelel fathered Mathuselah, and Ma-
Gen 5:1-26 thuselah fathered Enoch.[c]

18 [1]*Concerning Enoch:* After Enoch was born, he became a good and reli-
gious man, fulfilling the wishes of God. [2]He was unswayed by the counsels of
Gen 6:4 the giants, for at that time there were giants. [3]And Enoch was translated by the
Gen 5:24 command of God, and no one witnessed his translation.

19 [1]*Concerning Noah*: At the time when the giants among them were loath to
glorify God, there was born a man named Noah. (p. 197) [2]A religious and God-
fearing man, he was unswayed by the counsels of the giants, in the same way as
Enoch. [3]Seeing that he was righteous, God said to him, "You are pleasing before
Gen 7:1 me, because I saw that you are righteous in this generation. [4]*I will establish my*
Gen 6:18 *covenant with you, for my spirit will not abide among these men because they are*
Gen. 6:4 *flesh* (that is, lovers of fleshly desires). [5]Build for yourself, then, an ark from
sturdy wood. [6]This is the way you shall construct it: three hundred cubits in
length, fifty cubits in width, and three hundred cubits in height,[d] and on it you
shall construct lower, second and third decks in the empty space,[e] and this is the
way you shall make it and finish it to a cubit above. [7]You shall make a door on
the side, and you shall bring in with you from all [the animals and all the birds
and all] the reptiles that crawl on the earth by sevens, male and female. [8]And you
shall bring them into the ark with you and from all the kinds of food of which
there is to eat, they shall be there for you to eat. [9]And you shall bring in with you
from all the animals and all the reptiles so as to leave offspring on the face of all
Gen 6:15-21 the earth. [10]And in this way you shall build the ark in 120 years."[f]

20 [1]Noah did everything that the Lord God commanded him. [2]The giants
heard that the righteous Noah was building an ark because of the flood of water
and began to laugh at him. [3]But Enoch, who was still around, said to the giants,

---

a. Beginning as early as the fourth century, most Christian interpreters understood "the sons of God" and "daughters of men" of Genesis 6 as, respectively, the offspring of Seth and Cain. Although the *Palaea* identifies the "daughters of men" with the daughters of Cain, the identity of the "sons of God" is not specified.

b. Andrew of Crete, *Canon* (PG 97.1344A): "I have imitated those who were licentious in Noah's time, and I have earned a share in their condemnation of drowning in the flood."

c. Cf. Gen 5:21, according to which Enoch fathered Methuselah.

d. Cf. Gen 6:15: thirty cubits high (= Slav.).

e. Cf. Slav.: "and make a small ark inside the ark with second and third decks."

f. For explanation of the 120 years for the building of the ark, see below, note to 20.9.

"The earth will be consumed either by water or by fire." 4And the righteous Enoch
was doing nothing else except to occupy himself recording on marble and on brick
the mighty acts of God from the beginning. 5He would say, "If the earth is consumed by fire, the brick tablets will be preserved, and they will serve as a memorial
[to succeeding generations] of the mighty acts of God from the beginning. And if
the earth is consumed by water, the tablets of marble will be saved."[a] (p. 198) 6Even
though Enoch bore witness at length to the giants, they remained intransigent and
implacable, nor were they willing to glorify the Creator.[b] 7Instead, each [of them]
continued in their own fleshly desire. 8Therefore, God grew angry with them and
gave strength to Noah. 9He completed the ark in one hundred years, <removing[c]>
twenty years because the giants refused to glorify their Lord God.[d] 10After Noah
completed the ark and covered it on the inside and outside with pitch, he brought
into the ark from all the animals, just as the Lord God had commanded [him]. 11By
his command, all the animals came to him, and the righteous Noah received them
and brought them into the ark. Gen 7:8-9

21 1*Concerning the ark*: After the righteous Noah completed [all these
things] that had been ordained by God, the Lord said to him, "Go into the
ark, you and your sons and the wives of your sons and your wife. 2*For, behold,* Gen 7:1
I am bringing down rain on the earth to destroy whatever flesh is on the earth,
from man to cattle, and [reptiles and] birds of the sky." 3Noah entered into the Gen 6:17
ark which was under heaven, [he] and his sons and [his wife] and the wives
of his sons with them. 4The Lord God shut the ark from without, and rain
[was poured out on the earth from the sky]. 5The waterfalls of heaven were
opened, and the abyss gave forth [water in very great quantities, and the]
water [rose] on the land fifteen cubits above the highest mountains. 6And
every offspring [of men and animals] which was under heaven was blotted
out. 7Every man who was under the dry earth died, and the water continued
to rain on the earth for forty days. 8After 150 days, God remembered Noah
and all those who were with him on the ark. 9The rain abated, and (p. 199) the
water diminished from the land after 150 days. 10Concerning this ark, a wise Gen 7:11-24
man spoke figuratively,[e] "There was heaven, but there was not earth; there
was a place, but it did not have a road."[f]

---

a. For discussion of the two tablets motif, see the Introduction.

b. On Enoch's witness to the sinning pre-flood generations, see *1 Enoch* 12–16; *Jub.* 4:22 (to the Watchers).

c. Text: *ephexerisen,* apparently a meaningless corruption of *huphexērēsen.*

d. Underlying this statement about the reduction of the years from 120 to 100 is a celebrated problem in biblical chronology. Because biblical patriarchs after the flood lived longer than 120 years, the divine decree of Gen 6:3 was sometimes understood to refer to the years left remaining for the sinning pre-flood generations to repent; see Tg. Onq. *ad loc.* "I will give them an extension of time, 120 years, to see if they will repent." For other sources, see Kugel, *Traditions,* 183-85. But if the order to build the ark occurred in Noah's 500th year, at the time of the birth of his three sons (Gen 5:32), and the flood occurred in the 600th year of Noah's life (Gen 7:11), then the ark would have been built in 100, not 120 years. To account for the missing twenty years, interpreters concluded that God reduced the number of years to 100; see George Mon. 1.48.1-5; Jerome, *Heb. Quaest.* (on Gen 6:3), ed. P. Antin (CC 72; Turnholt, 1959).

e. Omit "saying."

f. Unknown source.

Gen 8:1 **22** [1]The Lord God brought a wind to the earth and scattered the water.
[2]After this, the ark came to rest on the mountain of Ararat near the Bactrians,
between the Assyrians and those known as the Amanites.[a] [3]When Noah realized that the ark had come to rest, he opened the door of the ark that he had
built and sent out the raven to see if the water had receded from the face of the
earth. [4]After the raven had left, it did not return to the ark, but after finding
the bodies of the deceased, it fed on [them] and did not return to Noah and
the ark.[b] [5][Noah] waited for seven days and sent out the dove. [6]When the dove
did not find rest for its feet, it returned to Noah and the ark. [7]Noah stretched
out his hand from the ark and received it into the ark. [8]Again after seven days,
he sent out the dove, and the dove was gone until evening. [9]But [the dove]
returned with an olive twig in its mouth. [10]And the righteous Noah knew that
Gen 8:6-13 the water had receded from the face of the earth. [11]Concerning this dove, a wise
man spoke figuratively, "A mute messenger brings <back[c]> an unwritten book,
having failed to obtain a staff."[d]

23 [1]*Concerning the dove*: After waiting in this way for seven days, Noah
opened the ark and took from the clean cattle and offered a pure sacrifice to
Gen 8:20 the Lord God. [2]Righteous Noah took the matter of the sacrifice seriously, for
he did not dare to make an offering from the (unclean) animals that were in
the ark. [3]And after making a sacrifice from the clean cattle, he set it before
God, entreating him for his favor and saying, "We offer to you what is yours
from that which is yours in all and for all."[e] [4]That is to say, "The offerings
are not ours, but rather that part of your possessions that was saved by your
command we offer to you, O Lord." (p. 200) [5][And his sons replied,] "We
sing of you, we bless you, we give thanks to you, Lord, and we pray to you,
our God." [6]This means, "We sing of you who formed us and brought us from
non-existence into existence. [7]We bless you, [the one] who brought[f] such a
torrential flow of water and utterly destroyed the whole world together with
our ancestors. [8]We pray [to you, our God,] that we not be destroyed with
our ancestors, and that we might not see another flood like this on the earth;
but let us be protected by your mercy." [9]The Lord [God] smelled the aroma
of the sweet smell, and the Lord [God] said to Noah and his sons, "Behold,
I lift up my covenant [for you] for everlasting generations, behold [I am the
one] who has given you everything, as I did the green herbs; but you shall not
Gen 8:21; 9:3-4, 9 eat flesh with the blood of life." And Noah said to the Lord, "I fear that I will
somehow again come to grief in the same way [that my fathers did]." [10]The
Lord God said to Noah, "I place my bow in the cloud, and in days of rain it
will come to pass that I will show it to the sons of men. [11]They will know that

---

a. Bactria is an area in northern Afghanistan and Pakistan. The "Amanites" may refer to the Ammonites (see below 126.1), a Canaanite tribe dwelling to the east of the Jordan.

b. On the tradition that the raven fed on human corpses, see R. W. L. Moberly, "Why Did Noah Send Out a Raven?" *VT* 50 (2000): 345-56.

c. Text: *polin* ("city"). Emended to *palin* ("back").

d. Text: *baktēran*, probably a variant spelling of *baktērian* ("staff").

e. The prayers of Noah and his offspring are adapted from the Divine Liturgy of Basil of Caesarea (in PG 31.1637D). For discussion, see the Introduction.

f. Text: *anagonta* ("raised up") With Vas., emended to *agonta* ("brought").

I will remember my covenant that I made with you, so that I will never bring
a flood on the earth." [12]And God repented of the act that he had done, and
made a covenant with Noah not to bring a flood upon the earth to destroy all
flesh. [13]Noah said to his sons, "Do you know what your ancestors have gone Gen 9:12-17
through, how they were utterly destroyed? Now you pay attention so that you
might not experience a disaster like this." [14]Noah divided the whole world
among his three sons, just as described in the division of the earth contained
in the book of Josephus,[a] as the discussion will explain below.

24 [1]*Concerning the building of the tower:* After [an increase] of the human
population and people became numerous on the earth, they moved from the
east and found a plain in the land of Shinar (p. 201). [2]They settled there, *and all* Gen 11:2
the earth was one voice and one tongue. [3]*Each said to his neighbor, "Come, let us* Gen 11:1
bake bricks and burn them with fire." [4]The single brick structure that they had Gen 11:3
was like a rock. [5]*"And let us make for ourselves a city and a tower, whose crown*
reaches to heaven. [And let us make for ourselves a name] before we are scattered
over the face of the entire earth." [6]They began to build the tower and the city. [7]*The* Gen 11:4
Lord God said, "Look, there are one people and one tongue, and they have begun
to do this, and now nothing will fail from them until they undertake to do it. [8]*But*
come, let us descend and confuse their tongues there, so that each person might not
understand the voice of his neighbor." [9][And the Lord God confused the tongue Gen 11:6-7
of all the earth. And there was given to them an understanding of the twelve
tribes, that is of the seventy-two languages.[b] [10]Those building the tower and the
city ceased their work, because each person did not understand the voice of his
neighbor]. [11]They were scattered over every place under the sun, and in this way
were dispersed over the face of all the earth. Gen 11:8-9

25 [1]*Concerning Nimrod:* After this, Nimrod became king, a giant of a man
who founded Babylon the great and reigned over it for eighty-five years. [2]This Gen 10:9-10
Nimrod measured all the universe, both the land and the sea, and he discovered
the middle of the world in Palestine.[c] [3]From that point, they began to practice
idolatry, and humankind began to worship created things, from their first-born
sons and daughters to snakes and wild creatures.[d] [4]There was not a person on
the earth who called upon [the name] of the Lord God.

26 [1]*Concerning Abraham:* In those days, [a man] was born [by the name]

---

a. See 27.9-13. Josephus's narrative of the post-diluvian migrations in his *Antiquities* (1.109-12) does not recount Noah's division of the earth. For Noah's allocation of the habitable earth among his three sons, see *Jub.* 8:11–9:15.

b. On the widespread tradition linking the seventy-two languages of the world to the seventy-two nations sprung from the sons of Noah (cf. Gen 10), see, for example, Clem., *Strom.* 1.21.142, ed. O. Stählin (GCS 15; Leipzig, 1906); Aug., *Civ.* 16.6. Flusser ("Palaea," 52 n. 20) suggests that the reference to "twelve tribes" may be linked in some way to the activity of the twelve apostles and the seventy disciples described in Luke 10:1.

c. Other sources commonly identify Jerusalem as the *omphalos mundi* ("navel of the world"); see, for example, *Jub.* 8:19; Jos., *War* 3.51-52. See P. S. Alexander, "Jerusalem as the *Omphalos* of the World: On the History of a Geographical Concept," *Judaism* 46 (1997): 147-58.

d. On Nimrod and the beginnings of idolatry, see ps.-Clement, *Homilies* 9.5; George Mon. 11.1-15. For discussion, see K. van der Toorn and P. van der Horst, "Nimrod before and after the Bible," *HTR* 83 (1990): 22-29.

of Abraham. [2]He was given the name by his father and was taught astronomy.[a]
[3]He used to seek for God the creator of heaven and earth and the stars, the sun
and the moon (p. 202), but he was unable to find knowledge of him. [4]Now his
father was an idolater. [5]When Abraham saw the gods of [his] father, he said
[to] himself, "Why is my father, who builds homes for gods and invents new
ones, unable to explain to me about the creator of heaven and earth, as well as
the sun, moon and stars?"[b] [6]While turning these questions over in his mind, he
was in deep reflection. [7]Then one day he rose up early in the morning and set
fire to the building where the gods of his father were housed; and the building,
together with the gods, went up in flames. [8]Terah,[c] who was his brother and the
father of Lot, got up and retrieved his so-called gods. [9]He was consumed in the
flames, he together with his gods. [10]When the Lord God saw Abraham's zeal and
that he alone yearned to become a friend of God, he appeared to him through
his holy angel, telling [him], "*Go forth from your land and from your kinfolk and*
Gen 12:1 *from your father's house and to the land that I will show you.* [11]I will appear to
you there, and I will make you into a great and populous nation. [12]I will bless
you, and your offspring will inherit the cities of your enemies, and the one who
Gen 12:2-3 blesses you is blessed, and the one who curses is cursed."[d]

27 [1]Abraham said to his father, "You know, father, [that] I have found God,
the creator of heaven, the sun, moon and stars. He told me that I should go out
from this land and to another land that he himself will show to me, for there he
says that he will give me rest." [2]And his father told him, "Son, you know that I
have grown old, and your mother has passed away, and your brother was consumed in the fire. All the hope of my old age has been placed upon you. [3]Everything that the God whom you have discovered has told you, you must do out of
piety to him, and you must do everything that is pleasing before him. [4]Do not
go astray, my son, and do not follow the empty gods that I have followed and
from which I have found no benefit." (p. 203) [5]Abraham arose and took with
him his father and his nephew Lot and came to Mesopotamia of Syria, which
is called Arabia Felix; there his father died. [6]He settled in [the land of] Haran.
Haran in the language of the Syrians means "excrement."[e] [7]After his father died,
an angel of the Lord appeared to him and said, "Rise up and go to the land to
Gen 12:1 which the Lord [your] God has summoned you." [8]Abraham arose, taking with
him his wife Sarah and his nephew Lot, and arrived in the land of Palestine.
[9][Although this was the inheritance of Shem, the Canaanites,] the offspring of
Ham, [were dwelling in] this [land]. [10]For because the land to the south that
fell to Ham's lot was parched, his descendants rose up and seized the land of
Palestine, which was Shem's inheritance. [11]They retained possession of it for

a. For a similar account of Abraham's renunciation of idolatry and its aftermath, see *Jubilees* 12.

b. Cf. *Jub.* 12:1-5, where Abraham openly confronts his father about his idolatry.

c. Cf. *Jub.* 12:14. The text confuses Abraham's brother Haran with his father Terah.

d. Cf. Gen 12:1-3, according to which God issued this directive only after Abraham had already arrived in Haran. The *Palaea* describes two divine calls, first in Ur (26.10-12), and again in Haran (27.7).

e. Possibly Syriac *khry'* ("dung"); see Liebermann, "Zenihin," 52-53.

four hundred years.[a] [12]Although God was long-suffering, Ham's descendants would not ever repent and restore the land to the offspring of Shem. [13]When after four hundred years they had not returned the land, God enforced the oaths and brought Abraham, of the offspring of Shem, out from the land of the Chaldeans —[this, so that the offspring of Abraham might inherit this land and satisfy the oaths] that Noah had imposed on his sons, that one brother was not to trespass on the inheritance of the other.[b]

28 [1]When Abraham arrived and saw the Canaanites, he was extremely fearful and told his wife Sarah, "You know, my wife, that you are truly beautiful in appearance, but I am deformed and unsightly and fear that I might perhaps die because of you."[c] [2]Sarah came up with a clever solution to this problem and told him, "I too am aware of this. [3]Let us say that you are my brother. They will keep me for themselves,[d] but you will live." [4]When they came to the Canaanites, [they went up to Ephron], and Ephron the son of Chet was king of that land.[e] [5]When they entered the city, the Canaanites saw them (p. 204) and inquired of them, "Where do you come from?" [6]And they said, "From the land of the Chaldeans." (For the people of that time were unacquainted with travel abroad.) [7]They went in and spoke to their king about them. Ephron sent and asked Abraham, "Who is the woman with you?" [8]And he said, "She is my sister." [9]When evening fell, Chet sent and took Sarah and sent her off to his bed-chamber. [10]After having his dinner, Chet got up and went into his bed-chamber. [11]And he saw an angel standing before him, near his bed and holding in his hand an outstretched sword. [12]When Chet saw him, he grew fearful and started to tremble. [13]Casting a piercing glance at him, the angel said, "Where are you going?" "To my consort(," he answered).[f] [14]Chet trembled with fear and said to his servants, "Summon this man." [15]So they summoned Abraham, and when he entered, Chet said to him, "Tell me, Sir, who is this woman with you?" [16]Abraham said, "She is my wife. But out of fear of the Canaanites, I said, 'She is my sister.'" [17]So he gave her back to him, saying to his servants, "[Give this man a place to sleep], so that he and his wife might have their rest."

Gen 12:10-12; 20:2

Gen 20:2-7

29 [1]Abraham took his wife Sarah and rested for that night. [2]But Ephron the son of Chet remained the whole night afflicted with trembling. [3]He arose early in the morning and in the company of his friends, said, "Summon Abraham." [4]When Abraham arrived, he ordered him to be seated and said to him, "Tell us the truth, Sir, whence have you come here? From what place and for what reason have you come here?" [5]And he said, "I set out from the land of

a. Cf. Gen 15:13, where God tells Abraham that his descendants will be sojourners in a foreign land for four hundred years.

b. On Canaan's violation of the oath sworn by Noah's sons, see *Jub.* 10:28-33.

c. The Genesis story told about Pharaoh and Abimelech (12:11-20; 20:1-18) has been transferred here to Ephron the Hittite. The purpose of the story is to demonstrate the Canaanites' assent to Abraham's acquisition of the land (see below 29.17).

d. Or possibly, "they will keep me alive." The sense seems to require the other meaning.

e. In the narrative that follows, there is unclarity about proper names. Because the author seems to understand "*ho Chettaios*" (lit. "the Hittite") as a proper name, we have translated it as "Chet." In some cases, however, the king of the city is named "Ephron, son of Chet," in other cases simply "Chet."

f. For the sake of the meaning, the translation has repunctuated the text.

the Chaldeans. I was searching to find God the creator of [the] heaven and the
earth and [the] sea, the sun and the moon and the stars. [6]After I found him,
he explained to me that he had come to settle[a] in this place. [7]He ordered me to
go out from my land and from my kinfolk (p. 205), and when I arrived I would
find him in this land, where he has come to dwell." [8]Upon hearing this, the
son of Chet grew fearful and said to his friends, "He is a terrifying god, for I
saw him and am gripped with fear. [And] I believe that he is a terrifying god."
[9]He said to Abraham, "And how do you appease him when you see him?" [10]He
said, "I make a sacrifice to him, and in this way he becomes kindly disposed to
me." [11]And so Chet said to him, "Take twelve rams from my house [and] seven
heifers [and] offer a sacrifice to the Lord your God, propitiating him for me so
that he might not kill me." [12]Abraham took the animals and came to a high land
and offered them up as a sacrifice to God.[b] [13]An angel of the Lord appeared to
him and said, "Traverse [this] land over its length and width because I will give
it to you, and I will cause you to multiply exceedingly, and your offspring will
inherit this land [and the cities of your enemies]. [14]And I will not abandon you
Gen 22:17 until I accomplish everything that I have said to you." [15]From that day, Chet
gave Abraham seventy heifers, forty bulls, one hundred sheep and ten servants.
[16]And he told him, "In seven days (I want) you to take a tithe from my house
and offer this as a sacrifice to the Lord your God."[c] [17]And he said, "All the land
before you is yours. Wherever it is pleasing to you, settle with your wife and
children and cattle and everything that belongs to you, for behold we are your
servants."

30 [1]Abraham went and settled at the oak of Mabri,[d] which means "cold
water." [2][For translated into Greek, this is what "*Mabri*" means in the Syriac
language: "water" in Syriac is called "*mga*,"[e] the "oak" is called "*mebere*," and
"cold" is called "*Mabri*."[f]] [3]So Abraham, after traversing the land in its length
Gen 13:18 and width, settled at the oak of Mabri, taking full advantage of the hospitality.
[4]Abraham then said to Lot, "Look, [my] son, the land is before us. (p. 206)
Choose from all the land and settle where it is pleasing to you." [5]Now Lot saw
that the land of Sodom was more bountiful than all the rest of the land, [and]
had fresh water with [the river] Jordan flowing through it, and all kinds of
fruit-bearing trees. [6]Put simply, it was like the paradise of God, and it was not
possible for anyone to experience adversity there. [7]When Lot saw that it was
bountiful, he asked to dwell there. [8]Now the inhabitants of Sodom were wicked
and sinners before the Lord. [9]When Lot arrived, he settled in their midst [and
Gen 13:8-13 took a wife from their number].

31 [1]After Lot had separated from him, the Lord told Abraham, "Behold, I
am raising up my covenant with you for everlasting generations, and I will bless
you, and you will be blessed, and your name will be Abraham, which means

a. Reading with Vas. Text: "he has settled him."

b. Reading with Vas. Text: "to your God."

c. For the significance of this act, see below 38.6-8.

d. That is, Mamre. Because of the etymology that follows, we have transliterated the Greek.

e. *Mga* is probably a transliteration of the Syriac word *my'* ("water"); see Lieberman, "Zenihin," 53.

f. The meaning of this etymology is obscure.

'father of a multitude,' 'chosen father,' and 'our father'. 2Your name will not be
Abram. [Your name] will be Abraham instead, because I have made you father
of many nations. 3I will cause you to increase, and I will cause you to multiply
exceedingly. 4Now, then, saddle up your donkey and take with you costly rai- Gen 17:1-7
ment, bread, wine, and a razor. 5Go up to Mount Tabor and stand on the rock
and shout three times, 'Man of God!' 6There will come up from the northern
side [of the mountain] a wild-looking man. 7His finger-nails are a cubit long,
and the hair of his head and his beard reach down to his feet. 8Don't be afraid of
him. Rather stay and cut his nails [and hair and give to him], and he will eat and
drink, and you will receive a blessing from him, and you will be blessed."

32 1*Concerning Melchizedek:*[a] This Melchizedek is called fatherless and
motherless [and] without genealogy and in the likeness of the son of God.[b] Heb 7:3
2His mother was named Salem, according to the name of his city. And his
father was called Josedek. 3Josedek fathered two sons: one he called Sedek,
the other Melchi.[c] 4And they and their city were given over to idols,[d] (p. 207)
for [they] were descendants of Nimrod.[e] 5They thus remained in the palace
built[f] by Nimrod, and continued their rule up to the reign of Archisedek,
king of Babylon.[g]

33 1One day, king Josedek said to his son Melchi, "Son." And he said, "What is it, father?" 2He told him, "Go out to our ox-stall in Galilee and bring me seventy bulls so that I might make an offering to the great god Cronus and the rest of the gods, because [I am planning to go out into battle." 3When Melchi heard this, he stayed awake that night,] wanting to carry out his father's order. 4Now it was a full moon that night, and the stars were shining. 5When Melchi saw them, he was awe-struck and said to himself, "I can see that the creator of heaven [and] the heavenly bodies is at rest in them. I will tell my father, and we shall offer to him the sacrifice that I am about to bring." 6[When he came in, he said to his father, "Father, hear me. The sacrifice that I am about to bring,] let us offer it to the God of heaven." 7His father became angry and swore an oath, telling him, "By the greatest gods, because you have wanted to make me a stranger to the greatest gods, may [the gods] not get angry with me and kill me. 8So now let me without delay offer you as a sacrifice to the gods, even as you have acted wantonly against the gods and against me."[h] 9While Melchi was on his way to Galilee, his father came in and said to the queen Salem, "Look, I have decided to sacrifice one of my sons to the greatest gods." 10Now the queen loved Melchi more than Sedek,

a. For discussion of the various versions of this story about Melchizedek, see the Introduction.

b. Cf. Heb 7:3, which includes the words "he has neither beginning of days nor end of life." The *Palaea*'s omission of this statement is in line with the narrative that follows, which presents Melchizedek as a mortal human being, orphaned after God's destruction of his ancestral home.

c. Melchi is later renamed Melchizedek. Cf. ps.-Athanasius (PG 28.525A), which identifies the father as Melchi and calls his two sons Melchi and Melchizedek.

d. Reading with P. Cf. ps.-Athanasius (PG 28.525A). The reading of V. is corrupt.

e. On Nimrod and the beginnings of idolatry, see above 25.1-4.

f. Reading with P. Text: "settled."

g. Cf. P.: "And they were ruling when the kingdom of Babylon was in power."

h. Contrast the hostile response from Melchi's father with the earlier blessing that Abraham receives from his father after learning of the one true God (27.2-4).

and was in grief, saying, "Do you absolutely want to sacrifice my beloved son?"[a] [11]The king replied to her, "Not necessarily. But let us cast lots." [12]They cast lots, and the lot fell to her younger son.[b] [13]When she learned that he was coming from Galilee, Salem said to her first son Sedek, "Look, your brother is about to die [and] become a sacrifice offered up by your father. [14]Get up and go out to meet him and tell him [what to do], that he should run away to another land and escape his father's plan." (p. 208)

34 [1]Sedek arose and went away to meet Melchi. [2]Now his father said to his grandees, "Look, I have issued a decree to sacrifice my son Melchi." [3]When his grandees heard this, they too issued an order to sacrifice their children to their gods, because it was a royal decree. [4]As soon as his brother met up with him and told him what to do, Melchi immediately mounted his horse, removed the garment that he had on, placed it upon [his] horse, [and told his brother, "Take the horse] and the garment, and the animals and our men, and depart to our parents. [5]As for me, I will move to another land, attired like a hermit, where no one knows me. And there I will be a beggar, only a bitter death will I escape."

35 [1]His brother Sedek took these things and departed [for home]. [2]Now Melchi stopped to hear the lamentation arising in the city over the boys whom they were about to sacrifice; and there was great lamentation among all the people. [3]After they gathered up all the boys, eighty in number, they stopped and waited for the king so that after he sacrificed his son, then they too would sacrifice their sons. [4]Melchi stood opposite the city in the mountain now called the Mount of Olives.[c] [5]He was the one who conferred this name on this mountain because he found mercy there.[d] [6]As he heard the lamentation that was going on and the wailing of the city, he groaned loudly and lifted his gaze to heaven. [7][He soaked the ground with his tears and cried out with his eyes directed to heaven, and said, "You are the God who created the heaven and the earth] and the sun and the moon and the stars, and I believe that you are just and greater than all the other gods, because your deeds manifest your power. [8]You are truly the one God, who rests above the heavens (p. 209). [9][If] you want me to be your servant, may you not overlook my request. [10]But hear me this very hour and let this city with its gods and all those who worship them be plunged under the earth." [11]As soon as he said this, [there was an earthquake in the city of Salem, and] the whole city of Salem was submerged, together with all its inhabitants. For the earth completely swallowed them up.

36 [1]When Melchi saw that awesome act, he was astounded and feared God the creator of heaven and [the] earth. [2]He got up and went away to Mount

a. No explanation is given here as to why the queen assumed it was Melchi. In ps-Athanasius (PG 28.527A), the queen immediately recognizes from the king's question that he planned to kill Melchizedek (= Melchi), because he had reproached his father about making sacrifices to the gods.

b. Cf. ps.-Athanasius (PG 28.527A), which states that the king allowed the queen to make the choice; she selects Melchizedek's brother for sacrifice.

c. Ps.-Athanasius (PG 28.528C) situates this episode on Mount Tabor.

d. The author connects the word for "olives" in "Mount of Olives (*oros elaiōn*)" with the Greek word for "mercy" (*eleos*).

Tabor[a] and entered into the northern part of the mountain into a ravine. [3]He remained there for forty years, with no human contact and not leaving that spot. [4]He ate [wild] plants and drank only water up until the time when Abraham was dispatched to him, in accordance with the Lord God's instruction to him to saddle his donkey and take fine raiment, and bread and wine and a razor.[b] [5]For this is what the angel of the Lord said to him, "Go up to the mountain, stand on the rock, and cry out three times, 'Man of God!' [6]And a wild-looking man will come out[c] to you. [7]The hair of his head and beard extend down to his feet, and his nails are a cubit long. [8][Don't be afraid of him, but rather get up and cut his nails and hair] and clothe him with the cloak and give to him, [and] he will eat and drink. [9]You will receive a blessing from him, and you will be blessed, because he is priest of God the Most High; and Melchizedek is the man's name."

37 [1]When Abraham had done this, the wild-looking man came out to him and said, "Who are you?" [2]Abraham replied, "I am a man sent from God to cut your nails and hair." [3]And he said, "What is the nature of the God who sent you?" [4]Abraham replied, "The God who made the heaven and the earth and the moon and the stars, the sea and all that is in it, he is the one who commanded me to seek for you." [5]And Abraham fell to the ground and made obeisance to the Lord, saying, "Lord God, maker of heaven (p. 210) and earth, be propitious to me, because I have seen an extraordinary marvel in this man." [6]Then Melchizedek saw Abraham and approached him; and Abraham laid hold of his head, cut his hair and nails, clothed him with the robe, embraced him and said to him, "Let us bring bread, wine and oil so that we might partake of them, because I have received this command from God." [7]Melchizedek said in response, "For forty years I allowed myself to be on this mountain, and I saw no one other than you on this day. Nor did bread come into my mouth. [8]And since you say, 'God ordained it,' please do as you say; but first make an offering from them to the Lord my God, and then let us partake." [9]After bringing him to an opening in the rock, he received bread [and wine, and he poured out oil on them and set them aflame], and both worshipped the Lord—Abraham and Melchizedek—and they ate and rejoiced.[d]

38 [1]Abraham inquired of him about his origins and his city and his arrival at the mountain, how he went into it. [2]Melchizedek told him everything about himself. ["I named the mountain called Salem[e] the 'Mount of Olives,' because," he said, "I found mercy on it."[f]] [3]After hearing all these things, Abraham worshipped the Lord, saying, "It is no great thing for me to have come from the [land] of the Chaldeans. [4]I have found a God who performs wonders. For be-

a. Lit.: Taburion.

b. Cf. Num 6:1-8, in connection with the Nazirite requirements to abstain from wine and the cutting of hair. For other sources depicting Melchizedek as a Nazirite, see Robinson, "Melchizedek," 35-36.

c. Reading with P. Text: "will come in."

d. Cf. Gen 14:18, which states that Melchizedek supplied the loaves and wine. This is also the version of events found in ps.-Athanasius (PG 28.529C) and 46.4 below.

e. Cf. P.: "the mountain adjacent to Salem."

f. See above note to 35.5.

hold, because of what has happened here, I have been taught not to have a high
opinion of myself. [5]Indeed, God does not receive benefactions from humans;
rather he is the benefactor." [6]And Abraham arranged to give Melchizedek tithes
from his household. [7]For this reason, the blessed Paul recalls this, saying, "*Re-*
Heb 7:9 *ceiving tithes, he paid tithes*." [8]For Abraham received a tithe from the house of
Chet, and he in turn paid a tithe to Melchizedek.[a]

39 [1]*Concerning Christ*: In this way Christ as well, who is the creator of everything and receives offerings of everything, did himself offer a pair of doves as
Luke 2:24 an offering according to the law.[b] [2]And these things have been said about Christ
[and entirely in reference to him].

40 [1](p. 211) Melchizedek blessed Abraham, [invoked him by name], blessed
him as a son, and on his own[c] foretold a blessing on his offspring; from that day
Abraham continued coming to be blessed by Melchizedek. [2]Abraham returned
to his house rejoicing and glorifying God. [3]Abraham moved camp and settled
Gen 20:2 in Gerara, where Abimelech was the king. [4]The servants of Abraham contended
<with[d]> the Gerarites over the wells; for the Gerarites would not permit the ser-
vants of Abraham to provide water for their animals, and great contention arose
between them. [5]They thrashed camels and other animals, and many Gerarites
Gen 21:25 died in the conflict as well.

41 [1]*Concerning Abimelech*: Abimelech, the king of the Gerarites, went out in
pursuit of Abraham's servants and despoiling their bodies; [but] Abraham came
and brought a peaceful end to the conflict.[e] [2]After he built a well, both sides,
Abraham and the citizens of Gerara, swore an oath not to create contention
Gen 21:27-31 from that day on. [3]For that reason, the well was named the "well of [the] oath."[f]

42 [1]Abraham made an offering to the Lord God after the offering at the
well, that is the "well of the oath," and the Lord God appeared to him, saying,
"Do not fear, Abraham. Your reward will be exceedingly great." [2]And Abraham
said, "Lo, I am about to die childless." [3]The Lord God said to him, "It will not
be so." [4]And Abraham returned [to his house]. [5]After this, his wife Sarah said
to him, "See, I have grown old, and I am about to die childless from you. Take,
then, Hagar my maidservant and have intercourse with her, so that perhaps you
might raise offspring from her, and they will be heir to your entire household."
[6]Now Abraham was unwilling, until he went away to Melchizedek and told him
about the matter. [7]Melchizedek said to him, "Act [in accordance with] your
wife's word, for I see two peoples arising from you, one bright and fragrant, the
other dark and fetid." (p. 212) [8]And Abraham had intercourse with Hagar, and
Gen 16:1-16 begot from her Ishmael.

43 [1]*Concerning Ishmael*: After Abraham begot Ishmael, [the] Lord said to
him, "Abraham, [Abraham]." And he said, "Here I am." [2]The Lord said to him,
"From all the other nations on the earth, I desire to form a bond with you, and

---

a. See above, 29.16. According to Heb 7:9, Levi, not Abraham, received tithes.

b. According to Luke, Jesus' parents made the offering.

c. Vas.: "the righteous one."

d. Text: *me* ("me"). Emended with Vas. to *meta* ("with").

e. Cf. Gen 21:25, according to which Abraham reproved Abimelech because his servants had taken away the waters of the well.

f. This is based on Gen 21:31 LXX (= Hebrew "Beer-sheba").

I want you to be sealed with an eternal seal. Circumcise yourself in Melchizedek.[a] [3]You shall circumcise every male in your household, and also Ishmael
and all those born in your house. Not one of your males will be uncircumcised.
[4]For I want your offspring to have a seal, because through them all the nations,
as many as are on the earth, are blessed." [5]Abraham went away and did just as Gen 17:10-14
the Lord God had told him. [6]He circumcised every male in his household, and
there was not a male in it who remained uncircumcised. [7]Abraham led out his Gen 17:23-27
entire household, and Melchizedek blessed it because the Lord told him to.
[8]And Abraham was rejoicing with his servants. [9]When he came to the well of
the oath, he made an offering to the Lord God. [10]The Lord [God] appeared to
him and said to him, "Behold, I have established my covenant with you, and
your offspring will be glorified for everlasting generations, and I will multiply
you exceedingly." Gen 17:2, 19

44 [1]*Abraham said to the Lord, "[Lord], what will you give to me? For I am
going to perish childless, and my household slave will be my heir."* [2]And the Lord
[said] to him, "*He will not be your heir, [but rather] another one will issue forth
from you, and this is the one who will be your heir." [3]Abraham said, "How will I* Gen 15:2-4
*know this?" The Lord said to him, "Bring me a heifer three years of age, a goat of
three years, a ram of three years, a turtledove and a pigeon." [4]He split them open
down the middle, but he did not split open the birds. [5]And the birds descended on
the bodies that had been severed in half, and came to rest on them. [6]Around sunset,* Gen 15:9-11
a trance descended on Abraham. [7]A great dark fear descended on him, and a voice Gen 15:12
came to him, saying, "Cast your gaze up to heaven, and look, if (anyone) is able
to count (p. 213) the stars of the sky, you will be able to count your offspring. [8]*But* Gen 15:5
*have this knowledge that your offspring will be a foreigner in a land not their own,
and they will enslave and [oppress] them for four hundred years.* [9]The people to
whom they will *be enslaved I will judge. [10]And after this, they will come forth to
this place with many belongings, and you will depart to your ancestors [in peace],
after having grown up to a good old age."*[b] Gen 15:13-15

45 [1]*Concerning the captivity of Lot*: His nephew Lot was in Sodom. [2]The five
kings, after conferring with one another, departed and despoiled all the land of
Sodom and Gomorrah and took them captive. [3]Lot was also taken captive with
his entire household, and they were all taken captive. [4]When Abraham heard
that his nephew Lot had been taken captive, he numbered the servants born in
his own household as 318. [5]And he pursued them as far as Dan, attacked them
at night, smote them with swords, and recovered the entire cavalry of Sodom,
and Lot his nephew, and [the] wagons, the women and the people. [6]Concerning Gen 14:1-16
these kings, the psalmist makes mention with these words, *"like Oreb and Zeeb,
Zebah and Zalmunna, all their princes."* Ps 82(83):11

46 [1]Abraham [routed all of them and] turned the kings away, (for the kings
of the nations were five in number), just as it was said, *"After Abraham returned
from the slaughter of Chodologomor."* [2]This is to be interpreted as referring to five Gen 14:17

a. The expression "circumcise yourself in Melchizedek" is unknown elsewhere. Christian writers usually claimed that Melchizedek was uncircumcised; see, for example, Just. Mart., *Dial.* 19.4; 33.2.

b. In Genesis, these events occur before the birth of Ishmael.

kings. [3]The letters "*chi* and *omicron*" stand for Chaldeans; "*delta* and *omicron*"
stand for Domites; "*lambda* and *omicron*" stand for Lydians; "*gamma* and *omicron*" stand for Gasphinoi, and "*mu*, *omicron* and *rho*" stand for Moraioi. This is
what "Chodologomor" means, [that is] "five kings." [4]When Abraham returned
from the slaughter of Chodologomor, Melchizedek king of Salem came out, [for
Scripture makes mention of the name of the ancestral house of Melchizedek
and says, "The king of Salem went out] to meet Abraham *and brought out bread*
Gen 14:18 *and wine, for he was priest of God the Most High*."[a] [5]Hence, the psalmist makes
this prophecy concerning Christ, (p. 214) "*You are priest forever according to the*
Ps 109(110):4 *order of Melchizedek*." [6]["*He is without mother, without father, without geneal-*
Heb 7:3 *ogy*." [7]Again another passage]: "Just as Melchizedek made a sacrifice of bread
Gen 14:18 and wine to the Lord God," in the same way, Christ, in place of the body and
the blood, gave us bread and wine with which to make an offering. [8]So much
regarding Melchizedek.

47 [1]*Concerning the Holy Trinity*: Abraham returned [and] encamped at the oak of Mamre, where previously he had enjoyed the hospitality.[b] [2]Now that he had advanced to old age, reaching the age of eighty, he did not want to partake of bread unless a stranger was keeping company with him. [3]But because of malice from the devil, who despises good, he blocked the roads to prevent any stranger from coming to Abraham. [4]Abraham did not send out a servant or any of his household to watch the road. [5][For he said that if he were to send out any of his slaves or his household to observe the road,] he would not notice when strangers happened to be passing through. [6]He would instead lie down and fall off to sleep, and fail to see anyone who might be passing through. [7]So he sat down by the road himself, watching the road lest perchance strangers might be passing through. [8][If he were to find a stranger, he would receive him], and he would come and eat with him. [9]Now the devil, the hater of good, begrudged his good intentions. [10]So what does he do? He blocked the roads so that no one could pass through that road. [11]The patriarch spent the whole night like a highly skilled hunter, sitting there watching the road. [12]He spent one whole day without lunch or dinner and for most of the second day. [13]Sarah told him to partake of bread. But he would not allow it. [14]The second day also passed, and the patriarch Abraham remained up to the third day neither eating nor drinking.

48 [1]*Manifestation of the Holy Trinity:* When the Lord God saw his good intentions, there appeared to him the Father, the Son and the Holy Spirit, like three men traveling along the road, wayfarers coming from a long trip. [2]When he saw them, he rejoiced with great joy. [3]Falling to the ground, he made obeisance to them and said, (p. 215), "[My] lords, if I am worthy, come into my hut." [4]But they were unwilling, offering the excuse that they were traveling on a long journey. [5]So Abraham became extremely downcast and kept urging them more persistently not to disregard his request. [6]After a little while, because they saw him in anguish, they reclined in his hut [and he rejoiced with exceedingly great joy]. [7]He went in and told his wife Sarah, "Mix three measures of wheat flour

a. For a different version of the meeting between Abraham and Melchizedek, see above 37, where Abraham is said to have provided the bread and wine.

b. See above, 30.1-3.

and bake bread, and prepare warm water, and let them wash their feet. 8 I for
my part will go to the cattle stall. After bringing a calf and offering a sacrifice,
I will make merry with these men." 9 Sarah got up and did as Abraham had
instructed her. 10 He went into the cattle stall, brought a gentle little calf, and
boiled it as a sacrifice. 11 He also brought [the] bread and placed it on a table,
and they began to eat. Gen 18:1-8

49 1 As they were eating, one of them said to Abraham, "Do you have a
son?" And he said, "No." 2 And they said to Abraham, "I shall return to you
this time next year, at the due time, and you will have a son." 3 Sarah laughed
presumptuously and said, "[If] my master is an old man, and I am a barren old
woman, how will I give birth to a son?" 4 She found what he said beyond belief.
5 His tablemate said to Abraham, "Why [is it] that Sarah laughed? What I am
telling you is true." 6 After they had the meal, they wanted to leave the table.
7 And behold, the calf's mother appeared, crying out and searching for the calf
that belonged to her. 8 When they arose from the table, the slaughtered calf also
got up and followed its mother.[a] 9 When Abraham saw this, he fell to his face,
unable to make eye contact with the men. 10 And the men continued on to the
land of Sodom. Gen 18:9-15

50 1 *Concerning Sodom and Gomorrah*: Abraham got up and followed behind them. 2 Laying hold of them, he fell down at their feet and said, "My lords,
tell me, your servant, 'Who are you, and where are you going?'" 3 And the Lord
said, "I will not conceal it from my servant Abraham. 4 *The shouting from Sodom
and Gomorrah has been increased* (p. 216) *to me, and their transgressions are
extremely great.* 5 *So I will go down and see whether they have done altogether
according to their outcry which is coming to me; and if not, that I may know
for myself.*" 6 Abraham stood before the Lord [and said to the Lord, "May you Gen 18:20-21
not pronounce judgment, and I will speak before you,] and may you not be
angry with me. 7 If [there are] fifty righteous people (in) the city, would you
destroy them, and will the righteous be as the impious? 8 And will you not ex-
ecute [justice][b] on behalf of the fifty righteous men? [By no means should you,
the Judge, act unjustly.]"[c] 9 The Lord said to Abraham, "If I should find fifty
righteous people, I will spare the entire place for their sake." 10 Abraham said
to [the] Lord, "[Lord], please may I speak once more? If the fifty are reduced
to forty[-five]?" 11 [The Lord] said, ["If I find there forty-five], I will spare the
whole place for their sake." 12 [Abraham said], "If thirty are found [there]?"
13 And [the Lord] said, "[If I find thirty there,] I will spare the entire place."
14 Abraham said, "If twenty are found there?" 15 And he said, "I will spare the
place for twenty." 16 And Abraham said, "If ten are found there?" 17 And he said,
"I will spare it for ten." 18 The Lord departed when he ceased speaking with

a. Cf. *Testament of Abraham* 6, which records the same tradition about the calf that was restored to life after Abraham had sacrificed it. The story of the calf's restoration may have been intended to show that the three heavenly visitors did not really partake of the calf's flesh; for the same idea, see below 132.11; 166.8. For discussion, see D. Allison, *Testament of Abraham* (Berlin: de Gruyter, 2003), 164-67; Kugel, *Traditions*, 344; Flusser, "Palaea," 60.

b. Text: *ouk anuseis* [*krisin*]; cf. Gen 18:24 (LXX): *ouk anēseis panta ton topon* ("will you not spare the whole place"?).

c. The text has been emended in accordance with Gen 18:25.

Abraham. 19[Abraham] returned to his house; and the men departed for Sod-
Gen 18:20-33 om and entered into the house of Lot.

51 1The Gomorrosodomites[a] arrived and were searching for the men, saying, "Give us the strangers who have come here today." 2For these Gomorrosodomites were wicked and sinners before the Lord God, and they stood there demanding the men. 3But Lot did not want to hand them over [to them], and they thronged around the house, seeking to enter. 4Lot said to them, "Take my daughter and leave the men alone." 5But they refused. They crowded around the doors of the house, intending to break them down and enter and seize them. 6The men went to the gate-house, and one of them wanted to open the door of the courtyard of the house. 7But Lot did not allow them, saying, (p. 217) "Sir, please don't open the door for them and let these wicked men seize you." 8In response, he said to Lot, "Allow me to open it, and you will see the means I have to deal with them." 9When he opened the gate, he released a fire-bolt and consumed them in flames. 10When Lot beheld this extraordinary marvel, he fell at their feet [and said to them], "Tell [me], good sirs, who are you?" 11And they said to him, "Gather up your belongings and flee to the mountain, because, look, just as with the conflagration you have seen, we have come to incinerate this country because of their sins and licentiousness. 12Now then [flee this disaster, and let not one of you turn around] and watch the wrath coming to pass; [for] the city [will not survive it
Gen 19:1-13 and will be entirely destroyed]."

52 1*Concerning the flight of Lot:* In great haste, Lot saddled [his] asses, took bread and wine, [and] traveled along the road with his wife and two daughters. 2He kept urging the men not to leave him. But they said to him, "Go, for we are with you." 3Now near the mountain, there was a field called Zoar. 4Lot appealed [to the men] not to set it aflame, so that he might come through safely on it. They yielded to his request. 5In Sodom continuous thunder and fire rained down, and the earth gushed with bubbling pitch and brimstone. 6It consumed the people and the animals and spared no one, utterly burning up everyone instead. 7Lot's wife, upon hearing the loud cry going forth, lost control of her feelings and turned around to look at her native land. 8She was immediately turned
Gen. 19:16-27 to stone. She became a pillar of salt, not stone, but salt. 9And if you don't believe it, the writer in the hymns attests to my words when he says: "Do not be a pillar of salt."[b] Salt is called a pillar {…}.[c]

53 1Only Lot and his two daughters made it through. (p. 218) 2After they settled in Zoar, they supposed that the whole world was destroyed and that not a person was left in the world. 3The two daughters of Lot made an agreement. "Look," they said, "the whole world is destroyed, and no one is left in the world. 4Who will raise up offspring for us, since there is not a man left in the world? 5Come on, let us give our father unmixed wine to drink. He will have relations with us and will produce offspring, and we will populate the world." 6So after making this plan, they gave their father unmixed wine. 7He became

---

a. A description of the inhabitants of the region unique to the *Palaea*.

b. Andrew of Crete, *Canon* (PG 97.1344CD): "Do not be a pillar of salt, my soul, by turning back; but let the example of the Sodomites frighten you, and take refuge up in Zoar."

c. The meaning of the Greek word *harmyra* is unknown.

drunk and had intercourse with his older daughter, and did not know what happened. [8]He did the same thing once again with the other daughter as well. And his two daughters conceived from him. [9]And Kyr Theodore the Studite alludes Gen 19:30-38
to this when he says, "No one who drinks water acts foolishly, but Noah appeared naked, after trying wine. And Lot produced offspring of evil as a result."[a] [10]The blessed John Chrysostom says in his work *Concerning the consumption of wine*, "Lot became a husband to his daughters because of his drunkenness. And the man was both father and grandfather."[b] [11]And scripture in many places reproaches his carelessness.[c]

54 [1]When not a few days had passed, they realized that only Sodom and Gomorrah had been incinerated. [2]Lot arose and went to Abraham and told him everything, how he had been deceived and committed the transgression. [3]Abraham was aggrieved upon hearing this and said to Lot, "Listen to me, son; go to the river Nile that flows out from Paradise and bring me three firebrands." [4]Lot arose and made his way through trackless and arid wilderness. [5][For] Abraham had made the judgment that Lot would either be killed by a wild beast or [die] a bitter death from thirst and [in this way] be delivered from this transgression. [6]But Lot survived by the protection of God and went off to the river Nile that flows out from Paradise and found three firebrands in the wilderness: pine, cedar and cypress. (p. 219) [7]He fetched them and returned to Abraham.[d]

55 [1]When Abraham saw him, he was exceedingly joyous and embraced him as if he had received him back from the dead. [2]He took the wood and together with Lot brought them to the top of a wilderness [mountain] and planted the [three] pieces of wood facing each other, each a cubit from the other in the form of a triangle.[e] [3]He instructed him to leave for the Jordan River, bring back water, and water the pieces of wood planted on the cliff. Now the Jordan was twenty-four miles away. [4]Thus Lot through his struggles watered the pieces of wood and they became entwined [with each other.[f]] [5][When Abraham arrived at the place and saw that not only had the pieces of wood sprouted leaves], but that

---

a. Theodore the Studite (ca.759-826), theologian and hymnographer. The work to which the *Palaea* refers is unknown.

b. The reference is not attested in the writings of Chrysostom. Cf. ps.-Basil of Caesarea, *Sermo 11 (sermo asceticus et exhortatio de renuntiatione mundi)*: "Lot became a husband to his daughters, his own son-in-law and father-in-law, a father and grandfather" (PG 31.640CD). See Vasiliev, XLVII.

c. While an exaggeration, the comment that scripture reproaches Lot's carelessness "in many places" is consistent with the *Palaea*'s understanding of biblical figures as exemplars of sin and penitence; see the Introduction.

d. Isa 60:13 (LXX) speaks of the cypress, pine and cedar trees that will "glorify my holy place." Christian interpreters in the East understood this as a reference to the wood both of Solomon's temple and of the cross. The story about Lot that follows explains the origins of the tree that produced this wood. By having Abraham tell Lot to retrieve fire-brands, the *Palaea* highlights the tree's miraculous origins from three dried-out pieces of wood. For origins of this legend and its relationship to similar stories told about other biblical figures, see the Introduction.

e. Presumably a symbol of the Trinity; see the Introduction.

f. The unexplained allusion to Lot's struggles may refer to his contest with Satan when he returned from the Jordan with water for the tree. Other versions of the story tell how Satan, disguised as an exhausted pilgrim, tried to thwart Lot's efforts by drinking the water that he

they were entwined with each other, he made obeisance to the Lord and said, "This tree will be the abolition of sin." [6]The tree was growing and had roots that divided into three from the top down, but the trunk of the tree was smooth and did not separate the one from the other. [7]The tree was standing up to the reign of Solomon. But we will explain about this tree at another time.[a] [8]So Abraham, fully assured about Lot's repentance and the change[b] caused by the conflagration, gave thanks to God.

56 [1]*Concerning Isaac and his circumcision*: At that time, Abraham's wife Sarah gave birth to a male child and named him Isaac. [2]Abraham circumcised him, and he and his entire household rejoiced [at the birth of Isaac]. [3]When Isaac was seven years of age, he was playing with Ishmael, his brother from Hagar, and Ishmael was thrashing Isaac. [4][When Sarah saw that Ishmael was beating Isaac], she was wounded in her soul and quarreled with Abraham, saying, "Drive away [my] maid-servant with her son."[c] [5]Although Abraham found this course of action grievous, (p. 220) Sarah kept pressuring him more, saying, "Drive the maid-servant away. For I cannot bear to see her and her son." [6]So Abraham inquired of the Lord, "Shall I banish the maid-servant?" [7]And the Lord answered him, "If this is what Sarah is telling you, do it. For I will never abandon your offspring. [8]But I will cause them to multiply like the stars of the sky and like the sand by the edge of the sea. Your offspring will inherit the cities of your enemies, and all
Gen 21:9-13; 22:17 the tribes of the earth will be blessed in your offspring."

57 [1]After coming from the offering, Abraham gave Hagar a skin of water and as much bread as he could, and led them out of his house. [2]With Ishmael at her side, Hagar made her way through the wilderness. [3]When the water was used up, the boy was thirsting, because there was no water in that place. And lo, Ishmael was on the verge of dying. [4]When his mother [Hagar] saw this, [and because she did not want to witness the death] of her son, she withdrew from the boy about the distance of a stone's throw. And she was bewailing his death. [5]Her son Ishmael was groaning from thirst and had only death before his eyes, rather than life. [6]As Hagar was wailing and lamenting over the bitter and violent death] of her son, an angel of the Lord appeared before her and said, "Get up, take your son and follow me. For I will show you [water] for you and [your] son to drink." [7]So she got up in haste and took her son, and the angel of the Lord showed her water for them to drink. [8]The angel of the Lord said to her, "Take your child,

---

was carrying from the Jordan; see J. E. Hanauer, *Folklore of the Holy Land* (London: Sheldon Press, 1907), 34-36.

a. The conclusion to the story is supplied in the parallel version found in one of the manuscripts of Michael Glycas' *Annales*, 254.38–255.33 (*lectiones variae*) (ed. I. Bekker; CSHB: Bonn, 1836). It describes how the hybrid tree was cut down for use in Solomon's temple. By divine providence, however, the hewn wood was not used and later became the wood of the cross.

b. Text: *alloiōseōs* ("change" or "conversion"). The meaning in this context is unclear. Cf. Vas.: *halōseōs* ("capture").

c. Gen 21:9 says only that Ishmael was "playing" with Isaac. Later Jewish sources understood this meant that Ishmael mocked or abused Isaac in some way, even shooting arrows in his direction; see *Gen. Rab.* 53.11.3. According to Jos., *Ant.* 1.215, Sarah urged Abraham to send Hagar away because she feared that Ishmael would harm Isaac. For Ishmael's persecution of Isaac, see also Gal 4:29. See further Ginzberg, *Legends*, 5.246 n. 211.

for he will become a great nation. For the Lord God will not ever abandon the
offspring of Abraham." Gen 21:14-19

58 [1]*Concerning the sacrifice of Abraham*: When Isaac was eighteen years of
age,[a] God tested Abraham and told him, "Abraham, [Abraham]." [2]And Abraham
said, "Here I am, Lord." [3]He said, "Take your beloved son Isaac whom you have
loved, (p. 221) and present him as a whole burnt-offering on one of the mountains
of which I will tell you." [4]Because he heard this from God, Abraham saddled his Gen 22:1-2
ass and put on it wood that he had split for the whole offering. [5]He took with
him two servants and his son Isaac. [6]With fire and a knife in hand, he got up
and journeyed forth; on the third day he came to the place about which God had
spoken to him. [7]Abraham lifted up his eyes and saw the place far off and told his
slaves, "Stay here with the ass. I and the boy will continue up to that place, and
after making obeisance to God, we will return to you." [8]So he took the wood for
the whole burnt-offering and laid it on his son Isaac. [9]He took hold of the fire and
the knife, and the two went on together. [10]*Isaac said to his father, "Here are the* Gen 22:2-5
fire and the wood. But where is the sheep for the whole burnt-offering, [Father]?"
[11]*Abraham said, "God will provide for you a sheep for a whole burnt offering, my
son."* [12]He arrived at the place called the "rock of the skull"[b] and made [there] an Gen 22:7-8
altar. [13]*Then Abraham bound together the feet of his son Isaac and laid him on the
altar over the wood.* [14]*Abraham reached out his hand to take the knife [and slay his
son].* [15]But an angel of the Lord called him and said to him, "Abraham, Abraham." Gen 22: 9-10
And he said, "Here I am." [16]*And the angel said to him, "Do not lay* the knife[c] *on the* Gen 22:11
*boy or do anything to him. [For] now I know that you do fear God and for my sake
would not spare your beloved son.* [17]*And I swore to myself,"* said the Lord, *"blessing* Gen 22:12
*I will bless you, and multiplying I will multiply your offspring like the stars of the sky
and the sand that is by the edge of the sea."* [18]*Abraham lifted up his eyes and looked* Gen 22:17
and behold, there was a ram caught by his horns in a sabek plant. [19]Now the sabek, Gen 22:13
which means "forgiveness,"[d] is the "*chrysolachanos*" in Greek.[e] [20]Abraham took the
(p. 222) ram and sacrificed it instead of his son Isaac; and [he] took his son, still
alive, and returned to his household. Gen 22:13

59 [1]When Isaac came of age, Abraham summoned one of his servants—
the eldest one who was named Andrew—[f], and said to him, "Place your hand

---

a. Genesis does not provide Isaac's age. Most later sources assume than he was a grown man; see Jos. *Ant.* 1.227 (twenty-five years old); *Jub.* 17:15 (twenty-three years); *Seder 'Olam* (thirty-seven years).

b. In reference to Golgotha.

c. Text: *tēn machairan*. Cf. Gen 22:12 (LXX): *tēn cheira* ("your hand").

d. Cf. Gen 22:13 (LXX), which refers to the "plant of sabek" (= Heb. "thicket"), in which the ram was caught by its horns. The interpretation of "sabek" as "forgiveness" (and thus a prefiguration of the cross) assumes a derivation of the word from the Aramaic/Syriac root ŠBQ ("loose" or "forgive"). For this interpretation of "sabek," see, for example, Melito, *Fragmenta* 12 (ed. O. Perler; SC 123; Cerf, 1966); ps.-Athanasius, *Quaestiones in scripturam sacram* (PG 28.740BC).

e. The chrysolachanos is a plant also known as the "atriplex rosea" or the "red orach." For the identification of the sabek plant as the chrysolachanos, see also ps.-Zonaras, *Lex. s.v.* "Sabek," ed. J. A. H. Tittmann (Leipzig: Crusius, 1808).

f. Gen 24:2 does not identify the servant by name. In Jewish sources, he is sometimes named Eliezer (cf. Gen 15:2); see Ginzberg, *Legends*, 5.259.

on your thigh." And he did so. [2]Abraham said to him, "I adjure you by oath
[to God] the creator of heaven and earth, that you will not give my son Isaac
a wife [from the Canaanites among whom I dwell, but that[a] you bring him a
Gen 24:2-4 wife from my land and my lineage]." [3]When Abraham's servant heard this, he
arose, saddled his camels, took servants with him, and went away to the land
of the Chaldeans, saying to himself, "Because I do not know who is of noble
lineage and who is of dual lineage, I will sit at the spring and find out everything from the maidens." [4]After he sat down near the well, he saw a number
of maidens coming and inquired of them, saying, "Who among you will give
me water to drink?" [5]Rebekah replied, "I will, Sir. Bring up your camels [too]
and we will give them water to drink." [6]After she gave them water, he said
to her, "Is there in your father's house a place for animals to rest?" [7]And she
said, "Sir, there is a place for them to rest, [and provisions], and fodder for
Gen 24:10-25 [your] camels."

60 [1]They followed her and went into her father's house and sat down. [2]They
brought out a table for them to have lunch. [3]Andrew said to the lord of the
house, "I am a servant of Abraham who comes from the land of the Chaldeans."
[4]And he said to him, "He is our kinsman." [5]And Andrew said, "I have come to
offer a pledge of money from my master in exchange for a wife for his son. [6]At
the well, I saw your daughter Rebekah, and I was very eager to offer a pledge
for her for my master. [7]If you are willing to give her to me, I will also eat your
bread; if not, I will not eat." [8]After conferring with his wife, they agreed to give
her to him. [9]So they ate and agreed on the terms of the payment of the pledge
(p. 223). [10]They drew up contracts and terms according to the rules[b] of the
Chaldeans, and received the young girl and her dowry along with her servants
and maidservants and everything that [her] parents had given her: beasts and
camels, mules and asses. [11]After taking all these things, they set out. [12]When
they drew near to their own land, Rebekah asked, "Where is the one to whom
I am betrothed?" [13]As they were getting near, they found Isaac playing in the
field, and he pointed him out to her. [14][Rebekah said, "Get me down from the
camel." And he took her down.] [15]She came into Isaac's presence and made
obeisance to him. [16]Taking her by the hand, he came to his father, and Abraham
Gen 24:32-67 blessed them.

61 [1]Some time later Abraham's wife [Sarah] died,[c] and Abraham said to
Chet,[d] "Give me a place to bury my dead." [2]Chet said to him, "Look, we are your
servants, and there is a burial plot in the country before you. Bury your dead
wherever you like." [3]Abraham did not want to, however, and said only, "Sell me
a [plot] to bury my dead, for I do not want a gift to bury my dead." [4]Chet said
to him, "You have the whole land at your disposal. Bury your dead wherever
you like." [5]Abraham said, "Sell me the cave located at the oak of Mamre, along
with the surrounding [land]." [6]And Ephron said to him, "That whole piece of

---

a. Lit.: "unless."

b. Vasiliev's printed text is not legible, but this meaning was probably intended.

c. Genesis 23 puts Sarah's death before the marriage of Rebekah and Isaac, described in the following chapter.

d. On the name Chet, see above note to 28.4.

land is worth four hundred didrachms."[a] [7]And Abraham took out four hundred
didrachms and handed them over, and purchased the double cave, together with
the surrounding area. And this is where they buried Sarah. Genesis 23

62 [1]Isaac fathered two sons, first Esau and then Jacob. [2]Esau received the
rights of the first-born, as, for example, what are called the "first-fruits." [3]One
day, when [Esau and Jacob] sat down for the midday meal, they gave (p. 224)
them a dish of lentils and a ration of bread. [4]While Esau immediately ate the ration of his bread along with the lentils, Jacob did [not] eat his. [5]Esau said to him,
"Give me the lentils and your bread." [6]And Jacob said to him, "Give me your
rights as the first-born, and you can have my meal." [7]Esau got up from his seat
and gave it to Jacob, and Jacob sat down on it. [8][So Esau ate Jacob's meal]. And
Jacob continued fasting until the next day. [9]Esau lost the rights of the first-born
because of his gluttony, handing them over to Jacob.[b] Gen 25:29-34

63 [1]*Concerning Jacob*: Jacob was a good man who was loved by [his] mother
and father. [2]He therefore earned their blessing, as it is written[c] in Genesis. [3]For
this reason, he was envied and persecuted by his brother. [4]On the advice of [his]
parents, he journeyed to the land of [the] Chaldeans, fleeing from the hands of
his brother Esau. [5]So when he was leaving the presence of his parents, he was in Gen 27:41–28:5
great affliction because of it and pondered how he came to be separated from
them. [6][When] he fell asleep, he saw a ladder stretched from the earth up to
heaven, and the angels of God were ascending and descending on it. [7]*The Lord* Gen 28:11-12
stood upon it and said to him, "I am the God of Abraham and the God of Isaac
your father. [8]*Do not be afraid. The land on which you lie I will give to you and to*
your offspring, and your offspring will be like the sand of the earth and will extend
to the sea and to the west and to the north and the east. [9]I will not forsake you, Gen 28:13-14
but I will return you to this land, and I will do for you everything that I said to
you." [10]*[Jacob] awoke from his sleep and said, "The Lord is in this place and I did* Gen 28:15
not know it." [11]*He was afraid and said, "How terrifying is this place.* [12]*This is none*
other than the house of God. And this is the gate of heaven." Gen 28:16-17

64 [1]Jacob got up and went away to [the] land of the Chaldeans (p. 225), and
dwelt with Laban and received his two daughters for wives. [2]This is how he received them: He loved Rachel, because she was beautiful in appearance. [3]Laban
agreed to give her to him. But because Leah was the first-born, he misled Jacob
at her wedding feast and brought Leah to him. [4]When Jacob realized what had
happened, he was aggrieved [and said to him, "Why did you do this?"] [5]Laban
said to him, "Be my servant for her, and you will receive her as well." [6]And he
served [him] for seven years: three [for] Leah and four [for] Rachel.[d] Gen 29:1-29

65 [1]Laban reached an agreement with Jacob: "Among the cattle that I own
in my house, the ones that are born white will be your wage." And the ones
that were born were all white. [2]And he said, "Whatever are born {…}." And so
they were. [3][Each year he spoke of his every need, and whatever he spoke of

---

a. Reading with O, omitting the preceding word "denarius."

b. For the idea that Esau's transgression was gluttony (cf. Heb 12:16), see Tertullian, *Jejun.* 17.2; Basil Caes., *De jejunio (homilia 1)* (*PG* 31.171A). See further, L. Ginzberg, *Legends*, 5.277 n. 45.

c. Lit.: "he writes."

d. Cf. Gen 29:24-29 (seven years for Leah, and seven years for Rachel).

Gen 30:32-43 came to pass.] [4]And Jacob became rich, while Laban was brought low. [5]And
the Lord said to Jacob, "Return to the land of your birth, and I will be with
you." [6]Jacob took with him his two wives and everything that he had acquired
in the house of Laban, and came to the land of his birth. [7]Jacob fathered
twelve sons: Reuben, Symeon, Levi, Judah, Issachar, Zebulun, Nephthali, Dan,
Gad, Asher, Joseph and Benjamin, (the last two) from Rachel. [8]As for the
remaining sons, Reuben, Symeon, Levi, Judah and Is(s)achar [were] from
Leah. And Zebulun, Nephthali and Dan [were from] Zilpah. Gad and Asher
were from Bilhah. [9]Zilpah was a maid-servant of Leah, whereas Bilhah was a
Gen 30:1-14 maidservant of Rachel.

66 [1]The ten brothers were jealous of Joseph and sold him to the Ishmaelites,
who led him away to Egypt. His value was a measure of gold worth 5,500 de-
Gen 37:11, 25-36 narii.[a] [2]They were afraid to bring this money home because of their father, lest
perchance it be discovered by him. [3]They went away and hid it underneath the
three-peaked tree[b] at its root, covering it up with a mound of soil (p. 226) [which
they brought with[c] camels; for there was no soil at that site, but it was rocky
instead]. [4]When a famine arose, they departed to Egypt to buy grain and found
Genesis 42 that Joseph was reigning in Egypt.

67 [1]*Concerning the reign of Joseph*: When they arrived, they had their father
Gen 46:1-27 with them and entered Egypt with seventy-five people.[d] [2]The money from the
sale of Joseph, however, was left behind under the three-peaked tree. [3]Now Joseph reigned in Egypt and took as a wife Asenath, the daughter of his master
Gen 41:45, 50-52 Potiphera,[e] and begot from her two sons, Ephraim and Manasseh. [4]When Jacob
had gotten old, he lost his eyesight; as he was nearing death, he said to his son
Joseph, "Bring me your sons, so that I might bless them." [5]Joseph presented his
sons before his father and placed the elder one to his right and the younger one
to his left. [6]But Jacob crossed his outstretched hands in the shape of a cross, and
placed his right hand on the younger son and his left on the first-born. [7]Joseph
said to him, "Father, put your hand where the elder son is standing." [8]Jacob answered, "I know (where he is standing), but the younger one receives the bless-
Genesis 48 ing." [9]Jacob did not change his hands, nor did he release the sign of the cross.
[10]Concerning this, the hymnographer[f] writes, "Wearied by age and worn out
by sickness, Jacob is restored in strength and crosses his hands, summoning the
power of the life-bringing cross." [11][And elsewhere:] "The godly Israel placed
his hands on the youths in the sign of the cross and showed that the people who
worship the law, under suspicion of deceiving the honor due to the elder, did not
alter the life-bringing symbol."[g] [12]So much for this subject.

68 [1]*Concerning the death of Joseph*: When Joseph had died, another king arose over Egypt, who did not know Joseph (p. 227), and they began to oppress

---

a. Cf. Gen. 37.28 (LXX): "twenty (pieces of) gold."

b. The significance of this episode, mentioned again below (67.2), is unclear.

c. Reading with Slav. rather than the corrupt *me* ("me") of the Greek text.

d. Gen 46:27 (LXX); cf. MT: "seventy."

e. Text: "Pentephri."

f. The source of the two quotations that follow is uncertain.

g. The meaning of the sentence is not altogether clear. On Jacob's blessing as a foreshadowing of the cross, see Tertullian, *On Baptism*, 8.5-10; Ephrem Syr., *Comm. on Gen.* 41.4.

the Hebrew nation. [2]Distress came upon them,[a] because they had grown extremely numerous. [3]And Pharaoh said to his servants, "Come, let us deal cleverly with the Hebrew nation and {...} to be slaughtered." [4]When the mother Exod 1:1-10
of Moses heard this, she became fearful that Moses, who was still an infant,
would perhaps be slaughtered by the Pharaoh's servants. [5]So she fashioned a
basket, smeared it with pitch on the inside and outside, and watched closely for
an opportune time when the Pharaoh's daughter was going to bathe in the river
during the hot time of the day. [6]She then tossed the basket into the river with
the baby inside. [7]When the Pharaoh's daughter saw the basket during the heat of
the day, she sent out Aura[b] and fetched it. [8]Upon opening [it], she beheld in the
basket a crying child, and Pharaoh's daughter felt compassion for[c] it and said,
"This child is from the Hebrews." [9]His sister said to Pharaoh's daughter, "Do you
want me to summon for you a wet-nurse from the Hebrews who will breast-
feed the child for you?" [10]Pharaoh's daughter said to her, "Go do it." [11]When the
young women arrived, Pharaoh's daughter called the child's mother and said to
her, "Look after this child for me, [and nurse him for me], and I will pay you a
salary." [12]The woman took the child and breast-fed him. [13]When the child had
matured, she brought him to Pharaoh's daughter. [14]And he became like a son to
her, and she named him Moses, saying, "From the water I fetched him." [15]And Exod 2:1-10
he was loved by the Pharaoh.

69 [1]One day Moses was brought before Pharaoh, and there were also with
him his grandees.[d] [2]Pharaoh took his diadem from his head and placed it on
Moses' head. But Moses took it and trampled on it.[e] [3]The Pharaoh's grandees became angry at this, and Pharaoh gave orders to toss Moses into the river. [4]But a
certain sage told the Pharaoh, "The infant is being killed unfairly." [5]And he said,
"Bring [me] gold and burning wax. If Moses reaches for the gold, he knows what
he did, but if he reaches for the flame, (p. 228) what he did he did innocently."
[6]When he did this, Moses grabbed the torch, and after sticking it in his mouth
burnt his tongue. This is how he was rescued from death.[f] [7]Once again the Pharaoh picked him up, and (Moses) grabbed at his beard. [8]Again Pharaoh became
angry with him. [9]Once again the sage said, "Don't be angry at him without rea-

---

a. Emending the corrupt "under him."

b. Cf. Exod 2:5(LXX): "And having seen the basket in the ooze, she sent her maid (*habran*), and she took it up." The author apparently misunderstood the Greek word for "maid" as a proper name.

c. Text: *emphusato* ("implanted"). Emended to *epheisato* (cf. Exod 2:6).

d. The story that follows combines two traditions, one first told in Josephus about Moses' trampling on Pharaoh's crown, the other about his playful attempts on his beard.

e. Cf. Jos., *Ant.* 2.234-36. Josephus's version refers only to Moses' trampling on Pharaoh's crown. When a scribe, who had interpreted this childish act as a bad omen, tried to kill him, Pharaoh's daughter Thermuthis stepped in to rescue him. The *Palaea*'s own narration of events combines this story with another tradition about a series of tests designed by a court sage to establish Moses' innocence. For discussion of the various later elaborations of this story, see Flusser, "Palaea," 63-67; Kugel, *Traditions*, 510-11; Ginzberg, *Legends*, 5:402 n. 65.

f. Other versions of this tradition (including the Slavonic *Palaea*) ascribe Moses' speech impediment to this event; see, for example, *Exod. Rab.* 1.26. The *Palaea* has not fully integrated this story into the episode recorded in Josephus about Moses' trampling on Pharaoh's crown. The sage establishes Moses' innocence by demonstrating that he was attracted to the crown because it was a shiny object. It would not explain, however, why he cast it to the ground.

son, my Lord King, for Moses does not know what he did." [10]Pharaoh asked him, "How might you demonstrate this to us?" [11]And he said, "Bring me, my King, a golden crown and an unsheathed sword. [12]If he grabs hold of the crown, let him be put to death. But if he seizes the [unsheathed] sword, you should not allow it." [13]When they did this, Moses grabbed hold of the sword, and [again] he was rescued from death, now for a second time.[a]

70 [1]When he reached manhood, Moses performed many acts of valor for the Pharaoh. [2]The Indian Ocean bordered Egypt, and the Egyptians endured many sea battles with the Indians. [3]When Pharaoh ordered him to go into battle against the Indians, Moses cleverly decided to fight them on land. [4]But because of the huge number of snakes on the land, they were completely incapable of crossing overland to India. [5]So Moses issued an order, and they brought him [a throng] of storks, around 3,000 in number. [6]After bringing [the men] to a halt, he instructed them to march as a unit. [7]And the storks walked about in front of the camp for a day's journey, devouring the snakes. [8]In this way, Moses passed across the Egyptian border.[b] [9]Now the Indians feared the Egyptians coming by sea; but since they had the snakes as a barrier, they were not afraid of the Egyptians coming over land. [10]So Moses attacked them unawares and after crossing over the border plundered all their cities. [11]He captured the entire country of the Indians, despoiled their cities and brought victory to the Egyptians, of a kind that the king of Egypt had never before had. (p. 229) [12]India, however, had never experienced so much plundering. [13]Moses returned with a great victory, bringing an enormous quantity of spoils to the king of the Egyptians. [14]And Moses was treated fondly by the Pharaoh and his grandees.

71 [1]One day Moses went out and found an Egyptian [beating a Hebrew],
Exod 2:11 and he struck him and concealed his body in the sand. [2]A [few] days later, he
went out and again found two Hebrews quarreling and said to the one doing
the wrong, "*Why are you beating your neighbor?*" [3]*And he said to him, "Who
made you ruler and judge over us? Do you want to kill me in the way you killed
the Egyptian yesterday?"* [4]*When the king heard about this matter, he sought to kill
Moses.* [5]*So Moses fled in fear from the face of Pharaoh and arrived in the land of*
Exod 2:13-15 *Midian.* [6]He came to Reuel the priest of Midian and dwelt with him. And Reuel
gave Moses his daughter Zipporah [as] a wife. [7]Moses fathered a son, giving him
Exod 2:15-22 the name Gershom and named the second son Eliezer. [8]*And Moses said, "The
Exod 18:4-5 God of my father is my helper, and he rescued me from the land of Pharaoh."* [9]And
Moses was in the land of Midian with Reuel.

---

a. By reaching for the unsheathed sword, Moses shows that he was attracted to shiny objects like the Pharaoh's crown. But this would not prove that he meant no harm in tugging on Pharaoh's beard. As with the previous episode, the author seems to have incompletely blended two different traditions: one about Moses' grabbing at Pharaoh's beard, the other about his reaching for his crown.

b. Cf. Jos., *Ant.* 2.243-47, which states that ibises (not storks) kept in wicker baskets enabled Moses to destroy the snakes blocking a land invasion against Ethiopia. The *Palaea*'s statement that Moses invaded India, not Ethiopia, may have arisen from the belief, common in Byzantine sources, that the Axumite kingdom of Ethiopia was "inner India"; see P. Mayerson, "A Confusion of Indias: Asian India and African India in the Byzantine Sources," *JAOS* 113 (1993): 169-74. For the identification of the birds as storks, see also *Divrei ha-Yamim shel Moshe Rabbeinu*, in *Bet ha-Midrash*, ed. A. Jellinek (2nd ed.; Jerusalem: Bamberger & Wahrmann, 1938), 2:6-7.

72 [1]*Concerning the bush that Moses beheld*: Moses went out to the mountain
of Horeb where he was tending sheep. [2]He saw that a bush was burning and
was not consumed by the flames. [3]*And Moses said, "I will pass by and look at* Exod 3:1-2
this great sight, because the bush is burning and is not consumed in the flames."
[4]*When the Lord saw that he was going forth to see, the Lord called him from the*
bush and said, "Moses, Moses, do not draw near to this place. Untie the sandal
from your feet, for the place where you stand is sacred." [5]Moses was afraid to look Exod 3:3-5
at the Lord. *And [the Lord] said to Moses, "I am the God of your fathers, the God*
of Abraham, the God of Isaac, and the God of Jacob; [do not be afraid]." [6]Moses Exod 3:6
replied to him, "Why are you sitting idle in this bush, while [your] people are a
slave in Egypt?" [7]*The Lord said, "I [have seen]* (p. 230) *the oppression of my people*
in Egypt, and I have heard their cry caused by the taskmasters, and I have come
down to deliver them.. And [now] I want you to go off to Egypt and lead out my Exod 3:7-8
people from Egypt."

73 [1]Moses replied [to the Lord] and said to him, "I am unable to go off to
Egypt, because I am weak." [2]And the Lord said to him, "Throw your staff on
the ground," and [when he did so], it became a serpent. [3]When Moses saw this,
he became fearful, and the Lord said to him, "Fear not, stand up [and] grab its
tail." [4]After he took hold of it, it became a staff again. [5]And he said to him, "With
this staff, you shall lead out my people in Egypt." [6]Moses said to him, "I am not
able, because I am slow of speech." [7]And the Lord said to him, "You have Aaron
your brother and Hur.[a] When they hear what you say, they will go in and report
it to the Pharaoh." [8]Moses said, "[And] if they should say to me, 'What is his
name?,' what shall I tell them?" [9]And he said to him, "I am who I am." [10]"And if
the people should say to me, 'Who sent you here?', how shall I answer?" [11]And
the Lord said to him, "Tell them, 'The God of our fathers sent me,' and you shall
perform signs with the staff, so that they will believe that I sent you." [12]And the
Lord said to him, "Put your hand into your bosom." And he did so. [13][And he
said to him, "Remove it."] [14]When he removed it, it was whitened. [15]And the
Lord said to him, "Put it back into your bosom." [16]After he put it into his bosom,
he removed it and it was in its natural state. [17]And the Lord said to him, "Be off,
fulfill the plan that I ordered you to do." Exod 4:1-17

74 [1]Moses departed and told his father-in-law, "Father, I have found the
God of my fathers, and he told me to depart for Egypt." [2]Reuel said to him,
"Whatever the God of your fathers has told you, do it." [3]Moses got up and
saddled his ass and took with him his wife and two sons and journeyed forth to
Egypt. (p. 231) [4]He came to his brothers the (sons) of Israel and said to them, "I Exod 4:18-20
have found the God of our fathers in the mountain of Horeb, and he appeared
to me in the bush." [5]When they were all gathered, he performed the signs of
his hand and the staff. [6]And [the] sons of Israel beheld the wonders of God and
worshipped the Lord. [7]After this, he came to the Pharaoh, and it was reported Exod 4:29-31
that Moses had arrived. [8]He told the Pharaoh, "Release the people of the Lord
so that they might sing the praises of their God on the [mountain] of Horeb."
[9]Pharaoh said, "[And] who is the God of the people?" [10]Moses said, "God is on
high, God is fearsome, God is eternal." [11]Pharaoh replied, "How will we know Exod 5:1-2

a. Exod 4:10-17 does not mention Hur, one of Moses' aides, in connection with this event.

that you are speaking truthfully?" [12]And when Moses cast down the staff, it be-
Exod 7:9-10 came a serpent. [13]When Pharaoh saw this, he became fearful and said to Moses,
"Let this be stopped until I can consider."[a] [14]Moses went away to his brothers
the sons of Israel and reported everything Pharaoh had said.

75 [1]When Pharaoh heard these things, he assembled his chieftains and told
them about what Moses had said and the wonder of the staff. [2]Now Jannes and
Jambres[b] answered and said to the Pharaoh, "What manner of God is more powerful [than] the gods of Egypt? If we should see Moses, he will tell us and we, for
our part, will show him the power of the gods of Egypt." [3]So when Moses came
to Pharaoh, his attendants Jannes and Jambres [also] came and disputed with
Moses. [4]Moses stretched out [his] hand and cast down his staff, and it became a
serpent. [5]When Jannes and Jambres saw this, they also stretched out staffs they
were holding themselves, and they too became serpents. [6]And the staff of Moses
turned and became a dragon and choked the staffs of the magicians. [7]Then Moses put his hand into his bosom, and it became like snow. [8]When they saw this,
the magicians were at a loss. [9]Moses said to the Pharaoh, "Send forth the people
of the Lord so that they might worship their God (p. 232) on the mountain of
Horeb, that is Sinai." [10]Although the Pharaoh wanted to do this, his attendants
Exod 7:1-13; 2 Tim 3:8 Jannes and Jambres, the chief magicians, would not allow him.[c]

76 [1]And Moses stretched out his hand and said: [*Concerning the ten plagues*:[d]
I]. Let there be darkness that can be felt over all of Egypt. And it was [so].
[2]While the Egyptians were without light, the Hebrews, wherever they happened
Exod 10:21-23; to be, did have light. [3]Pharaoh told his servants, "Tell Moses to restore light to
Ps 104(105):28 Egypt, and I will let the people go." [4]And when Moses spoke, there was light.[e]
[5]And again Pharaoh's attendants prevented him from letting the people of the
Lord go.

77 [1]Moses said, [II], "Let the waters of Egypt turn to blood." And it was so,
Exod 7:19-25; and there was no potable water. [2]Pharaoh said to Moses, "Return the water to
Ps 104(105):29 its natural state [and I will let the people go." [3]Through the hand of Moses, the
waters turned into their natural state.] [4]Pharaoh's servants said, "Let the men
go, but let them leave behind the women, along with their children, sojourners
and their cattle." [5]Moses said, "I will leave behind here neither an old man nor a
child, nor anyone infirm [or] maimed or disabled, because it is by the order of
my God." [6]And they did not listen to him.

---

a. The Exodus account of Moses' first meeting with the Pharaoh (Exod 5:1-2) does not include the miraculous transformation of the staff into a serpent.

b. Unnamed in the Exodus account, the magicians are commonly identified in later tradition as Jannes and Jambres. For discussion, see the Introduction.

c. Noticeably missing from the *Palaea's* account are any references to God's hardening Pharaoh's heart. Most of the blame is assigned to his servants, who prevent him from honoring Moses' requests.

d. The Greek text includes a number for each of the ten plagues, which are indicated in the translation with Roman numerals. The sequence and description of the plagues in the *Palaea* do not strictly follow the book of Exodus. In places, it adheres more closely to the sequence enumerated in Ps 104 (105):29-36. For a comparison of the *Palaea* with Exodus and other ancient sources, see A. Pietersma, *The Apocryphon of Jannes and Jambres the Magicians*, 160-62. See also H. Jacobson, "The Egyptian Plagues in the *Palaea Historica*," *Byzantion* 47 (1977): 347.

e. Cf. Exod 10:21-23; Ps 104(105):28 (darkness).

78 1Moses said [III], "Let their land bring forth frogs, and let them[a] consume
the Egyptians."[b] And this is what happened. 2And Pharaoh's servants became Exod 8:2-7;
hardened and did not allow [the Pharaoh] to let the people go. Ps 104(105):30
79 1Moses said, [IV], "Let a plague of dog-flies come, and let them consume
the Egyptians." 2And this is what happened, [and Pharaoh's servants] were hard- Exod 8:21-24;
ened, and thus did not yield and release the people of the Lord. Ps 104(105):31
80 1Moses was aggrieved because of their hard-heartedness, and stretched
out his hand and said, [V] "Let gnats come and afflict the Egyptians." And this
is what happened. 2But Pharaoh did not find it in his heart to let the people go. Exod 8:16-18
81 1Moses became angry and aggrieved and said, [VI] "Let hail come down,
and let it burn up their vines and their trees."[c] And this is what happened. 2And Exod 9:18-26;
Pharaoh said to his servants, "Let us release the people [p. 233], because Egypt is Ps 104(105):32
being scourged on account of them." 3Pharaoh's servants replied, "Let the gods of
the Egyptians withstand Moses." 4They ascribed the blame to the time of year,[d]
and convinced the Pharaoh not to let the people go.
82 1Moses said, [VII] "Let fire come down and burn up Egypt." 2When fire Exod 9:23
rained down, it burned up the Egyptians, and the Egyptians were being consumed in flames. 3Pharaoh said, "Summon Moses [to me]," and when he came
he said to him, "For how long will you cause trouble for Egypt?" 4Moses said,
"For how long will you provoke the anger of the God of Israel, by <not>[e] re-
leasing his people, so that they might worship their God in the mountain of
Horeb?" 5And Pharaoh said, "Take the people and go [and] serve [the Lord]
your God, but [leave behind] the animals together with the sojourners in the
land of Goshen."[f] 6And Moses said, "I will not leave here a hair of a goat or a
lame sheep, but I will put them on a wagon so that they might be blessed by their
God." 7And Pharaoh did not hearken to his request to let them go.
83 1Moses said, [VIII] "Let the locust come and devour their crop." 2The
locust did come and devoured the lands of the Egyptians. 3And again he would Exod 10:4-15;
not release the people. Ps 104(105):34
84 1Moses said, [IX] "Let the caterpillar come and devour what has been left
behind by the locust." 2But Pharaoh's servants, the superintendents of the works,
made life for the Jews difficult with the labors for which they had enslaved them.
3They came to Moses wailing and inveighing against him, "From the time when
you came, we have not received [respite] from the harsh labor; they have instead
withheld the straw from us, and we have been consumed by the severity of the
labor." 4And Moses became extremely distressed and asked the Lord God. 5The Exod 5:6-7
Lord God told him, "See, I will spend my arrows upon Egypt. But the Egyptians Deut 32:23

---

a. Lit.: "Let it consume."

b. Cf. Exod 8:2-7 (gnats); Ps 104 (105):30 (frogs).

c. According to Exod 9:18-26, the seventh plague consisted of hail, along with thunder and flaming fire. Cf. Ps 104 (105):32, which also states that the sixth plague was hail and "flaming fire" that burnt the vine and fig-trees. Although the *Palaea* separates hail and flaming fire into separate plagues, the influence of the Psalms is evident in the statement that the hail "burnt up" up the vines and leaves.

d. Reading with Vas. Text: "they bring the dead of a year." Cf. Slav.: "Let the gods of the Egyptians fight Moses and create visible miracles."

e. The missing word "not" is required by the sense.

f. Text: Gersem. Cf. Exod 9:26 (LXX): "Gesem" (= Goshen).

will not be taught their lesson in this way, and I will scourge them with another scourge because they have preferred [the] gods of the Egyptians over me. (p. 234). [6]I will for the last time destroy them, and in all the nations I will cause them to sing of their downfall; for they do not want me to be their God, [but preferred their own gods instead], and they do not know that I am the God who is chastising them and restoring them to health."

85 [1]*Concerning the Passover:* The Lord told Moses, "Speak to the whole
assembly of the sons of Israel. [2]Let each of them take a lamb with all his household, a male lamb for the household, a lamb without blemish, each year; and
let the whole assembly of the sons of Israel slaughter them, and in the evening
let them rub some of their blood, and let them place it [on] the two doorposts
and on the lintel. [3]And the whole assembly of the sons of Israel shall eat them
roasted in fire, and they shall eat unleavened bread with bitter herbs; they shall
eat them in this way: your loins girded, your sandals on your feet, [and your
staffs in your hands]; and you shall eat them in haste. They are the Passover of
the Lord. [4]And you shall rub some of its blood on the two doorposts and on the
lintel and in the houses in which you will eat them. [5][X] For behold, I am sending forth an angel to destroy every first-born in the land of Egypt, from humans
to beast, but he will not enter into the house wherever he finds the blood. [6]And
then I will show to the Egyptians who is the living God of Israel who performs
wonders. [7]And let ten people in number eat.[a] [8]And if the household is too small
Exod 12:1-20 for a lamb, then he shall take with him his neighbor." [9]When Moses heard this
from the Lord, he went out and spoke to all the assembly of the sons of Israel.
[10]And they performed the Passover, eating it towards evening. [11]By the command of the Lord God, an angel of the Lord arrived, and wherever he did not
find blood he went in and killed every firstborn in that house. [12]There was
great lamentation among the Egyptians. For there was not a house in which
there was not lamentation. [13]All of Egypt assembled and cried against Pharaoh
himself, (p. 235) "Release this people from here, because we are perishing on
Exod 12:21-30 account of them."

86 [1]As they were making ready to depart from the land of Egypt, the Lord
said to Moses, "Let no one from among you go out empty-handed. [2]Rather a
woman shall go to her neighbor and ask for her adornments and raiment, saying, 'Give this to me so that I might wear an adornment before my God, and I
will return it to you.' [3]And let the men do [likewise], and let them receive every
adornment of Egypt for themselves and all their wealth; do not go forth empty-
handed from them, but take with you every adornment of Egypt with you." [4]This
Exod 3:21-22 is what they did, taking with them all the adorned clothing of Egypt. [5]They took
the bones of their brother Joseph with them, because this is what he instructed
them at his death, saying, "God will surely visit you, and you will go forth from
Gen 50:24; Exod 13:19 the land of Egypt and you shall carry my bones from here." [6]This is what they
did, and the entire twelve tribes of Israel moved their quarters from there and
went out. [7]*The Lord told Moses, "Speak to the sons of Israel, let them turn back*

a. Emending the text, which reads "from the number." For the Jewish custom of serving the Paschal lamb to numbers not less than ten (lacking in the Exodus text), see Jos., *War* 6.423; *b. Pesah.* 64b; *Tg. Ps.-J.* (to Exod 12:4). See further Flusser, "Palaea," 68-69.

and encamp before the village, between Migdol and the sea. Let them turn around
and encamp." [8]When Pharaoh heard about this, he said, "[The] sons of Israel Exod 14:2
are wandering, for the wilderness has hemmed them in." [9]The Pharaoh yoked Exod 14:3
[his] chariots and his viziers over all the cavalry of Egypt, and with the chariots
and viziers over all of them, and six hundred chosen chariots [and viziers], he
chased[a] after them. Exod 14:7

87 [1]The sons of Israel were advancing with a strong hand and an uplifted
arm. [2]The Lord guided them for the entire night in a pillar of fire and the whole
day with a cloud and led them forward. [3]By day the pillar of the cloud did not
depart from all of Israel. [4]As they were journeying on, they found themselves Exod 13:21- 22
drawn up[b] next to the sea, and the people murmured against Moses, saying
(p. 236), *"Because there are no graves in Egypt, have you led us into this wilder-*
ness to kill us?" [5]Moses told them, "Take heart, stand firm [and] do not fear. Exod 14:11
You will see the salvation from the Lord which he will do for us this day." [6]*The* Exod 14:13
Lord said to Moses, "Why do you cry out to me? [7]*Speak to the sons of Israel, and*
let them move out. And you lift up your staff and stretch out your hand over the
sea and divide it. [8]*And let [the] sons of Israel go through the middle of the sea on*
dry land. [9]*Behold, I will harden the heart of Pharaoh* and his attendants[c] *and all*
the Egyptians, and he will go in after them. [10]*I will be glorified in Pharaoh and*[d] *in*
[his] chariots and horses." Exod 14:14-17

88 [1]*Moses stretched out his hand [over the sea and the Lord brought down*
upon the sea] a violent south wind for the whole night and dried up the sea. Exod 14:21
[2]*And [the] sons of Israel entered into the middle of the sea on dry land, and they*
had the water as a wall on the right and a wall on the left. [3]*The Egyptians pur-*
sued after them, along with the entire cavalry of Pharaoh and horsemen, into the
midst of the sea. [4]At the morning watch, the Lord looked upon the camp of the Exod 14:23
Egyptians and bound the axles of their chariots and impeded their advance. Exod 14:24-25
[5]*The Egyptians said, "Let us flee from the face of Israel because the Lord is fight-*
ing the Egyptians on their behalf." [6]The Lord told Moses, "Now make the sea Exod 14:25
return to the way it was before." [7]When Moses returned his hand and the staff Exod 14:26
to the original position, the water returned and submerged Pharaoh's chariots
and the riders in the middle of the sea and Pharaoh's entire cavalry. Not one of
them was left. [8]*But the sons of Israel advanced over dry land through the middle* Exod 14:27-28 | Exod 14:29
of the sea. [9][The] sons of Israel beheld the great and mighty hand that the Lord
displayed, who delivered Israel from the hand of the Egyptians, and saw [their]
enemies thrown up by the shore of the sea. [10]And Moses' sister Miriam took the Exod 14:30-31
timbrel in her hand, and she, her brother Moses, and [the] sons of Israel sang
[p. 237] this song to the Lord: *"Let us sing a song to the Lord, for he has been very*
greatly glorified, horse and rider. . . ."[e] Exod 15:1; Exod 15:21-22

---

a. Following O. Text: "they chased." The sentence is both ungrammatical and repetitious.

b. Text: *parabeblēkotas*. Cf. Exod 14:9: *parembeblēkotas* ("encamped").

c. The words "and his attendants" are missing in Exod 14:17 (LXX). Here as elsewhere the *Palaea* partly faults Pharaoh's advisors for his intransigence; see 75.10.

d. Cf. Exod 14:17: "I will be glorified in Pharaoh, and in all his army, and in his chariots and horses."

e. In the Exodus verse (15:1), the words "he has thrown into the sea" follow "horse and rider." Readers would have had little difficulty recognizing the source of this citation. It is the

89 [1]*Concerning Amalek:* After [the] sons of Israel made their way from the
Red Sea through the wilderness, they came to Mount Sinai. [2]When Amalek
heard that [the] sons of Israel had taken with them the wealth of the Egyptians,
he came to do battle with them with thousands and tens of thousands, saying,
"They are unarmed, and I will take them in the wilderness and reap the wealth
of the Egyptians which they seized for themselves." [3]Amalek came with his
thousands and tens of thousands and engaged the Hebrews in battle. [4]Moses
ascended the mountain and on the mountain stretched out his hands in prayer.
[5]When [Moses] raised his hands, Amalek was routed; but when Moses' hands
grew numb and they were lowered, the people of Israel were routed. [6]When
Moses again raised his hands, Amalek was routed. And the battle they had
joined continued to be extremely fierce. [7]When Aaron and Hur observed that
when [Moses] raised his hands Amalek was routed, one came from the right,
the other from the left, and held up Moses' hands. [8]In this way they put Amalek
to flight, and he was completely destroyed. [9]In them was fulfilled the verse: "In
Ps 9:17 [LXX] the works of his hands, the sinner was taken."[a] [10]For although Amalek wanted
to plunder Israel, he himself was plundered. [11]When Israel entered, they plundered the cities of Amalek and looted them and seized their property and cut
Exod 17:8-16 them to pieces.

90 [1]After this, [the] sons of Israel removed from the Red Sea and came to
the wilderness of Shur. [2]*They were journeying for three days in the wilderness,
not finding water fit for drinking;* for the water from Marah was bitter.[b] [3]*For this
reason, the name of that place was called "bitterness."* [4]*The people were murmuring against Moses, saying, "What are we to drink?"* [5]*Moses cried out to the Lord*
(p. 238)*; and the Lord showed him a tree. They threw it*[c] *into the water, and the water became sweet.* [6]*In that place, the Lord God established [for him] ordinances and
judgments, and there he tested them, saying, "If you will diligently hear the voice of
the Lord your God, and do that which is pleasing before him, and give heed to his
commandments and keep all his statutes, I will put none of the diseases upon you
which I put upon the Egyptians; for I am the Lord, your healer."* [7]*And they came to
Elim, and there were twelve springs of water there and seventy stems of palm trees.*
Exod 15:22-27 *And the whole assembly of the sons of Israel encamped there.*

91 [1]*Concerning the twelve springs*: The twelve springs of water prefigure the
twelve apostles. [2]Why, [then], were twelve springs of water discovered? So that
each tribe might procure for itself its own spring and not be in strife. [3]And why
were there seventy stems of palm-trees? The twelve apostles are palm trees, and
Luke 10:1, 17 the seventy disciples are their stems.[d]

---

first verse from the Song of the Sea (Exod 15:1-9), the first of the nine canticles of Byzantine hymnody.

a. For a text virtually identical to 89.2-9, see Michael Glycas, *Annales (lectiones variae)*, 295.18–296.1.

b. Cf. Exod 15:23: "And they came to Marah and were not able to drink from Marah; for it was bitter."

c. Cf. Exod 15:25: "he threw it."

d. On the twelve springs and seventy palm trees as prefiguring the twelve apostles and the seventy disciples (Luke 10:1, 17), see, for examples, George Cedrenus, *Compendium historiarum*, 137.8-15 (ed. I. Bekker; CSHB; Bonn, 1838): ps.-John Chrysost., *In illud: Memor fui dei* (PG

92 [1]After encamping there by the water, they departed from Elim, and [the] whole assembly of the sons of Israel came to the wilderness of Shur which is between Elim and Sinai. And they encamped under the mountain. [2]After Moses made an offering to God, the Lord said to him, *"Come up to me in the mountain, and I will give you stone tablets,*[a] *the law and precepts that I have written for them to have as laws."* [3]And Moses arose early in the morning and ascended to the mountain, and he was there for forty days and forty nights. [4]And he ordered the people, "See, I am going up to the mountain of the Lord and *look, Aaron and Hur* [my brothers are with you].[b] [5]*If there is any judgment to be made for anyone, have them go to them.* [6]And observe a fast for forty days, [until I come down from the mountain."[c] [7]But while there were some who would not observe the command and keep a fast] until Moses came back down, Aaron would not allow them, and told [them], "Keep the fast until Moses returns from the mountain." [8]But they would not have it, and Aaron (p. 239) was grieved about the people.

Exod 24:12

Exod 24:14

93 [1]The people kept pressuring Aaron, saying, "Give us a god so that we might worship him and break the fast. As for Moses, we do not know what has become of him." [2]Aaron became cross and told the people, "Bring me the jewelry of Egypt that you have taken out from there, and let us cast it into the fire. Whatever god is made to appear, this is the one we shall serve." [3]Aaron said this, because he wanted to restrain their eagerness, that they might feel sorrow about smelting the gold and silver, and keep the fast. [4]But some, because of their insatiable gluttony, brought out [their] silver [and gold], and Aaron lit a fire and threw them into it. [5]And the smelted stuff took the form of a calf. When all the people beheld it, they worshipped it.[d] [6]And on the mountain, Moses became aware of what had happened, the disobedience of the people, and he was grieved. [7]The Lord said to Moses, "Let me destroy them, *and I will make you into a great nation.*" [8]Moses, however, found this unbearable, and said to the Lord, "If you want to destroy them, destroy me along with them, lest the foreign nations boast, saying, 'Where is their God?'" And that is what he said.

Exod 32:23

Exod 32:1-6

Exod 32:10

Exod 32:7-14

94 [1]Moses went up on the mountain, and the law was given to him as a guide so that they might learn the precepts of the Lord and his ordinances. [2]The Lord told Moses, "These are the ordinances that I am giving to you. [3]You shall sanctify the seventh day and call it a sabbath, nor shall you initiate[e] any work with your hands. [4]But on this day, your ox, your yoke animal, your sojourner, and your slave shall rest and all those in your household shall rest. [5]And they will say,

---

61.693); Theodoret, *Interpretatio in Psalmos* (PG 80.1464AB); Tert., *Marc.* 4.13.4; Aug., *Faust.* 12.30.

a. The text is corrupt. Emended in accordance with Exod 24:12.

b. The parallel passage in Exodus does not include the description of Aaron and Hur as Moses' "brothers." Cf. Jos., *Ant.* 3.54, which states that Hur was the husband of Miriam. In rabbinic tradition, Hur was son of Miriam and thus Moses' nephew.

c. Exod 24:14 does not include Moses' directive to the Israelites to keep a fast for forty days.

d. The author assumes that when Moses fasted on Mount Sinai for forty days (Exod 34:28), he also directed the Israelites to do the same. But because some of them were unable to keep the fast, they implored Aaron to provide them with a "god," to whom they could make the necessary offerings before sitting down to the feast. For discussion, see the Introduction.

e. Text: *ou proesthai*. Cf. Exod 20:10: *ou poiēseis* ("nor shall you do").

'This is the day called holy to the Lord.' This will be an everlasting ordinance
for every sabbath, prescribed by law; and you shall do no work with your hands
on the day of the sabbath (p. 240), but you shall go forth to the sanctuary to the
priest in the tabernacle, whomever your brothers declare.[a] [6]You will be taught by
Exod 20:10-11 him and learn the law and the commandments."

95 *Concerning the (Mosaic) legislation:* [1]"*You shall not receive a vain report.*
[2]*You shall not agree with unjust men to become an unjust witness.* [3]*You shall*
Exod 23:1-2 *not be <with[b]> the multitude in evil.* [4]*You shall not spare a poor man in judg-*
Exod 23:3 *ment.* [5]*You shall not distort a judgment for the poor.* [6]*You shall abstain from*
every unjust judgment. [7]*You shall not slay the innocent and the unjust.*[c] [8]*You*
shall not justify the wicked for the sake of gifts, for gifts blind the eyes of the see-
Exod 23:6-8 *ing and corrupt righteous words.* [9]*You shall not act unjustly in judgment.* [10]*You*
shall not be partial to the poor person, nor shall you admire the mighty person.
Lev 19:15 [11]*You shall judge your neighbor in righteousness.* [12]*A slave shall not commit*
fornication[d] *in your people, and the land shall not be supported from the blood*
Lev 19:16 *of your neighbor.*"[e]

96 *Concerning the decalogue of the law:*[f]

[1]*I am the Lord your God who led you out from the land of Egypt, from the*
house of slavery. You shall have no other gods besides me.

[2]*You shall not fashion for yourself idols or any other likeness of anything in the*
heaven above and the earth below; you shall not bow down to them [nor shall you
Exod 20:2-5 *serve them].*

[3]*You shall not take the name of the Lord your God in vain, nor will the Lord*
Exod 20:7 *acquit him who holds his name in vain.*

[4]Remember the day of the sabbath to sanctify it. [After doing all your works
in six days], on the day of the Sabbath you shall do nothing, not you, not your
son, not your daughter, not your maid-servant, not your beast of burden, [not
your cow with suckling calf], not your ox, [not the sojourner dwelling in your
Exod 20:8-10 home,] and no one bought with silver; rather they will [all] rest in your home,
[and they will say, "This day is called holy to the Lord" and they will glorify the
Lev 23:3 Lord your God, all of them in your home]. You yourself will depart for the sanctuary and learn the law and the commandments, and you will be blessed by the
priest (p. 241) and [receive] release from (the) transgressions of the six days of
the week and you will be blessed.

[5]*Honor your father and mother so that it might be well with you* from them
and make entreaty to receive a prayer from your father and mother as an inheri-
Exod 20:12 tance *so that you may live a long life to old age.*

---

a. Vas's emendation would produce the following: "with whomever your brothers deal."

b. Emending me ("me") to meta ("with").

c. Cf. Exod 23:7: "just."

d. Text: *ou porneusei doulos*. Cf. Lev 19:16: *ou poreusē dolō* ("You shall not walk in deceit").

e. Cf. Lev 19:16: "You shall not rise up against the blood of your neighbor."

f. By compressing the prohibition against adultery, stealing, murder and false witness into a single commandment (96.6), the *Palaea* accommodates an additional three commandments at the end, which are drawn from other verses in the Pentateuch. The additional commandments deal largely with honoring elders and parents.

[6]You shall not commit adultery or murder, nor shall you make dishonest
prosecution against your neighbor; you shall not steal or make false witness. Exod 20:13-16

[7]You shall not covet your neighbor's wife or his son or daughter, or his field,
[his oxen], his yoke-animal, or any of his property or whatever belongs to your
neighbor. Exod 20:17

[8]*The Lord said to Moses, "Speak to the sons of Israel, and you will tell them,
'A man who curses his God will take a great transgression upon himself. He who
curses the name of [his] Lord*[a] *shall surely be put to death; the whole assembly of
the sons of Israel will stone him with stones.* If a sojourner or a poor man curses
the name of the Lord God, he will die.'"[b] Lev 24:15-16

[9]*You shall rise up before the hoary head, and honor the face of an old man, and
you shall fear the Lord your God. [For I am the Lord your God.]* Lev 19:32

[10]*Whenever a man strikes his mother or father, he shall surely be put to death;* Exod 21:15
for he is liable to death. *Fathers are not to be put to death for their sons, and sons
are not to be put to death for fathers. For each person dies for his own transgression. Whoever strikes his father or mother, let him be put to death;*[c] for he is a Deut 24:16
murderer." Exod 21:15

97 [1]God gave these and [many] other laws to Moses. [2]Moses was on the
mountain for forty days and forty nights. [3]But when the people assembled, [they
made an offering to the calf] which the gold had made in the furnace. [4]Aaron
told them, "Behold, sons of Israel, this is the God who delivered you from the
land of Egypt."[d] (p. 242) [5]And the sons of Israel made an offering to the calf in
the name of God, and they ate from the offerings for twenty days until the time
when Moses came down from the mountain. [6]When he came down, Aaron and
Hur and some of the elders of the sons of Israel met with him. [7]Asked by Moses [concerning the people] and how they were doing, they told him about the
situation. [8]Moses was filled with wrath, and shattered the tablets written by the
hand of God. [9]A wise man attests to my words, when he says, "In anger Moses Exod 32:4-19
shattered the divinely-wrought tablets written by the divine spirit."[e] [10]So when
these things happened, Moses was enraged at the people, and his face became
more luminous than the sun. [11]The sons of Israel were unable to cast their gaze
at Moses' face. [12]After Moses hung his veil inside and sat down, [the] sons of
Israel received his words through Aaron because they were unable to cast their
gaze upon the face of Moses. [13]Consider [then] those who are feasting and the
one is fasting, how the Jews were feasting, while Moses was fasting and his face
was illuminated. [14]For this reason, Moses asked for another set of legislation.
[15]After ascending into the mountain, he received another set of legislation similar to the first. Exod 34:1-4, 29-35

98 [1]After this, the Lord said to Moses, "Build for me a tabernacle according
to the pattern of heaven." [2]By the command of God, the clouds lifted, and the Exod 25:40
pattern of heaven appeared in pure form to Moses. [3]The Lord told him, "Make

---

a. Cf. Lev 24:16: "he who names the name of the Lord."

b. Cf. Lev 24:16: "Whether he be a stranger or a native, let him die for naming the name of the Lord."

c. Emending "to be put to death" in the text.

d. Cf. Exod 32:4: "these are your gods who have brought you up out of the land of Egypt."

e. Source unknown.

a tabernacle like this for me, and inside it present offering-services to me. [4]For
I do not want you to make sacrifices on hills and rocks and valleys, but rather
inside of the tabernacle, which is a representation of heaven. [5][You shall make
the tabernacle in this way: Make it of one storey according to the representation
of heaven], and you shall make it with three precincts separated by two curtains:
one outside of the tabernacle accessible to everyone (p. 243), one in the middle
of the tabernacle accessible to the pure, and one inside the tabernacle, accessible
Exod 26 only to the priests. [6]Let anyone who wants to enter into the tabernacle be washed
with pure water before the tabernacle, and let him in this way enter [into the
tabernacle]. [7]After this make [for me] a sacred robe and put it on Aaron [your
Exod 28:1-14 brother] and let him come into the sanctuary, into the interior of the tabernacle.
[8]He will make atonement for the tabernacle and the whole world [and the air
Exod 30:10 and the storms and kings and rulers and the people and the whole world.] [9]In
the tabernacle you will make for me two altars, one inside the holy of holies,
the other in the middle of the sanctuary. [10]And let the altar on the outside receive bread [and flesh] and wine. And let the altar on the inside receive incense
Exod 27:1; 30:1-10 only." [11]Moses did all the things that had been ordered him by God. [12]After this,
the Lord God said to Moses, "Give heed to me here, and observe what I am
commanding you. Tell Aaron your brother not to enter into the sanctuary at all
times, lest he die." [13]And the Lord God ordained ordinances for Moses and also
described the birth of all the things created by God and the release from transgressions and the atonements for men who transgress.

99 [1]*Concerning the dedication of the tabernacle*: It came to pass that when the
tabernacle of witness was being dedicated, the Lord descended in a cloud [and
Exod 40:17-36 the cloud covered] the tabernacle. [2]Now Moses happened to be inside the tabernacle by himself, [and the sons of Israel could not enter into the tabernacle.]
[3]The other tribes beheld the glory of Moses and Aaron; seized with jealousy,
they murmured against the two of them, saying, "Are we not also Jacob's offspring? Did [God] not also bring us across the Red Sea? Why has Moses not
given us too a share of the priesthood (p. 244), and not just his brother Aaron?"
[4]And they rose up against Moses, and Moses was grieved and asked the Lord
about this. [5]And the Lord said to him, "Go out and take twelve staffs, one staff
for each tribe [of the twelve tribes of Israel] and bring them into the tabernacle; and go out and distribute the staffs to them. I, for my part, will show them
my wonders." [6]Moses acted in accordance with the order of the Lord God, and
went out from the tabernacle and found all the people of Israel waiting for him
around the tabernacle. [7]He gave them the staffs, [one for each tribe,] and there
was no sign in them. [8]He next gave Aaron his own staff, and immediately [the
staff] blossomed and sprouted leaves and three nuts. [9]When the people saw the
Num 17:1-9 wonder, they glorified the God of Israel. [10]And the one who writes in the hymns
attests to my words, as follows,[a] "The staff is to be interpreted as a type of the
divine mystery, for with the sprouting shoot, it determines who should be the
priest,"[b] that is, the sprouting staff selected Aaron as priest.

100 [1]Aaron was serving as priest [in the tabernacle] in accordance with

a. Unknown source.

b. The meaning of the Greek phrase is unclear.

the command of [the] Lord. 2Again men arose from the tribe of Reuben of
the assembly of Dathan, and they rose up in revolt against Moses and Aaron,
saying, "Why don't we also offer incense to God, rather than Aaron alone? Did
God appear only to Aaron? [Haven't all of us also seen him on Mount Sinai?]
Aren't we also Jacob's offspring, and don't we also make up the twelve tribes?"[a]
3And they took the censers and spread incense and made smoke. 4Now the
Lord seethed with anger against them, and the earth opened, swallowed up
the assembly of Dathan, and even began to consume the assembly of Abiram.
5There was not a little lamentation and wailing over them, and the sons of Israel
began to wail over this calamity. 6When Moses heard this, he came running at
full speed and discovered that the slaughter had also enveloped the assembly
of Abiram [for by the command of God the censers that they were holding
and with which they were making smoke ignited and burnt them up.] (p. 245)
7Moses then stretched out his hands and made supplication to God, and the
flame stopped consuming them. 8[And the Lord said to Moses, "Let me keep
them in this wilderness, and I will make you king over a great people, because
this is a rebellious and twisted people." 9And Moses continued appealing to
God on their behalf.] 10The psalmist makes mention of this slaughter, when he Numbers 16
says, "*The earth opened and swallowed up Dathan, and covered the assembly of
Abiram; and fire broke out in their assembly, a flame burned them up.*" 11Like- Ps 105(106):17-18
wise, on the day of the sabbath, some came to cut wood, and a flame coming
from heaven burnt them up.[b] Num 15:32-36

101 1Although it is possible to say many other things about the giving of the
law and his[c] deeds, we are making the narrative of these things in cursory form,
describing only things befitting our purpose. 2He says {...}. 3And after this the
sister of Moses spoke out against his Ethiopian wife and immediately was made
leprous; and her brother Moses was grieved on account of his sister. 4After he
petitioned God, God healed her. Numbers 12

102 1*Concerning the ark that Moses made:* The Lord said to Moses, "Make an
ark from myrtle wood five and a half cubits in length and one and a half cubits
in width, and you will overlay it with pure gold on the inside and outside, and
inside of it you will place the rod of Aaron and your own rod. 2You will make a Exod 25:10-11
golden jar, and you will put manna in it, and it will be carefully guarded by their
offspring so that they might know of the wonders that I did with their fathers. Heb 9:4
3Place the tablets of the law inside of the ark, and you will record the oracles of
the law on untouched parchments.[d] 4You will read them on every sabbath for all Deut 31:26
the people to hear, so that the whole house of Israel might learn the commands
of the law. 5When you are about to move out from here,[e] you will make a small
wagon and put (p. 246) upon it the ark on a seat. 6You will yoke young bulls,
one-year old and innocent of the yoke, to pull the wagon of the ark. 7[Let no one

a. Cf. Num 16:1, which numbers Korah, a Levite, among the rebels. The *Palaea*'s version describes only the revolt of Dathan and Abiram, from the tribe of Reuben.

b. Cf. Num 15:36, which states that the Israelites stoned to death the man found gathering wood on the sabbath day.

c. Reading with V. Text: "their."

d. Emendation. The text is corrupt.

e. Text: *endothen* ("from within"). With Vas. emended to *enthen*.

touch] the bulls [or the wagon] except for the priests and Levites only. Let them
be the ones to serve the ark. [8]But if someone else dares to draw near either to
the wagon of the ark or to the holy ark, he will be condemned to death. [9][But let
Num 4:1-15; 7:1-9 only priests and Levites serve the holy ark and everything belonging to it.] [10]You
will also make a golden censer and have it to make incense for the holy ark [and
Exod 30:1-10; Heb 9:4 everything belonging to it].

103 [1]Moses prepared everything just as the Lord God had commanded him.
[2]The sons of Israel arose from Mount Sinai and continued on until they reached
the wilderness of Kadesh. [3]It was full of serpents, and the serpents were biting the sons of Israel, and they were dying. [4]Previously, they remembered the
meats of Egypt and the garlic and the onions;[a] but when the serpents began to
bite, it drew their attention to the misfortune caused by the biting serpents. And
they stopped fighting with Moses. [5]The serpents biting them were deadly, and
Num 21:4-6 lamentation fell upon the sons of Israel. [6]The psalmist explained this by saying,
Ps 28(29):8 "*And the Lord shakes the wilderness of Kadesh.*" [7]Moses besought the Lord God
[about this] and the Lord God said to him, "Make a bronze serpent and at day-
break set up a wooden pole of fifty cubits. [8][After you stretch the bronze serpent
crossways at the top], the serpents will stop biting. [9][When Moses did this, the
serpents did stop biting. [10]Moreover, whoever happened to be bit by the venom-
Num 21:7-9 ous serpents was delivered from death after casting their gaze on the pole]. [11]A
certain wise man recalls this story in his hymns, when he says, "As an antidote
for a lethal and venomous bite, Moses set up {on a pillar} a pole, which is a type
of the cross," and so on.[b] For the word "*enkarsion*" means "placed sideways." [12]In
2 Kgs 18:4; John 3:14 many places in divine scriptures, you will find out about this story.

104 [1]After they were delivered from this evil ordeal and (p. 247) drew near
to the land of the promise as far as the brow of the mountain, they did not want
to enter into it. [2]Instead, they said to Moses, "Send out quick-witted and able-
bodied men to reconnoiter the land that God promised [to give] to our fathers.
And if it is good, we shall dwell there, with the natives in fear of us."[c] [3]Moses told
them, "You choose for yourself those whom you want from the twelve tribes,
and I will send my own men [and let them reconnoiter the land.] [4]When everyone was assembled, they sent around fifty men, and Moses sent out [Joshua]
Num 13:1-6 son of Nun and Phinehas.[d] [5]They got as far as the brow of the mountain and
discovered fruits from trees, pomegranates and quince [and] clusters of grapes
of the kind that do not exist anywhere else; for they were unnaturally huge. [6]The
two men fetched a cluster of grapes, likewise pomegranates and quinces [of the
kind that are actually citrons]. [7]But when the fifty men came back, they found
Num 13:23-33 fault with the land. [8]And there was not a little lamentation in the camp, with
them saying, "We made a mistake by following Moses, and look, we will be at
risk in this strange place. [9]For we made a mistake [by saying] that we will follow

---

a. Slav. adds: "But they were eating moths (or worms) now."

b. Unknown source.

c. Cf. Num 13:2-3, which states that God himself ordered Moses to spy out the land of Canaan. According to the *Palaea* (105.3), Moses' decision to do this was in defiance of God's wishes.

d. Cf. Num 14:6, which numbers Joshua and Caleb (not Phinehas) among the spies that were sent out.

God, when there is no God. [10]It were better to dwell in Egypt and serve Egyp- Pss 13(14):1; 52(53):2
tians than to become a laughing-stock to the Canaanites." [11]When Moses heard
their weeping, he questioned [Joshua] the son of Nun [and Phinehas. [12]And they
praised the land] and its fruit. As for the Canaanites dwelling on that land, they
reckoned them "as ants before us." Num 14:1-10

105 [1]Moses inquired of God, and the Lord responded to him with these
words: "You did this and reconnoitered my land which I promised to give to the
offspring of Abraham for an eternal possession. [2]You along with them showed
yourself stiff-necked in reconnoitering my land. [3]Instead of heeding my voice,
you listened to those who were disobedient [to me. Because they disobeyed] me,
I will not lead them into[a] the land of the promise. (p. 248) [4]They will not go in,
nor will you yourself, or anyone from their generation, because they failed to
remember my wonders that I did with them in Egypt: [5]I scourged the Egyptians
because of them, I led them out with silver and gold, I delivered them from
slavery in Egypt, I divided [the] sea, I brought them across it, and I utterly destroyed their enemies. [6]But they were hard of heart and did not remember how
they routed Amalek by my strength. [7]Instead, they made a golden calf in Horeb
and did not keep my commandments, but rather chopped wood on a sabbath.
[8]I rained down fire [from heaven] to burn them up. [9]And they did not take care
to sanctify the sabbath day, but walked in their own will instead. [10]They preferred the meats of Egypt over [the fruit and] heavenly bread that [I] gave them.
[11][And], see, they provoked me, and you with them. [12]You will not enter into
my land, neither you nor them. [13]I will lead their offspring into my land instead,
and Joshua and Phinehas, because instead of finding fault with my land, they
praised it."[b] [14]And the Lord seethed with anger against them. [15]The psalmist Num 14:10-35
makes mention of this, speaking in the person of the Lord, "*They did not know
my ways, so I swore in my anger that they shall not enter into my rest.*" Ps 94(95):10-11

106 [1]In this way, [the] sons of Israel provoked God, and ignorance was
given to them. [2]They continued forward, tested [and encamped in the wilder-
ness] for forty years until that generation who had provoked him was blotted
out. [3]Concerning this, the psalmist says, "*[If] today you hearken to his voice,
do not harden your hearts, as at the Provocation,*" and the rest of the psalm:
"*[On the day of the testing, when your fathers tested me, and they put me to the
proof, though they had seen my works for forty years, I loathed that generation
and said, 'They err in their heart, and they did not know my ways* (p. 249), *so
I swore in my anger that they shall not enter my rest.*"] [4]As a result of this oath, Ps 94(95):7-11
then,—because they provoked God by reconnoitering the land—[the wicked]
suffered a wicked death, 600,000 men, excluding women and children. [5][The
psalmist makes mention of this: "*And he caused them to wander on a trackless
way and not on a road.*"] Ps 106(107):40

107 [1]After arising from there, they passed through [on a trackless way, and
not on a road], with young oxen innocent of the yoke pulling the holy ark
containing the tablets of the law inside, just as I said previously. [2]When they

a. Omitting "(they) are not to go."

b. Cf. Num 14:24, according to which God makes this promise to Caleb only.

reached a certain place, the young ox became agitated. [3]Zan[a] came and placed
his hand on the loop attached to the yoke. [4]His hand immediately withered,
2 Sam 6:3-7 [and he was tested because of his willfulness.][b] [5][For] no one dared to touch
the holy ark containing the sacred objects, except for the priests and Levites.
[6]There was no provision [in] the law for the unholy to make contact with the
ark, but only the priests and the Levites [would tend to the oxen and all the
things belonging to the ark.] [7]But Zan, while neither a priest nor a Levite, dared
to make contact with the sacred objects.[c] [8]For this reason, he was tested by the
wrath [of God], and all [the unconsecrated] were taught a lesson through him
[not to dare to touch the holy things.] [9]Therefore, the wise man writes as follows, "When the ark was being carried on the wagon, that one Zan, when the
ox balked, simply touched it and experienced [God's] wrath."[d] [10]That is, when
it sensed that the road[e] was ascending, the ox became agitated and hesitated.
[11]By placing his hand on the yoke-loop, Zan merely intended to support the
ox. [12][But God wished to punish the violation of the command of the law and
stayed] his hand. [13]In this way, others would learn not to deal impudently with
untouchable objects, but rather honor divine things and not behave disdain-
fully to them.

108 [1]*Concerning manna*: Because the sons of Israel were short of food as they
were making their way in the wilderness, Moses besought God (p. 250), and he
rained down upon them manna from heaven. [2]Each day they would collect it
[early in the morning, make it into bread], boil and eat it. [3][They did not have
manna as a source of sustenance when they happened to be in a wilderness location.] [4]If, however, they entered into a country of the gentiles, they had manna
Exod 16:1-4; Num 11:1-9 as a steady supply of food, lest they be defiled by the food of the gentiles. [5]They
were passing through from [country to] country, wiping out the countries of
the gentiles, destroying all their armies [and devouring their countries]. [6]When
Balak the king of the Moabites heard about this, he became afraid and trembled
in fear. [7]His heart sank and he was in great turmoil about this.

109 [1]*Concerning Moab*: Moab heard about the Jewish nation, that they had
a great God, that their God is able to divide the sea, stop the flow of water, dry
up rivers and marshes, move mountains, crush kings and rulers and shatter the
necks of sovereigns, and that he is a powerful God, a God of armies, and a God
who does wonders. [2]Balak the king of the Moabites was in grief and fear, his
commanders having melted away in large numbers. [3]So the king of the Moabites
Num 22:1-6 asked Balaam the seer to enter into an alliance with them.

110 [1] [This Balaam was descended from the line of Esau.[f] Esau fathered Re-

---

a. Uzzah according to 2 Sam 6:3; on the origin of the name Zan, see below note to 107.9. The *Palaea* transfers this episode from the reign of David to the time of the Israelites' wandering in the wilderness.

b. According to 2 Sam 6:7, Uzzah's transgression led to his death.

c. Lit.: "the uninitiated things."

d. Andrew of Crete, *Canon* (PG 97.1369B). The citation from Andrew of Crete explains the origin of the corrupted name "Zan." The Hebrew name Uzzah in Andrew's hymn is "Ozan." The text of the *Palaea* apparently understood the omicron as a definite article.

e. Emendation. The text is corrupt.

f. Flusser ("Palaea," 70) suggests that Balaam's descent from Esau originated in an identifi-

uel and Reuel Zerah and Zerah Job,[a] and Job Salmon, and Salmon Neri, and Neri Adem.[b] [2]Childless, Adem approached Baal their god with the appeal that if he would make him the father of a child, he would hand him over to minister to him. [3]The wife of this <A>dem did indeed conceive and bore a son. She named him Balaam, as if he had been begotten from Baal. [4]When he was four years of age, his father Adem offered him as a servant to Baal. [5]The young child Balaam was raised in the house of Baal and (p. 251) trained in magic and divination. [6]This was a pursuit practiced by the Persians for education in the science of magic and divination. [7]There was nothing to be studied here apart from the practice of astrology, and both the magical and divinatory branches of this art.[c] [8]Balaam advanced in every magical art based on astral motion and made a business of divination.] [9]This Balaam, then, was so efficient in the magical arts that whomever he blessed prospered and whomever he cursed was in peril.

111 [1]Realizing this, [Balak] the king of the Moabites, [after hearing that Balaam had an aptitude for magic and having a need of his services,] sent emissaries to him with gifts to induce him to come and curse the God of Israel. [2]When Balaam the seer saw the emissaries from [Balak] the king [of the Moabites] coming to him with gifts, he said, "Why have you, men from a foreign land and a people who speak a different language, come to me?" [3]They replied, "Balak, king of the Moabites, sent us to you." [4]And he said, "And what is the reason for your visit? Have his commanders and governors planned an uprising against him, or has he lost a part of his kingdom?" [5]They answered, "No, but we have learned that a powerful nation has come forth from Egypt with a mighty God, who is strong and unshakeable, and does deeds that are great and awesome, glorious and extraordinary beyond number. [6]He scourged Egypt with ten plagues, he divided a sea and led them across, he annihilated Amalek with his tens of thousands, [and he wiped out Philistia]. [7]Quite simply, [anything his people said] their God brought to pass. [8]And look, they have reached us [and want to plunder our city too]. [9]We have been sent from our king to petition [you] to come and help us. [For] you have received authority from the gods, and they are working with you in everything. [10][There is no one who stands against you, but (p. 252) he who is blessed by you will be blessed, and he who is cursed by you will be cursed. [11]For this reason, we appeal to you to come and help us, lest we be pillaged and perish."]

112 [1]As soon as Balaam the diviner heard this and set his eyes on the gifts, he said to them, "I will look into the decrees of my god Baal. If he tells me to go, I am going; if not, I am staying." [2]When he examined his oracular books, there was nothing said to him about his leaving. [3]And Balaam told the servants of the king of Moab, "I cannot go, because [neither] my horoscope nor my oracular

---

cation of Balaam the son of Beor (Num 22:5; 24:3, 15; 31:8; Deut 23:4; Jos 13:22; 24:9) with Bela the son of the Edomite Beor, a descendant of Esau (Gen 36:32; 1 Chr 1:43).

a. Cf. Gen 36:33, which names "Jobab" as the son of Zerah.

b. On Adem as a possible corruption of Edom, see Flusser, "Palaea," 71.

c. To establish the connection between Balaam's prophecy and the star of David (see below, 115), the *Palaea* makes Balaam an adept in the Persian science of astrology, of which magic and divination are branches. For Balaam's representation as an astrologer and magus in Jewish and Christian tradition, see below note to 115.4.

books permit me to.” 4And the men returned unsuccessful to Balak king of
Moab, reporting the words of the seer, “I cannot go,” and so forth. 5The king
of Moab was distressed. [The Israelites were nearing his country,] and there
was [great] distress [among the Moabites and inconsolably great tribulation.]
6King Balak again sent out other emissaries to appeal to Balaam to come and
curse the people of Israel. 7When Balaam once again examined his oracular
books, they did not encourage him to leave, and again his emissaries returned
Num 22:5-14 without success.[a]

113 1Now the people of the Lord had encamped near the country of the
Moabites, and [the Moabites], lacking the power to withstand them, trembled
before the face of Israel. 2Again the king of Moab dispatched [his grandees] to
Balaam the seer, this time with a letter [from him] and copious gifts, with a
promise as well of half of his kingdom. So Balaam, blinded by the gifts, left with
Num 22:15-20 them. 3When he came up to the mountain, he saw the camp of the sons of Israel. 4After he made an offering of bulls, calves and rams and performed all
his magical works, he stood upon the rock and opened his mouth to curse the
people of the Lord. 5But when he opened his mouth (p. 253), he said things he
did not mean to say. Instead of a curse, he blessed them [twice and three times,
Numbers 23 and it was not possible for him to say what he wanted to say]. 6In great distress,
the king's men again brought him bulls, rams and calves. 7Again he made an offering, and with greater determination began to speak so as to curse the people
of Israel. 8But when he reached their camp, he said, “*How fair are your houses,
O Jacob, [(and) your tents, O Israel, like shady valleys, like gardens beside rivers,*
Num 24:5-7 *like tents that the Lord has pitched, like cedar trees beside waters.* 9*A star shall rise
from Jacob,] and a man shall rise up from Israel, and he shall shatter the chiefs of
Moab and plunder the sons of Seth.* 10*Edom shall be (his) inheritance (and) Esau*
Num 24:17-18 *his enemy, and Israel performed an act of power.*”

114 1As Balaam the diviner was saying these things, the king's men began to
make a great lament, telling him, “What have you done to us? We brought you
here to curse them and bless us, and you did the opposite. Them you blessed,
and us you cursed.” 2Now Balaam said, “What are the words that I spoke?” 3And
they pointed out to him the words that they had recorded. 4When he saw them,
he became angry with himself and mounted his ass and returned [home] to
consult his magic books so that he might perform other acts of magic against
the Jews. 5After he left and entered through the walls of a vineyard, behold an
angel of the Lord stood in the middle of the road. The ass saw the angel, but
Balaam did not see him. 6When the ass saw the angel, it became fearful and did
not continue forward. 7So Balaam struck the ass to make it go on, but the ass,
constrained by the angel, crashed against the wall and crushed Balaam's foot.
8So Balaam began to beat the ass violently, and by the will of God, the ass began
to speak in a human voice (p. 254), saying, “Sir, why are you thrashing [me]?”
9Balaam said to him, “Why did you crush my foot?” 10The ass replied and said
to him, “Don't you see the angel of God standing there and not allowing me to
continue on?” 11At that point, the eyes of Balaam were opened, and he saw the

a. Cf. Num 22:9-20, which states that Balaam sought guidance from God, who initially refused to let him go, but then agreed on condition that Balaam does what he commands.

angel of God. [12]Falling to the ground, he made obeisance to him and said, "Who
are you, Sir?" [13]And the angel of the Lord God said to him, "I am an angel of the
[Lord] God, and I have come to accuse you: how did you dare to seek divina-
tions against the people of the Lord and curse them? Now cease this effort lest
you die." [14]And Balaam said to the angel, "I did this out of ignorance. Please
forgive me, Sir." [15]And the angel departed from him, and Balaam went on his
way.[a] [16]Hence, the wise man says, "The fearsome angel appeared to an ass and Num 22:21-35
accused Balaam the diviner on his return of disobeying the ineffable and divine
decrees of God made long ago. In displaying an animal with the ability to speak,
a wondrous act, he altered [a characteristic feature of its nature]." [b]

115 [1]Concerning his statement, "*A star shall rise from Jacob [and a man shall
rise up from Israel] and he shall shatter the chiefs of Moab*": [2][The Persians and Num 24:17
their astronomers] recorded this statement, [supposing that the diviner spoke
more truthfully than anyone else. [3]As they were expecting the star to shine
forth,] at each and every season they would look for it. [4]When Christ was born,
Balaam was proved truthful.[c] [5]The wise man alludes to this in his hymns, when
he states, "Filling with joy the wise astronomers, initiates into the secret teaching
of Balaam the diviner of old, a star arose from Jacob, Lord."[d] [6]That is to say: "See
how the words of the diviner (p. 255) have been fulfilled, when the star arose and
the Messiah appeared." [7]So much for this subject.

116 [1]After failing with magic, Balak, [the] king of the Moabites, was inspired
with a plan from the devil: [2]"Because the Jewish people [have] a mighty God, a
fearsome God, and a God who hates injustice, I will cause them to be defiled.
[3]And if they are defiled, they will be despised by their God, and then I will attack
them and wage war against them." [4]Balak pitched tents before them on the road
by which the warriors of the Jews were planning to pass through. [5]In the tents he
put comely and unchaste[e] women, and set up next to them tables with meats and
wine and an idol of Baal in front of the tents.[f] [6]They went into them and ate from
their offerings and drank wine and worshipped Baal, that is Cronus. [7]This is the
translation of Baal, who is called Cronus by the Greeks. [8]They had relations with
the women, and the Lord was enraged against them and turned his face from
them. [9]The Moabites attacked them and found them drunk in the tents and cut
them to pieces. [10]This [is what] the psalmist says, "*Then they joined to the Baal of* Num 25:1-3; Rev 2:14
Peor, and ate sacrifices of the dead." That is to say, (they ate) sacrificial meat of the Ps 105(106):28
idol Baal in the place of Peor. [11]And (the psalmist states) [that "they ate sacrifices

---

a. Cf. Num 22:21, according to which the incident with the encounter with the angel occurred before Balaam reached Balak. The quotation from "the wise man" that follows explains why the *Palaea* places the event after his departure.

b. Unknown source.

c. For the connection of Balaam's prophecy with Matthew's narrative (2:1-2) about the magi and the star of David, see, for example, Iren., *Haer.* 3.9.2; Origen, *Cels.* 1.59.14-22; Ambrose, *Expositio Evangelii Lucae* 2.48, ed. C. Schenkl (CSEL 32/4; Vienna, 1902). For discussion of the sources, see J. R. Baskin, *Pharaoh's Counsellors: Job, Jethro, and Balaam in Rabbinic and Patristic Tradition* (BJS 47; Chico, Calif.: Scholars Press, 1983), 101-113.

d. Unknown source.

e. Literally "free." Cf. Slav.: "And in the tents he put very beautiful prostitutes."

f. For the idea that Balak tempted the Israelites with an idolatrous banquet and fornication, see Rev 2:14.

of the dead,"] for those associated with Cronus are dead.[a] [12]These words also
Num 25:8-9 allude to the plague that befell the Jews.

117 [1]Moses dispatched Phinehas to see what had happened. [2]When Phinehas
arrived, he found a Jew having sex with a Moabite woman. [3]After doing away
with them by piercing both of them with a spear (that is a "*kontarion*"[b]), he
prayed [to God] that it not be counted for him as a transgression. [4]After his
Num 25:5-9 prayer, the destruction subsided. [5][This is also what the psalmist says: "*Then
Phinehas stood up and made atonement and the plague subsided.] And it has been
Ps 105(106):30-31 reckoned to him as righteousness from generation to generation for ever.*" [6]After
(p. 256) Phinehas exacted retribution, they were empowered by the Most High.
[7]They plundered [the] Moabite people, cut their armies to pieces, [despoiled
and] burned their cities, and gained dominion over all the Moabites and the
country of Edom. [8]At that time what was said by Moses was fulfilled: "*Then the
commanders of Edom and the leaders of the Moabites hastened, trembling seized
Exod 15:15 them, [and all the inhabitants melted away]*."

118 [1]After annihilating the country of the Moabites, they then arose from there and continued on to another place. [2]As they were continuing on, they came into a wilderness place, both trackless and waterless. [3]They did not discover potable water, and began to cry out against Moses. [4]Moses was heavy of heart when he saw them crying out, and when he took hold of the staff with his hand, he struck the rock with wrath, saying, "How am I to give you water from this rock?" [5]Rather than say, "God is blessed," he struck a staff on the rock with bitterness. [6]Immediately the rock was split, and water instantaneously gushed out in copious quantity—which Moses beheld with astonishment. [7]Now although Moses struck the rock in bitterness, because the staff had its power by divine command, it accomplished the miracle. [8]It was an extraordinary wonder to behold. As the rock was being carried on the wagon, water gushed out, providing [potable] water for [all] the people [and their animals]. [9]And the drinking of [that] water succeeded in slaking thirst and was more nourishing than any food. [10]The water was extremely sweet, sweeter than honey and any
Num 20:2-11 kind of water on earth.

119 [1][The] sons of Israel continued making their way from there for many days, plundering the towns of the gentiles as they were passing through. [2]For forty years, they kept moving [from country to] country [and to wilderness places] until all those who had spoken out in opposition to the land of the promise were gone. [3]And this was more remarkable, seeing that for forty years (p. 257) they did not want for clothing or sandals or shelter, but whatever they sewed together for themselves in the exodus from Egypt was intact. [4]The rock itself
was a figure of Christ, just as the divine apostle states, "*For they drank from the
1 Cor 10:4 supernatural rock that followed them, and the rock was Christ.*" [5]That the water
was nourishing, hear what a certain wise man writes: "{…} bitter drink, those who suckled the honey from a rock for the one who worked wonders in the

---

a. For the association of the "sacrifices of the dead" with the cult of Cronus, see also ps.-Athanasius, *Expositiones in Psalmos* (PG 27.448C).

b. The *kontarion* is a lance of around 12 feet in length used by the Byzantine army.

wilderness."[a] 6Do you see that because it was nourishing, he called it honey? 7But
the psalmist also speaks about it in this way, *"And he fed them with honey from a
rock."* 8And [in the song] of Deuteronomy, he says the following, "*Oil out of hard* Ps 80(81):16
rock." 9[And see how everyone attests that the water had acquired the capability Deut. 32:13
to be used as any kind of food.]

120 1After [that] whole generation of the disobedient had died and their
offspring had risen up and reached adulthood, Moses was the sole survivor from
that generation. 2And God told him, "Teach the sons of the disobedient [of Is-
rael] my commandments, [and make them remember my wonders] and write
for them the following song: "*Give ear, O heaven, and I will speak; and let the* Deut 31:19
earth hear the words from my mouth." 3[This is also where this second song was Deut 32:1
arranged.[b] "And let them be taught and know this song. 4If someone does not
know this song from memory and does not have it on the tip of his tongue, let
him be cut off from the people. 5But let the sons of Israel record this song, and let
them recite and master it, so that through this song are taught the wonders that
I have done with them, and how much their fathers provoked me.] 6Because of
the oaths that I established with Abraham, I did not deny them my benefactions.
7Teach them all the things I desire, which I enjoined upon you on the mountain."
8And Moses spoke to the people all these words.

121 1*Concerning the death of Moses*: Moses said to Joshua son of Nun, "Let
us go up on the mountain." 2After they ascended, Moses saw the land of the
promise and told him (p. 258), "Go down to the people and report to them that
Moses has died." 3Joshua went down to the people, and Moses reached the end
of his life. 4Sammael attempted to bring down his body to the people so that they
might deify him. 5But Michael, the captain of the Lord's host, on the command
of God came to get the body and remove it. 6Sammael opposed him, and they
fought. 7So the captain of the host became incensed and rebuked him, saying,
"The Lord rebukes you, Devil." 8In this way, the adversary was defeated and took
flight. 9The archangel Michael removed the body of Moses to a place ordered by
Christ our God, [and no one saw Moses' tomb].[c] Deut 34:1-9; Jude 9

122 1*Concerning Joshua son of Nun*: Joshua the son of Nun took the people
of the Lord with him and came to the Jordan, intent on entering into the land of
the promise. 2There was a city near the Jordan on the west, with its tower-wall
constructed entirely from what is called the magnet stone. 3When Joshua heard
about this, he sent out spies to look over the city and reconnoiter. 4After the spies
entered the city, they were recognized by the citizens of Jericho and fled away.
5They came to an inn and found Rahab the harlot and began to entreat her to
hide them. 6She asked them, "Who are you?" And they said, "[We are] Jews."
7And Rahab said, "[I] have heard that you have a great God and that you are in
fact servants of a great God. So now go your way without fear, for I will drive
off the Jerichoites." 8Rahab let them out through the wall and showed them the
way. 9When the Jerichoites arrived, she showed them another way, saying, "They

a. Cf. Slav.: "A bitter drink was brought you by those who suckled the honey from the rock." The source of the quotation is unknown.

b. In the Byzantine canon of nine odes or canticles, Deut 32:1-43 constitutes the second song of Moses (after Exod 15:1-19).

c. For discussion of the source of this legend, see the Introduction.

left this way." This is how the spies made it out safely. [10]When the spies had left,
they told everything to Joshua son of Nun, [how they were recognized by the
Josh 2 citizenry and how (p. 259) they were delivered by the harlot Rahab.]

123 [1]After they were near the Jordan, the Lord told Joshua son of Nun, "*On
this day, I am coming*[a] *to exalt you before all the sons of Israel so that they might
know that just as I was with Moses, so will I also be with you.* [2]*Now direct the
priests bearing the ark of the covenant* of the Lord to go forth and stand in the
Josh 3:7-8 Jordan." [3]For the Jordan River is not passable by people on foot; one must swim
across instead. [4]And the priests came and stood in the middle of the water of the
Jordan. [5]*Now the Jordan River overflows all its banks around the day of the wheat
Josh 3:15 harvest.* [6]This river itself originates half from the sea of Tiberias and half from
the lake of Gennesaret; the [one part] is called "Jor," and the other "Dan." [7]When
the two tributaries flow together downstream, it is called the Jordan.[b] [8]So when
the priests of God carrying the ark went in, *the water receded and the waters
flowing down from above stopped, into one solid heap very far off*, from the city
of Dan[c] *up to the region of Kiriathjearim.* [9]*The lower part flowed down to the sea
Josh 3:16 of Araba, the sea of salt, until it finally failed.* [10]All the people passed through the
Jordan on dry land and in this way launched the battle of Jericho.

124 [1]*Concerning the manifestation of the captain of the Lord's host:* The
people of Jericho began to engage in combat, and it was an unrelenting battle.
[2]The combatants were locked in battle and when they were [un]able to crush
the Jerichoites, Joshua became distraught. [3]One day, while they were joined in
combat and Joshua was encouraging and supporting the people, the captain
of the Lord's host appeared to him [standing on the right of the battle with a
drawn sword in his hand. [4]When Joshua saw him, he came to him and said,
Josh 5:13 "*Who are you?*] *Are you one of ours* (p. 260) *or one of our enemies?*" [5]And the
captain of the host [told him, "*I am the captain of the host*] *of the Lord, and
Josh 5:14 now I am* here to help you." [6]Joshua fell down in obeisance, and said to him,
"*Sir, what do you command to your servant?*" [7]*The captain of the host said to
Josh 5:15 him,* "*Loosen the sandal from your feet.* For the Lord God will deliver [to you]
the Jerichoites into your hand. [8]But you will not take from them [any spoils,[d]
but guard against them] lest you ever worship their gods and be in conflict
Josh 6:18 with the law of the Lord; for the law of God is the means of salvation." [9]And
the captain of the host said, "Let the priests take seven trumpets, and let them
encircle the walls of Jericho for seven days, (and) let them sound the trumpets
around Jericho, and the walls will fall." Then the captain of the host departed.
[10]After the priests did this, the walls of Jericho collapsed on the seventh day,
Josh 6:1-16 the entire city collapsing with it. [11]When this happened, Joshua told the people, "Do not take anything from this city, [even a single obol],[e] nor let anyone

---

a. Text: *erxomai*. Cf. Jos 3:7: *arxomai* ("I am beginning").

b. For witnesses to this popularly known theory about the sources of the Jordan, see the Introduction.

c. Text: Damēn. Read: Danēs, presumably in reference to the northern frontier village of Dan, located at the source of the Dan River.

d. Emendation. The text is corrupt.

e. Cf. Josh 6:19, where Joshua makes an exception for silver and gold, and vessels of bronze and iron.

remain from them except for Rahab the harlot, she who delivered the spies
from danger." [12]Now a man by the name of Achan,[a] a Judahite by lineage, was Josh 6:17-19
discovered to have stolen armlets and wedges, many in number. [5]In this way Josh 7:1
they captured the city of Jericho.

125 [1]*Concerning Jericho and Ai:*[b] After they captured the [city of] Jericho,
they ascended the mountain [to] a small stronghold called Ai. [2]The people of
Ai ambushed them and slew their armed [fighters], thirty in number. [3]Joshua
was distraught, and his face fell, and [the] angel of the Lord said to him, "Look,
inquire of the people [of the Lord], because they have transgressed your order
[through Achan]. For this reason, the people of Ai have outmanned them." [4]Af-
ter conducting an investigation, Joshua discovered that Achan had stolen [their
(p. 261) goods[c] and done additional things]. [5]And Joshua ordered that [Achan
be stoned to death.] The whole house of Israel stoned him, <destroyed[d]> his
flocks [and destroyed his entire line]. [6]After exacting this retribution, they then Josh 7:2-26
went up and seized the [land of] Ai and wiped it out. [7]They saved nothing from
Ai except for animals, and from Jericho Rahab the harlot. [8]The psalmist recalls Josh 8:3-29
this, saying, *"I will remember Rahab and Babylon to them that know me* [that is, Ps 86(87):4
those who have feared me"]. [9]The Canaanites heard of the approach of the Jews
and they melted away. [10]At that time the saying was fulfilled, "*All those dwelling
in Canaan melted away*." For the Canaanites were dwelling in this land. Exod 15:15

126 [1]Now the Gibeonites heard that a mighty people of God were coming against them and said, "Their God divided the sea and led them across;
he routed and annihilated Amalek, overpowered the Assyrians, wiped out the
Moabites, mastered Edom, overpowered the country of Midian, did away with
Uz,[e] reduced the Ammonites[f] to nothing, eradicated the country of the Salt
(Sea), split the Jordan in half, and led them across over dry land. [2]There is simply
nothing that can stand up to them, no river, no sea, no military encampments,
not the walls of Jericho; they have instead collapsed by the power of their God."
[3]After taking account of all of this, the Gibeonites devised the following scheme:
They outfitted themselves with filthy garments and wrinkled tunics, old wine-
skins, rotten wine, dried-out bread and old sandals. [4]After this makeover, they
came into the camp, went to the leaders and Joshua son of Nun, fell down before
him and said to him, "Sirs, we have come to make obeisance to you, so that you
will at some time not wipe us out." [5]And the leaders said to them, "Where have
you come from?" [6]And they said, "We have come from a far-away country, to
see you and sue for peace with you. [7]Do you see the old tunics that we are wearing? They were unused when we put them on, and the bread we took was newly
boiled; we have come seeking peace." [8]They thus duped the leaders, and Joshua
son of Nun, who made peace with them just as they asked (p. 262). [9]They were
deceived, because even though they lived nearby, they said that they came from
afar. [10]And the Gibeonites left for home, without a care. Josh 9:3-15

a. Text: Achar (= 1 Chr 2:7 [LXX]).

b. Text: Gai (= LXX).

c. Lit.: "words."

d. Text: *katekapsan* ("gulped down"). Emended to *kateskapsan* ("destroyed").

e. Text: Ausis (= LXX).

f. Text: Amanites.

127 [1]Now the Jews went out to plunder the surrounding cities, and came to Gibeon. [2]The Gibeonites, the ones who had come seeking peace, came out to meet them. [3]The Jews recognized them and said to them, "Is this your city?" And they said, "Yes it is." [4]And they said to them, "Why did you mislead us, saying, 'We have come to you from a distant country'?" [5]All the people rose up against Joshua and the leaders, saying, "Instead of asking God, why did you take an ill-advised and inappropriate course of action?" [6]So then the Gibeonites came out to meet Joshua and fell at his feet. [7]Joshua said to them, "You misled us by saying, 'We have come from a distant country,' when you were actually near to us. [8]So in accordance with our oath, I will now not do you any harm, but you will be wood and water carriers in the camp of the sons of Israel." [9]By doing this, he
Josh 9:16-27 reduced them to servitude. [10]Concerning this, a wise man writes, "Rise up and like Joshua son of Nun, battle against the sensations of the flesh, ever conquering the Gibeonites, deceptive notions,"[a] that is, the evil notions that are forever deceiving us. [11]Just as the Gibeonites deceived Joshua son of Nun and the leaders of the Jews, in the same way does evil argument (deceive) us because we do evil as if we are doing good, and we do not realize it. [12]For this reason, the wise man (prays) to conquer deceptive arguments.]

128 [1]*Concerning Endor:*[b] Joshua son of Nun held power for twenty-one years, and after him the elders ruled.[c] [2]When the kings of the Persians came and did battle against them, they gained dominion over them, and the Jews became subjects of the Chaldeans. [3]A man arose among the Jews named (Endor). He became indignant that his fathers were enslaved to the Chaldeans and began to work to free the country, saying to the Jews, "What will you do for me, if I free the country from the land[d] of the Chaldeans?" [4]The Jews then told him, (p. 263) "We shall make you our leader." [5]And he said to them, "Give me gifts so that I might leave with them for Got,[e] the king of the Persians." [6]For this Got was at that time king of the Persians, Chaldeans, Medes and Gazarenes, and as ruler also had control of the Jewish nation.

129 [1]So Endor took [the gifts] and departed for Got king of the Persians. After making obeisance, he gave him the gifts, saying, "These were sent to you, my Lord, by your servants the Jews." [2]Blinded by the gifts, Got gladly welcomed him. [3]After his arrival, Endor rested at his camp. For he brought with him 3,000 warriors, ready for battle, who took what they needed from Got's palace. [4]Now [Endor] wanted to return home and told the king, "I would like to have a word with you in private." [5]Got said, "Let us go into the interior of the palace, [where

a. Andrew of Crete, *Canon* (PG 97.1360B).

b. Text: Aedor (Aendor below). The story that follows is a fanciful elaboration of Ps 82 (83):10: "They were utterly destroyed at (*en*) Endor." The *Palaea*, as it does elsewhere, understood "*en*" to mean "by" and imagined that a fictional character named "Endor" was responsible for their destruction; see below 129.13. The author may have placed this episode after the death of Joshua, because the preceding verse of the Psalm describes events occurring at the time of the judges. The details of the story bear some similarities to the account of Ehud's killing of Eglon king of Moab in Judg 3:16-26; see Flusser, "Palaea," 75.

c. Reading with Vas. V.: "prayed."

d. Vas.: "from the hand of."

e. Flusser ("Palaea," 75) suggests that "Got" is a corruption of "Lot." Ps 82 (83):8 refers to the nations coming to the aid of "the children of Lot."

you can tell me these things.]" [6]When they went in and were alone, Endor
plunged a dagger he was secretly carrying into the king's belly. [7]After he slashed
him, he hurled his mute corpse to the ground. [8]When he came out, he shut the
door behind him, saying to the attendants, "The king is asleep, and he gave me
instructions to shut the door behind me, so that he might not be disturbed."[a]
[9]After Endor said this to the attendants, he headed off to the Jews and told them,
"Make ready. After we plunder the Persians, let's get out of here." [10]After making
ready, they began to plunder the Persians. [11]When they saw what had happened,
Got's princes removed the doors of the palace, [went in and] saw Got lying there
dead. [12]Now Endor took an enormous quantity of loot and departed for the Jews
in Jerusalem. [13]David makes mention of this when he curses his enemies, "*They*
were utterly destroyed by Endor." Ps 83:11 (Evv 83:10)

130 [1]"[My soul], make an offering of praise to God, offer action (p. 264) as
a daughter [purer than Jephthah's, and slay your carnal passions as a sacrifice
to your Lord."][b] [2]*Concerning Jephthah*: This Jephthah, from the tribe of Dan,
was expelled [from] his tribe because he was illegitimate. [3]His mother gave
birth to him after sexual misconduct with her servant. For the twelve tribes
of Israel did not have relations with each other; rather each tribe held its own
allotment. [4]For this reason, the psalmist says, "*portion of inheritance,*" and else- Ps 104(105):11
where, "*in a portion of inheritance.*" [5]Now Jephthah, driven away from his tribe, Ps 77(78):55
ascended [the] mountain and settled there alone.[c] [6]And the sons of Israel were
subjugated by the gentiles, and they had no respite. [7]The sons of Israel were
troubled, and because they lacked a leader, they [were in great hardship,] for
they did not have a leader. [8]They approached Jephthah, urging him [to come]
to their aid. [9]But he declined, telling the Jews, "Because I am banished from
my tribe, I am unable to fight on your side in battle." [10]So they swore an oath
[with him] to make him leader of the whole Jewish nation, on condition that
he fight on their side and prevail in battle. [11]When Jephthah heard the words Judg 11:4-11
of the people and the leaders, he went out for battle. [12]As he was departing,
he[d] made an oath not to take spoils from the enemy. [13]"Likewise," (he said), "if
someone happens to meet me on my return from victory, I will make that person an offering to the Lord my God." [14]After departing for battle, he returned Judg 11:30-31
in triumph. [15][Upon his return,] his daughter heard that her father had arrived
from battle victorious, and she went out to meet him. [16]When Jephthah saw
his daughter, he began to wail. [17]His daughter inquired about the reason for his
lamentation. And [Jephthah] said to her, "My child, I have arranged to make
you an offering to the Lord God." (p. 265) [18]His daughter told him, "My lord,

---

a. Although the meaning of the Greek text of the last phrase is unclear, the translation is suggested by the context.

b. Andrew of Crete, *Canon* (PG 97.1365C). The same citation from Andrew appears at the end of this episode (130.22).

c. Cf. Judg 11:1-2, according to which Jephthah, the son of Gilead, was cast out by his half-brothers because his mother was a harlot. According to the *Palaea*, Jephthah's father was an unnamed servant of his mother. The *Palaea*'s reference to the psalms also suggests that Jephthah was driven out because his mother and her servant were from different tribes.

d. Emending plural to singular with Vas.

grant me a period of three months[a] to make merry with the young girls of my
age, and then do to me whatever you order." [19]Her father acted in accordance
with her wish. [20]She spent the three-month period passing from place to place,
gathering mountain flowers with her peers, and sampling the delights of this
world.[b] [21]After the period of three months had expired, she came to her father,
who made a pure offering of her to the Lord God. [And it was not reckoned to
Judg 11:34-40 him as a transgression.] [22]For this reason, the wise man recalled this story, "My
soul, make an offering of praise," he said.[c]

131 [1]*Concerning Manoah*: "Do you hear, my soul, of Manoah of old, the
one who saw God in a vision, the one who at that time received from a barren
woman the fruit of the promise? Let us imitate his piety."[d] [2]It so happened that
this Manoah, from the tribe of Asher, was childless. [3]Manoah, in anguish that
he had not fathered offspring, used to pray to have a child. [4]One day, when
Manoah was plowing in his field, an angel of the Lord came to his house and told
his wife, "Woman, from this day on, observe whatever instructions I give you.
[5]May neither meat enter through your mouth nor anything impure, and may
you not drink strong drink or wine. [6]Rather, from this day (observe everything)
that I command you, because you will conceive a child and you will give birth to
a son, and the boy is a Nazirite of God." [7]The angel departed from her. [8]When
her husband arrived in the evening, she told him these things, and her husband
Manoah said to her,[e] "Why didn't you tell me so that I might also see the man
for myself? But now have supper with me, and whenever he comes back, let me
know so that I too might see him." [9]The woman did as her husband directed her.
Judg 13:1-7 For Manoah and his wife were devout. (p. 266)

132 [1]On the next day, the angel came to the woman and said to her, "Did I
not tell you, woman, to keep away from anything impure, and not drink wine
and strong drink, and that a razor shall not come on his head, because the child
is a Nazirite of God?" [2]And the woman said to the angel, "Sir, if your words are
true, stay seated here until I tell my husband." And the angel said to her, "Go
ahead." [3]The woman departed in haste {... }[f] her husband. [4]He found the angel
sitting down and said to him, "Are you the man of God who came yesterday
to my home and said these things to my wife?" [5]And the angel said, "Yes I am,
and see, I am telling <them> to you now.[g] [6]Your wife will become pregnant
and give birth to a male child. [7]May she not drink wine or strong drink, nor
will a razor come on his head because the child is a Nazirite of God." [8]When
Manoah heard this, he said to the angel of God, "Sir, if your words are true,
accept {...},[h] and I will go and bring a kid-goat and make an offering and you

---

a. Cf. Judg 11:37 (two months).

b. Cf. Judg 11:38, according to which Jephthah's daughter spent her final months on the mountain bewailing her virginity.

c. Andrew of Crete, *Canon* (PG 97.1365A).

d. Andrew of Crete, *Canon* (PG 97.1366A).

e. Emending "of her" to "to her" with Vas.

f. Something is missing. Cf. Slav.: "And the woman departed in haste to retrieve her husband."

g. Something is missing.

h. Something is missing. Cf. Slav.: "Sir, if your words are true, sit and wait until I go ahead and bring a goat ...."

will eat." [9]And the angel said to him: "Go ahead." [10]Manoah hurried to his
flocks and brought a kid from his goats and made an offering of it. [11]And the
angel told him, "Put it on the rock. If you roast it, let us not eat it. But if you
make it an offering to the Lord your God, it will be for you as a propitiatory
offering." [12]And Manoah made an offering of the sacrificial victim on the rock.
[13]When the angel stretched out the tip of the staff that he was carrying in his
hand, there came forth from it a flame, which consumed the burnt offering.
[14]And the angel became a flame of fire and disappeared.[a] [15]When Manoah saw
this extraordinary wonder, he fell to the ground and told his wife, "We have
perished, woman, for we have seen God." [16]For Manoah had a vision of God,
and he was afraid lest he die. Judg 13:9-22

133 [1]After this incident, Manoah's wife conceived and gave birth to a son,
whom she named Samson.[b] [2]He was a powerful man as long as he had self-
control as a companion. [3]When the child reached manhood and had achieved
many victories for Israel, this is what happened to him: [4]His enemies, 12,000 in
number, found him on the plain, like a child in the field. (p. 267) [5]Because he did
not have available to him a chariot, a sword, (or any other) form of armament
to aid him in battle, he found in the plain a dry jawbone of an ass. Taking it in
his hands, he routed the 12,000. [6]Parched from the battle, he prayed to God, and
even though it was dry, he squeezed the jawbone, and water flowed from it. [7]He
drank his fill, and his thirst was quenched. [8]The man was mighty (and) well- Judg 15:15-19
pleasing to God, observing God's commandments. [9]Therefore, the wise man
makes mention of him with these words of praise:[c] "The one who previously
conquered the Philistines with the jawbone of the ass was now found to be the
refuse of passionate intercourse."[d]

134 [1]*Concerning Samson*: This Samson accomplished many feats for Israel
and achieved many triumphs. And he erected many trophies. [2]Now the Philistines, overpowered by his feats of courage, (began) to set upon him with artifice,
so that they might destroy him. [3]They began to have drinking bouts with him.
[4](Samson) began to get drunk with them and did not obey the wishes of his
mother to take a woman from his own tribe. He was eating with the Philistines
instead. [5]One day, when he had became drunk from wine, the Philistines shack-
led him in irons, and put seven collars on him.[e] For they feared[f] to touch him
when he was fasting. [6]By putting him in irons they assumed that when he became sober from the wine, he would make an agreement with them not to fight

---

a. Although lacking in the Judges account, this detail about the angel's staff igniting the offering is also found in Jos., *Ant.* 5.284 and ps.-Philo, *Bib. Ant.* 42:9. Cf. Judg 6:21, where the angel of the Lord touches a rock with his staff, from which bursts forth fire that consumes the offering.

b. The life of Samson that follows is substantially different from the account found in Judges 14–16. The chief purpose of the story is to explore the consequences of Samson's laxity and his continual violations of his Nazirite vow, especially in his repeated bouts of drunkenness with the Philistines.

c. Andrew of Crete, *Canon* (PG 97.1366B).

d. Emending *lachnias* ("wooliness") to *lagneias*.

e. For this detail about the seven collars, lacking in the Judges account, cf. Judg 16:6, where Delilah tries to subdue Samson with seven bowstrings.

f. Emendation. Text: "For they did not fear."

with them or make war. [7]Samson awoke in the middle of the night, and released
from the wine, realized that he was chained. [8]He came to, broke the bonds, and
utterly crushed the seven chains. [9]He then got up, went and found the gates of
the city closed. [10]By shoving up against them with his shoulders, he tore out the
city gates, along with the tower, from their foundations. [11]He then picked them
Judg 16:1-3 up, went up and placed them atop the mountain. [12]In an act of retaliation against
them, Samson found a big pack of cats,[a] caught them, tied their tails together,
and burned them with wax, it being the harvest season at the time; he then re-
Judg 15:1-5 leased them into the fields and reduced their fields to ashes.

135 [1]Now the Philistines came up with a plan to give him a woman from
their own tribe (p. 268), which they in fact did. [2]After the matrimonial bond was
made, he came to see the woman to whom he was <betrothed[b]>; lo and behold,
he came upon a lion on the way and smote it. [3]As he was passing through the
place a few days later, he found a swarm of bees nesting in the skull of the lion,
and he partook of the honey. [4]When the younger men of the Philistines arrived,
they <ate[c]> with him, around thirty of them. [5]When they became drunk, Samson told them, "I will ask you a riddle. If you find the answer to it, I will give you
thirty robes; but if you don't, I will take your robes." [6]And they said, "Say what
you please." Samson said, "What is food from that which eats[d] and sweet from
that which is bitter?" [7]Now when the sons of the Philistines heard this, they did
not know the answer and requested a recess of fifteen days. [8]He granted them
the recess that they wanted. [9]They went in and said to Delilah, the wife of Samson, "You are for sure one of us; that is why we gave you Samson, that bravest
of men. Now you go ask him, and he will explain the riddle to you, and you will
pass it on to us." [10]After conferring with her, they departed. [11](So) Delilah said
to Samson, "Why don't you teach me some of your riddles, so that when I spend
time with my lady friends,[e] I might receive {…}?"[f] [12]And Samson said to her,
"What do you want me to tell you?" [13]And she said, "The one that you told the
sons of the Philistines." [14]And he said to her, "One time when I was coming here,
I slew a lion. A few days later I ate honey that I found in its skull and brought
some to you as well." [15]This villainous woman, after learning the explanation of
the riddle from him, told it to the sons of the Philistines. [16]When the appointed
time arrived, Samson demanded their robes, thinking that they did not know
the answer to the riddle. [17]And they said to him, "You killed a lion. A swarm
of bees was nesting in its exposed skull, and you ate some of the honey." [18]And
Samson said, "If you had not coerced Delilah, you would not have known the
Judg 14:5-18 answer to my riddle."

136 [1]This most admirable Samson the Philistines conspired against in the
following way: [2]The Philistines (p. 269) encouraged Delilah to learn all there
was to know about his courage and the circumstances of his birth. [3]Initially he
refused, but later, under great pressure from her, he explained everything to her,

a. According to Judg 15:4 (= Slav.), the animals were foxes.

b. Reading with Vas.; the Greek text is corrupt.

c. Reading with Vas.; the Greek text is corrupt.

d. Emendation. Text: "that which does not eat." Cf. Judg 14:14.

e. Lit.: "women of my age."

f. The meaning of this Greek word is uncertain. Cf. Slav.: "I might receive honors."

that "an angel of the Lord told my mother that a razor shall not come upon my
head, and the essence of my power is this: the seven locks of hair on my head."
[4]When Delilah heard this, she passed it on to the Philistines. [5]When he had become drunk from wine and then sobered up, he found that he was weaker than
all other men.[a] [6]Then the Philistines came up to him and gouged out his eyes.
[7]It was a terrible sight to behold, <the one before whom>[b] thousands and tens of
thousands cowered exposed as a plaything of a woman. [8]In lamenting this, the Judg 16:4-21
wise man writes as follows: "Emulating the laxity of Samson."[c]

137 [1]*On the death of Samson*: But let us not skip over his death. [2]He had
someone to serve him after he lost his sight. [3]He would bring him water and
pour it on the locks of his head. [4]They began to grow, and he recovered his
strength. [5]He found an opportune time when Delilah was eating and drinking
with her paramours in the house that Samson had built and which was supported on one column.[d] [6]He told the young man guiding him, "Lead me near
the column supporting my house." [7]He led him there, and Samson told him,
"Get far away from the house." [8]The young man fled and stood far off. [9]Samson
leaned on the column with his shoulders and heaved it to the ground. [10]This
is what he then said: "My soul, you too must go away with the Philistines."
[11]When this happened, all who were in the upper part of the house perished,
Samson himself along with them. Judg 16:22-30

138 [1]*Concerning the prophetess Hannah*[e]: A [certain] woman by the name of
Hannah was from the tribe of Asher. She was barren and childless. [2]She went
away to the temple of the Lord, and she was praying with silent lips. Not a sound
was heard from her. [3]The son of Eli the priest came in and said to her, "Why
have you entered into the temple of the Lord to seek an oracle?" [4]She could not
bear the reproach and with a groan wept and said [to herself], "As the Lord God
[Sabaoth] lives, (p. 270) if I give birth to [a child], I will present him as a gift [to
the Lord God in] the temple of the Lord, and he will perform services there all
the days of his life." [5][Her prayer] was heard and she gave birth to a son. [6]And 1 Sam 1:1-20
she [glorified the Lord God and] prayed with this song: *"My heart is established
in the Lord. [My] horn is exalted in my Savior, [my mouth is enlarged over my
enemies."* [7]And she recited this song in its entirety.[f] [8]The Cretan recalls this when 1 Sam 2:1
he says]: "Chaste Hannah when praying [moved her lips in supplication, but her
voice did not sound forth. But while completely barren, she gave birth to a son
worthy of her prayer."[g]]

139 [1]When Samuel was three years old, he was given by his mother to the
temple of the Lord. [2][A woman by the name of Armathem[h] was the one who

a. For Samson's drunkenness (lacking in Judges), see Jos., *Ant.* 5.309.

b. Text is corrupt here.

c. Andrew of Crete, *Canon* (PG 97.1365A).

d. Cf. Judg 16:29 (two columns).

e. For Hannah as a prophetess, see, for example, Philo, *Somn.* 1.254; *Tg. Ps-J.* (to 1 Sam 2:1-2). Hannah is also known as a prophetess in the Eastern Orthodox tradition. Hannah's stated connection with the tribe of Asher, a detail lacking in 1 Samuel, may have been influenced by Anna, the daughter of Phanuel, described in Luke 2:36 as a "prophetess... of the tribe of Asher."

f. In Byzantine hymnody, Hannah's song is the third in the canon of nine canticles.

g. Andrew of Crete, *Canon* (PG 97.1368A).

h. See the following note for explanation of this name.

raised Samuel. [3]When he reached maturity, he became a priest of God and a
1 Sam 2:11 judge of the people. [4]He was the one who anointed Saul as king and likewise
David and censured Saul for his transgressions. [5]Concerning this, the Cretan
says: "The offspring of Hannah, the great Samuel, was called among the judges,
whom Armathem raised in the house of the Lord," and so forth.[a]

140 [1]He (Eli) was priest of the Most High. This Eli had five sons and although he taught them the precepts of the law, he did not train them to keep
these precepts. [2]Instead, his sons partook of the sacrificial offerings before the
1 Sam 2:12-17, 22-25 priest blessed them. And the people were extremely distressed. [3]Samuel was being raised in the temple of the Lord], and an angel of the Lord came and said to
Samuel, as if in a trance, "Samuel, Samuel." [4]Samuel, supposing that it was his
teacher,[b] went off to him and said, "Why did you call me, Sir?" [5]And he said, "I
didn't call you, my son." [6]Again the angel spoke to him, and again he went off,
and said to his teacher, "Why did you call me, Sir?" [7]And he said, "I did not call
you, my son. But if the one speaking to you should speak to you once again, answer him, 'Here I am, [Sir,] and what do you command your servant?'" [8]When
the angel came again, Samuel said. "Why did you call me, Sir? Here I am." [9]And
the angel told him, "Get up and say to Eli, 'Why won't you discipline your sons?
(p. 271) [10]They are violating the temple offerings by consuming the bread and
the meat and the wine before the priest blesses them. [11]Do you not read what
has been written in the law of the Lord? [12][No one is to touch anything offered
in the temple by the people until the priest blesses them.] [13][For] you will give
[their] first-fruits to your Lord God, and in this way the priest will make atonement to [the Lord]. [14]After the atonement he will bless them, and so shall you
eat from them.'" [15]Samuel arose [in the morning] and told this to Eli the priest,
but Eli did not accept it. Instead, his sons continued to behave brazenly in the
same way. [16][Again Samuel told him about this, but Eli did not himself admon-
ish his sons to abandon the wicked deed that they were committing. [17]He was
1 Sam 3:4-18 lenient with them instead and did not discipline them.] [18]God therefore became
angry against him and his sons and brought down a nation upon the country,
which devoured everything in [the] hills of Jerusalem and slew the sons of Eli by
the edge of the sword. [19][Eli the priest learned about the death of his children,
because] they brought him their heads. [20]When he saw them, he sat down on a
seat and breathed his last [, and great lamentation could be seen in Israel.] And
1 Sam 4:1-18 much of the population died along with them. [21]For this reason, the wise man
writes: "You, my soul, for lack of understanding have drawn upon yourself the
priest Eli's condemnation, by allowing the passions to act lawlessly in you, just
as he allowed his children."[c] [22]If therefore Eli had disciplined his sons, a great
number of the people would also not have perished along with them.

141 [1][*Concerning Jael*]: "You know, my soul, of Jael's bravery, who impaled

---

a. Andrew of Crete, *Canon* (PG 97.1368A). According to 1 Sam 1:1, 19, Arimathea (Gr.: Armathaim) was Samuel's birth-place. The *Palaea*'s identification of "Armathem" as Samuel's nursemaid arose from a misunderstanding of Andrew's *Canon*: "Hannah's child, the great Samuel, was reckoned among the judges, and *Arimathea raised him* in the house of the Lord."

b. Cf. 1 Sam 3:4-8, which identifies the teacher as Eli.

c. Andrew of Crete, *Canon* (PG 97.1366C). See below 141.14.

Sisera of old."[a] 2 *Concerning Sisera*: This Sisera was king of Tyre and often
despoiled the country of Palestine. (p. 272) 3 One day he rose up with a countless multitude and laid waste to all the countryside of the city of Jerusalem.
4 Barak, who was judge of Israel at that time, was unable to withstand Sisera.[b]
5 He went off, made an offering in the temple of the Lord, prayed and went out
to do battle with Sisera. 6 The Lord said to him through the prophet, "Go forward, your victory will be with a woman."[c] So Barak arose to fight with Sisera.
7 Sisera, the king of the gentile nations, left his army, went out on his own and
was walking around by himself through the hills. 8 A woman by the name of
Jael came out from her tent and saw king Sisera walking around alone in the
heat of the day. 9 For he had witnessed the battle, and, left on his own for a
while, was walking about, suffering with the heat. 10 Jael said to him, "Sir, look,
we are your servants, get down from your horse, come into the tent, take a rest
from the heat, and have some butter and milk to eat." 11 [And Jael gave him
butter and milk.] He ate, and she gave [him] wine as well, which he drank.[d]
12 He took a nap on the ground, because there was dew on the ground and
it was hot. 13 [And] Jael took a tent-peg and thrust it into the neck of Sisera,
killing him. 14 Salvation came to Israel on that day. Because of this, the wise Judg 4:1-22
man wrote profoundly, "You know, my soul, of Jael's bravery, who impaled
Sisera of old [and wrought salvation; do you hear of the tent-peg by which
the Cross is typified to you."] [e] 15 That is, just as the tent-peg, a piece of wood,
killed Sisera, in the same way was the Cross, a piece of wood, stuck into the
heart of Beliar, the adversary, [and] it killed him.

142 1 *Concerning the Levite, one of the judges*:[f] This Levite, who happened to
be one of the judges, took a wife [from] the tribe of Reuben.[g] 2 For the tribes of
Reuben were dispersed among the twelve sons of Israel. 3 These were the twelve
patriarchs [and their scepters were the twelve scepters of Israel, and] they were
also called the twelve tribes. 4 For every tribe, there was a particular position in
the marching order (p. 273). When they were making their way through Egypt,
each tribe would move along its own way. 5 But when the Red Sea was divided,
[the width into which it was divided was such] that they were unable to cross
without being hemmed in. 6 [They thus had an order for marching, some in the

---

a. Andrew of Crete, *Canon* (PG 97.1366B).

b. Cf. Judges 4, according to which Sisera was the captain of the army of Jabin, king of Hazor. When Jael killed him, Sisera was fleeing from Barak, whose forces had already destroyed Sisera's army. The *Palaea*'s retelling of the Judges narrative magnifies the glory of Jael's triumph. The *Palaea* makes Sisera the king of Tyre, whose enormous army was ravaging Palestine before his death at Jael's hands.

c. Cf. Judg 4:14, which identifies the prophetess as Deborah.

d. Judges says nothing about wine.

e. Andrew of Crete, *Canon* (PG 97.1365B).

f. Emending with Vas. Text: "Concerning the judge Levi." As told in the *Palaea*, the Levite is made to bear a share of the blame for the outrage committed against his wife. Because of his laziness, the Levite was slow in departing from the home of his in-laws. He was thus forced to spend the night in a town of the Benjaminites, a tribe notorious for its depravity. The quotation from Andrew of Crete provided at the conclusion of the story (144.17) summarizes the overall point of the story.

g. Cf. Judg 19:1-2, which describes the woman as a concubine from Bethlehem, of the tribe of Reuben.

back, some in the front, one on the right, another on the left. [7]For this reason, when the sea was divided, it was divided with sufficient width so that] each tribe [might have] its own way across. [8][Likewise] when they returned to the land of the promise, each tribe [received in this way] an allotment of land. [9]Drawing the boundaries with a measuring line, each of the <tribes[a]> received its division
of land. [10]For this reason, scripture mentions this everywhere: "*And he made*
Ps 77(78):55 *them to inherit by a line of inheritance.*" [11]And elsewhere: "*your own allotment of*
Ps 104(105):11 *inheritance*,"[b] [for each tribe had its own apportionment of land.]

143 [1]This Levite, then, who happened to be one of the judges, took a wife from another tribe. [2][The] tribe of Benjamin was in between when he traveled back and forth. [3]Now [the tribe of] Benjamin was really profligate, sodomites, pederasts, corrupters of children, adulterers, practitioners of incest and murderers. They used to commit every wicked act hateful to God. [4]The Levite, then, took his wife and went off to see his in-laws.[c] [5]As he was about to return home, he was inattentive in the morning about getting started on his journey. [6][His departure was lazy, and they did not take care to make their way quickly] so as to avoid tarrying in the cities of Benjamin as they passed through them. [7]He idly took his wife [along with his ass] and set out. [8]When [the] day waned, the evening took him to the city of Benjamin, where he lodged in a man's house.[d] [9]When it had become evening, the residents, [those] of the offspring of Benjamin, came looking for the stranger, saying, "Give us the stranger who has arrived here." [10]When the lord of the house resisted, [they descended upon the house like wild animals. [11]And the lord of the house appealed to them not to do anything to the man], saying (p. 274), "He is one of ours." But they did not listen to him. [12]And he gave them [his] own little daughter. [13]But [they cried out against him], demanding the stranger's wife. [14]When he[e] saw their wicked plan, he gave them his own little daughter and the wife <of the wayfarer[f]>. They violated her[g]
throughout the entire night. [15]She could not bear the lawless abuse of her body.
Judg 19:1-26 In the morning, she was found dead.

144 [1]When <the wayfarer[h]> saw the dead body of his wife, he put her on the ass and led her away to her parents. [2]When her parents saw the crime that had

a. Text: *physeis* ("natures"). Emended to *phylai* ("tribes").

b. The same psalm verses are quoted above in connection with Jephthah; see above 130.4.

c. Cf. Judg 19:2-3, which states that the Levite traveled to the parents of his concubine after she had left him.

d. According to Judg 19:5-15, the Levite delayed his departure only because his father-in-law kept urging him to stay another day. After he did leave, he intentionally chose to spend the night in the Benjaminite town of Gibeah in order to avoid having to lodge in Jebus, a city of the Jebusites. By blaming the delay on the Levite himself, the *Palaea* adapts the narrative to the appended quotation from Andrew of Crete (144.17).

e. The text specifies the Levite as the subject but the context suggests that after the townsmen rejected the initial offer of his daughter, it was the master of the house who complied with their request to hand over the Levite's wife as well. See also Judg 19:24, according to which the master of the house, not the Levite, made the offer.

f. Text: *Hodētē*. Emended to *hoditou* ("wayfarer"). Either the author or a copyist appears to have assumed that *hoditēs* ("wayfarer") was a proper name.

g. Emendation. Text: "herself."

h. Text: *Hosdētēs*. Emended to *hoditēs* (see above note to 143.14). The Greek text of this sentence has been rendered freely.

taken place, he gave his wife to them (after cutting her up) in eleven pieces[a]; and he sent to the eleven tribes, saying, 3"Do you see the hateful act that has taken place among our brothers? Does not Benjamin also belong to the offspring of Jacob? Are we not all brothers? 4Now look, because of them are we not going to be a laughing-stock to [the] Canaanites and to all the nations? 5So come on, let us wipe them out from our midst, [lest the Lord ever become angry at us because of them] and deliver us into the hands of the nations." 6[Everyone was incited to indignation by the Levite at what had happened,] and the eleven tribes joined together and began to wage war against the tribe of Benjamin, with the intention of rooting out the hateful act that had occurred. 7The devil, however, evil through and through, cooperated instead with the evil-doers. 8They crushed the ranks of the eleven tribes, [8,000 men. 9Again on the next day they engaged in battle and 12,000 men] from the eleven tribes [were cut down]. 10On the third day, after pursuing the matter among themselves, they said, "It is from the evil one that one tribe, while wicked, is superior in battle to the eleven tribes. 11Let us go to the temple of the Lord, and let us pray, and the glory of God will come upon us." 12After being sanctified, they went out and engaged in combat. 13With almighty God working on their side, the offspring of Benjamin were defeated. The eleven families utterly destroyed them. (p. 275). 14They completely laid waste their homes, and massacred all of them by the tip of the sword. 15From them, they spared not a person or an animal, nor was there a city that they did not strip from its foundations. 16These were the offspring of Benjamin, the last
son of Jacob. 17And for this reason, the wise man says, "The Levite among the Judg 19:29–20:48
judges, <by negligence[b] >. . . ." Add to this another passage from Jeremiah: "Ra-
chel mourning for her children."[c] 18In this story are found the very voices of Kyr Jer 38:15 [LXX]; Matt 2:18
Andrew and the prophet Jeremiah.

145 1*Concerning Deborah:*[d] This Deborah was the first of the aristocracy of the city of Jerusalem. 2And it so happened that Artasyris king of the Persians came, completely surrounded the city of Jerusalem and the countryside, attacked it, and was attempting to enter into it. 3The inhabitants of the city resisted as long as they could. 4But when they were no longer able to and lacked the power to resist the forces of the Persians, they reached an agreement to hand over this city to him. 5But Deborah arose and said to the leaders of Jerusalem, "Why have you decided to give the holy city into the hands of the gentiles? Put it off until tomorrow." 6So when they heard this, all of them suspended action for that day. 7Deborah got up, adorned herself, and took with her two maidservants carrying all kinds of fruits and two others carrying choice aged wine,

a. According to Judg 19:29, the Levite sent the twelve dismembered parts of his concubine throughout the land of Israel.

b. Text: *dia melian* ("by ash-wood"). Emended to *dia amelian* ("by negligence"). See Andrew of Crete, *Canon* (PG 97.1365D): "The Levite among the judges, by negligence, divided his wife among the twelve tribes, my soul, in order to proclaim the lawless outrage of Benjamin."

c. The *Palaea*'s citation from Jeremiah is closer to the wording of Matthew (Matt 2:18) than it is to the Greek text of Jeremiah.

d. The following story of Deborah's exploits has no parallel in the Judges narrative (Judges 4-5). The inspiration for the story appears to be the book of Judith's account of Judith's triumph over Holophernes.

bread and <an earthenware vessel[a]>. [8]When she had gone out of the city, she set out for Artasyris and his camp; it had now become evening. [9]When Artasyris set eyes on her, he was awestruck. For her appearance was lovely. [10]She entered and (said to) him, "I have found you well, mighty and most glorious king." [11]He welcomed her in and said to her, "You have come well, my blossoming red-rose of the field. Come in and take a seat." [12]When Deborah was seated, king Artasyris said to her, "From where have you come to us, you ray of sunshine?" [13]And she answered, "I am a nursling of this city and this day its leading lady. I have just heard about your valor (p. 276) and have come to keep company with you and deliver to you this city into your hands."

146 [1]When king Artasyris heard this, he halted his army's siege of the city. Those inside the city thus got a reprieve. [2]Because it was already evening, Artasyris sat down for dinner. [3]After cajoling him with her words, Deborah next delighted him with a variety of different foods. [4]By giving him wine to drink in abundance, she got him intoxicated and spoke these words to him: "I will make merry with lord Artasyris, with my own hands I will mix the wine for him, the overseer of my city. [5]Like a queen, I will make merry with him, my lord, for I do not know a man like you. [6]But right now it is my custom to worship my God, seven times at night without interruption. [7]Let your majesty issue an order, then, that no one might approach him this night, so that only Deborah might serve him and that no one is to impede her from {...},[b] and it will be done." [8]When this decree was issued {...}[c] of Artasyris, he rested and was left alone with Deborah and her house servants. [9]After the clever Deborah made Artasyris drunk with much wine, he fell off to sleep. [10]Once she found it safe to do so, she took a sword and cut off his head. She took the head and went out from the camp at night. [11]When she reached the city, she knocked on the gates of the city, imploring them, "Open the gates." They opened the gates for her and brought her inside. [12]She presented them with the head of Artasyris, and they rejoiced with exceedingly great joy. They took it and hung it on the wall of the city. [13]At that time, Deborah delivered Israel from the hand of the gentiles and became a woman of manly mind.[d] [14]Divine grace thus operates sometimes through men, at other times through women.

147 [1]*Concerning Saul:*[e] This Saul was poor and had a father named Kish, with
1 Sam 9:1-2 whom he lived doing manual labor.[f] [2]Priests and elders were serving as judges of the Israelites. [3]The people were distressed about the many onslaughts of the enemy and petitioned God to have a king. (p. 277). [4]The one serving as judge at that time was Samuel, whose extraordinary birth of old was from a barren and

---

a. Text: *aphrakeramida* ("plaster vessel"[?]). Emended to *keramida*.

b. Vas. states that the text is illegible here. Cf. Slav.: "that no one is to impede her from what she has to do."

c. Vas. suggests a lacuna here. Cf. Slav.: "After listening to what he ordered, all of the king's commanders and servants rested."

d. A possible allusion to Andrew of Crete, *Canon* (PG 97.1365B): "Barak and Jephthah, military leaders, with manly-minded Deborah, were promoted to be judges of Israel."

e. In the quotation from Andrew of Crete cited below (148.9), Saul is said to have gained the kingdom "incidentally." To explain this statement, the *Palaea's* narrative emphasizes the fortuitous, almost random, nature of Saul's rise from poverty to power.

f. According to 1 Sam 9:1, Kish was a man of wealth.

aged woman. He was judge of Israel at that time. [5]Now the people ill-advisedly
were not content to be under the administration of the just Samuel, but under
duress petitioned God for a king. [6]In his petition, Samuel spoke about the will of
the people. And the Lord told him, "Because they are not content to be guided
by you, and wish instead to be like the nations, I will give them a king according
to the desire of their hearts." [7]And the Lord told him, "Go off and shut the gates 1 Samuel 8
of the city. The one who is found by the gate the first thing in the morning, he is
your king." [8]And Samuel closed the gates of the city.

148 [1]Now Saul, who was feeding his father's asses, lost track of them. [2]He
ran around in circles for a long time, but was unable to locate them. [3]When it
was in the dark of the evening, he arrived at the city, found the gates closed,
and fell asleep before the gate of the city. [4]As soon as the gates opened, he went 1 Sam 9:3-10
inside, and Samuel walked up to him, took hold of him and said to the people,
"Here is your king." [5]Samuel brought the horn of oil and anointed him, and
all the people made obeisance to him. [6]Saul was one-eyed, and when he took 1 Sam 9:17–10:1
power,[a] he began to subjugate all the people. [7]Some he killed, for others he
gouged out their eyes,[b] and others he subjected to all kinds of punishments,
and he did not cease from testing the people of the Lord. [8]So the Lord grew
angry with him and delivered him over to an evil spirit. [9]The wise man recalls 1 Sam 16:14
this with these words: "When Saul once lost his father's asses, my soul, he incidentally found the kingdom."[c]

149 [1]Saul, possessed by a wicked spirit, sought for some medical treatment
to be set free of it, but he did not find it. [2]The Nazarene[d] sorcerers, who have
experience in chasing out spirits of evil, came and told him, "If you find a young
boy strumming the harp and singing a song, the spirit will flee from you." [3]Saul
searched for a young boy, but was unable to find him. [4]Now it was made known
to him that Jesse had a young boy who strummed the harp and sang a song. And
king Saul told him to bring him. [5]They went off to Jesse (p. 278), and inquired
of him, "Do you have a young boy who plays the harp and sings?" And they told
him, "King Saul has need of him." [6]And Jesse said, "Tomorrow he is coming
from the sheep-fold, and I will take him to him." And the emissaries left. [7]The
following day Jesse took rabbits, lambs, hares, birds and all kinds of winged creatures, and conducted David to the king. [8](He told him), "I have found you well,
my king." [9]And he said, "Is this one your son, who strums the harp and sings
songs?" And Jesse said, "Yes he is." [10]And Saul said, "I need him to remain with
us." [11]And Jesse said, "He will be your servant, my lord king. For I have six other
sons, and they will serve in my house." And David stayed in the palace. [12]When
the spirit would begin to torment Saul, David would arrive and strum the harp
and stop the evil spirit. [13]In this way, Saul had rest from the evil spirit and peace
from the wrath sent to him from God. [14]When this was taking place, David was 1 Sam 16:14-23

---

a. Emendation with Vas. Text: "and he did not take power."

b. 1 Samuel says nothing about a one-eyed Saul or his blinding of his subjects. Cf. 1 Sam 11:1-2, which describes how the Ammonite king Nahash demanded to gouge out the right eyes of the Jabesh-Gileadites in return for a peace treaty.

c. Andrew of Crete, *Canon* (PG 97.1367CD). The quotation from Andrew would make better sense after 147.8.

d. Text: *Nazōrēnoi*. Read: *Nazarēnoi*.

living in the palace of Saul. [15]And Saul's son Jonathan said to his father, "Father,
let us give David my sister Michal[a] as a wife. Let us make him a son-in-law, and
let him remain with us." [16]This is what they did. Saul gave him his daughter as a
1 Sam 18:20-26 wife, and David became a son-in-law to Saul.

150 [1]At that time, a war broke out, and Saul went to Samuel and asked him
to find out from the Lord whether he should go out in battle. [2]Samuel said, "Go
ahead, God is telling you that you will prevail in the battle. But do not take anything from them, even so much as the hair of a ram." [3]Saul went out in battle and
prevailed, but he did not keep the Lord's commandment, taking instead animals
and various things. [4]And Samuel went out to meet Saul and told him, "You have
fared well in conquest, but I hear a sound of animals in my ears." [5]And Saul
said, "I have taken the animals to raise them." [6]And Samuel became angry and
told him, "Because you transgressed the law of the Lord and denied the commandment of the Lord, God says to you, 'My spirit (p. 279) shall not abide in
you. [7]Your kingdom will instead be taken from you, and I will give it to the one
who carries out my wishes. No longer shall you see my face as long as you live.'"
1 Samuel 15 [8]Samuel turned his face from Saul and fled from him. [9]Saul was stripped of his
kingdom, and the spirit hearing the harp fled from him. [10]And David departed
for the house of his father and was tending his flocks.

151 [1]*Concerning the kingdom of David:* The Lord told Samuel, "Go out to
the house of Jesse and anoint David his younger son as king, because I have
found him after my heart, and he will carry out my wishes." [2]Samuel went to
the house of Jesse and said to him, "Give me your son so that I might make
him king, because Saul has provoked the Lord God, who has snatched his
kingdom away from him." [3]Jesse brought his first son, and Samuel said to him,
"The Lord has not found him pleasing." [4]He brought him the second, nor was
he pleasing, and likewise the third, similarly for all the sons of Jesse. And God
was not pleased with any of them. [5]Now David had come from the sheep-fold,
and as he was coming up to his father's house, he found the horn of oil and
was anointed by him.[b] [6]When Samuel saw (him), he arose and made obeisance to him (saying), "Here is the king of Israel; he will do everything that is
1 Sam 16:1-13 pleasing to the Lord God." And Samuel returned to his house in Arimathea.
[7]Saul was in great distress over his kingdom and went out to a procuress.
[8]To keep from being recognized, he was wearing the clothes of a commoner.
[9]He asked that she might conduct an inquiry for him. (The procuress) told
him, "You are the king. Why have you come here to mislead me?" [10]And Saul
{....}.[c] [11]And she said to him, "I see a man wearing a robe and cursing you."
And Saul said, "I know this man." [12]When the procuress, that is the diviner,
pointed at him, he saw Samuel from the looking glass, saying, "The Lord God
has stripped you of the kingdom because you provoked him." [13]Seized with
dread, he collapsed in trembling fear on a couch, where he remained until
the afternoon. [14]And the woman who was the procuress said to him, "Lord

a. Text: *Melcho* (cf. LXX: *Melchol*).

b. Presumably Samuel (see 1 Sam 16:13).

c. Something is missing. Cf. Slav.: And Saul told her, "Throw (dice?) for me, and she threw and said to him...."

King, get up, eat and (p. 280) get strong. Return to your house. For that man who appeared to you has given your kingdom to someone else." [15]Saul ate and departed to his house in anguish. 1 Sam 28:7-25

152 [1]David, a most gentle man, was not exalted in his mind, either as the king's son-in-law or as nobility. [2]He observed the highest degree of humility; he never left his father's flocks, but was always with them. [3]He used to go off to Saul's house, and when the spirit agitated Saul, David would come and strum his harp, and would stop the spirit. [4]Jonathan, Saul's son, loved David, but Saul hated him because of his fitness to rule the kingdom.[a] [5]When he was in good health, he was always persecuting David, but when the spirit was agitating him, he would summon him, and David would chase away the spirit by strumming the harp. 1 Sam 16:23; 18:1-3, 10

153 [1]It so happened that at that time a nation came to plunder the countryside of Palestine, and everyone was in great despair. [2]They had a mighty combatant named Goliath who, confident in his own manliness, chided the living God. [3]They gained control of the entire region. [4]Every man shuddered before his face, and Goliath was making a show of his manliness. [5]David went to his father-in-law Saul and said to him, "Why is my lord king anguished and why has his countenance fallen?" [6]And Saul said, "I am in anguish because of the nation that has come into our midst. Look, the kingdom was given to you, but you are a mere lad, and I do not know what you will do." [7]David said to him, "Let me go out to fight him man to man." [8]And Saul said, "Take chariots and a horse of your choosing." [9]David replied, "I have no need for chariots. When I used to tend my father's flocks and a lion or a bear would come along, I would smite them. So let this man be like (one of) those wild beasts." [10]David went into battle, and when he got up to the battle-line, he said to Goliath, "Who are you to come here chiding the living God, plundering the people of the Lord, and meaning to completely devour all of us? [11]Get out of here unless you want me to deliver up your flesh as food for the beasts of the earth and the birds of the sky. (p. 281) [12]The dogs will lap up your blood because the Lord God of Israel is with us." [13]Goliath answered him, "Lad, what has deluded you, that you should speak this way to me? [14]I am not going to pull out a spear or a sword against you; I'll smite you instead with my bare hand and hand you over as food for the birds. [15]I will level this city to the ground and utterly annihilate everyone. [16]The God in whom you have trusted will not avail you at all, for my gods are mightier than any other god. [17]Get away from here, lad, lest you lose your life, and bring grief to your parents." [18]When David heard this, he invoked the name of the Lord God and after placing three stones in his sling, hurled them at the face of Goliath, telling him, "Behold the power of my God." [19]As soon as he shot the sling, it struck Goliath in his face and killed him. [20]Deliverance came to Israel on that day. David took his sword, cut off his head, and brought it to king Saul. 1 Samuel 17

154 [1]David was proclaimed king. But Saul pursued David, wanting to kill him. [2]When (David) came <to Hebron[b]>, they made him their king, and he

---

a. Lit.: "because of the business of the kingdom." Cf. Slav.: "because of his calm rule."

b. Text: *eucherōn* ("reckless"). Emended with Vas. to *en Cheurōn* ("to Hebron").

2 Sam 2:1-11 reigned over them for seven years up to the death of Saul, his father-in-law.[a] [3]But
Saul pursued him from city to city. [4]Now one day, Saul learned that David was in
Methel.[b] [5]He came and encamped near Methel, looking for David. [6]That night,
David opened the gates of the city and led out his people. [7]He himself entered
Saul's camp and took from him his scepter and cushion. [8]When (Saul) could
not find them, he said that David had carried them off. [9]And David came into
the middle of the road and stood atop the rock. [10]As Saul (was approaching), he
cried out after him, "Why does my lord pursue a stinking dog?[c] [11]Those of you
who are guarding my lord the king are hardly acting vigilantly. [12]Wasn't the one
who took away his scepter and cushion also able to cut off his head? But by no
means would I lay a hand on the Lord's anointed." (p. 282). [13]And he returned
1 Samuel 26 the scepter and cushion (to Saul).[d] [14]David escaped to a wilderness place with
three hundred men, and they did not find anything to eat. [15]David came to the
house of God during the night and said to Abiathar the priest, "Is there bread
for the servants of God to eat?" [16](Abiathar replied), "I do not have bread except for the shew-bread. Are the servants pure enough to eat it?" [17]David said,
1 Sam 21:1-6; Mark "They have gone three days without touching a woman." [18]And Abiathar the
2:25-26 high priest said, "Let them eat." And they all ate and drank.[e] [19]A Syrian man by
the name of Doeg[f] got up and went away, and told Saul, "Lord King, the priests
of the Lord love David, and they are giving him oracles from the Lord." [20]When
Saul heard this, he sent out and killed three hundred priests of the Lord God.[g]
1 Sam 22:9-23 But Abiathar the high priest departed with David. [21]Saul did many other things
to David, and brought ordeals to the people until the day of his death. And Saul
1 Samuel 31 lost his life in battle.

155 [1]*Concerning Uriah's wife and his death:* David took control of the kingdom and was in the palace. [2]One day he was walking around in his chamber and
saw a woman bathing.[h] [3]After learning who she was, he sent for her, brought
her to him, and began to spend time with her. [4]Uriah, the woman's husband,
happened to be in battle. He was summoned through a letter by Joab his commander. [5]The king told him, "Return to your home, Uriah, and leave tomorrow."
And Uriah departed for his home. [6]Because he had made an agreement with his
comrades not to touch his bed, he did not sleep with his wife, saying, "Are my
comrades at this very moment to keep watch in battle, while I sleep on my bed?

---

a. Cf. 2 Sam 2:4, which states that Saul was already dead at the time of David's anointing as king in Hebron.

b. The place is unknown. Cf. Slav.: "Bethel." According to 1 Sam 26:3, Saul encamped on the hill of Hachila (= Echela [LXX]).

c. The meaning is unclear.

d. In the parallel account told in 1 Samuel 26, David removed Saul's spear and a jar of water while he slept in his camp at Ziph.

e. According to 1 Sam 21:1-6, Ahimelech, not Abiathar, was the priest, and there is no mention of him serving in the "house of God." But cf. Mark 2:25-26, which describes how David went "into the house of God in the days of Abiathar the high priest."

f. Text: Doiki; cf. 1 Sam 21:7 (LXX): Doēk. Greek authors following the Septuagint text of 1 Samuel *ad loc.* call Doeg a Syrian, not an Edomite (= MT). The two words look almost identical in Hebrew.

g. Cf. 1 Sam 22:18 (MT): eighty-five priests; (LXX): 305; Jos., *Ant.* 6.268: 300.

h. Bathsheba remains unnamed throughout the narrative.

Let the sight of my home suffice." So he slept on a mat. [7]Now his wife, who was
pregnant from David, disclosed this to the king, saying, "Let my lord the king
know that my husband did not sleep with me, and I am pregnant from you. If
he should return from battle, he will certainly have my head." [8]When David
heard this, he wrote Joab his commander, (p. 283), "When the battle has broken
out, station Uriah on the other side of the battle so that he will be killed." [9]And
he handed Uriah the letter describing his own death, who delivered it to Joab.
[10]When Joab read the letter, Uriah was ordered to go into combat, and he was
slain in the battle. [11]King David thus committed both adultery and murder. 2 Sam 11:2-27

156 [1]So the Lord said to Nathan the prophet, "Go out and reprove king David for having committed adultery." [2]The prophet said to the angel, "I am afraid
lest perchance the king will not accept my rebukes and put me to death." [3]The
angel of the Lord told him, "Go ahead, for you will see me before you." And the
prophet left for king David. [4]As he was going in, he saw the angel holding in his
hand the drawn sword and standing before the king. [5]If he planned to resist the
rebuke, the angel would kill him.[a] [6]So the prophet said, "I have a case to make
to you, my king." And the king said, "State your case." [7]The prophet had the following reply: "A certain man owned ninety-nine lambs, and he sat with them
and enjoyed being with them. [8]But a poor man lived near him, who had only
one lamb, which ate from his table, drank from his cup, and slept at his knees.
[9]Now that wealthy man left behind the ninety-nine lambs that he owned and
enjoyed, and took the one lamb of the poor man. I bring this case before you, my
king." [10]And the king replied, "If the one who did this in my kingdom is found,
I'll have his head." [11]And the prophet answered, "You are the one, my king, who
did this." [12]So the most gentle king immediately arose from his throne and made 2 Sam 12:1-12
obeisance saying, "*I have sinned against my Lord,* I have sinned." [13]When at that 2 Sam 12:13
time the prophet saw the angel turn his sword away, he told the king, "The Lord
has taken away your transgressions." [14]At that time he also wrote down the fiftieth psalm.[b] [15]And the angel delivered an oracle, saying, "A sword shall not leave
from your house."[c] 2 Sam 12:1-13

157 [1]*Concerning Ahithophel*: David fathered seven sons: two with the wife
of Uriah, three with Michal, Saul's daughter, (p. 284) and two with Magaia[d] the
daughter of Naua. His first-born son was Absalom.[e] [2]At that time, there hap- 2 Sam 3:2-5; 1 Chr 3:1-9
pened to be a counselor named Ahithophel. He harbored all along a grudge
against David, and sought an opportunity to kill him, but failed to find it. [3]When
Absalom reached manhood, Ahithophel found an opportune time and told to
him, "Why have you no interest in your father's kingdom? [4]Solomon, the bastard

a. The immediate inspiration for this story originates in the quotation from "the wise man" given below (161.16), which describes how David stopped "your angel smiting the people with the sword." The image was probably generated by Nathan's statement to David in 2 Sam 12:10 that, because of his murder and adultery, "the sword shall never depart from your house." Cf. also 1 Chr 21:16.

b. The reference to this penitential psalm (Psalm 50 [51]), commonly sung in the Orthodox liturgy, shows how David's penitence forestalled God's wrath.

c. According to 2 Sam 12:10, Nathan delivered this oracle.

d. Possibly a reference to Maacah (= [LXX] Mōcha), the mother of Absalom (1 Chr 3:2) and Hanan (1 Chr 11:43).

e. Cf. 2 Sam 3:2-3, which states that Absalom was the third son born to David in Hebron.

son, is going to inherit it, but the kingdom is yours and belongs to you. [5]So you
should set your mind on taking it. For God has expelled your father from his
2 Sam 15:12 kingdom, and given it to you." [6]Upon hearing this, Absalom got carried away in
his thinking. [7]Ahithophel offered him advice about the kingdom, and Absalom
agreed to usurp it from his father. [8]But Ahithophel was seized by fear that, because of Absalom's love for his father, he would himself be condemned to be sold
into slavery.[a] [9]And he said to him, "I cannot be confident that you will supersede
your father unless you do what I tell you." [10]And (Absalom) said, "Whatever it
is that you want, I will do." And he said, "I want you to sleep with one of your
father's concubines; then I will put my trust in you."[b] [11]Ahithophel's actions instigated an irreconcilable[c] conflict between father and son. [12]Absalom, won over
by Ahithophel's most vile advice, took one of his father's concubines and slept
2 Sam 16:20-23 with her. [13]When a conflict arose as a result, Absalom took as many as he wanted
to involve in their plot and went out with Ahithophel to the region of Hebron,
leaving David alone by himself. [14]And David mourned, weeping constantly over
the transgression that Absalom had committed. David was in mourning, left all
2 Sam 15:1-30 alone.

158 [1]There was a wise man named Hushai. He kept company with David,
mourning with him. [2]Seeing him overwhelmed with grief, he said to him,
"Why are you so downcast and weighed down by grief?" [3]The king said, "My
friend, you see the disaster that befalls me from this, and yet you say to me,
'Why are you in anguish?' [4]Do you see that I, alone with you, have been abandoned, without a supporting hand? [5]My army is stationed on the other side of
the Jordan in the valley of salt (p. 285), and I do not know what will happen
to it, along with Joab my commander-in-chief. [6]If they were here with me, I
would be released from this great despair." [7]And Hushai said to him, "How
long before your servant is able to return from the valley of salt?" David said,
"Another ten days." [8]Hushai said, "I am leaving for your son Absalom, and I
will make sure that they won't come against you for another ten days. [9]Only
don't be angry with me, because I will have much to say against you." [10]And
David said to him, "Go ahead, only keep them away for ten days. I will explain
things in a letter to Joab my commander-in-chief, and he will come and go
2 Sam 15:32-36 to war against them." [d]

159 [1]Hushai got up and took his men along with horses and mules and left
for Absalom and Ahithophel in Hebron.[e] [2]And they stood up and said to him,
"Why have you come to us? What is the reason for your arrival?" [3]And he said,
"The kingdom has been given to you. The Lord has chosen you and rejected
your father. [4]Look, everyone will go with you, my lord Absalom, for you will
fulfill the precepts of the Lord." [5]When Absalom heard the words of Hushai and

---

a. Cf. Slav.: "he would himself be sentenced because of this child."

b. According to 2 Sam 16:21-22, Absalom had sex with his father's "concubines" (plural), ten of whom had been left behind by David (2 Sam 15:16).

c. Text: "unreasonable."

d. In the account in 2 Samuel, David, not Hushai, is the author of this plan. 2 Samuel says nothing about the ten days needed for Joab to return.

e. According to 2 Samuel, the meeting between Hushai and Absalom took place in Jerusalem, not Hebron.

his son Emene,[a] he was joyful in his heart, welcomed Hushai, and let him rest. [6]Now the camp had become full, with people gathered together from every city, region and village. [7]And Ahithophel told him, "Let us go out and take control of the cities and our kingdom, lord Absalom." [8]Absalom said, "Let us also ask Hushai, because the man is a fine advisor." [9]And they said to Hushai, "What do you think? Shall we depart for Jerusalem or not?" [10]Hushai said, "Why is my lord Absalom in such a rush? You are going after a gnat. [11]Let my lord stay put and rest for another ten days, and the elders of the twelve tribes will come to make obeisance to you; for you do not have a fight with anyone." [12]And Absalom said, "Hushai's advice is better than Ahithophel's." [13]And Absalom ordered that there be a pause for ten days. 2 Sam 17:1-14

160 [1]In the meantime, Joab arrived with his army and found David in sackcloth and mourning his own isolation. [2]Joab said to him, "Are the enemies from the nations not enough for me? With your bastard offspring as well, are we going (p. 286) to be oppressed, constrained by evil men?"[b] [3]With a groan David began to cry out: "My son has risen up against me." [4]And taking his camp and all its armament with him, Joab went out against Absalom. [5]After calling upon the name of the Lord our God, he joined battle and routed all of them by the power of the God of Israel. [6]Absalom, the only one of them left, turned in flight. As he was fleeing on horseback, the locks of his head got tangled in the tree, and he was left suspended, as his horse continued running. [7]One of the soldiers saw him hanging, extended his bow and shot him. [8]With him still breathing, he cut off his head and brought it to his father David. [9]And his father took hold of it and grieved for the transgression that he had committed.[c] [10]Concern- 2 Samuel 18
ing this transgression, the wise man says: "You have heard of Absalom, (my soul, how)...."[d] [11]We have spoken previously about the transgression of David and his murder; and he says the following: "David once joined lawlessness to lawlessness."[e]

161 [1]*Concerning the census*: When David, then, found a timely moment and a respite from warfare, he decided that he would register his people. For at that time, a census did not exist. [2]He said to Joab, his commander-in-chief, "I want

a. For the name "Emene," unmentioned in 2 Samuel, see the heading to the Greek version of Psalm 7: "Psalm of David which he sang to the Lord because of the words of Hushai, the son of Iemeni" (translating the Hebrew word *ben*, which means son, as though it were not part of the tribal appellation "Benjaminite"). The *Palaea* apparently understood the Greek text "*Chousi uiou Iemeni*" to mean "Iemeni, son of Hushai," and hence the story about Hushai and his son "Emene."

b. Or possibly "evil things," "misfortune."

c. The story departs from the account in 2 Samuel in several particulars. According to 2 Samuel, Joab and ten of his armor-bearers killed Absalom, who was riding on a mule when his hair became entangled in the tree. 2 Samuel, which says nothing about David receiving Absalom's severed head, states only that Absalom's body was cast into a pit. A Cushite messenger then discreetly informed David of Absalom's fate.

d. Andrew of Crete, *Canon* (PG 97.1370B): "You have heard of Absalom, how he rose against nature. You know his accursed deeds and how he insulted the bed of his father David. But you have imitated his passionate and pleasure-loving cravings."

e. Andrew of Crete, *Canon* (PG 97.1369A): "David once joined sin to sin, for he mixed adultery with murder, yet he immediately offered double repentance. But you, my soul, have done things more wicked without repenting to God."

you to register the people of Israel, so that we might know how many soldiers we have, and how many farmers, and how many are in the whole community." [3]Joab replied to the king, "I am unable to do this, because it is written in the law of the Lord, 'You shall not number the people of the Lord.'"[a] [4]And (David) instructed another man by the name of Achria[b] (to register the people of the Lord), and he went out and began the registration. [5]When they were doing the count over nine months and twenty days, {...} and in the census they found 800,000 men capable of wielding a sword, and for the tribe of Judea alone 500,000 men in arms.[c] [6]The Lord was angry with David and said, "Behold, let there come a famine upon your land for three years. [7]Either that, or for three months you will be in flight from enemies, or for three days there will be death upon your land and your people." (p. 287) [8]When David heard this, he was struck dumb, unable to speak. [9]And the angel of the Lord said to him, "Speak up, because the divine wrath is urging me on." [10]And David answered the angel of the Lord, "It is impossible to flee from the hands of the Lord my God. Let it be the punishment of death." [11]As soon as the king said this, the angel of the Lord departed and began to smite them. There was great mourning over all Judea. [12]And David donned sack-cloth and was mourning and lamenting, saying: "I am the one you should kill, because I am the one who transgressed, not the people. [13]Be merciful, Lord, to your people, and let not the sinless one be angry, O Lord." [14]As David was lamenting over this, the Lord God saw his weeping and felt pity on his people. And the Lord's wrath ceased from the people. [15]When David counted up the numbers, he found that in three hours 70,000 men had perished from
2 Samuel 24; 1 Chronicles 21
the people. [16]The wise man has made mention of this when he says, "To David your prophet, how you stopped your angel smiting the people with the sword."[d] [17]These and many other things are told about David. Let us put these stories aside in our summary and send up glory to Christ.

162 [1]*Concerning king Uzziah:* "Having emulated Uzziah, my soul, you have his leprosy in you doubled."[e] [2]When Uzziah was king of Judea, he entered into the temple of the Lord God. [3]When the priest went in to burn incense, king Uzziah said, "Give me incense to burn." [4]And the priest answered, "You are not allowed to burn incense." [5]And Uzziah said, ["Why am I not allowed to burn incense?] Am I not a priest? [Do I not wear the purple?]"[f] [6]The priest answered, "You are indeed king. But you are not allowed to burn incense." And he returned the censer to its place. [7]But the king reached out and took the censer in his hand and burnt incense. [8]The Lord became angry with him and gave him leprosy on his forehead. [9]It was a custom for the Jews to remove outside

a. The biblical source of this prohibition against the census is unclear. According to 2 Sam 24:3-4, Joab, while initially hesitant, finally agreed to conduct the census.

b. This name is unknown in the account told in 2 Samuel. The name is possibly related to the Greek word "*achreia*" ("useless").

c. These numbers agree with 1 Sam 24:9; but cf. 1 Chr 21:5 (1,100,000 men in Israel and 470,000 in Judah).

d. Unknown source. The quotation summarizes the point of the *Palaea*'s narrative about David's kingdom: namely how repentance for his transgressions (first for adultery and murder, and then for disobedience) turned away God's wrath.

e. Andrew of Crete, *Canon* (PG 97.1375B).

f. For discussion, see the Introduction.

the city anyone who happened to be a leper among them. [10]But out of respect
for him, they did not take him outside the city. [11]And the Lord became angry 2 Chr 26:16-23;
with them (p. 288) and did not give a word to Isaiah until the death of Uzziah. 2 Kgs 15:5
[12]But after the death of Uzziah, the Lord appeared to him. For this reason, he
writes with exceeding joy: "*In the year in which Uzziah the king died, having
seen the Lord sitting...*" Isa 6:1

163 [1]*Concerning Bit:*[a] This Bit was taken captive during the captivity of the
Hebrews in Nineveh. [2]A pious and very just man in adherence to the law, he
would bury the bodies of his fellow countrymen who were dying in the captivity, when he saw their bodies treated with contempt and unburied. [3]One day, Tob 1:17-19
then, he returned from this {...} from his work pleasing to God. [4]After putting
away his shovel and spade, he lay down outside his house, because he had been
defiled according to the law at that time. For anyone who touches a corpse is impure until morning. [5]That night, a sparrow flying by defecated on his eyes from
above. [6]He immediately became blind, even though he had never blasphemed,
but always gave thanks to the Lord for his forgiveness. [7]He summoned Tobias Tob 2:9-10
his son and said, "Look, as you can see, my son, I am blind and an old man, and
I have become poor because of my transgressions. [8]So now I will send you to my
powerful relative in Judea, for before the captivity I left with him a talent of gold
in trust.[b] [9]Now go there and bring it back for the nourishment of our bodies and
as comfort for our misfortunes. [10]But you are not entirely familiar with the way
there, my son, for it is long. [11]So let us find a man who does know the way, and
who fears God, and let us pay him a fitting wage. [12]Let him guide you with God
and bring you back to my darkened eyes safe and sound." [13]And indeed the sort
of man they were looking for did appear to them—it was the divine archangel
Raphael in the form of a man, pretending to be a hired worker. [14]And he told
them, "Pay me a fair wage and I will bring him through safely with God, for I
do in truth know about all these things, both about the region and about this
relative of yours." Tobit 4–5

164 [1]And the angel having made him(self) into the form of a hired worker
(p. 289) and with much prayer from the hands of the old man, they traveled
without stumbling for a considerable number of days, with a little dog from the
house also following them.[c] [2]When they reached the Tigris river, the lad Tobias
sat down to wash his feet. [3]He saw a fish leaping up and charging at him, so
as to devour him. And the lad cried out. [4]The angel, his traveling companion,
told him, "Do not be afraid, but be of good courage." [5]When this happened,
he again said to him, "Cut it open in its heart, and keep its liver safe in a jar.
[6]The old man to whom we are going has a daughter with an unclean spirit,
called Asmodeus, who because of his love for her has choked to death seven
men betrothed to her. [7]I will speak to the old man about a marriage contract.
[8]After he provides us with the sum of gold in his safekeeping, I will see to it that

a. The narrative about Tobit, Daniel and Habakkuk is missing in O; see Vas. note *ad loc.*

b. Cf. Tob 4:1, which states that Tobit had left the sum of money (ten talents of silver) in trust with Gabael at Rages in Media.

c. Although only an incidental character in the Greek version of *Tobit*, the dog plays a more central role in the *Palaea* narrative; see below 166.1-2.

you receive from him his daughter as a wife. [9]And make it[a] from the liver and
the heart, and Asmodeus, the homicidal demon, will flee to the lowest part of
Egypt, where he will be bound with unbreakable bonds. [10]At that very moment
{...}[b], you will not die and she will return with you to your house, along with
Tob 6:1-8 great abundance."

165 [1]To put it briefly, this is what actually happened. [2]The boy kept the heart,
the gall-bladder and the liver, and ate the rest of the fish. [3]They set off and were
welcomed with exceeding joy by the old man. [4]After they received the money
in safekeeping and brought up the subject of a marriage contract, the old man
demurred, mainly out of fear about his marrying her.[c] [5]He showed them graves
of the seven men, but he was ultimately won over. [6]After performing the wedding rites and seeing him still alive, just as his travel companion had promised
him on the journey, he gave effusive thanks to God. [7]The old man gave her to
Tobias as his wife and half of his wealth and sent them on their way with great
joy. [8]And they returned, along with her and her maid-servant and servants and
Tobit 7–9 an immense sum of money.

166 [1]As they drew near to the house of Bit, the dog recognized the house.
[2]He ran ahead and entered the house and licked Bit's feet all around.[d] [3]When
he knew from him that his son had returned, he got up eagerly (p. 290) to meet
him. [4]Since he couldn't see, the old man stumbled this way and that against the
wall. [5]And the travel-companion said, "Take the gall-bladder of the fish, and
when you reach your father's door, anoint his eyes before embracing him, and
his vision will be immediately restored." [6]When this happened, and the old man
immediately had his sight restored, they stood for a long time in amazement,
Tobit 11 praising God for all the good things that had come their way. [7]They wanted the
fellow traveler, the one they believed to be a man for hire, to be compensated
generously, and were eagerly willing to give him half of the money they had
brought. [8]So the archangel of the Lord revealed himself to them and said, "I am
Raphael, one of the seven archangels who carry prayers of the righteous up to
God. I have neither eaten nor drunk, even if you yourselves believed I did. [9]You,
then, should always give thanks to the Lord and acknowledge him in gratitude."
Tobit 12 [10]And after saying these things, he was removed from their sight.

167 [1]*Concerning the prophet Daniel*: When Daniel the servant of God was
thrown into the lions' pit {...}. [2]Following the reign of other kings after Nebuchadnezzar, Daniel, the divinely inspired interpreter of their dreams, was favored by all of them. [3]The Babylonians, stirred by jealousy of him at that time,
as they had previously been when Darius, the son of Cyrus, was their king, told

---

a. Presumably referring to incense. Cf. Tob 6:16, according to which the angel instructed Tobias to chase away Asmodeus, by burning incense from ashes sprinkled with parts of the fish's liver and heart.

b. Vas. suggests some words have been omitted here.

c. According to the book of Tobit, Tobias and Raphael arrived in Ecbatana, and were greeted there by Raguel and his wife Edna. After Raphael left for Rages to obtain the money being held by Gabael, they both returned to Ecbatana for the marriage celebration. The *Palaea* collapses Gabael and Raguel into a single unnamed figure, described here only as a "powerful relative."

d. For this detail about the dog, lacking in the Greek text of *Tobit,* see also the Latin Vulgate version of Tob 11:8: "then the dog, who had been with them on the way ran on ahead, and as if bringing the news, showed his joy by fawning and by wagging his tail."

him, "Allow us to put Daniel to death, because he shattered our god Baal, slew
the sacred serpent and murdered our priests and enchanters. [4]But if you don't,
we shall kill you and your household for having favored a Jew."[a] [5]When the king
saw that they were bearing down on him forcefully, under pressure he delivered
Daniel over to them. [6]They cast him into the lions' pit, where he remained for
six days. The lions were there in the pit above. [7]And the archangel of the Lord
sealed their mouths, and they did not bother Daniel. [8]When the king came to
mourn for Daniel on that seventh day in the pit, he found the seals that he had
fixed were intact. [9]When he opened them, he saw Daniel standing upright, with
his hands outstretched, and saying, "Blessed is the God who sent your angel and
stopped up the mouths (p. 291) of the lions, who did not injure me." [10]Praising
God, the king then brought Daniel out of the pit unharmed. [11]Amazed at this
wonder, he made obeisance to him. [12]But the men who were accusing Daniel
he cast into the lions' pit. [13]They did not even reach the floor of the pit, before
the lions overpowered them, lapping up their blood and grinding down their
bones greedily. [14]And this man Daniel, as he was burning incense {…} and the
all-hallowed name of the archangel Michael displayed to us that he was named
Michael and a soldier from God. Dan 6:10-28; Bel 1–32

168 [1]*Concerning Habakkuk the prophet*: When Habakkuk the prophet was in
Judea, <he boiled pottage[b]> and sustained his reapers with bread, by going out
and bringing it to them. [2]An angel of the Lord seized Habakkuk by the crown
of his head and carried him by the gust of the wind and took him from Judea to
Babylon. [3]With the provision of lentils,[c] the angel brought him to the lions' pit,
where the seals had been loosened. [4]And Daniel, the servant of the Lord, ate.
[5]Michael, the same angel, again returned Habakkuk to his own place. He arrived
there within the hour, and while feeding his reapers as he had before, delivered
a meal to them in greater abundance.[d] Bel 1:33-42

169 [1]*Concerning the giving of the law:*[e] [Then the Lord said to Moses], "You
shall not make any idol nor shall you worship any likeness, [whatever things]
are in heaven above or on the earth below." [2]As for you, [O] Jew, why did you Exod 20:4
worship[f] the idol of Baal in the place of Peor? [3]You are allowed to eat from your Num 25:3; Ps
field and your vineyard and the produce [of] all your labors. [4]After six years, 105(106):28
on the seventh you will have a release, and let the poor eat the works of your
hands. [5]Everything brought into your house, let it be divided among the poor
and the needy of the orphans and widows, because in [six] days all the works are
collected, and there is a remission on the seventh. (p. 292) [6]Because of this, you

a. Lit.: "Juda." The narrative more closely aligns with Bel than with the parallel version in Daniel 6. According to Daniel 6, Daniel was cast into the pit because he violated a recently enacted decree prohibiting pleas or prayers to anyone other than the king himself. The king at the time was either Darius the Mede (Daniel 6) or Cyrus the Persian (Bel and the Dragon).

b. Emending with Bel 33.

c. For Daniel's diet of vegetables, see Dan 1:12.

d. The Greek text is difficult to understand here. For the story about Habakkuk's return to Judea in time to feed his reapers (lacking in Bel), see the pilgrimage report of Abbot Daniel, in Wilkinson, *Jerusalem Pilgrimage*, 149. According to Daniel, a chapel to the south of Bethlehem was the site of the field where Habakkuk fed his reapers.

e. On the purpose of this final chapter, see the Introduction.

f. Lit.: "why do you worship?"

shall bless the seventh year, which is called a "remission." [7]Anyone who does not keep this will be wiped out from the people. [8]But the one who keeps this, "I will give him a blessing and I will multiply his fruits and all his revenue in order that he might fulfill the year of release." [9]Whence, O Jew, do you have hope for the remission of transgressions? [10]Where do you have a scape-goat {…}[a] it writes as follows, "If someone falls into this transgression, take two goats to him, and you shall offer the one, and the other you shall lead away into the wilderness because it is called a scape-goat."

Exod 23:10-11; Lev 25:1-7; Deut 15:1-6; 31:1-13

Lev 16:10

a. The Greek text is corrupt here.

Quotations from Lost Books in the Hebrew Bible

A New Translation and Introduction, with an Excursus on Quotations from Lost Books in the New Testament

by James R. Davila

Quotations from and references to lost Old Testament pseudepigrapha—books attributed (probably fictionally) to biblical characters or set in the biblical period—appear in the Hebrew Bible itself. The biblical books refer not infrequently to lost song collections, historical chronicles, and priestly and prophetic works. This chapter collects all of these references. In addition, the New Testament quotes or alludes to a number of lost Old Testament pseudepigrapha, some of which have their own entries in these volumes. A brief excursus discusses these.

Contents

The quotations from the Hebrew Bible collected here are of otherwise lost literary works attributed to a biblical character or presented as having been written in the biblical period. I have limited the translated citations to those that I judge have a reasonable chance of once having existed as a separate source apart from the document that cites it, although in this introduction I do briefly note all potentially relevant citations in the Hebrew Bible. The fragments are quoted in the order of their appearance in the Bible, except that passages that refer, or may refer, to the same work are grouped together with the first appearance of the work. The Book of Numbers has a poetic quotation from the Book of the Wars of Yahweh, as well as quotations of two other poetic fragments that may come from the same source. First Samuel quotes a lament attributed to David which comes from the Book of the Righteous. Poetic fragments in Joshua and 1 Kings may come from the same source. In 1 Samuel there is also mention of a didactic work of guidance for kings which was attributed to the prophet Samuel. In 1-2 Kings we find a reference to sapiential and scientific observations of Solomon, the Book of the Acts of Solomon, and numerous citations of the Chronicles of the Kings of Israel and the Chronicles of the Kings of Judah, which seem to have been annalistic works with parallels in Mesopotamian literature. In 1-2 Chronicles there are numerous prophetic source citations, most of which probably came from a single compendium of a combination of the two annalistic works cited in 1-2 Kings, perhaps with some additions. The Chronicler also cites annalistic or genealogical and priestly sources attributed to the time of David and Solomon, as well as a collection of laments assigned to the prophet Jeremiah and others. Each of these lost documents is discussed briefly below.

Manuscripts and Versions

For the text of each of the quotations I have consulted the standard text of the Hebrew Bible (the Masoretic Text or MT) and the ancient Greek translation (the Septuagint or LXX). Unfortunately, none of the biblical manuscripts from Qumran preserve material from any of these passages. On rare occasions I cite other ancient translations when they offer a reading of particular interest.

The Texts

Lost Books Cited in the Pentateuch

There are three quotations of lost works in Numbers 21. The first is a truncated four-line poetic excerpt from the Book of the Wars of Yahweh, which excerpt contains some obscure geographical information. The context is the wandering of the Israelites near the border of Moab (21:10-13) after a conflict with the Canaanites (21:1-3) and the punishment of the Israelites with fiery serpents after their grumbling about their rations (21:4-9). The citation begins with "therefore," implying that the context of the quoted poetic fragment is the same as that of vv. 10-13. Not enough of the quoted poem survives for us to speculate usefully on its genre, but the title of the book implies that it was an epic recounting of battles fought by the Israelites.

The second quotation follows immediately after the first, reporting that in a place called "Beer" ("Well") "then Israel sang this song." The song itself is a work song that celebrates the digging of a well, and it may have been traditional for this purpose. No source is cited, but given its proximity to the quotation from the Book of the Wars of Yahweh, it is reasonable, if inconclusive, to assume that it came from this book as well.

The third quotation comes after the account of a devastating defeat of Sihon, king of the Amorites, by the Israelites (21:21-25). The account notes that Sihon had inflicted a similar defeat on an unnamed Moabite king (21:26), then introduces the quotation with "therefore the poets say" (21:27a). Remarkably, the quoted poem appears to be an Amorite victory song celebrating the defeat of the Moabites, quoted here to underline the accomplishment of the Israelites in vanquishing such a formidable foe as Sihon.[1] This song too may come from the Book of the Wars of Yahweh, but there is no way to be sure.

Lost Books Cited in the Deuteronomistic History

The Deuteronomistic History is the prose account of the history of Israel from the time of Joshua to the destruction of the kingdom of Judah (Joshua, Judges, 1-2 Samuel, 1-2 Kings, not including Ruth). This work was written by a single author or school much influenced by the Book of Deuteronomy. Several lost documents are quoted in it.

The Book of the Righteous (The Book of Jashar) or The Book of the Song

This book is quoted at least once, and perhaps two or three times in the Bible. The meaning of the adjective translated as "righteous" is uncertain in this context. Its basic meaning is "straight" and by extension "upright," "just," or "righteous." What or who is straight or righteous is unclear: perhaps either the heroic figures featured in it or the people of Israel as a whole, or even the God of Israel. The certain quotation is found in 2 Sam 1:17-18, which reports that the beautiful lament over the death of Saul and Jonathan attributed to David (1:19-27) comes from this book. The archaic language of the poem and its very specific subject matter are evidence that this could really be a piece of poetry from the hand of David himself.

Another archaic poetic passage is quoted in Joshua 10:12-13a and attributed in the Hebrew text to the Book of the Righteous. It is understood by the Deuteronomistic Historian

1. The classic biblical example of a victory song is Judges 5.

to describe a miracle in which God stopped the motion of the sun for a day to allow the Israelites to conquer their Amorite enemies (10:13b-14). It is likely, however, that this is a misunderstanding of the cryptic poetry, probably already ancient in the time of the Deuteronomistic Historian. The placement of the moon is important in these lines as well and the most plausible understanding of the fragment is that in it Joshua calls on the sun and moon to be aligned in the sky at the same time in an oppositional arrangement propitious for the Israelites to face battle (v. 12), and then we are told that this balance of the sun and the moon occurred and caused the Israelites to defeat their enemies (v. 13a). The Mesopotamian omen literature demonstrates that periods when the sun and moon stood in the sky together in opposition were regarded as either beneficial or harmful, depending on the day of the month on which this occurred.[2]

This is an important quotation from an early Hebrew poem, but unfortunately its derivation from the Book of the Righteous is not entirely certain, since the sentence "Is it not written in the Book of the Righteous?" is missing in the LXX. It is possible that this omission is inadvertent, but the context has nothing that would make it easy for a scribe accidentally to leave the phrase out (a "haplography") and there would be no motivation for a scribe deliberately to delete a source attribution. On the contrary, if there was no source attribution in the verse originally, it might have been very tempting for a scribe to add one, either because the scribe had genuine information about the source, the scribe had spurious information about the source, or even that the scribe made an educated guess that the source was the same as the piece of archaic poetry quoted in 2 Sam 1:17-27.

A third passage that may quote from the Book of the Righteous is found in 1 Kgs 8:12-13 in the MT, but after 8:53 in the LXX. It attributes a brief poetic passage to King Solomon, a passage that is better preserved in the LXX than in the MT. The LXX, but not the MT, concludes with the statement, "Behold, is this not written in the Book of the Song?" It has been pointed out that in Hebrew the word "song" contains the same three letters as the word "righteous," raising the distinct possibility that the Hebrew text behind this Greek sentence originally read "the Book of the Righteous" and was either miscopied before it reached the translator or was misread by the translator.[3] As with the quotation in Joshua, there is no haplographic trigger that would explain the loss of the source attribution in the MT and we must reckon with the possibility that this attribution too is a secondary addition that was found in the manuscript used by the LXX translator.

Minimally, we can say that the Book of the Righteous or the Book of the Song included poetic material that was ancient in the time of the Deuteronomistic Historian (perhaps the late seventh or the sixth century B.C.E.), including a funeral dirge that may well have come from the time and even the hand of David (tenth century B.C.E.).[4] If all three quotations come from this work, it apparently also contained battle poetry attributed to Joshua[5] which was archaic enough that its original meaning was not understood

2. Holladay, "The Day(s) the *Moon* Stood Still."

3. Contrawise, if the citation of the Book of the Righteous in Joshua 10:13 is secondarily dependent on 2 Sam 1:18, it is possible that the original name of the work was "the Book of the Song" and the title in 2 Samuel is the one with the error, which was copied by the scribe who inserted the reference into Joshua. The title the Book of the Song would be very appropriate for the surviving quotations.

4. See 2 Sam 3:33-34 for another funeral dirge.

5. There is too little of the poem for us to be sure of its genre, but it appears to be a victory song.

by the Deuteronomist. It also included a poem about the dedication of the Temple attributed to Solomon.[6]

A number of compositions in the Middle Ages and later have been published under the name of the Book of the Righteous (the Book of Jashar), but they have no connection with the original Book of the Righteous cited in the Hebrew Bible.[7]

A Book on the Conduct of the Kingship

In 1 Sam 8:1-22; 10:17-27; and 12:1-25 we read of the prophet Samuel's very reluctant acceptance of the new institution of kingship in Israel and of Saul as the first king. We are told in 10:25 that Samuel wrote a book on "the conduct of the kingship" which he deposited "before Yahweh," presumably in the sanctuary where the Ark of the Covenant was found. The Deuteronomistic Historian or one of the Deuteronomist's sources may have known or heard of a work attributed to Samuel concerning the kingship. If the book existed, something like its content may be reflected in 1 Sam 8:11-18; 12:6-15, as well as in the more constructive code of conduct in Deut 17:14-20.

The Sapiential Works of Solomon

The passage praising the wisdom of King Solomon in 1 Kgs 5:12-13 (Evv 4:32-33) may refer to lost literary and scientific works attributed to Solomon. There is no explicit reference to written documents; the text says that Solomon "spoke" numerous proverbs and songs and "spoke about" plant, animal, and aquatic life. These traditions may have been entirely oral, but we have other grounds for believing that the Deuteronomistic Historian had access to at least one written document attributed to Solomon with similar interests (see the next section), so it is reasonable to explore the possibility that some of the material referred to in this passage was written.

The reference to the sapiential works of Solomon comes in the paragraph in 5:9-14 (Evv 4:29-34) devoted to establishing that the wisdom that God granted to Solomon was all-surpassing and all-encompassing. It was greater than that of Egypt, whose reputation for wisdom stretches to dimmest antiquity and survives today. The identity of the "easterners" who were also surpassed by Solomon is less clear. The phrase *bene qedem* refers to tribes in the Syrian-Arabian desert (cf. Judg 6:3, 33) but the meaning may at times extend as far as Mesopotamia (cf. Gen 29:1).[8] Solomon was also wiser than several named sages. These four men, Ethan, Heman, Calcol, and Dara (Darda) appear in 1 Chr 2:6 as brothers (with a fifth brother, Zimri), sons of Zerah and grandsons of the patriarch Judah (cf. Gen 38:30). It may well be, however, that the Chronicler lifted the four names from our passage in 1 Kings and placed them here, treating the term Ezrahite and the name Zerah as the same name (probably erroneously—see below). It is thus significant that another list in Chronicles mentions Levitical musicians from the time of David named Ethan and Heman, kinsmen of Asaph (1 Chr 15:17, 19; cf. 6:42) and that the heading to Psalm 88 attributes the psalm to the Levitical sons of Korah, specifically to Heman the Ezrahite, and the heading to Psalm 89 names Ethan the Ezrahite. The meaning of the term "Ezrahite"

6. Again, too little of the poem remains for its genre to be certain, but it is certainly a royal song, and evidently one celebrating the founding of a sanctuary (cf. Psalm 132).

7. Christensen, "Jashar, Book of," 647.

8. The phrase could perhaps also mean the "ancients," that is, people of the distant past (cf., e.g., 2 Kgs 19:25). This meaning, however, is not attested elsewhere for the phrase *bene qedem* and in any case a geographical sense fits better here with the immediately following mention of Egypt.

is uncertain, but may indicate a pre-Israelite native inhabitant of the land of Canaan. The traditions about these men do not seem entirely consistent or coherent, but it is clear that they were remembered for their musical skill, one aspect of ancient wisdom.

Solomon's compositions are broken down into several categories. His reputation for proverbs is well illustrated by the late attribution of the entire book of Proverbs to him in Prov 1:1. More relevant is the note in Prov 25:1, which indicates that chapters 25–29 were proverbs of Solomon transcribed in the court of King Hezekiah. This verse suggests that written collections of Solomonic proverbs were known in the pre-exilic period. Solomon's connection with songs is best known by the ascription to him of the collection of love poems in the biblical Song of Songs. As noted above, a Temple-dedication song, perhaps part of the Book of the Righteous, is also assigned to him in 1 Kgs 8:53a (LXX). It seems unlikely that the Deuteronomist actually knew written documents containing three thousand proverbs or a thousand and five songs authored by Solomon (4:32). The numbers themselves look like general terms for an unspecified but very large number; compare *The Thousand and One Nights*. Nevertheless, some of them may have been written down.

The other Solomonic compositions involve the natural world, specifically, plants, animals, birds, "crawling things" (i.e., insects and reptiles), and fish or aquatic creatures. The use of living things for illustration in sapiential instruction is well known in the biblical tradition. See, for example, Jotham's fable of the trees in Judg 9:7-15; King Jehoash's fable of the thorn bush (2 Kgs 14:9-10); the sayings involving animals, crawling creatures, and birds in Prov 30:24-31; and the summary statement involving animals, birds, plants, and fish in Job 12:7-9. Such sayings may have been in mind in this verse. But the systematic listing of elements in the natural world suggests an additional possibility, not mutually exclusive with the first. A genre of wisdom literature called "onomastica" or "lists of nouns," known from ancient Egypt, consisted of long lists of related objects, including plants and animals. Onomastica evidence an early scientific interest in categorizing and classifying the diverse elements that make up reality. Not surprisingly, no examples of onomastica are preserved in the Hebrew Bible, but passages such as Job 38–39 and Psalm 148 may indicate familiarity with the genre. It is possible, then, that the Deuteronomist knew of Solomonic sayings involving nature, Solomonic onomastica focusing on the natural world, or both. These traditions could have been oral or written, but it seems more likely that onomastica would be transmitted in written form. We have no way of knowing whether Solomonic traditions known to the Deuteronomist, who lived centuries after the time of Solomon, were genuine or pseudepigraphic.[9]

The Book of the Acts of Solomon

The Book of the Acts[10] of Solomon is cited in 1 Kings 11:41 and we are told that it contained "the rest of the acts of Solomon and all that he did and his wisdom." This brief note is less

9. For additional discussion of this passage see Mulder, *1 Kings*, 198-205.

10. The word translated "acts" (except in "acts of covenant loyalty," where the whole phrase translates a different Hebrew word) can mean either "acts" or "words" according to context and its meaning is not always clear in the titles of the sources quoted here. Most of the time it clearly refers to the acts of this or that king, but the titles in 1-2 Chronicles which refer to prophets could usually be taken either to mean their acts or their words. I have generally assumed (in accordance with the discussion below) that the Chronicler was referring to the accounts of the careers of the prophets in the larger source on the kings of Israel and Judah and have translated the word as "acts." But in a few cases "words" seemed a more appropriate meaning and I have translated accordingly.

informative than we might wish, but it does imply that some of the material in 1 Kings 1–11 came from it, since the biblical text gives both an account of Solomon's deeds and accomplishments and illustrations of his wisdom (3:3-28; 5:9-14 [Evv 4:29-33]; 10:1-10, 23-25). It also indicates that the Book of the Acts of Solomon dealt with Solomon's wisdom as well as his deeds, which may imply that it was of a folkloric rather than, or as well as, of an annalistic nature.[11]

The Book of the Chronicles of the Kings of Israel

The Book of the Chronicles[12] of the Kings of Israel is cited eighteen times in 1-2 Kings. The structure of the passages that cite it is broadly consistent. They always begin with (a) "and the rest of the acts of (the king in question)...." The acts are sometimes filled out with vague phrases such as "and all that he did" or "and all his might" or more specific accomplishments or actions such as "and the ivory house that he built and all the cities that he built" (Ahab) or "and the conspiracy that he plotted" (Zimri, Shallum). Next (b) is an indication of the source, either "behold they are written in the Book of the Chronicles of the Kings of Israel" or "are they not written in the Book of the Chronicles of the Kings of Israel?" More information on the king may be added after this citation. We are then told (c) that the king slept with his fathers. Usually, but not always (d) his place of burial is given. Finally, (e) where relevant (i.e., when the dynasty was not overthrown in the king's generation and the king had a son), we are told that a named son succeeded the father on the throne.

The most natural reading of these citations would take them to say that at least some of the preceding material on the king in question is derived from this source and that the reader may go to the source to find additional information. This understanding is borne out by a close look at the contents of the citations in context. Some of the specific accomplishments and actions mentioned in the citations go over ground covered in the preceding section on the king: the conspiracies of Zimri and Shallum; Ahab's mighty warmaking (cf. 1 Kings 20); the conflict between Joash of Israel and Amaziah of Judah; and the recovery of Damascus and Hamath for Judah by Jeroboam II (Damascus is only mentioned in the citation, but its recovery is implied in 2 Kgs 14:25). But other specific details in the citations do not appear in the preceding material: the battles fought by Jeroboam I; the mighty acts of Baasha; and the ivory house and cities built by Ahab. This lost source thus clearly contained more information than is preserved in our books of 1-2 Kings.

The Book of the Chronicles of the Kings of Judah

The Book of the Chronicles of the Kings of Judah is cited fifteen times in 1-2 Kings. The citation format is similar but not identical to that of the Book of the Chronicles of the Kings of Israel. The citations begin with (a) "and the rest of the acts of" the king, again, sometimes expanded a little with the same bland additions and sometimes with a few

---

11. Liver argues that the Book of the Acts of Solomon was composed by a scribal sage in the reign of Solomon's son, Rehoboam ("The Book of the Acts of Solomon"). But he bases this conclusion on the assumption that he can determine which parts of 1 Kings 1–11 came from this source and he offers no genre parallels from cognate ancient Near Eastern writings to the document he claims to reconstruct. Given our lack of positive evidence for the contents of the Book of the Acts of Solomon, I do not believe that firm conclusions can be drawn about its contents or genre.

12. "Chronicles" is the generally accepted interpretive translation of the Hebrew phrase "the acts of the days."

substantive details such as "and the cities that he built" (Asa) or "and that he made the pool and conduit and he brought the water into the city" (Hezekiah). Then comes (b) the indication of the source, always "are they not written in the Book of the Chronicles of the Kings of Judah?" Notes with additional information about the king may come after the source citations. Then we are told (c) that he slept with his fathers. Usually (d) it is specified that he was buried in the city of David (i.e., Jerusalem), but there is no mention of Hezekiah's burial place; Manasseh and Amon are said to have been buried in a "garden of Uzza"; and Josiah's burial place is given as his tomb in Jerusalem. Finally, (e) it is always reported that the king was succeeded by a named son (the dynastic chain of the line of David was never broken during this period, although it came close).

Our evidence indicates that the nature of the Book of the Chronicles of the Kings of Judah was essentially the same as that of the Book of the Chronicles of the Kings of Israel. Some elements in the citations repeat ground covered in the preceding passage on the king, such as the cities that Asa built and the sin that Manasseh committed. Other elements are not found in the preceding passage, including the might shown by Jehoshaphat and the building projects of Hezekiah. Again, the author of 1-2 Kings seems to have used this work as a source but did not include all of the information that was in it.

Our positive evidence for the contents of these two books is limited and this fact in turn limits our ability to locate their genre. But they narrated the deeds of the kings, their military conflicts, regicidal plots against some of them, and their building projects.[13] The Chronicle of the Kings of Judah evidently also made reference to sins of Manasseh. Unfortunately, no royal annals from kingdoms that spoke cognate Northwest Semitic dialects and languages (such as Moab, Ammon, Edom, and Syria/Aram) survive, but the Mesopotamian annalistic tradition does offer points of comparison.[14] The best parallel to these sources in 1-2 Kings is found in the Chronicle of the Kassite Kings, a copy of which survives from the Late Babylonian Period, but this may be part of a Babylonian copy of the Assyrian Synchronistic Chronicle, three copies of which survive from the seventh century B.C.E. The Chronicle of the Kassite Kings deals with the much earlier conflicts between Assyria and the Kassite dynasty of Babylon in the fourteenth and thirteenth centuries B.C.E. This Chronicle describes royal military conflicts, regicidal plots, and royal building

13. Bin-Nun argues in "Formulas from Royal Records" on the basis of internal evidence in 1-2 Kings that the writer used a different source for the information on the kings of Israel and the kings of Judah, which supports the understanding of the Chronicles of the Kings of Israel and the Chronicles of the Kings of Judah as two separate books. She also concludes that the Deuteronomistic Historian made use of king lists for Israel and Judah.

14. It should be noted, however, that some of the surviving Northwest Semitic royal inscriptions inscribed on stone do show a similar range of interests. The Mesha Stele, written in a Moabite dialect similar to biblical Hebrew and dating to the second half of the ninth century B.C.E., deals with King Mesha's military campaigns and his building projects. He attributes past oppression by Israel to the anger of the Moabite national god Chemosh, and his own military successes to the favor of Chemosh. The stele of Bir Rakib about his father Panamuwa, erected around 730 B.C.E., gives an account in an Aramaic dialect (Samalian) of the coup in which Panamuwa's father and brothers were killed and how Panamuwa restored the dynasty because the gods looked favorably on his right conduct. A stele erected by King Zakkur of Hamath contains an Aramaic royal inscription from about 800 B.C.E. in which Zakkur reports that during a siege of his city "prophets and seers" assured him (correctly in the event) that the city would be delivered from the siege. The stele also lists some of Zakkur's building projects. (See Parker, *Stories in Scripture and Inscription*, 44-58, 83-89, 106-12.) It may be that some of the conventions of the lost chronicles of the Northwest Semitic kingdoms are preserved indirectly in these inscriptions as well as in the brief notices of the contents of the sources of 1-2 Kings.

projects, and it also offers theological reflections on royal sin and divine punishment.[15] It seems likely that the Chronicle of the Kings of Israel and the Chronicle of the Kings of Judah were annalistic works similar to the Chronicle of the Kassite Kings.[16]

Lost Books Cited in 1-2 Chronicles[17]

The Book of 1-2 Chronicles is a retelling of the history of the world from Adam to the decree of Cyrus that ended the Babylonian Exile. The first nine chapters cover the period from Adam to the career of Saul in the form of genealogies and very brief notes. The rest of the work is an annalistic account of the history of Israel from the reign of Saul to the Exile. It draws on genealogical material in the Pentateuch and narrative material in 1-2 Samuel and 1-2 Kings. The date of 1-2 Chronicles is debated, with most dating it to somewhere in the fourth century B.C.E or a little earlier or later. The Chronicler cites The Book of the Kings of Israel and Judah three times; the nearly identical title The Book of the Kings of Judah and Israel four times; the Book of the Kings of Israel twice; and the Midrash of the Book of the Kings and the Acts of the Kings of Israel once each.[18] Each of these is always cited exactly in the place that corresponds to a source citation in a passage in 1-2 Kings (either of the Book of the Chronicles of the Kings of Israel or the Book of the Chronicles of the Kings of Judah), raising the suspicion for some that the Chronicler is simply making up sources to give an appearance of verisimilitude. Moreover, the Chronicler rarely cites the Pentateuch (see below) and never cites the Deuteronomistic History, although both works were central sources for 1-2 Chronicles. But the Chronicler does present information not found elsewhere in the Bible and at least some of it has been shown to be historically accurate,[19] so it seems unduly pessimistic to assume that the lost sources cited in 1-2 Chronicles are imaginary. That said, the similarity to the titles of the lost sources in 1-2 Kings is suggestive and it seems probable that, first, these several sources cited by the Chronicler represent a single work and, second, that this work is a digest of the two separate documents used by the Deuteronomistic Historian in 1-2 Kings.

A number of other sources are associated with (usually) named prophets, seers, and visionaries: the Acts of Samuel the Seer, the Acts of Nathan the Prophet (listed twice), the Acts of Gad the Visionary, the Prophecy of Ahijah the Shilonite, the Visions of Jeddo the Visionary Concerning Jeroboam Son of Nebat; the Acts of Shemaiah the Prophet and Iddo the Visionary for Enrollment by Genealogy, the Midrash of the Prophet Iddo, the Acts of Uzziah that Isaiah the son of Amoz wrote, and the Words of the Visionaries. All of these prophets are known from 1-2 Kings, except for the prophet Jeddo/Iddo, who appears only in Chronicles. It is tempting to assume that each of these represents a separate source, perhaps a collection of prophetic oracles like those in the biblical prophetic books, but three considerations argue against this. First, all of these sources are said to cover the acts

15. Glassner, *Mesopotamian Chronicles*, 278-81.

16. If we are correct in deducing (see below) that the Chronicler's main source was a digest of these two works, the careers of a number of prophets may have figured in them as well, just as in the books of 1-2 Kings. This aspect is not paralleled in the Chronicle of the Kassite Kings, but unnamed prophets and seers figure in the Zakkur inscription (see n. 14 above). But it is also possible that the Chronicler's digest incorporated material from other sources as well.

17. For useful discussions of the surviving and lost sources of the Chronicler, see Japhet, *I & II Chronicles*, 14-23, and Knoppers, *I Chronicles 1–9*, 66-71, 118-28.

18. If we read with the LXX of 1 Chr 9:1, the Book of the Kings of Israel and Judah is cited four times and the Book of the Kings of Israel once.

19. Vaughn, *Theology, History, and Archaeology*.

of the reign of a particular king rather than the words of the prophet in question. Second, these prophetic sources are almost never cited alongside one of the general sources on the reigns of the kings. The only exception is the Words (or Acts) of the Visionaries (or perhaps the name "Hozai"), which is cited for the reign of Manasseh immediately after the Acts of the Kings of Israel (2 Chr 33:18). Third, two references to prophetic sources, "the Words (or Acts) of Jehu son of Hanani" (2 Chr 20:34) and "the Vision of Isaiah Son of Amoz the Prophet" (2 Chr 32:32) are explicitly said to be embedded in, respectively, the Book of the Kings of Israel and the Book of the Chronicles of Judah and Israel.[20] These factors make it likely that many or all of the prophetic sources are actually passages from the Book of the Kings of Israel and Judah, cited by their main content, a format known from elsewhere in antiquity.[21]

So our evidence indicates that most of the Chronicler's citations go back to a single comprehensive source on the Divided Monarchy rather than to the initially apparent multiplicity of sources. Nevertheless, some of the Chronicler's other citations seem to refer to additional sources. There are several set in the time of the united monarchy: the Book of the Chronicles of King David, of which we are told simply that partial census data gathered by Joab was not entered into it; King David's plan for the Temple, apparently revealed to him by God; and writings by David and Solomon pertaining to the divisions into which the Levites were grouped. All that we know about the Book of the Chronicles of King David is that one might plausibly have found census information in it. Such records could conceivably have survived to the Chronicler's time or, perhaps more likely, could have been reconstructed or concocted by that time. The Chronicler's insistence that David made extensive preparations for the Temple and handed them over to Solomon does not seem particularly historically plausible given the confusion over the succession indicated in 1 Kings 1–2. We have no way of knowing how ancient the organization of the clerical functionaries in the Jerusalem Temple was, but we should take the Chronicler's picture of one fully formed in all its details during the United Monarchy with at least a grain of salt. Nevertheless, it is entirely plausible that the priests and Levites of the Chronicler's time had written records about such matters which they attributed pseudepigraphically to David and Solomon and that the Chronicler consulted these records.

The one remaining source is the Laments over the fallen King Josiah, which were composed by Jeremiah (presumably the prophet) and unnamed male and female singers and which seem to have formed a standard liturgy in the Chronicler's time. These laments are clearly not to be identified with the biblical Book of Lamentations, since the latter are not about King Josiah. But there is no reason to doubt that such laments existed and that some of them were attributed to Jeremiah.[22]

Other Sources Cited in the Hebrew Bible

It is worth noting some other written sources mentioned in the Hebrew Bible but not translated here, because they dealt with day-to-day matters and thus were not, strictly

20. It should be noted, however, that the LXX of 2 Chr 32:32 makes the Vision of Isaiah a separate source from the Book of the Kings of Judah and Israel.

21. For example, Exodus 3 is cited in Mark 12:26 as "in the Book of Moses about the bush" and in Rom 11:2 Paul cites 1 Kings 19 as "what the scripture says of Elijah."

22. For the intriguing possibility that the prayer of Manasseh contained in the Acts of the Kings of Israel according to 2 Chr 22:18 has been partially preserved among the Dead Sea Scrolls in 4Q381 frag. 33, lines 8-11, see Schniedewind, "A Qumran Fragment."

speaking, literary works, or they are quoted in full and are thus not lost, or they are likely to be a composition by a biblical author rather than having existed previously on their own, or because the quotation may be from a surviving biblical book, or some combination of these reasons.

Numerous letters are quoted in the Hebrew Bible. These include the letter of David to Joab (2 Sam 11:14-15); the letters of Jezebel to the elders and nobles of Naboth's city (1 Kgs 21:8-10); the letter of the king of the Syrians to the King of Israel regarding Naaman (2 Kgs 5:5-7); the letters of Jehu to the rulers of Samaria (2 Kgs 10:1-3, 6); the letter of the King of Assyria to Hezekiah (2 Kgs 19:14//Isa 37:14; 2 Chr 32:17); the letters of the Babylonian king Merodoch-baladan to Hezekiah (2 Kgs 20:12//Isa 39:1); the letter of Jeremiah to the elders of the exiles and to the priests (Jer 29:1-23); the letters of Shemaiah to the people in Jerusalem and the priests (Jer 29:24-28); the letters of Ahasuerus proclaiming husbandly authority (Est 1:22); the letters of Haman against the Jews (Est 3:12-15; 4:8); letters of Mordecai in defense of the Jews (Est 8:5, 9-14); the letters of Mordecai and Esther establishing the holiday of Purim (Est 9:20-22, 27, 32); royal correspondence about the Jewish exiles in the Book of Ezra (Ezra 4:6, 7-16, 17-22; 5:6-17; 6:2b-12; 7:11-26); the letter of Sanballat to Nehemiah (Neh 6:5-7); the letter of Huram, king of Tyre, to Solomon (2 Chr 2:11-16); and a letter from the prophet Elijah to King Jeroboam (2 Chr 21:12-15).[23]

Other documents are mentioned as well. The Book of the Generations of Adam, cited in Gen 5:1, seems to be quoted in full and is probably a composition of the priestly writer, albeit based on earlier source material. In Exod 17:14 Yahweh has Moses write a book commemorating the annihilation of the Amalekites. In Josh 18:4, 8-10, a group of men from seven tribes of Israel wrote an account of the portion of the Land of Canaan that remained to be conquered at that point. In Josh 24:26, Joshua wrote an account of the renewed covenant at Shechem in the Book of the Law of God (see below). Three books containing prophetic oracles of Jeremiah are mentioned in the Book of Jeremiah. He gave one of these to his scribal assistant Baruch to read before King Jehoiakim, but the king destroyed it. Nevertheless, Jeremiah dictated its substance again and this new scroll may form part of the surviving Book of Jeremiah (Jer 36:1-28). The second book seems to consist of Jer 45:1-5, which was dictated to Baruch by Jeremiah. The third book had to do with "all the evil that is to come upon Babylon" and Baruch, at Jeremiah's behest, threw it into the Euphrates River (Jer 51:59-64).[24] But its contents may be preserved in Jer 50:1–51:58. The Book of Esther mentions the Book of the Chronicles (of the Kings of Media and Persia) in Est 2:23; 6:1-2; 10:2. Although the Persian Empire surely did keep royal chronicles (cf. Ezra 5:17–6:1), it is very doubtful that the author of Esther actually had access to them or that Mordecai figured in them. The Book of Nehemiah cites a work called the Book of Chronicles, of which it says, "The sons of Levi, the heads of the fathers, are written in the Book of Chronicles, even up to the days of Johanan son of Eliashib"[25] (Neh 12:23). The names of the Levites in Neh 12:24-25 were probably taken from the source cited in v. 23. Genealogical material had been preserved through the Exile,[26] so this source is not necessarily our 1-2 Chronicles, which does, however, contain much the same information in 1 Chr 9:14-17.

23. The letters found in the Hebrew Bible are discussed by Pardee et al. in *Handbook*, 169-82.

24. Jeremiah 25:11, 12 and 29:10 are also alluded to in Dan 9:2.

25. Eliashib was high priest in the time of Nehemiah (Neh 3:1). Johanan was actually his grandson (the word "son" in Hebrew can also mean "grandson"). See Neh 12:1, 10-11 for the high-priestly genealogy for this period.

26. Cf. Ezra 2:62//Neh 7:64.

In addition there are numerous references to a written Law of Moses:[27] Josh 1:7-8; 8:31 (cf. vv. 32-35); 23:6; 24:26a; 1 Kgs 2:3; 2 Kgs 14:6; 21:8; Mal 3:22 [Evv 4:4]; Dan 9:11, 13; Ezra 3:2; 6:18; 7:6; Neh 1:8-9; 2 Chr 17:9. A Book of the Law was reportedly discovered in the Temple in Jerusalem in Josiah's time (2 Kgs 22–23//2 Chr 23:18; 25:4), and Ezra read a Book of the Law to the returned exiles in Jerusalem (Nehemiah 8:1-18; 13:1). When some indication of the content of the Book of the Law is given, it usually corresponds to something in our Pentateuch, but the citation in Ezra 6:18 has to do with the priestly divisions and the Levitical courses, which are not mentioned in the Pentateuch. Likewise, the words attributed to God speaking to Moses in Neh 1:8-9 are not found in the Pentateuch, although the writer may be paraphrasing Deut 30:1-5. It is generally agreed that Josiah's Book of the Law had some connection with the Book of Deuteronomy. The exact relationship of Ezra's Book of the Law to our Pentateuch remains unclear. The Pentateuch went through a long and complicated editing process and differing sources and recensions were probably available to different biblical writers at different times.

Finally, there are a number of biblical passages that give the impression of being incorporated into their current position from an earlier context, although this is not explicitly stated. Many of these passages display archaic linguistic features or a discontinuity with their current context or both. They include: the Testament of Jacob (Gen 49:1-27); the Song of the Sea (Exod 15:1-18); the Song of the Ark (Num 10:35-36);[28] the Oracles of Balaam (Num 23:7-10, 18-24; 23:3-9, 15-19, 20-24); the Song of Moses (Deut 32:1-43); the Blessing of Moses (Deut 33:2-29); the Song of Deborah (Judg 5:1-30); the Song of Hannah (1 Sam 2:1-10); and the archaic poem in Habakkuk 3:1-16.

Bibliography

Bin-Nun, Shoshana R. "Formulas from Royal Records of Israel and of Judah." *VT* 18 (1968): 414-32.

Christensen, Duane L. "Chronicles of the Kings (Israel/Judah), Book of the." *ABD* 1:991-92.

__________. "Jashar, Book of." *ABD* 3:646-47.

__________. "Num 21:14-15 and the Book of the Wars of the Lord." *CBQ* 36 (1974): 359-60.

__________. "Wars of the Lord: Book of the." *ABD* 6:880.

Glassner, Jean-Jacques. *Mesopotamian Chronicles.* SBLWAW 19. Atlanta, Ga.: Society of Biblical Literature, 2004.

Hanson, Paul D. "The Song of Heshbon and David's *Nîr.*" *HTR* 61 (1968): 297-320.

Holladay, John S., Jr. "The Day(s) the *Moon* Stood Still." *JBL* 87 (1968): 166-78.

Japhet, Sarah. *I & II Chronicles.* OTL. London: SCM, 1993.

Knoppers, Gary N. *I Chronicles 1–9.* AB 12. Garden City, N.Y.: Doubleday, 2003.

Kraft, C. F. "Books, Referred to." *IDB* 1:453-54.

Liver, J. "The Book of the Acts of Solomon." *Bib* 48 (1967): 75-101.

Maisler, B. "Ancient Israelite Historiography." *IEJ* 2 (1952): 82-88.

Milgrom, Jacob. *Numbers.* JPS Torah Commentary. Philadelphia, Pa.: Jewish Publications Society, 1990.

---

27. Cf. the Book of the Covenant in Exod 24:7; and references to a written Law in Deut 17:18-19; and the Law of the Lord in 2 Kgs 10:31; 17:13; 1 Chr 16:40; and 2 Chr 12:1; 17:9.

28. A medieval Jewish tradition claims that the Song of the Ark is quoted from the *Prophecy of Eldad and Modad* (see Bauckham, "Eldad and Modad" in this volume).

Mulder, Martin J. *1 Kings*, Volume 1: *1 Kings 1–11*. Historical Commentary on the Old Testament; Leuven: Peters, 1998.

Pardee, Dennis, et al. *Handbook of Ancient Hebrew Letters*. SBLSBS 15. Chico, Calif.: Scholars Press, 1982.

Parker, Simon B. *Stories in Scripture and Inscriptions: Comparative Studies on Narratives in Northwest Semitic Inscriptions and the Hebrew Bible*. Oxford: Oxford University Press, 1997.

Schniedewind, William M. "A Qumran Fragment of the Ancient 'Prayer of Manasseh'?" *ZAW* 108 (1996): 105-7.

__________. "The Source Citations of Manasseh: King Manasseh in History and Homily." *VT* 41 (1991): 450-61.

Vaughn, Andrew G. *Theology, History, and Archaeology in the Chronicler's Account of Hezekiah*. SBLABS 4. Atlanta, Ga.: Scholars Press, 1999.

Excursus: Quotations from Lost Books in the New Testament

A number of Old Testament pseudepigrapha are quoted or alluded to in the New Testament. The best-known such quotation is a passage from the Book of the Watchers (*1 Enoch* 1:9) which is quoted in Jude 14-15 as a prophecy of the biblical patriarch Enoch.[29] The Book of the Watchers survives complete in an Ethiopic translation and a Greek translation, and fragments of it in Aramaic were found among the Dead Sea Scrolls. Awareness of Enochic traditions may also be reflected in 1 Peter 3:19.[30] There is a reference to opponents of Moses named Jannes and Jambres in 2 Tim 3:8. A *Book of Jannes and Jambres* is attested in two poorly preserved Greek manuscripts as well as other quotations and allusions.[31] Neither of these pseudepigrapha, therefore, count as lost.[32] But as many as three other Old Testament pseudepigrapha may be quoted in the New Testament, all three arguably lost apart from quotation fragments.

The Apocalypse or Apocryphon of Elijah?

Paul quotes a passage in 1 Cor 2:9 using the rubric "it is written," which is normally used of scriptural citations, but the passage does not appear in the Old Testament. The third-century church father Origen attributes it to the *Apocryphon of Elijah* and in the late fourth or early fifth century Jerome reports that it is found in both the *Apocalypse of Elijah* and the *Ascension of Isaiah*.[33] The passage is also found elsewhere, including in the Coptic *Gospel of Thomas* 17, and was a free-floating saying used in numerous works.[34] In addition a text is quoted in Eph 5:14 with the rubric "therefore it is said," which may be used for a scriptural quotation in Eph 4:8.[35] In the third century Hippolytus assigns the quote in Eph 5:14 to Isaiah; in the fourth century, Epiphanius attributes it to Elijah; and George Syncel-

29. See Bauckham, *Jude and the Relatives of Jesus*, 137-41, 191-201, 210-18, 225, 288-90.

30. Achtemeier, *1 Peter*, 242, 252-62.

31. For translations of the surviving material from the *Book of Jannes and Jambres*, see Pietersma and Lutz, "Jannes and Jambres."

32. Quotations of Greek philosophers are also found in Acts 17:28 and Titus 1:12, but these are not Old Testament pseudepigrapha and do not concern us here.

33. The quotation is found in the surviving Latin and Greek fragments of the Ascension of Isaiah, and appears also as "an insignificant variant" in the Slavonic. See Stone and Strugnell, *The Books of Elijah*, 44-45.

34. Stone and Strugnell, *The Books of Elijah*, 41-73.

35. The quotation in Eph 4:8 is based on Ps 68:18, but it has alterations consistent with mystical traditions about an ascent to heaven by Moses and appears in a similar but not identical form in the *Targum to the Psalms* on this verse. This quotation may also be of a lost pseudepigraphon, but we have no other information on it. See Lincoln, *Ephesians*, 242-44.

lus (died after 810) assigns it to the *Apocrypha of Jeremiah*.[36] The New Testament writers may have quoted the passages from one of these lost pseudepigrapha.[37]

The Book of Eldad and Modad?

In James 4:5 an odd quotation is introduced with the rubric "the scripture says," but the quote itself does not appear in the Old Testament. The Greek quotation itself is very difficult and there is no consensus on its meaning. A straightforward translation would be "the spirit that dwells in us longs for envy," but this hardly makes sense. Bauckham has made the intriguing suggestion that the Greek is a mistranslation of a Hebrew original that read "the spirit that dwells in us abhors envy." He further notes that this statement fits the context of the story of Eldad and Modad in Num 11:25-29 and that there is a quotation from an apocryphal Book of Eldad and Modad in the *Shepherd of Hermas* (*Herm. Vis.* 2:3:4), a text that shares a number of other interesting parallels with the quotation in James. We have seen above that there is independent evidence for a Hebrew *Book of Eldad and Modad* and it is possible that the quotation in James is a Greek translation from that work.[38]

The Assumption or Testament of Moses

In Jude 9 we read a laconic account of a conflict between the archangel Michael and the devil over the body of Moses. This story does not appear in the Old Testament, but a number of later writers report that it comes from a work entitled either the *Assumption of Moses* or the *Testament of Moses*. Bauckham has collected all the surviving references to these works and has concluded that Jude knew a Jewish *Testament of Moses*, a substantial part of which also survives in an untitled Latin manuscript of a work about Moses. The *Assumption of Moses* was a later Christian work with gnosticizing tendencies, perhaps a reworking of the Testament.[39] I have argued that the Latin Moses fragment is a different work from either the Testament of Moses (which Jude quotes) or the Assumption of Moses.[40] If so, Jude's quotation is from a lost pseudepigraphon.

Bibliography

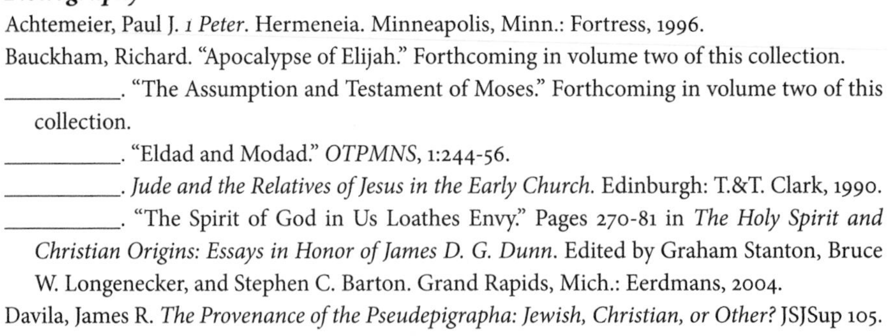

Achtemeier, Paul J. *1 Peter*. Hermeneia. Minneapolis, Minn.: Fortress, 1996.

Bauckham, Richard. "Apocalypse of Elijah." Forthcoming in volume two of this collection.

__________. "The Assumption and Testament of Moses." Forthcoming in volume two of this collection.

__________. "Eldad and Modad." *OTPMNS*, 1:244-56.

__________. *Jude and the Relatives of Jesus in the Early Church*. Edinburgh: T.&T. Clark, 1990.

__________. "The Spirit of God in Us Loathes Envy." Pages 270-81 in *The Holy Spirit and Christian Origins: Essays in Honor of James D. G. Dunn*. Edited by Graham Stanton, Bruce W. Longenecker, and Stephen C. Barton. Grand Rapids, Mich.: Eerdmans, 2004.

Davila, James R. *The Provenance of the Pseudepigrapha: Jewish, Christian, or Other?* JSJSup 105. Leiden: Brill, 2005.

36. Stone and Strugnell, *The Books of Elijah*, 75-81.

37. The fragments of the *Apocalypse of Elijah* will be covered by Bauckham in "Apocalypse of Elijah."

38. Bauckham, "The Spirit of God in Us Loathes Envy" and "Eldad and Modad," in this volume.

39. Bauckham, *Jude and the Relatives of Jesus*, 235-80. Bauckham has also collected the quotations of and allusions to the *Assumption* and *Testament of Moses* in "Assumption and Testament of Moses."

40. Davila, *Provenance of the Pseudepigrapha*, 149-54. The Latin Moses fragment is translated by Priest in "Testament of Moses."

Lieman, Sid Z. "The Inverted *Nuns* at Numbers 10:35-36 and the Book of Eldad and Medad." *JBL* 93 (1974): 348-55.
Lincoln, Andrew T. *Ephesians*. WBC 42. Dallas, Tex.: Word, 1990.
Pietersma, A. *The Apocryphon of Jannes and Jambres the Magicians: P. Chester Beatty XVI (with new editions of Papyrus Vindobonensis Greek inv. 29456+29828 verso and British Library Cotton Tiberius B. v f. 87)*. Religions in the Graeco-Roman World 119. Leiden: Brill, 1994.
Pietersma, A., and T. R. Lutz. "Jannes and Jambres." *OTP*, 2:427-42.
Priest, J. "Testament of Moses." *OTP*, 1:919-34.
Stone, Michael, and John Strugnell. *The Books of Elijah Parts 1-2*. SBLTT 18/SBLPS 8. Missoula, Mont.: Scholars Press, 1979.

Quotations from Lost Books in the Hebrew Bible

The Book of the Wars of Yahweh

[14]Therefore it is said in the Book of the Wars of Yahweh:

Waheb in Suphah and the seasonal streams,
the Arnon [15]and the base of the seasonal streams,
which extends to the seat of Ar
and leans toward the territory of Moab.[a]

[16]And from there to Beer.[b] It is the Beer where Yahweh said to Moses, "Gather
Num 21:4-9 the people that I may give them water." [17]Then Israel sang this song:[c]

"Rise, O well—you all sing to it!
[18]The well the princes dug,
which the nobles dug,
with scepter,
with their staves." (Num 21:14-18a)

Excerpt from an Amorite victory song

[27]Therefore the poets say:[d]

Enter Heshbon, let it be built,
let the city of Sihon be founded.
[28]For fire came out of Heshbon,
flame from the town of Sihon.
It consumed Ar of Moab,
swallowed[e] the high places of the Arnon.
[29]Woe to you, Moab;

---

a. The quotation appears to consist of these two poetic couplets. The context is the description of the movements of the Israelites in the wilderness before the conquest of Canaan. The words "Waheb" and "Suphah" appear to be place names, but are not otherwise known. The Arnon is the river that marks the border between Israel and Moab to the east of the Dead Sea. Ar seems to have been a city near the Arnon. My translation of this passage is sparing of emendations, but Christiansen offers a not implausible reconstruction making freer use of them in "Num 21:14-15."

b. The meaning of "Beer" is "well."

c. It is uncertain whether the quoted song was also found in the Book of the Wars of Yahweh, but the proximity of this quotation to the previous one leaves this as a distinct possibility.

d. This seems to be an ancient poem that was not well understood by either the Masoretic vocalizers or the Greek translator. I have at times translated the consonantal Hebrew text differently from either.

e. "swallowed" LXX; "the masters of" MT

You have perished, people of Chemosh!
He has made his children into refugees,
put his daughters into captivity,
to the Amorite king, Sihon.
Their yoke has perished
from Heshbon as far as Dibon.
30It is devastated as far as Nophah.
which is as far as Medeba.[a] (Num 21:27-30)

The Book of the Righteous (Book of Jashar)

12Then Joshua spoke to Yahweh on the day Yahweh gave over the Amorite before
the children of Israel, and he said before the eyes of Israel,
"Sun, be still in Gibeon,
and moon, in the Valley of Aijalon." Hab 3:11
13And the sun was still
and the moon stood
until the nation avenged itself on its enemies.
Is it not written in the Book of the Righteous?[b] (Josh 10:12-13a)

17Then David composed this lament for Saul and for Jonathan his son. 18And he
determined to teach it to the sons of Judah (for the use of the) bow.[c] Behold, it is
written in the Book of the Righteous.
19Is the gazelle of Israel
slain on your high places?[d]
How the warriors have fallen!
20Do not tell it in Gath!
Do not proclaim it in the streets of Ashkelon!
Lest the daughters of the Philistines rejoice.
Lest the daughters of the uncircumcised triumph.
21O mountains of Gilboa,
let there be no dew and no rain upon you
nor groundswells of the deep.[e]
For there the shield of warriors was polluted;
the shield of Saul, not anointed with oil.
22From the blood of the slain,
from the fat of warriors,
the bow of Jonathan did not turn back,
and the sword of Saul did not return empty.

---

a. "Medeba" MT; "Moab" LXX. The last two lines of the poem seem to be corrupt and their meaning is very uncertain.

b. "Is it not ... Righteous?" MT; omit LXX

c. "bow" MT; omit LXX

d. "Is the gazelle ... slain?" MT; "Set up a monument, Israel, over those who died on your high places, wounded" LXX. The MT gives the more likely text.

e. "groundswells of the deep"; emending the Hebrew text, which reads "fields of offerings," to a graphically similar and contextually more appropriate phrase found in Ugaritic. See A. A. Anderson, 2 *Samuel* (WBC 11; Dallas, Tex.: Word, 1989), 18.

[23]Saul and Jonathan,
beloved and pleasant;
in their life and in their death
they were not parted.
They were faster than eagles,
they were mightier than lions.
[24]Daughters of Israel, weep for Saul,
who clothed you in luxurious scarlet,
who put decoration of gold on your clothing.
[25]How the warriors have fallen,
Jonathan in the midst of the battle,
slain on your high places.
[26]I am troubled over you, my brother;
Jonathan, you were very pleasant to me.
more wonderful was your love to me
than the love of women.
[27]How the warriors have fallen
and the implements of war have been destroyed! (2 Sam 1:17-27)

[12]Then Solomon said,
"Yahweh has placed the sun in the heavens[a]
(yet) He said He would tabernacle in deep darkness.
[13]Surely I have built an abode for You;
a foundation for You to stay in forever."
Behold, is this not written in the Book of the Song?[b]
(1 Kgs 8:12-13 MT//1 Kgs 8:53a LXX)

A book on the conduct of the kingship

And Samuel spoke to the people the conduct of the kingship and he wrote it in a book and he placed it before Yahweh. And Samuel sent away all the people, each to his home. (1 Sam 10:25)

The sapiential works of Solomon

[9]And God[c] gave very much wisdom and understanding to Solomon, and breadth of mind like the sand that is on the seashore. [10]And the wisdom of[d] Solomon was greater than the wisdom of all the easterners[e] and all the wisdom[f] of Egypt. [11]And he was wiser than anyone—than Ethan the Ezrahite, and Heman and Cal-

---

a. "Yahweh has placed (another reading is 'made known') the sun in the heavens" LXX 1 Kgs 8:53a; omit MT

b. "Behold ... Song" LXX; omit MT. The Hebrew words for "righteous" or "upright" and "song" are written with the same three consonants in a different order and it is possible that the LXX has misread the title of the book and it should be "The Book of the Righteous."

c. "God" MT; "the Lord" LXX

d. "the wisdom of" MT; omit LXX

e. Or, less likely, "the ancients." See the Introduction, p. 676 n. 8.

f. "the wisdom" MT; "the sages" LXX

col and Darda the dance masters,[a] and his fame was among the surrounding nations.[b] 12And Solomon spoke three thousand proverbs and his songs[c] were a thousand and five.[d] 13And he spoke about the trees,[e] from the cedar that is in Lebanon to the hyssop that emerges from the wall. And he spoke about animals and birds and crawling creatures and fish. 14And there came some from all the peoples[f] to hear the wisdom of Solomon, from[g] all the kings of the earth who had heard of his wisdom. (1 Kgs 5:9-14 [Evv 4:29-34])

1 Chr 2:6; 6:42; 15:17, 19; Pss 88:1, 89:1

The Book of the Acts of Solomon

And the rest of the acts of Solomon and all that he did and his wisdom, are they not written in the Book of the Acts of Solomon? (1 Kgs 11:41)[h]

The Book of the Chronicles of the Kings of Israel

And the rest of the acts of Jeroboam that he fought and which he carried out as king, behold they are written in the Book of the Chronicles of the Kings of Israel. (1 Kgs 14:19)[i]

And the rest of the acts of Nadab and all that he did, are they not written in the Book of the Chronicles of the Kings of Israel? (1 Kgs 15:31)[j]

And the rest of the acts of Baasha and that which[k] he did and his mighty acts,[l] are they not written in the Book of the Chronicles of the Kings of Israel? (1 Kgs 16:5)[m]

And the rest of the acts of Elah and all that he did, are they not written in the Book of the Chronicles of the Kings of Israel? (1 Kgs 16:14)[n]

And the rest of the acts of Zimri, and his conspiracy that he plotted, are they not written in the Book of the Chronicles of the Kings of Israel? (1 Kgs 16:20)[o]

---

a. It seems better to take *bene mahol* as a noun phrase, "sons of dance," hence "dance masters," than as "sons of Mahol," referring to an otherwise unknown person by that name.

b. "and his fame ... nations" MT LXX MSS; om LXX (Lucianic stratum)

c. "his songs" LXX; "his song" MT

d. "a thousand and five" MT; "five thousand" LXX

e. The word translated "trees" seems to have a range of meaning that includes both trees and smaller plants, as here.

f. "And there came some from all the peoples" MT LXX; "And all the peoples came" LXX

g. "from" MT LXX MSS; "and he received gifts from" LXX (Lucianic stratum)

h. An account of the reign of Solomon is found in 1 Kings 1-11.

i. An account of the life and reign of Jeroboam I is found in 1 Kgs 11:26–14:20.

j. An account of the reign of Nadab is found in 1 Kgs 15:25-32.

k. "that which" MT; "all that" LXX

l. "mighty acts" LXX; "might" MT

m. An account of the life and reign of Baasha is found in 1 Kgs 15:27–16:6.

n. An account of the reign of Elah is found in 1 Kgs 16:6-14.

o. An account of the conspiracy and reign of Zimri is found in 1 Kgs 16:8-20.

And the rest of the acts of Omri which[a] he did and his might that he did,[b] are they not written in the Book of the Chronicles of the Kings of Israel? (1 Kgs 16:27)[c]

And the rest of the acts of Ahab and all that he did and the ivory house that he built and all the cities that he built, are they not written in the Book of the Chronicles of the Kings of Israel? (1 Kgs 22:39)[d]

And the rest of the acts of Ahaziah which he did, are they not written in the Book of the Chronicles of the Kings of Israel? (2 Kgs 1:18)[e]

And the rest of the acts of Jehu and all that he did and all his might,[f] are they not written in the Book of the Chronicles of the Kings of Israel? (2 Kgs 10:34)[g]

And the rest of the acts of Jehoahaz and all that he did and his might,[h] are they not written in the Book of the Chronicles of the Kings of Israel? (2 Kgs 13:8)[i]

And the rest of the acts of Joash and all that he did and his might[j] that he fought with Amaziah, king of Judah, are they not written in the Book of the Chronicles of the Kings of Israel? (2 Kgs 13:12)[k]

And the rest of the acts of Jehoash[l] which he did and[m] his might and[n] that he fought with Amaziah, king of Judah, are they not written in the Book of the Chronicles of the Kings of Israel? (2 Kgs 14:15)[o]

And the rest of the acts of Jeroboam and all that he did and his might[p] that he fought and that he returned Damascus and Hamath to Judah in Israel,[q] are they not written in the Book of the Chronicles of the Kings of Israel? (2 Kgs 14:28)[r]

---

a. "which" MT; "and all" LXX

b. "his might that he did" MT; "his might" LXX

c. An account of the reign of Omri is found in 1 Kgs 16:16-28.

d. An account of the reign of Ahab is found in 1 Kgs 16:28–22:40.

e. An account of the reign of Ahaziah is found in 1 Kgs 22:40, 51-53; 2 Kgs 1:1-18.

f. "might" MT; + "and the conspiracy that he plotted" LXX (cf. 1 Kgs 16:20)

g. An account of the reign of Jehu is found in 2 Kgs 9:1–10:36.

h. "might" MT; "acts of might" LXX

i. An account of the reign of Jehoahaz is found in 2 Kgs 10:35; 13:1-9.

j. "might" MT; "acts of might" LXX

k. An account of the reign of the Israelite King Joash (Jehoash) is found in 2 Kgs 13:9-13.

l. "Jehoash" MT LXX; + "and all" Syriac

m. "and" MT; "in" LXX

n. "and" MT; omit LXX

o. The entry in 2 Kgs 14:15 is essentially a duplicate of the one in 2 Kgs 13:12 apart from the different spellings of the name.

p. "might" MT; "acts of might" LXX

q. "to Judah in Israel" MT LXX; "to Israel" Syriac

r. An account of the reign of Jeroboam II is found in 2 Kgs 13:13; 14:16, 23-29.

And the rest of the acts of Zechariah, behold they are written in the Book of the Chronicles of the Kings of Israel. (2 Kgs 15:11)[a]

And the rest of the acts of Shallum and the conspiracy that he plotted, behold they are written in the Book of the Chronicles of the Kings of Israel. (2 Kgs 15:15)[b]

And the rest of the acts of Menahem and all that he did, are they not written in the Book of the Chronicles of the Kings of Israel? (2 Kgs 15:21)[c]

And the rest of the acts of Pekahiah and all that he did, behold they are written in the Book of the Chronicles of the Kings of Israel. (2 Kgs 15:26)[d]

And the rest of the acts of Pekah and all that he did, behold they are written in the Book of the Chronicles of the Kings of Israel. (2 Kgs 15:31)[e]

The Book of the Chronicles of the Kings of Judah

And the rest of the acts of Rehoboam and all that he did, are they not written in the Book of the Chronicles of the Kings of Judah? (1 Kgs 14:29)[f]

And the rest of the acts of Abijam and all that he did, are they not written in the Book of the Chronicles of the Kings of Judah? (1 Kgs 15:7a)[g]

And the rest of all[h] the acts of Asa and all his might and all[i] that he did and the cities that he built,[j] are they not written in the Book of the Chronicles of the Kings of Judah? (1 Kgs 15:23a)[k]

And the rest of the acts of Jehoshaphat and his might that he did and that he fought,[l] are they not written in the Book of the Chronicles of the Kings of Judah? (1 Kgs 22:46 [Evv 45])[m]

And the rest of the acts of Joram and all that he did, are they not written in the Book of the Chronicles of the Kings of Judah? (2 Kgs 8:23)[n]

---

a. An account of the reign of Zechariah is found in 2 Kgs 14:29; 15:8-12.
b. An account of the conspiracy and reign of Shallum is found in 2 Kgs 15:10-15.
c. An account of the reign of Menachem is found in 2 Kgs 15:14-22.
d. An account of the reign of Pekiah is found in 2 Kgs 15:22-26.
e. An account of the conspiracy and reign of Pekah is found in 2 Kgs 15:25-31.
f. An account of the reign of Rehoboam is found in 1 Kgs 11:43–12:24; 14:21-31.
g. An account of the reign of Abijam is found in 1 Kgs 14:31–15:8.
h. "all" MT; omit LXX
i. "and all" MT; omit LXX Syriac
j. "and the cities that he built" MT; omit LXX
k. An account of the reign of Asa is found in 1 Kgs 15:8-24.
l. "and that he fought" MT; omit LXX
m. An account of the reign of Jehoshaphat is found in 1 Kgs 15:24; 22:1-51 [Evv 1-50].
n. An account of the reign of the Judean King Joram (Jehoram) is found in 2 Kgs 8:16-24. There is no mention of a source for the reign of his son Amaziah (cf. 2 Kgs 9:27-28).

And the rest of the acts of Joash and all that he did, are they not written in the Book of the Chronicles of the Kings of Judah? (2 Kgs 12:20 [Evv 12:19])[a]

And the rest of the acts of Amaziah,[b] are they not written in the Book of the Chronicles of the Kings of Judah? (2 Kgs 14:18)[c]

And the rest of the acts of Azariah and all that he did, are they not written in the Book of the Chronicles of the Kings of Judah? (2 Kgs 15:6)[d]

And the rest of the acts of Jotham which he did, are they not written in the Book of the Chronicles of the Kings of Judah? (2 Kgs 15:36)[e]

And the rest of the acts of Ahaz[f] which he did, are they not written in the Book of the Chronicles of the Kings of Judah? (2 Kgs 16:19)[g]

And the rest of the acts of Hezekiah and all his might and that he made the pool and the conduit and he brought the water into the city, are they not written in the Book of the Chronicles of the Kings of Judah? (2 Kgs 20:20)[h]

And the rest of the acts of Manasseh and all that he did and the sin that he committed, are they not written in the Book of the Chronicles of the Kings of Judah? (2 Kgs 21:17)[i]

And the rest of the acts of Amon[j] that he did, are they not written in the Book of the Chronicles of the Kings of Judah? (2 Kgs 21:25)[k]

And the rest of the acts of Josiah and all that he did, are they not written in the Book of the Chronicles of the Kings of Judah? (2 Kgs 23:28)[l]

And the rest of the acts of Jehoiakim and all that he did, are they not written in the Book of the Chronicles of the Kings of Judah? (2 Kgs 24:5)[m]

---

a. An account of the life and reign of the Judean King Joash (Jehoash) is found in 2 Kgs 11:1–12:20 [Evv 12:21].

b. "Amaziah" MT; + "and all that he did" LXX

c. An account of the reign of Amaziah is found in 2 Kgs 12:22 [Evv 12:21]; 14:1-20.

d. An account of the reign of Azariah (Uzziah) is found in 2 Kgs 14:21-22; 15:1-7 (cf. Isa 1:1; 6:1; Amos 1:1; Zech 14:5).

e. An account of the reign of Jotham is found in 2 Kgs 15:7, 32-38.

f. "Ahaz" MT MSS LXX MSS; + "and all" MT MSS LXX (Lucianic stratum) Syriac

g. An account of the reign of Ahaz is found in 2 Kgs 15:38–16:20.

h. An account of the reign of Hezekiah is found in 2 Kgs 16:20; 18:1–20:21.

i. An account of the reign of Manasseh is found in 2 Kgs 20:21–21:18.

j. "Amon" MT MSS LXX MSS; + "and all" MT MSS LXX (Lucianic stratum) Syriac

k. An account of the reign of Amon is found in 2 Kgs 21:18-26.

l. An account of the reign of Josiah is found in 2 Kgs 21:24, 26–23:30. No source is given for the reign of Jehoahaz (2 Kgs 23:30-34).

m. An account of the reign of Jehoiakim is found in 2 Kgs 23:34–24:6.

The Book of the Kings of Israel and Judah

And the rest of the acts of Jotham and all his wars[a] and his ways, behold they are written in the Book of the Kings of Israel and Judah. (2 Chr 27:7)[b]

[26]And the rest of the acts of Josiah and his acts of covenant loyalty according to what is[c] written in the Law of Yahweh [27]and his words,[d] first and last, behold they are written in the Book of the Kings of Israel and Judah. (2 Chr 35:26-27)[e]

And the rest of the acts of Jehoiakim and his abominations and what was found out about him,[f] behold they are written in the Book of the Kings of Israel and Judah.[g] (2 Chr 36:8a)[h]

The Book of the Kings of Judah and Israel

And behold, the acts of Asa, first and last, behold they are written in the Book of the Kings of Judah and Israel. (2 Chr 16:11)[i]

And the rest of the acts of Amaziah, first and last, are they not, behold, written in the Book of the Kings of Judah and Israel? (2 Chr 25:26)[j]

And the rest of his [Ahaz's] acts and all his ways, first and last, behold they are written in the Book of the Kings of Judah and Israel. (2 Chr 28:26)[k]

And the rest of the acts of Hezekiah and his acts of covenant loyalty, behold they are written in the vision of Isaiah son of Amoz the prophet[l] in the Book of the Kings of Judah and Israel. (2 Chr 32:32)[m]

---

a. "and all his wars" MT; "and the war" LXX

b. An account of the reign of Jotham is found in 2 Chr 26:23–27:9 (cf. 2 Kgs 15:36 above).

c. "according to what is" MT; omit LXX

d. Perhaps emend "words" to the similar looking "ways" (cf. 2 Chr 27:7 above)

e. An account of the reign of Josiah is found in 2 Chr 33:25–35:27 (cf. 2 Kgs 23:28 above).

f. "and his abominations ... about him" MT; "and all that he did" LXX (influenced by 2 Kgs 24:5)

g. "the Book of the Kings of Israel and Judah" MT; "the Book of the Chronicles of the Kings of Judah" LXX (influenced by 2 Kgs 24:5)

h. An account of the reign of Jehoiakim is found in 2 Chr 36:4-8 (cf. 2 Kgs 24:5 above).

i. An account of the reign of Asa is found in 2 Chr 14:1–16:14 (cf. 1 Kgs 15:23 above)

j. An account of the reign of Amaziah is found in 2 Chr 24:27–25:28 (cf. 2 Kgs 14:18 above).

k. An account of the reign of Ahaz is found in 2 Chr 27:9–28:27 (cf. 2 Kgs 16:19 above).

l. "prophet" MT; + "and" LXX

m. An account of the reign of Hezekiah is found in 2 Chr 28:27–32:33 (cf. 2 Kgs 20:20 above). For Isaiah son of Amoz see 2 Kgs 19:20-20:19//Isa 37:5–38:8; 39:3-8 (cf. 2 Chr 32:20) and Isaiah 1-33. It is unclear whether the biblical Book of Isaiah had any overlap with this vision of Isaiah in the Book of the Kings of Israel and Judah.

The Book of the Kings of Israel

And all Israel was enrolled by genealogy and behold they are written in the Book of the Kings of Israel. And Judah were exiled to Babylon for their unfaithfulness.[a] (1 Chr 9:1a)[b]

And the rest of the acts of Jehoshaphat, first and last, behold they are written in the Words of Jehu son of Hanani which is entered in the Book of the Kings of Israel. (2 Chr 20:34)[c]

The Book of the Chronicles of King David

[23]But David did not hold a census of those from twenty years old and above, for
Gen 22:17; 26:4 Yahweh promised to multiply Israel like the stars of the heavens. [24]Joab son of
Zeruiah began to count them up[d] but he did not finish, but by this there came about wrath upon Israel and he did not enter the number into the Book[e] of the Chronicles of King David. (1 Chr 27:23-24)[f]

King David's plan from Yahweh for the Temple

He (David) instructed (Solomon) in everything in a writing from the hand of Yahweh concerning it,[g] all the workmanship of the plan. (1 Chr 28:19)[h]

The Acts of Samuel the Seer, the Acts of Nathan the Prophet, and the Acts of Gad the Visionary

[29]And the acts[i] of David the king, first and last, behold they are written in the Acts of Samuel the Seer and in the Acts of Nathan the Prophet and in the Acts of Gad
the Visionary, [30]with all his reign and his might and the times that came upon him and upon Israel and upon all the kingdoms of the earth. (1 Chr 29:29-30)[j]

---

a. "Kings of Israel ... unfaithfulness" MT; "Kings of Israel and Judah after they were exiled to Babylon in their acts of lawlessness" LXX. The two readings reflect different interpretations of the same consonantal text. That of the MT makes more sense in that only Judah was exiled to Babylon, although the Chronicler does at times apply the name Israel to Judah as well. If we read with the LXX, this verse would go under the Book of the Kings of Israel and Judah.

b. 1 Chr 9:1 appears to be intended as a conclusion to 1 Chronicles 1–8. Those chapters derive much of their material from the Pentateuch and other biblical passages, but some of the material is not found elsewhere in the Bible and presumably comes from this source.

c. An account of the reign of Jehoshaphat is found in 2 Chr 17:1–21:1 (cf. 1 Kgs 22:45 above). For the prophet Jehu son of Hanani see 1 Kgs 16:1-4, 7, 12; 2 Chr 19:2.

d. "count them up" MT; "count the people" LXX

e. "Book" LXX; "number" MT (the two words are similar in Hebrew)

f. The episode of the abortive census is told in more detail in 1 Chr 21:1–22:1 (cf. 2 Sam 24:1-25).

g. "concerning it" emendation (cf. LXX?); "concerning me" MT

h. The writing apparently explained the "plan" (i.e., blueprint) for the Temple, which David gave to Solomon according to 1 Chr 28:11-18.

i. "the acts" MT; "the rest of the acts" LXX

j. An account of the reign of David is found in 1 Chr 10:14–29:30 (cf. the much longer account of his life and reign in 1 Sam 16:1–1 Kgs 2:11). For Samuel the seer/prophet see 1 Sam 1:1–12:25; 15:1–16:13; 19:18-24; 28:3-20. For Gad the seer/prophet see 1 Sam 22:5; 2 Sam 24:11-14//1 Chr 21:9-13; 2 Chr 29:25. For Nathan the prophet see 2 Sam 7:2-17//1 Chr 17:1-15; 2 Sam 12:1-15, 25; 1 Kgs 1:8-45; 2 Chr 29:25.

The Acts of Nathan the Prophet, the Prophecy of Ahijah the Shilonite, and the Visions of Jeddo the Visionary Concerning Jeroboam Son of Nebat

And the remainder of the acts of Solomon, first and last, are they not written in the Acts of Nathan the Prophet and in the Prophecy[a] of Ahijah the Shilonite and in the Visions of Jeddo[b] the Visionary Concerning Jeroboam Son of Nebat? (2 Chr 9:29)[c]

The Acts of Shemaiah the Prophet and Iddo the Visionary for Enrollment by Genealogy

And the acts of Rehoboam, first and last, are they not written in the Acts of Shemaiah the Prophet and Iddo the Visionary for Enrollment by Genealogy?[d] (2 Chr 12:15a)[e]

The Midrash of the Prophet Iddo

And the rest of the acts of Abijah and his ways and his words are written in the Midrash[f] of the Prophet Iddo. (2 Chr 13:22)[g]

The Midrash of the Book of Kings

And his (i.e., Joash's) sons and the multitude of oracles concerning him and the founding of the house of God,[h] behold they are written in the Midrash of the Book of the Kings. (2 Chr 24:27a)[i]

---

a. "Prophecy" MT; "Words" (or "Acts") LXX

b. "Jeddo" (= Iddo? Cf. 2 Chr 12:15a and 13:22 below) MT; "Joel" LXX

c. An account of the reign of Solomon is found in 1 Chr 28:1–2 Chr 9:31 (cf. the somewhat different account of his reign in 1 Kgs 1:1-11:43). For Nathan the prophet see above under 1 Chr 29:29-30. For Ahijah the Shilonite see 1 Kgs 11:29-39; 12:15//2 Chr 10:15; 1 Kgs 14:2-18. For Jeddo the visionary see perhaps on Iddo the visionary/prophet under 2 Chr 12:15a below. For Jeroboam son of Nebat see 2 Chr 10:2–11:15; 13:1-20 (cf. 1 Kgs 14:19 above).

d. "for Enrollment by Genealogy" MT; "and his ways" LXX (cf. 2 Chr 27:7; 28:26)

e. An account of the reign of Rehoboam is found in 2 Chr 9:31–12:16 (cf. 1 Kgs 14:29 above). For Shemiah the prophet see 1 Kgs 12:21-24//2 Chr 11:1-4; 2 Chr 12:5-8. For Iddo the visionary/prophet see 2 Chr 13:22 and perhaps 9:29.

f. "Midrash" MT; "Book" LXX. The term "midrash" occurs only here and in 2 Chr 24:27 (see below) in the Bible. In later Jewish tradition it means an exegetical comment or commentary on scripture, but it is unwise to read that meaning back into this much earlier context. The root of the word means "to seek, inquire," "to study," or "to seek a divine oracle." Possible meanings include "story," "commentary" (on the Book of the Kings of Israel and Judah?); "(historical) inquiry" (cf. 2 Chr 32:31); or "prophetic oracle" (cf. 2 Kgs 3:11).

g. An account of the reign of Abijah is found in 2 Chr 13:1-22 (cf. 1 Kgs 15:7 above). For Iddo the visionary/prophet see above on 2 Chr 12:15a.

h. "And his sons ... house of God" MT; "and all his sons and the five went to him. And the rest," LXX

i. An account of the life and reign of Joash is found in 2 Chr 22:10–24:27 (cf. 2 Kgs 12:20 [Evv 12:19] above). For the term "midrash," see above on 2 Chr 13:22.

The Acts of Uzziah

And the rest of the acts of Uzziah, first and last, Isaiah the son of Amoz the prophet[a] wrote. (2 Chr 26:22)[b]

The Acts of the Kings of Israel and the Words of the Visionaries

18 And the rest of the acts of Manasseh and his prayer to his God and the words of the visionaries who spoke to him in the name of Yahweh, the God of Israel, behold they are in the Acts of the Kings of Israel.[c] 19 And his prayer and the granting of his entreaty and all his sin and his unfaithfulness and the places where he built high places and set up Asherim and idols before he humbled himself, behold they are written in the Words of the Visionaries.[d] (2 Chr 33:18-19)[e]

Writings of David and Solomon on the Divisions of the Levites

And prepare by the houses of your fathers, according to their divisions, according to[f] the writing of David the king of Israel and according to the written document of[g] Solomon[h] his son. (2 Chr 35:4)[i]

The Laments

And Jeremiah lamented over Josiah and all the male and female singers have spoken in their laments about Josiah until today. And they made them a prescribed rite for Israel. And behold they are written in the Laments. (2 Chr 35:25)[j]

---

a. "Isaiah son of Amoz the prophet" MT; "Iessias the prophet" LXX

b. An account of the reign of Uzziah (Azariah) is found in 2 Chr 26:1-23 (cf. 2 Kgs 15:6 above). For Isaiah the prophet, see 2 Chr 32:32 above. This work cannot be the biblical Book of Isaiah, which does not narrate the acts or words of King Uzziah.

c. "of the Kings of Israel" MT; omit LXX

d. "Visionaries" MT one MS, LXX; Hozai MT. The name Hozai, which does not appear elsewhere in the Bible, is very similar to the Hebrew word "visionaries" and seems to be a copyist's error for it.

e. An account of the reign of Manasseh is found in 2 Chr 32:33–33:20 (cf. 2 Kgs 21:17 above).

f. "according to" MT MSS LXX; "in" MT MSS

g. "and according to the written document of" MT MSS; "and in the written document of" MT MSS; "and by the hand of" LXX

h. "Solomon" MT LXX MSS; "King Solomon" LXX MSS

i. The divisions of the priests, Levites, and other Temple personnel are given in 1 Chr 24–26.

j. For Josiah see 2 Chr 35:26-27 above. For Jeremiah (the prophet) see the Book of Jeremiah. The Laments mentioned here are not to be confused with the biblical Book of Lamentations, which does not mention Josiah.

Hebrew Visions of Hell and Paradise

A new translation and introduction

by Helen Spurling

The visions of hell and paradise (Visions) presented here were first selected and translated by Moses Gaster.[1] These medieval traditions present detailed descriptions of the fate of the righteous and the wicked, along with cosmological information on heaven, hell and paradise. Although of late date in their current form, they are important for their use of earlier apocryphal, pseudepigraphal and rabbinic material. There are also a number of parallels with early Christian apocalyptic tours of hell and paradise. Gaster did not identify the more commonly used titles of these texts, but these are used here, namely:

- *The Greatness of Moses* (*Gedulat Moshe*)
- *Legend of "Hear, O Israel"* (*Haggadat Shema' Yisra'el*)
- *History of Rabbi Yehoshua ben Levi* (*Ma'aseh de-Rabbi Yehoshua' ben Levi*)
- *Order of Gan Eden* (*Seder Gan 'Eden*)
- *Tractate on Gehinnom* (*Masseket Gehinnom*)
- *In What Manner Is the Punishment of the Grave?* (*Ketsad Din ha-Qever*)
- *Legend of Rabbi Yehoshua ben Levi* (*'Aggadat Rabbi Yehoshua' ben Levi*)
- *Treatise on the Work of Creation* (*Baraita de-Ma'aseh Bereshit*)
- *David Apocalypse*

Contents

The Greatness of Moses. This Hebrew work describes Moses' ascent through the seven heavens and his tour of hell and paradise. The vision begins with an account of Moses' first revelation of God on Horeb. His humility before God gains him the honour of ascending to heaven. Moses is transformed and Metatron leads him through the seven heavens during which he asks questions on the nature and role of the angels in each heaven. The greatest detail is given to the description of the seventh heaven with its angels and the Throne of Glory. Moses then visits Gehinnom (Hell) led first by Gabriel and then Nasargiel. He sees the punishment of the wicked in the different regions of hell, including punishment by hanging, worms, scorpions, fire and snow. Moses' tour continues with a visit to Gan Eden (the Garden of Eden) led primarily by Shamshiel. He sees the thrones

1. M. Gaster, "Hebrew Visions of Hell and Paradise," *JRAS* N.S. 25 (1893): 571-611, and reprinted in *Studies and Texts in Folklore, Magic, Mediaeval Romance, Hebrew Apocrypha and Samaritan Archaeology* (London, 1925-28), 1:124-64.

of the righteous and the four streams of Gan Eden. Moses' tour concludes with the announcement by a *Bat Qol*[2] that he will share in the rewards of the righteous.

Legend of "Hear, O Israel." This Hebrew vision is a first-person narrative by Moses of his ascension to heaven. Moses describes his ascent in the context of teaching Israel about his vision of God on Sinai. He outlines in turn the nature and role of the key angels in heaven, with focus on the angels around the Throne of Glory.

History of Rabbi Yehoshua ben Levi. This Hebrew work describes how Rabbi Yehoshua tricked the Angel of Death so that he could enter Gan Eden without having to die. Once there, Rabbi Yehoshua is commissioned by Rabbi Gamaliel to make a record of the proportions and contents of both Gan Eden and Gehinnom. The vision is then a first-person account by Rabbi Yehoshua of the seven compartments of Gan Eden, including description of their size, who lives in each one and who is appointed over them. The compartments of Gehinnom are treated similarly, although their number is not specified. The punishment of the nations of the world is particularly emphasized. The composition concludes with the completion of Rabbi Yehoshua's commission.

Order of Gan Eden. This Hebrew narrative presents a description of Gan Eden in the name of Rabbi Yehoshua ben Levi. The work describes the process of entry into Gan Eden by a righteous person, and follows with an outline of the four streams of Gan Eden, the canopies of the righteous, the transformations of the righteous and the trees of Gan Eden, including the Tree of Life. The vision concludes with a description of the seven compartments of the righteous and who dwells in each one.

Tractate on Gehinnom. This Hebrew work presents an account of the contents of Gehinnom and the fate of the wicked. The narrative opens with a description of the angelic guards and an explanation of the names of Gehinnom. The work describes the gates of Gehinnom and its fires, and then proceeds with an elaborate outline of the sentencing of the wicked, their punishments and ultimate fate. The sins of the wicked are described and punishments include torture by hanging, worms, fire and snow.

In What Manner Is the Punishment of the Grave? The beginning of this Hebrew text, as edited by A. Jellinek, is fragmentary, but what we have clearly describes some of the punishments dealt out in the grave before a person reaches Gehinnom. The vision provides a detailed outline of Gehinnom, its names, dimensions and divisions. This is followed by a description of the assessment of the deeds of the dead. The narrative continues with a tour of the five compartments of hell by Isaiah, with an outline of who is in each one and how the punishment they receive is appropriate to their sin. The composition concludes with the sentencing of Israel and the nations.

Legend of Rabbi Yehoshua ben Levi. This vision represents an Aramaic recension of the description of Gehinnom found in *History of Rabbi Yehoshua ben Levi.* It additionally describes the punishment of the nations of the world in each of the seven divisions of Gehinnom. For each division, the composition indicates which angel punishes the nations, and outlines those who are appointed over the nations and ultimately spared.

Treatise on the Work of Creation. These Hebrew traditions describe the different levels of earths, with particular focus on the seven divisions of hell on the level called Arqa, one of which is Gehinnom. The work outlines the dimensions of these seven divisions of hell and the fires found in each one. The vision also describes the punishment of the wicked by scorpions and rivers of fire and ice.

---

2. A *Bat Qol* (literally, "daughter of a voice") was a heavenly revelatory voice.

David Apocalypse. This work is found embedded in manuscripts of the mystical Hekhalot literature, usually in a work called the *Hekhalot Rabbati*, but it clearly is a separate composition. It is a first-person account by Rabbi Ishmael of a visionary experience in which the angel Sagansagel informs him of the future punishments for Israel. The shock makes Rabbi Ishmael unconscious, but he is revived by Hadraniel who shows him the future rewards for Israel and the glory of David.

Manuscripts and Versions

The printed editions of the Visions presented here are composed in Hebrew with the occasional use of Aramaic words. The main exceptions are the *Legend of Rabbi Yehoshua ben Levi*, which is composed primarily in Aramaic, and the *David Apocalypse*, which is mainly in Hebrew but contains a divine speech in Aramaic at 2:2-6. The Visions have a complicated textual history. They have been printed many times with variations in the material and under different titles, which is a reflection of the lack of final redactional unity to the traditions. The key editions and manuscripts of the Visions are listed below.

The Greatness of Moses

- The earliest printed edition is from Thessalonica in 1726-27 under the title *Gedulat Moshe*.
- *Sefer Gedulat Moshe* was printed in Frankfurt in 1733.
- The Thessalonica edition was reprinted in Amsterdam in 1753-54 with the title *Gedulat Moshe*.
- An edition of *Gedulat Moshe* was printed in Constantinople in 1799.
- Another edition was printed in Warsaw in 1848-49.
- S. A. Wertheimer published a version of the text with the title "Like an apple tree among the trees of the forest" in his *Batei Midrashot* (2nd ed.; Jerusalem, 1952-55), 1:273-85. He produced his edition of the text from a Yemenite manuscript available to him. This is the second edition of Wertheimer's collection and represents a revised edition of the text including variants in the apparatus from the Thessalonica 1726-27 edition.
- J. D. Eisenstein published the first edition of Wertheimer's text in his *Oẓar Midrashim* (New York, 1915), 1:262-64.
- An edition of the text in Judeo-Persian can be found in A. Netzer, "A Midrash on the Ascension of Moses in Judeo-Persian," *Irano-Judaica*, ed. S. Shaked and A. Netzer, vol. 2 (Jerusalem: Ben-Zvi Institute for the Study of Jewish Communities in the East, 1990), 105-143. Netzer lists all editions and manuscripts known to him and provides a critical edition, text and commentary. He entitles the text "Ascension of Moses."

Legend of "Hear, O Israel"

- This text is in the work of Menahem Tsiyyoni ben Meir published in *Tsiyyoni: Perush [Be'ur] 'al haTorah* (Karein, 1784-85), f.79a-c. *Tsiyyoni* was also published in Cremona in 1559-1560 and Lemberg in 1882 (reprinted Jerusalem 1963-64).
- A. Jellinek reproduced the text of *Tsiyyoni* in *BHM*, 5:165-66. For his bibliography, see 5:xl-xli.
- J. D. Eisenstein published the text in his *Oẓar Midrashim* (New York, 1915), 2:550-51. He refers to the edition of Jellinek and retains the title *Haggadat Shema' Yisra'el*.
- M. Gaster also identified a manuscript of the text in the Bodleian Library: MS. Oxford no. 1466,14, f.356 according to the catalogue of A. D. Neubauer.

History of Rabbi Yehoshua ben Levi (see also Legend of Rabbi Yehoshua ben Levi below)

- A. Jellinek published an edition of the text in *BHM*, 2:48-51. In his bibliography at 2:xviii-xx, he refers to the recension found in *Kol Bo* §120, which he notes was subsequently printed in Vilna 1802 and Lemberg 1850. Jellinek also refers to the text in the Bodleian Library as noted in M. Steinschneider's catalogue col. 610 from number 3882.
- J. D. Eisenstein published the text in *Oẓar Midrashim* (New York, 1915), 1:212-13. He provides bibliography at 1:210-11. Eisenstein's text represents another recension from that of Jellinek under the title *Iggeret Rabbi Yehoshua' ben Levi.*
- Y. Even-Shemuel, *Midreshe Ge'ulah* (Jerusalem, 1953-54), 307-308 provides an abridged text under the title *Be-Gan 'Eden*. He lists bibliographic details at 293-94.
- A manuscript of the text from the Cairo Genizah is in Cambridge University Library catalogued under Add.667.1. It is part of a larger collection of material similar to *Maḥzor Vitry*, and is dated to the thirteenth–fourteenth century. It consists of 229 folios written on vellum. The text is presented in two columns along with *Tractate on Gehinnom* on ff.177r-179r. *Order of Gan Eden* is also found here on ff.176v-177r.
- M. Gaster identified a version of the text in *Orḥot Ḥayim* which he found in cod. 52, Montefiore College, 281b-282b. He also located the text in cod. 28, Jews College London, 145b-147a.

Order of Gan Eden

- A. Jellinek published an edition of the text in *BHM*, 2:52-53. Jellinek provides bibliography at 2:xx-xxi. He refers to the texts in the Bodleian Library, as in M. Steinschneider's catalogue col. 611-12 number 3888. Steinschneider reports the titles *Seder Gan Eden*, *Pirqe Gan Eden* and *Massekhet Gan Eden*. The text is also in the Neubauer catalogue with the title *Pereq Gan Eden* no. 2274,5 f.29, which Neubauer states is dated to the early fifteenth century. Jellinek also mentions *Shebet Musar* (see below) and *Yalqut to Genesis* §20.
- J. D. Eisenstein published the text in *Oẓar Midrashim* (New York, 1915), 1:83-84 under *pereq rishon*. His sources are the edition of Jellinek and the end of *Baraita di-Shemuel* and he gives the title *Massekhet Gan 'Eden*. Eisenstein provides bibliographic details at 1:83.
- A manuscript of the text from the Cairo Genizah is in Cambridge University Library catalogued under Add.667.1 from the thirteenth–fourteenth century. See *History of Rabbi Yehoshua ben Levi* above. *Order of Gan Eden* is found here on ff.176v-177r.
- Gaster refers to a version of the text in Elia ha-Kohen, *Shebet Musar* (Constantinople, 1720), chap. 25 f.80-81a.

Tractate on Gehinnom

- A. Jellinek published an edition of the text in *BHM*, 1:147-149. In his bibliography at 1:xxv-xxvi, he refers to the text in *Reshit Ḥokmah* (see below), an edition of Vilna 1802, and cod. 21 of the Leipzig Raths-bibliothek under the title *Seder Gehinnom*.
- J. D. Eisenstein published the text in *Oẓar Midrashim* (New York, 1915), 1:91-92. He gives the title *Massekhet Gehinnom* and refers to the edition of Jellinek and *Reshit Ḥokmah*. Eisenstein presents his bibliography at 1:83.
- M. E. Stone and J. Strugnell, *The Books of Elijah, parts 1-2* (Atlanta, Ga., 1979), 16-20.

This contains part of the text along with translation and reference to a number of textual witnesses.

- The text is found in Elia de Vidas, *Reshit Ḥokmah* (Constantinople, 1736), 40a-b.
- The text is part of a larger "macroform," including material from *In What Manner Is the Punishment of the Grave?*, in the text of *Orḥot Ḥayim* located by Gaster in cod. 52, Montefiore College, 279a-b.
- A manuscript of the text from the Cairo Genizah is in Cambridge University Library catalogued under Add.667.1 from the thirteenth–fourteenth century. See *History of Rabbi Yehoshua ben Levi* above. *Tractate on Gehinnom* is found here on ff.177r-179r.
- M. Steinschneider's catalogue of the Bodleian Library reports the existence of the text in various recensions. See col. 602, from number 3844.

In What Manner Is the Punishment of the Grave?

- Jellinek published an edition of the text in *BHM*, 5:49-51. According to his bibliography at 5:xx-xxi, he took the text from a Halberstamm codex.
- J. D. Eisenstein used Jellinek's edition, which he published in *Oẓar Midrashim* (New York, 1915), 1:94-95.
- M. E. Stone and J. Strugnell, *The Books of Elijah, parts 1-2* (Atlanta, Ga., 1979), 20-24. This contains the description of Isaiah's tour including text and translation with reference to a number of textual witnesses.
- The text is part of a larger macroform, including material from *Tractate on Gehinnom*, in the text of *Orḥot Ḥayim* located by Gaster in cod. 52, Montefiore College, 279a-b.
- M. Steinschneider's catalogue of the Bodleian Library includes this text in col. 546, number 3527, 4 in an edition from Constantinople of 1570, and number 3528 in an edition from Prague of 1595-96.

Legend of Rabbi Yehoshua ben Levi (see also History of Rabbi Yehoshua ben Levi above)

- A. Jellinek published an edition of the text in *BHM*, 5:43-44. In his bibliography at 5:xx-xxi, he refers to Nachmanides' *Sha'ar haGemul* (see below).
- Nachmanides, *Sha'ar haGemul* (Ferrara, 1556), 11b, and (Warsaw, 1878), 10.
- M. Gaster identified a version of the text in *Orḥot Ḥayim* in cod. 52, Montefiore College, 282b-283a.

Treatise on the Work of Creation

- Abraham Azulai, *Ḥesed le-Avraham* (Amsterdam, 1685), *neharot* 7-9. The text gives the title *Baraita de-Ma'aseh Bereshit* and is accompanied by a commentary.
- S. A. Wertheimer, *Batei Midrashot* (2nd ed.; Jerusalem, 1952-55), 1:19-48, as part of *Seder rabbah di-Bereshit* chaps. 24-30 (1:32-38).
- P. Schäfer, et al., *Synopse zur Hekhalot-Literatur* (TSAJ 2; Tübingen: Mohr Siebeck, 1981), §446-49, §753-56 and §760-62. This work contains reference to all major textual witnesses.
- Gaster also refers to a version of the text in Elia ha-Kohen, *Shebet Musar* (Constantinople, 1720), chap. 26 f.84a.
- N. Séd, "Une cosmologie juive du haut moyen age: La Bāraytā dī Ma'aseh Berēšīt," *RÉJ* 123 (1964): 259-305; 124 (1965): 23-123. This presents a critical edition and French translation of a long and a short recension of this work.

David Apocalypse

- A. Jellinek published this text in *BHM*, 5:167-69 with some additional context from the *Hekhalot Rabbati*. He gives bibliographic details at 5:xli, including reference to *Siddur Amram* (Warsaw, 1865), 3b, 12b-13a.
- Gaster also referred to the text in *Massekhet Atziluth* (Warsaw, 1876), 54a-b.
- S. A. Wertheimer, *Batei Midrashot* (2nd ed.; Jerusalem, 1952-55), 1:63-136, as part of *Hekhalot Rabbati* chap. 6.3-7.2.
- P. Schäfer, et al., *Synopse zur Hekhalot-Literatur* (TSAJ 2; Tübingen: Mohr Siebeck, 1981), §122-26. This work contains reference to all major textual witnesses.

Genre and Structure

As the Visions are a collection of traditions, it is perhaps not surprising that the genre of the material varies from selection to selection. Broadly speaking, the Visions belong to the genre of apocalyptic literature or contain apocalyptic material and could be described as apocalypses on the fate of the dead.[3] The definition of "apocalyptic" is contentious, but this term is used of the Visions due to the primary concern with the fate of the dead and eschatological judgement, which are closely linked with cosmological descriptions of heaven, paradise and hell. The cosmic tour also features in a number of the traditions, where the visionary is given a tour of heaven or paradise and hell by an angelic guide.[4] Ultimately, however, each vision needs to be assessed individually.

The Greatness of Moses is best described as a cosmic tour, a form of the apocalyptic genre revealing details of the cosmos. Moses is led by an angelic guide through the seven heavens, followed by a tour of hell and paradise. The tour presents an interest in a number of subjects typical of this genre, including angelology, the Throne of Glory, cosmology, the punishment of the wicked and reward of the righteous. These topics are dealt with in a number of early apocalypses, such as 2 *Enoch*, *Testament of Levi* and *Apocalypse of Zephaniah*.[5]

The *Legend of "Hear, O Israel"* is a description of a cosmic tour. The vision is a first-person account given by Moses to Israel of his ascension to heaven to see the Throne of Glory. Moses does not mention his heavenly guide, or a visit to hell or paradise. The primary concern of the composition is angelology. It was considered by Gaster to be a shorter recension of *The Greatness of Moses*.[6] However, although the themes of the narrative are similar, namely the ascension of Moses and angelological concerns, the material differs substantially in content, which makes such a claim suspect.

History of Rabbi Yehoshua ben Levi belongs to the genre of haggadic narrative, but contains a description of a tour of hell. The vision contains much legendary material about Rabbi Yehoshua in Gan Eden, which is followed by a first-person narrative description by

---

3. The description of this genre with particular reference to the fate of the wicked is outlined in some detail by R. Bauckham, *The Fate of the Dead: Studies on the Jewish and Christian Apocalypses* (NovTSup 93; Leiden: Brill, 1998), 81-96.

4. For detailed discussion of the genre and development of the "tour of hell" see M. Himmelfarb, *Tours of Hell: An Apocalyptic Form in Jewish and Christian Literature* (Philadelphia, Pa.: University of Pennsylvania Press, 1983).

5. See Bauckham, *Fate of the Dead*, 65-66, for discussion of the genre of cosmic tour in relation to *The Greatness of Moses*.

6. This is indicated by Gaster's title for the text "The Revelation of Moses (B)," *Studies and Texts*, 141-43, with *The Greatness of Moses* called "The Revelation of Moses (A)," *Studies and Texts*, 125-41.

the Rabbi of paradise and hell. Rabbi Yehoshua searches Gan Eden by himself, but has an angelic guide for his visit to Gehinnom. The primary concerns of the narrative are the fate of the righteous and the wicked, but it also describes the structure of the compartments of paradise and hell. The Aramaic recension of the text, *Legend of Rabbi Yehoshua ben Levi*, is a first-person account by R. Yehoshua ben Levi of the compartments of Gehinnom, its structure and inhabitants.

Order of Gan Eden presents a description of paradise in the name of R. Yehoshua ben Levi. However, this account is a simple description of paradise without the viewpoint of a guide and visitor and is best described as an eschatological midrash due to the use of a number of proof-texts. Its primary concern is the fate of the righteous, but it also contains geographical information on the layout of Gan Eden, as is found in early ascent apocalypses such as *1* and *2 Enoch*. Both Gaster and Jellinek considered this text to be a recension of *History of Rabbi Yehoshua ben Levi*.[7] However, although the composition is introduced in the name of Rabbi Yehoshua, the material differs substantially from the *History of Rabbi Yehoshua ben Levi* and does not contain any of the legendary material about this figure.

Tractate on Gehinnom also belongs to the genre of eschatological midrash. It is a description of hell based on the teaching of a number of rabbis. It makes frequent use of scriptural proof-texts. Its interests focus on the fate of the wicked, but also include information on features of Gehinnom.

In What Manner Is the Punishment of the Grave? is a composite text including material belonging to the genre of midrash, haggadic narrative and the cosmic tour. The second chapter is a paraphrase of the opening and closing sections of *Tractate on Gehinnom*. Chaps. 6-10 contain a tour of hell by Isaiah. He does not have an angelic guide, but asks God questions about what he sees. The bulk of the vision is concerned with the fate of the dead, but also contains cosmological information about Gehinnom.

Treatise on the Work of Creation belongs to the genre of Jewish mysticism called *Ma'aseh Bereshit*. It is primarily concerned with cosmological details on the levels of earths, and the different divisions of hell including the location of Gehinnom. It also describes some of the punishments of the wicked. This material represents another recension of traditions found in *Seder Rabbah di-Bereshit*.[8]

The *David Apocalypse* is an apocalypse involving an otherworldly journey with cosmic eschatology. It describes Rabbi Ishmael's visionary experience which focuses on the fate of Israel, including the rewards and punishments reserved for them in the "chambers of chambers."[9]

Date and Provenance

Apocalyptic material is notoriously difficult to date, especially due to the repeated use of forms and motifs found in very early, even biblical, material. With regard to the Visions, there was a long process of transmission of the traditions found within the texts as we have them. Indeed, it is difficult to refer to a "text" of these traditions as the material circulated and was transmitted in different forms. This makes dating of the material problematic, as

7. See Jellinek, *BHM*, 2:xx; Gaster suggests this in his title for the text "The Revelation of R. Joshua ben Levi (B)," *Studies and Texts*, 149-51.

8. See the text of *Seder Rabbah di-Bereshit* in Schäfer, *Synopse*, §446-49 and §753-56 (which correspond to chaps. 1-3) and §760-62 (which corresponds to chap. 4).

9. The title *David Apocalypse* is noted by Townsend, "Minor Midrashim," 356 and 358.

it clearly existed in forms different from and earlier to that in the editions used as the basis for translation here. The dates suggested are therefore necessarily broad, and are based on the texts in the form we have them now, despite the presence of demonstrably early material. The Visions as we have them are clearly post-Talmudic, and on the whole represent work of the Geonic period.

Those who have discussed the dating of *The Greatness of Moses* have rightly not hazarded a proposed date beyond saying the text is "late" or medieval. R. Bauckham describes *The Greatness of Moses* as "a medieval Jewish apocalypse in Hebrew."[10] However, he supports the argument that the text contains much earlier material and states "whether or not it is a medieval version of an ancient apocalypse, it certainly preserves an ancient apocalyptic form and ancient apocalyptic traditions."[11] Bauckham refers particularly to the punishment in hell by hanging as an indication of the early nature of the material in this text.[12] C. Fletcher-Louis refers to *The Greatness of Moses* as "late" and S. Lieberman describes the text as "a late collection from several different works" although neither elaborates further.[13] *The Greatness of Moses* in its current form was clearly written after the seventh century due to the influence of material from the Babylonian Talmud, especially the famous description of the heavens in *b. Hag.* 12b-13b. The vision contains material found in the *Zohar*, although any literary relationship is unclear.

The dating of the *Legend of "Hear, O Israel"* has not been discussed elsewhere. Gaster considered this text to be an alternative recension of *The Greatness of Moses*, although, as noted, the material is sufficiently different to make such an assertion questionable.[14] The text has a number of close parallels with *3 Enoch*, which is itself often dated to the fifth or sixth century, although this is not generally accepted. Much of the material of the *Legend of "Hear, O Israel"* is found in a comparable form in *Pesikta Rabbati* 20.4, which may represent a parallel transmission of the legend, or have acted as a source for the text. There are also a number of parallels with material from the Babylonian Talmud. On the basis of this evidence, it seems safe to assume that the form of the text in Jellinek's edition is post-Talmudic. The text is also found in the Torah commentary of Menahem Tsiyyoni ben Meir from the fifteenth century, which provides a *terminus ante quem*.

The *History of Rabbi Yehoshua ben Levi* was also clearly composed after the seventh century due to the use of Talmudic motifs. Townsend claimed that the Hebrew *History of Rabbi Yehoshua ben Levi* was later than the Aramaic recension, which he dated to the seventh century or later.[15] The material in this text has a number of close parallels with *Midrash Konen*, which is generally dated to before the tenth or eleventh century. There is a manuscript of the text from the Cairo Genizah in Cambridge dated to the thirteenth or fourteenth century, which provides a *terminus ante quem*.

Order of Gan Eden exists in many different recensions and under different titles mak-

10. Bauckham, *Fate of the Dead*, 85.

11. Bauckham, *Fate of the Dead*, 85.

12. Bauckham, *Fate of the Dead*, 66.

13. C. H. T. Fletcher-Louis, *Luke-Acts: Angels, Christology and Soteriology* (WUNT 2/94; Tübingen: Mohr Siebeck, 1997), 48; S. Lieberman, "On Sins and Their Punishment," *Texts and Studies* (New York: Ktav, 1974), 29. Lieberman also argues for Muslim influence on *The Greatness of Moses*, which he sees evidenced in a link with the five compartments of Muslim purgatory.

14. See n. 6 above.

15. Townsend, "Minor Midrashim," 365. There is no discussion of how he arrived at this dating.

ing it difficult to speak of the date of this "text."[16] The vision as it stands in Jellinek's edition contains a number of popular Talmudic motifs, which dates the text to after the seventh century. *Order of Gan Eden* contains material also found in *Yalqut* 1.20 and has a number of parallels with material in the *Zohar*. Townsend accurately summarized the state of knowledge on the date of the recension translated here when he noted that it was composed "sometime after the Muslim conquest of Palestine and probably before Maimonides (1135-1204) who seems to allude to it."[17]

Tractate on Gehinnom has also been transmitted in different recensions and under a number of different titles.[18] Jellinek's edition clearly contains some Talmudic motifs, which dates the text to after the seventh century. Traditions found in this text are also paralleled in *Zohar* I, 78a, II, 205a. The text is found in the sixteenth-century *Reshit Ḥokmah*.

In What Manner Is the Punishment of the Grave? is a composite text taking material from a number of different sources. Interestingly, chap. 2 closely parallels material in *Tractate on Gehinnom*. The text follows a scheme for the divisions of Gehinnom similar to that found in *Erubin* 19a. The most that can be said of this text is that it is post-Talmudic.

Legend of Rabbi Yehoshua ben Levi is an Aramaic version of the description of Gehinnom in *History of Rabbi Yehoshua ben Levi*, with additional information on the seven compartments of hell. Townsend has stated of the vision that it is dated to the seventh century or later.[19] He claims that it is earlier than the Hebrew version of this midrash, as discussed above. The material is included in Nachmanides' *Sha'ar ha-Gemul*, which provides a *terminus ante quem* of the thirteenth century.

Treatise on the Work of Creation is taken from the seventeenth-century commentary of Abraham Azulai in *Ḥesed le-Avraham*. There are a number of parallels with *Midrash Konen*, which is generally dated to before the tenth or eleventh century. The text represents another recension of traditions from *Seder Rabbah di-Bereshit*, which itself is dated by Schäfer to the post-Talmudic or early Geonic era.[20]

The *David Apocalypse* survives embedded in Hekhalot manuscripts, usually in the *Hekhalot Rabbati*, but not always in the same place in that work. It also appears on its own in one Hekhalot manuscript. Townsend dated the *David Apocalypse* to the sixth century, but claimed it could be as early as the second century.[21] Whilst individual traditions from *Hekhalot Rabbati* may be dated much earlier, Schäfer dated the "macroforms" of the material to no later than the tenth century.[22]

Literary Context

The Visions have close links through themes, motifs and traditions with the early apocalypses of the Second Temple period onwards. However, it is difficult to assert direct literary dependence of the Visions on these apocalyptic texts or traditions, especially because of the transmission of this material in rabbinic traditions, which in turn have influenced the Visions. The Visions represent a late development of Jewish apocalyptic, reflecting

16. See Townsend, "Minor Midrashim," 354-55 for the various recensions, their titles and sources.

17. Townsend, "Minor Midrashim," 354.

18. Townsend, "Minor Midrashim," 353-54.

19. Townsend, "Minor Midrashim," 365.

20. P. Schäfer, "In Heaven as It Is in Hell," 233.

21. Townsend, "Minor Midrashim," 356. Again, Townsend does not give further detail on the basis for this dating.

22. P. Schäfer, *Übersetzung der Hekhalot-Literatur II* (Tübingen: Mohr Siebeck, 1987), xx-xxiii.

material influenced by the earliest apocalypses, rabbinic eschatological traditions and mystical writings. The following paragraphs draw attention to those early apocalypses that display a large number of parallels with the material found in the Visions.

Hebrew Bible. The midrashic use of "proof-texts" from many books of the Hebrew Bible is often found in the Visions to give support from Scripture to the descriptions of the heavens and the place of the wicked and the righteous. However, the Hebrew Bible serves only as support for the teachings and legends in the Visions, rather than providing a basis for biblical exegesis. There is particular use of the eschatological and angelological material in the books of Isaiah, Daniel and the Psalms through both explicit proof-text and allusion. The portrayal of the chariot in Ezekiel 1; 3:12-15, 22-24; 8:1-4; 10:1-22; and 43:1-7 has had an important influence on the descriptions of the divine Throne of Glory and associated elements.

1 Enoch. The Book of Watchers (*1 Enoch* 1–36) describes in some detail the ascension of Enoch to heaven where he receives a revelation of the heavens. It contains a number of motifs that are found in the Visions, which share its interest in cosmological geography, although there are also few direct parallels in the details of the motifs. The text describes the Throne of Glory at *1 En.* 9:4; 14:18 (cf. *Greatness of Moses* 1:7). There is a contrast between the fiery abyss for the wicked in *1 En.* 10:13; 21:7-8 (cf. *Greatness of Moses* 13:2) and the garden for the righteous with the Tree of Life and its special scent in *1 En.* 24:4–25:7 (cf. *Order of Gan Eden* 4). The angelology of the text has parallels with material in the Visions, namely, Enoch has an angelic guide in *1 En.* 22:6 (cf. *Greatness of Moses* 2:1), there are angels of fire in *1 En.* 17:1 (cf. *Greatness of Moses* 2:3) and guardian angels in *1 En.* 9:1 (cf. *Legend of "Hear, O Israel"* 1:2). Finally, *1 En.* 11:1 outlines the stores of blessings (cf. *David Apocalypse* 3:4).

The Similitudes of Enoch (*1 Enoch* 37-71) also contains a number of motifs found in the Visions. The Throne of Glory is described at *1 En.* 45:3; 47:3; 60:2; 62:2-5; 69:27 (cf. *Greatness of Moses* 1:7). The angelology of the text provides motifs also found in the Visions, namely, the angels of punishment in *1 En.* 53:3; 56:1; 62:11; 66:1 are similar to angels of destruction (cf. *Greatness of Moses* 16:1). See also the guardian angels in *1 En.* 40:2-10; 71:8-9 (cf. *Legend of "Hear, O Israel"* 1:2), and the numbers of angels in *1 En.* 40:1; 60:1; 71:8 (cf. *Greatness of Moses* 8:4). There is a strong similarity between the Visions and the Similitudes in terms of the question and answer conversations between the one who ascends and his angelic guide as in *1 En.* 52:3; 53:4; 56:2 (cf. *Greatness of Moses* 5:6). The places set aside for the wicked and righteous are also found in this text. The fiery abyss is in *1 En.* 54:1; 67:4 (cf. *Greatness of Moses* 13:2) along with description of chains for wicked angels and people in *1 En.* 56:1; 69:28 (cf. *Greatness of Moses* 13:10). The dwelling places of the righteous are described in *1 En.* 39:4-8; 41:2 (cf. *History of Rabbi Yehoshua ben Levi* 5:4).

The Astronomical Book (*1 Enoch* 72–82) is also worthy of note for its descriptions of the windows of heaven in *1 En.* 72:3; 72:7; 75:7 (cf. *Greatness of Moses* 3:2 ff.).

Testament of Levi. The Greek *Testament of Levi* outlines the ascent of Levi through the heavens. Levi is shown around the heavens by an angelic guide who answers his questions about the sights he sees. This text contains a number of motifs that are closely paralleled throughout the Visions. The common apocalyptic motif of the Throne of Glory is found in *T. Levi* 5:1 (cf. *Greatness of Moses* 1:7). A number of aspects of the angels are described similarly in this text and in the Visions, such as with the questions asked of the angelic guide in *T. Levi* 2:9 (cf. *Greatness of Moses* 5:6), angels of punishment in *T. Levi* 3:2 (cf.

Greatness of Moses 16:1), and the praise of the angels in *T. Levi* 3:8 (cf. *Legend of "Hear, O Israel"* 2:7).

The cosmological geography of the text also has parallels with the Visions, namely, in the plurality of heavens in *T. Levi* 2:7-3:10 (cf. *Greatness of Moses* 3-9), waters in the first heaven in *T. Levi* 2:7 (cf. *Greatness of Moses* 3:1-2) and the gates in *T. Levi* 5:1; 18:10 (cf. *Legend of "Hear, O Israel"* 1:3). The place of punishment for the wicked contains fire, snow and ice in *T. Levi* 3:2 (cf. *Greatness of Moses* 17:1-3) and it is filled with darkness in *T. Levi* 3:2 (cf. *Treatise on the Work of Creation* 1:4); the wicked have a dark face as an indicator of sin in *T. Levi* 14:4 (cf. *Tractate on Gehinnom* 7:3). The Tree of Life is described in *T. Levi* 18:11 (cf. *Order of Gan Eden* 4:4), and the righteous have garments in *T. Levi* 8:5; 18:14 (cf. *Order of Gan Eden* 1:3), crowns in *T. Levi* 8:2 (cf. *Order of Gan Eden* 1:4), and a branch in *T. Levi* 8:8 (cf. *Order of Gan Eden* 1:5).

Apocalypse of Zephaniah. The *Apocalypse of Zephaniah* describes the visions of that prophet about the fate of the righteous and the wicked and the places of their reward and punishment. The text is of primary interest for the Visions because of the descriptions of the sins and torments of the wicked. *Apoc. Zeph.* 10:4-14 outlines the torments of the wicked within a question and answer framework between visionary and guide (cf. *Greatness of Moses* 13:11-17). This question and answer format is also found in *Apoc. Zeph.* 3:4; 3:6; 6:16-17. *Apoc. Zeph.* 6:2 describes a sea of fire (cf. *Legend of "Hear, O Israel"* 3:1) with the angel in charge of the abyss and Hades in *Apoc. Zeph.* 6:15 (cf. *Greatness of Moses* 13:6). *Apoc. Zeph.* 10:5-7 describes sins of bribery and usury and their punishment (cf. *Greatness of Moses* 13:11). Fiery scourges are described in *Apoc. Zeph.* 4:4 (cf. *Legend of Rabbi Yehoshua ben Levi* 1:8).

With regard to the fate of the righteous, *Apoc. Zeph.* 5:1-6 describes the gates of a heavenly city (cf. *Legend of "Hear, O Israel"* 1:3) and Abraham, Isaac, Jacob, Enoch, Elijah and David are the key righteous figures in *Apoc. Zeph.* 9:4 (cf. *Greatness of Moses* 20:13 ff.). Finally, *Apoc. Zeph.* 4:8-10 outlines the protection of Zephaniah from fearsome angels (cf. *Greatness of Moses* 9:5-6).

2 Enoch. *2 Enoch* describes the ascent of Enoch with his vision of the different heavens. The angelology of the text is of particular relevance to material in the Visions, especially the angels around the Throne of the Lord. The throne is described in *2 En.* 18:4; 20:3 (cf. *Greatness of Moses* 1:7); *2 En.* 20:1 outlines a vision of the chariot and its retinue in the seventh heaven (cf. *Greatness of Moses* 10). The many-eyed six-winged cherubim and seraphim are described in *2 En.* 21:1 (cf. *Greatness of Moses* 10). The praise of the heavenly retinue is in *2 En.* 17; 20:4; 21:1 (cf. *Legend of "Hear, O Israel"* 2:7). In *2 En.* 12:2; 21:1 it is the role of the angels to do the will of God and not depart from him (cf. *Greatness of Moses* 4:6). Angels of fire are in *2 En.* 20:1; 29:3; 39:5 (cf. *Greatness of Moses* 2:3), with fire from the mouth of angels in *2 En.* 1:5 (cf. *Legend of "Hear, O Israel"* 4:3). An angel of ice is described in *2 En.* 37:1-2 (cf. *Greatness of Moses* 8:3). *2 En.* 1a:4; 1:5; 19:1 refer to the shining faces of heavenly beings (cf. *Order of Gan Eden* 1:2), and *2 En.* 12:2 outlines the measurements of angels (cf. *Greatness of Moses* 4:3). Fear of angels is mentioned in *2 En.* 1:7 (cf. *Greatness of Moses* 9:5).

Certain chapters of *2 Enoch* are also important for the Visions. The description of the throne and its retinue in chap. 20–21 is already noted above. *2 Enoch* 10 describes the place of torture in the third heaven, including merciless angels in 10:3 (cf. *Greatness of Moses* 16:2), with instruments of torture in 10:2 (cf. *Greatness of Moses* 16:2). The river of fire is in 10:2 (cf. *Legend of "Hear, O Israel"* 3:1), along with the fire that is never extinguished (cf. *Tractate on*

Gehinnom 5:3); 10:2 outlines darkness in the place of torture (cf. *Treatise on the Work of Creation* 1:4) along with fire and snow in 10:2 (cf. *Treatise on the Work of Creation* 3:8). *2 Enoch* 8 describes the righteous in paradise. 8:8 describes 300 angels in charge of paradise and they sing with a pleasant voice (cf. *Order of Gan Eden* 4:3). The trees of paradise, including the Tree of Life, are described with particular reference to their scent in 8:2-4 (cf. *Order of Gan Eden* 4). There are also four streams in *2 En.* 8:5 (cf. *Greatness of Moses* 20:29).

Ascension of Isaiah. The *Ascension of Isaiah* contains a tour through the seven heavens by an angel. Isaiah sees many angels in the different heavens and the praise that they offer to those in the higher regions. There are thematic similarities between *Ascension of Isaiah* and the Visions, but the details of the descriptions of the seven heavens vary considerably between the traditions. The following motifs represent key parallels between the *Ascension of Isaiah* and the Visions. The one who ascends has an angelic guide in *Ascen. Isa.* 6:13 (cf. *Greatness of Moses* 2:1). The angelic guide has a divine commission in *Ascen. Isa.* 8:8-9 (cf. *Greatness of Moses* 2:8). Strength is given to the one who ascends in *Ascen. Isa.* 7:3 (cf. *Greatness of Moses* 2:4). The transformation of the one who ascends is outlined in *Ascen. Isa.* 7:25 (cf. *Greatness of Moses* 2:10). Questions are asked by the one who ascends in *Ascen. Isa.* 7:3; 9:3; 9:24 (cf. *Greatness of Moses* 5:6), despite the fear they feel in *Ascen. Isa.* 9:1 (cf. *Greatness of Moses* 9:5). Praise is offered by the angels in *Ascen. Isa.* 7:15 ff. (cf. *Legend of "Hear, O Israel"* 2:7). Sammael the angel is mentioned in *Ascen. Isa.* 7:9 (cf. *Greatness of Moses* 9:9), and the Gate Keepers of heaven are described in *Ascen. Isa.* 10:24 ff. (cf. *Legend of "Hear, O Israel"* 1:3). The thrones, garments and crowns of the righteous are in *Ascen. Isa.* 7:22; 8:26; 11:40 (cf. *Order of Gan Eden* 1).

Apocalypse of Peter. The *Apocalypse of Peter* describes the apostle's ascent to heaven to see the punishments and rewards reserved for after death. Material of particular relevance to the Visions is found in the description of the sins of the wicked and their appropriate punishments. At the time of judgement, the world turns to fire in *Apoc. Pet.* 5:2-4, and there are a river of fire in *Apoc. Pet.* 5:8; 6:2; 12:4 (cf. *Legend of "Hear, O Israel"* 3:1) and pits of fire in *Apoc. Pet.* 7:3 (cf. *History of Rabbi Yehoshua ben Levi* 14:2). The fire does not go out in *Apoc. Pet.* 5:4; 5:8, a devouring fire is described in *Apoc. Pet.* 6:4 and an eternal fire in 6:9; 11:8 (cf. *Tractate on Gehinnom* 5:3). *Apoc. Pet.* 5:2 describes the world covered in darkness with abysses of darkness in *Apoc. Pet.* 6:5 and hell as a place of darkness in *Apoc. Pet.* 9:1 (cf. *Treatise on the Work of Creation* 1:4). Angels of punishment carry out the judgements in *Apoc. Pet.* 7:4 (cf. *Greatness of Moses* 16:1). Punishment is by coals of fire in *Apoc. Pet.* 5:3; 12:1 (cf. *Legend of "Hear, O Israel"* 3:4), fiery iron in *Apoc. Pet.* 9:3 (cf. *Legend of Rabbi Yehoshua ben Levi* 1:8), chains of fire in *Apoc. Pet.* 9:6 (cf. *Greatness of Moses* 13:10), a pillar of fire in *Apoc. Pet.* 9:5-6 (cf. *Greatness of Moses* 18:5), and beatings with lashes of fire in *Apoc. Pet.* 9:2 (cf. *Greatness of Moses* 16:1). This results in the wicked being half of fire in *Apoc. Pet.* 9:1 (cf. *Greatness of Moses* 17:1). Punishment by hanging is also found, including hanging by the hair for adultery and trying to seduce men in *Apoc. Pet.* 7:5-6 (cf. *Greatness of Moses* 13:10), hanging by the tongue for blasphemy in *Apoc. Pet.* 7:1-2 (cf. *Greatness of Moses* 13:13). The wicked are also tortured with worms in *Apoc. Pet.* 9:2 (cf. *Greatness of Moses* 14:3-4) and poisonous animals in *Apoc. Pet.* 7:9 (cf. *Greatness of Moses* 15:1-2). The wicked are forced to eat their own tongues in *Apoc. Pet.* 9:3; 11:8 (cf. *Tractate on Gehinnom* 5:8).

A number of motifs regarding the righteous are also found in this text and the Visions, namely, the Throne of Glory in *Apoc. Pet.* 6:1 (cf. *Greatness of Moses* 1:7) and similarly in the crown of God in *Apoc. Pet.* 6:2 (cf. *Legend of "Hear, O Israel"* 2:1 ff.). Clothing of the life above is in *Apoc. Pet.* 13:1 (cf. *Order of Gan Eden* 1:3), Patriarchs in heaven in *Apoc. Pet.*

14:2 and 15:1 (cf. *Greatness of Moses* 20:14 ff.), shining faces of heavenly beings in *Apoc. Pet.* 15:2 (cf. *Order of Gan Eden* 1:2), scent in paradise in *Apoc. Pet.* 16:2-3 (cf. *Order of Gan Eden* 4:5) and gates of heaven in *Apoc. Pet.* 17:5 (cf. *Legend of "Hear, O Israel"* 1:3).

Apocalypse of Paul. This Latin text describes the journey of Paul to heaven and hell, but the majority of the text focuses on the description of the rite of passage of death, and the trial and sentencing of a person upon death. The *Apocalypse of Paul* bears some similarity to the Visions in terms of the description of punishments delivered to the wicked. The one who ascends is granted a vision of both hell and paradise in *Apoc. Paul* 11 (cf. *Greatness of Moses* 12:4), and is led by an angelic guide in *Apoc. Paul* 11 (cf. *Greatness of Moses* 2:1), although there are angels without mercy in *Apoc. Paul* 11 (cf. *Greatness of Moses* 16:1). The wicked suffer punishment through hanging by the hair in *Apoc. Paul* 39 (cf. *Greatness of Moses* 13:10), by chains of fire in *Apoc. Paul* 39 (cf. *Greatness of Moses* 13:10), by worms in *Apoc. Paul* 36, 37, 39, 42 (cf. *Greatness of Moses* 14:3-4), by ice and snow in *Apoc. Paul* 39 (cf. *Greatness of Moses* 18:4), by river of fire in *Apoc. Paul* 31 (cf. *Legend of "Hear, O Israel"* 3:1), by cannibalism in *Apoc. Paul* 37 (cf. *Tractate on Gehinnom* 5:8), and by beatings in *Apoc. Paul* 35, 40 (cf. *Legend of Rabbi Yehoshua ben Levi* 1:8). The specific sins of the wicked are also outlined, including punishment for the sin of usury in *Apoc. Paul* 37 (cf. *Greatness of Moses* 16:5), the sin of adultery in *Apoc. Paul* 38 (cf. *Greatness of Moses* 13:11), and punishment for gossiping in *Apoc. Paul* 31 (cf. *Greatness of Moses* 13:13). There are pits for the wicked in *Apoc. Paul* 32 (cf. *History of Rabbi Yehoshua ben Levi* 14:2).

There are motifs about the righteous in this text that are similarly found in the Visions. There is a meeting with the patriarchs in heaven in *Apoc. Paul* 47 (cf. *Greatness of Moses* 20:14 ff.), four streams in paradise in *Apoc. Paul* 45 (cf. *Greatness of Moses* 20:29), the Tree of Life in paradise in *Apoc. Paul* 45 (cf. *Order of Gan Eden* 4), and a place for those who maintained chastity in *Apoc. Paul* 26 (cf. *Order of Gan Eden* 5:8).

3 Enoch. The Hebrew *3 Enoch* contains a large number of close parallels with material from the Visions, especially on angelological themes. In *3 En.* 1:4 Metatron Prince of the Divine Presence is the angelic guide of Rabbi Ishmael (cf. *Greatness of Moses* 2:1). Ishmael asks the identity of his guide in *3 En.* 3:1 (cf. *Greatness of Moses* 2:7) and Metatron is identified with Enoch in *3 En.* 4:2 (cf. *Greatness of Moses* 2:8). In addition to the Throne of Glory in *3 En.* 1:6; 7:1; 8:1; 15:1; 33:3 (cf. *Greatness of Moses* 1:7), and accompanying angels in *3 En.* chaps. 1, 7, 21–22, 33, 39 (cf. *Greatness of Moses* 10), a number of angels are mentioned in both *3 Enoch* and the Visions, including angels of destruction in *3 En.* 31:2; 32:1; 33:1; 44:2 (cf. *Greatness of Moses* 16:1), guardian angels in *3 En.* 18 (cf. *Legend of "Hear, O Israel"* 1:2), Erelim in *3 En.* 14:1 (cf. *Greatness of Moses* 5:7), Irin Qaddishin in *3 En.* 28:1-10 (cf. *Greatness of Moses* 8:5), Sammael in *3 En.* 14:2; 26:12 (cf. *Greatness of Moses* 9:9) and Galizur in *3 En.* 18:16-17 (cf. *Legend of "Hear, O Israel"* 4:1 ff.).

The angels also share a number of characteristics with those in the Visions, namely, angels of fire in *3 En.* 1:7; 2:1; 7:1; 39:2 (cf. *Greatness of Moses* 2:3), many-eyed ones at *3 En.* 9:4; 18:25; 22:8; 25:6; 26:6 (cf. *Greatness of Moses* 9:8), tongue of flame in *3 En.* 18:25; 22:4 (cf. *Greatness of Moses* 2:10), fire from mouths of angels in *3 En.* 22:4 (cf. *Legend of "Hear, O Israel"* 4:3), lightning out of the mouth in *3 En.* 18:25; 22:9 (cf. *Legend of "Hear, O Israel"* 4:3), horns of glory in *3 En.* 22:7; 22:13 (cf. *Greatness of Moses* 11:3) and measurements of angels in *3 En.* 9:2; 18:19; 21:1; 22:3; 25:4; 26:4 (cf. *Greatness of Moses* 4:3) including the size of wings in *3 En.* 18:25; 26:10 (cf. *Greatness of Moses* 10:4). The angels have many roles in *3 Enoch*, but the praise offered by the heavenly retinue is a major theme in *3 En.* 1:12; 20:2; 22:15-16; 26:8; 34:2; 35:4; 40:1-3 (cf. *Legend of "Hear, O Israel"* 2:7).

Images of the fate of the wicked are also paralleled in *3 Enoch* and the Visions. The fire of Gehinnom is in *3 En.* 44:3 (cf. *Greatness of Moses* 13:2-4). The river of fire is described in *3 En.* 18:19, 21 and 36:1 (cf. *Legend of "Hear, O Israel"* 3:1); it flows from under the Throne of Glory in *3 En.* 36:1, sim. 18:19 (cf. *Legend of "Hear, O Israel"* 3:1) and is made from fiery sweat in *3 En.* 18:25 (cf. *Legend of "Hear, O Israel"* 3:2). Angels bathe in the river of fire in *3 En.* 6:2; 47:1-2 (cf. *Legend of "Hear, O Israel"* 3:3) and it falls on the heads of the wicked in *3 En.* 33:4-5 (cf. *Legend of "Hear, O Israel"* 3:4).

This Translation

As this contribution is a new translation of the texts selected by M. Gaster, I have used standard editions that most closely represent the material he translated.[23] Where Gaster's selections were part of a larger "text," the entire tradition has been translated. The titles of the different Visions represent those cited in the editions used here. I have adopted my own division into chapter and verse where the editions do not include such information. Exceptions to this approach are noted and explained in the following.

- For this translation of *The Greatness of Moses*, I have used the text printed by S. A. Wertheimer in *Batei Midrashot*. I have retained Wertheimer's use of section divisions, but have added my own verse numbers which are not included in his edition. I have used the more well-known title *The Greatness of Moses* for this text.[24]
- *Legend of "Hear, O Israel"* is translated here from the edition of A. Jellinek in *BHM*, 5:165-66.[25]
- The translation of *History of Rabbi Yehoshua ben Levi* presented here represents the edition of Jellinek in *BHM*, 2:48-51.[26]
- *Order of Gan Eden* is translated from the edition of Jellinek in *BHM*, 2:52-53.[27]
- For the translation of *Tractate on Gehinnom* presented here, I have used the text printed by Jellinek in *BHM*, 1:147-49.[28] I have utilized the chapter divisions included by Jellinek after the introduction. However, the introductory part of the text is not numbered in his edition, and for this part I have maintained my own division into chapters and included my own verse numbers.
- The translation of *In What Manner Is the Punishment of the Grave?* represents the edition of Jellinek in *BHM*, 5:49-51.[29]
- *Legend of Rabbi Yehoshua ben Levi* is translated from the edition of Jellinek in *BHM*, 5:43-44.[30]
- For the translation of *Treatise on the Work of Creation*, I have used the material iden-

23. Unfortunately, it is not always clear from the information given by Gaster exactly which MSS and editions he used, and he apparently brought together different sources for his translation of each "text."

24. The text corresponds to that translated and entitled by Gaster as "The Revelation of Moses (A)," *Studies and Texts*, 125-41.

25. The text corresponds to that translated and entitled by Gaster as "The Revelation of Moses (B)," *Studies and Texts*, 141-43.

26. Cf. Gaster's text III "The Revelation of R. Joshua ben Levi (A)," *Studies and Texts*, 144-49.

27. Cf. Gaster's text IV "The Revelation of R. Joshua ben Levi (B)," *Studies and Texts*, 149-51.

28. This text corresponds to §1-9 and §20-24 of text V translated by Gaster under the title "Hell," *Studies and Texts*, 152-58.

29. This text corresponds to §10-19 of text V translated by Gaster under the title "Hell," *Studies and Texts*, 152-58.

30. This text corresponds to text VI translated and entitled by Gaster as "Hell," *Studies and Texts*, 158-60.

tifed by Gaster from Abraham Azulai's *Ḥesed le-Avraham* (Amsterdam, 1685), *neharot* 7-9.[31]

- The *David Apocalypse* is translated from the edition of Jellinek in *BHM*, 5:166-168, excluding the framing material from *Hekhalot Rabbati*.[32]

Bibliography

Bauckham, R. *The Fate of the Dead: Studies on the Jewish and Christian Apocalypses*. NovTSup 93. Leiden: Brill, 1998.

Buchholz, D. D. *Your Eyes Will Be Opened: A Study of the Greek (Ethiopic) Apocalypse of Peter*. Atlanta, Ga.: Scholars Press, 1988.

Eisenstein, J. D. *Oẓar Midrashim*. New York: s.n., 1915.

Even-Shemuel, Y. *Midreshey Ge'ulah*. Israel: Mosad Byalik al-yede 'Masadah', 1959.

Gaster, M. "Hebrew Visions of Hell and Paradise." *JRAS* N.S. 25 (1893): 571-611 (reprinted in *Studies and Texts in Folklore, Magic, Mediaeval Romance, Hebrew Apocrypha and Samaritan Archaeology*. 3 vols. London: Maggs Bros, 1925-1928, 1:124-164).

Ginzberg, L. *The Legends of the Jews*. 7 vols. 11th ed. Philadelphia, Pa.: The Jewish Publication Society of America, 1982.

Himmelfarb, M. *Ascent to Heaven in Jewish and Christian Apocalypses*. Oxford: Oxford University Press, 1993.

__________. *Tours of Hell: An Apocalyptic Form in Jewish and Christian Literature*. Philadelphia, Pa.: University of Pennsylvania Press, 1983.

Hirschfelder, U. "The Liturgy of the Messiah: The Apocalypse of David in Hekhalot Literature." *Jewish Studies Quarterly* 12 (2005): 148-193.

Lieberman, S. "On Sins and Their Punishment." Pages 29-51 in *Texts and Studies*. New York: Ktav, 1974.

Netzer, A. "A Midrash on the Ascension of Moses in Judeo-Persian." Pages 105-143 in *Irano-Judaica*. Edited by S. Shaked and A. Netzer, vol. 2. Jerusalem: Ben-Zvi Institute for the Study of Jewish Communities in the East, 1990.

Odeberg, H. *3 Enoch or The Hebrew Book of Enoch*. Cambridge: Cambridge University Press, 1928.

Schäfer, P. "In Heaven as It Is in Hell." Pages 233-74 in *Heavenly Realms and Earthly Realities in Late Antique Religions*. Edited by R. Boustan and A. Yoshiko Reed. Cambridge: Cambridge University Press, 2004.

Schäfer, P., et al. *Synopse zur Hekhalot-Literatur*. Tübingen: Mohr Siebeck, 1981.

Stone, M. E., and J. Strugnell. *The Books of Elijah, parts 1-2*. SBLTT 18. Atlanta, Ga.: Scholars, 1979.

Townsend, J. T. "Minor Midrashim." Pages 331-92 in *Bibliographical Essays in Medieval Jewish Studies*. Edited by Y. Yerushalmi. New York: Anti-Defamation League of B'nai Brith, 1976.

Wertheimer, S. A. *Batei Midrashot*, 2nd ed. Jerusalem: Ktab Yad WaSepher, 1952-1955.

Wright, J. E. *The Early History of Heaven*. Oxford: Oxford University Press, 2000.

Wünsche, A. *Aus Israels Lehrhallen*. Leipzig: E. Pfeiffer, 1909.

31. Cf. Gaster's text VII translated and entitled by Gaster as "Hell," *Studies and Texts*, 160-61.
32. Cf. Gaster's text VIII translated and entitled by Gaster as "Paradise," *Studies and Texts*, 162-64.

The Greatness of Moses (*Gedulat Moshe*)

Moses Honoured by God

Cant 2:3 **1** [1]*As an apple tree among the trees of the wood, so is my beloved among the sons.*[a]
[2]This refers to Moses, our teacher, upon him be peace. [3]At the moment that the
Holy One, Blessed be He, was revealed to him on Horeb,[b] He said to him: "Go
and bring out my people, the children of Israel, from Egypt, for their cry has
come to me. [4]Also, I have remembered the covenant and the loving kindness
and the oath that I swore to Abraham, my servant,"[c] as it is said, *And also the*
Gen 15:14 *nation that they serve, I will judge.* [5]Moses, our teacher, upon him be peace, said
before the Holy One, Blessed be He: "Master of the World, *who am I that I should*
Exod 3:11 *go to Pharaoh, and that I should bring out the children of Israel from Egypt*?" [6]The
Holy One, Blessed be He, said to him: "You have said 'who am I?' and you have
humbled yourself.[d] By your life, I will honour you!" As it is said, *But the humble*
Prov 29:23 *of spirit gains honour.*[e] [7]"I will place all the princes into your hand. I will raise
you up to the heavens, and you will see my Throne of Glory,[f] and I will show to
you all the angels who are in the heavens."[g]

The Transformation and Ascent of Moses

2 [1]At that moment, the Holy One, Blessed be <He>,[h] commanded Metatron,[i] Prince of the Presence, and said to him: "Go and bring Moses, my servant, to the heavens. [2]Take with you 15,000 angels on his right, and 15,000 on his left, with rejoicing, songs, tambourines and choruses, and utter a song before Moses, my

---

a. This corresponds to Gaster's text I "The Revelation of Moses (A)."

b. Cf. Moses and the burning bush on Horeb in Exod 3:1-10.

c. Reference to the covenant between the pieces in Genesis 15 and the prophecy of slavery and redemption.

d. Cf. *Aseret ha-Dibrot*, *BHM*, 1:66; *b. Sotah* 5a.

e. Cf. *Num. Rab.* 13.3; *Pesiq. Rab.* 7.3.

f. For Throne of Glory cf. 1 Kgs 22:19; Isa 6:1; 66:1; Jer 3:17; 17:12; Ps 89:14; Rev 4:2-11; *1 En.* 9:4; 14:18; 45:3; 47:3; 60:2; 62:2-5; 69:27; *T. Levi* 5:1; *3 En.* 1:6; 7:1; 8:1; 15:1; 33:3; *Apoc. Ab.* 18:3; *2 En.* 1a:4; 18:4; 20:3; 22:2; *2 Bar.* 46:4; *Apoc. Pet.* 6:1; *Exod. Rab.* 33.4; *b. Pesah.* 54a; *b. Shab.* 152b; *Gen. Rab.* 1.4; *Midr. Prov.* 8. See also *Greatness of Moses* 10.

g. Cf. *L.A.B.* 19:10; *2 Bar.* 59:4-11.

h. The pronoun "He" is missing from Wertheimer's edition, but found in the Frankfurt 1733 edition.

i. For Metatron, see *b. Hag.* 15a; *b. Sanh.* 38b; *b. 'Abod. Zar.* 3b; *b. Yebam.* 16b; *3 En.* 1:4; for an angelic guide cf. *Ascen. Isa.* 6:13; *Apoc. Paul* 11; *1 En.* 22:6; *Apoc. Ab.* 10:16; Gk. *Apoc. Ezra* 4:7.

servant."[a] [3]Metatron said before the Holy One, Blessed be He: "Moses is not able to ascend [to][b] the angels, because there are princes of fire among the angels,[c] and he is flesh and blood." [4]After this, the Holy One, Blessed be He, commanded Metatron, and said to him: "Go, turn his flesh into flashes of fire so that his strength is like the strength of Gabriel."[d] [5]Metatron came to Moses. [6]When Moses saw him, immediately he was afraid. [7]He said to him: "Who are you?"[e] [8]He said to him: "I am Enoch,[f] son of Jared, father of your father. The Holy One, Blessed be He, sent me to bring you up to his Throne of Glory."[g] [9]Moses said to Metatron: "I am flesh and blood, and I am not able to look at the angels." [10]After this, he stood and turned his flesh into flashes of fire,[h] and his eyes into the wheels of the chariot.[i] His strength was like the strength of the angels, and his tongue became a flame.[j] [11]Then he raised Moses to the heavens,[k] and with him were the angels, 15,000 on his right and 15,000 on his left, and Metatron and Moses were in the middle.

Moses in the First Heaven

3 [1]Moses went to the first heaven,[l] which is like the first day of the week. [2]He saw the waters[m] standing in rows, and all of the heaven consists of windows.[n] [3]At each window, there the angels stand upon the waters on high in the greatness of the Holy One, Blessed be He. [4]Moses asked Metatron, he said to him: "What are these windows?" [5]He said to him: "These are the windows: windows of prayer, windows of supplication; windows of weeping, windows of joy; windows of plenty, windows of famine; windows of riches, windows of poverty; windows of war, windows of peace; windows of conception, windows of birth." [6]He saw windows until they were countless and without number.

---

a. Cf. *Gk. Apoc. Ezra* 4:8 where Ezra and his guides are accompanied by 34 angels.

b. Brackets are found in Wertheimer's edition.

c. For angels of fire cf. Ps 104:4; *1 En.* 17:1; *2 En.* 20:1; 29:3; 39:5; *2 Bar.* 21:6; *3 En.* 1:7; 2:1; 7:1; 39:2; *Pirqe R. El.* 4.

d. Isaiah is given strength to speak during his vision in *Ascen. Isa.* 7:3.

e. Cf. *3 En.* 3:1.

f. Cf. *3 En.* 4:2.

g. Cf. *Ascen. Isa.* 7:27; 8:8-9 for the angel being sent to bring Isaiah; *Apoc. Ab.* 10:6, 13, 16; *3 Bar.* 1:4.

h. Isaiah is transformed as he moves through the heavens in *Ascen. Isa.* 7:25; Enoch's face is changed in *1 En.* 39:14; *3 En.* 15:1 similarly describes the transformation of Enoch/Metatron.

i. Cf. Ezek 10:13; *3 En.* 19:2-7 describes the wheels of the chariot.

j. Cf. *3 En.* 18:25; 22:4.

k. Cf. *Ascen. Isa.* 6:11-12.

l. For plurality of heavens cf. *Ascen. Isa.* 7:8 ff.; *T. Levi* 2:7–3:10; *3 Bar.* 2:2 ff.; *2 En.* 3–21; *Apoc. Ab.* 19:4; 2 Cor 12:2f.; *3 En.* 17; *b. Hag.* 12b-13a; *Gen. Rab.* 19.7; *Song Rab.* 5.1; *Num. Rab.* 12.6; 13.2; *Lev. Rab.* 29.11; *3 En.* 17 also describes the seven angels in charge of each of the seven heavens.

m. For waters in the first heaven cf. *T. Levi* 2:7.

n. Cf. Gen 7:11; Mal 3:10; *1 En.* 60:12; 72:3; 72:7; 75:7; 83:11; 101:2; *2 En.* 13-16; *3 En.* 8:1 describes gates of different qualities; *Pirqe R. El.* 6; *y. Rosh. Hash.* 2.5, 58a; *Exod. Rab.* 15.22.

Moses in the Second Heaven

4 [1]Moses went to the second heaven, which is like the second day of the week. [2]He saw there one angel, and his name is Nuriel. [3]He is 300 parasangs[a] (high),[b] and fifty myriads of angels stand before him.[c] They are all made of fire and water.[d] [4]Their faces are directed upward, and they utter a song before the Holy
Ps 145:3 One, Blessed be He, as it is said, *Great is the Lord and greatly to be praised.* [5]Moses asked Metatron and said to him: "Who are these angels?" [6]He said to him: "These are the angels appointed over the trees, over the wind, and over the rains. They go and do the will of their Lord,[e] then return to their place and praise the Holy One, Blessed be He." [7]Moses said to Metatron: "Why are they standing, their faces on high directed towards the Holy One, Blessed be He?" [8]Metatron said to him: "From the day that the Holy One, Blessed be He, created them, so are they. They have not moved from their place."[f]

Moses in the Third Heaven

5 [1]Moses went to the third heaven, which is like the third day of the week. [2]He saw there one angel and his name is Noriel. [3]His height is a journey[g] of 500 years. [4]He has 70,000 heads, and each head has 70,000 mouths, and each mouth has 70,000 tongues, and each tongue has 70,000 utterances. [5]With him stand 70,000 myriads of angels, and they all are made of white fire, and give praise before the Holy One, Blessed be He. [6]Moses asked Metatron and said to him: "Who are these angels, and what is their name?"[h] [7]He said to him: "Their name is Erelim,[i] the ones appointed over the plants, over the trees, over the fruits and the grain.[j] They all go to do the will of their Lord, and return to their place."[k]

Moses in the Fourth Heaven

6 [1]Moses went to the fourth heaven, which is like the fourth day of the week. [2]He saw there the Temple rebuilt[l]—its pillars are of red fire. [3]He saw there the angels entering and praising the Holy One, Blessed be He, as David the King, upon him
Ps 103:20 be peace, said: "*Bless the Lord,* all[m] *his angels, mighty ones of strength.*" [4]Moses asked Metatron and said to him: "Who are these?" [5]He said to him: "These are

a. A parasang is a Persian unit of length equivalent to 3.88 miles.

b. Cf. measurements of angels in *2 En.* 12:2; *3 En.* 9:2; 18:19; 21:1; 22:3; 25:4; 26:4.

c. Cf. *3 En.* 17 for the angels accompanying each prince of the heavens.

d. Cf. the tension between fire and water in *2 En.* 29:1-2; *3 En.* 42:7, 33; *b. Hag.* 12a; *Gen. Rab.* 10.3; cf. *Greatness of Moses* 7:2.

e. Cf. *2 En.* 12:2; *3 En.* 5:2; 22:16 for angels doing the will of God.

f. For the angels who do not depart from their position cf. *1 En.* 14:23; *2 En.* 21:1.

g. *3 Bar.* 2:2; 3:2; 4:2 describe the dimensions of the heavens in terms of the days of a journey; cf. *b. Hag.* 12b-13a which describes the distance from earth to the first heaven as a journey of 500 years and the thickness of the first heaven as a journey of 500 years.

h. Cf. similar questions at *Ascen. Isa.* 7:3; 9:3; *1 En.* 52:3; *T. Levi* 2:9; *3 Bar.* 5:1; 16:5-6 (Slavonic); *Apoc. Zeph.* 3:6; 6:16-17.

i. The word Erelim is based on a word of uncertain meaning (translated "the valiant" by the NRSV) in Isa 33:7. Cf. *b. Ketub.* 104a; *3 En.* 14:1.

j. Cf. *2 En.* 19:4 for angels over fruits of the earth and grass in the sixth heaven.

k. Cf. *Greatness of Moses* 4:7.

l. Cf. *b. Hag.* 12b; *b. Zebah.* 62a; *b. Menah.* 110a; *Pesiq. Rab.* 20.3.

m. The word "all" is not found in the biblical text but is added in Wertheimer's edition.

the angels appointed over all land, and over the sun and the moon[a] and the stars[b] and the planets[c] and twenty-six celestial spheres.[d] All of them utter a song." 6He saw in it great stars,[e] and each and every star is as big as[f] all the land. 7The name of one is Nogah[g] and the name of the second is Ma'adim.[h] One is by the side of [the sun][i] and one is by the side of the moon. 8Moses asked Metatron, he said to him: "Why are they positioned one by the other?" 9He said to him: "This one is by the sun in summer so that it cools the world from its heat.[j] The other is by the moon in winter so that it heats the world from cold."[k]

Moses in the Fifth Heaven

7 1Moses went to the fifth heaven, which is like the fifth day of the week. 2He saw there angels made half of fire and half of snow[l]—snow from above and fire from below. 3The Holy One, Blessed be He, makes peace between them and one cannot extinguish its counterpart,[m] as it is said, *He makes peace in his high heaven.* 4All of them give praise before the Holy One, Blessed be He. 5Moses said Job 25:2
to Metatron: "What are these ones doing?" 6He said to him: "From the day that the Holy One, Blessed be He, created them, so are they." 7He said to him: "What is their name?" 8He said to him:[n] "Their name is Erelim,[o] the ones who are called Ishim." As it is said, *To you, O men,*[p] *I call.* Prov 8:4

Moses in the Sixth Heaven

8 1Moses went to the sixth heaven, which is like the sixth day of the week. 2He saw there one angel and his name is Uriel. 3His length is like a journey of 500 years, and all of his form is ice.[q] 4Many thousands and myriads[r] [of angels][s]

---

a. Sun and moon are in the fourth heaven in *2 En.* 11; *3 En.* 17:4 for the angel in charge of the sun; *3 En.* 17:5 for the angel in charge of the moon.

b. Cf. angels governing stars in the first heaven in *2 En.* 4:2; *3 En.* 17:7.

c. The Hebrew word can refer to either planets or constellations.

d. The Hebrew word can refer to wheels, also found on the divine chariot, or the sphere of the Zodiac in addition to the celestial spheres. Cf. *b. Hag.* 12b-13a which locates these in the first heaven, as does *2 Enoch* 4, but *3 Baruch* 7–9 locates them in the third heaven; cf. *3 En.* 14:3-4 which names the angels in charge of the elements and cosmos.

e. Cf. *2 En.* 11:3.

f. Lit. "full of."

g. Nogah means "light" but can also refer to the planet Venus; cf. *Pirqe R. El.* 6.

h. Ma'adim is the name often given to the planet Mars; cf. *Pirqe R. El.* 6.

i. The brackets are included in Wertheimer's edition.

j. Cf. *1 Enoch* 4.

k. Cf. *b. Ber.* 58b.

l. Cf. Iaoel's hair of snow in *Apoc. Ab.* 11:2.

m. I.e., God made it so both sides of the angels, snow and fire, could exist together within one angel without destroying the other. For God keeping peace between fire and water cf. *3 En.* 42:7.

n. "To him" is in Aramaic.

o. Cf. *Greatness of Moses* 5:7 where the Erelim are said to be in the third heaven. The Erelim of the fifth heaven are identified with the Ishim, and are also assigned a different task to those in the third heaven.

p. The Hebrew here is *'ishim* thus relating the biblical verse to the angels.

q. Cf. the angel in *2 En.* 37:1-2.

r. Cf. use of numbers such as this at *1 En.* 40:1; 60:1; 71:8; *Apoc. Zeph.* 8:2.

s. Wertheimer inserted "of angels" in his edition.

stand with him. They all give praise before the One who said "And the world
Ps 19:2 (Evv 19:1) was," as it is said, *The heavens declare the glory of God.*[a] [5]He said to him: "These are the angels who are called Irin and Qaddishin."[b]

Moses in the Seventh Heaven

9 [1]Moses went to the seventh heaven, which is like the day of the Sabbath. [2]He saw there two angels bound in chains[c] of fire that are hot and red. Each one is a journey of 500 years. [3]Moses asked Metatron, he said to him: "Who are these and what is their name?" [4]He said to him: "Their name is Af and Hemah.[d] The Holy One, Blessed be He, created them during the six days of creation to do the will of their Creator." [5]Moses said to Metatron: "I am afraid of these angels, and I am not able to look at their faces."[e] [6]Immediately, Metatron stood and embraced Moses. He said to him: "Moses, Moses, Beloved of the Lord, Servant of the Lord, do not be afraid and do not be dismayed on account of them." Immediately, the mind of Moses was pacified.[f] [7]After this, he saw one angel who is different in his form from all the angels. [8]His height is a journey of 500 years. He is girded about his loins in two places. From the sole of his foot to the crown of his head, he is full of eyes of fire.[g] Everyone who sees him falls upon their face on account of great fear. [9]Moses asked Metatron and said to him: "Who is this?" He said to him: "Sammael, the one who takes souls."[h] [10]Moses said to him: "To where is he descending?" He said to him: "To take the soul of Job, the righteous." [11]Moses said before the Holy One, Blessed be he, "Master of the World, may it be your will, O Lord, my God, and God of my fathers, that you do not deliver me into the hand of this angel."

The Angels at the Throne of Glory

10 [1]He saw the angels standing before the Holy One, Blessed be He. [2]Each one has six wings.[i] With two they[j] cover their face, with two they cover their feet and
Isa 6:2 with two they fly. With two they cover their face so that they[k] do not see the face of the Shekinah, with two they cover their bodies and with two they fly.[l] [3]They

---

a. Cf. *3 En.* 46:13; the edition of Thessalonica 1726-7, cited by Wertheimer, gives the following: "Moses asked Metatron and said: 'Who are these?'"

b. "Watchers" and "holy ones" – terms for angels used in Dan 4:10-17; *3 En.* 28:1-10. The Watchers also figure importantly in the Book of Watchers (*1 Enoch* 1–36).

c. For chained angels cf. *2 Bar.* 56:13; *1 En.* 10:4; 54:2-5; Rev 20:1-3.

d. "Anger and Wrath." Cf. *Apocalypse of Paul* 11 where Paul sees insane angels in heaven who are without mercy.

e. The motif of the fearsome appearance of angels is very common, e.g., *Ascen. Isa.* 9:1; *Apoc. Zeph.* 6:9; *2 En.* 1:7; *Apoc. Ab.* 11:4; cf. *b. Ned.* 32a.

f. Cf. *Apoc. Zeph.* 4:8-10 for protection of the ascender from fearsome angels.

g. For angels with many eyes cf. Ezek 1:18; 10:12; *Apoc. Ab.* 17:15; 18:3; *2 En.* 1a:4; 21:1; *3 En.* 9:4; 18:25; 22:8; 25:6; 26:6; Rev 4:8; for eyes of fire cf. *2 En.* 1:5; Rev 1:14; 2:18.

h. Cf. *Ascen. Isa.* 7:9; *T. Ab.* 17; *3 En.* 14:2; 26:12; *Deut. Rab.* 11.10; *Tg. Ps.-J.* Gen 3:6; *Pirqe R. El.* 13-14.

i. For angels with six wings cf. *2 En.* 11:4; 16:7; 19:6; 21:1; *Apoc. Ab.* 18:6-7; Rev 4:8; *3 En.* 26:9; *Pirqe R. El.* 4.

j. The Hebrew gives a singular verb, used in a collective sense, for the verbs of the next line.

k. The plural verb returns from this word.

l. Cf. *Pirqe R. El.* 4 for this tradition.

minister before the Holy One, Blessed be He, and say: "*Holy, holy, holy is the Lord
of hosts, all the earth is full of his glory.*"[a] [4]Each wing is a journey of 500 years, and
its width goes from one end of the world to the other.[b] [5]Moses asked Metatron
and said to him: "What is their name?" He said to him: "Seraphim[c]—they stand
above." [6]He saw four angels lifting the Throne of Glory.[d] Moses said to Metatron:
"What is their name?" He said to him: "The Holy Living Creatures."[e]

The Torah in Heaven

11 [1]After this, Moses saw one angel, his name is Zagzagel.[f] [2]He teaches Torah to
souls in seventy languages, and they all say the halakhah of Moses from Sinai,
as it is said, *The court sat in judgement and the books were opened.* [3]The word Dan 7:10
"judge"[g] refers to Zagzagel, who is Prince of Torah and Wisdom.[h] He has the rays
of glory.[i] [4]Moses sat before him and learnt all the ten secrets. [5]Afterwards, he
said before the Holy One, Blessed be He: "I will not go down from here until you
give me a good gift." [6]The Holy One, Blessed be He, said to him: "I have given
you the Torah, which they will call after your name," as it is said, *Remember the
Torah of Moses, my servant.* Mal 3:22 (Evv 4:4)

Moses Permitted to See Gan Eden and Gehinnom

12 [1]From where do we know that Moses ascended on high? As it is said, *God
ascended with a shout, the Lord with the sound of a trumpet.*[j] [2]The word "God" Ps 47:6 (Evv 47:5)
refers to Moses, as it is said, *God*. The interpretation of "God" is "judge," and Ps 47:6 (Evv 47:5)
the word "judge" means Moses, as it is said, *And Moses sat to judge the people.* Exod 18:13
[3]Therefore, it is said, *As an apple tree among the trees of the wood.*[k] [4]Afterwards, Cant 2:3
a *Bat Qol*[l] went out and said to Moses: "Moses, you have come and seen my
Throne of Glory. Thus, you are worthy of seeing two enclosures—one of Gan
Eden and one of Gehinnom."[m]

---

a. Cf. the Qedushah in *1 En.* 39:12; Rev 4:8; *3 En.* 1:12; 20:2; 40:1-3; *Pirqe R. El.* 4. For angels who say "holy" and "blessed" cf. *3 En.* 34:2; 35:4.

b. Cf. *3 En.* 18:25; 26:10.

c. For the Seraphim cf. Isa 6:2-3, 6-7; *1 En.* 20:7; 61:10; 71:7; *3 En.* 1:7; 26:8-12; 33:3.

d. Cf. *3 En.* 33:3.

e. For the living creatures and the chariot cf. Ezek 1:4-28; 10; *1 En.* 14:18; *2 En.* 20:1; *2 Bar.* 51:11; *Apoc. Ab.* 18; *b. Hag.* 13b; *Gen. Rab.* 78.1; *Midr. Ps.* 103.16; *Pirqe R. El.* 4; *3 En.* 1:5-12; 21; 39:1-2. The term "Holy Living Creatures" is often found in Hekhalot literature, e.g., *3 En.* 22:13, 33:4.

f. Edition of Thessalonica 1726-27, cited by Wertheimer, gives: "in the heaven called Araboth, the seventh heaven."

g. The word *dayyān* "judge" is not found in Dan 7:10 which instead has *dîna'* "the court."

h. Edition of Thessalonica 1726-27 gives: "And he had another name, they call him Yefifiyah with reference to Yofiel Prince of Torah."

i. Cf. *3 En.* 22:7, 13.

j. Cf. *3 En.* 5:14.

k. Thessalonica 1726-27 gives: "as he is Moses, teacher of all the prophets."

l. See Introduction, n. 2.

m. Cf. *Apoc. Paul* 11 where Paul is told that he will see the place of the just and the place for the souls of sinners.

Descent of Moses to Gehinnom and Punishment by Hanging

13 [1]After this the Holy One, Blessed be He, sent for Gabriel and said to him: "Go with Moses and open Gehinnom."[a] [2]Moses came, and Gabriel opened Gehinnom.[b] Moses saw a burning fire.[c] [3]Moses said to Gabriel: "I am not able to enter Gehinnom on account of the fire." [4]He said to him: "There is another fire greater than this and the fire of Gehinnom cannot damage (it)." [5]When Moses entered Gehinnom, Gehinnom fled before Moses. [6]Nasargiel Prince of Gehinnom[d] came and said to Moses: "Who are you?" He said to him: "I am Moses, son of Amram." [7]He said to him: "This is not your place—but your place is in Gan Eden!" He said to him: "I have come to see the greatness of the Holy One, Blessed be He." [8]The Holy One, Blessed be He, said to Nasargiel, Prince of Gehinnom: "Go with Moses and show him Gehinnom, and how the wicked are in its midst." [9]After this, Moses went after Nasargiel and they came to the beginning of Gehinnom. [10]Moses saw people hung by their eyes and hung by their ears and by their hands and by their feet and by their tongue. The women were hung[e] by their breasts and by their hair[f] and by their feet with chains of fire.[g] [11]Moses said to Nasargiel: "Why are they hung by their eyes?"[h] He said to him: "Because they looked with evil at a married woman and at the money of their neighbours.[i] [12]They are hung by their ears because they listened to idle words and words of vanity, and turned[j] their ear from hearing words of Torah.[k] [13]The ones who are hung by their tongue, they are the ones who told gossip and spoke idle words.[l] [14]They are hung by their feet because they listened to[m] the gossip of their neighbour,[n] and did not walk[o] for a religious purpose and go to the synagogue to pray to their Creator. [15]They are hung by their hands because they stole the money of their neighbours with their hands, and killed[p] their neighbour.[q] [16]The women are hung by their breasts because they lifted their breasts and fed

a. On the seven names of hell cf. *b. 'Erub.* 19a.

b. Cf. 2 Chr 28:3; 33:6; 2 Kgs 23:10; Jer 7:30-34; *b. Pesah.* 54a; *b. Tamid* 32b; *b. B. Bat.* 84a; *b. 'Erub.* 19a.

c. For fiery abyss cf. *1 En.* 10:13; 21:7-8; 54:1; 67:4; 90:24; 98:3; 100:9; *4 Ezra* 7:36; *Apoc. Ab.* 15:6; *Gk. Apoc. Ezra* 1:9; *3 En.* 44:3; world turns to fire *Apoc. Pet.* 5:2-4; lake of fire Rev 20:14-15; 21:8; *b. Ber.* 57b states that normal fire is a sixtieth of the fire of Gehinnom; *b. Hag.* 13b; *T. Zeb.* 10:3 describes fire emptying upon the heads of the wicked in Gehinnom; *t. Ber.* 6:7 claims that the fire of Gehinnom will never go out.

d. Cf. angel in charge of the abyss and hades in *Apoc. Zeph.* 6:15.

e. *Gk. Apoc. Ezra* 5:2 describes the punishment of women who are suspended.

f. Cf. *Apoc. Paul* 39 and *Apoc. Pet.* 7:5-6 for punishment through hanging by hair for adultery.

g. For punishment of the wicked by chains cf. *Apoc. Pet.* 9:6; *Apoc. Paul* 39; *1 En.* 69:28.

h. Cf. Gk. *Apoc. Ezra* 4:23-24 for punishment through hanging by eyelids for the sin of incest.

i. Cf. *Apoc. Paul* 37 for sins of lending money; 38 for adultery; *Apoc. Zeph.* 10:5-7 describes punishment by chains for sins of bribery and usury; *Apoc. Pet.* 9:7; 10:1.

j. Hebrew is singular used collectively.

k. Cf. Prov 28:9.

l. Cf. *Apoc. Pet.* 7:1-2 for punishment of hanging by tongue for blasphemy.

m. Lit. "walked in" gossip and thus they are hung by their feet.

n. This sin is punished by a stream of fire in *Apoc. Paul* 31.

o. Hebrew is singular used collectively.

p. Hebrew is singular used collectively.

q. Cf. the punishment of those who killed in *Apoc. Pet.* 7:9-10.

their children, and the young men could see and come into the power of impure imagination."[a] [17]After this, Gehinnom cried a great and bitter cry, and said to Nasargiel: "Give to me, as I am hungry!" [18]He said to it: "What shall I give you?" It said to him: "Give me the souls of the righteous." [19]He said to it: "The Holy One, Blessed be He, will never give you the souls of the righteous."

Punishment by Worms in Aluqah

14 [1]Afterwards, Moses descended to another place. [2]He saw two of the wicked
hung. Their heads are below and their feet are above.[b] [3]From the sole of their
feet to the crown of their heads, they are all affixed with black worms.[c] Every
worm is 500 parasangs.[d] [4]The wicked cry out on account of them and say: "Give
death to us that we may die!" As it is said, *The ones who long for death and it does
not happen.*[e] [5]Moses asked Nasargiel: "What were the deeds of these ones?" He Job 3:21
said to him: "They <swore>[f] a false oath. They are the ones who profaned Sabbaths and appointed times. They are the ones who despised scholars. They are
the ones who oppressed orphans and widows. They are the ones who testified
false testimony. Therefore, the Holy One, Blessed be He, delivered them to the
worms." [6]Moses said to Nasargiel: "What is the name of this place?" He said to
him: "Aluqah."[g]

Punishment by Scorpions in Tit Ha-yaven

15 [1]Moses went to another place. He saw two of the wicked lying down. Two
scorpions were attached to them.[h] [2]Each scorpion has 70,000 heads, and each
head has 70,000 mouths, and each mouth has 70,000 (vessels of)[i] poison and
venom. [3]All these scorpions swelled their bodies, and their eyes were sunken on
account of fear of the scorpions, as it is said, *But the eyes of the wicked will fail.* Job 11:20
[4]Moses asked Nasargiel: "What were the deeds of these ones?" He said to him:
"They are the ones who consumed the wealth of Israel. They are the ones who
exposed their neighbour in public. He is the one who cast additional fear upon
the community but not for the sake of heaven. They are the ones who delivered
the people of Israel or their officers into the hand of gentiles. He is the one who
ignored the Torah of Moses, our teacher, upon him be peace. He is the one who

---

a. Cf. *Apoc. Zeph.* 10:4-14 for a description of the torments of the wicked within a question and answer framework between visionary and guide; *Gk. Apoc. Ezra* 4:9-24; 5:1-6, 24-25 includes hanging punishments; *2 En.* 7:1 describes prisoners hanging up in the second heaven along with questions and answers in 7:2-3; *2 En.* 10:4-6 and 60:1-5 describe the sins of the wicked; 52:1-5 lists both wicked and righteous deeds.

b. I.e., they were hung upside-down.

c. For punishment by worms cf. *1 En.* 46:6; *Apoc. Paul* 36, 37, 39; *Apoc. Pet.* 9:2; *Gk. Apoc. Ezra* 4:20; 6:24. The inspiration for the idea seems to come from Isa 66:24.

d. *Apoc. Paul* 42 describes the worms as one cubit long.

e. Cf. Rev 9:6.

f. The word has been misspelt in Wertheimer's edition. The corrected form is translated here.

g. Aluqah means "leech"; cf. Prov 30:15.

h. Cf. Rev 9:5; *Apoc. Pet.* 7:9 for poisonous animals.

i. Omitted in Wertheimer's edition, but "vessels of bitter poison and venom" is found in the Frankfurt 1733 edition.

said that the Holy One, Blessed be He, did not create the world. The Holy One, Blessed be He, delivered all of these to the scorpions." [5]Moses said to Nasargiel: "What is the name of this place?" He said to him: "Tit Ha-yaven."[a]

Punishment by the Angels of Destruction

16 [1]Moses looked and saw two of the wicked from their navel upwards[b] in mud. [2]Angels of destruction[c] stand over them and strike them with chains of fire, and smite them with stones of fire.[d] [3]They break their teeth from morning until evening. In the evening they lengthen their teeth, then in the day they break them,
Ps 3:8 (Evv 3:7) as it is said, *You break the teeth of the wicked.*[e] Do not read "you break" but "you lengthen."[f] [4]These wicked ones cry out on each and every day. [5]Moses asked Nasargiel and said to him: "What were the deeds of these ones?" He said to him: "They are the ones who consumed *nevelot* and *terephot*[g] and dishes of the gentiles. They are the ones who converted to heathenism. He is the one who put his money into usury and profit out of Israel. He is the one who wrote names on an amulet on account of the gentiles. He is the one who practised deceit on the balances and with weighing. He is the one who stole the wealth of Israel. He is the one who ate on Yom Kippur. He is the one who ate fat, blood, creeping things, and reptiles, and did not prohibit himself from these things. Therefore, the Holy One, Blessed be He, delivered them into the hand of angels of destruction."

Punishment by Fire and Snow

17 [1]He saw other wicked ones, half of fire[h] and half of snow—snow from above and fire from below.[i] [2]At night the fire comes in place of the snow, and during the day the snow comes in place of the fire. [3]Moses asked Nasargiel, he said to him: "Why are they half in the midst of the fire and half in the midst of the snow?" He said to him: "Because they left the way of good and went on the path of evil."

Overview of Moses in Gehinnom

18 [1]Nasargiel said to Moses: "Go and see how the wicked are in Gehinnom, and how they burn them." [2]He said to him: "I am not able to go." [3]He said to him: "The light of the Shekinah will rest before you, and do not be afraid for the fire

---

a. Tit Ha-yaven means "mirey mud." Cf. Ps 40:3 [Evv 40:2].

b. Frankfurt 1733 edition of *Greatness of Moses* gives "downwards" here.

c. For angels of punishment cf. *1 En.* 53:3; 56:1; 62:11; 66:1; *T. Levi* 3:2; *Apoc. Pet.* 7:4; angels of destruction cf. *3 En.* 31:2; 32:1; 33:1; 44:2; *b. Shab.* 55a; 88a; *b. Pesah.* 112b; *b. Ketub.* 104a; *b. Sanh.* 106b; merciless angels cf. *2 En.* 10:3; *T. Ab.* 12:1-3.

d. For torture by the angels and their methods cf. *2 En.* 10:3; *T. Ab.* 12:1; *Apoc. Pet.* 9:2. Angels receive the beatings in *3 En.* 20:2; 28:10.

e. Cf. *1 En.* 46:4.

f. In Hebrew this is a pun on the word "you break." Cf. *b. Ber.* 54b; *b. Meg.* 15b; *b. Sotah* 12b.

g. *Nevelot* is meat that has died without proper slaughter and is therefore forbidden; cf. Deut 14:21. *Terephot* also refers to ritually unfit meat; cf. Exod 22:30 (Evv 22:31).

h. For the wicked made half of fire cf. *Apoc. Pet.* 9:1.

i. *T. Levi* 3:2 describes fire, snow and ice in the lowest heaven; *2 En.* 5:1 outlines storehouses of snow; *Exod. Rab.* 51.7 states that Gehinnom is half fire and half hail; *b. Sanh.* 29b describes snow in Gehinnom.

of Gehinnom will have no power over you," as it is said, *Even though I walk in*
the valley of deep darkness, I fear no evil. [4]Moses went and saw wicked ones half Ps 23:4
of fire and half of snow, and worms descending and ascending on their bodies.
[5]A pillar of fire[a] is on their necks and angels of destruction strike them and they
do not have any rest. [6]Concerning them Scripture says: *For their worm will not*
die, and their fire will not be extinguished.[b] [7]Moses asked Nasargiel and said to Isa 66:24
him: "What were the deeds of these ones?" He said to him: "He is the one who
committed adultery. He is the one who had sexual relations with a menstruating
woman. He is the one who had sexual relations with his sister. He is the one who
had sexual relations with men. He is the one who practised idolatry.[c] He is the
one who shed blood unreasonably. He is the one who cursed his father or his
mother or his teacher. He is the one who said 'I am God,' like Nimrod, Pharaoh,
Nebuchadnezzar, Hiram King of Tyre and similar to these." [8]Moses asked Nasargiel: "What is the name of this place?" He said to him: "Tit Ha-yaven."[d] [9]He
saw wicked ones who steal the snow and place (it) under their elbows when they
enter Gehinnom. [10]This is what our teachers, may their memory be for blessing, said: "The wicked who are by the entrance of Gehinnom do not return in
repentance."

Moses Intercedes for Israel

19 [1]Afterwards, Moses ascended from Gehinnom and said: "May it be your will,
O Lord, my God, and God of my fathers, that you save your people, Israel, from
this place." [2]The Holy One, Blessed be He, said to Moses: "Moses, there is no
partiality before me, and never bribery. Whoever does good will be in Gan Eden
and whoever does evil will be in Gehinnom," as it is said, *I, the Lord, search the*
heart and test the mind.[e] Jer 17:10

Moses Enters Gan Eden

20 [1]After this, Moses lifted his eyes and saw Gabriel, and Moses bowed and went
out. [2]The Holy One, Blessed be He, said to Gabriel: "Go with Moses and show
him Gan Eden." [3]Moses came and entered Gan Eden.[f] [4]Two angels came before
him and said to him: "Has your time arrived that you have come here?" He said:
"My time has not arrived, but I have come to see the reward of the righteous in
Gan Eden." [5]They began and said: "Happy are you, Moses, that you were found
worthy of coming here! Happy are the people to whom such a man belongs!
Happy are the people whose God is the Lord!" The word "such" by gematria[g]

---

a. Cf. *Apoc. Pet.* 9:5-6.

b. *Apoc. Paul* 39 describes punishment by burning chains on the neck (cf. *Greatness of Moses* 13:10), bare feet in a place of ice and snow, and consumption by worms (cf. *Greatness of Moses* 14:3); 42 describes punishment by worms one cubit long with two heads, and snow.

c. For the sin of idolatry cf. *Apoc. Pet.* 10:2-6.

d. Cf. the compartment called Tit Ha-yaven in *Greatness of Moses* 15:5.

e. Cf. *2 En.* 46:3 for judgement without favouritism.

f. Cf. Jer 31:12; Joel 2:3; Ezek 28:16; 36:35; *b. Ber.* 34b; *b. Hag.* 14b-15a; *b. B. Bat.* 84a; *b. 'Erub.* 19a; *b. Pesah.* 54a.

g. "Gematria" is a form of creative exegesis in which the numerical values of the letters of a Hebrew word or phrase are added up and then the word is interpreted by another word or phrase whose letters total to the same numerical value.

refers to Moses. [6]When Moses entered Gan Eden, he saw one angel who was sitting under the Tree of Life. His name is Shamshiel, Prince of Gan Eden.[a] [7]Moses
came to him. He said to him: "Who are you?" He said to him: "I am Moses son
of Amram." [8]He said to him: "Why have you come here?" He said to him: "I have
come that I may see the reward of the righteous in Gan Eden." [9]The Holy One,
Blessed be He, said to Shamshiel: "Go with Moses and show him Gan Eden."
[10]After this, he took hold of the hand of Moses[b] and led him before him. [11]Moses
looked and saw seventy thrones[c] fixed one with the other. All of them are made
of precious stone and jewels. Their feet are made of fine gold, and gold, emerald,
sapphire, and diamond.[d] Each throne has sixty ministering angels attending it.
[12]Among them is one throne greater than the rest of them and 120 angels minister to it. [13]Moses asked Shamshiel: "To whom does this throne belong?"[e] He
said to him: "To Abraham, your father." [14]Moses came to Abraham.[f] [15]He said to
him: "Has your time arrived that you have come here?" He said to him: "No, but
I have come that I may see the reward of the righteous in Gan Eden." [16]Abraham
began and said: "*Give thanks to the Lord, for he is good, for his loving kindness*
Ps 106:1 *is forever*." [17]He came to Isaac, and he answered him similarly. [18]He came to Jacob, and he answered him similarly. [19]Moses asked Shamshiel and said to him:
"What is the length of Gan Eden?" He said to him: "It is innumerable and without number." [20]He returned him to Gan Eden and the thrones. Each throne has
sixty ministering angels ministering to it, and one is not like another. Thrones of
silver and of jewels are among them. [21]He said to him: "To whom does a throne
of jewels belong?" He said to him: "To scholars who trouble themselves with
Torah." [22]"And to whom does a throne of chalcedony belong?" He said to him:
"To the perfectly righteous." [23]"To whom does a throne of gold belong?" He said
to him: "To those who repent." [24]"To whom does a throne of silver belong?" He
said to him: "To the true proselytes." [25]"And to whom does a throne of bronze
belong?" He said to him: "To whoever is wicked but his father is righteous, or
to whoever is righteous but his father is wicked. [26]For the Holy One, Blessed be
He, gives Gan Eden to him through the merit of the son[g]—just as with Terah,[h]
to whom the Holy One, Blessed be He, gave Gan Eden on account of the merit
of Abraham, and seated him upon a throne of bronze," as it is said, *And* [i][*you*
Gen 15:15 *will come to your fathers in peace*. [27]He saw one spring of living water going out

---

a. Cf. 2 *En.* 8:8 which describes 300 angels in charge of paradise.

b. Cf. *Ascen. Isa.* 7:3; *1 En.* 71:3.

c. For thrones of the righteous cf. *Ascen. Isa.* 7:14 ff.; 7:22; 8:26; 9:11-12; 10:40; *1 En.* 108:12; Rev 3:21; 4:4; *b. Hag.* 14a; 3 *En.* 10:1.

d. *nophek*, *sapir* and *yahalom* cf. Exod 28:18.

e. Cf. similar question at *Ascen. Isa.* 9:24.

f. *Ascen. Isa.* 9:7 refers to all the righteous from the time of Adam onwards in the seventh heaven; in *Apoc. Paul* 47, Paul meets Abraham, Isaac and Jacob; souls of patriarchs in *3 En.* 44:7-10; *Apoc. Pet.* 14:2; 15:1; Abraham, Isaac, Jacob, Enoch, Elijah, and David are the key righteous figures in *Apoc. Zeph.* 9:4.

g. Cf. *Sifre Deut.* 328; *b. Sanh.* 104a; 2 *En.* 53:1-4.

h. Cf. *Gen. Rab.* 38.12.

i. Wertheimer has taken the bracketed material (from here to the end of the text) from the Thessalonica 1726-27 edition of *Gedulat Moshe*.

from under the Tree of Life, and it goes up and is divided into four portions.[a] [28]It comes from under the Throne of Glory[b] and they all surround Gan Eden from its beginning to its end. [29]Under every throne flow four rivers—one of honey, the second of milk, the third of wine and the fourth of pure balsam.[c] [30]They all flow from under the feet of the righteous who are sitting upon the thrones, etc. [31]When Moses, our teacher, saw all these desirable and good things, he rejoiced with a great joy, and Moses said: "*How great is your goodness that you have stored up for those who fear you, which you have done for those who take refuge in you, in front of everyone*."[d] [32]Moses, our teacher, went out and went from there. [33]At Ps 31:20 (Evv 31:19)
that moment, a *Bat Qol* went out and said to Moses, our teacher, upon him be peace: "Moses, Servant of the Lord, Faithful of His House, just as you have seen the reward of the righteous that is reserved for them for the future, so you are worthy of seeing the life of the world to come. You and all the righteous will be in the building of the Temple at the coming of the King Messiah to see the beauty of the Lord and to enter into His palace."]

a. Cf. Rev 22:1; *Apoc. Ab.* 21:6; *Apoc. Paul* 45 for the river originating in Eden.
b. Cf. Rev 22:1.
c. For streams of honey, etc., cf. 2 *En.* 8:5; *Apoc. Paul* 23.
d. Cf. 4 *Ezra* 7:77 for a store of good things.

Legend of "Hear, O Israel" (*Haggadat Shema' Yisra'el*)

Moses Ascends to See the Guardian Angel

Deut 6:4 **1** [1]*Hear, O Israel, the Lord our God the Lord is One.* [2]Moses,[a] our teacher, upon
him be peace, said to Israel: "Hear, O Israel, all the nation, I have ascended on
high,[b] and I have seen all the guardian angels.[c] [3]I have seen Qemuel, the gate-
keeper, the angel appointed over 12,000 angels of destruction standing at the
gates of heaven.[d] [4]I have seen Hadraniel who is higher than Qemuel by sixty
myriads of parasangs. [5]Every utterance that goes out of his mouth is (accompanied by) 12,000 fiery lightning bolts.[e] [6]I have seen Sandalphon the Prince who
is higher than Hadraniel by a journey of 500 years, and Ezekiel said concerning
him: *And behold, one wheel was on the earth beside the living creatures, one for*
Ezek 1:15 *each of the four of them.* [7]This is Sandalphon, who adorns crowns for his Lord."[f]

The Heavenly Crown

2 [1]"At the moment that the crown[g] goes out over the armies of heaven, all of
them writhe and shake.[h] [2]The Holy Living Creatures are struck dumb and the
Holy Seraphim roar like lions and answer and say: '*Holy, holy, holy is the Lord of*
Isa 6:3 *hosts, all the earth is full of his glory.*' [3]When the crown comes to the Throne of
Glory,[i] the wheels of the chariot are immediately rolled and the rests of the foot-
stool are shaken, and all the heavens are seized with anguish. [4]When the crown
passes onto the Throne of Glory to sit in His place, all the armies of heaven open
their mouths towards the Seraphim and say: '*Blessed be the glory of the Lord*
Ezek 3:12 *from His place*,' because they do not recognise 'His place' as something tangible.[j]
[5]When the crown reaches His head, He gratefully accepts the crown from His

---

a. This parallels the beginning of Gaster's translation II "The Revelation of Moses (B)" §1 ff.

b. Cf. *Ma'yan ha-Ḥokmah, BHM*, 1:58-61; *Pesiq. Rab.* 20.4.

c. For guardian angels cf. *1 En.* 9:1; 40:2-10; 71:8-9; 100:5; *4 Ezra* 7:85, 95; *T. Levi* 3:5; *2 Bar.* 59:11; *3 En.* 18; *Pirqe R. El.* 4.

d. For gates or doors of heaven cf. *T. Levi* 18:10; *3 Bar.* 2:2; 3:1; 4:2; 6:13; 11; *Apoc. Zeph.* 5:1-6; *T. Ab.* 11; *Apoc. Pet.* 17:5. For guardians of the gates cf. *Ascen. Isa.* 10:24 ff.; *T. Levi* 5:1; *2 En.* 42:4; *Pesiq. Rab.* 20.4; guardian of the gates of hell cf. *1 En.* 42:1; mouth of hell cf. *2 Bar.* 59:10.

e. Cf. *Pesiq. Rab.* 20.4; *3 En.* 18:25; 22:9.

f. Cf. *3 En.* 22:11; *b. Hag.* 13b; *Pesiq. Rab.* 20.4; *Midrash Konen, BHM*, 2:26.

g. For the crown of God cf. *3 En.* 29:1; *Apoc. Pet.* 6:2; *b. Hag.* 13b; *Pesiq. Rab.* 20.4.

h. For heavenly commotion cf. Isa 13:13; *T. Levi* 3:9; *1 En.* 1:5; *Apoc. Ab.* 7:8; *2 Bar.* 59:3; *3 En.* 22:2; 38; *Pesiq. Rab.* 20.4.

i. Cf. *Greatness of Moses* 1:7; 10.

j. I.e., no one can see the abiding place of God, so they turn to the Seraphim.

servants. [6]All the Living Creatures, the Seraphim, the wheels of the Chariot, the Throne of Glory, the armies of heaven, the Hashmalim[a] and the Cherubim[b] are glorified and made mighty and exalted. [7]They give praise and glory to the Creator, and they acknowledge Him as King over them and say unanimously: '*The Lord was King, the Lord is King, the Lord will be King forever and ever.*'"[c] Ps 93:1 | Ps 10:16 | Exod 15:18

Rigyon—The River of Fire

3 [1]"I have seen Rigyon, the river of fire[d] that goes out from before the Holy One, Blessed be He, from under the Throne of Glory.[e] [2]It is made from the sweat of the four Living Creatures who support the Throne.[f] They drip fire on account of fear of the Holy One, Blessed be He, and it is explicitly stated concerning it, *A river of fire streamed and flowed out from before him, a thousand thousands ministered to him and a myriad myriads stood before him, the court sat in judgement and the books were opened,*[g] as the Holy One, Blessed be He, sits and judges Dan 7:10
the ministering angels.[h] [3]When they come for judgement they change turns and bathe in that river of fire.[i] [4]Afterwards, that river is conducted into a channel, and it flows with burning coals[j] and they are cast upon the head of the wicked in Gehinnom, as it is said, *Behold, the tempest of the Lord! Anger has gone out, and a whirling storm, it will burst upon the head of the wicked.*"[k] Jer 23:19

The Role of Galizur

4 [1]"I have seen Galizur,[l] the one who corresponds to Raziel, who stands behind the curtain[m] and hears what is decreed and announces (it). [2]He delivers the proclamation to Elijah, and Elijah announces (it) to the world upon Mount Horeb. [3]The wings of Galizur the Prince are spread and positioned to receive the breath of the mouths of the Living Creatures, as, if not for this, all the ministering angels would be burned from the breath of the mouths[n] of the Living Creatures."[o]

---

a. Hashmal is a word of uncertain meaning found in Ezek 1:27 (the NRSV translates as "gleaming amber") which later Jewish tradition interpreted as a type of angelic being. Cf. *3 En.* 26:4; *b. Hag.* 13a.

b. Cf. *1 En.* 14:18; *3 En.* 7; 22:13-15.

c. For praise of the heavenly retinue cf. *1 En.* 61:10-11; 71:7; *2 En.* 17; 20:4; 21:1; *Ascen. Isa.* 7:15 ff.; 10:1 ff.; *T. Levi* 3:8; Rev 5:11-14; *3 En.* 1:12; 22:15-16; 26:8.

d. For a river of fire cf. *1 En.* 17:5; 23:2; *2 En.* 10:2; *3 En.* 18:19, 21; 36:1; *Apoc. Zeph.* 6:2 describes a sea of fire; *Apoc. Pet.* 5:8; 6:2; 12:4; *Pesiq. Rab.* 20.4; *Gen. Rab.* 78.1; *Lam. Rab.* 3.8; *Apoc. Paul* 31.

e. As in *1 En.* 14:19; *3 En.* 18:19; 36:1; see also *Tractate on Gehinnom* 7:6.

f. Cf. *3 En.* 18:25; *b. Hag.* 13b; *Gen. Rab.* 78.1; *Lam. Rab.* 3.8; *Pirqe R. El.* 4.

g. Cf. *3 En.* 18:19.

h. Cf. the divine judgement in *3 En.* 28:7-9; 30:1-2.

i. For angels in a river of fire cf. *1 En.* 67:7; *3 En.* 36:2; 47:1-2; *Maʿyan ha-Ḥokmah, BHM*, 1:59.

j. For coals of fire cf. *Apoc. Pet.* 5:3; 12:1; *3 En.* 47:1.

k. For punishment of the wicked by a stream of fire cf. *3 En.* 33:4-5; *Apoc. Paul* 31; *b. Hag.* 14a.

l. Cf. *3 En.* 18:16-17; *Pirqe R. El.* 4; *Pesiq. Rab.* 20.4.

m. Cf. *3 En.* 45; *b. Yoma* 77a; *b. Ber.* 18b; *b. Hag.* 15a; 16a; *b. Sanh.* 89b; *b. Sotah* 49a; *b. B. Mesiʿa* 59a; *Pirqe R. El.* 4.

n. Fire from the mouth of angels cf. *2 En.* 1:5; *3 En.* 22:4.

o. Cf. *Pesiq. Rab.* 20.4; *Pirqe R. El.* 4.

God Protects Moses from the Angels

5 [1]"I have seen Michael, the Great Prince, standing on the right of the Throne and Gabriel standing on the left. [2]Yefifiyah,[a] the Prince of the Torah, stands before him, and Metatron, the Prince of the Presence, stands before the entrance of the palace of the Holy One, Blessed be He. [3]He sits and judges all the heavenly armies according to the judgement of the one standing before the King, and the Holy One, Blessed be He, passes sentence and he does (it).[b] [4]I have seen a band of angels of fear who surround the Throne of Glory that are mightier and stronger than all the angels.[c] [5]All these that I saw sought to burn me with the breath of their mouth,[d] but, due to fear of the King of Kings of Kings, the Holy One, Blessed be He, they did not have power to injure me for they were all afraid and writhed and shook because of fear of Him."[e]

Vision of Sinai and Statement about God

6 [1]"Also, you[f] saw in the wisdom of your heart and your understanding and your soul, how He was revealed by the sea (as a sage, may his memory be for blessing, said: 'The handmaid saw by the sea what prophets did not see')[g] and how the upper heavens inclined and His glory descended upon Mount Sinai with a chariot of two myriads, thousands upon thousands.[h] [2]You saw that all the host of heaven were afraid to speak His holiness. [3]The earth trembled on account of Him, and the heavens overflowed. [4]The mountains danced and all the people were amazed and afraid on account of Him. [5]Every creature of the earth and every bird of the heavens was struck dumb and trembled because of fear of Him. [6]The sea was torn open, the earth shook, the sun and moon were brought to a standstill. [7]As a consequence, O Israel, all the holy nation, you have an obligation to hear, to understand, and to know that the Lord is our God, that his name is called by us in the special declaration 'One Lord.' [8]He does not have a second, a likeness, a comparison, a partner or assistance—not in heaven, not on earth and not in the deeps, not in this world and not in the world to come."

---

a. Cf. *Greatness of Moses* 11:1-4.

b. For an angelic judge cf. Rev 20:4; *3 En.* 16:1-2; 28:7-9; cf. Abel the judge *T. Ab.* 12.

c. *Pesiq. Rab.* 20.4.

d. Cf. *Legend of "Hear, O Israel"* 4:3.

e. This parallels the end of Gaster's text II "The Revelation of Moses (B)" §9.

f. The use of the plural here indicates that Moses is addressing Israel.

g. Brackets inserted in Jellinek's edition. This statement is attributed to R. Eliezer in *Mek. de-R. Ishmael Beshallah* 3 to Exodus 15:2; cf. *Deut. Rab.* 7.8; *y. Sotah* 5:6, 16c.

h. Cf. Ps 68:18.

History of Rabbi Yehoshua ben Levi (*Ma'aseh De-Rabbi Yehoshua' ben Levi*)

Rabbi Yehoshua Enters Gan Eden

1 [1]Legend of Rabbi Yehoshua ben Levi,[a] may his memory be for blessing. [2]Rabbi[b] Yehoshua ben Levi was a completely righteous person. [3]When his time arrived to depart from the world, the Holy One, Blessed be He, said to the Angel of Death:[c] "Do for him anything he needs, whatever he asks of you."[d] [4]He went to him and said: "Your time has arrived to depart from the world, but any matter that you ask of me, I will do for you." [5]When Rabbi Yehoshua heard this, he said to him: "I ask of you that you show me my place in Gan Eden."[e] [6]He said to him: "Go with me, and I will show it to you." [7]He said to him: "Give me your sword so that you do not terrify me with it." [8]Immediately, he gave him the sword, and the two of them walked until they came to the walls of Gan Eden. [9]When they came to the walls of Gan Eden, outside of the wall, the Angel of Death took Rabbi Yehoshua and raised him and set him upon the wall of Gan Eden. [10]He said to him: "See your place in Gan Eden." [11]Rabbi Yehoshua ben Levi jumped from the wall and fell into Gan Eden, but the Angel of Death seized the shoulder of his robe. [12]He said to him: "Get out from there!" Rabbi Yehoshua swore by Ha-Shem that he would not go out from there, and the angel did not have authority to enter there.[f]

The Ministering Angels Investigate Rabbi Yehoshua

2 [1]The ministering angels said before the Holy One, Blessed be He: "Master of the World, see what ben Levi has done—he took his portion in Gan Eden by force." [2]The Holy One, Blessed be He, said to them: "Go and investigate whether he has sworn before for such a purpose, and has broken his oath; if so, he will break (it this time) also." [3]They went out and investigated and said: "During his

a. A renowned Palestinian Amora of the early third century. Rabbi Yehoshua was famous for his dealings with the Angel of Death; cf. *b. Ber.* 51a; *Der. Er. Zut.* 1.

b. This parallels the beginning of Gaster's translation III "The Revelation of R. Joshua ben Levi (A)" §1.

c. Cf. *b. Ber.* 51a; for Angel of Death cf. *2 Bar.* 21:23; *T. Ab.* 16-20.

d. Cf. *T. Ab.* 9.

e. Cf. *Der. Er. Zut.*1; *b. Ketub.* 77b outlines Rabbi Yehoshua's dealings with the Angel of Death and Elijah corresponding to the legend found in chaps. 1-4 of this composition.

f. 2 *Alphabet of Ben Sira* 28b lists eleven people who entered paradise during their lifetime: Enoch; Serah the daughter of Asher; Bithiah the daughter of Pharaoh; Hiram king of Tyre; Abraham's servant Eliezer; Elijah; Jabez; Ebedmelech; Jonadab the Rechabite; Rabbi Yehudah ha-Nasi's servant; and R. Yehoshua.

lifetime he has never transgressed his oath." [4]The Holy One, Blessed be He, said to them: "If so, he will never go out from there!"

Work of the Angel of Death

3 [1]As soon as the Angel of Death saw that he could not bring him out, he said to him: "Give me the sword." [2]But Rabbi Yehoshua did not want to give (it) to him until a *Bat Qol* went out and said: "Give him the knife as it is needed for human beings." [3]Rabbi Yehoshua said to him: "Swear to me that you will not show it to human beings at the moment that you take the soul of a person." [4]Before, wherever he was found, he slaughtered him in the presence of everyone like an animal, and even at the breast of his mother. [5]At that moment, he[a] swore to him and he[b] gave it to him.

Rabbi Yehoshua and the Rainbow

4 [1]Elijah began to announce before Rabbi Yehoshua and said to the righteous: "Empty a place for ben Levi." [2]He went and found him with Rabbi Shimon ben Yohai, who was sitting upon the thirteen <compartments>[c] of the righteous. [3]He said to him: "Are you ben Levi?" He said to him: "Yes." He said to him: "Have you seen the rainbow during your lifetime?" He said to him: "Yes." He said to him: "If that is so, then you are not ben Levi." [4]But the matter was not so, because the rainbow had not appeared during his lifetime. [5]Why did he say to him that it had appeared? So that he would not assume goodness for himself. [6]Why did he ask him about the rainbow? Because it is a sign of the covenant between the Holy One, Blessed be He, and the land. [7]Every time that the rainbow appears, the Holy One, Blessed be He, has compassion over his world, and every time that there is a righteous person in the world, the world does not need a rainbow, as the world stands through the wisdom of one righteous person, as it is said, *The righteous one is the foundation of*
Prov 10:25 *the world.* Therefore, he asked him about the rainbow.

Rabbi Yehoshua Commissioned to Investigate Gan Eden and Gehinnom

5 [1]The Angel of Death went to Rabbi Gamaliel and said to him: "Rabbi Yehoshua ben Levi did so and so to me." [2]Rabbi Gamaliel said to him: "He dealt with you correctly. But come and I will send you to him; say to him: 'I beg of you that you search through all of Gan Eden and Gehinnom and their treasuries,[d] and write about them and send them to me—whether there are gentiles in Gan Eden, or from the people of Israel in Gehinnom.'" [3]The Angel of Death went, and Rabbi Yehoshua said to him: "I will do so." [4]Rabbi Yehoshua went and searched through the whole of Gan Eden, and he found seven compartments

---

a. I.e., the Angel of Death.

b. I.e., Rabbi Yehoshua.

c. Uncertain word. The spelling can be emended to give "compartments."

d. Cf. chambers for the elements in *1 En.* 41:1-5; 69:23; *4 Ezra* 5:37; *2 Enoch* 5 describes treasuries of snow, ice and clouds in the first heaven; for treasuries of snow and storehouses of cold and wind cf. *2 En.* 40:10; *T. Levi* 3 allocates fire, ice and snow to the first heaven; *Gk. Apoc. Ezra* 5:23 describes the storehouses of ice as a punishment; cf. *3 En.* 10:6 for treasuries in the heavenly heights.

in Gan Eden.[a] [5]Each compartment is twelve myriads of miles in length, and in width it is twelve myriads of miles—the measure of their length is proportioned according to their width.[b]

The First Compartment of Gan Eden

6 [1]"The[c] first compartment corresponds to the first entrance into Gan Eden.[d] [2]The proselytes who are in Israel—who converted of their own accord, not by force—dwell in it. [3]Its walls are built of glass, and its beams are cedar. [4]When I came to measure it,[e] all the proselytes stood and sought to prevent (me). [5]Obadiah the righteous, who is appointed over them, answered and said to them: 'What are your merits that this one should sit with you?' Immediately they allowed me to measure it."

The Second Compartment of Gan Eden

7 [1]"The second compartment corresponds to the second entrance into Gan Eden. [2]It is built of silver, and its beams are cedar. [3]Those who have repented dwell in it, and Manasseh,[f] son of Hezekiah, is appointed over them."

The Third Compartment of Gan Eden

8 [1]"The third compartment corresponds to the third entrance which is in Gan Eden. [2]It is built of silver and gold. [3]Abraham, Isaac and Jacob[g] dwell in it, and all Israel that went out from the land of Egypt, and all the generation of the wilderness, and all the sons of the King except Absalom. [4]David and Solomon are there, and Chileab[h] the son of David, still alive. [5]He is there and all the kings of the house of Judah are there except Manasseh the son of Hezekiah, who is appointed over all those who have repented. [6]Moses and Aaron are appointed over them. [7]All the desirable vessels of gold and silver are there, and all the good things, and oils, stones, canopies, beds, thrones, candlesticks of gold and of precious stones and jewels. [8]I said: 'For whom are these things designated?' David answered and said to me: 'All those who dwell in the world from which you have come.' [9]I said to him: 'Perhaps there is someone from the gentiles there, even from the children of Esau my brother?' [10]He said to me: 'No, as any good that they do in the world, the Holy One, Blessed be He, pays them their reward during their lifetime in that world.[i] In the end they inherit Gehinnom, but, with respect to Israel, each wicked person who is among them suffers in this world during his lifetime, but is worthy of the world to come.' As it is said, *And repays those who hate him, etc.*" Deut 7:10

---

a. Cf. dwelling places of the righteous in *1 En.* 39:4-8; 41:2.

b. Cf. *Greatness of Moses* 20:19.

c. The text now changes to a first person account by Rabbi Yehoshua ben Levi.

d. Cf. *Midrash Konen, BHM*, 2:28-30 for the compartments of Gan Eden similarly described.

e. Cf. *1 En.* 70:3 where the angels measure the place of the righteous for Enoch; Rev 11:1; 21:15-17.

f. Cf. 2 Chr 33:10-13; *Pr. Man.*; *Ascen. Isa.* 11:41-43; *2 Bar.* 64.

g. Cf. *Greatness of Moses* 20:13-18.

h. Cf. 2 Sam 3:3.

i. Cf. *1 En.* 103:6-7.

The Fourth Compartment of Gan Eden

9 [1]"The fourth compartment corresponds to the fourth entrance into Gan Eden. [2]It is beautifully built, like Adam, and its beams are made of olive trees. [3]The perfect and faithful righteous ones are in it. [4]Why is it made of olive trees? Because their days were bitter like an olive."

The Fifth Compartment of Gan Eden

10 [1]"The fifth compartment is built from silver, gold, fine gold,[a] gold,[b] glass and *bedolah*.[c] [2]The river Gihon flows into its midst. [3]Its beams are gold and silver, and (perfume) rises better than all the scent of Lebanon. [4]The covers (of) beds of silver, gold and spices are of violet and purple wool woven by Eve, and scarlet yarn and goats (hair) woven by the angels. [5]The Messiah ben David and Elijah, may his memory be for blessing, dwell in it (in) a litter made of the wood of Lebanon. [6]Its pillars <are made>[d] of silver, its seat of gold, its saddle of purple, and the Messiah, who is the love of the daughters of Jerusalem, dwells in the midst of the litter; its midst is crowded with love. [7]Elijah, may his memory be for blessing, takes the head of the Messiah and rests it on his breast. He[e] said to him: 'Be silent, for the end is near!' [8]The Fathers of the World, all of the tribes, Moses, Aaron, David, Solomon, every king of Israel and from the house of David come to him on every second and fifth (day) and every Sabbath and holy day, and they weep with him and encourage him and say to him: 'Be quiet and rely on your
Num 16 Creator, for the end is near!' [9]Even Korah and his assembly, Dathan, Abiram and Absalom[f] come to him every fourth day, and ask him: 'When will be the end of (our) particular[g] (punishment), and when will you bring our resurrection from the depths of the earth (and) our ascent?' [10]He says to them: 'Go to your Fathers and ask them.' When they hear this, they are ashamed and do not ask the Fathers. [11]When I came to the Messiah, he asked me and said to me: 'What are Israel doing in the world from which you have come?' [12]I said to him: 'They are waiting for you every day.' Immediately, he raised his voice in weeping."

The Sixth Compartment of Gan Eden

11 [1]"The sixth compartment: those who died in performance of a good deed dwell in it."

The Seventh Compartment of Gan Eden

12 [1]"The seventh compartment: those who died of illnesses on account of the iniquities of Israel dwell in it."

---

a. Cf. *b. Yoma* 45a.

b. Cf. Ps 45:10 (Evv 45:9).

c. A type of jewel: cf. Gen 2:12; Num 11:7; *Gen. Rab.* 2.12.

d. Lit. "he made."

e. Elijah said to the Messiah.

f. The estranged son of David who led an unsuccessful revolt against his father (cf. 2 Sam 13–18).

g. Or: "the wonders."

Rabbi Yehoshua Gains Access to Gehinnom

13 [1]Furthermore, Rabbi Yehoshua ben Levi said:[a] "I asked to measure Gehinnom and to see it, but He did not give authority to me because the righteous should not see Gehinnom. [2]I sent for that angel whose name is Qomam that he may write (about) all of Gehinnom for me.[b] But he was not able (to do so), as at that moment Rabbi Ishmael the High Priest and Rabbi Shimon ben Gamaliel and ten righteous people were killed. [3]The news came and I was not able to go with that angel to Gehinnom. [4]Another day I stood and met with Qinor the angel. [5]The light went with me until I came to the gates of Gehinnom. [6]They were open and the wicked who were there saw the light, and they rejoiced and said to each other: 'This light will bring us out of here.'"

Compartments of Gehinnom

14 [1]"I saw compartments. Their length is ten miles by five miles.[c] [2]Many pits of fire[d] are open and they rise up and consume the wicked.[e] [3]After they consume them, they rise up on their feet from the fire and fall down and are burned (again). [4]In that compartment are ten nations from the nations of the world. [5]Absalom the son of David is appointed over them. [6]The nations say to each other: 'If we have sinned because we did not accept the Torah, then what is your sin?' They answer them: 'We are also like you.' [7]They say to Absalom: 'You and your fathers, you accepted the Torah, why (are you punished)?' He says to them: 'Because I did not listen to the commandments of my father.' [8]Angels stand here with their staffs and throw them upon the fire and all of them are burned. [9]After this, they run to Absalom and want to strike him and burn him in the fire, but a *Bat Qol* says to them: 'Do not strike him and do not burn him, as he is from the seed of Israel who said before me "we will do and we will listen" and he is the son of David my servant.' [10]Therefore, they set him upon his throne and seat him with the glory of the King. [11]After this, they bring the wicked out of the fire as though they were burned, but the fire had not touched them at all. [12]Then they burn them again, and thus they do to them seven times—four by day and three by night. [13]But Absalom is saved from all these things because he is the son of David."

Rabbi Yehoshua Fulfils His Task

15 [1]Rabbi Yehoshua said: "When I saw all these things, I returned to Gan Eden and wrote down all the things.[f] [2]I sent them to Rabbi Gamaliel and the elders of Israel, and told them all that I saw in Gan Eden and in Gehinnom.[g] [3]May God,

---

a. 13:1–14:13 corresponds to *Legend of Rabbi Yehoshua ben Levi* chap. 1.

b. Cf. the recording of such secrets by Uriel in *1 En.* 23:4.

c. Cf. 2 *Bar.* 59:5; *1 En.* 18:11; 21:7-10 for the depths of the abyss.

d. Cf. *Apoc. Pet.* 7:3.

e. *Apoc. Paul* 32 describes pits for the souls of the wicked that are 3000 cubits in depth.

f. Cf. 2 *En.* 23; 40; 43:1; 47:1-2 for Enoch's writing about his vision and what he has measured and recorded.

g. This parallels the end of Gaster's translation III "The Revelation of R. Joshua ben Levi (A)" §22.

in his compassion, deliver us from the punishment of Gehinnom and give us a portion in the world to come with the righteous and the pious.[a] Amen."

End of the History of Rabbi Yehoshua ben Levi.

a. Cf. *Greatness of Moses* 19:1; *In What Manner Is the Punishment of the Grave?* 1:8.

Order of Gan Eden (*Seder Gan 'Eden*)

The Righteous Person Enters Eden

1 [1]Rabbi[a] Yehoshua ben Levi said: "There are two gates of carbuncle in Gan Eden. [2]Sixty myriads of ministering angels are above them, and the glory of every one of their faces is like the light of heaven[b] shining.[c] [3]At the moment that the righteous person comes to them, the clothes that he was buried in are stripped from him,[d] and they dress him in eight garments made of the clouds of glory.[e] [4]They put two crowns[f] upon his head—one of precious stones and jewels and one of Parvaim gold.[g] [5]They put eight myrtle branches[h] in his hand and they give praise and say to him: '*Go, eat your bread with joy.*'"[i] Eccl 9:7

Canopies of the Righteous

2 [1]"They bring him to a place of rivers of water surrounded by 800 roses and myrtle branches. [2]Each one has his own canopy according to his honour,[j] as it is said, *For over all the glory is a canopy.* [3]Four rivers flow from it—one of oil, one Isa 4:5
of balsam, wine and honey.[k] [4]Every canopy has a vine of gold above it, and thirty jewels are hanging on it. Every one shines with splendour like the splendour of Nogah.[l] [5]Every canopy has a table of precious stones and jewels in it. [6]Sixty angels stand over the head of every righteous person, and they say to him: '*Go, eat honey with joy*, because you have worked at the Torah,' as it is said, *Sweeter* Eccl 9:7

---

a. This parallels the beginning of Gaster's translation IV "The Revelation of R. Joshua ben Levi (B)" §1.

b. For light of heaven see *Ascen. Isa.* 8:20-25; 9:6.

c. For shining faces of heavenly beings cf. *2 En.* 1a:4; 1:5; 19:1; Rev 1:16; 10:1; *Apoc. Pet.* 15:2; *Apoc. Zeph.* 6:11.

d. Cf. *2 En.* 22:8; *Ascen. Isa.* 9:7 describes the righteous stripped of their robes of flesh.

e. For garments for the righteous cf. *1 En.* 62:15-16; *2 En.* 22:8-9; 2 Cor 5:1-5; *3 En.* 12:1-2; 18:22; *T. Levi* 8:5; 18:14; Rev 6:11; 7:9, 13; *Apoc. Pet.* 13:1; *Ascen. Isa.* 7:22; 8:14, 26; 9:9-10, 18, 24-26; 10:40.

f. For crowns for the righteous cf. *Ascen. Isa.* 7:22; 8:26; 9:11-12, 18, 24-25; 10:40; *3 En.* 12:3-5; *5 Ezra* 2:42-48; *T. Levi* 8:2; *Gk. Apoc. Ezra* 6:21; *2 Bar.* 15:8; *b. Ber.* 17a.

g. Cf. *Ascen. Isa.* 8:14; 9:9, 24. For Parvaim gold cf. *b. Yoma* 45a; *Num. Rab.* 11.3; *Treatise of the Vessels* §VII.

h. Levi receives a branch of olive wood in *T. Levi* 8:8.

i. Cf. the rejoicing of the angels at the arrival of the righteous in *2 En.* 42:4.

j. For seven canopies cf. *b. B. Bat.* 75a; *Pesiq. Rab.* 37.1; for habitation according to merit cf. *2 En.* 61:2; John 14:2; *Ruth Rab.* 1.16; *b. Shab.* 152a; *b. B. Bat.* 75a.

k. Cf. *Greatness of Moses* 20:29.

l. Nogah means "light" but can also refer to the planet Venus; cf. *3 En.* 25:6; 26:4; *Pirqe R. El.* 4.

Ps 19:11 (Evv 19:10) *than honey*, [7]'and drink wine which was kept in its grapes from the six days of
creation,[a] because you worked at the Torah which is like wine,' as it is said, *I*
Song 8:2 *would give you spiced wine to drink*."

The Transformations of the Righteous Man

3 [1]"The ugliest one among them has the likeness of Joseph or Rabbi Yohanan or
the blossoms of a silver pomegranate brought towards the sun, and night does
not go near them, as it is said, *And the* light *of the righteous is like the light of*
Prov 4:18 *splendour*.[b] [2]A change comes over them during three watches. [3]The first watch:
he is made into a child and he enters the division of children, and he rejoices
with the joy of[c] children. [4]The second watch: he is made into a young man and
he enters the division of young men, and he rejoices with the joy of young men.
[5]The third watch: he is made into an old man and he enters the division of old
men, and he rejoices with the joy of old men."

The Tree of Life in Gan Eden

4 [1]"There are eighty myriads of kinds of trees in Gan Eden.[d] [2]In every corner,
the smallest among them is praised more than all the trees of spices.[e] [3]In every
corner, there are sixty myriads of ministering angels singing with a pleasant
voice.[f] [4]The Tree of Life[g] is in the middle, and its trunk covers all of Gan Eden.[h]
[5]There are 500,000 tastes in it, and the taste of one is not like another, and the
scent of one is not like another.[i] [6]Seven clouds of glory are above it. [7]Winds
strike it from the four (corners) and its scent spreads from one end of the world
to the other.[j] [8]The scholars are under it explaining the Torah, and each one has
two canopies—one of stars and one of the sun and moon. Between each canopy
is a curtain of clouds of glory."[k]

The Seven Compartments of the Righteous

5 [1]"The Eden that contains 310 worlds is inside it, as it is said, *To cause those*
Prov 8:21 *that love me to inherit substance*. The word "substance" is by gematria[l] 310.[m] [2]In

a. Cf. *b. Sanh.* 99a; *b. Ber.* 34b; *Tg. Eccl.* 9:7; *Num. Rab.* 13.2.

b. The citation has adapted "the path of the righteous" to "the light of the righteous"; for light of the righteous cf. *2 Bar.* 51:3; *Sifre Deut.* 10; 47; *Lev. Rab.* 28.1; *Pesiq. Rab. Kah.* 8.1; *Pesiq. Rab.* 18.1; *Eccl. Rab.* 1.3.1; 1.7.9; *Midr. Ps.*11.6.

c. Cf. *Zohar* I, 140a.

d. Cf. 2 *En.* 8:4.

e. Cf. *1 En.* 32:3 ff.; *Apoc. Ab.* 21:6.

f. Cf. 2 *En.* 8:8.

g. Cf. Gen 2:9; 3:22-24; *1 En.* 25; *2 En.* 8:3; *Apoc. Paul* 45; *T. Levi* 18:11; *Gk. Apoc. Ezra* 5:21; Rev 22:2, 14, 19; also see *Greatness of Moses* 20:27.

h. Cf. 2 *En.* 8:4.

i. Cf. *Apoc. Pet.* 16:2-3; *1 En.* 29:2; 32:3; *2 En.* 8:2.

j. Cf. the scent of the Tree of Life in *1 En.* 24:4–25:7; *5 Ezra* 2:12; *2 En.* 8:3.

k. Cf. *4 Ezra* 8:52.

l. "Gematria" is a form of creative exegesis in which the numerical values of the letters of a Hebrew word or phrase are added up and then the word is interpreted by another word or phrase whose letters total to the same numerical value.

m. Cf. *b. Ber.* 34b; *b. Sanh.* 99a-100a.

its midst are the seven compartments of the righteous.[a] [3]The first: the martyrs are there such as Rabbi Aqiba and his associates.[b] [4]The second: those who were drowned in the sea.[c] [5]The third: Rabbi Yohanan and his disciples.[d] What was his strength? That he said: 'If all the heavens are sheets for writing, all the world are scribes, and all the forests are writing pens, they would not be able to write down what I have learned from my teachers, and I am no less than a dog that laps at the sea.' [6]The fourth group: these are the ones upon whom the cloud descended and covered them. [7]The fifth group consists of those who have repented.[e] In the place where those who have repented stand, (even) the perfectly righteous may not stand. [8]The sixth group consists of single men who have not tasted the taste of sin during their lifetime.[f] [9]The seventh group consists of the poor, who still had among them Scripture, Mishnah and morality.[g] Scripture says concerning them: *And let all who take refuge in you rejoice, let them shout for joy forever.* Ps 5:12 (Evv 5:11)
[10]The Holy One, Blessed be He, sits between them and explains the Torah to them, as it is said, *My eyes will be on the faithful of the land that they may dwell with me.* [11]The Holy One, Blessed be He, has not divulged the glory that is pre- Ps 101:6
pared for them more and more,[h] as it is said, *No eye has seen any God besides you, who acts for the one who waits for him.*"[i] Isa 64:3

End of Order of Gan Eden

---

a. Cf. *Sifre Deut.* 10; 47; *Midr. Tannaim* 6; *Lev. Rab.* 30.20; see also *History of Rabbi Yehoshua ben Levi* chaps. 6–12.

b. Cf. *b. B. Bat.* 10b.

c. Cf. *b. Git.* 57b.

d. Cf. *b. Hag.* 14b.

e. Cf. *History of Rabbi Yehoshua ben Levi* 7:3.

f. Cf. *Apoc. Paul* 26; *b. Ber.* 34b; *b. Pesah.* 113a.

g. Lit. "way of the land."

h. For the goodness that is prepared for the righteous cf. *1 En.* 103:3; *2 Bar.* 44:13-15; 52:7; 54:4.

i. This parallels the end of Gaster's translation IV "The Revelation of R. Joshua ben Levi (B)" §6.

Tractate on Gehinnom (*Masseket Gehinnom*)

Introduction to Gehinnom

1 [1]It is written, *Who can stand before his indignation, and who can endure the*
Nah 1:6 *heat of his anger?* [2]Rabbi Zeira opened with: *The leech has two daughters, "Give!*
Give!" [3]Rabbi Eliezer said: Two bands of angels stand over the entrances of Gehinnom. They say "Give! Give! Bring! Bring!" [4]Why is it called Gehinnom? Because the sound of its shrieking[a] goes from one end of the world to the other. [5]Why is it called Tofteh?[b] Because everyone enters there through being enticed by the evil inclination.[c]

The Gates of Gehinnom

2 [1]The first chapter: [2]Rabbi[d] Yohanan began with: *As they pass through the val-*
Ps 84:7 (Evv 84:6) *ley of Baca, they make it a place of springs, also the early rain covers it with pools.*
[3]This teaches that the wicked person confesses just as the leper confesses and says: "I, so-and-so, son of so-and-so have committed a certain transgression in a certain place on a certain day against so-and-so in the presence of so-and-so and so-and-so." [4]There are three gates into Gehinnom[e]—one is in the sea, one is in the desert, one is on the inhabited land. [5]Where do we learn about that
which is in the sea? As it is said, *From the belly of Sheol I cried out, you heard my*
Jonah 2:3 (Evv 2:2) *voice.* [6]Where do we learn about that which is in the desert? As it is said, *And*
Num 16:33 *they went down (etc.) alive to Sheol.* [7]Where do we learn about that which is on
the inhabited land? As it is said, *Says the Lord, whose light is in Zion and whose*
Isa 31:9 *furnace is in Jerusalem.*

The Fires of Gehinnom

3 [1]Five kinds of fire are in Gehinnom[f]—a fire that consumes and absorbs,[g] one that absorbs but does not consume, one that consumes but does not absorb, one

---

a. The word "its shrieking" is vaguely reminiscent of the word "Gehinnom."

b. This is a word of uncertain meaning (NRSV translates "his burning place") in Isa 30:33. It also sounds like the word Tofet, a place of child sacrifice (cf. Jer 7:31-32). Cf. *b. 'Erub.* 19a; *Lam. Rab.* 1.9. The word "enticed" is vaguely reminiscent of the word Tofteh.

c. For 1:2-5 cf. *In What Manner Is the Punishment of the Grave?* 2:1-4.

d. This parallels the beginning of Gaster's translation V *"Hell"* §1.

e. Cf. *History of Rabbi Yehoshua ben Levi* 13:5.

f. Cf. *Greatness of Moses* 13:1-4; *History of Rabbi Yehoshua ben Levi* 14:2-3, 11; *Tractate on Gehinnom* 4:1-2; 5:3.

g. Lit. "eats and drinks."

that does not consume or absorb, and there is a fire that consumes fire. [2]There
are coals in it[a] like mountains, there are coals[b] in it like hills, there are coals in it
like the Sea of Salt, there are coals in it like large stones. [3]There are rivers of pitch
and sulphur in it flowing and boiling with many brooms.[c]

The Sentence of the Wicked

4 [1]The sentence of a wicked person: Angels of destruction push him on his face,
and others take him from them and push him before the fire of Gehinnom. [2]Its
mouth opens wide and swallows him,[d] as it is said, *Therefore Sheol has enlarged
its appetite and opened its mouth without limit. Her nobility and her multitude
descend, her throng and the one who exults in her.* [3]This happens to whoever has Isa 5:14
not done a single good deed that decides him towards the scale of merits,[e] but
whoever possesses Torah and good deeds and many trials come upon him, he is
delivered from the punishment of Gehinnom, as it is said, *Even though I walk in
the valley of deep darkness,* I do no evil, *etc., your staff and your rod, they comfort
me.*[f] [4]"Your staff": these are the trials. "And your rod": this is the Torah. Ps 23:4

The Punishments of Gehinnom

5 [1]The second chapter: [2]Rabbi Yohanan expounded: *But the eyes of the wicked
will fail and escape will be gone from them, their hope will become a last breath
of the soul.* [3](This refers to) a body which has not been destroyed[g] and its soul Job 11:20
goes out into the fire that is never extinguished.[h] [4]Concerning them, Scripture
says, *For their worm will not die and their fire will not be extinguished.* [5]Rabbi Isa 66:24
Yehoshua ben Levi said: One time I went on a journey and I found Elijah the
prophet, may his memory be for blessing. [6]He said to me: "Is it your desire that
I place you upon the gate of Gehinnom?" I said to him: "Yes!" [7]He showed me
people who are hung by their noses, and people who are hung by their hands,
people who are hung by their tongues and people who are hung by their feet.
[8]He showed me women who are hung by their breasts, and he showed me people
who are hung by their eyes.[i] He showed me people that are forced to eat their
(own) flesh,[j] and people that are forced to eat the coals of broom,[k] and people
sitting alive while worms[l] eat them. [9]He said to me: "These are the ones concerning whom it is written, *For their worm will not die.*" [10]He showed me people Isa 66:24

a. I.e., Gehinnom.

b. Cf. *Legend of "Hear, O Israel"* 3:4.

c. The fiery coals are often said to be from the broom plant; cf. *Tractate on Gehinnom* 5:8.

d. Cf. *1 En.* 56:8.

e. For the scales of judgement cf. *2 En.* 44:5; 52:15; *T. Ab.* 12:13; 13:10, 14; *2 Bar.* 41:6; *3 En.* 18:20.

f. "I fear no evil" has been replaced with "I do no evil."

g. I.e., "failed" which is the same verb from Job 11.

h. For fire that does not go out cf. *1 En.* 67:12; *2 En.* 10:2; *Apoc. Pet.* 5:4, 8; 6:4, 9; 11:8; *3 En.* 42:3.

i. For these punishments by hanging cf. *Greatness of Moses* 13.

j. Cf. *Apoc. Paul* 37 where people who disparaged the word of God are forced to eat their own tongues; sim. *Apoc. Pet.* 9:3; 11:8.

k. Eating coals of broom is a common means of punishment for the wicked; cf. *b. 'Arak.* 15b; *Midr. Ps.* 120:4; *Gen. Rab.* 98.19.

l. Cf. *Greatness of Moses* 14; 18:4.

who are forced to eat fine sand. They were forced to eat against their will and
their teeth were broken.[a] [11]The Holy One, Blessed be He, says to them: "Wicked
ones, when you ate the fruits of robbery, it was sweet in your mouth, but now
you do not have the strength," to confirm what is said, *You break the teeth of the*
Ps 3:8 (Evv 3:7) *wicked.*[b] [12]He showed me people who are cast from the fire into snow, and from
the snow into fire,[c] like this shepherd who shepherds his flock from mountain
to mountain, and concerning them Scripture says, *Like sheep they are appointed*
for Sheol, death will be their shepherd. The upright have dominion over them in the
Ps 49:15 (Evv 49:14) *morning, their form to decay in Sheol, far from their habitation.* [13]Rabbi Yohanan
said: Each angel is appointed to punish a particular sin. A certain one comes and he[d] punishes him and he goes, and thus it is with the second and the third. Thus it is with all of them until they pay for all the sins they have committed. [14]A parable: To what is the matter like? To a creditor who had many creditors, and they brought him to the king. The king said to them: "What can I do for you? Go and divide him between you." [15]At that moment, his soul is delivered into Gehinnom to the cruel angels, and they divide it between them.[e]

Those Who Receive Permanent Punishment

6 [1]Chapter three: [2]It is taught: Three descend into Gehinnom and do not ascend—the one who commits adultery,[f] the one who exposes his neighbour in public[g] and the one who swears falsely[h] in the name of the Lord. [3]There are those who say: also the one who glorifies himself through the disgrace of his neighbour,[i] and the one who becomes entangled between a man and his wife in order to bring strife between them.[j] [4]On every eve of the Sabbath, they are brought to two mountains of snow[k] and left there. [5]At the end of the Sabbath, they are brought back to their place. An angel goes out and pushes them and returns them to their place in Gehinnom. [6]Some of them take snow and they put (it) under their armpits in order to cool them during the six days of the week.[l]
[7]The Holy One, Blessed be He, says to them: "Wicked ones, woe to you who steal
even in Gehinnom," as it is said, *Just as drought and heat steal snow waters, so*
Job 24:19 *does Sheol with those who have sinned.* [8]This means: "Even in Sheol they sinned."

---

a. Cf. *Greatness of Moses* 16:3.

b. Cf. *Apoc. Paul* 39 for those denied sustenance; *Exod. Rab.* 1.23; *Pirqe R. El.* 48; *b. Ber.* 54b; *b. Meg.* 15b.

c. Cf. *Greatness of Moses* 17; 18:4.

d. I.e., the angel appointed for the particular sin.

e. Cf. *Greatness of Moses* 13:11; 15:4; 16:5 for sins connected to finance.

f. Cf. *Greatness of Moses* 13:11; 18:7.

g. Cf. *Greatness of Moses* 15:4.

h. Cf. *Greatness of Moses* 14:5.

i. Cf. *Apoc. Paul* 31; *Greatness of Moses* 13:13-14.

j. This parallels the end of Gaster's translation V *"Hell"* §9. In §10-19, Gaster translates the text *In What Manner Is the Punishment of the Grave?* which is translated following *Tractate on Gehinnom* in this contribution. The text of *Tractate on Gehinnom* is continued in Gaster's translation V from §20.

k. Cf. mountains of snow in *3 En.* 42:4.

l. Cf. *Greatness of Moses* 18:9.

The Ultimate Fate of the Wicked

7 [1]The fourth chapter: [2]Every twelve months[a] they are made into dust and the wind scatters them under the feet of the righteous, as it is written, *You will trample the wicked for they will be ashes under the soles of your feet.* [3]Afterwards, their soul returns to them and they go out from Gehinnom, but their faces are black like the bottom of a pot.[b] [4]They declare the punishment upon them to be right, and they say: "Rightly you have decreed concerning us, rightly you have judged us.[c] Righteousness belongs to you, O Lord, and shame belongs to us as this day."[d] [5]But the nations of the world, idolaters, are punished in the seven divisions of fire, and in each division for twelve months. [6]The river Dinor[e] goes out from under the Throne of Glory, and flows down upon them, and goes from one end of the world to the other. [7]There are seven divisions in Gehinnom.[f] [8]In each division there are 6,000 compartments, and in each compartment there are 6,000 windows, and in each window there are 6,000 vessels of poison. They are all designated for scribes and judges. [9]Regarding that moment, Solomon said, *You will groan at your end when your flesh and your body are consumed, etc.* [10]Not one of them will escape, unless he possesses Torah and good deeds.[g] [11]After all this, the Holy One, Blessed be He, has compassion over his creatures, as it is said, *For I will not contend forever and I will not always be angry, for the spirit would grow weak before me and souls I have made.*[h]

Mal 3:21 (Evv 4:3)

Prov 5:11

Isa 57:16

The end of Tractate on Gehinnom.

---

a. Cf. *t. Sanh.* 13:4-5.

b. Cf. *Apoc. Paul* 38; *b. Meg.* 11a; *b. Shab.* 30a; *b. Sanh.* 107b; *b. Rosh. Hash.* 16b; *1 En.* 63:11; *3 En.* 44:6; *T. Levi* 14:4; *3 Bar.* 13:1.

c. Cf. *b. 'Erub.* 19a.

d. Cf. *Apoc. Pet.* 7:11; 13:6.

e. Dinor is Aramaic for "of fire." Cf. Dan 7:10 and *Legend of "Hear, O Israel"* 3.

f. Cf. *Midr. Ps.* 11.7; *b. Sotah* 10b; *History of Rabbi Yehoshua ben Levi* 14:1.

g. Cf. *Tractate on Gehinnom* 4:3.

h. This parallels the end of Gaster's text V *"Hell"* §24.

In What Manner Is the Punishment of the Grave? (*Ketsad Din Ha-Qever*)

Fragments Outlining the Punishment of the Grave

1 [1]His disciples asked Rabbi Eliezer: "In what manner is the punishment of the grave?" [2]He said to them: [...] and half of iron and strikes him. [3]One time his limbs were taken apart [...] and from his tongue [...] and revile people, and so it is with all of them. [4]Rabbi Meir says: The punishment suffered in the grave is worse than the punishment of Gehinnom. [5][...] from this originates what the sages said: The generation comes [...] even the generation in Babylon. [6]The one who dies on the eve of the Sabbath does not see the punishment of the grave. [7][...] from the womb, this is the punishment of Gehinnom. [8]May God,[a] in his compassion and his loving kindness, deliver us from punishment and set our portion with the righteous in Gan Eden.[b]

Introduction to Gehinnom

2 [1]Rabbi Hiyya expounded: *The leech has two daughters, "Give! Give!"* [2]Rabbi Elazar said: Two bands of angels of destruction stand over the entrance of Gehinnom and say: "Give! Give! Bring! Bring!" [3]Why is it called Gehinnom? It is a valley where all its dead walk from one end of the world to the other.[c] [4]Why is Gehinnom also called Tofteh? Because everyone who is enticed by his inclination enters there.[d] [5]Rabbi Yohanan began with:[e] There are seven divisions in Gehinnom. [6]Each division has thousands of compartments, and in each compartment there are seven windows. [7]In each window there are thousands of vessels of poison. [8]They are all destined for the officers, the scribes, the judges, the heretics and the apostates. [9]Not one of them will escape unless he possesses Torah and good deeds. [10]After this, He has compassion over his creatures, as it is said, *For I will not contend forever and I will not always be angry, for the spirit*
Isa 57:16 *would grow weak before me and souls I have made.*[f]

---

a. I.e., "The Place."

b. Cf. *Greatness of Moses* 19:1; *History of Rabbi Yehoshua ben Levi* 15:3.

c. The biblical place named Gehinnom (Josh 15:8; cf. Jer 7:31-32) was a site for child sacrifice and became a metaphor for Hell (e.g., Mk 9:43-47). The pun here is based on the fact that it sounds like the Hebrew phrase "the valley of look at them."

d. For 2:1-4 cf. *Tractate on Gehinnom* 1:2-5.

e. Jellinek references *Tractate on Gehinnom* in his edition.

f. Cf. *3 En.* 43:3; for 2:5-10 cf. *Tractate on Gehinnom* 7:7-11.

Those Who Receive Permanent Punishment

3 [1]Seven[a] descend into Gehinnom and these are they: the judge, the butcher, the clerk, the physician, their scribes and the teachers of young children. [2]If they do (their duty) for the sake of heaven, they all descend and ascend, except three who descend but do not ascend—the one who exposes his neighbour in public, the one who calls his neighbour a name and the one who commits adultery.[b]

Names and Dimensions of Gehinnom

4 [1]Gehinnom has seven names and these are they: Sheol,[c] Abaddon,[d] Beer Shaon,[e] Beer Shahat,[f] Hatsar Mavet,[g] Bor Tahtiyah[h] and Tit Ha-yaven.[i] [2]Sheol is a journey of 300 years and so are its length and its width.[j] [3]So it is with all of them; consequently, the length of Gehinnom is a journey of 2,100 years.

The Sentencing of the Dead

5 [1]At the time that a person is convicted for punishment, they deliver him to angels of destruction. [2]They seize him and lead him to the court of death, darkness
and shade, as it is said, *May their way be dark and slippery.* [3]Not only this, but Ps 35:6
they push him into the midst of Gehinnom, as it is said, *And the angel of the Lord*
pursues them. [4]When a person dies and is put on a bed, the ministering angels Ps 35:5
walk before him, and people walk behind him. [5]If people say about him: "Happy
was so-and-so, this one was good and praiseworthy in his lifetime," the ministering angels say to him: "Write it down," and he writes it down and they sign. [6]Not
only this, but two ministering angels escort a person at the moment of his death
and they know whether he stole or withheld or denied a debt.[k] [7]Not only this,
but the beams and stones of a person's house testify against him, as it is said, *A*
stone from the wall will cry out, etc.[l] [8]Whoever repented is brought to Gan Eden, Hab 2:11
but if he died without repentance, he is brought to Gehinnom.[m] [9]When a person
dies, they bring him to Abraham and Isaac and they say to him: "My son, what
have you done in the world from which you have gone out?" [10]He says to them:
"I bought fields and vineyards and laboured in them all my days." [11]They say to
him: "Fool! Did you not learn from David the King who said, *The earth is the*
Lord's and the fullness of it?" [12]They lead him out and bring in another, and they Ps 24:1

---

a. This parallels Gaster's translation of text V *"Hell"* §10-19.

b. Cf. *Tractate on Gehinnom* 6:1-3.

c. The Underworld; cf. Jonah 2:3 (Evv 2:2); *3 En.* 44:2-6.

d. "Destruction"; cf. Ps 88:12 (Evv 88:11); Rev 9:11.

e. "Pit (or 'Well') of desolation"; cf. Ps 40:3 (Evv 40:2).

f. "Pit (or 'Well') of ruin"; cf. Ps 16:10.

g. "Courtyard of death."

h. "Lowermost pit."

i. "Mirey mud"; cf. Ps 40:3 (Evv 40:2).

j. Cf. *Treatise on the Work of Creation* 2.

k. For revelation of a person's deeds cf. *Apoc. Paul* 14; *2 En.* 61:2; *4 Ezra* 7:35; *3 Bar.* (Gk) 11:9. For books of deeds cf. Dan 7:10; *Ascen. Isa.* 9:21-22; *Apoc. Paul* 17; *1 En.* 103:2; *4 Ezra* 6:20; *Apoc. Zeph.* 3:6-9; 7:1 ff.; *2 En.* 19:5; 22:11; 50:1; 52:15; 53:2-3; *T. Ab.* 12:4-18; 13:9; *2 Bar.* 24:1; Rev 20:12-13; *3 En.* 18:19, 24; 28:7; 44:9; *Apoc. Pet.* 6:3.

l. Cf. *Apoc. Paul* 12.

m. For no possibility of repentance after death cf. *2 En.* 62:2-3; *2 Bar.* 85:12; *4 Ezra* 7:82; 9:12; *Apoc. Pet.* 13:5.

ask him the same. 13 He says: "I acquired silver and gold." 14 They say to him:
"Fool! Did you not learn from the first prophets who said: *The silver is mine and*
Hag 2:8 *the gold is mine*?" 15 When they bring scholars to them, they say to them: "My
sons, what have you done in the world from which you came?" 16 They say: "We
toiled over the Torah all the days of our lives." 17 They say to him: "*He enters into*
Isa 57:2 *peace, they rest on their beds*."[a] 18 Also, the Holy One, Blessed be He, receives him
with a friendly countenance.

First Compartment of Gehinnom

6 1 Five compartments[b] of punishments are established in Gehinnom. 2 Isaiah saw all of them. 3 He entered the first compartment and found there two men who hold containers of water upon their shoulders, and they fill them and throw them into the midst of the pit, but the pit is never full. 4 Isaiah, upon him be peace, said before the Holy One, Blessed be He: "Revealer of Secrets, reveal this secret to me."[c] 5 The Holy Spirit answered him: "These are people who covet from their neighbours, therefore they are punished for this."

Second Compartment of Gehinnom

7 1 He entered the second compartment and found there two people hung by their tongues.[d] 2 He said to the Holy One, Blessed be He: "Revealer of Secrets, reveal this secret to me." 3 He said to him: "These are people who slandered[e] and therefore they are punished in such a way."

Third Compartment of Gehinnom

8 1 He entered the third compartment and found there people who are hung by (their) nakedness. 2 He said to Him: "Revealer of Secrets, etc." 3 He said to him: "These are people who left their wives alone and were faithless with the daughters of Israel, and therefore they are punished in such a way."

Fourth Compartment of Gehinnom

9 1 He entered the fourth compartment and found there two women who are hung by their breasts.[f] 2 He said to him: "Revealer of Secrets, etc." 3 He said to him: "These are women who uncovered their head, tore their hems, sat in the street and nursed their children in the street in order to incline the heart of people to them and cause them to sin, and therefore they are punished in such a way."

Fifth Compartment of Gehinnom

10 1 He entered the fifth compartment and found the compartment there full of smoke. 2 He found there the governors, the chiefs and the managers, and Pharaoh the wicked sits over them and guards the entrance of Gehinnom. 3 He says

a. Cf. 2 *En.* 42:3; 2 *Bar.* 73:1 for the "rest" of the righteous in Eden.

b. Cf. *In What Manner Is the Punishment of the Grave?* 4; *Tractate on Gehinnom* 7:7.

c. Cf. 2 *Bar.* 48:3; 54:5; 3 *En.* 11:1-3.

d. Cf. *Greatness of Moses* 13:10, 13.

e. Cf. *Greatness of Moses* 13:13.

f. Cf. *Greatness of Moses* 13:10, 16.

to them: "Did you not learn from me, when I was in Egypt?" [4]And still he sits and guards every entrance of Gehinnom.[a]

The Sentencing of Israel and the Nations

11 [1]Rabbi Eliezer the Great says: The house of Israel is the vineyard of the Holy
One, Blessed be He, as it is said, *For the vineyard of the Lord of Hosts is the house*
of Israel. [2]They are delivered by the Holy One, Blessed be He, as it is said, *Israel* Isa 5:7
is delivered by the Lord with everlasting salvation. [3]The Holy One, Blessed be He, Isa 45:17
says to the nations of the world: "Stay away from the glory of Israel. You will not
partake in their glory, you will not profit along with them, and you will not eat
from their fruits, but if you do, you will be banished from the world," as it is said,
Israel is holy to the Lord, the first fruits of his harvest. All who eat of it are guilty,
evil will come upon them, says the Lord. [4]The word "evil" refers to Gehinnom, as Jer 2:3
it is said, *Happy is the one who considers the poor. The Lord will deliver him on the*
day of evil. [5]When the Holy One, Blessed be He, judges Israel, he does not judge Ps 41:2 (Evv 41:1)
except by standing, as it is said, *God stands in the divine council.* [6]When he judges Ps 82:1
the nations, he does not judge them except by sitting, as it is said, *For there he*
sits, etc.[b] [7]At the time that they judge the person, they do not judge him in the
estimation of a creature in the world, but in the estimation of his Father only.
[8]Three do not enter for judgement—(those who go through) the sufferings of
poverty or sickness of the stomach and the dispossessed. [9]There are those who
say: also the one who has an evil wife. [10]Rabbi Eleazar said: Poverty is harder
for a person than the punishment of Gehinnom, as it is said, *Did I not refine*
you, etc., I tested you in the furnace of poverty:[c] [11]because the Holy One, Blessed Isa 48:10
be He, recovered every good reward to give them to Israel, but he did not find
anyone learning Torah except the poor who are in the midst of poverty.[d] [12]None
of them have anything to eat and because of this they are afraid of the Holy One,
Blessed be He.[e]

---

a. This parallels the end of Gaster's translation of text V *"Hell"* §10-19.

b. This verse is cited as a proof-text, but does not correspond to anything in the MT.

c. The proof-text from Isaiah does not correspond exactly to the MT which reads "Behold, I have refined you, but not as silver, I have chosen you in the furnace of poverty/affliction."

d. Cf. *Order of Gan Eden* 5:9.

e. Cf. the fate of the poor in 2 *Enoch* 63.

Legend of Rabbi Yehoshua ben Levi (*'Aggadat Rabbi Yehoshua' ben Levi*) Aramaic Recension

The First Compartment of Gehinnom

1 [1]Rabbi[a] Yehoshua ben Levi said: "When I measured the first compartment, which is in a division of Gehinnom, I found that it is 100 miles in length and fifty miles in width. [2]There are many pits and lions of fire rise up there. When people fall there, the lions consume them. [3]After the fire destroys them, they rise up as before and are cast into the fire of every compartment of the first division. [4]I measured the second compartment, which is in the second division, and I found that it is like the first. [5]I asked about the first compartment, and they said: 'In the first compartment are ten nations and with them is Absalom.' [6]Each nation says to another: 'If we sinned because we did not accept the Law, of what are you guilty?' They say: 'We are like you, we have sinned.' [7]They say to Absalom: 'Have you not accepted (the Law)? Your fathers accepted (the Law), so why are you punished like this?' He says to them: 'Because I disregarded my father.' [8]One angel is standing (there) and he strikes each and every one with rods of fire.[b] [9]Qushiel is the name of the one who strikes them. [10]He says: 'Cast them and cast them' and they are burnt in the fire, and they raise up others and he strikes them and throws them into the fire. And so on with each and every one until he places all the sinners. [11]After this they raise up Absalom to strike him. A *Bat Qol* goes out and says: 'Do not strike him and do not burn him, because he is from the
Exod 24:7 children of my beloved, who said at Sinai "we will do and we will listen."'' [12]After the wicked were placed to be struck and burnt, they went out from the fire as though they were not burnt, but again they return and strike them, and so they do to them seven times by day and three times by night. [13]But Absalom is spared from all these things because he is a son of David."[c]

The Second Compartment

2 [1]"In the second compartment, which is in the second division, are ten nations and they are punished like this.[d] [2]Doeg is with them. [3]Lahatiel is the name of the one who strikes them. [4]Doeg is spared from all these things because he is a
Exod 24:7 descendant of those who said at Sinai '*we will do and we will listen.*'"

a. This parallels the beginning of Gaster's translation of text VI "*Hell*" §1.

b. For rods of fire cf. *Apoc. Zeph.* 4:4; *3 En.* 16:5; 44:3; *Apoc. Pet.* 9:3. Cf. *Apoc. Paul* 35 and 40 for beating by an angel.

c. For 1:1-13 cf. *History of Rabbi Yehoshua ben Levi* 14.

d. I.e., like the punishment of the first compartment.

The Third Compartment

3 [1]"In the third compartment are ten nations, and they are punished like this. [2]Shaftiel is the name of the one who strikes them. [3]Korah and his assembly are spared from all these things because they said *'we will do and we will listen.'*"

The Fourth Compartment

4 [1]"The fourth compartment: they are punished like this. [2]There are ten nations in it and Jeroboam is with them. [3]Maktiel is the name of the one who strikes them. [4]Jeroboam is spared from all these things because he worked at the Law, and he is from the children of Israel who said at Sinai *'we will do and we will listen.'*"

The Fifth Compartment

5 [1]"The fifth compartment: they are punished like this. [2]Ahab is with them. 1 Kgs 21:25-26
[3]Hutriel is the name of the one who strikes them. [4]Ahab is spared from all these things because he is from the children of Israel who said at Sinai *'we will do and we will listen.'*"

The Sixth Compartment

6 [1]"The sixth compartment: they are punished like this. [2]Micah[a] is with them. [3]Pusiel is the name of the one who strikes them. [4]Micah is spared from all these things, because they said at Sinai *'we will do and we will listen.'*"

The Seventh Compartment

7 [1]"The seventh compartment: like this. [2]Elisha ben Abujah[b] is with them. [3]Dalqiel is the name of the one who strikes them. [4]Elisha is spared because he is a descendant of those who said at Sinai *'we will do and we will listen.'* [5]Regarding all the seven thousands who are in every division: they punish all the wicked with the former punishment. [6]They cannot see each other on account of the darkness, which is of all that darkness that was there before the world was created."[c]

---

a. The reference is probably to the Micah of Judges 17–18.

b. A rabbi usually dated to the end of the first century and the beginning of the second century in Palestine. He is one of four rabbis said to have seen paradise (cf. *b. Hag.* 14b).

c. This parallels the end of Gaster's translation of text VI *"Hell"* §7.

Treatise on the Work of Creation (*Baraita De-Maʿaseh Bereshit*)

The Levels of Earths up to Arqa

1 [1]On the punishment of Gehinnom, we[a] read in the Treatise on the Work of Creation:[b] [2]Upwards from Yabashah[c] is Tehom,[d] and upwards from Tehom is Bohu.[e] Upwards from Bohu is Yam.[f] Upwards from Yam is Mayim.[g] Upwards from Mayim is Arqa[h] and upon Arqa[i] is Sheol, Abaddon, Beer Ha-shahat, Tit Ha-yaven, Shaare Mavet, Shaare Tsalmavet and Gehinnom.[j] [3]The wicked are in them and angels of destruction are appointed over them. [4]Darkness[k] as thick as a wall of a city is there. [5]The punishments of the wicked are prepared there; dif-
1 Sam 2:9 ficult and bitter,[l] as it is said, *But the wicked will be silenced in darkness.*

The Divisions of Arqa

2 [1]The upper division is Sheol.[m] Its height is a journey of 300 years. Its width is a journey of 300 years. Its diameter is a journey of 300 years.[n] [2]The second division is Beer Shahat. Its height is a journey of 300 years. Its width is a journey

---

a. This parallels the beginning of Gaster's translation of text VII *"Hell"* §1.

b. Sections 1 and 2 correspond to *Nehar* 7 of Azulai's commentary. This treatise is almost identical to sections of *Seder Rabbah di-Bereshit*: §446-49 and §753-56 correspond to chaps. 1-3, and §760-62 corresponds to chap. 4. Cf. also *Midrash Konen, BHM*, 2:35-36.

c. "Dry land."

d. "Abyss."

e. "Emptiness."

f. "Sea."

g. "Waters."

h. "Earth" (Aramaic). For the seven earths cf. *ʾAbot R. Nat.* A 37; *ʾAbot R. Nat.* B 43; *Midr. Prov.* 8; *Lev. Rab.* 29.11; *Midrash Konen, BHM*, 2:35-36; *Seder Rabbah di-Bereshit* §429-36; §440-62; §743-76; §832-54. Tehom and Bohu are in the layer surrounding the seventh earth in *Seder Rabbah di-Bereshit* §748.

i. In *Seder Rabbah di-Bereshit* §439, Arqa is positioned as the third earth (Heled, Tevel, Arqa, Yabashah, Haravah, Adamah, Eretz).

j. For these seven names, see *Tractate on Gehinnom* 1:2-5 and *In What Manner Is the Punishment of the Grave?* 1:1-4; 4:1. The seven divisions of Gehinnom on Arqa are described in *Seder Rabbah di-Bereshit* §754-55; *b. ʿErub.* 19a; *Midrash Konen, BHM*, 2:30, 35. The Vision here follows the scheme also found in *Midrash Konen, BHM*, 2:35 and *Seder Rabbah di-Bereshit* O1531, although the order of divisions changes in chapter 2 of this text.

k. For darkness in the place of the wicked cf. *T. Levi* 3:2; *2 Bar.* 53:5; 58:1; 60:1; *2 En.* 7:1; 10:2; *Apoc. Pet.* 5:2; 6:5; 9:1; *Legend of Rabbi Yehoshua ben Levi* 7:6.

l. Cf. *T. Ab.* 13:12.

m. Note differences in the names and their order from chapters 1 and 3.

n. For dimensions of thickness and width cf. *3 Bar.* 2:4 (of heaven).

of 300 years. Its diameter is a journey of 300 years. [3]The third division is Tit Ha-yaven. Its height is a journey of 300 years. Its width is a journey of 300 years. Its diameter is a journey of 300 years. [4]The fourth division is Shaare Mavet. Its height is 300 years. Its width is 300 years. Its diameter is 303 years. [5]The fifth division is Abaddon. Its height is 300 years. Its width is 300 years. Its diameter is 300 years. [6]The sixth division is Shaare Tsalmavet. Its height is 300 years. Its width is 300 years. Its diameter is 300 years. [7]The seventh division is Gehinnom. Its height is 300 years. Its width is 300 years. Its diameter is 300 years. [8]Consequently, the journey of Gehinnom is 6,300[a] years.[b]

The Fires of the Seven Divisions of Arqa

3 [1]We read there:[c] [2]The fire of Gehinnom is strong. It is one sixtieth of the fire that is in Shaare Tsalmavet. [3]The fire that is in Tsalmavet is strong. It is one sixtieth of the fire that is in Shaare Mavet. [4]The one that is in Shaare Mavet is strong. It is one sixtieth of the fire that is in Tit Ha-yaven. [5]The fire that is in Tit Ha-yaven is strong. It is one sixtieth of the fire that is in Beer Shahat. [6]The fire that is in Beer Shahat is strong. It is one sixtieth of the fire that is in Abaddon. [7]The fire that is in Abaddon is strong. It is one sixtieth of the fire that is in Sheol.[d] [8]Sheol is half fire and half ice.[e] When the wicked who are in its midst go out from the midst of the fire, ice presses them, and when they go out from the ice, the fire presses and burns them. [9]The angels who are appointed over them preserve their soul in their body, as it is said, *For their worm will not die and their fire will not be extinguished, etc.*[f] Isa 66:24

Punishment by means of the Rivers and Scorpions

4 [1]We read there:[g] [2]The Holy One, Blessed be He, created seven Gehinnoms.[h] [3]Every Gehinnom has seven divisions in it, and every division has seven rivers of fire and seven rivers of ice in it. [4]Each one is 1,000 cubits wide, its depth is 1,000 cubits and its length is 300 cubits. Each one flows out one after the other. [5]Every wicked person passes through them and is burnt in their place, but the 1,000 angels of destruction appointed over them restore and revive them and stand them on their feet and proclaim to them all their deeds that are evil, and all their deeds and ways that are corrupt.[i] [6]They say to them: "Also now, pass before us into the rivers of fire, and into the rivers of ice, and into the rivers of lightning[j]

---

a. The numbers given actually add up to 6303, but the additional 3 years in the diameter of the 4th division is probably a textual error.

b. Azulai quotes the start of the next line "The fire of Gehinnom," etc., before beginning his commentary on the passage translated.

c. This section marks the beginning of *Nehar* 8 in Azulai's commentary.

d. Cf. the measures of fire in *2 Bar.* 59:5; *b. Ber.* 57b.

e. Cf. *2 En.* 10:2; *Exod. Rab.* 51.7 states that Gehinnom is half fire and half hail; *b. Sanh.* 29b describes snow in Gehinnom; *Greatness of Moses* 17; 18:4.

f. *Seder Rabbah di-Bereshit* §755 describes the strength of the fires in the compartments of Arqa. For the use of this proof-text cf. *Greatness of Moses* 18:6; *Tractate on Gehinnom* 5:4, 9.

g. This is from *Nehar* 9 in Azulai's commentary.

h. Cf. *Seder Rabbah di-Bereshit* §759-64; *Tractate on Gehinnom* 7:7.

i. Cf. *In What Manner Is the Punishment of the Grave?* 5:4-7.

j. Cf. *2 Bar.* 59:11 for splendour of lightnings.

and into the rivers of snow because you transgressed[a] the words of Torah and commandments that he gave to you on Sinai. [7]You were not afraid of the fire of Gehinnom[b] or of the punishment of Abaddon—come and receive[c] account of your deeds!" [8]Not only this, but there are in every division 7,000 cracks. Each crack has 7,000 scorpions[d] in it. Every scorpion has 300 limbs, and every limb has 7,000 vessels of venom hanging on it, and seven rivers of deadly poison flow out from it. [9]A person who touches it immediately bursts open, and each limb that is on him immediately falls from the midst of his body. His stomach bursts open and he falls upon his face. [10]Angels of destruction stand and take every limb and revive them and stand them upon their feet[e] and punish them (again).[f]

---

a. They "passed over" the Torah just as they must now "pass" through the streams.

b. Cf. 2 *Bar.* 59:2.

c. Or "give."

d. Cf. *Greatness of Moses* 15.

e. Cf. *History of Rabbi Yehoshua ben Levi* 14:2-3, 11-12; *Legend of Rabbi Yehoshua ben Levi* 1:2-3, 10, 12.

f. This parallels the end of Gaster's translation of text VII *"Hell"* §4.

David Apocalypse

The Future Punishments for Israel

1 [1]Rabbi Ishmael said:[a] "Sagansagel Prince of the Presence told me and said to me: 'My beloved, sit on my lap and I will tell you what will happen to Israel.' [2]I sat on his lap and he was looking at me and weeping.[b] His tears were dripping from his eyes and falling on my face. [3]I said to him: 'Glorious Heavenly Splendour, why are you weeping?' He said to me: 'Come and I will introduce you and make known to you what is reserved for Israel, my holy people.' [4]He took me and led me to the chambers of chambers and to the treasuries of treasures. [5]He took the writing tablets and he opened and showed me documents. Troubles that were different from each other were written (in them).[c] [6]I said to him: 'For whom are these?'[d] He said to me: 'For Israel.' [7]I said to him: 'Will Israel be able to endure them?' He said to me: 'Come tomorrow and I will make known to you troubles different from these.' [8]The next day he led me to the chambers of chambers and he showed me troubles that were worse than the first ones: who is destined for the sword, who is destined for hunger, who is destined to become spoil and who is destined for captivity. [9]I said to him: 'Glorious Heavenly Splendour, have Israel only sinned?' [10]He said to me: 'On each day, troubles worse than these are newly established, but when they assemble at the synagogues and say "May His great name be blessed," we do not allow them[e] to go out from the chambers of chambers.'"

The Destruction of Jerusalem

2 [1]"At the moment that I descended before him, I heard a voice speaking in Aramaic, and thus it was saying: [2]'The holy sanctuary is destined to become a ruin and the palace is destined to be a burning fire. [3]The compartment of the King is reserved for destruction and young women and young men are destined to become spoil. [4]The sons of the King are destined for the death penalty. [5]The pure altar is to be made unclean, and opponents will make spoil of the table that he has prepared. [6]Jerusalem is destined to become a ruin, and the land of Israel a commotion.'"

---

a. This parallels the beginning of Gaster's translation of text VIII *"Paradise."*

b. Cf. *Apoc. Paul* 20; *History of Rabbi Yehoshua ben Levi* 10:7-12.

c. Cf. *In What Manner Is the Punishment of the Grave?* 5:4-7.

d. Cf. similar questions at *1 En.* 53:4; 56:2; *Apoc. Zeph.* 3:4.

e. I.e., the troubles.

3 1"When I heard this loud voice, I shouted out and I was overcome by sleep and I fell backwards until Hadraniel the prince came and put strength and spirit into me.[a] 2He stood me upon my feet and said to me: 'My Beloved, what has happened to you?' 3I said to him: 'Glorious Heavenly Splendour, is there no possibility of a remedy for Israel?' 4He said to me: 'My Beloved, come and I will introduce you to the treasuries of consolations and salvations[b] for Israel.'"

The Future Rewards for Israel

4 1"He brought me and I saw bands of ministering angels sitting and weaving garments of salvation. 2They make crowns of life[c] and fix precious stones and jewels on them,[d] and perfume them from all kinds of spices and all good things in the world. 3I said to him: 'For whom are these?' He said to me: 'For Israel.' 4I saw one crown that is different from all the crowns. The sun and moon and twelve constellations are fixed on it. 5I said to him: 'To whom belongs this praiseworthy crown?' He said to me: 'To David King of Israel.' 6I said to him: 'Glorious Heavenly Splendour, show me the glory of David.' 7He said to <me>:[e] 'My beloved, wait[f] three hours until David comes here and you will see him in his greatness.'"

5 1"He took hold of me and sat me on his lap. 2He said to me: 'What do you
see?' I said to him: 'I see seven lightning bolts[g] that are running as one.' 3He
said: 'Squeeze your eyes shut, my son, so that you are not frightened. These
are going out to meet David.' 4Immediately, all the Ophannim,[h] Seraphim, Holy
Living Creatures, stores of snow,[i] clouds of glory, planets, stars and ministering
Ps 19:1 | Ps 19:2 angels trembled and said: '*To the leader, etc., The heavens declare, etc.*'[j] 5I heard
(Evv Ps 19:1) the voice of a great earthquake that came from Eden and said: '*The Lord will be*
Exod 15:18 *King forever and ever.*'[k] 6Behold, David King of Israel was at the head, and all the
kings of the house of David (followed) after him. 7Each one had his crown on his
head, but the crown of David was more distinguished and praiseworthy than all
the crowns. Its splendour goes from one end of the world to the other.[l] 8David
ascended to the Temple that is in heaven[m] and prepared for him there is a throne
of fire which is forty parasangs in height and its length and its width are double."

6 1"As soon as David came and sat himself on that throne which is prepared for him opposite the throne of his Lord, all the kings of the house of David sat

---

a. For fainting cf. *1 En.* 60:3-4; 71:11; *4 Ezra* 10:29-31; *Apoc. Ab.* 10:1 ff.; Rev 1:17; *3 En.* 1:7-9.

b. For stores of blessings cf. *1 En.* 11:1.

c. Cf. *Legend of "Hear, O Israel"* 1:7.

d. Cf. *3 En.* 12:3 where Metatron is given a crown fixed with jewels.

e. Lit. "him," but should be amended to "me" as this fits in with the narrative pattern of the text.

f. Cf. Enoch's instruction to wait for revelation in *1 En.* 52:5.

g. Cf. lightning and stars accompanying Enoch in *1 En.* 14:8.

h. Cf. Ezek 1:15 ff.; *3 En.* 25:5-7; 33:3.

i. Cf. *History of Rabbi Yehoshua ben Levi* 5:2.

j. Cf. the use of this biblical verse at *Greatness of Moses* 8:4.

k. Cf. the use of this verse at *Legend of "Hear, O Israel"* 2:7.

l. Cf. *3 En.* 14:5 which describes the splendour of Metatron's crown.

m. Cf. *Greatness of Moses* 6:2; 20:33.

before him, and the kings of Israel stood behind him. 2 Immediately, David stood
and uttered songs and praises that no ear has ever heard.[a] 3 As soon as David
began and said: '*The Lord will be King forever, etc.*,' Metatron and all his minis- Ps 146:10
ters began and said: '*Holy, holy, holy is the Lord of hosts, etc.*'[b] 4 The Holy Living Isa 6:3
Creatures praise and say: '*Blessed be the glory of the Lord from His place.*'[c] 20 The Ezek 3:12
heavens say: '*The Lord will be King forever.*' 5 The earth says: '*The Lord was King,*[d] Ps 146:10 | Ps 93:1
the Lord is King.'[e] 6 All the kings of the house of David say: '*And the Lord will be* Ps 10:16
King over all the earth.[f] *On that day the Lord will be one and his name one.*'"[g] Zech 14:9

---

a. David sings psalms before Jesus in the seventh heaven in *Apoc. Paul* 29.
b. Cf. *Greatness of Moses* 10:3; *Legend of "Hear, O Israel"* 2:2.
c. Cf. *Legend of "Hear, O Israel"* 2:4.
d. Cf. *Legend of "Hear, O Israel"* 2:7.
e. Cf. *Legend of "Hear, O Israel"* 2:7.
f. This parallels the end of Gaster's translation of text VIII *"Paradise."*
g. Cf. the Rosh Hashanah Shaharit service; cf. *3 En.* 48A:10.

Index of Modern Authors

The indexes were prepared by Dr. Elizabeth Tracy.
Citations to footnotes are represented by superscript letters and numbers.

Index of Scripture and Other Ancient Texts

NEW TESTAMENT

DEAD SEA SCROLLS AND TEXTS FROM THE JUDEAN DESERT

JOSEPHUS

PHILO OF ALEXANDRIA

CLASSICAL AND GRECO-ROMAN LITERATURE

NEW TESTAMENT APOCRYPHA

COPTIC GNOSTIC TEXTS FROM THE NAG HAMMADI LIBRARY

GREEK MAGICAL PAPYRI (see also *Moses, Eighth Book of* and *Moses, Tenth Book of*)

RABBINIC LITERATURE

MISHNAH

BABYLONIAN TALMUD (BAVLI)

OTHER RABBINIC WORKS

OTHER HEBREW AND ARAMAIC LITERATURE

PATRISTICS/ CHURCH FATHERS

Apostolic Fathers

Ante-Nicene Patristic Works

QUR'AN

MEDIEVAL AND RENAISSANCE

MISCELLANEOUS LITERATURE